MARRIAGES
and
FAMILIES

MARRIAGES
and
FAMILIES

**Changes,
Choices, and
Constraints**

FOURTH EDITION

Nijole V. Benokraitis
University of Baltimore

Prentice
Hall

Upper Saddle River, New Jersey 07458

Library of Congress Cataloging-in-Publication Data

Benokraitis, Nijole V. (Nijole Vaicaitis)
    Marriages and families : changes, choices, and constraints /
Nijole V. Benokraitis.—4th ed.
        p.   cm.
    Includes bibliographical references and index.
    ISBN 0-13-034177-0
    1. Family—United States. 2. Marriage—United States. I. Title
HQ536.B45 2001
306.8'0973—dc21   2001032737

VP, Editorial Director: Laura Pearson
Publisher: Nancy Roberts
Senior Acquisitions Editor: Christopher DeJohn
Editorial Assistant: Christina Scalia
Developmental Editor: Maggie Barbieri
VP, Director of Manufacturing and Production:
    Barbara Kittle
Executive Managing Editor: Ann Marie McCarthy
Production Liaison: Fran Russello
Project Manager: Linda Cupp/Lithokraft II
Prepress and Manufacturing Manager: Nick Sklitsis
Prepress and Manufacturing Buyer: Mary Ann Gloriande
Creative Design Director: Leslie Osher

Interior and Cover Design: Carmen DiBartolomeo
Cover Art: Jose Ortega/Stock Illustration Source
Director, Image Resource Center: Melinda Lee Reo
Manager, Rights & Permissions: Kay Dellosa
Interior Image Specialist: Beth Boyd
Photo Researcher: Christine Pullo
Art Manager: Guy Ruggiero
Artist: Mirella Signoretto
Marketing Manager: Christopher Barker
Director of Marketing: Beth Gillette Meja
Senior Media Editor: John J. Jordan
Media Production Manager: Maurice Murdock

This book was set in 10/11 Sabon by Lithokraft II and was printed and bound by World Color. The cover was printed by Lehigh Press, Inc.

Printed in the United States of America
10 9 8 7 6 5 4 3 2 1

ISBN: 0-13-034177-0

Pearson Education LTD., London
Pearson Education Australia PTY, Limited, Sydney
Pearson Education Singapore, Pte. Ltd
Pearson Education North Asia Ltd, Hong Kong
Pearson Education Canada, Ltd, Toronto
Pearson Educación de Mexico, S.A. de C.V.
Pearson Education—Japan, Tokyo
Pearson Education Malaysia, Pte. Ltd
Pearson Education, Upper Saddle River, New Jersey

To Andrius and Gema

BRIEF CONTENTS

CONTENTS

BOXED FEATURES

PREFACE

Welcome to the fourth edition of *Marriages and Families: Changes, Choices, and Constraints.* As we embark on the new millennium, we are experiencing unprecedented changes that affect marriages and families. The shift in the racial and ethnic composition of the U.S. population is transforming families. As the number and variety of immigrants increase, the way we relate to each other becomes both more interesting and more complex. Medical technology continues to alter life spans. As this book goes to press, for example, a premature infant weighing only four ounces is thriving. At the other end of the life course, the number of people age 65 and over is surging. Living longer means that many of us will enjoy multigenerational families but will also have numerous elderly relatives who will need caregiving.

Other recent changes have also affected families. A booming economy during the 1990s has propelled some families into higher socioeconomic brackets but left many others poorer than ever. Though some complain about the "information overload," widespread access to the Internet has connected family members across the states and overseas. There has also been a groundswell of supporters who oppose divorce as well as a concerted effort to identify unwed fathers and enforce their financial child-support obligations.

Marriages and Families offers students a comprehensive introduction to these and other issues facing families in the twenty-first century. Although written from a sociological perspective, the book incorporates material from other disciplines—history, economics, social work, psychology, law, biology, and anthropology. Moreover, the research that supports this edition, most from the mid-1990s to early 2000s, encompasses both quantitative and qualitative studies. Nationally representative and longitudinal data are supplemented with insights from clinical, case, and observational studies.

A Continuity of Major Themes on the Contemporary Family

Marriages and Families continues to be distinguished from other textbooks in several important ways. It offers comprehensive coverage of the field, allowing instructors to select chapters that best suit their particular needs. It balances theoretical and empirical discussions with practical examples and applications. It highlights important contemporary changes in society and the family. It explores the choices that are available to family members as well as the constraints that often limit our choices. It examines the diversity of U.S. families, using cross-cultural and multicultural material to encourage students to think about the many critical issues that confront the family of the twenty-first century.

More Changes

Changes that are affecting the structure and functioning of today's family inform the pages of every chapter of this book. Also, several chapters focus on some major transformations in American society. Chapter 12, for example, examines the growing cultural diversity of the United States, focusing on African American, American Indian, Latino, Asian American, and interracial marriages and families. Chapter 17 discusses the ways in which the rapid "graying of America" has affected adult children and grandchildren, family members' roles as caregivers, and family relations in general. And Chapter 18 analyzes some of the social policy changes that affect the family.

More Choices

On the individual level, family members have many more *choices* today than ever before. People feel freer to postpone marriage, to cohabit, or to raise children as single parents. As a result, household forms vary greatly, ranging from commuter marriages to those in which several generations live together under the same roof. As reproductive technology becomes increasingly sophisticated, many infertile couples can now have children. Some states offer "covenant marriages" and mediation to stem the high divorce rates. And as the U.S. population continues to age, many elderly family members are implementing innovative housing arrangements (such as senior communes) and demanding legislation that allows them to die with dignity. Although some of these issues are highly controversial, they increase the options that family members have now and will enjoy in the future.

More Constraints

Although family members' choices are more varied today, we also face greater macro-level *constraints.* Our options are increasingly limited, for example, by government policies that ignore national health insurance coverage for families and child-care resources for middle-class and lower socioeconomic households. Economic changes often shape family life and not vice versa. Political and legal institutions also have a major impact on most families in terms of tax laws, welfare reform, and even in defining what a family is. Because laws, public policies, and religious groups affect our everyday lives, I have framed many discussions of individual choice within the larger picture of the institutional constraints that limit those choices.

Cross-Cultural and Multicultural Diversity

Because contemporary American marriages and families vary greatly in terms of structure, dynamics, and cultural heritage, discussions of gender roles, class, race, ethnicity, age, and sexual orientation are integrated throughout this book. To further strengthen students' understanding of the growing diversity among today's families, I have also included a series of boxes that focus on families from many cultures. Both text and boxed materials are intended to broaden students' cultural "pool of knowledge" (as one of my college professors used to say) and to encourage you, the student, to think about the many forms families may take and the different ways in which family members interact.

New and Expanded Topics

In most chapters "a global view" adds new material to either the *Data Digest* or text. In addition, many chapters include more examples from the popular culture (television, videos, movies) to which students relate. Specifically, new, updated, and expanded coverage includes the following:

- Updated and streamlined section on demographic changes, social class and racial-ethnic variations in using technological innovations, and the rise of social movements such as communitarianism, father's rights, and "saving marriages" (Chapter 1)

- More emphasis on applied research in family studies, Internet-based research, and updates on ethical issues (Chapter 2)

- New material on misconceptions about slavery (Chapter 3)

- Updates on the nature–nurture debate and the gender division of family labor, and new material on the effects of violent video games and the recent interest in raising boys in "toxic environments" (Chapter 4)

- New material on cyberstalking, narcissistic love, arranged marriages, and romance among older persons (Chapter 5)

- Recent research on the genetics and politics of sexual orientation, sexual scripts among racial-ethnic families, teen–parent lack of communication about sexual behavior, changing attitudes about gay rights, and HIV/AIDS among gays and heterosexual black women and Latinas (Chapter 6)

- New material on personal classified ads, Filipina mail-order brides, cyber romances, new rape drugs, and dating infidelity among college students (Chapter 7)

- Civil unions in Vermont, cohousing communities, singles penalty taxes, life satisfaction of older, never-married people, cohabitation by race-ethnicity, and recent cultural shifts that encourage cohabitation (Chapter 8)

- New data on marital satisfaction, domestic work, and interpersonal communication (Chapter 9)

- New material on first-time parents, international adoptions, open adoptions, the decline of unmarried teen births, updates on reproductive technology, fatherhood, and variations in unmarried births by race, ethnicity, and age (Chapter 10)

- New material on parental responsibility statutes, psychological aggression as a form of discipline, day care, and parenting during a child's early years (Chapter 11)

- Section on American Indians revised extensively, new material on intergenerational relationships, the model minority myth, and parenting in black families (Chapter 12)

- New material on middle-class families and work, a discussion of the "old economy" and the "new economy" and their effect on families, stay-at-home dads, black commuter marriages, and the increasing gender wage gap (Chapter 13)

- Recent research on sibling abuse and elder abuse, domestic violence against women worldwide (including honor killings), intimate violence by race-ethnicity and marital status, and suicide among American Indian youth (Chapter 14)

- New information on technology and getting a divorce, child support by race-ethnicity and gender, changing attitudes about divorce, and divorced parents who act like peers (Chapter 15)

- Recent research on lesbian stepfamilies, successful stepfamilies, and longitudinal studies on remarriage (Chapter 16)

- New material on centenarians, aging stereotypes (especially about women), grandparenting styles, grandparents' visitation rights, funeral rip-offs, and variations in racial-ethnic caregiving (Chapter 17)

- Revised and updated sections on national health insurance, the Canadian health care system, the 1996 welfare reforms, and some results of Oregon's assisted suicide legislation (Chapter 18)

Features in the Fourth Edition

Much of *Marriages and Families* has been revised to incorporate new research (both in print and on the Internet), recent surveys, and current examples and illustrations from the media. I have maintained several popular features such as the *Data Digest* and the author's files quotations. In response to student and reviewer comments, I have revised many figures and end-of-chapter materials, including the *Taking It Further* sections.

Data Digest

I introduced the *Data Digest* in the second edition because "all those numbers" from the Census Bureau, empirical studies, and demographic trends often overwhelm students (both mine and others'). Because this has been a popular feature, I've updated the U.S. information and have included data from other countries. The *Data Digest* that introduces each chapter not only provides students with a thought-provoking overview of current statistics and trends but makes "all those numbers" more interesting and digestible.

The first question from my students is usually, "Will this stuff be on the exam?" Not in my classes. I see the *Data Digest* as piquing student curiosity about the chapter rather than for memorizing a lot of numbers they can look up. Some faculty tell me that their students have used the *Data Digest* to develop class presentations or course papers.

Material from the Author's Files

Many faculty who reviewed previous editions of *Marriages and Families*, and many students as well, liked the anecdotes and personal experiences with which I illustrate sometimes "dry" theories and abstract concepts. In this new edition I weave more of this material into the text. Thus, many examples from discussions in my own classes are included (cited as "from author's files") to enliven theoretical perspectives and abstract concepts.

Figures

Many students tend to skip over figures (or tables) because they're afraid of numbers, don't trust statistics (see Chapter 2), or the material seems boring or complicated. Regardless of what textbooks I use, and in *all* the courses I teach, I routinely go over a number of figures in class because, as I tell my students, a good figure or table may be more important (or at least more memorable) than the author's explanation. To encourage students' looking at data, I have streamlined many figures and often provide brief summaries to accompany the figures.

Taking It Further

A common question from my own students has been, "Can't we do something about [issue X]?" And sometimes students have asked me for practical information—for example, "How can I find a good child-care center?" or "Can anyone help my sister get out of an abusive marriage?" The *Taking It Further* section addresses such questions and concerns. It tells students how to get information on particular topics; how to get personal assistance—such as counseling or therapy—for themselves or others; how to contact organizations that deal with specific problems; and provides URLs for a wealth of Internet sites that delve deeper into topics discussed in each chapter. Some of the Websites are fun (like love and dating), some provide up-to-date information (especially many of the Census Bureau and Centers for Disease Control sites), and others offer practical advice and community resources on the workplace, family research, aging, sex and sexually transmitted diseases, gender, sexual orientation, and many other family-related topics.

What is on the Internet today may be gone tomorrow. I have tried, therefore, to include only the Websites that have been around for a while and will not vanish overnight.

Pedagogical Features

The pedagogical features in *Marriages and Families* have been designed specifically to capture students' attention and to facilitate their understanding and recall of the material. Some of these features are familiar from the earlier editions but some are new. Each has been carefully crafted to ensure that it ties in clearly with the text material, enhancing its meaning and applicability.

Informative and Engaging Illustration Program

Many chapters contain figures that, in bold and original artistic designs, demonstrate such concepts as the exchange theory of dating, romantic versus lasting love, and theories of mating and that present simple statistics in innovative and visually appealing ways. More than a third of the photographs are new. We have taken great care to select substantive photographs (rather than what I call "pretty postcards") that illustrate the text.

Thought-Provoking Box Series

Reflecting and reinforcing the book's primary themes, three categories of boxes focus on the changes, choices, and constraints that confront today's families. A fourth category discusses cultural differences, and a fifth, self-assessment quizzes, helps students evaluate their own knowledge and acquire insights about family life.

- **Changes boxes**—some historical, some anecdotal, and some empirically-based—show how marriages and families have been changing or are expected to change in the future. For example, a box in Chapter 13 describes how the role of the working mother has evolved over the years.

- **Choices boxes** illustrate the kinds of decisions families can make to improve their well-being, often highlighting options of which family members may be unaware. In Chapter 10, for instance, a box shows what mothers and fathers can do to increase the likelihood of having healthy babies.

- **Constraints boxes** illustrate some of the obstacles that limit our options. They highlight the fact that although most of us are raised to believe that we can do whatever we want, we are often constrained by macro-level socioeconomic, demographic, and cultural factors. For example, a box on the ten biggest myths about the African American family reveals some of the stereotypes that black families confront on a daily basis.

- **Cross-Cultural/Multicultural boxes** illustrate the richness of varying family structures and dynamics, both within the United States and in other countries. For example, one box contrasts the American style of dating with arranged courtship and marriage in Muslim societies.

- **Ask Yourself** Self-assessment quizzes not only encourage students to think about and to evaluate their knowledge about marriage and the family but help them develop guidelines for action, both on their own and others' behalf. For example, "If This Is Love, Why Do I Feel So Bad?" helps the reader evaluate and make the decision to leave an abusive relationship.

Outlines

Each chapter contains an opening outline. The outlines help students organize their learning by focusing on the main topics of each chapter.

Key Terms and Glossary

Important terms and concepts, boldfaced and defined in the text, are listed at the end of each chapter. All key terms and their definitions are repeated in the Glossary at the end of the book.

Supplements

The supplements package for this textbook is of exceptional quality. Each component has been meticulously crafted to amplify and illuminate materials in the text itself.

Study Guide

This carefully written guide helps students better understand the material presented in the text. Each chapter consists of chapter summaries, definitions of key terms/concepts, critical thinking exercises geared to the questions in the text, a self-test questions page referenced to the text, and *Study Tips* written by the author.

Instructor's Manual with Tests

This essential instructor's tool includes detailed chapter outlines, teaching objectives, discussion questions, and classroom activities. Prepared by Lee Frank of Community College of Allegheny County, this manual also includes over 1900 test questions to include multiple choice, true/false, and essay questions—all page referenced to the text.

Prentice Hall Test Manager

This computerized software allows instructors to create their own personalized exams, to edit any or all test questions, and to add new questions. Other special features of this program, which is available for Windows and Macintosh, include random generation of an item set, creation of alternate versions of the same test, scrambling question sequence, and test preview before printing.

Sociology on the Internet: Evaluating Online Resources

This guide provides a brief introduction to navigating the Internet, along with references related specifically to the discipline of sociology. This supplementary book is free to students when packaged with Marriages and Families.

ContentSelect Research Database

Prentice Hall and EBSCO, the world leader in online journal subscription management, have developed a customized research database for students of sociology.

The database provides free and unlimited access to the text of over 100 peer-reviewed sociology and family publications when a ContentSelect Access Code is packaged with a new textbook. Please contact your local Prentice Hall representative for more information on ordering ContentSelect.

ABCNEWS ABC News/Prentice Hall Video Library for Marriage and the Family

Video is the most dynamic supplement you can use to enhance a class, but the quality of the video material and how well it relates to your course still make all the difference. Prentice Hall and ABC News are now working together to bring you the best and most comprehensive video ancillaries available in the college market.

Through its wide variety of award-winning programs—*Nightline, Primetime Live, This Week,* and *World News Tonight,* ABC offers a resource for feature and documentary-style videos related to the chapters in *Marriages and Families: Changes, Choices, and Constraints.* The programs have extremely high production quality, present substantial content, and are hosted by well-versed, well-known anchors.

Prentice Hall and its authors and editors provide the benefit of having selected videos and topics that will work well with this course and text and include notes on how to use them in the classroom.

The New York Times Supplement

The *New York Times* and Prentice Hall are sponsoring *Themes of the Times,* a program designed to enhance student access to current information relevant to the classroom. Through this program, the core subject matter provided in the text is supplemented by a collection of timely articles from one of the world's most distinguished newspapers, *The New York Times.* These articles demonstrate the vital, ongoing connection between what is learned in the classroom and what is happening in the world around us. To enjoy the wealth of information of *The New York Times* daily, a reduced subscription rate is available. For information, call toll-free: 1-800-631-1222.

Prentice Hall and *The New York Times* are proud to co-sponsor *Themes of the Times.* We hope it will make the reading of both textbooks and newspapers a more dynamic, involving process.

PH Marriages and Families PowerPoint Slides

Created by Roger J. Eich of Hawkeye Community College, this PowerPoint slide set combines graphics and text in a colorful format to help you convey principles in a new and exciting way. Created in PowerPoint, an easy-to-use widely available software program, this set contains over 200 content slides keyed to each chapter in the set.

Companion Website™ www.prenhall.com/benokraitis

More than an online study guide, the Prentice Hall *Companion Website™* to accompany *Marriages and Families: Changes, Choices, and Constraints* is a truly integrated text-specific resource, written and maintained by the text author, Nijole V. Benokraitis. The site offers

- **Self-grading quizzes** where students can test their knowledge of key concepts and obtain instant feedback.

- **Web destinations** with chapter by chapter hotlinks that will help launch your students' exploration on the Web.

- **Key Word searches** that are easy to use with built-in search engines.

- **Census Updates** to reflect the release of statistics from Census 2000 and links to relevant census Websites.

- **Polling feature** which allows students to delve more deeply into where they stand on issues facing the family.

Distance Learning Solutions

Prentice Hall is committed to providing our leading content to the growing number of courses being delivered over the Internet by developing relationships with the leading course management platforms. Please visit our technology solutions Website at http://www.prenhall.com/demo for more information or contact your local Prentice Hall representative.

Acknowledgments

A number of people have contributed to this edition of *Marriages and Families: Changes, Choices, and Constraints.* First, I would like to thank my students. Their lively exchanges during class discussions helped me refocus much of my research and writing. Linda Fair, our departmental guru, is always good-natured and responsive in solving everyday office-related glitches and facilitating correspondence.

Many thanks to the reference and circulation staff at the University of Baltimore's Langsdale Library for their continuous support. Carole Mason, Mary Atwater, Brian Chetelet, and Tammy Taylor kept track of hundreds of books checked out from a dozen Maryland system libraries, always facilitated my research, and resolved all problems patiently and graciously.

Carol Vaeth is continuously extraordinary in accessing materials from a variety of academic and public libraries when I have only partial (and often incorrect) references. Carol's amazing interlibrary skills have provided me with many of the articles and books I've needed to research and revise this edition of *Marriages and Families*. Also in the Reference Department, Steve LaBash routinely sends me information from discussion lists and other sources that are related to both my teaching and research. Other reference librarians—Lucy Holman, Randy Smith, Mary Schwartz, and Susan Wheeler—have always been responsive. They have trained my students on Internet usage, have spent hours helping me track down elusive information, and have *always* willingly provided instruction when I ran into Internet or online problems.

Colleagues play a critical role in revisions. For this edition, I received valuable input from Donna Altepeter (University of Wisconsin, Oshkosh), John P. Bartkowski (Mississippi State University), Susan Blackwell (Delgado Community College), Theodore N. Greenstein (North Carolina State University), Kim M. King (Hiram College), Hadley G. Klug (University of Wisconsin, Whitewater), Barbara Seater (Raritan Valley Community College), and Glenna M. Van Metrie (Wichita State University).

At Prentice Hall, Chris DeJohn, sociology editor, responded quickly and resolved a variety of snags.

Christina Scalia, Chris's superb administrative assistant, handled a variety of tasks efficiently and enthusiastically. Maggie Barbieri, development editor, provided helpful suggestions during the book's revision. Linda Cupp, production editor, orchestrated the myriad and endless day-to-day tasks required to produce this textbook. I am grateful to Mary Louise Byrd, copy editor; Kathleen Karcher, permissions editor; Carmen DiBartolomeo, designer; and Christine Pullo, photo researcher, for their high-quality contributions.

I thank my family for their unfaltering patience and sense of humor throughout life's little stresses, especially my research and writing. Throughout our 35 years of marriage, Vitalius, my husband, has always been a steadfast friend and a sympathetic sounding board. He and our son, Andrius, keep my computer humming. I'm especially grateful to Andrius for responding very quickly (no matter where he is during numerous business trips) to my exasperated whining and whimpering when my computer hiccups, wheezes, or goes into a coma. Gema, our daughter, has finally convinced me to turn off the PC once in a while and take time to smell the flowers. And the flowers smell mighty good, Gema. Thanks very much.

Last, but not least, I have benefited greatly from the thoughts and suggestions of faculty and students who have contacted me through e-mail or snail mail. I have incorporated many of their reactions in the fourth edition and look forward to future comments.

Thank you, one and all.

Nijole V. Benokraitis, professor of sociology at the University of Baltimore, has taught the Marriage and Family course for 18 years and says it's her favorite class, although her courses in Racial and Ethnic Relations and Gender Roles run a close second. Professor Benokraitis received a B.A. in Sociology and English from Emmanuel College, a M.A. in sociology from the University of Illinois at Urbana, and a doctorate in sociology from the University of Texas at Austin. She is a strong proponent of applied sociology and requires her students to enhance their study of course topics through interviews, direct observation, and other hands-on learning methods. She also enlists her students in community-service activities, such as tutoring and mentoring inner-city high school students, writing to government officials and other decision makers about specific social problems, and volunteering research services to nonprofit organizations.

Professor Benokraitis, who immigrated to the United States from Lithuania with her family when she was six years old, is bilingual and bicultural. She has authored, co-authored, edited, or co-edited *Contemporary Ethnic Families in the United States: Characteristics, Variations, and Dynamics* (Prentice Hall, 2002), *Feuds about Families: Conservative, Centrist, Liberal, and Feminist Perspectives* (Prentice Hall, 2000); *Subtle Sexism: Current Practices and Prospects for Change* (Sage, 1997); *Modern Sexism: Blatant, Subtle, and Covert Discrimination*, 2nd Edition (Prentice Hall, 1995); *Seeing Ourselves: Classic, Contemporary, and Cross-Cultural Readings in Sociology,* 5th Edition (Prentice Hall, 2001); and *Affirmative Action and Equal Opportunity: Action, Inaction, and Reaction* (Westview Press, 1978).

Professor Benokraitis has published numerous articles and book chapters on such topics as

The author (left) with her mother

institutional racism, discrimination against women in government and higher education, fathers in two-earner families, displaced homemakers, and family policy. She has served as both chair and graduate program director of the University of Baltimore's Department of Sociology and has chaired numerous university committees.

The recipient of grants and fellowships from many institutions, including the National Institute of Mental Health, the Ford Foundation, the American Educational Research Association, the Administration on Aging, and the National Endowment for the Humanities. She has for some time served as a consultant in the areas of sex and race discrimination to women's commissions, business groups, colleges and universities, and programs of the federal government, and she has made several appearances on radio and television on gender communication differences and single-sex educational institutions. She currently serves on the editorial board of *Women & Criminal Justice.*

Professor Benokraitis lives in Maryland with her husband, Dr. Vitalius Benokraitis, Chair of the Computer and Information Sciences Department at Shepherd College, West Virginia. They have two children, Gema and Andrius.

The author looks forward (and always responds) to comments on this 4th Edition of *Marriages and Families: Changes, Choices, and Constraints.* She can be contacted at

University of Baltimore
Division of Criminology,
    Criminal Justice,
    and Social Policy
1420 North Charles Street
Baltimore, MD 21201
Voicemail: 410-837-5294
Fax: 410-837-5061
E-mail:
    nbenokraitis@ubmail.ubalt.edu

The Changing Family

OUTLINE

DATADIGEST

■ The **"traditional" family** (where the husband is the breadwinner and the wife is a full-time mother) declined from 45 percent in 1972 to 26 percent in 1998.

■ In 1998, almost 14 million persons aged 25 to 34 years had **never been married,** representing 35 percent of all persons in that age group.

■ The median **age at which people marry** for the first time was higher in the mid-1990s than at any time during the past century: 26.7 years for men, 25.0 years for women in 1998.

■ The proportion of ever-married **adults who have been divorced** doubled from 17 percent in 1972 to about 34 percent in 1998.

■ The percent of children under age 18 and **living with one parent** rose from 11 percent in 1970 to 28 percent in 1998. About 41 percent of these children lived with mothers who had never been married.

SOURCES: T. W. Smith, 1999; Lugaila, 1998; Pamuk et al., 1998; U.S. Census Bureau, 1999a.

TWO generations ago, the typical American family consisted of a father, a mother, and three or four children. In a recent survey on what constitutes a family, in contrast, a woman in her 60s wrote the following:

> My boyfriend and I have lived together with my youngest son for several years. However, our family (with whom we spend holidays and special events) also includes my ex-husband and his wife and child; my boyfriend's ex-mother-in-law and her sister; his ex-wife and her boyfriend; my oldest son who lives on his own; my mom and stepfather; and my stepbrother and his wife, their biological child, adopted child, and "Big Sister" child. Needless to say, introductions to outsiders are confusing. (Cole, 1996: 12,14)

Clearly, contemporary family arrangements are more fluid and more transitory than stereotypes suggest. Does this shift reflect changes in individual preferences, as people often assume, or are other forces at work here? As this chapter shows, although individual choice has brought about some alterations in family structure, many of these changes reflect adjustments to larger societal transformations. We will also see that, despite both historical and recent evidence to the contrary, we continue to cling to a number of myths about the family. Before we examine these issues, however, we need to define what we mean by marriage and family.

What Is Marriage?

Although the concept of **marriage** has become more complex, a currently accepted definition—a socially approved mating relationship—is very broad. Marriage forms vary across many different societal and cultural groups because the members of the society construct our **norms,** or culturally defined rules for behavior. Among the norms that help define marriage are formal laws and religious doctrines. To be legally married, for example, U.S. citizens must meet specified requirements (e.g., minimum age) in every state. Although the laws are rarely enforced, 28 states prohibit marriage between first cousins. And because the Catholic Church prohibits the dissolution of what it considers the holy sacrament of marriage, devout Catholics may seek annulments but not divorces.

Despite numerous societal and cultural variations, marriages in most Western industrialized countries have some common characteristics. In general, married couples are expected to share economic responsibilities, to engage in sexual activity only with their spouses, and to bear and raise children.

In the United States, laws governing marriage have changed more rapidly than have social customs or regional practices. For example, although the U.S. Supreme Court declared miscegenation laws, which prohibit interracial marriages, unconstitutional in 1967, local customs and attitudes among many groups continue to discourage such unions (see Chapter 12). Furthermore, as violent outbursts in white neighborhoods in Massachusetts, New York, and New Jersey in recent years have shown, intolerance of interracial dating is not limited to the South or to rural areas.

Marriages in the United States are legally defined as either ceremonial or nonceremonial. A *ceremonial* marriage is one in which the couple must follow procedures specified by the state or other jurisdiction, such as buying a license, getting blood tests, and being married by an authorized official. Some states also recognize the *nonceremonial,* or **common-law marriage,** which is established by *cohabitation* (living together) and/or evidence of *consummation* (sexual intercourse). Common-law marriages are recognized as legal in 14 states and the District of Columbia. In both kinds of marriage, the parties must meet minimal age requirements, and they cannot engage in **bigamy**; that is, they cannot be married to a second person while a first marriage is still legal.

When common-law relationships are dissolved, unless there is a written contract, the legal repercussions can be complex. Even when common-law marriage is considered legal, marriage provides more rights (such as health benefits). In a number of states, however, children born to common-law partners have the same legal rights as children born to partners in a ceremonial marriage.

What Is a Family?

Although it may seem unnecessary to define familiar terms like *family,* meanings vary among groups of people and change over time. Moreover, such definitions have important consequences for policy decisions, often determining what rights and obligations of family members are recognized by legal and other social institutions. Under Social Security laws, for example, only the worker's spouse and dependent parents and children can claim benefits based on the worker's record. Other "nontraditional" family members, such as siblings and grandchildren, cannot claim benefits no matter how financially dependent they may be on the worker's income. As another example, in most cases of adoption, the child is not legally a member of the adopting family until both social service agencies and the courts have approved the adoption. Thus, definitions of family affect people's lives by limiting their options.

Traditionally, the family has been defined as a unit made up of two or more people who are related by blood, marriage, or adoption and who live together, form an economic unit, and bear and raise children. The U.S. Census Bureau defines the family simply as two or more people living together who are related by birth, marriage, or adoption. Because these descriptions exclude a multitude of diverse groups who also consider themselves families, such traditional definitions have been challenged in recent years. Social scientists have asked: Are childless couples families? What about cohabiting couples? Foster parents and their charges? Elderly sisters living together? Gay and lesbian couples, with or without children? Communal households in which child rearing is assumed by people other than the child's parents?

Our definitions of family become even more complicated if they're at odds with "official" designations of family membership when people seek greater rights. Grandparents, for example, have considerable legal privileges to maintain contact with minor grandchildren

Friends, a popular sitcom, portrays close friends and a brother and sister as a non-traditional "family."

in all 50 states. On the other hand, a 2000 Supreme Court decision limited some of these rights (see Chapter 17). Moreover, and unlike foster parents, large numbers of grandparents find themselves raising grandchildren without any financial assistance from the government (Treas, 1999). Similarly, many cohabitors demand to register their unions with employers to cover their partners' medical benefits (see Chapter 8). Yet there is no evidence that most cohabiting couples are willing to pay for the partners' rental costs, credit-card charges, or other expenses when the relationship breaks up. Are such behaviors and expectations contradictory? Or should courts, employers, schools, and other institutions expand their definitions of family to accommodate many groups' changing notions of family life?

As yet, social scientists have been unable to answer these questions; contemporary family arrangements are very complex (Cowan et al., 1993). Because we need a working definition, however, here we define **family** as an intimate environment in which two or more people: (1) live together in a committed relationship; (2) the members see their identity as importantly attached to the group; and (3) the group shares close emotional ties and functions. Be warned that not all social scientists will agree with this definition because it does not explicitly include legalized marriage, procreation, or child rearing. Definitions may become even more complicated—and more controversial—in the future. For instance, laws and medical technology have made it possible for a child to have more than two parents after birth through open adoption or in vitro fertilization (see Chapter 10).

Some believe that definitions of the family should emphasize affection and mutual cooperation among people who are living together. Particularly in African American and Latino communities, ties with **fictive kin,** or nonrelatives who are accepted as part of the family, may be as strong as or stronger and more lasting than the ties established by blood or marriage (Dilworth-Anderson et al., 1993). A recent variation of fictive kin among Unitarian congregations is "intentional families" made up primarily of white, professional people who are separated by distance or estrangement from their own relatives but who hope to achieve familial closeness. Intentional families live apart but meet regularly for meals, holidays, and milestones. They also plan outings together, help each other during crises, and sometimes find stand-in grandparents (E. Graham, 1996).

Family Structure

Many social scientists are contesting traditional definitions because the **nuclear family**—made up of a husband, a wife, and their biological or adopted children—ignores many other prevalent household forms. One researcher, for example, has identified 23 types of family structures and some include only friends or group-home members (Wu, 1996). Diverse family households are more acceptable today than ever before, as reflected in many television shows (see *Table 1.1*). At the same time, this lineup of shows is rarely representative of "real" families. For example, at least five shows highlight single-father households, but only two portray single-mother households. The star of the one show that featured an unwed mother—*Murphy Brown*—was white, upper middle class, and a successful professional. In some shows, such as *Home Improvement* during the late 1990s and *Everybody Loves Raymond* more recently, the fathers are lovable but emotionally "under construction." And while the numbers of traditional families have decreased since the 1970s (see Data Digest), such programs have increased during prime time during the early 2000s (e.g., *The Hughleys, Baby Blues, 7th Heaven, Yes, Dear, The PJs*).

Functions of the Family

Although family structures differ, most contemporary families fulfill similar functions. There are four major tasks that today's family is expected to perform:

legitimizing sexual activity, bearing and raising children, providing emotional support to family members, and establishing members' places in society.

Families in preindustrial societies continue to fulfill other traditional functions, such as educating their children, serving as an important economic unit, taking care of their elderly, and providing religious instruction to family members. Some families in industrialized societies—especially American Indians, Latinos, Asian Americans, and the Amish—also perform some of the latter functions.

Legitimizing Sexual Activity

Every society has norms regarding who may engage in sexual relations with whom and under what circumstances. One of the oldest rules is the **incest taboo,** which forbids sexual intercourse between close blood relatives, such as brother and sister, father and daughter, or mother and son. No one really knows where, when, or why incest taboos arose. Many people believe that they were created to avoid the birth of physically and/or emotionally deficient individuals as a result of inbreeding (Nimkoff, 1961).

Although sexual relations between close relatives can increase the incidence of inherited genetic diseases and abnormalities, incest taboos have primarily social bases. They probably arose to maintain the family in several ways. First, they minimize jealousies and destructive sexual competition that might interfere with the functioning of the family circle. Second, they are maintained because incest is impractical—it jeopardizes the group's survival. If members lose interest in each other, for example, they may avoid mating. Related to this explanation, primitive peoples' lives were so short and survival of progeny so difficult that it was rare for a child to be able to mate with its other-sex parent. Third, incest taboos ensure that mating will take place outside the family, thus widening the circle of people who will band together in cooperative efforts or in the face of danger (Ellis, 1963). Fourth, incest bans may reflect ritualistic and religious-dominated practices—although the reasons still remain a mystery—that originated among primitive peoples (Sagarin, 1963).

Finally, some analysts suggest that incest taboos reflect businesslike transactions in patriarchal societies. In a **matriarchy,** women control cultural, political, and economic resources and, consequently, have power over men. In a **patriarchy,** in contrast, men hold the positions of power and authority—political, economic, legal, religious, educational, military, and domestic. Males are considered heads of the household and dominate the economic, social, and domestic spheres of the family. In preindustrial societies, especially, if girls are not virgins, they are much less desirable as "barterable" merchandise between families or clans. Marry a virgin off well, Janeway (1981) argues, and the male head of household could gain powerful

TABLE 1.1

Family Structure According to 1990s and Early 2000s Television

You may not even remember some of the shows that have come and gone during the 1990s. Some, such as *Married . . . with Children, Mad About You, Home Improvement, The Nanny,* and *The Bill Cosby Show* are now syndicated. On the one hand, the 1990s shows have portrayed a wide variety of family structures. On the other hand, how many of these programs are really representative of most U.S. families today? Or of your own family?

Family Structure	Television Show
Married couple with children; father as breadwinner	*Married . . . with Children, The Simpsons, Dave's World, Everybody Loves Raymond, 7th Heaven, The Hughleys, Baby Blues, The PJs, Family Guy*
Married couple with children; two earners	*The Cosby Show, Roseanne, Home Improvement, Mad About You, Malcolm in the Middle, Bette*
Married couple with no children	*Dharma and Greg, King of Queens*
Married couple with children and related adults	*Under One Roof, All-American Girl, Family Matters*
Male householder with children	*Soul Man, The Geena Davis Show*
Male householder with children and unrelated adults	*Full House, The Nanny*
Male householder with children and related adults	*Me and the Boys, The Gregory Hines Show*
Male householder with children and grandchildren	*Thunder Alley*
Male householder with unmarried adult children	*Empty Nest, Providence*
Female householder with children	*Grace Under Fire, Cybill, Gilmore Girls*
Married couple with children from a previous marriage	*True Colors, Major Dad*
Married couple with biological and stepchildren	*Step By Step*
Children, no adults present	*On Our Own, Party of Five*
Unmarried mother	*Murphy Brown*
Related adults	*Head over Heels, Between Brothers, Charmed*
Related and unrelated adults	*Frasier*
Unrelated adults	*Living Single, Friends, 3rd Rock from the Sun, George and Leo, Men Behaving Badly*
Single-person households	*Seinfeld, Ellen*
Retired couple or roommates	*Cosby, The Golden Girls*

allies, a chance at inheriting valuable property, or a friend at court. According to Janeway, the incest taboo controlled the mother's sexuality so that no questions could be raised about the legitimacy of her offspring and about the property rights or titles within or between families. The incest taboo also guaranteed that daughters who were delivered to their husbands as virgins would prevent conflict or doubts about the future legitimacy of the daughters' heirs. Thus, by forcing people to have sexual relationships outside their immediate family, incest taboos forged political and economic ties with other families.

Most social scientists maintain that the existence of some sort of incest taboo is universal. There have

been exceptions, however. It is believed that the rulers of the Incan empire, the native Hawaiian royalty, the ancient Persian rulers, and the Ptolemaic dynasty in Egypt practiced incest while it was forbidden to commoners. Cleopatra, for example, was purportedly the issue of at least 11 generations of incest and married her younger brother. Some anthropologists speculate that wealthy Egyptian families practiced sibling marriage to prevent losing or fragmenting their agricultural land. If a sister married a brother, the property would remain in the family in cases of divorce or death (Parker, 1996). More recently, a nomadic tribe of ten families in Malaysia has reportedly been repopulating itself through incestuous relationships, even though

The family provides love, comfort, and emotional support that children need to develop into happy, healthy, and secure adults.

outside partners were readily available (Twitchell, 1987).

Two other rules define the "right" marriage partner: The principle of **endogamy** requires that people marry and/or have sexual relations within a certain group, such as Jews marrying Jews or African Americans marrying African Americans. **Exogamy** requires marriage outside the group, such as not marrying one's relatives. Even in those countries where marriages are not arranged—including the United States—intensely felt societal, religious, subcultural, and familial rules, however implicit, usually govern our choice of sexual and life partners (see Chapter 7).

Procreation and Socialization of Children

Procreation is an essential function of the family. Although some married couples choose to remain childless, most plan to raise families, and some go to great lengths to have the children they want. Today couples who are unable to conceive naturally for various reasons (e.g., a woman's fallopian tubes may be blocked; a man's sperm count may be too low) have increasing numbers of options (see Chapter 10). Once a couple becomes parents, the family embarks on another critical function, that of socialization. Through **socialization**, children acquire the language, the accumulated knowledge, attitudes, beliefs, and values of their culture and learn the social and interpersonal skills needed to function effectively in society. Some of the socialization is unconscious and may be unintentional, such as teaching culturally accepted stereotypical gender traits (see Chapter 4). Much of the socialization is both conscious and deliberate,

however, such as carefully selecting preschoolers' playmates or raising children in a specific religion.

We are socialized through **roles**, the obligations and expectations attached to a particular situation or position. Families are important role-teaching agents because they define relationships between mothers and fathers, siblings, parents and children, and among relatives and nonfamily members. Some of the rights and responsibilities associated with our roles are not always clear because family structures shift and change. If, for example, you or your parents have experienced divorce or remarriage, have some of the new role expectations been fuzzy or even contradictory? As a later chapter on stepfamilies illustrates, children are often torn between their allegiance to a biological parent and a stepparent because stepparent–stepchild roles are often ambiguous.

Some argue that the family is less powerful today in socializing its young than it was in the past because of changes in other institutions. With more mothers of young children in the work force, child-care centers and preschool programs are playing an increasing role in socialization. Moreover, in states that have extended the length of the academic year, school-age children are spending even less time with their parents. Especially on such politically charged issues as sex education, some parents feel that schools have become too intrusive in socializing their children and have undermined parental authority. These debates are presented in Chapter 6.

Emotional Support

American sociologist Charles Horton Cooley (1864–1929) explored the concept of **primary groups,** characterized by close, long-lasting, intimate, and face-to-face interaction. Later writers introduced the notion of **secondary groups,** characterized by relatively impersonal and short-term relationships and where people work together on common tasks or activities. The family is a critical primary group because it provides the nurturance, love, and emotional sustenance that people need to be happy, healthy, and secure.

In contrast, secondary groups have few emotional ties and its members typically leave the group after attaining a specific goal. While you're taking this course, for example, you, most of your classmates (except for a few close friends, perhaps), and your instructor reflect a secondary group. You've all come together for a quarter or a semester to study marriage and the family. Once the course is over, most of you—especially if you try hard enough—may never see each other again. You might discuss the course with other secondary groups, such as co-workers. They might listen politely, especially if you're the boss, but they probably won't care how you feel about the course. Such primary groups as your family and close friends, in contrast, will usually listen attentively, drive you to class when your car breaks down, offer to do your laundry during exam week, and console you if you don't get that much-deserved "A." There's a simple "test" that distinguishes my primary and secondary groups. I don't hesitate to call the former at 3:00 A.M. to pick me up at the airport, for example, because I know they'll be happy (well, at least willing) to do so.

Social Class Placement

Many scholars characterize the United States as a highly stratified society where *structured social inequality* "defines a social arrangement patterned socially and historically, which is rooted in an ideological framework that legitimates and justifies the subordination of particular groups of people" (Aguirre and Baker, 2000: 4). As a result of this inequality, many women, people at lower socioeconomic levels, and racial and ethnic groups are systematically excluded from full and equal participation in major social institutions such as politics, education, and employment. This exclusion limits *social mobility,* the transition from one social position or social class to another.

To a great extent, our position in society is acquired through our family. We are born into a certain social class, ethnic or racial group, or religious affiliation. Although we can later change some of these memberships, our family shapes our initial definition of who we are (and are not) and our place in society. Social class affects many aspects of family life. Middle-class couples are more likely than their working-class counterparts to share more equally in housework and child rearing, for example (see Chapters 9 and 11). Many studies show—as you will see in the chapters on racial-ethnic families, work, and raising children—that families on the lower rungs of the socioeconomic ladder face a greater risk (than their middle-class counterparts) of adolescent nonmarital childbearing, dropping out of high school, committing street crimes, and neglecting their children.

Although family violence is not limited to low-income families, wife abuse is more likely to occur in low-income than middle-income or upper-income families (see Chapter 14). Men who are employed part time or who are chronically unemployed have high rates of wife battering because they may feel frustrated by not fulfilling society's expectation that men are the family providers (Gelles, 1997).

Diversity in Marriages, Families, and Kinship Systems

Although the basic family functions we have described are common to most cultures, each society has its own norms that specify acceptable marriage and family forms. Thus, there is considerable diversity among families both across and within cultures.

Social scientists often differentiate between a **family of orientation**—the family into which a person is born—and a **family of procreation**—the family a person forms later by marrying and having or adopting children. Each type of family is part of a larger **kinship system,** or network of people who are related by blood, marriage, or adoption. In much of the preindustrial world, which contains most of the world's population, the most common family form is the **extended family,** in which two or more generations (such as the family of orientation and the family of procreation) live together or in adjacent dwellings.

Some researchers are predicting that in industrialized societies where single-parent families are on the increase, extended families may become more common. Such families can make it much easier for a single parent to work outside the home, raise children, and perform needed but time-consuming household tasks. Because remarriage rates are high, however, it remains to be seen whether or not extended families will become widespread.

A variety of formal laws and informal norms regulate inheritance rights, define the pool of eligible marital partners, and determine whether the children will take the surname of the father's, the mother's, or both sides of the family. There are also worldwide variations in the types of marriages and residential patterns that characterize families and kinship systems.

Types of Marriage

There are several types of marriage that are accepted by most societies. In **monogamy,** one man is married to one woman. Because divorce and remarriage are common in the United States and in many European countries, residents of these countries are said to practice **serial monogamy.** That is, they marry several people, but one at a time—they marry, divorce, remarry, redivorce, and so on. **Polygamy,** in which a man or woman has two or more spouses, is subdivided into *polygyny*—one man married to two or more women—and *polyandry*—one woman with two or more husbands. In group marriage, two or more men and two or more women live together and have sexual relations with each other. One anthropologist concluded that only about 20 percent of societies are strictly monogamous. Others permit either polygamy or combinations of polygamy and monogamy (Murdock, 1967). Anthropologists believe that polygyny is common in human societies, especially in Africa and South America, but observe that "accurate censuses of polygyny are generally unavailable" (Hern, 1992: 504).

Although industrial societies forbid polygamy, small pockets of polygynous groups sometimes ignore state laws. The Mormon Church banned polygamy in the late 1800s, but an estimated 50,000 fundamentalists

in the Rocky Mountain states and Canada live in households made up of a man with two or more wives and practice polygamy in accordance with nineteenth-century Mormon religious beliefs. Most law enforcement officials say it is difficult to prosecute bigamy. Marriages are often performed in secret ceremonies and evidence can be skimpy or nonexistent.

Contemporary plural families that consider themselves fundamentalist Mormons are quite diverse on a number of characteristics. In a study of 24 fundamentalist Mormon families, Altman and Ginat (1996) found that, on the average, a plural family had 27 children and 4 wives. Besides working on a full-time basis, some of the men had more than one job to support their large families. Some of the wives worked as receptionists, telephone operators, elementary school teachers, and nurses. The employed wives were also responsible for managing the homes and caring for the children. Most women choose their own marriage partners. In other cases, the girl's family arranges the marriage, or the church president, who is regarded as a prophet with powers of divine revelation, may decide who marries whom even though the people have never met (Johnson, 1991). Families live in three general dwelling arrangements: dyadic arrangements, in which wives and their children live in separate homes, apartments, or areas of a home; communal living arrangements, in which wives live together and share kitchens, living rooms, and other areas but have their own bedrooms or sleeping areas; and mixed dyadic and communal arrangements (Altman and Ginat, 1996).

Polygynous husbands usually follow some type of rotational system in visiting their wives and children. It is the husband, as religious and social patriarch, who theoretically decides with which family he spends time. Most families, however, prefer a flexible system that allows a husband to be with a particular wife and

family on special occasions, such as birthdays and anniversaries, or to deal with problems that require immediate attention. Several explicit norms govern sexual relations: each husband–wife pair "seals off" information about its intimate life from the other wives, and no one snoops into the others' matters:

> Charlotte said that she never discusses with other wives the intimate details of her relationships with Hal, including their sexual relationship. Hal believes it is also important for a man not to disclose intimate things about his relationship with one wife to another wife. A husband needs to be trusted by each wife, he said, and each wife must be confident that her husband will keep their personal affairs and "secrets" private. (Altman and Ginat, 1996: 352)

If these expectations are violated, jealousy, conflict, and even divorce may result. While children and their mothers are strongly attached to each other, fathers have somewhat detached and distant relationships with their children. According to a lawyer who is one of nine wives of a man in Big Water, Utah, polygamy is an idyllic family form:

> I see it as the ideal way for a woman to have a career and children. . . . In our family, the women can help each other care for the children. Women in monogamous relationships don't have that luxury. As I see it, if this life style didn't already exist, it would have to be invented to accommodate career women. (Johnson, 1991: A22)

Despite such accolades, wives who have recently escaped from plural families have raised allegations of forced marriage, sexual abuse, pedophilia, and incest ("Child abuse trial . . . ," 1999; Egan, 1999).

CROSSCULTURAL

The Outside Wife

Temi, 38 years old, is a British-trained doctor in private practice in Lagos, Nigeria. Her father (now retired) was a university professor and her mother was a high school teacher. Temi's first church marriage, in which she had two children, ended in divorce. She is now an outside wife of an eminent businessman, with whom she has a child. She lives in a flat rented by her "husband" on Victoria Island, said to be where the who's-who of Nigeria live.

Temi sees no contradiction in her way of life:

Look, I lived in England for years and I know there you are expected to be monogamously married. Well, I am not in England now, am I? (She laughs.) My first husband was a fine gentleman, but, let's face it, he had no money. Most of our spare time was spent bickering over who was going to pay the bills. It was intolerable. In the

end I decided to quit. Financial straits for me are history. My children are in school abroad. My husband recently bought me a Mercedes Benz, and I am building a house here in Lagos with his help. We also plan to buy a home in the U.S.

Temi's "husband" has two other wives. The church, or inside wife, is a doctor like herself; the other outside wife is an attorney who practices and lives in Lagos (Karanja, 1987: 255–56).

Polygynous marriages can be either formal or informal. In a study of marriage forms in Nigeria, Karanja (1987) differentiates between an inside wife and an outside wife. An "inside wife," who marries a Nigerian man in a church or civil ceremony, typically subscribes to the Christian ideal of monogamy in marriage. Under native law and custom, however, her husband may also "marry" (no official ceremony is performed) an "outside wife." As the box "The Outside Wife" shows, the outside wife has regular sexual relations with her "husband," is financially maintained by him, establishes an autonomous residence, and has children whose paternity is acknowledged by the man. Outside wives, however, have limited social recognition and status and considerably less political and legal recognition than do inside wives. Outside wives are the town-dwelling sweethearts while legal wives run the rural households. When a well-known Nigerian businessman and politician died at age 60 a few years ago, he had four official wives because "under Muslim law, a man may have four wives," and over 40 unofficial wives (Vick, 1998). Some African families that immigrate to Europe continue to live in polygynous families (Randle, 1998).

The very rare practice of polyandry is illustrated by the Todas, a small pastoral tribe that flourished in south India until the late nineteenth century. The Toda woman who married one man became the wife of his brothers—including brothers born subsequent to the marriage—and all lived in the same household. When one of the brothers was with the wife, "he placed his cloak and staff outside the hut as a warning to the rest not to disturb him" (Queen et al., 1985: 19). Marital privileges rotated among the brothers, there was no evidence of sexual jealousy, and one of the brothers, usually the oldest, was the legal father of the first two

or three children. Another brother could become the legal father of children born later. Some anthropologists suggest that polyandry exists in societies where property is difficult to amass because there is a limited amount of available land and the kinship group is more likely to survive in harsh environments if more than one husband contributes to the production of food (Cassidy and Lee, 1989).

Group marriage is also rare, although there are documented cases among the Reindeer Chukchee of Siberia and the Siriono, wandering hunters of the Bolivian jungles (Stephens, 1963). Some groups in the United States like the Oneida community, formed in the mid-1800s, and the countercultural communes formed between 1965 and 1975, experimented with group marriage, but these communities were short-lived (Kephart, 1987).

Residential Patterns

Families also vary in terms of where family members live. The three most common ways in which families establish a residence are patrilocal, matrilocal, and neolocal. In the *patrilocal* residential pattern, newly married couples live with the husband's family. In a *matrilocal* pattern, newly married couples live with the wife's family. A *neolocal* residence is one in which the newly married couple sets up its own residence. Around the world families tend to be extended rather than nuclear, and the most common pattern is residence with the husband's family.

In industrial societies, married couples typically establish their own residences. Since the early 1990s, however, there has been an increasing tendency for young married adults to live with the parents of either the wife or husband or sometimes with the

Like these Nebraska homesteaders, many families in the so-called "good old days" lived in dugouts like this one, made from sod cut from the prairies.

grandparents of one of the partners. About half of all families starting out cannot afford a medium-priced house because they don't have the cash for a down payment and the closing costs (Savage and Fronczek, 1993). Divorced mothers and their children also frequently live with parents or grandparents because of economic reasons (see Chapters 11 and 15).

You see, then, that there is much diversity in family arrangements both in the United States and around the world. As families change, however, we sometimes get bogged down with idealized images of what a "good" family looks like. As the next section shows, our unrealistic expectations can result in dissatisfaction and anger. Instead of enjoying our families, we might waste a lot of time and energy searching for family relationships that exist only in fairy tales.

Myths about Marriage and the Family

There are five common myths that shape our beliefs about marriages and families: (1) families were happier in the past; (2) marrying and having children are the "natural" things to do; (3) "good" families are self-sufficient; (4) every family is a bastion of love and support; and (5) we should all strive to be a "perfect family."

Myths can be *dysfunctional* when they result in negative (although often unintended) consequences that disrupt a family. For example, the myth of the perfect family can make us miserable because we feel there is something wrong with us if we do not live up to some ideal scenario. Instead of accepting our current families, we may put off really living our own

lives while we wait for the perfect mate, or for our children to become what we want them to be, or for our in-laws to accept us. We may become very critical of family members or withdraw emotionally because they don't fit into a mythical mold.

Myths can also divert our attention from widespread social problems that create family crises. If people blame themselves for the gap they perceive between image and reality, they may not recognize the external forces, such as social policies, that create difficulties on the individual level. For example, if we believe that only bad, sick, or maladjusted people beat their children, we will search for solutions at the individual level, such as counseling, support groups, and therapy. As you will see in later chapters, however, many family crises result from large-scale problems such as racism, poverty, and unemployment.

Not all myths are harmful, however. Some are *functional* because they bring people together and promote social solidarity (Guest, 1988). If myths give us hope that we can have a good marriage and family life, for example, we won't give up at the first sign of problems. Myths thus help us maintain our emotional balance during crises. Myths can also free us from guilt or shame. For instance, "We fell out of love" is a more acceptable explanation for getting a divorce than "I used bad judgment" or "I realized that I prefer to live alone."

The same myth may be both functional and dysfunctional. A belief in the decline of the family has been functional, for example, in generating social policies (such as child-support legislation) that try to keep children of divorced families from sinking into poverty. But this same myth is also dysfunctional if people become unrealistically preoccupied with finding self-fulfillment and happiness.

CHANGES

Diary of a Pioneer

Many scholars point out that life on the old frontier was anything but romantic. Malaria and cholera were widespread. Pioneer cabins, because of their darkness, humidity, and warmth, as well as their gaping windows and doors, created ideal environments for mosquitoes. Women and children have been described as doing household tasks with "their hands and arms flailing the air" against hordes of attacking mosquitoes (Faragher, 1986: 90).

Historian Joanna Stratton examined the letters, diaries, and other documents of pioneer women living on the Kansas prairie between 1854 and 1890. The following selection is from a diary of a 15-year-old girl:

A man by the name of Johnson had filed on a claim just west of us and had built a sod house. He and his wife lived there 2 years, when he went to Salina to secure work. He was gone 2 or 3 months and wrote home once or twice, but his wife grew very homesick for her folks in the east and would come over to our house to visit mother.

Mother tried to cheer her up, but she continued to worry until she got bedfast with the fever. At night she was frightened because the wolves would scratch on the door, on the sod, and on the windows, so my mother and I started to sit up nights with her. I would bring my revolver and ammunition and ax and some good-sized clubs.

The odor from the sick woman seemed to attract the wolves, and they grew bolder and bolder. I would step out, fire off the revolver, and they would settle back for a while when they would start a new attack. I shot one through the window and I found him lying dead in the morning.

Finally the woman died and mother laid her out. Father took some wide boards that we had in our loft and made a coffin for her. Mother made a pillow and trimmed it with black cloth, and we also painted the coffin black.

After that the wolves were more determined than ever to get in. One got his head in between the door casing, and as he was trying to wriggle through, mother struck him in the head with an ax and killed him. I shot one coming through the window. After that they quieted down for about half an hour, when they came back again. I stepped out and fired at two of them but I only wounded one. Their howling was awful. We fought these wolves five nights in succession, during which time we killed and wounded four gray wolves and two coyotes.

When Mr. Johnson arrived home and found his wife dead and his house badly torn down by wolves he fainted away. After the funeral he sold out and moved away. (Stratton, 1981: 81)

Rebecca Bryan Boone, wife of the legendary pioneer Daniel Boone, endured months and sometimes even years of solitude when Boone hunted in the woods or went on trading trips. Besides household chores, she chopped wood, cultivated the fields, harvested the crops, and hunted for small game in the woods near her cabin. Although Rebecca was a strong and resourceful woman, she told a traveling preacher that she felt "frequent distress and fear in her heart" (Peavy and Smith, 1994: xi).

Myths about the Past

We often hear that in the "good old days" there were fewer problems, people were happier, and families were stronger. Because of the widespread influence of movies and television, many of us cherish romantic notions of the frontier days. These highly unrealistic images of the family have been portrayed in John Wayne films; the antebellum South of *Gone with the Wind;* and the strong, poor, but loving rural family presented in such television series as *The Waltons* and *Little House on the Prairie* during the 1970s and *Dr. Quinn, Medicine Woman* during the late 1990s.

Many historians maintain that such golden ages never, in fact, existed, and we glorify them only because we know so little about the past (Coontz, 1992). Even in the 1800s, many families experienced desertion by a parent or the births of illegitimate children (Demos, 1986). Family life in the "good old days" was filled with deprivation, loneliness, and physical dangers, as the box "Diary of a Pioneer" illustrates. Families worked very hard and were often decimated by accidents, illness, and disease. Until the mid-1940s, a much shorter life expectancy meant that parental death often led to child placements in extended families, foster care, or orphanages. Thus, the chances of not growing up in an intact family were actually greater in the past than they are now (Walsh, 1993).

The "nostalgia bug" seems to vary by both age and social class. A national survey found, for example, that most people aged 30 to 44 (and especially those who were raising young children) defined the 1970s of their youth as the "good old days" while those aged 60 and older yearned for the 1940s and 1950s. In addition, people with more education and money felt that yesterday was less alluring than today. For example, 44 percent of college graduates compared to 65 percent of people who didn't graduate from high school preferred the past over the present (Crispell, 1996). Thus, the past may be more enticing than the present for two

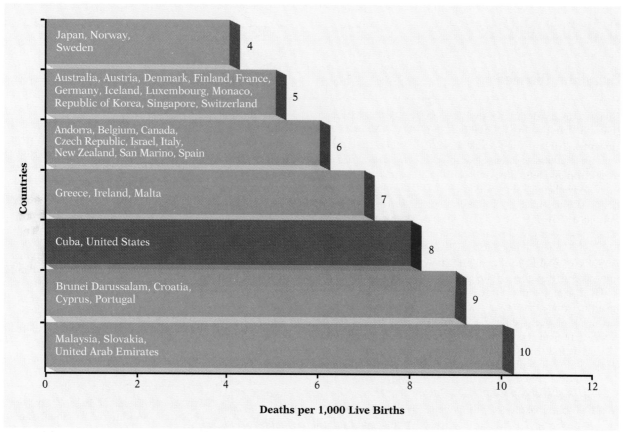

FIGURE 1.1 A Global View: Rates at Which Children Under Age 5 Die, 1998. The under-5 mortality rate is defined as the probability that a child will die between birth and 5 years of age. This statistic reflects many factors, including mother's nutritional health and health knowledge, the availability of prenatal, maternal, and child health services, family income and food intake, and the quality of water and general sanitation (United Nations Children's Fund, 2000).

groups of people: those with lower educational levels whose lives haven't turned out as they had hoped and for older generations who may be feeling prematurely old because of the rapid changes in technology, family structures, and gender roles.

Myths about What Is Natural

Many people have strong opinions about what is natural or unnatural in marriages and families. Although remaining single is more acceptable today than in earlier times, there is still a lingering suspicion that something is wrong with a person who doesn't marry (see Chapter 8). Also, we sometimes have misgivings about childless marriages or about other committed relationships, thinking that "It's only natural to want to get married and have children" or that "Gays are violating human nature." Other beliefs, also surviving from so-called simpler times, claim that family life is a "natural" fact and that women are natural mothers.

The problem with such thinking is that if motherhood is natural, why do many women choose not to have children? If homosexuality is unnatural, how do we explain its existence since time immemorial? If getting married and creating a family are natural, why do millions of men refuse to marry their pregnant partners and then abandon their children?

Myths about the Self-Sufficient Family

Some of our most cherished values in the United States idealize individual achievement, self-reliance, and self-sufficiency. The numerous best-selling books on such topics as parenting, combining work and marriage, and having "good sex" also reflect our belief that we can improve ourselves, that we can pull ourselves up by our bootstraps.

Although we have many choices in our personal lives, few families, past or present, have been entirely self-sufficient. Most of us need some kind of help at one time or another. For example, because of unemployment, underemployment, and recession, the poverty rate has increased by 40 percent since 1970; in the early 2000s, about one in six families lives in poverty. Many of the "working poor" are two-parent families (see Chapter 13). Even though the United States is one of the wealthiest countries in the world, its child poverty rate is two to three times higher than that in Sweden, Switzerland, Norway, West Germany, Canada, Australia, and the United Kingdom (Children's Defense Fund, 1995).

The United States also has a higher infant mortality rate than many other countries. As *Figure 1.1* shows, among a large group of industrialized countries, the United States ranks only twenty-ninth in terms of child well-being and has slipped from its twentieth rank since this book's publication a few years ago. The plight of black children is even worse. Here the United States ranks fortieth, lower even than such developing countries as Costa Rica, Poland, Malaysia, Chile, Sri Lanka, Bulgaria, and Colombia (Children's Defense Fund, 1994). Among industrialized countries, the United States ranks first in terms of military technology, the number of millionaires and billionaires, health technology, and defense spending but seventeenth in low birthweight births, eighteenth in the income gap between rich and poor children, and *last* in protecting children against gun violence (Children's Defense Fund, 2000a). Thus, millions of families are far from being self-sufficient in maintaining their own or their children's well being. (We discuss the effects of poverty in Chapters 11 and 13.)

The middle class isn't self-sufficient either. Historian Stephanie Coontz (1992) points out, for example, that during the 1950s and 1960s many middle-class families were able to prosper not because of family savings or individual enterprise but as a result of federal housing loans, education payments, and publicly financed roads that provided suburbanites with inexpensive travel to their jobs in the city.

The Myth of the Family as a Loving Refuge

The family has been described as a "haven in a heartless world" (Lasch, 1977: 8). Although one of the major functions of the family is to provide love, nurturance, and emotional support, the home can also be one of the most physically and psychologically brutal settings in society. As Chapter 14 shows, an alarming number of children suffer from physical and sexual abuse from family members, and there is a high rate of violence between marital and cohabiting partners.

Many parents experience stress while balancing work and family responsibilities. Moreover, concern about crime, drugs, and unemployment has made many parents pessimistic about their children's future.

In one recent national poll, 33 percent of those surveyed said they expect their children to have a lower quality of life and to be worse off financially than they, the parents, are (Ladd, 1999). The worry that underlies such responses is bound to affect family dynamics. Sometimes family members are unrealistic about the daily strains that they encounter. If, for example, people expect family interactions to be without conflict or disagreements, the level of tension may surge even when routine problems arise. And especially for families with health or economic problems, the home may be loving, but it's hardly a "haven in a heartless world."

Myths about the Perfect Marriage, the Perfect Family

Here's how one woman described the clash between marital expectations and reality:

> *Marriage is not what I had assumed it would be. One premarital assumption after another has crashed down on my head. . . . Marriage is like taking an airplane to Florida for a relaxing vacation in January, and when you get off the plane you find you're in the Swiss Alps. There is cold and snow instead of swimming and sunshine. Well, after you buy winter clothes and learn how to ski and learn how to talk a new foreign language, I guess you can have just as good a vacation in the Swiss Alps as you can in Florida. But I can tell you, doctor, it's one hell of a surprise when you get off that marital airplane and find that everything is far different from what one had assumed. (Lederer and Jackson, 1968: 39)*

Even if partners live together and feel they know each other, many couples may find themselves in the Swiss Alps instead of Florida after tying the knot. Many marriages dissolve because we cling to mirages about conjugal life. After the perfect wedding, the perfect couple must be everything to one another—good providers, fantastic sexual partners, best friends, sympathetic confidantes, stimulating companions, and spiritual soulmates (Rubin, 1985). How realistic are such expectations?

Fables about the perfect family are just as pervasive as those about the perfect marriage. According to historian John Gillis (1996), we all have two families, one that we live *with* (the way families really are) and another we live *by* (the way we would like families to be). Gillis maintains that humans have been imagining and reimagining family throughout recorded history—at least since the late Middle Ages—because the families we are born into and marry into have been too fragile to satisfy most people's need for a sense of continuity, belonging, unity, and rootedness.

Family Values: Three Perspectives on the Changing Family

We introduced this chapter with several definitions of the family, and we discussed the functions of the family, the ways families vary, and some myths about family life. Now we are ready to look at the major theme of this chapter—how the family is changing.

A number of writers have suggested that the family is falling apart. Quite commonly, journalists and scholars refer to the "vanishing" family, "troubled" marriages, and "appalling" divorce statistics as sure signs that the family is disintegrating. Popenoe (1996) contends, for example, that the decline of marriages has been a disaster for fatherhood. Blankenhorn (1995) claims that the most urgent social problem confronting U.S. society is the disappearance of many fathers. Sowell (1996) feels that love has become a meaningless four-letter word because it rarely results in a marital commitment. And if you watch talk shows, you probably wonder whether there are *any* normal families or marriages left in America.

Although many parents worry about the future of their children, some surveys suggest that the general population is optimistic about the family. In a national study of high school seniors, for example, 76 percent said that having a good marriage and family life was "extremely important," up from 73 percent in 1976 (*Public Perspective,* 1994). Another national survey of adults found that "almost 8 out of 10 married Americans said they would give their marriage an A grade, with the bulk of the rest saying they would give their marriage a B" (Newport, 1996: 18). There were few Cs, Ds, or Fs. As you will see in later chapters, however, many people's attitudes and beliefs may reflect the myths we have been discussing and may not always be consistent with their behavior. Some of the most passionate advocates of family life (like many of the divorced authors who pen how-to-succeed-in-marriage books discussed in Chapter 2) may themselves be unwilling to make the personal and job sacrifices that family cohesion often requires.

The status of the family continues to spark debate among three schools of thought. One group contends that the family is deteriorating; a second argues that the family is changing but not deteriorating; and a third, smaller group maintains that the family is stronger than ever.

The Family Is Deteriorating

More than 100 years ago, the *Boston Quarterly Review* issued a dire warning: "The family, in its old sense, is disappearing from our land, and not only our institutions are threatened, but the very existence of our society is endangered" (cited in Rosen, 1982: 299). In the late 1920s, E. R. Groves (1928), a well-known social scientist, warned that marriages were in "extreme collapse." Some of his explanations for what he called the "marriage crisis" and high divorce rates have a surprisingly modern ring: hedonism, too much luxury, independence, financial strain, and incompatible personalities.

Even those who were optimistic a decade ago have become more pessimistic in recent years because recent data on family "decay" are more compelling. Some of these data include an increase in divorces, high rates of children born out of wedlock, millions of "latchkey children," an increase in the number of people deciding not to get married, unprecedented numbers of single-parent families, and a decline of parental authority in the home.

Why have these changes occurred? Those who feel the family is in trouble echo Groves, citing such reasons as lack of individual responsibility, lack of commitment to the family, and just plain selfishness. Many conservative politicians and influential academics argue that the family is deteriorating because most people put their own individual needs over family duties (see Benokraitis, 2000, for a discussion of these perspectives). This school of thought claims that many men and women are unwilling to invest their psychological and financial resources when they have children or give up on marriages too quickly when there are problems (Flanders, 1996; Gallagher, 1996; Popenoe, 1996).

Many of those who believe that the family is deteriorating are headed by *communitarians,* who are politically somewhat more moderate than conservatives on some family issues (such as accepting the idea that many mothers have to work outside the home for economic reasons). Communitarians are an organized social movement group that has enjoyed much media attention since the mid-1990s. Communitarians claim that a relentless pursuit of career goals and financial success diminishes the attainment of marital and parental goals. They contend that there has been a general increase of a sense of entitlement (what people believe they should receive from others) and a decline of a sense of duty (what people believe they should give to others). If married people focus almost exclusively on their personal gratification, according to communitarians, such traditional institutional functions of marriage as early care and socialization of children become a lower priority (Glenn, 1996).

Although few people would discourage adults from pursuing individual happiness within marriage, the family-decline adherents point out that marriage exists for the sake of the children and not just adults. Simply telling children we love them is not enough. Instead of wasting our money on divorce, the argument goes, we should be investing in children by maintaining a stable marriage:

A large divorce industry made up of lawyers, investigative accountants; real estate appraisers and salespeople; pension specialists; therapists and psychologists; expert witnesses; and private collectors of child support has sprung up to harvest the fruits of family discord. However necessary their services, these professionals are the recipients of family income that might, in happier circumstances . . . [be] invested in children. (Whitehead, 1996: 11)

Others feel that educators and scholars generate distorted information about the family. For instance, contemporary philosophers are accused of emphasizing friendship, compatibility, and interpersonal love and being indifferent to the children who are traumatized by divorce and become vulnerable economically (Sommers, 1989), an issue discussed in Chapters 15 and 16. In an evaluation of 20 marriage and family textbooks published during the 1990s, Glenn (1997a) criticized almost all of the books for giving a negative image of marriage, for paying little attention to the beneficial effects of marriage on individuals or society, for devoting little space to the adverse effects of marital disruption and solo parenting on children, and for emphasizing liberal perspectives while ignoring more conservative positions or moderate views on family issues.

Some blame many of the family's problems on mothers who work outside the home. If mothers stayed at home and took care of their children, these writers maintain, we would have less delinquency, fewer high school dropouts, and more children who are disciplined (see Chapters 11 and 13). Other "it's-the-employed-mother's-fault" arguments are more subtle. Gallagher (1996: 184) notes, for example, "Today the young woman who contemplates dropping out of the workforce to care for her own baby, even temporarily, must fight strong cultural forces that seek to keep her tied to the workplace." And, if women had good provider husbands, they could choose "to devote their talents and education and energy to the rearing of their children, the nurturing of family relationships, and the building of community and neighborhood." The implication is that the deteriorating family could be shored up if fathers were breadwinners and mothers were homemakers.

Although many parents worry about their children's welfare (see Chapters 11 and 12), several recent polls suggest that many people don't see family decline as a major societal dilemma. According to the Pew Research Center, for example, in 1994 about 31 percent of the respondents cited crime as a critical problem and 10 percent felt that morality and family values were disintegrating. In 2000, however, respondents were most concerned about education (12 percent), health care and the economy (11 percent in each category), and taxes (7 percent). Only 3 percent felt that morality and family values were problematic (Walczak et al., 2000). Similarly, in a recent Pew poll nearly three-quarters of respondents said they were satisfied overall with the way things were going in their communities. When asked to identify the biggest problems, 18 percent cited urban sprawl and traffic—the same percentage as those citing crime. In contrast, only 6 percent felt that child and teen issues were a major concern (Knickerbocker, 2000). On the one hand, perhaps the family-is-deteriorating proponents are too pessimistic. On the other hand, and as you'll see in Chapters 10, 11, and 13, perhaps many parents are too busy negotiating congested roads, worrying about economic issues, and being anxious about the quality of public education to be concerned about the family's daily life.

The Family Is Changing, Not Deteriorating

Other writers argue that the family has not deteriorated as much as we think, and the changes we are experiencing are extensions of long-standing family patterns. Although more mothers have entered the labor force since 1970, the mother who works outside the home is not a new phenomenon. Mothers sold dairy products and woven goods during colonial times, took in boarders around the turn of the twentieth century, and held industrial jobs during World War II (Chafe, 1972). The number of married women in the labor force doubled between 1930 and 1980 but *quadrupled* between 1900 and 1904 (Stannard, 1979). Some family scholars contend that family problems such as desertion, illegitimacy, and child abuse have *always* existed. Family literature published during the 1930s, for example, included studies that dealt with such issues as divorce, desertion, and family crises due to discord, delinquency, and depression (Broderick, 1988).

Similarly, single-parent families have always existed. The percentage of single-person households has doubled during the past three decades, but this number *tripled* between 1900 and 1950 (Stannard, 1979). Divorce began to be more common during the eighteenth century, when parents could no longer control their adult married children, the importance of romantic love began to grow, and women began to have greater access to divorce (Cott, 1976). There is no question, however, that a greater proportion of people divorce today than in the past (see Data Digest) and that more early marriages are ending in divorce (see Chapter 15). As a result, the decision of many singles to postpone marriage until they are older, more mature, and have stable careers may often be a sound one (see Chapter 8).

There is little empirical evidence that family change is synonymous with family decline. Houseknecht and Sastry (1996) examined the relationship between family decline and child well-being in four industrialized countries—Sweden, the United States, the former West Germany, and Italy. Family decline was a composite of eight variables (which included nonmarital birth rates, divorce rates, and percent of mothers in the labor force with children under 3 years of age). Child well-being included such variables as the percent of children in poverty, deaths of infants from presumed abuse, and juvenile delinquency rates. Houseknecht and Sastry found that children are better off when they live in a society, such as Italy, in which nonmarital birth rates and divorce rates are low. Sweden, however, which has the highest family decline score, also has high child well-being scores. The researchers concluded that generous social and economic policies that are family- and child-oriented alleviate the stress of nontraditional families and their related problems. Thus, family relationships deteriorate not because they are changing but because the changes are not softened by supportive societal policies. Many families are especially fragile during periods of rapid economic change and recessions in the United States, most Western countries, and the rest of the world (Schoettler, 1994).

The Family Is Stronger Than Ever

Do our nostalgic myths about the past misinterpret the contemporary family as weak and on the decline? Some writers think so and assert that family life today is much more loving than in the past. Consider the treatment of women and children in colonial days. If they disobeyed strict patriarchal authority, women and children were often severely punished. And, in contrast to some of our sentimental notions, only a small number of white, middle-class families enjoyed a life that was both gentle and genteel:

> *For every nineteenth-century middle-class family that protected its wife and child within the family circle . . . there was an Irish or a German girl scrubbing floors in that middle-class home, a Welsh boy mining coal to keep the home-baked goodies warm, a black girl doing the family laundry, a black mother and child picking cotton to be made into clothes for the family, and a Jewish or an Italian daughter in a sweatshop making "ladies'" dresses or artificial flowers for the family to purchase. (Coontz, 1992: 11–12)*

Some social scientists argue that, despite myriad problems, families are healthier today than in the past because of the increase of multigenerational relationships: Many people have living grandparents, feel closer to them, and often receive both emotional and economic support from these family members. The current growth of the older segment of the population has produced four-generation families early in the twenty-first century. On the one hand, more adults in their 60s are caring for 80- to 90-year-old parents. On the other hand, more children and grandchildren grow up knowing and enjoying their older relatives (see Chapter 17).

Thus, extended families may be the norm in the future and may strengthen intergenerational family ties.

Whether or not people feel that the family is strong varies across ethnic groups and their length of residence in the United States. In a national study of Latinos and non-Latinos, for example, the researchers found that half of the Latino immigrants surveyed said families were stronger and had greater family unity in the countries they came from. The Latino respondents differed, however, in terms of their degree of assimilation (measured by English-language use and proficiency). For example, while 27 percent of the non-Latino population felt that "in general, the husband should have the final say in family matters," only 38 percent of the Latinos surveyed agreed with this statement. Within the Latino group, however, there were differences by the degree of assimilation. About 23 percent of the "highly assimilated" Latinos agreed with this statement compared to 50 percent of recent immigrants (Deane et al., 2000).

Each of the three schools of thought on the status of the family provides evidence for its position. How, then, can we decide which perspective to believe? Is the family weak, or is it strong? The answer depends in large part on how we define, measure, and interpret family "weakness" and family "strength"—issues we address in Chapter 2. For better or worse, the family has never been static and continues to change.

Trends in Changing Families

It is clear that the family is changing. But how? And why? Changes in the demographic mix in our country, shifts in the racial and ethnic composition of families, and economic transformations have all played a role in these changes.

Demographic Changes

Two demographic changes have had especially far-reaching consequences for family life. First, fertility rates have declined. Since the end of the eighteenth century, American women have been bearing fewer children, having them closer together, and finishing child rearing at an earlier age. Second, the median age of the population has risen from 17 in the mid-1800s to nearly 36 in 2000. Both these shifts mean that a larger proportion of the U.S. population now experiences the so-called "empty-nest syndrome"—the departure from the home of grown children—at an earlier age, as well as earlier grandparenthood and prolonged widowhood. We see other changes in the composition of households, the numbers of singles and cohabitants, the rates of marriage and divorce, the rise of one-parent families, the growth of working mothers, and the rapid increase in the number of stepfamilies (see *Figure 1.2*). All of these changes will be examined more closely in later chapters.

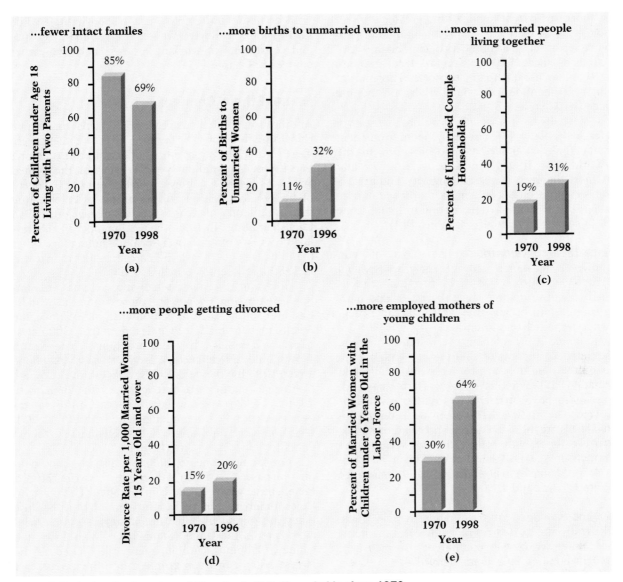

FIGURE 1.2   An Overview of Changes in U.S. Households since 1970

SOURCES: Lugaila, 1998; U.S. Census Bureau, 1999c; Pamuk et al., 1998; Labor Force Statistics, stats.bls.gov/news.release/famee.t04.htm (accessed August 5, 2000)

Changes in Family and Nonfamily Households   The Census Bureau divides households into two major categories: family and nonfamily. A *family household* consists of the two or more persons living together who are related through marriage, birth, or adoption. A single parent with one or more children also comprises a family household. *Nonfamily households* consist of two or more unrelated people who share living quarters. The count of unmarried-couple households is intended mainly to estimate the number of cohabiting couples, but it also includes the small number of households with a roommate, boarder, or paid employee of the opposite sex. An estimated 66 percent of households in 1998 were either nonfamily households or families with no children under age 18, a substantial increase from 55 percent in 1970 (U.S. Census Bureau, 1999c).

As *Figure 1.2a* shows, the percent of children under age 18 living with two parents has decreased from 85 percent in 1970 to 69 percent in 1998. On the other hand, the percent of children under age 18 living in one-parent families has more than doubled during this same period (see Data Digest). Part of the increase in one-parent families is due to the surge of births to unmarried women (see *Figure 1.2b*).

Singles and Cohabitants   Singles make up one of the fastest-growing groups. The decrease in household size is due, among other reasons, to fewer children per family, more one-parent families, and greater age segregation—that is, the tendency of young and old people to live separately. The numbers of cohabitants have also climbed since 1970 (see *Figure 1.2c*) and are expected to increase due to greater societal acceptance of living together and many young adults' postponing marriage (see Chapters 7 and 8).

The percentage of people living alone has grown considerably since 1970. For baby-boom women in particular (**baby boomers** are people born in the post–World War II generation between 1946 and 1964), more divorces, increased longevity, and precarious retirement incomes could mean that fewer midlife and older women will have the option of living alone even if this is their preference (Chalfie, 1995).

Marriage-Divorce-Remarriage As most of you know, divorces have increased over the years (see *Figure 1.2d*). One out of every two first marriages is expected to end in divorce. Teen marriages and marriages entered into because the woman became pregnant are especially likely to unravel.

Stepfamilies are becoming much more common. An estimated 25 percent of children live with a stepparent by the time they are 16 years old (Miller and Moorman, 1989). Whether or not a couple has children seems to have little effect on either divorce or remarriage. The finding that women with lower educational levels are more likely to divorce and/or remarry than are those with college degrees suggests the importance of age and maturation in lasting marriages. We examine marriage, divorce, and remarriage in Chapters 9, 15, and 16.

One-Parent Families As more adults remain single into their 30s and as divorce rates increase, the number of children living with one parent also increases. One-parent families have almost tripled—from 9 percent in 1960 to nearly 28 percent in 1998 (U.S. Census Bureau, 1999c). The proportion of children living with a divorced parent decreased slightly between 1980 and 1990, but those living with a never-married parent have increased considerably—from around 4 percent in 1960 to nearly 37 percent in 1998. Of all one-parent families, 84 percent are mother–child families (Lugaila, 1998). One-parent households are discussed in several later chapters.

Employed Mothers The increased participation of mothers in the labor force has been one of the most important changes in family roles. Two-earner couples with children rose from 31 percent in 1976 to 62 percent in 1998 (U.S. Census Bureau, 1999c). Almost 60 percent of all mothers with children under 1 year of age are in the labor force. In addition, six out of every ten married women with children under 6 years old are in the labor force (see *Figure 1.2e*). This means that a substantial number of families is now coping with domestic and employment responsibilities while raising young children. We explore the characteristics and constraints of working mothers and two-earner couples in Chapter 13.

Racial-Ethnic Changes

Another source of change reflects the racial and ethnic transformations of U.S. families. In 1990, there were more than 130 distinct ethnic or racial groups among the almost 250 million people living in the United States. As *Figure 1.3* shows, by 2025 almost 40 percent of the U.S. population will be people of color. More than 16 million Americans speak a language other than English at home. In 1990, the total number of U.S. residents 5 years old and over speaking a language other than English at home was 38 percent higher than it was in 1980 (U.S. Census Bureau, 1993).

Some of the fastest-growing groups of non-English-speaking people are those from the Middle East and Southeast Asia. Nationwide, for example, the Asian-language market includes more than 300 newspapers (92 dailies), 50 radio programs, 75 television shows, and miscellaneous products such as phone directories. By the mid-1990s one Orange County, California, station was broadcasting in Vietnamese 18 hours a day and another southern California station was entirely Korean-language (Trumbull, 1995). One company publishes a Chinese-language Yellow Pages for New York City (Dortch, 1997).

For the first time, in 2000, Spanish-speaking people surpassed African Americans as the largest racial/ethnic group in the United States. There are no exact numbers for the Latino population because many are "undocumented immigrants"—people who have entered the United States illegally. In 1990, the Chinese, Filipinos, and Japanese still ranked as the largest Asian American groups. Since then, Southeast Asians, Indians, Koreans, Pakistanis, and Bangladeshis have registered much faster growth. Mexicans, Puerto Ricans, and Cubans were the dominant groups among Latinos, but people from mostly Central and South American countries—such as El Salvador, Guatemala, Colombia, and Honduras—have been immigrating in very high numbers. We examine ethnic families in every chapter, especially Chapter 12.

Why Are Families Changing?

Clearly, we are seeing changes in the family, and these changes reflect both the choices people make (such as choosing to marry later or to divorce) and the constraints that limit those choices (such as economic problems or caring for elderly parents). To study people's choices, social scientists often take a **micro-level perspective**, focusing on small-scale patterns of individuals' social interaction in specific settings. To understand the

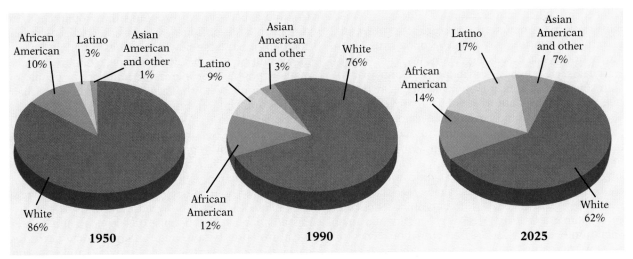

FIGURE 1.3   U.S. Racial and Ethnic Composition, 1950–2025

Sources: Population Reference Bureau, 1988; U.S. Bureau of the Census, *http://www.census.gov/population/www.pop-profile/nat-proj.html*, (October 24, 1997).

constraints that limit people's options, social scientists use a **macro-level perspective,** focusing on large-scale patterns that characterize society as a whole. Both perspectives and how they interface are crucial in understanding the family.

Micro-level Influences on the Family

Consider the following scenario: Two students meet in college, fall in love, marry after graduation, find well-paying jobs, and live the good life—feasting on brie and lobster, driving a Corvette, and the like. Then they have an unplanned child. The wife quits her job to take care of the baby, the husband loses his job, and the wife goes to work part time. She has difficulty balancing her multiple roles of mother, wife, and employee. The stress and arguments between the partners increase, and the marriage ends. When asked what went wrong here, most of my students take a micro viewpoint and blame the individuals: "They should have saved some money." "They didn't need a Corvette." "Haven't they heard about contraceptives?" and so on.

On the one hand, there's much to be said for micro-level perspectives. As you will see throughout this book, some of the biggest societal changes that have had a major impact on families began with the efforts of one person who took a stand on an issue. For example, Mary Beth Whitehead's refusal to give up her right to see the baby she bore as a surrogate mother and the ensuing court battles created national debates about the ethics of the new reproductive technologies. As a result, many states have instituted surrogacy legislation.

On the other hand, micro explanations should be kept in perspective. Many marriage and family

textbooks stress the importance of individual choices, but some give short shrift to the importance of macro-level variables. Micro analyses are limited, and they cannot explain some of the things over which families have very little control. For these broader analyses, we must turn to macro explanations.

Macro-level Influences on the Family

Constraints such as economic forces, technological innovations, popular culture, social movements, and family policies limit our choices. These are broad social issues that require macro-level explanations.

Economic Forces   The Industrial Revolution and urbanization brought about widespread changes that affected the family (see Chapter 3). By the late eighteenth century, factories replaced the domestic industries that had employed large numbers of women and children. As family members became less self-sufficient and worked outside the home, parents' control over their children diminished. In the latter half of the twentieth century, many manufacturers moved their companies to third world countries to increase their profits. Such moves resulted in relocations and unemployment for many U.S. workers. Job dissatisfaction, unemployment, and financial distress disrupted many marital relationships and families.

Many African Americans have been concerned that immigration, another external factor, is diminishing their job opportunities. As you've seen in the previous section, Latinos and people from Asian countries constitute the fastest-growing groups in the United States as we move into the twenty-first century. Because a large proportion of African Americans are still employed in skilled and semiskilled blue-collar jobs, the influx of new immigrants, who are also competing for such jobs, constitutes a serious economic threat to many working-class African Americans and, consequently, to their families (see Chapters 12 and 13).

In some areas, concern among whites is rising. In 1994, for example, California voters approved Proposition 187, which would have denied schooling, medical care, and other welfare benefits to undocumented immigrants. Proposition 187 died in 2000 after Governor Gray Davis decided not to appeal a federal court ruling that the proposition was unconstitutional. Despite the setback, some politicians feel that most Californians want a measure that prohibits undocumented immigrants from receiving benefits and may launch another effort in 2001 (as this book goes to press). At that time, however, demographers predict that California will become the first big state in the nation in which Latinos outnumber whites and other racial groups. Other big states with large Latino populations—like Texas, Florida, New York, and Illinois—will not catch up with California's diversity until around 2050 ("White majority fading . . . ," 2000). If large numbers of Latinos register to vote, a state's policies on providing services to both legal and undocumented immigrants may change quite a bit.

As the U.S. economy has shifted, millions of low-paying service jobs have replaced higher-paying manufacturing jobs. This has wrought havoc with many families' finances and has contributed to the rise in the number of employed mothers. At the other end of the continuum, the booming high-tech sector requires people to spend more time learning the new technologies. Other effects have included postponing marriage, postponing having children, or both.

Technological Innovations Advances in medical and other health-related technologies have led both to a decline in birth rates and to a prolongation of life. On the one hand, the invention and availability of the birth-control pill in the early 1960s meant that women could prevent unwanted pregnancies, pursue a higher education, and seek long-term jobs. Improved methods of pre- and postnatal care have released women from the need to bear six or seven children so that one or two will survive. On the other hand, because the average man or woman can now expect to live into his or her 70s and beyond, poverty after retirement is more likely. Medical services can eat up savings, and the middle-aged—sometimes called the "sandwich generation"—cope with both raising their own children and helping their aged parents (see Chapters 11 and 17).

Televisions, videocassette recorders (VCRs), microwave ovens, and personal computers have also affected families. The effects have been both positive and negative. On the negative side, for example, multiple television sets in a home may dilute parental control and supervision of programs that young children watch. In addition, the "Internet addicted"—whether children or parents—may interact less often with family members. On the positive side, computers have made it possible for increasing numbers of people to work at home, with the result that they may see their spouses and children more often.

Some observers feel that electronic mail (e-mail) and discussion lists are intrusive because enthusiasts, especially, might replace close offline relationships with superficial but time-consuming online relationships (see Wellman, 1997). College students who spent four to seven hours a day online for nonacademic reasons may experience low grades and the risk of dismissal, poorer health because of sleep loss, and greater social isolation because high Internet usage decreases participation in extracurricular activities and opportunities to meet new people (Reisberg, 2000). In the general population, people who spent more than ten hours a week on the Internet reported a decrease in social activities and less time talking on the phone to friends and family (Nie and Erbring, 2000). On the other hand, e-mail has encouraged long-distance conversations between parents, children, and relatives that would otherwise wilt because of busy schedules or high telephone costs. Family members who are scattered coast to coast, for example, can now exchange photos on their own Web pages (including background music and voice commentary), organize family reunions, and track down distant relatives or trace one's ancestral roots (Brady, 1999; Kanaley, 2000).

In the mid-1990s, several observers noted a racial "digital divide" because white households were more likely than minority families to have computers and Internet access. More recently, however, studies are finding that the digital divide reflects social class and generational differences rather than race, ethnicity, or gender. In a recent survey of 80,000 U.S. households, for instance, the researchers found that almost 80 percent of people with college educations had Internet access compared to 30 percent of those with a high school education. As might be expected, people over 65 were considerably less likely to use computers than those under age 40. In terms of race and ethnicity, 69 percent of Asian households were online compared to 47 percent of Latinos, 43 percent of whites, and 33 percent of blacks. Most of these households were middle class and earned $50,000 and over per year (Walsh et al., 2000).

Popular Culture Popular culture—which includes television, pop music, magazines, radio, advertising, sports, hobbies, fads, fashions, and movies—is one of our major sources of information and misinformation about our values, roles, and family life. Television is especially influential in transmitting both facts and fictions. According to TV–Free America, a national nonprofit organization, in a 65-year lifetime, the average

American will spend nine years in front of a TV set (Holmstrom, 1997).

In their studies of how people in the United States use time, Robinson and Godbey (1999) found that television viewing increased from 10.4 hours a week in 1965 to 15.1 hours a week in 1985 while reading decreased from 3.6 hours a week to 2.8 hours a week. In 1985, the average American adult spent 40 percent of her or his free time watching television and 17 percent of the time (the next highest category) socializing, in the form of visits, meals, parties, receptions, and other informal activities. People said they spent the least amount of time in religious activities and at cultural events (.9 hour each per year). Robinson and Godbey also reported that teenagers (aged 12 to 17) watch television more than 17 hours a week and children aged 3 to 11 average over 19 hours a week. During the "family hour" (between 8 and 9 P.M.), 6 million children aged 2 to 11 watch television—more children than view Saturday morning or weekday afternoon programs (Zurawik, 1996).

Compared to even five years ago, today there is a sizable number of programs on black families. Even though Asian and Latino families are huge consumers of prime-time television, they're virtually invisible, except for an occasional role or two (such as Jimmy Smits's past character on *NYPD Blue*). According to a study by the Center for Media and Public Affairs, Latinos were less visible in prime time in the 1990s than they were in the 1950s (Gerbner, 1993). In the music industry, some Latino singers like Ricky Martin, Marc Anthony, Jennifer Lopez, and Shakira are "hot." Of the several dozen new comedies and dramas presented by the four major networks during the 1999/2000 season, however, not one had a Latino in a leading role (Haubegger, 1999). Not only do Latinos comprise only 1 percent of all characters portrayed on television, but they are more likely than any other group to be depicted as poor or criminal (Mittelstadt, 1994). There are, however, an increasing number of television series dominated by African American characters (see *Table 1.1*). Some see this as progress; others have blasted the shows for caricaturing black households.

Consider, also, how television portrays working-class families, especially some of the most recent and long-running hit series. On the one hand, such shows as *Roseanne, The Simpsons, King of the Hill,* and *Everybody Loves Raymond* depict the families as valuing close family ties and dealing with such real-life problems as paying bills, facing unemployment, and responding (although nervously) to their children's sexual development. On the other hand, the husbands are typically manipulated by their more intelligent wives (or ex-wives as in *Grace Under Fire,* now in syndication), hang around with dim-witted pals, and have little authority in the home. In *Married . . . with Children,* one of the longest-running and popular working-class sitcoms, the family members are empty-headed and crude. They lie, steal, cheat, manipulate, connive, and constantly insult each other. Is this what most working-class households are really like? Or are such programs hackneyed Hollywood images of working-class families?

Television portrayals of families are little more than fiction, of course. The problem is that most children can't differentiate between fiction and reality (see Chapter 4). Many people report that after watching a music video, listening to the song later frequently brings up visual images from the video (Jhally, 1995). Isn't it even more difficult for young children to separate stereotypical clutter from authentic representations of ethnic or working-class families? If *Married . . . with Children* is a spoof of sappy middle-class family sitcoms of the past (such as *Leave It to Beaver*), how many young children can distinguish between farce and fact?

Social Movements Over the years, a number of social movements have changed family life. The civil rights movement of the 1960s had a considerable impact on most U.S. families, black and white. Because of affirmative action legislation, many African Americans and Latinos were able to take advantage of educational and economic opportunities that improved their families' socioeconomic status (see Chapter 12).

The women's movements, in the late 1800s and especially during the 1970s, transformed many women's roles and, consequently, family life. As women gained more rights in law, education, and employment, many became less financially dependent on men and started questioning traditional assumptions about gender roles. The upside of this is that women—particularly white, middle-class women—enjoyed increased personal and professional options and provided their children with less stereotypical female role models. The downside, according to some observers, is that when women became sexually "liberated," they entered willingly into nonmarital sexual relationships (see Chapter 6). The result was more out-of-wedlock children who were not supported by their biological fathers.

The gay rights movement that began in the 1970s challenged discriminatory laws in such areas as housing, adoption, and employment. Although many lesbian women and gay men (as well as sympathetic heterosexuals) feel that the challenges have so far resulted in very minimal changes, some shifts have in fact occurred. Children with a gay or lesbian parent, for example, are less likely to be as stigmatized as they were a decade ago (see Chapter 11). As later chapters show, homophobia is still widespread in U.S. society. Some companies, however, are providing benefits to the gay or lesbian partners of employees; many community colleges, colleges, and universities offer courses in gay and lesbian studies; and a number of adoption agencies now assist lesbians and gays who want to become parents. Increasingly, moreover, city governments and some states are recognizing civic unions as legitimate. As a result, many gay partners now enjoy

On Mother's Day in May, 2000, hundreds of thousands of women across the United States and across all walks of life converged on Washington, D.C. for the Million Mom March. The purpose of the march was to protest lenient gun-control laws that result in the deaths of children and teenagers through suicide, accidents, and homicides in urban neighborhoods and shooting sprees in suburban schools.

the same (or similar) legal and economic rights as their heterosexual counterparts (see Chapters 7–11).

When the last edition of this textbook was published in 1999, the Promise Keepers, a small but influential group of (mostly white male) evangelical Christians, dominated the mainstream media. Among other things, the Promise Keepers sought to be faithful to their wives, to not pursue sex without love, and to participate more equally in child care. Since then, the Promise Keepers have been replaced by several other grassroots social movements that seek to decrease high cohabitation and divorce rates and the father's absence from the family.

Divorce rates have declined since the 1980s (see Chapter 15). Nonetheless, people who are alarmed by marital dissolution and the increase in cohabitation rates buoy the Marriage Movement. In its *Statement of Principles*, for example, the Marriage Movement pledges to "turn the tide on marriage and reduce divorce and unmarried childbearing, so that each year more children will grow up protected by their own two happily married parents, and so that each year more adults' marriage dreams will come true" (*Marriage Movement . . .*, 2000: 3). Among other things, the Marriage Movement seeks to repeal no-fault divorce laws, to reduce both the rates of and state benefits for out-of-wedlock children, to promote abstinence among young people, to increase funding on marriage-supportive research, and to embrace women's homemaker roles. In addition, the Marriage Movement encourages proponents to lobby lawmakers to pass state "covenant marriage" laws that require couples to take mandatory pre-marital counseling

classes and "marital skills" programs (*States ponder . . .*, 1999).

A related grassroots movement that has received much media attention is the National Fatherhood Initiative. While this group encourages all fathers—regardless of marital status—to be involved in parenting, the organization's founder and president argues that people "need to be honest that the best situation for a child to grow up in is within the context of their two continuously married parents" (Gardner, 2000: 13). Although countermovements have emerged that promote divorce as in the best interest of the child (see Chapter 15), the National Fatherhood Initiative has received much attention from the print and television media (see, for example, "Dads lacking . . ." 1999).

Communitarians, a group that you met earlier in this chapter, support the Marriage Movement, the National Fatherhood Initiative, and similar organizations. Some communitarians, however, are more accepting than the other groups in developing quality child-care facilities and services to help working parents and in implementing pro-family economic policies. Many communitarians believe, however, that most of our current social problems (like juvenile delinquency, high divorce rates, and high out-of-wedlock birth rates) could be solved by promoting "traditional" family values. These values include enhancing marital stability, reinforcing parental responsibility, reining in children's premature sexualization, and curbing the excessive society-wide individualism that endangers many children's well-being (see Elshtain et al., 1993). In contrast to many liberals, communitarians claim that many family problems are not due to macro-level variables, such as government policies that subsidize middle-class families but penalize poor and working-class families. Instead, communitarians maintain, family decline is due to micro-level variables such as "self-absorbed baby boomers" and a "me-first" attitude that has eroded family loyalty and responsibility.

Family Policies Government policy affects practically every aspect of family life. Thousands of rules and regulations, both civil and criminal, at the local, state, and federal levels, govern domestic matters: laws about when and whom we can marry, how to dissolve a marriage, how children will fare after a divorce, how we treat one another within the home, and even how we dispose of our dead. Families do not just passively accept policy changes, however. Parents themselves have played critical roles in such major social policy changes as the education of handicapped children and joint custody of children after divorce. Chapter 18 and sections of several other chapters examine the effects of government policy on families in greater detail.

A Cross-Cultural and Global Perspective

This textbook includes material both on U.S. subcultures (American Indians, African Americans, Asian Americans, and Latinos) and on cultures in other countries for a number of reasons. First, unless you are a full-blooded American Indian, your kin were slaves or immigrants to this country. They contributed their cultural beliefs and practices to the shaping of current North American family institutions. U.S. families today are a mosaic of many cultural, religious, ethnic, and racial groups. A traditional white, middle-class model is not adequate for understanding our marriages and families.

A second reason for this cross-cultural approach is that the world is shrinking. Compared to even ten years ago, more people are traveling outside the United States, more students from abroad attend North American colleges and universities, and more exchange programs for students and scholars are offered at all educational levels. Furthermore, the dramatic events of the 1990s in Eastern Europe, South Africa, and Central America have enabled oppressed countries that had been closed to the rest of the world since 1940 to become independent and to open up to trade, travel, and education. We should be aware of family practices and customs in other cultures.

A third reason for the text's perspective is that U.S. businesses are beginning to recognize the importance of understanding cross-cultural differences. Since the late 1980s, more companies have been requiring their employees to take crash courses about other cultures before they are sent abroad. For example, one of my students who won a job with a Fortune 500 company felt she had gained an edge over some very tough competition because of her knowledge of Portuguese and of Brazil's cultural institutions.

Business is not the only sector that has learned to appreciate diversity. Many educators believe that a multicultural perspective is becoming essential to the professional preparation of researchers, faculty, counselors, and therapists who will study and interact with people from many different social, economic, and national backgrounds during the twenty-first century. Increasingly, moreover, U.S. higher education institutions are forming ties with their counterparts or with private industry in other countries to exchange information about technology, to sponsor research in disease control and prevention, or to establish cooperative networks in business ventures (Chapman and Claffey, 1998).

Finally, understanding other countries challenges our notion that U.S. marriage forms are "natural" or inevitable. According to Hutter (1988), "Americans have been notorious for their lack of understanding and ignorance of other cultures. This is compounded by their gullible ethnocentric belief in the superiority of all things American and not only has made them unaware of how others live and think but also has given them a distorted picture of their own life." Hutter's perspective—and that of this book—is that understanding other people helps us understand ourselves.

Conclusion

Families are transforming themselves rather than destroying themselves. Although there have been *changes* in family structures, families of all kinds desire relations that are caring, supportive, comforting, and enduring. There is nothing inherently better about one type of family form over another. Family structures don't appear by themselves. People create families that meet their needs for love and security.

These greatly expanded *choices* in how families are structured and function mean that the definition of family no longer reflects the interests of any one social class, gender, sex group, or racial group. This fluidity makes some people nervous because it generates new questions. Who, for example, will ensure that our children will grow up to be healthy and responsible adults if both parents must work outside the home? Or, is it possible to pursue personal happiness without sacrificing our obligations to other family members?

Our choices are often limited by *constraints*—especially at the macro level—due to economic and political policies. Dealing with changes, choices, and constraints requires our having as much information about the family as possible. The next chapter shows how family scientists conduct research on families, gathering data that make it possible for us to track the trends described in this and other chapters and to make informed decisions about our choices.

SUMMARY

1. Although the nuclear family—composed of husband, wife, and children—is still predominant in U.S. society, the definition of family has been challenged to include such less traditional arrangements as single parents, childless couples, foster parents, and siblings sharing a home. Advances in reproductive technology have opened up the possibility of still more varied redefinitions of the family.

2. The family continues to fulfill such basic functions as producing and socializing children, providing family members with emotional support, legitimizing and regulating sexual activity, and placing family members in society.

3. Marriages, families, and kinship systems vary in terms of whether marriages are monogamous or polygamous; whether familial authority is vested in the man or in the woman or both share power; and whether a new family resides with the family of the man or of the woman or creates its own home.

4. The many deep-rooted myths about the family include erroneous beliefs about how the family was in "the good old days"; the "naturalness" of marriage and family as human interpersonal and social arrangements; the self-sufficiency of the family; the family as a refuge from outside pressures; and the "perfect family."

5. Social scientists generally agree that the family is changing, but they disagree as to whether it is changing in drastic and essentially unhealthy ways, whether it is simply continuing to adapt and adjust to changing circumstances, or whether it is changing in ways that will ultimately make the family stronger.

6. A number of changes are occurring in U.S. families: There is more racial and ethnic diversity; membership is more varied than that of the traditional nuclear family; and there are more single-parent families, stepfamilies, and families in which the mother works outside the home.

7. The reasons for changes in the family can be analyzed on two levels. Micro-level explanations emphasize individual behavior—the choices that people make and the personal and interpersonal factors that influence these choices. Macro-level explanations focus on large-scale patterns that characterize society as a whole and may constrain individual options. Some constraints arise from economic factors, technological advances, the popular culture, social movements, and government policies that affect families.

8. Understanding the family requires an appreciation of racial, ethnic, religious, and cultural diversity, both at home and around the world.

KEY TERMS

marriage   2
norm   2
common-law marriage   2
bigamy   3
family   3
fictive kin   4
nuclear family   4
incest taboo   4
matriarchy   4

patriarchy   4
endogamy   6
exogamy   6
socialization   6
roles   6
primary groups   6
secondary groups   6
family of orientation   7
family of procreation   7

kinship system   7
extended family   7
monogamy   7
serial monogamy   7
polygamy   7
baby boomers   18
micro-level perspective   18
macro-level perspective   19

Examine U.S. and Global Family Trends

Does your instructor want you to compare family trends and patterns in the United States and worldwide? Here are a few sites to get you started:

International Data Base at the U.S. Census Bureau offers a variety of country-level data, including marital status, family planning, ethnicity, religion, labor force, and employment.

www.census.gov/ftp/pub/ipc/www/idbnew.html

Statistical Abstract of the United States, also from the U.S. Census Bureau, provides a wealth of information about marriage, remarriage, family characteristics, living arrangements, divorce, and hundreds of other variables.

www.census.gov/statab/www

The Population Reference Bureau maintains four sites that may be valuable in your research:

www.prb.org, the main Website, offers excerpts or full text of many of the Population Reference Bureau's publications on U.S. and international issues

www.popnet.org allows the visitor to view a clickable world map and provides a comprehensive directory of population-related Websites

www.ameristat.org gives summaries—in graphics and text—of 14 demographic characteristics of the U.S. population, including marriage and family, income and poverty, fertility, and race and ethnicity.

www.measurecommunication.org is devoted to disseminating information and data on population, health, and nutrition in developing countries.

The **Internet Scout Project,** an invaluable research resource, offers weekly summaries of recent sites on many family-related issues.

scout.cs.wisc.edu

And more . . . If your instructor assigns a "do-whatever-interests-you" project, look at www.prenhall. com/benokraitis for Websites that include Asian and Latino URLs, black communities, social movements (such as the women's movement, communitarianism, and the Marriage Movement), global statistics, the social and economic implications of information technologies, groups that endorse and denounce polygamy, and an online comic strip of a middle-class Latino family.

Studying Marriage and the Family

DATA DIGEST

■ Of all marriage and family research studies, **more than 65 percent rely on surveys;** fewer than 5 percent use the observation method.

■ **A typical interview can cost about $75 an hour,** including training, pretesting, transportation, wages, and follow-up interviews.

■ The **return of census questionnaires** has decreased over the years: 78 percent in 1970, 75 percent in 1980, 65 percent in 1990, and 65 percent in 2000.

■ During the 2000 census, the **cost per individual mailing was $2.00 compared to**

$36.00 every time a census worker visited a nonrespondent's home as part of a follow-up when the form wasn't filled out.

■ **People are less trusting of some types of surveys** than of others. In a recent study, 81 percent of respondents were willing to rely on scientific studies that describe the causes of disease, 63 percent believed consumer survey reports of how many people like a particular product, but only 54 percent said they trusted the results of general public opinion polls.

SOURCES: Nye, 1988; Crossen, 1994; Edmonston, 1999; Libbon, 2000.

Most of you probably remember the national media attention in the case of Elián González, a six-year-old boy who survived while his mother drowned during an escape from Cuba. The boy's relatives in Miami fought to keep him in the United States. After about six months of negotiations and court rulings, the U.S. Attorney General's Office "broke into" the relatives' home and took Elián. In its weekly online poll of various issues, *Newsweek* magazine published the following results:

"Did the U.S. go too far by forcibly taking Elián?" (39,167 responses)

68% No, it was the only choice

11% No, but the display of guns was excessive

14% Yes, the Feds should have given the talks more time

7% Yes, the boy should stay with his family in Miami (*Newsweek,* 2000: 6)

Do you see any problems with this question? How neutral, for example, are such words as "go too far" and "forcibly"? Although precoded responses ("yes" or "no") are easy to key into a computer, do such black-and-white choices capture respondents' complex, moderate, or "don't know" views? In addition, are such online polls and their results representative of the U.S. population in general?

Scholarly publications are usually "refereed"— that is, peers review the research before it is published. In contrast, the mass media are relatively immune to criticism, even when their reports are biased, simplistic,

or wrong (Gans, 1979). As a result, many people who rely exclusively on the media for information often get a very skewed picture of marriages and families, as well as of other aspects of life.

This chapter will help you evaluate the enormous amount of information we encounter on a daily basis. It will also help you to understand how the information in this text was gathered. We begin with a discussion of why a basic understanding of family theory and research is important.

Why Are Theories and Research Important in Our Everyday Lives?

The very words *theory* and *research* often intimidate people. Many of us may distrust statistics because they often challenge generally accepted beliefs. Most of my students, for example, believe that cohabitation decreases the chance of divorce. When we examine the studies that show this is not the case (Chapter 8), they are surprised. There are two very practical reasons why theory and research are important to us: They can help us understand ourselves and our families, and they can make us better informed "consumers" as we negotiate our way in our own marriages and families.

They Help Us Understand Our Family Life

Theoretical perspectives and research can illuminate many aspects of our everyday family lives. For example, does spanking correct bad behavior? Suppose a 2-year-old throws a temper tantrum at a family barbecue.

An adult comments, "What that kid needs is a good smack on the behind." Another person immediately disagrees: "All kids go through this stage. Just ignore it." Who's right? In fact, empirical studies show that neither ignoring a problem nor inflicting physical punishment stops misbehavior (see Chapter 11).

Theory and research are also important to family practitioners. If counselors, clinicians, and other professionals who work with families rely exclusively on anecdotal and personal experiences, their effectiveness will be limited. Instead, successful intervention requires understanding cultural variations, the wider context in which the family is embedded, and a firm grasp of research results that enhance the efficacy of service providers in the helping professions (McGoldrick and Giordano, 1996; Hanson, 1998).

They Help Us Become Knowledgeable Consumers of Information

Our world is becoming more quantitative. It is rare to pick up a magazine or newspaper and not see numbers that affect some aspect of our lives. Medical researchers numb us with the probabilities of dying earlier than expected because of our genetic inheritance, lifestyle, or environment. We are inundated with information on the importance of exercising, lowering cholesterol levels, and not smoking. We hear frightening statistics about the possibility of being mugged, robbed, raped, or having our children abused by a caretaker, relative, or family member.

One of the largest growth industries is parenting magazines. An estimated 108 parenting magazines compete for 5 million subscribers. Some of the information we get is sound, but some is biased or generated by unlicensed, self-proclaimed "experts" who know less about family life than you do. As the box "Popular Magazines and Self-Help Books: Let the Reader Beware" shows, one of the best ways to protect yourself against quacks, charlatans, and con artists is to be informed.

Students in family courses where faculty incorporate research methods may feel that they and their instructors are on different planets. I've heard my students grumble at the beginning of a semester, for example, that "I took this course to find out how to avoid a divorce after I get married. Who cares about divorce studies!" By learning to evaluate empirical evidence, however, you will be able to make more informed decisions about finding a suitable mate and, quite possibly, protecting against a future divorce. In addition, writes one sociology professor, knowing something about *how* social scientists study families will enhance your ability to think more critically and to vote intelligently on public policy issues concerning families:

I'd like to think that students carry with them some of the sociological perspectives we discussed and some knowledge about the limitations of data and the importance of comprehensive information. When they hear that the American family is disintegrating, I hope that some will respond: "How are you measuring 'disintegration'? . . . Let me see your data." (Watkins, 1996: A72)

This chapter is not meant to transform you into a researcher, but it will help you ask some of the right questions when you are deluged with popular nonsense. To learn how to evaluate biased polls like the one cited at the beginning of this chapter and how reputable social research is conducted, you need to understand something about the most influential theories of marriage and the family that guide social science investigation.

Theoretical Frameworks for Understanding Families

Someone once observed that "I used to have six theories about parenting and no children. Now I have six children and no theories." This quip suggests that there is no relationship between theory and practice. As you saw in Chapter 1, however, theories about families are often translated into policies and laws that affect all of us. Ideas have consequences. Those who theorize that the family is disintegrating might propose such micro-level solutions as cutting off welfare benefits for unmarried mothers. In contrast, those who theorize that the family is changing might propose such macro-level remedies as providing girls and young women with access to good schools and jobs that discourage early sexual involvement and childbearing.

As people struggle to understand family-related processes, they develop theories. A **theory** is a set of statements that explains why a phenomenon occurs. Theories guide our research, help us to analyze our findings, and, ideally, offer solutions for social problems.

Wesley Burr (1995) compares the nature of theories to the fable of the six blind men who felt different parts of an elephant and arrived at different explanations of what elephants were like. For example, the man who felt the side of the elephant compared it to a massive and immovable wall, while the man who felt the trunk thought the elephant was like a rope that could move large objects. Similarly, Burr notes, different theories explain different aspects of the elephant. In this chapter we look briefly at eight of the most influential theories in the study of marriage and the family: four macro-level theories (ecological, structural-functional, conflict, and feminist perspectives) and four micro-level theories (symbolic interaction, social

CHOICES

Popular Magazines and Self-Help Books: Let the Reader Beware

People who write self-help books are extremely well-adjusted folks, free of phobias and anxieties, and bursting with self-esteem. Right? Wrong, says an editor of a company that specializes in publishing self-help psychology books. A best-selling book on phobias, for example, lacks the author's photo because the author has a phobia about having his picture taken, and many manuscripts come from people who claim that God dictated the words to them (Quick, 1992). A husband and wife who co-authored a two-volume textbook on divorce and other aspects of family law have been involved in "'the divorce from Hell'—a very public, increasingly bitter blizzard of litigation that has spawned nearly 400 legal filings . . . covering everything from the dissolution of their law firm to ownership of a low-number auto tag" (Ringle, 1999: C1). Some of the most ardent Marriage Movement (see Chapter 1) leaders have been divorced at least once. And Dr. Benjamin Spock, a best-selling baby-book author and family expert for at least 50 years, agreed with his estranged sons and admitted just before he died at age 94, that he had been too career-driven to spend much time with his family (Maier, 1998).

A major weakness of many self-help books and articles in popular magazines is that they are based on personal opinion and experience rather than scholarly research. Rosenblatt and Phillips (1975) maintain that although the single best thing about the magazine articles is that most of them encourage people to believe that they can change their lives, they also "violate commonly accepted standards of scholarship." Self-help books and articles can lead to four serious problems:

1. **They can threaten relationships.** Many articles encourage the reader to make new demands on a spouse or on children. Although this kind of assertiveness may improve an individual's life, making such changes unilaterally can increase conflict that the family may be unable to handle.
2. **They can make partners feel inadequate.** Many popular writers tie a person's feelings of adequacy to his or her relationships with family members. This ignores the satisfaction and self-confidence that people can get from work, friendships, participation in organizations, and solitary pursuits.
3. **They may oversimplify complex problems.** Many popular writers gloss over complex factors in family relationships. For example, in pointing out that a reduction in sexual activity can lead to depression, they may ignore the fact that depression can be caused by many other factors, such as menopause and "the change of life" (Chapter 6), the birth of a new baby (Chapter 11), poverty and unemployment (Chapter 13), or bereavement (Chapter 17).

4. **They may make irresponsible recommendations for professional help.** Many people are not equipped to evaluate the qualifications of counselors or therapists. Writers who simply recommend that people seek help without providing guidelines for distinguishing between high-quality and low-quality professionals do the public a great disservice. In one study, for example, the researchers found that 51 percent of the 267 respondents reported negative experiences in their stepfamily therapy (Visher and Visher, 1996).

Readers of popular articles and books about the family should ask themselves the following basic questions:

- Does the writer cite research and/or clinical experience or only anecdotal material as sources? If the writer cites himself or herself, are the references scholarly or only personal stories?
- Does the book or article describe only a few families with problems but then generalize the findings to all families?
- Does the writer make it sound as though the world is exceedingly simple and easy to understand (such as following ten steps for marital happiness)? Family interaction and behavior are considerably more complex than throwing a few ingredients into the pot and stirring.

exchange, developmental, and family systems perspectives) (see *Figure 2.1*). Although researchers typically use more than one theory in examining any marriage and family topic, and the theories overlap, as you will see, for the sake of clarity we'll look at each perspective separately.

The Ecological Perspective

The word *ecology* (which means "place of residence") was coined in 1873 by a German biologist. It was first applied to the study of plants, then to the study of animals, and still later to the study of human communities.

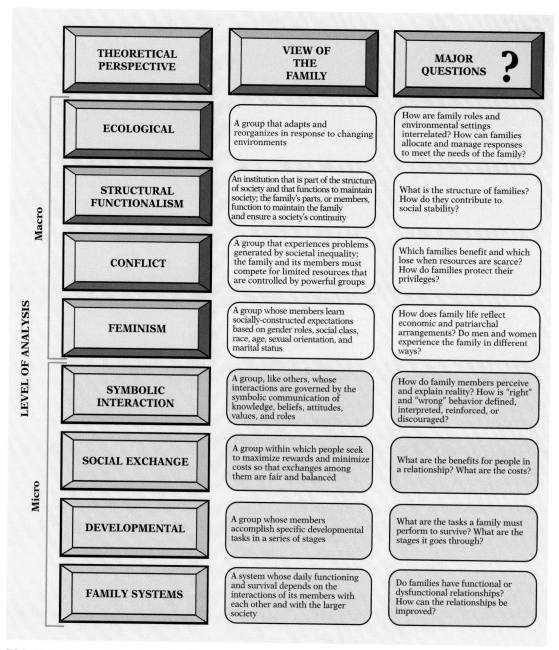

FIGURE 2.1 **Major Theoretical Perspectives on Marriage and the Family**

In sociology, ecology is the study of the relationship and adaptation of human groups, such as families, to their physical environment.

In the United States, the earliest urban ecology studies were conducted from the early 1920s to the late 1940s by a group of sociologists at the University of Chicago. They used Chicago neighborhoods as the "laboratory" and observed how communities and individuals changed because of urbanization, industrialization, and immigration. More recently, theorists and researchers have used ecological perspectives to

explain how the family is embedded in larger kinship networks, how the family reorganizes in response to changes in the economy, and how micro- and macro-level variables intersect as people develop over the life course.

According to an ecological model developed by Bronfenbrenner (1979), human development is shaped by both "immediate" and "remote" environments. The *microsystem* is made up of the interconnected behaviors, roles, and relations that influence the person's daily life (such as the linkages between home and school). The *exosystem* consists of settings or events that people do not experience directly but that affect their development (such as parents' employment). The *macrosystem* reflects complex ideological systems (such as beliefs and values) within a culture or subculture that also affect the individual. For example, a parent's self-evaluation of being a good (or bad) parent (the microsystem) is related to such external factors as job flexibility and adequacy of child-care arrangements (the exosystem), as well as the availability of supportive cultural settings that provide quality health services for a child or family (the macrosystem).

Ecological theory proposes, then, that individuals' roles and environmental settings are highly interrelated. Bogenschneider (1996) contends, for example, that one of the reasons that efforts to decrease teenage alcohol and drug abuse have been unsuccessful is because many communities have not incorporated ecological models in their prevention programs. He maintains that successful drug-prevention programs must be multifaceted: They must understand the teenager's specific family dynamics, address the unique needs of a particular neighborhood, and involve all the citizens (such as local churches, businesses, as well as colleges and universities) to offer alternatives to high-risk behavior. Such alternatives include not selling alcohol to adolescents, providing parent education and family support, and involving youth in meaningful community projects.

Critique While many family scientists endorse ecological perspectives, others note several weaknesses. According to Klein and White (1996), for example, while ecological theories seek to explain how growth comes about because of changes in the environment, explanations of decay or disintegration (such as aging) are "notably absent." Also it is not always apparent, they contend, exactly how and when environments produce changes in individuals and families. In addition, it is unclear how the interactions between microsystems, exosystems, and macrosystems affect such nontraditional family groups as stepfamilies (Ganong et al., 1995), gay and lesbian households, or intergenerational families living under one roof.

The Structural-Functional Perspective

Structural-functional theory examines the relationship between the family and the larger society. When social scientists study family structure, they examine how the parts work together in fulfilling the functions or tasks necessary for the family's survival.

Sociologist Talcott Parsons (1902–1979) was the leading proponent of the structural-functional perspective throughout the 1950s and into the 1960s. According to Parsons and his colleagues, adult family tasks are best accomplished when spouses carry out distinct and specialized roles—one called *instrumental,*

the other *expressive* (Parsons and Bales, 1955). The husband and/or father, the "breadwinner," plays the **instrumental role.** Playing the instrumental role means providing food and shelter for the family and, at least theoretically, being hardworking, tough, and competitive. Assuming the **expressive role,** the wife and/or mother is the homemaker. Playing the expressive role means providing the emotional support and nurturing qualities that sustain the family unit and support the husband/father. The homemaker does the housework, cares for the children, and bolsters the husband's/father's ego by listening, encouraging, and supporting his efforts whenever possible. Not surprisingly, these family roles characterize what social scientists refer to as the *traditional family,* a family form that many conservative groups would like to resurrect (see Chapter 1).

These and other roles that family members may play are functional. That is, they preserve order, stability, and equilibrium and provide the physical shelter and emotional support that can ensure the health and survival of family members. Anything that interferes with these family tasks is seen as dysfunctional because it jeopardizes the smooth functioning of the group. For example, the abuse of one member by another is dysfunctional because the negative physical and emotional consequences threaten the family's ability to function and even to survive.

There are two kinds of functions. **Manifest functions** are intended and recognized; that is, they are present and clearly evident. **Latent functions** are unintended and unrecognized; they are present but are not immediately obvious. Consider the marriage ceremony. The primary manifest function of the marriage ceremony is to publicize the formation of a new family unit and to legitimize sexual intercourse. Its latent functions include the implicit communication of a "hands-off" message to past or future suitors, the outfitting of the new couple with household goods and products, and the redefinition of family boundaries to include in-laws or stepfamily members.

Finally, structural functionalists note that the family affects and is affected by such other interrelated institutions as law, politics, and the economy. For example, politicians (many of whom are lawyers and businessmen) play a major role in setting policies that determine, among other things, whether or not a marriage is legal, how much a family is taxed, and how the family is defined in claiming Social Security payments (see Chapter 1).

Critique During the 1970s and 1980s, much of the sociological writing about the family challenged or refuted functionalist perspectives. Structural functionalism has come under attack for being so conservative in its emphasis on order and stability that it ignores social change. For example, this perspective typically sees high divorce rates as dysfunctional and as signaling the disintegration of the family rather than indicating change (such as people leaving an unhappy situation). Nor does this perspective show how families interact on a daily basis, "up close and personal." Structural functionalism has also been criticized for seeing the family narrowly, through white, male, middle-class lenses (Andersen, 2000).

And some feel that structural-functionalist terms like "equilibrium" are unclear and difficult to measure (McIntyre, 1981). Despite such criticisms, structural-functional perspectives continue to frame many sociological analyses. In a study of marriage and family textbooks that had at least four editions published throughout the 1980s and into the 1990s, for example, the researchers concluded that "structural functionalism still governs major assumptions and debates in family sociology" (Mann et al., 1997: 340).

The Conflict Perspective

A third macro theory, the conflict perspective, has a long history. It became popular during the late 1960s when African Americans and feminists started to challenge structural functionalism as the dominant explanation of marriage and the family. **Conflict theory** examines the ways in which groups disagree, struggle over power, and compete for scarce resources (such as wealth and prestige). In contrast to structural functionalists, conflict theorists see conflict and the resulting changes in traditional roles as natural, inevitable, and often desirable.

According to conflict theory, many family difficulties are the result of widespread societal problems. For example, shifts in the U.S. economy that led to a decline in manufacturing resulted in the loss of many well-paying blue-collar jobs. This has had a profound influence on many families, sending some into a spiral of downward mobility. Racial discrimination has a negative impact on many families, diminishing access to health services, education, and employment. And, as you will see in Chapter 14, many researchers argue that it is society's acceptance of male dominance over women and children that has made the family one of the major settings for violence in our culture.

Conflict theorists see society not as cooperative and stable but as a system of widespread inequality. There is a continuous tension between the "haves" and the "have-nots"; the latter are mainly children, women, people of color, and the poor. Much research based on conflict theory focuses on how those in power—typically white, middle-aged, wealthy, Protestant, Anglo-Saxon males—dominate political and economic decision making in American society.

Critique Conflict theorists have been criticized for overemphasizing conflict and coercion at the expense of order and stability. Some feel that conflict theory presents a negative view of human nature and neglects

the importance of love and self-sacrifice, which are essential to family relationships. Because it examines institutional rather than personal opportunities and constraints, this perspective is sometimes seen as less useful than others in explaining everyday individual behavior.

Feminist Perspectives

Conflict theories provided a springboard for feminist theories, the fourth macro approach discussed in this section. **Feminist theories** include a wide range of perspectives and research procedures. The theories examine, for example, the ways in which socially constructed categories of sex (our biological characteristics) and gender roles (expectations about how men and women should behave) shape relations between women and men in such institutions as politics, the economy, religion, education, and the family. Prior to the 1960s women's movement, for example, very little was written about the relationships between mothers and daughters, women's sexuality, parenting arrangements, and many other family-related topics (Osmond and Thorne, 1993).

Despite some widespread misconceptions, feminists are not always women or lesbians. Any person, male or female, straight or gay, who believes that men and women should have equal political, economic, and social rights and who endorses liberating changes for *both* sexes is a feminist. A second misconception is that feminists hate men. Many feminists are angry about the injustices perpetrated against women in the workplace and the family and have proposed such "radical" changes as equal pay for equal work and men's greater participation in raising children.

There are many "feminisms" (see, for example, Elliot and Mandell, 1995; Kemp and Squires, 1997; Lindsey, 1997). "Liberal feminism" emphasizes social and legal reform to create equal opportunities for women. "Radical feminism" considers patriarchy (see Chapter 1) to be the major cause of women's inequality. "Global feminism" focuses on how the intersection of gender with race, social class, and colonization has exploited women in the developing world. Whether we identify ourselves as feminist or not, most of us are probably liberal feminists because we endorse equal opportunities for women and men in the workplace, politics, and education.

Feminist theory has had a significant impact on our understanding of family life. Since the early 1980s, feminist scholars (women and men) have contributed to family theory and social change in several ways:

- They have shown that the structural-functionalist notion of the traditional family where the father is the breadwinner and the mother is the full-time homemaker is neither "natural" nor characteristic of most U.S. households. Feminists have pointed out that family life is diverse and that our notion of "the family" should be expanded to encompass families from many cultures and racial groups, including those with single heads of households, lesbian and gay families, stepfamilies, and grandparent–grandchild households.

■ Feminist theorists have promoted legislation on family violence by showing that adult women and children are more often the victims of domestic assaults than are adult men and the latter are often immune from prosecution because of men's dominance in families.

■ They have emphasized patterns of inequality and conflict between spouses, viewing husbands and wives as equal partners in marriage. Feminist scholars have questioned why employed women still do most of the housework and child care and have worked for legislation that provides employed women and men with a modicum of parental leave rights (see Chapters 4 and 13).

■ They have refocused much of the research to include fathers as involved, responsible, and nurturant family members who have a profound effect on children and the family (see, for example, Thorne, 1982; Ferree, 1990; Thompson and Walker, 1995; Baca Zinn, 1996; Okin, 1997).

Critique Feminists have challenged discriminatory peer review processes that have routinely excluded women who are not part of the "old boy network" (Wenneras and Wold, 1997). One of the criticisms, however, is that many feminists are part of an "old girl network." This network has not always welcomed conflicting points of view from African American, Latina, Asian American, American Indian, Muslim, lesbian, working-class, and disabled women in both research and therapeutic settings (Almeida, 1994; Lynn and Todoroff, 1995; S.A. Jackson, 1998).

Another criticism is that much feminist research uses qualitative methods to the exclusion of quantitative methods. In **quantitative research**, researchers assign numbers to qualitative (i.e., nonnumeric) observations by counting and measuring attitudes or behavior. In Chapter 1, for example, all of the figures are based on quantitative research. In **qualitative research**, researchers rely on observation and interviews and report their data from the respondents' point of view. While quantitative research presents useful overall snapshots of families, qualitative approaches "provide rich and informative insights on the fluid aspects of family structure as they are experienced in day-to-day family life" (Jarrett and Burton, 1999: 177–78). Some of the most insightful studies on the everyday behavior of dual-earner couples and poor mothers' struggles to stay off welfare, for instance, come from qualitative

analyses (see Hochschild and Machung, 1989; Edin and Lein, 1997).

Many feminists maintain that quantitative methods, which emphasize detachment and "objectivity," fail to convey the respondents' experiences on such topics as everyday communication and gender power differences. Some critics argue, however, that findings based on quantitative methods have important political implications (Maynard, 1994). For example, policy makers are more likely to take feminist research seriously if the studies show the widespread prevalence—rather than just the subjects' personal feelings—of such problems as wife abuse, the negative effects of poverty on children, and sex discrimination in the workplace.

The Symbolic Interaction Perspective

In contrast to the structural-functionalist, macro ecological, conflict, and feminist theories, **symbolic interaction theory** is a micro-level theory that looks at the everyday behavior of individuals. It can be defined as a theory of human interaction as governed by the symbolic communication of knowledge, ideas, beliefs, and attitudes and how people interpret situations. To the symbolic interactionist, for example, a father's batting practice with his daughter is not simply batting practice. It is an interaction that conveys such messages as "I have time for you," "I enjoy spending time with you," or "Girls can be good baseball players."

This theory looks at subjective, interpersonal meanings and at the ways in which we interact with and influence each other by communicating through *symbols*—words, gestures, or pictures that stand for something. If we are to interact effectively, our symbols must have *shared meanings,* or agreed-upon definitions. One of the most important of these shared meanings is the *definition of the situation,* that is, the way we perceive reality and react to it. We learn our definitions of the situation through interaction with **significant others**—people in our primary groups, such as parents, friends, relatives, and teachers—who play an important role in our socialization.

According to symbolic interaction theory, each family member plays more than one role. For example, a man may be a husband, father, grandfather, brother, son, uncle, and so on. Roles are also *reciprocal.* Even before a baby is born, the prospective parents begin to take on parenting roles (see Chapter 11). Roles require different behaviors both within and outside the family, and people modify and adjust their roles as they interact with other role players. For example, a woman's interactions with her husband will be different from her interactions with her children. And she will interact still differently when she is teaching a class of students, talking to a colleague in the hall, or addressing a professional conference.

At age 77, actor Tony Randall and his 27-year-old wife had their first child. A few years later, they had a second child. Such marriages usually reflect an exchange of the man's money and fame for the woman's youth, physical attractiveness, and ability to bear children.

Critique One of the most common criticisms of symbolic interaction theory is that because it emphasizes micro relationships, it ignores the impact on family relationships of macro-level factors such as economic forces and social movements. The Promise Keepers movement, for example, has encouraged men's dominance over gender equality in the family (see Chapter 1). If such views are accepted by large numbers of men, marital relationships may become more strained because many women already complain that many men aren't doing their share of the housework (see Chapter 4).

Some feel that symbolic interaction theory has limited utility because it has ignored the irrational and unconscious aspects of human behavior (LaRossa and Reitzes, 1993). That is, people don't always consider the meaning of their actions or act as reflectively as symbolic interactionists assume. And because symbolic interactionists often study only white, middle-class families—those most likely to cooperate in research—

the findings of such studies are rarely representative of a wide range of racial-ethnic and lower socioeconomic groups (Winton, 1995).

The Social Exchange Perspective

The fundamental premise of **social exchange theory** is that any social interaction between two people is based on the efforts of each person to maximize rewards and minimize costs. As a result, individuals will continue in a relationship only as long as it is perceived as more rewarding than costly to do so. People bring various resources to a relationship—some tangible, some intangible—such as energy, money, material goods, status, intelligence, good looks, youth, power, talent, fame, or affection. These resources can be "traded" for more, better, or different resources that another person possesses. And as long as costs are equal to or lower than benefits, the exchanges will be seen as fair or balanced.

From the social exchange perspective, when the costs of a marriage outweigh the rewards, there may be a separation or divorce because one or both partners feel that they're not getting anything out of the relationship. On the other hand, many people stay in unhappy marriages because the rewards seem equal to the costs: "It's better than being alone"; "I don't want to hurt the kids"; "It could be worse." Although some of our cost–reward decisions are conscious, others are not. For example, much of the research on wife abuse shows that women stay in abusive relationships because their self-esteem has eroded after years of criticism, put-downs, and ridicule by both their families of orientation and their spouses or partners ("You'll be lucky if anyone marries you," "You're dumb," "You're ugly," and so on). As a result, abused girls and women rarely recognize that they have the right to expect a rewarding relationship.

Critique Exchange theorists have been accused of putting too much weight on rational behavior. People do not always calculate logically and carefully the potential cost and reward of every decision. For example, Linda, one of my students, spent every Saturday, the only day she wasn't working or in class, driving from Baltimore to Philadelphia to visit a grandmother who was showing early symptoms of Alzheimer's disease. Linda's mother and several nurses' aides were giving the grandmother, who often didn't recognize Linda, good care. Nonetheless, Linda gave up her "dating evening" because "I just want to make sure Grandma is OK." In this and other cases, genuine love and concern for others can override "sensible" cost–benefit considerations.

Exchange theory is also limited to explaining behavior that is motivated by immediate costs or rewards. In many cultural groups, in contrast, family responsibilities take precedence over individual rights and rewards. Traditional Asian cultures stress filial piety, whereby children are expected to make sacrifices for the well-being of their parents, and children are socialized to conform to family and societal expectations rather than pursuing personal interests (Hurh, 1998; Do, 1999). Instead of balancing individual costs and benefits, children are taught to make long-term sacrifices on behalf of the family.

The Developmental Perspective

A third micro-level perspective, **developmental theory,** examines the many ways in which families change over time. The **family life cycle** refers to the transitions that a family makes as it moves through a series of stages and events from the early days of marriage to the death of one or both partners. As family members progress through the various stages and events, they accomplish **developmental tasks;** that is, they learn to fulfill role expectations and responsibilities such as showing affection and support for family members and socializing with people outside the family.

Many family development tasks are important to keep the group going. In the film *What's Eating Gilbert Grape,* for example, an obese mother is unable to cook, clean, shop, or prepare birthday parties for her children because she can barely move around the house. Gilbert spends his adolescence parenting his younger brother, and all three older children run the household. Only after the mother dies are the children "freed" to develop such age-appropriate developmental tasks as dating and socializing with their peers.

We learn many developmental tasks in response to a community's pressures for conformity. Teachers, for example, expect that even very young children will have accomplished such developmental tasks as paying attention and obeying the teacher. As a child gets older, a failure to comply with school standards—skipping classes or being disruptive—can give parents a bad reputation and lead to intervention by public authorities such as the police (Aldous, 1996).

Among the several variations of the family life cycle that have been proposed, one of the earliest and best known is Duvall's (1957). According to classic developmental theory like Duvall's, the family life cycle begins with marriage and continues through having and raising children, seeing the children leave home, retirement, to the death of one or both spouses (see *Table 2.1*). Over time, developmental theories became more sophisticated. Theorists now acknowledge, for example, that developmental stages and tasks vary in different kinds of families, such as single-parent families, childless couples, and grandparent–grandchild families. Also, the complex situations and problems that confront families in an aging society are multigenerational rather than one-generational (Jerrome, 1994). If a couple divorces, for example, the ex-spouses aren't the only ones who must learn new

TABLE 2.1
The Classic Portrayal of the Family Life Cycle
Does this model illustrate your family of orientation? What about your family of procreation? If not, how have the stages been different?
Stage 1 Couple without children
Stage 2 Oldest child younger than 30 months old
Stage 3 Oldest child between 2-$\frac{1}{2}$ and 6 years old
Stage 4 Oldest child between 6 and 13 years old
Stage 5 Oldest child between 13 and 20 years old
Stage 6 Period starting when first child leaves family until the youngest leaves
Stage 7 Empty nest to retirement
Stage 8 Retirement to death of one or both spouses

developmental tasks in relating to their children and each other. Grandparents and even great-grandparents may also have to forge different ties with their grandchildren, an ex-son-in-law or an ex-daughter-in-law as well as grand-stepchildren if either of the divorced partners remarries.

Finally, the nature of the family life cycle may differ greatly among poor, racial-ethnic, and white, middle-class families. As the box "Kinscripts: Ensuring Family Survival in Tough Situations" shows, to keep their members together throughout the life cycle, poor families must be more creative than others.

Critique Developmental theories have generated a great deal of research, especially on the internal dynamics of marital and family interaction. Critics, however, point out several limitations. First, some feel that the stages are artificial because "the processes of life are not always so neatly and cleanly segmented" (Winton, 1995: 39). Second, despite the recent work on kinscripts and extended families, developmental theories are generally restricted to examining nuclear and stable families. Third, gay and lesbian households are generally excluded from family life cycle stages (Laird, 1993). Fourth, some question why developmental theories ignore sibling relationships, which are among the most important emotional resources we have throughout life and especially after the last parent dies (McGoldrick et al., 1993). Thus, according to Burr (1995: 81), even as a micro theory, family development theory "deals with a fairly small part of the elephant."

The Family Systems Perspective

Family systems theory views the family as a system, a functioning unit that solves problems, makes decisions, and achieves collective goals (Day, 1995). The

CHOICES

Kinscripts: Ensuring Family Survival in Tough Situations

Family life cycle patterns differ markedly in terms of needs, resources, gender roles, migration patterns, education, and attitudes toward family and aging (McGoldrick et al., 1993). Studying low-income African American families, Burton and Stack (1993) have proposed the concept of the *kinscript* to explain the life courses of many multigenerational families. The kinscript arises in response to both extreme economic need and intense commitment by family members to the survival of future generations, and it requires family interaction in three domains: kin-work, kin-time, and kin-scription.

Kin-work is the collective labor that families share to endure over time. It includes family help during childbirth, intergenerational care for children or dependents, and support for other relatives. For example, a 76-year-old widower parented three preschool children after their mother started "running the streets":

There ain't no other way. I have to raise these babies, else the service people will take 'em away. This is my family. Family has to take care of family else we won't be no more. (Burton and Stack, 1993: 105)

Kin-time is the shared understanding among family members of when and in what sequence kin-work should be performed. Kin-time provides for learning developmental tasks during such transitions as marriage, childbearing, and grandparenthood and includes temporal guides for assuming family leadership roles and caregiving responsibilities. A woman receiving assistance from her mother and other female kin describes the complex but cooperative pattern that characterizes the care of her child:

Well, on the days Damen has school, my mother picks him up at night and keeps him at her home. And then when she goes to work in the morning, she takes him to my grandmother's house. And when my little sister gets out of school, she picks him up and takes him back to my mother's house. And then I go and pick him up. (Jarrett, 1994: 41–42)

Kin-scription is the process by which kin-work is assigned to specific family members, most often women and children. Women often find it difficult to refuse kin demands. One woman, who had lost her first love 14 years earlier at the age of 21, provides an example of the interplay of family power, kin-scription, and the role of women:

When Charlie died, it seemed like everyone said, since she's not getting married, we have to keep her busy. Before I knew it, I was raising kids, giving home to long-lost kin, and even helping the friends of my mother. Between doing all of this, I didn't have time to find another man. (Burton and Stack, 1993: 107)

Many people believe that poor families or those on welfare are doomed to pass dependency down from generation to generation (Hill et al., 1993). As the kinscript framework suggests, however, many low-income, multigenerational families have well-defined family scripts that enable family members to survive by depending on kin rather than on public assistance.

Rebecca Anderson, 54 years old and battling lupus, became a mother again when she took in five nieces and nephews whose three sets of parents could not care for them. Anderson's husband, Alton, who does not live with Rebecca, helps with the children occasionally but provides no financial support.

emphasis is not on individual family members but on how the members interact within the family system. Much of the research and therapeutic models, then, emphasize communication processes, how family patterns evolve, and how individual personalities affect family members (Rosenblatt, 1994).

Family systems analysts are interested in the implicit or explicit rules that hold families together. How, for example, do family members influence each other during stressful times, such as illness, unemployment, and the death of a loved one? Because such environments as schools and communities affect families, researchers are also interested in the rules that maintain a boundary between the family and the outside world. As the boundaries of the family change—through birth or remarriage, for example—the focus of the analysis may shift from family members to the relationship between family members and outside groups (Broderick, 1993).

You may have noticed that the systems approach is compatible with symbolic interaction theory. In fact, those who rely on symbolic interaction—clinicians, counselors, and social workers—often use systems theory to examine family interaction patterns. They study the way spouses and children relate to each other, which interaction patterns are most destructive in interpersonal relations, and how family members can be taught to change everyday behavior that is dysfunctional for the family over the life course.

Critique Some critics have argued that general systems theory has generated a lot of terminology but little insight into how the family functions (Holman and Burr, 1980; Nye and Berardo 1981). Some concepts and the usage of mathematical models, for example, render family systems theory very abstract and too general to explain specific family processes. Because the perspective originated in the study of dysfunctional families in clinical settings, some question whether the theory can be applied to healthy families. Finally, since some of the findings on boundaries and interaction patterns come from case studies, the generalizability of the results is limited (Day, 1995).

Conclusion

Although we've discussed the eight major theories of marriage and the family separately, researchers and clinicians often combine several of these perspectives to interpret data or decide on intervention strategies. For example, a counselor who is helping a couple with marital problems might draw on social exchange, symbolic interaction, developmental, and systems theories to shed light on the couple's situation. Or, as Bernier and Siegel (1994) note, counselors who work with children with attention-deficit hyperactive disorders (ADHD) should combine ecological and family systems perspectives in assessments and intervention. Instead of simply focusing on the child or the family, clinicians would observe the child in his or her natural environment, recruit the child's teacher in the helping process, and educate grandparents about ADHD.

Clinicians would also locate or create community-based social skills groups, train educators and child-care providers who have contact with ADHD children, and encourage community agencies to lobby for services for children with this disorder. It is not realistic to expect a counselor or clinician to fulfill more than a few of these tasks, of course. The point, however, is that both researchers and practitioners often rely on several theories in explaining or responding to family-related issues.

You've now had an introduction to some of the most influential theoretical perspectives that guide researchers and practitioners in their work. We turn next to a consideration of the ways that people, guided by these theoretical perspectives, design studies and collect information about marriages and families.

Methods and Techniques in Family Research

Probably the first systematic collection of data about the family was compiled by French social scientist Frederick LePlay. His detailed analyses of the family budgets of 36 working-class families, published in 1855, led eventually to the "minimum standard of living" concept that welfare agencies still use to determine a family's economic needs (Broderick, 1988). Since LePlay's time, data on marriages and families have come primarily from five major sources: surveys, clinical research, observation, secondary analysis, and evaluation research.

Surveys

Researchers use **surveys** to systematically collect data from respondents either by a mailed questionnaire or an interview. Ideally, researchers would like to study all the units or elements of the population in which they are interested—say, all adolescents who abstain from sexual intercourse. In social science research, a **population** is any well-defined group of people about whom we want to know something specific. For several reasons, however, obtaining information from populations is problematic. The population may be so large, for example, that it would be too expensive and time-consuming to conduct the research. In other cases—such as obtaining the membership lists of religious groups or social clubs—it may be impossible even to identify the population we would like to study.

Researchers, therefore, typically draw a **sample,** a group of people (or things) that are representative of

CHANGES

The Prospects and Pitfalls of Internet Surveys

Several hundred World Wide Websites invite visitors to participate in a variety of scientific studies or those that resemble scientific research, including personality tests and opinion surveys. The Internet is a powerful research tool, and one of its greatest benefits is the ability to reach large numbers of people at a very low cost. How scientific are the studies, however? Should you or your family members—especially children under age 18—participate?

In terms of the latter question, a nationally representative study of 1,305 parents and their children (aged 10 to 17) found that almost two out of three of the children (65 percent) are willing to divulge private information to online marketers in exchange for a free gift (like a sweepstakes prize). Some of the information children say they would provide includes the names

of their parents' favorite stores, what their parents do on weekends, how many days of work a parent has missed in the past year, and whether or not the family drinks beer or wine with dinner (Turow and Nir, 2000).

The Children's Online Privacy Protection Act now bars sites from collecting information from users under age 13 without their parents' consent. Enforcement is practically nonexistent, however. In addition, many preteens can probably figure out ways to get around such precautions or even forge their parents' permission electronically.

What about legitimate academic Internet surveys—should you or your family members participate? Empirical studies conducted on the Internet, though scientific, reflect a variety of problems. In face-to-face or telephone interviews, for example, researchers

can see or sense if participants have a negative reaction to an item. The researcher can stop the interview or answer a respondent's questions. Internet surveys, in contrast, can't provide such safeguards, even if there are "warnings" that some of the questions may be sensitive or intrusive.

While an Internet researcher can keep information confidential, computer hackers can easily intercept participants' responses to online studies. In addition, institutional review boards try to ensure that paper-and-pencil studies comply with legal and ethical standards (a topic we address later in this chapter). So far, however, many institutions and government agencies have not established guidelines for online research (Hamilton, 1999). In effect, then, Internet users should check out the data collection site before participating even in scientific studies.

the population they wish to study. In drawing a sample, researchers must decide whether to use probability or nonprobability sampling. In a *probability* (or representative) sample, each person (or thing) has an equal chance of being selected because the selection is random. In a *nonprobability* (or nonrepresentative) sample, researchers use other criteria such as convenience or the availability of respondents.

Television news, newsmagazines, and entertainment shows often provide a toll-free number or an Internet site and encourage viewers to "vote" on an issue (such as the Elián González example at the beginning of this chapter). How representative are these voters of the general population? And how many enthusiasts "stuff the ballot box" by voting more than once? According to one observer, most Internet polls are "good for a few laughs" but are little more than "the latest in a long series of junk masquerading as indicators of public opinion because the participants aren't representative of everyone's opinion" (Witt, 1998). But, you might think, almost 40,000 people cast their vote about Elián. Aren't such large numbers meaningful in reflecting how people think? No. Because the respondents are self-selected,

the pollster simply has "junk" from a very large number of people.

Since the mid-1990s, the amount of social science research—including polls—has boomed. Are the studies legitimate? The box "The Prospects and Pitfalls of Internet Surveys" examines some of the benefits and costs of online research that relies on surveys to collect data.

Questionnaires and Interviews   Researchers collect survey data using questionnaires, face-to-face or telephone interviews, or a combination of these techniques. Questionnaires can be mailed, used during an interview, or self-administered to large groups of respondents. Student course evaluations are good examples of self-administered questionnaires.

In interviews, the researcher and the respondent interact directly, either face to face or by telephone. The latter approach is becoming increasingly popular because it is a relatively inexpensive way to collect data. Representative samples can be obtained through *random-digit dialing*, which involves selecting area codes and exchanges followed by four random digits. In the procedure called *computer-assisted telephone*

Modern census taking is often difficult and time consuming. In 1870, however, when this Pierce City, Idaho, census was recorded, it was even more difficult to count heads. Miners, ranchers and their cooks, and even farmers were often out on the land or in the mountains for days, weeks, and even months at a time.

interviewing (CATI), the interviewer uses a computer to select random telephone numbers and then types the respondents' replies into the computer.

Focus Groups Marketing companies have traditionally used *focus groups* to pretest people's reactions to consumer goods or to get reactions to a new or a "new and improved" product. Recently, however, family researchers have been using focus groups to explore issues before launching a large survey project (Morgan, 1993; Krueger, 1994). Usually 6 to 12 members of a focus group participate in a guided discussion of a particular topic. Although a focus group can become a relatively unstructured bull session, it often provides important information. In a study using 11 focus groups across the country, for example, Stone and Waszak (1992) found that teenage participants, aged 13 to 19, had strong opinions about the topic of abortion but said that their parents or teachers had never discussed the students' attitudes about abortion. The researchers also found that, compared to a 1972–1973 study of adolescents, teenagers in the 1990s didn't know that a first-trimester abortion was safe, that having an abortion would not make the woman sterile, and that other people could not tell if a woman had ever had an abortion. Regardless of how one feels about abortion, Stone and Waszak noted that the focus groups were invaluable in exploring sensitive issues that had been largely untapped by previous studies.

Strengths Surveys are usually inexpensive, simple to administer, and have a fast turn-around rate. With assurance that their answers will remain anonymous, respondents are generally willing to answer questions on such sensitive topics as income, sexual behavior, and the use of drugs.

Face-to-face interviews have high response rates (up to 99 percent) compared to other data-collection techniques. Interviewers can also record the respondent's body language, facial expressions, and intonations, which can sometimes be as useful as the verbal response. Moreover, if a respondent does not understand a question or is reluctant to answer, the interviewer can clarify, probe, or keep the respondent from digressing. An astute interviewer can also gather information on such variables as social class by observing the respondent's home and neighborhood.

Like questionnaires, telephone surveys are relatively inexpensive and a quick means of gathering information. Telephone interviews provide a nearly unlimited pool of respondents (more than 98 percent of all homes have at least one telephone), and they often elicit more honest responses on controversial issues than face-to-face interviews. Respondents are less likely to be affected by interviewer bias in this type of survey, and researchers have more control over interviewer procedures (such as probing a respondent's vague answers).

Weaknesses One of the major limitations of surveys that use mailed questionnaires is a low response rate, often well under 50 percent. If the questions are unclear, complicated, or offensive, a respondent may simply throw the questionnaire away. A number of

© Benita Epstein, 1994.

studies have found that anywhere from a third to half of survey respondents offer opinions on subjects they know nothing about, such as fictitious legislation or nonexistent political figures (see Bishop et al., 1980).

Moreover, those who respond to questionnaires may be very different from those who do not. Some of the least representative surveys tap self-selected respondents such as readers of particular magazines. How many times, for example, have *you* taken the time to complete and return such questionnaires? Norman Bradburn of the National Opinion Research Center has termed these surveys SLOPS, for "Self-Selected Opinion Polls" (cited in Tanur, 1994).

Another problem with surveys is that people may skip or lie about questions that they feel are "too nosy." During the 2000 census, for example, a third of the people who received the 53-question long form felt that none of the questions was too personal. However, 53 percent viewed questions about income as intrusive and 32 percent felt the same way about questions on physical or mental disabilities (Cohn, 2000). If respondents lie or omit questionnaire items about their income or other family characteristics, the data will be invalid or the researcher may have to scrap a key variable (such as income).

Unlike questionnaires and telephone surveys, face-to-face interviewing can be very expensive (see Data Digest). Even trained interviewers sometimes misinterpret answers because of their own prejudices, or they elicit biased answers by their own body language. Men may be less candid with female interviewers than with male interviewers, and vice versa (Herod, 1993; Kane and Macaulay, 1993). And the interview environment itself can affect responses. For example, women may be less willing to admit they have been raped if questioned by men, by interviewers of different racial or ethnic backgrounds, or in the presence of family members (Marcus, 1990).

In the *George Burns and Gracie Allen Show,* a popular television program during the 1950s, George, the straight man, and Gracie, cast as his scatterbrained wife, are discussing Gracie's cousin Gallop Allen, a pollster. Gracie says that Gallop's most successful survey was the one he took for the telephone company. He had to find out how many people had telephones, and the answer was 100 percent! "A hundred percent?" George asks incredulously. "Yes," Gracie responds enthusiastically, "everyone he called had one." This anecdote illustrates one of the problems with telephone surveys: Only people who have phones—or, these days, who answer their telephone calls—are included in surveys. Because people have become oversaturated with marketing research, many use answering machines to screen or avoid all telephone surveys. And if a researcher does succeed in getting through to a respondent, there is great pressure to keep the interview brief; bored or tired respondents may hang up before the interview is completed.

As surveys become increasingly computerized, researchers are finding that there are trade-offs. According to a national study of 15- to 19-year-old males, for example, Turner and his associates (1998) found that surveys on embarrassing subjects, such as adolescent homosexual experiences, may be more accurate when the survey is conducted on a computer rather than with a traditional paper questionnaire. In this study, the participants wore headphones, a laptop computer played audio recordings of the questions, and the respondents keyed in their answers. Compared to their counterparts who answered an identical paper-and-pencil questionnaire, the adolescents who were surveyed by computer were 3 times more likely to say that they had had sex with a prostitute, over 4 times more likely to report that they had ever had sex with another male, and 17 times more likely to acknowledge that at least one of their partners had used intravenous drugs. The researchers concluded that computer answers to sensitive questions about risky behavior are more accurate than written ones because teenage boys worry less about survey takers' reactions or members of their family seeing their responses. The disadvantage of such surveys, however, is that buying and programming laptops to pose the questions and record the answers is considerably more expensive than paper-and-pencil questionnaires.

Because the survey is the research approach you will encounter most often, it is important to be an informed consumer. As the box "Can I Trust This Survey?" shows, you can't simply assume that the survey is accurate or representative of a larger population.

Clinical Research

Unlike survey research, which explores large-scale social processes and changes, **clinical research** studies individuals or small groups of people who seek help

CHOICES

Can I Trust This Survey?

Surveys are often used in public opinion polls and are reported on television and in newspapers. Asking a few basic questions about the survey will help you evaluate its credibility:

- *Who sponsored the survey?* A government agency, a nonprofit partisan organization, a business, or a group that's lobbying for change?

- *What is the purpose of the survey?* To provide objective information, to promote an idea or a political candidate, or to get attention through sensationalism?

- *How was the sample drawn?* Randomly? Or was it a SLOP (see text)?

- *How were the questions worded?* Were they clear, objective, loaded, or biased? If the survey questions are not provided, why not?

- *How did the researchers report their findings?* Were they objective or did they make value judgments?

for both physical and social problems from mental health professionals and other scientists (Miller and Crabtree, 1994). Many clinical researchers focus on conflict in family relationships, intervene in traumatic situations such as marital rape and incest, and try to change dysfunctional system networks such as hostile communication patterns between spouses or the family situations surrounding eating disorders.

Clinical research is based on the *case-study method,* a traditional approach used by social workers, psychologists, clinical sociologists, and marriage counselors. Clinical practitioners work with families or individuals on a one-to-one basis using several techniques, including interviews, analysis of records, and direct observation. The written report of the research, the case study itself, provides in-depth information and can generate detailed and vivid descriptions of family life. (Ralph LaRossa's *Family Case Studies: A Sociological Perspective* presents excellent examples of case studies across the life course.)

Strengths   A major strength of clinical research and case studies is that they are typically linked with long-term counseling, which is useful for many individuals or families. Useful intervention strategies can be disseminated fairly quickly to thousands of other practitioners. Also, clinicians may offer insights about family dynamics that can enrich theories such as symbolic interaction or general systems perspectives and that can be examined in larger populations through surveys or focus groups.

Weaknesses   Clinical research and case studies are usually time-consuming and expensive. They are based on individuals or small groups of people, and clinicians typically see only those with severe problems or people who are willing and financially able to seek help. Thus, the results are not representative of the average family or even of other troubled families.

Despite numerous methodological problems, the media, especially, often embraces the "findings" of studies based on small clinical groups and reports the results to the general public as "definitive" conclusions. In the late 1980s, for example, clinical psychologist Judith Wallerstein and Sandra Blakeslee, a science writer, published *Second Chances: Men, Women, and Children a Decade after Divorce* (Wallerstein and Blakeslee, 1989). The book became "a best seller and probably the most widely read book on divorce ever published" (Cherlin, 1999: 422). The findings were based on 60 troubled families (where many of the parents had histories of mental illness) who had sought help at Wallerstein's divorce clinic. Wallerstein concluded that divorce *causes* long-term negative effects on children. Although several methodologically respected studies have shown that Wallerstein's conclusions were invalid (see Chapter 15), journalists, pro-marriage social movements (see Chapter 1), and even some social scientists continue to cite *Second Chances* as an authoritative and landmark "scientific" study on the negative effects of divorce on children.

Observation

In **observation,** researchers collect data by systematically observing people in their usual surroundings. In *participant observation,* researchers interact naturally with the people they are studying but do not reveal their identities as researchers. For example, if you quietly examined interaction patterns between the "stars" and the "black sheep" during a Thanksgiving dinner, you would be engaging in participant observation. In *nonparticipant observation,* researchers study phenomena without being part of the situation. For example, child psychologists, clinicians, and sociologists often study young children in classrooms through one-way mirrors. (For a discussion of other variations in observation research, see Adler and Adler, 1994.)

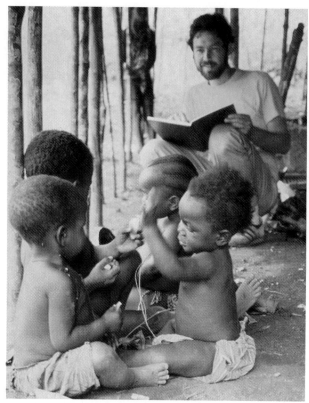

Researchers often study child development by observing children in natural settings.

Although they are conducted in natural settings, observational studies are usually highly structured. The research typically involves carefully designed projects where the data are recorded and then converted to quantitative summaries. The studies examine complex communication patterns, measure the frequency of acts (such as the number of nods or domineering statements), and note the duration of a particular behavior (such as the length of eye contact) (Stillars, 1991). Thus, observational studies are much more complex and sophisticated than they appear to be to the general public or an inexperienced researcher.

In many studies, researchers combine both participant and nonparticipant observation. Sociologist Elijah Anderson, for example, has devoted much of his research to examining households in West Philadelphia, an inner-city black community with high crime rates. Although Anderson teaches at the University of Pennsylvania, he "hangs out" in West Philadelphia to collect the data. Anderson's nonparticipant observer role has included watching and interacting with "decent" and "street" family members to explain how and why some poor residents take extraordinary measures to conform to mainstream values (such as

maintaining a strong family life) while others engage in crime and violence (Anderson, 1999). Over the years, however, Anderson has become personally involved with some of his research subjects. Instead of being a detached observer, for example, Anderson has hired an ex-drug dealer as a part-time research assistant, finds community members lawyers or jobs, encourages his respondents to stay out of crime, and even lends them money (Cose, 1999).

Strengths Studies that use observation often provide a deeper understanding of behavior than "one-shot" data-collection methods because the phenomena are studied over time. Observation is also more flexible than some other methods because the researcher can modify the research design even after data collection has begun. For example, the researcher can decide to interview (rather than just observe) key people after the research has started.

Most important, observation does not disrupt a "natural" situation. Thus, the respondents are not influenced by the researcher's presence. For example, Phillip Davis (1996) and some of his graduate research assistants have observed adults' verbal aggression and corporal punishment of children in such public settings as indoor shopping malls, zoos, amusement parks, flea markets, city streets, rapid transit stations, bus depots, department stores, and toy stores. They listened for statements in which adults threatened children with physical punishment or harm. When they heard a threat, they watched to see what happened. They then went to a nearby spot and recorded what was said on a coding sheet.

Weaknesses If a researcher needs elaborate recording equipment, must travel far or often, or lives in a different society or community for an extended period of time, observation research can be very expensive. Researchers who study other cultures must often learn a new language. For example, anthropologist Jean Briggs (1970) spent months living with an isolated Eskimo band in the Arctic before she even learned to communicate with her subjects. Besides learning a new language, researchers have to adjust to different cultural norms. Diane Freedman (1986), another anthropologist, reports that the Rumanians were "scandalized" by her and her husband's egalitarian division of household labor because they violated the villagers' traditional attitudes that housework was inappropriate for men. (See also Garland, 1999, for an experiential discussion of doing fieldwork in a country that's experiencing civil wars and where the researcher may be abducted or killed.)

It also may be very difficult to balance the role of participant and observer, even if the researcher wants to do so. In a study of black men in a Chicago community, sociologist Mitchell Duneier (1992) found that the men sometimes turned to him for advice or involved him in political discussions about the neighborhood. The researcher may bias the research by succumbing to the impulse to fix a problem and to protect respondents from harm by "making everything right" (Fine, 1993). Thus, in both the Duneier study and that of Anderson cited earlier, the mere presence of an observer can have unwanted effects on the study.

The researcher may have little control over selecting samples or collecting the desired data. Homeless and battered shelters, for example, are usually—and understandably—wary of researchers' intruding on their residents' privacy. Even if the researcher has access to a group, an ongoing problem with field research is the observer's ability to recognize and address her or his biased points of view. Because observation is very personal and subjective, it is often difficult to maintain one's objectivity while collecting and interpreting the data.

Secondary Analysis

Besides using surveys, clinical studies, and observation, researchers rely heavily on secondary analysis. **Secondary analysis** examines data that have been collected by someone else. Such data may be historical materials (such as court proceedings), personal documents (such as letters and diaries), public records (such as federal information on immigration, state or county archives on births, marriages, and deaths), and official statistics (such as Census Bureau publications). As you will see, many of the statistics throughout this textbook rely on such official sources of information as the U.S. Census Bureau.

Strengths In most cases, secondary analysis is accessible, convenient, and inexpensive. Census Bureau information on such topics as marriage, the number of children in single-parent families, and divorce is readily available at public and college and university libraries and, most recently, on the Internet (see the "Taking It Further" section in Chapter 1). Also, many academic institutions buy tapes or CD-ROMS—containing national, regional, and local data—which can then be used for faculty/student research or for class-related projects. Because secondary data are often *longitudinal* (information collected at two or more points in time) rather than *cross-sectional* (information collected at one point in time), there is the added advantage of examining trends (such as age at first marriage) over time.

Weaknesses Secondary data may not have the information you need. For example, some of the statistics on remarriages and redivorces have been collected only since the early 1990s. Thus, it is impossible for a researcher to make comparisons over time. Further, it may be difficult to gain access to historical

In some isolated locations, census takers must often travel to places that are inaccessible by road or without conventional postal addresses. In the 2000 census, for example, Harold Johnson transported Census Director Kenneth Prewitt into town by dog sled. Unalakdeet, a village of about 800, is on the Bering Sea 400 miles northwest of Anchorage.

materials because the documents may be fragile, housed in only a few libraries in the country, or part of private collections. In addition, it may be very hard to determine the accuracy and authenticity of historical materials. Also, if the materials do not include information the researcher is looking for, she or he may have to change the direction of the research or exclude important variables. If you wanted to examine some of the characteristics of stepfamilies, for example, you'd find very little national data. Consequently, you'd have to rely on studies with small and nonrepresentative samples (see Chapter 16) or collect such data yourself.

Evaluation Research

Evaluation research, which relies on all of the standard methodological techniques described in this section, assesses the efficiency and the effectiveness of social programs in both the public and private sectors. Many government and nonprofit agencies provide services that affect the family both directly and indirectly.

Housing programs, programs to prevent or deal with teenage pregnancy, work-training programs, care for infants with AIDS, and drug rehabilitation programs are examples. Because local and state government budgets have been cut since the early 1980s, service-delivery groups have become increasingly concerned about the effectiveness and efficiency of their programs.

Like clinical research, evaluation research is *applied*; it assesses the efficiency and effectiveness of a specific social program for a specific agency or organization, evaluating that program's achievements in terms of its original goals (Weiss, 1998). The findings of the research are generally used to make decisions that are intended to improve the operations of the program—decisions that affect both the sponsoring agency and the people the program helps.

Strengths and Weaknesses Evaluation research is one of the most interesting, and frustrating, research designs. It is interesting because it examines actual efforts to deal with problems that confront many families. If new data are not collected, the expenses can be low. And the research findings can be very valuable to program directors or agency heads. The research helps managers keep a program on course because the findings highlight discrepancies between the original objectives and how the program is actually working (Peterson et al., 1994).

Evaluation research can be frustrating, however, because politics plays an important role in what is evaluated, for whom the research is done, and how the results are appraised. Even though supervisors typically solicit the research, they are not happy if the results show that the program is excluding the most needy group, that the administrators are wasting money, or that caseworkers are making serious mistakes. Also, if staff members have to be trained to change their behavior to meet the program's objectives, the costs may escalate beyond the agency's budget.

Conclusion

Researchers have to weigh the benefits and limitations of each research approach in designing their studies (see *Table 2.2*). Often, they use a combination of strategies to achieve their research objectives. Despite the researcher's commitment to objectivity, ethical debates and politically charged disagreements can influence much of the family research.

Ethical and Political Issues in Family Research

Researchers work in environments in which they interact with people from many backgrounds and, often, people with very strong opinions about family issues. There is also considerable pressure in universities, for example, to supplement decreasing education budgets with outside funding sources. It is not surprising, then, that researchers may encounter ethical and political dilemmas.

TABLE 2.2

Five Common Data-Collection Methods in Family Research

Method	Strengths	Weaknesses
Surveys	Questionnaires are fairly inexpensive and simple to administer; interviews have high response rates; findings are often generalizable	Mailed questionnaires may have low response rates; respondents may be self-selected; interviews are usually expensive
Clinical research	Helps subjects with family problems; offers insights for theory development	Usually time-consuming and expensive; findings are not generalizable
Observation	Flexible; offers deeper understanding of family behavior; usually inexpensive	Difficult to quantify and to maintain observer/subject boundaries; the observer may be biased or judgmental; findings are not generalizable
Secondary analysis	Usually accessible, convenient, and inexpensive; often longitudinal and historical	Information may be incomplete; some documents may be inaccessible; some data can not be collected over time
Evaluation research	Usually inexpensive; valuable in real-life applications	Often political; may require training many staff members

---

TABLE 2.3

Some Basic Principles of Ethical Family Research

Family scientists are expected to be respectful of others, show sensitivity to the dignity of all humans, and avoid all forms of exploitation. They should protect confidentiality in their professional role as family scientists, whether it be in teaching, service, public speaking, writing, or consulting activities. When subjects are discussed in a course or class, including controversial issues, family scientists should encourage an open, respectful, and thoughtful atmosphere that acknowledges and respects a diversity of values, beliefs, and attitudes.

All researchers are responsible for the ethical behavior of everyone involved in their research, including themselves. Among other professional organizations, the National Council on Family Relations and the American Sociological Association publish a detailed set of Ethical Code guidelines for researchers. The key elements of these codes are the following:

- Researchers must obtain all subjects' consent to participate in the research and their permission to quote from their responses and comments, particularly if the research concerns sensitive issues or if subjects' comments will be quoted extensively;

- Researchers may not exploit subjects or research assistants involved in the research for personal gain;

- Researchers must never harm, humiliate, abuse, or coerce the participants in their studies, either physically or psychologically. This includes the withholding of medications or other services or programs that might benefit subjects;

- Researchers must honor all guarantees to participants of privacy, anonymity, and confidentiality;

- Researchers must use the highest methodological standards and be as accurate as possible;

- Researchers must describe the limitations and shortcomings of the research in their published reports;

- Researchers must identify the sponsors who funded the research;

- Researchers must acknowledge the contributions of research assistants (usually underpaid and overworked graduate students) who participate in the research project; and

- Researchers must make the details of their studies and the findings available to people who request them.

Ethical Issues

In 1996, the U.S. Public Health Service's Office of Research Integrity (ORI) found a professor of obstetrics and gynecology at Harvard University's medical school guilty of altering information in patient medical records, falsifying research notes, and making up notes for clinical visits that had not taken place. The physician admitted to falsifying and fabricating 80 percent of the data in his research published in two prestigious medical journals (Walker, 1996). In 1997, a research coordinator at the Johns Hopkins Oncology Center admitted to federal investigators that, in a national study, she invented facts about the status and health complaints of patients previously treated for breast cancer. In a second study, she failed to update the status of breast cancer patients, leading to erroneously favorable data on the outcomes of their treatment (Roylance, 1997).

More recently, a researcher at the University of Illinois at Chicago admitted that she had fabricated research data and submitted the false information to the director of a study on prenatal care (Campbell, 1999). One of the world's most influential medical journals, *The New England Journal of Medicine*, recently acknowledged that nearly half of the drug reviews published since 1997 were written by researchers who had ties with drug companies that sponsored the research ("Correspondence . . . ," 2000).

As these examples illustrate, some researchers—even those at such privileged institutions as Harvard University and Johns Hopkins University—engage in unethical behavior. According to the ORI, 30 percent of the 1,000 scientists it has investigated since mid-1992 have been found guilty of fraud or other unethical research practices (Walker, 1997). For the most part, however, research errors are unintentional. They result from ignorance of statistical procedures, simple arithmetic mistakes, or inadequate supervision. These kinds of honest errors are often caught by referees who review academic articles and books before publication or by scholars who evaluate funding requests.

Because so much research relies on human subjects, the federal government and many professional organizations have devised codes of ethics to protect research participants. Common to most of these codes, and regardless of the discipline or type of research method used, are several minimal rules for professional conduct. These rules are summarized in *Table 2.3*.

Some data-collection methods are more susceptible to ethical violations than others. Surveys are less vulnerable than observation, for example, because in many surveys researchers do not interact directly with

CONSTRAINTS

The Politics of Sex Research

Research on sexual behavior is important because it "lifts the pluralistic ignorance [about sex] and tells us what people are doing" (Udry, 1993: 105). Some groups prefer not to know about sexual behavior, however, and accuse researchers of legitimating "nontraditional" sexual behavior.

In 1991, both the U.S. Secretary for Health and Human Services and the Congress got involved in the politics of sex research by blocking $40 million research projects on adolescent and adult sexual behavior that had already been peer-reviewed, approved, and funded by the National Institutes of Health (NIH). Why and how did this happen? The following is a brief account of how social, political, and religious factors interacted to bring about the demise of such projects:

- In early 1988, the National Institute of Child Health and Human Development and the National Institute of Mental Health approved two studies of human sexual behavior. One study focused on adult behavior; the other, referred to as the American Teenage Study, examined adolescent behavior.
- As these studies were gearing up in 1991, Louis Sullivan, secretary of Health and Human Services, appeared on a Christian Action Network talk show and was asked

why he was funding the American Teenage Study. He said he knew nothing about it.

- A few days later, the front page of the *Washington Times* carried both a story about the secretary's talk-show appearance and an article quoting the head of the (conservative) Family Research Council as opposing the American Teenage Study. C-SPAN and every major newspaper in the country carried the story.
- Shortly thereafter, both Pat Robertson of the Christian Coalition and the Concerned Women of America, a conservative group, encouraged "outraged" Christians to write their congressional representatives to protest the proposed research.
- The Christian Action Network then circulated petitions to NIH to cancel the study. Viewers also inundated local school boards with letters demanding that the study not be carried out in local communities and enclosed a letter in which then-Congressman William Dannemeyer (R–California) condemned the study.
- In Congress, Congressman Dannemeyer and Senator Jesse Helms led the opposition to the two studies. According to Helms, "These sex surveys . . . have not been concerned with legitimate scientific inquiry as

much as they have been concerned with a blatant attempt to sway public attitudes in order to liberalize opinions and laws regarding homosexuality, pedophilia, anal and oral sex, sex education, teenage pregnancy and all down the line."
- In 1992, Congress withdrew the funds for both studies.

Research on teenage sexual behavior is valuable because it provides information that health agencies and schools can use to prepare and disseminate information about sexually transmitted diseases, such as AIDS, and contraception. Nonetheless, local jurisdictions have also refused to let social scientists study adolescent sexual behavior. For example, the Centers for Disease Control and Prevention developed a questionnaire to measure major health problems of adolescents, including drug and alcohol abuse, unsafe sexual practices, physical inactivity, poor eating habits, and smoking.

Maryland school officials initially approved the survey and planned to send it to 3,000 randomly selected ninth- and eleventh-grade students at 30 public high schools. The survey was scrapped, however. Parents in several counties felt that the study might make the school systems look bad (if a high incidence of drug use or pregnancy were reported). The parents also felt that the research violated student privacy (Fiester, 1993; Udry, 1993).

subjects, interpret their behavior, or become personally involved with the respondents.

Political Pressures

Senator William Proxmire became famous (or infamous, some feel) for his "Golden Fleece" awards to social research projects that he ridiculed as wasting taxpayer money. Some of the most recent examples include studies on stress and the content of dreams (Neuman, 1994). The legitimacy of social science

research becomes especially suspect to political and religious groups when the studies focus on sensitive social, moral, and political issues (Stanfield, 1993).

One of the most controversial research topics is human sexuality. Alfred Kinsey and his colleagues carried out the first widely publicized research on sexuality in the late 1940s and early 1950s. Although there were methodological limitations (see Chapter 6), many social scientists consider Kinsey's research to be the major springboard that launched scientific investigations of human sexuality in the following decades.

Many people are still suspicious of research on sex, however. As "The Politics of Sex Research" box shows, research authorizations may be rescinded and funding may be withdrawn because studies on sex—*especially* studies of adolescent sexual behavior—are opposed by conservative religious groups, school administrators, or politicians who feel that such research undermines "traditional family values."

Policy makers also play a major role in encouraging or restricting many types of research. Although research on in vitro fertilization (see Chapter 10) in private fertility clinics is largely unregulated, Congress has banned the use of federal funds for embryo research. In 1997, for example, NIH canceled several multimillion-dollar research grants at Georgetown University when it learned that the research involved storing fetal tissue and performing other human embryo studies (Weiss, 1997).

This and similar studies raise such unresolved questions as whether embryo research is ethical if the results protect millions of still unborn children from inherited disorders. Should fetal tissue be transplanted if it helps people who suffer from Huntington's or other diseases? Another important question is whether deception is justifiable if the findings will be used "for the greater good."

Conclusion

As this chapter shows, understanding marriage and the family is *not* an armchair activity that is dominated by ivory-tower philosophers. Quite to the contrary, and like the family itself, the study of the family reflects *changes* in the evolution of theories and *constraints* due to the limitations of research designs. There has been considerable progress in the family field, and researchers have more *choices* as to methodology. At the same time, "there is plenty of reason for marriage and family scholars to be modest about what they know and humble about what they do not" (Miller, 1986: 110). Research explanations are sometimes inadequate because social scientists ignore the historical context that has shaped the contemporary family. In the next chapter we will look at some of these historical processes.

SUMMARY

1. Although many people are suspicious of statistics, data of all kinds are becoming increasingly important in our daily lives. Information derived from social science research affects much of our everyday behavior, shapes family policy, and provides explanations for social change.

2. The most influential theories of marriage and the family include four macro-level perspectives: ecological, structural-functional, conflict, and feminist theories, as well as four micro-level theories: symbolic interaction, social exchange, developmental, and family systems. Researchers and clinicians often use several theoretical perspectives in interpreting data or in choosing intervention strategies.

3. The survey is one of the most common data-collection methods used in social science research. Surveys rely on questionnaires, interviews, or a combination of the two. Both questionnaires and interviews have advantages and limitations that researchers consider in designing their studies. Focus groups are often used to explore ideas before a survey is launched.

4. Clinical research and case studies provide a deeper understanding of behavior because phenomena can be studied intensively and over time. However, such research is also time-consuming and limited to small groups of people.

5. Observation offers a deeper understanding of behavior and is usually inexpensive. The results of this type of research are difficult to quantify, however, and the researcher may experience difficulty in maintaining a balance between observation and participation.

6. Secondary analysis uses data collected by other researchers (such as historical documents and official government statistics). It is usually an accessible, convenient, and inexpensive source of data. One primary limitation of this method is that existing data may not provide information on the variables that a researcher wants to examine.

7. Evaluation research, an applied research technique, is often used to assess the effectiveness and efficiency of social programs that offer services to families.

8. All social scientists are expected to adhere to professional ethical standards, both in conducting research and in reporting the results. Because political issues often affect research, however, collecting data is not as simple as it seems.

KEY TERMS

theory 28
ecological theory 31
structural-functional theory 31
instrumental role 31
expressive role 31
manifest functions 31
latent functions 31
conflict theory 32
feminist theories 32

quantitative research 33
qualitative research 33
symbolic interaction theory 33
significant others 33
social exchange theory 34
developmental theory 35
family life cycle 35
developmental tasks 35
family systems theory 35

surveys 37
population 37
sample 37
clinical research 40
observation 41
secondary analysis 43
evaluation research 43

TAKING IT FURTHER

Do Your Research Online

Here are some Internet sites that are especially germane to this chapter:

WWW Virtual Library: Sociology is a comprehensive site that offers a good overview of many sociology resources, including chat rooms that discuss family issues.

www.mcmaster.ca/socscidocs/w3virtsoclib/resource.htm

Social Science Information Gateway contains an excellent Internet catalog that includes thousands of online resources, browsable or searchable by subject topics such as *family, theory,* and *research methods.* Its Social Science Search Engine—sosig.ac.uk/harvester.html—indexes a database of over 50,000 social science Web pages.

sosig.ac.uk

Academic Survey Research Centers provides links to and information about survey research centers in the United States and other countries. Many of the sites include full reports on family studies.

www.princeton.edu/~abelson/xsrcs.html

Bill Trochim's Center for Social Research Methods "is for people involved in applied social research and evaluation." Besides covering many research topics, this site offers an online statistical adviser and links to Internet data and research methods sites.

trochim.human.cornell.edu/index.html

Human Development & Family Life Education Resource Center offers research and practical information for professionals, educational resources, reviews of information technology developments that affect family life education, and online bulletins on evaluating family life Websites.

www.hec.ohio-state.edu/famlife

And more . . . www.prenhall.com/benokraitis provides URLs for feminist theory sites, practical tips for evaluating a variety of online resources, a "dictionary" of nonverbal communication, sites for searching full-text U.S. Internet government periodicals, studies of human development across the life span, and a number of online journals on qualitative research, cybersociology, and "mundane" behavior.

The Family In Historical Perspective

DATADIGEST

- During the **Great Depression,** the Southern Pacific Railroad threw more than half a million transients—200,000 of whom were adolescent males—off its boxcars in a single year.

- The fathers of **nearly 183,000 children were killed during World War II.**

- Of the almost 7 million women who **worked outside their homes** during the war, 75 percent were married.

- African American women made some of the greatest **employment gains** during World War II. Those working as servants fell from 72 to 48 percent, while the proportion employed in factories grew from 7 percent to almost 20 percent.

- **Divorce rates surged** from 321,000 in 1942 to 610,000 in 1946, after the end of the war. By 1950, a million veterans had been divorced.

SOURCES: Chafe, 1972; Tuttle, 1993; Mergenbagen, 1996.

gnoring the past leaves large gaps in our understanding of the present. We sometimes think that the modern family is in trouble. Social scientists are showing, however, that "the good old days" never existed for most people. This raises some interesting questions: Were the colonists as virtuous as we were taught in grade school? Did people really pull together to help each other during the Depression? Were the 1950s as fabulous as many people say? Penetrating the stereotypes about the past helps us understand family life today.

Much of this chapter focuses on American Indians, African Americans, Mexican Americans, and European immigrants—four groups that were especially exploited from the seventeenth through the nineteenth centuries. This chapter also shows how the Great Depression, World War II, and the decade of the 1950s, the so-called Golden Fifties, affected the American family. In Chapter 12 we will examine the contemporary experiences of the groups we discuss here as well as those of others.

The Colonial Family

The diversity that characterizes families today also existed in colonial times. Although colonial families differed from modern families in terms of social class, religious practices, and geographic dispersion, such factors as family roles and family structure were very similar.

Family Structure

The nuclear family was the most prevalent family form both in England and in the first settlements of New England. An elderly grandparent or an apprentice sometimes lived for a while with or near the family, but few households were made up of extended families for long periods of time (Goode, 1963; Laslett, 1971). Although families typically raised six or seven children, high infant mortality rates made household sizes small, with large age differences between children. The Puritans—Protestant colonists who adhered to strict moral and religious values—believed that the community had a right to intervene in families that did not perform their duties properly. In the 1670s, for example, the Massachusetts General Court directed towns to appoint "tithingmen" to oversee every 10 to 12 households. The tithingmen were to ensure that marital relations were harmonious and that parents disciplined unruly children (Mintz and Kellogg, 1988).

Unlike later times, few individuals survived outside the family during the colonial period. Most of the settlements were small—fewer than 100 families—and each family was considered a "little commonwealth" that performed a variety of functions. The family was a self-sufficient *business* that produced and exchanged commodities; all family members worked together to meet the family's material needs. At the same time, the family was a *school* that taught children to read. It was a *vocational institute* that taught children specific skills and prepared them for jobs through apprenticeships.

The family also served as a miniature *church* that taught its members daily prayers, personal meditation, and formal family worship in the community. It was a *house of correction;* the courts sentenced idle or criminal people to live as servants in the families of more reputable citizens. Finally, the family served as a *welfare institution* because each family was expected not only to give its members medical and other care but to provide a home and care for other relatives who were orphaned, aging, infirm, or homeless (Demos, 1970). As we shall see later in this chapter, all of these functions changed considerably with the onset of industrialization.

Sexual Relations

The Puritans tried to prevent premarital intercourse in several ways. One was **bundling,** a New England custom in which a young man and woman, both fully dressed, spent the night in a bed together, separated by a wooden board. The custom was adopted because it was difficult for the young suitor, who had traveled many miles, to return home the same night, especially during harsh winters. Because the rest of the family shared the room, it was considered quite proper for the bundled young man and woman to continue their conversations after the fire was out (McPharlin, 1946).

Premarital and extramarital sex were not uncommon. According to some historians, between 20 and 33 percent of colonial women were pregnant at the time of marriage (Hawke, 1988; Demos, 1970). Keep in mind, however, that sexual activity was generally confined to engaged couples. The idea of a casual meeting that included sexual intercourse would have been utterly foreign to the Puritans. On the other hand, among young women who immigrated to the southern colonies as indentured (contracted) servants, out-of-wedlock births were not uncommon. Female indentured servants typically came to the United States alone because they were from families whose lower socioeconomic status meant they could not all migrate together. Because these often very young (under 15) women were alone and vastly outnumbered by men in the colonies, they were vulnerable to sexual attacks by their employers and other men (Harari and Vinovskis, 1993).

In the Puritan community, the primary offenses of adultery and illegitimacy were condemned because they threatened the family structure. Sometimes a straying spouse was denounced publicly:

> CATHERINE TREEN, *the wife of the subscriber, having, in violation of her solem vow, behaved herself in the most disgraceful manner, by leaving her own place of abode, and living in a criminal state with a certain William Collins, a plaisterer, under whose bed she was last night, discovered, endeavoring to conceal herself, her much injured husband, therefore, in justice of himself, thinks it absolutely necessary to forewarn all persons from trusting her on his account, being determined, after such flagrant proof of her prostitution, to pay no debts of her contracting. (cited in Lantz, 1976: 14)*

Few records document men's extramarital affairs because, although frowned upon, a husband's infidelity was considered "normal." Moreover, because the courts did not enforce a father's economic obligation to a child born out of wedlock, it was women, and not men, who paid the costs of bearing and raising illegitimate children (Ryan, 1983). As you can see, the so-called double standard (which we discuss later) is not a modern invention.

Illustrated Edition **25c**

LITTLE KNOWN FACTS ABOUT

BUNDLING

IN THE NEW WORLD

•

By A. MONROE AURAND, Jr.
Member:
Pennsylvania German Folklore Society, &c.

THE OLD-FASHIONED CENTER-BOARD
The Pennsylvania Germans invented all kinds of ways and means to get the courting couples together — and all kinds of knick-knacks to keep them apart when they got together! Girls were safer in the old days, in bed with their beaux, than they are today roaming the world over in search of adventure!

The Pennsylvania Germans invented various ways of keeping courting couples apart when they were together. What do you suppose might have happened to the "centerboard" shown in this sketch after the young woman's parents went to bed? The couple could hope that the family members—who typically slept in the same room—were sound sleepers.

Husbands and Wives

Husbands and wives worked together to make sure that the family survived. Colonial America, like modern society, expected spouses to have strong personal as well as economic relationships. Inequalities, however, were very much a part of early American family life.

In Personal Relationships In general, women were subordinate to men, and the wife's chief duty was obedience to her husband. New England clergymen often referred to male authority as a "government" that the female must accept as "law," and in the southern colonies, husbands often denounced assertive wives as "impertinent" (Ryan, 1983). A woman's social status as well as her power and prestige in the community came from the patriarchal head of the household—either her husband or her father.

At the same time, according to a writer in 1712, the "well-ordered" family was based on a number of mutual spousal responsibilities (Benjamin Wadsworth, cited in Scott and Wishy, 1982). Husbands and wives were expected to love each other and to show "a very great affection." They should be chaste and faithful to each other, and they were encouraged to be patient and to help each other: "If the one is sick, pained, troubled, distressed, the other should manifest care, tenderness, pity, compassion, & afford all possible relief and succour" (p. 86).

In Plymouth, women had the right to transfer land. In 1646, for example, when one man wanted to sell his family's land, the court called in his wife to make sure that she approved. The courts also sometimes granted liquor and other business licenses to women (Demos, 1970). And they sometimes offered a woman protection from a violent husband. The Plymouth court ordered a whipping for a man for "abusing his wife by kiking her of from a stoole into the fier" (Mintz and Kellogg, 1988: 10). Such protections were not typical in the colonies outside of Plymouth, however.

In a few cases, the local courts permitted divorce. The acceptable grounds were limited to desertion, adultery, bigamy, and impotence. Incompatibility was recognized as a problem, but not serious enough to warrant divorce. It was not until about 1765, when romantic love emerged as a basis for marriage, that "loss of affection" was mentioned as a reason for divorce (Cott and Pleck, 1979).

At Work and in the Economy Although men were expected to be industrious, hardworking, and ambitious and were held responsible for the family's economic survival, husbands and wives were not segregated into rigid work roles. Men, women, and children all produced, cultivated, and processed goods for the family's consumption. When necessary, men would care for and discipline the children while women worked in the fields. Much of women's work was nevertheless directed toward meeting the needs of others. In his 1793 *Female Guide*, a New Hampshire pastor defined a woman's role as "piety to God—reverence to parents—love and obedience to their husbands—tenderness and watchfulness over their children—justice and humanity to their dependents" (quoted in Cott, 1977: 22–23).

Although prosperity and industry were praised in both sexes during colonial times, men were expected to initiate economic activity, and women were expected to support men and to be frugal. In 1692, Cotton Mather, an influential minister and author, described women's economic role as being only "to spend (or save) what others get" (Cott, 1977).

In some cases, unmarried women, especially widows and those who had been deserted by their husbands, turned their homemaking activities into self-supporting businesses. Some used their homes as inns, restaurants, or schools. Some sold homemade foods or performed domestic tasks for others. Women living outside of town could make a living by washing, mending, nursing, midwifery, or producing cure-all and beauty potions. Some widows continued their husband's business in such "masculine" areas as chocolate and mustard production, soap making, cutlery, coach making, rope making, publishing, printing, horseshoeing, net making, whaling, and running grocery stores, bookstores, drugstores, and hardware stores. And some of these businesswomen placed ads, on a regular basis, in the local newspapers (Matthaei, 1982).

However, women's, especially wives', economic roles were generally severely limited. Women had little access to credit, could not sue to collect debts, were restricted from owning property, and were less likely to be chosen as executors of wills, especially if their husbands had complicated estates (Ryan, 1983).

Children's Lives

Poor sanitation, crude housing, limited hygiene, and dangerous physical environments characterized colonial America. Infant and child mortality rates were high. Between 10 and 30 percent of all children died before their first birthday and fewer than two out of three children lived to see their tenth birthday. Cotton Mather fathered fourteen children, but only one outlived his father; seven died shortly after birth, one died at age 2, and five died in their early 20s (Stannard, 1979).

Children in colonial times were dominated by the concepts of repression, religion, and respect (Adams, 1980). The Puritans believed that children were born with original sin and were inherently stubborn, willful, selfish, and corrupt. The Reverend John Robinson, a leading preacher among the Pilgrims, wrote: "Surely there is in all children . . . a stubbernes and stoutnes of minde arising from naturall pride which must in the first place be broken and beaten down, that so the foundation of their education being layd in humilitie and tractableness, other virtues may in their time be built thereon" (quoted in Earle, 1899: 192).

The entire community—parents, school, church, and neighbors—worked together to keep children "in their place." Compared to contemporary standards, colonial children were expected to be extraordinarily well disciplined, obedient, and docile (see *Figure 3.1*). Within 40 years of their arrival in Plymouth, however, many colonists worried that their families were disintegrating, that parents were becoming less responsible, and that children were losing respect for authority. Ministers repeatedly warned parents that their children were frequenting taverns, keeping "vicious company," and "tending to dissoluteness (unrestrained and immoral behavior)" (Mintz and Kellogg, 1988: 17).

Wealthy southern families were more indulgent with their children than were well-to-do families in

OF CHILDREN'S BEHAVIOR WHEN AT HOME

1. Make a Bow always when you come Home, and be immediately uncovered [take off your hat].

2. Never Sit in the Presence of thy Parents without bidding, tho' no Stranger be present.

3. If thou art going to speak to thy Parents, and see them engaged in discourse with Company, draw back until afterwards; but if thou must speak, be sure to whisper.

4. Never speak to thy Parents without some Title of Respect, as Sir & Madam.

5. Approach near thy Parents at no time without a Bow.

6. Dispute not, nor delay to Obey thy Parents' Commands.

7. Go not out of Doors without thy Parents leave, and return within the Time by them limited.

8. Quarrel not nor contend with thy Brethren or sisters, but live in love, peace, & unity.

9. Grumble not nor be discontented at anything thy Parents appoint, speak, or do.

10. Bear with Meekness and Patience, and without Murmuring or Sullenness thy Parents' Reproofs or Corrections: Even tho' it should so happen that they be causeless or undeserved.

FIGURE 3.1   Rules for Colonial Children (Adapted from Wadsworth, 1712, in Scott and Wishy, 1982).

the northern colonies, but child labor was nearly universal throughout the colonies at other levels of society. Even very young children worked hard in their own homes or as indentured servants or slaves. For example, several shiploads of "friendless boys and girles," evidently kidnapped in England, were sent to the Virginia colony to provide cheap and docile labor for the American planters (Queen et al., 1985).

Because girls were expected to be homemakers, their formal education was meager. The New England colonies educated boys, but girls were generally banned from education. They were commonly admitted to the public schoolhouse only during those hours and seasons when boys were occupied with other affairs or were needed in the fields. As one farmer stated, "In winter it's too far for girls to walk; in summer they ought to stay at home to help in the kitchen"

(quoted in Earle, 1899: 96). Women who succeeded in getting an education were often ridiculed:

> *One woman who dared to write a theological treatise was rudely rebuffed by her brother: "Your printing of a book is beyond your sex and doth rankly smell." John Winthrop—the first governor of the Massachusetts Bay Colony—maintained that such intellectual exertion could even rot the female mind. He attributed the madness of Ann Hopkins, wife of the Connecticut governor, to her intellectual curiosity: "If she had attended her household affairs and such things as belong to women and not gone out of her way to meddle in the affairs of men whose minds are stronger, she'd have kept her wits and might have improved them usefully." (Ryan, 1983: 57)*

Social Class and Regional Differences

The colonial family's experiences were not the same across all groups; there were a number of regional and social class variations. In a study of Salem families between 1790 and 1810, Farber (1972) found three social classes with very different socialization patterns that supported the economic structure. In the *merchant class,* or the upper class, the patriarchs typically were shipping and commercial entrepreneurs. The oldest son continued the commercial enterprises and invested the family's profits in other high-paying ventures. There was no need to inculcate strong motives for upward social mobility because the family businesses were inherited and partnerships were expanded through first-cousin marriages. Highly skilled occupations, apprenticeship systems, and cooperation among relatives characterized the *artisan class,* or the middle class. Children were encouraged to be upwardly mobile and to achieve security in a livelihood. The *laboring class,* or the working class, was made up mainly of migrants in the community. These people, who had no voting privileges and little education, provided much of the necessary unskilled labor for the merchant class.

Colonial families also differed across regions. Whereas in the northern colonies people settled in villages, in the southern colonies people settled on isolated plantations and farms. There was an especially rigid stratification system among wealthy families, poor whites, indentured servants, and black slaves in the southern colonies.

Early American Families from Non-European Cultures

European explorers and settlers who invaded the North American continent in the sixteenth and seventeenth centuries pushed the American Indians, the original inhabitants, out of their territories. Large numbers of these peoples succumbed to starvation, illnesses, and European epidemics. Except for people who arrived in the colonies as servants—and in general they *chose* to indenture themselves—African Americans are the only people who did not come to America voluntarily. A third group of people who were instrumental in the economic growth of the United States was the Mexican Americans, who were treated as outsiders even though, as we shall see, they were an important source of labor in an expanding economy. The experiences of these three peoples were quite different. Some families and/or tribes fared better than others, and there was considerable diversity within each group.

American Indians

Many anthropologists believe that American Indians migrated, in three waves, from northeastern Asia to North America over a period of 30,000 years (Greenberg and Ruhlen, 1992). By the time European settlers arrived, there were almost 18 million Indians living in North America, speaking approximately 300 languages (John, 1988). Over 100 distinct languages are still spoken in the United States (Trimble and Medicine, 1993). American Indians were enormously diverse racially, culturally, and linguistically. This variation was reflected in kinship and family systems, as well as in interpersonal relations.

Kinship and Family Systems   The Indian societies in North America included bands (Arctic, Subarctic, Great Basin, and Plateau), tribes (Northeast, Plains, Southwest, and the West Coast), and chiefdoms (Southeast and Canadian west coast). *Bands* were characterized by equality between men and women, little polygyny, and small residential households. *Tribes,* which had some egalitarian characteristics and more polygyny, often built large residential structures, like the pueblos in the Southwest. *Chiefdoms* had class structures that often included slaves at the bottom; they were polygynous, and lived in elaborate houses (Price, 1981).

Family structures and practices varied across regions. For example, polygyny was practiced in more than 20 percent of marriages among Indians of the Great Plains and the northwest coast, whereas monogamy was practiced almost exclusively among such agricultural groups as the Hopi, Iroquois, and Huron. Among the agricultural tribes in eastern and southwestern America, where women played a major role in food production, inheritance through the mother's side was common, and young couples lived more often with the woman's family. In most American Indian groups, the most important stages of the life cycle were birth, puberty, marriage, and death. Again, however, there were many variations—some formal and some more casual—that governed marriage, relations with in-laws, and religious rituals.

Approximately 25 percent of North American Indian tribes were **matrilineal,** which meant that children traced their family descent through their mother's line rather than the father's (**patrilineal**). The women owned all the houses, the household furnishings, the fields and gardens, the work tools, and the livestock—and all of this property was passed on to their female heirs (Mathes, 1981). Some groups, such as the Creek society, allowed polygyny. Few men took more than one wife, however, because only the best hunters could support more than one wife and set of children (Braund, 1990).

Some historians tell us that Indian women were better off than their white counterparts in many instances. In contrast to filmmakers' stereotypes of the passive Indian woman and docile "squaw," Indian women actually wielded considerable power and commanded respect in many bands and tribes. The box

CROSS**CULTURAL**

Multicultural: American Indian Women: Chiefs, Physicians, Politicians, and Warriors

Before they were forced onto reservations, where they adopted many customs and practices of the larger society, many American Indian women and men had egalitarian relationships. Besides being wives and mothers, many Indian women were also chiefs, physicians, politicians, and warriors.

Chiefs: In some cases, women became chiefs because of their achievements on the battlefield. In other cases, they replaced husbands who died. Like men, female chiefs could declare war, resolve disputes in the community, and punish offenders.

Physicians: Women could be medicine women, or *shamans,* the Indian equivalent of doctors. Among the Zuñi and other Pueblo cultures, for example, women were members of the Rain Priesthood, the most important religious group. Among the Anishinaabe, Blackfoot, Chilula, and Dine tribes, women also played crucial spiritual leadership roles.

Politicians: Because many tribes were matrilineal and matrilocal, many women were powerful politically. Among the Lakota, for example, a man owned nothing but his clothing, a horse for hunting, weapons, and spiritual items. Homes, furnishings, and other property belonged to wives. In many tribes, women were influential decision makers in the community.

Warriors: Among the Apache, some women warriors were as courageous, daring, and skillful as the men, and Cheyenne women fighters distinguished themselves in war. Lakota women maintained four known warrior societies of their own, and among the Cherokee, one of the fiercest warriors was a woman who also headed a women's military society. Women could stop—and they did stop—war parties by refusing to supply the necessary food for the journey. An Iroquois woman could initiate a war party because she was entitled to demand

Delaware Nation council chief and educator Linda Poolaw was asked to choose works for an exhibition for the Smithsonian's National Museum of the American Indian. Poolaw's ancestors once lived on Manhattan Island in New York.

that a captive replace any murdered member of her clan. Creek women were often responsible for raising "war fervor" against enemies (Mathes, 1981; Braund, 1990; Stockel, 1991; Jaimes and Halsey, 1992).

"American Indian Women: Chiefs, Politicians, and Warriors" describes some of the societal roles that Indian women of colonial times played.

Marriage and Divorce Most American Indians married at a young age. Women typically married between the ages of 12 and 15, after reaching puberty. Men married at slightly older ages, between 15 and 20, usually after they had shown an ability to hunt or to provide for a family. Some families arranged their children's marriages; others allowed young men and women to choose their own spouses.

Family structures and customs also varied. Among the Shoshone there were no formal marriage ceremonies; the families simply exchanged gifts. Also, there were no formal rules of residence. The newly married couple could live with the family of either the groom or the bride or establish its own independent unit.

Mohave marriages were similarly casual—there was no dowry, gift exchange, or wedding ceremony.

The only rules were designed to prevent incest. A man could not marry a woman to whom a direct blood relationship could be traced either through his mother or father or who was a member of his own clan. The married couple took up residence with the husband's parents. Divorce was simple—either partner could initiate the separation—and fairly common among young adults, who remarried easily.

Among the Zuñi of the Southwest, marriages were arranged casually, and the groom moved into the bride's household. The Zuñi and other groups made divorce easy. If a wife was fed up with a demanding husband, all she had to do was put his belongings outside their home, and they were no longer married. The man, though he might be unhappy, accepted the dismissal and returned to his mother's household. If a husband sought a divorce, he would tell his wife he was going hunting and then never return (Stockel, 1991).

In the Great Plains, most Teton parents arranged marriages but some were based on romantic love.

Marriages were often lifetime associations, but divorce was easy and not uncommon. A man could divorce a wife for adultery, laziness, or even excessive nagging. Both parties usually agreed to divorce, but a man could humiliate a wife by casting her off publicly at a dance or other ceremony. A truly generous husband who had evidence of adultery would—instead of cutting off his wife's nose (literally) and demanding a payment from her lover—force the couple to leave the band and even provide them with a horse and other property to show his magnanimous nature.

Children   Most Indian families were small because of high infant and child death rates and because mothers nursed their children for several years, often abstaining from sexual relations until the child was weaned. Throughout most American Indian groups, childhood was considered to be a happy time, and parents were generally kind and loving. Mohave parents, for example, were indulgent; childhood was a carefree time, and disciplinary methods, only rarely invoked, were mild. Similarly, the Zuñi treated children with kindness and little physical restraint. Children were taught to be polite and gentle. Unruly children were frightened into conformity by stories of religious bogeymen rather than by physical punishment. The grandparents on both sides of the family took an active part in the education of the children and told stories that inculcated the tribe's values.

In general, children were greatly desired and welcomed. Adults fussed over the babies; they were gentle and permissive in weaning and toilet-training practices and imposed few responsibilities.

Puberty   In most Indian societies, puberty rites were more elaborate for girls than for boys. Among the Alaskan Nabesna, for example, the menstruating girl was secluded, observed strict food taboos, was forbidden to touch her own body with her hands (lest sores break out), and was forbidden to travel with the tribe. Among the Navajo, girls underwent elaborate rites with an all-night "sing" on the fourth ceremonial night. In contrast, among the Mohave, the observance of a girl's puberty was a private family matter that did not include any rituals.

The Zuñi celebrated rites of passage for boys twice—between ages 5 and 9 and again between 11 and 14. Each time the ceremony included purification and exorcism rites. Among the Teton, a boy's puberty was marked by a series of events, such as his first successful bison hunt, his first war party, his first capture of enemy horses, and other deeds, all of which were commemorated by his father with feasts and gifts to others.

Also of great importance in some tribes was the *vision quest*—a supernatural experience in which a "familiar spirit" suggested the course the boy's adult life would take and which involved fasting, isolation, and self-torture (such as gashing his arms and legs).

The young boy fasted for four days before leaving the tribe's camp and took ritual purifying sweat baths in a small dome-shaped sweat lodge. On leaving the camp, the boy found an isolated place—frequently a butte top or other elevated spot—where he waited for four days and nights or until he experienced a vision in which a supernatural being instructed the boy on his future responsibilities (Spencer and Jennings, 1977).

The Impact of European Cultures   The French, Spanish, Portuguese, and British played a major role in destroying much American Indian culture. Missionaries, determined to convert the "savages" to Christianity, were responsible for some of this destruction. With no understanding of the crucial importance in the normal functioning and survival of the native societies, missionaries tried to eliminate religious ceremonies and such practices as polygyny and matrilineal inheritance (Price, 1981). Most exploitation was economic, however. Europeans saw the opportunities for exploiting the abundant North American resources of gold, land, and fur.

Indian tribes coped with military slaughter, enslavement, forced labor, land confiscation, coerced mass migration, and involuntary religious conversions (Collier, 1947). In addition, by the end of the seventeenth century, staggering numbers of American Indians in the East had died from such new diseases as influenza, measles, smallpox, and typhus. The Plymouth colony was actually located in a deserted Indian village whose inhabitants had been devastated by epidemics brought by Europeans. By the 1670s, only 10 percent of the original American Indian population of New England had survived. At least 50 tribes became extinct as a result of disease and massacre. During the eighteenth and nineteenth centuries, the diversity of American Indian family practices was reduced even further through missionary activities, intrusive federal land policies, poverty on reservations, marriage with outside groups, and federal government relocations of American Indians to urban areas (John, 1988).

African Americans

One colonist wrote in his journal that on August 20, 1619, at the Jamestown settlement in Virginia, "there came . . . a Dutch man-of-warre that sold us 20 negars." These first African Americans in the North American colonies were brought over as indentured servants. After their terms of service, they were free to buy land, marry, and hire their own labor. These rights were short-lived, however. By the mid-1660s, the southern colonies had passed laws prohibiting blacks from testifying in court, owning property, making contracts, traveling without permission, congregating in public places, and marrying. The slave trade grew in both the northern and the southern colonies over several decades.

CONSTRAINTS

A Slave Auction

In the mid-1970s, Alex Haley, a journalist who had taught himself to read and write during a 20-year career in the U.S. Coast Guard, was catapulted to fame when his book *Roots* became a best-seller and was made into one of the first mini-series on television. In the book, Haley traced the six generations of his ancestors, the first of whom was abducted at the age of 16 from Gambia, West Africa, in 1767. The following excerpt is an equally powerful description of how African families were destroyed by slavery:

During the day a number of sales were made. David and Caroline were purchased together by a Natchez planter. They left us, grinning broadly, and in a most happy state of mind, caused by the fact of their not being separated. Sethe was sold to a planter of Baton Rouge, her eyes flashing with anger as she was led away.

The same man also purchased Randall. The little fellow was made to jump, and run across the floor, and perform many other feats, exhibiting his activity and condition. All the time the trade was going on, Eliza was crying aloud and wringing her hands. She besought the man not to buy him, unless he also bought herself and Emily. She promised, in that case, to be the most faithful slave that ever lived. The man answered that he could not afford it, and then Eliza burst into a paroxysm of grief, weeping plaintively. Freeman turned round to her, savagely, with his whip in his uplifted hand, ordering her to stop her noise, or he would flog her. He could not have such work—such sniveling; and unless she ceased that minute, he would take her to the yard and give her a hundred lashes. Yes, he would take the nonsense out of her pretty quick. . . . Eliza shrunk before him and tried to wipe away her tears, but it was all in vain. She wanted to be with her children, she said, the little time she had to live.

All the frowns and threats of Freeman could not wholly silence the afflicted mother. She kept on begging and beseeching them, most piteously, not to separate the three. Over and over again she told them how she loved her boy. A great many times she repeated her former promises—how very faithful and obedient she would be, how hard she would labor day and night, to the last moment of her life, if he would only buy them all together. But it was of no avail; the man could not afford it. The bargain was agreed upon, and Randall must go alone. Then Eliza ran to him, embraced him passionately, kissed him again and again, told him to remember her—all the while her tears falling in the boy's face like rain.

Freeman damned her, calling her a blubbering, bawling wench, and ordered her to go to her place, and behave herself, and be somebody. He swore he wouldn't stand such stuff [but] a little longer. He would soon give her something to cry about, if she was not mighty careful, and that she might depend on.

The planter from Baton Rouge, with his new purchase, was ready to depart.

"Don't cry, mama. I will be a good boy. Don't cry," said Randall, looking back, as they passed out of the door.

What has become of the lad, God knows. It was a mournful scene indeed. I would have cried myself if I had dared. (Adapted from Solomon Northrup, cited in Meltzer, 1964: 87–89)

Some early statesmen, like Thomas Jefferson, publicly decried the institution of slavery but supported it privately. While drafting the Declaration of Independence in 1776, Jefferson denounced the king of England for allowing the importation of slaves. In 1809, however, Jefferson maintained that "the Negro slave in America must be removed beyond the reach of mixture" for the preservation of the "dignity" and "beauty" of the white race (Bergman, 1969). At the same time, Jefferson had a slave mistress and fathered children with her. Inconsistent to the end, he freed five of his slaves in his will but left the rest to his heirs.

Marriage   Throughout the colonies, it was difficult for a slave to find a spouse. In northern cities, most slaves lived with their masters and were not allowed to associate with other slaves. In the southern colonies, most slaves lived on plantations that had fewer than ten slaves. Because the plantations were far apart and the sex and age ratios were skewed, it was difficult for slave men and women to find a spouse of roughly the same age. In addition, overwork and high death rates due to widespread disease meant that marriages did not last very long (Mintz and Kellogg, 1988).

After the importation of slaves into the United States was prohibited in 1807, breeding increased in importance. To ensure that slaves would remain on the plantations, many owners recognized familial relationships among slaves, encouraged them to have large families, and provided living quarters. Yet slave marriages were fragile institutions. As the box "A Slave Auction" shows, owners often separated slave families for economic reasons. Studies of slave families in Mississippi, Tennessee, and Louisiana show that between

35 and 40 percent of marriages were terminated by such actions (Gutman, 1976; Matthaei, 1982).

Family Structure   Until the 1970s, sociologists and historians maintained that slavery had emasculated black fathers, forced black mothers to be family matriarchs, and destroyed the African American family. Historian Herbert Gutman (1983) dispelled many of these beliefs with his study of 21 urban and rural communities in the South between 1855 and 1880. Gutman found that 70 to 90 percent of African American households were made up of a husband and wife or a single father. Furthermore, most women who were heads of households were alone because their husbands had died, not because they had never married, and they usually had only one or two children. Thus, according to Gutman, black families were surprisingly stable and intact during the nineteenth century.

Husbands and Fathers   Several black scholars have also noted that the slave family structure has been misrepresented by white, male, middle-class historians and sociologists (McAdoo, 1986; Staples, 1988). One example of such misrepresentation is the portrayal of slave husbands and fathers. In contrast to popular conceptions of the African American male as emasculated and powerless, adult male slaves provided important role models for boys:

> *Trapping wild turkeys required considerable skill; not everyone could construct a "rabbit gum" equal to the guile of the rabbits; and running down the quick, battling raccoon took pluck. For a boy growing up, the moment when his father thought him ready to join in the hunting and to learn to trap was a much-sought recognition of his own manhood. (Genovese, 1981: 239–40)*

These activities reduced families' nutritional deficiencies and supplemented monotonous and inadequate diets. In addition, even though the intervention was often fatal, there are numerous slave narratives documenting men's attempts to save their daughters, mothers, and wives from sexual exploitation by their masters (Genovese, 1981; Staples, 1988).

African male slaves often served as surrogate fathers to many children, blood relatives and others. Black preachers, whose eloquence and morality commanded the respect of the entire community, were also influential role models. Men made shoes, wove baskets, constructed furniture, and cultivated the tiny household garden plots allotted to families by the master (Jones, 1985). Some male slaves were also apprenticed in skilled jobs, promoted to better jobs, and granted cash bonuses for loyal service (Ryan, 1983). They were excluded, however, from political, economic, and educational institutions.

Wives and Mothers   Images of strong slave mothers and wives have dominated portrayals of black families both in films and in print. Many historical documents describe African American women as survivors who resisted the slave system. For example, one proud daughter recalls, "My mother was the smartest black woman in Edes . . . she would do anything. She made as good a field hand as she did a cook. She was a demon, loud and boisterous, high-spirited and independent. I tell you she was a captain" (quoted in Ryan, 1983: 162–63).

Mothers reared the children, cooked the food, maintained the slave cabin, and worked in the fields. Because the African American woman was often both a "mammy" to the plantation owner's children and a mother to her own, she experienced the exhausting *double day*—a full day of domestic chores plus a full day of work outside the home—at least a century before middle-class white women coined the term. Black women got little recognition for this grueling schedule and were often subjected to physical punishment; even pregnant and nursing mothers did not escape such abuse. Pregnant slaves were sometimes forced to lie facedown in a specially dug depression in the ground, which protected the fetus while the mother was beaten, and some nursing mothers were whipped until "blood and milk flew mingled from their breasts" (Jones, 1985: 20).

In the South, only a few female slaves worked in the master's house, known as "the big house." Most females over 10 years of age worked in the field, sunup to sundown, six days a week, and struggled to maintain a semblance of family life:

> *A female field hand might be granted a month off for childbirth or be allowed to return from the fields three or four times a day to nurse a newborn infant. Occasionally, women were permitted to leave the fields early on Saturday to perform some chores around the slave quarters. Their homes were small cabins of one or two rooms, which they usually shared with their mate and their children, and perhaps another family secluded behind a crude partition. . . . Slave women were often responsible for manufacturing soap, candles, and clothes for their families, as well as cooking crude meals. (Ryan, 1983: 159)*

Popular films like *Gone with the Wind* often portray house slaves as doing little more than adjusting Miss Scarlett's petticoats and announcing male suitors. In reality, domestic work was as hard as fieldwork. Fetching wood and water, preparing three full meals a day over a smoky fireplace, and pressing clothes for an entire family was backbreaking labor. Female servants sometimes had to sleep on the floor at the foot of the mistress's bed. They were also often forced into sexual relations with the master. Injuries were common,

minor infractions met with swift and severe punishment, and servants suffered abuse ranging from jabs with pins to beatings that left them disfigured for life (Jones, 1985).

Economic Survival *Ethnic Notions,* a memorable documentary, shows that many Hollywood movies, books, and newspapers have portrayed slaves as helpless, docile, and dependent people who couldn't care for themselves. Recent evidence is shattering such stereotypes. An archaeological team excavating Virginia plantations, for example, has found that some enslaved Africans were "entrepreneurs": They exchanged fish and game for children's toys, dishes, and other household items. Also, many slaves hid important personal possessions and items stolen from plantation owners in underground storage areas (Wheeler, 1998). Several historians, similarly, argue that slaves were hardly passive or submissive. Instead, slaves used such effective tactics as breaking tools to slow their pace of work and negotiated with masters over assigned tasks (Berlin, 1998; Morgan, 1998).

After Emancipation After slavery was abolished, many mothers set out to find children from whom they had been separated many years earlier (King, 1996). Numerous slaves legitimized their marriages, even though the one-dollar fee for the marriage license cost about two weeks' pay for most. In Hinds County, Mississippi, 15 years after emancipation, African Americans bought 75 percent of the marriage licenses issued, even though they constituted less than 75 percent of the population between 15 and 44 years of age. A legal marriage was an important status symbol, and a wedding was a festive event (Degler, 1981; Staples, 1988).

Even where slavery had destroyed many families, kinship networks survived. After slavery's end, African American families began naming children after blood relatives—uncles, aunts, siblings, and grandparents—thus preserving these kinship ties.

Some writers have claimed that the African American family, already disrupted by slavery, was further weakened by urban migration to the North in the late 1800s (Frazier, 1939; Moynihan, 1970). Many black migrants, however, tried to maintain contact with their kin and families in the South. When black men migrated alone, "A constant flow of letters containing cash and advice between North and South facilitated the gradual migration of whole clans and even villages" (Jones, 1985: 159). Others returned home frequently to join in community celebrations, or to help with planting and harvesting on the family farm. Thus, many African American families remained resilient despite difficult conditions.

Mexican Americans

Mexican American families are very heterogeneous. Some trace their roots to the Spanish and Mexican settlers in the Southwest before the arrival of European immigrants; others migrated to North America from Central and South America at the beginning of the twentieth century.

The United States annexed territory that was originally Mexican in 1848 after 30 years of war and conflict. Despite the provisions of the Treaty of Guadalupe Hidalgo, which guaranteed security of their property, Mexican landowners had their lands confiscated or were defrauded by land speculators. By the mid-nineteenth century, in spite of treaty promises, old land grants were ignored and many Mexican families lost their land to the U.S. government. Most of the Mexicans and their descendants became landless laborers. The dispossession of land and the depletion of their economic base have had long-term negative effects on Mexican American families (see Chapter 12).

Work and Gender Whether they lived and grew up in the United States or migrated from Mexico, Mexican laborers were essential to the prosperity of southwestern businesses. Mexican migrants were assigned to particular jobs by gender. Even though many had done skilled work in Mexico, employers purposely refrained from hiring them for skilled jobs because "they are available in such [great] numbers and . . . they [would] do the most disagreeable work at the lowest wages" (Feldman, 1931: 115).

During the 1800s, most women and children worked as almond pickers and shellers. Men typically worked on the railroads and in mining or in agricultural, ranching, or low-level urban occupations (such as dishwasher). Women worked as domestics, cooks, live-in house servants, and laundresses, in canning and packing houses, and in agriculture (Camarillo, 1979). By the 1930s, Mexican women made up a major portion of the labor pool of the garment manufacturing sweatshops in the Southwest. Even though American labor codes stipulated a pay rate of $15 a week, Mexican women were paid less than $5, and some earned as little as 50 cents a week. If the women protested, they lost their jobs. Illegal migrants were especially vulnerable because they were intimidated by threats of deportation (Acuna, 1988). Despite the economic exploitation, many Mexican families preserved traditional family structure, child rearing, and family roles.

Family Structure   Mexican society was characterized by **familism**; that is, family relationships took precedence over individual well-being. (As you will see in Chapter 12, familism still characterizes much of Mexican American culture.) Moreover, the nuclear family embraced an extended family of several generations, including cousins, where the relationships were both emotionally and financially supportive (Moore and Pachon, 1985).

A key factor in conserving Mexican culture was the concept and practice of *compadrazgo,* in which close relationships were established and maintained among parents, children, and the children's godparents. The *compadres,* or co-parents, were godparents who enlarged family ties, similar to the fictive kin described in Chapter 1. Godparents were close family friends who had strong ties with their godchildren throughout life and participated in such rites of passage as baptism, confirmation, first communion, and marriage. The godparents in the *compadrazgo* network provided both discipline and support. They expected obedience, respect, and love from their godchildren, but they were warm and affectionate and helped the children financially whenever possible. Among poor or rural families, godparents also provided trips away from home. For girls, who led cloistered and protected lives, visiting godparents' families was a major form of recreation (Williams, 1990).

Children   The handful of available diaries, letters, and other writings suggests that, at least in middle- and upper-class families, children were socialized according to gender. Although boys did some chores that might have been labeled "women's work," they also had considerably more freedom than girls. Young girls were severely restricted in their social relationships outside the home. The overwhelming concern was that a girl should learn how to be a good mother and wife—a refuge for the husband, a virtuous example for her children, and the "soul of society" (del Castillo, 1984: 81).

A diary kept by a teenage girl who lived on the outskirts of San Antonio from 1889 to 1892 indicates that her brother was responsible for helping with such family tasks as laundry and chopping wood. He was allowed to go into town on errands and to travel around the countryside on his horse. In contrast, she was not allowed to go into town with her father and brother or to attend chaperoned dances in the town. She could not visit neighbors, and she attended only one social event in a six-month period when her family traveled into town to visit her aunt at Christmastime (del Castillo, 1984).

Many middle-class Mexican American children who were born in the United States had a prolonged adolescence, living with their parents until young adulthood. This was because, in general, Mexican American families believed in protecting children as long as possible. The practice was more common among affluent families, where children stayed at home to learn to take care of inherited land and wealth. In contrast, working-class children left home earlier to seek wage-paying jobs.

Much of the children's socialization was based on religious teachings and parental role models. It was not uncommon for children to memorize long passages from the catechism. Although the upper classes were more permissive, all children were taught respect for their parents and elders. In California, parents even took their children to public executions (until the 1870s, when such executions were banned) to teach them the fatal consequences of evil acts.

Family Roles   Even though many mothers were forced by economic necessity to work outside the home, women were the cultural guardians of family traditions. In spite of the disruptions caused by migratory work, women nurtured Mexican culture through folklore, songs, baptisms, weddings, and celebrations of birthdays and saints' days (Garcia, 1980). In the traditional family, women defined their roles primarily as homemakers and mothers.

In the Mexican American family, the male head of the family had all the authority. Masculinity was expressed in the concept of *machismo,* which stresses such male attributes as dominance, assertiveness, pride, and sexual prowess. (Some of the controversy surrounding the interpretation of *machismo* is discussed in Chapter 12.) This notion of male preeminence carried with it the clear implication of a double standard. Men could engage in premarital and extramarital sex, for example, but women were expected to remain virgins or faithful to their husbands and to limit their social relationships, even after marriage, to family and female friends (Mirande, 1985; Moore and Pachon, 1985).

The European Influence Although they suffered less physical and cultural destruction than American Indians, Mexican Americans endured a great deal at the hands of European frontiersmen, land speculators, and politicians. Anglos (a term originally used by many Mexicans to mean whites of non-Mexican descent; now sometimes used to mean people of Anglo-Saxon descent) justified taking over Mexican land by describing Mexicans as having a "distinctly low mental caliber," being incapable of self-government, and working cheaply (Carlson and Colburn, 1972). By the mid-1800s, when most Mexican Americans were beginning to experience widespread exploitation, new waves of European immigrant families were also harnessed under the yoke of industrialization.

Industrialization, Urbanization, and European Immigration: 1820 to 1930

The lives of many U.S. families changed considerably from about 1820 to 1930 due to two massive waves of immigration from Europe. More than 10 million immigrants—mostly English, Irish, Scandinavian, and German—arrived during the first wave, from 1830 to 1882. During the second wave, 1882 to 1930, immigrants were predominantly Russian, Greek, Polish, Italian, Austrian, Hungarian, and Slavic.

The Industrial Revolution brought about extensive mechanization, which shifted home manufacturing to large-scale factory production. As the economic structure changed, a small group of white, Anglo-Saxon, Protestant (often referred to as WASP), upper-class families prospered from the backbreaking labor of Mexicans, Asians, European immigrants, and many American-born whites. For millions of other families, the economic changes brought poverty, family dislocations, and enormous hardships. European immigrants endured some of the most severe pressures on family life.

Family Life

As farming became large scale and commercial and as factories developed, families lost many of their production functions. Most family members had to work outside the home to purchase goods and services. Although it is not clear exactly how it happened, family life changed.

In the middle classes, husbands and wives developed separate spheres of activity. The husband went out to work (the "breadwinner"), and the wife stayed home to care for the children (the "housewife"). Couples had more freedom in choosing partners on the basis of compatibility and personal attraction because

romantic love became the basis for marriage. As households became more private, ties with the larger community became more tenuous, and spouses now turned to each other for affection and happiness. New attitudes about the "true woman" became paramount in redefining the role of the wife as nurturer and caregiver rather than workmate. In the lower socioeconomic classes, many mothers worked outside the home in low-paying jobs. Children often dropped out of school to work and help support their families, and most spouses had little time to display love and affection.

The Debut of "True Womanhood"
By the late eighteenth century, a small group of northern merchants had monopolized the import business, and wealthy southern planters had greatly expanded their landholdings and crop production. The wives and daughters of these elite business leaders devoted much of their energy to "a conspicuous display of personal adornment and social graces." The women spent much of their time socializing, throwing lavish parties, and adorning their homes and themselves. "The upkeep of her appearance might involve preparation of the cosmetic base, aqua vitae, a potion requiring 30 ingredients, 2 months' cultivation, and an impossible final step: 'shake the bottle incessantly for 10 to 12 hours'" (quoted in Ryan, 1983: 85–86).

By the early 1800s, most men's work was totally separated from the household, and family life became oriented around the man's struggle in the economy at large. The "good" wife made the home a comfortable retreat from the pressures that the man faced in the workplace. Between 1820 and 1860, women's magazines and religious literature defined the attributes of *true womanhood*. Women were judged as "good" if they displayed four cardinal virtues: piety, purity, submissiveness, and domesticity (Welter, 1966). As the box "Characteristics of 'True Womanhood'" demonstrates, working-class women were not considered capable of being "true women" because, like men, most worked outside the home.

Children and Adolescents
Fathers' control over children began to erode even before the onset of the Industrial Revolution. By the end of the seventeenth century, fathers had less land to divide among sons. This meant that fathers had less authority over their children's (especially sons') sexual behavior and choice of a marriage partner. The fact that the percentage of women who were pregnant at the time of marriage shot up to more than 40 percent by the middle of the eighteenth century (Mintz and Kellogg, 1988) suggests that parents had become less effective in preventing premarital intercourse.

Because a marriage became less likely to involve agreements about the distribution of family land and property, children were less dependent on their fathers

CHANGES

Characteristics of "True Womanhood"

One author describes nineteenth-century working-class women as "without corsets, matrons with their breasts unrestrained, their armpits damp with sweat, with their hair all over the place, blouses dirty or torn, and stained skirts" (Barret-Ducrocq, 1991: 11). The expectations of the "true woman" of the upper classes (and whom middle-class women tried to emulate) were quite different.

The loss of purity was worse than death. Mrs. Eliza Farrar, in *The Young Lady's Friend* (1837), gave practical advice about staying out of trouble: "Sit not with another in a place that is too narrow; read not out of the same book; let not your eagerness to see anything induce you to place your head close to another person's."

Men were the movers, the doers, and the actors. Women should be gentle, passive, submissive, childlike, weak, dependent, and protected. They should work silently, unseen, and only for affection, not for money or ambition. Women should marry, but not for money. They should choose "only the high road of true love and not truckle to the values of a materialistic society" (Welter, 1966). A woman should stifle her own talents and devote herself "to sustain her husband's genius and aid him in his arduous career." Domesticity was a woman's most prized virtue. One of the most important functions of woman as comforter was her role as nurse. The sickroom needed her "higher qualities" of patience, mercy, gentleness, and housewifely arts (Welter, 1966).

Home was supposed to be a cheerful place, so that brothers, husbands, and sons would not go elsewhere for a good time. Women were not only the "highest adornment of civilization" but were supposed to keep busy at "morally uplifting tasks." Housework was seen as uplifting. For example, making beds was good exercise, the repetitiveness of routine tasks inculcated patience and perseverance, and proper management of the home was a surprisingly complex art: "There is more to be learned about pouring out tea and coffee than most young ladies are willing to believe" (Welter, 1966).

The true woman was expected to love flowers, to write letters, "an activity particularly feminine since it had to do with the outpourings of the heart," to practice singing and playing an instrument, or even to read. Because women were dangerously addicted to novels, however, they should avoid them because they interfered with "serious piety." If a woman had to read, she should choose spiritually uplifting books from a list of "morally acceptable authors," preferably religious biographies (Welter, 1966).

for economic support. Moreover, new opportunities for nonagricultural work and a shortage of labor allowed many children to leave home and escape strict fathers.

Perhaps the biggest change was that, largely in the middle class, children began to be perceived and treated not just as small adults but as individuals in a particular stage of life. Around 1800, the concept of original sin—which decrees that children are inherently bad—gave way to the notion that children were innocent creatures with the capacity for either good or bad. Children began to spend more time playing than working, and adolescence gained recognition as another stage of life that had no adult responsibilities. More books for and about children were published, and people began to recognize children's individuality by giving them names that were different from their father's or mother's. In the nineteenth century, people began for the first time to celebrate birthdays, especially those of children. There was also a marked decline in the use of corporal punishment, and physicians and others now recognized the early onset of sexual feelings in children (Aries, 1962; Degler, 1981; Demos, 1986).

Among the working classes and the poor in the nineteenth century, however, child labor was widespread, and children made a critical contribution to their families' income. In a Massachusetts survey of working-class families in 1875, for example, children under age 15 contributed nearly 20 percent of their families' income (Mintz and Kellogg, 1988).

The Impact of Immigration and Urbanization

Immigration played a key role in the Industrial Revolution in the United States. Immigrants provided a large pool of unskilled and skilled labor that fueled emerging industries and gave investors huge profits. In the first large waves of immigration during the late 1800s, paid middlemen arranged for the shipment of immigrants to waiting industries. For example, Asians were channeled into the western railroads, Italians were funneled into public works projects and used

These Pennsylvania miners and "breaker boys"—youngsters who sorted the mined coal into traded categories—worked as many as fourteen hours a day for very low pay. Like most miners of this period, they were immigrants who provided backbreaking labor during the U.S. Industrial Revolution.

as strikebreakers, and Hungarians were directed toward the Pennsylvania mines. Later immigrants followed these established paths into industrial America (Bodnar, 1985).

Work Very few immigrant families escaped dire poverty. Because men's wages were low, most married women also worked. Many were not counted by the census, however, because they worked outside of organized industries. Some, for example, worked at home making flowers, threading wires through tags, or crocheting over curtain rings. Some were cleaning women or seamstresses, did laundry, or sold cakes (Weatherford, 1986). Others took in boarders and lodgers, especially after their children had left home (Hareven, 1984). And, like the men, women of different ethnic groups tended to move into specific jobs. Italian women, for example, were more likely than Polish or Greek women to reject domestic labor, which would take them out of the Italian community and into other people's homes. Consequently, they were more likely to work as seasonal laborers for fruit-and-vegetable processing companies. In this way, they also avoided competing for work with their frequently unemployed husbands (Squier and Quadagno, 1988). By the turn of the century, as *Figure 3.2* shows, a woman's occupation seemed to be associated with her race and ethnicity.

By 1890, all but 9 of the 369 industries listed by the U.S. Census Bureau employed women. Many of these industries were especially eager to hire "greenhorns" and women "just off the boat" who would work for low wages. Greenhorns were often underpaid or not paid at all. In some cases, employers delayed wage payments for several months and then closed up the shops, disappearing overnight (Manning, 1970). By the turn of the century, some Irish girls as young as 11 began leaving home to work as servants; 75 percent of all Irish teenage girls were domestic servants (Ryan, 1983). Many had to perform child-care tasks even though they were hired only to do housekeeping, were sexually assaulted by the male employers, and were not paid their full wages.

Most manufacturing jobs were segregated by sex. In the tobacco industry, for example, even though cigar rolling traditionally had been a woman's task in Slavic countries, men filled this well-paying job. Immigrant women were relegated to damp and putrid basement rooms where they stripped the tobacco that was then rolled by men who worked "upstairs" under better conditions. In the metal trades, men who had gone through apprenticeships worked with lighter and more intricate sand cores (devices used in molding steel) and had high-paying jobs. In contrast, immigrant women hauled heavy sand cores through dusty shops to fuming ovens (Ryan, 1983).

Housing One of the biggest problems for immigrant families was the lack of decent housing in densely populated cities. One Philadelphia tenement house, for example, housed 30 families in 34 rooms. A Lithuanian couple and their five children lived in a tiny closet of a home that contained only slightly more air space than the law required for one adult. New York City police, enforcing health department orders, found many immigrants' rooms of less than 13 square feet that slept 12 men and women, most of them on the floor. The buildings themselves were jammed together so that the population of an immigrant city block was equal to that of an entire town; women increased their kitchen wall space by reaching out the window and hanging utensils on the outside of the house next door (Weatherford, 1986).

Epidemics and disease were rampant among immigrant families. A cholera epidemic that barely touched the rest of New York City killed nearly a fifth of the residents of a crowded immigrant neighborhood. Because a third of tenement rooms had no windows or ventilation, many immigrants contracted tuberculosis. In Lawrence, Massachusetts, where the population was 90 percent immigrant, a third of the spinners in the textile mills died of respiratory diseases, such as pneumonia and tuberculosis, before they had worked ten years. These diseases were triggered by the lint, dust, and machine fumes of the unventilated mills. Further, the excruciating noise of the mills

FIGURE 3.2   Women and Work in Nineteenth-Century America. As you can see, women who worked outside the home in the 1800s tended to cluster in certain low-paying jobs. Only those who spoke English well were hired as office workers or teachers.

often resulted in deafness, and many workers were injured by faulty machines (Weatherford, 1986).

Dilapidated urban housing and epidemics were not the only problems the immigrant family faced. In a study of Polish immigrants, Thomas and Znaniecki (1927) found that people suffered many of the ills that come with poverty and isolation in a strange and often hostile new environment—a breakdown of marital and family relations, crime, delinquency among their children, and general demoralization. Living quarters shared with relatives put additional pressures on already-strained conjugal ties.

Prejudice and Discrimination   Like American Indians and African Americans before them, white immigrants, no matter what their country of origin, met with enormous prejudice, discrimination, and economic exploitation. The prejudice and discrimination were often fostered by high-ranking, highly respected, and influential people who had been educated in the most prestigious colleges and universities in the United States (see the box "Stereotypes about European Immigrants"). Despite the prejudice and discrimination, however, most white immigrant and racial-ethnic families overcame enormous obstacles. Rarely complaining, they worked at low-status jobs with low-paying wages and encouraged their children to achieve and move up.

The "Modern" Family Emerges

The economic depression of the 1930s, World War II of the 1940s, the baby boom of the 1950s, and the increasing economic and political unrest of the years since the 1960s have all influenced the American

CROSSCULTURAL

Stereotypes about European Immigrants

On October 28, 1886, President Grover Cleveland dedicated the Statue of Liberty in New York Harbor on whose pedestal are inscribed Emma Lazarus's famous welcoming words: "Give me your tired, your poor, your huddled masses yearning to breathe free. . . ." As the following examples show, however, Lazarus's poem did not reflect the reality:

1886—The U.S. consul in Budapest advised that Hungarian immigrants were not "a desirable acquisition" because, he claimed, they lacked ambition and they would work as cheaply as the Chinese, which would interfere "with a civilized laborer's earning a 'white' laborer's wages."

1891—Congressman Henry Cabot Lodge called for a restriction of immigration because (referring especially to Jewish and Polish immigrants) the immigrants represented the "lowest and most illiterate classes" which were "alien to the body of the American people."

1910—The eugenics movement was devoted to improving the human species by controlling hereditary factors in mating. Its members believed that immigration, through intermarriage, would contaminate the "old stock" with feeblemindedness, criminality, and pauperism. Many eugenicists were located in privileged eastern universities. Robert DeCourcey Ward, for example, a Boston-born Harvard graduate and professor, helped form the Immigration Restriction League in 1894.

1914—Edward A. Ross, a prominent sociologist at the University of Wisconsin, considered himself one of the nation's immigration watchdogs. He wrote: "That the Mediterranean people are morally below the races of northern Europe is as certain as any social fact."

1922—Kenneth L. Roberts, a Cornell graduate, served as a correspondent for the *Saturday Evening Post* on immigration questions. He warned that

"if a few more million members of the Alpine, Mediterranean, and Semitic races are poured among us, the result must inevitably be a hybrid race of people as worthless and futile as the good-for-nothing mongrels of Central America and Southeastern Europe."

1946—After World War II, the immigration of displaced persons revived old fears. Influential senators, like Pat McCurran and James Eastland, argued that political immigrants should not be permitted to enter the United States because of their "alien philosophies" and "biological incompatibility with Americans' parent stocks."

1963—Harvard sociologists Nathan Glazer and Patrick Moynihan described Puerto Rican Americans as weak, disorganized, and "sadly defective" in their culture and family system (Glazer and Moynihan, 1963: 88–90; Carlson and Colburn, 1972: 311–50).

family—sometimes for better, sometimes for worse. By the beginning of the twentieth century, what came to be called the companionate family was on the rise (Burgess et al., 1963).

Rise of the Companionate Family (1900–1930)

The turn of the twentieth century saw married couples increasingly stressing the importance of sexual attraction and compatibility in their relationships. Particularly in the middle classes, the notion of companionship, or the *companionate family*, encompassed a couple's children. Affection between parents and children was more intimate and more openly demonstrated, and adolescents enjoyed greater freedom from parental supervision. This new independence generated public criticism, however. Many of the popular magazines, such as *The Atlantic Monthly, The Ladies' Home Journal,* and the *New Republic,* worried about "young people's rejection of genteel manners, their defiant clothing and hairstyles, their slang-filled lan-

guage, and their 'lewd' pastimes . . . (such as smoking, attending petting parties, and going out on school nights). Public condemnation and moral outrage were widespread" (Mintz and Kellogg, 1988: 119). Do any of these complaints about young people sound familiar?

The Great Depression (1929–1939)

Many of us have heard stories about how families either coped or collapsed during the widespread unemployment and poverty that characterized the Great Depression. In fact, families had a great variety of experiences, influenced largely by such factors as residence, social class, sex, and race.

Urban–Rural Residence Among tenant farmers, many people who farmed the land owned by others could not pay the rent either in cash or in a share of the crops. Husbands sometimes left their families to search for jobs. Some women who could not cope with such desertion took drastic steps to end their misery.

In 1938, for example, a Nebraska farm mother of 13 children committed suicide by walking into the side of a train because "she had had enough" (Fink, 1992: 172). Even when husbands remained at home, some families lost their land and personal possessions. Parents made enormous sacrifices to feed their children. As one jobless Oregonian father stated: "We do not dare to use even a little soap when it will pay for an extra egg or a few more carrots for our children" (cited in McElvaine, 1993: 172).

To help support their families, many young men and women raised on farms moved to cities to find work. Young women were more likely to find jobs because there was a demand for low-paying domestic help. What they sent home from their $10 or so a week helped their families buy clothes and other near-necessities.

Social Class The Depression had the most devastating impact on working class and poor families. More than half of all women were employed in low-paying jobs, such as domestic and personal service and apparel and canning factories. The poorest states—South Carolina, Mississippi, Louisiana, Georgia, and Alabama—had the highest proportion of married working women (Cavan and Ranck, 1938; Chafe, 1972).

In contrast to the middle classes, children from working classes did not have carefree teenage years during the 1930s. Boys, especially, were expected to work after school or to leave school entirely to supplement their family's meager income. When mothers found jobs, older children, especially girls, looked after their younger brothers and sisters and often had to drop out of school to do so (McElvaine, 1993). Some children became part of the "transient army" that drifted from town to town looking for work. Most of the transients slept in lice-ridden and rat-infested housing when they could afford to pay the 10 or 15 cents for a urine-stained mattress on the floor. Others slept on park benches, under park shrubbery and bridges, in doorways, in packing crates, on construction sites, or in abandoned automobiles (Watkins, 1993).

As blue-collar employment in the male-dominated industrial sectors decreased, white-collar clerical and government jobs expanded. Women took many of these jobs. The wages of white, middle-class women enabled their families, even during the Depression, to maintain the standard of living and consumer habits that had been established during the affluent 1920s (Ryan, 1983).

Families in the upper-middle classes fared even better. Although many incomes decreased, fairly affluent families made only minor sacrifices. Some families cut down on entertainment, did not renew club memberships, and decreased such outside family services as domestic help. Few women reported problems in food budgets, and many of these families continued to take summer vacations. In fact, there was even an increase in the number of families that owned radios, musical instruments, and new cars (Morgan, 1939).

Race Although the Depression was an economic disaster for many people, African Americans suffered even more greatly. Unemployment was much higher among blacks than whites. As layoffs began in late 1929 and accelerated in the following years, blacks were often the first to be fired. By 1932, unemployment among African Americans had reached approximately 50 percent nationwide. As the economic situation deteriorated, many whites demanded that white workers in such occupations as garbage collector, elevator operator, waiter, bellhop, and street cleaner replace blacks.

In some government jobs, an unofficial quota of 10 percent black enrollment was set, on the theory that this represented, roughly, the percentage of blacks in the general population. In fact, though, the government employed only about 6 percent. Even those who were able to keep their jobs faced great hardship; a 1935 study in Harlem found that from the onset of the Depression, skilled black workers experienced a drop of nearly 50 percent in their wages (McElvaine, 1993; Watkins, 1993).

Gender Roles In many families, unemployment wreaked havoc on family roles. Because the position of the husband and father was based on his occupation and his role as provider, if he lost his job he often suffered a decline in status within the family. Men, understandably, were despondent: "Sometimes the father did not go to bed but moved from chair to chair all night long" (Cavan and Ranck, cited in Griswold, 1993: 148). Men who could not provide for their families became depressed, preoccupied, abusive, drank more, or spent much of their time searching for jobs. As fathers became physically and emotionally distant, their authority in the family and their children's respect often decreased. Adolescents became more independent and more rebellious (Griswold, 1993).

In 1932, a federal executive order decreed that only one spouse could work for the federal government. The widespread unemployment of men thus put pressure on women, especially married women, to resign from some occupations. School boards fired married female teachers, and some companies dismissed married women. More than 77 percent of the school districts in the United States would not hire married women, and 50 percent had a policy of firing women who married (Milkman, 1976; McElvaine, 1993). When women did work, the federal government not only permitted lower pay rates for women than men but promoted sex discrimination as well. For example, men on Works Progress Administration (WPA) projects were paid $5 per day; women received only $3.

World War II (1939–1945)

World War II triggered even greater changes in the lives of families. These changes, which began to be felt in 1941, after the United States entered the war, affected both work roles and family life.

Work Roles When the United States entered World War II, there was a scarcity of workers, especially in the defense and manufacturing industries, because many able-bodied men were drafted. Initially, employers were not enthusiastic about recruiting women for traditionally male jobs, and many women (especially white middle-class women) were unwilling to violate traditional gender roles. In 1942, employers—prompted by both the Women's Bureau of the U.S. Department of Labor and organized women's groups—attempted to fill many jobs, especially those in nontraditional positions, with women. The government, supported by the mass media, was enormously successful in convincing both men and women that a "woman's place is in the workplace" and not the home:

> They created "Rosie the Riveter," who became the lauded symbol of the woman temporarily at work. In all the media, women at work were pictured and praised, and the woman who did not at least raise a "victory garden" or work as a volunteer for the Red Cross was made to feel guilty. . . . Even the movies joined in. The wife or sweetheart who stayed behind and went to work . . . became as familiar a figure as the valiant soldier-lover for whom she waited. (Banner, 1984: 219)

Millions of women, including middle-aged mothers (and even grandmothers), worked in shipyards, steel mills, and ammunition factories (see Data Digest). They welded, dug ditches, and operated forklifts. African American women, who, for the first time, were recruited into high-paying jobs, made some of the greatest economic gains. Hundreds of thousands of domestic servants and farm workers left their jobs for much better paying positions in the defense and other industries. In the superb documentary film *The Life and Times of Rosie the Riveter,* black women describe the pride and exhilaration they felt in having not only well-paying jobs but jobs they genuinely enjoyed doing.

Because of the labor shortages, this was the only time when even working-class women were praised for working outside the home. Two of the best-selling magazines, the *Saturday Evening Post* and *True Story,* supported the government's propaganda efforts before, during, and shortly after World War II by casting working-class women in very positive roles:

> Stories and advertisements glorified factory work as psychologically rewarding, as emotionally exciting, and as leading to success in love. Both

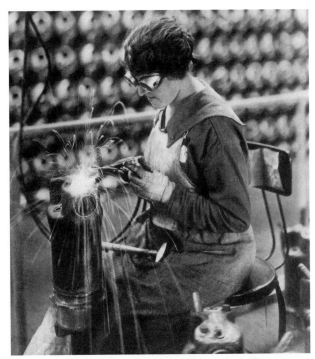

Many women worked in American factories, steel mills, and shipyards during World War II. Although many women found it hard to give up their new-found jobs and financial independence, most were replaced by men who returned from the war in 1945.

> magazines combated class prejudice against factory work by portraying working-class men and women as diligent, patriotic, wholesome people. . . . Working-class women were resourceful, respectable, warmhearted, and resilient. In *True Story,* characters experienced pride in their working-class origins and were glad to be an important part of the nation. (Honey, 1984: 186–87)

Family Life Although divorce rates had been increasing slowly since the turn of the century, they hit a new high in 1946, a year after the end of World War II. The war had a direct, negative effect on many families. Some wives and mothers who had worked during the war enjoyed their newfound economic independence and decided to end unhappy marriages. In other cases, families disintegrated because of the strains brought about by the return of a partially or completely incapacitated husband. But it was alcoholism, which was rampant among veterans, that was believed to be the major cause of the upward spiral of postwar divorces (Tuttle, 1993).

For some people, the war deferred, rather than caused, divorce. Some couples, caught up in war

CHANGES

"Daddy's Coming Home!"

Soldiers returning from World War II encountered numerous problems, including unemployment and high divorce rates (Mowrer, 1972). Historian William M. Tuttle, Jr. (1993), solicited 2,500 letters from men and women, then in their 50s and 60s, who were children during World War II. What most of these people had in common were the difficulties they and their families experienced in adjusting to the return of their fathers from military service.

Some children feared that their fathers would not stay and thus avoided becoming too attached. Some were bitter that their fathers had left in the first place. Others, especially those who were preschoolers at the time, were frightened of the strange men who suddenly moved into their homes. One woman remembered watching

"the stranger with the big white teeth" come toward her; as he did, the 4-year-old ran upstairs in terror and hid under a bed.

Some people recalled anger because their fathers disrupted their lives. Grandparents had often pampered children they helped to raise. In contrast, the returning father, fresh from military experience, was often a strict disciplinarian and saw the child as "a brat." If the children were very close to their mothers, they became resentful of fathers for displacing them. Other children were disappointed when the idealized images they had constructed of "Daddy" did not match reality. Or fathers who had been described as kind, sensitive, and gentle returned troubled or violent.

Readjustment was difficult for both children and fathers. Although some

The "G.I. Bill" enabled many World War II veterans to go to school and improve their job opportunities. But for many vets with families, like William Oskay, Jr., and his wife and daughter, daily life required many sacrifices and hardships.

households adjusted to the changes, in many families the returning fathers and their children never developed a close relationship.

hysteria, courted for a very short time and married impulsively before the man was shipped out (Mowrer, 1972). In other cases, when the husband was away for a prolonged period of time, both the bride and the young soldier matured, changed, and had little in common when they were reunited.

Perhaps one of the most difficult problems faced by families with returning war veterans was the reaction of children to fathers they barely knew or had never even seen. As the box "Daddy's Coming Home!" shows, despite widespread rejoicing over the end of the war, a father's return was unsettling for many children in a variety of ways.

The "Golden" Fifties

After World War II, when women were no longer needed in the workplace and returning veterans needed jobs, the propaganda about family roles changed almost overnight. "Rosie the Riveter" advertisements were replaced by ads depicting happy housewives totally engrossed in using vacuum cleaners and the latest consumer products. Heroines in short stories and women's magazines were no longer the nurses dying at the front, but mothers who devoted themselves

exclusively to cooking, caring for their children, and pleasing their husbands.

Movies and television shows celebrated two stereotypical portrayals of women—sweet, innocent virgins, like Doris Day and Debbie Reynolds, or sexy bombshells like Marilyn Monroe and Jayne Mansfield. Television applauded domesticity on such popular shows as *I Love Lucy, Ozzie and Harriet, Leave It to Beaver,* and *Father Knows Best.* Full skirts, big bosoms, tiny waists, and very high heels replaced the mannish, work-oriented clothes worn by women during the war. Countless marriage manuals and childcare experts, like Dr. Benjamin Spock, told women to be submissive and stay at home to raise their children. By the mid-1950s, 60 percent of female undergraduates were dropping out of college to marry (Banner, 1984).

As you saw in Chapter 1, the post–World War II generation experienced a baby boom. Family plans that had been disrupted by the war were renewed. Although women continued to enter the job market, many middle-class families, spurred by the mass media, sought a traditional family life in which the husband worked and the wife played the domestic role. The editor of *Mademoiselle* echoed a widespread belief that women in their teens and twenties should avoid careers and instead choose to raise as many children as the "good Lord gave them." Many magazines and newspaper articles encouraged families to participate in "creative" activities such as outdoor barbecues and cross-country camping trips (Chafe, 1972).

Suburbs mushroomed, accounting for nearly two-thirds of the population increase in the decade of the fifties. The interest in moving to the suburbs reflected structural and attitudinal changes. The federal government, fearful of a return to economic depression, underwrote the construction of homes in the suburbs (Rothman, 1978). Low-interest mortgages were made available to the general public, and veterans were offered the added inducement of purchasing a home with a $1 down payment.

Massive highway construction programs enabled people to commute from the city to the suburbs. Families wanted more room, seclusion, and an escape from city noise, crime, dirt, and crowding. The larger space offered more privacy for both children and parents: "The spacious master bedroom, generally set apart from the rooms of the children, was well-suited to a highly sexual relationship. And wives anticipated spending many evenings alone with their husbands, not with family or friends" (Rothman, 1978: 225–26).

The suburban way of life added a new dimension to the traditional role of women:

> *The duties of child-rearing underwent expansion. Suburban mothers volunteered for library work in the school, took part in PTA activities, and chauffeured their childr'en from music lessons to scout meetings. Perhaps most important, the suburban wife was expected to make the home an oasis of comfort and serenity for her harried husband. (Chafe, 1972: 217–18)*

Were such changes desirable? And did they really take place in most families? Some writers have argued that many of these presumed shifts in people's beliefs and behavior are actually myths, not reality. "Contrary to popular opinion," notes historian Stephanie Coontz, "*Leave It to Beaver* was not a documentary." In fact, the "golden fifties" were riddled with many family problems, and people had fewer choices than they do today. Here are some examples:

- *Consumerism* was limited primarily to middle and upper-class families. In 1950, a supermarket stocked an average of 3,750 items; in the 1990s, most markets carried more than 17,000 items. Until the 1990s, *many prepared foods were loaded with lard, salt, sugar, and harmful preservatives.*

- Black and other ethnic families faced *severe discrimination* in employment, education, housing, and access to recreational activities.

- *Domestic violence and child abuse,* though widespread, were invisible (see Chapter 14).

- Many young people were forced into *"shotgun" marriages* because of premarital conception; young women were pressured to give up their babies for adoption.

- About 20 percent of mothers had *paying jobs.* Although child-care services are still inadequate, they were practically nonexistent during the 1950s.

- Many people tried to escape from their unhappy lives through *alcohol or drugs.* The consumption of tranquilizers was virtually unheard of in 1955, but by 1958 had reached 462,000 pounds per year and in 1959 soared to almost 1.2 million pounds annually (Coontz, 1992; Crispell, 1992; Reid, 1993).

The Family since the 1960s

In this chapter we have laid the groundwork for the remaining chapters of the book. Beginning with Chapter 4, we shall examine marriage and the family in recent decades. In the 1970s, for example, families had lower birth rates and higher divorce rates, and larger numbers of women entered colleges and graduate programs. In the 1980s, more people over 25 years of age postponed marriage, and many of those who were already married delayed having children. Out-of-wedlock births, especially among teenage girls, declined during the late 1990s, but one-parent households increased precipitously (see Chapters 6 and 8). Two-income families and adult children who continued to live at home with their parents because of financial difficulties burgeoned (see Chapter 11).

Conclusion

If we examine the family in a historical context, we see that *change,* and not stability, has been the norm. Furthermore, the family differed by region and social class even during colonial times. We also see that the experiences and *choices* open to American Indians, African Americans, Mexican Americans, and many European immigrants were very different from those of "middle America," experiences that were romanticized by many television programs during the 1950s. Families were also affected by such macro-level constraints as wars and shifting demographic characteristics. Many families survived despite enormous hardships, disruptions, and dislocations. They are still coping with such macro-level constraints as an unpredictable economy and such micro-level variables as greater *choices* in family roles, however. The next chapter, on gender roles, examines some of these choices and constraints.

SUMMARY

1. Historical factors have played an important role in shaping the contemporary family. The early exploitation of American Indian, African American, and Mexican American families has had long-term economic effects on these groups in U.S. society.

2. The colonial family was a self-sufficient unit that performed a wide variety of functions. Children were part of the family work force and were expected to be docile and well behaved. Premarital sex was not uncommon, wives' work was subordinate to the husbands', and family practices varied across social classes and geographic regions.

3. American Indian families were extremely diverse in function, structure, sexual relations, puberty rites, and child-rearing patterns. European armies, adventurers, and missionaries played major roles in destroying many tribes and much of American Indian culture.

4. Contrary to popular belief, many African American households had two parents, men played important roles as fathers or surrogate fathers, and most women worked as hard as the men did in the fields. Instead of succumbing to subordination, many slaves were resourceful and resilient in maintaining their families.

5. Mexican American families were dispossessed of their lands, which were taken over by European American settlers. Despite severe economic exploitation, many families survived through cohesive family networks and strong family bonds.

6. By the nineteenth century, industrialization had changed some aspects of the family. Marriages were based more on love and choice rather than on economic considerations, parental roles within the family became more sex-segregated, and in the middle class the "true woman," who devoted most of her time to looking beautiful and pleasing her husband, emerged.

7. Millions of European immigrants who worked in labor-intensive jobs at very low wages fueled the rapid advance of industrialization. Many immigrants, including women and children, endured severe social and economic discrimination, dilapidated housing conditions, and chronic health problems.

8. Working-class families felt the most devastating effects of the Great Depression. While middle-class families cut back on luxuries, working-class men experienced widespread unemployment and their wives took jobs in the most menial and low-paying jobs.

9. World War II had a mixed effect on families. For the first time, many women, especially black mothers, found jobs that paid a decent salary. Death and divorce, however, also disrupted many families.

10. After the war, suburbs boomed and birth rates surged. The family roles of white middle-class women were expanded to include full-time nurturance of children and husbands. Husbands' roles were largely limited to work. The "golden fifties" reflects a mythical portrayal of the family during that decade.

KEY TERMS

bundling   *51*
matrilineal   *54*

patrilineal   *54*
familism   *60*

compadrazgo   60
machismo   60

TAKING IT FURTHER

Research Your Family Tree

The Web is full of genealogy sites. Here are some of the best I've found, in alphabetical order:
www.ancenstry.com
www.CyndisList.com
www.familyhistory.com
www.familysearch.com
www.gendex.com
www.genealogy.com
www.geneanet.org
www.genhomepage.com
www.kindredkonnections.com
www.myfamly.com
www.nara.gov

www.ngsgenealogy.org
www.rootsweb.com
www.switchboard.com
www.yourpastconnections.com

And more . . . www.prenhall.com/benokraitis provides sites on topics that include a bibliography on North American Indians, interviews with former slaves, a Women of the West Museum, documentary materials from the original Plymouth Colony, photographs and oral histories on American Indian traders in the Southwest, key events in the history of slavery, World War II posters featuring women, and techniques for evaluating American Indian Websites.

Gender Roles and Socialization

DATADIGEST

- Two-thirds of the estimated 876 million **illiterate people in the world** are women.

- Women make up **11 percent of the national legislatures worldwide.** Some 1998/1999 statistics include the following: Sweden, 43 percent; Denmark, 41 percent; South Africa, 30 percent; United Kingdom, 24 percent; United States, 13 percent; France, 12 percent; Mexico, 5 percent; and *none* in most African countries and Asian countries such as the United Arab Emirates, Vietnam, Israel, Saudi Arabia, and Turkey.

- In 1995, only **17 percent of the world's news "actors"** (people interviewed, quoted, or described in detail in the news) were women.

- White men make up **33 percent of the U.S. population** but 86 percent of the U.S. House of Representatives, 87 percent of the U.S. Senate, 90 percent of state governors, 85 percent of tenured professors, 85 percent of partners in law firms, 90 percent of daily-newspaper editors, 95 percent of Fortune 500 CEOs (chief executive officers), and 97 percent of school superintendents.

SOURCES: World's Women . . . 2000; *Time,* 1997; Benjamin, 1998; www.senate.gov (accessed January 3, 2000).

COMEDIAN Jerry Lewis recently remarked that he doesn't like female comedians. They "set me back a bit," Lewis said, because "I think of her as a producing machine that brings babies in the world." Such blatant and public sex stereotyping by a celebrity is relatively rare. Instead, much sexism is considerably more subtle.

The evening before a football game in Boston several years ago, for example, Houston Oilers tackle David Williams decided to stay at the hospital with his wife after their son was born. The Oilers' managers were angry and docked Williams a week's pay: $125,000. The incident caused much controversy. Was Williams really letting his teammates down? Is a football game more important than being with one's wife and child during the first days of an infant's life?

We keep hearing that "things are really different now" because both men and women have a lot of options. Even if these options exist, their consequences, as Williams's experience shows, may be so negative that, in reality, there are really very few choices for most women and men. This chapter examines gender roles: how they are learned and how they affect our everyday relations in marriage and the family. We begin with a look at gender myths and some of the unresolved nature–nurture debates that often fuel such myths.

Gender Myths and Biological Puzzles

According to a Gallup poll (*Table 4.1*), many Americans think that men and women have quite different personality characteristics. Men are often seen as aggressive, strong, and independent, whereas women are described as emotional, sensitive, and affectionate. When you examine this list of characteristics, do most of the traits characterize your female and male family members and friends? Probably not. For example, your mom may be aggressive and strong and your dad emotional and talkative. Or both may be aggressive, strong, emotional, or talkative, *depending on the situation.* And either or both parents may change over the years.

In capitalistic, patriarchal societies (see Chapter 1), we tend to associate stereotypically female characteristics with weakness and stereotypically male characteristics with strength. We may criticize women for being "emotional," for example, but praise men for being "aggressive." Again, whether such traits are desirable or not depends on the situation. An authoritarian drill sergeant may be very effective. An authoritarian parent, however, may produce rebellious children (see Chapter 11). According to some research, the most successful organizational leaders are both tough and soft. They have "business smarts" in negotiating deals and "people skills" in being sensitive to co-workers' feelings (Kabacoff, 1998).

Why, then, do these stereotypes persist? Largely because we don't differentiate between sex and gender, many of us believe that "anatomy is destiny." As a result, we may ignore the importance of the social context that produces and maintains these stereotypes. All of these misconceptions promote and sustain cultural gender myths that are detrimental to both men and women.

The Difference between Sex and Gender

Sex and *gender* are not synonymous. **Sex** refers to the biological characteristics with which we are born—chromosomal, anatomical, hormonal, and other

---

TABLE 4.1

The Top Ten Personality Characteristics Ascribed to Men and Women

Terms Most Often Used by Men and Women to Describe Men		Terms Most Often Used by Men and Women to Describe Women	
Aggressive	64%*	Emotional	81%*
Strong	61	Talkative	73
Proud	59	Sensitive	72
Disorganized	56	Affectionate	66
Courageous	54	Patient	64
Confident	54	Romantic	60
Independent	50	Moody	58
Ambitious	48	Cautious	57
Selfish	47	Creative	54
Logical	45	Thrifty	52

*Percentage of those surveyed.

SOURCE: Adapted from DeStefano and Colasanto, 1990: 29.

---

physical and physiological attributes—that determine whether we are male or female. Biology, for example, determines whether or not you're able to bear children. **Gender,** on the other hand, refers to learned attitudes and behaviors that characterize people of one sex or the other; gender is based on social and cultural expectations rather than on physical qualities. Thus, whereas we are *born* either male or female, we *learn* either to be women or men because we associate conventional patterns of behavior with each sex.

If you've shopped for baby cards, for example, you might have noticed that the baby cards for girls are typically pink and white while those for boys are blue and white. The cards usually portray the baby girls as playing with their toes, in a bubble bath, or gazing at a mobile above their cribs. The cards for boys typically use artwork that includes sports (such as holding a baseball), playing with toys such as train sets, and even using laptops. Note, also, how many baby cards describe female infants as "dear," "sweet," "cute," or "cuddly" while the male infants are described as "a special joy," "a pride," and "a precious gift." What's the message in these cards—that female infants are passive and ornamental and male infants are active and more valued?

As you saw in Chapter 1, one of the functions of the family is to teach its members appropriate social roles. Among the most important of these are **gender roles**—characteristics, attitudes, feelings, and behaviors that society expects of females and males. We learn to become male or female through interaction with family members and the larger society. In most societies, for example, men are still expected to

provide physical shelter, food, and clothing for their family members; women are expected to nurture their children and to tend to the family's everyday needs. Social scientists often describe our roles as *gendered.* Gendered refers to the process of treating and evaluating males and females differently because of their sex:

> . . . *to the extent that women and men dress, talk, or act differently because of societal expectations, their behavior is gendered. To the extent that an organization assigns some jobs to women and others to men on the basis of their assumed abilities, that organization is gendered. And to the extent that a professor treats a student differently because that student is a man or a woman, their interaction is gendered. (Howard and Hollander, 1997: 11)*

The Nature–Nurture Debate: Is Anatomy Destiny?

Most social scientists differentiate among sex, gender, and gender roles. If gender roles are learned, these scientists argue, they can also be unlearned. Some social scientists and biologists, on the other hand, believe that observed differences in the ways women and men behave are attributable to their innate, biological characteristics, and not to social and cultural expectations. This difference of opinion is often called the "nature-nurture debate " (see *Table 4.2*). Today the issue is viewed not so much as nature *or* nurture but as the relative importance of nature *and* nurture.

How Important Is Nature? There *are* some established biological differences between men and women. Here are some examples:

- Infant mortality rates are higher for boys, and, on average, women live seven years longer than men do.
- Boys are afflicted with more genetic disorders, such as night blindness, myopia (nearsightedness), hemophilia, and glaucoma.
- Females have more acute senses of smell and taste than males, and women's hearing is better and lasts longer than men's.
- While women are better than men at warding off viral and bacterial infections, they are much more susceptible to autoimmune diseases such as lupus.
- While alcoholism is twice as prevalent in men as in women, alcoholic women are at much greater risk for death from drinking and cirrhosis of the liver.
- Women have a higher risk than men of developing diabetes (a major contributor to endometrial cancer, adult blindness, and cardiovascular disease), and a heart attack is more likely to be fatal for a woman than for a man (McDonald, 1999; see also Sugg, 2000).
- Some diseases such as migraine headaches predominate in women while others, including some kinds of skin cancer, are more common to men (Montagu, 1974; Legato, 1998; McDonald, 1999).

Scientists don't know why women and men differ but believe that hormones provide part of the explanation. All males and females share three sex **hormones**—chemical substances secreted into the bloodstream by glands of the endocrine system. They are *estrogen* (dominant in females and produced by the ovaries), *progesterone* (present in high levels during pregnancy and also secreted in the ovaries), and *testosterone* (dominant in males, where it is produced by the testes). All of these hormones are produced in very small quantities in both sexes before puberty.

After puberty, different levels of these hormones in males and females produce different physiological changes. For example, testosterone, the dominant male sex hormone, strengthens muscles but threatens the heart. It triggers production of low-density lipoprotein, which clogs blood vessels. Thus, males are at twice the risk of coronary heart disease as are (premenopausal) females. The dominant female sex hormones, especially estrogen, make blood vessels more elastic and strengthen the immune system, giving females more resistance to infection (Boston Women's Health Book Collective, 1992).

The presence of male or female sexual anatomy and hormones does not in itself make a man a man or a woman a woman. **Gender identity** refers to a person's emotional and intellectual awareness of being either male or female. Gender identity, which typically corresponds to a person's biological sex, is learned in early childhood and is believed to remain fixed throughout life. In some cases, however, such as transsexualism, gender identity may be inconsistent with a person's physical sex.

Transsexuals are people who feel that their gender identity is out of sync with their anatomical sex. Transsexuals often describe themselves as feeling "trapped in the wrong body." In one of the earliest and most publicized cases during the 1970s, Richard Raskind, a married man with two children who was a highly ranked tennis player and a respected ophthalmologist, underwent surgery and became Renee Richards.

According to some estimates, about one person in 350,000 believes she or he was born the wrong sex (Gorman, 1995). Some undergo surgery (which costs about $60,000), but others opt for only hormonal treatments. There is little research in this area but several studies have found that between 60 and 80 percent of the patients have no problems in sexual adjustment after they undergo a sex-change operation and do not regret their decision (Sorenson, 1981; Mate-Kole et al., 1990). No one knows the reasons for transsexualism, but autopsies of six male-to-female transsexuals showed that a tiny structure deep within a part of the brain that controls sexual function was more like women's than men's (Zhou et al., 1995). The researchers suggested that structures in the brain, or nature, probably account for transsexualism and help explain why there are more male-to-female than female-to-male transsexuals. Devor (1997), who conducted intensive interviews with 46 female-to-male transsexuals, describes the transsexuals as women who felt "ill suited to being females, girls, and women" throughout childhood and adolescence: "They felt neither female nor male; they felt stuck as women who should have been men" (p. 601).

TABLE 4.2

The Nature–Nurture Debate

Nature	Nurture
Differences in male and female beliefs, attitudes and behavior are:	Differences in male and female beliefs, attitudes and behavior are:
Innate	Learned
Biological, physiological	Psychological, social, cultural
Due largely to heredity	Due largely to environment
Fairly fixed	Very changeable

CHOICES

The Case of John/Joan

In 1963, twin boys were being circumcised. The penis of one of the infants was accidentally burned off. Encouraged by John Money, a medical psychologist at Johns Hopkins Hospital, the parents agreed to reassign and raise "John" as "Joan." Joan's testicles were removed a year later to facilitate feminization and further surgery would construct a full vagina when Joan was older. Medical texts and social science writings reported, for many years, that masculine and feminine behavior could be altered despite a person's genes at conception and anatomy. Money had reported that the twins were growing into happy, well-adjusted children of the opposite sex. The case set a precedent for sex reassignment as the standard treatment for 15,000 newborns with similarly injured genitals (Colapinto, 1997).

In the mid-1990s, however, Milton Diamond, a biologist at the University of Hawaii, and Keith Sigmundson, a psychiatrist with the Canadian Ministry of Health, conducted a follow-up of Joan's progress and showed that the sex reassignment had not been successful. Almost from the beginning, Joan refused to be treated like a girl. When Joan's mother dressed her in frilly clothes as a toddler, Joan tried to rip them off. She preferred to play with boys and stereotypical boys' toys such as machine guns. People in the community said that she "looks like a boy, talks like a boy" (Colapinto, 1997: 70). Joan had no friends and no one would play with her. "Every day I was picked on, every day I was teased, every day I was threatened" (Diamond and Sigmundson, 1997: 300).

When she was 14, Joan rebelled and stopped living as a girl: ". . . she refused to wear dresses and now favored a tattered jean jacket, ragged cords and work boots. Her hair was unwashed, uncombed and matted" (Colapinto, 1997: 73). She urinated standing up, refused vaginal surgery, and decided she would either commit suicide or live as a male. When her father finally told her the true story of her birth and sex change, John recalls that "all of a sudden everything clicked. For the first time things made sense and I understood who and what I was" (Diamond and Sigmundson, 1997: 300). Joan had a mastectomy at the age of 14 and underwent several operations to reconstruct a penis. He is able to ejaculate but experiences little "erotic sensitivity." At age 25 he married a woman several years older than him and adopted her three children.

In contrast to Money's theories, then, Diamond and Sigmundson maintain that John's case is evidence that gender identity and sexual orientation are largely inborn. Nature, they argue, is stronger than nurture in shaping a person's sexual identity.

Some scientists point to unsuccessful attempts at sex reassignment as another example favoring the nature-over-nurture argument. Since the 1960s, John Money, a highly respected psychologist at Johns Hopkins University, has published numerous articles and books which maintain that gender identity is not firm at birth but is determined as much by culture and nurture as it is by hormones (see, for example, Money and Ehrhardt, 1972). Recently, however, several scientists have challenged such conclusions. As the box "The Case of John/Joan" shows, Money's most famous sex reassignment experiment does not appear to support his contention that infants born as biological males can be raised successfully as females.

A Global View: How Important Is Nurture?   Most social scientists believe that nature and nurture interact to explain gender roles. They maintain, however, that cultural influences shape biological factors. Nature-over-nurture adherents often point to cross-cultural data and successful sex assignment cases to illustrate the importance of cultural conditioning on gender roles and identities.

Anthropologist Margaret Mead (1935) studied three tribes that lived within short distances of each other in New Guinea. She found three combinations of gender roles. Among the Arapesh, both men and women were nurturant with their children. The men were cooperative and sensitive, and they rarely engaged in warfare. The Mundugumors were just the opposite. Both the men and women were competitive and aggressive. Neither parent showed much tenderness and both often used physical punishment to discipline the children. The Tchumbuli demonstrated the reverse of Western gender roles. The women were the economic providers, and the men took care of children, sat around gossiping, and spent a lot of time decorating themselves for tribal festivities. Mead concluded that attributes long considered either masculine or feminine (such as aggression) were culturally, not biologically, determined.

Mead's findings were supported by research on the Tasaday of the Philippines. Tasaday men are rarely angry or hostile, and they do not punish their children physically or fight with neighboring tribes. Indeed, the Tasaday's language does not even include words for "enemy," "fight," "weapon," "murder," or "war" (Nance, 1975).

If men were innately aggressive, we would find that they commit violent acts such as homicide across all societies. This is not the case, however. As you can see from *Figure 4.1*, the rates of homicide in which the assailant is male vary considerably among a number of countries, and the rate for the United States is by far the highest in the Western world. Is it possible that American men are genetically more aggressive than men in other countries? Because the United States is a nation made up of people from many nations, races, and cultures, a genetic explanation seems unlikely.

According to Miedzian (1991), U.S. society encourages and rewards male aggression socially, culturally, legally, and politically. Miedzian argues, for example, that U.S. political leaders typically use war and force in countries around the world, sports and violence often go hand in hand, films and videos often glorify murder and cruelty, and the boys' sections of toy stores look like a military arsenal.

This does not mean that all men are aggressive and all women are nonviolent. Recently, for example, archaeologists have excavated burial mounds of fifth century B.C. nomads in Russia and found that 14 percent of the graves were those of women buried with daggers, arrowheads, swords, and other artifacts. Both the artifacts and bent arrowheads in some of the women's body cavities suggest that the women were warriors and some had been killed in battle (Davis-Kimball, 1997). As we discuss in Chapter 14, females abuse children and engage in domestic violence. Some campuses have suspended *sorority* chapters because hazing incidents have included beating and physically injuring pledges (Geraghty, 1997). In addition, 10 percent of those arrested for murder and nonnegligent manslaughter are women (U.S. Census Bureau, 1999c). Overall, however, female violence is very low compared to male violence.

Male violence and aggression are most likely in patriarchal societies to the degree that they are male-dominated, male-identified, and male-centered (Johnson, 1997). Patriarchal societies are *male-dominated* in that men have a monopoly of authority in political, economic, religious, and educational institutions (see Chapter 1 and Data Digest). Men as a group become identified with superiority even though most men may not be powerful in their individual lives. Patriarchal societies are *male-identified* in that core cultural ideas about what is considered good, preferable, or normal are associated with how we think about men and masculinity. The simplest example of a male-identified society, Johnson notes, is "the still widespread use of

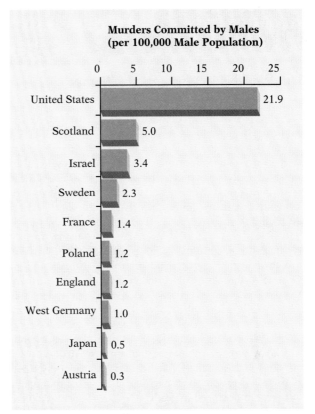

FIGURE 4.1 Incidence of Deadly Assault by Males in Selected Industrialized Countries. Although the incidence of male violence varies considerably worldwide, one of the highest rates is in Colombia, South America, where of every 100,000 men, 79 have committed murder. Among industrialized countries, however, the highest rate is in the United States (*Newsweek,* 1990, p. 7; Brooke, 1994, p. A6).

male pronouns and nouns to represent people in general. When we routinely refer to human beings as 'man' or to doctors as 'he,' we construct a symbolic world in which men are in the foreground and women in the background, marginalized as outsiders and exceptions to the rule" (p. 6). Patriarchy is also *male-centered*, which means that the focus of attention is primarily on men and what they do. Although many men may not feel at the center of things, they are rewarded—by success and wealth, for example—if they are competitive, tough, and forceful.

A result of patriarchy is the exclusion of most women from major areas such as religion, education, professional jobs, and political power. As the box "The Worldwide War against Women" shows, patriarchal societies practice discrimination and violence against women because cultural and religious values, customs, and laws promote women's second-class citizenship.

CONSTRAINTS

The Worldwide War against Women

According to a United Nations report, women make up half the world's population, do two-thirds of the world's work, earn one-tenth of the world's income, and own one-hundredth of the world's property. Women are widely mistreated in many countries around the world.

- *Afghanistan:* Since the militia group known as the Taliban seized control in 1996, girls are not permitted to attend schools or universities, and women are forbidden to work or appear in public unless accompanied by a close male relative. A woman who has been raped may be publicly punished for adultery. Women suspected of pre- or extramarital relations can be stoned to death.
- *China:* A culture that values boys more than girls, China has used advances in sonogram technology to help prospective parents identify—and abort—female fetuses. Despite official government condemnation of the practice, the gap between the number of male and female births is widening.
- *Nigeria:* The penal code allows a man to "correct" his wife as long as the "correction" does not leave a scar or require a stay of 21 days or more in the hospital.
- *India and Pakistan:* If a groom and his family decide a bride's dowry is too small, she may be persecuted or burned to death. In 1992, for example, India had more than 4,700 "dowry deaths." Aborting female fetuses is also widespread in India.
- *Kuwait:* Although Kuwaiti women are now allowed to drive and no longer have rigid dress codes, they still cannot vote. Household maids, many from the Philippines, are often victims of "unintentional" abuses and murders.
- *Latin America:* A macho culture pervades most countries in Latin America, unofficially condoning wife abuse, rape, and other forms of violence against women.
- *Morocco:* If a woman commits adultery, the law permits the husband to maim or kill her as punishment. Adulterous husbands, on the other hand, are not punished at all.
- *Norway:* Even though women dominate the political scene, they are still hired last, fired first, paid less than men, and held back from the top jobs.
- *Russia:* Wife-beating is not against the law; husbands kill approximately 15,000 wives each year.
- *Saudi Arabia:* A divorced woman may keep her children until they are 7 years old. Although she may visit them, the father's relatives then raise the children.
- *South Africa:* A woman is raped every 83 seconds. Domestic work is the primary occupation for black women, and the average salary is about $80 a month.
- *Thailand:* Young rural women are kidnapped or bought from their parents for prostitution. An estimated 1 million women work in Thai brothels.
- *United States:* On average, women earn 75 percent of what men in the same jobs earn, and a woman with a college degree earns about the same as a man who has completed one year of high school. Among single mothers, about 60 percent live in or near poverty.
- In war-torn countries around the world, hundreds of thousands of women and children have been victims of mass rape and torture. Mass rapes, torture, and genital mutilation have been reported in *Bangladesh, Burundi, Cambodia, Liberia, Peru, Rwanda, Somalia,* and *Uganda.* Reports of large-scale organized rape in recent years have come from the countries that made up the former Yugoslavia, where at least 20,000 women and girls were raped during the first few months of the war that followed the country's dissolution in 1992.

SOURCES: MacFarquhar et al., 1994; Seter, 1994; Berry, 1997; Neft and Levine, 1997; Goodsmith, 2000.

Just as men are not innately violent, women are not innately nurturant. There is no scientific evidence that "parenting comes more naturally to mothers than to fathers" even though many judges think so and often award custody of the children to mothers (or even aunts and grandmothers) in divorce cases (see Chapter 15). If mothers are natural parents, why are hospitals teaching mothers how to "bond" with their infants? Further, why do some mothers abuse or even kill their children?

Although, as you saw earlier, some scientists cite the John/Joan case as evidence of the biological imprint on gender role and identity, others posit that the *successful* sex assignments of hermaphrodites offer convincing evidence of powerful cultural effects.

Hermaphrodites—also known as intersexuals—are people born with both male and female sex organs (internal and/or external). The incidence of ambiguous genitalia—where the sex of the newborn is not immediately apparent—is about 1 in every 8,000 to 10,000 births (O'Mara, 1997). Typically, parents choose a sex for the child and pursue surgical and hormonal treatment to change the ambiguous genital organs. The parents raise the child in the selected gender role: The name is male or female, the clothes are masculine or feminine, and the child is taught to behave in gender-appropriate ways. Such sex assignments suggest that socialization is more important than biology in determining a child's gender identity.

What Can We Conclude about the Nature–Nurture Debate? What does all this information tell us, ultimately, about the nature–nurture debate? Several things. First, although women and men show some sex-related genetic differences in health and illness, there is no evidence that a person's hormones *cause* physical maladies or his or her being good at math rather than writing. Second, the research on other cultures suggests much variation on the personality and cultural characteristics, like aggression, that are typically ascribed to women and to men (see *Figure 4.1*).

Finally, the nature–nurture controversy isn't subsiding. In 1998, for example, Judith Harris's *The Nurture Assumption* (1998), a best-selling and hotly debated book, argued that genetics and peer influences (more about this later), rather than parents, shape a child's development. Harris maintains that heredity, not environment, determines a child's life outcomes. If a child is innately rambunctious while a sibling is innately pleasant, for example, parenting reactions will differ. The same genetic tendencies that elicit resignation from a parent, Harris claims, are also the same tendencies that make a child a runaway, a dropout, or a delinquent.

Many critics dismissed *The Nurture Assumption* as unscientific, ignoring data that supported the importance of environmental factors and oversimplifying parental influence like parents' moving to a particular neighborhood or sending a child to a particular school (Begley, 1998; Williams, 1998). Researchers who have used longitudinal studies (see Chapter 2) argue that parenting has a strong effect on children's genetic proclivities and behavior. For example, a child with a difficult temperament—irritability, hostility, or aggressiveness—can become more sociable and learn self-control if parents are continuously patient, affectionate, and loving. In effect, many researchers contend, genes are turned on or off by socialization factors: "A particular gene can have a different effect, depending on the environment" (Sapolsky, 2000: 68).

The Importance of Social Context

When looking at gender and gender differences, it is important to keep in mind that research shows that there are more similarities than differences between the sexes. Males and females have similar cognitive skills and abilities and perceive the world visually in similar ways. They have similar memory abilities and similar processes for storing and retrieving information. Despite stereotypes to the contrary, language and mathematical scores on the Scholastic Aptitude Test (SAT) are virtually the same for both sexes after controlling for such factors as the number of math and literature courses taken and young people's attitudes about their strengths in these areas (Fausto-Sterling, 1985). In addition, males and females display similar abstract problem-solving skills, and parents express affection and love to their children in very similar ways (Golombok and Fivush, 1994). Sex differences, on almost every psychological trait measured, are either nonexistent or very small (see Rowe, 1994, for a different perspective).

There are greater differences between men *as a group* and between women *as a group* than there are between women and men overall. Individual boys, for example, might not like math and conclude that they have no mathematical abilities. Individual girls might excel in sports and surpass many of their male and female peers. There can be considerable dissimilarities even among same-sex twins in terms of their personalities and behavior (Cherro, 1992). One of my colleagues tells the story about his twin girls who received exactly the same dolls when they were 3 years old. When the parents asked the girls what they would name the dolls, one twin chattered that the doll's name was Lori, that she loved Lori, and would take good care of her. The second twin muttered that "Her name is Stupid" and flung the doll into a corner.

An emphasis on gender differences overlooks the importance of the social context in which women and men live. Regardless of our personal preferences or abilities, most of us accommodate our behavior to gender-role expectations, in a process that West and Zimmerman (1987) call "doing gender."

We "do gender," sometimes consciously and sometimes unconsciously, by adjusting our behavior and our perceptions depending on the gender and age of the person we are working or talking with. In a review of the studies on child development, for example, Eleanor Maccoby (1990) found that children as young as 3 years typically modify their behavior depending on the gender of the child they are playing with. Girls may compete with each other over toys in same-sex play groups but tend to let the boys monopolize the toys in mixed-sex play groups. Many little girls play a subordinate role not because they are "innately passive" but because they have probably

Cooking with his dad teaches a young boy that domestic work is an acceptable activity for a man. Such activities also increase interaction and closer relationships between fathers and their children.

already learned that little boys are "the boss" and have "first pick" of the toys.

Maccoby's research suggests that men and women do not have fixed masculine and feminine traits but that our behavior often varies depending on the situation. By young adulthood, many women are uncomfortable about traveling or living alone, not because they are less adventurous than men are but because they fear being attacked by violent males. Note, also, that under some conditions the qualities that we label feminine or masculine are seen as desirable for *both* sexes:

> *In the family . . . the positive qualities of tradition-al femininity—compassion, nurturance, warmth, and so on—are associated with marital satisfaction in both sexes. Naturally; everyone wants a spouse who is affectionate and caring. And at work, the positive qualities of masculinity—assertiveness,*

competence, self-confidence—are associated with job satisfaction and self-esteem in both sexes. Naturally; everyone wants a co-worker who is capable. (Tavris, 1992: 293)

Even though many social scientists agree that there are more similarities than differences between men and women, there are vast societywide gaps on the macro level—such as unequal incomes, unequal responsibilities in child care, and significant differences in access to political power. Why aren't women organizing revolts to change the status quo? Gender socialization theories provide some of the answers.

How We Learn Gender Roles

A common misconception is that the gender roles we learn at an early age are carved in stone and do not change after about age 4. In fact, gender roles can—and do—change throughout the life cycle. Before we can understand how such change occurs, however, we need to examine, briefly, some of the major perspectives on gender-role learning: social learning theory, cognitive development theory, and gender schema theory.

Social Learning Theory

The central notion in **social learning theory** is that people learn new attitudes, beliefs, and behaviors through social interaction, either by reinforcement of their behavior or by imitating others. Consequently, we learn some gender-role behaviors by direct reward or punishment. A little girl who puts on her mother's makeup may be told she is cute, but her brother will be scolded ("boys don't wear makeup"). We also learn gender roles through indirect reinforcement. For example, if a little boy's male friends are punished for crying, he will learn that "boys don't cry."

We also learn gender roles through imitation or role modeling of same-sex significant others. In principle, because parents are available and emotionally important to children, they are the most powerful role models, but other role models include caregivers, friends, and even television characters. Behavior and attitudes change as the situations and expectations in the environment change. Thus, books and television programs play an important role in expanding or constricting gender-role expectations. Social learning theories see behavior not as fixed at an early age but as changing throughout the life cycle (Bandura and Walters, 1963; Lynn, 1969).

Cognitive Development Theory

Cognitive development theory, based on the work of Jean Piaget (1950, 1954), sees learning as an active process in which children interact with their environment and then, using mental processes such as thinking, understanding, and reasoning, interpret and apply the information they have gathered. According to Lawrence Kohlberg (1969), children learn gender-role identity by understanding and accepting perceived reality rather than by being reinforced for certain behaviors or modeling them. For example, in contrast to a social learning sequence ("the boy wants rewards, the boy is rewarded by boy things, therefore, he wants to be a boy"), cognitive theory assumes a different sequence: "The boy asserts he is a boy. He then wants to do boy things; therefore, the opportunity to do boy things and the presence of masculine models is rewarding" (Kohlberg, 1969: 432).

In contrast to social learning theories, the cognitive development perspective argues that the child acquires basic female or male values on her or his own. According to this theory, children pass through developmental stages in learning gender-appropriate attitudes and behavior. By the age of 3 to 4, the girl knows she is a girl and prefers "girl things" to "boy things" simply because she likes what is familiar or similar to herself. After masculine/feminine values are acquired, the child tends to identify with same-sex people. The age at which a child moves through the developmental stages varies with the child's cognitive, intellectual, and maturity level (Kohlberg, 1969; Maccoby, 1990). By age 5, however, most children anticipate disapproval from their peers for playing with opposite-sex toys and don't do so (Bussey and Bandura, 1992).

Carol Gilligan's (1982) work has challenged Kohlberg's (and others') conclusions about men's and women's psychological development. Whereas men are socialized to be independent, women are expected to establish connections to other people and to develop social ties. Gilligan has argued that while males are more interested in individual rights and playing by the rules in determining what is fair, females are more concerned with issues of self-sacrifice and responsibility in preserving interpersonal relationships. According to Gilligan, then, women tend to reason in a "different voice." Men attach greater priority to formal rights and competition while women value caring relationships and cooperative interaction.

Gender Schema Theory

Elements of cognitive development theory have been incorporated into a newer perspective, known as gender schema theory. **Gender schema theory** focuses on how children actively construct for themselves what it means to be female or male. *Schema* are cognitive (or mental) information-processing categories that organize and guide a person's perceptions of a vast array of

©Judy Horacek from *Life on the Edge* (Melbourne: Spinifex Press, 1992).

cultural stimuli (Bem, 1983). For example, when girls realize that cultural expectations of being feminine include being affectionate, understanding, and emotional, they incorporate these perceptions into their emerging gender schema and adjust their behavior accordingly. The same is true of boys, who incorporate such male gender schema as being brave, forceful, and tough.

Children use gender schema to evaluate the behavior of others as gender appropriate ("good") or gender inappropriate ("bad"). Because most cultures polarize gender characteristics into rigid categories, children become gender schematic themselves without even realizing it. Eventually, children become conventionally sex-typed because they evaluate different ways of behaving in terms of the cultural definitions of gender appropriateness and reject any way of behaving that does not match their sex (Bem, 1993).

Gender schema may become more rigid during adolescence, when young people often feel compelled to conform to peers' **gender-role stereotypes**—the belief and expectation that both women and men display rigid traditional gender-role characteristics—but may become more flexible again during adulthood (Stoddart and Turiel, 1985). Generally, however, people who have internalized sex-typed standards tend to expect stereotypical behavior from others or to ignore nonstereotypical behavior that is incongruent with their gender schemas (Hudak, 1993; Renn and Calvert, 1993).

These three perspectives—social learning theory, cognitive development theory, and gender schema theory—are often used together. One perspective is no better than another, just different. Note, however, that almost all of the theories are based on very nonrepresentative samples. While Kohlberg's research was based only on males, for example, Gilligan's conclusions were drawn from a very small sample of upper-middle-class white students. It is not clear, then, whether these theories are applicable to ethnic or non-middle-class families.

Parents are important socialization agents. This three-year-old may be inspired to follow in his father's occupational footsteps.

Who Teaches Gender Roles?

Theorists try to explain how we learn gender roles. The next question is who does the teaching. The most important teachers are parents (and other adult caregivers), peers, teachers, and the popular culture.

Parents

Parents are usually the first and most influential source of learning about gender roles. Many children are raised in sex-stereotyped physical surroundings and often parents begin to treat infants differently from birth. Girls are held more gently and cuddled more, whereas boys are jostled and played with more roughly. Parents are more likely to put females in a nearby high chair and male infants on the floor or in a playpen. Thus, girls are kept closer to a parent and in a more confined area. Boys are frequently given toys that demand more space (such as trains and car sets), whereas girls receive dolls or dollhouses, which require less space. Also, toys that boys receive (such as footballs and basketballs) encourage leaving the home; girls' toys (such as play vacuum cleaners, play ovens) are designed to be used within the home (Knapp and Hall, 1992). Even when children in kindergarten and elementary school request gender-atypical toys (as sports equipment for girls or arts and crafts for boys), parents usually give gender-typical toys, such as cars and trucks to boys and dolls or miniature kitchen sets to girls (Etaugh and Liss,

1992). Thus, both toys and the usage of space encourage traditionally gender-appropriate behavior, activities, and interests.

Parents often communicate differently with boys and girls, starting at a very early age. Both mothers and fathers use more words about feelings and emotions when speaking with girls than when speaking with boys. Fathers tend to use more directives ("Bring that over here") and more threatening language ("If you do that again, you'll be sorry") with their sons than with their daughters. Mothers ask for compliance rather than demand it—"Could you bring that to me, please?" By the time they start school, boys use threatening, commanding, and dominating language ("If you do that one more time, I'll sock you"). In contrast, girls emphasize agreement and cooperation ("Can I play, too?") (Shapiro, 1990).

Promoting sex-stereotypical behavior continues into childhood. If parents *expect* their daughters to be better in English and their sons to excel in math and sports, they provide the support and advice to enable them to do so. This encouragement builds up the children's confidence in their abilities and helps them master the various skills (Eccles et al., 1990).

The larger culture reinforces parents' sex-typed socialization. In *Reviving Ophelia*, for example, clinical psychologist Mary Pipher observes that many of the adolescent girls she sees in therapy have lost their sense of self because our "girl-poisoning" patriarchal culture stifles their creativity and destroys their self-esteem at every turn:

Girls complain that they do more chores than their brothers. Or that they make less money baby-sitting than their brothers do mowing lawns. Or that parents praise brothers' accomplishments more than theirs. An athlete complained that her track coach spent more time with the boys. Another noted that only the female gymnasts had to weigh in at practices. A softball player complained that sports coverage was better for men's events than for her own. A musician noticed that most rock stars were male. (Pipher, 1994: 41–42)

Adolescent boys are also "poisoned," however. Many parents expect their sons to be bigger, better, stronger, faster, and braver than their peers. Although the traditional male norm of aggression may be changing somewhat, most boys are still learning to be tough and aggressive: "It's through fighting, conquering, dominating, and intimidating that they earn the respect and approval of other males" (Levant and Kopecky, 1995: 83). "Manhood" rituals for coming of age still involve sex, drugs and alcohol, and exerting control over others, especially women (Kimmel and Messner, 1995). Young black males, who are especially vulnerable to experiencing daily racism and inequality, may establish their male identity through what Majors and Billison (1992: 5) refer to as "cool pose":

By acting calm, emotionless, fearless, aloof, and tough, the African-American male strives to offset an externally imposed "zero" image. Being cool shows both the dominant culture and the black male himself that he is strong and proud. . . . It provides a mask that suggests competence, high self-esteem, control, and inner strength. It also hides self-doubt, insecurity, and inner turmoil.

Being cool is an effective coping strategy in the face of danger and discrimination because it helps the young black male to deal with the closed doors and negative images of himself. The negative side of this survival technique, according to Majors and Billison, is that the cool pose masks the male's true feeling and interferes with establishing strong bonds with family and friends.

Although there is a range of socialization practices across families, black and other ethnic parents may be torn between helping their children succeed in a white society while maintaining their group's cultural identity and gender-role expectations. On the one hand, for example, many low-income Latino parents are proud of their children who go to college. On the other hand, if the children—especially daughters—live on campus, parents may fear that a lack of parental supervision will create problems. One Mexican American student remarked, for instance: "My stepdad thought I was just going to get pregnant and drop out of school.

They didn't know why I had to go so far away [a three-hour drive from home]. We had so many arguments over this" (Reisberg, 1999: A43). Other female students at the same college said that their mothers expect them to come home every weekend to help with housework, to run errands, or to care for younger children. Male Latino students did not experience the same demands on their time.

Toys, Play, and Peer Interaction

Play is generally sex-typed. Boys are still more likely than girls to play with warlike toys, to participate in warlike games and sports, and to react aggressively to (real or imagined) verbal, personal, or physical threats (Colburn, 1991). Toys for boys encourage exploring spatial dimensions and have step-by-step instructional styles that develop the use of logic and concepts that children will need in science and mathematics (Cargan, 1991).

Girls' sections of both catalogs and toy stores are swamped with cosmetics, dolls and accessories, arts and crafts kits, and housekeeping and cooking wares. In contrast, boys' sections feature sports equipment, building toys, workbenches, and construction equipment. Boys' toys tend to emphasize activity, mobility, and problem solving, whereas girls' toys tend to foster passivity, domestic skills, and imaginative play. War, violence, aggression, and sexism have been the hallmarks of many computer games geared to young boys. Whereas boys' toys—including educational video games—encourage competition and following strict rules, girls' toys usually foster nurturance and emotional expressiveness (Morse, 1995).

Some of the most popular video software aimed at young men in their late teens emphasizes "a nasty streak of violence" that includes blood, gore, and "mature sexual themes." The purpose of *Carmageddon*, for example, is "to waste contestants, pedestrians and farmyard animals for points and credits." *Carmageddon 2: Caropocalyse* promises "pedestrian splatting action." Another big seller, *Diablo 2*, boasts "an advanced combat system that incorporates class-specific fighting techniques and spells" (Blasko, 2000).

Mattel, a toy manufacturer, estimates that 99 percent of all U.S. girls between the ages of 3 and 10 own at least one of its Barbie dolls, and the average girl owns a total of eight (Greenwald, 1996). Barbie's accessories (which include thousands of tiny outfits, dozens of pieces of pink furniture, Hollywood hot tubs, and sleek racing cars) bring in almost a billion dollars a year for Mattel.

The problem with Barbie dolls, according to many critics, is that they idealize unrealistic body images (such as enormous breasts, a tiny waist, and extremely long legs) that many girls and women try to achieve through diets and cosmetic surgery (Lord, 1994; Tosa, 1998; M. F. Rogers, 1999; see also Chapter 14).

Mattel has manufactured a few Barbie dolls with more realistic physical proportions (such as the Rosie Barbie based on talk-show hostess Rosie O'Donnell). These dolls, however, may reflect little more than a marketing attempt to derail some of the growing criticism.

The only acceptable dolls for boys—and they're called "action figures"—are *Star Wars* and commercial wrestling characters and GI Joe, which was manufactured by Hasbro in 1964 to compete with Mattel's Barbie dolls for girls. GI Joes are rugged, macho fighting men and come with a wardrobe of Army fatigues and such accessories as M–1 rifles. Over 400 million GI Joes have been sold since 1964. The creator of GI Joe has described it as "a doll that's okay for boys to play with" because "even dads don't mind" (Oldenburg, 1996).

Some researchers note, however, that male action figures have grown increasingly muscular over the years. GI Joes, for example, have biceps that are twice as large as those of a typical male and larger than those of any known bodybuilder (Pope et al., 1999). Action figures (and comic-strip heroes) put boys at risk of developing the "Barbie syndrome"—unrealistic expectations for their bodies. As a result, some researchers maintain, increasing numbers of men may become obsessively preoccupied with working out and taking dangerous drugs, such as anabolic steroids (see Chapter 14).

Many parents encourage sports among both daughters and sons because athletic activities are healthy, give children a chance to develop team skills, and provide a chance at college athletic scholarships. There are certainly more women's teams in middle schools and high schools today than in the past. Over 2.3 million high school girls are active in sports today compared to only 300,000 in 1971, for example (Richey, 1997). Except for some of the Olympic competitions, however, women's athletics are still not taken very seriously. Girls' teams may not have uniforms or travel budgets, they frequently get inferior athletic equipment, and they are often discouraged from participating in traditionally male sports (Cahn, 1994). Some parents' groups have even sued municipal and county recreation and parks departments for providing boys' softball teams with first-class facilities and a choice of playing times while girls' teams play on "scruffy fields" and have little choice of playing times (Blair, 1998).

The share of women among all intercollegiate athletes increased from 33 percent in 1991 to almost 40 percent in 1998. Despite such increases, female athletes still play in inferior facilities, stay in lower-caliber hotels on the road, eat in cheaper restaurants, get smaller promotional budgets, and have fewer assistant coaches (Zimbalist, 2000). In addition, women's athletic accomplishments are often diminished and sexualized. Many viewers were thrilled, for example, when the U.S. women's soccer team won the World Cup in 1999. As one sportswriter observed, "Anyone who watched even a few minutes of the World Cup saw a U.S. team made up of highly skilled, disciplined players, who seemed to glide across the field, the ball never leaving their feet" (Hyman, 1999). What was splashed across many newsmagazine and newspaper covers? A photo of Brandi Chastain, one of the team members, who "celebrated" by peeling off her jersey (to reveal only a sports bra), a practice that is common to male soccer players but virtually unreported.

Teachers and Schools

Gender-role socialization also takes place in schools. Teachers often treat boys and girls differently in the classroom. Even when their behavior is disruptive, "problem girls" often receive less attention than do either "problem boys" or "nonproblem boys." Moreover, teachers tend to emphasize "motherwork" skills for girls, such as nurturance and emotional support. Although both girls and boys are evaluated on academic criteria, such as work habits and knowledge, teachers are more likely to evaluate girls on such nonacademic criteria as grooming, personal qualities such as politeness, and appearance (American Association of University Women, 1992).

Boys are given more time to talk in class, are called on more often, and are given more positive feedback. Teachers are more likely to give answers to girls or to do the problems for them, but to expect boys to find the answers themselves (Sadker and Sadker, 1994). Expecting more from boys increases their problem-solving abilities, decision-making skills, and self-confidence in finding answers on their own.

In high school, guidance counselors, who play an important role in helping students make career choices, are particularly guilty of sex stereotyping. Even well-intentioned counselors often steer girls into vocational training, such as secretarial work or data processing, rather than college preparatory programs. Girls who are in college preparatory programs are often encouraged to take courses in the social sciences and humanities rather than mathematics or the sciences (Renzetti and Curran, 1995). Even talented young women may be squeezed out of the "science achievement pipeline" because they are less likely than their male counterparts to have fathers who keep track of their progress in school and parents who attend PTA meetings and parent–teacher conferences (Hanson, 1996). Such research findings suggest that adolescent males and females may be steered into stereotypical career choices despite their talents or interests if counselors and parents adhere to traditional gender-role expectations.

Peer groups help maintain gender stereotypes. Both boys and girls engage in behavior that promotes rigid gender-role expectations. One study found that boys conveyed the importance of toughness through

CONSTRAINTS

Textbooks Are Still Male

A few years ago a teacher in an affluent and progressive suburban high school in Maryland invited me to discuss gender issues with an advanced class of juniors. I examined their history textbook to see what issues had received the least coverage. To my surprise, the textbook offered only two paragraphs on women: one discussed the women's rights movement in the 1960s; the other described the Equal Rights Amendment.

Many textbooks in colleges and professional schools also ignore women or present them in stereotypical ways. Mendelsohn and her associates (1994) analyzed more than 4,000 illustrations in 12 anatomy and physical diagnosis textbooks used in medical schools. The anatomy textbooks used illustrations of male bodies more than twice as often as female bodies. In the texts on physical diagnosis, the illustrations of women were largely confined to chapters on reproduction, falsely implying that female and male physiology differs only in respect to their reproductive organs. The researchers concluded that "women are dramatically underrepresented in illustrations of normal, nonreproductive anatomy" and that "males continue to be depicted as the norm or the standard. As a result, students may develop an incomplete knowledge of normal female anatomy" (p. 1269).

In an analysis of law school materials, Frug (1992) identified several ways in which presumably gender-neutral law courses and casebooks on contract law are gendered. First, men not only monopolize the majority of the cases but also the cases that involve women. Second, men represent many different occupations and roles while the few cases that include women are limited to domestic relations and sex discrimination issues. In addition, because casebooks rely almost exclusively on the work of male judges and male legal commentators, women were practically invisible in the broader legal culture.

---

insults such as "fag," "wimp," "sissy," and "girl" to boys who were not aggressive. These labels—that associated a boy's not being tough with femininity or homosexuality—reinforced traditional masculine behavior. The boys' focus on girls' appearance as the most important characteristic in being popular or not "losers" also preoccupied many of the girls' informal conversations. Girls gossiped about or teased other girls who were perceived as overweight, under- or over-developed physically, or "ugly." The researchers note that such stereotypical language limits both the girls' and the boys' ability to view themselves as more complete human beings (Eder et al., 1995).

Books and Textbooks

For years, studies of children's books and textbooks consistently reported two findings: (1) Women were much less visible than men, and (2) when women were depicted, they were not as important as men. Recent studies have found that females are now more likely to be included as characters in books but in roles that do not reflect the actual behavior of females or males in our society. Female characters, for example, are still overwhelmingly portrayed as using household objects (cooking utensils, brooms, sewing needles), whereas male characters are expected to master outside-the-home tools (pitchforks, plows, construction equipment) (Crabb and Bielawski, 1994).

Nonstereotypical books are more readily available, especially for preschoolers, than ever before. Very young children are generally open to stories that describe nontraditional male roles, such as boys playing with dolls (K. Taylor et al., 1993). If parents or teachers tend to stereotype gender roles, however, children will not be exposed to these resources. Early exposure to gender-neutral information is critical in removing gender blinders because many educational materials still depict men's and women's roles very narrowly. As the box "Textbooks Are Still Male" shows, for example, many high school and college textbooks are still very stereotypical. Like television, books and textbooks shape our self-concept, beliefs, values, and aspirations during the socialization process. If children and adolescents don't see role models or don't identify with the images they see in books, they will feel invisible, unimportant, or marginalized (see Berry, 1998).

Popular Culture and the Media

Media myths and unrealistic images of everyday life assault our gender identity on a daily basis. The research in this area has boomed during the last

TATJANA CAN'T WAIT TO TEST THE CORSA'S ALL ROUND SAFETY CAGE.

Much of the advertising in the United States and other western countries uses sexy images of women to sell everything from cars to toothpaste. As the graffiti on this London poster illustrates, many people are offended by stereotypical advertising that demeans women.

decade and is too extensive to discuss fully here. However, a few examples from advertising, newspapers and magazines, television, and music videos will amply illustrate how the media reinforce sex stereotyping during both childhood and adulthood.

Advertising Much of the advertising aimed at children bolsters stereotypes. Although girls are sometimes included in advertisements for educational toys, typically they are featured in doll and housework toy ads. Most of the advertising aimed at children uses blond, blue-eyed, freckled children. Ethnic children are often a face in a crowd or they are used to promote a product as "cool" or trendy. Black children routinely appear in commercials that plug sports and music, reinforcing the stereotype that African Americans are "natural" in sports and music—and, by default, "not natural" in educational and other pursuits. The few exceptions include some makers of preschool-age toys where manufacturers use black, Asian American, and white children together in their ads. McDonald's, also, has cast a variety of kids (including Latinos, African Americans, and Asian Americans) in its commercials (Seiter, 1993).

Do children *really* pay attention to ads? Although older children are affected by ads, as you'll see shortly, they may be more sophisticated than their younger counterparts in understanding that advertising is motivated by profits rather than a concern for the child's well-being. According to a study of Latino preschoolers in northern California, however, young children are much more vulnerable: 63 percent of the children asked for toys they had recently seen on

television (Barbie toys and cosmetics for girls and remote cars and action figures for boys); 55 percent wanted food or drinks that were advertised (Squeeze Its fruit drinks and Kellogg's cornflakes); and 67 percent nagged their mothers to go to a specific store or fast-food restaurant (Borzekowski and Poussaint, 1998). To decrease advertisers' influence on children under age 12, Sweden, Norway, Austria, and parts of Belgium ban ads before, during, and after children's television programs. Greek TV forbids toy ads altogether. Many other European governments are considering similar restrictions on ads that promote toys, games, candy, breakfast cereals, fast foods, and unhealthy snacks (Ford, 1999).

Advertising, in both magazines and television, has changed somewhat in its implicit message about adult roles. A few years ago, women were told that their kitchen floors should be spotless and that "ring-around-the-collar" was one of life's worst disasters. Today the ring-around-the-collar commercials are usually limited to daytime television. Even if the viewers are full-time homemakers, however, the voice-overs (voices narrating off-camera) are typically men's and not women's. The message here is that women's voices are not authoritative enough to persuade homemakers that Cheerios are better than Rice Krispies. Commercials during televised sporting events are especially sex-stereotypical. Beer commercials, for example, routinely present images of one-dimensional women and men. Most of the male characters are shown in leisure wear or work clothes, and female characters are usually in skimpy swimwear. Half of the camera shots of women focus on their bodies—

especially their breasts, buttocks, and crotches—instead of their entire bodies (Hall and Crum, 1994).

Media critics maintain that magazine ads are more sexist than ever. Some feature bondage. An ad in a computer magazine for hardware, for example, shows actress Goldie Hawn in a bondage pose, and perfume ads show a woman tied to a bed. Many ads, including those for energy bars, display parts of women's bodies but not their heads or faces. The ability to alter photographs with computers—to elongate bodies or put one woman's head with another woman's body—makes the "perfect woman" even less attainable (Kilbourne, 1999). Almost all ethnic models—male and female—have white features. This sends the message that beauty is synonymous with whiteness. An ad reviewer notes, moreover, that "beer commercials are slowly going back to babes" and that another advertising theme involves men making fun of women's obsession with their bodies—which ads helped to create in the first place (Gardner, 1999b). *Teen Voices,* a national magazine written by and for young women, runs columns that criticize ads about women's appearance that are damaging to teens. Such awareness is rare, however.

Stereotypical advertising is not limited to television commercials and magazines. In a study of medical advertisements in three prominent medical journals (*Journal of the American Medical Association, New England Journal of Medicine,* and *Annals of Internal Medicine*), the researchers found that although heart disease is the leading cause of death in women, males vastly outnumbered females in cardiovascular drug ads. In addition, the facial expressions of men were more likely to be serious, whereas those of women were often pleasant. The researchers suggest that such depictions may contribute to physicians' perceptions of male medical problems as being more serious: Smiling people are probably healthier than those who are serious or scowling (Leppard et al., 1993).

Newspapers and Magazines Even mainstream news organizations promote gender stereotypes. When the U.S. Senate confirmed Madeleine Albright's nomination as secretary of state in 1997, a *Baltimore Sun* article noted that Ambassador Albright "looked slimmer, blonder, and more elegant than when she first appeared before Congress four years ago" and that she wore "a navy blue suit" to the hearing. One of the readers blasted the article for being preoccupied with Albright's physical characteristics rather than her foreign policy accomplishments and her credentials:

> The [Baltimore] Sun *could have informed readers that Ms. Albright holds her Ph.D. from Columbia University, was a professor at Georgetown University and speaks five languages. . . . Instead, the Sun seems unsure whether the person third in line for presidential successor belongs on the front page or the fashion page. (Cusimano, 1997: 12A)*

A study of newspaper coverage of the 1998 gubernatorial campaigns in five states found that both female and male reporters included personal and family data (such as marital status, age, appearance, and even hair color) about female candidates much more often than about their male opponents. Reporters were more likely to highlight men's but not women's positions on issues (such as education, transportation, and taxes). The report concluded that coverage of women as personalities, not leaders, is a barrier for women seeking election to public office (Women's Leadership Fund, 1999).

Newspapers routinely ignore women who are not running for political offices as well. A recent survey of the front-page stories of 20 national and local newspapers found that although women make up 52 percent of the population, they show up just 13 percent of the time in the prime newspaper coverage. Even the stories about breast implants quoted men more often than women. Two-thirds of the bylines on front pages were male, and three-quarters of the opinions on op-ed pages were by men. Fewer than a third of the photographs on front pages featured women. Because the old "women's sections" are now more unisex and focus on both men and women, news about and by women has actually lost space even in these lifestyle sections (Goodman, 1992; Overholser, 1996).

Most magazines reinforce gender stereotypes. Magazines aimed at male adolescents, for example, emphasize success in sports and improving their mechanical and computer skills, but those for adolescent girls are full of articles and ads on being more popular, thin, and beautiful. Almost 61 percent of all female teens (and 76 percent of Latina teens) read such beauty magazines as *Seventeen* on a regular basis (Weissman, 1999a). Are many young women internalizing messages that achieving a Barbie-like physical appearance and "male validation" is, or should be, one of life's top priorities?

Television and Other Screen Media Children spend considerably more time in front of the television set and other screen media (video games, videotapes, computers, and movies) than they do interacting with parents, family members, teachers, or friends. According to two national studies, the typical American child spends 5.5 to 6.5 hours a day consuming media outside of school. Watching television accounts for more than half of all media use. Across all income levels, black children spend an average of almost 4 hours a day watching television, compared to just over 3 hours for the average Latino child and 2.5 hours for the average white child. Twenty-eight percent of preschool children aged 2 to 5 have television sets in their bedrooms; 60 percent of adolescents have them. About

According to some researchers (see text), some of the Walt Disney G-rated animated films, such as Aladdin, portray high levels of violence.

58 percent of children said that the TV is usually on during meals, 49 percent said there are no household rules about watching TV, and 42 percent said the TV is on in their homes "most of the time." Ethnic children are also more likely to live in a home where the TV is on "most of the time"—56 percent of black children, 42 percent of Latino children, and 39 percent of white children (Roberts et al., 1999; Woodard and Gridina, 2000).

Television molds children's views of how the sexes should behave. Some studies have found that the more television children watch, the more they subscribe to male–female stereotypes (Lips, 1993). Some feel that gender and race stereotypes are probably at their worst in children's television programming. Even on the highly acclaimed *Sesame Street*, the best-known characters are male: Big Bird, Kermit, Bert, Ernie, Snuffalupugus, Grover, and Cookie Monster. Two female puppets, Betty Lou and Prairie Dawn, are less interesting and do not appear regularly.

Middle-class white boys are often at the center of children's programming, whereas children of color and girls of all races play peripheral roles as companions (Seiter, 1993). Some of this programming is slowly changing, however. Fox and UPN, for example, broadcast a number of shows that include black children (see Chapter 1). There are also half a dozen series on network and cable television that feature young women who are capable, self-assured, and intelligent; *Sabrina the Teenage Witch, Buffy the Vampire Slayer, Daria,* and *Moesha* are examples. Critics point out, however, that such programming is the exception rather than the rule.

In a study of 118 characters in the top eight network Saturday morning cartoon shows, Spicher and Hudak (1997) found that the male/female character ratio was 4 to 1. Male characters tended to be at the center of the action, and the occupations or roles of characters were highly stereotypical (males dominated a variety of occupations such as scientists, paramedics, doctors, and helicopter pilots while female characters were typically housewives, princesses, reporters, and nurses). In addition, Latino, Asian, and American Indian characters—whether in cartoons or other programs—are almost nonexistent (Espinosa, 1997).

Films and videocassettes provide an important source of entertainment, especially for young children. Young children (aged 2 to 7) spend nearly 2 hours per day watching television and an additional half hour per day watching commercially prerecorded videotapes (Roberts et al., 1999; see also Stanger, 1997).

What do young children see when they watch these movies and videotapes? A study of 74 animated movies rated G (for general audiences), released between 1937 and 1999 and available on videocassette, concluded that these materials expose children to significant amounts of violence. The researchers defined *violence* as "intentional acts (e.g., to cause harm, to coerce, or for fun) where the aggressor makes some physical contact that has potential to inflict injury or harm." The findings showed that the amount and duration of violence had increased, especially in the films released during the 1990s. The total duration of violent acts ranged from 6 seconds (*My Neighbor Totoro,* 1993) to 24 minutes (*Quest for Camelot,* 1998). Films that depicted 10 or more minutes of violence included *Aladdin, Mulan, Hercules,* and *The Hunchback of Notre Dame* (Yokota and Thompson, 2000). Although the researchers didn't specify assailants and victims by sex, according to my informal observations, most of the films cast male characters as the aggressors.

There is no evidence that viewing violence in the media *causes* aggressive behavior. Researchers are finding, however, that such material desensitizes children to violence and makes it seem "normal." According to some recent studies, playing violent video games like *Doom*, *Wolfenstein 3D*, or *Mortal Combat* can increase a person's aggressive thoughts, feelings, and behavior both in laboratory settings and in actual life. Violent video games may be more harmful than violent television and movies because they are interactive, very engrossing, require the player to identify with the aggressor, and teach "aggression-related scripts" to solve real-life conflict situations. Violent video games also encourage male-to-female violence because much of the violence is directed at women (Dietz, 1998; Dill and Dill, 1998; Anderson and Dill, 2000).

The entertainment media affect our lives. What roles and behaviors children and adults consider appropriate come, in part, from the images we see in video games, television, and the movies. How do children react to gender and ethnic diversity portrayals in the media? A national study of 1,200 children and nine focus groups—Asians, Latinos, blacks, and whites—between the ages of 10 and 17 found that whites overwhelmingly appear in positive roles compared to other groups. As *Figure 4.2* shows, children believe that Latinos, especially, are portrayed in negative ways. Across all races, the children felt that white characters on television were portrayed as having lots of money, being well educated, being a leader, doing well in school, and being intelligent. In contrast, ethnic characters—especially blacks and Latinos—were typically portrayed as breaking the law, having a hard time financially, being lazy, and "acting goofy." An Asian boy commented, for example, that "the shows with white people, they don't fight a lot. But with black and Latino people, they're always fighting or arguing." One teenage Asian girl complained that when Asians do appear, they are shown as "kind of book smart . . . wearing thick glasses and taking notes . . . Or they're like the Kung Fu Master" (Children Now, 1998).

A study of focus groups with American Indian children (aged 9–17) from more than 20 tribes in Oklahoma City, Albuquerque, and Seattle found, also, that American Indian children felt that media stereotypes were widespread. They saw themselves characterized as "poor," "drunk and beating up on each other" "living on reservations," "selling fireworks," and "fighting over land." The children also said that on TV "black people are always funny" and "white people are all rich and stuff" (Children Now, 1998).

How does television depict gender roles? In a national survey, 78 percent of the children described boys and men on television as strong and as problem solvers. Ninety-eight percent felt that boys and men on television were funny, but primarily because they often

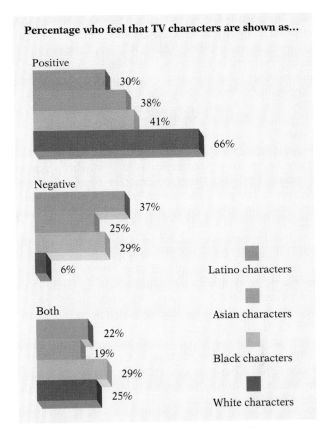

Percentage who feel that TV characters are shown as...

FIGURE 4.2   **How Children View Racial Groups on TV.** Percentage of children aged 10–17 who responded to the question "Are TV characters shown in a mostly positive way, a mostly negative way, or both?"

Source: Based on Children Now, *A Different World: Children's Perceptions of Race and Class in the Media, 1998,* www.childrennow.org/redesigns/media/mc98/MC98page6.html (accessed August 24, 2000).

acted dumb, as in *The Simpsons* and *Martin*. Further, 91 percent of the children polled believed that men on television are usually portrayed as confident and athletic. The same study examined entertainment content of 25 prime-time television programs with the highest ratings among adolescent boys. The researchers found that male characters are more often shown at their place of work while female characters are more frequently shown at home. Male characters are more likely to be shown in higher status occupations, such as an executive/CEO, a doctor, or a business owner, and are also more frequently cast in traditionally male-dominated fields like politics, the military, and law enforcement. The female character is more likely to be shown in traditionally female occupations, such as teacher, student, homemaker, or clerical worker ("Boys to men . . . ," 1999).

The portrayal of ethnic characters and women has improved slightly during the last few years. The four biggest networks (ABC, CBS, NBC, Fox), for example, now feature more black men and black women during prime-time shows and cast them in primary and strong supporting roles. In programs like *The Practice, Spin City, City of Angels,* and *Walker, Texas Ranger,* black characters are more likely to be competent and successful than some of their white counterparts in both sitcoms and dramas. Nonetheless, black characters are more likely to appear in situation comedies than in dramas. The few Latino characters often play secondary rather than primary roles, and American Indians are virtually invisible (Heintz-Knowles et al., 2000).

Finally, how we watch television also reflects gender differences. In a study of couples who view television together, for example, Walker (1996) found that men tend to dominate program selection, rarely consider their partner's interests, and monopolize remote control devices. In the study, men used the remote control to avoid commercials, to watch more than one show at a time, and to check what else was on—even when such behavior frustrated their partners. If the couple didn't have a video recorder, the women tried to minimize conflict by backing off or not watching their favorite programs.

Music Videos Another dominant source of much sex-stereotypical programming is music videos. Over the years, a number of researchers have found that music videos are a powerful transmitter of gender stereotypes, and current research continues to support this observation. For example, a recent content analysis of 20 music videos that were most requested on Music Television (MTV) found that 62 percent of the music characters were men (54 percent white, 42 percent black, 4 percent "other"). More than 25 percent of the videos emphasized female breasts, legs, or torsos. Almost two-thirds of the videos featured females as props, like background dancers. While half of the female props were semi-nude or dressed in revealing clothes, 75 percent of the male props were fully dressed ("Boys to Men . . . ," 1999).

About 10 percent of children aged 8 to 18 report watching music videos every day. Of these, almost twice as many are girls as boys, and black girls are more likely to view music videos as are white or other ethnic girls (Roberts et al., 1999). Although 10 percent may seem like a low figure—especially compared to figures for children who watch TV or play video games—remember that this percentage represents millions of kids and adolescents. Thus, some of the research has focused on the damaging effects of these stereotypes. For example, adolescent females who are very unhappy with their family environment may be especially likely to engage in the sexually permissive (and risky) behavior that many music videos portray (Signorielli et al., 1994; Strouse et al., 1995).

Traditional Views and Gender Roles

Many women, including those who work outside the home, enjoy at least some of their domestic tasks. A survey of European and U.S. women found that 85 percent and 88 percent, respectively, were responsible for taking care of family members. About 56 percent of both the European and U.S. women said that they would not give up even "some" of their family responsibilities (Whirlpool Foundation, 1996). In a U.S. survey, approximately 7 out of 10 men *and* women agreed with the statement: "When it comes to housework and childrearing, women still want to be in charge" (Roper Starch Worldwide, 1996: 88).

Instrumental and Expressive Roles

As you saw in Chapter 2, many social scientists describe traditional gender roles as instrumental or expressive. Although there is a great deal of variation in everyday life and all of the characteristics of instrumental and expressive role players may not correspond exactly to every single case, they are useful in understanding some of the differences between traditional and nontraditional gender roles. Conceptually, *instrumental role players* (husbands and fathers) must be "real men." A "real man" is a procreator, a protector, and a provider. He must produce children because this will prove his virility, and having boys is especially important to carry on his family name. The procreator must also be a protector. He must be strong and powerful in ensuring his family's physical safety. The provider keeps working hard even if he is overwhelmed by the requirements of multiple roles, such as "the breadwinner," "the dutiful husband," and "the dutiful son" (Gaylin, 1992; Betcher and Pollack, 1993).

If the traditional male is a "superman," the traditional female is an only slightly more modern version of the "true woman" you met in Chapter 3. Many women have internalized gender expectations and try to live up to them. In a study of two coeducational middle schools in northern California, for example, Orenstein (1994) found that intelligent female students, regardless of social class and across all racial groups, lived up to the traditional definition of girls: pretty and polite but not too aggressive, not too outspoken, and not too smart. If young women want to be popular with both male and female peers they often "dumb down" to them and to teachers as well.

Expressive role players (wives and mothers) provide the emotional support and nurturing qualities that sustain the family unit and support the father/husband. They are warm, sensitive, and sympathetic. For example, the expressive role player consoles a teenage daughter when she breaks up with her boyfriend, encourages her son to try out for the Little League baseball team, and is always ready to comfort a husband who has had a bad day at work.

A good example of women's expressive roles is that of kinkeeper. The role is often passed down from mother to daughter. Kinkeepers are important communication links between family members. They spend a lot of time writing to or e-mailing family members, visiting friends and families, and organizing or holding family gatherings during the holidays or for special events like birthdays and anniversaries. They also often act as the family helper, problem solver, or mediator (Rosenthal, 1985).

The Benefits and Costs of Traditional Gender Roles

Traditional gender roles have both benefits and costs. These roles may be chosen consciously, or they may be a product of habit, custom, or socialization. Remember, too, that traditional relationships vary. In some, partners feel loving and committed; in others, people feel as though they are trapped or sleepwalking.

Benefits Traditional gender roles promote stability, continuity, and predictability. Because each person knows what is expected of him or her, rights and responsibilities are clear. Men and women do not have to argue over who does what: If the house is clean, she is a "good wife"; if the bills are paid, he is a "good provider." Using the exchange model (see Chapter 2), if the costs and benefits of the relationship are fairly balanced and each partner is relatively happy, traditional gender roles can work well. As long as both partners live up to their role expectations, they are safe in assuming that they will take care of each other financially, emotionally, and sexually.

Some women stay in traditional relationships because as long as they live up to the idealized role, they don't have to make autonomous decisions or assume responsibility when things go wrong. An accommodating wife or mother can enjoy both power and prestige through her husband's accomplishments. As a good mother, she not only controls and dominates her children but can also be proud of guiding and enriching their lives (Harris, 1994).

When a traditional husband complained about his traditional wife's spending more money than he approved, the wife composed the following "help wanted" ad that she gave him and sent to Ann Landers. The ad provides a good description of how men benefit from traditional marriages:

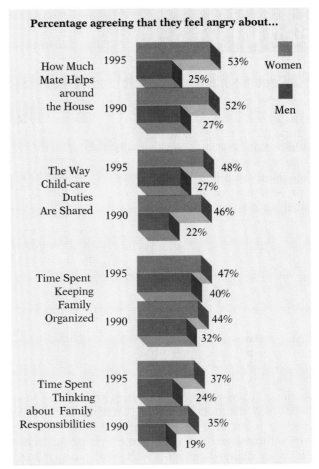

Percentage agreeing that they feel angry about...

How Much Mate Helps around the House
1995: Women 53%, Men 25%
1990: Women 52%, Men 27%

The Way Child-care Duties Are Shared
1995: Women 48%, Men 27%
1990: Women 46%, Men 22%

Time Spent Keeping Family Organized
1995: Women 47%, Men 40%
1990: Women 44%, Men 32%

Time Spent Thinking about Family Responsibilities
1995: Women 37%, Men 24%
1990: Women 35%, Men 19%

FIGURE 4.3 Sources of Resentment When Wives Are Employed. Note that women are twice as likely as men to feel angry about how much their mate helps around the house and the way child care is shared. Men's resentment rose between 1990 and 1995, even though women say they do the bulk of the household chores and child care. (Adapted from the 1995 Virginia Slims Opinion Research Poll conducted by Roper Starch Worldwide, 1996, p. 82.)

I need someone full time who is willing to be on call 24 hours a day, seven days a week. Sick leave only when hospitalization is required. Must be able to cook, clean house, do laundry, care for children, feed and clean up after dog, do yard work, mow lawn, shovel snow, do shopping, do menu planning, take out trash, pay bills, answer phone and run errands. Must be able to pinch pennies. Also must be a friend and companion. Must be patient and cannot complain. If you are interested, please leave a message. I will contact you when I feel like talking. Speak only when you have something to say that might interest me. Otherwise, shut up and get to work.—C. L. in Utah. ("Want ad proves . . . ," 1997)

CHOICES

College Seminars for (Male and Female) Sexists

During the last few years, a number of messages have appeared on e-mail either challenging or reinforcing gender-role stereotypes. Some Net lists have suggested that colleges establish a graduation requirement of specific and parallel seminars for men and women. Here are some of the suggested courses:

Seminars for Men

1. You, Too, Can Do Housework
2. Easy Laundry Techniques
3. Get a Life—Learn to Cook
4. Spelling—Even You Can Get It Right
5. How to Stay Awake after Sex
6. Garbage—Getting It to the Curb
7. How to Put the Toilet Seat Down
8. Combating Stupidity

Seminars for Women

1. You, Too, Can Change the Oil
2. Elementary Map Reading
3. Get a Life—Learn to Kill Spiders Yourself
4. Balancing a Checkbook—Even You Can Get It Right
5. How to Stay Awake during Sex
6. Shopping—Doing It in Less Than 16 Hours
7. How to Close the Garage Door
8. Combating the Impulse to Nag

As this ad suggests, traditional wives protect their husbands from the pressure of doing domestic work while meeting job-related responsibilities. In addition, the wives themselves don't have the tension of being pulled in many directions. Such clearly demarcated responsibilities decrease both partners' stress.

But traditional roles are changing. Many men have lost their jobs to downsizing and more women are working to pursue their own professional interests as well as to help out financially. Black fathers, especially, are losing well-paying low-skilled manufacturing jobs that are eliminated by automation and global job restructuring (see Chapters 12 and 13). As a result, black and other ethnic fathers who were primary breadwinners are now sharing this role with their wives (Bowman and Forman, 1997). This has created more strain at home. Although husbands of employed wives may be doing more of the household tasks than their fathers did, there is some evidence that men's resentment about the division of labor may be growing. As *Figure 4.3* shows, for example, both employed wives and their mates were more dissatisfied with their share of family responsibilities in 1995 than 1990.

Costs   Traditional gender roles have their drawbacks. As one historian notes, "Not all men, contrary to the rhetoric of masculinity, can be at the top of the pyramid" (Coontz, 1997: 22). Today, many husbands depend on their wives' income to make ends meet. In 1980, for example, only 19 percent of all employed women said they worked to support the family. By 1995, this number had increased to 44 percent

(Whirlpool Foundation, 1996). Adhering to a traditional view in these circumstances can make men feel like failures. Although many traditional families probably scale down their standard of living, a sole breadwinner is under a lot of economic pressure. A traditional wife, similarly, can expect little relief from never-ending tasks that may be exhausting, monotonous, and boring. She may also be taken for granted by her husband and children. And what are her options if she's miserable? If she's been out of the work force for a number of years, she might be worse off after a divorce (see Chapter 15).

Another cost of traditional gender roles is loneliness. A strong but unemotional male may be hard to live with if he does not communicate. Sometimes the seemingly unemotional male is quiet because he is continuously worried about the family's economic well-being (Kaufman, 1993). The dutiful worker, husband, and father may feel overwhelmed by his responsibilities and may be unhappy with his life. A traditional male may believe that he never quite lives up to the standard of manhood. Although he has not failed completely, he may feel that he has not succeeded, either (Gaylin, 1992).

On the female side, the responsibilities suddenly thrust on a woman in her role as wife or mother can create problems if she is dependent on her spouse for economic support and insecure about her roles as a good wife and mother. Moreover, such traditional values as being nurturant, dependent, and submissive can discourage some women from leaving abusive relationships (see Chapter 15).

Gender-role stereotypes reflect another cost of traditional roles. The box "College Seminars for (Male and Female) Sexists" offers a tongue-in-cheek look at such stereotypes. Traditional roles have been idealized for so long that many of us think they are normal.

There are several reasons why traditional gender roles persist. First, they are profitable for business. The unpaid work that women do at home (such as domestic labor, child rearing, and emotional work) means that companies don't have to pay for child-care services or counseling for stressed-out male employees. And if there is only one breadwinner, many men may work extra hours without additional pay to keep their jobs. Thus, companies increase their profits. If women are convinced that their place is in the home, they will take part-time jobs that have no benefits, will work for less pay, and will not complain. This increases the corporate world's pool of exploitable and expendable low-paid workers (Eitzen and Baca Zinn, 1994; Kendall, 1999).

Second, traditional roles maintain male privilege and power. If women are seen as not having leadership qualities (see *Table 4.1*), men can dominate political and legal institutions and shape the laws and policies that maintain their vested interests without being challenged by women who are unhappy with the status quo. Finally, traditional roles save taxpayers money. After decades of demands by the National Housewives' Federation, Italy's government announced that it would start a state-aided pension plan for housewives and househusbands at age 57 provided they pay five years' social security contributions ("Italy promises . . . ," 1996). Such progressive legislation for full-time housewives is not even being discussed in the United States.

A Bubbling Contradiction about Traditional Gender Roles?

In a national survey, many people wanted to return to the romanticized "good old days": 42 percent of the women and 35 percent of the men felt that it would be "better for the country if men and women went back to the traditional roles they had in the 1950s." About two-thirds of both women (68 percent) and men (69 percent) embraced the idea that, although mothers often *have* to work for economic reasons, it would be better if they stayed at home and took care of the house and kids (Hugick, 1999).

In contrast to such perspectives, a recent survey of boys and girls aged 13 to 17 found that many teenage girls "envision a family-work model that stands tradition on its head." On the one hand, twice as many girls as boys saw themselves staying home to raise their children (52 percent of girls compared to 25 percent of boys). This suggests that many adolescent girls still perceive raising children as "women's work." On the other hand, while half of the teenage boys expected that their wife will stay home with the kids, 38 percent of the girls believed *it will be their husband* who stays home with the children while the girls work outside the home (Roper Youth Report, 1999).

These surveys suggest an interesting dilemma. While parents (and grandparents) might encourage

Increasing numbers of women are attending college part time while working and raising their children. Others are pursuing college degrees in their later years.

their offspring to reclaim traditional gender roles, nearly two in five teen girls expect their future spouses to be househusbands. As Chapter 13 shows, there is no evidence that househusbands have ever represented more than a minuscule number of fathers. Nonetheless, some of these surveys suggest that, in the future, there may be a significant gap between the roles that women and men expect their partners to play in the home.

Contemporary Gender Roles in Adulthood

Many of us believe that adults have more options than ever before to "do gender" any way they want. Certainly, there have been many changes, especially in women's roles. Nearly three out of four married mothers were in the labor force in 1998 compared with two out of four in 1970. Women now earn 38 percent of business administration degrees, 44 percent of law degrees, 41 percent of medical degrees, and 41 percent of all doctorates (U.S. Census Bureau, 1999c). Although the numbers are still very low, some women are U.S. Senators, CEOs, and tenured professors (see Data Digest). By the mid-1990s, almost 8 million women owned businesses in the United States that generated $1.4 trillion in revenue (Myers, 1996).

Despite such changes, or because of them, men—especially working-class and middle-class white men—feel that they are being attacked from all sides. Such complaints are not supported by the data, however. White males make up just 33 percent of the population but they hold most of the power (see Data Digest). Large proportions of both sexes feel that men have more advantages than women. In 1995, for example, 39 percent of women and 33 percent of men said that there are more advantages in being a man. Most cite such job-related reasons as better-paying jobs, more opportunities and choices in jobs, and quick promotions. In contrast, only 7 percent of women and 10 percent of men felt that there were more advantages in being a woman (Roper Starch Worldwide, 1996).

Gender Roles at Home: Who Does the Work?

Because many mothers work outside the home today, there is more pressure on fathers to share in child rearing and housework. As you saw in *Figure 4.3,* a number of fathers aren't very enthusiastic about their new responsibilities. Growing numbers, however, are eager participants. Some fathers have reported that it took them some time to become concerned about child safety or to be more "tuned in" to their children. Others have become more understanding of the drudgery involved in housework and are more willing to buy expensive appliances (such as self-cleaning ovens) to make the work easier (Coltrane, 1998).

Men today have "permission" that they didn't have a generation ago to care for their children. There are several organizations, such as the National Fatherhood Initiative, that encourage fathers—and especially divorced fathers—to be more involved in their children's upbringing. Many fathers think they're doing a better parenting job than their fathers did. In a *Newsweek* poll, for example, 55 percent of fathers said being a parent is more important to them than it was to their own fathers, 61 percent said they understand their children better compared to their own fathers, and 70 percent said they spend more time with their children than their fathers spent with them (Adler, 1996). Despite the positive self-evaluations, a *Good Housekeeping*/Roper survey of American families reported that husbands might be doing less around the house than they think they do. For example, 70 percent of fathers of children aged 8 to 17 said they prepare dinner for the family but fewer than half of the children agreed (Dortch, 1994).

In most cases, one of the major sources of tension is that many fathers do not participate in the "second shift"—household work and child care after coming home from work. Increasingly, more couples say that they share tasks, especially cooking and grocery shopping, about equally. In these and other areas, however, there's quite a discrepancy in women's and men's perceptions of their domestic contributions. As *Figure 4.4* shows, for example, many men don't feel that women have as much responsibility for household tasks as women say they do. Such differing perceptions might explain why husbands and wives are increasingly dissatisfied with their family lives (see *Figure 4.3*). Conflict over who does how much may also lead to communication problems or, ultimately, to separation and divorce (see Chapters 9 and 15).

Even when men share some of the work, women feel more responsible for caring for the home and children:

> More women than men kept track of doctor's appointments and arranged for kids' playmates to come over. More mothers than fathers worried about a child's Halloween costume or a birthday present for a school friend. They were more likely to think about their children while at work and to check in by phone with the babysitter. (Hochschild and Machung, 1989: 24)

In addition, women sometimes complain that men's participation is peripheral and superficial:

> I'm always amused when my husband says that he'll "help" me make our bed. I guess he "helps" because he feels making the bed is my

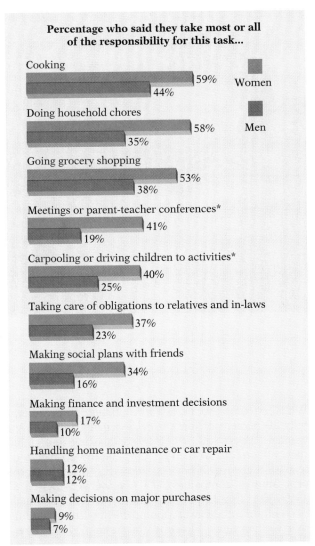

Percentage who said they take most or all of the responsibility for this task...

Cooking
Women 59%
Men 44%

Doing household chores
58%
35%

Going grocery shopping
53%
38%

Meetings or parent-teacher conferences*
41%
19%

Carpooling or driving children to activities*
40%
25%

Taking care of obligations to relatives and in-laws
37%
23%

Making social plans with friends
34%
16%

Making finance and investment decisions
17%
10%

Handling home maintenance or car repair
12%
12%

Making decisions on major purchases
9%
7%

FIGURE 4.4 **She Says, He Says.** Question: "Thinking of your relationship with your spouse or partner, I'd like to ask you about your roles with respect to a number of responsibilities in your relationship. For each item I read, please tell me whether you take all the responsibility for that item, you take most but not all the responsibility, or your spouse or partner takes all the responsibility . . ."

Note: All questions were asked of respondents who are part of a couple in a household.

*Asked of respondents who are part of a couple in a household and they have children.

Source: Survey by Peter D. Hart Research Associates for Shell Oil, January 7–13, 2000. Adapted from table in *Public Perspective*, July/August 2000, p. 27.

responsibility, not his, even though we both sleep in it. When I mow the lawn, it's no big deal. But when he occasionally helps make the bed or does the dishes, he expects a litany of thank-you's and hugs. (author's files)

Housework combined with full employment means that women often experience greater stress than men. Because they have either more responsibility or a greater share of the domestic work, women are often doing two things at once, such as writing checks while returning phone calls. In addition, women do more of the tedious household chores, such as scrubbing the toilet, whereas men prefer to tend to their children and do "fun" things with them, like going to the movies or playing video games.

Fathers may feel very close to their children and be affectionate with them, but they are still less involved in child care. Fathers spend an average 45 minutes a day caring for their children by themselves compared to more than 10 hours daily by mothers (Adler, 1996). Some men believe child care is simply not their job. Chapter 11 will examine the division of labor in the home more closely.

The number of full-time fathers seems to fluctuate with economic conditions, downsizing, and temporary layoffs. In 1991, for example, 20 percent of U.S. fathers were taking care of young children in the home. Two years later, as the economy improved, that proportion dropped to 16 percent (Adler, 1996). Full-time fathers may become primary caregivers by default after a layoff or by choice, as when wives outearn their husbands and it's more cost-effective not to pay for day care and the husband's job-related expenses. Still, full-time fathers may feel guilty about not earning money, may be ostracized by friends, peers, and relatives who are suspicious of any man who does "women's work," or may complain that their breadwinner wives aren't doing their share of the housework. Despite such problems, many full-time fathers report that they are "just blown away by the depth of the emotions they feel for their children, which they had no idea were there" (Gardner, 1995a: 12).

Gender Roles in the Workplace

A few years ago Air Force Colonel Eileen Collins, age 42 and a mother of a young child, became the first woman astronaut to command a space shuttle, *Columbia*. Although many people praised Collins's achievement, some men grumbled, "They're not going to let her land it, are they?" ("1st woman prepares . . . ," 1999: 4a). This anecdote illustrates the hostility that women, especially employed mothers, still encounter.

While there has been progress, many gender roles in the workplace affect both men and women negatively. The average male employee does not have options for flexible schedules, paternity leaves, or extended absences for "household" matters. Women may feel they have to postpone or forgo having children to pursue a career. In a study of female college graduates who got degrees between 1966 and 1979,

As more women enlist in the military forces, gender roles are changing. In Parris Island, South Carolina, for example, women recruits in the U.S. Marine Corps trudge through mud and rain, carry 50 pounds of gear, and respond to "barking drill instructors" during daily training maneuvers.

for example, Goldin (1997) found that only 13 to 17 percent (compared to 60 percent of their male counterparts) had reached midlife with both a family (defined as having at least one child) and a career. Many of the women in this cohort who had achieved a career did so by delaying having a family. For most women, Goldin notes, "that which is delayed is often not achieved." We'll examine family and work roles at some length in Chapter 13. In this section, we consider, briefly, sex discrimination and sexual harassment—two work-related gender inequities that affect women, men, their partners, and families.

Sex Discrimination   Recently, one of *TV Guide*'s cover stories, "How Women Took Over the News," announced that women now enjoy gender equity in the newsroom. "Women are on every beat, in every aspect of news, as fixtures in jobs traditionally held by men," the author wrote. She concluded, happily, that, no longer held back by institutional sexism, female journalists have come "a long way, baby" (Murphy, 1999: 23).

Several things are wrong with this picture. First, focusing on a handful of very visible women on major and cable networks hardly proves that women have attained journalistic gender parity. In response to the *TV Guide* article, for example, Fairness & Accuracy in Reporting (FAIR), a national media watch group, pointed out that female news reporters made up only one-third of the correspondent corps and covered only 28 percent of stories in 1998. Male journalists outnumber their female counterparts by two-to-one.

When it comes to newswomen behind the camera, only 20 percent of local television news directors are women. Worse still, a 1998 Broadcasting and Cable survey found no women heading the top 25 media or television groups, broadcast networks, or major cable programming companies ("*TV Guide* cover story . . . ," 1999; see also http://www.fair.org/activism/national-press-club.html). The second problem with concluding that women have "made it" in an employment area, like the newsroom, by pointing to a few women ignores the larger landscape. As the FAIR comment noted, how many women are in decision-making roles? Finally, we can't generalize from a few cases (such as journalists Katie Couric, Barbara Walters, and Diane Sawyer) who are either single, or past their childbearing years, or can spend enormous amounts of money to hire nannies or other domestic help.

Unlike national news anchors, most women are in low-paying, low-status occupations that have little autonomy or power (see Chapter 13). Often even women in managerial or professional jobs are denied the opportunities and benefits offered to men in comparable jobs. One example of the glass ceiling is a highly publicized case at the Massachusetts Institute of Technology's School of Science. A female professor of molecular biology spent several years collecting information on the unequal resources provided to male and to female scientists—including salaries, research funds, laboratory space, assignments to important committees, and participation in departmental decision-making processes. The university admitted that the discrimination existed but that it had not been "conscious or deliberate" and implemented such remedies as salary increases for women scientists, more desirable teaching assignments, and greater support for research (Wilson, 1999).

In another recent case, the University of Rhode Island settled a faculty grievance in which three female engineering faculty complained of discrimination, harassment, and a hostile working environment. The women asserted that, among other things, they were given heavier teaching loads than their male colleagues, were not provided with laboratory facilities and equipment that they had been promised, and had been subjected to demeaning statements by male professors about their appearance or personal lives (Wilson, 2000).

Female physicians are more likely than their male counterparts to teach in medical schools but are less likely to be promoted (Nonnemaker, 2000). While individual circumstances explain being stuck at the junior ranks for particular people—female or male—many researchers believe that much of the disparity in advancement is due to one's sex. Women's child-rearing obligations are one barrier to their advancement (De Angelis, 2000). As long as women have the primary (and often nearly total) responsibility for the care of children, even generous maternity leaves will not enable women to catch up to male colleagues who have been focusing all of their attention on their careers.

Sexual Harassment Another area where gender roles intersect with the workplace is the issue of sexual harassment. **Sexual harassment** is any unwelcome sexual advance, request for sexual favors, or other conduct of a sexual nature that makes a person uncomfortable and interferes with her or his work. Harassment includes touching, staring at, or making jokes about a person's body, nonreciprocated requests for sexual intercourse, and rape. A landmark Supreme Court decision in 1986, *Meritor Savings Bank* v. *Vinson,* ruled that sexual harassment violates federal laws against discrimination and is unlawful. Sexual harassment in the workplace had a generally low profile, however, until the Senate confirmation hearings of Clarence Thomas, a candidate for the U.S. Supreme Court. In October 1991, sexual harassment got national coverage when Anita Hill, a law professor at the University of Oklahoma, testified that in the early 1980s Thomas had sexually harassed her while he was her supervisor and the director of the Equal Employment Opportunity Commission (EEOC).

In 1996, the EEOC brought a lawsuit against Mitsubishi Motor Corporation alleging that pervasive sexual harassment at the plant affected as many as 500 women. According to one employee, the men would gather around her, grabbing her breasts and reaching between her legs to touch her crotch. The men drew pictures of her engaging in sexual activities with them and placed them on the cars as they moved through the assembly line. Some men openly admitted the harassment because they felt that "there was nothing wrong with it."

At a food processing plant in Baltimore, Maryland, the female workers—all recent immigrants from Central America—said that male managers and co-workers subjected them to unwanted groping and explicit requests for sexual favors over several years. One supervisor locked a woman in a freezer after she turned down his sexual requests. Plant managers gave other women menial or difficult work assignments after the women rejected sexual propositions ("EEOC obtains $1 million . . . ," 2000). At a large construction company based in New Jersey, black and female employees charged that they had experienced ongoing sexual harassment that included racist and sexist graffiti in portable toilets at constructions sites ("$1.3 million settlement . . . ," 2000).

Sexual harassment is unlawful regardless of the sex of the victim or the harasser. In 1999, 15,222 sexual harassment charges were filed with the EEOC, up from 10,532 cases in 1992 ("Sexual harassment charges . . . ," 1999). Men filed 10 percent of these cases, but breakdowns by the offender's sex are not available. One of the largest settlements ($500,000) to date on same-sex harassment involved a major Colorado auto dealership. According to the suit, ten former salesmen allegedly carried on persistent same-sex harassment that included the touching and grabbing of genitals, exposing of a manager's penis in the workplace, crude sexual language and jokes, referring to male employees in obscene and derogatory terms, presenting sexual materials at sales meetings, and tolerating offensive sexual conduct in the workplace ("EEOC settles same-sex . . . ," 2000).

Some men say that they are confused about what sexual harassment is. They claim that they don't see the difference between flirting or complimenting someone and what is being called sexual harassment. Actually, the difference is quite clear: If someone says "stop it" and you don't, it's sexual harassment. We discuss the prevalence, consequences, and legal ramifications of sexual harassment in more detail in Chapter 13.

Gender and the Consumer Marketplace

Consumer problems are typically more common and more serious for women than for men. Women are often overcharged for car and home repairs, even when they have some expertise in these areas. They routinely pay more and get less as consumers in many everyday transactions. Women are charged, on average, over 27 percent more than men to dry-clean a basic white cotton shirt and 25 percent more than men for a basic shampoo, cut, and blow-dry. Women rarely get free alterations when they purchase expensive clothing in the same stores that do not charge men for alterations on their clothing purchases (Whittelsey, 1993).

Millions of women invest in stocks or bonds and, again, experience unequal treatment. Stockbrokers are four to six times more likely to tell men about a wide range of investments (such as corporate bond funds, money market funds, and IRAs). They are twice as likely to explain investments to men and to urge men to open accounts (because they assume women will be confused by explanations and have less money to invest), and they ask men more probing questions about their finances (Wang, 1993).

Women typically spend more on health insurance than men. The justification is that women's reproductive systems are more complex than men's and that women are more likely to require annual medical "maintenance" such as Pap smears and mammograms (even though screening for colon cancer is increasing among men over age 50) (Myers, 1996). Whether or not they have health insurance, women pay—financially, physically, and emotionally—for two of the most commonly performed and unnecessary surgeries. Wolfe (1991) estimates that one in four hysterectomies and half of all cesarean sections performed in the United States could be avoided. Furthermore, most contraceptives are female-based and women often bear the financial burden for birth control.

Two exceptions to women's paying more as consumers are in automotive and life insurance premiums. Young men pay more for car insurance because their driving records, on average, are worse than women's. At age 30, men and women pay the same life insurance premiums. At age 40, however, men's payments at a typical life insurance company may be $451 per year compared to $414 per year for women. For those who wait until age 50 to buy life insurance, men pay $845 and women $733 (Myers, 1996). Men pay a price, literally, for their shorter (on average) life expectancy.

Language and Communication

Language enables us to communicate, to interpret and organize our environment, and to give meaning to our everyday experiences. On the other hand, language can also limit our ideas and thought processes.

In *You Just Don't Understand,* sociolinguist Deborah Tannen (1990) proposes that women and men have distinctive communication styles that include different purposes, different rules, and different ways of interpreting communications. For example, Tannen says, women are more likely than men to use "rapport-talk," a way of establishing connections and negotiating relationships. They are most concerned with how people feel and with making people feel comfortable. In contrast, men are more likely to use "report-talk," a way

Many women endure sexual harassment in the workplace because they're afraid of complaining and losing their jobs. Some, such as these demonstrators outside a Mitsubishi car dealership in Watertown, Massachusetts, have challenged sexual harassment through public protests. Others have won lawsuits against several major corporations.

TABLE 4.3

Are Women More Critical of Men Today?

Beliefs about Male Attitudes and Behavior	Percentage of Women Agreeing	
	1970	1995
Most men think only their own opinions about the world are important.	50%	52%
Most men find it necessary for their egos to keep women down.	49	43
Most men look at a woman and immediately think how it would be to go to bed with her.	41	45
Most men are interested in their work and life outside the home and don't pay much attention to things going on at home.	39	50
Most men are basically kind, gentle, and thoughtful.	67	53
Men are basically selfish and self-centered.	32	38

Note that many women's positive opinion of men increased on only one item between 1970 and 1995—"Most men find it necessary for their egos to keep women down." Are men becoming more macho? Are women demanding too much from men? Or are there other explanations?

SOURCE: Adapted from Roper Starch Worldwide, 1996, p. 90.

of exhibiting knowledge and skill and holding center stage through verbal performance such as storytelling, joking, or giving information. For example, if a man comes home and his (female) partner asks, "How was your day?" she probably expects rapport-talk in response (such as office gossip). Often, however, she will get report-talk: "Fine. Had some problems but got 'em straightened out." Not hearing what she expects, the woman may be miffed, and her partner will probably not understand why she's upset. Julia Wood (1994) has suggested other differences between women's and men's communication patterns which we discuss in Chapter 9.

Current Gender-Role Changes and Constraints

As you saw earlier, although men feel that they are better parents than their fathers were, they would prefer to do less housework and child care. According to one nationwide survey, women seem to be angrier about the current imbalances between men's and women's juggling family and work roles and more critical of men than they were 25 years ago. As *Table 4.3* shows, women today seem more dissatisfied in their relationships with men compared to women a generation ago. Some attribute such strain to role conflict. Others

argue that our society, especially feminists, is waging a war against boys and men.

Role Conflict

Whether it is men or women who are changing, many people are bound to encounter serious **role conflict**—the frustration and uncertainties a person experiences when confronted with the requirements of two or more roles that are incompatible with each other. Role conflict can produce tension, hostility, aggression, and stress-related physical problems, such as insomnia, headaches, ulcers, eating disorders, teeth grinding, anxiety attacks, chronic fatigue, nausea, weight loss or gain, and drug and alcohol abuse (Weber et al., 1997).

According to one national survey, mothers who work full time said time pressures were the most difficult problems they faced and almost half said that finding a job with a schedule flexible enough to let them meet family responsibilities is a serious problem ("Motherhood today . . . ," 1997). Such role conflict may explain why many women's attitudes about men have become more negative (see *Table 4.3*). Some men complain, however, that their wives' housecleaning standards are too high, that women add unnecessary "finishing touches" (such as rewiping the kitchen table after the husband has cleaned it), or that women grumble that the husbands "dressed the kids funny" (Coltrane, 1996). As a result, men may feel unappreciated or inadequate and assume fewer house-work and child-care responsibilities.

Are We Waging War against Boys and Men?

With a few exceptions (such as *Reviving Ophelia*, discussed earlier), material about girls, women, or sex inequality usually garners little media attention. In contrast, a number of recent books about boys' and men's lives have been highly publicized by newspapers, newsmagazines, and talk shows. This attention to boys and men may reflect a greater societal concern about white, middle-class boys who are violent—like the ones responsible for the killing spree at Columbine High School, Colorado, in 1999—as well as boys' development (see Canada, 1997; Garbarino, 1999; Kindlon et al., 1999; Nikkah and Furman, 2000). Some argue, however, that the recent emphasis on males signals a backlash against some of the gains that girls and women made in education and the workplace during the 1990s.

A Rising Concern about Men and Boys' Development In *Real Boys*, clinical psychologist William Pollack (1998) maintains that "boys today are in serious trouble, including many who seem 'normal' and to be doing just fine" (p. xxi). Pollack feels that "many boys are deeply troubled." Among other things, they make up 67 percent of special education classes, are more likely than girls to suffer from attention deficit disorders, lag behind girls in reading scores, create more disciplinary problems in school, and are more likely than girls to be both perpetrators and victims of crime.

In a similar vein, Christina Hoff Sommers (2000) claims that U.S. culture ignores and dismisses boys. Sommers blames feminists, especially, for turning "masculinity into a politically incorrect idea" by spending too much time worrying about how girls are treated, in schools especially, and neglecting boys. According to Sommers, girls outshine boys in school: They get better grades, have higher educational aspirations, read more books, and are less likely than boys to be involved in crime, alcohol, and drugs.

Anthropologist Lionel Tiger (1999) contends, also, that "these are perilous times for men." He claims that sex equality ignores the biological differences between women and men and that the widespread use of the Pill by women has lessened men's virility, as evidenced by lower sperm production (a topic addressed in Chapter 10). Tiger is troubled by two-career couples who decide to be childless. He also worries that blue-collar workers can't find jobs in an "increasingly feminized workplace." He concludes that the rising confidence and power of women has led to a corresponding erosion in the confidence and power of men (see also Faludi, 1999).

A Backlash against Girls' and Women's Progress Critics of such perspectives feel that accusations of antimale cultural biases are unwarranted and unsupported. The traditional gender gap in the national mathematics and science scores of 17-year-olds has narrowed, although males still outperform females (Campbell et al., 2000). If girls are doing better in the classroom, many researchers claim, it's probably because they spend more time than boys on homework rather than playing video games, watching television, or working after school.

While many girls are succeeding in school, they are twice as likely as boys to suffer from depression, they comprise 90 percent of the teens with eating disorders, and are catching up with boys in smoking, taking drugs, and drinking alcohol (see Chapter 14). Interviews with 2,000 girls aged 11 to 17 found that pressure to have sex begins at age 12 and comes from both boys and girls. White and Asian girls, especially, report increasing pressure to fit in, do drugs, drink, and be popular and cool (Haag, 1999).

Instead of girl- and women-bashing, many researchers suggest, we should look at the evidence. Among full-time workers, for example, females with bachelor's degrees earn $30,119 per year compared to $28,307 for males with only a high school degree (U.S. Census Bureau, 1999c; see also Chapter 13). From one-fourth to one-third of girls are sexually victimized (ranging from sexual harassment to rape) by the time they finish high school (Phillips, 1999). There is also increased discussion among some Protestant denominations to forbid women to continue to serve as pastors. Gender-role expectations are especially problematic in many ethnic families. Recent immigrants try to maintain traditional values, which often include a double standard, while adjusting to a new environment in the United States where gender roles are more permissive (see Chapters 6, 7, 12, 14, 15, and 17).

Is Androgyny the Answer?

Some social scientists feel that androgyny may be the solution to sexist attitudes about gender roles. In **androgyny,** both culturally defined masculine and feminine characteristics are blended within the same person. According to Bem (1975), who did much of the pioneering work on androgyny, our complex society requires that people have both kinds of abilities. Adults must be assertive, independent, and self-reliant, but they must also relate to other people, be sensitive to their needs, and provide them with emotional support. Theoretically, androgyny allows people to play both roles.

Martin (1990) has suggested that androgyny might be especially beneficial for men. Many males might stop being workaholics, relax on weekends, refrain from engaging in risky sexual behavior (to demonstrate their sexual prowess), live longer, and stop worrying about being "real men." If we were more comfortable when children display nontraditional traits, according to Martin, assertive girls and nonaggressive boys would be accepted. And because society frowns more deeply when boys reject traditional roles than when girls do so, androgyny might take some of the pressure off men, giving them more freedom to be and do whatever they want. Would androgyny relax some of our rigid views of men's roles? Or would androgynous men be dismissed as wimps and sissies?

A Global View: Variations in Gender Roles

Each culture has its own gender-role norms and values, and the degree of equality between men and women differs widely across societies. As we saw in the research by Margaret Mead discussed earlier, cross-cultural variations constitute some of the best evidence that gender roles are learned and not inherited.

At one end of the continuum are many societies, primarily in the Middle East and in developing countries, where most women are almost totally dominated by men. According to the Qur'an (sometimes transliterated as "Koran"), the sacred book of Muslims, men and women are fully equal in the eyes of God. Muhammad, the founder of Islam, abolished such sex-discriminating practices as female infanticide and introduced concepts guaranteeing women the right to inherit and bequeath property and to control their own wealth (Shaaban, 1995). According to much of the data, however, Muhammad's revolutionary innovations are rarely practiced in most countries today. There is a great deal of variation across Islamic societies in women's roles in the family, education, politics, and employment opportunities. Each country interprets women's rights under Islam somewhat differently, and within each country social class is a determining factor in women's rights (Sabbagh, 1996).

In the Arab world, overall female literacy is slightly over 50 percent, but it ranges from a low of 20 percent in Yemen and Morocco to a high of 89 percent in Lebanon. Religious laws often play an important role in defining women's educational and employment opportunities. In some Middle Eastern countries, including Kuwait and Saudi Arabia, thriving sex industries are fed by a steady supply of young women—mostly from Bangladesh, India, the Philippines, Sri Lanka, and other poor countries where the women cannot find employment. The unsuspecting women are told they are accepting overseas jobs as maids or domestic laborers. Instead, they work as prostitutes. Those employed as domestics are often subjected to physical and sexual abuse by their employers, who keep them virtual captives by withholding their salaries and confiscating their passports and other travel documents (see Chapter 14).

Islamic women's roles are complex, however. On the one hand, women have challenged some of the most repressive Islamic laws and practices of Muslim fundamentalists that limit women's participation in education and the economy. According to Haq (1996), Muslim fundamentalist men compete with educated urban women over limited educational resources and shrinking employment opportunities. On the other hand, many women often reject the West's permissive sexual attitudes and what they see as a lack of cooperation between males and females in the family. In addition, many Islamic women feel safe and protected by being "veiled" and clothed in garments that cover the woman's entire body (Sabbagh, 1996; Najab, 1997).

In India, most women are under the authority of fathers, brothers, husbands, or husbands' families and are often considered property (epitomized by the dowry that the bride's family pays to the groom's). If a husband or his family is not satisfied with the bride's dowry in Bangladesh, India, and other countries, they may physically harass her, kill her, or drive her to suicide. In 1986, the government of India passed a special amendment to the penal code stating that the husband or in-laws will be presumed responsible for a wife's unnatural death during the first seven years of marriage if there is sufficient evidence of cruelty or harassment. Despite this law, the number of dowry deaths has continued to climb (see Chapter 14).

In China's traditional family, a new wife spends most of her time in the service of her mother-in-law. A wife can be divorced if she fails to bear children, and she has no property rights after a divorce. Confucian values dictate that a woman is always under male authority—first her father's, then her husband's, then her sons'. This outlook has not changed in much of China. After the 1995 United Nations World Conference on Women in Beijing, national newspapers began to publish more articles on such issues as female stereotypes seen in television advertisements. In addition, grass-roots movements have pressed for funding for women's health care and to include more women in the government's training programs for new farming techniques (L. Johnson, 1996).

In Central and South America, there is a great deal of variation in women's progress. In terms of literacy rates, for example, in Chile 95 percent of the women are literate compared to 73 percent of the women and 89 percent of the men in Bolivia. In Colombia, 37 percent of all administrative and managerial positions are filled by women compared to only 7 percent in Argentina. Their husbands abuse about 80 percent of women in Chile. In Bolivia, the government estimates that 100,000 acts of violence against women are committed every year, 95 percent of which go unpunished

(Neft and Levine, 1997). A double standard in wives' and husbands' roles is widespread:

> . . . in Brazil and much of Latin America a man may be excused for killing his wife if he catches her in the act of having sexual relations with another man. This is commonly called a defense of honor, and it is often successful in cases where the husband can prove that he acted spontaneously in order to defend his honor. In some cases the husband may only have to suspect his wife's infidelity to qualify for a defense of honor. (The law does not provide such exoneration of a wife who kills her husband under the same circumstances.) (Neft and Levine, 1997: 154)

Families at lower socioeconomic levels encounter considerably greater perils. In northern Mexico, for example, numerous young women in Juárez leave their homes to work for $4 a day in factories. Since 1993, more than 80 young women—most in their teens—have been murdered. Because the victims are poor, young, and labeled as "promiscuous" by the local police because they're not supervised by their mothers, most of the killings have been ignored by the local authorities (LaFranchi, 1997).

Since the dissolution of the Soviet Union in 1991, women's status has eroded. Women have been hit hardest by crime and unemployment, and three out of four jobless Russians are women (Hockstader, 1995). The World Health Organization reports that Russian women are murdered at a rate four times higher than women in most of Europe, but the police ignore the murders because the women are blamed for promoting the battering. There are no shelters for battered women (Hockstader, 1995).

At the other end of the gender-role continuum are those societies, like France, Germany, and Sweden, which are considered more progressive than the United States. Sweden has very generous maternity and paternity leave policies, for example. All families with newborn babies are given an 18-month leave from work at 90 percent compensation and a government subsidy per child every year for child care. In Germany, mothers receive 100 percent of earnings for 15 weeks.

Many other societies, such as Japan, are in the middle of the continuum. Japan is often described as a father-absent, achievement-oriented society, where men devote most of their lives to the company and work-related activities. Employed wives do double duty, spending more than three hours a day on housework when the average man puts in only eight minutes, and spending most of their "free" time checking on homework and escorting their children to extracurricular activities.

Some changes are taking place, however. According to one writer, the Japanese woman today "is equally likely to be single, married, living with a partner, or divorced; to have children or be childless; and to be working part- or full-time" (Iwao, 1993). Increasing numbers of women are challenging their traditionally submissive roles. They are pursuing higher education, entering the labor force, and moving into fields that were once considered exclusively male, such as engineering. Finally, although entrusting childcare to strangers was once unthinkable, today child-care centers are experiencing a booming business in Japan (Shimomura, 1990; Takayama, 1990).

Conclusion

There is no doubt that the last 20 years have seen *changes* in some aspects of gender roles. More people today say they believe in gender equality, and unprecedented numbers of women have entered the labor force. But do most people really have more *choices*? Women are becoming increasingly resentful of the burden of both domestic and economic jobs, especially in a society that devalues them and their labor. Men, although often freed from the sole-breadwinner role, feel that their range of choices is narrowing as women compete with them in more sectors of society. Many men are proud of their increased parenting roles. At the same time they are also unhappy about the increased burdens of domestic responsibilities.

Significant change in gender roles elicits *constraints* at every level: personal, group, and institutional. Those who benefit from gender-role inequality will resist giving up their privileges and economic resources, although—as conditions in some other countries show—changes in ideology, socialization practices, work, and family structures are possible. In the next chapter we examine how changes in gender-role attitudes and behavior affect love and intimate relationships.

SUMMARY

1. Sex and gender are not interchangeable terms. Sex refers to the biological characteristics we are born with. Gender refers to the attitudes and behavior society expects of each sex.

2. Scholars continue to debate how much of our behavior is a reflection of nature (biology) and how much of nurture (environment). Although biology is important, there is little evidence that women are naturally better parents, that men are naturally more aggressive, or that men and women are inherently different in other than anatomy and physiology.

3. Traditional gender roles are based on the beliefs that women should fulfill expressive functions and that men should play instrumental roles.

4. Playing traditional roles has both positive and negative consequences. On the positive side, men and women know what is expected of them. On the negative side, traditional roles often create stress and anxiety and seriously limit choices.

5. Many theoretical perspectives try to explain how we learn gender roles. Social learning theory posits that gender roles are learned by reward and punishment and by imitation and role modeling. Cognitive development theory assumes that children learn gender identity through interacting with and interpreting the behavior of others. Gender schema theory proposes that children organize their experience by developing information-processing categories, or schema, that they use to develop a gender identity.

6. We learn gender expectations from many sources—parents, peers, teachers, and the media. Many of these socializing influences continue to reinforce traditional male and female gender roles.

7. During much of our adult life, our activities are sex-segregated. Typically, men and women play different roles in the home, in the workplace, and as consumers.

8. Many men and women communicate differently. These differences are often unintentional, but they may create misunderstandings.

9. Some writers contend that boys are ignored and devalued while girls are supported. Others argue that girls' and women's progress in closing gender gaps has been exaggerated.

10. There is considerable variation across cultures in terms of equality between men and women. Many societies are male-dominated; others are considerably more progressive than the United States.

KEY TERMS

sex   *73*
gender   *74*
gender roles   *74*
hormones   *75*

gender identity   *75*
social learning theory   *80*
cognitive development theory   *80*
gender schema theory   *81*

gender-role stereotypes   *81*
sexual harassment   *97*
role conflict   *99*
androgyny   *100*

TAKING IT FURTHER

Gender Roles and Socialization Material Online

There are hundreds of gender-related Internet resources. Some of the most comprehensive and interesting Websites include the following:

Women's Studies/Women's Issues WWW Sites offers hundreds of women-related e-mail lists, Websites around the world, and dozens of topical subsections on gender topics.

www.umbc.edu/wmst/links.html

The Men's Bibliography provides a thorough introduction to material on men, masculinities, and sexualities.

www.anu.edu.au/~a112465/mensbiblio/mensbibliomenu.html

Women of Color Web focuses on issues related to feminisms, sexualities, and reproductive health and rights, as well as writing by and about women of color in the United States.

www.hsph.harvard.edu/grhf/WoC

International Gender Resources offers general and specific bibliographies and filmographies on issues pertaining to women and gender in Africa, Asia, Latin America, the Middle East and Arab world, and among minority cultures in North America and Europe.

globetrotter.berkeley.edu/GlobalGender

WWWomen! The Premier Search Directory for Women Online includes topics such as women in business, feminism, lesbian visibility, publications, women's resources, science and technology, women's sports, and women throughout history.

www.wwwomen.com/

Women's Leadership Fund Resource Center includes dozens of links to women and politics, international women's agencies and global statistics, girls' education resources, and advocacy and academic organizations.

www.womensleadershipfund.org/resource/index.html

And more . . . www.prenhall.com/benokraitis offers, for example, The Movie Mom's Guide to Family Movies, Girl Tech sites, men's movement periodicals, several international sites, sexual harassment resources, and a gallery of the most negative ads about women, and invites you to calculate how much unequal pay will cost you over your lifetime.

Love and Loving Relationships

DATA DIGEST

■ **Love is great for business.** On Valentine's Day, Americans spend more than $400 million on roses, purchase more than $600 million worth of candy, and send 900 million cards (compared to 150 million on Mother's Day). Romance novels constitute almost 60 percent of all paperback fiction sales.

■ Having **money may facilitate love.** Among people earning less than $20,000 a year, 36 percent said they were in love; among those earning $50,000 or more a year, 51 percent said they were in love.

■ On the other hand, **money can't buy love.** In a national survey of affluent Americans (those with annual incomes of $100,000 or more),

72 percent said that family and friends provide the greatest satisfaction in their lives. Just 1 in 20 said that their wealth gave them the greatest satisfaction.

■ **Would you marry someone with "all the right qualities" if you didn't love her or him?** A study of college students from ten countries found a lot of variation. About 85 percent of the American and Brazilian students said "no," compared to about 75 percent in Mexico, England, and Australia. About 60 percent in Japan and the Philippines said "no," while only 24 percent in India said "no."

SOURCES: Levine, 1993; Cowherd, 1994; Smith, 1994; Kephart, 1996; "Deck the box," 1999; "Romance writers . . . ," 2000.

OVE—as both an emotion and a behavior—is essential for human survival. The family is usually our earliest and most important source of love and emotional support (see Chapter 1). Babies and children deprived of love have been known to develop a wide variety of problems—for example, depression, headaches, physiological impairments, and neurotic and psychosomatic difficulties—that sometimes last a lifetime. In contrast, infants who are loved and cuddled typically gain more weight, cry less, and smile more (Bowlby, 1969). By 5 years of age, they have been found to have significantly higher IQs and to score higher on language tests (Klaus and Kennell, 1976).

Oxygen, warmth, and food are an infant's most basic necessities. The human being's potential for learning during the first year of life is enormous. At birth, the human brain weighs about 350 grams, but by the end of the first year it has more than doubled in size; at 825 grams, it has reached nearly 60 percent of the weight of the adult brain. To thrive and grow emotionally and intellectually, the child needs constant care by loving people (Gaylin, 1986).

Much research shows that the quality of care infants receive affects how they later get along with friends, how well they do in school, how they react to new and possibly stressful situations, and how they form and maintain loving relationships as adults. It is for these reasons that people's early intimate relationships within their family of origin are so critical. As you saw in Chapter 1, children who are raised in impersonal environments (orphanages, some foster homes, or unloving families) show emotional and social underdevelopment, language and motor skills retardation, and mental health problems.

Love for oneself, or self-love, is also essential for our social and emotional development. Actress Mae West once said, "I never loved another person the way I loved myself." Although such a statement may seem self-centered, it's actually quite insightful. Social scientists describe self-love as an important basis for self-esteem. Among other things, people who like themselves are more open to criticism and less demanding of others. Fromm (1956) saw self-love as a necessary prerequisite for loving others. People who don't like themselves may not be able to return love but may constantly seek love relationships to bolster their own poor self-images (Casler, 1974). But just what is love? What brings people together?

What Is Love?

Love is an elusive concept. We have all experienced love and feel we know what it is; however, when asked what love is, people give a variety of answers. According to a 9-year-old boy, for example, "Love is like an avalanche where you have to run for your life." What we mean by love depends on whether we are talking about love for family members, friends, or lovers. As the box "The Breadth and Depth and Height of Love" illustrates, love has been a source of inspiration, wry witticisms, and even political action for many centuries.

Love has many dimensions. It can be romantic, exciting, obsessive, and irrational. It can also be platonic, calming, altruistic, and sensible. Many researchers feel that love defies a single definition because it varies in degree and intensity and across

CHANGES

The Breadth and Depth and Height of Love

Throughout the centuries many writers have commented on the varieties, purposes, pleasures, and pain of love. Love is universal; it is a focus of concern in all societies.

- Jesus (4 B.C.–A.D. 29): "A new commandment I give unto you, that ye love one another."
- I Corinthians 13:4–7: "Love is patient and kind; love is not jealous or boastful; it is not arrogant or rude. Love does not insist on its own way; it is not irritable or resentful; it does not rejoice at wrong, but rejoices in the right. Love bears all things, believes all things, hopes all things, endures all things."
- William Shakespeare (1564–1616): "To say the truth, reason and love keep little company together nowadays" (from *A Midsummer Night's Dream*).
- Hindustani proverb: "Life is no longer one's own when the heart is fixed on another."

- Duc François de La Rochefoucauld (1613–1680): "True love is like ghosts, which everyone talks about but few have seen."
- Abraham Cowley (1618–1667): "I love you, not only for what you are, but for what I am when I am with you."
- Ninon de Lenclos (1620–1705): "Much more genius is needed to make love than to command armies."
- Irish saying: "If you live in my heart, you live rent-free."
- Elizabeth Barrett Browning (1806–1861): "How do I love thee? Let me count the ways. I love thee to the depth and breadth and height my soul can reach."
- Henry Wadsworth Longfellow (1807–1882): "Love gives itself; it is not bought."
- Japanese saying: "Who travels for love finds a thousand miles only one mile."

- William Thackeray (1811–1863): "It is best to love wisely, no doubt; but to love foolishly is better than not to be able to love at all."
- Robert Browning (1812–1889): "Take away love and our earth is a tomb."
- Benjamin Disraeli (1804–1881): "The magic of first love is our ignorance that it can ever end."
- Marlene Dietrich (1901–1992): "Grumbling is the death of love."
- Turkish proverb: "When two hearts are one, even the king cannot separate them."
- Che Guevara (1928–1967): "The true revolutionary is guided by a great feeling of love."
- Cher (1946–): "The trouble with some women is that they get all excited about nothing—and then marry him."

social contexts. At the very least, three elements are necessary for a love relationship: (1) a willingness to please and accommodate the other, even if this involves compromise and sacrifice; (2) an acceptance of the other person's faults and shortcomings; and (3) as much concern about the loved one's welfare as one's own (Safilios-Rothschild, 1977). And, as you will see shortly, people who say they are "in love" emphasize caring, intimacy, and commitment.

In any type of love, caring about the other person is essential. Although love may involve passionate yearning, respect is a more important quality. Respect is inherent in all love: "I want the loved person to grow and unfold for his own sake, and in his own ways, and not for the purpose of serving me" (Fromm, 1956: 23–24). If respect and caring are missing, the relationship is not based on love. Instead, it is an unhealthy or possessive dependency that limits the lovers' social, emotional, and intellectual growth (Peele and Brodsky, 1976).

Love, especially long-term love, has nothing in common with the images of love or frenzied sex that we get from Hollywood, television, and romance novels. Because of these images, many people believe a variety of myths about love. These misconceptions often lead to unrealistic expectations, stereotypes, and disillusionment. (To test your general knowledge about love, see the box "How Much Do You Know about Love?") In fact, "real" love is closer to what one author called "stirring-the-oatmeal" love (Johnson, 1985). This type of love is neither exciting nor thrilling but is relatively mundane and unromantic. It means paying bills, putting out the garbage, scrubbing toilet bowls, being up all night with a sick baby, and performing myriad other "oatmeal" tasks that are not very sexy.

Some partners take turns stirring the oatmeal. Others seek relationships that offer candlelit gourmet meals in a romantic setting. Whether we decide to tie the knot or not, what brings people together? And does "falling in lust" lead to "falling in love"?

ASKYOURSELF

How Much Do You Know about Love?

The following statements are based on the material in this chapter.

	Fact	Fiction
1. There is an ideal mate for every person; just keep looking.	❑	❑
2. Women are more romantic than men.	❑	❑
3. Love conquers all.	❑	❑
4. Men's and women's love needs are different.	❑	❑
5. Real love lasts forever.	❑	❑
6. Everybody falls in love sooner or later.	❑	❑
7. Love brings happiness and security.	❑	❑
8. Love endures and overcomes all problems.	❑	❑
9. Men are more interested in sex than in love.	❑	❑
10. Love and marriage go together like a horse and carriage.	❑	❑

(The answers to these questions appear on page 110.)

What Brings People Together?

What attracts individuals to each other in the first place? Many people believe that "there's one person out there that you're meant for" and that destiny will bring them together. Such beliefs are romantic but untrue. Empirical studies show that cultural norms and values, not fate, bring people together. We will never meet millions of potential lovers because they are "filtered out" by formal or informal rules on partner eligibility due to factors such as age, race, distance, social class, religion, sexual orientation, health, or physical appearance (see Chapter 7 on dating).

Beginning in childhood, parents encourage or limit future romantic liaisons by selecting certain neighborhoods and schools. In early adolescence, peer norms influence the adolescent's decisions about acceptable romantic involvements ("You want to date *who*?!"). Even during the preteen years, romantic experiences are *cultured* in the sense that societal and group practices and expectations shape romantic experiences. Although romance may cross cultural or ethnic borders, criticism and approval teach us what is acceptable romantic behavior and with whom (Brown, 1999; Coates, 1999). We might "fall in lust" with someone. These yearnings, however, will not lead most of us to "fall in love" if there are strong cultural or group bans.

Do Lust and Love Differ?

Regan and Berscheid (1999) differentiate among sexual arousal (or lust), sexual desire, and love—especially romantic love. They describe *sexual arousal* as getting "turned on" physically rather than emotionally, a state that may occur consciously or without conscious awareness (see Chapter 6). *Sexual desire,* in contrast, is a psychological state in which one wants "to obtain a sexual object that one does not now have or to engage in a sexual activity in which one is not now engaging" (p. 17). Sexual desire may or may not lead to *romantic love* (which the authors equate with passionate or erotic love). Regan and Berscheid posit that sexual desire is the essential ingredient for igniting and maintaining romantic love: "If at any time sexual desire disappears, a person is no longer said to be in a state of romantic love" (p. 115). Once desire dissipates, disillusioned and disappointed lovers will wonder where the "spark" in their relationship has gone and may reminisce regretfully (and longingly) about "the good old days."

You should not conclude, however, that sexual desire *always* culminates in sexual intercourse or that romantic love and love are synonymous. As a later section in this chapter shows, married partners may love each other even though they rarely, or never, engage in sexual intercourse. In addition, there are some notable differences between love—especially long-term love—and romantic love that we'll address shortly.

Arranged marriages provide a good example both of how prospective lovers are brought together and how cultural values and practices limit the choice of partners (see "A Global View" at the end of this chapter). Healthy, loving relationships, whether sexual or asexual (such as love for family members), reflect a balance of caring, intimacy, and commitment.

Caring, Intimacy, and Commitment

As you will see later in this chapter, people fall in love for many reasons—physical attraction, shared interests, companionship, or simply because romance is fun. For love to survive, however, key words are caring, intimacy, commitment, and change. Accepting changes in oneself and one's partner is addressed in Chapters 8 and 9. Here we focus on caring, intimacy, and commitment.

Caring

Most concepts of love include *caring*, defined here as wanting to help the other by providing aid and emotional support whenever needed (Cutrona, 1996). People use such metaphors for love as "I'm crazy about you" or "I can't live without you." These terms of endearment may not be translated into such ongoing, everyday behavior as valuing your partner's welfare as much as you do your own, however. Caring means being responsive to the other person's needs. If over time a person does not see evidence of responsiveness and supportiveness, there will be serious doubts that a partner *really* loves her or him. This doesn't mean that a partner should be submissive or docile. Instead, people who care about each other will bolster each other's self esteem and will offer encouragement when there are problems. When an individual is responsive to the needs of his or her partner, the relationship will become more intimate.

Intimacy

While the definitions vary from writer to writer, all definitions of intimacy emphasize feelings of closeness. In his analysis of couples, for example, P. M. Brown (1995: 3) refers to an intimate pairing when people

- experience a mutual emotional interest and bonding;
- have some sort of history together;
- are mutually interdependent;
- have a distinct sense of identity as a dyad;
- hold a shared commitment to a continued relationship; and
- share hopes and dreams for a common future.

Still other writers distinguish among three kinds of intimacy—physical (sex, hugging, and touching), affective (feeling close), and verbal (self-disclosure)—and point out that physical intimacy is usually the least important (Piorkowski, 1994). **Self-disclosure** refers to open communication where one person offers his or her honest thoughts and feelings to another person in the hope that truly open communication will follow. Within intimate relationships, people feel free to expose their weaknesses, idiosyncracies, hopes, and insecurities without fear of ridicule or rejection (P. M. Brown, 1995). Lovers, for example, will reveal their innermost thoughts and marital partners will feel comfortable in venting their frustrations because their spouses are considered trustworthy, respectful, and best friends or confidantes. Although children, parents, and siblings may have very close and affectionate ties, Prager (1995) suggests that such relationships are not necessarily intimate because the interactions and interdependence typically (and normally) decrease over time. In adult love relationships, intimacy increases as people let down their defenses, learn to relax in each other's company, and can expect reciprocal support during good and bad times (Josselson, 1992). Caring and intimacy, in turn, foster commitment.

Commitment

Commitment refers to a person's intention to remain in a relationship no matter what happens—for better or for worse (Cutrona, 1996). Mutual commitment can arise out of (1) a sense of loyalty and fidelity to one's partner; (2) a religious, legal, or moral belief in the sanctity of the marriage; (3) a continued optimism about the potential future rewards—emotional, financial, sexual, or otherwise; and (4) strong emotional attachments, dependence, and love (P. M. Brown, 1995). Many people end their relationships, though they still love each other, if they feel that commitment is not increasing (Sprecher, 1999).

In a healthy relationship, commitment has many positive aspects such as affection, companionship, and trust. Each partner looks forward to staying together and is available to the other not only during times of stress but day in and day out. Commitments generate responsibilities that support rather than threaten love. These responsibilities remain in the background but surface in times of conflict, temptations to be unfaithful, or mood fluctuations. In this sense, commitments reinforce, not replace, caring (Martin, 1993).

Commitment in secure relationships is not "hearts and flowers" but behavior that demonstrates repeatedly and across a variety of situations that "I'm here, I will be here, I'm interested in what you do and what you think and feel, I will actively support your independent actions, I trust you, and you can trust me to be here if you need me" (Crowell and Waters, 1994:

32). In a dysfunctional or abusive relationship, in contrast, partners who define commitment as a lifelong tie can experience "a crushing burden of obligation, entrapment, and limited options" (Brown, 1995: 152). Unhealthy relationship commitments are examined in Chapter 14.

Some Theories About Love and Loving

Why and how do we love? Biological explanations tend to focus on the why of love, whereas psychological, sociological, and anthropological approaches try to deal with the how as well as the why.

The (Bio)Chemistry of Love

You might say that biologists, psychobiologists, and biological anthropologists look at love under the microscope, while social scientists use a wide-angle lens. These distinctions parallel the nature–nurture debate we discussed in Chapter 4.

Biological perspectives maintain that love is grounded in evolution, biology, and chemistry. Biologists and others see romance as serving the evolutionary purpose of drawing males and females into long-term partnerships, which, as we've seen, are essential to child rearing. On open and often dangerous grasslands, one parent could care for offspring while the other foraged for food.

When lovers claim that they feel "high" and as if they are being swept away, it's probably because they are literally flooded by chemicals. A meeting of eyes, a touch of hands, or a whiff of scent sets off a flood that starts in the brain and races along the nerves and through the bloodstream. The results are familiar: flushed skin, sweaty palms, and heavy breathing (Ackerman, 1994). Natural amphetamines like dopamine, norepinephrine, and phenylethylamine (PEA) are responsible for these symptoms. PEA is especially effective; it revs up the brain, causing feelings of elation, exhilaration, and euphoria:

No wonder lovers can stay awake all night talking and caressing. No wonder they become so absent-minded, so giddy, so optimistic, so gregarious, so full of life. Naturally occurring amphetamines have pooled in the emotional centers of their brains; they are high on natural "speed." (Fisher, 1992: 53)

PEA highs don't last long, though, which may explain why passionate or romantic love is short-lived.

What about love that endures beyond the first few months? According to the biological perspective, another set of chemicals helps maintain relationships. As infatuation wanes and attachment grows, another group, called endorphins, which are chemically similar

- -

Answers to How Much Do You Know about Love

All ten statements are myths. Eight or more correct answers indicate that you know a myth when you hear one.

1. We can love many people, and we can love many times. This is why some people marry more than once. We typically marry someone we grew up with, lived close to, or met in college or on the job (see, also, Chapter 7).

2. Men fall in love more quickly, are more romantic, and suffer more intensely when their love is not returned.

3. Because almost one out of two marriages ends in divorce, love is not enough to overcome all problems and obstacles. Differences in race, ethnicity, religion, economic status, education, and age can often stifle romantic interest.

4. Both men and women want trust, honesty, understanding, and respect.

5. A love can be genuine but not last eternally; good marriages do not always last a lifetime. People today live much longer, the world is more complex, and partners change as they mature and grow older.

6. Some people have deep-seated emotional scars that make them suspicious and unloving; others are too self-centered to give love.

7. Love guarantees neither happiness nor security. In a study of college students and adults who said they were in love, only 56 percent described themselves as secure. The others reported feeling generally insecure or anxious.

8. People who love each other make sacrifices, but emotional or physical abuse should not be tolerated. Eventually, even "martyrs" become unhappy, angry, depressed, and resentful.

9. During the romantic stage, both women and men may be more interested in sex than in love. As love matures, both partners value such attributes as faithfulness, patience, and making the other person feel wanted.

10. As many arranged marriages in countries around the world show, love is not an indispensable ingredient in a happy marriage. Other factors, such as similar values, complementary life goals, comparable attitudes toward money, and parallel child-rearing philosophies are equally (if not more) important. In general, love should be one criterion, but not the only one, in deciding whom and when to marry.

to morphine and reside in the brain, takes over. Unlike PEA, endorphins calm the mind, eliminate pain, and reduce anxiety. This, biologists say, explains why people in long-lasting relationships report feeling comfortable and secure (Walsh, 1991; Fisher, 1992).

Remember that there is no hard evidence for biological theories. One observer has noted, for example, that these evolutionary perspectives are "exceeding the limits of knowledge, scientific method, and credulity" (Swedlund, 1993: 1053). Nonetheless, they provide food for thought.

Psychological and *sociological perspectives* claim that culture, not PEA, is Cupid. The social science theories that can help us understand the components and processes of love include attachment theory, Reiss's wheel theory of love, Sternberg's triangular theory of love, and Lee's research on the styles of loving.

Attachment Theory

Attachment theory posits that "our primary motivation in life is to be connected with other people—because it is the only security we ever have. Maintaining closeness is a bona fide survival need" (Johnson and Marano, 1994). In the 1960s the work of British psychiatrist John Bowlby and his colleagues and students sparked revolutionary changes in hospitals and in the care of institutionalized children (Bowlby, 1969, 1984). For example, mothers are encouraged to spend a lot of time with their hospitalized children and to perform basic caring tasks such as feeding. Fathers are now present at births, and both fathers and siblings are encouraged to interact with the mother and the new infant while they are still in the hospital (Feeney and Noller, 1996).

American psychologist Mary Ainsworth (1978), one of Bowlby's followers, assessed infant–mother attachment through the "strange situation" procedure. In both natural and experimental situations, Ainsworth created mild stress for the infant by having the mother leave an unfamiliar room temporarily while a friendly stranger was left with the infant.

Ainsworth then observed the infant's behavior toward the mother when she returned and the mother's responsiveness to the infant's signals and needs such as crying or clinging.

Ainsworth identified three infant–mother attachment styles. About two-thirds were characterized as *secure* in their attachment, with sensitive and responsive mothers. They showed some distress when left with a stranger, but when the mother returned, the child clung to her for just a short time and then went back to exploring and playing. When mothers were inconsistent—sometimes affectionate, sometimes aloof—about 19 percent of the infants displayed *anxious/ambivalent* attachment styles. They showed distress at separation but rejected their mothers when they returned. The remaining 21 percent of the infants, most of whom had been reared by caregivers who ignored their physical and emotional needs, displayed *avoidant* behavior when their mothers returned from an absence.

Some of the infant attachment research has been criticized for relying almost exclusively on laboratory instead of natural settings and for not capturing cross-cultural differences in child-rearing practices (see Feeney and Noller, 1996). Despite such criticisms, researchers propose that adult love often reflects these three attachment styles. Using a "love quiz" based on the three attachment styles identified by Ainsworth, Cindy Hazan and her associates administered the quiz to 108 college students and 620 adults in the surrounding community who said they were in love (Hazan and Shaver, 1987; Shaver et al., 1988). The respondents were asked to describe themselves within their "most important romance" using three measures:

- *Secure*: I find it relatively easy to get close to others and am comfortable depending on them and having them depend on me. I don't often worry about being abandoned or about someone getting too close to me.
- *Avoidant*: I am somewhat uncomfortable being close to others; I find it difficult to trust them

completely, difficult to allow myself to depend on them. I am nervous when anyone gets too close, and lover partners often want me to be more intimate than I feel comfortable being.

- *Anxious-ambivalent*: I find that others are reluctant to get as close as I would like. I often worry that my partner doesn't really love me or won't want to stay with me. I want to merge completely with another person, and this desire sometimes scares people away.

In addition, the respondents were asked whether their childhood relationships with their parents were warm or cold and rejecting.

Secure adults (about 56 percent of the sample), who generally described their parents as having been warm and supportive, were more trusting of their romantic partners and more confident of a partner's love. They could be intimate in their relationships and reported trusting and happy relationships that lasted, on average, about ten years. Anxious/ambivalent adults (about 20 percent) had a tendency to fall in love easily and wanted a commitment almost immediately. Avoidant adults (24 percent of the sample) reported little trust for other people, had the most cynical beliefs about love, and were not very good at either intimacy or making a commitment.

Despite the popularity of attachment theory, critics contend that the studies by Hazan and her colleagues were based on small, nonrandom samples. And because they were not longitudinal, there is no direct evidence that the mother–child attachments of the respondents really influenced their experiences in adult love. Critics argue, moreover, that much of the research relies on dysfunctional families. The studies often reflect serious methodological flaws and ignore data that find little support for attachment theory. They also perpetuate the belief that parenting young children is the mother's, not the father's, responsibility. Events like divorce, disease, and financial problems are far more important in shaping a child's well-being by age 18 than any early bonding with his or her mother (Lewis, 1997. For some summaries and critiques of attachment theory, see Goldberg, 1983; Eyer, 1992; Franzblau, 1999; Watson, 1997; de Wolff and van Ijzendoorn, 1997; Hays, 1998; and Birns, 1999).

Reiss's Wheel Theory of Love

Sociologist Ira Reiss (1960; Reiss and Lee, 1988) has proposed a "wheel theory" of love (see *Figure 5.1*) that generated much research for several decades. Reiss describes four stages of love: rapport, self-revelation, mutual dependency, and personality need fulfillment. In stage one, the partners establish *rapport* based on similar cultural backgrounds, such as upbringing, social class, and education. (As you saw in Chapter 1, families and kin groups typically have

FIGURE 5.1 **The Wheel Theory of Love.** Reiss likened his four stages of love to the spokes of a wheel. As the text describes, a love relationship begins with the stage of rapport and, in a lasting relationship, continues to build as the wheel turns, deepening rapport, fulfillment, and mutual dependence and increasing the honesty of self revelation (Based on Reiss, 1960: 139–45).

strong endogamous rules that discourage relationships with people from different ethnic, racial, religious, and socioeconomic groups.) Without this rapport, according to Reiss, the would-be lovers would not have enough in common to establish an initial interest.

In stage two, *self-revelation* brings the couple closer together. Because each person feels more at ease in the relationship, he or she is more likely to discuss hopes, desires, fears, and ambitions, and to engage in sexual activities. As the couple becomes more intimate, the partners' *mutual dependency* increases in stage three, and they exchange ideas, jokes, and sexual desires. In the fourth and final stage, the couple experiences *personality need fulfillment*. The partners confide in each other, make mutual decisions, support each other's ambitions, and bolster each other's self-confidence.

Like spokes on a wheel, these stages can turn many times—that is, they can repeat themselves over and over. For example, partners build some rapport; then they reveal bits of themselves; then they build more rapport; then begin to exchange ideas, and so on. And the spokes may keep turning indefinitely to produce a deep and lasting relationship. Or the wheel may stop after a few turns during a fleeting romance. The romantic wheel may "unwind"—even in one evening—if the relationship is weakened by arguments, a lack of self-disclosure, or competing interests.

Sociologist Dolores Borland (1975) modified the wheel theory, proposing that love relationships be viewed as "clocksprings," like those in a watch. Like clocksprings, associations can wind and unwind several times as love swells or ebbs. Tensions, caused by events like pregnancy and the birth of a child, may wind the spring tightly, but if the partners communicate and work toward a common goal, such tensions may solidify rather than weaken a relationship. On the other hand, relationships can end abruptly if they are so tightly overwound that they cannot grow or if one partner feels threatened by increasing or unwanted intimacy.

Albas and Albas (1987) note that both the wheel theory and the clockspring theory ignore the variations in intensity among the stages of a relationship. People may love each other, but the intensity of their feelings may be high on one dimension and low on another. For example, where a couple stays together for the sake of their children, the intensity of personality need fulfillment might increase while the intensity of their rapport might decrease significantly.

Sternberg's Triangular Theory of Love

Instead of focusing on stages of love, psychologist Robert Sternberg and his associates (1986, 1988) have proposed that there are three important components of love—intimacy, passion, and commitment. *Intimacy* encompasses feelings of closeness, connectedness, and bonding. *Passion* leads to romance, physical

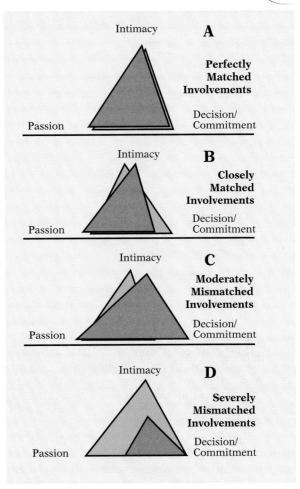

FIGURE 5.2 **Sternberg's Triangular Theory of Love.** This theory of love allows us to see how people can be very close on some dimensions but very far apart on others (Adapted from Sternberg, 1988).

attraction, and sexual consummation. *Decision/commitment* has a short- and a long-term dimension. In the short term, partners make a decision to love each other; in the long term, they make a commitment to maintain that love over time.

According to Sternberg, love can vary in its mix of intimacy, passion, and commitment. Relationships thus range from nonlove, in which all three components are absent, to consummate love, in which all the components are present. Even when all components are present, they may vary in intensity and over time for each partner. In his triangular theory of love, Sternberg presents these three components as forming a triangle (see *Figure 5.2*). In general, the greater the mismatching, the greater the dissatisfaction in a relationship. Let's use Jack and Jill to illustrate this model. If Jack and Jill are "perfectly matched" (*Figure 5.2A*), they will be equally passionate, intimate, and committed, and their love

TABLE 5.1		
Lee's Six Styles of Love		
Meaning		**Major Characteristics**
Eros	Love of beauty	Powerful physical attraction
Mania	Obsessive love	Jealousy, possessiveness, and intense love dependency
Ludus	Playful love	Carefree quality, casualness; fun-and-games approach
Storge	Companionate love	Peaceful and affectionate love based on mutual trust and respect
Agape	Altruistic love	Self-sacrificing, kind, and patient love
Pragma	Practical love	Sensible, realistic

SOURCES: Adapted from Lee, 1973; and Lee, 1974, pp. 46–51.

will be "perfect." Even if the degree to which they want intimacy and commitment varies a little, they may still be closely matched (*Figure 5.2B*). However, if both are about equally passionate, but Jack wants more intimacy than Jill does, and Jill is unwilling to make the long-term commitment that Jack wants, this couple will be "moderately mismatched" (*Figure 5.2C*). And if they want to marry each other (make a commitment), but Jill is neither as intimate nor as passionate as Jack, they will be severely mismatched (*Figure 5.2D*).

Like the other perspectives we've discussed, the triangular theory of love has limitations. For example, "perfectly matched" love is found only in Disney movies. Also, Sternberg calls a relationship that is committed but neither intimate nor passionate (see *Figure 5.2D*) "empty." How do you think people who care for severely ill spouses or partners over many years would respond to this description? Finally, some researchers suggest that intimacy, passion, and commitment often overlap; that the validity of the measures is questionable; and that Sternberg's theory has always been "tested" on unmarried college students rather than noncollege students—especially married samples (Lemieux and Hale, 1999).

Lee's Styles of Loving

One of the most widely cited and studied approaches to love was developed by Canadian sociologist John A. Lee (1973, 1974). Although not a full-fledged theory, Lee's approach was built on his collection of more than 4,000 statements about love from hundreds of works of fiction and nonfiction. The sources ranged from the literature of ancient Greece (which recognized *agape* and *eros* as two kinds of love) and the Bible through the work of medieval, Victorian, and modern writers. Lee administered a 30-item questionnaire based on this research to people in Great Britain and Canada. From the responses he derived six basic

styles of loving: eros, mania, ludus, storge, agape, and pragma (see *Table 5.1*), all of which both overlap and vary in intensity in real life.

Eros   Eros (root of the word *erotic*) is the love of beauty. Because it is also characterized by powerful physical attraction, eros epitomizes "love at first sight." This is the kind of love often described in romance novels, where the lovers are immediately love-struck and experience palpitating hearts, light-headedness, and intense emotional desire.

Erotic lovers want to know everything about the loved one—what she or he dreamed about last night and what happened on the way to work today. Erotic lovers often like to wear matching T-shirts, identical bracelets, and matching colors, to order the same foods when dining out, and to be identified with each other as totally as possible (Lasswell and Lasswell, 1976).

Mania   Characterized by obsessiveness, jealousy, possessiveness, and intense dependency, **mania** may be expressed in anxiety, sleeplessness, loss of appetite, and headaches. Manic lovers are consumed by thoughts of their beloved and have an insatiable need for attention and signs of affection (Lee, 1974).

Often irrational, manic lovers may even consider suicide because of real or imagined rejection. Because of their high level of anxiety, manic lovers frequently have sexual problems. Mania is probably associated with low self-esteem and a poor self-concept, and as a result, manic people are typically not attractive to those who have a strong self-concept and high self-esteem (Lasswell and Lasswell, 1976).

Ludus   Ludus is carefree and casual love that is considered "fun and games." Its pleasure comes more from playing the game than from winning the prize. Physical appearance is less important to ludic lovers than self-sufficiency and a nondemanding partner.

They try to control their feelings and may have several lovers at one time. They are not possessive or jealous, largely because they don't want lovers to become dependent on them. Ludic lovers have sex for fun, not emotional rapport. Indeed, in their sexual encounters they are typically self-centered and may be exploitative because they do not want commitment, which they consider "scary."

Storge Storge (pronounced "stor-gay") is a slow-burning, peaceful, and affectionate love that "just comes naturally" with the passage of time and the enjoyment of shared activities. Storgic relationships lack the ecstatic highs and lows of despair that characterize some other styles; sex occurs late in this type of relationship, and the goals are usually marriage, home, and children. Even if they break up, storgic lovers are likely to remain good friends (Lee, 1974).

The storgic lover finds routine home activities relaxing and comfortable. Because there is mutual trust, temporary separations are not seen as a problem. Occasions like anniversaries, birthdays, and Valentine's Day are not important to storgic lovers and may be forgotten or overshadowed by other matters (Lasswell and Lasswell, 1976). Storgic love may also be called conjugal love; affection develops over the years, as in many lasting marriages. Passion may be replaced by spirituality, respect, and contentment in the enjoyment of each other's company (Murstein, 1974).

Agape The classical Christian type of love, **agape** (pronounced "ah-gah-pay") is altruistic, self-sacrificing, and directed toward all humankind. It is a self-giving love in which partners help each other develop their maximum potential without considering the advantages or costs to themselves. Agape is always kind and patient, never jealous or demanding, and does not seek reciprocity. Lee points out, however, that he has not yet found an unqualified example of agape during his interviews.

Intense agape can border on masochism. For example, an agapic person might wait indefinitely for a lover to be released from prison or from a mental hospital, might tolerate an alcoholic or drug-addicted spouse, or might be willing to live with a partner who engages in illegal or immoral activities (Lasswell and Lasswell, 1976).

Pragma According to Lee, **pragma** is rational and based on practical considerations, such as compatibility and perceived benefits. Indeed, it can be described as "love with a shopping list." A pragmatic person seeks compatibility in such things as background, education, religious views, and vocational and professional interests. If one love does not work out, the pragmatic person moves on, quite rationally, to search for someone else.

Pragmatic lovers are realistic about their own assets, decide on their "market value," and set out to get the best possible "deal." If the assets of either partner change, a pragmatic lover may feel that his or her contract has been violated and may search for another partner. Pragmatic lovers look out for their partners, encouraging them, for example, to ask for a promotion or to finish college. They are also practical in divorce; for example, a couple might stay together until the youngest child finishes high school or until

Agape, or altruistic love, includes kindness, self-sacrifice, compassion, and patience. Actor Christopher Reeve of the popular Superman films was confined to a wheelchair after a riding accident. Reeve's wife, Dana, has cared for him since the accident and has supported his lobbying Congress on such issues as raising the lifetime spending caps on catastrophic insurance policies.

TABLE 5.2

Some Items from the Love Attitudes Scale

If you're dating, you can use this scale to examine your own and your partner's feelings. If you've never been in love or have no partner now, answer in terms of what you think your responses might be. Keep in mind that there are no wrong answers to these statements; they're designed simply to increase your understanding of different types of love. For each item, mark a "1" for "strongly agree," "2" for "moderately agree," "3" for "neutral," "4" for "moderately disagree," and "5" for "strongly disagree."

Eros

❑   **1.** My partner and I were attracted to each other immediately after we first met.

❑   **2.** Our lovemaking is very intense and satisfying.

❑   **3.** My partner fits my standards of physical beauty/handsomeness.

Ludus

❑   **4.** What my partner doesn't know about me won't hurt him/her.

❑   **5.** I sometimes have to keep my partner from finding out about other partners.

❑   **6.** I could get over my partner pretty easily and quickly.

Pragma

❑   **7.** In choosing my partner, I believed it was best to love someone with a similar background.

❑   **8.** An important factor in choosing my partner was whether or not he/she would be a good parent.

❑   **9.** One consideration in choosing my partner was how he/she would affect my career.

Agape

❑   **10.** I would rather suffer myself than let my partner suffer.

❑   **11.** My partner can use whatever I own as she/he chooses.

❑   **12.** I would endure all things for the sake of my partner.

Storge

❑   **13.** I expect to always be friends with the people I date.

❑   **14.** The best kind of love grows out of a long friendship.

❑   **15.** Love is a deep friendship, not a mysterious, passionate emotion.

SOURCES: Lasswell and Lasswell, 1976, pp. 211–24; Hendrick and Hendrick, 1992a, 1992b; and Levesque, 1993, pp. 219–50.

---

both partners find better jobs (Lasswell and Lasswell, 1976).

Researchers have developed dozens of scales to measure the constructs of love and intimate relations that Lee proposed (see Tzeng, 1993). *Table 5.2* presents some items from the Love Attitudes Scale that was originally developed by the Lasswells and modified by later researchers.

Functions of Love and Loving

Love is the core of healthy and well-functioning relationships and families and fulfills many purposes. First, love ensures *human survival*. In a tongue-in-cheek article, one writer suggested that romantic love is a "nuisance," "an evolutionary device," and "a nasty trick played upon us by nature to keep our species going," especially during the childbearing years (Chance, 1988: 23). In fact, love *does* keep our species going. Because children can be conceived outside of love and marriage, there is no guarantee that those engaging in sexual intercourse will feel an obligation to care for their offspring. Unlike sex, love implies a commitment. Thus, by promoting interest in caring for helpless infants, love ensures the survival of the species.

Second, love *prolongs life*. As noted earlier, studies have shown that infants who do not receive love may grow up emotionally handicapped. Perhaps the most dramatic example of love's impact is suicide. People who commit suicide often feel socially isolated, unloved, or unworthy of love (Hendin, 1982; Osgood, 1985). Suicide is far more prevalent among the divorced than it is among married people. Divorced people also tend to suffer more serious illnesses and more chronic disabling conditions than do married couples (Kiecolt-Glaser et al., 1987). Although these studies do not suggest a causal relationship between marriage and health, it appears that those who are in loving relationships may experience fewer health problems.

Third, love improves the *quality of our lives.* Whether parental or between adults, love is a primary source of feeling anchored, and it fosters the development of self-esteem. From the solid basis of loving family relationships, children acquire the confidence to face the world outside the family (Bodman and Peterson, 1995). Terminally ill patients, AIDS victims, and paraplegics report that they can accept death or cope with their disabilities when they are surrounded by supportive, caring, and loving family members and friends. Failure to have a secure base of love, on the other hand, can lead to aggression, hostility, diminished self-confidence, and emotional problems. At least half of all teenage runaways are escaping a lack of love as evidenced by violence, abuse, or incest. Battered wives become suspicious, fearful, and bitter.

Fourth, love *inspires* us not to give up because life can get better. Some of the most popular love stories— *Romeo and Juliet, West Side Story, Camelot,* and *Love Story,* for example—are tragedies. Nevertheless, "they inspire a soaring hope within us that we will find the same magic power of love that has transformed the lives of our tragic heroes and heroines" (Douglas and Atwell, 1988: 274). There are many examples of children, parents, and spouses who perform heroic feats or undergo enormous sacrifices because they are motivated by love.

Fifth, love is *fun.* Without love, life is "a burden and a bore" (Safilios-Rothschild, 1977: 9). Even though love can be extremely painful, it is also enjoyable. Love can be pleasurable and exciting. It is both comforting and fun to plan to see a loved one, to travel together, to write and receive letters, cards, and presents, to talk about personal activities, to have someone care for you when you are sick or grumpy, and to know that someone will pick you up if your car breaks down. Love is reassuring and comfortable, a diversion from mundane, day-to-day activities.

Finally, social scientists often describe love as a social exchange process (see Chapter 2). Romantic and long-term love relationships represent social exchanges in the sense that they provide rewards and costs to each participant. If the initial interactions are reciprocal and mutually satisfying to both people, interdependence will continue. If, however, our needs are mismatched (see *Figure 5.2*) or change drastically over time, our love interests may wane or shift. Exchange theory is especially helpful in explaining

why romantic love, especially among adolescents, is short-lived. As we mature, socially and cognitively, our perceptions of rewards and costs usually change. We might decide that nurturing a relationship with someone who's patient and confident, for example, outweighs the benefits of being with someone who's "a good catch" or "a knockout" but is controlling and self-centered (see Laursen and Jensen-Campbell, 1999).

We consider the costs and benefits of romance later in life as well. A national survey asked men and women over age 60 what qualities they sought in a romantic partner. Ninety percent of respondents of both sexes said they wanted high moral character, a pleasant personality, and a good sense of humor and intelligence in a prospective mate. There were several distinct differences between men and women, however. More women (85 percent) than men (56 percent) sought financial security in a partner. More men (72 percent) than women (46 percent) wanted partners who were interested in sex. Men (67 percent) were more likely than women (48 percent) to express a preference for a partner with an attractive body ("Half of older Americans . . . ," 1998). Because women, especially older women, are less likely than men to be affluent, financial security may be a more important consideration than sex or physical appearance (see Chapters 4, 14, and 18).

Some scientists argue that one of the most important functions of love and intimacy is physical well-being: "When you feel loved, nurtured, cared for, supported, and intimate, you are much more likely to be happier and healthier. You have a much lower risk of getting sick and, if you do, a much greater chance of survival" (Ornish, 1998: 24). They argue that anything that promotes feelings of love and intimacy is healing. Anything that promotes isolation, loneliness, hostility, anger, depression, and similar feelings often leads to suffering, disease, and premature death from many causes.

Experiencing Love

For most people, men and women alike, caring, trust, respect, and honesty are central to love. There are some differences, however, in the ways men and women conceive of love and in the ways they express it. In addition, although both heterosexuals and homosexuals share many of the same feelings and behaviors, there are also some differences in their experiences of love.

Are Women or Men More Romantic?

Contrary to popular opinion, many men seem to fall in love faster and are more romantic than women. In one of the earliest studies on this topic, Hobart (1958) administered a romanticism scale to college students and found that, in general, men were more romantic than women. Agreement with such statements as "To be truly in love is to be in love forever" and "A person should marry whomever he loves regardless of social position" was scored as "romantic." Being "nonromantic" meant agreeing with such statements as "Lovers ought to expect a certain amount of disillusionment after marriage" and "Most of us could sincerely love any one of several people equally well." In another well-known study, the researchers found that although men tended to fall in love more quickly, women were more intense, more euphoric, and more likely to idealize the love object (Kanin et al., 1970).

Replications of Hobart's research have yielded similar results. Knox and Sporakowski (1968) concluded that women were more practical because they had more at stake in the relationship: (1) Women were more pressured by parents and relatives to marry "wisely"; (2) women were more dependent on men for economic security; and (3) women were more family-oriented and thus concerned about having a successful marriage. Because they themselves are often discriminated against in the workplace, women are more concerned about a potential mate's social, occupational, and economic status; a woman's own economic status frequently still depends on the man's (see Chapter 13). In contrast, because they are rarely dependent on a woman's financial status, men are generally freer to be more spontaneous and romantic. They may complain about the women they date, saying, "The first thing she wants to know is where I work, what kind of car I drive, and how much money I make." Such statements imply that women may be more concerned about a man's socioeconomic status than about love.

In their research on loving styles, Hendrick and Hendrick (1992b) found that, in general, men are more ludic, or game playing, whereas women tend to be more storgic and pragmatic. One of women's biggest complaints is that the men who profess to love them are reluctant to marry. Women sometimes belittle men for being "commitment dodgers," "commitment phobics," "paranoid about commitment," and "afraid of the M word." Given the tremendous costs of unprotected sex—sexually transmitted disease, pregnancy and childbirth—it is not surprising that many women are angry when their lovers refuse to marry (Crittenden, 1999).

In a review of the literature on love and romance, Hatfield (1983) concluded that women love more than they are loved in return and are willing to sacrifice more for love than men are. Women also seem to work harder on love than men do, spending more time on trying to understand, express, and manage their feelings (Rubin, 1973). On the other hand, women are usually the ones who decide when to break off a relationship. And after the breakup, men are more likely than women to be sad, lonely, depressed, and unwilling to accept the situation; they are also more violent and possessive than women are when a relationship ends (Herman, 1989; see also Chapter 14).

Are Women or Men More Intimate?

We often hear that men are less intimate than women. As you saw earlier, there are many possible definitions of intimacy, including the intensity of a relationship and sexual expression (Brehm, 1992). When women complain about a lack of intimacy, they usually mean that the man doesn't communicate his thoughts or feelings. Many men believe that such expectations are unfair because they show their intimacy through sex. While many women want to feel close emotionally before being sexual, many men use sexual activity to bring about emotional closeness (Piorkowski, 1994).

A few years ago advice columnist Ann Landers sparked a nationwide controversy when she reported that many women prefer being touched, hugged, cuddled, and kissed over having sexual intercourse. In general, men and women in loving relationships may see intimacy differently and engage in sexual activity for different reasons. A wife complains: "I think being close means sharing. He thinks being close means screwing! When he's anxious or insecure, he wants sex; it reassures him." The husband, however, feels that his wife should accept sex as a substitute for intimacy:

> I think women have this need to analyze everything, talk it through down to every little detail, no matter how private it might be. Just because I come home and don't immediately start spilling my guts about everything that happened at work doesn't mean I don't love her. She gets all over me for not being "feeling," whatever that means. Women need all this feeling, emotion stuff from relationships. Men don't. It just means that men are different from women and need different things. (McGill, 1985: 190–91)

Love relationships and intimacy are complex, however. The more traditional the couples, for example, the more stereotyped their patterns of communication. Less traditional women and men have been found to be fairly relaxed about discussing such personal matters as friends and their strengths and weaknesses (Roberts and Krokoff, 1990). There is also some evidence that black newlywed couples find it easier than their white counterparts to disclose their intimate feelings and to talk openly about many sensitive issues (Oggins et al., 1993). In addition, the gender gap in intimacy may widen after marriage. For wives, intimacy may mean talking things over. For husbands, as the box "Do I Love You? I Changed Your Oil, Didn't I?" shows, men may feel that doing things (such as taking care of the family cars) shows their love.

CHOICES

"Do I Love You? I Changed Your Oil, Didn't I?"

We often hear that men are less loving than women because they equate love with sex and never talk about their feelings. Several social scientists disagree. According to Francesca Cancian (1990: 171), the fault lies not in our men but in our definitions of loving, which ignore masculine styles of showing affection:

We identify love with emotional expression and talking about feelings, aspects of love that women prefer and in which women tend to be more skilled than men. At the same time we often ignore the instrumental and physical aspects of love that men prefer, such as providing help, sharing activities, and sex.

Cancian calls excluding men's ways of showing affection as the "feminization of love." Because of this bias, men rarely get credit for the kinds of loving actions that are more typical of them. According to Carol Tavris (1992: 255):

What about all the men . . . who reliably support their families, who put the wishes of other family members ahead of their own preferences, or who act in a moral and considerate way when conflicts arise? Such individuals are surely being mature and loving, even if they are not articulate or do not value "communication."

Thus, a man who is a good provider or who changes the oil in his wife's car or fixes his child's bike is showing just as much love as the wife who tells her husband she loves him and shares her innermost thoughts and feelings with him. Actions may not "speak louder than words," but perhaps they have an equal impact.

There are several negative consequences of the "feminization of love." First, it assumes that women need love more than men and are more dependent on men for emotional satisfaction. Second, emphasizing only the expressive side of love ignores or diminishes the importance of women's instrumental activities, such as working inside and outside the home. Finally, the feminization of love intensifies the conflicts over intimacy between women and men. As the woman demands more verbal contact, the man feels increased pressure and withdraws. The woman may then intensify her efforts to get closer. This leads to a vicious cycle where neither partner gets what she or he wants. As the definition of love becomes more feminized, men and women move farther apart rather than closer together (Tucker, 1992). One way to break this vicious cycle is to give both men and women credit for the things they do to show their love for each other and for their families.

Although some of the research suggests that men may be more romantic than women and that the sexes may show their affection differently, there are probably more similarities than differences between the love attitudes of women and men. In a study based on Lee's love typology (see *Table 5.1*), Montgomery and Sorell (1997) analyzed the love attitudes of people aged 17 to 70 in four groups—college-age youth; young, childless, married adults; married adults with children living at home; and married adults with launched children. The researchers found that the young singles were more likely than the married groups to have manic (obsessive) and ludic (playful) attitudes and less likely to endorse agapic (self-sacrificing) attitudes. Across all groups, however, *both* women and men prized passion (eros), friendship/companionship (storge), and self-sacrifice (agape). Although Montgomery and Sorell note that their data were limited to white, middle-class adults, they question the shallow approaches of recent popular books (such as Gray's *Men Are from Mars, Women Are from Venus*), which have trumpeted "the radical differences in men's and women's approach to partnering relationships" (p. 60).

Same-Sex Love

During the nineteenth century, friendships were almost exclusively same sex because women's and men's social spheres were rigidly defined (Swain, 1992). Although most of these friendships were not sexual, some were. They were referred to as "romantic friendships" until the twentieth century, when medical circles began to use such terms as "homosexual" or "lesbian." Today, many gay men openly admit they are lovers and talk about loving each other (in contrast to having loveless one-night stands). Lesbians are more likely to describe a variety of relationships ranging from romantic but asexual relationships to passionate, sexual love (see, for example, Rothblum and Brehony, 1993).

Heterosexual and same-sex love is very similar. Regardless of sexual orientation, most partners want to be emotionally close, expect faithfulness, and often plan to grow old together (Clark, 1999). Breakups are generally as painful for same-sex partners as they are for most heterosexual couples. A few years ago, for example, one of my best students was devastated when his partner left. The student's grades suddenly plum-

The family is usually our earliest and most important source of love and emotional support.

meted because he was unable to concentrate on his courses; he became depressed and wanted to drop out of college. With some counseling and enormous fortitude, he finished his senior year and graduated with honors.

One of the biggest differences between heterosexual and same-sex love is that lesbians and gay men are usually criticized for showing their affection in public. As you will see in Chapter 6, differences between men and women in expressing sexual love are greater than the differences between heterosexual and same-sex love.

Barriers to Experiencing Love

Any number of obstacles can impede our way to love. Some barriers are macro-level—for example, the impersonality of mass society, demographic variables, our culture's double standard for men and women, and its emphasis on individualism. Other barriers are micro-level—for example, certain kinds of personality characteristics and family experiences. Understanding some of these obstacles can give us more choices and more control; it can also help us accept some constraints that we can't change.

Mass Society and Demographic Factors Mass society's bureaucratic systems, along with burgeoning technologies like answering machines, fax machines, electronic mail, and telemarketing services, decrease the opportunities for face-to-face interaction among people and tend to dehumanize interpersonal communication. In response, as you will see in Chapter 7, a

"love industry" has mushroomed. Computerized matchmaking, Internet chat rooms, personal ads, singles bars, dinner clubs, and dozens of books promise singles that they can find love and counteract the isolation and impersonality of our society.

Something as unromantic as demography plays a role in love. In one study, students who perceived that members of the opposite sex were relatively scarce expressed more desire for commitment than did students who thought that members of the opposite sex were plentiful. The researchers concluded: "In the face of scant opportunities for new relationships, people seem to learn to love the one they are with: They invest more in their romantic relationship, like it more, and are more committed to it" (Jemmott and Ashby, 1989: 1209).

Such demographic variables as age, income, and occupation also play an important role in love. In one study, for example, 40 percent of the men but only 9 percent of the women over age 54 were involved in romantic relationships. Why? There is a shortage of older males, the researchers pointed out, and a super-abundance of young females. In the same study, almost 90 percent of the African American women aged 55 and older said that they were not married or romantically involved. This is an age group in which relationships may simply be more costly for women than they are for men. An elderly man may expect housekeeping from his partner as well as caretaking if he becomes ill. An elderly woman, especially if she is financially secure, may be unwilling to be burdened with more housework because she is looking forward to a more relaxed lifestyle (Tucker and Taylor, 1989).

The Double Standard As you saw in Chapter 4, there is still a great deal of social inequality between men and women. The double standard is one of the most damaging forms of inequality because it often discourages the development of love. The fact that our society still implicitly condones men's having sex without love but labels women who "sleep around" as "sluts" and "tramps" makes many women angry and resentful of men. This creates a lack of mutual trust and often leads to playing power games in which men may perceive women as manipulative and demanding, and women may see men as sex-crazed, irresponsible, and domineering.

"Me-First" Individualism Our cultural values encourage individualism and competition rather than community and cooperation. This emphasis on the individual leads to a preoccupation with self (Bellah et al., 1985; Kass, 1997). In the 1980s we heard statements like "Look out for Number One" and "If it feels good, do it." We have been steeped in narcissistic messages that preach self-improvement, self-actualization, self-aggrandizement, and self-serving behavior, often at the expense of the couple or the family (Lasch, 1978). Measuring love solely in terms of feeling good leaves us unequipped to handle its hard, painful, or demanding aspects, such as supporting a partner during unemployment or caring for a loved one who has a long-term illness.

Individual Personality Characteristics Sometimes personality traits or family history get in the way of finding love. Many children, especially girls, whose parents have undergone hostile divorces, report that they are cynical about love or are afraid to fall in love (Wallerstein and Blakeslee, 1989; Rodberg, 1999).

As you saw earlier, some psychiatrists and psychologists believe that attachment problems during childhood are replayed in adulthood. Some of these problems include a fear of commitment and doubts about one's ability to inspire love in another. For example, a child who has grown up in a cold and unloving family may be suspicious in adulthood of potential partners who are warm and loving ("I wonder what she's after") because she or he finds it hard to believe themselves to be lovable. Or a child who was molested by a family member or relative may be distrustful of future relationships (see Chapter 14). Some parents may be so suffocating that even adult children may not become independent enough to pursue love or marry people who don't meet parental approval.

When Love Goes Wrong

The topic of a recent talk show was something like "Do You Use Jealousy to Keep Your Lover?" The panelists were women in their 20s and 30s who regaled the audience with stories of how they used jealousy to jolt their inattentive husbands or to get even with a boyfriend's "wandering eye." The implication was that making someone jealous or using other forms of manipulation not only is acceptable but may be a particularly desirable way to spark or maintain a relationship. Such tactics often backfire, however. They are usually unhealthy and even hazardous to our emotional and physical well-being.

Jealousy: Trying to Control Love

Typically, people experience *jealousy* when they believe a love relationship is being threatened, usually by a rival, for the affections of their lover. The jealous person is suspicious of his or her partner, often obsessive, and frequently angry and resentful. Some people are also jealous of their partner's spending time with family members, relatives, or hobbies (Brehm, 1992). Although some researchers have suggested that jealousy has a positive function in helping people identify those relationships that are truly important to them, writer Ayala Pines disagrees: "Jealousy is like a hot pepper. Use it mildly, and you add spice to the relationship. Use too much of it and it can burn" (quoted in Maggio, 1992: 175).

Love flourishes when it is based on trust and respect for the other's individuality. In contrast, jealousy is usually an unhealthy manifestation of insecurity, low self-esteem, and possessiveness (Douglas and Atwell, 1988; Farrell, 1997). Both males and females who report high jealousy tend to depend heavily on their partners for their own self-esteem, consider themselves inadequate as mates, and feel that they are more deeply involved in their relationship than their partners are. A study of college students found that, whether the parents were married or divorced, the students who had grown up in homes with continuous interparental conflict or rejecting, overprotective parents were most likely to report jealousy and fears of abandonment in their love relationships (Hayashi and Strickland, 1998). In addition, people who are jealous often have been or are still unfaithful (White and Mullen, 1989). All these findings strongly suggest that jealousy is a serious threat to love.

Some jealous lovers become obsessed. They constantly daydream about the person with whom they are obsessed, make numerous phone calls, send flowers, cards, gifts, and love letters, or continuously check up on their partner's whereabouts. Males tend to act out violently by hurting or killing their lovers; women are more likely to damage or destroy property, like scratching a lover's car or spraying it with paint (Tuller, 1994). Jealous females can also be violent. Recently, for example, two model adolescents—he was at the Air Force Academy and she was at the Naval Academy—were convicted of murdering a high school schoolmate. According to the young man's confession, he and his fiancée killed the young woman because his fiancée wanted vengeance after he and the victim had had sexual intercourse one evening.

Jealousy and Stalking In recent years, stalking by a jealous lover has been recognized as a serious problem. California passed the first anti-stalking law in 1990. Many people believe the legislation was the result of the shooting death of television actress Rebecca Schaeffer. Schaeffer had received numerous love letters and death threats from a male fan, but she ignored both. The fan eventually tracked down her address and shot her in front of her home. By the mid-1990s, all 50 states had adopted anti-stalking laws. Unfortunately, these laws rarely discourage suitors (almost always men) from threatening, harassing, or even killing those who reject them.

Although people who stalk celebrities—like the man who scaled the 8-foot wall around pop star Madonna's property—make the headlines, most stalking cases involve ordinary people who either were once married to each other or had dated one another. One in 12 women and one in 45 men have been stalked at some time in their life. According to the best available statistics, 70 to 80 percent of all stalking cases involve men who hound women ("Stalking," 2000). *Cyberstalking*, a relatively new phenomenon, involves threatening behavior or unwanted advances toward someone using the Internet and other forms of online communications. Many cyberstalking situations evolve into offline stalking, and a victim may experience abusive or harassing phone calls, vandalism, threatening or obscene mail, trespassing, and physical assault ("Cyberstalking," 2000).

Is Jealousy Universal? Although it is apparently widespread, jealousy is not universal. Surveying two centuries of anthropological reports, Hupka (1991) found two types of cultures: one in which jealousy was rare—for example, the Todas of southern India—and one in which jealousy was commonplace—for example, the Apache Indians of North America. Toda culture did not encourage possessiveness of either material objects or people. It placed few restrictions on sexual gratification, and it did not make marriage a condition for women's social recognition. In contrast, Apache society prized virginity, paternity, and fidelity. While an Apache man was away from home, he had a close relative keep secret watch over his wife and report on her behavior when he returned. Based on the variations he found across cultures, Hupka concluded that jealousy is not innate but learned. In addition, jealousy is common in many modern-day societies.

In a recent study of several Western countries, Buss and colleagues (1996) found that twice as many men as women reported being more upset imagining their partners' "enjoying passionate sexual intercourse"

with other people than imagining their partners' "forming a deep emotional attachment." The researchers explain the gender differences in evolutionary terms. That is, men worry more about sexual infidelity than emotional infidelity because if they are cuckolded they might unknowingly end up raising someone else's child rather than passing down their own genes. Women, in contrast, worry more about their partners' emotional entanglements because a loss of emotional commitment could decrease their children's chances of survival. Others argue that gender differences reflect cultural, not genetic or evolutionary, influences. Since, for example, men in the United States are more likely to be jealous of their partners' sexual infidelity than men in Germany or the Netherlands, such variations suggest that in some countries there is more tolerance of sexual dalliances and men are less likely to be jealous (DeSteno and Salovey, 1996).

Other Types of Controlling Behavior

Jealousy is not the only type of unhealthy, controlling behavior in love relationships. Threatening the withdrawal of love or creating guilt feelings can be deeply distressing to a partner; inflicting severe emotional and physical abuse can be devastating.

"If You Loved Me . . ." One of the most common pressures for sex (especially by men) is based on the threat of the loss of a love relationship: "If you really loved me, you'd show it." People use the loss or withdrawal of love to manipulate other behavior as well. Faculty tell many stories about students who choose majors they hate because they don't want to disappoint parents who insist that they become a doctor, a lawyer, an accountant, and so on. Many women drop out of college because their husbands or boyfriends accuse them of placing more importance on earning their degrees than on maintaining their homes, preparing dinner, and being free on weekends to spend time with them.

Essentially, controlling people want power over others. They use "love" to manipulate and exploit those who care about them. With pressure and ultimatums, they force partners to sacrifice their own interests. Whether such control is well intentioned or malicious, it is designed to ensure the controller's happiness, not the happiness of the person being manipulated.

Controllers are not all alike: "A wealthy executive may use money and influence, while an attractive person may use physical allure and sex" to manipulate another (Jones and Schecter, 1992: 11). Moreover, as the box "If This Is Love, Why Do I Feel So Bad?" shows, controllers use a variety of strategies in dominating a relationship. And they may switch strategies from time to time to keep the controlled person off balance or because the controller sometimes has fleeting regrets about being manipulative.

ASK YOURSELF

If This Is Love, Why Do I Feel So Bad?

If you feel bad, what you're experiencing may be control, not love (see Clarke, 1990). Controllers use whatever tactics are necessary to maintain power over another person: nagging, cajoling, coaxing, flattery, charm, threats, self-pity, blame, insults, humiliation. In the worst cases, controllers may physically injure and even murder people who refuse to be controlled. As you read this brief list (based on Jones and Schecter, 1992: 16–22), check any items that seem familiar to you. Individually, the items may seem unimportant, but if you check off more than two or three, you may be dealing with a serious controller.

❏ My partner calls me names: dummy, jackass, whore, creep, bitch, moron.

❏ My partner always criticizes me and makes even a compliment sound like a criticism: "This is the first good dinner you've cooked in months."

❏ Always right, my partner continually corrects things I say or do. If I'm five minutes late, I'm scared my partner will be mad.

❏ My partner withdraws into silence, and I have to figure out what I've done wrong and apologize for it.

❏ My partner is jealous when I talk to new people.

❏ My partner often phones or unexpectedly comes by the place I work to see if I'm "okay."

❏ My partner acts very cruelly and then says I'm too sensitive and can't take a joke.

❏ When I try to express my opinion about something, my partner either doesn't respond, walks away, or makes fun of me.

❏ I have to account for every dime I spend, but my partner keeps me in the dark about our bank accounts.

❏ My partner says that if I ever leave he or she will commit suicide and I'll be responsible.

❏ When my partner has a temper tantrum, he or she says it's my fault or the children's.

❏ My partner makes fun of my body.

❏ Whether my partner is with us or not, he or she is jealous of every minute I spend with my family or other relatives or friends.

❏ My partner grills me about what happened whenever I go out.

❏ My partner makes sexual jokes about me in front of the children and other people.

❏ My partner throws things at me, hits, shoves, or pushes me.

The Guilt Trip People use guilt to justify actions that have nothing to do with love. It is not uncommon for parents, in particular, to invoke the love/guilt complex to influence children's behavior: "If you cared about me, you'd go to college. I've made a lot of sacrifices to save up for your education"; or "If you marry that Catholic [or Jew or Protestant], how can I face Rabbi Katz [or Mr. Beirne or Father Mulcahey] again!" Objectively, the parents might be right because a college education is a good investment, and marriage outside of one's religious group often presents problems. The danger, however, is that the parents may be more concerned about their own needs than their children's.

The guilt trip can be used by many family members and does not end at adulthood. Older parents and relatives sometimes use guilt to manipulate middle-aged children. One of the most disabling guilt trips is the "affection myth," where children are taught that love is synonymous with caregiving. Thus, children and grandchildren may feel that, no matter what their own circumstances are, they must care for the older family members at home. As a result,

younger family members sometimes endure enormous stress, when often their elderly relatives might actually get much better medical care at a skilled nursing facility (Jarrett, 1985).

Emotional and Physical Abuse Love is sometimes used to justify severe emotional or physical neglect and abuse, but violence is *never* a manifestation of love (see Chapter 14). A partner who is sarcastic or controlling, a parent who severely spanks or verbally humiliates a child—such people are not expressing love for the child's "own good," as they often insist. They are simply being angry and brutal. According to Gelles and Cornell (1990: 20), "the most insidious aspect of family violence" is that children grow up unable to distinguish between love and violence and believe "that it is acceptable to hit the people you love." The film *What's Love Got to Do with It?*, based on singer Tina Turner's biography, dramatically portrayed the effects on Turner of enduring violence for years because she believed that doing so proved her love and commitment to her husband, Ike.

Unrequited Love

In unrequited love, another person does not reciprocate one person's romantic feelings. Why does this happen? There are several reasons. First, a person may "fall upward" in love. That is, someone who is less physically attractive may fall in love with someone who's gorgeous. As you will see in Chapter 7, there is a tendency for people of similar degrees of attractiveness to date and marry. Thus, love for someone who is much more attractive may go unrequited. The rebuff is even more painful if the person being rejected senses that physical appearance is the major reason for being cast aside (Baumeister and Wotman, 1992). We often hear both women and men complain that the object of their affections "never took the time to get to know me," implying that such things as personality, intelligence, and common interests should be more important than looks.

Unrequited love may also be the outcome when only one of the partners wants to move from casual dating to a serious romance. Realizing that the person one is dating, and perhaps having sexual relations with, is in it "just for the fun of it" (ludic lovers) and does not want to become more serious or exclusive can be very distressing.

People who are rejected after entering into a sexual relationship are especially likely to feel that they were led on and then dumped. Although the castoffs tend to see rejecters as aloof, "teases," or even sadistic heartbreakers, in fact, they usually are "ordinary, well-meaning people who find themselves caught up in another person's emotional whirlwind and who themselves often suffer acutely as a result" (Baumeister and Wotman, 1992: 203). Rejecters often agonize over how to disengage themselves from their admirers without hurting them.

Jealousy, insecurity, and controlling behavior illustrate some of the reasons why affection "unwinds." Wheel theories of love note that relationships can be "rewound." If partners want to stay together, they can implement "repairs" at various stages of dissolution. Early in the relationship, for example, people can discuss concerns about emotional problems or personality differences rather than assume that the other partner will change or that the situation "is bound to get better" (Duck, 1998).

How Couples Change: Romantic and Long-Term Love

Because romantic love permeates literature, the theater, films, and television, as well as the fine arts, it is worthwhile examining this often-fleeting form of love. Romantic love can be both exhilarating and disappointing. It is long-term love, however, that provides security and constancy.

Some Characteristics of Romantic Love

According to Tennov (cited in Hatfield, 1983: 114) romantic love is usually a passionate and dizzying experience:

- Lovers find it impossible to work, to study, or to do anything but think about the beloved.
- Their moods fluctuate wildly; they are ecstatic when they hope they might be loved, despairing when they feel they're not.
- They find it impossible to believe that they could ever love again.
- They fantasize about how their partners will declare their love.
- They care so desperately about the other that nothing else matters; they are willing to sacrifice anything for love.
- Their love is "blind," and they idealize each other.

Thus, romantic love is idealized, emotional, passionate, and melodramatic. Romantic love might also be self-absorbed and self-serving. Narcissists, for example, may woo partners who admire them and who are always positive and caring rather than people who offer a potential for intimacy (W. K. Campbell, 1999). Thus, narcissistic romantic love relies on enhancing one's self-esteem rather than expressing interest in the other partner ("Tell me what else you like about me" versus "How are *you* doing?").

People from other cultures may see it as bizarre and frivolous, but Western countries take romantic love very seriously. It is considered the most legitimate reason for living together, getting married, or getting a divorce ("the spark is gone"). Romantic love thrives on two beliefs—love at first sight and fate.

Love at First Sight Romantic love was less common in the United States during the 1800s than it is today for three reasons: Life expectancy was short; living in isolated towns and homes made it difficult to meet a variety of people; and most people did not live long enough to fall in love more than once. Today, with increased life spans, geographic mobility, and high divorce rates, we may fall in love with many people during our lifetime.

It's not surprising that people fall in love at first sight. Unlike most of our everyday feelings, such love is fun, exciting, and has an air of mystery. In addition, love at first sight typically overtakes people who not only are very lonely and starved for physical affection but who have had little experience with love and sex (Douglas and Atwell, 1988). Finally, people fall in love with love itself through romantic stories in movies, television, novels, and magazines.

Experience, however limited, may dampen beliefs about love at first sight. In a study of 184 undergraduates, for example, Knox and his associates (1999)

© 1997 Creators Syndicate, Inc.

found that young college students (age 19 and under) were significantly more likely to believe in love at first sight and "love conquers all" than older students (age 20 and over). There's no evidence, however, that the college students in this study or people in larger populations ignore love at first sight as one of the primary reasons for dating, cohabiting, or marrying.

Fate   Fate is often seen as an important component of romantic love. Songs tell us that "you were meant for me" and "that old black magic has me in its spell." In reality, fate has little to do with romantic love. In several studies of college students, romantic love was ignited not by fate but by such factors as similar socioeconomic background, physical attractiveness, and a need for intimacy (Shea and Adams, 1984; Benassi, 1985).

Love in Long-Term Relationships

Many characteristics of romantic love overlap those of long-term love (some combination of eros, ludus, storge, agape, and pragma). In a review of the literature on love and romantic love, Fehr (1993) found a common core of feelings in both types of love. As *Figure 5.3* shows, there is considerably more overlap than one might expect. Both value such characteristics as trust, understanding, and honesty. There are also some striking differences, however. First, romantic love is simple, whereas lasting love is more complicated. It takes much less effort to plan a romantic evening than to be patient with a partner day after day, year after year. Second, romantic love is self-centered, whereas long-term love is altruistic. For example, romantic lovers are often swept away by their own fantasies and obsessions, but lasting love often requires putting the other before self and making the partner feel wanted.

Almost all of the research on romantic love shows that it is short-lived because love changes over time,

and flaws that seemed "cute" during a whirlwind courtship may become unbearable a year after marriage. For example, his dumpy furniture may have seemed quaint until she realized that he refused to spend any money on home furnishings. And values, especially religious values, become increasingly important after the birth of the first child (Trotter, 1986). While long-term love usually grows and matures, romantic love is typically immature. For example, romantic lovers often feel insecure about themselves or the relationship. As a result, one of the partners may demand constant attention, a continuous display of affection, and daily "I love you" reassurances (Dilman, 1998). Most of us appreciate tokens of love, verbal or behavioral. Never-ending and self-absorbed commands such as "prove to me that you love me," however, can become tedious, exasperating, and alienating.

It's easier to fall in love than to stay in love. There is no one formula for sustaining a long-term relationship. Many variables play a role in maintaining love. Consider, for example, socioeconomic status. Analyzing the findings of two national polls that asked people whether they were in love, Smith (1994) found an association between money and love: "The pattern suggests that having enough income to be out of poverty may alleviate financial problems enough to reduce stress and thereby facilitate feelings of love" (p. 34). So, although money may not buy love, a lack of money may encourage falling out of love.

And consider style of loving: There's some evidence that storgic, or companionate, love may be the most productive of long-term love relationships. Hecht et al. (1994) interviewed 144 women and men who said they were in love with each other. Those who were the happiest described their love as companionate (feeling of togetherness, of connectedness, sharing, and supporting each other) or committed. Committed lovers, ruled by the head as much as the heart, were faithful to each other and were planning their future

Unique to Romantic Love	Common to Both	Unique to Long-term Love
• Romantic Walks • Obsession • Longing • Candlelit Trysts • Going Out For Dinner • Picnics and Sunsets • Playfulness • Fantasy • Physical Attraction • Loss of Sleep • Ecstasy	• Trust • Caring • Communication • Honesty • Friendship • Respect • Understanding • Having Fun Together • Passion (but More Intense in Romantic Love)	• Patience • Independence • Putting Other before Self • Possibility of Marriage • Making Other Feel Wanted

FIGURE 5.3   Romantic Love and Long-term Love: Similar but Different. Try to rate your own relationship, if you are currently involved with someone, according to the characteristics shown here. Is your relationship one of romantic love? Or long-term love? Try to rate other relationships between people you know as well. (Based on Fehr, 1993, pp. 87–120).

together. Piorkowski (1994: 286) describes healthy, long-term love as follows:

> *Happy couples have similar values, attitudes, interests, and to some degree, personality traits. They also share a philosophy of life, religion, vision, or passion that keeps them marching together in spite of minor differences. In addition, they are autonomous, fair-minded, emotionally responsive individuals who trust one another and love spending time together, especially in communication with one another. Because they are separate selves, they also enjoy spending time apart to solidify their own individuality without feeling threatened by potential loss or abandonment. Moments of separateness and union are balanced, one following the other as naturally as night follows day.*

For more thoughts on how to achieve a satisfying, lasting relationship, see the box "Helping Love Flourish."

A Global View

If we look at love in other countries and cultures, we find many variations. In societies like India, love is not necessarily a prerequisite for marriage. Even highly educated Indian men and women who date non-Indians while living in Western countries often consent to arranged marriages. Respect for parents' wishes, family traditions, and duty to the kin group are more important than love. According to an economics student at Delhi University:

> *This whole concept of love is very alien to us. We're more practical. I don't see stars, I don't hear little bells. But he's a very nice guy, I get along with him fine, and I think I'm going to enjoy spending my life with him. (Bumiller, 1989: 93)*

Most middle- and upper-middle class women in India can marry whomever they want. Many, however, prefer arranged marriages and have veto power over undesirable candidates. Arranged marriages are attractive because they offer more stability than love. According to one highly educated woman in Calcutta who has been happily married for three years to a man she had met just three times before their engagement, love isn't essential for marital happiness: "I met a lot of people I liked, but no one was suitable for marriage, because I was looking for practicality also. Love is important, but it's not sufficient" (Lakshmanan, 1997: 2A).

Anthropologists Jankowiak and Fischer (1992) found evidence of romantic love in 89 percent of the 166 cultures they studied and concluded that romantic love is not a product of Western culture but constitutes "a human, universal, or at the least a near-universal" phenomenon. A number of studies suggest that romance is least important in societies where kin relationships take precedence over conjugal relationships. In this research, which largely studied college students, students in Burma and India were found to be the least romantic. In another traditional society, college students in one Mexican university said that storgic, agapic, and pragmatic love were more desirable than manic, erotic, and ludic love styles (Leon et al., 1994).

American and German students were more likely to say that romance is very important in love than were Japanese students, although the latter were more likely to believe that true love lasts forever. Japanese students were also more likely to state that marriage may result in disillusionment (Simmons et al., 1986).

It is not clear why the Japanese students felt that true love lasts forever but that marital love may be disappointing. It could be that most young people (such as these college students) idealize romantic love (see Hatfield and Rapson, 1996) but are more pragmatic about not expecting passionate love in marriage.

Despite images of French men as being flirtatious and romantic, Murstein and his associates (1991) found that American college students were more likely to endorse manic, emotional love while French students emphasized agapic, or compassionate and self-sacrificing love. The researchers suggested that the predominance of Catholics in the French sample might have accounted for their higher scores on agape.

Attitudes toward love may also vary by gender. A study of university students and others in Sydney, Australia, found that whereas women ranked the most important romantic act as "hearing or saying I love you," men gave the highest rank to "making love" (Hong and Faedda, 1994). In a study of 223 Korean students at a Seoul college, R. A. Brown (1994) found that the men were more romantic than women. For example, they were more likely to believe in love at first sight and to say that common interests are not important in marriage. In contrast, most of the female students in the study said that "love is just an emotion, but marriage is reality" (p. 188).

Conclusion

Love can be a many-splendored thing. When it is healthy, love *changes* how we feel about others and ourselves. It can inspire us and motivate us to care for friends, lovers, and family members. Love also creates *choices* in finding happiness during dating, marriage, and old age. There are *constraints,* however, because we sometimes confuse love with jealousy or controlling behavior.

Love is essential to human growth and development, but it is often shrouded in myths and surrounded by formidable barriers. For those who are willing to learn and to work at it, love is attainable and can be long-lasting. Do love and sex go together? Not always. We examine this and other issues related to sexuality in the next chapter.

CHOICES

Helping Love Flourish

Although they do not guarantee ever-lasting love, several practitioners (Hendrix, 1988; Osherson, 1992) have suggested some "rules" for creating a loving environment:

- Relationships do not just happen; we create them. Good relationships are the result of conscious effort and work.
- One partner should be pleased, rather than threatened, by the other partner's successes or triumphs.
- A lover is not a solution to a problem. Love may be one of life's greatest experiences, but it is not life itself.
- Love is about acceptance—being sympathetic to another's flaws and cherishing the person's other characteristics that are special and lovable.
- Lovers are not mind readers. Open communication is critical.

- It is not what you say; it is what you do. Quite often, communication is used to manipulate, induce guilt, or place blame, even though it is presented as positive and loving. Communication can be, and very often is, a weapon.
- Stable relationships are always changing. We must learn to deal with both our own changes as individuals and the changes we see in our mates.
- Love is poisoned by infidelity. If a loved one is deceived, it may be impossible to reestablish trust and respect.
- Blame is irresponsible. It discourages communication, makes people feel angry, and damages self-esteem.
- Giving is contagious. People who feel loved, accepted, and valued are more likely to treat others in a similar manner.

- Love does not punish; it forgives. It may be difficult to forget cruel words or acts, but forgiveness is essential in continuing a healthy relationship.
- Even though partners are very close, they must respect the other person's independence and his or her right to develop personal interests and other friendships.

SUMMARY

1. Love is a complex phenomenon. Because it varies in degree and intensity among people and across social contexts, love is difficult to define. Minimally necessary for a loving relationship are the willingness to please and accommodate the other, acceptance of the other's shortcomings, and have as much concern about the other's well-being as about one's own.

2. Caring, intimacy (including self-disclosure), and commitment form the foundations of love.

3. There are many approaches to understanding love and loving. Attachment theory posits that warm, secure, loving relationships in infancy are essential to emotional health and to the formation of self-esteem and loving relationships in adulthood. Reiss described four stages of love: rapport, self-revelation, mutual dependency, and personality need fulfillment. Borland suggested that love winds and unwinds as tensions build and are resolved. Sternberg focused on the interrelationships among passion, intimacy, and decision/commitment; and Lee described six styles of loving in relationships.

4. Love serves many functions, and people fall in love for a variety of reasons. Simple availability of partners is one determining factor; others include a wish to have children, survival, quality of life, inspiration, and just plain fun.

5. In contrast to popular beliefs, men are typically more romantic than women and suffer more when a relationship ends. Women are more prone to express their love verbally and to work at a relationship, but they are also more pragmatic about moving on when love goes awry. There are more similarities than differences, however, in women's and men's attitudes about love.

6. There are many obstacles to love. Macro-level barriers include the depersonalization of mass society, demographic factors, a double standard, our society's emphasis on individual achievement and advancement, its negative view of gay and lesbian love, and family expectations and pressures. Micro-level obstacles include personality characteristics and childhood experiences.

7. Several kinds of negative and controlling behavior can kill love. Jealousy is not a healthy sign of love but is usually destructive and sometimes even dangerous. Other harmful forms of love include threatening loved ones with the withdrawal of love, using guilt trips, and hurting them physically and emotionally.

8. In our society, romantic love is generally the basis for cohabitation, marriage, and divorce. Although romantic love can be exhilarating, it is often short-lived and can be very disappointing. In contrast to romantic love, long-term love is secure, constant, and reflects adaptation over the life course. There is a great deal of variation in love attitudes cross-culturally. While some societies embrace love, others see love as less important than marrying someone who is economically stable and from one's own social class.

KEY TERMS

self-disclosure *109*
eros *114*
mania *114*

ludus *114*
storge *115*
agape *115*

pragma *115*

TAKING IT FURTHER

Love and Romance in Cyberspace

Want to find out how romantic you are? If you and your partner are compatible? Here are a few self-assessment and other sites that you might enjoy:

Romance on the Air provides an *Interactive Romantic Survey* to see how romantic and sensitive you really are. It also includes *Romantic Stories for Some Inspiration,* a humor section, and an advice column.

members.aol.com/wakkarotti/romance.htm

Words of Love has an interesting array of Shakespeare's sonnets, songs, and witticisms about love.

www.randomhouse.com/wordsoflove

Valentines on the Web is "Dedicated to the One I Love." Netters can send Valentine cards that include both Websites and personal messages.

www.aristotle.net/valentines

Love Test, constructed by Betty Harris and Jim Glover, will remind you of Sternberg's and Lee's measures of love. You can take the *Concept of Love* quiz, the *Experience of Love* questionnaire, or both, and will receive an "analysis" of your (and your partner's) love styles after you submit the answers. It's fun!

www.topchoice.com/~psyche/lovetest

And more . . . www.prenhall.com/benokraitis provides numerous other sites on the topics covered in this chapter. Some, like *The Stalking Victim's Sanctuary,* offer resources for people who are victimized by "love." Others are great diversions when you need a break from studying or writing that paper: love quizzes, a matchmaking service "exclusively for graduates of top universities," Valentine's Day and greeting-card sites to send romantic gems, a collection of Victorian valentines, and several anti-Valentine's Day URLs.

CHAPTER 6

Sexuality and Sexual Expression throughout Life

DATADIGEST

- The percentage of men who say it is **easy to talk about sex with a partner** increased from 59 percent in 1984 to 71 percent in 1994. The proportion of women feeling this way remained the same: 86 percent.

- According to a recent survey, 2.8 percent of men and 1.4 percent of women **identified themselves as gay or bisexual.**

- Between 1988 and 1997, the percentage of women 15 to 19 years of age **who had ever had intercourse** declined from 53 percent to 48 percent. The rates for never-married males in this age group who had ever had intercourse declined from 60 percent to 55 percent during the same period.

- According to a national study, the percentage of high school students who had **initiated sexual intercourse** before 13 years of age was 9 percent. Male students (13 percent) were more likely than female students (5 percent) to have done so.

- A recent national survey found that over 80 percent of adults expressed concern about the **portrayal on television** of verbal references to sex, visual images of nudity or seminudity, premarital sex, and extramarital sex.

SOURCES: Clements, 1994; Laumann et al., 1994; Centers for Disease Control and Prevention, 1996; Impoco et al., 1996; Kann et al., 1996; Santelli et al., 2000.

SEX plays a bigger part in the lives of some people than others. Several years ago, for example, the late basketball star Wilt Chamberlain announced that he had slept with about 20,000 women. According to Chamberlain, that "equaled out" to having sex with 1.2 women a day, every day since he was 15 years old. In contrast, basketball player A. C. Green, a forward for the Dallas Mavericks, was still single and a virgin at age 33 and said he planned to be celibate until marriage. Green also encouraged adolescents to abstain from sex and to spend their energy developing leadership and academic skills.

Was Chamberlain sexier than Green? No. Sex involves much more than counting how often we use our genitals. Our sexuality provides an opportunity to express loyalty, passion, affection, and pleasure. As this chapter shows, culture shapes our sexual development, attitudes, and actions. Sexual behavior changes throughout life and varies over the years. In addition, cross-cultural research shows that there is great latitude in defining what is "normal" or acceptable.

Sexuality and Human Development

Our sexuality is considerably more complex than most people realize. It is the product of our sexual identity, sexual orientation, and the influence of sexual scripts. Our *sexual identity*—awareness of ourselves as male or female and how we express our sexual values, attitudes, feelings, and beliefs—is part of how we define who we are and what roles we play. Sexual identity involves placing oneself in a category created by society (such as

female and heterosexual) and learning, both consciously and unconsciously, how to act.

Sexuality is a multidimensional concept that incorporates psychological, biological, and sociological components such as sexual desire, sexual response, and gender roles (Bernhard, 1995). *Sexual desire* refers to the sexual drives that we learn through sexual experiences and feelings of enjoyment or dissatisfaction during sexual activity (see Chapter 5). *Sexual response* encompasses the biological aspects of sexuality that include experiencing pleasure or orgasm (as we will discuss shortly). *Gender roles* reflect the behavior that women and men enact according to culturally prescribed expectations (see Chapter 4). In a typical situation, for example, a man may be aroused by a woman's cleavage because breasts are considered sexy in our society (sexual desire), experience an erection (sexual response), and may take the initiative in having sexual intercourse with a woman he finds attractive (gender roles). What if, however, the man is aroused by other men and would prefer to initiate sexual activities with men rather than women?

Sexual Orientation

Our sexual identity incorporates a **sexual orientation** so that people prefer sexual partners of the same sex, of the opposite sex, or of either sex. A **homosexual** (from the Greek root *homo*, meaning "same") is a person who is sexually attracted to people of the same sex. In contrast, **heterosexuals,** often referred to as *straight,* are attracted to partners of the opposite sex. Male homosexuals prefer to be called gays; female homosexuals are called

CROSSCULTURAL

Homosexuality in Non-Western Cultures

In their classic studies, Ford and Beach (1972) examined data on 190 societies in Oceania, Eurasia, Africa, North America, and South America. They suggested three generalizations about homosexual behavior: (1) There is a wide divergence of social attitudes toward homosexuality; (2) homosexuality occurs in all societies regardless of societal reactions; and (3) males seem more likely to engage in homosexual activity than females.

Bisexual behavior has been documented in many cultures. In several non-Western societies, homosexual behavior during boyhood and adolescence is a rite of passage before the male switches to heterosexuality in adulthood. Among the Sambia of Papua New Guinea, from birth until somewhere between ages 7 and 10, boys interact frequently with females and live in heterosexual households. The Sambia believe that fellatio is essential for the boys to grow big and live a long life. The young initiates are told to ingest semen as if it were food.

In time, a boy's taking semen supposedly causes puberty and makes him manly enough to inseminate women. In their late teens or early 20s, young men are expected to find a wife and turn to heterosexuality. They are expected to be close, sensitive, and sexually proficient partners for their wives and to have children (Herdt, 1984; Baldwin and Baldwin, 1989).

During the eighteenth and nineteenth centuries, missionaries, travelers, anthropologists, and colonists ignored same-sex relationships in many African countries or described them as "the foulest of crimes" among "savages." Despite many attempts to repress homosexuality and to "save the natives," homosexuality is not uncommon today in many parts of Africa. For example, woman-to-woman marriage has been documented in more than 30 African populations, including at least 9 groups in present-day southern Africa (Carrier and Murray, 1998).

According to Hinsch (1990), both homosexuality and bisexuality in China

date back to at least the Bronze Age. Because marriage was seen as the bonding of two families rather than the romantic union of two individuals, both upper-class and peasant men sometimes maintained a heterosexual marriage and a homosexual liaison. Heterosexual marriages were important for both groups because children played a vital role: For the rich, they ensured progeny to continue the family line; for the poor, they provided agricultural labor and caretaking during old age.

Most Chinese have maintained that in China homosexuality is rare. Recently, however, Chinese researchers have estimated that there are about 40 million to 50 million homosexuals in a population of 1.2 billion. Homosexuality is still officially considered a perversion by the medical establishment. Nonetheless, China decriminalized sodomy in 1997 (which is still outlawed in 20 American states), several magazines are devoted to gay life in China, Internet chat rooms are burgeoning, and some gay men and lesbians have celebrated "wedding ceremonies" (Pomfret, 2000).

lesbians. **Bisexuals,** sometimes called *bis,* are sexually attracted to members of both sexes.

Sexual orientation is more complicated than "simply" identifying oneself as homosexual, heterosexual, or bisexual. Kinsey and his colleagues (1948) devised a 7-point rating scale to describe an individual's overt sexual experiences and psychological reactions (such as fantasies). The continuum ranged from people who identified themselves as exclusively heterosexual to those who said they were exclusively homosexual. The five categories in between included people who identified themselves as heterosexual but had had homosexual experiences, bisexuals, and gays who had had heterosexual experiences. Although heterosexuality is the predominant adult sexual orientation, homosexuality occurs in nearly all known societies (see the box "Homosexuality in Non-Western Cultures"). Many gay men and lesbians deny or try to suppress their sexual preference, however, because our society is still characterized by *heterosexism,* a belief that heterosexuality is superior to and more "natural" than homosexuality,

and Judeo/Christian religious beliefs that homosexuality is immoral.

Transgendered people are a small (2 percent of Americans) but increasingly visible group. *Transgendered* refers to people who live as the opposite sex. Some are transsexuals who have undergone sex change surgery (see Chapter 4); others are transvestites, also known as cross-dressers. Transgendered people include gays, heterosexuals, and bisexuals.

What Determines Sexual Orientation? No one knows why we are heterosexual, gay, or bisexual. *Biological theories* argue that genes, sex hormones, or anatomy determine sexual preference (see Burr, 1996, for a discussion of the biological research). Studies of gay men with twin brothers and lesbian women with twin sisters have reported that a significantly greater proportion of identical than fraternal twins were gay or lesbian (Bailey and Pillard, 1991; Bailey et al., 1993). LeVay (1993) found that the hypothalamus, an organ deep in the center of the brain that is believed to regulate the sex drive, differed in size between heterosexual and homosexual men. In another study, scientists took blood samples from 40 pairs of gay brothers and searched the family genes that might pass on sexual orientation. While 33 pairs of the brothers had in common a particular region of the X chromosome (a "marker"), which presumably revealed a "gay gene," 7 pairs of brothers did not possess the marker (Hamer et al., 1993). Most recently, Rice and his colleagues (1999) replicated Hamer's study, focusing on the same region of the X chromosome. Their investigation, based on a larger sample of 52 gay men and their brothers, found no evidence of a genetic influence on homosexuality. The researchers suggested that the genes governing sexual orientation may or may not exist elsewhere on the human genome.

Social constructionist theories hold that sexual orientation is largely the result of social and environmental factors. According to this theory, culture plays a large role in encouraging or discouraging heterosexual or homosexual behavior. In a study of adults who had been raised in lesbian families, Golombok and Tasker (1996) found—and consistent with several previous studies (see, for example, Bailey et al., 1995)—no evidence that parents have a significant impact on their children's sexual orientation. The majority of the children identified themselves as heterosexual. The parents' greater acceptance of lesbian and gay relationships enabled some of their children to pursue same-sex relationships without feeling guilt or shame, however. Environmental factors such as parental openness about sexual orientation might facilitate the development of either homosexual or heterosexual identities but doesn't *cause* them.

So far, none of the studies has shown conclusively that there is a "gay gene" or that the environment determines sexual orientation. At this point many researchers speculate that a combination of genetic and cultural factors probably shapes our sexual orientation.

The Politics of Sexual Orientation Research   While researchers are interested in determining the roots of sexual orientation for scientific reasons, many gay men and lesbians have mixed feelings about the studies. On the one hand, establishing that sexual orientation is genetic would disprove those who say that homosexuality is perverse and who instruct gays to seek counseling for a "cure" (see Socarides, 1995). Like eye or skin color, sexual orientation would be accepted as an innate characteristic. This would challenge denying gay men positions as teachers, for example, for fear that they would "recruit" heterosexual children. It would also rid parents of guilt feelings that, somehow, they were responsible for their children's gay sexual orientation.

On the other hand, some lesbians and gay men fear that genetic proof of a person's homosexuality could lead to new forms of discrimination. Insurers, for example, might refuse health coverage to someone who is tested as gay because he might be seen as a high risk for contracting AIDS. Others are concerned that antigay groups would seek eugenic solutions during prenatal screening: "One can imagine a pregnant mother and father being told, 'Your baby is going to be queer. Do you want it?'" (Watson et al., 1996: 96).

Like their heterosexual counterparts, most gay and lesbian parents are proud of their children and offer loving homes. In this Gay Pride Parade in New York City, fathers demonstrate their committed role as parents and affirm their identity as homosexuals.

Sexual Orientation and Gender Many researchers assert that gender is a more powerful distinguishing factor among people than sexual orientation is—that is, there are more similarities between straight and gay men than between lesbians and gays. First, lesbians and heterosexual women usually have monogamous relationships; gays and heterosexual men are more likely to have more than one lover at a time. A second difference is that for lesbians and heterosexual women, love and sex usually go hand in hand; many gays and heterosexual men often separate emotional intimacy and sex. Third, lesbians and heterosexual women are much less likely to be aroused by visual stimuli than are gays and heterosexual men. The size of the pornography market, which caters largely to men, suggests that many gay and heterosexual men see sex as a commodity. Fourth, both lesbians and heterosexual women are considerably less interested in sex with strangers (or in public places) than are many gays and heterosexual men. Both groups of men cruise for sexual partners; most women don't. Fifth, whereas many gays and heterosexual men want as much sexual variety as possible, most women seek long-term partners and less exotic experimentation. Finally, it is heterosexual and homosexual men who are the mainstay of such industries as prostitution, pornography, topless or gay bars, escort services, and adult bookstores (Brehm, 1985; Goode, 1990).

A study of bisexuals in San Francisco found clear gender differences in the nature of the sexual experience as well as the nature of relationships and the choices people make within their relationships. Both women and men said that in sexual acts women were more affectionate, personal, tender, caring, nurturing, comforting, and loving. As one woman noted, "Women care about satisfying you sexually and emotionally." The clearest male–female difference in a relationship was the ability to express emotions. Both women and men thought it was more difficult for men to reveal their feelings. Finally, the researchers found that the choices both women and men made often reflected institutionalized gender scripts rather than behavior that seemed unique to bisexuality. Men preferred attractive partners rather than unattractive ones, for example. Both men and women turned to women when they wanted an emotional involvement and to men when they sought "intellectual sharing" (Weinberg et al., 1994).

Don't be misled into thinking that such analyses are "male bashing." These researchers are simply pointing out that gender roles may be considerably more important than sexual orientation in shaping our sexual behavior and sexual scripts.

Sexuality and Sexual Scripts

In the late 1940s, social norms emphasized that love, sex, and marriage were deeply intertwined. By the early 1960s, however, the so-called sexual revolution questioned such assumptions. Greater openness about sexuality made sex less shameful and mysterious. Reproductive sex was replaced by a growing acceptance of recreational sex largely because the birth-control pill ("the Pill") meant that, for women, sex and childbearing could be separated. Finally, the sanctions against premarital sex were greatly reduced. By the mid-1970s, the fear of pregnancy, the concepts of sin and guilt, and the value of virginity had changed considerably, especially for teenagers (Bell and Coughey, 1980).

The sexual revolution encouraged more open communication about sex. There were also costs, however, especially for women. Women "were pressured more than ever [by men] to be sexually liberated . . . and then were accused of being uptight and puritanical if [they] didn't want sex" (Elshtain, 1988: 41). Women became more vulnerable because greater sexual freedom was not accompanied by greater economic equality. As women became "free sexual agents," men were released from responsibility in marriage or parenthood (Ehrenreich et al., 1986; Crittenden, 1999).

Although we like to think that our sexual behavior is spontaneous, even our erotic feelings are conditioned by the society we live in. Sexual activity occurs within the framework of sexual scripts that tell people how to behave and think in particular situations. A **sexual script** specifies the formal or informal norms for legitimate or unacceptable sexual activity, the eligibility of sexual partners, and the boundaries of sexual behavior in terms of time and place. For example, U.S. culture prohibits sexual intercourse with children, discourages relationships with same-sex partners, and frowns upon sexual activities in public places. As you will see in Chapter 7, these expectations also shape dating and mate-selection processes.

Traditional Sexual Scripts Men and women have different sexual scripts. In traditional sexual scripts, men were expected to take the initiative in sexual encounters, and women were expected to give pleasure. Men were supposed to be assertive, confident, and aggressive while women were expected to be accommodating and receptive. Sex was for orgasm, not intimacy, and the man was always in charge, always ready for sex, and always able to have an erection. Any physical contact was a sign for sex, especially intercourse.

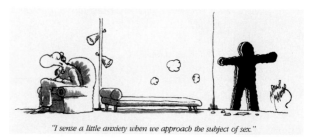

"I sense a little anxiety when we approach the subject of sex."

Scott Arthur Masear.

By dressing to "look sexy" and frequenting many nightclubs, women often feel that men will be drawn to them as future dates. Many men assume, however, that such dress and behavior are "cues" for sexual intercourse.

And, for men, the more often the orgasms, the better the sex. In contrast, women were expected to be compliant and responsive and to make the man happy. Engaging in sex without being in love was wrong. Sex was for men, love was for women, and women must be romanced to get them into bed (see Chapter 5).

Contemporary Sexual Scripts
Despite the sexual revolution, modern and traditional scripts are not very different. For example, a girl may wear tight jeans because they are in style, but a boy may think she is trying to be seductive. A girl may go to a boy's house just to talk, but the boy may assume she is consenting to sex.

Some authors feel that male scripts still reflect dominance rather than intimacy with female sex partners. According to Brooks (1995), the "centerfold syndrome" represents "one of the most malignant forces in contemporary relationships between men and women" because it objectifies women:

> *Women become objects as men become objectifiers. As the culture has granted men the right and privilege of looking at women, women have been expected to accept the role of stimulators of men's visual interest, with their bodies becoming objects that can be lined up, compared, and rated. Objective physical aspects are critical: size, shape, and harmony of body parts are more important than a woman's human qualities. . . . Men talk of their attraction to women in dehumanizing terms based on the body part of their obsession—"I'm a leg man," or "I'm an ass man." (pp. 3–4)*

Brooks notes that one of the most harmful effects of such idealization and objectification is that real

women are bound to seem less appealing, and even ugly, compared to airbrushed, eternally youthful models: "Stretch marks, varicose veins, sagging breasts, and cellulite-marked legs, common phenomena for real female bodies, may be viewed as repugnant by men who see women as [sex] objects" (p. 5). Women, too, can suffer from this syndrome. Plastic surgery and eating disorders are two ways that women—especially white, middle-class women—surrender to and reinforce the notion that aging and being natural are offensive.

Not all men fixate on female body parts or objectify women, of course. Some men admit that they are searching for emotional intimacy and not just sex. When there are sexual problems, men are increasingly willing to seek help for the difficulties (Osherson, 1992). Furthermore, some men encourage women to be more aggressive, and they follow women's directives about providing greater sexual pleasure.

The Double Standard Revisited
The double standard emerged during the nineteenth century and still shapes the behavior of many women and men (see Chapters 3, 4, and 5). Some believe that the sexual double standard—in which sexual intercourse outside marriage is acceptable for men but not women—is eroding but has not disappeared. In some families, especially Asian, Latino, and Middle East, because of "gendered notions of propriety," parents monitor their daughters' sexual behavior but allow sons considerable freedom (Toro-Morn, 1995; Leonard, 1997; Hojat et al., 1999; Posadas, 1999).

People are generally more tolerant of men who engage in casual sex than of women who do so. A number of college men, for example, think it's fine for them but not for women to have sex on a first date or in a casual relationship (Hatfield and Rapson, 1996). Even in committed relationships, such as love or engagement, women are expected to be more faithful than are men (Hyde, 1996).

One indicator of the double standard is the increasing rate of rape and other sexual assaults on women (see Chapter 7). After the annual Puerto Rican Day Parade in New York City a few years ago, a mob of men went on a rampage in Central Park. Yelling "Get the bitches," the men chased and attacked at least 50 women, yanking off the women's shirts, squeezing their breasts, ripping their shorts, groping them, and using "digital penetration." When some of the panicked victims reported the attacks, the police officers in Central Park ignored the complaints. One policeman, for example, said he didn't have a radio to ask for help (Campo-Flores and Rosenberg, 2000). Critics saw the police inaction as an example of a double standard. In this case and others, much sexual violence is still dismissed as masculine misbehavior rather than as a criminal assault (Quindlen, 2000).

In June, 2000, at least 47 women reported that they were raped, their breasts grabbed, and their clothes ripped off by male participants in the National Puerto Rican Day Parade in New York City. As this book goes to press, only three of the attackers had been arrested.

Viagra, the male impotence pill, got front-page coverage when it came on the market in 1998. Insurance companies immediately covered the costs of Viagra, about $10 per pill, but still do not pay for female contraceptions, such as birth-control pills, which typically cost $20 to $30 per month. The American College of Obstetricians and Gynecologists accused insurance companies of promoting a discriminatory double standard. While aging men "have an inalienable, and insurable, right to their sexual health" to get erections, "women have an enduring responsibility to take care of these things alone. And quietly, please" (Cocco, 1998). Nationwide, more women (43 percent) than men (31 percent) suffer from sexual difficulties that include an inability to achieve orgasm or experiencing pain during sexual intercourse (Laumann et al., 1999). Nonetheless, much pharmacological research focuses on erectile dysfunctions.

Finally, the double standard is not limited to the Western world. Many observers believe that female circumcision, still practiced extensively in Africa, Southeast Asia, and the Middle East, reflects a double standard that allows men to mutilate women under the guise of making them more marriageable. Men have no comparable restrictions. With increased emigration from Africa and the Middle East, female genital mutilation is now also practiced in the United States (Kaplan et al., 1993).

Female circumcision generally involves extensive damage to the sexual organs and causes lasting health problems for women. In 1979, the World Health

Organization denounced female circumcision as indefensible on medical and humane grounds. The Kenyan government banned female mutilation in 1990, but the procedure is still widely performed in Kenya and many other countries. As the box "Tradition or Torture? Female Genital Mutilation" shows, millions of girls are still subjected to these procedures.

Why We Have Sexual Relations

Sex, especially the first experience of intercourse, doesn't "just happen." It is usually not spontaneous but progresses through such stages as approaching each other, flirting, touching, or asking directly for sex. Though usually a passionate act, sex for the first time in a particular relationship typically occurs after some planning and thought (Sprecher and McKinney, 1993).

People have different reasons in deciding to have sex the first time. For some, it is an expression of affection and a means of communication. Others experience physical arousal or receptivity to sexual advances. One partner may feel an obligation to have intercourse for fear of hurting the other's feelings or losing the other's interest. Partners may also be pressured to have sex by peers who already engage in intercourse. Curiosity is another reason. Inexperienced partners may be curious about sex itself; some people may be interested in how it would be to make love to a particular person. Finally, the reason may be circumstantial: People may take advantage of someone who loses control after consuming alcohol or other drugs, for example (Christopher and Cate, 1984).

Once people have committed to a relationship, they may have a number of reasons to continue having sexual relations. Reviewing some of the literature on sex in close relationships, Sprecher and McKinney (1993) concluded that sex serves many functions (see *Figure 6.1*). Sex can be an expression of *love* and *affection*. It can increase *intimacy*, a feeling of closeness that is emotional (allowing the expression of feelings), social (encouraging the sharing of friends), intellectual (promoting the sharing of ideas), and recreational (leading to a sharing of interests and hobbies). Sex can encourage *self-disclosure*: Learning how to tell a partner what feels good in sexual activity can promote *disclosure* in other ways (see Chapter 5). Sex also fosters interdependence because the partners depend on each other for sexual satisfaction. Most importantly, of course, many people have sex because they want children.

Once a close bond develops, sexual and other physical expressions of intimacy are important in *maintaining the relationship,* although there are many other ways (and perhaps even more important ones) such as communicating with one another, respecting each other, and making sacrifices for a partner. Finally, both love and sex provide an *exchange of resources* in an intimate relationship (see the discussion of social exchange theory in Chapter 2). Such an exchange may

CROSS CULTURAL

Tradition or Torture? Female Genital Mutilation

Over 94 percent of women in some African countries (such as Mali and Eritrea) and Egypt have experienced female genital mutilation (Chalkley, 1997). In 1997, an Egyptian court overturned a government ban on female genital mutilation in order to "preserve virginity until marriage" (Cooperman, 1997).

Several types of female circumcision are practiced in Africa and the Middle East. The two most common, which remove all or parts of the female's external genitalia, or vulva (see Appendix A), are excision and infibulation. In *excision,* part or all of the clitoris is removed in a procedure called a clitoridectomy, and part or all of the labia minora is removed as well. This operation often results in scar tissue that blocks the vaginal opening. *Infibulation* combines removal of the clitoris and labia minora with excision of the inner layers of the labia majora. The raw edges of these inner layers are then sewn together with cat gut or acacia thorn. Three or four of these thorns pierce what remains of the vaginal lips, holding them together. A sliver of wood or straw is inserted into the tiny opening that remains, allowing for the slow, and often painful, passage of urine and the menstrual flow. When the female marries, her husband manually and with his penis enlarges the opening for intercourse, and the opening must be further enlarged for childbirth. In many cases, the opening is then closed in another excision or infibulation, and the cycle begins again.

The age at which the mutilations are carried out varies from area to area. Among the Jewish Falashas in Ethiopia

and the nomads of the Sudan, the girl may be only a few days old; in Egypt and many countries of central Africa, she may be anywhere from 3 to 9 years old. The younger the girl, the less likely she is to know what's going to happen to her and, therefore, the less likely she is to resist. The circumcision usually involves immobilizing the little girl by tying her arms behind her back and the women participants (sometimes including her mother) holding the child's thighs apart. The "operator," an old village woman, cuts off the clitoris and then scrapes the flesh from the labia lips even though "the little girl howls and writhes in pain." The procedure lasts from 15 to 20 minutes, depending on the ability of the woman performing the circumcision and the resistance of the child.

Female mutilation is still carried out at all levels of society—from members of the elite and professional classes to the simplest villagers. In rural areas, the instruments include razor blades, scissors, kitchen knives, or pieces of glass. Antiseptic techniques and anesthesia are generally unknown.

A number of immediate and long-term complications are associated with female circumcision: The girl can hemorrhage and die; the bad eyesight of the operator or the resistance of the child can cause cuts in other organs (such as the urethra or bladder); a rupture of the internal division between the vagina and the bladder or the vagina and the rectum may cause a continual dribbling of urine or feces for the rest of the woman's life; women feel severe pain during intercourse; women sometimes become sterile due to infections that ascend into

the reproductive organs; their husbands may use razors, knives, or other instruments to enable them to penetrate the vagina; and during childbirth, even if the opening is made wider for the baby's birth, the woman may experience perineal tears or may even die because the baby cannot push through the mutilated vulva.

In cultures that practice female circumcision, it is generally believed that women are highly sexual and by nature promiscuous. Circumcision curbs their wild sexual desires and a constricted vagina ensures virginity. Because of social pressure, even mothers who disapprove of their daughters' circumcision participate in the practice because if they refuse, their daughter(s) would be ostracized, remain unmarried, and consequently become financially destitute. Thus, disabling women makes them more marriageable, more dependent on their husbands for economic survival, and, consequently, available for any sexual, emotional, or domestic demands made upon them. As a reward, the young girls who undergo circumcision receive special clothes and good food associated with the event and often feel proud of being like everyone else (Herbert, 1989; Lightfoot-Klein, 1989; Dorkenoo and Elworthy, 1992; Kaplan et al., 1993; Kamara, 1998).

Female genital mutilation seems barbaric to most Americans. But what about comparable practices in the United States and other Western countries? Even though they are voluntary, are silicone breast implants, collagen injections, and liposuction any more "civilized" in making women's bodies more acceptable to men?

be sincere; for example, a shy person may like a partner who is assertive during lovemaking. In other cases, however, an exchange may be manipulative; for example, a sexually desirable person may use sex as a weapon or a tool for acquiring power, status, or money (Flores, 1994).

Besides these sociological and psychological reasons for having sex, biologists maintain that there is an essential evolutionary connection between sexual pleasure and reproduction. As anthropologist Meredith Small (1995) notes, for example, sexual pleasure is a physical reaction that evolved over millions of years to make the

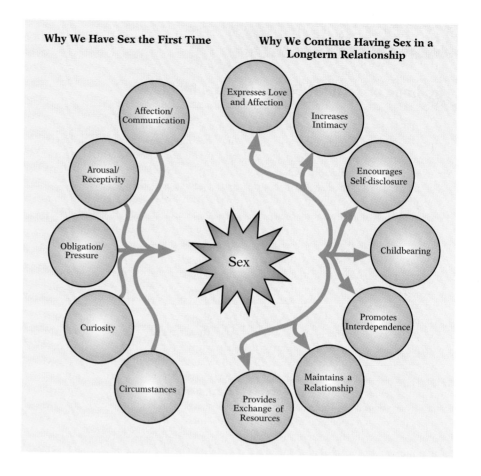

FIGURE 6.1   Why We Have Sex.

genitals sensitive and the body able to experience orgasm. Without pleasure, we wouldn't be driven to have sex. And without sex, procreation could plummet.

How We Learn about Sex

John Barrymore, the noted American actor, once said: "The thing that takes up the least amount of time and causes the most amount of trouble is sex." If sex causes a lot of trouble, it is probably because most of us know very little about it. In a national survey, the Kinsey Institute found that 55 percent of U.S. adults failed a sex knowledge test (similar to the one in the box titled "How Much Do You Know about Sex?" based on Reinisch and Beasley, 1990).

What we see as normal sexual behavior is neither "natural" nor "instinctive" but is learned in a societal context. In at least eight known societies, for example, kissing is seen as repulsive:

When the Thonga first saw Europeans kissing they laughed. . . . "Look at them—they eat each other's saliva and dirt." The Siriono never kiss, although they have no regulation against such

behavior. The Tinguian, instead of kissing, place the lips near the partner's face and suddenly inhale. (Ford and Beach, 1972: 49)

We become sexual over time. In the *normative* stage, children learn gender roles and related values and norms about both appropriate and inappropriate sexual expression. Parents (or other caretakers) and popular culture have considerable control over the types of influences to which the child is exposed. In the *informational* stage, in early adolescence, young people learn about sexual anatomy and physiology primarily from peers, but also from sex education programs in schools. In the *behavioral* stage, in late adolescence and young adulthood, people engage in sexual activity and learn the behavioral aspects of sexuality from a partner (DeLamater and McCorquodale, 1979; Turner and Rubinson, 1993).

From Parents

Parents can be very influential in how children think and feel about sexuality. As you saw earlier, parents affect our sexual scripts by what they say (or don't

ASK YOURSELF ?

Ask Yourself: How Much Do You Know about Sex?

After reading each question, circle one answer.

1. What do you think is the age at which the average, or typical, American first has sexual intercourse?
   - a. 11 or younger
   - b. 12–13
   - c. 14–15
   - d. 16–17
   - e. 18–19
   - f. 20
   - g. 21 or older

2. Out of every ten married American men, how many would you estimate have ever had an extramarital affair—that is, have been sexually unfaithful to their wives?
   - a. Fewer than one out of ten
   - b. One out of ten (10%)
   - c. About two out of ten (20%)
   - d. About three out of ten (30%)
   - e. About four out of ten (40%)
   - f. About five out of ten (50%)
   - g. About six out of ten (60%)
   - h. More than six out of ten

3. A person can get AIDS by having anal (rectal) intercourse even if neither partner is infected with the AIDS virus.
   ❑ True ❑ False

4. Petroleum jelly, Vaseline Intensive Care lotion, baby oil, and Nivea are good lubricants to use with a condom or diaphragm. ❑ True ❑ False

5. About 10 percent of the U.S. population is exclusively homosexual. ❑ True ❑ False

6. A woman or teenage girl can get pregnant during her menstrual flow (her period). ❑ True ❑ False

7. A woman or teenage girl cannot get pregnant if the man withdraws his penis before he ejaculates. ❑ True ❑ False

8. Unless she is having sex, a woman does not need to have regular gynecological examinations. ❑ True ❑ False

9. Which of the following STDs do experts call "the silent epidemic"?
   - a. scabies
   - b. genital herpes
   - c. syphilis
   - d. chlamydia

10. Menopause, or change of life, causes most women to lose interest in having sex. ❑ True ❑ False

11. What do you think is the length of the average man's erect penis?
    - a. 2–4 inches
    - b. 5–7 inches
    - c. 8–9 inches
    - d. 10–11 inches
    - e. 12 inches or longer

12. Which of the following groups is at greatest risk for STDs?
    - a. men under 25
    - b. women under 25
    - c. men 25–40
    - d. women 25–40

(Answers are on page 140.)

say) about sex. Ideally, parents (or guardians) should be the first and best sex educators because they are experienced and have children's interests at heart. In reality, this is rarely the case.

Most children get very little information about sex from their parents. Many parents feel uncomfortable talking about sex because they themselves may have little knowledge about sexuality. Sex education pro-

•••

Answers to "How Much Do You Know about Sex?"

Scoring the test: Each question is worth 1 point. Score each item and add up your total number of points.

Correct answers: 1. d, 2. c, 3. false, 4. false, 5. false, 6. true, 7. false, 8. false, 9. d, 10. false, 11. b, 12. b

A score of 11 or 12 is an "A"; 9 or 10 a "B"; 8 a "C"; 7 a "D"; and fewer than 7 points an "F."

•••

grams were unavailable when they were youngsters, and sexuality was deemed an inappropriate topic of discussion in the home (Brock and Jennings, 1993; Kyman, 1995).

One study of 700 males and females ranging in age from 9 to 73 years found that parents were *never* reported as the primary source of sexuality instruction. In fact, those age 19 and older said that siblings were typically twice as likely as parents to provide information on such topics as reproductive anatomy (Ansuini et al., 1996). A national study of adolescents aged 14 to 16 by Clea Sucoff and her associates found that 39 percent of the boys and 28 percent of the girls said that their mothers discussed sex "not at all" or "somewhat." In addition, 64 percent of the males and 77 percent of the females had never recommended a specific form of birth control (cited in "Moms . . . ," 1999; see also Hutchinson and Cooney, 1998).

Many parents seem to overestimate the role they actually play in their children's sex education. Tucker (1989) found that although mothers said that they were their daughters' primary source of information about the menstrual cycle, intercourse, and contraception, most of the daughters felt that their mothers gave little information on such topics as male and female anatomy and the availability or correct use of contraceptives. In a study of 110 adolescent Latinas, similarly, the mothers reported higher rates of mother–daughter communication about sexuality issues than did their daughters (O'Sullivan et al., 1999).

Many adolescents think their parents are old-fashioned and often lapse into "adultspeak": telling them what to do without discussing the implications of various behaviors, such as the long-term responsibilities involved in raising a child (Fullilove et al., 1994). Teenagers may be reluctant to discuss sex with their parents because they don't want to disappoint, hurt, or shock them. Many teenagers feel that parents see them in an unrealistically innocent light, and they do not want to tarnish this idealized image:

> *16-year-old girl: "They have so much faith and trust in me. It would just kill them if they found out I had made love before. There's a lot of pressure on me to be good since I'm the most successful of my brothers and sisters. They feel I'm a reflection of all their efforts and their ideal child." (Hass, 1979: 168)*

Even though the Hass research was published almost two decades ago, the reasons for not talking to parents about sex are similar today. Sometimes, for example, parents want to "protect" their children from sex-related information. A parent of a 4-year-old daughter stated: "I want the innocence to last as long as I can. Just be a kid and have fun and don't think about this kind of stuff." Parents may be protecting themselves from their own discomfort rather than the child in not discussing sex-related topics. Both mothers and fathers were also uneasy in responding to what they viewed as gender-inappropriate sexual behavior. A mother said:

> *My son did that [played with his penis]. It was alright. I didn't have any problem with it. If he didn't want to let go, I'd just put him down on the floor without his diaper. But my daughter, I felt uncomfortable with her doing that, I just really had to walk away from the situation because for some reason I was very uncomfortable with her exploring herself. (Geeasler et al., 1995: 187)*

Many youth have little accurate information about reproductive anatomy and functioning or about contraception (contraceptive methods are discussed in Appendix D). A health educator who visits eighth-graders says that, although some of the children are sexually active, most don't know what sexually transmitted diseases are, how they can be prevented, when a girl can get pregnant, or how birth control works. One teen asked: "Can masturbation kill you?" (Reimer, 1999). A number of college students also have information gaps about sex. Some believe, for example, that a woman cannot get pregnant if the man drinks alcohol before intercourse because the sperm become "drunk" and cannot swim straight. Others assume that they are safe from contracting AIDS if they are in monogamous relationships (Henken and Whatley, 1995). In fact, monogamy is only safe during unprotected intercourse if the partner is not infected. Being monogamous with an infected partner can be fatal.

Communication between parents and children may not always postpone the first sexual experience. Several studies suggest, however, that such discussions, as well as parental supervision of teenagers' activities, often result in safer sexual behaviors (such as using condoms) and fewer sexual partners across all racial and ethnic groups (see Miller et al., 1999; Schreck, 1999; Lehr et al., 2000; Whitaker et al., 2000).

Besides not talking with children about sex, sex educators contend, many parents are poor role models. They themselves may "sleep around," initiate sexual intercourse with young teens, have out-of-wedlock births, condone sleepovers that they suspect include sexual activity, and oversexualize 5- to 6-year-old girls by encouraging them to wear makeup and adultlike clothes (Haffner, 1999; Saltzman, 1999).

From Peers

Peers are the most common sources of knowledge about sex. Because peers typically are misinformed about sex, however, the instruction is similar to the blind leading the blind. In a study of Flemish senior high school and college students, Buysse (1996) found that many males and females knew little about such topics as the proper use of condoms, women's fertile periods, and contraceptives. The students were disinterested in obtaining more information, however, because they assumed that their peers had given them all the facts.

Peers can provide positive socialization, however. For example, often they are more open about discussing sexuality issues, offer support when a friend feels insecure about visible signs of maturing (such as the growth of breasts or facial hair), and encourage friends to seek information about birth control if parents are unwilling to talk about contraception (Gecas and Seff, 1991).

From Popular Culture

Because parents rarely talk about sex, young people often get their information from the popular culture. Television, movies, music, magazines, romance novels, and sometimes pornographic materials have become powerful sources of information—or misinformation—about sex.

Movies Examining 17 films aimed at adolescents during the 1990s (such as *Cooley High, Risky Business, Weird Science,* and *Bill and Ted's Bogus Journey*), Whatley concluded that almost all deemphasized the dangers of unprotected sexual intercourse: "Pregnancy is rarely a fear; contraceptives are almost never mentioned; and disease transmission, even in the age of AIDS, is nearly absent as a concern" (1994: 191). Because rating systems are not strictly enforced (few moviegoers are stopped from seeing R-rated films, for example) and videos are accessible to most age groups, it is not unusual for adolescents or even younger children to get much of their sex information from movies.

Television Television also has a significant impact on our attitudes about sex. Young children and teenagers spend much of their time in front of television sets (see Chapter 4). What images do they get of sex and intimate relationships?

Ward (1995) examined the content of the 12 most popular prime-time television programs during the mid-1990s starring children aged 2 to 11 (such as *Full House, The Simpsons,* and *Family Matters*) and adolescents aged 12 to 17 (such as *Fresh Prince of Bel Air, Roseanne, Beverly Hills 90210,* and *Home Improvement*). She found sexual content in more than one of every four interactions, and nearly 50 percent of the interactions between characters contained statements related to sexuality in some of the programs. Ward points out that such an exceptionally high content "paints a false impression of the degree to which sexuality is discussed in everyday life" (p. 610). She notes that frank discussions of sex on television may be healthy but that the content of these discussions is still traditional and sex-stereotypical. For example, many television shows stress the importance of physical appearance for women and of "scoring" for men, portray sex as an exciting competition involving deceit and manipulation, and suggest that the purpose of sex is almost exclusively recreational rather than procreative.

Most recently, researchers examined a composite week of 1,351 shows—excluding news and sports shows—aired on ten broadcast and cable channels between October 1997 and March 1998, measuring six categories of sexual behavior, from flirting to depictions of intercourse. More than two-thirds (67 percent) of all network prime-time shows contained sexual content and averaged more than five sex scenes per hour. Of all shows with sexual content, just 9 percent—including *Chicago Hope, Felicity,* and *Party of Five*—mentioned the possible risks or responsibilities of sexual activity or contraception, protection, or safe sex (Kunkel et al., 1999).

Besides gaining few insights about sexuality from regular programming, the average U.S. teenager views almost 15,000 sexual jokes, innuendoes, and other references on TV each year. Fewer than 170 of these references deal with responsible sexual behavior such as self-control, birth control, abstinence, the risk of sexually transmitted diseases (STDs), pregnancy, and HIV. In addition, the typical teenager watches 20,000 commercials per year with implicit messages that sex is fun, sex is sexy, and everyone out there is constantly "doing it" (Strasburger, 1997).

From Sex Education

Because most parents do *not* teach their children about sex, and popular culture deluges viewers with unrealistic portrayals of sexuality, many schools and community organizations have assumed the responsibility of teaching children and adolescents about human

At King Junior High School in Berkeley, California, the 9th-grade "social living" class includes instruction in sexual anatomy. Do you think teachers should provide this information? Or should parents be responsible for educating their children about sexuality?

sexuality. About 90 percent of U.S. adults approve of schools giving sex education, an increase from the 65 percent who favored it in 1970 (Squires, 1995). Despite such general approval, a very vocal minority of parents, headed primarily by conservative religious groups, has opposed sex education in the schools. These groups argue that sex should be taught only in the home and that sex education in the schools will put ideas into young children's heads and increase promiscuity. As a result, some counties refuse to fund any program in the schools that counsels unmarried people about contraceptives. In 1997, the federal government funded $50 million for abstinence-only sex education programs, even though participation in such programs doesn't decrease pregnancy rates (Haffner, 1997). "Just say no" approaches probably don't work because many teens are already sexually active and because such promises are easily broken.

Which sex education programs are the most effective? Probably those that endorse more than one approach in communicating with young people. In a review of numerous school-based programs, Kirby and associates (1994) found that the most effective curricula had six common characteristics. First, they taught youth how to resist peer pressure to engage in sex. Second, they focused on specific issues such as delaying the initiation of intercourse or using protection. Third, through experiential activities they conveyed information on the risks of unprotected sex and how to avoid those risks. The most successful programs were active and personalized: Students participated in small group

discussions, games or simulations, role playing, and brainstorming, and in real-world exercises such as locating contraceptives in local drugstores and visiting family planning clinics. Fourth, effective programs included activities that addressed the problem of social and media pressure to have sex (such as the use of sex in advertising to sell products or the "lines" that people typically use to persuade someone to have sex). Fifth, they reinforced age- and experience-appropriate individual values and group norms against unprotected sex. For example, instruction about postponing sexual intercourse was aimed at middle school–age students; information about how to use condoms was directed at older students. Finally, through role playing and other techniques, the best programs developed skills in communication, negotiation, and refusal to bow to pressure. The most influential sex education programs train adolescents to serve as peer counselors. They also discuss sexual feelings and behavior as a normal part of human development rather than focusing narrowly only on danger and disease (Ehrhardt, 1996; Rust, 2000).

Sexual Behaviors

Most of us have fairly conventional sex lives according to a national survey of 3,432 U.S. adults aged 18 to 59 (cited hereafter as the "Sex Survey"). A large percentage of people had one or no sex partners over the year of the study, more than 85 percent said they were happy with their sexual relationships, and the median number of partners the respondents had had since age 18 was relatively "average" (see *Figure 6.2*). It's important to keep in mind, too, that sex is not just sexual intercourse; the expression of sexuality encompasses many other behaviors—including sexual fantasies, masturbation, petting, and oral sex.

Sexual Fantasies

Most of us, regardless of our age or marital status, have sexual fantasies. We fantasize differently, though, depending on whether we're male or female. Males' and females' different sexual scripts lead young girls, for example, to have elaborate fantasies that often focus more on activities leading up to intercourse, whereas boys tend to envision very specific sexual acts (Hass, 1979). Gender differences in sexual fantasies often mirror differences in gender roles. Women's fantasies are typically more romantic, passive, and submissive than are men's. Even when women fantasize about "unusual" sex practices, they are less likely to act them out. For example, in a survey of 2,000 adults, twice as many men as women said that they had actually realized such fantasies as incest, sex with defecation, sadomasochism, or sex with an animal (Patterson and Kim, 1991).

A. Number of Sexual Partners during Preceding Year

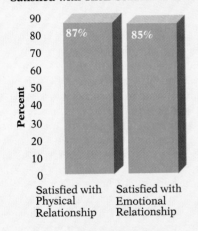

One
71%

Two-four
14%

None
12%

5 or more
3%

B. People Who Said They Were "Extremely" or " Very" Satisfied with Their Sexual Partners

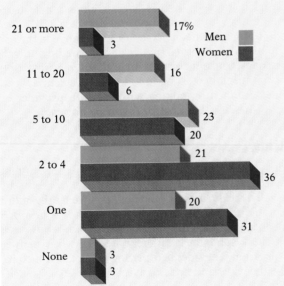

C. Number of Sexual Partners since Age 18

FIGURE 6.2 **Sex Survey Findings: Sex is Largely Monogamous and Very Satisfying.** These findings from the 1994 nationwide U.S. survey of sexual behavior surprised some observers. Nearly three-quarters of respondents said they had had only one sexual partner in the preceding year (A); more than 85 percent said they were both physically and emotionally satisfied with their partners (B); and two-thirds of men had had no more than 10 partners since the age of 18 (the comparable figure for women was 90 percent) (Based on Laumann et al., 1994: 177–180; 369).

Most scientists who study sexual behavior maintain that sexual fantasies are emotionally and psychologically healthy. Fantasies can provide a safety valve for pent-up feelings or a harmless escape from boring, everyday routines: "To be covered in whipped cream and wrestle my lover, then the loser has to lick it off," or "Having sex on the 50-yard line at a sold-out football game" (Patterson and Kim, 1991: 79). Fantasies can also boost our self-image because we need not worry about penis size, breast size, or weight. Because we have total control in producing and directing the fantasy, we can change or stop it anytime we want. In some cases, fantasies are mental rehearsals for future sexual experiences (Masters et al., 1992).

Masturbation

In his film *Annie Hall,* Woody Allen described masturbation as "having sex with someone I love." When asked about sex in the future, Robin Williams responded: "It's going to be you—and you." **Masturbation** refers to sexual self-pleasuring that involves some form of direct physical stimulation. It may or may not result in orgasm. Masturbation typically involves rubbing, stroking, fondling, squeezing, or otherwise stimulating the genitals, but it can also be self-stimulation of other body parts, such as the breasts, the inner thighs, or the anus.

Early in the twentieth century masturbation was branded as a source of damage to the brain and nervous system. It was believed to cause a variety of problems, such as bad breath, blindness, deafness, acne, and heart murmurs. In 1918, for example, one woman wrote that masturbation had "worn out [her] sexual organs . . . before they were put to their proper use." Some physicians treated masturbation with recommendations for prayer or exercise. Others went much farther:

"Treatment" for boys included piercing the foreskin of the penis with wire, applying leeches to the base of the penis, or cutting the foreskin with a jagged scissors. "Treatment" for girls included

Reprinted with special permission of King Features Syndicate.

applying a hot iron to the thighs or clitoris or removing the clitoris in an operation called a clitoridectomy. Adults could buy various commercial devices, such as metal mittens, an alarm that went off when the bed moved, rings with metal teeth or spikes to wear on the penis at night, or guards worn against the female's vulva. Some of these horrors were so popular that they were advertised in the Sears-Roebuck catalog. (Wade and Cirese, 1991: 46)

Masturbation often begins in childhood and occurs commonly throughout the life cycle. Prepubertal children may stimulate themselves without realizing that what they are doing is sexual. For example, one girl learned when she was 8 years old that she could produce an "absolutely terrific feeling" by squeezing her thighs together (Nass et al., 1981). Thus, many teenagers discover masturbation accidentally.

The Sex Survey found that more than a third of male respondents and over half of female respondents said they had never masturbated. The study also found large differences by race and ethnicity. Black men (60 percent) were twice as likely as whites, Latinos, and Asians to say they never masturbated. The differences among women who said they had never masturbated were less striking: 56 percent for white women, 68 percent for black women, and 66 percent for Latinas (Laumann et al., 1994). Masturbation rates among black men may be lower than among other ethnic groups of men because black men have traditionally viewed masturbation as an admission of an inability to seduce a woman (Belcastro, 1985).

Frequency of masturbation, like that of other sexual activities, declines with age. One-third of women and 43 percent of men in their 70s reported masturbating about three times a month (Brecher, 1984). Note, however, that these estimates may be low; many older adults are reluctant to discuss their sexual behaviors. Questions such as "How often do you

masturbate?" may be intimidating and even guilt-inducing to people now in their 60s and 70s who grew up when masturbation was surrounded by the myths we discussed earlier (Laumann et al., 1994).

In fact, masturbation fulfills several needs: It can relieve sexual tension, provide a safe means of sexual experimentation (avoiding disease and unwanted pregnancy), increase sexual self-confidence, and may ultimately transfer valuable learning to two-person lovemaking. Masturbation can be as sexually satisfying as intercourse, and it does not hinder the development of social relationships during young adulthood or create problems in a marriage (Leitenberg et al., 1993; Kelly, 1994). Although masturbation is not essential in people's sexual lives, it does not lead to mental illness, homosexuality, or a decrease in the production of semen. Each person must decide whether or not to masturbate based on her or his religion and values. Long-term guilt and worry about masturbation can cause negative feelings and low self-esteem. If such feelings are intense, talking with a health provider or other professional counselor might be advisable.

Petting

Petting, which includes touching, stroking, mutual masturbation, and fondling various parts of the body, especially the breasts and genitalia, is generally more acceptable than intercourse because it is less intimate and does not result in pregnancy. In the past, researchers sometimes differentiated between petting and necking. They defined petting as sexual touching below the waist and necking as any other sexual touching, including kissing. More recently some researchers are including oral sex in definitions of petting.

By the early 1950s (when, theoretically, at least, no one had sex until after marriage), 81 percent of boys and 84 percent of girls had had experience with petting by the age of 18. Approximately 23 percent of the men and 32 percent of the women between the ages of 16 and 20 had petted to orgasm (Kinsey et al., 1953). More recently, interviews with first-year college students about their high school sexual experiences showed that 40 percent of the women and 50 percent of the men reported having experienced orgasm during petting (Masters et al., 1986). By the age of 18, more than 75 percent of teenagers had engaged in heavy petting (Roper Starch Worldwide, 1994).

Oral Sex

Oral sex includes several types of stimulation. **Fellatio** (from the Latin word for "suck") refers to oral stimulation of a man's penis. **Cunnilingus** (from the Latin words for "vulva" and "tongue") refers to oral stimulation of a woman's genital organs. Fellatio and cunnilingus can be performed singly or simultaneously. Simultaneous oral sex is sometimes referred to as "69," indicating the physical positions of the partners.

Although many adolescent couples stop at petting, there may also be oral-genital contact either preceding intercourse or instead of it. One survey of 17- to 18-year-olds found that 41 percent of the women and 33 percent of the men had performed oral sex on a member of the opposite sex (Haffner, 1993). A national study of men between 20 and 39 years of age reported that almost 80 percent of those who were currently married had either performed or received oral sex (presumably with their spouses). The same study found substantial overall differences by race. Among white men, 79 percent had performed oral sex, compared with 73 percent among Latino men and 43 percent among black men (Billy et al., 1993). Belcastro (1985) suggests that the infrequent reporting of fellatio among black women is probably largely due to their perception of fellatio as an unclean and demeaning act. In contrast, white females often reported using fellatio as a method of birth control.

Some people find oral sex pleasurable or engage in it to please their partner. Others complain about the odors (although bathing solves the problem for both sexes), do not enjoy it, or find it revolting. When Wade and Cirese (1991: 334) asked their students what bothers them about oral sex, they got the following responses:

One woman wrote, "I can't swallow his semen! Choke! Choke!" Another wrote, "I always want to say "Well, would you like me to blow my nose in your mouth?' That's how I feel about it; I'm not trying to be rude."

Engaging in oral sex, as in many other sexual behaviors, depends on personal preference. Many people don't realize, however, that sexually transmitted diseases can be transmitted orally ("Primary HIV infection . . . ," 2000).

Sexual Intercourse

Most people understand sexual intercourse to mean heterosexual, vaginal-penile penetration, but the term actually refers to any sort of sexual coupling, including oral and anal. *Coitus* specifically means penile-vaginal intercourse, and unless noted otherwise, we will use sexual intercourse to refer to coitus.

Some adolescents begin to be sexually active in their early teens (see Data Digest). On average, however, the first heterosexual intercourse takes place between ages 16 and 17 among both men and women. By age 65, men report that they've had sex with an average of 15 women; women have had sex with an

FIGURE 6.3 **How Often Do I Love Thee? Frequency of Sexual Intercourse over the Life Course** (Adapted from Clements, 1994, 1996).

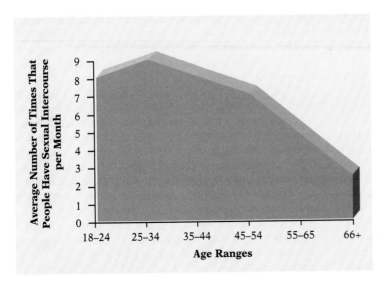

Average Number of Times That People Have Sexual Intercourse per Month

Age Ranges: 18–24, 25–34, 35–44, 45–54, 55–65, 66+

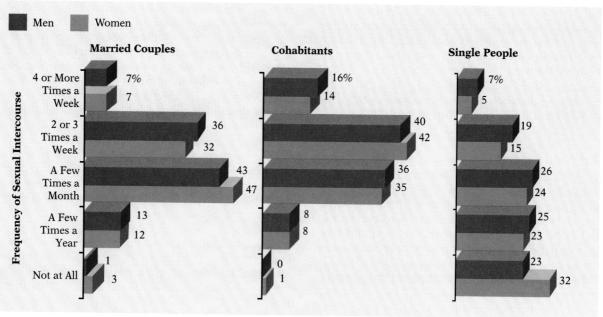

FIGURE 6.4 **Cohabitants and Married Couples Have More Fun Than Singles.** As the text points out, married couples and people who live together have sexual intercourse considerably more often than single people (Based on Laumann, et al., 1994:88–89).

average of 8 men (Clements, 1994). As *Figure 6.3* shows, average monthly sexual intercourse peaks between ages 25 and 34 and then declines over the years. This pattern suggests that, with time, people develop other interests besides sex that become high priorities in maintaining a family or a relationship.

Married couples and cohabitants have considerably higher rates of sexual intercourse than single persons do (see *Figure 6.4*). Such figures challenge popular perceptions of "swinging singles." Several studies also report that married people are happier with their sex lives than either single people or cohabitants (Billy et al., 1993; Clements, 1994; Laumann et al., 1994). These findings support the notion, discussed in Chapter 5, that sexual intercourse is more than just the sexual act—it also involves intimacy, commitment, and love.

Overall, African Americans have sex with a partner about as often as whites, although Latinos have slightly higher rates. About a third each of black and white women reported having sex with a partner a few times a year or not at all, however. Level of education does not affect the frequency with which women have sex with a partner, although the more education men have, the less likely they are to have had little or no sex. Similarly, Protestants, Catholics, and nonreligious people are very similar in the frequency with which they have sex (Billy et al., 1993; Laumann et al., 1994).

Why are people so similar in sexual experience? Michael et al. (1994) propose that it is our many myths about racial and religious groups that lead us to expect otherwise. In reality, there is nothing about being a member of a particular racial or religious group or being at a particular educational level that translates into more or less sexual desire or sexual opportunity. Having an easily accessible partner, such as in marriage or cohabitation, seems to have the largest impact on the frequency of sexual activity.

Sexual Response Fantasies, sounds, smells, touch, sexy pictures, dreams, hearing the person we love say "I love you," and a variety of other sources can arouse our sexual feelings. Our physiological reaction to sexual stimulation is sometimes called **sexual response.** Although our sexual responses can vary greatly by age, gender, and health, some scientists suggest that the sexual response cycle consists of desire, excitement, orgasm, and resolution (Masters et al., 1992; Kaplan, 1979).

Desire is a psychological phase that can lead to physical response. Sexual fantasies or other stimuli can lead to sexual arousal so that an individual is emotionally receptive to sexual intercourse. Because the brain sparks desire, there are cross-cultural variations in what people deem sexy or a turn-off. As noted earlier, kissing may be seen as repulsive in some cultures.

During the second, *excitement phase,* both men and women experience an increase in blood pressure, pulse rate, and breathing. In the male, the first responses to sexual stimulation are the swelling and erection of the penis and partial elevation of the testes. Female excitement results in vaginal lubrication, and clitoral swelling, and the nipples may become erect and hard. During this phase, the penis may emit several drops of fluid that are not semen but may contain sperm cells. If this fluid is discharged while the penis is in the vagina, a woman can be impregnated. Thus, withdrawal before ejaculation, commonly used as a means of contraception, is often totally ineffective in preventing conception.

Sexual tension reaches its peak, or *climax*, during orgasm and is suddenly discharged. This third stage of sexual response lasts only a few seconds. In the male, it is characterized by three or four major contractions of the entire length of the urethra and the spurting of semen during ejaculation. Women may feel contractions in the vagina, uterus, and rectum.

What many people don't realize is that ejaculation and orgasm are not the same phenomenon. They can be experienced independently of each other because they are affected by different neurological and vascular

systems. Because penile erections, ejaculations, and orgasms do *not* occur simultaneously, men who argue that a penile erection must be followed by ejaculation during sexual intercourse lest they suffer dire consequences are, quite simply, wrong. There is no scientific evidence that any man has ever died of a "terminal erection."

Do you believe that women and men experience orgasm differently? Read the box "How Do Orgasms Differ by Gender?" before continuing with this paragraph. Actually, the major difference between male and female orgasms is that women can have multiple orgasms within a very short space of time, whereas most men cannot. Although some men can become erect again almost immediately after ejaculation and orgasm, most need at least 20 minutes if not more to become erect again (Coote, 1991).

There are many individual variations in reaching orgasm. Some people may skip stages, experiencing

ASK YOURSELF

How Do Orgasms Differ by Gender?

Read each of the following descriptions of orgasm. Is the speaker a man or a woman?

	Man	Woman
1. For me, orgasm feels like a building wave of emotion. First I notice a pulsing sensation that is quite localized, then it spreads through my whole body. Afterwards, I feel tired but also superrelaxed.	❑	❑
2. My anxiety about sex definitely inhibits my orgasm. There are times when I feel some intense sensations, but usually I am too inhibited to really let myself go. If I am not very comfortable with my partner, it is very difficult to come. I have orgasms most easily when I masturbate.	❑	❑
3. Basically, I feel a glow which starts in my genitals and then spreads through my whole body. Sometimes one orgasm is enough, and other times it is not completely satisfying.	❑	❑
4. I think orgasm is overrated. I sometimes spend over an hour getting turned on, and then the orgasm takes only a few seconds. I'd like to learn how to make the feeling of orgasm last longer.	❑	❑
5. I concentrate all my attention on the sensations in the genitals [then] I completely lose contact with everything around me. My body feels incredibly alive and seems to vibrate. Afterwards, I just want to hold my lover and be very still.	❑	❑

Answers

All of the descriptions of orgasm are by men.

SOURCE: Based on Vance and Wagner, 1976: 87–98.

orgasm, for example, in the excitement stage. And women may experience different kinds of orgasms: clitoral, uterine (which is characterized by involuntary breath holding due to a contraction in the muscle at the back of the throat), and a combination of clitoral and uterine. Many women prefer or require clitoral stimulation to reach orgasm. Response patterns are the same regardless of the source of sexual stimulation. That is, an orgasm that comes from rubbing the clitoris can't be distinguished physiologically from one that results from breast stimulation alone or from intercourse. Many partners are fully satisfied with tender sexual activities that do not necessarily include orgasm.

After orgasm, in the *resolution phase,* the fourth and last stage of the sexual response cycle, the male's penis begins a rapid loss of swelling and erection. In the female, the clitoris returns to its normal position, followed by a slower reduction in the size and level of swelling. Breathing, heart rate, and blood pressure return to normal in both partners. Both partners may experience physical and mental relaxation and a sense of well-being.

Myths about Sexual Response   One of the biggest concerns expressed by men is that their penises are not big enough to stimulate women during intercourse (Reinisch and Beasley, 1990). There is no association between clitoris, breast, or penis size and orgasm. Similarly, there is no evidence for the belief that, compared to white men, black men have larger penises, a greater sexual capacity, or an insatiable sexual appetite.

A second misconception about sexual response is that the male can always tell if his female partner had an orgasm. To appease or please their partners, women sometimes fake orgasms (Hite, 1987). Except in the movies, women's orgasms are rarely accompanied by asthmatic breathing and clutching of the bedposts. Response can be explosive or mild, depending on a woman's emotional or physical state, stress, alcohol consumption, and a variety of other factors.

Finally, the idea that simultaneous orgasm (both partners experiencing orgasm at the same time) is the ultimate peak in sexual pleasure became popular in the 1950s and was advocated enthusiastically in numerous marriage manuals. Many people tried to fine-tune the timing of their responses, but working so hard at sex usually resulted in a loss of spontaneity (Masters et al., 1986). Although simultaneous orgasm can be exhilarating, so can independent orgasms.

Sexuality throughout Life

We are not sexually involved with most of the people we love; with some we are. There may be many sexual relationships during the life course and a diversity of sexual unions. There is also an option: abstinence.

Virginity and Abstinence

The terms "abstinence" and "virgin" have several meanings, ranging from absence of all types of sexual activity, which many religious groups endorse, to people who have never had vaginal intercourse, the standard definition used in the scientific literature (and in this chapter). As you saw earlier, large numbers of teenagers have engaged in heavy petting or have experienced fellatio and/or cunnilingus. Of those teens who are virgins nearly one-third reported that they had engaged in heterosexual masturbation of or by a partner, 10 percent had participated in oral sex, and 1 percent had participated in anal intercourse (Schuster et al., 1996).

Although health professionals advocate abstinence from sexual intercourse for adolescents and teenagers, they note that some form of sexual behavior is "almost universal" among U.S. adolescents (Haffner, 1997). Even though many young people are sexually active, one school district in three teaches abstinence as the only option outside of marriage. Districts in the South are almost five times as likely as those in the Northeast to have an abstinence-only policy. Discussions of contraception are either prohibited entirely or permitted only to emphasize its shortcomings (Landry et al., 1999).

Although sexual activity appears widespread, virginity is not a cultural dinosaur. Nearly 20 percent of adolescents do not have intercourse at all during their teenage years (*Sex and America's Teenagers,* 1994). A study of 697 early adolescents (eighth through tenth grade) attending 20 schools across the state of Missouri found three broad reasons for teens' abstaining from sex. The first was fear of getting AIDS or other diseases, along with fear of becoming pregnant or getting someone pregnant. The second reason represented "emotionality and confusion" which included fears about pain, embarrassment, and parental or peer disapproval. The third most common reason for postponing sex reflected religious values about waiting to have sex until marriage (Blinn-Pike, 1999).

According to a recent national survey, about 12 percent of all women were married when they had their first intercourse (comparable numbers are not available for men). Women who lived with both of their parents throughout their childhood were more likely than other women to have been married to their partner at first intercourse (Abma et al., 1997). This may reflect greater parental supervision or a combination of other factors (see *Table 6.1*).

Situational necessities can also encourage abstinence. Someone whose energy is consumed by work, family, or other obligations may not even notice the loss of sexual activity. In addition, some people are abstinent because they are between relationships. Unlike food, sleep, and shelter, sex is not a prerequisite for physical survival. Sexual relationships can

TABLE 6.1

What Factors Are Related to Early Sexual Intercourse among Adolescents?

- Use of alcohol or other drugs, such as marijuana, hashish, cocaine, crack, heroin, angel dust, tranquilizers, barbiturates, or amphetamines

- Delinquent behavior, such as stealing, hitting an adult at school, getting into physical fights with peers, or selling drugs

- Dating before age 16 or involvement in a committed relationship (such as "going steady")

- Having a low grade point average; dropping out of school

- Frequent geographic moves, which decrease parental supervision while parents are involved in the mechanics of the move or in finding new jobs; children sometimes use sex to establish new friendships or combat loneliness

- Lack of parental support; an adolescent may feel that a parent doesn't care about him or her, is not available, or does not include the children in important decision making

- Experiencing parental divorce during adolescence

- Poverty

- Sexual abuse

- Minimal parental monitoring of the adolescent's activities and friends

- Permissive parental values toward sex, which includes a parent who cohabits or entertains overnight guests

- A lack of neighborhood monitoring, such as "keeping an eye on what teens are up to" or reporting unacceptable behavior to parents

certainly be satisfying and rewarding, but neither virginity nor abstinence is fatal.

Sex and Adolescence

The first sexual experience can be happy and satisfying. It can also be a source of worry, disappointment, or guilt:

> *My first time was very unpleasant. The boy I was with rushed and fumbled around and then came so fast it was over before it started. I thought, "What's so great about this?" For weeks afterward, I was afraid I had V.D. and had bad dreams about it. (Masters et al., 1992: 226)*

When a large sample of college students was asked about their first sexual intercourse experiences, both sexes reported more pleasure when sex occurred in a close relationship than in a casual one. When the first premarital sexual intercourse experience with a partner is satisfying, it has a positive effect on relationships for both females and males (Cate et al., 1993). The strongest emotion for both sexes, however, was anxiety. Men experienced more anxiety than women did possibly because they were more likely to be the planners and/or initiators. Women felt less pleasure and had stronger feelings of guilt than men. Probably this was because women may still feel there is something wrong about losing their virginity and also have high standards about their first intercourse that are rarely met. In addition, many more men (79 percent) than women (7 percent) had an orgasm the first time. The researchers suggest that these differences may be due to men's greater freedom to enjoy sex because of sexual scripts or because early masturbation habits and prior petting experiences allow more men than women to be orgasmic. As a result, they are more pleased with the first intercourse experience (Sprecher et al., 1995).

The tasks adolescents face as they navigate through unknown sexual waters are formidable: They must forge an identity that includes culturally dictated gender-role expectations. They must learn about sexual and romantic relationships. They must develop a personal set of sexual values. Many adolescents have sexual intercourse before accomplishing these tasks. At age 15, 21 percent of females and 27 percent of males have had sexual intercourse ("Teen sex and pregnancy," 1999). By age 19, almost half of all high school students have had sexual intercourse. The rates are higher for black and Latino students than for their white counterparts. While 16 percent of high school students have had four or more sex partners by age 19, the highest rates are among black and Latino males (see *Figure 6.5*) (Kann et al., 2000).

Reasons for Adolescent Sex "Raging hormones," the old explanation for adolescent sex, is more fiction than fact. Although adolescents who mature early are more likely to become sexually active at a younger age, the degree of interest in sex varies among young people. For young girls, sex still occurs most often in the context of close, romantic relationships, whereas many boys see sex as an end. Less than 3 percent of teenage women aged 15 to 19 had their first intercourse experience with a man they had just met. Instead, about 73 percent were "going steady" and 3 percent were engaged to the man they had intercourse with for the first time (Abma et al., 1997).

One reason for early premarital sex, especially for boys, is *peer pressure*. Boys as young as 13 brag about their sexual prowess (though most are lying) and ridicule friends who have not "scored." Boys may even challenge a friend to "prove his manhood." Girls are

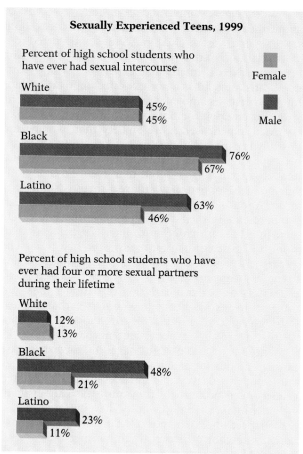

FIGURE 6.5   Sexually Experienced Teens, 1999

SOURCE: Based on Kann et al., 2000, Table 30.

more likely to have fewer partners and to engage in sex to keep or to please boyfriends (Sprecher and McKinney, 1993). When an obstetrics and gynecology professor asked 1,000 girls in Atlanta what subject they most wanted to learn about in sex education classes, 82 percent answered, "How to say no without hurting the other person's feelings" (Besharov, 1993: 57).

Parental and environmental factors also play an important role in early premarital sex. A study of mothers and adolescents found that young teens (those between ages 14 and 16) were less likely to engage in sexual intercourse and with fewer partners if the mothers monitored their children's activities, maintained positive communication patterns, and had nonpermissive attitudes about adolescent sex (Miller et al., 1999; Rodgers, 1999). Teens who are more likely to engage in sexual activities are those who live in single-parent or remarried families, have more opportunity for sex (as in steady dating), associate with delinquent peers, use alcohol and other drugs, or have been sexually abused (Perkins et al., 1998; Upchurch et al., 1999; Whitbeck et al., 1999; Lindberg et al., 2000).

Halpern and her associates (2000) found that, compared with teenagers of average intelligence, the brightest and the least intelligent adolescents tend to put off having sex (including kissing and light petting). The researchers speculated that parents and other adults may be protecting less intelligent teens from compromising situations while the above-average teens tend to avoid sex because they are focused on future goals, such as college, and invest their energy in getting good grades. It might also be the case that middle-class parents (whose children score higher on "intelligence tests" because they've enjoyed more educational resources) keep their children busy. Beginning with preschool and throughout high school, middle-class children are more likely to have demanding schedules that include music lessons, sports, summer camps, and family trips, all of which are supervised leisure activities.

Cultural attitudes and expectations also influence early sexual experiences. As *Figure 6.5* shows, young Latino males are considerably more likely than their female counterparts to report that they've had sexual intercourse and with more partners. The double standard that we discussed earlier and in Chapters 4 and 5 probably explains some of the differences by gender. Two concepts common in Latin American culture promote female premarital abstinence: *verguenza* ("shame"), which connotes embarrassment about body parts and the notion that "good" girls should not know about sexuality; and *marianismo* (from the name of the Virgin Mary), which reflects values relating to chastity, purity, and virtue. If young Latinas agree with their parents about these values, they are more likely to delay sexual activity (Liebowitz et al., 1999).

Despite these traditional cultural expectations, sexual behavior among young Latinas is changing. About 22 percent of Latinas under 16 years old report having had voluntary intercourse (Abma et al., 1997). As immigrants assimilate into U.S. culture, their children often internalize peer values and behaviors. A study of Cuban families highlighted this generation gap in attitudes about daughters' virginity. Although mothers still taught their daughters that virginity was a highly regarded virtue, one teenager said, "If you are a virgin, you are a nerd . . . an oddity." Based on a "silent agreement," young Cubans had premarital sex and parents pretended not to know (Prieto, 1992).

Involuntary Intercourse   About two-thirds of girls who had their first (voluntary) intercourse before they were 16 had partners who were under 18 years of age (Abma et al., 1997). Adult men, then, are not seducing the majority of teenage girls (see Elo et al., 1999). Some premarital sexual experiences are coerced, however. In the Sex Survey, 12 percent of the women and 6 percent of the men reported they had had unwanted sex with an adult by the time they were 13 years of age (Laumann et al., 1994).

Nationwide, almost 13 percent of female and 5 percent of male high school students said they have had sex against their will. Black and Latino students (12 percent and 11 percent, respectively) were significantly more likely than white students (7 percent) to have been forced to have sexual intercourse (Kann et al., 2000). The most common factors associated with a young girl's being forced to have sex include her mother's having an abusive boyfriend, illicit drug use (by the parent, victim, or the nonparental abuser), lack of parental monitoring in the home, a history of sexual abuse in the victim's family, and the victim's living apart from parents before the age of 16 (Small and Kerns, 1993).

Sex and Young Adults

Since the mid-1960s, premarital intercourse has increased considerably among young adults in their early to mid-20s, especially among women. The post–high school years represent a transitional phase for most young adults. High school graduates who take jobs, enroll in vocational training programs, or join the military services have more opportunity and money for recreational pursuits that may include sex. Many young adults who go on to college find themselves free from parental monitoring for the first time. This first experience of independence among people of the same age and social class provides a fertile environment for courting and mating.

Who Initiates Sexual Contact? Traditional sexual scripts dictate that the man should initiate sexual contact because "nice girls don't." Some young women are becoming much more assertive, however. For example, instead of sitting and waiting for the phone to ring, they frequent singles bars or call men they're interested in. In other ways, such as going to a man's apartment or dorm room, they put themselves in situations that invite sexual contact. In steady dating relationships, women may touch or stroke a partner or make sensuous comments about his appearance to arouse him (O'Sullivan and Byers, 1993).

Men and women may define initial sexual contact differently, however. Anderson and Aymami (1993) found that male college students reported female encouragement of sexual contact more often than female students reported initiating such contact. Attributing this discrepancy to traditional gender roles, the researchers suggested that if women see men as "always ready and interested in sex," they may view their own behavior as simply giving the man what he already wants, rather than as initiating something that they want. It's also possible that the notion of a woman initiating sexual contact is still contrary to many men's expectations and they exaggerate such behavior when they recall and report it.

Adolescent sex sometimes results in unwanted pregnancy. This can be highly traumatic for a teenage girl and her partner and may result in the young mother dropping out of school and living in poverty.

Do Women and Men Have Different Motives? College-aged males and females may engage in sex for different reasons. Women typically describe their first sexual experience as being with someone they love or within the confines of a serious relationship. For example, almost 70 percent of the women aged 20 to 24 who had voluntary sexual intercourse were going steady and another 3 percent were engaged (Abma et al., 1997). Today's young women may rationalize intercourse in the same way that earlier generations justified petting ("It's O.K. if I love him"). In contrast, men are more likely to have had their first sexual experience with someone they considered "just a friend" or with someone they had just met (Christopher and Cate, 1988). Across racial and ethnic groups, parents appear to be more tolerant of premarital sex in sons than in daughters (Padilla and O'Grady, 1987; Prieto, 1992). The growing number of women who are having intercourse when "just dating," however, suggests that these traditional views may be changing.

Women are still more likely than men to have sex only in a committed relationship. Many young women, however, such as these college students during a Spring Break, have more opportunities than in the past to initiate sexual activity.

There is some evidence that casual sex is being viewed less favorably—at least among college students. A national survey conducted among first-year students since the mid-1960s found that 40 percent said they believed that "if two people really like each other, it's all right for them to have sex even if they've known each other for a short time." A decade ago, half of the respondents agreed with this statement. In 1990, in contrast, 60 percent of the students (53 percent of the men and 30 percent of the women *disagreed* with this statement ("Attitudes and characteristics . . . ," 2000).

But will you respect me tomorrow? Not if we're having casual sex, according to some researchers. Several studies report that many men still have a double standard about sex and commitment. They often judge sexually permissive women as acceptable or even desirable for casual dates or as regular sexual partners but unacceptable for long-term commitments or as marriage partners. In contrast, the women in these studies viewed sexually permissive men as less desirable both for casual dates or as long-term partners (Sprecher et al., 1991; Oliver and Sedkides, 1992). As more women have premarital sex, it's not clear where people are going to find partners with little sexual experience.

Sex and Married Life

Compared to premarital and especially extramarital sex, marital sex has elicited very little attention from scholars. Several recent studies report that most married couples are happy with their sex lives.

Frequency of Sex As you saw earlier, the Sex Survey found that about 40 percent of married people have

sex with their partner two or more times a week and about half of all married people have sex with their spouses several times a month. This rate is much higher, as *Figure 6.4* showed, than the rate for noncohabiting single people.

Marital sexual activity typically decreases with both partners' age and longevity of the marriage. As a marriage matures, concerns about earning a living, making a home, and raising a family become more pressing than lovemaking. Changes in leisure time can also reduce sexual activity. As we will see in later chapters, economic conditions have forced many families into the two-paycheck mold, adding the stress of double days to many women's lives. That sex is less important for both men and women than managing finances, spending time together, communicating, and sharing household duties should come as no surprise (see *Figure 6.6*).

Although the frequency of sex decreases, the longer people are married the more likely they are to report that they are very satisfied with their current sex life (Mattox, 1994). Remember that there is a broad range of behavior. Among some couples, the frequency of sexual intercourse may remain constant or even increase over the years. Among others, sexual expression may change: Intercourse may decrease, but fondling and genital stimulation (with or without orgasm) may increase.

Is the importance of marital sex exaggerated? The false notion that most Americans have unhappy sex lives has become big business. Magazines, books, movies, television programs, psychiatrists, counselors, sex clinics, and massage parlors all benefit financially by convincing us that we need more or better sex.

Society has become so obsessed with this subject that sex manuals are constantly on best-seller lists. As we have seen, however, less frequent sex is not unusual, abnormal, or distressing. Even young married couples report that companionship is often more important than sexual passion. As one man stated:

I think it's very important, but I don't think it's number one or even number three on the list. On my list it would come fourth. Marriage, as far as I'm concerned, is friendship and companionship; that ranks first. Then there's consideration for one another, and then trust, and then fourth I'd say your physical relationship. And those three that come before hopefully enhance what you experience in your physical relationship. (Greenblatt, 1983: 298)

Spouses in Middle Years As we mature, our sexual interests, abilities, and responses change. **Menopause**— the cessation of the menstrual cycle and the loss of

FIGURE 6.6 What People Would Most Like to Change in Their Relationships. In this Roper survey of married couples, both men and women rated sex only sixth among aspects of their relationships they would like to change. Interestingly, the only issue on which they disagreed widely was the performance of household chores (Roper Organization, 1990).

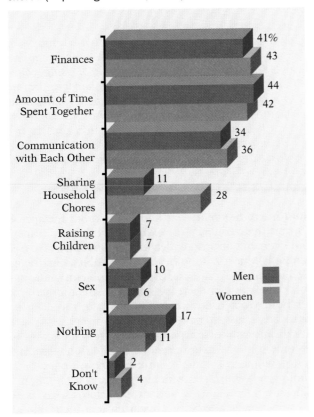

reproductive capacity—has been studied seriously only recently. Early in the twentieth century many women died, often in childbirth, long before they could experience "the change of life," as it was once called. Now gynecologists study not only all the stages of the menstrual cycle but also *perimenopause*, a phenomenon that precedes menopause itself and has many of the same symptoms. Whereas menopause typically begins in a woman's mid-40s to early 50s, perimenopause can begin in the late 30s. The symptoms of both perimenopause and menopause include "hot flashes" (sudden experience of overall bodily heat, sometimes accompanied by sweating), irregular menstrual cycles with uncharacteristically heavy or light bleeding, mood changes, vaginal dryness, fatigue, migraine headaches, backaches, insomnia, loss or increase of appetite, diarrhea or constipation, urinary incontinence, and more frequent urinary tract infections (Smith, 1993).

Not all women experience these phenomena, and some hardly notice that they are going through menopause. Hot flashes affect only about 10 percent of all women, and they usually last only a minute or so. Rarely will a woman experience a "drenching sweat" or be awakened from sleep. Most women do not consider menopause a time of crisis, and many enjoy sex more because they are no longer bothered by menstruation, the need for contraception, or the fear of pregnancy (Fausto-Sterling, 1985).

According to some social scientists, the subjective experience of menopause may reflect cultural as well as biological influences. Compared to North American women, for example, Japanese women report a considerably lower incidence of such problems as hot flashes, fatigue, irritability, feelings of depression, and stiffness in the joints (Lock, 1993). Because most Japanese women have extensive family responsibilities, which often include caring for elderly parents or relatives as well as young children, they may regard complaining about menopause as "pure self-indulgence" and thus report fewer problems. This doesn't mean that they don't experience the same physiological changes—only that they endure them quietly.

Whether there is a **male climacteric,** or change of life analogous to female menopause, is not known for sure. Although testosterone production does decline with age, unlike women, men do not lose their reproductive capacity. Some men have fathered children in their late 70s. Only a small percentage of men complain of nervousness, depression, decreased sexual desire, inability to concentrate, irritability, and other emotional reactions in middle age. Research on the male mood cycle has been only suggestive (see Gould et al., 2000). It may be that the male "change of life" is a more general "midlife crisis," in which men look back over their lives and feel distress at not having achieved all that they might have.

Although some spouses in their middle years may be dissatisfied with sex in marriage, problems such as

GEECH®

by Jerry Bittle

a loss of interest in sex have a negative effect on only a minority of marriages (Edwards and Booth, 1994). Couples who have no children living at home and need not care for elderly parents are freed from time-consuming responsibilities. They have more time, energy, and privacy for talking, intimacy, and sex. Thus, "the empty nest may actually be a love nest" (Woodward and Springen, 1992: 71).

Sexuality and Later Life

As with other age groups, the sexual lives of older persons are not homogeneous. There is considerable variation in the way people are affected by cultural, social, psychological, and medical factors. Generally, however, many men and women remain sexually active into their 60s, 70s, and beyond.

Sexual Activity   In the later years, sexuality encompasses a wide range of acts and feelings, from hugging and holding hands to sexual intercourse. In a study of the sexual practices of 202 men and women aged 80 to 102 (that's right, 102!), 47 percent of the respondents were having sexual intercourse and 34 percent engaged in oral sex. Also, 88 percent of the men and 71 percent of the women still fantasized or daydreamed about the opposite sex (Bretschneider and McCoy, 1988). A national survey sponsored by the American Association of Retired Persons (AARP) found that sexual activity among older people declines but doesn't evaporate. About half of the 45-through 59-year olds reported having sex at least once a week. Among 60- through 74-year-olds, the proportion dropped to 30 percent for men and 24 percent for women (Jacoby, 1999; see also *Figure 6.3*). Despite the decline in sexual intercourse, many seniors say that they are happy and satisfied with their sexual lives.

Sexual Activity and Satisfaction   Experiencing sexual activity changes in later life within the context of

a loving, committed relationship is likely to be much less problematic than in situations where partners have little rapport (Marsiglio and Greer, 1994). Lowered activity—as well as inactivity—is not a problem if both partners are satisfied with their sex lives (Marsiglio and Donnelly, 1991; Matthias et al., 1997). Among those aged 70 and over, for example, the strongest predictors of a satisfying relationship are being sexually active (which may or may not include intercourse) and having good mental health, such as feeling happy, calm, and peaceful (Matthias et al., 1997). As a 71-year-old woman noted, sex can improve because partners are emotionally closer:

> My husband, Gerald, and I probably enjoy sex more now than we did in our 50s, because when you're younger, you worry about pleasing yourself. As you age, you're more knowledgeable and more aware of your partner's needs. When you're younger, I don't believe you really realize what sex is all about. It's not just about physical contact, it's about love and commitment. . . . There's laughter to sex, too. Some of those positions are pretty funny. (Clements, 1996: 5–6)

Health and Sexuality   It's not until about the age of 70 that the frequency of sexual activity, in both men and women, begins to decline significantly. This is generally due to poor health and habits. Smoking, alcoholism, heart disease, prostate problems, and vascular illnesses can decrease sexual desire and activity for both women and men. For women, the drop in estrogen levels after menopause can decrease sexual desire and make sex painful because vaginal walls become thin and cause dryness. In addition, especially for women, a complex mix of stress, anger, or a cooling relationship can dampen sexual desire. Some illnesses, like diabetes and arteriosclerosis, as well as some medications for hypertension (high blood pressure), can cause impotence in older men (Butler and Lewis, 1993; McKinlay and Feldman, 1994).

A higher percentage of older men (53 percent) than women (32 percent) report having sexual difficulties. Among women, the major limitations are a low sex drive, difficulty in achieving orgasm, and self-consciousness during sex (Clements, 1996). The most common sexual problems among men include an inability to maintain an erection, a low sex drive, and premature ejaculation. Despite these difficulties, older men and women engage in and enjoy sex. When a 90-year-old woman who married an 18-year-old man was asked by a reporter, "Aren't you afraid of what could happen on the honeymoon? Vigorous lovemaking might bring on injury or even a fatal heart attack!" she smiled and replied, "If he dies, he dies!"

Double Standards and New Sexual Scripts   Whereas gray-haired men in their 60s are considered "distinguished," their female counterparts are just "old." Men are not under the same pressure to remain young, trim, and attractive. When comparing her own public image to that of her actor husband Paul Newman, actress Joanne Woodward remarked: "He gets prettier; I get older."

The aging process may enhance a man's desirability because he is seen as more distinguished and has more resources and power. An older woman, in contrast, may be regarded as an asexual grandmother: "Because attractiveness is associated with feelings of well-being, a perceived decline in appearance can be particularly devastating for women. Women who have undergone a mastectomy or hysterectomy are especially vulnerable to feelings of sexual unattractiveness and reduced desirability" (Levy, 1994: 295–296). As in earlier stages of life, male sexual scripts seem to connect intimacy with intercourse, orgasm, and physical expression. Older women are more interested in relational and nongenital activities, whereas older men are more interested in genital sexual behaviors (Johnson, 1996).

As people age, the biggest impediment to sex, especially for women, is a "partner gap." For every 100 females over age 65, there are only 69 males. Because our culture frowns on liaisons and marriages between older women and younger men but smiles on matches between older men and younger women, older women have a further reduced pool of eligible sexual partners (see Chapters 5, 8, and 17). In contrast, married women over age 70 report being both sexually active *and* sexually satisfied (Matthias et al., 1997).

Extramarital Sex

Husband: Honey, if I died, would you remarry?
  Wife: Well, I suppose so.
Husband: Would you and he sleep in the same bed?
  Wife: I guess we would.
Husband: Would you make love to him?
  Wife: He would be my husband, dear.
Husband: Would you give him my golf clubs?
  Wife: No. He's left-handed.

What Is Extramarital Sex?

People use the terms *affair, infidelity, adultery,* and *extramarital sex* interchangeably. For our purposes, *extramarital sex* refers to sexual contact with someone other than a person's spouse. Pittman (1989: 20) put it more succinctly by defining its opposite, *sexual exclusivity*: "The genitals stay out of the hands or whatever of outsiders."

In one of the earliest studies on extramarital sex, Hunt (1969) reported that a number of men he interviewed said that having sexual relations with a call girl while away from home, for example, was not "real infidelity" because it did not include caring for the woman or seeing her on a regular basis. In contrast, 20 years later a *People* magazine survey found that 70 percent of respondents felt that a sexual act is not necessary for a person to be unfaithful; lust was enough to qualify (cited in Frenkiel, 1990). This suggests that many people may be defining extramarital sex more broadly than in the past. What's most devastating about extramarital sex is not that it's "just" about sex but also about violating trust, intimacy, and commitment. When political consultant Dick Morris's year-long affair with a call girl was exposed, for example, his wife said she was hurt and angry because Morris had been "my best friend for 20 years" (Clift, 1996).

Extramarital sex is *not* a common occurrence. Although it makes great fodder for talk shows, national surveys have shown that most Americans are faithful, and that extramarital sex rates have even decreased slightly since 1991 (see *Table 6.2*). When researchers asked people who were either married or had been married at one time whether they had *ever*

TABLE 6.2

Married People Who Admitted Having Extramarital Sex during the Preceding Year, 1988–93

	All Respondents	Men	Women
1988	3.9%	5.0%	2.8%
1989	3.6	5.8	1.7
1990	3.8	5.3	2.3
1991	4.4	5.4	3.4
1993	2.9	4.1	1.9

SOURCES: Cited in Morin, 1994.

committed adultery, 16 percent said yes (21 percent of men, nearly 13 percent of women).

Why Are Spouses Unfaithful?

Popular magazines routinely imply that it's a woman's fault if her husband is unfaithful. The articles offer advice on how to please a husband, such as not nagging, having cosmetic surgery, losing weight, buying sexy lingerie, and preparing romantic dinners. Magazines very rarely advise a husband to please his wife so that *she* will not be tempted to have an affair.

The complex reasons for adultery include both macro and micro explanations. Although they overlap and are often cumulative, I present them separately for the sake of clarity.

Macro Reasons Among the many macro explanations for extramarital sex, four are especially significant:

1. *Economic recessions and depressions* place strains on families. Underemployment (employment below a person's level of training and education), layoffs, and unemployment can create pressures that may increase the incidence of extramarital affairs. Husbands and wives who must work different shifts or who live in different cities may develop intimate relationships with others.

2. The *purpose of marriage* has changed for many people (see Chapter 1). Although procreation is still important, many couples today marry primarily for companionship and intimacy. When these needs are not met, outside relationships may develop.

3. The *anonymity of urban life* provides the opportunity for socially disapproved behaviors like adultery to be concealed more easily than in small towns where more people know each other.

4. Because today people have greater *longevity,* marriages can last as long as 50 to 60 years, increasing the chances for conflict, dissatisfaction, and infidelity.

Micro Reasons There are also a number of micro explanations for extramarital sex:

1. *Social roles,* especially women's roles, are changing. Even happily married women may have sex outside of marriage in response to more liberal sexual attitudes. Some continue an adulterous relationship even when they recognize that it may wreck their marriage. Since there are more women in the workplace, they have more contact with men—there is *greater opportunity* for extramarital sex today. If their marital relationships are not satisfying, women may become closer to and

emotionally involved with a co-worker (Greeley, 1994).

2. The *need for emotional satisfaction* or, conversely, the *need to escape emotional isolation* may propel a married partner into extramarital sex. Sometimes people get involved in extramarital relationships to counteract sexual deprivation caused by a spouse's long-term illness. And when people are separated from their spouses because of military duty or constant business trips, they may have "flings" to decrease loneliness. Finally, as people grow older, some may try to prove to themselves that they are still physically and socially desirable. An extramarital relationship can make someone feel more desirable, more attractive, and more loved. Women who engage in extramarital sex often do so because they feel that their husbands do not communicate and have no time for them except in bed:

A 28-year-old from Kansas, who has been having an affair for two years, wrote, "My sex life with my husband was good, very good. But . . . we shared nothing but sex. He never wanted to talk to me about his work, or about mine, or go anywhere, or do anything. It . . . was like going to bed with a stranger." (Wolfe, 1981)

Ironically, husbands and wives often appear to be having affairs for complementary reasons: While women complain that their husbands do not talk to them, men often say that they are looking for someone to talk to and someone who will listen to them (Bass, 1988).

3. People may be tempted to try *different sexual experiences.* An extramarital affair may offer an opportunity for sexual experimentation (such as oral sex); the lover may be more physically appealing or may provide feedback that supports a positive sexual self-image for the partner (Weil and Winter, 1993). Some happily married men may seek "novelty" through extramarital sex (Walsh, 1991). Others have extramarital affairs for fun; even women admit being unfaithful "just for the sport of it" (Krance, 1993).

4. People sometimes have extramarital sex as a form of *revenge or retaliation* against a spouse for involvement in a similar activity or "for some sort of nonsexual mistreatment, real or imagined, by the other spouse" (Kinsey et al., 1953: 432).

5. An extramarital relationship may provide *a way out of marriage.* Women, especially, can find the courage to leave an unsatisfying marriage if they realize they have better options. Some people might even deliberately initiate an affair

as an excuse to dissolve an unhappy marriage (Walsh, 1991).

When Affairs End

Men involved in extramarital affairs are generally older and have much higher incomes than their female partners. Often they may be a woman's boss or mentor. Women are usually less powerful and more dependent in an affair; and the more dependent a woman is, the more likely that the man will end the relationship and that she will suffer pain and humiliation when it ends.

In a recent case, a North Carolina woman was awarded $1 million by a jury when she sued her husband's lover for luring away her husband of 18 years. The lawsuit claimed "alienation of affection"—basically breaking up a marriage—which is a legal basis for adulterous lawsuits in ten states. Although the husband married his mistress in this case, only about 10 percent of adulterous relationships end in marriage (Lawson, 1988), and the average length of an affair is a year (Patterson and Kim, 1991). In other words, affairs most often end rather than endure.

Consequences of Extramarital Sex

One clinician describes the discovery of a spouse's affair as the "emotional equivalent of having a limb amputated without an anesthetic" (McGinnis, 1981: 154). The injured spouse typically feels deceived, betrayed, even devastated, at the discovery of a partner's infidelity. The aggrieved person may suffer from doubts about his or her own desirability, adequacy, or worth. There is some evidence that men and women respond differently to the discovery of an extramarital affair. Whereas men tend to focus their jealousy and anger on the rival male ("I'll kill him"), women experience a more generalized sense that they have lost their partner's attention, caring, and concern (Scarf, 1987). Women are thus more likely to distrust the adulterous spouse in general. Both men and women, however, may be justifiably concerned about pregnancy, sexually transmitted diseases, and especially AIDS.

Clinicians point out that most extramarital affairs devastate the entire family. They can have an especially negative impact on children, who often feel insecure and confused, particularly if the marriage collapses because of the affair. Very young children are self-centered, so they may feel that they are somehow to blame for what has happened (see Chapter 15). Extramarital sex also has broad structural implications for society as a whole. Group solidarity is necessary for a society's survival. As we saw in Chapter 1, family members depend on one another for emotional support, and the unity and cohesiveness of the family can be threatened by intruding outsiders.

Gay, Lesbian and Bisexual Sex

As you saw earlier, homosexuality has generated numerous research studies and speculations about the origin of sexual orientation. Although the percentage of gays and bisexuals is small, their sexual activities have triggered a wide range of public reactions. We begin with a look at the prevalence of homosexuality in the United States.

Prevalence of Homosexuality

How many gay men, lesbians, and bisexuals are there? No one knows for sure, largely because it is difficult to define and to measure homosexuality. For example, are people homosexual if they have *ever* engaged in same-sex sexual behavior? What about people who have other-sex partners and desire same-sex partners but are afraid to come out? Furthermore, what about men and women who identify themselves as heterosexuals but can be sexually aroused only when they fantasize about same-sex intercourse? Because of these complicating issues, most researchers generally measure the prevalence of homosexuality by simply asking people whether they identify themselves as heterosexual, homosexual, or bisexual.

In the Sex Survey, 1.4 percent of women and 2.8 percent of men identified themselves as bisexual or exclusively homosexual. Of the self-identified homosexuals, about 0.7 percent of men and 0.3 percent of women reported having had both male and female sexual partners in the 12 months preceding the survey. (Similar ranges have been reported in Kinsey et al., 1953; Billy et al., 1993; and Clements, 1994.)

Homosexual couples do many of the same sexual things as do heterosexuals, with the exception of penile-vaginal intercourse. All other feelings and activities are basically the same, including kissing, caressing, hugging, nipple stimulation, and other nongenital touching or foreplay, as well as oral and anal sex. Lesbian sexual activities include cunnilingus, manual masturbation, body-to-body rubbing of breasts or clitorises, and slow, sensual body caressing. While some lesbians report using dildos, the most popular activities include nongenital acts such as kissing and oral sex (Casler, 1993; Van Gelder and Brandt, 1996). Like heterosexuals, homosexuals use a variety of positions to achieve sexual satisfaction, and not all couples participate in or enjoy all sexual activities (Reinisch and Beasley, 1990).

Societal Reactions to Homosexuality

Societies vary greatly in their responses to homosexuality. As you saw earlier, some societies are punitive, some tolerate and/or even encourage homosexuality either in adulthood or in childhood, and some require

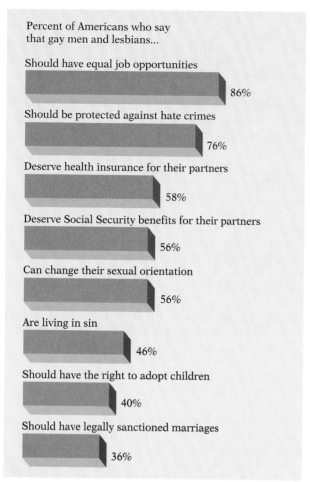

Percent of Americans who say
that gay men and lesbians...

Should have equal job opportunities
86%

Should be protected against hate crimes
76%

Deserve health insurance for their partners
58%

Deserve Social Security benefits for their partners
56%

Can change their sexual orientation
56%

Are living in sin
46%

Should have the right to adopt children
40%

Should have legally sanctioned marriages
36%

FIGURE 6.7 **Attitudes about Gay and Lesbian Rights.**

SOURCES: Based on material in Leland, 2000; "Considering Alternative Lifestyles," 2000.

limited homosexual activities during puberty ceremonials. In the United States, societal reactions include both homophobia and a growing acceptance of gays and lesbians.

Homophobia The fear and hatred of homosexuality, **homophobia**, has several sources. Many social scientists consider homophobia an expression of a deeply rooted insecurity about a person's own sexuality and gender identity. Homophobic people often have a strong fundamentalist religious orientation and typically know little about gay and lesbian life.

Many people still believe that homosexuality is a conscious choice or a contagious disease that can be "caught" through seduction, infection, or role modeling. For example, the Utah legislature banned gay student clubs in high schools to curb homosexuals from "recruiting" others into "a lifestyle that can kill them" ("Utah legislature bans . . . ," 1996). Some Roman

Catholic institutions have fired openly gay administrators or faculty ("Roman Catholic College . . . ," 1997). In addition, a federal appeals court, in order to "preserve community values and character," upheld a Cincinnati voter initiative that allowed the city discriminatory practices against gay people (Biskupic, 1997). Gay men, especially, are often targets of hate crimes by male heterosexuals.

Increasing Acceptance Many Americans have ambivalent feelings about homosexuals. While, on the one hand, they oppose legalizing homosexual relations, a large number (86 percent) feel that gay men and lesbians should have equal rights in job opportunities and protection against hate crimes (76 percent) (see *Figure 6.7*).

Since the late 1980s, there has been an increased acceptance of homosexuality. Many municipal jurisdictions, corporations, and smaller companies now extend health-care coverage and other benefits to the partners of its gay and lesbian employees. Many states allow gay partners to jointly adopt children on the same basis as unmarried couples. In addition, numerous colleges and universities offer health and other benefits to gay and lesbian couples, offer courses or programs in gay and lesbian studies, and provide funding for gay student clubs. In late 1999, the Vermont state supreme court ruled that unions between homosexuals should be afforded the same benefits and protections that married heterosexual couples enjoy. Though the court refused to give homosexuals the legal right to marry, it supported same-sex partnerships. Some of the rights that the court granted include joint ownership of homes and other property, a right to financial support from a partner, a share of the partner's medical or life insurance, and a right to inheritances and to survivors' benefits if the other partner dies.

Some observers feel that commercial television has also come a long way in its portrayal of gays and lesbians. For example, in the popular 1970s show *Marcus Welby, M.D.*, in one episode Dr. Welby advised his patient to suppress his homosexual tendencies and he'd be a good husband and father. During the 1990s, Ross's ex-wife Carol married her lesbian lover on *Friends;* Jamie, on *Mad about You*, had a lesbian obstetrician; Carter, on *Spin City*, is the mayor's no-nonsense aide who constantly challenges gay stereotypes; and Ellen DeGeneres came out as a lesbian—both on the *Ellen* show and in real life. Currently there is a multitude of homosexual characters in major or secondary roles on prime-time TV: *Will & Grace, Dawson's Creek, Chicago Hope, ER, The Simpsons* and *Nash Bridges*, among others.

Some observers see such programming as progress while others are offended by it (see De Moraes, 1999). Many people's ambivalence is especially evident in religious institutions. Some denominations have welcomed gays as members and as ordained ministers. Others—Episcopal, Lutheran, Methodist, Presbyterian, and United Church of Christ—find themselves polarized and divided over homosexuality. Further, as you will see in Chapters 7 and 8, ethnic gay men and lesbians face additional hurdles in their families and communities due to cultural, religious, and generational variations.

Sexually Transmitted Diseases, HIV, and AIDS

Sexual expression is not always a smooth and carefree process. Appendix B provides information on sexual problems, dysfunctions, and their treatment. Here we discuss diseases, infections, and illnesses that are conveyed almost solely through sexual intercourse before turning to an examination of the human immunodeficiency virus (HIV) and the acquired immunodeficiency syndrome (AIDS). HIV and AIDS are transmitted through sexual contact, but they may also be contracted by use of contaminated intravenous drug needles and, more rarely, by transfusions of infected blood.

STDs

Sexually transmitted diseases (STDs) are infections that are spread by contact, sexual or nonsexual, with body parts or fluids that harbor specific microorganisms (generally bacterial or viral). The term *sexually transmitted* indicates that sexual contact is the most common means of transmission. An estimated 12 million people acquire a sexually transmitted infection each year in the United States. *Figure 6.8* presents the reported cases of some of the most common sexually transmitted diseases for 1998, the most recent year for which such data are available.

STDs affect women and men of all backgrounds and economic levels. They are most prevalent among teenagers and young adults. Nearly two-thirds of all STDs occur in people younger than 25 years of age. Most of the time, STDs cause no symptoms, particularly in women. Even when a STD causes no symptoms, a person who is infected can pass the diseases on to a sex partner.

The oldest known STDs—syphilis and gonorrhea—have now been joined by more than 20 other diseases that can cause cancer, birth defects, miscarriages, and death (see Appendix E for more information on some of these diseases, symptoms, and their treatment). Today *syphilis* is the least common STD; the most common is *chlamydia,* a bacterial infection. Even if there are no symptoms, untreated chlamydia can cause permanent damage to the reproductive organs, such as infertility in women and sterility in men.

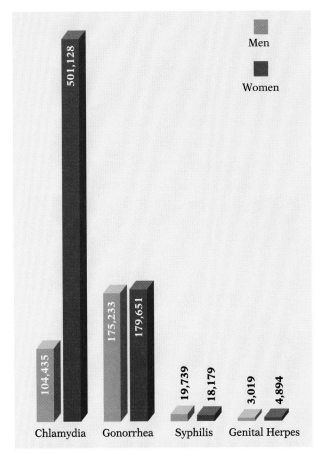

FIGURE 6.8 Reported Cases of Selected STDs in the United States, 1998. These figures are conservative because many people don't realize they're infected and don't seek medical care. Although only 607,602 people reported chlamydia in 1998, for example, at least 4 million are believed to be infected annually. For some STDs, like genital herpes, data are available for a limited number of states.

SOURCE: Based on Table 2, Division of STD Prevention, 1999.

When present, the symptoms of chlamydia are often similar to those of *gonorrhea*. Gonorrhea can result in infertility for men. A baby born to an infected mother may become blind. Without early screening and treatment, 10 to 40 percent of women with gonorrhea will develop pelvic inflammatory disease (PID), which can result in infertility in women and life-threatening pregnancy when, for example, the fertilized egg implants itself in the fallopian tube rather than the uterus. The tube can rupture and cause death. *Human papillomavirus (HPV)* causes *genital warts*. Genital warts infect an estimated 1 million Americans each year. In addition to genital warts, certain types of HPV cause cervical cancer and other genital cancers (see, for example, Mount and Papillo, 1999). There's no cure for herpes or genital warts.

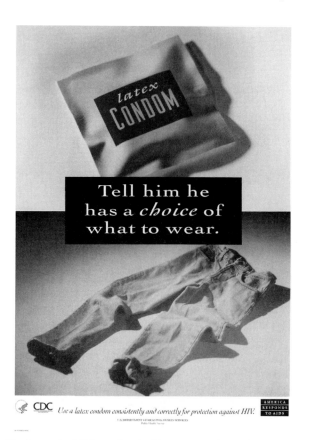

Most people fall in and out of love many times during the life course. In contrast, an HIV/AIDS infection is forever. As this poster by the Centers for Disease Control and Prevention notes, using condoms and acting responsibly is the best protection against HIV/AIDS as well as other STDs (see text).

There are considerable infection variations by race. African Americans account for about 79 percent of all reported cases of gonorrhea and about 86 percent of all reported cases of syphilis. Syphilis in Latinos is about three times that in whites. The reasons for the race differences include lower access to quality health care, less likelihood of seeking medical treatment, living in communities with a high prevalence of STDs, having multiple sexual partners, and engaging in unprotected intercourse (Centers for Disease Control and Prevention, 1996).

HIV and AIDS

One of the most serious (and still fatal) STDs is the **human immunodeficiency virus (HIV)** that causes **acquired immunodeficiency syndrome**, or **AIDS**, a degenerative condition that attacks the body's immune system and renders it unable to fight a number of diseases, including some forms of pneumonia and cancer. First reported on June 5, 1981, AIDS had taken the lives of almost 380,000 Americans by September 1997. An estimated 242,000 people are living with AIDS, and 650,000 to 900,000 Americans are now living with HIV. At least 40,000 new HIV infections occur each year (Centers for Disease Control and Prevention, 1998).

In 1996, and for the first time in the history of the HIV/AIDS epidemic, the number of Americans diagnosed with AIDS declined and was second to accidents as the leading cause of death for Americans between the ages of 25 and 44 (Brown, 1997). The decrease in AIDS deaths has been attributed to a number of factors: advances in the treatment of HIV infection—especially such potent antiviral drugs as protease inhibitors which are used in combination with other drugs ("drug cocktails")—that prolong peoples' lives; better treatments that slow the rate at which infected people develop full-blown AIDS; success of HIV prevention and education efforts; better access to medical care; and increased financing for AIDS research and treatment by the federal government.

Although AIDS deaths have been decreasing, some populations have become more vulnerable. As *Figure 6.9* shows, since 1985 the AIDS epidemic has grown among intravenous users and heterosexuals, has become more prevalent among blacks and Latinos, and has increased among women.

Women and AIDS AIDS is now spreading fastest among heterosexuals and especially among heterosexual women (see *Figure 6.8*). In mid-1997, 44 percent of female adolescents and adult women with AIDS were injecting drugs and another 17 percent were having intercourse with male drug users. About 53 percent of the women got AIDS from heterosexual men who were neither bisexual nor drug users (*HIV/AIDS Surveillance Report*, 1997).

Heterosexual women are more than twice as likely as men to become infected with HIV for a number of reasons. First, the genital surface exposed to the virus is much more extensive in women than in men. Second, it is believed that vaginal secretions from an HIV-infected woman are less potent than an infected man's semen, which is capable of packing high concentrations of the virus. Third, a man's exposure to the virus is limited to the duration of sex, but semen remains in a woman's body after intercourse (Nicolosi et al., 1994).

Latinas and black women are the most likely to contract HIV/AIDS. The most vulnerable groups are low-income women who use both contaminated needles during drug use and engage in prostitution with unprotected sex. Prostitutes often exchange sex for drugs, such as cocaine. Cocaine lowers inhibitions and unprotected sex is more likely. Being infected with HIV is largely a reflection of poverty or dependence for economic security on a male partner who is a drug user and has unprotected sex (Jemmott et al., 1995).

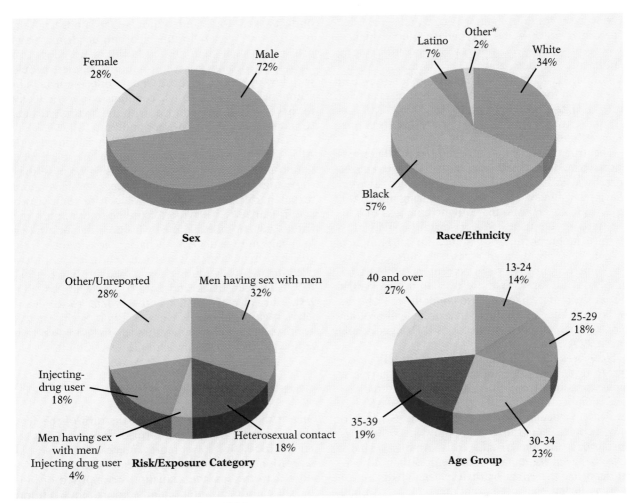

FIGURE 6.9   HIV Characteristics, 1999.

*Includes Asian Pacific Islanders, Native American, and unknown race/ethnicity

Source: Centers for Disease Control and Prevention, 1999.

Latinas are believed to have high HIV and AIDS rates, especially from heterosexual contact, for several reasons. First, both adolescents and adults know less and have more misconceptions about HIV transmission than do non-Hispanic whites. For instance, many Latinas still believe the myth that one can discern an HIV person by the way he or she looks. Second, many Latinas continue to think that HIV and AIDS affect only gay people or drug users. Third, with the exception of Cubans, Latinas are younger, poorer, and less educated than non-Hispanic women. They suffer from problems often associated with poverty, such as unemployment and illicit drug use. Fourth, they are less likely than non-Hispanic women to use condoms during intercourse (Fernandez, 1995). Finally, those who speak little or no English have less access to educational materials about HIV and AIDS. All of these reasons increase the incidence of HIV and AIDS.

One widespread misperception is that midlife women are relatively immune to HIV infection. According to the Center for Women Policy Studies (1994), the life situations of midlife and older women increase their possible risk for infection. For example, because more older women than men are unmarried, they may be sexually involved with men who may not admit that they are using drugs or are having sexual relations with other women or men. In addition, older married women may be less assertive than younger women and feel they cannot insist on using condoms. Or they feel that they cannot refuse the sexual demands of their husbands, who may be infected, for unprotected sex.

Sexual Orientation and AIDS   Almost 65 percent of all AIDS-infected people are gay and bisexual men. The largest number of male adult and adolescent HIV infection cases result from unprotected male–male sex: 62 percent among whites, 31 percent among blacks, 39 percent among Latinos, 51 percent among Asian/Pacific Islanders, and 51 percent among American Indians/Alaska Natives. The next highest source of HIV infection for male adolescents and adults is use of injected drugs—especially among black males (18 percent) and Latino males (20 percent) (*HIV/AIDS Surveillance Report*, 2000).

The drug cocktails that revolutionized AIDS treatment have made some gay men more willing to engage in risky sex. San Francisco health authorities reported a sharp jump in new HIV infections during mid-2000. Health officials believed that the increase was due, in large part, to a return of risky sexual behavior. For example, the proportion of gay men in San Francisco who said they always used a condom during sex fell from 70 percent in 1994 to 54 percent in 1999 ("AIDS rising . . . ," 2000). Even those who do not have HIV reported being less likely to use condoms than in the past because they're confident that drugs will prolong their lives or even prevent infections ("Drug cocktails . . . ," 1999).

Heterosexuals with the highest risk for HIV infection are teenagers, adults with multiple sex partners, people who suffer from other sexually transmitted diseases, and people who live in areas where AIDS is prevalent, particularly the South and the Northeast. Many people, even those who know how AIDS is transmitted, continue to take risks. Among sexually active college students, for example, less than 30 percent reported that they or their partner had used a condom during the last sexual intercourse. Among males, black students (52 percent) were significantly more likely to use condoms than white (33 percent) and Latino (36 percent) students (Centers for Disease Control and Prevention, 1997).

Race, Ethnicity, and AIDS AIDS is disproportionately high among people of color (see *Figure 6.9*), in part because of educational, socioeconomic, and cultural factors. In states where sex education is allowed but not required, for example, schools with predominantly minority enrollments are less likely to devote time to HIV/AIDS education (Denson et al., 1993). If

budgets are low and schools are understaffed, resources are generally funneled into academic areas rather than such "luxuries" as health or sex education classes. According to several national studies, people with low incomes and those who do not complete high school are less likely to use condoms and more likely to have sexual intercourse with high-risk partners (Catania et al., 1992; Mosher and Pratt, 1993).

The majority of gay men now being diagnosed with AIDS are either black or Latino, not white. Black and Latino infection rates may be increasing because they engage in sexual behavior at a young age, have more sexual partners (see *Figure 6.5*), or are uninformed about their risky behavior. According to one study, the Latino gay and bisexual men who were the most likely to engage in sexually risky behavior were in their early 20s, had frequent sex with casual partners, and were likely to use drugs during sexual activity (Diaz et al., 1999). Further, black and Latino men who have sex with other men are less likely than whites to see themselves as gay or bisexual (Morales, 1996). Such a stance, health experts believe, may hinder disease-prevention campaigns in their communities (Brown, 2000).

Conclusion

One of the biggest *changes* since the turn of the century is that we are better informed about human sexuality. Today we have more *choices* in our sexual expression, and most people recognize that sexuality is more than the sex act; sexuality is comprised of biological, emotional, intellectual, spiritual, and cultural components. But there are also a number of *constraints*. We are often unwilling to provide young people with the information they need to make thoughtful decisions about sex. Gay men and lesbians still face discrimination and harassment because of their sexual practices. And our health and lives and the lives of our children are threatened by the rising incidence of STDs and HIV infection. These changes have significant effects on both women and men in their search for suitable marriage partners and other long-term relationships. We will look at some of these issues in the next several chapters.

SUMMARY

1. Our sexual lives affect our families and marriages from birth to death. Regardless of age or marital status, sexual expression plays an important role throughout life.

2. Human sexuality is complex and incorporates components such as sexual identity, sexual orientation, and gender roles. Biological theories maintain

that genes and sex hormones determine sexual preference, whereas social constructionist theories emphasize social and environmental factors.

3. Although we like to think that our sexual behavior is spontaneous, sexual scripts shape most of our sexual activities, attitudes, and relationships.

4.   Most of us do not learn about sex in the home. Much of our information, and misinformation, comes from peers and the popular culture. Although there are variations, many sex education programs are still limited to discussing the dangers and negative consequences of sex.

5.   Sexual activity encompasses many behaviors other than sexual intercourse, such as fantasies, masturbation, petting, and oral sex.

6.   Adolescent girls are more likely to romanticize sex, whereas adolescent boys typically see sex as an end. The reasons for early premarital sex include early pubertal changes, peer pressure, environmental factors, and cultural expectations.

7.   Marital sex typically decreases over the course of a marriage, but married couples enjoy sex as well as a variety of other sexual activities besides intercourse.

8.   Despite many stereotypes about sexuality and aging, people who are 70 years old and over continue to engage in sexual activities, including intercourse, masturbation, and sexual fantasy.

9.   Gay and lesbian partners experience many of the same feelings as do heterosexuals and face some of the same problems in their relationships. Major factors that differentiate gay and lesbian couples from heterosexual couples are society's disapproval of homosexual practices and their consequent lack of legal rights in many areas.

10.   Although today more people are informed about STDs, HIV infection, and AIDS, many still engage in high-risk sexual behavior, such as sharing needles while injecting drugs, having sex with many partners, and not using condoms. The rates for new HIV infections are especially high among male–male couples, people of color, and heterosexual women.

KEY TERMS

sexual orientation   *131*
homosexual   *131*
heterosexual   *131*
bisexual   *132*
sexual script   *134*
masturbation   *143*
petting   *144*

fellatio   *145*
cunnilingus   *145*
sexual response   *146*
menopause   *153*
male climacteric   *153*
homophobia   *158*

sexually transmitted diseases (STDs)   *159*
human immunodeficiency virus (HIV)   *160*
acquired immunodeficiency syndrome (AIDS)   *160*

TAKING IT FURTHER

Everything You've Ever Wanted To know about Sex . . .

National Abstinence Clearinghouse offers resources and material that encourages premarital abstinence.

www.abstinence.net

Centers for Disease Control and Prevention Home Page offers health information, publications, international data, and links to numerous health-related sites on HIV, AIDS, and other sexually transmitted diseases.

www.cdc.gov

SIECUS (Sexuality Information and Education Council of the United States) Home Page develops and disseminates information on sexuality education and responsible sexual choices.

www.siecus.org

The STD Home Page includes a STD quiz, statistics, and photos of STD symptoms.

www.grin.net/~sycamore/std

And more . . . www.prenhall.com/benokraitis includes numerous sites on safer sex, world statistics and maps on HIV and AIDS, decreasing teen pregnancy, a museum of menstruation, AIDS and the elderly, female genital mutilation, and men's and women's health.

Choosing Others:
Dating and Mate Selection

DATADIGEST

- In 1998, 30 percent of all **never-married adults** were between the ages of 30 and 34. Another 22 percent were 35 to 39.

- Some nations had a **shortage of marriageable women** in the mid-1990s. For example, in India there were nearly 133 single men for every 100 single women, and in China there were nearly three single men for every two single women.

- In 1997, there were 3,000 **dating services** in the United States with an annual revenue of $1 billion. The annual revenue from **newspaper and magazine personal ads** for the same year was $500 million.

- Nationwide, 26 percent of women college students reported being confronted with **alcohol-related unwanted sexual advances.**

Sources: Neville, 1997; Shenon, 1994; U.S. Census Bureau, 1999c; Wechsler, 1995.

SOME of the most popular television programs include *The Dating Game, Blind Date, Change of Heart,* and *Friends or Lovers.* Why are these shows so popular? Some opine that "Americans are voyeuristic and nosy" about other people's real-life dating difficulties. Others feel that viewers identify with people who are still searching for that "love connection" but are at a crossroads in their relationship, as in *Change of Heart.* The producer of *Blind Date* says that many viewers tune in to learn how to be better dates (Tan, 2000).

Despite the advantages of singlehood, most of us seek intimacy with a lifelong partner. Regardless of what words we use—"dating," "going out," "hooking up," "having a thing," or "seeing someone"—mate selection is a process that, most of us hope, will result in pairing off and finding an intimate other or marriage mate. As the box "Courting throughout History" shows, we have more choices today than in the past. Someone once joked that dating is the process of spending enormous amounts of money, time, and energy to get better acquainted with a person you don't especially like in the present and will learn to like a lot less in the future. Although such a "definition" of dating seems cynical, it suggests that finding *the* right person is not as easy as it seems. Dating is romantic and enjoyable; it is also a serious enterprise.

Why Do We Date?

The reasons for **dating**—the process of meeting people socially for possible mate selection—seem self-evident, but dating is considerably more complicated than just going out or having fun. Sociologists describe the dating process as a **marriage market,** in which prospective spouses compare the assets and liabilities of eligible partners and choose the best available mate. In this sense, everyone has a "market value," and whom a person "trades" with depends on what resources each

brings to the exchange (Coltrane, 1998). People weigh their costs and benefits in this exchange to "catch" someone who is often their equal in terms of physical characteristics, education, social class, age, and so on (see Chapter 2).

People differ in their objectives as they choose a sex partner. "Trading" in the marriage market, then, varies depending on one's goals. Those who seek recreational sex, for example, may expend fewer resources—such as time, energy, and money—than people who are looking for a marriage partner who wants to raise children. Like many other choices we make, dating involves taking risks with the resources we invest. The more valuable the "catch," the more likely we are to invest our time and money in looking attractive, accommodating the partner's personality or interests, or getting along with her or his family and friends, for example (Laumann et al., 1994). "One-night stands," in contrast, require taking few risks (assuming the partners don't contract STDs or the woman doesn't become pregnant) and investing few resources.

Note, also, that people might use their resources differently depending on whether the relationship is new or "settling in." As one of my students observed, people may invest more time than money in a relationship if they are no longer in the "trading" stage in the marriage marketplace:

> *It's very expensive to date. When two people are in a comfortable relationship, they tend not to go out as much. The quiet nights at home are considerably less expensive than extravagant nights on the town. The longer you date someone the less of a need there is to impress that person with fancy dinners and costly dates. (Author's files)*

Dating fulfills a number of specific functions that enhance people's sociopsychological development and, ultimately, promote a society's continuity. These functions vary according to a person's age, social class, and

CHANGES ••

Courting throughout History

Historians have found a remarkable continuity in some courtship patterns. Contrary to what we might think, young people in colonial America were often given a surprising degree of freedom in sexual expression. For example, a young suitor in Towanda, Pennsylvania, wrote in his diary that, after the family members went to bed, "my beloved and I went down, made a fire, and sat down to talk and kiss and embrace and bathe in love" (Rothman, 1983: 396). And a young woman wrote passionately to her lover:

O! I do really want to kiss you. How I should like to be in that old parlor with you. I hope there will be a carpet on the floor for it seems you intend to act worse than you ever did before by your letter. But I shall humbly submit to my fate and willingly too, to speak candidly. (Rothman, 1983: 401)

There were also practical considerations. In colonial New England, the engaged woman's parents would conduct economic negotiations, and most young men could not even think about courtship until they owned land. They were advised to "choose by Ears, as well as Eyes" and to select women who were industrious, hardworking, and sensible. Affection was expected to blossom into love *after* marriage.

Some women were very down-to-earth about courtship. A New York woman wrote: "I am sick of all this choosing. If a man is healthy and does not drink and has a good little handful of stock and a good temper and is a good Christian, what difference can it make to a woman which man she takes?" (Ryan, 1983: 40–41).

Before the Industrial Revolution, most courtship activities took place within the hustle and bustle of community

life. Young people could meet after church services, during picnics, or at gatherings like barn raisings, corn huskings, and dances. The buggy ride was especially popular: There was no room for a chaperone, and "the horse might run away or lose a shoe so that one could be stranded on a lonely country road" (McPharlin, 1946: 10).

With the advent of bicycles and telephones, parlor sofas and front-porch swings were quickly abandoned. At the turn of the twentieth century people began to use the term *dating*, which referred to couples setting a specific date, time, and place to meet. When the automobile came into widespread use in the early 1920s, dating took a giant step. "The car provided more privacy and excitement than either the dance hall or the movie theater, and the result was the spread of petting" (Rothman, 1984: 295). Young people had the mobility to meet more frequently, informally, and casually.

---

sex. Dating functions can be either *manifest*—the purposes are visible, recognized, and intended—or *latent*—the purposes are unintended or not immediately recognized (see Chapter 2). Keep in mind that these functions often overlap.

Manifest Functions of Dating

One of the most important functions of dating is *recreation*. Dating should be fun. Waller (1937) saw dating as "pure thrill seeking." Although recent studies suggest that dating has become more serious and marriage-oriented, it is still fun. And as more people postpone marriage, dating has become an important recreational activity in its own right.

Another important manifest function is *companionship*. Especially as people age, dating may be important for developing and maintaining long-term friendships rather than just for recreation or "thrills" (McCabe, 1984). Dating can be a valuable source of companionship, especially after retirement, when leisure hours increase.

Finally, whether people admit it or not, dating is usually a step in *mate selection*. Adolescents often become angry if their parents criticize their dates with

such remarks as, "We don't want you to marry this guy" or "She's not good enough for you." The teenager's impatient rebuttal is usually, "I'm not going to *marry* him (her). We're just dating!" Parents are often critical, however, because they recognize that dating *can* lead to marriage. Young people are "comparison shopping," acquiring knowledge of what sorts of people they are attracted to and may want to marry (Whyte, 1990). In contrast, there is little need for dating in cultures where parents control their children's mate selection, where values focus on the needs of the family rather than on those of the individual, or where love is not the basis for marriage (see later sections of this chapter).

Latent Functions of Dating

The manifest purpose of "meeting new people" tends to obscure a function of dating that is less visible but equally important—that of *socialization*, in which people learn to adjust and adapt their own behavior to that of others. Through dating, people learn about expected gender roles; they learn about family structures that are different from their own; and they learn about new attitudes, beliefs, and values. This kind of learning may be especially vital for high school students, who can test and hone their self-confidence and their communication skills in a one-on-one setting (Ramu, 1989; Berk, 1993).

Gaining social status is another important latent function of dating. In the mid-1930s Waller found that college students tried to date the "most desirable" people on campus. Dating a very attractive coed or the son of wealthy parents enhanced one's status and prestige. This function has not changed. It is not unusual, for example, to hear someone brag about dating the captain of the football team or cheerleading squad, a vice president of a prestigious company, or a successful physician.

A related function of dating is *fulfilling ego needs.* Being asked out on a date or having one's invitation accepted boosts a person's self-esteem and self-image. If the date goes well, or if the partner is understanding, flattering, or attentive, self-confidence is enhanced.

Finally, dating provides *opportunities for sexual experimentation and intimacy.* As you saw in Chapter 6, many teenagers learn about sex during dating.

Manifest and latent functions of dating may change over time. Roscoe et al. (1987) examined dating patterns at three developmental stages: early adolescence (sixth grade), middle adolescence (eleventh grade), and late adolescence (college). These researchers found that early and middle adolescents were most interested in recreation, romantic intimacy, and status. Late adolescents cited sexual intimacy, companionship, and learning socialization skills as the most important aspects of dating. In addition, whereas early adolescents emphasized such things as fashionable dress and peer approval, late adolescents were more interested in the dating partner's future goals and job prospects. Thus, as people mature, their expectations about dating change.

The Dating Spectrum

About 3 percent of the U.S. population never marries (U.S. Bureau of the Census, 1999c). Most of us will marry at least once during our lifetimes. Between adolescence and the altar, speaking symbolically, most people initially get an overview of the marriage market by getting together in groups of prospective partners, then pairing off, and ultimately going off with one person. Although traditional dating is still widespread, there are a number of newer forms of getting together, as well as some combinations of traditional and contemporary dating. As partners become more serious, they compare expectations and habits, look for compatibility or complementarity in their personality traits, search for similarities in their beliefs and values, develop trust, and express loyalty, acceptance, admiration, and support for each other (Sterling, 1992).

Dating during the middle of the twentieth century was more structured than it is today. Although casual dates weren't unheard of, formal dates ruled by codes of dress and behavior were commonplace.

Traditional Dating

In traditional dating, males and females follow clearly defined expectations in meeting and spending time with each other. The *traditional date,* which is the form that dominated up through the 1970s at least among the middle classes, is a fairly formal way of meeting potential spouses. The girl waits to be asked out, the boy picks her up at her home, and she is almost always late, giving Mom and Dad a chance to chat with the boy. The boy has specific plans for the evening, the couple has a good time, and he brings her home by curfew. Some television reruns like *Happy Days* and *The Brady Bunch,* although idealized, portray this type of date. The downside of the traditional date is the expectation that because the boy pays for the date, the girl must show her gratitude in some way, usually through a goodnight kiss, petting, or intercourse.

Cultural Variations on Traditional Dating   The continuing popularity of traditional dating is particularly noticeable in such formal events as *coming-out parties,* where young women—usually of the upper classes—are "introduced to society" at debutante balls. Other cultural rites-of-passage celebrations include the *bas mitzvah* for girls and the *bar mitzvah* for boys in the Jewish community. These rituals mark the end of puberty and readiness for adult responsibilities and such rights as dating.

In some Latino communities, the *quinceañera* (translated loosely as "fifteen years") is a coming-out party that celebrates a girl's entrance into adulthood. The *quince* (pronounced KEEN-say), an elaborate and dignified religious and social affair given by the girl's parents, begins with a Catholic mass, followed by a reception at which 14 couples (each couple represents one year in the girl's life before the quince) serve as her attendants. The event includes a traditional waltz in which the young woman dances with her father, a champagne toast, and the tossing of a bouquet to the boys to determine who wins the first dance with the young woman. The girl may be allowed to date boys after her quince (Leff, 1994). In Cuban American neighborhoods in Miami, middle-class and affluent parents pay between $30,000 and $50,000 for a quince. Parents of modest means pay as much as $10,000: ". . . factory workers, an auto body shop manager. . . . They save up for years for their daughters" (McLane, 1995: 42). There is no comparable rite of passage for Latino boys.

Going Steady Going steady and "getting pinned" were common during the 1930s and became especially popular after World War II. A couple was "pinned" when a male gave his fraternity pin to his girlfriend to show his affection and commitment to the relationship. *Going steady*, which often meant that the partners were seeing only each other, usually came after a couple had had a number of dates, and it preceded engagement (Tuttle, 1993). Going steady was not necessarily expected to result in marriage. As one teenage girl explained: "Going steady doesn't have to mean you're madly in love. . . . It just means you like one boy better than the rest" (quoted in Breines, 1992: 116). Going steady eliminated many of the anxieties associated with traditional dating but allowed emotional and sexual intimacy without a long-term commitment. It did, however, give a "hands-off" message to possible competitors.

It is not clear how widespread going steady is today, but a "modern" version may be "goin' with" or "going together." For many junior high school students, "goin' with" signals their transition from childhood to adolescence (Merten, 1996). Although the couples are not planning to get engaged, they are also not seeing other partners. "Goin' with" sometimes starts before puberty, even though the relationships of fourth-, fifth-, and sixth-graders usually last only a few weeks (Thorne, 1993). For older children, "goin' with" may last months or even years.

The advantage of "goin' with" is having a stable relationship when many other things around the young person are changing and unpredictable (physiological changes, divorcing parents, preparation for college or a job). The disadvantage is that such a relationship discourages meeting new people during a developmental stage when adolescents experience many changes in their attitudes and interests within relatively short periods of time.

Contemporary Dating

Contemporary dating falls into two general categories: *casual dating*, which includes hanging out, getting together, and "pack dating"; and *serious dating*, which can lead to cohabitation, engagement, and marriage.

In one ritual of the Latino "quince," the young woman's father slips on her first pair of high heels. In the Miami Cuban community, some families spend as much as $50,000 on a daughter's quinceañera.

Hanging Out Parents and adolescents in many American homes engage in a familiar dialogue:

Parent:	Where are you going?
Teenager:	Out.
Parent:	What will you do?
Teenager:	Just hang out.
Parent:	Who will be there?
Teenager:	I don't know.
Parent:	When will you be back?
Teenager:	I'm not sure.
Parent:	Leave a phone number, please.
Teenager:	We'll be moving around a lot.

Whether *hanging out* occurs on a neighborhood street corner, a pizza parlor, or in a mall, it is a time-honored adolescent pastime. A customary meeting time and place may be set, with people coming and going; or once a group gets together and the members decide what they want to do, the information is spread (at amazing speed) by telephone or e-mail. Hanging out is possible both because many parents respect their teenagers' privacy and independence and because most 16- and 17-year-olds have access to cars.

Getting Together *Getting together* implies a more intimate and structured event than hanging out. A group of friends meet at a friend's house, a club, or a party. Because most people do not come with dates, there can be a lot of mixing. Either males or females can organize the initial effort, and the group often pools its resources, for the use of alcohol or other drugs may be part of the activities. Because participants are not formally dating, there is a lot of flexibility in meeting new people and initiating relationships.

The typical characteristic of getting together is "floating." The group may meet at someone's house for a few hours, decide to go to a party later, spend a few hours at a pizza place, and wind up at another party. Young adults see getting together as normal and rational—"You get to meet a lot of people" or "We can go someplace else if the party is dead"—but it concerns parents. Even if teenagers call from the various locations to tell parents where they are (although it is easy to forget to do so), parents worry that the gatherings can become unpredictable or dangerous.

Getting together is a popular form of dating for several reasons. Because the activities are spontaneous, there is little anxiety about preparing for a formal date or initiating or rejecting sexual advances. It is also a less threatening emotional experience because the participants do not have to worry about finding a date or getting "stuck" with someone (like a blind date) for the whole evening. It also relieves females of sexual pressure because the women may help organize the get-together, share in the expenses, and come alone or with friends (not as part of a couple). People may pair off, participate in the group as a couple, or gradually withdraw to spend more time together, but there is less pressure to have a date as a sign of popularity. Finally, getting together decreases parental control over the choice of one's friends. Parents usually don't know many of the adolescents and are less likely to disapprove of the friendships or to compare notes with other parents.

"Pack Dating" While traditional dating and early marriages are not uncommon on many campuses, especially in the South and Midwest, many undergraduates socialize in unpartnered groups, or *pack dating*:

> They go out to dinner in groups, attend movies in groups and at parties dance in a circle of five or six. The packs give students a sense of self-assurance and identity, but keep them from deeper, more committed relationships. (Gabriel, 1997: 22)

Pack dating may be popular for several reasons. If college students don't expect to marry until their 30s, socializing in small groups provides recreation without feeling pressured to make a commitment or get romantically involved. Since, also, increasing numbers of students hold down jobs while taking high course loads, many may feel that they don't have the time and energy to find dates or maintain one-on-one relationships. Finally, if some of the participants "hook up" (which can range from petting to sexual intercourse), pack dating may be an attempt to deal with the risk of disease: "If sex partners are drawn from a small circle of friends, whose histories and habits are known to all members of the group, the risk of exposure is theoretically lower" (Gabriel, 1997: 22).

Traditional–Contemporary Combinations

Several dating patterns incorporate both traditional customs and contemporary innovations. Today it is more acceptable for either sex to initiate dates or to invite a partner to a prom or dinner, but many of the gender scripts (see Chapter 4) remain remarkably traditional.

Proms and Homecoming Parties *Proms and homecoming parties* continue to be among the most popular dating events. As in the past, they are formal or semiformal. Women get corsages, men are typically responsible for transportation and other expenses, and females, especially, invest quite a bit of time and money in preparing for these events:

> She spends $196 for a dress; begins looking 12 weeks before the prom; shops at 11 different stores; and tries on 36 different dresses before finding the perfect frock. He spends $162 on accessories and tuxedo rental or purchase and reserves his duds six weeks before the prom. (Weissman, 1999b: 80)

Contemporary changes include occasional invitations by women to men instead of the reverse; attending these events in small groups of friends rather than with partners; and extending an event by holding sleepovers (presumably chaperoned by parents), staying out all night and returning after breakfast, or continuing the festivities into the weekend at a nearby beach or other recreational place.

Dinner Dates One of the most traditional forms of dating, the *dinner date* is still popular today, especially among adults. One observer has noted that there is no more widespread courtship ploy than offering food in the hope of gaining sexual favors: "Around the world men give women presents prior to lovemaking. A fish, a piece of meat, sweets, and beer are among the delicacies men have invented as offerings" (Fisher, 1993: 43).

Dinner dates, and especially first dates of any kind, are still highly scripted. For example, in a study of college students, Rose and Frieze (1993) found considerable gender typing on the first date. Men typically initiated the date, drove the car, opened doors, and started sexual interaction (such as kissing good night or making out). Women spent a good deal of time on their appearance, depended on the men to make the plans, and often responded to men's sexual overtures instead of initiating them. The researchers concluded that making a "good impression" early in the dating relationship is still largely synonymous with playing traditional gender roles.

In contrast to the past, the dinner date or the first date does not always involve "paying off" with sex. The rise of the women's movement in the 1970s led to the custom of *going Dutch*, in which men and women split the costs of a date. Sharing dating expenses frees women to initiate dates and, at the same time, relieves them from feeling they are expected to reciprocate a man's financial generosity with sexual favors.

Perhaps the least gender-typed dating, at least on first dates, is between same-sex partners. In a study of lesbians and gay men, Klinkenberg and Rose (1994) found little gender typing compared to heterosexual dating: Both partners participated more equally in orchestrating the date, maintaining the conversation, and initiating physical contact. There was also less concern about appearance.

Meeting Others

The quest for love reflects a variety of creative strategies. Singles bars have been popular for a number of years. A matchmaking dry-cleaning owner in Washington, D.C., has devoted a wall for customers who leave photos and phone numbers (Makinen, 1997). An especially determined, never-married, college-educated elderly woman contacted a research scientist at the University of Michigan to find states with "the highest concentration of retired, single gentlemen who are well-educated and healthy" and the ratio of men with these attributes to all women over age 65 (Dortch, 1995). The scientist suggested Nevada because it had 156 educated, retired, and single men for every 100 elderly women. A growing number of cities have gay neighborhoods where men and women easily meet potential partners at the grocery store, the library, and church groups (Huston and Schwartz, 1995).

There are many other avenues for finding a mate—including clubs, college classes, matchmaking by your sister-in-law, and recreational activities such as hiking, bicycling, and bowling groups. Others include personal classified ads, mail-order brides, and marriage bureaus. Recently, advances in computer technology have added to the methods available today, all of which promise (but do not necessarily provide) options for meeting a prospective spouse.

Personal Classified Advertisements

Personal classified advertisements used to be published in the back pages of "smutty" magazines. Now mainstream newspapers include "personals" in their daily or weekend issues. Similarly, many suburban, religious, and local newspapers also carry personal ads.

Men are twice as likely as women to place personal ads. In addition, the ads seek companions with stereotypical gender characteristics: Male advertisers tend to emphasize such traits as appearance and attractiveness in the women they hope to meet, whereas women advertisers look for intelligence, a college degree, and financial status in the male (Davis, 1990). While 50 percent of the male advertisers in one study used terms such as "curvaceous," "pretty," or "gorgeous," only 34 percent of the females used comparable terms such as "handsome," "hunk," or "athletic." When specifying their requirement in a mate, women were four times more likely than males to use terms like "college-educated," "homeowner," and "professional" (Dunbar, 1995).

The researchers of a recent study of personal columns noted that the ad placers are very "selective" (rather than dishonest) in their self-descriptions because both sexes "are quite conscious of the cultural scripts" that females and males expect. Because, for example, women know that men want attractive partners, they emphasize their appearance and femininity. Men, similarly, aware of women's expectations, describe their success, professional status, or being a "caring" and "sensitive" person (Raybeck et al., 2000).

These findings suggest that most women and men barter with the qualities that they see as most important in the marriage market. Because (as you saw in Chapters 4, 5, and 6), many women cannot provide for children by themselves and many males value youth and attractiveness, women tend to rank the status and earning potential of a prospective mate higher than men do, while men rate physical appearance more highly.

The advantages of classified ads include anonymity, low cost and time savings, and numerous applicants. A major disadvantage is that advertisers often exaggerate their desirable attributes (such as attractiveness). As one of my male students said, "I called her because she said she was devastatingly gorgeous and intelligent. She was neither." In addition, "selective truth telling" is commonplace. For example, single women often omit mentioning having children in the ads because the men might not be willing to support children from a previous marriage (Ahuvia and Adelman, 1992).

A recent variation is the "voice personal," which promises to "put you together with someone who shares similar interests, dreams, and goals." For example, a person can place a 20-word classified ad in the newspaper and record a personal voice greeting as well. People responding to the ad can browse through the voice greetings, make selections, and leave advertisers a message.

Mail-Order Brides

Some American men seeking wives patronize mail-order services that publish photographs and descriptions of women, usually from Russia and poor countries in Asia or Latin America. Women's rights activists view men who seek mail-order brides as "losers" who want sock-sorters or live-in nurses. Although the men do not deny that they want housekeepers, they complain that American women are self-centered or promiscuous:

> American girls left me really disappointed. . . .
> They're pushy, spoiled rotten, and they talk like
> sailors. They're not cooperative, but combative—
> and they never appreciate what you do for
> them. . . . They're not psychologically together.
> They just don't seem to know what they want.
> (Krich, 1989: 385, 387)

Many American men look for Asian mail-order brides:

> The American men imagine the [Asian] woman as
> the epitome of the traditional wife: submissive,
> subservient, eager to please men and easy to please,
> erotic, exotic, a good housekeeper, contented with
> a nice home, faithful, loyal, and not inclined to
> divorce her husband. (Ordoñez, 1997: 123)

Such stereotypes and expectations, however, may clash with reality. In the case of Filipinas, for example, the brides come from a strong matriarchal culture and the wife may not be submissive. Instead, she may demand more and more authority over family finances and decision making. Contributing to the economic advancement of family members left behind is a major obligation. If a husband doesn't allow his wife to send money back home, she may find a job to have her own income. Conflict arises if she neglects the housework or doesn't live up to the husband's idealized visions of marital happiness (Ordoñez, 1997).

Mail-order brides are usually 20 years younger than their prospective husbands. At home, they often live in poverty, are unwed or abandoned mothers, or may be unacceptable to the men in their own countries. Frequently, they see marriage as the fastest way to enter the United States legally (Randolph, 1996). Some are subjected to mental or physical abuse by the men they marry yet fear to seek help lest they be deported.

Marriage Bureaus

In some countries, classified ads and especially marriage bureaus have replaced the old-fashioned, community-based matchmaker (see the box "Modern Arranged Marriages in India"). In the United States, prices, services, and personal attention vary according to the needs of the client. In one case, the retired director of a nonprofit health agency charges $65 for two introductions and another $40 for additional matches (based on "an old lady's gut feeling"). At the more expensive Meet the Elite dating service in New York City, clients pay at least $10,000 for a more rigorous selection process in which all subscribers are investigated by detectives, undergo medical examinations and handwriting analysis, and are analyzed by the company's psychologist (Polk, 1988).

For $9,600, another entrepreneur in New York doesn't introduce women to any men but provides a six-month "intensive husband-hunting program." The program includes a talk with an interior designer on how to make the women's homes or apartments man-friendly, 9 hours of learning to move gracefully, 8 hours of wardrobe consultations, 26 hours of talking with a "relationship coach," and a field trip to a bridal shop where women try on dresses and visualize their wedding day (Marder, 2000). One-on-one services where a matchmaker searches for someone who is "just right for you" can cost up to $25,000 (Tennesen, 1993).

Computer Dating on the Internet

Many people find computer-dating services appealing because they are busy at work, have less time to date or look for eligible partners, or are disenchanted with singles bars. Nevertheless, many are disappointed by the results.

Computer-dating services typically use 5- to 10-minute videotapes, where the candidates talk about themselves and their interests. This method is not very effective because data on too many prospective partners can create an information overload and result in poor

CROSSCULTURAL

Modern Arranged Marriages in India

In India, the loyalty of the individual to the family is a cherished ideal. To preserve this ideal, marriages are carefully arranged to avoid selecting inappropriate mates; brides and grooms rarely choose their own spouses. In some cities, people are combining traditional aspects of arranged marriages with very nontraditional methods of finding prospective spouses.

Among the literate classes, newspaper advertisements and computer services are replacing traditional matchmakers. Every Sunday the newspapers are filled with classified ads inviting inquiries about "smart, well-educated, professional boys" and "really beautiful, homely, university graduate girls." ("Homely" in India does not mean unattractive but that a woman would make a good home-maker.)

This style of mate selection is not confined to Indians living in India. For example, Sanjit, a 34-year-old engineer, has lived in the United States since he was 12. Sanjit's family received 103 responses when they placed the following ad in *The Times of India*: "Alliance invited for smart, Bengali Hindu engineer, 34, 185 cms [6 feet], settled in the United States, music addict, no encumbrances." Sanjit's family narrowed the list down to seven women and then started negotiations, writing or calling the women's families. Sanjit said he hoped his family would find the right woman so he could get married on his next trip to India ("Seek spouse . . . ," 1989).

A 1976 study of upper-middle-class north Indian women found that 39 percent said love was essential for marital happiness. Two decades later, that figure had fallen to 11 percent. Among urban professionals polled in another survey, 81 percent said their marriages had been arranged, and 94 percent rated their marriages "very successful" (Lakshmanan, 1997).

Although educated, upper-middle-class women are allowed to marry whomever they fall in love with, many opt for arranged marriages. One young woman explained: "Love is important, but it's not sufficient." She asked her parents to research and solicit proposals from parents of men with good earning potential and a higher education and who were refined, intellectual, and good human beings. She is reportedly happily married to a man she had met just three times before their engagement.

Arranged marriages persist, also, because of family ties. Even financially independent couples usually live with the husband's parents. As a result, similar backgrounds and compatibility with in-laws are more important than in the West. The advantage is that there tends to be much family support if a marriage runs into trouble. As one young woman noted: "In the United States, you go to your shrink. Here, we go to our family" (Lakshmanan, 1997: 2A).

---

decision making (Woll and Young, 1989). And even when clients find attractive possibilities, a match is not guaranteed because videotapes and written summaries are simply not accurate predictors of personality traits, values, and long-term behavior (see Ahuvia and Adelman, 1992, for a review of some of this research). Many people believe that finding dates through computer services is safer than picking them up in bars, but all dating involves the risk of such serious problems as sexual pressure, aggression, and violence.

The most recent computer cupids are electronic networks. People can subscribe to discussion groups and chat rooms, "meet" hundreds of other people, and discuss anything from radishes to romance. Match.com, for instance, charges members $40 a month to match members with others whom the computer deems compatible. Jdate.com caters to Jewish singles. Singleswithscruples.com is "an Internet dating site for people who have morals and a sense of honor."

One of the advantages of electronic liaisons is that people use code names and remain anonymous or they can get involved. Because physical appearance recedes into the background, attraction and intimacy can sometimes lead to enduring relationships or marriage. Some networks have even had weddings online. In one case, the happy couple typed their vows on one computer terminal while the minister typed his lines on another, and more than 75 subscribers "witnessed" the wedding (Catalfo, 1994).

Electronic romances can also be deceptive and superficial. As in classified personal ads, people may not be honest or may have an exaggerated notion of their good qualities. One critic notes that "you can learn more [about a person] from two minutes at a party than from months of e-mail communication" (Herbert and Hammel, 1999: 56). A cyber-romance can also become offensive, intimidating, or dangerous. Rejected suitors may start stalking or harassing their love interests (Plotnikoff, 1994). Lovers who quarrel or break up might send hundreds of vindictive and hostile messages to the person who has spurned them before the network management closes the offender's account (Catalfo, 1994). In addition, people who use the Internet to find real-life sex partners are much more likely to have had sexually transmitted diseases or to have engaged in risky behavior. As a result, people who seek sex using the Internet are at greater risk for STDs and HIV infection (McFarlane et al., 2000).

Choosing Whom We Date: Choices and Constraints

Many people believe that "This is America. I can date anyone I want." Compared to even ten years ago, people *do* have more dating and mate-selection options today. As the discussion in this section on heterogamy shows, more of us are dating and marrying across ethnic, racial, religious, and age boundaries. Most of us, however, select dating partners and marry people like ourselves in many ways. As you will see shortly, much of the available research shows that marrying people like ourselves often results in stable relationships. There is little research evidence indicating, however, that dating and marrying people different from us result in unhappy unions. We begin with an examination of the filtering process that shapes our choices; we demonstrate that a person doesn't simply "date anyone I want." Then we look at partners who are expanding their marriage market perimeters.

Homogamy and Filter Theory: Narrowing the Marriage Market

Theoretically, we have a large pool of eligible dating partners. In reality, our field of potential partners is limited by our culture. **Filter theory** suggests that people searching for partners tend to go through a process of sifting eligible people according to specific criteria and thus narrow the pool of potential partners to a relatively small number of candidates (Kerckhoff and Davis, 1962). *Figure 7.1* depicts the filter theory of mate selection.

The major filtering mechanism is homogamy. Often used interchangeably with the term *endogamy* (see Chapter 1), **homogamy** refers to dating or marrying someone who possesses similar social characteristics such as ethnicity and race, religion, age, and social class. The reasons for dating and marrying homogamously are unclear. These tendencies may reflect pressure from family and friends, personal preferences, the pool of eligible partners, or a combination of these and other factors. Although the reasons for homogamy are inconclusive, some of the most important filtering variables include geographic proximity, and physical attractiveness, as well as similar social characteristics.

Propinquity Geographic closeness, or **propinquity**, is one of the first filters that shapes whom we meet, see often, get to know, interact with frequently, and subsequently date and marry. Despite the mushrooming business in personal ads, singles bars, and Internet services, most people meet their prospective spouses in high school, in college, at work, or in community activities. According to a national study, 66 percent of married couples were introduced by family and friends, co-workers, classmates, and neighbors; 32 percent introduced themselves but in "preselected" circumstances—they were at a party given by a mutual friend or they were at a social organization or club

Computer-dating services typically use short videotapes where candidates talk about themselves and their interests. Although such matches rarely lead to marriage, computer-dating customers feel that these services are safer than meeting eligible partners at bars or through classified ads.

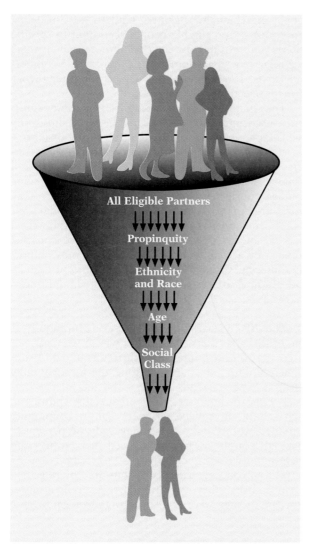

FIGURE 7.1 **The Filter Theory of Mate Selection.** According to filter theory, most of us narrow our pool of prospective partners by selecting people we see on a regular basis who are most similar to us in terms of such variables as age, race, values, social class, sexual orientation, and physical attractiveness.

(Laumann et al., 1994). Thus, we meet sexual and marriage partners, typically, through physically close social networks of people who are very similar to us.

As more women enter the labor force, workplaces offer many possibilities for meeting a prospective mate. Although a romantic relationship between a supervisor and a subordinate can decrease performance and morale, 70 percent of employers say they have no policies or guidelines regarding office romances. In addition, 76 percent of the respondents in a recent survey saw nothing wrong with intra-office dating ("Taboo no more . . . ," 2000). In some situations, however, the workplace dampens opportunities

for making a love connection. Some of the high-tech pockets, like Silicon Valley in northern California, for instance, have among the biggest single-man surpluses of any place in America. Some of these men are willing to pay as much as $10,000 for a matchmaking service to help find them a potential bride (Conlin, 2000).

With a few exceptions (such as publications targeted at specific religious or ethnic groups), the most successful publishers of singles magazines feature local—whether rural or urban—rather than national eligible partners (Enrico, 1993; Freiberg, 1996). Most people do not have the time and resources to maintain long-distance romances, although computer-based communication, as you saw earlier, might facilitate such relationships in the future (see also Rohlfing, 1995; Merkle and Richardson, 2000).

Physical Attractiveness A number of studies show that men and women choose partners whose level of physical attractiveness is similar to their own (see Berscheid et al., 1982). Physically attractive people benefit from a "halo effect"; they are *assumed* to possess other desirable social characteristics as well, such as warmth, sexual responsiveness, kindness, strength, modesty, sensitivity, poise, sociability, and good character. They are also seen as likely to have more prestige, happier marriages, more social and professional success, and more fulfilling lives in the future (Dion et al., 1972). Despite such perceptions, life satisfaction is much the same for very attractive and not so attractive people (Brehm, 1992).

In an examination of five decades of research on the topic, Hatfield and Sprecher (1986) found that physical attractiveness is more important for men than for women in choosing dating and marriage partners. Other studies have confirmed such findings (see, for example, Bolig et al., 1984; Woll and Young, 1989). You will recall that several recent studies of personal ads found, similarly, that male advertisers emphasized attractiveness in the women they hoped to meet. Women advertisers, moreover, were much more likely than were men to describe themselves as attractive.

Perceptions of beauty vary across cultures. Several Nigerian communities prize hefty women and "hail a woman's rotundity" as a sign of good health, prosperity, and allure. Many believe that a thin girl will be sickly and unable to bear children. Teenage girls spend several months in a "fattening room" eating starchy food such as yams, rice, and beans. The fattening room is a centuries-old rite of passage from girlhood to womanhood. The months are spent in gaining weight and supplemented by daily visits from elderly matrons who offer tips on how to cook and be a successful wife and mother (Simmons, 1998).

In the United States and many other Western countries, in contrast, and especially for women, attractiveness is synonymous with slimness and eternal youth. The pressure to "look good" begins as early as middle school (see Chapter 14). Although teens (mostly girls) accounted for only 3.1 percent of nearly 3 million cosmetic procedures performed in the United States in 1998, teenage cosmetic surgeries nearly doubled between 1996 and 1998, from about 14,000 to almost 25,000. Most of the surgery involved breast enlargement or reduction, nose and ear reshaping, and liposuction (Austin, 2000).

Businesses are delighted with our obsession about our looks. According to one marketing analyst, "Anything with the words 'age defying' sells." As a result we can be seduced into believing we've halted or slowed the aging process by a variety of products, and most targeted at women. A few of these products include Rembrandt Age Defying toothpaste, Age Defiance hosiery, Clairol's Revitalizing Age-Defying Color System, Oil of Olay Age Defying Daily Renewal Cream, Pond's Age Defying Lotion, Revlon's Age Defying eye color, and Clinique's Stop Signs Anti-Aging Serum (Mayer, 1999).

While a pleasant physical appearance is usually a desirable trait in both women and men, physical attractiveness may not always enhance one's chances of finding a suitable partner. In a study of black women, for example, some of the respondents felt that being attractive sometimes had negative consequences. A good-looking woman might make a man feel so insecure that he will not approach her: "People assume you already have enough candidates." Many of the women also felt that "the guys want to show you off because an attractive woman increases a man's status in his friends' eyes" (Sterk-Elifson, 1994: 108). If some men treat attractive women as trophies instead of serious marriage candidates, the women may have a large pool of dating partners but few serious suitors.

Men assign more importance to physical attractiveness than women do, but both sexes tend to choose partners whose degree of attractiveness closely matches their own.

Ethnicity and Race   Films like *Jungle Fever, The Bodyguard,* and *Mississippi Masala* romanticized interracial relationships and sex, but in real life, interracial dating is still highly controversial. For example, a high school principal in Alabama threatened to cancel the senior prom if interracial couples planned to attend. Although he later withdrew the threat, the principal's initial action led to lawsuits, angry exchanges between white and black parents in the community, and, ultimately, the torching of the high school (Gross and Smothers, 1994). In 2000, a straight A student and talented football player who was a high school junior was found hanging from a tree just steps from his front door. Although a coroner's report concluded that the young man had committed suicide, many people in the small Mississippi town felt that he was lynched by someone who disapproved of his dating white girls.

On some college campuses, black female students resent interracial dating between white women and black men. The black women say that such interracial romances decrease the already modest pool of eligible black men and make them feel rejected by black men,

who "naively succumb to standards of beauty drawn from mainstream magazines and movies, which present blonde, blue-eyed women as the ideal" (Gose, 1996: A47; see also St. Jean and Parker, 1995; and Kiecolt and Fossett, 1997). Outside of college campuses, many black women avoid interracial dating because it creates conflict with their relatives, friends, and colleagues and decreases the survival of the race by having interracial babies (Sterk-Elifson, 1994). Black journalists like Ellis Cose (1995) have criticized black women who date white men instead of cherishing the millions of black males who are hardworking contributors to society despite negative stereotypes and "expectations of failure on every side."

Within the black community, skin hue and features can also be a political issue: "Blacks often judge each other on the basis of the skin color of those . . . they date and mate. The black man who goes out exclusively with light-skinned women may be accused of having a color complex" (Russell et al., 1992: 107). According to researcher Robert L. Douglas, the more strongly a man identifies with his African heritage, the

MULTICULTURAL

Why I Never Dated a White Girl

Although interracial and interethnic dating is on the rise, many people consider such coupling inappropriate or outrageous. For instance, Lawrence Otis Graham (1996: 36–56) gives six reasons why he never dated a white woman and why his grounds for doing so reflect many blacks' opposition to interracial relationships:

- **Objection 1:** When black leaders or advocates marry outside the race, such decisions demonstrate less commitment to black people and our causes.
- **Objection 2:** We fear that intermarrying blacks are making a statement to black and white America that black spouses are less desirable partners—and are, therefore, inferior.
- **Objection 3:** Interracial marriage undermines our ability to introduce our black children to black mentors and role models who accept their racial identity with confidence and pride.
- **Objection 4:** Because it diffuses our resources, interracial marriage makes it difficult to build a black America that has wealth, prestige, and power. This makes it harder to empower black America and to erase the stereotypes of a weak and impoverished black community.

- **Objection 5:** We worry that confused biracial children will turn their backs on the black race once they discover that it's easier to live as a white person.
- **Objection 6:** Today's interracial relationships are a painful reminder of a 250-year period in black American history when white people exploited our sexuality.

Interracial and interethnic couples encounter numerous obstacles on a fairly regular basis. One of the most common negative experiences is stares by others, particularly in public places. In the service sector, waiters or waitresses, gas station attendants, convenience store clerks, sales staff in retail outlets, or even other customers at these places often express their hostility ("Sometimes the service stinks or takes too long") (McNamara et al., 1999). Other unpleasant, sometimes frightening expressions of disapproval come from passers-by:

We were in Sausalito a couple of years ago. . . .We were walking down the street, just sightseeing, and doing what tourists do. And this guy's coming up the street, and . . . as he approached us, he kind of said under his breath, "White girl, wake up" (Rosenblatt et al., 1995: 128).

Some of the literature on Asian intermarriage (research on interracial and interethnic dating is practically nonexistent) reflects several factors that might also explain dating outside of one's ethnic group. First, Asian American men born in the United States are far more likely to marry women who are white (19 percent), of other Asian origins (23 percent), or another racial minority (6 percent) than more recent immigrants (Pan, 2000). Such statistics suggest that assimilation blurs interracial dating boundaries. Second, because their economic and educational achievements are high, Asian Pacific Islanders might be seen as attractive marriage partners (see Chapter 12). Some observers suggest, finally, that Asian American men are now portrayed as sexy, cool, and desirable in such films as *Anna and the King* and *Lethal Weapon 4*. This "new wave of Asian actors and action heroes—Chow Yun Fat, Rick Yune and Jet Li—are showing that Asian stars can be objects of lust as well as the next guy" (Pan, 2000: 51). Despite such positive images, Asian (and Latino) women and men are often pressured to marry within their own group to maintain the family's cultural values and traditions.

less likely he is to be attracted to light-skinned black women (cited in Russell et al., 1992). Thus, and as the box "Why I Never Dated a White Girl" discusses, homogamy influences dating behavior *within* as well as across racial and ethnic lines.

Religion Religion can play a major role in dating and mate selection. All three of the major religions in the United States—Catholicism, Protestantism, and Judaism—have traditionally opposed interfaith marriages.

Jews, who constitute about 3 percent of the total U.S. population, have one of the lowest birth rates and one of the "oldest" populations. About 40 percent of Jews are over the age of 45, compared to 30 percent of the general population. Thus they consider intermarriage a serious threat to Jewish identity and culture. Some Jews actively discourage intermarriage, and some parents arrange marriages for their children (Hartman, 1988). Dozens of synagogues have started Jewish dating services and singles programs, and even Reform Jews are encouraging non-Jewish spouses to convert (Gruson, 1985).

Most religions oppose interfaith marriage because of the belief that it weakens individual commitment to the faith. Church leaders, for example, often advise

Mormon adolescents to date only within their own religion. One reason is that only Mormons are allowed to participate in the highly valued marriage ceremony in a Mormon temple (Markstrom-Adams, 1991). In the Roman Catholic Church, interfaith couples must sign a premarital agreement promising to raise the children as Catholics.

Religion often sets clear standards regarding "respectable family styles." In black and other communities, religiously similar spouses typically share basic beliefs about child rearing and other family issues and hold compatible views of marriage and commitment to marital and familial roles (Ellison, 1997). If religions differ, especially in the case of interracial and interethnic marriages, a couple may be the brunt of gossip instead of being embraced by the clergy and church members.

Age Americans tend to marry within the same age group; the man is typically two to three years older than the woman. If there are large age differences, and especially if the woman is the older dating partner, families and friends are likely to disapprove. Large age differences may also lead to generation gaps in attitudes about lifestyle, such as music preferences, recreation, and family activities. Furthermore, a much older man may be unwilling to have children, especially if he has a family by a previous marriage or is expected to share in the child-rearing responsibilities. Even if he wants to raise a second family, he may not have the energy or patience to deal with high-spirited or rambunctious progeny (see Chapter 16).

Social Class Most people marry within their social class because they share similar attitudes, values, and lifestyles. Even when people from different ethnic groups intermarry, they usually belong to the same social class (Mindel et al., 1988). Despite the popularity of films like *Pretty Woman* in which a powerful business mogul marries a prostitute, very few of the rich and powerful marry outside their social class. The *New York Times* wedding page provides a good example of our class-consciousness. According to Brooks (2000), the *Times* emphasizes four things about a person—college degrees, graduate degrees, career path, and parents' professions. And, of course, marriages among couples from lower socioeconomic levels shouldn't expect to see their engagement or wedding announcement in the *Times* or other national newspapers. The Harlequin romance novels are probably popular, in part, because they reflect many people's fantasies about breaking out of the boundaries imposed by our rigid mate-selection rules and expectations.

Some studies suggest that parents play a minimal role in direct courtship (Leslie et al., 1986), but remember that parents have already influenced the field of eligibles by choosing where to live. Parents may not feel the need to exert pressure on their children to marry someone of "their own kind" because communities are typically organized by social class; schools, churches, and recreational facilities reflect the socioeconomic levels of neighborhoods. It is highly unlikely that children living in upper-class neighborhoods will even meet those in middle-class, much less working-class, families. Eckland (1968) referred to colleges and universities as "matrimonial agencies" that are arranged hierarchically; students at Ivy League, private, state-supported, and community colleges have few chances to meet one another. Because they influence their children both by encouraging them

Although endogamy continues to be a strong force in choosing a mate, interracial and interethnic marriages are becoming more common.

to go to college and by advising them on selecting a particular college or university, many parents further narrow dating choices in terms of social class.

Finally, social class interacts with other variables to promote homogamy. Blue-collar and white-collar workers rarely interact in the workplace because they occupy different physical spaces and have different schedules. At colleges and universities, for example, staff and maintenance workers are often housed in different buildings or floors and rarely talk to each other. Social class also overlaps with age and race. In the study of African American women cited earlier, for example, Sterk-Elifson (1994) found that younger women (aged 21 to 44) dated men primarily because of sex, while older women (aged 45 and over) dated people primarily to meet a lifetime companion. In addition, whereas lower-class women (those whose annual incomes were $20,000 or lower) considered it acceptable for a woman to approach a man for a date, middle-class women "were inclined to label all behaviors other than making eye contact as flirtatious" (p. 120). If we add gender, religion, and personality traits to this mix of variables, homogamy would reduce eligible dating partners even further.

Hypergamy is often defined as a woman's "marrying up" to improve her overall social standing (see Coltrane, 1998). Japan has run marriage bureaus since 1933. When applicants fill out the forms, hypergamy is evident: "The women ask for university graduates, making at least $40,000 to $50,000, not previously married, working as a bureaucrat. The men ask for high school graduates who are young. Period" (Tanaka, 1994: 2A).

Increasing numbers of college-educated men and women in the United States expect that their partners will be similar to themselves in intelligence, ability, success, education, and income. Nevertheless, a sizable percentage still expects that the husband will make significantly more money, have a higher educational level, and be more intelligent and more successful than the wife (Ganong and Coleman, 1992).

Despite such evidence that women are hypergamous, increasing numbers of educated women make more money than their dating partners and spouses (see Chapter 13) and do not have to rely on marriage for financial security or upward mobility. It is curious, moreover, that sociologists have not coined a term for males who seek to improve their social standing by marrying up.

Values   Mate-selection methods may have changed, but has there been a corresponding change in the values that shape our choices? College students' responses as to what they wanted in a future mate in three widely spaced studies—1939, 1956, and 1967—didn't change much (Hudson & Henze, 1969). Students wanted partners who were dependable, emotionally stable, intelligent, sociable, and good-looking. They

TABLE 7.1		
The Most Important Qualities in a Mate		
Order of Priority	**Married couples**	**Unmarried students**
1	Good company	Kind and understanding
2	Considerate	Exciting personality
3	Honest	Intelligent
4	Affectionate	Physically attractive
5	Dependable	Healthy
6	Intelligent	Easygoing
7	Kind	Creative
8	Understanding	Wants children
9	Interesting to talk to	College graduate
10	Loyal	Good earning capacity

SOURCE: Buss and Barnes, 1986.

sought pleasing dispositions, good health, and similar religious background and social status, as well as evidence of mutual attraction. The researchers concluded that "social change in the area of mate selection has not been as great as indicated by the press, feared by the parent, and perhaps hoped by . . . youth" (p. 775).

The characteristics of the "ideal partner" had not changed very much by the late 1980s, either. In one study, the most important traits cited by undergraduates were honesty, trust, communication, sharing, thoughtfulness, intelligence, understanding, wit, openness, patience, gentleness, kindness, and a sense of humor (Laner, 1989). As *Table 7.1* indicates, after marriage, qualities related to compatibility, such as being considerate and good company, become more important than having an exciting personality or being physically attractive.

Homogamy narrows the pool of eligible partners. Increasing numbers of people, however, are expanding their marriage markets by selecting dating partners and marrying through *heterogamy*.

Heterogamy and Permanent Availability: Expanding the Marriage Market

As U.S. society becomes more diverse and multicultural (see Chapter 1), many people are dating and marrying across traditionally acceptable religious, ethnic, racial, and age confines. Although many of these crossovers are still stigmatized, some are becoming more acceptable. Whether we decry the changes or encourage them, mate-selection processes *are* changing due to the permanent availability of partners through heterogamy.

The Permanent Availability Model   In the early 1960s, sociologist Bernard Farber challenged traditional explanations of mate selection and marriage with his *permanent availability model.* Farber (1964) argued, essentially, that adults are "permanently available" for marriage with anyone and at any time. Farber proposed that because individuals' needs and desires change over time, they "may not suffice to maintain the marriage." Because divorce and remarriage rates were increasing, and youth and glamour were becoming more important, Farber felt that "playing the field" would prepare people for change better than settling on a spouse at an early age.

The permanent-availability model is probably more applicable today than it was three decades ago. Although still bound by homogamy, mate-selection options are growing for many people, and they are increasing throughout the life cycle rather than just during early adulthood (see Chapter 16).

Heterogamy   Often used interchangeably with the term *exogamy* (see Chapter 1), **heterogamy** refers to dating or marrying someone from a social, racial, ethnic, religious, or age group different from one's own. Most societies, for example, prohibit dating or marriage between siblings and between parents and children, aunts and uncles, or first cousins. Many states in the United States don't allow marriage between half-siblings. About half the states forbid marriage between in-laws and between stepchildren and stepparents. In some societies, such as India, exogamy rules may forbid marriage between individuals of similarly named clans, even though the families have never met and live several hundred miles apart (Gupta, 1979).

Denmark, Norway, Sweden, and France recognize same-sex unions as "legitimate" (but not as marriages) in the sense that partners can enjoy the same legal benefits as heterosexual couples (see Chapter 8). In the United States, Vermont has provided gay partners with many of the same rights as their heterosexual counterparts (see Chapter 6). Also, some Protestant denominations are allowing religious marriage ceremonies for gay and lesbian partners. Despite these changes, all societies still define a marriage as valid only between members of the opposite sex.

Interfaith Relationships   Historically, religion has been an important factor in dating and mate selection in the United States and many other countries. Although the data are not recent, one of the best available studies estimates that 82 percent of Catholics, 88 percent of Jews, and 93 percent of Protestants in the United States are married to people with the same religion (Glenn, 1982). Later studies have estimated that 52 percent of Jewish-born U.S. adults had intermarried by 1990 (Van Biema, 1997).

Since these numbers included people who had switched religions to match those of their partners, and shifts across Protestant denominations were defined as endogamy rather than exogamy, interfaith marriages—and especially interfaith dating—may be considerably more widespread than these numbers suggest. As *Table 7.2* shows, for example, only 56 percent of long-term partnerships and 72 percent of marriages are between

TABLE 7.2

Sexual Relationships in Dating and Marriage

Characteristic	Percentage in Relationships with Persons of Similar Background			
	Marriages	Cohabitations	Long-term Partnerships	Short-term Partnerships
Racial/ethnic	93	88	89	91
Age	78	75	76	83
Education	82	87	83	87
Religion	72	53	56	60

On which characteristic are marriage partners most similar? Most dissimilar? Do the characteristics differ for short-term dating, living together, and marriage? Why are the people we pick as partners for purely sexual relationships so similar to ourselves? Does this reflect random occurrences? Conscious choices? Factors that shape our choices?

Notes: Sexual relationships include both heterosexual and same-sex couples.

Marriages and *cohabitations* include only those that began within the past ten years.

Short-term partnerships are sexual relationships that lasted one month or less and involved no more than ten instances of sexual activity; all remaining partnerships are considered long term.

Age similarity is defined as a difference of no more than five years between the partners' ages.

Educational similarity is defined as a difference of no more than one educational category (less than high school, high school graduate, vocational training, four-year college, and graduate degree).

SOURCE: Adapted from Laumann et al., 1994: 232, 255.

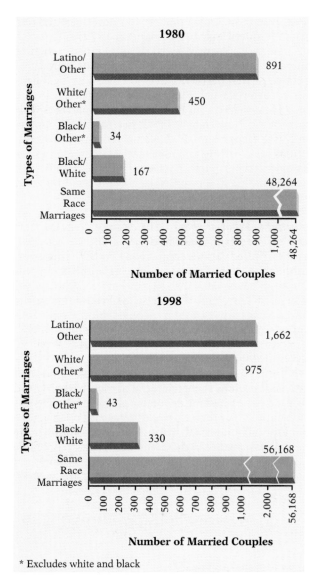

FIGURE 7.2   Interracial and Interethnic Married Couples, 1980–1998.

NOTE: All figures are in thousands; 891, for example, represents 891,000.

SOURCE: Adapted from U.S. Census Bureau, 1999C, p. 58.

people with the same religious affiliations. As these data indicate, religion is less influential than race and ethnicity, for example, in determining whom we date and marry. In addition, it appears that interfaith dating relationships are more prevalent than interfaith marriages. Once again, in marriages the religious similarity may be slightly inflated because some people might have switched faiths to match those of their spouses.

Interracial and Interethnic Relationships Interracial/interethnic marriages have increased slowly, from 3 percent in 1980 to about 5 percent in 1998. In 1998,

28 percent of married Latinos were married to non-Latinos, 10 percent of blacks had a spouse of a different racial group, and about 5 percent of whites had mixed marriages. In addition, black–white unions were much lower than those between whites and partners who were Asian or another race (see *Figure 7.2*). Thus, despite much publicity about black–white dating, there are considerably more marital unions between partners of white and nonblack races. About 64 percent of black–white marriages in 1998 involved black men married to white women compared to 73 percent in 1980 (U.S. Census Bureau, 1999c). These figures challenge the general perception that black men are rejecting black women as marital partners (as you saw earlier). In fact, increasing numbers of black women are marrying white men.

Blacks and Latinos intermarry for several reasons that will be discussed in greater detail in Chapter 12. Since black women, as a group, are more likely than their male counterparts to obtain college and graduate degrees, they have a smaller pool of educated male partners. Because many Latinas and black women are employed, they are often likely to meet men from other races and ethnic groups who are potential marriage partners (propinquity). Discrimination and racism create strain between partners of the same race that most white spouses, especially men, don't have to deal with. A black woman married to a white man observed, for example, that white men get more respect because it is their world: "My husband walks out of the door, and he knows the taxi is going to stop for him. It isn't a thing he has to think about" (Cose, 1995: 66). Finally, interracial marriages are more acceptable than they were in the past. In a recent study of 620 students, the researchers found that one-fourth had dated interracially and almost half of the students were open to becoming involved in an interracial relationship (Knox et al., 2000). As racial and ethnic populations increase (see Chapter 1), interracial and interethnic dating and marriage may become more commonplace.

Why We Choose Each Other: Mate-Selection Theories

Sociologists have offered various explanations of mate-selection processes (see Cate and Lloyd, 1992, for a summary of several theoretical perspectives). None is perfect, but each perspective offers insights about the dating process. As you saw earlier, filter theory proposes that our social structure limits our opportunity to associate with people who are significantly different from ourselves. In this sense, the sifting process that narrows our pool of eligibles is largely unconscious and often beyond our control. What influences our decision to stay in the relationship or to move on? Exchange theory and equity theory suggest that satisfaction is a key factor in weighing our mate-selection investments and our liabilities.

Dating as Give and Take: Social Exchange Theory

Recall from Chapters 2 and 5 that, according to social exchange theory, people are attracted to prospective partners who they believe will provide them with the best possible "deal" in a relationship. This may not sound very romantic, but social exchange theorists propose that it is the basis of most relationships.

Arguing that every relationship carries both rewards and costs, social exchange theory posits that people will begin (and remain in) a relationship if the rewards are high and the costs are low. Rewards may be intrinsic characteristics (intelligence, a sense of humor), directly rewarding behavior (sex, companionship), or access to desired resources (money, power). Costs, the "price" paid, may be unpleasant or destructive behavior (inattentiveness, insults, violence) or literal losses (money, time). The box "Am I Seeing the Wrong Person?" offers advice from practitioners for filtering out undesirable candidates as you look for a long-term relationship.

Historically, because women were expected to bear children and be homemakers, physical attractiveness was one of the few assets they could offer in an exchange. Men, on the other hand, had a variety of resources to offer, including money, education, and power, and thus had more dating options. Today, as more women earn college degrees and establish careers, they are increasing their assets and thus can be more selective in dating relationships. As this happens, however, the pool of eligible partners for both sides is reduced.

As more women compete for jobs, and as the economy worsens, women's values about desirable traits in men are changing. Although they are interested in men who are competent workers and who are high earners, women today are more concerned about a partner who will share housework and child-rearing responsibilities (see Chapter 4). Thus, economic security may be less important than companionship and communication. Men who do not think such characteristics are important will be seen as less desirable partners.

Dating as a Search for Egalitarian Relationships: Equity Theory

Equity theory, an extension of social exchange theory, tries to predict when individuals will perceive injustice and how they will react when they find themselves enmeshed in inequitable relationships (Walster et al., 1973). Equity theory advances several basic propositions:

- Individuals try to maximize their outcomes, which are defined as rewards minus costs.

- When people find themselves in an inequitable relationship, they become distressed. The greater the inequity, the greater the distress.

- People in an inequitable relationship will attempt to eliminate their distress by restoring equity. The greater the inequity, the harder they will try to restore equity.

Equity theory reflects the American sense of "fair play," the notion that one has a right to expect a reasonable balance between costs and benefits in life. When costs exceed benefits, people try to regain some of their benefits. If we receive more than our "fair share" of benefits, we might feel guilt. In each case we experience dissatisfaction with the relationship, and will try to reduce it, either by demanding that our partner does more or by doing more ourselves (Miell and Croghan, 1996).

Consider Tim and Tammy, who were initially happy with their dating relationship. Among other cost–benefit outcomes, she helped him with his calculus and he helped her write a paper on contemporary American novelists. Tim and Tammy began having sexual intercourse, spent as much time as possible together, and shared similar extracurricular interests. Their relationship at this point appeared egalitarian. By the end of the semester, however, Tammy was still helping Tim with his calculus assignments, but Tim was no longer available to help Tammy with her English papers because he had joined the swim team. According to equity theory, Tim might feel guilt and increase his help, or Tim and Tammy will have to "renegotiate" their costs and benefits if the relationship is to continue.

A Global View: Desirable Mate Characteristics and Selection

You saw earlier that many of our values about desirable marital mates have remained fairly constant. Although there are some differences—such as men's emphasis on physical attractiveness in women—most of us seek prospective spouses who are kind, understanding, and personable (see *Table 7.1*). What about other countries that differ from the United States culturally, racially, religiously, and ethnically? Do desirable mate traits and selection methods differ across countries? Or are they universal?

Preferred Mate Characteristics

To identify valued characteristics of potential mates worldwide, Buss (1990) and 59 other researchers interviewed almost 10,000 people in 37 cultures drawn from

ASK YOURSELF

Am I Seeing the Wrong Person?

Our habits, personalities, attitudes, and values don't usually change dramatically after marriage, but because often "love is blind," many people overlook serious flaws and marry Mr. or Ms. Wrong. Here are some red flags that should alert you to possible problems.

- **Don Juans and other sexual predators.** Men, who are more likely than women to expect sex in casual dating, admit using a variety of lines to persuade women to have sex. These Don Juans will *declare their love for you* ("I love you," "I don't want to have sex with you—I want to make love to you"); attempt to *gain your sympathy or flatter you* ("You're one of the most beautiful women I've ever seen, and I would be honored to spend the night with you," "I never met anyone like you before"); *make meaningless promises* ("Our relationship will grow stronger," "I'll respect you even more," "I swear I'll get a divorce"); *threaten you with rejection* ("If you don't have sex, I'll find someone who will," "Our relationship really needs to move on," "If you loved me, you would"); *put you down* if you refuse ("You're really old-fashioned"); or *challenge you to prove you're "normal"* ("Are you frigid?" "Are you gay?").
- **Incompatibility of basic values.** Initially, it may be exciting to be with someone who's very different. In the long run, however, serious differences in values may jeopardize a relationship. If your partner spends a lot

of time at the office and attends an endless round of meetings and receptions, whereas you look forward to gatherings of family or friends or to quiet times at home, you may have difficulty making a relationship work. If your partner wants you to be a full-time homemaker and raise children, but you want a career, there may be strain. If your partner likes to curl up with a mystery novel, but you want to entertain friends or go out every weekend, you may be in for trouble.

- **Carrying around emotional baggage.** If you can't have a conversation without a partner's talking about an ex-spouse—comparing you to her "saintly" dead husband or talking about his past lovers—she or he is living in the past instead of getting to know you.
- **Extreme jealousy and violent tendencies.** Stay away from someone who is possessive, jealous, or violent. Such characteristics as a bad temper, frequent angry outbursts, constant criticism, and excessive argumentativeness will not decrease in the future.
- **Substance abuse.** The person addicted to alcohol or other drugs is the wrong choice for a mate. Watch for such things as slowed responses, slurred speech, glassy eyes, extreme mood swings, unexplained absences, or failure to keep dates.
- **Excessive time spent with others.** Does your partner spend several nights a week with other friends or with family members while you

spend time alone? If your partner is always on the phone with family members or friends, or if family "emergencies" frequently come before your needs, there will probably be similar conflicts in the future.

- **Mr. Flirt and Ms. Tease.** If you are a woman whose partner constantly flirts with your sister and girlfriends, or a man whose girlfriend is a big tease, watch out. Flirting might seem cute at first, but not over the long run.
- **Lack of communication.** Good communication is critical for a good relationship. Talking about one's feelings, needs, desires, aspirations, and fears increases intimacy. Feelings of boredom, evidence of your partner's disinterest, or finding that you have little to talk about may signal serious communication problems.
- **Control freaks.** Does your partner always try to control you or the relationship? Do you constantly feel criticized, judged, scrutinized, and corrected, especially in public? Stay away from partners who are determined to change you.
- **Trouble holding a job.** In a bad economy, people get laid off or have to find new jobs, but if your partner never seems able to keep a job, blames someone or something else for this failure, and expects you to pay the bills, think twice about continuing the relationship. You may end up supporting a "ne'er-do-well" for the rest of your life.

SOURCES: Powell, 1991; Collison, 1993; Kenrick et al., 1993.

---

33 countries on 6 continents and 5 islands. The researchers drew several conclusions from this study. First, culture appears to have substantial effects on mate preferences. The most pervasive difference between cultures appears to be a "traditional" versus a "modern" orientation about a prospective partner's characteristics. At one end of this continuum, China, India, Iran, and Nigeria place a great value on chastity, good house-

keeping, and a desire for home and children. At the other end of the continuum, Netherlands, Great Britain, Finland, and Sweden emphasized different characteristics. Dutch respondents placed a higher value on political similarity, the British emphasized education and political background, Finns valued creativity and artistry in potential mates, and Swedes desired mates who are politically similar, dependable, and healthy.

In spite of these significant cultural differences, nearly all groups placed mutual attraction-love (which the researchers interpreted as a mutually satisfying relationship rather than romantic love) as the top-rated characteristic. Dependability, emotional stability and maturity, and kindness-understanding were the next most highly valued mate traits. The researchers noted that such similarities imply that humans share "a degree of psychological unity" that transcends geographical, racial, political, ethnic, and sex diversity. It is interesting, however, that across cultures there are significant differences in mate-selection criteria by sex:

> *An important sex difference appeared in nearly every sample in the study: More than females, males prefer mates who are physically attractive. More than males, females prefer mates who show ambition-industriousness and other signs of earning potential. These differences appear to be the most robust psychological sex differences of any kind to be documented across cultures. (Buss et al., 1990: 37)*

Why are there such "robust" sex differences between women and men in most cultures and regardless of traditional versus modern industrial values? Buss (1989) posits that different evolutionary selection pressures on females and males "signal" different valued mate characteristics. Females desire ambition and industriousness in men because it signals their financial capacity to provide for children, increased status and protection for the family unit, and even "good genes" that pass to the woman's offspring. Buss notes that the male may not be *willing* to devote these resources to a female and her offspring, but most women see a capacity to be a good provider as an important trait. Males, in contrast, value physical attractiveness and relative youth in potential mates more than do females because these characteristics signal a high reproductive capacity.

Because women's childbearing years are limited (despite the technological innovations we discuss in Chapter 10), older men who have a high status and financial resources have an edge in the marriage market, as you saw at the beginning of the chapter. In addition, in societies that deem paternity identification as important for social, political, religious, or economic reasons (see Chapter 1), chastity is an important mate-selection criterion for many males. To a great extent, then, mate-selection preferences reflect women's and men's efforts to maximize their personal benefits and minimize their personal costs in their social, cultural, and ecological settings (see Eagly and Wood, 1999).

Variations in Mate-Selection Methods

Most countries do not have the "open" courtship systems common in Western nations. Many factors promote traditional mate-selection arrangements, including

"Mine was a marriage of convenience. I wanted desperately to get married and Hank was convenient."

Reprinted with permission from the September/October 1998 *Upscale* Magazine.

religion, a country's rate of industrialization, the economic status of women, and family structure. Some societies are trying to maintain their traditional mate-selection values; others are changing.

Traditional Societies   In some Mediterranean, Middle Eastern and Asian societies, the **dowry**—the money, goods, or property a woman brings to a marriage—is still an important basis for mate selection. Women with large dowries have a competitive edge in attracting suitors (Gaulin and Boster, 1990).

As in India (see the earlier box on arranged marriages), in many countries parents still arrange marriages for their children. For example, in Egypt arranged marriages are more common in the villages than in the cities, but they occur among all social classes and account for between 50 and 75 percent of all marriages (Cowell, 1988).

In Saudi Arabia, Islamic (Muslim) society regulates the lives of its women strictly. During the Persian Gulf War in 1991, Saudis had little concern that American and European soldiers would father children or bring home Saudi brides, as was so common in World War II and the Korean and Vietnam wars, because in Saudi Arabia, the groom must be Muslim. Most Saudi women cover themselves in black, are forbidden to drive or drink, accept arranged marriages, and live with their parents, who act as chaperones. The box "Matchmaking in Muslim Societies" provides a closer look at the criteria that many Muslim parents use in selecting partners for their children.

Although small groups of Saudi and other Middle Eastern women are challenging some strict dating restrictions (see Chapter 4), many Muslim women, including those living in the United States, believe in arranged marriages. Listen to a Muslim mother from Sierra Leone describe the arranged marriages of her sons and daughter:

CROSSCULTURAL

Matchmaking in Muslim Societies

No matter where they live—North America, South Asia, or the Mideast—many Muslim families preserve family consistency and continuity through arranged marriages. Marriage in Islamic society is basically a family rather than an individual affair, and both sons and daughters are raised to expect arranged marriages. Although children do have veto power, the norm is to let the parents and other kin initiate and decide the matter. Thus, even college-educated youth in countries like Pakistan do not think it's necessary for them to meet their future spouses before they marry (Ba-Yunus, 1991).

What criteria do parents use in choosing a son- or daughter-in-law? Although priorities vary across families, two of the most important criteria for a future son-in-law are competence and education or training that will provide their daughter with economic and social assets equal to or better than those of her parents, and close ties between the son-in-law and the daughter's family, whether or not they live near the latter's family. In addition, according to one mother, "We look for wisdom, patience, good sense, not qualities that may be more exciting, but which soon disappear" (Alibhai-Brown, 1993: 29).

For a prospective daughter-in-law, the major criterion is her ability to be integrated into the son's existing family, including, if possible, patrilocal residence for the young couple. Because in Muslim society the man is expected to be the provider, his wife's education is more of a social enhancement than an essential socioeconomic asset (Qureshi, 1991).

Islamic societies forbid dating and "other illicit meetings of the sexes" but allow polygyny. To reduce the number of unmarried middle-aged women, matchmakers in Saudi Arabia have set up services that provide wives for husbands who seek more than one wife. These services have apparently been flooded with telephone calls and faxes from devout Muslims in Sweden, the United States, and countries in the Middle East. One matchmaker, who has a half-dozen computer-terminal assistants to store data and keep up with the demand, is helped by his own four wives in assessing possible matches. Despite the protests of some Saudi housewives who do not want their husbands to acquire additional wives, the matchmaking business is thriving (Boustany, 1994).

As in the semiarranged matches in India, most women are practical and religious: "I am a Saudi woman, 36, finished elementary school and have never been married. I wish to marry a man who fears God and heeds him and who will treat me to God's satisfaction, and who will also help me memorize the Koran and attend religion lessons, not younger than 40" (Boustany, 1994: A14).

We are saved from the evils of teen-age pregnancy that you see nowadays. We are saved from AIDS. We are saved from all sorts of different diseases, all sorts of evil vices being practiced, especially by the teenagers of America. (Somerville, 1994: 4B)

Many young Asian Muslims who live in the United States agree with their parents about the benefits of arranged marriages. When a journalist interviewed nine teenage Muslim girls at a school in Birmingham, Alabama, three were envious of girls who had the freedom to go out and fall in love. But the other six were either ambivalent or very critical of the way this freedom was used against the girls by boys who picked them up and discarded them without any concern for their self-respect. One of the girls described her best friend, who is "always tortured about whether her boyfriend likes her or not, if she is fat, attractive, how many silly Valentine's cards she gets. I couldn't go through all of that. It's crazy" (Alibhai-Brown, 1993: 29).

Societies in Transition Some countries in Asia are also experiencing changes in the way people meet and select mates. In some cases, these changes are the result of a shortage of women; in others, the rising number of women who pursue higher education and careers has led to the postponement of marriage for many.

Both India and China have recently experienced a glut of single men and a scarcity of single women (see Data Digest). In both countries the preference for boys has led to the killing of millions of female infants and to the deaths of many others as a result of neglect—poor nutrition, inadequate medical care, or desertion. An unmarried woman has thus become a scarcity. China has responded by implementing some Western-style mate-selection methods that include newspapers and magazine columns on finding the ideal mate (Hershatter, 1984).

Finding partners through personal advertisements is also popular in China. The desirable attributes differ quite a bit from those in the United States, however. Linlin (1993) compared previous studies of Chinese and American researchers in this area and found some striking cultural differences:

- All the Chinese advertisers were marriage-minded and family-oriented, whereas many of their counterparts in the United States wanted someone to have fun with.

■ Chinese advertisers emphasized health, both because health of both spouses is very important in a lasting marriage and because physical health implies good mental health.

■ Because most male advertisers expect their future spouses to be virgins, marital status got close attention.

■ Chinese women expect the husband to be the major decision maker. Thus, signs of being resolute and career-minded were important.

■ Chinese advertisers rarely asked about humor or communication because these qualities are seen as important in public life rather than in marriage and family life.

■ Male suitors with apartments were seen as particularly attractive because there is a housing shortage in China.

In Japan and Korea the mating game has also changed, in part because more women are acquiring a college education, finding jobs, postponing marriage, or preferring to remain single. Japan has one of the highest average ages of marriage—28.4 years for males and 25.8 years for females. It also has one of the most severe labor shortages. To retain the loyalty of unmarried employees in the under-40 age bracket, several companies are including marriage in their benefit packages and have engaged matrimony brokerage firms to act as matchmakers. Men are less successful than women in finding mates because the pool of single women has been diminishing; 60 percent of all Japanese between the ages of 20 and 39 are single men. Matchmaking companies are thriving because they teach men how to date, court, and select a wife (Shearer, 1990). A recent innovation includes a bank of videophones where singles can talk one-on-one with every online member of the opposite sex for $100 to $150 per session (Thornton, 1994).

In Korea, in the 25 to 29 age bracket, the ratio of eligible men to women is almost four to one. Moreover, as Korea has become more industrialized and urbanized, many women have moved to cities. Women who are used to the urban lifestyle refuse to accept the monotony of rural life, physical labor, sharing a home with aged or aging in-laws, and husbands who are reluctant to help wives do home chores such as cooking and baby-sitting (Hoon, 1993). As a result, villagers and farmers have difficulty finding wives. Marriage bureaus such as Seoul's Committee to Help Find Brides for Farm Bachelors report only modest rates of success; the committee matched only 44 couples in almost three years.

Harmful Dating Relationships: Power, Control, and Sexual Aggression

So far we have focused on the positive side of dating— how people meet each other and what qualities they look for in marital partners. Dating also has a dark side. It can be disappointing and even dangerous. This section examines some major problems in dating, such as control and manipulation that may turn to violence, suggests how to recognize risk factors for sexual aggression and date rape, and proposes some solutions for avoiding dating violence.

Power and Control in Dating Relationships

Sociologist Willard Waller's (1937) *principle of least interest* is useful in explaining the balance of power in the traditional male–female dating relationships. Why do so many women still sit around waiting for their "boyfriends" to call even when they are in steady dating relationships or cohabiting? According to Waller, the male continues to have more power than the female because he is usually the partner with the least interest. The person with more power is less dependent on others, less interested in maintaining the relationship, and as a result, has more control (Lloyd, 1991). Conversely, the person with less power, usually the female, is more likely to be dependent, to try to maintain the relationship, and, often, to be exploited as a result (Sarch, 1993).

Women can also dominate and manipulate a relationship. When the control is nonviolent and nonsexual, women may be more likely than men to try to control a relationship. For example, in a national study of single, never-married people between the ages of 18 and 30, Stets (1993b) found that women were more likely than men to keep tabs on their partners, to make their partners do what they themselves wanted rather than what the partners wanted, and generally to set the rules in the relationship.

Women's manipulation and control of men was the topic of *The Rules* (Fein and Schneider, 1996). The authors encourage women to scheme and to manipulate men to get marriage proposals. Some of "the rules" include not calling the man, rarely returning his calls, and always ending phone calls first to maintain control of the relationship. Such maneuvers presumably entice men into pursuing the hard-to-get female. Since *The Rules* was a best-seller, one might conclude that women are trying, desperately, to get married even if dating involves conniving and manipulating men. Tricks and dishonesty are *not* the bases for marriage or a long-term relationship for either men or women, however (see Chapter 5). Applying the least interest principle, do women feel a greater need to manage or control a relationship because they have less power and are more dependent on their partners?

CONSTRAINTS

How Abusers Control Dating Relationships

Both men and women try to control relationships. Although the following categories are based on the experiences of women who have been victims, men are also subject to abusive dating relationships.

- **Blaming:** Blaming is often based on jealousy; almost anything the partner does is considered provocative. For example, a man may criticize his partner for not being at home when he calls or for talking to another man. He may say he loves her so much that he can't stand for her to be with others, including male friends.

- **Emotional Abuse:** Coming from a person the victim thinks she or he loves, emotional abuse is very powerful. Insults, which attack a person's feelings of independence and self-worth, are generally intended to get a partner to accede to an abuser's demands ("Don't wear your skirt so short—it makes you look like a hooker" or "No one else will ever want you"), denigrate the

victim, and imply she had better do what the partner wants or be left without anyone.

- **Coercion, Intimidation, and Threats:** Abusers may coerce compliance with their demands by threatening to expose embarrassing secrets, often about the partner's sexual behavior, to family or friends. Coercion may also be used to get partners to engage in illegal acts, such as shoplifting, drug dealing, or prostitution, usually to get money for the abuser. A controller may intimidate a partner, just to show "who's boss": "We'd be lying in bed and he'd just decide to kick me out of the house and make me leave, no matter what time it was—3 A.M., whatever—and I'd have to get out." Threatening to commit suicide or to attack a partner's family is not uncommon among abusers.

- **Isolation:** Typically, abusers spend a lot of time and energy watching their victims. For example, one man got his friends to find out what his girlfriend's daily activities were;

then he forced her to stay at home or punished her if she wasn't home when he called. In another case, a student elected the same major as his girlfriend's, home economics, just to monitor her behavior. If these isolating techniques work, they break the partner's ties with other friends and increase dependence on the abuser.

- **Physical Abuse:** Violent acts range from slaps and shoves to beatings, rape, and attacks with weapons. Many abusers manage to convince a partner, on each occasion of abuse, that "I really love you" and "This will never happen again"—but it does. And in some cases, the last time the abuser strikes, he or she kills.

- **Sexual Abuse:** Conflicts about sex often lead to violence. Often a male abuser decides whether to have sex, which sex acts are acceptable, and whether or not the couple should use condoms or other contraceptive devices to prevent AIDS and other STDs.

SOURCES: Gamache, 1990: Rosen and Stith, 1993.

The box on "How Abusers Control Dating Relationships" examines some coercive tactics in more detail.

Aggression and Violence in Dating Relationships

For both men and women, the desire to have control often increases as a relationship progresses from casual to more serious dating (Stets, 1993a). Men are much more likely than women to use physical force and sexual aggression as a means of getting their own way or of intimidating or "striking fear" into a partner (Stets and Pirog-Good, 1990). Women are also physically and emotionally abusive, however.

Dating Violence Because dating violence is underreported by both men and women, it is much more serious than the figures indicate (Ward et al., 1991). A study of 185 adolescents in the sixth to eighth grades found that 42 percent had experienced dating violence

and 66 percent of these students reported that the violence was mutual (Gray and Foshee, 1997). One study has estimated that 30 percent of high school students have experienced physical or sexual violence in dating relationships (Gardner, 1994). In a survey of almost 21,000 students in grades 8 through 12, Kreiter and Krowchuck (1999) found that 2 percent of the females and 4 percent of the males reported that their last (physical) fight was with a boyfriend, a girlfriend, or a dating partner. A national sample found that 37 percent of the men and 35 percent of the women had inflicted some form of physical aggression on their dating partners (White and Koss, 1991). In a sample of 623 college women, 27 percent reported having experienced physical abuse in a six-month period and 77 percent reported some form of psychological abuse such as insults and intimidation (Neufeld et al., 1999).

Dating violence is rarely a one-time event. Only about 50 percent of couples end relationships after the first violent act; others go on seeing one another despite continuing violent occurrences (Henton et al., 1983). Whereas nonviolent men believe that violence would end a relationship, violent men use violence to win in arguments (Riggs and Caulfield, 1997). Aggression and violence can be "instrumental" because they are used to attain some goal; injury may occur, but injury is not the goal in and of itself (Muehlenhard et al., 1994). Apparently, many women interpret the violence as evidence of love. According to a domestic violence counselor, "With so little real-life experience, girls tend to take jealousy and possessiveness to mean 'he loves me'" (L. Harris, 1996: 6).

A study of college students reported that, on average, students had known the person who abused them for almost a year before the violent incident occurred (Muehlenhard and Linton, 1987). The incidence of violence may be higher in long and serious relationships because issues of control and power become more central. Dissatisfaction with the amount of power one has in a relationship and unmet expectations may erupt in more intense, negative reactions (Stets, 1993a; Ronfeldt et al., 1998). In some cases, couples who stay in abusive relationships seem to have accepted violence as a legitimate means of resolving conflict. It is almost as if they are testing the strength of their relationship, as if they are saying, "If we can survive this, we can survive anything" (Lloyd, 1991).

Acquaintance and Date Rape

During 1999, almost 9 percent of high school students were hit, slapped, or physically hurt on purpose by their boyfriend or girlfriend. Black female students (12 percent) were more likely than white female students (7 percent) to report dating violence (Kann et al., 2000). Nationwide, over 20 percent of female college students and almost 4 percent of male college students reported that they had been forced to have sexual intercourse against their will during their lifetime (Centers for Disease Control and Prevention, 1997b).

Women are especially vulnerable to acquaintance and date rape. **Acquaintance rape** refers to rape of a person who knows or is familiar with the rapist. Acquaintance rapists may include neighbors, friends of the family, co-workers, or people the victim meets at a party or get-together. **Date rape** is unwanted, forced sexual intercourse in the context of a dating situation; the victim and the perpetrator may be on a first date or in a steady dating relationship. A number of research studies conducted on campuses reveal that an average of between 13 and 25 percent of the participating females reported being raped or had been taken advantage of when they were incapacitated by alcohol or other drugs (Koss and Cook, 1993; Abbey et al., 1996). One of the reasons date rape is so common, and one of the reasons it comes as a great shock to the victim, is that, typically, the rapist seems to be "a nice guy"—polite, clean-cut, and even a leader in the community or on campus.

Factors Contributing to Date Violence and Date Rape

There are many reasons for dating violence and date rape. Some of the most important explanations include family violence and gender-role expectations, peer pressure, and secrecy.

Family Violence and Gender-Role Expectations

In December 1989, a gunman who called women "a bunch of feminists" massacred 14 female students at the University of Montreal and then killed himself. Some attributed the murders to *misogyny*, the hatred of women. Most aggressors are not necessarily misogynous, however. A number of researchers have found an association between family violence and dating violence. Witnessing family violence, being hit by an adult and learning that aggressive responses to conflict produce desired outcomes increases the likelihood of being both an assailant and a victim during courtship (see, for example, White and Humphrey, 1994; L. Harris, 1996; Foshee et al., 1999).

Dating violence and date rape are also ways of striking out against women (especially independent and self-confident women) who challenge men's right to control women. Generally speaking, men who commit date rape hold traditional views of gender roles, seeing themselves as in charge and women as submissive. They initiate the date, pay the expenses, and feel that women lead them on by dressing suggestively (Hannon et al., 1995). Women who date traditional men (see Chapter 4) may find themselves in a Catch-22 situation:

> If she allows him to pay for the date then he may infer sexual interest. Alternatively, if she contributes to the cost of the date, he may feel threatened and may be more likely to be sexually aggressive as a means of regaining control of the situation. . . . If she accepts an invitation from him for a date, [he may] arrange the circumstances of the date in a manner that could be conducive to sexual overtures. On the other hand, if she asks him out on the date, then she may be perceived as liberated, assertive and hence, wanting to have sex. (Szymanski et al., 1993: 33)

Traditional men can be sexually aggressive and not feel guilty because "She deserved it," or "Women enjoy rough sex" (Walker et al., 1993).

Women are more likely than men to take the blame for courtship violence. In a study of college students, for example, LeJeune and Follette (1994: 137) concluded that women were more likely than men to blame themselves for dating violence because "females are socialized to accept more responsibility for relationship conflict than males are" (see also Lloyd and Emery, 2000). In addition, acquaintance rape is often seen as less serious than stranger rape. Both male and female college students in one study saw the woman as encouraging or being responsible for acquaintance rape (Szymanski et al., 1993) because women should "know better" than to visit men in their apartments or to "lead men on" through heavy petting.

Some charge that "date-rape hysteria" has been fanned by feminist propaganda (see Sanday, 1996, for a review of these accusations). Camille Paglia (1990), for example, claims that sexual aggression is natural in a man. She has proposed that women who can't deal with male sex and avoid violence are immature, naive, or ignorant. Katie Roiphe (1993: 52) argues that feminists have greatly exaggerated the breadth of campus sexual violence and that there have been no more than "one or two shadowy instances of rape." According to Paglia, Roiphe, and others, many women cry rape the morning after consensual sex, are responsible for their own behavior if they use alcohol or drugs, and can take care of themselves in sexual encounters because they aren't victims. A counterargument is that if these charges are true, why do women undergo public humiliation by prosecuting alleged rapists?

Peer Pressure and Secrecy Peer pressure is one of the major reasons why people are violent and why many partners stay in abusive dating relationships. "The pressure to date is fierce" and having any boyfriend is better than having none. Teens who date are seen as more popular than those who don't (L. Harris, 1996). Peer pressure may be even more important in college. In a study of fraternity members, for example, Sanday found that many of the men saw sexual behavior as a "hunt" in which the most successful hunter is the one who traps the largest number of prey:

> [According to one fraternity man], when a man has many partners, he is not only admired by other men, but he believes that women will think he is an incredible lover. Many men get bothered if they are having sex with only one woman because it makes them question their attractiveness and masculinity in the eyes of other women. This man was so worried . . . that he set quotas. . . . Once he decided to have intercourse with 13 new and different girls before the end of the semester. (Sanday, 1990: 114)

In some cases, men admit that their strategies include getting women drunk to get them into bed (Martin and Hummer, 1993).

Men can also be the recipients of sexual coercion. In a survey of 165 men and 131 women—all of them new members of fraternities or sororities—34 men and 36 women said they had experienced unwanted sexual contact. Most of the male victims reported giving in to sexual arousal or verbal pressure by women. The women were more likely to have been subjected to physical force or plied with alcohol or drugs (Larimer et al., 1999).

Secrecy also protects abusers. Most teenagers remain silent about abusive relationships because they don't want to be pressured by their friends into breaking up. They rarely tell parents because either they are afraid of losing the freedom they have, they don't want their parents to think they have poor judgment, or they are trying to figure out what to do on their own (M. Harris, 1996). Racial-ethnic women may endure dating violence for several interrelated reasons. Young Asian/Pacific women, for instance, may be divided between duty to their family values of virginity and accommodating the men they are dating. When violence occurs in a secret dating relationship, there is additional pressure to keep both the violence and the dating relationship itself secret from parents. The secrecy intensifies the woman's feeling of being responsible for the violence. If the abuser is of the same cultural background, men and women alike share the cultural value of enduring and suffering problems without complaint—to save face and to prevent family shame in the community (Yoshihama et al., 1991).

Use of Alcohol and Other Drugs The use of alcohol and other drugs often accompanies aggression and date rape (see Data Digest). Many college students, including fraternity and sorority members, see no relationship between alcohol consumption and sexual aggression. The men say they would exercise sexual restraint and the women feel they could resist attempts of unwanted sex (Cue et al., 1996; Nurius et al., 1996). However, alcohol lowers inhibitions against violence and it also reduces a woman's ability to resist. Among fraternity men who want to coerce women into having sex, the use of alcohol or other drugs is common. If the situation escalates into sexual activity, fraternity men may watch one another perform various sexual acts with the drugged woman and then brag about it afterward (Boeringer et al., 1991).

Since the mid-1990s, a growing number of college women have reported being raped after their drink was spiked with Rohypnol (also known as "roofies," "rope," and "roach"). Rohypnol is a sedative prescribed by physicians in 80 countries outside the United States to treat patients with sleep disorders. Although Rohypnol is not marketed in the United States, it is widely available and inexpensive ($1 to $5 a pill). When slipped into any beverage, Rohypnol's sedating effects begin within 20 to 30 minutes of ingestion and usually last six to eight hours. Rohypnol has been called the "date-rape drug" and the "forget pill" because women who have been knocked out with roofies have blacked out, been raped, and had no memory of what had happened (Lively, 1996). When mixed with alcohol or narcotics, Rohypnol can be fatal.

A more recent "rape drug" is GHB, or gamma hydroxybutyrate, a liquid or powder made of lye or

In urban centers, the cocktail party provides a favorite meeting ground for singles, but drinking too much may pave the way for trouble later in the evening.

drain-cleaner that's mixed with GBL, gamma butyro-lactone, an industrial solvent often used to strip floors. GHB is an odorless, colorless drug that knocks the victim out by depressing her central nervous system. Often she loses consciousness after sipping a spiked drink and falls into a coma within half an hour (Cannon, 1999).

Consequences of Dating Violence and Date Rape

Most dating violence and date rapes occur in situations that seem safe and familiar. This is why these behaviors often come as a great shock to victims, who often cannot believe what is happening.

Violence and rape violate both body and spirit; they can affect every aspect of the victim's life. Women who are raped may not only lose their ability to trust others but may also lose confidence in their ability to judge people's characters. *Even though they are not responsible for the attack,* they may feel ashamed and blame themselves for the rape. Fear of men, of going out alone, and of being alone become part of their lives, as do anger, depression, and sometimes inability to relate to a caring sexual partner. *Table 7.3* lists other consequences of courtship violence and date rape.

Some Solutions

Because violent behavior and rape are learned behaviors, they can be unlearned. We need remedies on three levels: individual, organizational, and societal.

On the *individual* level, women, as the primary victims, must become more "savvy" and avoid risky

dating situations. One of these situations, drinking, can be prevented by both sexes.

Much can be done on the *organizational* level as well. In 1992, Antioch College in Ohio required verbal consent before any sexual act—from kissing to intercourse. Some ridiculed the policy, charging that it's ridiculous to seek consent before a kiss and that such rules are impossible to enforce. Increasingly, however, colleges and universities across the country have adapted student codes to get explicit consent from partners before sex to prevent sexual assault, particularly date rape. In addition, many higher education institutions offer men-only workshops, have set up special hotlines and counseling centers, and require first-year students and fraternity pledges to attend "peer education" classes on dating violence. If colleges and law enforcement agencies prosecuted sexual violence, it would probably decrease.

Finally, to make a serious dent in the incidence of dating violence and date rape, we must change *societal* attitudes and beliefs about male and female roles in dating, about sexual behavior, and about violence. The traditional notion that it is the woman's job to maintain the tone of relationships often leads women to blame themselves when things go wrong and to overlook, forgive, or excuse sexual aggression.

There has been some movement toward legal remedies. The Student Right-to-Know and Campus Security Act of 1990 requires colleges to report crimes, and the Higher Education Reauthorization Act of 1992 requires reporting of rape. Students can have assaults investigated by local police, not just college security. Victims of sexual assault have many new rights, such as the right to have someone of their

TABLE 7.3

Emotional and Behavioral Difficulties Experienced by Female and Male Victims of Courtship Violence or Date Rape

- General depression: Some signs are changes in eating and sleeping patterns and unexplained aches and pains. Depressive symptoms may prevent women from attending classes, completing course assignments, or functioning effectively on the job.

- Dissatisfaction with a particular course, a major, or college in general or with the victim's job.

- A sense of powerlessness, helplessness, vulnerability, shame, and sadness.

- Loss of self-confidence and self-esteem, which may increase the likelihood of future sexual assaults.

- Changes in the victim's attitudes toward sexual relationships in general and in her behavior within an intimate relationship.

- Irritability with family, friends, or co-workers.

- Generalized anger, fear, or anxiety.

- Inability to concentrate, even on routine tasks.

- Development of dependency on alcohol or drugs.

Sources: Benokraitis and Feagin, 1995; Larimer et al., 1999

choosing present at a hearing, to learn the outcome of judicial hearings, and to be offered options for changing academic and living situations.

Breaking Up

Most dating relationships break up before marriage (for a good summary of the literature on the dissolution of relationships, see Cate and Lloyd, 1992). The reasons for breakups include arguments, pressure from parents, geographic separation, deception, avoidance of open communication, and boredom. A major reason for relational dissolution may be an unequal commitment on the part of each partner. According to a study of college students in northern California, for example, 40 percent admitted to having cheated on their partners. Males and females had similar cheating rates. However, while women said they considered all forms of betrayal as equally destructive, men felt that betraying a friend was a greater offense than sexual infidelity (Feldman et al., 2000). Such strikingly different views on cheating can lead to a breakup.

Classic songs warn us that "breaking up is hard to do." It is, sometimes. It can also be a great relief to end an unsatisfying relationship. Those with the greatest investments in a relationship—people who feel they have few desirable alternatives, as you saw earlier in this chapter—may suffer the most. Having the support of friends and family may go a long way toward easing the pain. This explains, in large part, why breaking up may sometimes be more traumatic for gay men and lesbians, who often feel that they cannot discuss their romantic breakups with anyone (Martin, 1993).

Breaking up a dating or cohabiting relationship is much less complicated than breaking up a marriage (see Chapter 15). You'll recall that Farber's permanent-availability model suggests that we have no predestined partners. Instead, one of the important functions of dating and courtship is to filter out unsuitable prospective mates. Thus, breaking up is a normal process (see Chapter 5). If anything, it should probably occur more often than it does. Ending dating relationships provides people with opportunities to find mates that may be more suitable for marriage, opens up a larger pool of eligible and interesting partners as we mature and become more self-confident, and gives us time to reflect on past experiences before getting married.

Conclusion

We have more *choices* in mate selection today than ever before. A broad dating spectrum includes both traditional and contemporary ways to meet other people. These choices emerge within culturally defined boundaries, or *constraints,* however. Factors that determine who selects whom for a partner come into play long before a couple marries and despite our romantic views expressed as "I can date anyone I want." Besides the pressure to date and mate with people who are most similar to us in race, religion, ethnicity, and socioeconomic status, some partners must also deal with aggression and violence. One response to today's array of choices and constraints in mate selection is to postpone marriage. In fact, a significant *change* today is the decision of many people to stay single longer, the subject of the next chapter.

SUMMARY

1. Sociologists describe the dating process as a marriage market, in which prospective spouses compare the assets and liabilities of eligible partners and choose the best available mate. In this sense, we "trade" with others depending on what resources can be exchanged.

2. Dating fulfills both manifest and latent functions. Manifest functions include recreation, companionship,

fun, and mate selection. Latent functions include socialization, social status, sexual experimentation, and meeting intimacy and ego needs.

3. Dating forms have changed over the years. Although people still engage in traditional dating, many adolescents and young adults, especially, have forsaken traditional dating for more informal methods like "getting together" and "pack dating."

4. Adults use a variety of mate-selection methods to meet a potential spouse, including personal classified ads, marriage bureaus, computerized services, and the Internet.

5. Much of our dating and mate-selection behavior is shaped by homogamy rules that define appropriate mates in terms of race, ethnicity, religion, age, social class, and values.

6. Our field of eligibles is expanded when people seek mates from dissimilar religious, racial, or ethnic groups.

7. Social exchange theory and equity theory suggest that partners seek a balance of costs and benefits in a relationship; the relationship is most satisfying when it is seen as egalitarian.

8. Unlike the United States and some other Western nations, most countries around the world do not have "open" courtship systems. Rather, marriages are often arranged by families and restricted to members of the same culture, religion, or race. The selection methods are changing in some traditional societies, however.

9. Although dating is typically fun, there are also many risks and problems. Women, especially, are often victims of sexual pressure and aggression, violence, and date rape. The reasons for such victimization include power differentials between men and women, peer pressure and secrecy, and the use of alcohol and other drugs.

10. Ending a relationship may be painful, but it also provides opportunities for finding a more suitable mate.

KEY TERMS

dating *165*	propinquity *173*	dowry *183*
marriage market *165*	hypergamy *178*	acquaintance rape *187*
filter theory *173*	heterogamy *179*	date rape *187*
homogamy *173*	equity theory *181*	

TAKING IT FURTHER

Meeting People Online and Avoiding Date Violence on Campus

Here are a few sites that are free, offer a free trial membership, or include interesting links to a variety of national, international, religious, and travel sites for "single and romance-minded individuals":

Meet Me Online—The 100% Free Single's Site

www.meetmeonline.com

Single Sites Directory of . . . WWW sites, Chat, Forums, Anonymous E-mail

www.singlesites.com

Yahoo Personals

personals.yahoo.com

The following sites provide valuable information on campus crime statistics and prevention of campus violence, contain links to acquaintance and date rape sites, and offer a variety of resources to assist victims of violence:

Sexual Assault Information Page

www.cs.utk.edu/~bartley/saInfoPage.html

Security on Campus, Inc.

www.campussafety.org

National Victim Center

www.nvc.org

And more . . . www.prenhall.com/benokraitis contains sites on interracial/intercultural relationships, research on egalitarian dating, self-defense tactics for women, and several URLs on breaking up-—politely or more bluntly—if she or he "just doesn't get it."

Singlehood, Cohabitation, and Other Nonmarital Living Arrangements

DATADIGEST

- The number of **unmarried adults** (never married, divorced, and widowed) increased from 37.5 million in 1970 to 79.6 million in 1998.

- The **never-married make up the largest and fastest-growing segment** of the unmarried population. The proportion of adults who have never been married rose from 15 percent in 1972 to 23 percent in 1998.

- In 1998, 26 percent of the 103 million households were one-person households; one in every nine adults **lived alone.**

- The number of **unmarried-couple households has grown.** Cohabitors represented only 1.1 percent of couples in 1960 compared to 7 percent in 1997. Almost 24 percent of women aged 15 to 44 cohabited before their first marriage.

- An estimated 145,000 households are made up of **same-sex partners.**

SOURCES: Laumann et al., 1994; Saluter, 1996; T. W. Smith, 1999; U.S. Census Bureau, 1999c.

A COUPLE who had been dating for several years went out to a Chinese restaurant for dinner one evening. After studying the menu, the man turned to the woman and asked, "How would you like your rice—fried or boiled?" She looked him straight in the eye and replied, "Thrown." Sound corny? Maybe not. Television programs like *The Dating Game* and *Blind Date* have high viewer ratings. Most people eventually make that "love connection" and marry but until then—or if the relationship fizzles—there is more freedom today than ever before to pursue other alternatives.

Marriage has become an option rather than a necessity in many Western countries. Consider, for example, how many of the reasons for getting married have changed over the years. Even 30 years ago, marriage legitimated having sex, served as the most important marker of adulthood and respectable status, provided children with biological parents, and determined the roles that men and women played at home and in public. Today, in contrast, premarital sex is commonplace (Chapter 6), a good job is a better indicator of adulthood than is a marriage license, only half of U.S. children live in families with both biological parents present, and there is a greater overlap between women's and men's domestic and economic roles (Chapter 4). Many of us seek happiness, love, leisure companions, and intimacy (Chapters 1 and 5). Marriage is just one selection from a smorgasbord of relationship possibilities in trying to meet such needs.

Because nearly 93 percent of all Americans eventually marry, marriage is still the norm. A growing number of people maintain nontraditional families, however. This chapter examines four nontraditional living arrangements: singlehood, cohabitation, gay households, and communal residences. Other nonmarital

households, such as single parents raising children and the widowed, will be discussed in later chapters.

Being Single

Although marriage rates have remained high, household size has been shrinking. The average number of people per household was 2.6 in 1998, down from 3.7 in 1940. This decrease reflects several factors, such as falling birth rates overall and the lower number of children in married-couple families. Another major reason for the decreasing household size is the growing number of people living alone (see *Figure 8.1*).

Why are larger numbers of people living alone? A major reason is that many of us are postponing marriage. Instead of moving from parental homes to their own marital homes in early adulthood, many people are pursuing college educations, preparing for jobs or careers, and spending more time pursuing recreational or other activities before "settling down." As *Figure 8.2* illustrates, the median ages of nearly 27 for men and 25 for women reflect the oldest ages at first marriage ever recorded by the Census Bureau. (Remember that the *median* represents the midpoint. Thus, half of all men were 27 or older and half of all women were 25 or older the first time they got married.)

From a historical perspective, however, our current tendency to delay marriage is the norm, especially for men. As *Figure 8.2* shows, men's median age at first marriage in 1890 was only slightly lower than in 1998. The median for women, however, has increased more noticeably, especially since 1960. For both sexes, the younger age at first marriage during the 1950s and 1960s was a historical exception rather than the rule.

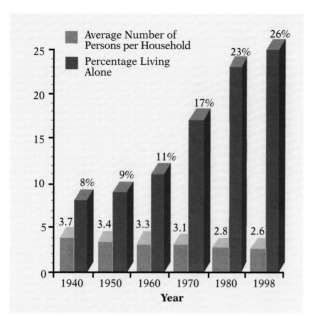

FIGURE 8.1 **The Shrinking Household.** Both the decline in the average number of people per household and the rapidly rising numbers of people living alone have contributed to the smaller contemporary household (Rawlings, 1994, A1, A2; U.S. Census Bureau, www.census.gov/population/projections/nation/hh-fam/table1n.txt, accessed September 12, 2000).

The unmarried population in the United States, which has almost doubled since 1970 (see Data Digest), constitutes a very diverse group of singles.

The Diversity of Singles

As the Data Digest indicates, there are several kinds of singles—those postponing first marriages, the small percentage who will never marry, the currently unmarried who are divorced or widowed but may be looking for new partners, and singles such as lesbians and gay men who are legally prohibited from marrying. In addition, the living arrangements of particular people may vary greatly—from living alone during all of one's adult life, to cohabiting with different partners over time, to forming long-term common-law marriages which may not be recognized by state laws (see Chapter 1).

With the exception of the widowed (Chapter 17) and the divorced (Chapter 15), there is strikingly little recent research on singles. Especially lacking is information on the characteristics, beliefs, values, and behaviors among singles and variations by age, race, ethnicity, or socioeconomic background. The reasons for such empirical neglect are unclear. Given time and budget constraints, some might argue that topics such as economics and communication are more central in

analyzing families. One wonders, nonetheless, whether the research is modest because sociologists and other social scientists *don't* take nonmarital relationships very seriously.

Despite the empirical chasms, the existing literature shows that singlehood reflects more dimensions than simply being "not married." Stein (1981), for example, suggests that being single can be freely chosen or unintentional as well as enduring or short term:

- *Voluntary temporary singles* are open to marriage but place a lower priority on searching for mates than on other activities, such as education, career, politics, and self-development. This group includes men and women who cohabit.
- *Voluntary stable singles* include people who have never married and are satisfied with that choice, those who have been married but do not want to remarry, those who are living together but do not intend to marry, and those whose lifestyles preclude the possibility of marriage, such as priests and nuns. Also included are single parents—both never married and formerly married—who are not

FIGURE 8.2 **At What Age Do Men and Women First Marry?** As the text points out, the median age of first marriage for men was almost the same in 1998 as in 1890, but the median for women shows a generally rising trend since 1960 (Based on data from Saluter, 1994, Table B; Saluter, 1996, Table A-33; and U.S. Census Bureau, www.census.gov/population/projections/nation/hh-fam/table6n.txt, accessed September 12, 2000).

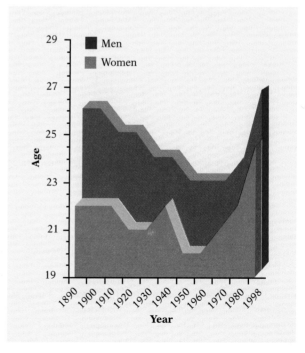

seeking mates and who are raising their children alone or with the help of relatives or friends.

- *Involuntary temporary singles* are those who would like to be married and are actively seeking mates. This group includes those who are widowed or divorced and single parents who would like to get married.

- *Involuntary stable singles* are primarily older divorced, widowed, and never-married people who wanted to marry or remarry but did not find a mate and now accept their single status. This group also includes singles who suffer from some physical or psychological impairment that prevents them from being successful in the marriage market.

A person's position in these categories can change over time. For example, voluntary temporary singles may marry, divorce, and then become involuntary stable singles because they are unable to find another suitable mate. In this sense, the boundaries between being single and married are fairly fluid for most people. For a much smaller number, singlehood is constant either because it is freely chosen or because individuals have little to trade on the marriage market (see Chapter 7).

Why People Are Remaining Single Longer

Many Americans will tell you they are single because they are not in love and are still looking for "the right person." Despite what people *say* are their reasons for marrying or being single (see *Figure 8.3*), staying single reflects a complex interplay of micro-level, demographic, and macro-level variables.

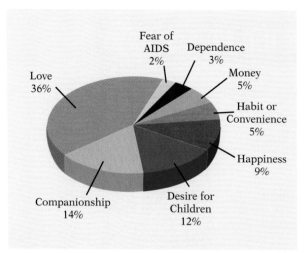

FIGURE 8.3 **Why We Marry.** Over a third of the people sampled in this study said they married for love. As the text and this figure show, there are many other reasons for getting married (based on Patterson and Kim, 1991).

Individual Choices and Constraints in Being Single

On the individual level, there are many factors in the decision to marry. While there are many benefits in marriage, there are usually parallel incentives for being single (see *Table 8.1*). An important reason for marrying is *to have children*. A couple may marry because they plan to raise a family and want their children to be legitimate. Or they may decide to marry because the woman becomes pregnant. Among white women in their 20s who are cohabiting, pregnancy often leads to marriage (Manning, 1993). On the other hand, mothers with

---

TABLE 8.1

The Benefits of Marriage and the Benefits of Being Single

Benefits of Getting Married	Benefits of Being Single
Companionship	Privacy, few constraints, independence
Faithful sexual partner	Varied sexual experiences; cohabitation
Dependability, love	Exciting, changing lifestyle
Sharing mutual interests	Meeting new friends with different interests
Pooling economic resources	Economic autonomy
Social approval for "settling down" and producing grandchildren	Freedom from responsibility to care for spouse or children
Becoming a part of something larger than self	Basic need for independence

Sources: Based on Stein, 1981; Carter and Sokol, 1993.

CHOICES

Gender Differences in How Singles Spend Their Free Time and Money

There are several interesting (but probably not surprising) differences between men and women in terms of spending patterns. First, single women spend more on food consumed at home, housing, apparel, health care, personal care services, and reading material. In contrast, single men spend more on eating out, alcohol, transportation, entertainment, tobacco, and retirement, pension, and contributions to Social Security.

Second, women who live alone spend only half of what bachelors spend on entertainment but more than men do on pets and home-centered entertainment products. When single men "play," they are likely to spend money on fees and admissions to events and on sporting goods and electronic equipment (such as stereos and computers).

A third difference is that women spend more on others than on themselves. For example, single women spend 20 percent of their entertainment money on toys for family members' children, whereas only 10 percent of a single man's entertainment dollar is spent on children's toys (Exter, 1990).

It appears that single women devote much of their time and money to pleasing others. They take care of aging parents and relatives, and they provide numerous supportive services to the extended family:

I believe I was born for a certain purpose here on earth. My purpose has been to take care of all these kids that have come along. Of course, they call me their second mother. I'm not as close as they would have been to their real mother, but I take care of those kids. If my sister wanted to go out someplace, she just called me and I'd usually stay with them. (Allen and Pickett, 1987: 524)

Caring for sick family members, serving as surrogate mothers, and ensuring that the family is cohesive and functioning are often full-time responsibilities. Thus, many single women have less leisure time for recreation than do single men.

---

children born out of wedlock and even of different fathers face much less ostracism today than in the past. Moreover, some men don't want to participate in child care and other activities that many women now expect them to share (see Chapter 4).

Another reason for getting married is *companionship,* or its mirror image, *avoiding being alone.* Young adults may feel left out when their married friends start excluding them from social functions. Living with someone may not only prevent loneliness but, in traditional relationships, provide a man with a housekeeper or a woman with economic resources. Older people sometimes look for caretakers. An elderly man may want a wife who will cook, clean, and care for him if he becomes frail or sick (see Chapter 17).

Because cohabitation is more widely accepted, people feel less pressure to get married, regardless of age. According to a recent survey, 58 percent of the single adults in their late twenties and early thirties said that their social life and having fun was a high priority, compared to only 38 percent of their married friends (Phillips, 1999). Getting married doesn't end having fun or an active social life, of course. Singles who are delaying marriage, however, rely on peers rather than a spouse for support and companionship.

Although companionship and having someone to talk to are important, one of the biggest advantages of remaining single is independence. Singlehood provides privacy and autonomy for both men and women. Women may feel liberated from doing a disproportionate share of domestic work; men are freed from the economic responsibilities of providing for a spouse and children.

Many people marry *to satisfy emotional needs.* Singles in their early 30s sometimes feel they are "missing something" in their lives and expect marriage and children to fill the gap. For men, who may be reluctant to confide in friends or colleagues, wives may be important "sounding boards" (Tannen, 1990). For both women and men, marriage can create kin "out of strangers"; marriage ensures that there will be more relatives around to help out or to consult when things go wrong (Murray, 1994). However, many singles are quite involved in family life. Women, especially, devote much of their time and resources in supporting other family members (see the box "Gender Differences in How Singles Spend Their Free Time and Money").

Marriage is sometimes an *escape* from a bad situation. As one woman stated: "I came from an abusive family . . . he offered stability and comfort and that's all I wanted" (Barreca, 1993: 139). Marriage is an attractive alternative to living at home for some young adults, especially for those whose parents or stepparents are seen as rejecting or authoritarian (see

Chapters 11 and 16). Women particularly may feel that marriage will provide them with greater freedom and autonomy and an escape from parental supervision. On the other hand, disruptive family relationships such as divorce or prolonged years of conflict between parents can have a negative effect on young adults' perceptions of marriage and motivate them to stay single as long as possible (Goldscheider and Goldscheider, 1993).

Social pressure is often an important factor in marriage. Although being single is becoming more acceptable, many people still get married because it is expected of them. Some of my students complain, for example, that "if you're not married by the time you're 30, people think there's something wrong with you. My family and friends are constantly telling me to get married." Unmarried women, especially, often dread family get-togethers because they will be asked over and over again whether they are dating "someone special." The older they are, the more often friends and relatives "badger" singles about marriage plans.

Finally, *physical attractiveness* may play an important role in the decision to marry. Physical appearance strongly affects dating and mating. It is often assumed that people who are physically attractive are also sexually responsive, warm, interesting, kind, and outgoing (see Chapters 5 and 7).

Demographic Influences Demographic shifts, such as the sex ratio and the marriage squeeze, also help explain the large proportion of singles. The **sex ratio,** expressed as a whole number, refers to the ratio of men to women in a country or group. A ratio of 100 means that there are equal numbers of men and women; a ratio of 110 means there are 110 men for every 100 women.

Because both women and men are postponing marriage (see *Figure 8.2*), there are large numbers of never-married singles in all age categories until the midlife years (see *Figure 8.4*). If we add to the pool another 8 million men and 11 million women who were unmarried due to divorce during 1998, the marriage market appears very large. As you saw in Chapter 7, however, homogamy narrows the pool of eligibles to those of the same race, ethnicity, education, and other factors. In addition, since women on average marry men three or more years older than themselves, this may create a **marriage squeeze,** a sex imbalance in the ratio of available unmarried women and men. Because of this imbalance, members of one sex can be "squeezed" out of the marriage market. The squeeze may be due to wealth, power, status, level of education, age, or other factors that diminish the pool of eligible partners in the marriage market.

Many countries are experiencing a marriage squeeze. Men in China, India, Korea, Taiwan, Africa, the Middle East, and other regions face a scarcity of young, single women because of skewed sex ratios.

QUALITY TIME Gail Machlis

The *Quality Time* cartoon by Gail Machlis is reprinted by permission of Chronicle Features, San Francisco, California.

For example, the sex ratio is 119 in China, 112 in India, and 114 in South Korea (Tefft, 1995). The low ratios of women are due to such factors as a cultural preference for boys who will carry on the family name, care for elderly parents, inherit their property, and play a central role in the family and family rituals. As a result, hundreds of thousands of female infants have died yearly because the use of ultrasound scanners that disclose the sex of the child may lead to abortion, as well as neglect, abandonment, murder, and starvation (see Chapter 4). Some countries, like China, are trying to change the sex ratio by changing the attitudes toward female infants and upgrading women's economic and social status. Population experts say, however, that cultural attitudes that devalue daughters and women will be hard to change despite marriage squeezes (Tefft, 1995).

Since there are more never-married men than women in most age groups (see *Figure 8.4*), why do so many women complain that "there's nothing out there"? One reason is that some men simply don't want to get married:

Ed . . . is a charming, handsome, 48-year-old Washington, D.C., lobbyist who plans evenings that most women just fantasize about. His dates

FIGURE 8.4 Percent of Never Married Men and Women, 1998. Of the almost 95 million U.S. men in 1998, 26 percent were never married, 59 percent were married, 3 percent were widowed, and 8 percent were divorced (the respective numbers for 102.4 million women were 21 percent, 59 percent, 11 percent, and 11 percent). What happens to the marriage pool as people age? For example, if a woman is 30 to 34 years old and is probably seeking someone several years older, what happens to the pool of available men? Is dating younger men a viable option? (Adapted from U.S. Census Bureau, 1999c, Table 62).

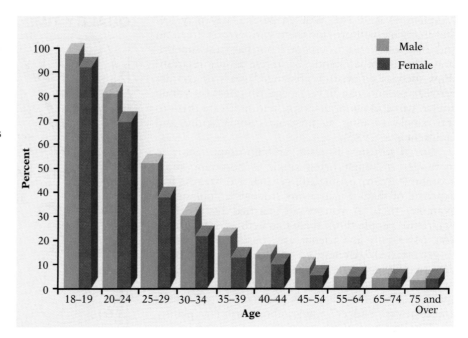

may involve box seats at a performance of Tosca, champagne served during the intermission, dinner at the best Italian restaurant. . . . What Ed is not planning is a long-term relationship: "I have had four very important relationships," he says. "Each one lasted about three years, but at a certain point the woman wanted marriage and I didn't." (Szegedy-Maszak, 1993: 88)

Many single men view marriage as a major economic responsibility that they don't want to undertake. Stagnant wages in many employment sectors have led many men to put off marriage. Because of the increase in premarital sex, most men can have sex without getting married (see Chapter 6).

As gender roles change, marriage is no longer the primary vehicle in determining our domestic and public roles. With the advent of washing machines, frozen foods, wrinkle-resistant fabrics, and 24-hour one-stop shopping, for example, "a man does not really need a woman to take care of cooking, cleaning, decorating, and making life comfortable" (Coontz, 1997: 81). Women aren't rushing into marriage either. Since the stigma once attached to "living in sin" has largely vanished, young women have more alternatives to cohabit and have babies outside of marriage. Some women feel that they can't have both a career and a family at the same time and choose to advance their professional lives before marrying and starting a family. Because some men are unsympathetic to a woman's need to combine career and family, many educated and professional women have little incentive to marry or stay married (Bennett et al., 1988; Collette, 1993).

Macro-Level Variables Macro-level phenomena and events like *war, technology,* and *social movements* often shape decisions about marriage. For example, marriage rates tend to drop slightly during wartime and to rise after a war (Rodgers and Thornton, 1985). Although out-of-wedlock children are more acceptable now than in the past, advances in contraceptive technology have decreased unplanned pregnancies and "shotgun marriages." The women's movement opened new educational and occupational opportunities for women, giving them career options outside marriage. The gay rights movement encouraged homosexuals to be more open about their sexual preferences and relieved the pressure some felt to marry.

Economic factors also play an important role in delaying or encouraging marriage. Economic depressions and unemployment tend to postpone marriage for men (Ogburn, 1927; Rodgers and Thornton, 1985). In 1973, for example, the typical male high school dropout found a regular job at about age 22. Today, it can take until age 26 for a dropout to find a full-time job that can support a family. Even then, supporting a family may be difficult because the average annual earnings of dropouts have been cut in half since 1973 (Amott, 1993). The well-paid blue-collar jobs that once enabled high school graduates to support families are mostly gone. The economic situation for many college-educated men is also worsening rather than improving (see Chapter 13). In contrast, economic opportunities, as well as a belief that a person has access to those opportunities, encourage men to marry (Landale, 1989; Landale and Tolnay, 1991).

The effects of employment on women's tendency to marry are somewhat contradictory. On the one hand, being employed increases a woman's chances of meeting eligible men and may enhance her attractiveness as a potential contributor to a household's financial resources (see Chapter 7). In a national study of women under age 29 who decided to marry, Oropesa et al. (1994) found that white and black women who were successful in the labor market (were employed and had high incomes) were more likely to marry than their nonemployed counterparts, despite the shortage of eligible men. On the other hand, if employed women seek a higher-earning spouse, it will take longer to find a suitable mate (Raley and Bratter, 2000). Employed women who are breadwinners may decide not to marry if they don't find the right partner.

Parental resources also affect men and women differently. Inherited income gives men a more stable economic base for marriage, but women are more likely to use inheritances to delay marriage (Goldscheider and Waite, 1986).

Living at home with parents encourages marriage, whereas moving out of the parental home delays marriage. In general, those who move out very early in young adulthood are the most likely to postpone marriage. This is especially true for women. Women gain more independence than men do when they're single because men, as a group, are less likely to be supervised and monitored by parents (see Chapter 4). Women also typically lose more independence than men do when they marry, especially if the woman is responsible for much of the domestic work. In addition, women are more integrated into social networks, so that loneliness is not as much of a problem for them as it is for men (Goldscheider and Waite, 1986). Living independently encourages marriage only when people—usually men—both leave home early and accumulate resources, usually through full-time work (Goldscheider and DaVanzo, 1989; McLaughlin et al., 1993).

Latino and African American Singles

The unmarried population has increased among many groups. *Figure 8.5* compares data on whites, blacks, and persons of Hispanic origin since 1970 (there are no similar data on Asian Americans). The biggest changes characterize African Americans and Latinos for 1970 and 1998. In 1998, for example, 39 percent of black adults over the age of 18 had never been married, up from 21 percent in 1970. The proportion of Latino adults over 18 who had never married rose from 19 to 30 percent during the same period.

Latinos Singlehood is increasing among Latinos. Because there has been less research on Latino singles than on black singles, we have less information about the reasons for these changes. There are several possible explanations, however. For example, the Latino

population is much younger than the non-Latino population. As a result, a higher percentage of Latinos have not yet reached an age appropriate for marriage. Moreover, large numbers of young people who are migrating for economic reasons may be postponing marriage until they can support a family (Becerra, 1988). The Cuban community, which has always emphasized the importance of marriage and children, has been assimilating Americanized values and behaviors, and second-generation Cuban Americans are more likely to postpone marriage for the same reasons as whites (Szapocznik and Hernandez, 1988). Finally, Puerto Rican women tend to have more children out of wedlock than do either Mexican American or Cuban American women. Because they also have extensive kinship networks both in the United States and in Puerto Rico, Puerto Rican women may be less

FIGURE 8.5 **Changes in Marital Status, by Race and Latino Origin, 1970 and 1998.** The percentage of people who are married has decreased while the percentage of divorced and never married has increased, especially among blacks. Persons of Latino origin may be of any race (Saluter, 1994, vi; U.S. Census Bureau, 1999c, Table 62).

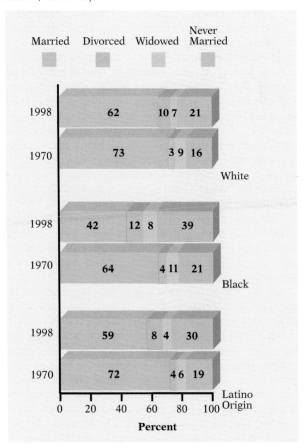

dependent on having a husband to help raise the children (Sanchez-Ayendez, 1988; Toro-Morn, 1998).

Researchers point out, however, that Latino men expect to marry even if they don't do so. South (1993) found, for example, that more than either white or black men, Latino men wanted to marry. South suggests that, for Latino men, "marriage and parenthood may be important signals of achievement, visible to the family of origin and the wider community" (p. 368).

African Americans Large numbers of African Americans are also postponing marriage, but an even higher proportion may never marry (Saluter, 1996). Both structural factors and personal attitudes are behind this change. A major reason is the shortage of marriageable men among African Americans. Some estimate that there are eight black men for every ten black women (Amott, 1993; Anders, 1994). This makes a marital commitment unnecessary in the eyes of some men.

The economy also plays a role. When there are plenty of jobs available, African American men and women are likely to marry and have children (Fossett and Kiecolt, 1993). In regions where unemployment rates for black men are the highest, marriage rates are the lowest (Wilson, 1987). During the 1980s, as U.S. corporations started closing factories and moving their facilities to developing countries, numerous women were absorbed into low-paying jobs in both the private and public sectors. Many men who lost their jobs became reluctant to commit themselves to marriage and the support of children.

Deteriorating employment conditions often discourage young African American men from getting married. This is especially true when over 50 percent of black men in a given area are jobless, employed only part time, or working at poverty-level wages (Lichter et al., 1991). Discrimination in employment contributes to this problem, making many black males poor economic providers (see Chapter 12). And at all age levels, an unemployed or underemployed man may be a liability rather than an attractive marital partner (Horton and Burgess, 1992; Blake and Darling, 1994). A study of black women age 55 and over found, for example, that many of the women were not interested in marrying or remarrying because they perceived an unemployed man as a potential "drain on their own finances" (Tucker et al., 1993).

Black men also have a lower life expectancy than their white counterparts. Occupational hazards in dangerous jobs have claimed many men's lives. Mortality rates for heart disease are almost three times higher for blue-collar workers—many of whom are black—than for managerial and professional groups, at least in part because of a lack of preventive medical care (Schulman et al., 1999). Urban black males face a 10 percent chance of being killed in street crimes, compared to a 2 percent chance for white males. The "war on drugs" has led to the incarceration of increasing numbers of

men who are disproportionately black or Latino. In 1999, almost 1 in 3 (32 percent) young black males in the 20–29 age group were incarcerated, on probation, or parole compared to 1 in 15 white males and 1 in 8 Latino males in the same age group (The Sentencing Project, 2000). An estimated 28 percent of black males will enter state or federal prison during their lifetime (U.S. Department of Justice, 1997).

Unfavorable social and economic conditions have exacerbated the eligibility problem for educated, middle-class, black women as well. As a group, black men earn more than black women in almost every occupation (see Chapter 13). There are more college-educated black women than black men, however. In 1998, for example, 16 percent of black women compared to 14 percent of black men had completed four years or more of college (U.S. Census Bureau, 1999c). Many middle-class men are already married, and women are reluctant to "marry down." In a memorable scene in *Waiting to Exhale,* the black women lament their marriage squeeze (though not in those words) and consider the merits of marrying hard-working black men in lower socioeconomic levels.

In reality, however, homogamy generally limits the pool of eligibles in terms of social class and regardless of race (see Chapter 7). Some of my black, "thirty-something," female students have stated emphatically, for example: "I'm making a lot of sacrifices to be in college while working full time. I don't think a man will appreciate what I've accomplished unless he's gone through the same [expletive deleted]!" Many middle-class black women are also unwilling to give up their hard-won financial independence. One national study concluded that although never-married black women see marriage as a preferable state, they delay matrimony because they expect a husband to support a family without depending, almost entirely, on the wife's income (Bulcroft and Bulcroft, 1993).

Because of their advantage in numbers, some middle-class black men may simply screen out assertive, independent, or physically unappealing women because they enjoy a large pool of eligible romantic partners (Davis et al., 2000). According to some, many successful black men have internalized white, middle-class, male values such as working long hours and having more than one sexual partner. As a result, many black women feel they can't find mates who want a committed relationship and who are supportive and affectionate (Chapman, 1994). And, like many whites, blacks from divorced families tend to shun marriage (Bulcroft and Bulcroft, 1993).

Social mobility also affects singlehood. Many parents of girls from lower-middle-class and middle-class black families tend to emphasize educational attainment over early marriage. As a result, black women who pursue higher education may place a higher priority on academic achievement than on developing personal relationships (Holland and Eisenhart, 1990).

Others have tight social schedules because they devote most of their time to successful businesses they own and to community activities (Jones, 1994).

Single Adults in Later Life

For older singles who date and want to marry or remarry, the double standard still favors men. Aging women are typically seen as "over the hill," whereas aging men are often described as "mature" and "distinguished." Because more women are becoming financially independent, however, they are less likely to depend on successful, "mature" men for their economic stability. There is also a greater tendency, as one grows older, to become choosier. At the same time, there are fewer choices because the most desirable people are already married (Hendrick and Hendrick, 1992a). Older women are also more likely than older men to remain single because they have caretaker responsibilities for relatives, primarily aging parents (see Chapter 17).

In their later years, women are more likely than men to live alone (see *Figure 8.6*). On average, women live about eight years longer than men. If women enjoy relatively good health and have enough income to stay out of poverty, they can care for themselves into their seventies and eighties (see Chapter 17). The sex ratio also squeezes many women out of the marriage market because older men seek *younger* wives, while marriage matches between older women and younger men are still stigmatized (see Chapters 4 and 7).

Some researchers suggest, however, that the impact of the sex ratio probably varies by both age and ethnicity. In a national study of black women and men aged 55 and over, for example, Tucker and Taylor (1997) found that males were more than five times more likely than females to want a romantic involvement that might end in marriage. The researchers felt that a disproportionate difference between the sexes outweighed an imbalanced sex ratio and the tendency for older men to marry significantly younger women. Instead, Tucker and Taylor suggest, older black women don't want romantic relationships because the costs and rewards differ by gender: ". . . men are likely to be served in such relationships whereas women are likely to be required to serve" (p. 93).

There is little research on older people who have never married, probably because fewer than 5 percent of men and women age 65 and over fall into this category (Saluter, 1996). Few never-marrieds marry in old age; first marriages constitute less than 10 percent of all marriages of elders (Barrow, 1996). The never-married are a diverse group—some are isolated; others have many friends. Some wish they were married; some are glad they're single.

Never-married people are more likely than their married counterparts to develop the self-reliance to cope with aging (Hooyman and Kiyak, 1991). Some

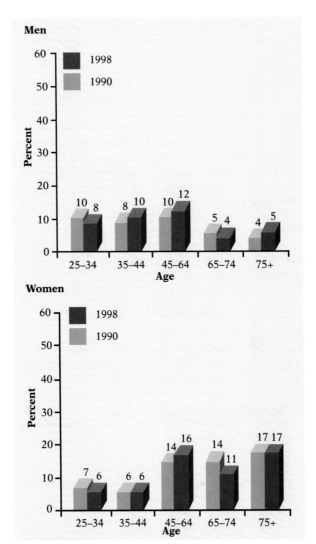

FIGURE 8.6   Living Alone: 1990 and 1998. As these data show, older women are much more likely than their male counterparts to be living alone in their midlife and later years, especially after age 74. How would you explain these differences?

SOURCE: Based on U.S. Census Bureau, 1999c, Table 87.

see the never-married elderly as lonely and as enduring many problems. A commitment to another person may be satisfying, but it also means making compromises and limiting one's own freedom:

> When I was a little girl and, later on, an adolescent, it never occurred to me that I would not meet the man of my dreams, get married, and live happily ever after. Now, at fifty-four, it seems unlikely, though not impossible, that this will happen. Not only do I live alone but I actually like it. I value my space, my solitude, and my independence

enormously and cannot [imagine] the circumstances that would lead me to want to change it. (Cassidy, 1993: 35)

Never-marrieds do not have to deal with the desolation of widowhood or divorce. Many develop extensive social networks among friends and relatives. They work, date, and engage in a variety of hobbies, volunteer work, church activities, and lasting relationships. As people age, however, the supportive social ties of never-married people aged 60 and older diminish compared to those of their married or divorced counterparts. Older never-married singles are likely to have the closest relationships with parents or older sibling. When these family members die or become physically impaired, the never-married lose confidants and caregivers and report lower life satisfaction (Barrett, 1999; Keith et al., 2000).

Myths and Realities about Being Single

Being single has many advantages, but some of the benefits have been exaggerated or romanticized. Here are some of the most popular myths about singlehood (Cargan and Melko, 1982):

1. *Singles are tied to their mother's apron strings.* In reality, there are few differences between singles and marrieds in their perceptions of and relationships with parents or other relatives.
2. *Singles are selfish and self-centered.* In reality, singles often make more time for friends than married people do, and they tend to be more active in community service.

3. *Singles are well-off financially.* A number of single professionals and young college graduates in high-tech jobs are affluent, but more singles than marrieds live at or below the poverty level. In general, married couples are better off financially because both partners work. In fact, our taxes support singles rather than married couples (see the box "The Marriage Penalty or a Singles Penalty?").
4. *Singles are happier.* Although singles spend more time in leisure activities such as attending movies, eating in restaurants, and going to clubs, they are also more likely to be lonely, to be depressed when they are alone, and to feel anxious and stressed.
5. *There is something wrong with people who do not marry.* There is nothing wrong with being or staying single. Many singles simply feel that the disadvantages of marriage outweigh the benefits.

In terms of personal well-being, single men have the *most* problems, married men the *fewest*. Compared to married men, single men have higher mortality rates and a higher incidence of alcoholism, suicide, and mental health problems (Coombs, 1991; Rowe and Kahn, 1997). This may be due to the fact that married men have less time and money to engage in high-risk behavior (such as using alcohol or other drugs) because of greater family responsibilities. In addition, they often have wives who urge them to have annual physical checkups, who prepare healthier meals, and who may generally be more concerned about preventing illness.

On a day-to-day basis, however, single women encounter more problems than do single men. Because

CONSTRAINTS

The Marriage Penalty or a Singles Penalty?

Using the logic that two can live more cheaply than one, the federal government has historically taxed married couples at a higher rate than single people (Gage, 1994; Crenshaw, 1994). In 1999, about 25 million couples, nearly half of those filing joint returns, incurred an average marriage penalty of $1114 (Tyson, 2000).

The marriage penalty varies, however, depending on whether or not both spouses are employed and how much each partner earns. Consider a man with a taxable income of $50,000. As a

single, he'd pay $10,712 in federal taxes. If he married and his wife didn't work, he'd pay $8502, a tax cut of 21 percent. The marriage penalty is greatest for two-earner couples whose incomes are similar. They pay more as a couple than they would as two singles. Take two people with taxable incomes of $30,000 and $20,000. As singles, their tax would total $7508. As a $50,000 couple, they'd pay $8502. Some argue that singles generally pay taxes at a higher rate and are penalized for not marrying. On a $50,000 taxable

income, for example, their tax comes to $10,712, which is $2210 more than many married couples have to pay (Quinn, 1999).

In 2000, Congress voted to eliminate much of the marriage penalty tax. Arguing that the plan would be too costly and eat up too much of the budget surplus, President Clinton vetoed the proposed legislation (Francis, 2000b). Because the marriage/singles penalty has been controversial since the early 1990s, we'll probably hear about it again in the future.

Single women and men often work long hours at their jobs, sometimes because they want to advance their careers but sometimes because they're perceived as being less burdened with home and family responsibilities.

of the rising incidence in recent years of rape and other violent crimes against women, single women, who often live alone, are more likely than their married counterparts to be mugged, burglarized, or raped. Professional women who travel have encountered problems in hotel accommodations and must often take extra safety precautions because they are more vulnerable than single men.

Unmarried people of both sexes face a number of prejudices. They are often accused of being "immature" or "flighty" ("When are you going to put down roots?" "Are you ever going to settle down?"). In addition, they may be given more responsibilities at work because they are viewed as having more free time. For example, some single professional women complain that they are often expected to do the "little extras" at work: "To serve on more committees, volunteer for more overtime, or to give up more holidays and weekends—because they are perceived as having nothing better to do" (Cejka, 1993: 10).

As you can see, singlehood has both advantages and disadvantages for adults of all ages. Because there are many incentives for remaining single, both singlehood and cohabitation are becoming increasingly acceptable ways of life.

Cohabitation

Cohabitation is a living arrangement in which two people who are not related and not married live together and usually have a sexual relationship. Cohabitants are sometimes called **POSSLQs** (pronounced "posselkews"), meaning "persons of the opposite sex sharing living quarters." Until 1995, the Census Bureau inferred cohabitation rates based on information on household composition that included roommates and other non-cohabitors, such as tenants. Since then, POSSLQ households have been identified as households with two and only two adults (age 15+) who are unrelated to the opposite sex and with or without the presence of children under 15 years old (Casper and Cohen, 2000; Cohen, 1999).

Since 1950, the number of unmarried-couple households in the United States has increased tremendously—from an estimated 50,000 households in 1950 to almost 5 million in 1997 (Saluter, 1994; Casper and Cohen, 2000). Keep in mind, however, that only 7 percent of the population is cohabiting at any point in time (U.S. Census Bureau, 1999c). Cohabitation usually postpones marriage (or remarriage); it rarely replaces marriage permanently.

Types of Cohabitation

There are several types of cohabitation. The most common are part-time/limited cohabitation, premarital cohabitation, and cohabitation that is a substitute for a legal marriage.

A form of cohabitation that people "drift" into gradually is called **part-time/limited cohabitation** (Macklin, 1974). A couple that spends a great deal of time together may eventually decide to move in together. The decision may be based on a combination of reasons, such as convenience, sharing expenses, and sexual accessibility. There is no long-term commitment, and most often, marriage is not the couple's goal. A large majority expects to marry someone in

MULTICULTURAL

Multicultural Love Is More Color-blind Than Marriage

As you saw in *Table 7.2* and the related discussion, most marriages are between couples with the same racial and ethnic backgrounds and similar educational levels. Before marriage, however, many people are likely to live with a partner of another race or ethnic group. Analyzing 1990 U.S. Census Bureau data for black, white, Asian, and Latino couples aged 18 to 30, Harris and Ono (2000) found that intimate partnerships between the races are much more common than interracial and interethnic marriages. In general, whites and blacks were much more likely than Asians and Latinos both to marry and to cohabit with their own racial group. But within each racial group, cohabitation patterns varied by gender. For example,

- While almost 96 percent of married white women have white husbands, only 8 percent of white women cohabit with nonwhite men. White women are almost four times as likely to live with black men as to be married to them and they're also more likely to live with than marry Asians and Latinos.
- About 96 percent of married black women are married to black men compared with about 94 percent of cohabiting black women who live with black men. But while black women are more likely to live with than marry white and Latino men, they are no more likely to marry Asian men than to live with them.
- About 80 percent of married Latino women have Latino husbands, but

only 73 percent of cohabiting Latino women have Latino partners. About 22 percent of Latino women are living with white men, compared with 17 percent who are married to white men.

- Asian women are the most likely to live with and marry non-Asian men (see *Table 8.2*).

The researchers noted: "Our findings suggest that there is much greater intimate contact between the races than marriage data imply," even though most people still marry within their own racial and ethnic groups.

---

their lifetime, but not necessarily their current partner. Cohabitants may feel that living together provides more intimacy than singlehood but less of a commitment than marriage (Rindfuss and VandenHeuvel, 1990). One or both partners may be divorced or may be involved romantically but not interested in remarriage. One or both might recognize that the relationship may be short-lived, but they benefit economically by pooling their incomes (Griffin, 1995). In the case of young adults, sometimes one or both partners use cohabitation to distance themselves from parental values and influence (Clarkberg et al., 1995).

For many people, premarital cohabitation is "a new step between dating and marriage" (Gwartney-Gibbs, 1986). In **premarital cohabitation,** the couple is testing the relationship before making a final commitment. In this sense cohabitation may be a *trial marriage*. If a trial marriage does not lead to formal marriage, the couple will usually end the relationship. Such first phases of marriage may be especially attractive to partners who doubt that they can deal successfully with problems that arise from differences in personalities, interests, age, race, or previous marital status.

A **substitute marriage** is a long-term commitment between two people without a legal marriage. Motives for substitute marriages vary widely. For example, one

or both partners may still be legally married to someone else or may be divorced and reluctant to remarry. In some cases, one partner may be highly dependent or insecure and thus prefer any kind of relationship to being alone. In other cases, partners may feel that a legal ceremony is irrelevant to their commitment to each other (see Chapter 1).

There is also some evidence that partner choices differ depending on the kind of cohabitation relationship that people seek. That is, those who expect a long-term relationship (premarital cohabitation) are much more likely to choose partners who are similar in age, race, and religion than those who expect a short-term relationship (part-time/limited cohabitation) (Schoen and Weinick, 1993).

Who Cohabits and Why

Cohabitation isn't a passing fad. More than half of marriages are preceded by periods of cohabitation (up from 10 percent three decades ago). What are the characteristics of cohabitors? And why has cohabitation become so common?

Characteristics of Cohabitants By 1995, half of all U.S. women in their thirties had cohabited outside of marriage (Bumpass and Lu, 2000). A third of all

TABLE 8.2

Whom Young Asian Women Marry and Live With

Race/Ethnicity of Partner	Married Asian Women	Cohabiting Asian Women
Asian	69%	42%
White	25	45
Latino	4	6
Black	2	5

SOURCE: Based on Harris and Ono (2000), Figure 1A.

married Americans cohabited with their spouses before marriage. About half of those aged 18 to 29 said that they lived with their husband or wife before getting married and 27 percent of those aged 50 to 64 had done so (Newport, 1996). The large numbers, especially among those 45 and older, suggest that cohabitation is a widely accepted living arrangement. As the box "Multicultural Love Is More Color-blind Than Marriage" shows, cohabitation outside of one's own racial or ethnic group is fairly prevalent, especially among young Asian women.

Living together is more common in large cities, in the U.S. Northeast and especially on the West Coast, and among people who are politically liberal and less actively religious (Thornton, 1991; Newport, 1996). Low educational attainment is strongly related to cohabitation, contradicting the widespread perception that the highly educated are the most likely to live together. Cohabitation rates are higher for women than for men and most common for those with low socioeconomic status who grew up in divorced homes or in families that depended on welfare (Bumpass et al., 1991). Those who are less educated are more likely to cohabit. As *Figure 8.7* shows, 60 percent of the

women with no high school diploma or general equivalency diploma (GED) had cohabited compared to 38 percent of the women with a bachelor's degree or higher. Cohabitation may be more common at lower socioeconomic levels because partners can combine resources and they can avoid the legal costs associated with a possible future divorce. Because, however, almost 40 percent of the women who have cohabited have at least a college degree (see *Figure 8.7*), it is not likely that economic constraints alone are a key factor in explaining high cohabitation rates (Bumpass and Lu, 2000).

Most cohabiting relationships are relatively short-lived, with a median duration of 15 to 18 months. When these relationships end, about 60 percent result in marriage and 40 percent in a breakup. As cohabitation becomes more and more accepted, living together may include a greater proportion of couples with less serious commitments who decide to cohabit as a matter of temporary convenience rather than as a prelude to marriage (Bumpass and Lu, 2000). On the other hand, and especially for black couples, cohabitation often serves as a long-term alternative to marriage (S. L. Brown, 2000). As we discussed earlier, postponing matrimony or not marrying often reflects financial circumstances that weaken the odds of marriage (S. L. Brown, 2000; Gorman, 2000). The probability of cohabitation dissolution decreases when household earnings increase. Men who are employed full time, especially those in professional and semiprofessional occupations, are more likely to marry than are unemployed men (Wu and Pollard, 2000).

Why Has Cohabitation Become So Common? The first cohabitation is more likely to result in marriage for white and Asian women (about 61 percent) than for Latinas (54 percent) and African American women (41 percent) (Abma et al., 1997). Although social scientists know little about how or why racial-ethnic cohabitation differs, it could be that the stagnant earning

© 1996 United Feature Syndicate, Inc.

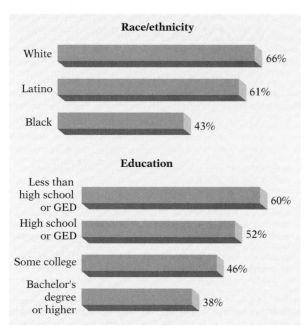

FIGURE 8.7 **Percent of U.S. Women Ages 15 to 44 Who Have Ever Cohabitated: 1995.**

SOURCE: Based on U.S. Census Bureau, 1999c, Table 66.

prospects for ethnic males, especially black men, encourage cohabitation—which involves less commitment and responsibility—rather than marriage (see Chapter 12). In addition, black and white cohabitors are less likely to marry when women are earning more than men. Such financial differences may lead to competitiveness and insecurity about one's decision-making power, a reluctance to make joint investments, and a resulting erosion of commitment to the relationship (Smock and Manning, 1997; Brines and Joyner, 1999; Cohen, 1999).

Family experiences and values may also be important factors in the decision to cohabit. Young people whose mothers approve of cohabitation marry at significantly later ages than young people whose mothers disapprove of cohabitation (Axinn and Thornton, 1993). Cohabitors are more likely than their married counterparts to have parents who divorced or remarried, to regard their parents' marriage as unhappy, and to have poorer relationships with their parents. In addition, cohabitors have their first sexual intercourse earlier and have sex with more partners than noncohabitors (Cunningham and Antill, 1995). Although researchers have not focused on the reasons for such differences, factors such as family instability and conflict might distinguish cohabitors from single and married people of similar ages.

Some suggest that cohabitation is just one component of a constellation of longer-term changes in family patterns that have been occurring in the United States and Europe. Cultural values have emphasized the importance of individual attainment (Smock, 2000). Women who plan to complete a four-year college degree or more, for example, are likely to delay marriage and cohabit instead (Barber and Axinn, 1998a). Intragenerational attitudes may also be causing cohabitation rates to escalate. Young men whose mothers want them to have four or more children enter any type of co-residential union—either marriage or cohabitation—at a much higher rate than men whose mothers want them to have one child (Barber and Axinn, 1998b).

Finally, much of the stigma associated with cohabitation and out-of-wedlock births has diminished. According to national surveys, for example, in 1972 only 19 percent of 45- to 54-year-olds believed it was okay to have sex before marriage. This number mushroomed to almost 50 percent in 1998 (Stapinski, 1999). In addition, as Bumpass and Lu (1999) observe, if children grew up in cohabiting households, parents are "unlikely to have much moral force" in arguing that their children should abstain from either unmarried sex or cohabitation.

The Benefits of Cohabitation

Not surprisingly, cohabitants generally favor cohabitation. It can provide couples with the emotional security of an intimate relationship but at the same time allow them to maintain their independence in many areas. They can dissolve the relationship without legal problems, or they may marry with a feeling that they have established a sound foundation (J. F. Crosby, 1991). Simply postponing marriage can contribute to marital stability because a later age is one of the best predictors of a stable marriage (see Chapter 15).

Cohabitation often encourages people to establish a meaningful relationship instead of playing superficial dating games. Long periods of intimate contact afford an opportunity for self-disclosure and may foster emotional growth and maturity. Living with someone can be annoying at times, but cohabitants may gain a deeper understanding of their partners' needs, expectations, and weaknesses. They may gain self-confidence as they learn to deal with each other on a daily basis.

Cohabitation may prevent unhappy marriages that end in divorce if it gives partners a more realistic view of each other and forces them to recognize and deal with opposing values, opinions, and ideas (Bumpass and Sweet, 1989). And it can help people find out how much they really care about each other when they have to cope with some unpleasant realities such as a partner who doesn't pay overdue bills or has different hygiene standards. Cohabitants who plan to marry report more frequent interaction with their partners than do marrieds (Brown and Booth, 1996). Among unmarried persons age 60 and over,

Many cohabitants like this couple in Moscow, Russia, are 45 years old or older and tend to live in large cities rather than rural areas.

cohabitation may increase the chances of receiving caregiving that is usually provided by spouses (Chevan, 1996). Thus, cohabitation might be an alternative to living alone rather than a prelude or alternative to marriage.

The Disadvantages of Cohabitation

Unlike married couples, cohabitants enjoy few legal rights. In addition, cohabitants often face the same kinds of problems as married couples (see Chapters 9–11). Some partners experience a loss of identity or a feeling of being trapped. They may feel restricted from participating in activities with friends. One or both partners may dislike being dependent on the other. If cohabitants are sexually intimate (and most cohabiting couples are), they can experience the same kinds of difficulties that married couples encounter, including a lack of sexual interest, failure to achieve orgasm, fear of pregnancy, and susceptibility to infections. Most important, if people are not honest about their sexual histories, partners can contract sexually transmitted diseases, HIV infection, or AIDS (see Chapter 6).

Although some women think that cohabitation will promote egalitarian gender roles, this is rarely the case. Women in cohabiting relationships still do more of the cooking and other household tasks traditionally assigned to women. Several studies suggest that cohabiting arrangements exploit women economically. When both partners are working, some cohabiting men insist that women pay half of all expenses, even though women earn much less than men (Khoo, 1987).

Several researchers have found that cohabitors, compared to married couples, have a weaker level of commitment to their relationship and lower levels of happiness and satisfaction, report more alcohol problems, and are more likely to be unfaithful (see, for example, Horwitz and White, 1998; Treas and Giesen, 2000; Waite, 2000). These and other problems may reflect a general fuzziness about a cohabitor's responsibilities and rights. Because marital commitment is embodied in law, it takes some effort to terminate a marriage (see Chapter 15). In contrast, "strong consensual norms or formal laws" don't govern nonmarital unions (Nock, 1995). As a result, the social and legal costs of not working on a cohabiting relationship or exiting from it are relatively negligible.

About 36 percent of cohabiting couples have children under age 15 in the household, a substantial increase over the 27 percent in 1980 (U.S. Census Bureau, 1999a). One reason for this increase may be that women in lower socioeconomic levels postpone divorce because it is expensive but continue to increase their families by having children with cohabitants (Loomis and Landale, 1994). Children in cohabiting households—whether they are biological offspring or not—might enjoy some of the benefits associated with two-parent families. Even at lower socioeconomic levels, for example, children can reap some economic advantages by living with two adult earners instead of a single mother. Children may also experience more violence than their counterparts in married households. Cohabiting women report two times greater abuse than married women due to such factors as the cohabiting men's lower investment in the relationship, patriarchal values, and low deterrence because the women typically tolerate the assaults. The violence and sexual abuse perpetrated by cohabiting partners have a negative effect on the mental health of children in such households (Cunningham and Antill, 1995).

Even when children in cohabiting households aren't targets of violence, they are more likely than their counterparts in married homes to experience greater family instability. An estimated two-fifths of all children will spend some time in a cohabiting household before age 16 (Bumpass and Lu, 2000). Moreover, there may be several cohabiting unions, or what Popenoe and Whitehead (1999) call "serial cohabitation." In serial cohabitation, divorces and remarriages may lead to numerous family disruptions that "do not bode well for children's well-being" (Smock, 2000).

Does Cohabitation Lead to Better Marriages?

Many couples who live together contend that cohabitation leads to better marriages. Some research shows, however, that marriages that follow cohabitation have a higher dissolution rate than do marriages between noncohabitors (Krishnan, 1998).

Why does living together not lead to better marriages? According to social scientists, people likely to cohabit differ from those who do not in ways that predispose them to eventual divorce, known as the *selectivity* or *unconventionality hypothesis*. Some cohabitors were poor marriage risks before they married, in terms of a higher incidence of drug problems, inability to handle money, trouble with the law, unemployment, sexual infidelity, and personality problems (Bumpass and Sweet, 1989; Teachman et al., 1991). These risk factors increase the likelihood of divorce after marriage. In addition, cohabitors are less likely than noncohabitors to have more doubts about their partner or the institution of marriage (Cunningham and Antill, 1995).

For young people, especially, cohabitation may be a way of avoiding the responsibilities of marriage. As a result, cohabitors may make less effort to communicate with one another and to work out problems. There is also a difference between cohabitants who intend to marry their partners and those who do not. The latter put less effort into the relationship, are less likely to compromise, and tend to have poorer communication skills for solving interpersonal problems. Thus, "those who cohabit with no intention of marrying are ill equipped for a lasting relationship" (Stets, 1993b: 256).

Couples who cohabit usually expect more from marriage than others and are less likely to adapt to traditional marital role expectations. Most cohabitants believe, for example, that any relationship should be ended if either partner is dissatisfied. In contrast, adults who do not cohabit may hold the more traditional view that the marriage bond is sacred (Cherlin, 1992). Or the experience of cohabitation itself may lead to instability: Cohabitants used to having more autonomy may be quick to leave a marriage (DeMaris and MacDonald, 1993). In addition, former cohabitants may be less able to weather the storms that some complex family structures (such as those involving stepchildren) encounter (Teachman and Polonko, 1990).

Cohabitation and the Law

Unmarried couples have very little legal protection (Stone, 1993; Seff, 1995). In a recent case in Sacramento, California, a state appeals court ruled that a landlord had the right to refuse to rent an apartment to an unmarried heterosexual couple because the owner considered sex outside of marriage sinful. Thus, renting the apartment would violate the religious freedom of the apartment owner. The presiding judge noted that because the California legislature had not passed laws giving cohabitants the same housing rights as those of married couples, there was no basis for extending the same housing-rights protection to unmarried couples as to married couples (*New York Times*, 1994).

According to many legal experts, cohabitants' best protection in financial matters is to maintain separate ownership of possessions. Partners should not have joint bank accounts or credit cards. They should prepare a written agreement about debts and how bills are to be paid. Shared leases should also be negotiated before moving in together. If partners buy real estate together they should spell out carefully, in writing, each person's share of any profit. Homeowners' and renters' insurance policies should carry both partners' names so that the possessions of both are clearly covered. Cars should not be registered in a woman's name just to escape the high insurance premiums commonly charged men under 25. If there is an accident, the woman will be liable even if the man was driving.

Health insurance plans that cover a spouse almost never extend to an unmarried partner. If either partner is not covered by a group health plan at work, unmarried couples should buy their own protection against catastrophic medical costs. A medical power of attorney will permit an unrelated person not only to visit a critically ill partner but also to make medical decisions for him or her.

If a partner dies and leaves no will, relatives, no matter how distant, can claim all of his or her possessions. The cohabiting partner has no claim at all. Cohabiting couples' best course is to put everything possible in writing. If a couple has children, both unmarried parents must acknowledge biological parenthood in writing to protect the children's future claims to financial support and inheritance (see

Chapter 16). Partners can name each other as beneficiaries in life insurance policies. To make sure their wishes are carried out in probate (the process by which a will is certified as genuine) and that no kin inherit undeserved assets, an unmarried couple should prepare wills. Few pension plans allow unmarried partners to receive survivor retirement benefits, something elderly unmarried couples must consider carefully (see Chapter 17).

It may seem unromantic to discuss legal matters when we are talking about people who love each other. When a cohabiting relationship ends, however, the legal problems can be overwhelming. Many attorneys recommend that cohabitants draw up a contract similar to a premarital document. Appendix F describes some of the complex issues that cohabitants are likely to encounter.

A Global View: Cohabitation

Cohabitation has been rising almost everywhere but has been climbing most rapidly and is most prevalent among the industrialized countries. In Sweden, for example, 99 percent of married couples live together before marriage and as many as one in four couples are not legally married; in Denmark, 80 percent cohabit. Other European countries with high rates of cohabitation (and higher than in Australia, Canada, and the United States) include Austria, France, Germany, and the Netherlands. Cohabitation is common in Latin America and the Caribbean—especially in Cuba, the Dominican Republic, Ecuador, Panama, and Venezuela—and less common in Africa and Asia. In China, an estimated one-third of all couples cohabit. About two-thirds of these unions occur in the countryside and constitute "early marriages" between adolescents who are below the legal minimum age for marriage—20 for women, 22 for men (Neft and Levine, 1997).

Why these high rates? Many countries' governments offer single women economic security. In Sweden, for example, birth-control information and some contraceptive devices are free. Moreover, since 1976, Swedish women have been able to obtain an abortion on request up to the eighteenth week of pregnancy. All parents, married or unmarried, receive a children's allowance from the state, and divorced and single mothers are entitled to cash advances on child-support payments if a child's father fails to pay. Norway's social policies are similar (Blanc, 1987; Haas, 1992).

As more and more couples live together either before marrying or instead of marrying, some governments are extending cohabitors some of the same rights that were previously provided only to married couples. Argentina, for example, grants pension rights to spouses in common-law marriages, and Canada extends insurance benefits to cohabiting partners. Other countries, including Australia, require a distribution of property when cohabiting relationships break up (Neft and Levine, 1997).

Gay and Lesbian Households

Regardless of sexual orientation, most of us seek an intimate relationship with one special person. Because homosexuals are denied marriage by law, they must turn to cohabitation.

Gay and Lesbian Couples

Both homosexual and heterosexual couples want close and loving relationships (see Chapter 5). Most homosexuals desire stable partnerships with someone they love. And, like heterosexuals, gays must work out issues related to effective communication, power, and household responsibilities (Meyer, 1990; Kurdek, 1998). If there are children from previous marriages, gay and lesbian partners, like heterosexual parents, must deal with custody or child-rearing issues (see Chapter 11).

Gay and lesbian relationships, like those of their heterosexual counterparts, are not always harmonious. For example, in a study of 75 gay, 51 lesbian, and 108 heterosexual couples who did not reside with children, Kurdek (1994) found that all cohabitants, whether heterosexual or homosexual, experienced similar degrees of conflict in four areas—power, personal flaws, intimacy, and personal distance. In terms of *power,* all subjects were equally likely to report arguments about finances, lack of equality in the relationship, and possessiveness. They were also equally likely to complain about such *personal flaws* as smoking or drinking, driving style, and personal grooming. There was no significant difference in the numbers of reports from both groups of dissatisfaction in *intimacy,* especially in sex and not showing enough affection. Finally, both groups were equally likely to complain that their partners were *physically absent,* usually because of job or school commitments.

Gay and heterosexual groups did differ in two ways, however. According to Kurdek, the heterosexual couples were more likely to argue over personal values, social and political issues, and relationships with the partner's parents, whereas the gay and lesbian couples reported greater distrust, especially over previous lovers. In addition, Kurdek suggests that suspicion may be a more common phenomenon among gay and lesbian cohabitants because their previous lovers are likely to remain in their social support networks, increasing the likelihood of jealousy and resentment.

In contrast to past accounts of gay life being divided into "butch" and "femme" roles, most lesbians and gay men are in "dual-worker" relationships, so that neither partner is the exclusive breadwinner or homemaker. If one partner usually performs most of the "feminine" activities such as cooking and the other performs most of the "masculine" tasks such as car repair, the specialization is typically based on individualistic factors, such as skills or interests, rather than traditional husband-wife or masculine-feminine roles (Peplau, 1993).

As you saw in Chapter 6, there are probably more differences between men and women than there are between homosexuals and heterosexuals. Gay men, like heterosexual men, tend to separate love and sex and to have more brief relationships, whereas both lesbian and heterosexual women are more interested in integrating sex with emotional intimacy. Power and equity issues are also gendered rather than shaped by sexual orientation. For most heterosexual and gay male couples, for example, the person who makes more money has more power in terms of both decision making and getting out of housework. Most lesbians and many heterosexual women, in contrast, see money as a means to avoid dependence on one's partner. In addition, gay and heterosexual men are more career-oriented because our culture equates affluence with success. Most lesbian and heterosexual women, in contrast, are less competitive and more relationship-oriented (Huston and Schwartz, 1995).

Despite these positive characteristics, gay and lesbian cohabitation is far from idyllic. Researchers estimate, for example, that the incidence of battering in lesbian and gay couples is about the same as it is for heterosexual couples—approximately 25 to 33 percent of all such couples (Brand and Kidd, 1986; Lundy, 1993). Moreover, much of the abuse tends to be recurrent. Renzetti (1992) found, for example, that 54 of the 100 respondents in her study stated that they experienced more than ten abusive incidents during the course of the relationship. More recently, a national survey found that although gay men and lesbians experienced violence rates with intimate partners that were comparable to those of heterosexual cohabitants, the violence was more prevalent among gay men than either lesbian or heterosexual cohabitants. Almost 16 percent of same-sex cohabiting men reported being raped and/or physically assaulted by a male partner while 11 percent reported such violence by a lesbian partner. Moreover, gay male cohabitants were twice as likely to report being raped and/or physically assaulted by a male partner than were heterosexual male cohabitants (15 percent and 8 percent, respectively). The researchers concluded that violence is more prevalent among gay male couples than either lesbian or heterosexual couples (Tjaden et al., 1999).

Although it's not clear why the violence rates among gay male cohabitants are so high, one explanation may be that gay men have internalized the notion that aggression is an acceptable "male" way of solving conflict in intimate relationships. Another reason may be that gay men are more likely than lesbians to be rejected by their family and friends and to strike out against intimate partners.

Gay and lesbian couples often perceive less social support from family members than do married or cohabiting couples. The greatest rejection may come from racial-ethnic families, whose attitudes tend to be more traditional and conservative. Traditional values about marriage and the family are often reinforced by religious beliefs. In some faiths homosexual behavior is considered aberrant or a sin. Family members are expected to marry and to continue the traditional family structure. A related reason is that racial-ethnic families have strong extended family systems. A gay family member may be seen as jeopardizing not only the intrafamily relationships but also the extended family's continued strong association with the ethnic community (Morales, 1996; Liu and Chan, 1996; Mays et al., 1998).

Scholars are increasingly emphasizing that there is a rich diversity of same-sex relationships that still remains unexplored because such factors as ethnicity, social class, and age variations are just beginning to be considered (Peplau, 1993). Despite the diversity, one of the problems that all gay and lesbian couples face—regardless of the position they might take—is the lack of institutional recognition that heterosexuals enjoy through the marriage ceremony.

Same-Sex Marriages

Same-sex marriages have been described as registered partnerships rather than official marriages. They were first legalized in Denmark in 1989, then in Norway in 1993, Sweden in 1994, and France in 1998 as "civil solidarity pacts." Although the partners cannot be married in church, they have many of the same rights as heterosexual couples. Recently, however, Dutch lawmakers approved legislation that gives gays rights beyond those offered in any other country. When the law takes effect in 2001, same-sex couples will have the right to marry, adopt, and divorce. The bill stipulates that same-sex marriages are allowed only for citizens or people with residency permits ("Dutch gays . . . ," 2000).

In October 1996, President Clinton signed the Defense of Marriage Act, which states that no U.S. state or territory has any legal duty to respect a marriage between homosexuals, even if such a marriage is valid in any other state. The act also bans any form of federal aid to a married couple unless the couple is in "a legal union between one man and one woman as husband and wife." That would rule out any use in the future by a married homosexual couple of tax or other benefits tied to marriage. Between 1993 and 1999, 30 states passed similar laws that prohibit same-sex marriages.

In December 1999, Vermont's state supreme court was the first to approve same-sex civil unions. According to the legislation, Vermont gay and lesbian couples can apply for a civil union license. Once certified by a judge, justice of the peace, or clergy member, they can

Lesbian mothers who work outside the home often have to struggle, just as heterosexual parents do, for quality time with their children.

take advantage of more than 300 benefits previously available only to married couples, such as the ability to make medical decisions for their partners and inherit property. If they want to end their union, the couple must go to family court (Marks, 2000). Some states, cities, and many major corporations offer medical and other benefits to the partners of gay and lesbian employees but not to unmarried heterosexual couples. About 18 percent of all U.S. employers have some form of domestic partner benefits that include health care (Swoboda, 2000).

Some feel that recognizing same-sex marriage would be only a symbolic act that might even have deleterious economic or legal effects. For example, lesbian mothers now have the same tax benefits for children as do other couples or single mothers. Social Security benefits are usually irrelevant because both partners in most gay and lesbian couples work and have accrued their own retirement benefits. If same-sex marriage were legalized, tax-withholding forms might reveal information that could result in even greater discrimination for a gay or lesbian in the workplace. Brownsworth argues that "just because straight people and heterosexual society do something does not mean we should strive to do it too" (1996: 97). According to Brownsworth, the marriage contract is a pact with the state, rather than an expression of love for one's partner. It has historically maintained social

control over women and children, defined women as property, and legitimized "divisions of paid and unpaid labor within the society (male labor is paid, female labor is unpaid)."

Others argue that denying same-sex marriages a legal status deprives gays of "a litany of benefits and protections, rights and responsibilities" (Wolfson, 1996: 83). If gay marriages were legal, for example, family members and relatives could not contest inheritance. Current rent-control regulations that define "family" in traditional terms can prevent access by gay families to housing. Furthermore, like heterosexual cohabitants, gay families are not entitled to the hospitalization or bereavement leaves that married couples enjoy. Family courts are sometimes reluctant to give custody of children or even visiting rights to lesbian mothers or gay fathers because of the fear that the children might become homosexual (Dean, 1991). Not being able to marry, Wolfson (1996) maintains, excludes same-sex couples from receiving *federal* out-of-state benefits and protections, such as Medicare, immigration laws, and joint filing of tax returns. These federal penalties remain in effect even when a state adopts domestic partnership laws or a company *voluntarily* provides health plans or other employee perks. Most important, Wolfson contends, legalizing same-sex marriages would provide the fundamental freedom of having "the equal right to choose whether and whom to marry."

Communal Living Arrangements

Communes are collective households in which children and adults live together. The adults may be married or unmarried. Some communes permit individual ownership of private property; others do not. There is a great deal of variation in the amount of sharing of economic, sexual, and decision-making rights.

Communes are not a modern invention. They are believed to have existed since 100 B.C. Today there are an estimated 1000 communes in the world. The popularity of communal living has fluctuated in the United States, but its membership has never exceeded more than a tenth of 1 percent of the entire population.

Both nineteenth-century and contemporary communes have differed widely within their respective time periods in terms of structure, values, and ideology (Kantor, 1970). In the nineteenth century many such communities wrestled with the issue of monogamy and had very different solutions. One group, the Icarians, made marriage mandatory for all adult members. Others, such as the Shakers and Rappites, required everyone, including husbands and wives, to live celibate lives. The Mormons, in emphasizing group rather than individual well-being, adopted polygyny. Others practiced free love, where sexual intercourse was permissible to all members and was

CHOICES

Senior Communes

Some communities offer care for the elderly and their families in communal settings (see Chapter 17). For instance, adult day-care programs provide meals and activities in which elderly clients share jointly. Geriatric foster-care programs place nonrelated elderly people in private residences where they usually receive assistance with the tasks of daily living but may also join in tasks and activities of the family whose home they share (Conner, 1992).

In some states, the elderly play an active role in communal residential life. For example, in the private residences maintained in Florida by the Share-A-Home Association, elderly residents make all the important decisions. Their authority ranges from hiring and firing staff and voting on new members to choosing menus and

organizing entertainment. Started in 1960 as a nonprofit organization, Share-A-Home enables older people to live together as a family, sharing expenses and functioning as a single household unit. In this environment the members not only fulfill their basic needs but also provide one another with companionship and emotional support.

A case involving a Share-A-Home group in Winter Park, Florida, gave a new legal definition to the concept of family. In 1971, the Orange County Board of Commissioners filed a suit against a Share-A-Home facility, claiming that it was a boardinghouse and as such was in violation of the single-family zoning ordinance in its neighborhood. The Share-A-Home group in question consisted of 12 older people,

aged 61 to 94, who had formed a communal type of family and were living in an old 27-room house. The Orange County code defined a family as "one or more persons occupying a dwelling and living as a single housekeeping unit." Although this definition did not stipulate that the persons living as a unit must be related, the plaintiff's main argument for not recognizing the elderly group as a family was the fact that they were not related. The court ruled, however, that the group met the legal definition of a family: "any group that pools its resources with the intention of sharing the joys and sorrows of family life is a family." Because these seniors were living in the same household, sharing the same kitchen, splitting living costs, and giving one another support and understanding, they were a bona fide family (Harris, 1990).

---

not regulated by norms about marriage or monogamy (Muncy, 1988).

The Oneida Community, founded in New York State in the 1840s by John Humphrey Noyes, practiced "complex marriage," in which every adult was theoretically married to every other member. Much older men initiated Oneida girls into sexual intercourse shortly after their first menses (menstruation). Communal child care presumably freed mothers to pursue their highest calling—serving God. According to some sources, mothers had the greatest difficulty with the idea that community adults, not biological parents, were responsible for raising children (Dalsimer, 1981).

Contemporary communes vary in terms of parent–child arrangements. On an Israeli kibbutz, for instance, parents often see their children only during meals and in the evenings. There are strong emotional parent–child ties, and parents are very involved in the decision making concerning their child's future (O'Kelly and Carney, 1986). Today, however, many kibbutz-raised children are opting to raise their own children in a nuclear family structure to be able to spend more time together (Kaffman, 1993).

Heiss (1986) maintains that both the historical communes and the rural, "hippie" communes of the

1960s were "notorious for the burdens carried by women." Women typically did their traditional tasks and participated in men's work as well. Contemporary urban communes have come the closest to an equitable division of labor. The purpose of urban communes is to create a collective household and a shared home rather than a countercultural attack on the current system. Both men and women often work in traditional 9-to-5 jobs, make about equal financial contributions, and share the routine household functions. Most of the child care, however, still rests with the mother.

Most communes have been short-lived (W. L. Smith, 1999). Often, the members are unwilling to give up their autonomy or private property. In a society that emphasizes individuality and competition, it is difficult to subordinate individual rights and privileges "for the greater good." There may be conflict and jealousy regarding sexual relationships (Zablocki, 1980). Furthermore, communes that practiced polygamy or free love "drew the wrath" of a culture that believed that sexual relations outside of marriage and monogamy are evil (Muncy, 1988). Other groups are dwindling because of a lack of new membership. For example, the Shakers have only a handful of members left in one "family" in Maine. The members are quite elderly, and most of the buildings and grounds have now been turned into tourist attractions (Kephart and Zellner, 1991).

Communal living is common on many college campuses. For example, fraternities, sororities, and houses that are rented and shared by five or six students fulfill many of the social and economic functions that characterize all communes. At the other end of the continuum, a growing proportion of older people is experimenting with communal living as an alternative to moving in with children or living in a nursing home. As the box "Senior Communes" illustrates, the communal movement is not only providing emotional and financial support for some elderly but is also changing the traditional definition of the family.

There are about 40 co-housing communities in the United States. They are usually single-family town houses where residents arrive at decisions through consensus and create a supportive, extended family environment. The families participate in the planning and design of the community and contribute to such purchases as a neighborhood playground. A "common house" may include a large dining area (for those who choose to eat together), kitchen, lounges, meeting rooms, recreation and child-care facilities, library, and workshops. Some people feel that decisions reached through consensus are tedious and time-consuming. Most residents, however, are enthusiastic about the closeness and warm friendships that develop in collaborative communities (Holmstrom, 2000).

Conclusion

There have been a number of *changes* in relationships outside of, before, and after marriage. Some of our *choices* include staying single longer, cohabiting, forming same-sex households, participating in communal living arrangements, or not marrying at all. Thus, larger numbers of people are single for a greater portion of their lives. Our choices are not without *constraints,* however. For example, many U.S. policies do not encourage or protect most of these relationships under the law. Despite the growing numbers of unmarried people, marriage is not going out of style; it is merely occupying less of the average adult's lifetime. Although there is less pressure to marry, most of us will do so at least once in our lifetime. In the next chapter we examine the institution of marriage.

SUMMARY

1. Diverse lifestyles have always existed, but in the past 20 years, many alternative family forms have increased, including singlehood, cohabitation, gay households, and communal living arrangements.

2. Household size has been shrinking since the 1940s. A major reason for the decrease is the growing number of people who are postponing marriage and living alone.

3. People are postponing marriage more often because there is a greater acceptance of cohabitation and of children born out of wedlock.

4. Singles constitute an extremely diverse group. Some have been widowed, divorced, or separated; others have never been married. Some singles choose their status, whereas others are single involuntarily.

5. There are many reasons why the numbers of singles have increased since the 1970s. Some of the reasons are macro, some are demographic, such as the marriage squeeze, whereas others reflect personal choices. African Americans, especially educated black women, are the most likely to postpone marriage or never marry.

6. Cohabitation has boomed since the 1970s. Although most cohabitation is short-lived, in some cases it is a long-term substitute for legal marriage.

Cohabitation is not restricted to the young. Most cohabitants have been divorced or have children in the home. As with other living arrangements, cohabitation has both advantages and disadvantages.

7. There is no evidence that cohabitation leads to more stable or happier marriages. Cohabitors have higher divorce rates than noncohabitors, and men typically benefit more than women do from cohabitation.

8. Legal factors sometimes dictate living arrangements. Because same-sex marriage is illegal in all states except Vermont (which allows same-sex civil unions), gay and lesbian partners have fewer options than do heterosexuals. There are also some differences between gay and lesbian households that are influenced more by gender roles than by sexual orientation.

9. Communal living arrangements have changed since the turn of the twentieth century and even since the 1970s. They are less numerous and less popular today, but they still fulfill the economic and social needs of many adults.

10. A growing number of elderly people are choosing to live in communal residences rather than move in with their children or live in retirement or nursing homes.

KEY TERMS

sex ratio *197*

marriage squeeze *197*

cohabitation *203*

POSSLQ *203*

part-time/limited cohabitation *203*

premarital cohabitation *204*

substitute marriage *204*

TAKING IT FURTHER

Learn More about Nonmarried Living Arrangements

There are a number of informative Internet sites on heterosexual cohabitation, same-sex households, and communal living arrangements. Here are a few:

Cohabitation-Living Together offers numerous sites that include financial advice, national polls, and the pros and cons of living together before or instead of marriage.

http://dating.about.com/people/dating/msubcohab.htm

Queer Resources Directory contains almost 26,000 files that include links to "Queers and Their Families."

www.qrd.org

The Cohousing Network provides information on "collaborative housing that attempts to overcome the alienation of modern subdivisions."

www.cohousing.org

Law.com is a valuable source of information about cohabitation rights, prenuptial agreements, and many other nonmarital issues.

www.law.com/index.html

And more . . . www.prenhall.com/benokraitis includes sites to national organizations that encourage or discourage cohabitation, information about the status of same-sex marriage legislation, collaborative housing options, and lists of government, higher education institutions, and private sector employers that offer domestic partnership benefits.

Marriage and Communication in Intimate Relationships

DATADIGEST

- In a national study of first-year college students, 72 percent said that **raising a family was an "essential" or "very important"** objective.

- Between 1984 and 1994, the average cost of a typical American wedding quadrupled, to **over $16,000 for a formal wedding.** In Las Vegas, where in 1994, 4 percent of Americans got married, the ceremony can take as little as seven minutes and cost $30.

- On the average, wives who work outside the home still do **over 80 percent of the household work.**

- In 1998, **married couples** accounted for 60 percent of all U.S. households.

- In a recent survey, 30 percent of the respondents nationwide said that **working women generally are worse mothers than women who don't work outside the home.**

SOURCES: "Attitudes and characteristics . . . ," 2000; Dogar, 1997; U.S. Census Bureau, 1999c; "Mothers work," 2000.

WHEN a journalist interviewed couples celebrating their fiftieth or greater wedding anniversaries, she found some common characteristics: mutual respect, common goals, supportive spouses, and a focus on communication and problem solving rather than winning battles. There were disagreements, but they were toned down. As a 77-year-old woman said about her husband:

> In all our 55 years, he has rarely gotten angry. If I get angry about something, we have a little argument, and he'll say something funny to me and I'll have to laugh and there goes the argument. Laughter has always been a big part of our life. (Licht, 1995: 19)

As you saw in the last chapter, people marry for a variety of reasons (see *Table 8.1*). The single greatest attraction in marriage is the continuous and intimate companionship with a loved one. As this chapter shows, enduring marriages are not born during the marriage ceremony but are the products of much thoughtful effort and years of cooperation, involving both mutual enjoyment and mutual sacrifices. One of the keys to enduring intimate relationships is the ability to communicate, a process that involves listening to one's partner and learning to express one's feelings constructively.

Marriages are highly personal, but they don't take place in a vacuum. Social pressures and societal constraints such as economic fluctuations affect every marriage. Some people become disillusioned with marriage because they have misconceptions and unrealistic expectations about married life that are deeply ingrained in our culture. A marriage will indeed be short-lived if the relationship is based on myths and misinformation. Before reading the rest of this chapter, take "A Marriage Quiz" on the next page. It should encourage you to think more critically about some of our assumptions about marriage.

We begin with a look at marital expectations and marriage rituals, consider various types of marriages and how they change over the years, and examine communication processes that can strengthen or undermine intimate relationships within and outside of marriage.

What Do We Expect from Marriage?

In Western societies, most women and men marry because they long for the certainty of secure love. As you will see shortly, many wedding rituals and practices reinforce the idea that marriage is a fusion of lovers who vow a lifelong commitment to each other. Although marriage is typically seen as a free choice based on affection, enduring marriages more often reflect a partnership, not unlike in business, where both people must compromise and cooperate in living up to a contract. In general, as you will see later in this chapter, the greater the gap between two people in terms of attitudes, values, habits, recreational activities, and temperaments, the greater is the likelihood that they will find themselves incompatible and unable to form a workable relationship.

Our Marriage Rituals

Marriage is a critical rite of passage in almost every culture. The major events that mark the beginning of a marriage are engagement, showers and bachelor parties, and the wedding itself.

Engagement Traditionally, an **engagement** formalized a couple's decision to marry and usually was signaled by an *engagement ring* given by the man to the

ASK YOURSELF

A Marriage Quiz

To respond to each statement, circle either True or False.

	Fact	**Fiction**

1. A husband's marital satisfaction is usually lower if his wife is employed full time than if she is a fulltime homemaker.   True   *(False)*

2. Marriages that last many years almost always have a higher level of satisfaction than marriages that last only a few years.   *(True)*   False

3. In most marriages, having a child improves marital satisfaction for both spouses.   True   *(False)*

4. The best single predictor of overall marital satisfaction is the quality of the couple's sex life.   True   *(False)*

5. Overall, married women are physically healthier than married men.   True   *(False)*

6. African American women are happier in marriage than are African American men.   True   *(False)*

7. Marital satisfaction for a wife is usually lower if she is employed full time than if she is a full-time homemaker.   True   *(False)*

8. "If my spouse loves me, he/she should instinctively know what I want and need to make me happy."   True   *(False)*

9. In a marriage in which the wife is employed full time, the husband usually shares equally in housekeeping tasks.   True   *(False)*

10. "No matter how I behave, my partner should love me because he/she is my spouse."   True   *(False)*

11. Anglo husbands spend more time on household work than do Latino husbands.   *(True)*   False

12. Husbands usually make more lifestyle adjustments in marriage than do wives.   True   *(False)*

13. "I can change my spouse by pointing out his/her inadequacies and bad habits."   True   *(False)*

14. The more a spouse discloses positive and negative information to his/her partner, the greater the marital satisfaction of both partners.   True   *(False)*

15. For most couples, maintaining romantic love is the key to marital happiness over the life span.   True   *(False)*

Scoring the Marriage Quiz

All of the items are false. The more "true" responses you gave, the greater your belief in marital myths. The quiz is based on research presented in this chapter and on Larson (1988: 8–9).

woman. Engagement was the last step in the courtship process leading to marriage. Before "popping the question," the man typically asked the woman's parents for their approval (or blessing), and the couple generally refrained from sexual intercourse until the wedding night. The bride's parents usually covered the wedding expenses, and the couple often planned a romantic, expensive honeymoon for which the groom's parents sometimes paid. According to the *Guinness Book of Records,* the longest engagement was between Octavio

In recent years, it's become more common for couples to break from tradition in planning their weddings. Here, the bride and groom marry at a "baseball wedding" at Kobe Green Stadium, Japan.

Guillen and Adriana Martinez of Mexico, who took 67 years to make sure they were right for each other. Most engagements are at least 65 years shorter.

Today many couples cohabit before they get married, and as a result engagements are often casual and informal. If couples are older when they marry, and if both partners work, they may purchase engagement and wedding rings jointly. They may also dispense with formal wedding announcements in the local newspapers and forgo the honeymoon. Despite the changing attitudes toward premarital sex and the rise of cohabitation, a recent national study reported that 12 percent of women aged 15 to 44 said they were virgins on their wedding night (Abma et al., 1997).

Whether or not the couple follows traditional customs, an engagement serves several functions. First, it sends a message to others to "keep their hands off" the future bride and bridegroom. Second, it gives both partners a chance to become better acquainted with their future in-laws and to strengthen their identity as a couple. Third, it provides each partner with information about a prospective spouse's potential or current medical problems (through blood tests, for example). Fourth, it legitimates premarital counseling, either secular or religious (such as Catholic engagement-encounter weekends), especially if the partners are of different races, religions, or ethnicities. Finally, if the couple has been living together (and/or has had a child out of wedlock), the engagement signals the intent to make the union legal.

In the traditional view, women enter marriage enthusiastically, but men are unsuspecting victims who have been "caught" or "trapped" into marrying. These mythic notions have been institutionalized in the bridal shower and bachelor party that for years

have been part of most young couples' prewedding activities. Today, however, there is a growing tendency in middle-class America for *both* women and men to attend engagement parties to celebrate the future marriage. These parties often supplant the two more traditional events: the *bridal shower,* at which female friends and relatives "shower" a bride with both personal and household gifts and commemorate the beginning of a new partnership, and the *bachelor party,* at which the groom's friends typically lament their friend's imminent loss of freedom and celebrate one "last fling."

Many men are becoming more involved in the wedding preparations. They are attending bridal shows, participating in flower consultations, producing original wedding invitations, and making choices about the menus. There are many reasons for men's taking an active role in the wedding plans. Some are sharing the costs of the wedding and "like to know where the money is going." Others are used to cooking and have opinions about the china, silver, and crystal. Those who are remarrying want to involve their children in the ceremony (Mathias, 1997).

The Wedding Recent years have seen some atypical weddings. In 1994, for example, the first wedding by videoconference hookup took place in New York City at PC Expo, a computer convention and exhibition. The bride and bridegroom were attending the convention, and the judge officiated from California. In 2000, in an annual single ceremony in Seoul's Olympic Stadium, the Reverend Sun Myung Moon, founder of the Unification Church, married 20,000 couples from more than 100 countries, including the United States. Reverend Moon matches the couples, all of whom are

total strangers, by age and education. The divorce rate of these couples is estimated to be about 75 percent (Baker, 2000).

Most weddings are more traditional. Even when the partners are very young—as is still common in some countries, like India, where the average marriage age is 19 for women and 23 for men—a wedding marks the end of childhood and the acceptance of the responsibilities of adulthood. Often the ceremony is performed in a religious setting, like a church or synagogue, where a cleric such as a priest, a minister, or a rabbi officiates. Although most ceremonies follow prescribed language, many modern couples write their own vows and recite them at the ceremony. The ceremony generally reinforces the idea that the marriage commitment is a sacred bond "till death us do part." The presence of family, friends, and witnesses affirms the acceptance and legitimacy of the union by both immediate relatives and the larger community.

In Western society a number of ritual acts and activities have come to be associated with the celebration of a marriage. The box on "Some Cherished Wedding Rituals" illustrates the historical origins of some of our current marriage rituals.

Love and Prenuptial Agreements

Prenuptial agreements are not uncommon among the very rich (such as Donald Trump and Marla Maples), but generally people do not draw up a prenuptial agreement because it seems unromantic and because little property is involved at the start of most marriages. Prenuptial agreements were common practice during the seventeenth and eighteenth centuries, however. For example, in 1683, John French and Eleanor Veazie signed a marriage contract in which John agreed "not to meddle with or take into his hand" any part of the estate that Eleanor had inherited from her former husband and "the new end of the dwelling

In 2000, in an annual single ceremony in Seoul's Olympic Stadium, the Reverend Sun Myung Moon, founder of the Unification Church, married 20,000 couples. Brides and grooms who could not be present were represented by photographs held by their future spouses. Reverend Moon conducts such mass marriages every year.

CHANGES •••

Some Cherished Wedding Rituals

Most of our time-honored customs associated with engagement and marriage, like rings and honeymoons, originally symbolized love and romance (Ackerman, 1994; see also Bulcroft et al., 1999). Many were designed to ensure the fertility of the couple and the prosperity of their household. Some, however, also reflected the subordinate position of the woman in the union. For example, the Anglo-Saxon word *wedd,* from which "wedding" is derived, meant the groom's payment for the bride to her father. Thus a wedding was literally the purchase of a woman. Here are some others:

- The *best man* was a warrior friend who helped a man capture and kidnap a woman he desired (usually from another tribe).
- Carrying the bride *over the threshold* is not simply a romantic gesture. Originally, it symbolized the abduction of the daughter who would not willingly leave her father's house.
- After a man captured or bought a bride, he disappeared with her for a while in a *honeymoon,* so that her family couldn't rescue her. By the time they found the couple, the bride would already be pregnant. In America, around 1850, the honeymoon was usually a wedding trip to visit relatives. A better economy, safety, and comfort of railroad and ocean travel popularized more distant and independent honeymoon trips (Kern, 1992).
- The *engagement ring* symbolized eternity. The medieval Italians favored a diamond ring because of

their superstition that diamonds were created from the flames of love.

- It was the soldiers of ancient Sparta who first staged *stag parties:* "The groom feasted with his male friends on the night before the wedding, pledging his continued loyalty, friendship, or love. . . . The function of this rite of passage was to say goodbye to the frivolities of bachelorhood, while swearing continued allegiance to one's comrades. It was important for the groom to reassure his friends that they wouldn't be excluded from his life now that it included a family" (Ackerman, 1994: 270).
- Sometime in the 1890s, the friend of a newly engaged woman held a party at which a Japanese parasol filled with little gifts was turned upside down over the bride-to-be's head, producing a shower of presents. Readers of fashion pages, learning of this event, then wanted bridal *showers* of their own.
- In medieval times the wedding party's *flower girl* carried wheat to symbolize fertility. Perhaps for symmetry, the *ring bearer* also appeared in the Middle Ages.
- Although in biblical times it was the color blue that symbolized purity, in 1499 Anne of Brittany set the pattern for generations to come by wearing a *white wedding gown* for her marriage to Louis XII of France. The white bridal gown came to symbolize virginity and is still worn by most first-time brides, even though many are not virgins. Today,

even women who remarry sometimes wear white, but they are advised by etiquette experts to forgo pure white as well as other symbols of virginity such as a veil, a train, and orange blossoms.

- The first *wedding ring* was probably made of iron, so it wouldn't break. The Romans believed that a small artery or "vein of love" ran from the third finger to the heart and that wearing a ring on that finger joined the couple's hearts and destiny.
- The ancient Romans baked a special wheat or barley cake that they broke over the bride's head as a symbol of her hoped-for fertility. The English piled up small cakes as high as they could, and bride and groom tried to kiss over the cakes without knocking the tower over; success meant a lifetime of prosperity. The cakes evolved into a *wedding cake* during the reign of England's King Charles II, whose French chefs decided to turn the cakes into an edible "palace" iced with white sugar.
- *Tying shoes to the car bumper* probably came from ancient cultures. For example, the Egyptians exchanged sandals at a wedding ceremony to symbolize an exchange of property or authority. A father would give the groom his daughter's sandal to show that she was now in his care. In Anglo-Saxon marriage, the groom tapped the bride lightly on the head with the shoe to show his authority. Later, people began throwing shoes at the couple and somehow (perhaps a bride or groom protested this rather hostile activity) this evolved into the current practice.

---

house" after his death. He also promised to let her sell their apples and to give her a place for her garden plot (Scott and Wishy, 1982: 70–72). And in 1855, Lucy Stone and Henry Blackwell signed a marriage contract that protested such accepted practices as the husband's

control and guardianship of their children and the woman's taking the husband's name (McElroy, 1991).

Some of the arguments for and against prenuptial agreements are similar to those for cohabitation contracts, discussed in Chapter 8. Those who oppose pre-nuptial agreements feel that they set a pessimistic tone for the marriage and that disagreements about the contents might even derail wedding plans. Pre-nuptial agreements are not always binding in court, and if the contract is executed in a state other than where it was drawn up, the couple will experience legal problems. Further, because people change over time, their current viewpoints may no longer be reflected in the contract (Sloane, 1987).

Despite drawbacks, prenuptial agreements are drawn up for roughly 5 percent of all first marriages and 20 percent of remarriages (Stark, 1993). If there are children from a first marriage, or if one partner has considerable resources, the contract makes ending a bad marriage less complex and expensive. Even people entering their first marriage see contracts as useful if they come from broken homes and have unpleasant memories of their parents "slugging it out in court" (Deutsch, 1986). Because women—especially those who have not worked outside the home or have done so only on a part-time basis—are the ones who usually suffer financially after a divorce (see Chapter 15), a contract gives them some legal protection.

Attorneys recommend making a list of issues that could be potential problems, including each partner's financial condition, medical status, and prior marital involvements. The contract might also include a section on home life that discusses the allocation of household chores and expenses incurred in maintaining the home and automobiles as well as property rights. Couples are even cautioned to spell out what kind of birth control they will use, what the responsibilities of each partner are regarding children of either's previous marriage, who will pay for any career costs, and how a child's name will be selected (Swisher et al., 1990). Appendix F shows much of what a marriage contract can cover.

Characterizing Marriages

When a happily married couple was asked to what they owed their successful marriage of 40 years, the husband replied, "We dine out twice a week—candlelight, violins, champagne, the works! Her night is Tuesday; mine is Friday."

As this anecdote suggests, happily married couples are not joined at the hip. And those who are may not be happy. There is very little research on "happy" marriages. We will explore three studies in this section: Cuber and Haroff's classic typology of enduring marriages; Lavee and Olson's study of a larger sample of married couples in therapy; and Wallerstein and Blakeslee's classification of "good marriages." Note that *none* of these studies was based on representative samples of married couples. Instead, the sampling is highly skewed because it includes very self-selected respondents who don't represent the "average" married

When married couples work together on projects, they often learn better ways of communicating and of resolving difficulties. The seven years this couple spent building their California home may have helped them build their marriage as well.

couple (see Chapter 2). Until there is research based on representative samples, however, these studies offer some insight into the broad range of existing marriages.

The Cuber and Haroff Perspective

Until the mid-1960s, social scientists proposed fairly simple descriptions of marriage. A happy marriage was one that did not end in divorce and in which the husband and wife fulfilled the traditional instrumental and expressive roles (see Chapters 2 and 4). Cuber and Haroff (1965) studied 400 "normal," upper-middle-class marriages in which the partners ranged in age from 35 to 55 and identified five types of marriage: conflict-habituated, devitalized, passive-congenial, vital, and total. Some were happy and some were not, but all endured.

In a **conflict-habituated marriage**, the partners fight, both verbally and physically, but do not believe that fighting is a reason for divorce. They feel that fighting is an acceptable way to try to solve problems, and they thrive on the incompatibility. Usually the reason for the conflict is insignificant, and the partners seldom resolve their disputes.

The partners in a **devitalized marriage** are deeply in love when they marry, spend much of their time together, and have a strong, satisfying sex life. As time goes on, they continue to spend time together—raising the children, entertaining, and meeting community responsibilities—but begin to do so out of obligation,

CONSTRAINTS

Married Singles

An example of passive-congenial marriages might be characterized by what I call married singles. **Married singles** are married partners who, by choice or necessity, live under the same roof, may be good friends, and may or may not have sexual intercourse but who have in many ways drifted apart because of conflicting work schedules, interests, personality differences, or other reasons.

Although there has been no research on this concept, several writers have found a number of characteristics that may well describe such marriages. As Avna and Waltz (1992) have pointed out, some marriages are companionable even though the partners no longer engage in sexual intercourse. Both partners may have low sex drives, and over time they may engage in sex less and less or lose all interest in it. They may see other aspects of family life (such as raising children) as more important and time-consuming, and they may enjoy each other's company on a day-to-day basis.

In other cases, marital partners' jobs may force them to live in different cities (see Chapter 13). Such commuter marriages require men and women to establish separate residences and often prevent them from getting together more than once a week or even once a month. Commuter partners often develop separate friendships and live as singles most of the time.

Barreca (1993) suggests that some people purposely marry partners who will be absent: "I married him for better or worse, but not for lunch." In these marriages, an absent husband frees up his wife for other "adventures," both sexual and nonsexual. The wife has the advantage of a husband who legitimizes the couple's children and who is responsible for taking care of his family while the wife is generally free to do as she pleases. In many cases, however, it may be the husband rather than the wife who leads a "married single" life. If he is often on the road or at the office, the husband is free to live his life as he pleases while the wife may be at home (or both home and work) and caring for the children.

Finally, partners who live with alcoholics or other drug abusers must often function as singles. They have no spouse to talk to, they may not want to discuss their problems with family members, and they may feel isolated if the spouse refuses to change his or her behavior or seek help. Or the onset of a serious physical illness of one partner may plunge the other into solitude:

Ellen and Roy had been married for ten years when he was diagnosed with multiple sclerosis. The disease took its slow and predictable course, transforming Roy from a vital and handsome artist into a sullen and degenerating invalid. . . . While his courage helped them to adjust, his fatigue and limitations proved to be most difficult for Ellen. It was not merely that she sorely missed the healthy Roy, but she was overwhelmed by the huge amounts of time she was without him. When he slept, rested, or was in the hospital, Ellen found herself both lonesome for Roy and feeling very much alone in the world. She would wander the foyers of their apartment and haunt the hallways of the hospital beleaguered by a desperate sense of solitude. (Rosenzweig, 1992: 229–30)

---

not joy. They get along and see no alternatives to the marriage and, as a result, do not consider a divorce. Although one or both partners may be unhappy about the situation, they are both resigned to it.

A **passive-congenial marriage** is established by partners who marry with low emotional investment and minimal expectations that do not change. Fairly independent, the partners achieve satisfaction from other relationships, such as those with their children, friends, and co-workers, and they maintain separate spheres of activities and interests. Passive-congenial couples emphasize the practicality of the marriage over emotional intensity. A more "modern" version of the passive-congenial marriage is illustrated in the "Married Singles" box.

In the **vital marriage,** partners' lives are closely intertwined. They spend a great deal of time together, resolve conflict through compromise, and often make sacrifices for each other. They consider sex important and pleasurable. When a disagreement occurs, it is over a specific issue and is quickly resolved.

Finally, in the **total marriage,** which is similar to the vital marriage, the partners participate in each other's lives at all levels and have few areas of tension or unresolved hostility. Spouses share even more facets of their lives with each other—they may work together or share projects, friends, and outside interests. This type of marriage is more all encompassing than the vital marriage.

Finding that approximately 80 percent of the marriages they studied fell into the first three categories, Cuber and Haroff characterized these as **utilitarian marriages** because they appeared to be based on convenience. The researchers called the last two types **intrinsic marriages** because the relationships seemed to be inherently rewarding. In their sample, vital marriages made up 15 percent of the population, and total marriages accounted for only 5 percent.

Although the Cuber-Haroff typology has been widely cited, it has several limitations. The sample of upper-middle-class couples is hardly representative of most families. Note, also, that couples who report minimal conflict are classified as "vital" and "total," whereas the more typical couples who admit having problems are given such negative labels as "devital-ized" and "conflict-habituated." These labels may reinforce the idea that couples who argue or who have separate activities have inferior marriages.

The Lavee and Olson Perspective

In a more recent study, Lavee and Olson (1993) col-lected data on nine dimensions of marriage from 8385 couples who participated in either marital therapy or marital enrichment programs. The dimensions and the seven types of marital couples that the researchers iden-tified are presented in *Figure 9.1.* Although some of the types are similar to Cuber and Haroff's typology, Lavee and Olson reported more complexity and variety in marital relationship patterns. They found, for example, that traditional marriages (see Chapters 1 and 4) reflected problems in communication, conflict resolu-tion, sexual relationships, and parenting issues. And problems about parenting, family and friends, and reli-gious beliefs characterized even harmonious marriages.

Note, also, that the Lavee-Olson study was based on couples who *volunteered* for therapy and who may be very different from couples who don't seek counsel-ing or who are required to seek counseling during divorce mediation (see Chapter 15). Not surprisingly, then, the devitalized couples reported problems on *all* dimensions—from personality issues to conflicts over religious beliefs (see *Figure 9.1*). In contrast, couples

FIGURE 9.1   **How Marriages Differ.** Note that although the typologies offered by Lavee and Olson (shown here) and by Cuber and Haroff (see text) differ both in category content and in number of categories, their overall percentages paint a similar picture. That is, 75 to 80 percent of marriages are essentially based on convenience. Partners must also deal with such issues as personality differences, relationships with family and friends, and conflict resolution (based on data in Lavee and Olson, 1993, Figure 1, p. 332).

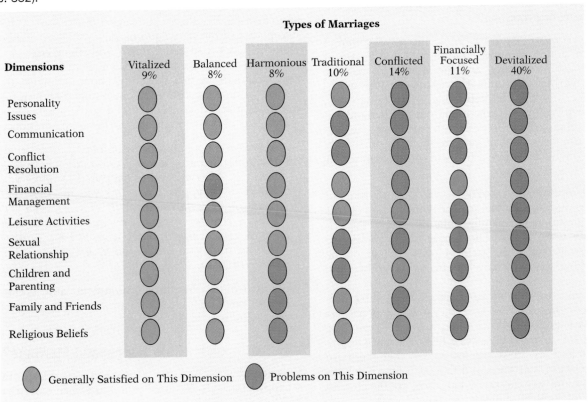

who have accepted some disagreements (such as pursuing different leisure activities) as normal or inevitable and who don't feel they need therapeutic intervention might present a different picture of married life.

The Wallerstein and Blakeslee Perspective

Wallerstein and Blakeslee (1995) interviewed 50 white, middle-class, and well-educated couples in northern California who had been married at least nine years (including second marriages) and came up with four types of "good marriages," each of which contains elements of "antimarriage," which may endanger the relationship:

■ The *romantic marriage* is a lasting and passionate sexual relationship. The couple retains a "glow" over the years based on the "sense that they were destined to be together." The "antimarriage" emerges when the romance freezes the husband and wife into a "self-absorbed childlike preoccupation with each other, turning its back on the rest of the world, including the children."

■ The *rescue marriage* provides comfort for past unhappiness and "the healing that takes place during the course of the marriage is the central theme." The rescue marriage, however, can provide a new forum for replaying earlier traumas because spouses "have the capacity to wound and abuse each other" and for suffering abuse without leaving or protesting.

■ The *companionate marriage,* the most common form among younger couples, reflected a core of friendship, equality, and the attempt to balance the partners' emotional investment in the workplace and the children. This type of marriage, however, "may degenerate into a brother-and-sister relationship" because both partners are invested primarily in their careers, see each other only fleetingly, and share a bed with little or no sex or emotional intimacy.

■ The *traditional marriage* has a clear division of roles and responsibilities. The woman takes charge of the home and family while the man is the primary wage earner. The danger of the traditional marriage is that the partners focus so much on the children they may have little in common otherwise.

As you've probably surmised, none of these perspectives—especially because they rely on nonrepresentative samples—tells us as much about "happy" or "successful" marriages as we'd like to know. Despite their limitations, these studies suggest that there are many types of marriages and that each type has both strengths and weaknesses. What, then, are the characteristics of stable and happy marriages?

Marital Success and Happiness

Researchers usually measure marital success according to marital "stability" and marital "satisfaction" (Noller and Fitzpatrick, 1993). *Marital stability* refers to whether or not a marriage is intact, if people ever thought the marriage was in trouble, if getting a divorce had ever crossed the wife's or husband's mind, and if the spouses had ever suggested divorce to each other (Holman et al., 1994). *Marital satisfaction* refers to whether or not a husband or wife (or both) see their marriage as good. In assessing the quality of relationships, researchers have used such concepts as adjustment, lack of distress, satisfaction, integration, happiness, and success. Often, these terms are used interchangeably (Fincham and Bradbury, 1987; Glenn, 1991). Because there is no generally agreed-upon definition, researchers describe the success or satisfaction of marriages based on the marital partners' own evaluations.

Are Married Couples Happy?

Since 1973, the University of Chicago's National Opinion Research Center has asked representative samples of married Americans to rate their marriages as "very happy," "pretty happy" or "not too happy." As *Figure 9.2* shows, the percentage saying "very happy" has fluctuated since 1973 (67 percent) and declined only moderately by 1998 (63.5 percent). Because happiness is a self-reported and highly subjective measure, however, it's impossible to know how respondents define happiness—a "vitalized marriage" (see *Figure 9.1*)? Acceptance of the status quo because "things could be worse"? Better than being alone? Something else?

While social scientists try to gauge marital happiness, others imply that questions about happiness are a waste of time. According to one family therapist, for example, married couples should grow up because marriage is about commitment rather than emotions:

> *Marriage is not about being in love. . . . It is something married grown-ups do no matter how they feel. . . . Marriage is not supposed to make you* **happy**. *It is supposed to make you* **married**, *and once you are safely and totally married, then you have a structure of security and support from which you are free to make yourself happy, rather than wasting your adulthood looking for a structure. (Pittman, 1999: 159, 160)*

What attributes, besides commitment and taking charge of one's own life, characterize a lasting, happy or successful marriage?

What's Important in a Successful Marriage?

Satisfaction with one's marital role is a critical factor in a happy marriage. National polls show that since the 1970s, what people consider to be very important in

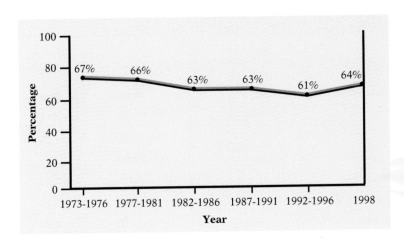

FIGURE 9.2   Percentage of Married Persons Age 18 and Older Who Said Their Marriages Were "Very Happy," by Period, United States

Source: Based on Smith, 1999, Table 9.

marriage hasn't changed much (see *Table 9.1*). In both 1974 and 1990, for example, both men and women considered love, sexual fidelity, and the ability to talk about feelings with each other the most important elements of a good marriage. Fewer men and women believed that having children was important. The fact that financial security has become more important than in the past probably reflects many people's concern about retirement expenses, medical care, and rising college costs.

Is there a recipe for an enduring and happy marriage? Researchers have been searching for an answer for decades. Unlike marital advice manuals, there are no ten, twelve, or twenty steps for living happily ever after. Social scientists have uncovered some features of marital relations, however, which help to produce relatively satisfying and stable marriages. In a study of 459 ever-married women in the Detroit area, for example, Whyte (1990) found that similar social backgrounds (such as ethnicity, religion, or educational level) were less important in marital quality than shared character traits (such as being tidy, outgoing, or hot-tempered), having similar values about raising children, doing things together and having common leisure activities, and enjoying supportive ties and interactions with parents and kin on both sides.

Couples who say they are happy in their marriages have described three main ingredients. First, each spouse must have a positive attitude toward the other and like the other "as a person" and a good friend. According to researcher Ted Huston (cited in Patz, 2000), couples whose marriages begin in romantic bliss are especially prone to divorce because such intensity is too hard to maintain. Couples in whirlwind courtships who marry are quickly disillusioned because they're saddled with fantasies and unrealistic expectations about married life (Pittman, 1999).

Second, both partners see marriage as a long-term commitment and a sacred institution in which the vow of "till death us do part" is taken seriously and

conflict is managed. For example, a salesperson who has been married 36 years advises, "Discuss your problems in a normal voice. If a voice is raised, stop. Return after a short period of time. Start again. After a period of time both parties will be able to deal with their problems and not say things that they will be sorry about later" (Lauer and Lauer, 1985). Partners who stay together are much less likely to insult or put a partner down from the very beginning of marriage (Notarius and Markman, cited in Schrof, 1994).

Finally, happily married couples often say that providing emotional support is more important than romantic love (see R. J. Erickson, 1993). A few years ago, the *Washington Post* conducted a survey of people who were happily married. Although the sample was highly self-selective, some of the comments about trust, privacy, and respect are instructive:

There are times when each of us needs to be alone, we need to have our space. It is very important in our marriage, to know that if he buries himself in a book or I in an old movie, we respect each other's privacy. (Married 9 years)

We like the personhood of the one each married, and we respect the capabilities of each other. . . . The undergirding strength of our marriage has been the trust that we have in each other. (Married 38 years)

He makes me feel smart, pretty, capable and cherished. (Married 21 years)

I asked my husband why he thought our marriage was a success, and he said it was because we don't "compete with each other" and because we "respect each other's independence." I agree. (Married 33 years) (Mathias, 1992: B5)

In contrast, partners in unhappy marriages keep trying to change one another to fulfill their own needs. They often become frustrated and angry when their

TABLE 9.1

What Makes a Good Marriage?

1974			1990	
Women	Men	Things Considered "Very Important"	Women	Men
90%	86%	Being in love	87%	84%
79%	70%	Spouse's sexual fidelity	85%	78%
88%	83%	Being able to talk together about feelings	84%	76%
71%	66%	Keeping romance alive	78%	76%
78%	70%	Being able to see the humorous side of things	76%	69%
74%	64%	Having similar ideas on how to raise children	72%	63%
77%	73%	Having a good sexual relationship	72%	74%
68%	61%	Having similar ideas on how to handle money	71%	65%
62%	52%	Spouse understanding what you do every day	67%	57%
68%	64%	Liking the same kind of lifestyle, activities, and friends	64%	62%
49%	49%	Financial security	63%	61%
51%	51%	Having children	48%	41%
28%	23%	Having similar backgrounds	34%	29%

SOURCE: Based on Roper Organization, 1990.

efforts fail (Quinn and Odell, 1998). Instead of cooling off and thinking a problem through, as the salesperson quoted earlier advises, the partners react when they are angry. For example, a 103-year-old man who recently celebrated an eightieth wedding anniversary advised, "When a woman is upset, keep quiet." Such advice is equally effective for a wife whose husband is angry. Hostile, sarcastic criticisms may lead to verbal or physical abuse. And, because people in unhappy marriages often spend minimal time together, there is little chance that their problems can be resolved through discussion or by sharing common activities or day-to-day interaction.

"His and Her Marriage"

Almost 30 years ago sociologist Jessie Bernard (1973) coined the phrase "his and her marriage" to show that many men and women experience marriage differently. Much recent research supports Bernard's observation that there are many gender differences in married life (see, for example, Nock, 1998).

Consider the process of **identity bargaining,** in which newly married partners readjust their idealized expectations to the realities of living together (Blumstein, 1976). In identity bargaining, partners negotiate adjustments to their new roles as husband and wife. In *foreclosure,* a type of adjustment in which one partner gives in to the new demands of the relationship by narrowing his or her own options, wives may accommodate their husbands' needs:

He wanted me home and a meal on the table when he came through the door, and he wanted everything in its place. He wanted to be out partying and with his friends. The first few years of marriage it was me trying to keep up with him. Of course, when I didn't have any children it was not a problem. But I'm not the cocktaily type person. I enjoy them, but I don't like doing it night after night. I don't drink. I like more educational, broadening type experiences. (Marks, 1986: 226)

Married life also increases the number of social roles each partner plays, thereby increasing the potential for role conflict. Women still play more roles in marriage than men. Most men and many women today are breadwinners but, as you'll see shortly, women are generally responsible for such additional roles as housekeeper, cook, and nanny, as well as for planning and coordinating a family's social activities and keeping in touch with extended family members. And some women must take on the most demanding role of all—that of mother—very quickly, because as many as 13 percent of women are pregnant at the time they marry (Abma et al., 1997).

Marriage and Health

A number of social scientists have found that married people are generally healthier and happier than are those who are single, divorced, or widowed (Horwitz et al., 1996; Keith, 1997; Murphy et al., 1997; Wickrama et al., 1997; see also Mastekaasa, 1994, for a 19-country study). Married people have lower rates of heart disease, cancer, stroke, pneumonia, tuberculosis, cirrhosis of the liver, and syphilis, and they less frequently attempt suicide and have fewer automobile accidents than singles. Married partners report less incidence of depression, anxiety, and other forms of psychological distress, and they are less likely to say they are sick, to be disabled, to visit the doctor, or to be hospitalized than unmarried people. Furthermore, married people have substantially lower mortality rates for almost all causes of death than do unmarried people of the same age and sex (Kaprio et al., 1987; Litwack and Messeri, 1989).

Why the general positive relationship between marriage and physical and psychological well-being? On the one hand, it may be that good health and happiness make people more desirable marriage partners. That is, fit and healthy people may be more likely to find and keep mates than those who have higher illness rates (Booth and Johnson, 1994). On the other hand, it may be that enjoying emotional, social, and physical support from a spouse improves one's general health and longevity. The feeling of security that such support brings may lower anxiety and prevent or lessen depression. It may also reduce risky activities and encourage healthy behavior. For example, married people are more likely to quit smoking and to maintain diets low in cholesterol, and they are less likely to drink heavily, get into fights, drive too fast, or take other risks that increase the likelihood of accidents and injuries. In addition, wives tend to encourage behaviors that prolong life, such as getting regular medical checkups. According to a recent national study, marriage introduces lifestyle changes that reduce heavy drinking and the recreational use of illicit drugs:

> *Being married involves new sets of responsibilities, mutual caring, intimacy, and increased adult contacts, as well as less time spent in bars and at parties frequented by singles—the "singles scene," where a lot of smoking, drinking, and illicit drug use tend to take place. (Bachman et al., 1997: 172)*

And when one partner does become ill, the physical and emotional support a spouse provides during recuperation after surgery or other medical treatment can help speed recovery. Finally, higher household incomes are correlated with good physical and mental health (Ross et al., 1991).

In a national study, Hahn (1993) found that married women rated their health higher than divorced, separated, widowed, and never-married women. According to Hahn, married women, whether or not they work outside the home, have a sense of security that their well-being is not entirely dependent on their own earnings. Whether they are full-time homemakers or work part time, married women are also more likely to have health coverage through their husbands' job benefits. All these economic factors provide access to health services and thus reduce the anxiety over possible illness. Whether married or not, however, poor women—especially ethnic women or those living in rural communities—are often less healthy than their middle-class counterparts (Baezconde-Garbanti and Portillo, 1999). As a result, disparities in health and health care access can have a negative effect on the quality of a marriage.

Besides greater financial strain, unmarried persons are more likely than their married counterparts to be socially isolated and to experience increased parental responsibilities that increase depression. Among midlife singles (those in their early fifties), men appear less likely than women to enjoy psychological well-being because they are less likely to have people in the family in whom they can confide private feelings and stressful concerns (Marks, 1996).

SALLY FORTH   **GREG HOWARD**

© 1995 Greg Howard. Distributed by King Features Syndicate.

Being married does not automatically guarantee better health, however. Several studies have found that married women are less healthy than married men. One factor that may contribute to the difference is the multiplicity of women's role responsibilities. Working women with young children in families in which both spouses' earnings are low are much more likely to report depression than married men, full-time homemakers, or employed married women who have no child-care or economic problems (Verbrugge, 1979; Gove, 1984; Anson, 1989).

If a marriage is unhappy and the partners try to "stick it out for the sake of the children," depression may result—especially if one of the partners is unsupportive, experiences role conflict, has low self-esteem, or a low level of mastery (e.g., "There is really no way to solve the problems that I have") (Cotten, 1999). Feeling that one has control over the good and bad aspects of a marriage also enhances marital satisfaction. Couples who believe that they can shape their marital quality through determination, hard work, and developing problem-solving skills are more likely to report that they have good marriages than couples who believe that relationships are a result of fate, luck, or chance (Myers and Booth, 1999).

Thus quality wins out: It is more important to be happily married than just to be married. In fact, studies have shown that people who have divorced and remarried successfully are less susceptible to health problems than are those who remain in unhappy marriages (see Ross et al., 1991). People who are unhappy in their marriages don't always end up in divorce court, however. **Marital burnout,** the gradual deterioration of love and ultimate loss of an emotional attachment between marital partners, can go on for many years (Kayser, 1993).

In marital burnout, even if spouses share housework and child care, one spouse may fail to provide the other with emotional support. A partner may complain that his or her partner is not confiding innermost thoughts and feelings, doesn't stick by the partner during bad times, or doesn't want to discuss problems (R. J. Erickson, 1993). Marital burnout can develop so slowly and quietly that couples are often not aware of it. Sometimes one partner will hide dissatisfaction for many years. At other times both partners may ignore the warning signs (see the box "Am I Heading toward Marital Burnout?"). Social exchange theory (Chapter 2) would suggest that when the costs in the relationship become much greater than the benefits, the couple will probably seek a divorce.

Domestic Work

Most women and men enjoy married life. If they don't, many will divorce and try again (see Chapters 15 and 16). Because marriage is an imperfect institution, even stable unions must deal with numerous pressures and changes, such as who will do the housework, who will care for children, and how marriage partners adapt to changing gender-role expectations.

Domestic work incorporates two major activities—housekeeping (cooking, cleaning, laundering, outdoor work, repairs) and child rearing. Some people might like housework; most don't (otherwise women wouldn't complain about being "saddled" with such chores). Child care is a more important part of domestic work than housekeeping. Although child rearing is highly rewarding, it's also a "24-7" job that's demanding, exhausting, and emotionally draining. Marital problems can arise if one person does most or all of the housekeeping and child care.

The Pleasures of Domestic Work

As you saw in Chapter 4, many fathers think they're doing a better parenting job than their father did and enjoy caring for their children. According to one national study, mothers of children under age 18 reported that the children (51 percent) and not the husband/partner (29 percent) were the most important source of personal happiness and fulfillment. Husbands/partners were a more significant source of satisfying relationships (44 percent) for mothers of adult children who, presumably, have left the home ("Motherhood today . . . ," 1997). Mothers with children under age 18 probably see their relationships with their children—especially with preschool children—as the most important aspect of their lives because the mother's parenting role is time-consuming and may not be shared equally with the husband (or partner).

The Pressures of Domestic Work

Although women and men experience much pleasure in marriage, there are also numerous pressures. Some of the tensions include sharing housework and child-rearing responsibilities when both parents are employed. Other emerging issues pertain to gender-role expectations in family life, as well as socioeconomic and racial-ethnic variations.

Employment and Family Care In a recent study on how Americans use their time, Robinson and Godbey (1997) concluded that "despite the events, technologies, and turmoil over the last thirty years," the broad outlines of American daily life are not that different from what they were in 1965. Men's housework hours have increased from about 5 hours in 1965 to more than 9 hours in 1995. Women's housework hours declined during the same period, from 27 hours to less than 16 hours. Although the cleaning gap has decreased, women's household chores declined in large part because *both* employed women and full-time housewives are simply doing less housework.

ASK YOURSELF ?

Am I Heading toward Marital Burnout?

All marriages have ups and downs, and checking off even as many as seven of the following items doesn't necessarily mean your marriage is in trouble. However, the more items you check, the wiser you may be to look further into these symptoms of burnout. The earlier you recognize symptoms, according to some practitioners, the better your chances of improving your marriage (based on Stinnett and DeFrain, 1985; Kayser, 1993).

❑ You've lost interest in each other.
❑ You feel bored with each other.
❑ There's a lack of communication; neither of you listens to the other.
❑ You seem to have little in common.
❑ You don't do things together, don't want to do things together, or can't find the time to do things together.
❑ Marriage is no longer your top priority; such things as careers, relatives, religion, friends, hobbies, and/or lovers are more important.
❑ Deep down, you want a divorce.
❑ Inflexibility: you can no longer compromise with each other.
❑ Minor irritations become major issues.
❑ You no longer try to deal honestly with important issues.
❑ You find yourself making family decisions alone.
❑ You have no desire for physical touching of any kind.
❑ Your relationships with other people are more intimate than your relationship with your spouse.
❑ The children have begun to act up; they have frequent trouble at school, get into fights with friends, or withdraw.
❑ "Small talk" dominates your conversations with your spouse.
❑ One of you controls the other through tantrums, violence, or threats of suicide or violence.
❑ You are both putting your own individual interests before the good of the marriage.
❑ You can't talk about money, politics, religion, sex, or other touchy subjects.
❑ You avoid each other.
❑ One or both of you subject the other to public humiliation.
❑ You are no longer concerned about how either you or your partner looks.
❑ You have increasing health problems, such as headaches, back pain, sleeplessness, high blood pressure, recurring colds, or emotional ups and downs.
❑ One or both of you is abusing alcohol or other drugs.
❑ Family functions, such as doing things together, decrease.
❑ One or both of you is irritable and sarcastic.
❑ You are staying in the relationship because it is easier than being on your own.
❑ You no longer have disagreements or arguments; it doesn't seem to matter.

According to the study, housework time varies by gender, employment, marriage, and parenthood. When women become employed, they do almost 7 hours less housework. If employed women marry, their housework increases by about 5 hours a week, while housewives show approximately a 12-hour increase over nonemployed women who are not married. In contrast, married employed men show only a 1-hour increase over unmarried men, although nonemployed men (a small minority) show a 9-hour increase. In effect, when women get married their housework increases by more than three times as much as that of men who get married (see also Gupta, 1999).

When there are children in the family, it is again the mothers whose schedules change the most: Women average about 3 hours more housework per day than when there are no children. Fathers, on the other hand, show almost no difference from nonfathers. In fact, some groups of men in the study reported less housework when there are children in the household than when there are no children. Only nonemployed married men put in more than 10 hours a week of housework. According to Robinson and Godbey, "the amount of housework time for women rises as more role responsibilities are added to their lives. For men, however, only marriage and lack of a job consistently increase their time on housework" but not child care (p. 334).

The number of young children at home and the average age of the couple typically have little effect on the relative proportion of housework each spouse does. In families with young children, employed wives spend longer hours in child care than do either their husbands or nonemployed wives. In particular, employed mothers with very young children spend 24 hours more a week in child-care activities than do their husbands. Because the husband's job typically takes priority over his wife's, she is the one who usually rearranges her work schedule when a child is sick. Nearly nine out of ten working mothers care for their children when they are sick, compared to only one out of ten working fathers (DeStefano and Colasanto, 1990; see also Chapter 13).

Gender-Role Expectations

Is men's lower participation in household tasks the result of long-accepted cultural views of men's and women's proper roles? Usually, but not always. Some studies have found that women's own attitudes may contribute to the imbalance between men's and women's sharing in domestic work. A recent U.S. survey found that seven out of ten men and women agreed with the statement: "When it comes to housework and childrearing, women still want to be in charge" (Roper Starch Worldwide, 1996). If women believe that work will not be done or that it will not be done competently unless they do it, other family members may avoid helping out. Fader (1985: 91) posits, for example, that women sometimes make themselves miserable because "we insist on the privileges of house power, then feel angry and overburdened when our husbands treat the responsibilities as 'our work.'" According to Fader, some women actively discourage their husbands' help by criticizing their work: "He uses too many pots when he cooks" or "He doesn't load the dishwasher right."

Responsibility and control are sometimes hard to give up. Several researchers refer to mothers' beliefs that fathers don't fit well in the domestic domain as "maternal gatekeeping." Although they are employed, maternal gatekeepers believe that women have the ultimate responsibility for family work and set standards necessary to complete a task "properly." In addition, maternal gatekeepers feel that doing family work affirms to themselves and to others that they are

good wives and mothers (Allen and Hawkins, 1999). Moreover, because American society is still generally suspicious of women who are not full-time homemakers (see Data Digest), and because these attitudes are often reflected in magazines, books, textbooks, and media images, it is not entirely surprising that many mothers are trying to be "supermoms."

Brines (1994) offers a different explanation. When a woman is a breadwinner, and especially when she earns more than her husband does, traditional gender-role expectations are overturned and the man's provider role is threatened. To compensate for not meeting cultural expectations of being the breadwinner, the husband may avoid "feminine" activities or avoid doing them competently. If the wife is sympathetic and doesn't want to threaten his masculinity further, she may do more of the housework to support his self-esteem. Greenstein (2000) describes such situations as "deviance neutralization." That is, couples violate traditional gender-role expectations if the wife's earnings are higher and the husband is economically more dependent on his wife. To neutralize such deviant identities, husbands may do less housework and wives do more than their share.

In most cases, a woman struggling to meet the challenges of work and family is responding to the generalized expectation that it is she and not her husband who must somehow manage to handle both work and family duties (Swiss and Walker, 1993). Even many men who consider themselves feminists are willing to share child care but still see housework as "women's work" (Deutsch et al., 1993). As a result, professional wives are often both self-critical and frustrated in trying to meet cultural expectations of doing well both at work and at home (Biernat and Wortman, 1991). In time, the frustration may result in the wife's dissatisfaction with the marriage (Piña and Bengston, 1993). In at least one case it resulted in an essay that has become a classic in its own time (see the box "Why I Want a Wife)."

Gender Roles, Domestic Work, and Marital Equality

The most durable relationships, according to Schwartz (1994), and especially in marriage, reflect a mix of *equity* (each person gives in proportion to what she or he receives) and *equality* (each person has equal status and is equally responsible for emotional, economic, and household duties). Women, particularly mothers, are often the least satisfied with their marriages when they have a disproportionate share of domestic responsibilities and child care, have little decision-making power, and do most of the "emotional work" to develop or maintain intimacy (Steil, 1997). As this section shows, wives' roles have expanded significantly since the 1970s while husbands' roles have remained essentially the same.

These role asymmetries are costly to both men and women. In Bird's (1999) study, the married women

CHANGES ••

Why I Want a Wife

The essay excerpted here has been reprinted more than 200 times in at least ten different countries (Brady, 1990). Written by Judy Brady [then Judy Seiters] in 1972, the article satirizes the traditional view of woman as wife and mother:

I am A Wife. . . . Why do I want a wife? . . . I want a wife who will work and send me to school . . . and take care of my children. I want a wife to keep track of the children's doctor and dentist appointments [and] . . . mine, too. I want a wife to make sure my children eat properly and are kept clean. . . . I want a wife who takes care of the children when they are sick, a wife who arranges to be around when

the children need special care because . . . I cannot miss classes at school. . . .

I want a wife who will take care of my physical needs. I want a wife who will keep my house clean . . . pick up after me . . . keep my clothes clean, ironed, mended, replaced when need be, and who will see to it that my personal things are kept in their proper place so that I can find what I need the minute I need it. I want a wife who cooks the meals, a wife who is a good cook. I want a wife who will plan the menus, do the necessary grocery shopping, prepare the meals, serve them pleasantly, and then do the cleaning up while I do my studying. I want a wife who will care for me when I am sick and sympathize with my pain. . . .

I want a wife who . . . makes love passionately and eagerly when I feel like it, a wife who makes sure that I am satisfied. And, of course, I want a wife who will not demand sexual attention when I am not in the mood. . . . I want a wife who assumes the complete responsibility for birth control, because I do not want more children. . . . And I want a wife who understands that my sexual needs may entail more than strict adherence to monogamy. . . .

When I am through with school and have a job, I want my wife to quit working and remain at home so that my wife can more fully and completely take care of a wife's duties.

My God, who wouldn't want a wife?

said they did about 70 percent of the housework. The sense of carrying an unfair burden (not the amount of work) created anxiety and reduced the women's emotional and psychological well-being. In another study of two-earner couples, the researchers found that marital dissatisfaction reflected wives' perceptions that they were doing an unfair share of housework (Wilkie et al., 1998). What are the costs to men? According to Greer (1999),

> If men want the pleasure of living with women and children they are going to have to shape up. All work and no play may have made Jill too dull to understand a football game but all play and no work will make Jack that most vulnerable of creatures, a redundant male. (p. 136)

Although such conclusions may seem anti-male, many women are not staying in marriages where the costs are significantly and continuously greater than the rewards (see also Chapter 4).

Variations in Domestic Work

Although there are some patterns in housework, child care, and gender-role expectations in domestic work, there are also a number of differences that reflect

demographic variations. Some of these variations include race-ethnicity and social class.

Effects of Race and Ethnicity Men's housework roles often vary by race and ethnicity. For example, a national survey of families found that employed Latino and African American men spend more time doing household tasks than employed white men, including such typically female tasks as meal preparation, washing dishes, and cleaning house (Shelton and John, 1993). Even so, men and women do not share equally in household work. Moreover, although black, Asian, and Latino women have a long history of full-time work outside the home, they still bear a disproportionate share of housework and child care (Billingsley, 1992; Pessar, 1995; Repak, 1995; Kim and Kim, 1998; Kim, 1999). In two-earner households, for example, black men do one-third as much household work as women (Kamo and Cohen, 1998).

In some racial-ethnic groups, many women can count on their kin to help raise and nurture their children. For example, whether married or single, black mothers are much more likely than their white counterparts to receive help with child care from supportive kin networks (Jayakody et al., 1993; see also Chapter 2, on kinwork). And although Latino wives have the major share of child-care tasks, some Latino husbands report being much more involved in child rearing than their own fathers were (Coltrane and Valdez, 1993; López, 1999).

Effects of Social Class The division of household labor also varies by social class. Although 14 percent of all Americans pay for outside help with household chores, working women are no more likely than non-working women to have cleaning help; it is a matter of who can afford it. Thirty percent of people who earn $50,000 or more a year have domestic help or employ a cleaning person, whether or not the wife works outside the home (DeStefano and Colasanto, 1990).

The higher a wife's socioeconomic status, the more likely it is that her husband will help with family tasks. Several studies have shown that wives who have achieved high levels of education and incomes get more help from their husbands than do wives who are employed at the lower end of the occupational scale (Moen, 1992; Perry-Jenkins and Folk, 1994). One or more of a number of factors may be at work here: Educated, professional women may have more authority in the home; women with high-powered jobs may be required to spend longer hours at work; and/or self-employed successful women may feel more comfortable asking for help from their spouses.

How Marriages Change Throughout the Life Cycle

Domestic work changes as the partners grow older. From the developmental perspective, family members will fulfill different roles and learn new tasks as families establish their own structure and identity. Throughout the life course, the members of different types of families must work together to attain specific goals and to deal with conflict.

The Early Years of Marriage

Newlyweds might keep romance alive by making love frequently, talking openly, and spending as much time as possible together. They also have to deal with several realities of married life, however. First, they need to put their mutual relationship before ties with others. In particular, they must strike a balance between their relationships with their in-laws and their marital bond as a couple (Sarnoff and Sarnoff, 1989; Chadiha et al., 1998). Parents, especially mothers, who fear losing contact with their married children sometimes create conflict by making frequent telephone calls and visits and "meddling" in the couple's life (Greider, 2000). One writer contends that new brides, in particular, face a "marriage shock." Unlike their husbands, many women must take on such "wifely" roles as pleasing the husband's family and friends and being the "emotional guardians" of the marriage (Heyn, 1997).

Most couples face numerous decisions, such as how to budget and how to divide up household tasks, and they may realize, for the first time, that they have different perspectives on many issues (Arnold and Pauker, 1987). On the other hand, the new couple also enjoys many benefits. They no longer have to play the dating game and can now relax with someone they love. If they want to conceive a child, preparing for parenthood can be an exhilarating experience (see Chapter 10). Finally, being married enhances a person's social standing as a mature adult.

The Family with Children

As you saw in Chapter 1, one of the most important functions of the family is to socialize children to become responsible and contributing members of society. Families with small children spend much of their time teaching rules, showing children how to live up to cultural expectations, and inculcating such values as doing well at school, following the rules, being kind, controlling one's temper, doing what one is asked, being responsible, getting along with others, and trying new things (Acock and Demo, 1994). Teaching values, rules, and expectations to their children takes enormous time and patience. If couples become parents during the first year, the time they spend talking to each other, even when the marriages are happy and low in conflict, declines about 20 percent—from about 80 minutes a day soon after marriage to about 60 minutes a day (Noller and Fitzpatrick, 1993).

This may explain why marital satisfaction tends to decrease once a couple has children. Both white and black parents experience more frequent conflicts after having children than before and more frequent conflicts than childless spouses (Crohan, 1996). Working parents may have to deal with heavy workloads, employment insecurity, career mobility, and geographic moves, with the result that they have neither the time nor the resources to perform either work or family functions adequately (see Chapter 13). Working-class mothers who work for low pay and have preschool children often have little time to discuss daily matters with their husbands, regardless of how caring and understanding their husbands are (Schumm and Bugaighis, 1986). Middle-class parents may be torn between competing demands at home, at work, and in the community (coaching children's sports during the weekends, attending neighborhood meetings or school functions during the evenings).

Family values that are held by most Americans, such as support, mutual respect, and communication, face their greatest test in families with adolescent children (Larson and Richards, 1994). Besides all the usual developmental tasks associated with the physical changes of puberty and emotional maturation, adolescents today face more complicated lives than ever before. Both parents and children may have to cope with divorce, parental unemployment, and such dangers as violence and drugs in their schools and neighborhoods.

The potential for conflict within the family often increases as adolescents begin to press for autonomy and independence. Conflict is sometimes brought on not by the children but by a dip in the parents' marital happiness as a result of marital burnout or communication problems. Sometimes changes occur suddenly, associated with geographic moves. Depending on the parent's (usually the father's) occupation and career stage, family members may have to adjust to new communities and build new friendships. We return to the adolescent years in Chapter 11.

The Middle-Aged Family

Social scientists used to characterize middle-aged parents, particularly mothers, as experiencing the *empty-nest syndrome*—depression and a lessened sense of well-being—when children left home. More recently researchers have suggested that marital satisfaction increases. The departure of children gives some married couples a chance to relax and enjoy each other's company:

> *Now that our . . . son is away [at college] we can talk about subjects that interest only us without having to consider whether he feels left out. We can talk about people he doesn't know without explaining who they are. . . . [Or we can] simply eat in companionable silence without the pressure to use mealtime for interacting with our kids.* (Rosenberg, 1993: 306–307)

A new phenomenon is the "boomerang generation." Because of a bad local economy, low income, divorce, or the high cost of housing, many young adults either don't leave their parents' home in the first place or move back. Parents try to launch their children but, like boomerangs, some keep coming back.

Boomerang kids can have either a positive or negative effect on their midlife parents' marital life. Mitchell and Gee (1996) found that such co-residence had a more negative influence on remarried parents than on first-married parents because there were still unresolved tensions in the home. As one mother stated:

> *I did like it [living together] when she was in a good mood and she was playful. This was far and few between, though. The stress caused by her relationship with her stepfather—it was disruptive to the family. (p. 446)*

Parents in poorer health were less able to cope with the strains of a returning child than were healthy parents. Marital satisfaction also diminished when a child returned home three or more times than just the first time, because the multiple returns prevented some parents from enjoying the greater intimacy, privacy, and freedom to pursue new interests they had expected. Marital satisfaction was enhanced, however, if the children had a good relationship with their mothers during co-residence. The children provided assistance, emotional support, advice, and companionship and improved the overall quality of family relationships. Parenting during the middle years can be enjoyable or problematic depending on such factors as a parent's health, psychological well-being, and work satisfaction (Willis and Reid, 1999).

The Family in Later Life

In retirement, some of the most difficult adjustments for older partners are the loss of an occupation and the necessity to be at home with a spouse all day long. Most people look forward to showering attention and affection on their grandchildren, but, as we shall see in Chapters 15 and 16, if children divorce, grandparents may be caught in the middle of the conflict. If one partner's health is poor, the couple must deal with wills and other estate management concerns. And if one spouse is widowed, she or he may have to forge new relationships. We look at these and other issues on the family in later life in Chapter 17.

A number of studies have found a curvilinear or U-shaped curve in marital satisfaction over the life cycle. Initially, romantic love produces a high degree of excitement and attraction in the marriage. Marital satisfaction decreases because of the strain caused by family life-cycle events, especially those related to having and raising children. When the children have left home, the marriage relationship improves at the end of the life cycle (Glenn, 1991). The U-shaped curve might vary by ethnicity, gender, and age, however. In a longitudinal study of three generations of Mexican Americans, for example, Markides and his colleagues (1999) found that marital satisfaction declined for midlife women but remained about the same for midlife men. After children leave home, the researchers suggest, midlife Mexican American women may feel something missing in their motherhood roles that were associated with fulfilling marriages. In addition, older Mexican American women often bear the burden of caring for extended family members. Thus, caretaking responsibilities may continue well past midlife and into old age.

Others suggest that in the final, empty-nest phase, conjugal relations settle into a pattern that is neither intensely positive nor negative. Women who are raising preschoolers report more problems in their conjugal relationship but also higher marriage quality than women who are raising teenagers. By the time adolescents have to be dealt with, the high quality and satisfaction of the early years of marriage have decreased (Whyte, 1990). In this sense, declining marital quality

Communication is a critical component in successful relationships. Body language conveys powerful messages about listening and being open to the other person's point of view.

is not necessarily a result of increasing child-rearing problems. There may be recurring power and communication issues, for example, which affect marital quality throughout the life cycle.

Communication: A Basic Key to Successful Intimate Relationships

Communication, verbal and nonverbal, is essential to any continuing relationship. A number of studies have found that, in general, satisfaction with communication is associated with marital satisfaction (Christensen and Shenk, 1991; Karney and Bradbury, 1995; Klinetob and Smith, 1996). Good communication is just as important for people in other close relationships, heterosexual and homosexual, including dating and cohabitation.

What Is Good Communication?

Because our most intimate relationships are in the family, being able to express what we think and feel and to expect that we will be listened to are critical components of family life and in all of our relationships. Whether the interaction is between people seeing each other, wives and husbands, or parents and children, communication can be either constructive or destructive. Let's consider some of the major goals of effective communication in intimate relationships.

Communication Goals Two of the major tools of effective communication include developing ways of communicating that are clear, nonjudgmental, and nonpunitive, and developing the ability to resolve

conflicts and disputes through problem solving rather than through coercion or manipulation. Very little can be gained "if someone tells us how we are *supposed* to feel, how we are *supposed* to behave, or what we are *supposed* to do with our lives" (Aronson, 1995: 404). In contrast, good communication conveys *what* we and others feel, and why different approaches may be equally legitimate (as in agreeing to disagree), and it establishes an atmosphere of trust and honesty that encourages exploring a variety of options in resolving, or at least decreasing, conflict. An important first step in effective communication is self-disclosure.

Self-Disclosure Self-disclosure means telling another person about oneself, honestly offering one's thoughts and feelings, and hoping that truly open communication will follow (see also Chapter 5). A consistent finding in the literature is that *reciprocity* is important if self-disclosure is to be effective in communication and conflict resolution. Many social scientists see self-disclosure as integral to exchange theory's model of family interaction. That is, reciprocal self-disclosure may increase partners' liking for and trust in each other, eliminate a lot of guesswork in the communication, and provide a balance of costs and benefits.

Women tend to disclose more than men do but hold back disclosure when they anticipate an uncaring, unemotional, or otherwise negative response. Men tend to disclose more to women than to men but to withhold disclosure when they feel they will get an emotional (rather than an objective and dispassionate) response. In nonmarital relationships, males disclose more fully to females than to other males, probably because they see women as nonthreatening in both work and social relationships (Arliss, 1991).

Disclosure can be either beneficial or harmful, depending on whether the reaction is supportive or worsens already negative feelings. Disclosure is beneficial under four conditions (Derlega et al., 1993):

1. *Esteem support* can reduce a person's anxiety about troubling events. If the listener is attentive, sympathetic, and uncritical, disclosure can motivate people to change significant aspects of their lives.

2. A listener may be able to offer *information support* through advice and guidance. For example, people under stress may benefit by knowing that their problems are not due to personal deficiencies.

3. Disclosure can provide *instrumental support* if the listener offers concrete help, such as shopping for food or caring for the discloser's children, if, for example, she or he is ill.

4. Even if a problem is not easily solved, listeners can provide *motivational support*. For example, if a husband is distressed about losing a job, his wife can encourage him to keep "pounding the pavement" and assuring him that "we can get through this."

When, on the other hand, is self-disclosure detrimental? If the feedback is negative, disclosure may intensify a person's already low self-esteem. (Disclosure: "I'm so mad at myself for not sticking to my diet." Response: "Yeah—if you had, you'd have something to wear to the party tonight.") Where self-esteem is strong, however, even negative feedback to self-disclosure will not be devastating. One of my students, in her mid-40s, said she was anxious about attending an honors' banquet for students with outstanding GPAs because "I'll look like everyone's grandmother." Expecting support, she asked her husband to attend the ceremony because she felt "out of place." He replied, "Well, just don't go. Everyone will wonder what an old lady is doing there and no one will hire you, anyway." (She attended alone, by the way, had a wonderful time and accepted a job offer by the end of the summer.)

Finally, self-disclosure does not work miracles overnight. In the short run, it may feel awkward and embarrassing. Over time, however, self-disclosure—if it is practiced by both partners and by parents and children—can decrease our tension and guilt feelings, increase our self-esteem, and enhance our ability to cope in stressful situations (Derlega et al., 1993).

Sex Differences in Communication

"Communication" has become a buzzword in recent years to summarize male–female relationship problems. This may explain why two of the best-selling books during the 1990s were Deborah Tannen's *You Just Don't Understand: Women and Men in Conversation* and John Gray's "borrowing" of Tannen's principles in the highly stereotypical (see Crawford, 1995) but popular *Men Are from Mars, Women Are from Venus*.

Some scholars, including Tannen, maintain that there are communication differences between women and men, although both styles are equally valid. Others counter that although women's and men's language sometimes differs, these differences are due, primarily, to how societal values and role expectations *shape* how we relate to our partner rather than to innate gender differences (see Chapter 4). First, we'll consider some of the studies which argue that men and women speak different languages. Then we'll examine some of the research which posits that communication gaps reflect role and power disparities and social context rather than gender differences.

Women's Speech Because women tend to use communication to develop and maintain relationships, *talk is often an end in itself*. It is a way to foster closeness and understanding. A second important characteristic of women's speech is *the effort to establish*

© 1997 United Feature Syndicate, Inc.

equality between people. Thus, women often encourage a speaker to continue by showing interest or concern ("Oh, really?" or "I feel the same way sometimes"). Or they may use affirmation, showing support for others ("You must have felt terrible" or "I think you're right"). Women often ask questions that *probe for a greater understanding* of feelings and perceptions ("Do you think it was deliberate?" or "Were you glad it happened?"). Women also do *conversational "maintenance work."* They may ask a number of questions that encourage conversation ("Tell me what happened at the meeting"). Another quality of women's speech is a *personal, concrete style:* Women often use details, personal disclosures, and anecdotes. By using concrete rather than vague language, women's talk clarifies issues and feelings so that people are able to understand and identify with each other. *References to emotions* ("Wasn't it depressing when . . .") personalize the communication but also make it more intimate than might be expected in public or professional settings.

A final feature of women's speech is tentativeness. This may be expressed in a number of ways. *Verbal hedges* ("I kind of feel you may be wrong") and qualifiers ("I may not be right, but . . .") modify, soften, or weaken other words or phrases. Men often give direct commands ("Let's go"), whereas women appear to show uncertainty by hedging ("I guess it's time to go"). *Disclaimers* weaken the message because they may suggest to the listener that the speaker is not serious, sincere, or very interested in the exchange. Women are more likely to use such disclaimers as "If you don't mind, could we . . . " or "Of course I don't know anything about politics, but I think. . . ." Women also use more *verbal fillers*—words or phrases such as "okay," "well," "you know," and "like"—to fill silences. *Verbal fluencies*—sounds like "mmh," "ahh," and "unhuh"—serve the same purpose. Women use fillers and fluencies much more frequently when they are talking to men than to other women (Pearson, 1985; Lakoff, 1990; Fitzpatrick and Mulac, 1995).

Men's Speech A prominent feature of men's speech is *instrumentality;* men tend to use speech to accomplish specific purposes ("Give me three reasons why I should . . ."). They often focus on problem solving: getting information, discovering facts, and suggesting courses of action or solutions. Thus, for men, speech is more often *a means to an end* than the end itself. Masculine speech is also characterized by *exerting control*—to establish, enhance, or defend their personal status and their ideas by asserting themselves and, often, challenging others ("I'll need more information to make a decision"). Men are much less likely than women to offer what women consider empathic remarks (such as "That must have been very difficult for you"), and they are less likely to express

sympathy or to divulge personal information about themselves.

Another feature of men's communication is *conversational dominance.* In most contexts, men tend to dominate the conversation, speaking more frequently and for longer periods of time. They also show dominance by interrupting others, reinterpreting the speaker's meaning, or rerouting the conversation. Men tend to express themselves in assertive, often absolutist, ways ("That approach won't work"). Compared with women, their language is typically more forceful, direct, and authoritative; tentativeness is rare. Finally, men are apt to *communicate more often in abstract terms,* a reflection of their more impersonal, public style (Tannen, 1990).

Gender Roles and Communication Differences

Some researchers consider the "female speech" and "male speech" dichotomy stereotypical and simplistic. According to Crawford (1995), for example, the notion that women and men come from "two cultures" (or, worse yet, from two planets) ignores power dimensions (as you'll see shortly). Nor should we assume that women are submissive or passive during marital conflict. Even during the early years of marriage, husbands may withdraw or distance themselves in response to a wife who is hostile, critical, or attacks her partner verbally (Roberts, 2000).

Nowinski (1993) speculates that most men don't communicate in intimate relationships because they are accustomed to being "stress absorbers" and stoics. Although the noncommunicative male is missing an opportunity for intimacy and connectedness, he is protecting his loved ones from "the disappointment, frustrations, and fears that are part and parcel of his daily work life" (p. 122). The expectation that unpleasant things are "no big deal," according to Nowinski, are reflected in many men's not reporting traumas, such as posttraumatic stress disorders after returning from wars or sexual abuse during childhood. Instead of focusing on disturbing feelings, many men may turn to alcohol or drugs.

The Venus/Mars dichotomy also ignores communication variations among many groups that separate people: social class, race, ethnicity, age, and sexual orientation. In terms of sexual orientation, for example, gay males and lesbians appear to be equally disclosing, equally "instrumental," and equally "expressive in their relationships" (Nardi and Sherrod, 1994).

Social context is also important in understanding gender communication styles. In a study that compared men and women as they interact with both strangers and spouses, Fitzpatrick and Mulac (1995) found that men are more likely to use "men's speech" when interacting with women in general than with their wives. Husbands tend to decrease the interaction distance between themselves and their wives by adopting a more "feminine" style in conversations. Women maintained the same "women's speech" with both husbands and men in general. This might reflect the power differential noted earlier.

Approach/Avoidance Communication in Marriage

People may be poor communicators, but they may also fear to speak openly and clearly for a variety of reasons. Rubin (1983) describes the lack of communication in marriage as "the approach-avoidance dance." Women, especially, she claims, want their husbands not only to communicate but to *want* to communicate—to want to know how their wives feel, what they think, and what they worry about. On the other hand, Rubin says, women are also sometimes relieved by a lack of communication because they can decide what is and isn't discussed (see also Barreca, 1993).

Goldberg (1987) feels that our demands for honest communication are not always genuine. Because we are defensive, Goldberg claims, we send contradictory messages to each other. For example, women want men to open up, but they don't want them to say anything that is weak or needy or will threaten women's sense of security. They tell men to share their feelings, but they don't want to hear anything that will make them feel anxious or attacked. According to Goldberg, although women want to be independent and assertive, they retreat to the "feminine-manipulative" approach because this will not scare off a man. Men, however, are also defensive. They want to be left alone emotionally, but they also want a woman to be there for them physically. They want a woman to be independent but, at the same time, they fear she may leave them or not need them.

Communication Problems

Even when people really do want to communicate, they may not be sure how to do so. Despite our best intentions, many of us communicate in ways that do not result in meaningful interaction. Since communication involves *both* partners, we can't control or change our partner's interaction. We can, nonetheless, recognize and do something about our own communication style. Some of the most common communication problems include a variety of issues ranging from not listening to using silent treatments.

Not Listening

Both partners may be so intent on making their point that they are simply waiting for their turn to speak rather than listening to the other person. Consider, for example, one of the nondiscussions between my husband and me while I was revising this textbook several years ago:

Me:	"I haven't had any time to do any Christmas shopping yet."
My husband:	"Your computer needs more memory. That's probably why you get all those error messages."
Me:	"And I'll probably be writing Christmas cards in February."
My husband:	"We should get 32MBs. That'll bring you up to 48MBs."
Me:	"What I need is a clone."
My husband:	"We better increase your disk space, too."
Me:	"I'll never finish these revisions on time."
My husband:	"Will the kids be home for dinner tonight?"

This isn't an earth-shattering example of noncommunication. It illustrates, however, the common pattern of partners talking but not communicating. One of the most important components in communication is *really* listening to the other person instead of rehearsing what we plan to say when he or she pauses for a breath (Noller, 1984). Listening and responding is especially critical when partners discuss relationship problems.

Not Responding to the Issue at Hand

If partners are not listening to each other, they will not address the problem. There are three common miscommunication patterns in unhappy couples. In *cross-complaining*, partners present their own complaints without addressing the other person's point:

Wife:	"I'm tired of spending all my time on the housework. You're not doing your share."
Husband:	"If you used your time efficiently, you wouldn't be tired" (Gottman, 1982: 111).

In *counterproposals*, a spouse ignores a partner's proposal for a solution and presents his or her own ideas (Krokoff, 1987). In *stonewalling*, which is more common among men than women, one of the partners turns into a stone wall: He or she may "Hmmmm" or "Uh-huh," but the partner neither really hears nor responds to the message, and there is a stony silence (Gottman, 1994). If the partner is addicted to alcohol or drugs, she or he might refuse to talk about the problem:

Whenever someone brings up the [alcohol] issue, he proclaims that they are making a big deal about nothing, are out to get him, or are just plain wrong. No matter how obvious it is to an outsider that the addict's life may be falling apart, he stubbornly refuses to discuss it. If that does not work, then he may just get up and walk out. (Nowinski, 1993: 137)

Blaming, Criticizing, and Nagging

Instead of listening and being understanding, partners may feel they are neglected or unappreciated. They feel their spouse or partner magnifies their faults, belittles them, accuses them unjustly, and makes them feel worthless and stupid. The criticism may escalate from specific complaints ("The bank called today and I was embarrassed about your two bounced checks") to more global and judgmental derision ("Don't you know *anything* about managing money?"). The blamer is a faultfinder who criticizes relentlessly and generalizes: "You never do anything right," "You're just like your mother/father" (Gordon, 1993: 82). In blaming and criticizing, the problem is *not* that a partner lacks communication skills, but that she or he uses sophisticated communication skills to emotionally wound a more vulnerable partner (Burleson and Denton, 1997). If I'm a "good" blamer, for example, I can probably convince you that our budget problems are due to *your* mismanagement rather than *my* low salary.

Using Scapegoats

Scapegoating is another way of avoiding true communication about a problem by blaming others for everything that goes wrong. It is often a way of trying to change our partners and not ourselves. We may be uncomfortable about being expressive because we had cold and aloof parents, or we might be suspicious about trusting people because we were taken advantage of by a best friend. However, blaming parents, teachers, relatives, siblings, or friends for our problems is debilitating and counterproductive (Noller, 1984).

Using Coercion or Contempt

Related to scapegoating, partners may be punitive and force acceptance of their point of view. If this works, coercive behavior can continue. Contempt can also be devastating in marriage. The most visible signs of contempt include insults and name-calling, sarcasm, hostile humor, mockery, and body language such as rolling your eyes, sneering, and curling your upper lip (Gottman, 1994). As you saw in the "Am I Heading toward Marital Burnout?" box, some of the red flags include a partner's or spouse's control through tantrums, violence, or threats of suicide or violence. In addition, a partner may subject the other to public humiliation.

Using the Silent Treatment

People communicate even if they are silent. Silence in various contexts, and at particular points in a conversation, means different things to different people. Sometimes silence saves many of us from "foot-in-mouth" problems. Not talking to your spouse or partner, however, is one of the best ways to build up anger and hostility. Initially, the "offender" may work very hard to make the silent partner feel loved and to talk about a problem. Eventually, however, the partner who is getting the silent treatment may get fed up, give up, or look for someone else (Rosenberg, 1993).

Power and Decision Making in Relationships

Power is an important factor in shaping communication patterns and decision making. Many of the dynamics in marriage and in nonmarital relationships are influenced by who has the power to make decisions. Sociologists define **power** as the ability to impose one's will on others. Whether we're talking about a dating relationship, a family, or a nation, some individuals and some groups have more power than others.

Theories of Power Some scholars use *resource theories* to explain family structures and marital power. Typically, the spouse with more resources has more power in decision making. Thus, a husband who earns more money than his wife or has more control over household finances has more power (Vogler and Pahl, 1994). Resources are often interrelated. For example, people with high incomes often also have more education and/or high occupational status. As you saw earlier in this chapter, as women increase their resources through paid work, they become less dependent on their husbands and more powerful in demanding that household chores and child care be shared.

Resource theory can combine with exchange theory to explain the trade-offs husbands and wives often negotiate. Spouses develop an explicit or implicit agreement to exchange such resources as time and money. The control of economic resources is a major, but not the only, determinant of who has the greater power in the family. Lips (1991) points out, for example, that even in families where the wives are doctors, professors, lawyers, or other professionals, the couple's decision making may be strongly traditional rather than based on "simple economics." In addition, men who are occupationally unsuccessful may be especially unlikely to see their wives' employment as a resource because it crushes their ego and identity as provider: "Sensitive to their husbands' feelings of failure, some wives respond by not resisting their husband's dominance to 'balance' his low self-esteem" (Pyke, 1994: 89).

Sources of Power Power is not limited to tangible things such as money. Love, for example, is an important source of power. As you saw in Chapter 7, the *principle of least interest* explains why, in a dating relationship, the person who is less interested is more powerful than the committed partner. In marriage, similarly, if you are more committed to your marriage than your spouse is, you have less power. As a result, you may refrain from expressing negative feelings, defer to your partner's wishes, or do things you don't want to do.

Other nonmaterial sources of power include access to information or having particular abilities or talents. For example, husbands often have more decision-making power about how to spend money on expensive things (such as houses or cars) because they are often more knowledgeable about financial matters, investments, and negotiating contracts. In traditional households, wives may have more power than their husbands in furnishing a home or raising children because they devote more time to reading informational material for homemakers and parents, to shopping, or are more familiar with neighborhood professionals, such as pediatricians, who provide important services.

Conflict and Decision Making

Power and conflict are normal and inevitable in close relationships. *Conflict* refers to discrete, isolated disagreements as well as chronic relational problems (Canary et al., 1995). Because we tend to see the family as a retreat from the problems of the outside world (Chapter 1), we may often suppress conflict: It seems inconsistent with an idealized picture of the family as a haven. All families, however, and no matter how supportive and caring they are, experience conflict (Roberts and Krokoff, 1990). A study of married couples, interviewed at two different points in time, three years apart, found that the majority of participants reported an average of one or two "unpleasant disagreements" per month (McGonagle et al., 1993). Comedian Phyllis Diller's quip, "Don't go to bed mad. Stay up and fight!" is actually insightful. Conflict is not in and of itself a bad thing. If families recognize conflict and actively attempt to resolve it, conflict can serve as a catalyst in deepening relationships (Rosenzweig, 1992). In this section we look first at some of the most common sources of conflict and then consider coping techniques and family counseling alternatives.

What Do Couples Fight About?   Couples fight about a variety of things. The most common disagreements are over gender roles, loyalty, money, power, sex, privacy, and children (Betcher and Macaulay, 1990).

- *Gender roles* and how they are filled can often cause disagreements; as we have seen, spouses often have different attitudes and beliefs about who should do what in a family. If they cannot come to an agreement, tension may rise and quarrels become more frequent. Today, when traditional husbands fail to meet their working wives' expectations that there should be greater equity in the division of household work, serious conflict can ensue (Lye and Biblarz, 1993).

- *Loyalty* is a common source of friction if relationship expectations are violated. For unmarried couples, the most frequent transgressions include having sexual intercourse outside the primary relationship, wanting to date others, and deceiving the partner (Metts, 1994). Although extramarital affairs are the most serious incidents of betrayal, couples argue about other violations of trust and commitment such as lies, two-timing, betraying confidences, and gossip (Jones and Burdette, 1994).

- *Sex* can also be a source of marital conflict. Women are more likely to equate sex with emotional intimacy and to resent partners who are affectionate only when they want sex (Oggins et al., 1993). The most serious problem may be unwanted sex. In a recent national survey, 9 percent of the wives reported being forced to have sex against their will at least once during the marriage (Schrof and Wagner, 1994). Most commonly, arguments over sex overlap with fidelity issues.

- *Money* is another common source of conflict. Arguments over money generally focus on how—or how not—to spend it. Conflicts over how money is spent may become particularly intense if a working wife has no input and feels that her husband's decisions are "unfair" (Blair, 1993). Although arguments typically erupt over specific expenditures, they are really based on different, sometimes opposing, value systems. For example, because Mary's family of origin is emotionally important to her, she spends a lot of money on long-distance telephone calls to them, which infuriates John because he thinks he and the children should be enough emotional support for Mary. John, on the other hand, spends a lot of money on stereo equipment because listening to music helps him to relax. But Mary thinks turning on the radio can produce the same effect and thus sees this as a waste of money.

- *Power* struggles can create conflict on several dimensions. Some antagonism may arise over economic power. Even when wives work, husbands may feel that the man should be the one to decide how the money should be spent. Couples may disagree about specific household rules. Whether they are explicit or implicit, rules about dealing with in-laws, making large purchases, disciplining the children, or entertaining friends may be sources of marital conflict. There are also differences in the ways partners exercise power. The person with less power may use manipulation (such as flattery), supplication (crying or acting helpless), or disengagement (sulking, playing the martyr, or not speaking). The more powerful person is more likely to be autocratic (for example, by claiming to be better informed) or to bully (through threats, insults, ridicule, or violence).

- *Privacy* in terms of space, time, emotion, and property is a crucial need of many partners. No matter how close a couple is, partners can run into problems if they do not respect each other's needs for privacy, including having space and time to be alone. A mother of young children, for example, may resent her husband's barging into the bathroom because it may be one of the few times during the day when she can be alone. Similarly, many men have workshops, not because they produce great furniture but because it gives them a chance for solitude. Many couples fight about privacy because they equate it with secrecy, but privacy and secrecy are not synonymous. For example, some couples never open each other's mail, not because they are afraid a partner may get a letter from a lover but because they respect each other's privacy.

■ *Children* may strengthen a marriage, but they are also a common source of conflict. In addition to the demands children make on parents, spouses may have different philosophies about such issues as discipline, the importance of teaching young children self-control, and the kinds of responsibilities a child should be given. Because many mothers work today, more parents are splitting child care, especially if the spouses have shift work (see Chapter 13). As more spouses collaborate in child rearing, there is more opportunity for clashes between different child-rearing approaches. For example, although a wife may expect her husband to take on more child-care tasks, she may also resent his insistence on making decisions about playmates, bedtimes, or curfews. As you'll see in Chapter 16, children are especially likely to be a source of conflict in remarriages.

Common Ways of Coping with Conflict   Conflicts are normal. What may not be normal or healthy is the way a family handles the conflict. Taping family interactions, Vuchinich (1987) found that families typically used four techniques to end—although not necessarily resolve—conflict: submission, compromise, standoff, and withdrawal.

1. *Submission.* One person submits to another; the conflict ends when the first person agrees with or goes along with the other.

2. *Compromise.* Partners find a middle ground between their opposing positions; each must give in a little to accept a compromise. The compromise can be suggested by a partner or by a third party.

3. *Standoff.* The disputants drop the argument without resolving it; they agree to disagree and move on to other activities. No one wins or loses, and the conflict ends in a draw.

4. *Withdrawal.* When a disputant withdraws, he or she refuses to continue the argument, either by "clamming up" or by leaving the room. Among the four techniques, withdrawal is the most disruptive of family interaction because there is no resolution.

Although many therapists recommend compromise as the best way to settle quarrels, Vuchinich found that family feuds ended in compromise only 14 percent of the time. In 61 percent of the cases he studied, fights ended in a standoff: Conflicts were allowed to "run their course," and family members moved on to other issues. This suggests that there are other peaceful methods, besides compromise, of resolving conflict.

Someone once noted that the difference between a good marriage and a not-so-good marriage is that in the latter a couple leaves about three or four things unsaid every day. That is, say what's on your mind, tell it like it is, and so on. One of the biggest myths about interpersonal relationships, however, is that it is okay to "let it all hang out." Some spouses unleash "emotional napalm" at their partners on the grounds that "if a man can't let down his hair at home and blow off some steam, he's likely to end up with stomach ulcers or have a heart attack." Displaced rage, unbridled attacks, and physical aggression are not normal ways of handling conflict, however (Lazarus, 1985).

Despite Lazarus's caution, some counselors instruct partners to confront each other openly and even bluntly. Such ventilation is helpful only if both partners are willing to listen. If both are cross-complaining, for example, neither will hear the other, and the hostility escalates. Increasing rage can lead to physical abuse. On the other hand, denying conflict can destroy a relationship. Couples who confront their problems may be unhappy in the short term, but such confrontations may result in better relationships in the long run. Couples who deal with issues as they arise are "not left with a legacy of unresolved problems" (Noller and Fitzpatrick, 1993: 178). Remember, however, that couples handle conflict differently. Gottman (1994: 136–37) found, for example, that some stable couples "seem to thrive on combat" and try to influence one another about almost everything: "This type of couple is quite passionate and emotionally expressive. They fight a lot, but they also laugh a lot. They have a wide range of emotional expression."

Family Therapy and Counseling   Because conflict is inevitable, and failing to deal with it can be destructive, family therapy and counseling have become a booming industry. Therapy and counseling are not always successful, however (Jacobson and Addis, 1993). In a 1995 *Consumer Reports* survey, marriage therapy ranked at the bottom of a poll of patient satisfaction with various psychotherapies. The magazine said part of the problem was that "almost anyone can hang out a shingle as a marriage counselor" (Kantrowitz and Wingert, 1999).

CHOICES

Ground Rules for Fair Fighting

Therapists, counselors, and researchers hold conflicting views as to whether and how marital partners and families should handle conflict. In general, however, many feel that arguing the issues is healthier than suffering in silence. The following suggestions are not derived from scientific research based on representative samples (see Chapter 2). Clinicians who deal with dissatisfied couples, however, offer advice on changing some of our most destructive interaction patterns:

1. Don't attack your partner. He or she will only become defensive and will be too busy preparing a good rebuttal to hear what you have to say.
2. Avoid ultimatums; no one likes to be backed into a corner.
3. Say what you really mean and don't apologize. Lies are harmful, and apologetic people are rarely taken seriously.

4. Avoid accusations and attacks; do not belittle or threaten.
5. Start with your own feelings. "I feel" is better than "You said. . . ." Focus on the problem, not the other person.
6. State your wishes and requests clearly and directly; do not be manipulative, defensive, or sexually seductive.
7. Limit what you say to the present or near present. Avoid long lists of complaints from the past.
8. Refuse to fight dirty:
   • No *gunnysacking,* or keeping one's complaints secret and tossing them into an imaginary gunnysack that gets heavier and heavier over time
   • No *passive-aggressive behavior,* or expressing anger indirectly as in criticism, sarcasm, nagging, or nitpicking
   • No *silent treatment;* keep the lines of communication open
   • No *name-calling*

9. Use humor and comic relief. Laugh at yourself and the situation—but not at your partner. Learning to take ourselves less seriously and to recognize our flaws without becoming so self-critical that we wallow in shame or self-pity can have a healing effect during fights.
10. Strive for closure as soon as possible after a misunderstanding or disagreement by resolving the issue. This prevents dirty fighting and, more important, it holds the partners to their commitment to negotiate until the issue is either resolved or defused (Crosby, 1991; Rosenzweig, 1992).

According to Hendrickson (1994), "a good fight is an essential ingredient" in building a good marriage. Do you agree? Or does keeping silent and side-stepping conflict increase love and respect?

Even credentialed therapists may use approaches that have no basis in empirical studies. According to some recent research, for example, the "active listening" models that many therapists promote are ineffective in resolving marital conflict. In active listening, people summarize each other's complaints and validate the other's feelings ("I'm hearing that you're angry"). Happily married couples don't use active listening exercises or validation. Instead, they try to prevent negativity from getting out of control, use humor as "repair attempts," and try to deescalate anger through soothing (Gottman et al., 1998).

In addition, many counselors have internalized cultural stereotypes about gender roles and may not be effective in diagnosing and treating particular problems (Wright and Fish, 1997). During the 1980s, for example, feminists challenged traditional family therapy models that tended to blame women for marital and family problems (Avis, 1985; Luepnitz, 1988). Furthermore, many people are not comfortable in

seeking advice. They may be embarrassed, can't afford the costs, deny they have a problem, want to find their own solutions, or do not trust "shrinks."

Offering alternatives to formal counseling, both researchers and practitioners have published books and articles of advice, including guidelines for "fair fighting" (see the box "Ground Rules for Fair Fighting"). Fights that humiliate, embarrass, browbeat, or demoralize the other person will not clear the air. Rules for fair fighting do not guarantee a resolution of conflict, but, because they are based on negotiation and compromise, they offer partners a better chance of developing more constructive ways of dealing with conflict.

Productive Communication Patterns

Over time, communication problems can erode intimate relationships. But it takes time to forge good communication networks. Psychologist John Gottman interviewed and studied more than 200 couples over 20 years and found that the difference between marriages that lasted and those that split up was a "magic ratio" of 5 to 1; that is, five positive interactions for every negative one:

> As long as there was five times as much positive feeling and interaction between husband and wife as there is negative, the marriage was likely to be stable over time. In contrast, those couples who were heading for divorce were doing far too little on the positive side to compensate for the growing negativity between them. (Gottman, 1994: 41)

According to researchers and practitioners, there are a number of ways that couples can increase positive communication and decrease negative interaction patterns:

- *Ask for information.* If your partner has a complaint ("I never get a chance to talk to you because you're always dealing with the kids"), address the issue. Don't be defensive ("Well, if you were around more often, we could talk"); find out why your spouse is upset.

- *Get inside the other person's world.* See things from the other person's point of view. When we disagree on an issue, it is not always because "I'm right and you're wrong." It is more likely due to the fact that we have different perspectives.

- *Create a caring communion.* Strong family members value each other and express their affection. As a result, positive self-concepts are reinforced, and a climate for continued effective communication is facilitated.

- *Keep the monsters in late-night movies.* Do not engage in "monster" behavior—do not criticize, evaluate, or act superior. Being supportive, attentive, and nonjudgmental increases a partner's desire to talk about problems.

- *Keep it honest.* Honesty not only means not lying, it means not manipulating others. Do not resort to bullying, outwitting, blaming, dominating, or controlling. Do not become a long-suffering martyr. Truthfulness and sincerity reinforce mutual trust and respect.

- *Make it kind.* Some people use "brutal honesty" as an excuse for cruelty. Maintain a balance of honesty and kindness.

- *Be specific.* A specific complaint is easier to deal with. "You never talk to me" is harder to manage than "I wish we could have 30 minutes each evening without television, the paper, or the kids."

- *Become allies.* Attack the problem rather than each other. If you treat each other as best friends and not as enemies, you have a better chance of resolving the problem.

- *Express appreciation.* Thanking your spouse for something he or she has done will enhance the relationship.

- *Share your hopes.* Sharing hopes is integral to a strong relationship. Hopes can range from the mundane ("I hope you don't have to work this weekend") to ambitious goals ("What if we invest our money to buy a condo near the mountains for our retirement?").

- *Use nonverbal communication to express your feelings.* Nonverbal acts, such as hugging your partner, smiling, and holding his or her hand, can sometimes be more supportive than anything you might say (Stinnett and DeFrain, 1985; Gold, 1992; Knapp and Hall, 1992; Gordon, 1993).

Conclusion

Someone once said that marriages are made in heaven, but the details have to be worked out here on earth. Working out those details is an ongoing process throughout a marriage. The biggest sources of conflict and *change* are disagreements over household work and communication. Different *choices* lead to different consequences. Deciding, for example, to have a more egalitarian division of domestic work and child-rearing responsibilities can diminish some of the *constraints* that many women (and some men) encounter as they juggle multiple roles. In addition, deciding to interact more honestly can result in more effective communication and greater interpersonal satisfaction. Despite the constraints, marriage is one of the most important rites of passage for almost all of us. Another is parenthood, on which we focus in the next two chapters.

SUMMARY

1. Marriage, an important rite of passage into adulthood, is associated with many traditions, rituals, and rules. Many of these rituals reflect historical customs.

2. There are several types of marriage. Most endure despite conflict over such issues as parenting, communication, finances, sex, and religious attitudes.

3. What people consider to be "very important" in marriage hasn't changed much over the years. Both men and women consider love, sexual fidelity, and the ability to talk about feelings with each other the most important elements of a good marriage.

4. Marriage generally increases a person's chances for good physical and mental health. Married women, however, are less likely to enjoy good health than are married men.

5. Men and women often experience marriage differently. Some of these differences reflect the differential status of men and women in society and the way household and child-care tasks are organized.

6. Marriages change throughout the life cycle. In general, having children decreases marital satisfaction, but satisfaction rises again when grown children leave the home. Throughout the life cycle, families adjust in raising young children, communicating with adolescents, and enjoying the empty-nest and retirement stages.

7. Communication is a basic key to successful intimate relationships. Self-disclosure is important to effective communication, but couples should recognize that disclosing all their innermost thoughts might be detrimental rather than helpful.

8. Most marriages break down not because of conflict but because couples fail to cope adequately with conflict. Such negative coping strategies as complaining, criticizing, being defensive, and stonewalling may lead to a partner's isolation or withdrawal.

9. Resource theories are commonly used to explain how power is distributed and used within a family. Power resides not only in such tangible things as money and property, but also in love, in having access to information, and in having particular abilities or talents.

10. Conflict is unavoidable and normal. Although it is unrealistic to expect communication to cure all marital problems, effective communication can decrease power struggles and conflict that can lead to marital dissolution.

KEY TERMS

engagement 216
conflict-habituated marriage 221
devitalized marriage 221
married singles 222
passive-congenial marriage 222

vital marriage 222
total marriage 222
utilitarian marriage 222
intrinsic marriage 222
identity bargaining 226

marital burnout 228
self-disclosure 234
power 238

TAKING IT FURTHER

Wedding Bells and Marriage Bytes

If you are planning to marry (or remarry), here is a sampling of informative sites:

Town and Country Wedding Registry has fashions, planning advice, and a free service that lets couples set up Web pages announcing their weddings and wedding registries.

tncweddings.com

Marriage Support offers information and encouragement to married and unmarried people who want to improve their relationship skills. The site includes bulletin boards, a relationship satisfaction quiz, and other resources.

www.couples-place.com

The following sites offer information on saving or improving marriages:

American Association for Marriage and Family Therapy Web Site

www.aamft.org

Marriage Builders

www.marriagebuilders.com

And more . . . www.prenhall.com/benokraitis offers numerous links on engagement and wedding sites (including one for same-sex marriages), honeymoon ideas, and several sites that scramble family names (as many as you want to key in) and provide a list of suggestions for those who want a "new" surname after marriage that reflects both sides of the family.

To Be or Not to Be a Parent: More Choices, More Constraints

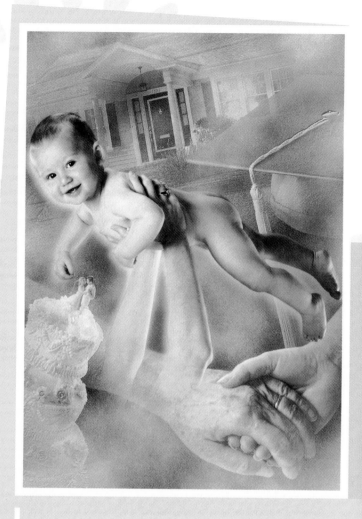

DATA DIGEST

- The **number of births** in the United States has decreased from about 4.2 million in 1990 to 3.9 million in 1999.

- In 1998, the **fertility rate** was 65.6 and varied by race and ethnicity: white, 57.7; black, 73.0; American Indian, 70.7; Asian or Pacific Islander, 64.0; and Latinas, 101.1.

- Between 1986 and 1991, the **teen birth rate** rose by one-fourth, peaking at 62.1 births per 1000 females aged 15 to 19 in 1991. Since 1991, the rate has declined by approximately 18 percent, to 51.1 in 1998.

The largest reductions occurred among young teenagers aged 15 to 17 and black teenagers.

- In 1998, there were 7,625 **multiple births,** up from 1034 in 1971. These figures don't include twins. In 1998, one in every six infants born to women 45–49 years of age and one in every three births to women 50-54 years of age were born in a multiple delivery.

SOURCES: Ventura, Martin et al., 2000; Ventura, Curtin et al., 2000; U.S. Census Bureau, 1999c.

A SUCCESSFUL psychiatrist in his fifties took his 80-year-old mother to a performance of the Metropolitan Opera in New York City. They were making their way out the lobby doors to the physician's Mercedes when his mother turned to him and checked: "Do you have to go to the bathroom, dear?"

As this anecdote suggests, a parent is forever. We may change colleges, buy and sell houses and cars, switch careers, and marry more than once, but when we become parents we form a lifelong, irreversible relationship. Although today we are freer to decide whether or not we want to have children, these choices are more complicated than ever before. Most people can decide whether and when to have children. We can postpone parenthood longer than was ever possible before, sometimes even after menopause. We can have children despite physiological problems that prevent normal conception or birth. And we can decide to remain childless altogether. We cover all these possibilities in this chapter, beginning with the choices facing the married-couple family.

Parenthood is a process rather than a single event. *Having* children—through childbirth or adoption—is not the same as *raising* children. This chapter focuses primarily on the biological, economic, and social aspects of *becoming* a parent (or not). The next chapter examines the child-rearing roles, activities, duties, and responsibilities in *being* a parent.

Becoming a Parent

We sometimes hear about mothers, most often teenage, who abandon their newborn infants. Overwhelmingly, however, most couples have children because they really want them. According to a recent national survey, for example, 79 percent of the respondents said that it was "very important" or "fairly important" to have children ("Americans on parenting," 1999). A couple may discuss family size before getting married, set up a savings account for their children's college education, enroll in a health plan that will cover pregnancy costs, and even buy a house to accommodate the family they plan. Almost half of all pregnancies in the United States are unintended, however (Henshaw, 1998).

Whether planned or not, a couple's first pregnancy is an important milestone. Pregnancies are "family affairs": Both parents may worry about the developing fetus's health, but they typically look forward to the baby's birth. The response of both partners to the news of pregnancy can vary, nonetheless, depending on a number of factors. Cowan and Cowan (2000: 33–45) have found four reaction patterns:

- *Planners* actively discuss the issue and make a joint decision to conceive a child. They anticipate an intimate relationship with their children, and they look forward to watching their children grow up. They are typically jubilant about becoming pregnant. As one wife said, "When the doctor called with the news that I was pregnant, I was so excited I wanted to run out in the street and tell everybody I met."

- *Acceptance-of-fate couples* are pleasantly surprised and quietly welcoming of a child, even though they have not planned a pregnancy. Often, these couples have engaged in a partly unconscious or unspoken agreement of becoming pregnant by using contraceptive methods only sporadically or not at all.

■ *Ambivalent couples* have mixed feelings before and after conception and even well into the pregnancy. As one wife noted, "I felt confused, a mixture of up and down, stunned, in a daze." Ambivalent couples decide to have the baby because one partner feels strongly about having a child and the other partner goes along. Or the pregnancy might be unintended, but one or both partners don't believe in abortion.

■ In *yes–no couples* one partner may not want children, even late in the pregnancy. For these couples, having a baby is one of many unresolved issues. Typically, the wife decides to go ahead with the pregnancy regardless of what her husband thinks, and the pregnancy sometimes causes a separation or divorce. In the case of unmarried teenage couples, as we'll discuss later in this chapter, the father may simply stop seeing the woman once she becomes pregnant.

The Benefits and Costs of Having Children

As the ambivalence just described indicates, parenthood has both benefits and costs. Some people weigh these issues before deciding to have a baby, but many do not. Emotions, after all, play a role, too. The desire to have a child is often deeply felt.

Benefits In a seven-nation study, some of the advantages of having children cited by both men and women were affection, close family ties, a feeling of immortality, and a sense of accomplishment. Being cared for during old age was an especially important reason for having children in nonindustrialized countries (Berelson, 1983). When a nationwide U.S. survey (Gallup and Newport, 1990) asked parents about the "greatest plus, or the thing you gain most, from having children," the most common responses were: Children bring love and affection; it is a pleasure to watch them grow; they bring joy, happiness, and fun; they create a sense of family; and they bring fulfillment and a sense of satisfaction. When asked how they felt about becoming a parent, 96 percent of the parents in another national survey said they were "in love" with their baby, and 91 percent reported being "happier than ever before" ("Bringing up baby," 1999).

Most couples place a high priority on raising healthy and happy children. Even new parents who are struggling with a colicky infant (whose abdominal distress causes the baby to cry frequently) delight in the baby's social and physical growth. It is not unusual for parents to say that having children brings a new dimension to their lives that is even more fulfilling than their jobs, their relationships with friends, or their leisure activities. Men, and especially men in higher socioeconomic positions, may be viewed as more "stable" and "reliable" when they become "family men" (Seccombe, 1991).

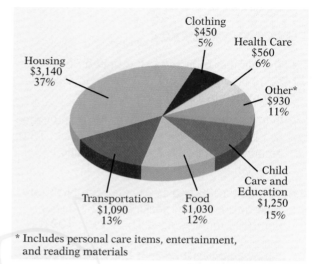

FIGURE 10.1 **What a Middle-Income Family Spends during the First Two Years of a Child's Life.** In 1999, families earning $36,800 to $61,900 spent about $8450 per year on each child under 2. These figures do not include the costs of prenatal care or delivery. (Based on Lino, 2000.)

Costs Parenthood isn't paradise. To begin with, raising children is expensive. Middle-income ($36,800 to $61,900 per year) families spend between 22 and 26 percent of their earnings on a child every year from the child's birth to age 17. *Figure 10.1* shows a typical year's expenses for a child 1 or 2 years old in husband–wife middle-income families. Child-rearing costs are much higher, especially in low-income families, if a child is disabled, chronically ill, or needs specialized care that welfare benefits don't cover (Lukemeyer et al., 2000).

Because of financial and other costs, many people restrict the size of their families. "What do you think is the ideal number of children for a family to have?" When the Gallup poll asked this question the first time in 1938, 66 percent of Americans said the ideal number was three or more children. This percentage increased to 73 percent in 1957 and to 80 percent in 1962 (during the "baby-boomer" years; see Chapter 1). In 1997, the percentage of people who felt that three or more children was the ideal family size declined to 31 percent. In the same year, however, 53 percent of respondents said that they would consider having three or more children if finances were not a problem (Kate, 1998; "Less is more," 1999).

Contrary to what many think, it is *not* selfish to consider economic costs before having a child (Folbre, 1994). In fact, it is selfish *not* to do so because a child raised in a poverty-stricken home may suffer lifelong disadvantages. One problem may be finding suitable housing. Large houses are expensive, and some rental units exclude children or limit their number. Families in the low-income range often have fewer housing options.

Children also carry emotional costs. While most parents report being "in love" with their baby, first-time parents, especially, experience anxiety or fatigue: 56 percent said they were stressed and worn out, 52 percent were afraid of doing something wrong, and 44 percent were unsure about what to do "a lot of the time" ("Bringing up baby," 1999). As the husband and wife become more focused on the child, interpersonal relationships may deteriorate. Many mothers report strain in balancing employment and household responsibilities (Walzer, 1998). Men, also, experience conflict with the birth of the first child. Although many would like to be involved fathers, men are still expected to participate fully in the economic sphere and to act as providers (Lupton and Barclay, 1997). New parents are likely to find that they have less patience with things (and people) that didn't annoy them before. They may take out their frustrations on each other: "For couples who thought that having a baby was going to bring them closer together, this is especially confusing and disappointing" (Cowan and Cowan, 2000: 18).

Pregnancy: Its Joys and Tribulations

Pregnancy can be exciting and a time of joy, particularly when it is planned or welcomed wholeheartedly. For both prospective parents it can deepen feelings of love and intimacy, and it can draw them closer in planning for the family's future. At the same time, pregnancy, especially the first pregnancy, can arouse anxiety such as knowing how to care for the baby properly and providing for the child economically.

The expectant mother may face numerous discomforts. In her first trimester (three-month period), she may experience frequent nausea, heartburn, insomnia, shortness of breath, painful swelling of the breasts, and fatigue. She may also be constantly concerned about the health of her *fetus* (the term for the unborn child from eight weeks until birth), especially if either she or the baby's father has engaged in any of the high-risk behaviors described in the box "Having Healthier Babies."

The second trimester can be very exciting because the mother begins to feel daily movements, or *quickenings*, as the fetus becomes more active. *Sonograms* (pictures taken by means of sound waves) can reveal an image of the baby and even, sometimes, indicate its sex. On the down side, backaches may become a problem, and fatigue tends to set in more quickly. In her third trimester, a woman may start losing interest in sex, which becomes awkward and difficult because of her growing abdomen. The pregnant woman begins to retain water during this period and may feel physically unattractive and clumsy. Once-simple, automatic tasks, like getting up from a sofa, turning over in bed, or picking something up from the floor, may now require planning and sometimes even assistance.

Vaginal births may be quick or they may be long and exhausting. Sometimes they are not possible and a *cesarean section* (surgical removal of the baby from the womb through the abdominal wall) is done, which is considerably more painful for the mother and requires a longer recovery. Both vaginal births and cesarean sections involve bloody discharge for several weeks. Infections and fevers are also common.

Parents have more birthing choices today that make delivery more pleasant and family-oriented. For example, many hospitals have *birthing rooms*, special areas that are brightly decorated and hospitable compared to the standard antiseptic hospital decor. Both parents usually remain in the same room during labor and delivery, and family and friends have greater privacy and intimacy in visiting the mother and baby.

Effects of Parenthood on Both Mother and Father

Parenthood is steeped in romantic misconceptions. And often we expect too much of mothers and ignore fathers. The infant responds to any person, mother or father, who is a consistent source of stimulation, love, attention, and comfort:

> The father is usually larger than the mother, his voice is deeper, his clothes are not the same and he moves and reacts differently. Furthermore, parents differ in odor and skin texture. The father and mother offer the child two different kinds of persons to learn about as well as providing separate but special sources of love and support. The infant also learns that different people can be expected to fulfill different needs. For example, the infant may prefer the mother when hungry or tired and the father when seeking stimulation or more active play. (Biller, 1993: 12)

Marital relationships also influence both parents' interaction with the baby. When fathers are supportive and encouraging—during the pregnancy and after the birth of the baby—most mothers feel more competent and are more responsive to their infants.

Mothers and Their Newborns   There is a widespread myth that there is instant "bonding" between the mother and the newborn baby (see Chapter 5). In reality, it is not only mothers but fathers, siblings, grandparents, and friends who have an effect on children. Historically, and in other cultures, children have been nurtured by many adults, not just mothers (Ambert, 1994). Because responsibility for caring for the baby tends to fall more heavily on new mothers, however, some women, particularly first-time mothers, feel frustrated or stressed out initially, not realizing that such

CHOICES

Having Healthier Babies

Most babies are born healthy. Some scientists believe that genes account for about 48 percent of the factors that determine IQ (Devlin et al., 1997). This suggests that the in utero environment and good prenatal care have a profound effect on the fetus's intelligence.

If high-risk behaviors are not controlled or eliminated, the baby can be unhealthy. Both smoking and poor nutrition have been linked with the risk of spontaneous abortion, premature birth, low birth weight, and illness in childhood. Low birth rate (which affects 7 percent of all newborns) increases the infant's chances of sickness, retarded growth, respiratory problems, infections, lower intelligence, learning problems, poor hearing and vision, and even death. Researchers estimate that 2800 of the annual infant deaths are due to low birth weight caused by pregnant mothers who smoke (Aligne and Stoddard, 1997). Even when the mother is a nonsmoker, men who smoke are 60 percent more likely than nonsmokers to have children who develop leukemia and 60 percent more likely to father children with tumors or brain cancer (Alvarado, 1991). Scientists believe smoking causes oxidation damage to sperm DNA, the carrier of genetic information.

Humans have a "brain growth spurt" that starts in the sixth month of gestation and continues for two years after birth. During the brain growth period, a single drinking binge—at least four hours or more—can permanently damage the brain of the unborn child (Ikonomidou et al., 2000).

Chronic drinking during pregnancy may lead to **fetal alcohol syndrome (FAS)**, a condition characterized by such physical abnormalities as congenital heart defects and defective joints and, often, mental retardation. Birth defects associated with prenatal alcohol exposure can occur in the first three to eight weeks of pregnancy, before a woman even knows she's pregnant. One out of every 29 women who know they're pregnant reports "risk drinking" (seven or more drinks per week, or five or more drinks on any one occasion) ("Fetal alcohol syndrome," 2000).

Each year in the United States between 1300 and 8000 children are born with FAS. Many more are born with *ARND, alcohol-related neurodevelopmental disorder* ("Fetal alcohol syndrome," 2000). As one report put it: "A pregnant woman . . . can hide her bottles, but in the delivery room she can't hold back the seriously underdeveloped child who often arrives steeped in pungent amniotic fluid that's really an 80-proof marinade" (Leerhsen and Schaefer, 1989: 57).

Mothers who use *illicit drugs* (heroin, cocaine, morphine, and opium) are likely to have infants who are addicted at birth. The baby may experience problems that include prenatal strokes, lasting brain damage, seizures, premature birth, retarded fetal growth, and malformations. Even common prescription drugs or drugs bought off the shelves can affect the fetus. Some of these include antihistamines, some antibiotics, tranquilizers, barbiturates,

and excessive amounts of vitamins A, D, B$_6$, and K (Boston Women's Health Collective, 1992).

Problems from *infectious diseases* are numerous. A woman who contracts German measles during the first three months of pregnancy may give birth to a deformed or retarded child. And some research suggests that men exposed to *toxic substances*, such as lead, alcohol, and some anticancer medications, as well as nuclear radiation and poisonous herbicides, could conceive children with serious physical and mental abnormalities (Purvis, 1990).

Sexually transmitted diseases are also dangerous to the unborn child. A woman with gonorrhea may have a child who becomes blind after passing through the infected vagina. Herpes or syphilis can result in a spontaneous abortion, a stillborn birth, or a baby born brain-damaged, deformed, blind, or deaf. Finally, and perhaps most serious of all, a parent with AIDS can pass the deadly disease on to the fetus.

Even spacing can affect a newborn's health. According to some medical researchers, women should wait 18 to 23 months after giving birth to get pregnant again. Mothers who become pregnant within six months after giving birth have a 30 to 40 percent chance of producing premature or undersize babies. Those who wait ten years for another child are twice as likely to have an unusually small baby, and 50 percent more likely to deliver prematurely (Zhu et al., 1999).

reactions are normal during the early months of parenting (Richardson, 1993).

Many women experience **postpartum depression**—"the blues" that appear after the birth of the baby. Some of this depression may be chemically caused. The sudden drop in the levels of estrogen and progesterone as the concentrations of these hormones in the placenta are expelled with other afterbirth tissue may have a depressive effect. And the high levels of the body's natural painkillers, called *beta-endorphins*, that the mother's body produces during labor also drop after birth. As a result the mother may "crash," contributing to the postpartum depression. Newborn infants require frequent feeding and almost constant care, which may contribute to fatigue and depression.

Some physicians and health practitioners suggest that our society is unrealistic in expecting women to recover during a six-week maternity leave. Half of all women experience one or more of a number of physical problems for some 12 months after childbirth: sinus problems, acne, hemorrhoids, vaginal discomfort, pain during intercourse, and difficulty reaching orgasm (Gjerdingen et al., 1993).

Despite the physical pain after childbirth, postpartum depression, and wondering if they'll ever get two hours of uninterrupted sleep again, most mothers are elated with their infants. If you're even minimally attentive, for example, most new mothers can spend hours describing the baby's eating schedule, every yawn and expression, and even the bowel movements of the "most beautiful baby in the world."

Fathers and Their Newborns According to Osherson (1992: 209), "Unlike career achievement or working, which we rehearse and practice for even as children, fatherhood is not a crucial part of our identities until we actually become fathers." Although men's readiness for fatherhood may vary, many men *do* think about becoming a parent. Shapiro (1987) interviewed both expectant and recent fathers, ranging in age from 18 to 60, and concluded that many men tend to experience several fears and concerns, which they usually keep to themselves. (Those who do talk to their partners about their feelings find that their relationships deepen.)

■ *Queasiness.* The most universal fear is of the birth process itself. Men may worry about helping their partners without fainting or getting sick.

■ *Increased responsibility.* Men are especially concerned about the financial responsibilities of parenting (Fox et al., 2000). Some take on two jobs, work overtime, or change to better-paying jobs, even though the change may result in more stressful employment conditions. As economic pressure mounts, some men worry whether they will be able to spend as much time with their children as they would like. According to Betcher and Pollack (1993: 140), they begin to realize, as the late Senator Paul Tsongas once phrased it, that "no man on his death bed ever said 'I wish I had spent more time with my work.'"

■ *Loss of spouse and/or child.* Almost every expectant father mentions fear that something will happen to his wife during delivery or that the child will be unhealthy or abnormal in some way.

■ *Feeling vulnerable.* Today's expectant fathers are more likely than are those of previous generations to know divorce—either their parents' or their own—firsthand. Some become concerned whether the marriage can survive the additional stress of a child.

Like mothers, many fathers worry about being good parents. And even when they feel anxious, many men feel that their task is to be calm, strong, and reassuring (another gender stereotype). Their tendency to keep their worries to themselves may increase the tension and distance between the partners. The couples who fare best are those who can listen sympathetically to each other without expecting immediate solutions (Cowan and Cowan, 1992).

Fatherhood often enhances maturity: "Being a father can change the ways that men think about themselves. Fathering often helps men to clarify their values and to set priorities" (Parke, 1996: 15). From a developmental perspective (see Chapter 2), fatherhood is an important transition in the life cycle. Some men react negatively to this transition. They may become abusive because of increased financial responsibilities, more emotional demands of new familial roles, and restrictions that parenthood brings (Schecter and Ganeley, 1995; see also Chapter 14). Most fathers, however, forge stronger links with their own parents who are supportive grandparents and have the opportunity to express loving and affectionate emotions to their children that "may be good for fathers as well as for babies" (Parke, 1996: 47). Although the mother may be more involved than the father in direct caregiving, a responsible father can get deep satisfaction by being available for the child and participating in child care (Johnson and Huston, 1998).

Married couples are not the only people who become parents, of course. Before we discuss other kinds of parents we need to consider, more generally, childbearing patterns during the last century.

Fertility Patterns in the United States

Except for the baby-boom "blip" during the 1950s, U.S. births have been declining steadily since the turn of the twentieth century. As *Figure 10.2* shows, the **birth rate**, or the number of live births per 1000 population, has decreased from 30.1 in 1910 to 14.6 in 1998. A more specific measure is the **fertility rate,** or the number of births per 1000 women in their childbearing years (aged 15 to 44). The U.S. fertility rate in 1998, for example, was 65.6 compared to 118 in 1960 (Ventura, Peters et al., 1997; Ventura, Martin et al., 2000). There are several other measures of population growth, but birth rates and fertility rates will suffice for our purposes here and in later chapters.

As *Figure 10.2* shows, people in the United States have been having fewer babies for a long time. Much

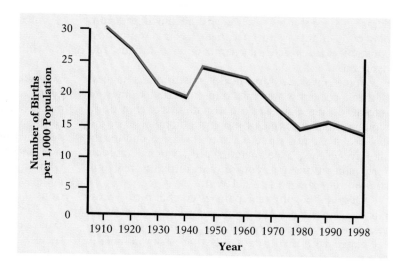

FIGURE 10.2 **Births in the United States, 1910–1998** (U.S. Census Bureau, 1999c; Ventura, Peters et al., 1997, Table 4).

of the decrease in the fertility rate is attributed to macro-level societal changes. Beginning with the Industrial Revolution in the mid-1800s, entry into paid employment allowed women to postpone motherhood (see Chapter 3). Improvements in the technology of contraception and greater opportunities in higher education gave women choices other than the traditional roles of wife and mother. Furthermore, advancements in medicine and hygiene decreased infant mortality rates. Families no longer had to have six children because three or four would die before their first birthday. And, as the Gallup polls cited earlier show, financial considerations limit the number of children that most parents have.

Fertility rates vary considerably by race and ethnicity. Within the Latino population, which has the highest fertility rates across almost all age groups (see *Figure 10.3*), fertility rates range from a high of 112 for Mexican American women to a low of 50 for Cuban Americans (Ventura, Martin et al., 2000). Some of the reasons for these variations reflect demographic and cultural differences. For example, most recent Mexican Americans have emigrated from rural areas that value large families. Children perform important economic functions, including contributing to the family income as migrant workers. In contrast, Cuban Americans are predominantly middle class, have low unemployment rates and higher education levels, and do not depend on children to augment family income.

Young Latino and black men and women typically begin sexual activities earlier than do their white counterparts, and they have more partners (see Chapter 6). As we will discuss later in this chapter, some black youth have babies purposely to fill emotional voids in their lives. Compared to white communities, black communities also tend to accept out-of-wedlock births and reject abortion. Although Asian/Pacific fertility rates are higher than those of whites (see Data Digest), they are lower than those of Latinos, American

Indians, and African Americans. In addition, the highest fertility rates among Asian/Pacific Islander women are between the ages of 30 and 39. This may be due to Asian women's—especially among Japanese and Filipina mothers—postponing childbearing until they've completed college and attained professional degrees.

The variations in fertility rates reflect, among other things, a mother's educational attainment. In terms of lifetime fertility, for example, black women and Latinas with 13 to 15 years of education have an average of 1.6 children compared to 4.1 for Latinas and 4.5 for black women with only a grade-school education (Mathews and Ventura, 1997). Such findings suggest that young women, especially teenagers, who expect to improve their lives through educational and earning opportunities are more likely to delay childbearing and to have few children over their lifetimes (Robinson and Frank, 1994; Trent, 1994).

Postponing Parenthood

Although it is still typical for a woman to have her first child before age 30, the numbers of first-time older mothers are rising. In the early 1970s, only 4 percent of American women having their first babies were 30 or older; by 1998, the number had increased to 23 percent (Ventura, Martin et al., 2000). Thus, women are beginning to postpone not only marriage (see Chapter 8) but parenthood as well.

Reasons for Postponing Parenthood

Both individual-level and macro-level factors affect the decision to postpone parenthood. As stated in Chapter 8, being single has many attractions, including independence, the opportunity to develop a career, and having more time for fun. Women, especially, have been enjoying the chance to achieve a higher level of education rather than marry right after high school, and they have been pursuing careers because they want financial independence. Moreover, the advances in reproductive technology that have made it possible for women to bear children successfully at older ages or to have children in other ways (see the section "Becoming a Parent Despite Infertility") have lessened women's concerns about biological clocks and finding mates.

On the macro level, disturbed by the current high rates of divorce (see Chapter 15), some young couples may be apprehensive about their own chances of marital success. Thus, they are delaying parenthood until they feel sure the marriage will work. In addition, economic recessions have encouraged many people to postpone parenthood. More young adults are living with their parents or returning to the nest because they don't have the resources to start a family (see Chapter 9). Young married couples living with their parents may postpone childbearing because they are reluctant to make already crowded living conditions even worse.

Characteristics of Older Parents

Older mothers tend to feel more self-assured, more ready for responsibility, and better prepared for parenthood than younger women; the latter sometimes feel trapped by having a baby at a young age (see Maynard, 1997). Compared to younger mothers, older mothers are more likely to be white, married, and highly educated. Moreover, they tend to work in professional occupations and to have high family incomes (Bachu, 1993).

Although older parents may be more patient, mature, and financially secure, there are some distinct drawbacks in deferred parenthood. Actor Tony Randall received enormous publicity when, at age 77, he and his 27-year-old wife had their first child. Randall's wife was young and healthy, and had a low risk for having a Down's syndrome baby compared to pregnant women in their forties. Even beyond health risks, however, consider some of the practical liabilities of becoming a parent at age 49:

FIGURE 10.3   Fertility Rates by Race, Ethnicity, and Age: 1998. How would you explain the high fertility rates of Latinas ages 25 to 29? Why do you think that the fertility rates of black women ages 30 and over are generally lower than those of most of the other groups? How, also, might you explain the much higher fertility rates of Asian and Pacific Islander women after age 29?

Source: Based on Ventura, Martin, et. al., 2000, Tables 3 and 9.

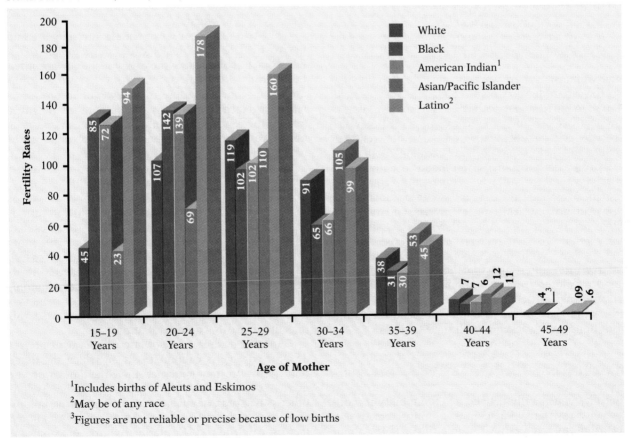

[1]Includes births of Aleuts and Eskimos

[2]May be of any race

[3]Figures are not reliable or precise because of low births

©Britt-Copley News Service

At 52, you'd be coming out of the "terrible twos" and hosting play groups for toddlers. As you turned 55, your child would start kindergarten and you'd qualify for dual memberships in the PTA and the American Association of Retired Persons (AARP). At 60, you and your spouse would be coaching soccer. . . . By the time you hit 70, you'd be buried under college tuition bills. And if your child delayed marriage and family like you did, you might be paying for a wedding when you were 80 and babysitting for your grandchildren at 90. (Wright, 1997: E5)

Some women who have waited to have children find that it is too late to have as many children as they wanted. Mature mothers, and especially those who have risen to powerful but demanding executive positions, may feel especially guilty about splitting their time between their families and their employers and "cheating" both.

Men who postpone parenthood usually enjoy more advantages and have fewer constraints than women. Most men do not face sex discrimination in the workplace, they earn higher salaries, and they have better health benefits. Thus, they are less likely to worry about not having the resources to raise children later in life. With fewer economic concerns, men remarry more often and sometimes, after a divorce, support children from two families (see Chapter 16). Because their careers are more established, older fathers may have more flexibility to spend their non-work hours and weekends with their families.

Involuntary Childlessness

Infertility is generally defined as the inability to conceive a baby after 12 months of unprotected sex. According to some estimates, infertility affects about 15 percent of all couples of reproductive age. The incidence of infertility increases, however, as childbearing is delayed. For example, the rate of infertility for couples between 30 and 34 years of age is more than 50 percent greater than the rate for those between 25 and 29 (Mosher and Pratt, 1991).

Infertility rates have remained fairly stable since the mid-1960s, but because more medical help is available, more couples are trying to overcome this problem. Since 1968, the demand for treatment of infertility has more than tripled: Every year more than a million American couples seek medical assistance. As a result, combating infertility has become a multibillion-dollar industry. Although some large employers offer medical benefits for the treatment of infertility, in most cases the couple must pay the costs themselves (DeWitt, 1993).

Reasons for Infertility

Infertility is attributable about equally to problems in males and females; each sex accounts for about 40 percent of cases and both together for about 20 percent. Until recently, however, most infertility research focused almost exclusively on women (Halpern, 1989). For years people believed that the major reason for female infertility was aging. Although it is true that reproductive organs age faster than other parts of the human body, the notion that infertility is a predictable "career woman's curse" is simplistic at best and stereotypical at worst.

The two major causes of female infertility are failure to ovulate and blockage of the *fallopian tubes*, which each month carry the egg, whether or not it has been fertilized by male sperm, from the ovaries to the uterus. A woman's failure to *ovulate*, or to produce a viable egg each month, may have a number of causes, among them poor nutrition, chronic illness, and drug abuse. Very occasionally, the lack of ovulation may be attributed to psychological stress (Masters et al., 1992).

The fallopian tubes can be blocked by scarring caused by **pelvic inflammatory disease (PID)**, an infection of the uterus that spreads to the tubes as well as to the ovaries and surrounding tissues. PID, in turn, is often caused by sexually transmitted diseases like chlamydia (see Chapter 6 and Appendix E for more information about sexually transmitted diseases). **Chlamydia,** a bacterial infection often referred to as "the silent epidemic" because it exhibits no symptoms in 75 percent of women and 33 percent of men, is a rapidly rising cause of PID today. Once diagnosed, this infection is easily cured with antibiotics.

Another leading cause of infertility in women over 25 years of age is **endometriosis,** in which the tissue that forms in the endometrium (the lining of the uterus) spreads outside the womb and attaches itself to other pelvic organs, such as the ovaries or the fallopian tubes. Endometriosis, caused by as yet unknown factors, can lead to PID, uterine tumors, and blockage of the opening to the uterus. *Table 10.1* summarizes the major reasons for infertility in women.

Male infertility is often due to "sluggish" sperm or a low sperm count. According to some recent research, since 1938 sperm counts of men in the United States and 20 other countries have plunged by an average of 50 percent (Swan et al., 1997).

Chemical pollutants are believed to play a major role in male infertility. Because for years men have been more likely than women to work in environments in which they come in contact with toxic chemicals or in which they are exposed to other environmentally hazardous conditions, their risks of infertility from these sources are high. Some substances and conditions that either have been found to affect male reproductive capacity or that are suspected of doing so are presented in *Table 10.2*.

Some scientists are skeptical about blaming pollutants for male infertility. If the sperm counts are low, they ask, why have infertility rates remained constant over the years? They also maintain that, so far, there has been no conclusive evidence that low sperm counts result from environmental toxins (Carpenter, 1996).

Other causes of low sperm counts include the following: injury to the testicles, or scrotum; infections such as mumps in postchildhood years; testicular varicose veins; undescended testes (the testes in the male fetus normally descend from the abdominal cavity into the scrotum in about the eighth month of prenatal development); endocrine disorders; and excessive consumption of alcohol, tobacco, marijuana, narcotic drugs, or even some prescription medications. There is some evidence that long-distance bicycle riding or tight-fitting underwear can lower sperm counts. Prolonged and frequent use of saunas, hot tubs, and steam baths may also have a negative effect because sperm production is sensitive to temperature. Male infertility can also result from such problems as an inability to ejaculate, ejaculation only outside the vagina, or inability to achieve or maintain an erection (Masters et al., 1992).

Finally, approximately 20 percent of infertile couples are diagnosed as having *idiopathic infertility*. In plain language, this means that doctors simply don't know what's wrong.

Reactions to Infertility

Although people respond in a number of ways, most couples are devastated by their infertility. In most societies, including the United States, two procreative cultural norms dominate. One is that all married couples *should* reproduce; the other is that all married couples should *want* to reproduce (Veevers, 1980). For many women, then, infertility becomes "an acute and unanticipated life crisis" that is characterized by stigma, grief, guilt, and a sense of violation. As one woman said, "It's a slap in the face. I feel like I'm isolated in

TABLE 10.1
Some Possible Causes of Female Infertility

Failure to ovulate, caused by poor nutrition, drug abuse, chronic illness, or, in rare instances, psychological stress

Blockage of the fallopian tubes, caused by pelvic inflammatory disease that results from infection with sexually transmitted bacteria or microorganisms

Endometriosis, which may cause infertility by blockage of the fallopian tubes by uterine tissue that migrates outside the uterus

Scarring, adhesions, and cysts around the ovaries and fallopian tubes that may be caused by sexually transmitted diseases (STDs) and pelvic inflammatory disease (PID)

Cervical mucus (from the cervix, the lower portion of the uterus) that is too thick for sperm to penetrate or that has an acid/alkaline balance harmful to sperm

Excessive exercise or rapid weight loss that may interfere with the production of reproductive hormones due to the loss of body fat

The regular use of douches and vaginal deodorants that may contain chemicals that either kill sperm or inhibit their movement

SOURCES: Fogel and Woods, 1995; DeLisle, 1997.

a prison; . . . no one understands how horrible this is" (Whiteford and Gonzalez, 1995: 29).

Disrupting generational continuity may reinforce a woman's feelings of being a "failure" when she doesn't conceive:

> *My husband is Italian and for the 10 years that we've been married, I have known that his having a son has been so important to him, and my not being able to deliver has been a real difficult thing for me to deal with. . . . My mother-in-law has been pushing for a grandchild since the day we got married. (Whiteford and Gonzalez, 1995: 34)*

Although well intentioned, potential grandparents' expectations exert pressure to carry on the family line. As the mother of one infertile woman asked, "Do you think that I will have a grandchild before I die?" (Daly, 1999: 18).

Many women, concerned that people will see them in a new and damaging light, engage in some sort of "information management." They may avoid the topic whenever possible, or they may attribute the problem to a disease like diabetes or kidney trouble, taking the focus off specific reproductive disorders. On the other hand, because male infertility may be considered a defect in one's masculinity, women will

TABLE 10.2

Some Chemical and Environmental Factors in Male Infertility

Risk Factors	Effects
Lead used in making storage batteries and paints	Fewer sperm, sperm that move more slowly than normal, and more abnormally shaped sperm
Ionizing and non-ionizing radiation: former found in nuclear plants and medical facilities; latter in high-voltage switchyards and communications facilities	Possible damage to sperm cells and lowered fertility
Anesthetic gases	Unexposed female partners may have higher than normal number of miscarriages
Vinyl chloride used in plastic manufacturing	Unexposed female partners may have more miscarriages and stillbirths
Pesticides like kepone, and the carbon disulfide used in the manufacture of viscose rayon and as a fumigant	Possible loss of sex drive, impotence, abnormal sperm, lowered sperm count
Heat stress found in foundries, smelters, bakeries, and farm work	Lowered sperm counts and sterility
Estrogen used in the manufacture of oral contraceptives	Possible loss of sex drive, abnormal sperm, lowered sperm counts
Methylene chloride used as a solvent in paint strippers	Possible very low sperm counts and shrunken testicles
EDB (ethylene dibromide) used as an ingredient in leaded gasoline and as a fumigant of tropical fruit for export	Possible lower sperm count and decreased fertility in wives of workers

SOURCE: Based on Kenen, 1993: 40–41.

often accept the responsibility for infertility themselves: "When I tell them we can't have children, I generally try to leave the impression that it's me. I may mutter 'tubes you know' or 'faulty plumbing'" (Miall, 1986: 36).

Still other women reveal their infertility because they fear they will be considered self-centered for not having children:

> I know at one point I overheard someone saying, "Oh, they're too selfish, they're too interested in going on fancy holidays. Material things, that's why they're not having children." It was so untrue and it hurt. (Miall, 1986: 37)

For many couples, infertility is socially isolating. As one woman remarked, "I feel sometimes like we're the only ones in the world who have this [problem]!" (Daly, 1999: 19). Some infertile couples, however, enjoy vicarious parenthood through contact with the children of relatives and friends. Others become increasingly involved in work-related activities, and in some cases even begin to regard their childlessness as advantageous. Some couples accept infertility as a fact of life and remain childless. A much larger group, however, tries to adopt a baby or turns to the many new reproduction technologies.

Becoming a Parent Despite Infertility

Traditionally, the solution to infertility was adoption. However, being a single, unmarried parent no longer bears the stigma it used to (see Chapters 6 and 8), and many unwed mothers are deciding to keep their babies instead of putting them up for adoption. Legal abortion has also reduced the number of available infants. Alternatively, many infertile couples are now exploring the various solutions that modern reproduction technology offers—artificial insemination, in vitro fertilization, embryo transplants, and surrogacy. We look first at the adoption alternative and then at some of the high-tech solutions.

Adoption: The Traditional Solution to Infertility

At one time, 80 percent of U.S. babies born out of wedlock were given up for adoption. Today, this rate has dropped to about 2 or 3 percent. At least 150,000 children were adopted in the United States in 1998 from foster care, private domestic sources, and other countries (Dunkin, 2000). Of the 560,000 foster children nationwide, 122,000 are legally eligible for adoption because the biological parents are dead or missing, have been found unfit, or have legally surrendered their rights to have their children returned ("Child welfare outcomes . . . ," 2000). Many of these children are hard to place, however, because they are perceived as "unsuitable"—they are sick, physically handicapped, biracial, nonwhite, emotionally disturbed, or "too old." Ironically between 100 and 500 U.S.-born children are adopted every year—primarily by Canadians but also by Europeans—because the United States has a large pool of available children and because there are long waits and delays in other countries ("At least 100 children . . . ," 1997).

Couples often have to overcome numerous barriers to adopt children. Some of the most controversial issues include the rights of biological fathers, transracial adoptions, and open adoptions. There are also some misgivings about for-profit orphanages and international adoptions.

The Rights of Biological Fathers   One issue that has gained recent prominence is the nature and extent of the rights of biological fathers. For years, fathers of out-of-wedlock children were rarely involved in adoptions. In 1993, however, in a highly publicized case, a child given up for adoption by her biological mother was returned to her mother and her biological father when the Iowa courts ruled favorably on a custody suit brought by the father.

In 1994, the Illinois Supreme Court ruled that a 3-year-old boy known as "Baby Richard" be returned to his biological parents. In this case, the biological father had been told by his former fiancée that the baby had died when the father was on a trip to his native country. When he learned that the baby was alive and had been placed for adoption, the father began legal action to stop the proceeding and married the baby's biological mother. In 1995 the biological parents won custody of the son. Two years later, the biological father moved out of the family home, leaving "Baby Richard" in the care of his mother.

Both of these cases expanded the rights of biological fathers in contested adoptions. They also raised concerns among advocates of adoption that such rulings may undermine the legitimacy of the adoption system if biological parents change their minds after a child is adopted. As a result, many groups have argued that to prevent such battles, uniform adoption laws should be implemented in all 50 states.

Transracial Adoptions   Another controversial issue is transracial adoptions. Advocates of transracial adoption claim that many black or biracial children—especially those with emotional or physical handicaps—would remain in foster homes until age 18 if white families did not adopt them. One study examined almost 3900 children in California who entered out-of-home care at age 6 or younger. The researcher found that, six years later, and regardless of the child's age, white children were five times more likely and Latino children almost three times more likely than black children to be adopted (Barth, 1997). The implication is that black children may languish in foster care or other homes longer than their white and Latino counterparts.

There is also evidence that when white adoptive families encourage children's participation in multicultural and multiracial activities, children in transracial adoptions have done well (Bagley, 1993; Simon and Altstein, 2000). If anything, some black adoptees complain, their white parents tried too hard to educate them about their heritage, turning dinner conversations into lectures on black history (Simon, 1993).

Despite findings that there is little difference in the self-concept or well-being between in-race and transracial adoptions, the National Association of Black Social Workers has strongly opposed transracial adoptions:

> *When children are removed from their ethnic environment, they tend to associate with their ethnicity negatively, because they are alienated from their culture of origin. Positive role models and orientations about the child's ethnicity may help, but they do not adequately address the loss of being dislodged from the ethnic community. (Kissman and Allen, 1993: 93)*

The Multiethnic Placement Act of 1994 makes it illegal to deny transracial adoption (see Curtis and Alexander, 1996). Many black (and some white) social workers, however, find ways to get around the law. They believe that it is the right of every child to find a permanent home with a family of the same race and that a white parent, "no matter how skilled or loving, could not avoid doing irreparable harm to the self-esteem of a black child" (Furgatch, 1995: 19).

On the one hand, proponents of transracial adoption argue that an insistence on in-race adoption has brought about a decrease of 90 percent in the adoption of black children (Furgatch, 1995). In addition, some critics imply that encouraging foster care instead of transracial adoptions protects many social service jobs: "the more kids in foster care, the more money states get from the federal government for their overall programs, since 50 percent of foster care funds go to administrative costs, including social worker salaries" (Spake, 1998: 31).

On the other hand, even successful and well-educated black professionals face daily racism and hostility (Cose, 1993; Feagin and Sikes, 1994; see also Chapter 12). It is not entirely surprising, then, that black social workers question the wisdom of placing black children with white parents who may not provide black adoptees with the strategies to deal with racism, prejudice, and discrimination.

Some organizations, like the National Adoption Center www.adopt.org), have turned to the Internet in placing children for adoption. Daniel, pictured here, was born in 1991, has "black hair, expressive brown eyes, and an endearing smile. He is soft spoken and displays good manners and enjoys drawing and coloring, especially space pictures."

Open Adoption   A third controversial issue is open adoption. **Open adoption** refers to the practice of sharing information and maintaining contact between biological and adoptive parents both during the adoption process and during the child's life. Currently, only Alaska, Kansas, and Oregon provide open access to adoption records. The open adoption movement began in the 1960s when adoptees sought to abolish the secrecy surrounding their sealed adoption records. Since then, the movement has been supported by numerous television shows (such as "Unsolved Mysteries" and almost all of the talk shows) that revel in reuniting adopted children with their biological parents, as well as articles in newsmagazines that applaud open reunions (see Purvis, 1997).

The general public has mixed feelings, however. For example, in a telephone survey of 640 randomly selected adults, Rompf (1993) found that only 52 percent either strongly or somewhat approved of open adoptions. And in a survey of 1268 adoptive parents in California, Berry (1993) found "considerable variation" in adoptive parents' willingness to be contacted by biological parents. The most guarded were adoptive parents of children who either were very young or who came from abusive backgrounds.

Some birth mothers filed suits against the state in 1998 when Oregon voted to approve Measure 58, a law that allows adults who were adopted as children to see their original birth certificates. The mothers claimed that such laws violate their right to privacy. A birth mother now in her late fifties said that the adoption "was the most searingly painful time of my life."

Being contacted by the biological child would renew past traumas that she has struggled to forget (Clemetson, 1999). Adopted children argue, however, that they have a right to information about their biological parents, even if the biological mother doesn't want to be contacted.

For-Profit Orphanages   For-profit orphanages can now compete for the billions of dollars that the government spends each year for nonprofit organizations to support poor children who were taken away from homes judged unfit. While some of the for-profit orphanages may be very good, others have been accused of mistreating children in their care, cutting staff to excessively low levels, and reducing labor costs by making children do more of the work ("For-profit orphanages . . . ," 1997).

International Adoptions   Because the waiting period required to adopt a child from overseas is only one or two years, as opposed to seven to ten years in the United States, Americans have increasingly turned to international adoptions. Of the roughly 150,000 children adopted in the United States in 1999, about 17,000 were from other countries. In 1999, over half of the foreign-born children adopted by Americans came from Russia and China, 13 percent from South Korea, and another 11 percent from Guatemala and Romania ("Immigrant visas issued . . . ," 2000).

A large number of the adoptions are successful because the adoptees are infants (as in China) or come from well-managed foster-care systems (as in South Korea). Although South Korean children are generally as healthy as U.S.-born children, many from other countries suffer from a variety of diseases and problems: parasites, rickets, malnutrition, exposure to tuberculosis, asthma, hepatitis B, neurological damage, and, especially in Russia, prenatal alcohol developmental lags (McGuiness and Pollansch, 2000; Oleck, 2000). Because there are no international adoption standards or accreditation criteria, prospective parents may face unexpected obstacles in the adoption process (see the box on "The Politics of International Adoptions").

Some Benefits and Limitations of Adoption   Compared to children raised in foster homes or by never-married mothers, adopted children are economically advantaged, are more likely to complete high school and hold a skilled job, and less likely to use drugs, to commit crimes, or to be homeless as adults (Bachrach et al., 1990; Spake, 1998). In a national study the researchers found that biological and adoptive parents were very similar. Both groups used positive rather than negative discipline (such as praising rather than spanking), emphasized desirable behavior in their children (such as doing well in school), and expected their children to complete college. The researchers concluded that adoptive parents functioned quite well and

CROSS CULTURAL

The Politics of International Adoptions

Although many international adoptions are successful, enthusiastic adopting parents are often uninformed and unprepared for some of the risks. Among these are the possibility that the child was obtained illegally by the agency handling the adoption; the presence of illnesses in the child that may range from mild to life threatening; and the necessity to wade through endless bureaucratic red tape to complete the adoption process (see K. Evans, 2000).

One of the recent barriers include U.S. immigration laws which require that children adopted abroad be vaccinated in their home countries before being allowed to enter the United States. Adoptive parents maintain that such requirements are unwarranted: They worry about the potential hazards of vaccines given abroad, including the possibility of a bad reaction,

infections from nonsterile needles, or the quality of available vaccines (Okie, 1997).

Mexican organizations estimate that a number of children destined for adoption by U.S. parents come from among the 500 to 20,000 children of lower socioeconomic classes that are kidnapped every year (Scott, 1994). In some countries, such as Russia, agencies will say that a child's health is fine, but American parents often find that their adopted child has one of a wide range of illnesses. These include hepatitis B, tuberculosis, intestinal parasites, congenital heart defects, brain damage, and other maladies that U.S. physicians find difficult to diagnose (Brink, 1994).

Even though there are thousands of orphans in Eastern Europe, they are not easy to adopt. Some couples describe "endless" bureaucratic obstacles and

legal systems that are hostile to intercountry adoptions. Agencies may "forget" about a promised adoption because of a last-minute higher offer from a flourishing black market baby industry. In addition, in some cases prospective parents have arrived in some East European countries only to find that adoption and immigration policies have been changed while they were en route. Prospective parents may have to pay bribes, called "contributions," to private agencies, religious groups, and government offices, both in the United States and abroad, that profit from adoptions. In some cases, attorneys or adoption agencies in the United States have collected up to $20,000 from parents, promising them, for example, a healthy baby from Eastern Europe—but have never delivered (Bogert, 1994; Tousignant, 1994; Borgman, 1995; Weir, 2000).

"at least as well as their biological counterparts" (Borders et al., 1998).

Most single parents are women who tend to adopt girls or older, nonwhite, or mentally retarded children. Because only two states, Florida and New Hampshire, have laws expressly barring homosexuals from adopting children, gay men and lesbians are increasingly adopting babies and older children (Selby, 1995). In 1997, New Jersey became the first state in the nation to allow gay partners to jointly adopt children on the same basis as unmarried couples. In a few states and the District of Columbia, gay couples can adopt children in a complex and expensive two-step process, where one partner is allowed to adopt and the second can then petition for joint rights (Havemann, 1997).

Some of the deterrents to adoption include societal beliefs that love and "bonding" in adoption are second-best, that adoptive parents are simply not "real parents," and that adopted children are second-rate because of their unknown genetic past. Adoptive parents sometimes worry that a teenage girl who has not had prenatal care and who may have poor nutritional habits or be a drug abuser could deliver a baby who may later have physical problems (Miall, 1987). In addition, adoptive parents must sort out their feelings

about having "your own" child versus becoming a parent. As one woman said, "I had to think about whether I was ready to accept all the things that an adopted child could throw at you" (Daly, 1999: 27).

Assisted Reproductive Technology

With the growth of genetic research, our ability to alter the course of nature has expanded greatly. The infertile couple now has many more options for having a child than before through **assisted reproductive technology (ART)**, a general term that includes all treatments or procedures that involve the handling of human eggs and sperm to establish a pregnancy (i.e., the blanket name for laboratory-assisted baby-making methods). This section discusses some types of ART such as IVT, GIFT, ZIFT, embryo cryopreservation, egg or embryo donation, and surrogate birth.

Many assisted reproductive techniques are risky, and success rates are modest at best. In this section you will also see that these new technologies have generated some difficult questions. Some are medical, involving the health of mother and baby. Some are legal, involving issues of custody and inheritance. And some are ethical.

Artificial Insemination Artificial insemination, sometimes called *donor insemination (DI)*, is a medical procedure in which semen is introduced artificially into the vagina or uterus about the time of ovulation. The semen, taken from the woman's husband or from a donor, may be fresh or it may have been frozen. Artificial insemination was first performed successfully in the 1970s and was followed by a normal pregnancy and birth (Matanoski, 1994).

Artificial insemination is the most common treatment for male infertility, but it has also been used in cases where husbands feared transmitting a genetic disease such as diabetes, cystic fibrosis, and muscular dystrophy. In addition, the artificial insemination process has been used to preserve the sperm of young men who are likely to be exposed to chemical and radioactive mutagens in the environment and the workplace so that they will still be able to father a child in the future. Men who undergo chemotherapy for cancer may store their sperm for future insemination in the event that the chemotherapy treatment makes them sterile.

For single women, artificial insemination offers a means of having children without waiting for Mr. Right. Some single women turn to artificial insemination because their partner has a serious hereditary disease. Other women prefer the mutual anonymity between the recipient and the donor to avoid legal and emotional complications after the baby's birth. It offers lesbians a way of conceiving a child without having to be sexually intimate with a man. According to one physician, men who decided to bank their sperm when the Persian Gulf War began in 1991 had a sense of some control "by leaving something of themselves behind that will live" (Ames et al., 1991). Some couples prefer artificial insemination to adoption because the mothers want to experience a pregnancy and birth, or one or both parents want to contribute to the child's biological/genetic makeup (Daniels, 1994).

Artificial insemination has its drawbacks. Because the identity of the donor is almost always concealed (unless it is the husband's sperm that is artificially introduced), and one donor may be used for as many as 15 pregnancies, inadvertent inbreeding may result. That is, two people might meet and mate not knowing that they share the same genetic father. Although such cases are presumably rare, a few years ago a prominent geneticist in the Washington, D.C., area used his own sperm to impregnate women who went to him for treatment of fertility problems. This man fathered at least 70 children without the mothers' knowledge or consent (Howe, 1991). Moreover, sperm banks that freeze sperm for later use can make mistakes. In 1990, for example, a Manhattan sperm bank was sued after a white couple gave birth to a black baby.

There are also emotional problems associated with artificial insemination. For example, if a couple

The use of fertility drugs—especially among white, educated, middle-class women—has resulted in multiple births, including quintuplets.

divorce, the father may become aloof with a child he never considered his own, threaten disclosure, or withhold child-support payments (Baran and Pannor, 1989). Furthermore, although many lesbians purposely distance themselves from information about the donor-fathers of their children, the children themselves may eventually seek information about their biological fathers.

Disclosure issues will probably increase in the future (Orenstein, 1995). For example, a young woman, age 19, who was conceived by donor insemination, feels frustrated because she has no idea of her father's biological roots:

With no records available, half my heritage is erased. I'll never know whose eyes I have inherited. I've searched family photo albums to no avail. . . . So, to couples seeking babies this way, I propose that you find out who your donors are, keep records and let your children know where they came from. And to a possibly brown-haired man who attended University of Tennessee Medical

School in 1974 and made a donation on my mother's behalf, I thank you for the gift of life. I think I have your eyes, your jaw and your personality. I just wish I could find out for sure. (M. R. Brown, 1994:12)

Despite such problems, national and international sperm industries are thriving. Denmark is one of the leaders in exporting "bulk amounts" of sperm to other countries. A sperm bank in Minnesota exports its product primarily to South America and Israel (Hartill, 2000). In the United States, a number of sperm banks advertise online. Some even specialize in donor types—sperm donors who have high IQs, are physically attractive, or have PhDs (Oldenburg, 1999). People with high IQs don't necessarily beget children with high IQs. As one sociologist observes, the "genius" sperm banks could produce progeny "who inherited the genius's nose, not his brain" (Rothman, 1999).

Fertility-Enhancing Drugs   Another of the less invasive ARTs is **fertility-enhancing drugs** that stimulate ovaries to produce eggs. In 1997, a couple from Carlisle, Iowa, became the parents of the first septuplets ever born alive in the United States and the only known living ones in the world. The mother had been taking a fertility drug, Pergonal. For religious reasons, the couple refused to undergo a process known as "selective reduction"—aborting some of the fetuses to give the others a chance to fully develop. It is estimated that about two-thirds of the triplets, quadruplets, and quintuplets born during 1998 (see Data Digest) were the result of increased use of fertility-enhancing drugs or a combination of drugs and other assisted reproductive techniques (Ventura, Martin et al., 2000).

In Vitro Fertilization   In vitro fertilization (IVF) involves surgically removing eggs from a woman's ovaries, fertilizing them in a petri dish (a specially shaped glass container) with sperm from her husband or another donor, and then reimplanting the fertilized eggs in her uterus. Louise Brown, the first in vitro baby (*in vitro* is Latin for "in glass") was born in England in 1978. Since then, more than 300 clinics have opened in the United States, and thousands of children worldwide owe their births to this procedure. More than one egg is usually implanted to increase the chances of success, and nearly half of all women using in vitro procedures have multiple births. Multiple birth babies are ten times more likely than single babies to be born prematurely and at low birth weight with poorly developed organs. This subjects them to medical risks that range from lung disease and brain damage to infant death (Brownlee et al., 1994; Bor, 1995).

There have been three recent variations in this procedure—**gamete intrafallopian transfer (GIFT)**, **zygote intrafallopian transfer (ZIFT)**, and **intracytoplasmic sperm injection (ICSI)** (see *Table 10.3*). In 1997, a 39-year-old Georgia woman was the first in the United States to become pregnant and give birth to twins using eggs that had been frozen for 25 months and then thawed and fertilized by her husband's sperm. Though similar to ICSI—where sperm are injected directly into an egg in a laboratory dish—the procedure is expected to revolutionize women's reproductive options. Women will be able to freeze healthy eggs in "egg banks," just as men are able to do with sperm, and save the eggs for future use. Although some researchers are concerned that the freezing and thawing process poses a greater risk of chromosomal abnormalities, the woman has sole ownership of the

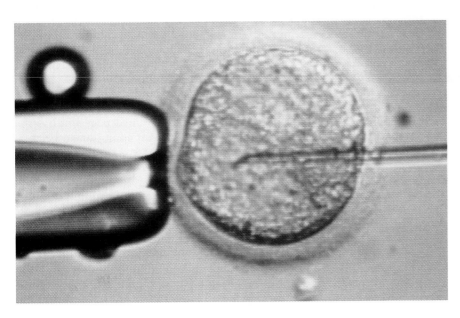

In ICSI (intracytoplasmic sperm injection, see text), a single sperm is inserted into an egg. A pipette holds the egg steady while the sperm is injected with a microneedle. Although some eggs don't survive ICSI due to needle damage, this new technique achieves high fertilization rates.

TABLE 10.3

Comparing Assisted Reproductive Technology (ART) Methods

About 15 percent of U.S. women have received some type of infertility service since the introduction of ART in 1981. Success rates vary by the woman's age, declining significantly after age 34, and the technique used. In 1997 fewer than three out of every five high-tech treatments administered at U.S. fertility clinics resulted in the birth of at least one child.

Method	How it works	First successful in humans	Cost per cycle*	Success rate
In vitro fertilization (IVT)	An egg and sperm are combined in a laboratory dish. If the egg is fertilized, the resulting embryo is transferred into the woman's uterus.	1978 (England)	$8000	28%
Gamete intrafallopian transfer (GIFT)	A doctor, using a laparoscope, inserts eggs and sperm directly into a woman's fallopian tube. Any resulting embryo floats into the uterus.	1984 (U.S.)	$6000 to $10,000	30%
Zygote intrafallopian transfer (ZIFT)	Eggs are fertilized in the laboratory and any resulting zygotes (fertilized eggs) are transferred to a fallopian tube.	1989 (Belgium)	$8000 to $10,000	28%
Intracytoplasmic sperm injection (ICSI)	A doctor, using a microscopic pipette, injects a single sperm into an egg.	1992 (Belgium)	$10,000 to $12,000	29%

*A cycle is the entire period of treatment, from the initial administration of ovulation-inducing drugs to harvesting eggs (or obtaining donor eggs), fertilizing them, and finally reimplanting them and monitoring the result. Typically, a complete cycle lasts about six weeks.

SOURCES: Centers for Disease Control and Prevention, 1997a; Grady, 1996; "1997 assisted reproductive technology . . .," 1999.

eggs and can fertilize them with a future partner (or partners) of her choice (Feldmann, 1997).

Which ART procedure is used most often? IVF was used in 72 percent of cycles carried out in the United States in 1997 (see *Figure 10.4*). Although IVF is a miracle come true for many couples, it has some drawbacks. It is expensive and time-consuming, and it can be emotionally exhausting. Halpern (1989: 148) describes women as "hostages" to the process:

> She will have her blood drawn on selected days until the twelfth day of the treatment cycle. She will be injected at least once—and often twice—a day with powerful hormones, before and after she ovulates, to stimulate egg production and help support early pregnancy. She will be subject to regular ultrasound examinations. She will probably lose time from work, even if her physician is near her workplace. If she chooses to venture farther afield, to one of the nationally known programs, she will have to live out of a suitcase, away from friends, workmates, and, often, family, until the sixteenth day of the cycle, when the fertilized eggs are transferred to the uterus.

Furthermore, success rates vary widely across clinics. Some clinics have never had a successful pregnancy resulting in a live birth. Others report rates of live deliveries ranging from 3 to 15 percent (after six consecutive attempts in the latter case). Some experts believe that eventually about half of couples will be successful within the first four attempts. Because repeated attempts are necessary, however, and each treatment can cost up to $15,000, in vitro fertilization is an expensive proposition (Brownlee et al., 1994).

Embryo Transplants For about $10,000 for each attempt, a fertilized egg from a female donor can be implanted into an infertile woman. The donor is paid an average of $2000 each time her eggs are removed. This technology is called **embryo transplant** (*embryo* is the term for the developing organism up to the eighth week of pregnancy). Each embryo is much smaller than a period on a printed page but has the potential for developing into an adult human being.

Donating eggs is much more difficult than donating sperm. A woman donor must undergo weeks of daily drug injections before the invasive medical procedure to extract the eggs. She must endure a series of hormonal treatments that routinely lead to a month or more of bloating and discomfort and culminate in painful suctioning of as many as two dozen eggs from her ovaries via a needle inserted through the vagina. On rare occasions, the procedure causes serious complications requiring hospitalization, and in a very few cases worldwide it has proven fatal (Weiss, 2000).

Thus, donors experience considerable risk to their own health. Moreover, the donation of eggs is far less successful than sperm donation; embryo transplant leads to the birth of a child in only 10 to 30 percent of cases.

Despite these difficulties and the expense, egg donation is a growing enterprise that is practiced at hundreds of clinics nationwide. Computer programs match the donors and recipients in terms of race, blood type, and hair and eye color. In 1999, a wealthy couple placed an ad in newspapers on the campuses of such universities as Harvard, Princeton, and Stanford. They offered to pay $50,000 for the eggs of a woman who was an "intelligent, athletic" egg donor, at least 5 feet 10 inches tall, had "no major family medical issues," and an SAT (Scholastic Aptitude Test) score of 1400 or higher. (Each of the verbal and mathematical sections of the SAT is scored on a scale from 200 to 800.) More than 200 college women responded to the ad. Some observers feel that college students are willing to accept the risks of donation both because they may be in debt and because they don't consider the risks involved (Rothman, 1999; Weiss, 2000).

In another controversial case, a 66-year-old proprietor of more than a dozen erotic Websites presented pictures of eight models and offered their eggs for sale to the highest bidder. Although the site apparently fizzled because of public pressure, there was a serious bid of $42,000 for the eggs. In addition, many site visitors paid $24.95 a month for the right to view pictures of the models and bid on their eggs (Weingarten and Hosenball, 1999). Although federal law forbids the purchase and sale of human organs, trafficking in sperm and eggs is legal.

Recently, even women who have gone through menopause have become pregnant using younger women's donated eggs that are fertilized with sperm from the older women's husbands or from other donors (see the box "Motherhood after Menopause"). This is possible because although a woman's ovaries shrivel up after menopause, her other reproductive organs remain viable.

Embryo transplants raise some troubling legal and moral issues: The resulting children are genetically unrelated to the mothers who bear them. Suppose the birth mother later decides that she does not want the child. Is the biological mother then responsible for it? Further, although the risk is less than in artificial insemination, embryo transplant does carry the possibility that genetically related children might one day marry each other.

There is also a question of ownership of the embryos. In 1989, a Tennessee couple that was divorcing went through a heated custody battle over seven frozen embryos that had been produced through IVF. The judge awarded the embryos to the woman. A few years later, however, the Tennessee Supreme Court ruled that the husband could prevent

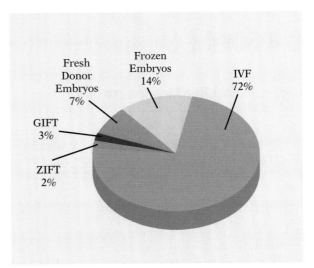

FIGURE 10.4 **Types of ART Procedures Used in the United States, 1997.** In 1997, 71,826 ART cycles (see the definition of a "cycle" in Table 10.3) were carried out in the United States. As this figure shows, most of these cycles (72 percent) used fresh embryos developed from a couple's own egg and sperm.

SOURCE: *1997 Assisted reproductive technology success rates . . . ,* 1999.

his ex-wife from using the embryos because he has the right not to procreate.

Another recent issue is what to do with the "leftovers." Should unwanted embryos be donated? If they are disposed of, is this comparable to abortion? Can the donors place restrictions on the recipients? In one case, for example, the owners of six unwanted embryos required that the recipients raise the baby as a Christian ("Couple wants to give . . . ," 1997). In another case, two fertility clinics in the University of California system were closed after 75 couples who were patients charged that their stored eggs or embryos had been "stolen"—given without their permission to other women, of whom at least 15 later gave birth. The university system agreed to a $14-million lawsuit settlement ("U. of Cal. Settles . . . ," 1997). In another recent case, a doctor mistakenly mixed embryos of two couples, resulting in one couple having twins—one white and one black. The black child was returned to his biological parents, although both sets of parents have agreed that the "twins" will maintain contact with one another ("Child of misplaced embryo . . . ," 1999).

Finally, can lesbian women both be biological parents? In 1999, for example, a lesbian fertilized her egg with the sperm from an anonymous partner. The fertilized egg was then transplanted to her partner, who bore the baby. Because both partners had biological ties to the fetus, a San Francisco court decreed that adoption wasn't necessary. Such rulings may become more

CHANGES ···

Motherhood after Menopause

The Census Bureau and the National Center for Health Statistics define the childbearing years as between 15 and 44, but in recent years, a number of women have had children after menopause:

- In 1992, a 53-year-old woman in California gave birth to a son after five embryos from younger women were fertilized and implanted.
- In 1994, a 59-year-old British woman who was artificially impregnated at a clinic in Italy gave birth to twins.
- In 1994, a 62-year-old Italian woman gave birth to a healthy boy after being implanted with a donated egg fertilized with her husband's sperm.
- In 1996, a 51-year-old Maryland woman gave birth to triplets after eggs, donated by her 31-year-old daughter, were fertilized by her husband and implanted.
- In the same year, a 63-year-old woman became the world's oldest known mother after an anonymous donor's egg was fertilized with sperm from her husband and implanted. The woman claimed to be ten years younger than she was to meet the University of Southern California's infertility clinic's under-55 criteria for assisted reproduction.

Public reaction to these events was mixed. Some people were delighted that older women have more options. Men, after all, can and do father children well into old age (remember the Tony Randall example?). Others felt childbearing at such late ages is selfish because both parents might die while the child is very young. In 1994, the French government passed a law barring postmenopausal women from artificial impregnation because it is "both immoral and dangerous for older women to be implanted with test-tube embryos." (Note that no government has required men over age 50 to have vasectomies.) In 1995, Italy's national association of physicians voted to deny artificial insemination to lesbians, single women, and women over 50. The association also banned surrogate motherhood and the use of frozen sperm of dead donors for artificial insemination, and prohibited married couples from seeking "designer babies" by choosing sperm based on a donor's physical attributes or social status.

---

common in the future. They raise prickly questions about parenthood, however, in societies that disapprove of *any* gay relationships (see Chapters 1 and 5 to 9). If the moms split up, for example, who can establish parenthood rights—the sperm donor, the egg donor, the mother who bears the child, or all three people?

Surrogacy   Surrogacy has a long history. In the Book of Genesis, Abraham's barren wife, Sarah, sends her husband to "lie with" the slave girl Hagar, hoping to "found a family." Jacob's wife, Rachel, makes a similar arrangement with her slave girl, Billah, "so that she may bear sons to be laid upon my knees" (Institute for Philosophy and Public Policy, 1989: 1). Today surrogacy is quite common even though the success rate is only 31 percent ("1997 Assisted reproductive technology . . . ," 1999).

In **surrogacy**, a woman who is capable of carrying a pregnancy to term serves as a surrogate mother for a woman who cannot bear children. Commonly, the surrogate is artificially inseminated with the sperm of the infertile woman's husband, and if she conceives, she carries the child to term. In some cases, the infertile couple's egg and sperm are brought together in vitro; and the resulting embryo is implanted in a surrogate who carries the child for them. Although the typical surrogate mother is 25 years old, married, and a high school graduate who agrees to surrogacy for a fee, some surrogates are family members. In 1991, for example, a 42-year-old woman in South Dakota served as a surrogate for her 22-year-old daughter who was born without a uterus. Eggs were removed from the daughter's ovaries, fertilized with her husband's sperm, and implanted in the mother's womb. When the mother gave birth to healthy twins she became the first grandmother to give birth to her own grandchildren. And in 1992, a woman in Buffalo, New York, underwent four implants of fertilized eggs from her son and daughter-in-law, ultimately giving birth to her grandson. Thus, surrogacy raises complicated questions about kinship.

One of the risks associated with surrogacy is that a surrogate mother might decide to keep the baby. In 1987, Mary Beth Whitehead delivered "Baby M," whom she bore after being impregnated through artificial insemination by William Stern. Stern and his wife, who said she could not bear a child, had hired Whitehead as a surrogate. Whitehead, however, refused to give up the baby girl after birth. In the court battles that followed she lost custody but was later granted visitation rights. In 1990, a surrogate mother in Garden Grove, California, also refused to give up custody of a baby boy who had been conceived in a petri dish using the biological parents' sperm and egg. Even though she was not genetically related to the baby, the surrogate mother said she had become emotionally attached to the fetus by the third month of pregnancy. A superior court judge denied her both custody and visitation rights (Walker, 1990).

Many people who object to surrogacy argue that it exploits poor women because rich couples can "rent a womb." According to some, Mary Beth Whitehead's contract with William Stern was extremely disadvantageous to her. She was obliged to assume all risks, including death and postpartum complications, and was offered no compensation in case of miscarriage and only $1000 if Stern demanded an abortion (Whitehead and Schwartz-Nobel, 1989). The typical surrogate mother is paid only about $10,000 for her services. The surrogate also risks pain, disease, surgery, and even death. Furthermore, the natural father is often not contractually obligated to accept custody of a "defective" baby (Chesler, 1988).

Genetic Engineering: Its Benefits and Risks   Genetic research and biotechnology have been a blessing for many couples, but some wonder if scientists are going too far (see the box "So What's Next? Pregnant Men?"). Although many people in the United States and other countries support in vitro fertilization, they also worry that genetic manipulation for a presumably good purpose could lead to interfering with nature in other ways that would be unethical and detrimental to society (Macer, 1994).

Consider the implications of prenatal testing designed to detect genetic disorders and biochemical abnormalities in the fetus. Two procedures that have become fairly common are **amniocentesis** and **chorionic villus sampling (CV)**. In amniocentesis, performed during the twentieth week of pregnancy, a needle is inserted through the abdomen into the amniotic sac, and the fluid withdrawn is analyzed for such abnormalities as Down syndrome and spina bifida (an abnormal opening along the spine). The same information can be produced at ten weeks by chorionic villi sampling, in which a catheter inserted through the vagina is used to remove some of the villi, or protrusions from the chorion that surrounds the amniotic sac. The chief advantage of detecting abnormalities early is that if parents decide on an abortion, a simpler technique can be utilized. Both these tests have risks such as spontaneous abortions and possible deformities, however (Boodman, 1992). Through a newer procedure, called *BABI (blastomere analysis before implantation)*, some couples have chosen to conceive several embryos in test tubes, keeping only the embryo that has no known defects.

CHANGES •

So What's Next? Pregnant Men?

In the movie *Junior*, a scientist (played by Arnold Schwarzenegger) loses funding for his research and implants a fertilized egg in his own body to test a wonder drug that ensures healthy pregnancies. According to Dick Teresi (1994: 54–55), we have all the technology we need right now to make a man pregnant.

Of course, there are some minor problems. Men don't produce the appropriate hormones. Men don't have ovaries and thus don't produce eggs. Men don't have wombs. However, hormones can be supplied by injection. In the first "test-tube" pregnancy, an egg was extracted from the mother and fertilized with the father's sperm in vitro, or in a laboratory dish, inserted back into the mother, and carried to term.

And as for wombs, they may not be totally necessary. Abdominal pregnancies—outside the womb—are rare, but they do happen about once in every 10,000 pregnancies.

An abdominal pregnancy may occur when the placenta, which is produced partly by the fetus, attaches to something other than the womb. In August 1979, for example, George Poretta attempted to perform an appendectomy on a Michigan woman suffering from stomach cramps. "I opened her up expecting to find an appendix," Poretta said, "and there was this tiny foot." The baby, a boy, weighed 3 pounds 5 ounces.

Both male and female abdomens offer a similar environment, including a membrane called the omentum that encloses abdominal organs and in which, theoretically, a fertilized egg could implant. Thus, Teresi suggests, fertilizing an egg in vitro and inserting the developing embryo through a small incision in the abdominal cavity could produce a male pregnancy. Luck would be required for the fertilized egg to implant in the omentum (a little bit of luck is needed even in normal pregnancies), but if it did and the placenta partly developed from the embryo, pregnancy could be under way. An endocrinologist could administer hormones to keep gestation going. Finally, the baby would be delivered via laparotomy, not unlike a cesarean section. A sci-fi dream? Or a sci-fi nightmare?

Both the advent of BABI and the 1993 decision of Congress to lift the ban on embryo development research (studying embryos outside of the womb to learn more about various diseases) have created controversy. Both technologies risk the destruction of embryos, an act that some people regard as abortion (which we discuss later in this chapter) and that some critics find unethical (Cowley et al., 1993; Zapler, 1995). There is also concern about such issues as parents' and scientists' right to "manufacture" babies, creating "designer babies" by choosing genes for a child's hair color and height, parents' right to reject imperfect fetuses, and the rights of both parents and embryos. Suppose, for example, both parents of a fertilized egg that has been frozen and held for future use die. Who is responsible for the frozen embryo? Should it be destroyed because the parents are dead? Given to relatives? Placed for adoption? Turned over to doctors for medical research?

Because of fertility drugs and ART, the annual number of multiple births has quadrupled (see Data Digest). Such drugs as Pergonal or Netrodin result in a woman's ovaries releasing as many as 40 eggs in one cycle instead of one egg during a normal cycle. Fertility drugs are more popular, at $2000 a cycle, than more expensive ART procedures (see *Table 10.3*). Since the birth of the Iowa septuplets, many fertility experts have become critical of physicians who don't limit the number of embryos implanted during IVF to three or four because "the human uterus is not meant to carry litters" (Cowley and Springen, 1997: 66).

Even if they're born alive, most multiple-birth babies are premature. Triplets, quadruplets, and quintuplets are 12 times more likely than other babies to die within a year. Many suffer from respiratory and digestive problems. They're also prone to a range of neurological disorders, including blindness, cerebral palsy, and mental retardation. At age 2, three of the Iowa septuplets were suffering serious health problems that included several forms of cerebral palsy, digestive problems that required feeding of high-calorie formula through tubes in the toddlers' stomachs, and an inability to walk or sit up without help ("McCaughey septuplets . . . ," 1999).

Finally, a recent advance has made it theoretically possible to help infertile women to conceive by using eggs or ovarian tissue from aborted fetuses or cadavers. British scientists who have successfully transplanted ovaries in mice and sheep believe the procedure could be carried out in humans. Thus, egg-bearing ovarian tissue from aborted fetuses might be transplanted into infertile women, or eggs or ovaries from women who have died suddenly could also be transplanted. Many infertile couples applaud such technological progress, but others condemn such research as bizarre or even ghoulish. As Robinson (1994) points out, some complicated interpersonal relationships might ensue from such activity. For example, how would you explain to your child that his or her biological mother had never even been born or had died before she could ever conceive?

In 1999, and the first known birth of its kind in the United States, a California woman had a baby using sperm retrieved from her husband 30 hours after he died unexpectedly of an allergic reaction. The reproductive specialist who extracted the sperm cells did so to allay the family's stress and grief. Medical ethicists wondered, however, if it's appropriate to bring a child into this world whose father is dead ("Woman gives birth . . . ," 1999).

Having Children Outside of Marriage

As we've seen so far, parenthood has benefits and costs, birth rates in the United States have decreased steadily since the turn of the twentieth century, many people have been postponing marriage, and those who are infertile have choices such as adoption and assisted reproductive options. Two other important topics in understanding the choices that people have and the constraints they encounter in becoming parents are nonmarital pregnancy and deciding to remain childless. We examine, first, how and why out-of-wedlock trends have changed. The last section focuses on voluntary childlessness.

Characteristics of Nonmarital Childbearing

In 1998, almost three of every ten births in the United States were to unwed mothers, an almost eightfold increase since 1940. Why have out-of-wedlock births increased? The reasons encompass a multitude of decisions and complex processes that stretch across a lifetime. We've seen, for example, that cultural values about nonmarital sex and out-of-wedlock child rearing have become more tolerant (Chapter 6) and that many people are postponing marriage, which increases the chances of premarital births (Chapter 8). As a 35-year-old public relations executive stated, "I decided I could live without a husband but I didn't want to go through life without being a mother" (Eckel, 1999). Well-educated and financially autonomous women, especially, may go forward with an unplanned pregnancy if their family and friends are supportive (Mannis, 1999).

Nonmarital childbearing is often accompanied by a decline of financial resources (Burton, 1995; Wu, 1996). If, however, a nonmarital birth is followed by marriage, the economic status of mothers who bore a child before or after marriage is very similar. The most economically disadvantaged mothers are those who never marry and who continue to have babies (Driscoll et al., 1999). Thus, economic outcomes are shaped by

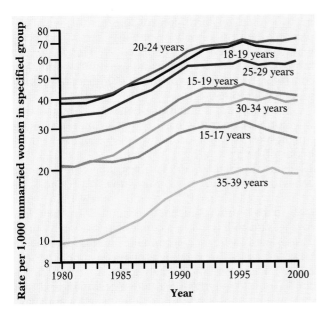

FIGURE 10.5   Birth Rates for Unmarried Women, by Age of Mother: United States, 1980–98

SOURCE: Ventura, Martin, et al., 2000, Figure 3.

birth and marriage, regardless of their order, rather than just nonmarital childbearing.

Variations by Age   Contrary to popular belief, unmarried teenagers have lower out-of-wedlock rates than older unmarried women. Since 1980, the highest birth rates for unmarried women were for women aged 18–19 and 20–24 years, followed closely by women aged 25–29 years. While teenage unmarried births started to decline in 1994, those for women aged 20–29 continued to increase (see *Figure 10.5*). Nonetheless, 79 percent of births to teenagers are out of wedlock (Moore et al., 1999).

There are a number of reasons for the declining unmarried teen birth rates. Several recent surveys indicate that teenagers are becoming less sexually active, while those who are active appear more likely to use contraceptives than in the past (Abma et al., 1997; Darroch and Singh, 1999; Ventura, Mosher et al., 2000). Another factor may be the long economic expansion in the 1990s. As more jobs with good pay became available, some teens postponed early pregnancy and parenthood (Ventura, Curtin et al., 2000). Community leaders feel that pro-abstinence organizations, churches, parents, and "blunt" school sex education programs also explain some of the reasons for the decline in teenage births (Shatzkin, 1999; Davis-Packard, 2000).

Variations by Race and Ethnicity   In terms of race and ethnicity, in 1998 the number of births for unmarried women was higher for white women (517,153)

than for black women (410,971) or Latinas (305,442) (Ventura, Martin et al., 2000). Proportionately, however, the number of out-of-wedlock births varies considerably across groups. As *Figure 10.6* shows, 16 percent of Asian/Pacific Islander births were to unmarried women compared to 60 percent for American Indian women and 69 percent for black women. In addition, there is much variation *within* groups. Among Asian/Pacific Islanders, for example, 6 percent of births were to unmarried Chinese women compared to almost 20 percent for Filipinas and 51 percent for Hawaiian women. And among Latinas, the births to unmarried women ranged from 60 percent for Puerto Rican women to 25 percent for Cuban women (Ventura, Martin et al., 2000).

Variations by Educational Attainment   Educational differences account for some of the differences in nonmarital childbearing among different racial and ethnic groups. Unmarried women with less than a high school diploma are at least three times as likely to have a baby as unmarried women with some college (Ventura, Bachrach et al., 1995). The finding that birth rates of college-educated women are lower than those of women with lower educational levels has led some researchers to conclude that the most effective way to reduce pregnancy, especially for teenagers, is to improve teenagers' educational and earning opportunities. If young people expect to work throughout their lives and find work worthwhile, it is argued, they will delay childbearing (Plotnick, 1993; Robinson and Frank, 1994; Trent, 1994). Educated women usually have more job opportunities, more awareness of family planning, and more decision-making power. They are also more likely to marry late, to postpone the first pregnancy, to leave more time between births, and to have fewer children (UNICEF, 1994).

FIGURE 10.6   Percent of Births to Unmarried Mothers, by Race and Ethnicity: 1998

SOURCE: Based on Ventura, Martin et al., 2000, Tables 13 and 14.

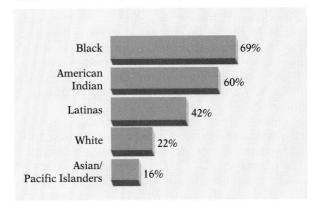

Drawing by Modell. © 1994 The New Yorker Magazine, Inc.

Some people believe that contraceptives and attitudes about abortion affect nonmarital childbearing rates. We begin with an examination of the impact of contraceptive practices.

Contraceptive Practices

Contraception, which is the prevention of pregnancy by behavioral, mechanical, or chemical methods, means different things in different social contexts. More than a quarter of nonmarital births occur to partners who cohabit, for example (Moore, 1995). Because most cohabiting relationships are short-lived, a lack of communication about or disagreement over contraceptive use may result in unintended pregnancy (Brown and Eisenberg, 1995). (Appendix D describes the most common contraceptives, including their usage, effectiveness, and possible problems.)

Adolescents and Parenthood Many young people view teenage parenthood negatively. In a recent national survey, for example, four out of five youths aged 18 to 22 said that becoming a teen parent is one of the worst things that could happen to a 16-year-old girl or boy. Only 15 percent of the births to girls aged 17 and younger are planned (Moore and Snyder, 1994). Why, then, is unmarried teenage pregnancy so common?

One of the primary reasons for teenage pregnancy is the failure of teenagers to use contraceptives: Nearly 15 percent of teenage women never use contraceptives (Abma et al., 1997). There are a variety of reasons: procrastination ("I just didn't get around to it"); fear that the family might find out; and not knowing where to get birth control information when it's not provided by schools or parents (Zabin and Hayward, 1993). According to Furstenberg (1991), for the most part, our society keeps information about birth control in "a plain brown wrapper" instead of making it accessible to teenagers.

Some teenagers intentionally have a baby to satisfy emotional or status needs. "Babies may become a sought-after symbol of status, of passage to adulthood, of being a 'grown' woman" (Anderson, 1990: 127; see also Sander, 1991). Regarding contraceptive behavior, Marsiglio (1993) found that black and Latino men aged 15 to 19 were more likely than white men to have discussed contraception with their last partner and to have used a condom at last intercourse. Those who were socioeconomically disadvantaged, however, tended to view paternity as a source of self-esteem. They were more likely to say that fathering a child would make them feel like a real man and that they would be pleased with an unplanned pregnancy.

Although economically and socially disadvantaged teenagers are three to four times more likely to bear children out of wedlock than are more advantaged teenagers, not all disadvantaged teenagers become pregnant. For example, in a study of poor black teenagers who ranged in age from 13 to 17, Freeman and Rickels (1993) found that those who successfully avoided childbearing had educational goals beyond high school and families that supported their goals and actively discouraged early childbearing.

There is one other important influence that cuts across these choices. A number of female adolescent sexual experiences are coercive (see Chapter 6). One national survey found that 24 percent of women aged 13 or younger and 10 percent of those aged 19–24 at the time of their first premarital intercourse reported that the experience was nonvoluntary. The same study found that women who as children have lived with a single parent from birth or had left home at ages younger than 16 were more likely than others to have experienced nonvoluntary first intercourse (Abma et al., 1998). Thus, there may be an important link between parental absence in the home, forced sexual experiences, and adolescent nonmarital births (B. C. Miller, 1995).

Family planning services are now less available to many teenagers, especially those in inner cities, than they were a decade ago. Between 1980 and 1992, total public expenditures for contraceptive services declined by 27 percent. Consequently, both family planning clinic personnel and state administrators report that, in response to reduction in funding for family planning during the past decade, they have charged higher fees, laid off staff, cut salaries, reduced hours, closed clinics, eliminated some services, and reduced education and outreach efforts (Moore and Snyder, 1994).

Many people claim that the availability of public assistance encourages out-of-wedlock births (see

CROSS CULTURAL

Contraceptive Policies in China

China makes up nearly 20 percent of the world's population. Since 1979 its government has maintained a strict policy of one child per family in order to limit the country's rapid population growth. The 1982 Chinese constitution made practicing birth control a civic duty. Some rural areas, however, are exempt from this regulation. The reinstitution of family farming under China's economic reforms encouraged farmers to have more children to help in the fields. Many affluent farmers are able to pay the fines imposed for having more than one child, and in many rural areas farmers whose first child is a girl are allowed to try again.

Most families are not exempt from family size restrictions, and some of the most populous areas in central China have enacted new rules and fines for illegal pregnancies. Fines for pregnancy can run as high as 33 percent of the average peasant's annual income, and if the woman refuses an abortion, the couple faces an additional fine of 20 percent for each of the child's first seven years. Local officials have also imposed sizable fines on women who have one child and who are not using an IUD and on healthy men or women who have two children and have not undergone sterilization.

Besides these sanctions, the government offers many incentives for practicing birth control: monthly bonuses; private plots of land; free medical, educational, and kindergarten facilities for the single child; and priority for jobs in rural industries. Although fertility rates started declining before the one-child policy, China has reduced its fertility rates from 6 births per woman in 1965 to 1.7 in 1994 (Cowell, 1994). In addition, an estimated 10 percent of couples of childbearing age, primarily those who are well educated and live in urban areas, are choosing not to have children (Zhou, 1994).

Some provinces in China are experimenting with policies to raise women's status, on the theory that if girls are seen as more desirable, couples with a daughter may stop trying for a son. For example, girls with no brothers attend the local school for free, while parents pay $7.50 a semester for boys. A girl's parents can enroll in a pension plan that will guarantee them nominal pensions in their old age. The parents also get preferential access to jobs in village enterprises. When the girls are old enough, they will get first access to the same jobs (Lawrence, 1994).

Some observers contend that China is losing its "war" on births because the one-child enforcement varies from town to town, province to province, and year to year. As a result, 80 percent of China's children have brothers or sisters, and many have both (Pomfret, 2000).

Moffitt, 1995). However, a team of researchers who studied 37 countries found that welfare support was much higher in all other Western countries. The countries surveyed provided extensive benefits for childbearing, food supplements, housing, and family allowances, as well as higher amounts than the average payments from Aid to Families with Dependent Children (AFDC) in the United States. Nonetheless, they still had lower teenage birth rates (Jones et al., 1986).

Contraception in Other Countries   Approximately 57 percent of couples throughout the world practice contraception. About 25 percent of the time one partner is sterilized, and about 6 percent of the time, it is the woman. Another 12 percent of couples use intrauterine devices, and 7 percent use the Pill. Another 13 percent use condoms, the rhythm method, or withdrawal (Neft and Levine, 1997).

China, which is confronting overwhelming population growth, has instituted a government policy that permits each family to have only one child. Despite its enormous size, great internal diversity, and relatively less advanced level of technological sophistication, China has been extremely successful in providing contraceptive information and technology to its people

and persuading them to use it (see the box on "Contraceptive Policies in China").

Japan's problem is the opposite of China's. Japan has the lowest fertility rate in the world; the average woman of childbearing age has only 1.38 children (compared to 1.87 for the United States), down from 4.54 in 1949 (Mosher, 2000). Demographers attribute the plunging rate to several factors. Although Japan has one of the strongest economies in the world and faces a labor shortage, almost half of the nation's salaried workers are dissatisfied with their quality of life. In particular, wives who live with their in-laws report discontent (Kamo, 1990). Individual housing is cramped, and there is a scarcity of neighborhood parks and playgrounds. Moreover, raising a child is very expensive because of the high costs of sending children to special cram courses or to the right private school to ensure their entry into an elite university. Women—41 percent of whom are in the labor force—are increasingly unhappy with traditional female roles. Even when women are employed, men do only about 6 percent of the housework and 11 percent of the work caring for children and old people (Gaouette, 1998; Butler, 1999). Finally, because of increasing educational and employment opportunities for women and the growing disenchantment with marriage, many women are postponing marriage or deciding to remain single (Klitsch, 1994).

Abortion

Abortion is a fiercely controversial issue in the United States. According to a recent Roper poll, only 40 percent of the respondents said that a woman should be able to get an abortion if she wants one, no matter what the reason. While 64 percent felt that abortion should be "generally legal" in the first three months of pregnancy, only 26 percent said it should be legal in the second trimester ("Abortion now divides Americans . . . ," 1998).

Abortion is the expulsion of the embryo or fetus from the uterus. It can occur naturally—as in a spontaneous abortion, or *miscarriage*—or it can be induced medically. Practiced by people in all societies, abortion was not forbidden by the Catholic Church until 1869 and was legal in the United States until the mid-nineteenth century. It became illegal not for moral or religious reasons but out of political, economic, and ideological considerations. According to Rothman (1989), physicians redefined abortion and childbirth as medical issues to eliminate competition from midwives and other nonmedical practitioners, most of whom were women. Furthermore, Mohr (1981) claims, when abortion became widespread among white, married, Protestant, American-born women in the middle and upper classes, concern that the country would be overpopulated by "inferior" new ethnic groups with higher birth rates led to the outlawing of this procedure during the late 1800s.

Abortion Laws and Reactions Anti-abortion laws went unchallenged until the 1960s and abortion remained illegal until 1973, when the *Roe v. Wade* decision made abortion legal. Since then, there have been a number of changes in abortion laws. Some states have cut or limited funds for clinics in low-income urban areas, and dozens of states have cut Medicaid funding for abortions. Teenagers in many states must now get approval from a parent, judge, or counselor before seeking an abortion.

Throughout the 1990s, some radical antiabortion organizations murdered several doctors, burned or bombed 39 clinics, and attempted 16 murders of physicians or staff who performed abortions. Others set up Internet "hit lists" of physicians, clinic owners and workers, and judges and politicians who supported abortion rights. The sites listed doctors by name, gave their home addresses, identified their spouses and children, and detailed the routes that doctors used to go to work every day. Doctors who had been murdered had a line crossed through their names. In 1999, a jury in Portland, Oregon, fined the Website $105 million, but the American Civil Liberties Union plans

to appeal the court decision (see Lafferty, 1999; Sanchez, 1999).

Because of pressure from antiabortion activists, few doctors in rural areas perform abortions. It is estimated that in 83 percent of counties in the United States, not a single physician is willing to provide abortion services. In some states, like the Dakotas, for instance, women have to travel hundreds of miles for proper medical attention (Goodman, 1993; Banisky, 1994). In addition, fewer hospitals offer abortion services or include such training during the obstetrics residency program for young physicians. As a result, fewer new physicians are skilled in performing abortions. Some seek such experience at local clinics, but many don't because they fear being picketed at home or even murdered by extreme antiabortion groups (Goldstein, 1998).

Characteristics of Women Who Seek Abortions
The number of abortions performed in the United States dropped from 1.6 million in 1990 to 1.2 million in 1996 (the most recent year for which data are available). Some reasons for this decrease include the greater use of condoms because of the fear of HIV/AIDS; the decision by more single women to keep their babies; and better contraceptive use, especially by teenagers (Vobejda, 1997). Nearly 33 percent of all pregnancies are terminated by abortion, and 91 percent of these within the first trimester. Abortion is most common among women who are young, white, and unmarried (see *Figure 10.7*), but black women are almost twice as likely as women of other racial groups to get an abortion. These variations are probably related to socioeconomic differences rather than to race. For example, women with annual incomes of less than $15,000 are four times as likely to have abortions as women with family incomes of $60,000 or above (Wagner, 1998).

Many people have the impression that the highest abortion rates are among teenagers. As *Figure 10.7* shows, however, women aged 20–24 obtain approximately one-third of all abortions. The decline in the unmarried birth rate we discussed in the previous section is *not* due to an increase in abortion. In fact, abortion rates for teenagers aged 15–19 declined by 22 percent between 1991 and 1996 (Moore et al., 1999). As you saw earlier, much of the decrease in unmarried teen births has been due to less sexual activity and an increase in the percentage of adolescent females who report using contraception.

Is Abortion Safe? Safety can be measured on two levels—physical and emotional. On the physical level, a legal abortion in the first trimester (up to 12 weeks) is safer than driving a car, using oral contraceptives, undergoing sterilization, or even continuing a pregnancy (see *Table 10.4*). For many black women, for instance, giving birth is more dangerous than getting

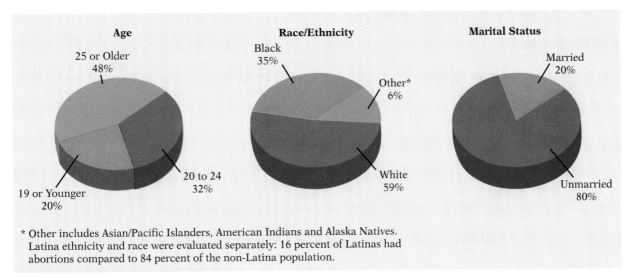

* Other includes Asian/Pacific Islanders, American Indians and Alaska Natives. Latina ethnicity and race were evaluated separately: 16 percent of Latinas had abortions compared to 84 percent of the non-Latina population.

FIGURE 10.7   Who Has Abortions?

SOURCE: Based on Koonin et al., 1999, Table 1.

an abortion. Nationally, the maternal death rate is 3.3 deaths per 100,000 live births, but the maternal death rates among black women are four times higher than those for white women (U.S. Census Bureau, 1999c). Researchers don't know for sure what is causing this gap. Some of the difference may be due to lifestyle differences (such as smoking) or medical complications, particularly hypertension. Even when black women receive the same level of medical care during pregnancy as white women, however, the maternal mortality gap persists.

As for emotional health, there is no evidence that abortion has long-term, negative psychological consequences. In the mid-1980s, C. Everett Koop, U.S. Surgeon General, outraged conservatives when he reported that the scientific research did not show that abortion has harmful effects. Several recent studies have drawn the same conclusions. In one study, women who underwent an abortion in the first trimester showed no later psychological distress (Raymond, 1990). A longitudinal study of unmarried black teenagers who were 17 years old or younger found that those who had abortions were more likely to graduate from high school and were less likely to become pregnant over the subsequent two years than were their counterparts who bore a child (Zabin et al., 1986). One study suggests that, without abortion, many young single mothers would have closely spaced children, which would increase economic stress and risk more child abuse and neglect (Russo et al., 1993).

This does not mean that women who have abortions never suffer from emotional problems. Anecdotal data suggest that some women have feelings of sadness, guilt, sin, or remorse. Women who have unplanned pregnancies report disliking themselves and their bodies right after the abortion. Some feel violated, unattractive, or like failures because they didn't control their reproduction. And the insistence by increasing numbers of biological fathers that women should not abort their offspring without their knowledge may increase the potential for feelings of guilt in some women and an initial disappointment with men in others (Kushner, 1997).

Attitudes about Abortion   To many, the basic conflict between abortion proponents and opponents seems clear-cut. Antiabortion proponents insist that the embryo/fetus is not just a mass of cells but a human being from the time of conception and therefore has the right to live. On the other hand, many abortion advocates believe that the organism at the moment of conception lacks a brain and other specifically and uniquely human attributes like consciousness and reasoning. Abortion proponents also believe that a pregnant woman has a right to decide what will happen in and to her body. These very different perspectives have resulted in political clashes over the development of abortion-type drugs. Sometimes called "morning-after" birth control, oral contraceptive pills taken within 72 hours after sexual intercourse prevent implantation of the fertilized ovum in the uterine wall. RU 486, a synthetic steroid, can be administered within six weeks after unprotected intercourse. It causes the uterus to shed its lining in which a fertilized egg must implant. Morning-after pills are controversial. Opponents claim they are *abortifacients*, substances that cause termination of pregnancy. Proponents maintain they are contraceptives because they prevent pregnancy and abortion.

TABLE 10.4

How Risky Is Abortion?

Activity	Chance of Dying
Motorcycling	1 in 1000
Illegal abortion	1 in 3000
Driving a car	1 in 6000
Power boating	1 in 6000
Legal abortion after 15 weeks	1 in 8700
Continuing a pregnancy	1 in 14,300
Oral contraception use (smoker)	1 in 16,000
Legal abortion between 13 to 15 weeks	1 in 23,000
Playing football	1 in 25,000
Sexual intercourse (risk of pelvic infection)	1 in 50,000
Oral contraception use (nonsmoker)	1 in 63,000
Tubal ligation	1 in 67,000
Legal abortion between 9 and 12 weeks	1 in 67,000
Using IUD	1 in 100,000
Vasectomy	1 in 300,000
Tampons (risk of toxic shock syndrome), ages 15–44	1 in 350,000
Legal abortion before 9 weeks	1 in 500,000

SOURCE: Hatcher et al., 1990.

Attitudes about abortion vary across and within ethnic and racial groups. White adults are more likely (52 percent) than black adults (45 percent) to support abortion (Benson and Herrmann, 1999). Although 40 percent of Latino adults feel that abortion should be legal in all or most cases, such support varies—from a low of 32 percent for Central and South Americans to a high of 60 percent for Puerto Ricans ("Differences within," 2000).

Many teenage mothers reject abortion. Black and Latino adolescents are more likely than white and Asian adolescents to feel that if they get pregnant, most of the people important to them would be against having an abortion (Adler and Tschann, 1993). Older black women are more likely than their white counterparts or younger black women to discourage abortion because of religious beliefs or the view that family planning is a form of black genocide (see Lynxwiler and Gay, 1994). Moreover, because many black communities place a high value on having children, they are more accepting of the out-of-wedlock child than are many white communities (see Chapter 6). Some observers also note that Latino teenagers are reluctant to seek information about contraception because of the Catholic Church's adamant opposition to contraception and abortion.

Abortion in Other Countries About 38 percent of the world's population lives in countries where abortion is available on request. Another 46 percent lives in countries where abortion is legal in certain situations, ranging from preserving the woman's mental health to cases where the fetus is physically impaired, or when the pregnancy resulted from rape or incest. The remaining 16 percent of the population lives in countries where abortion is legal only when it is necessary to save the woman's life. Since Islam and Catholicism strictly forbid abortion, the great majority of these countries—such as Guatemala, Iran, Ireland, Lebanon, Philippines, Syria, and Venezuela—are overwhelmingly Islamic or Roman Catholic. Only a few countries—Chile, Andorra, Djibouti, and Malta—do not allow abortion for any reason at all (Neft and Levine, 1997).

Every year an estimated 20 million women worldwide resort to unsafe, illegal abortions. The vast majority live in developing countries with strict abortion laws and strong cultural and religious prohibitions against the use of contraceptives. The highest incidence of illegal abortion is in South America, where an estimated 41 out of every 1000 women of childbearing age undergo this procedure each year. It is estimated that in many developing countries, complications from illegal abortions may account for as many as 70 percent of all gynecological hospital admissions (Neft and Levine, 1997).

Abortion is a highly controversial issue in many countries. In Australia, for example, bills have been introduced to restrict government health payments for abortion. In Israel, where abortion is relatively accessible, religious political parties are exploring ways to limit abortion. In Germany, antiabortionists are campaigning to make it virtually impossible for a woman to have an abortion unless her physical health is endangered. In England, lobby groups have tried to impose a shortened time limit for abortion.

Childless by Choice

Just as some couples make a conscious decision to have a child, others decide not to have children. The desire to have children is not universal. According to a 1990 nationwide survey, 4 percent of respondents said that they did not have children, did not want them, or were glad they had none (Gallup and Newport, 1990). Although by 1992 the proportion of couples who

Abortion continues to be a hotly-contested issue in many countries. In January, 1998, the National Abortion and Reproductive Rights League (NARAL) sponsored a rally to mark the 25th anniversary of the Roe v Wade decision that legalized abortion in the United States. Such rallies are usually well attended by anti-abortion protesters.

planned not to have children had reached 7 percent, childless families are still a minority (Bachu, 1993). A recent study found, however, that though a sizable proportion of both men and women intend to be childless, many change their minds and have children. In effect, then, some childless couples may be postponing rather than rejecting parenthood (Heaton et al., 1999).

The major reason that couples remain intentionally child-free is the freedom to do what they want:

Non-parents never have to budget for diapers or college educations. They can make decisions about where to live without worrying about the quality of local schools or which pediatricians offer weekend hours. They can even experience parenthood vicariously through nieces, nephews, and friends' children—but only if they choose to. (Crispell, 1993: 23–24)

This freedom may well be one of the reasons childless couples say they are very happy. Women report enjoying stimulating discussions with their husbands, sharing projects and outside interests, a more egalitarian division of household labor, devoting their passions to work and volunteering, and avoiding troubling child–parent relationships that they themselves encountered (Somers, 1993; Safer, 1996; Casey, 1998).

Some couples remain childless due to inertia. A national study found, for example, that when cou-

ples disagreed about having a child, the partner who wanted a child postponed further discussion, sometimes indefinitely (Thomson, 1997). People have different reasons for being childless. Some married later in life and decided not to have children. As one husband said: "I didn't want to be 65 with a teenager in the house" (Fost, 1996: 16). Some are teachers or other professionals who work with children but like to "come home to peace and quiet and a relaxing night with my husband" (May, 1995: 205). For others, marriage is a precondition for parenthood:

. . . a thirty-five-year old divorced Black attorney who had grown up in a "secure two-parent family" wanted to have children as a part of a committed relationship with "two on-site, full-time loving parents." She had two abortions because the men involved "weren't ready for the responsibility of fatherhood," and she did not want to be a single mother. (May, 1995: 193)

Today the general public is much more accepting of childless couples than in the past. Despite the shifts in societal attitudes toward the childless, some people are still suspicious of couples without children: "Throughout the culture, motherhood is celebrated while childlessness is promoted as a sorry state" (Morell, 1994: 1). Childless couples are often seen as self-indulgent, selfish, self-absorbed, workaholics, less well adjusted emotionally, and less sensitive and loving, and have even been stereotyped as "weirdos," "child haters," or "barren, career-crazed boomers" (Arenofsky, 1993).

Why do these stereotypes exist? Perhaps couples with children resent the childless because the latter have (or seem to have) more freedom, time, money, and fun. As you will see in the next chapter, raising children is not an easy task, and parents sometimes feel unappreciated. A childless lifestyle can sometimes look very attractive.

Conclusion

Attitudes about becoming a parent have *changed* considerably, even during the last generation. There are more *choices* today than in the past in postponing parenthood, becoming pregnant despite infertility, and having children outside of marriage. These choices are bounded by *constraints*, however, and many expectations are contradictory. We accept adults' postponing parenthood but are still somewhat suspicious of people who decide to remain childless. We recognize that most teenagers will encounter parenting problems, but reducing teenage pregnancy is still a low priority. We are developing reproductive technologies that help infertile couples become pregnant, but have many hazardous work environments that increase their chances of becoming infertile and of giving birth to infants with lifelong physical and mental disabilities. In addition, the high costs of reproductive technologies limit their availability to couples who are at the higher end of the socioeconomic scale. Even when the poor do not want babies, we cut off funds that provide information about contraception and restrict access to abortion services. Despite all these contradictions, most people look forward to raising children, which is the focus of the next chapter.

SUMMARY

1. Parenthood is an important rite of passage. Unlike other major turning points in our lives, becoming a parent is permanent and irreversible. People today have both more choices and more constraints in planning and having children than in the past.

2. There are both benefits and costs in having children. The benefits include emotional fulfillment and personal satisfaction. The costs include a decline in marital satisfaction, problems in finding adequate housing, and generally high expenditures.

3. Fertility rates in the United States have fluctuated in the past 70 years but are still low worldwide. Fertility rates are higher for Latinas than other women, but there are intragroup variations. For example, for several socioeconomic reasons, Mexican American women have much higher birth rates than do Cuban American women.

4. Postponing parenthood is a common phenomenon. On the one hand, remaining childless as long as possible has many attractive features, including independence and building a career. On the other hand, there are costs, such as finding it impossible to have children later in life.

5. Approximately 15 percent of all couples are involuntarily childless. The reasons for infertility include physical and physiological difficulties, environmental hazards, and unhealthy lifestyles.

6. Couples have a variety of options if they are infertile, including adoption, artificial insemination, in vitro fertilization, embryo transplants, and surrogacy.

7. Some emerging issues in the area of adoption include the rights of the biological father, transracial adoption, and open adoption.

8. Contrary to popular belief, women in their twenties have higher rates of unwed childbearing than do teenagers. The percentages of teenagers who are unmarried mothers have been decreasing, but vary by race and ethnicity. There are both micro- and macro-level reasons for the surge of out-of-wedlock children.

9. Improved contraceptive techniques and the availability of abortion have resulted in fewer unwanted births. The incidence of abortion has declined since 1990, but abortion continues to be a hotly debated issue in the United States and some other countries.

10. Couples who decide not to have children are still a minority, but remaining childless is becoming more acceptable.

KEY TERMS

fetal alcohol syndrome (FAS)   *248*
postpartum depression   *248*
birth rate   *249*
fertility rate   *249*
infertility   *252*
pelvic inflammatory disease (PID)   *252*
chlamydia   *252*
endometriosis   *252*
open adoption   *256*

assisted reproductive technology (ART)   *257*
artificial insemination   *258*
fertility-enhancing drugs   *259*
in vitro fertilization (IVF)   *259*
gamete intrafallopian transfer (GIFT)   *259*
zygote intrafallopian transfer (ZIFT)   *259*

intracytoplasmic sperm injection (ICSI)   *259*
embryo transplant   *260*
surrogacy   *262*
amniocentesis   *263*
chorionic villi sampling (CV)   *263*
contraception   *266*
abortion   *268*

TAKING IT FURTHER

Planning and Creating Families

There is a wealth of information about family planning issues on the Internet. Some of these sites include the following:

Child Trends, Inc. is a research organization that provides information on a variety of family-related issues including nonmarital birth.

www.childtrends.org

RESOLVE National Home Page provides information and support regarding infertility.

www.resolve.org

National Adoption Information Clearinghouse is a comprehensive resource for adoption statistics, a literature database, agency and support-group listings, and dozens of links to specific areas of adoption such as open adoption, transracial adoption, and the costs of adopting.

www.calib.com/naic

Nature magazine offers, among other topics, online articles on the legal and ethical issues surrounding reproductive technology.

www.nature.com

And more . . . www.prenhall.com/benokraitis provides sites on adoptions, sperm banks, planned parenthood, voluntary childlessness, and information on "the morning after" pregnancy prevention.

CHAPTER 11

Raising Children: Prospects and Pitfalls

 OUTLINE

DATA DIGEST

- Congress recognized Mother's Day as a **national holiday** in 1914. Father's Day became official in 1972.

- A survey in 30 countries found that **the most stressed people are full-time working mothers with children under the age of 13.** Nearly one in four (24 percent) reported feeling stressed out almost every day. A greater proportion of married women (21 percent) than married men (17 percent) experience daily stress.

- A 1994 national poll found that **67 percent of the respondents agreed that "a good, hard spanking" is sometimes necessary to**

discipline a child, down from 84 percent in 1986. Views of spanking vary regionally: 67 percent of northeasterners support spanking compared to 86 percent of southerners.

- A national survey found that **monthly fees for a 3-year-old child placed in a for-profit day-care center,** 5 days a week, 8 hours a day, ranged from a high of $640 in Minneapolis, Minnesota, to a low of $241 in Tampa, Florida, for essentially the same services.

SOURCES: Flynn, 1994; Runzheimer International, 1997; Libbon, 1999.

WANT to practice some parenting skills? For the "mess exercise," smear peanut butter on the sofa and curtains or place a fish stick behind the couch and leave it there all summer. Or, for the "grocery store exercise," borrow one or two small animals (goats are best) and take them with you as you shop. Always keep them in sight and pay for anything they eat or damage.

A Swahili proverb says that a child is both a precious stone and a heavy burden. Child rearing is both exhilarating and exhausting, a task that takes patience and sacrifice and a willingness to learn how to parent. There are many rewards but no guarantees. The transition to parenthood is an emotionally and physically stressful undertaking, but it is also one of the most satisfying and highly valued adult social roles.

This chapter discusses some of the central issues relating to child rearing, such as parenting across the life cycle, discipline, parental contributions to child development, and other issues that affect children's well-being. We begin with a look at how parenting has changed.

Changing Parental Roles

Even before they are born, children affect their parents. Most parents are emotionally and financially invested in planning for the arrival of a child. Months before the baby is born, prospective parents begin to alter their lifestyles. The mother will probably eliminate the Big Macs from her diet and will increase her intake of dairy products and vegetables. A nationwide study found that "parenthood effects" included significant reductions in the use of cigarettes, alcohol, and other drugs by pregnant women, and often by their spouses, that continued after the birth of the child (Bachman et al., 1997). The family will probably shop for baby clothing and nursery furniture and read books on how to raise children.

A Parent Is Born

Infants waste no time in teaching adults to meet their needs. Babies are not just passive recipients of care; they are active participants in their own development:

> The infant modulates, tempers, regulates, and refines the caretaker's activities. . . . By such responses as fretting, sounds of impatience or satisfaction, by facial expressions of pleasure, contentment, or alertness he . . . "tells" the parents when he wants to eat, when he will sleep, when he wants to be played with, picked up, or have his position changed. . . . From his behavior they learn what he wants and what he will accept, what produces in him a state of well-being and good nature, and what will keep him from whining. The caretakers, then, adapt to him and he appears content; they find whatever they do for him satisfying, and thus are reinforced. (Rheingold, 1969: 785–86)

People don't simply play parental roles but *internalize* them: "We absorb the roles we play to such a degree that our sense of who we are (our identities) and our sense of right and wrong (our consciences) are very much a product of our role-playing activities" (LaRossa, 1986: 14). Parental socialization and internalization begin early in life: Young children play house, older siblings may help a parent feed or care for a younger brother or sister, and teenagers often baby-sit within or outside the home. All of these experiences prepare us for parenting roles.

Parenting does *not* come naturally. It is neither instinctive nor innate. Especially with the first child, most of us muddle through by trial and error or turn to "experts" for advice. Some of the advice can be invaluable, especially on such topics as the baby's physical care and the stages of social development (which we will discuss shortly). In other instances, however, and as you'll see later in this chapter, even some "experts" have promoted myths that have become widely accepted.

How Infants Affect Parents

Expecting a baby is very different from *having* a baby. The first year of parenthood can be very demanding. Infants require what LaRossa (1986: 88) calls "continuous coverage:" "They need to be talked to, listened to, cuddled, fed, cleaned, carried, rocked, burped, soothed, put to sleep, taken to the doctor, and so on." Because there is always something parents have to do for their helpless charges, they are on call 24 hours a day. Such accessibility to an infant's care often results in a lack of privacy, minimal time to oneself, stress, and fatigue.

Since the 1980s there has been a trend back to breast-feeding. If the mother is healthy (she is not HIV positive, using drugs, or receiving cancer treatments, for example), her breast milk is rich in nutrients—such as protein, fat, lactose, vitamins, minerals—and antibodies that protect the infant from various infections. Breast-feeding has been promoted and supported by a variety of federal and professional groups. Some companies now provide lactation rooms for employees that are equipped with electric pumps. This emphasis on breast-feeding, although healthy for the infant, has increased the pressure on mothers to be available for the baby's feeding. In addition, if the mother is breast-feeding instead of pumping the milk or bottle-feeding, the father is less involved in the baby's care.

Infants communicate hunger or discomfort by crying and being "fussy." This may be another source of stress. Both mothers and fathers experience frustration when they cannot soothe a crying infant. Mothers, especially, may feel they're inadequate. Parents must recognize that crying is the most powerful way a baby can get attention. Babies cry during the first few months for a variety of reasons. They may be unable to digest cow's milk if they are bottle-fed; if they are breast-fed they may want to suckle even if they are not hungry; they may have ear or urinary tract infections; they may be allergic to juices; they may be wet; or they may simply want some company (Kitzinger, 1989).

Parents' own activities also change. As a father of newborn commented, "Going out for a quick beer, staying late at work, being spontaneous—all that stuff is history" (Blanchard, 1999–2000: 20). As the workload increases, parents have less time for each other. New parents may find themselves having sex rarely or even not at all for weeks or months at a time. Mothers, in particular, are often exhausted by child care. Mothers who are employed outside the home are tired and may temporarily lose interest in sex. It is not unusual for some women to view lovemaking differently after the baby's birth. According to one woman, "It has been hard to integrate the feelings of being a mother and being sexual. My breasts feel like they're the baby's for nursing and not for anyone else to touch" (Fishel, 1987: 76).

Although many parents experience strain, relationships can become richer. Many couples report being more in love than ever after the birth of a child. And as the baby starts sleeping through the night, and parents develop a schedule, life (including sex) gets back to normal. It just takes time.

Contemporary Parenting Roles

Just as there are benefits and costs in having children (Chapter 10), there are also benefits and costs in parenting:

> *Parenting can be an enormously satisfying, rewarding, enriching, and growth-promoting activity. It also can be frustrating, stress producing, isolating and lonely. For many (and perhaps most) parents, parenting varies, being enormously satisfying and seemingly easy at times as well as confounding, difficult, and burdensome at other times. (Arendell, 1997: 22)*

As society changes, so do expectations about parenting roles. As you saw in Chapter 3, for example, the rise of "true womanhood" during the nineteenth century and the emphasis on companionate marriage during the turn of the twentieth century—especially in white middle classes—put pressure on parents to provide children with greater emotional care and more freedom from direct parental supervision (see also Vinovskis and Frank, 1997). And, as you'll see later in this chapter, parents may have options or experience constraints because of economic circumstances, educational levels, race and ethnicity, family background, or sexual orientation.

The internalization of the parental role means that parenthood also changes both partners on an individual level. As people make the transition to parenthood, they help each other learn the role of parent, deal with the ambiguity of what constitutes a "proper" parental role, and share in the care of their child (Stamp, 1994).

Sociologists often use *role theory* to explain the interaction between family members. A *role*, you will recall, is a set of expected behavior patterns, obligations, and privileges. Theoretically, every role has both rights and responsibilities that are defined by a culture or group. In practice, however, role strain may occur as norms or role expectations change.

Many mothers and fathers experience problems in playing these seemingly natural roles. Some of the difficulties stem from our unrealistic and one-sided expectations of parenting roles. Most see parenthood as having less margin for error than other roles. Just as students accept the fact that some professors are better than others, most of us accept occasional mistakes from lawyers, ministers, social workers, and other professionals. Parents, however, expect and are expected to succeed with every child. Furthermore, because families today typically are smaller, parents may feel especially guilty if each child does not turn out "as expected" (LeMasters and DeFrain, 1989).

Another problem is that parents are faced with increasing responsibility but less authority. In recent court battles, parents have fought state laws regarding such things as the right to educate their children at home, to consent to a minor's abortion, or to take terminally ill children off life-support systems when there is no chance for recovery. Regardless of how we feel about these issues, their effect is that parental authority has decreased. Also, parents must often compete with television and movies in teaching children values about violence, sexual activity, and stereotypical images of gender roles, minorities, and the elderly (Chapter 4).

A third aspect of the role strain parents often experience is that being judged by professionals rather than by peers makes many parents feel insecure and guilty. If parents raised several children and one ran away from home, relatives and friends would feel that these "good" parents had had one "bad" child. In contrast, many psychiatrists, psychologists, academicians, lawyers, and social workers often automatically assume that "children do not run away from good homes." Therefore, they maintain, there must be something wrong with the parents. Increasingly, for example, some counties are passing "parental responsibility" statutes where parents can be sued for the sins of their children. That is, parents must pay for damages caused by their child, whether it's a minor offense such as graffiti or a serious offense such as homicide, because the parents are held liable for the child's offense (Schrof, 1999). This means that parents and not other influences, such as peers or the media, are accountable for a child's misbehavior.

Finally, parents have no training for their difficult role, yet they must live up to high standards. As many practitioners remind us, we receive more training to get a driver's license than to become parents. And parents today are being judged by higher standards of parental performance. Parents are expected to be informed about the latest medical technologies, to watch their children closely for early signs of physical or mental abnormalities, and to get their children to

This four-year-old girl seems as engrossed in filling her dump truck as she might be in dressing a doll. If parents and other caretakers don't steer children toward sex-stereotypical activities, little girls and little boys enjoy a variety of games and toys.

specialists immediately if they detect such things as problems in hearing or seeing or slowness in learning.

Motherhood: Ideal versus Realistic Roles

New mothers often face enormous pressures. The expectation that mothering "comes naturally" creates three problems. First, it assumes that a good mother will be perfect if she simply follows her instincts. Second, it implies that there is something wrong with a mother who does not devote 100 percent of her life to child rearing. Third, it discourages the involvement of other adults, such as fathers or other caretakers.

Today over 70 percent of mothers with children under 18 years of age are in the labor force (U.S. Census Bureau, 1999c). Nonetheless, mothers continue to do most of the work of raising children and the bulk of household labor (see Chapters 4, 9, and 14). Mothers who are employed full time are still expected to play active community roles, such as raising funds for Little League, organizing PTA activities, and providing a variety of services for religious organizations. This continuing emphasis on the mother–child relationship often leads researchers to "blame Mom" for adolescent problems, preschool misbehavior, and difficulties in school (Denham et al., 1991; Moorehouse, 1991).

There's no evidence to support such claims. In fact, a recent national study found that both working and stay-at-home mothers spend slightly more time caring for their children than their own mothers did, and dads spend almost twice as much time as their fathers did. Mothers spent an average of 5.5 waking hours a day with their children in 1998, compared with 5.3 in 1965, despite the fact that the percentage of mothers employed outside the home has nearly doubled in the last 30 years. Meanwhile, the time fathers spent with their children almost doubled, from 2.8 hours in 1965 to almost four hours a day in 1998. Fathers' increased participation in child care presumably compensates for reduced maternal time in the home due to employment. Contemporary mothers in general do less housework (see Chapter 9) but spend more time caring for children. Employed mothers report getting 5 to 6 fewer hours of sleep per week and have 12 fewer hours of free time per week than do nonemployed mothers (Bianchi, 2000).

If, however, many women feel guilty because they don't embrace motherhood as their life's calling, or if they insist that men do more nurturing, both men's and women's parenting roles will be limited and stressful. The greater the participation by the father, the greater the mother's satisfaction with parenting and the marriage (Levy-Schiff, 1994; Johnson and Huston, 1998).

Fathers' Increasing Participation in Child Care

Fathers, too, feel role strain. They may have very little opportunity to learn the necessary parenting skills, especially during the first year of a baby's life:

> An old joke for musicians goes like this: A young man asks an older musician, "How do I get to Carnegie Hall?" To which the older man answers, "Practice, my son, practice." You can say the same for fatherhood. It takes practice to know how to handle a crying baby in the middle of the night and to diaper a squiggly baby on a changing table. . . . But first-time fathers who work outside of the home . . . [are expected] to know how to be dads instantaneously, and this unrealistic expectation causes problems. (Marzollo, 1993: 10)

Fathers play an important role in a child's emotional, social, and intellectual development. Fathers can contribute to their children's intellectual growth, for example, simply by showing interest in their children's progress in school, which subjects they take, and even the kinds of occupations children choose (Parke, 1996). Constructive paternal involvement can help the mother become a better parent and person and can benefit the marital relationships because wives are happier if husbands are involved in child rearing (Biller, 1993; Kalmijn, 1999).

Gerson (1997) suggests that there are three types of fathers. *Breadwinner fathers* see themselves as primary earners even if their wives work. They view fatherhood mainly in economic terms and prefer a wife who is responsible for domestic responsibilities and child care. *Autonomous fathers* seek freedom from family commitments and distance themselves—usually after a marital breakup—from both their former spouses and children. An example of autonomous fathers is "deadbeat dads" who don't provide economic or emotional support after a marital breakup. *Involved fathers* feel that "good fathering" includes extensive participation in the daily tasks of child rearing and nurturing. Although these fathers don't necessarily have equally shared or primary responsibility for their children's care, they forge satisfying relationships with women and children.

The diversity of fatherhood patterns, according to Gerson, is the result of more women working outside the home and more alternatives to marriages (Chapter 8). In addition, employed mothers take some of the pressure off husbands who have experienced stagnating earnings or a decline in secure, highly paid jobs (Chapter 14).

When mothers work outside the home, economic factors play a major part in fathers' assuming the role of primary caregiver. As *Figure 11.1* shows, fathers are the single most important source of care for young children. Fathers are more likely to care for several preschoolers than just one (to eliminate high child-care costs). They are more likely to provide care if they work evening and weekend shifts or if they are unemployed. Fathers who work in service occupations such as maintenance, police, fire fighting, and security positions are twice as likely as fathers in other occupations to be taking care of the preschoolers. They are more likely to work nontraditional schedules than other fathers are, and they are more likely to be available for care. In addition, fathers in poor families are more likely to take care of their children than fathers in middle-class families because child-care costs constitute a large proportion of a poor family's budget—43 percent compared to 24 percent in higher income families (Casper, 1997).

In a historical analysis of fathering, Pleck (1990) describes the "new father" as one who is present at the birth, participates in day-to-day child care, and is involved with his daughters as much as his sons. Still, the father-as-breadwinner model continues to be dominant. In one survey, 56 percent of male employees said they were interested in flexible work schedules that would allow them more family time. In reality, fewer than 1 percent take advantage of the paternity leaves that about 33 percent of companies offer today. Most men still fear the career repercussions of taking paternity leaves (Fried, 1998). If fathers begin to care for young children, however, this pattern will continue even if they don't take paternity leaves (Aldous et al., 1998).

Many working-class and middle-class men feel that they show their commitment to parenthood by staying on their jobs (even jobs they hate) because doing so provides for their families (Cohen, 1993). Such fathers, for example, furnish the resources for

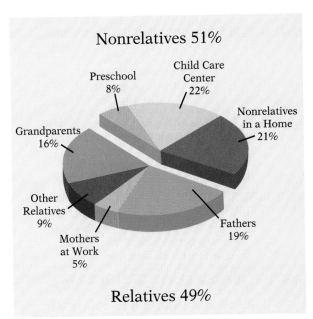

Nonrelatives 51%

Preschool 8%

Child Care Center 22%

Grandparents 16%

Nonrelatives in a Home 21%

Other Relatives 9%

Mothers at Work 5%

Fathers 19%

Relatives 49%

FIGURE 11.1 Primary Care Providers for Preschool Children while Mothers Work, 1994. "Mothers at Work" includes mothers working for pay at home or away from home. [Based on U.S. Census Bureau; Current Population Reports, Table A, January 14, 1998 (Internet release date) http://www.census.gov/p. . . child/p70-62/ tableA.txt (accessed January 26, 1998)].

children to pursue educational or cultural opportunities (and also weaken the detrimental influences of peers) by sending children away to camp or enrolling them in music lessons or sports activities (Ambert, 1997). Economically disadvantaged parents aren't able to provide such alternatives.

Parenting across the Life Cycle

Parents are the primary agents in a child's development and socialization until the children reach early adulthood. How do parents influence their children's development? We begin with a brief overview of some of the major theories of human development and then explore the years of childhood, adolescence, and the "empty nest," as well as some dynamics of only-children families and birth order.

Theories of Human Development

Social scientists have proposed a number of theories of human development. Some, like George Herbert Mead, focus on the influence of social interactions on the developing human being. Others, like Jean Piaget, are interested in the child's cognitive development—the ability to

think, reason, analyze, and apply information (see Chapter 4). And still others, like Erik Erikson, combine elements of psychological and sociological theories that encompass adulthood. Refer to *Table 11.1* as we look briefly at some of the major developmental theories.

Mead's Theory of the Social Self George Herbert Mead (1863–1931) saw the self as the basis of humanity and proposed that the *self* develops not out of biological urges but out of social interactions. For Mead, the infant was a "blank slate" (*tabula rasa*) with no predisposition to behave in any particular way. It is only as the infant interacts with other people in its environment, Mead said, that it begins to develop the attitudes, beliefs, and behaviors it needs to fit into society. The child learns first by imitating the behavior of specific individuals, such as parents, sisters, and brothers. As the child matures, he or she learns to identify with the generalized roles that these individuals and many others fulfill. When the child has learned the significance of roles, according to Mead, she or he has learned to respond to the expectations of society (see Chapter 4).

Piaget's Cognitive Development Theory Jean Piaget (1896–1980) was interested in the growing child's efforts to comprehend its world and to learn both how to adapt to that world and to develop its own independent identity. In his four major developmental stages, Piaget traced the child's acquisition of such abilities as differentiating itself from the external world and recognizing that objects in that world have an independent existence; learning to use symbols, such as language, to represent objects in the world; learning to take the perspective of another person; and learning to think and reason in abstract terms—as Piaget put it, to think "beyond the present and [to form] theories about everything" (Piaget, 1950: 48).

Erikson's Psychosocial Theory of Development Erik Erikson (1902–1994) is one of the few theorists whose conception of development encompassed the entire lifespan, not just childhood and adolescence. In each of Erikson's eight stages of development, the growing person faces a specific challenge that presents both opportunity and danger. The outcome of each "crisis" determines whether the person will move on successfully to the next stage. For example, the person may leave the first stage having learned to trust other people, such as parents or caregivers, or being burdened by the inability to place confidence in anyone. For Erikson, resolving each of these "crises" is essentially the responsibility of the individual, but successful resolution also reflects the person's social relationships with family members, peers, and others.

Because they are more influenced by situation than age, the stages postulated by Erikson may occur in a different sequence or at different ages than those

TABLE 11.1

Some Theories of Development and Socialization

Theory of the Social Self (George Herbert Mead)	Cognitive Development Theory (Jean Piaget)	Psychosocial Theory of Human Development (Erik Erikson)
Preparatory stage (roughly birth to 1 year) The infant does not distinguish between the self and others. Gradually, as it interacts with objects and people and begins to perceive others' reactions to itself, the infant builds the potential for a self.	**Sensorimotor stage (birth to $1\frac{1}{2}$ years)** The child develops a physical understanding of its environment through touching, seeing, hearing, and moving around. It learns the concept of object permanence, the fact that objects continue to exist even when they are out of sight.	**I. Trust versus mistrust (birth to 1 year)** The mother–child relationship is the basis for the child's development of trust both in others and in itself (i.e., in its ability to cope in its mother's absence). The danger is that a sense of abandonment may lead to mistrust.
Play stage (roughly $1\frac{1}{2}$ to 5 years) As the child begins to use language and continues to interact with significant others—parents, siblings, teachers, schoolmates—it learns that it has a self distinct from that of others, that others behave in many different ways, and that others expect the child to behave in certain specific ways. In other words, the child learns social norms.	**Preoperational stage ($1\frac{1}{2}$ to 7 years)** Children learn to use symbols. For example, they learn to represent a car with a block, moving the block around. They learn to use language, putting words together to express increasingly complex ideas. But they have difficulty seeing things from the viewpoint of another.	**II. Autonomy versus shame, doubt (1 to 3 years)** The child's desire for independence leads it to explore new territories and to oppose parental restraints. The danger is that parental shaming to control the child's willfulness may lead to self-doubt.
Game stage (roughly 6 years and beyond) As children grow older and interact with a wider range of people, they learn to respond to and to fulfill social roles. They learn to play different roles and to participate in organized activities.	**Concrete operational stage (7 to 12 years)** Children learn to discern cause and effect. They can anticipate possible causes of an action without having to try it out; they begin to understand the perceptions and views of others; they learn that quantities remain the same even when their shape or form changes (e.g., a fixed amount of liquid poured into a tall, thin glass and into a short, wide one is the same amount even though it looks different in the differently shaped containers).	**III. Initiative versus guilt (3 to 6 years)** A desire to learn and to master new tasks leads the child to pursue goals aggressively. The danger is a feeling of guilt for having attempted forbidden activities.
	Formal operational stage (12 years and beyond) Children can reason using abstract concepts. They can think in terms of future consequences and evaluate the probable outcomes of several alternatives. They can evaluate their own thoughts. They can think about major philosophical issues such as why pain and suffering exist.	**IV. Industry versus inferiority (6 to 12 years)** The child's eagerness to learn intensifies as she or he begins to shift interest from play to productive work. The danger is failure or the fear of failure.
		V. Identity versus identity confusion (12 to 20 years) Adolescents begin to sense their individuality and want to take their place in society. The danger is that the physiological changes of puberty and the need to make important decisions may lead to feelings of confusion or even to a feeling of being potentially bad or unworthy.
		VI. Intimacy versus isolation (20 to 30 years) Young adults seek intimate relationships with friends, coworkers, and lovers and are ready to develop the strengths they need to fulfill commitments to others. The danger is isolation if the person is unable to take chances by sharing real intimacy.
		VII. Generativity versus self-absorption (30 to 65 years) Adults want to establish and guide the next generation—their children—and/or to create and produce ideas and products. The danger is that not expressing this creative need may lead to stagnation.
		VIII. Integrity versus despair (65 years and beyond) The older adult contemplates his or her life and feels satisfaction and dignity in what has been achieved. The danger is that disappointment and unrealized goals may bring about despair.

specified in *Table 11.1*. The important point is that we mature by learning to deal with continuing new challenges. The child who feels loved and secure has a good chance of developing into a reasonably happy and productive member of society. You will recall that such socialization is one of the major functions of the family (Chapter 1).

Parenting during Childhood

Most of us learn about child rearing from parents, friends, relatives, self-help books, and even television talk shows. Much of the advice is more harmful than helpful, however, and, as one reviewer of this chapter noted, "can really mess parents up." According to Segal (1989), some of the ideas parents have about child development are myths that reflect considerable misinformation about the child's early years:

■ *Myth Number 1: You can tell in infancy how bright a child is likely to be later on.* On the contrary, a baby's early achievements, such as reaching, sitting, crawling, or talking, are not always good indicators of intelligence or predictors of later intellectual ability. For example, early agility in building with blocks or imitating words has virtually no relationship to later performance in school.

■ *Myth Number 2: The more stimulation a baby gets, the better.* Although it is true that a stimulating environment has a positive effect on babies' intellectual capacities (by influencing the brain's rate of growth), babies can be overstimulated, agitated, or even frightened into withdrawal by the relentless assault on their senses by the intrusive rattle, toy, or talking face.

■ *Myth Number 3: If a baby cries every time the mother leaves, it is an early sign of emotional insecurity.* Not at all. It is normal for babies 8 to 15 months of age to become agitated, to cry, or to show anxiety when separated from their mother or other steady caretaker. Moreover, both babies reared at home by their mothers and those who spend much of their early life at a day-care center are equally likely to show separation anxiety.

■ *Myth Number 4: Special talents surface early or not at all.* This is totally inaccurate. Many gifted children do not recognize or develop their skills until adolescence or even later. Innate talents may never surface if there are no opportunities for their expression. For example, jazz musician Louis Armstrong was a neglected and abandoned child. It was only years later, when Armstrong was living in the New Orleans Colored Waifs Home for Boys, that he was taught to play an instrument, and his talent was ignited.

These kindergartners seem very attentive to their teacher's instruction on how to use a computer. If they're loved and supported by their parents and families, children are more likely to meet this and other challenges successfully.

■ *Myth Number 5: An only child is likely to have problems relating to others.* As you will see shortly, this myth that single children are maladjusted and self-centered loners has very little basis in reality. Although only children tend to be somewhat less eager for social intimacy, they are also bright, successful, self-confident, and resourceful.

■ *Myth Number 6: Children who suffer early neglect and deprivation will not realize their normal potential.* Although early neglect and mistreatment often have devastating effects on children, even those who have been severely deprived until the age of 6 or 7 are capable of achieving normal functioning. Initial impairments are more likely to be linked to later problems in development only when combined with persistently poor environmental circumstances, such as chronic poverty, family instability, or parental illness. Although a highly unfavorable environment can be damaging, young children often prove to be resilient and capable of changing when circumstances change.

■ *Myth Number 7: Parental conflicts do not affect very young children.* Wrong. Even infants and toddlers recognize expressions of suspicion, anger, or contempt. Children as young as 18 to 24 months become sufficiently upset to try to break up their parents' fights, and they may act more aggressively toward their peers.

The dinner-hour myth in which family members relax with each other and share their day's experiences is often exploded when children—especially adolescents—and parents disagree over such things as where and with whom they have been, when they're going to clean up their rooms, or why they miss curfews.

Parenting is harder when adults believe these and other myths. Such fictions create unnecessary anxiety and guilt for many parents because they set up false expectations or unrealistic goals.

Many parents (and educators) believe that the first three years of a child's life is the critical learning period. As a result, millions of parents buy "enrichment" products such as *Brainy Baby* (to make the child smarter) and educational software for children as young as 6 months (Marcus et al., 1999). There are also "Ivy League" preschools—with an average tuition of $14,000 a year—where 3-year-olds are given French lessons, and the lunch menu consists of "salmon patties, garlic mashed potatoes, and legumes" (Barney, 1999). Many researchers contend that such obsession with "early child development" is little more than expensive marketing. Instead of organized activities and commercial gimmicks, what toddlers need most is adult attention and an opportunity to explore their environment (Gopnik et al., 1999).

Medical researchers are also concerned that, increasingly, physicians and parents are medicating children aged 2 to 4 with therapeutic drugs. In a study of 200,000 children, Zito and her colleagues (2000) found that as many as 1.5 percent of children were receiving stimulants (like Ritalin), antidepressants (like Prozac), or tranquilizers. These drugs were given as "quick fixes" for presumed emotional and behavioral problems such as attention deficit hyperactivity disorder (ADHD) and had tripled between 1991 and 1995. Scientists don't know the long-term impact of such drugs on the child's development and changes in the brain. It could be that "rambunctious" preschoolers are reacting to stressors like divorce, neglect, or poor child care rather than ADHD (Diller, 1998).

Other stressors might reflect frenetic schedules. Many children 12 and under lead very structured lives. Children today have 6 hours a week of free play time compared to almost 10 hours in 1981, for example (Karasik, 2000). As a result, many children have much more hectic schedules than in the past.

Parenting during Adolescence

A good parent–child relationship may change suddenly during adolescence. As children enter the seventh and eighth grades, for example, their relationships with their parents become more complex and their emotional experiences more mixed. Conflict over such issues as relationships, money, and access to peers often increases during puberty. As teenagers become more private and independent, parents may feel rejected and sometimes suspicious. The most difficult part of parenting adolescents, according to some mothers, is dealing with adolescents' changing moods and behavior:

One day around when she turned 12, she told you in no uncertain terms she didn't like the dress you were wearing. . . . She said . . . there was something wrong with everything you did. . . . By 14 she didn't hang around the kitchen after school anymore and tell you everything that happened. She endlessly told her friends on the phone instead. [Now] if you try to broach personal subjects, she leaves the room. . . . She slams the door to her room and stays there. . . . She used to chatter incessantly on car rides; now . . . "What's new in school today?" you ask. "Nothing," she answers. Now she's 15 and 16, and a boy comes over. They go up to her room and close the door.

You start to worry: If you set limits on them, won't they just find somewhere else to go? (Patner, 1990: C5)

Children, and especially adolescents, are active agents in the family. Adolescents are establishing their own identity and are testing their autonomy as they mature and break away from parental supervision, a healthy process in human development (see Erikson's stages in *Table 11.1*). It is not unusual, then, that many teenagers often complain that parents treat them like little children: "Have you done your homework?" "Did you brush your teeth?" "But you went out last weekend." How should parents behave? Two college freshmen advise parents not to embarrass their children. For example, don't cheer loudly for your kids when they're playing sports, don't call them by your pet nicknames in front of their friends, and don't tell your life story to the waiter or a store clerk (Elias and Goldman, 1999).

Variations in Parenting Adolescents In general, adolescent girls find the transition to puberty more difficult than boys do. Girls' self-esteem, or concept about self-worth, fluctuates more, and they tend to be more critical of their physical appearance and attractiveness (Jacklin and Baker, 1993). This is not surprising in light of the enormous cultural pressure on girls to be beautiful and popular (see Chapter 4). Self-esteem is important for all of us, regardless of sex or age. A positive self-image helps children to be more resilient to such family stressors as poverty and divorce and to avoid peer pressure that may result in behavior problems (Ambert, 1997). High self-esteem can help adults cope with family crises and other problems later in life.

Changes in social and economic circumstances have also altered the relationships between many adolescents and parents in a variety of ways. Adolescents being raised by single parents are more likely than their peers in two-parent families to leave home early even though they lack the economic and educational resources to succeed on their own (Cooney and Mortimer, 1999). In a national study of parents of children aged 15 to 18, Thomson et al. (1992) found that both male and female single parents set less restrictive rules for their children than married parents about such things as watching television and letting parents know where they were going. Compared to biological parents, stepparents engaged less frequently in activities with children such as shared meals, leisure activities away from home (like going to the movies), working at home on projects or playing together, and having private talks. Biological parents who are stressed at work sometimes bring this tension home with them (Small and Riley, 1990). They might be more impatient, verbally abusive, or too preoccupied to pay attention to the problems adolescents may be facing at school or with peer groups.

Despite such strains, a sense of closeness with parents protects many teenagers from engaging in risky behavior such as smoking, drinking, and fighting. Parents who let teenage children know they care about them and who share activities with adolescents play an important role in steering children away from trouble and into productive pursuits (Klein, 1997).

Gender Differences in Parenting Parents differ in their relationships with their children. Some children get along better with their mother, some with their father, and others report no difference. Although many studies find that adolescents generally feel closeness (feelings of warmth, acceptance, and affection) to both parents, many adolescents report feeling closer to their mothers than to their fathers. This may be because mothers are more likely than fathers to express love in terms of compliments, praise, and support (Hosley and Montemayor, 1997).

Fathers seem to have a stronger influence on adolescent self-esteem than do mothers (Ellis and Garber, 2000). This may be due to the father's greater power and authority in family and social relations. Because fathers are less likely than mothers to yield their authority as adolescents get older, fathers play an important leadership role, even though they may be less likely than mothers to understand their teenagers (Larson and Richards, 1994).

Since mothers spend more time monitoring their teens' lives, they are more likely than fathers to be on the "front line" over many issues. Also, because many girls typically have stronger ties with their mother than boys do, both positive and negative feelings toward mothers may be more intense (Larson and Richards, 1994). Many fathers have deeply satisfying relationships with their adolescent children. In many families, however, the father continues to fulfill traditional roles such as the economic provider, the disciplinarian, and the playmate. As a result, fathers may seem more distant emotionally than mothers to their teenage children (Hosley and Montemayor, 1997).

Racial-Ethnic Variations in Parenting When researchers examine parenting within similar socioeconomic levels, they usually find more similarities than differences. For example, both teenagers and their parents report that most arguments are over minor issues like clothes and helping around the house. In a study of white, African American, and Latino families, B. K. Barber (1994) found that all three groups reported daily conflict over such everyday matters as chores, family relations (like getting along with family members), clothes, and school. Parents and adolescents simply didn't discuss such crucial issues as sex and drug use.

In general, children living in continuously intact two-parent families will encounter fewer risks than children in single-parent, divorced, and remarried families. In intact households, family life is more stable (if there is little parental conflict), parents provide more resources, and there is greater parental involvement in their children's lives (Hetherington and Jodl, 1994). One exception, however, is stepfathers in black families. According to McLanahan and Sandefur (1994), for example, black male teenagers who live with stepfathers are significantly less likely to drop out of school, and black female teenagers with stepfathers are significantly less likely to become teen mothers than those in single-parent households. The researchers suggest that the income and role models that black stepfathers provide may be critical in communities with few resources or minimal adolescent supervision.

As racial and ethnic numbers have increased, adolescents in both white and minority groups have had to deal with prejudice, discrimination, and a diversity of cultural values. These changes have affected parent–child relationships both within the family and across peer groups. In immigrant families, adolescents must often shift between adherence to traditional family values and conformity to the values of peer groups. For example, when they are at home, teenagers in recent immigrant Chinese, Filipino, and Vietnamese families maintain formal relationships with their parents and suppress the expressions of individuality expected by their European American peers (Cooper and Cooper, 1992).

Only Children and Birth Order

Being an only child is no longer unusual; 20 percent of children today are "onlies." The general public's attitude toward only children hasn't changed much, however. In 1950, 71 percent of Americans said that being an only child was a disadvantage; 70 percent still said so in 1990 (Gallup and Newport, 1990). Although there is no hard evidence to support this view, many people believe that only children are spoiled, selfish, and self-centered (Boodman, 1995).

Only children sometimes wish they had had siblings. One grandmother remembers:

> Even though I loved being an only child, there was always this moment of loneliness when I walked home from school with my best friend and her sister. At the last corner they walked down one street to their house, and I had to walk down the other alone. I always wished I had a sibling to walk the rest of the way. (McCoy, 1986: 119)

Only children may also feel that "it's easier for two kids to argue against parents." They report feeling overprotected and think that routine family problems are sometimes magnified because they are always the center of attention or because parents have unrealistically high expectations. Parents of only children also see disadvantages. They feel that only children do

not learn important lessons in sharing, caring, and getting along, that they can't handle teasing from peers, and that they don't learn how to stand up for themselves (McCoy, 1986).

On the other hand, several studies have found that, for the most part, "onlies" are not very different from children who grow up with siblings. They are no more selfish or maladjusted and are as likely to be successful in college and careers, to have happy marriages, and to be good parents. They do well in school, have higher IQs, and tend to be more self-confident and popular among their peers. They are more likely to have better verbal skills and to finish high school and go to college (Blake, 1989).

In a review of 141 studies, Polit and Falbo (1987) concluded that the major difference between only children and children with siblings is that only children tend to have higher achievement motivation. Some famous onlies who have excelled in various fields include Hans Christian Andersen (writer), Leonardo da Vinci (artist–scientist), Albert Einstein (scientist), Clark Gable (actor), Elvis Presley (singer), and Jean-Paul Sartre (philosopher–writer). One of the reasons why only children may be more successful than children with siblings is due to financial assets. According to several national studies, parental resources are diluted because they must be divided among a larger number of siblings. As a result, these children often have lower levels of educational attainment and achievement (Travis and Kohli, 1995; Baydar et al., 1997).

Some researchers have claimed that birth order—regardless of age, sex, social class, or nationality—shapes personality. Sulloway (1996), for example, examined the lives and birth order of over 6,500 people who played influential scientific and political roles over the past five centuries. He concluded that first-borns (such as Franklin D. Roosevelt and Winston Churchill) tend to be more assertive, dominant, conservative, and ambitious because they identify with power and authority and seek their parents' approval. Later-borns, on the other hand (such as Copernicus and Susan B. Anthony), are more likely to have "revolutionary personalities," are open to new experiences and innovation because they aren't the parents' favorites and have less to lose by not espousing parental values.

Other researchers have found no association between birth order and personality. Nyman (1995) asked black and Latino college students at the City College of New York to list three words that described the personality traits of first-born, middle-born, last-born, and only children. Regardless of the respondents' birth positions, many of the adjectives overlapped. First-borns, for example, were viewed as aggressive, independent, intelligent, self-centered, and spoiled, but so were last-borns and only children. Older siblings who are harsh or aggressive (as well as kind and friendly) toward younger brothers and sisters

© 1997 Smith—Las Vegas Sun.

may be modeling parents' behavior toward younger children rather than reflecting personality differences due to birth order (Ambert, 1997).

Parenting in the Crowded "Empty Nest"

During the economic depression of the 1930s, it was not unusual for young adults 18 to 29 years of age to live with their parents. The numbers plunged by the 1960s, however. During the 1960s and 1970s, sociologists almost always included the "empty-nest" stage in describing the family life cycle. This is the stage when parents, typically in their 40s, find themselves alone at home after their children have married, gone off to college, or found jobs and moved out (see Burr et al., 1979). These descriptions were primarily confined to white, middle-class women, however. Black women and Latinas rarely experienced the empty-nest syndrome because they were in the labor force or involved in extended-kin networks (see Chapters 3 and 9).

The pendulum, however, is swinging back, especially for some middle-class, white families. More young adults are living at home longer, and there is a new group of young adults—called the **boomerang generation** by some—who move back with their parents after living independently for a while.

The Kids Are Back, with Their Kids Although most young adults leave the parental nest by age 23, the proportion of adults aged 25 to 34 who are living with parents increased from 9 percent in 1960 to nearly 13 percent in 1995 (U.S. Census Bureau, 1997a). Twice as many men as women in this age group are living at home (Thornton et al., 1993; Rawlings, 1994).

Among the middle classes, some of these boomerangers, especially men, are not moving out or are returning home because they are delaying marriage or because they enjoy the comforts of the parental nest: "They might even get maid service from mothers" (Quinn, 1993: 68). Women who leave their parents' home early in young adulthood see employment and privacy as more important than maintaining family bonds and obligations to kin. In contrast, remaining home until marriage or moving back later has little effect in changing sons' sense of commitment to caring for others or participating in the increased housework (Goldscheider and Lawton, 1998). Children with stepparents are less likely to return home than those who grew up in stable, two-parent homes (Goldscheider and Goldscheider, 1998). Not returning may reflect young adults' beliefs that their co-residence might create conflict (Chapter 16).

In general, however, structural, or macro-level, factors cause a larger number of young adults to stay or move home. Many young adults have found it difficult to find employment (or well-paid employment). Marital dissolution and unmarried motherhood have increased in the past decade, bringing single mothers and divorced sons and daughters back home. Because community colleges are near their parents' homes, and many students work part time, living with parents is both economical and convenient. Finally, changing norms regarding sexual relations outside of marriage have reduced the urgency to marry early. Although many parents look forward to an empty nest, few will

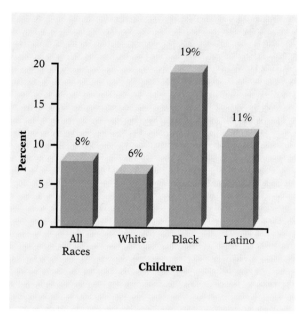

FIGURE 11.2 **Children under 15 Years Living in Extended Families.** (Based on Saluter, 1996, Table 3).

turn away a child in need of physical, emotional, or financial security (Mogelonsky, 1996).

In 1995, over 8 percent of all children under 15 years of age lived in extended families with a relative and at least one parent. African American children were three times as likely as white children and almost twice as likely as Latino children were to be living in such households (see *Figure 11.2*). Most of these children are in one-parent families, and they are more likely to move in with grandparents than with any other relatives (Furukawa, 1994).

Relations between Parents and Adult Children
How do adult children and parents get along, especially when they are under the same roof? Parents report a decrease of conflict and power issues with offspring who move out and live independently. If a child is occupationally and educationally successful, parent–child relations become closer and less contentious (Aquilino, 1997). In contrast, some parents report that they are tolerant of but unhappy with the return of their children. There is often conflict about clothes, helping out, the use of the family car, and the adult child's lifestyle (Clemens and Axelson, 1985). Pillemer and Suitor (1991) found that parents whose adult children suffered from mental, physical, or stress-related problems or who were unemployed or unwilling to help out with household expenses experienced greater depression than did parents whose children did not have these difficulties.

The biggest problems arose if the adult children were unemployed or if grandchildren lived in the home. Highly educated fathers reported especially

high hostility. This may be due in part to the fathers' higher expectations for their children's success (Aquilino and Supple, 1991). Single mothers with young children were less happy than those with adolescent children because grandparents were more likely to interfere with the mother's child-rearing practices (Stolba and Amato, 1993).

Other research shows that co-residence brings mutual benefits. For example, a national longitudinal study found that adult children who live with parents who are younger than 75 are likely to be the primary beneficiaries of the relationships in terms of such things as shared income and child care. The situation reverses, however, when the adult child reaches age 45; the child then provides assistance to the parent—cooking, for example, and doing housework (Speare and Avery, 1993). In a national study of parents whose children (aged 19 to 34) were living with them, most reported being very satisfied. They shared leisure time with their adult children and reported few conflicts (Aquilino and Supple, 1991). Much of the conflict can be avoided if both sides agree to set up and follow such ground rules as not engaging in activities parents don't approve of (such as bringing in sexual partners) and respecting each side's privacy (Estess, 1994).

Parenting Styles and Discipline

Parents differ greatly in the way they approach parenting. These differences reflect social class, racial or ethnic heritage, religious beliefs, attitudes toward gender, and the parents' own childhood experiences.

Social Class and Parenting Approaches

Parents use a variety of child-rearing techniques. Diana Baumrind (1968, 1989) has identified three broad approaches in interacting with and disciplining children (see *Table 11.2*).

Parents who use the **authoritarian approach** are very demanding, controlling, and punitive. They expect absolute obedience from their children and often use forceful measures to control behavior. Authoritarian parents, who tend to be working class, teach their children to respect authority, work, order, and traditional structure. Verbal give-and-take is not encouraged because the child is expected to accept parental authority without question. Authoritarian parents are typically not responsive to their children and project little warmth and supportiveness.

Authoritarian parenting styles may reflect stress due to low income in combination with other factors. For example, being poor, black, and/or an unmarried mother all bring added stress to the parenting experience because of discrimination and restricted economic opportunity (Giles-Sims et al., 1995). In addition, psychological factors such as depression (for white as

TABLE 11.2

Three Approaches to Parenting

Authoritarian: Highly demanding, controlling, and punitive: "You can't have the car on Saturday because I said so."

Permissive: Highly responsive and warm, not demanding, but sometimes manipulative: "You can't borrow the car next Saturday because Uncle Charlie said he'd drop by and you haven't seen him in a while."

Authoritative: Highly demanding, controlling, supportive, and responsive: "You can borrow the car after you've picked your brother up from soccer practice. And remember to be home by curfew."

well as black mothers in working and middle classes) increase the likelihood of punitive parenting styles (Jackson et al., 1998; Bluestone and Tamis-LeMonda, 1999).

In the **permissive approach** parents are warm, responsive, and nondemanding. They value a child's freedom of expression and autonomy. Permissive households are characterized by a lack of rules or regulations, and the parents, who are usually middle class, make few demands on their children for orderly behavior or performing household tasks. They use reason rather than overt power to accomplish their ends. The boundaries that permissive parents set are often subtle, but these parents can also be manipulative (see *Table 11.2*). Although permissive parents do not bully or tyrannize their children, their inculcation of moral and social responsibility does not give the children total freedom of choice.

Parents who use the **authoritative approach** are demanding and controlling but also responsive and supportive. These parents encourage autonomy and self-reliance, and they tend to use positive reinforcement and to avoid punitive, repressive discipline. They encourage verbal give-and-take and believe that the child has rights. Although they expect disciplined conformity, they do not hem the child in with heavy-handed restrictions. Instead, they are open to discussing and changing rules in particular situations when the need arises.

Although there are exceptions, a number of studies show that healthy child development is most likely in authoritative family settings, where parents are consistent in combining nurturance, monitoring, and discipline (Starrels, 1994; Fletcher et al., 1999; Gray and Steinberg, 1999; Barnes et al., 2000). Children from authoritative households have better psychosocial development, higher school grades, greater self-reliance, and lower levels of delinquent behavior than children raised in authoritarian or permissive homes (National Research Council, 1993). Both black and white adolescents whose parents are authoritative are

less swayed by antisocial peer pressure (to use drugs and alcohol, for example) than are adolescents whose parents are permissive or authoritarian (Mason et al., 1997; Collins et al., 2000).

Some researchers suggest that the authoritarian–permissive–authoritative parenting styles overlap in real life. Immigrant Chinese mothers, for example, reflect a combination of parenting roles that might seem authoritarian because of high expectations about academic success but are also warm, nurturing and supportive (Gorman, 1998).

Eight Parenting Styles

Parenting styles vary across families and may change over time. Moreover, they usually overlap; a particular family may use two or more styles at one time or another. Permissive and authoritarian methods of parenting are usually directed at the child, but other methods—typically those that are authoritative—often attempt to control the child's environment and relations with peers.

Influencing the Child Directly Parental roles that shape the child directly include the martyr, the pal, the police officer, the teacher, and the booster (LeMasters and DeFrain, 1989; Larson and Richards, 1994).

1. *The parent as martyr.* The parent as martyr sacrifices everything for the children, lets them do whatever they want, buys them everything they want, waits on them hand and foot, and tries to fulfill their every whim and wish. If children do not revolt against the martyr model, they run the risk of being emotionally crippled because they may never become self-sufficient.

2. *The parent as pal or buddy.* To overcome the generation gap, parents often let their children set their own rules because they want to be liked by their children and to be their pals. Parents, however, are responsible for rearing and guiding their children. If there is disagreement, a parent who is a pal will have little authority. And, as someone once said, "What child needs a 40-year-old for a buddy?"

3. *The parent as police officer or drill sergeant.* The parent who acts as a police officer or drill sergeant is authoritarian and punitive. Even minor offenses are punished. Although children may be submissive during the early years, they often rebel against this type of authority in adolescence and may demand more independence, socializing with peers from less restrictive households.

4. *The parent as teacher.* Fathers, especially, relish playing the role of teacher. They get enjoyment from helping children with their homework and are especially pleased when children ask for their advice or opinion.

CROSS CULTURAL

Parenting in Japan

Japan's approach to parenting is considerably different from that of the United States. Most Americans value individualism, independence, and initiative and raise their children to be self-reliant. From the Japanese viewpoint, these kinds of attitudes and behaviors are too narrowly goal-oriented. The Japanese value loyalty to the family and community over personal success. Respect for authority and obedience are taught early in the home, and they are reinforced in nursery school (Downs, 1994).

Japanese child rearing is based on a concept called *amae,* which is a sense of complete dependence based on the desire for love and caring. Mothers, who give them 24-hour love, instill *amae* in Japanese children. Many Japanese mothers typically spend every waking hour with their babies. They often take them into their beds at night, pick them up whenever they cry, and cater to their every whim. Most American parents think this kind of behavior will spoil a child and discourage independence and self-reliance. In contrast, the Japanese feel that keeping children happy will motivate them to be cooperative later in life. *Amae*-based care and guidance is continued in the school system, where children are rewarded for cooperative behavior and teamwork.

Although Japanese fathers are often absent from home, the father's authority is frequently reinforced in daily mother–child interaction:

"Since my husband is gone most of the time, my son really needs a role model to be a strong and responsible man. That's why I remind him constantly of what a diligent, dedicated, responsible, and great father he has. I also tell my daughter that it is important for her to find a hard-working man like her father who earns a comfortable living for the family."* This is from a homemaker-mother whose 9-year-old daughter and 6-year-old son see their father on the average of 4 minutes a day. (Ishii-Kuntz, 1993: 59)

Since provider and father roles are synonymous, co-workers or family members may criticize Japanese men who might choose to reduce work hours to be at home with their children. Because many fathers devote themselves to their jobs, mothers have complete authority in the home: "It's motherhood, not wifehood, which gives a woman a sense of accomplishment and it's the children around which the family revolves" (Diggs, 1998: 49).

---

5. *The parent as booster and promoter.* Both mothers and fathers enjoy their children's accomplishments. They may be especially proud when their children do well in school, in sports, or other activities. There may be conflict, however, if the children don't live up to the parents' expectations.

Shaping the Child's Environment Other parenting strategies include "managing" children's social development by influencing their social environments and their interactions with peers. These approaches include the parent as designer, mediator, or supervisor (Ladd et al., 1993).

■ *The parent as designer.* Parents act as designers when they try to influence the child's social environment, including the neighborhood, preschool, or child care. These social contexts may have an important impact on the nature of children's early peer experiences and, ultimately, the types of social skills that children develop during this period.

■ *The parent as mediator.* As mediators, parents try to influence the child's play opportunities and relationships with specific peers. For instance, parents might help young children find playmates and initiate and arrange play groups. Participation in play groups may provide children with the skills they need to function well in larger peer environments (such as the classroom or playground).

■ *The parent as supervisor.* A parent may be an observer or facilitator of the child's activities. For example, the parent might discourage or redirect objectionable behaviors or resolve conflicts between children. Or the parent might play a more active role by maintaining children's interest in peers or play or rewarding specific behaviors.

Some people believe that parenting in the United States is difficult because our cultural values (such as competition, independence, and success) encourage individuality rather than conformity. In contrast, the box on "Parenting in Japan" shows how societal expectations mold parental values that emphasize cooperation rather than independence.

Discipline

In 1994, a woman was shopping in a grocery store in Woodstock, Georgia, when her 9-year-old son, who reportedly was picking on his sister, talked back to his mother. The mother slapped him. Fifteen minutes later, in the parking lot, a police officer summoned by a store employee arrested the mother and charged her with cruelty to children, a felony that carries a jail sentence of 1 to 20 years. Many parents were outraged by the arrest. Why should the police intrude in a private family matter? And what's wrong with slapping or spanking kids? The incident fueled a national debate over how Americans should discipline their children.

Children must learn discipline because self-control is not innate. Many parents feel that both verbal and corporal punishment are legitimate forms of discipline. According to a recent Gallup poll, for example, over 80 percent of the parents said that the most effective form of discipline—and across all ages—was taking away children's privileges. About one in four parents reported that yelling at children was an effective disciplinary strategy. Half of the parents of children under age 6 felt that spanking worked ("What works?" 1999). How often, more specifically, do parents use verbal and physical aggression to discipline their children?

Verbal Punishment A national sample of 991 parents found that virtually all parents, and across all socioeconomic groups, used verbal and psychological aggression to control or change their children's behavior. Half of the parents yelled, screamed, and shouted at their infants and 1-year-old children. This percentage jumped to 90 percent of children aged 2 to 4 and stayed at that level through age 17. Roughly 25 percent of the parents sometimes cursed at their children in the previous 12 months, and 17 percent admitted calling a child a derogatory name (such as "dumb" or "lazy"). Almost a third of parents of teens swore at them and called them names, and about 20 percent threatened, at least once, to kick the child out of house. All of these figures are probably low because many parents either don't want to admit that they attack their children verbally or because the incidents have become so normal that parents have forgotten them.

The researchers noted that such psychological and verbal aggression is associated with higher rates of delinquency and psychological problems because parents criticize the child and not the child's misbehavior. The researchers observed, moreover, that the high prevalence of psychological aggression between adult partners shouldn't be surprising because almost all American children experience such violence from their parents and see it as normative (Straus and Field, 2000).

Corporal Punishment Many U.S. adults support spanking as a form of discipline (see Data Digest). Straus and Stewart (1999) found that 35 percent of parents had disciplined their infants by slapping their hand or leg, spanking their buttocks, pinching, shaking, hitting on the buttocks with a belt or paddle, or slapping the infant's face. These forms of corporal punishment reached a peak of 94 percent at ages 3 and 4 and declined after age 5. Over half of the parents hit their children at age 12, a third at age 14, and 13 percent at age 17. Parents who hit teenage children did so an average of about six times during the year. Severity, as measured by hitting the child with a belt or paddle, was greatest for children aged 5 to 12 (28 percent of such children). In addition, corporal punishment was more prevalent among black and low socioeconomic status parents, in the South, for boys, and by mothers. Similarly, Day and his colleagues (1998) found that boys are spanked more frequently than girls, mothers (and especially black mothers) spank more frequently than fathers, and older parents are less likely to use corporal punishment than their younger counterparts.

Does Corporal Punishment Work? A recent study of 2- and 3-year-olds found that parents who use reasoning and back it up with physical and nonphysical punishment will have well-behaved children (Larzelere et al., 1998; see also Holden et al., 1999). Most of the published research shows, however, that corporal punishment increases a child's aggression and misbehavior. In a recent study of preschool-age children, for example, children whose mothers threatened, insulted, spanked, or yelled at the children in response to defiant behavior were more likely to remain defiant and disruptive as they entered school (Spieker et al., 1999). Many researchers, pediatricians, and practitioners maintain that physical punishment is an ineffective disciplinary method (see the "Is Spanking Effective or Harmful?" box). Increasingly, child experts recommend nonphysical methods of punishment that have better long-term results, such as removing temptation for misbehavior, making rules simple, being consistent, setting a good example, praising good behavior, and disciplining with love and patience instead of anger (Gibson, 1991; Simons et al., 1994).

Variations by Race and Ethnicity Acceptable disciplinary measures appear to vary across racial and ethnic families. In a randomly selected sample of households in King County, Washington, for example, McDade (1995) found that 50 percent of the black parents thought spanking was acceptable compared to 10 percent of white parents, 7 percent of Asian/ Pacific Islander parents, and *none* of the American Indian or Latino parents. (Note that these were attitudes rather than actual behavior.) Instead, some researchers point out, ethnic parents often discipline their children by emphasizing self-control and doing well in school rather than using corporal or verbal punishment. Ethnic parents may be stricter—by placing greater demands and expectations on their children—because they feel that their children will face prejudice and discrimination (Julian et al., 1994; Ng, 1998).

CHOICES

Is Spanking Effective or Harmful?

A number of countries—Sweden, Finland, Denmark, Norway, Latvia, Italy, and Austria—have made it illegal for parents to spank their children. Other countries, such as Germany and Bulgaria, are considering similar bans (Ford, 2000). In contrast, many adults in the United States support spanking (see Data Digest). Advocates feel that spanking is effective, prepares children for life's hardships, and deters misbehavior (see Davis, 1994). Spanking proponents maintain that spanking is effective and desirable if it is age-appropriate, used selectively, and motivated by love for the purpose of teaching and correcting, not revenge or rage (Trumbull and Ravenel, 1999).

Some pediatricians feel that a "mild" spanking (one or two spanks on the buttocks) is acceptable when all other discipline fails, but even they find slapping a child's face abusive. Others argue that spanking and all other types of physical punishment are unacceptable. They maintain that children who are spanked regularly, from as early as 1 year old, face a higher risk of developing low self-esteem, depression, alcoholism, and aggressive and violent behavior, as well as of physically abusing their own spouses and children (Straus and Yodanis, 1996; Whipple and Richey, 1997; Swinford et al., 2000). Several researchers (Hunt, 1991; Segal and Segal, 1991) have offered a variety of reasons for not spanking or hitting children:

- *Children learn best by modeling their parents.* Physical punishment sends the message that hitting is an appropriate way to express one's feelings and to solve problems.
- *Physical punishment gives the message that it is okay to hurt someone who is smaller and less powerful.* Children also get the message that it is appropriate to mistreat younger or smaller children; and when they become adults, they feel little compassion for those less fortunate or less powerful than they are.
- *No human being feels loving toward someone who deliberately hurts her or him.* A strong relationship is based on loving feelings and grows through many examples of kindness and cooperation. Punishment, even when it appears to work, may produce only temporary and superficially "good" behavior based on fear.
- *Unexpressed anger is stored inside and may explode later.* Anger that has accumulated for many years may explode during adolescence and adulthood, when the individual feels strong enough to show this rage. The "good" behavior produced by punishment in the early years may disappear overnight.
- *Spanking can be physically damaging.* It can injure the spinal column and nerves and even cause paralysis. Some children have died after relatively mild paddlings due to other undiagnosed medical problems.
- *Physical punishment deprives the child of opportunities for learning effective problem solving.* Physical punishment teaches a child nothing about how to handle similar situations in the future. Loving support is the only way to learn true moral behavior based on strong inner values.

There is also some evidence that corporal punishment does not necessarily have a negative psychological effect on either white or black children if they perceive the punishment as just, not harsh, and administered by a caregiver (usually a mother) who is generally affectionate and loving (Rohner et al., 1996). In one study, harsh physical punishment was associated with more disciplinary problems and aggression among white children through the third grade, but black children tended to be better behaved (Deater-Deckard et al., 1996). The researchers speculated that while white children might interpret parental discipline such as spanking as hostility, black children saw it as an expression of concern.

In another study of preschool children, the researchers found that among those mothers who used "negative control" (such as spanking and yelling), black children were less prone to engage in defiant behavior than their white counterparts. The researchers suggested that verbal and physical discipline may be culturally more acceptable among black families than among families of other groups, and that black mothers may be more likely to temper negative control with "positive warmth" (Spieker et al., 1999; see also Mosby and Rawls, 1999). It appears, then, that effective disciplinary measures are associated with a number of factors, such as cultural attitudes, the harshness of the punishment, and a child's perception of a parent as loving or rejecting.

What's a Parent to Do? According to many family educators, it's important not to discipline too early. Many parents do not pick up crying babies because they are afraid of "spoiling" them. Several studies have shown that it is almost impossible to spoil a child who is under 1 year old. Crying is the only way a baby can "tell" its parents that it has a problem, such as hunger, discomfort, pain, or illness. Thus parents should pick up their baby as much as they want and not worry about discipline at such a young age (Kohn, 1991). Ignoring a newborn's cries sets off a vicious cycle that leads to more crying, which further discourages the parents from responding, which makes the baby even more irritable, and so on.

Effective discipline involves more than rewards and punishments. The most powerful parenting approaches include such activities as joint decision making, whenever possible, between parents and children (especially adolescents), consistent parenting, and creating special times together (such as celebrating holidays or special events). Whether a parent is single or married, monitoring children is crucial in discouraging young children and adolescents from associating with objectionable peer groups or using drugs and in encouraging them to

do well in school (National Research Council, 1993; Olson and Haynes, 1993). Children need three types of "inner resources" if they are to become responsible adults: (1) good feelings about themselves and others, (2) an understanding of right and wrong, and (3) alternatives for solving problems. *Table 11.3* lists 12 building blocks that parents can use to establish these inner resources in their children.

Parents' Contributions to Child Development

A 4000-year-old tablet discovered on the site of the biblical city of Ur was inscribed with the following: "Our civilization is doomed if the unheard-of actions of our younger generations are allowed to continue"

TABLE 11.3

Some Building Blocks of Discipline

1. **Show your love.** You can express your love not only through a warm facial expression, a kind tone, and a hug but also through doing things with your children, such as playing, working on a craft together, letting them help with grocery shopping, and reading their favorite books. When children feel loved, they want to please their parents and are less likely to engage in undesirable behavior.

2. **Be consistent.** Predictable parents are just as important as routines and schedules. A child who is allowed to do something one day and not the next can become confused and start testing the rules.

3. **Communicate clearly.** Ask children about their interests and feelings. Whenever possible, encourage them. Constant nagging, reminding, criticizing, threatening, lecturing, questioning, advising, evaluating, telling, and demanding make a child feel dumb or bad.

4. **Understand problem behavior.** Observe a problem behavior for several days and look for a pattern that may disclose its cause; for example, a child may become unusually cranky when tired or hungry.

5. **Be positive.** Sometimes children act up because they want us to notice them. Because children usually repeat attention-getting behavior, approval encourages them to repeat the positive behavior.

6. **Set up a safe environment.** Children are doers and explorers. Removing hazards shortens the lists of "no's," and changing play locations relieves boredom and prevents destructive behavior.

7. **Have realistic rules.** Set few rules, state them simply, and supervise closely. (Rules can become more extensive and abstract as toddlers become preschoolers.) Don't expect more than your child can handle; for instance, don't expect a toddler to sit quietly during long meetings.

8. **Defuse explosions.** Try to avert temper tantrums and highly charged confrontations (for example, guide feuding preschoolers into other activities).

9. **Teach good problem-solving skills.** Children under 4 years of age need very specific guidance in solving a problem and reinforcement for following suggestions.

10. **Give children reasonable choices.** Don't force them to do things that even you wouldn't want to do (such as sharing a favorite toy). Removing children from the play area when they misbehave and giving them a choice of other activities is often more effective than scolding or punishing.

11. **Seek professional help when needed.** Although most children outgrow common behavioral problems, some may need professional guidance, particularly if the parents themselves are experiencing a stressful time, such as divorce.

12. **Be patient with your child and yourself.** Parents may not always have enough control over their lives to be patient, but patience, love, and understanding are important for handling problems of all sizes (Harms, 1989; Goddard, 1994).

TABLE 11.4

Kids' and Parents' Rights

Kids Have the Right . . .	Parents Have the Right . . .
1. To be treated with respect	1. To be treated with respect
2. To say yes or no	2. To say no and not feel guilty
3. To be alone sometimes	3. To know where their children are, who their friends are, and who they are with at any time
4. To make mistakes	4. To make mistakes and/or change their minds
5. To ask questions	5. To ask questions and expect answers about all things that may affect their children
6. To be cared for when they're sick and well	6. To monitor all school-related activities: academic, behavioral, and social
7. To be safe from physical and sexual hurt from grown-ups and other kids	7. To know and consult with adults who influence their children's lives (such as coaches, employers, teachers, youth-group leaders, ministers, and counselors)
8. To be safe and protected	8. To know what is happening within their own homes, to set "house rules," and to know the identity of guests who come into their homes
9. To want and get attention and study time, affection	9. To promote time together as a family, which may include meals, outings, and other planned activities
10. To choose what they like and don't like	10. To be authoritative when logical explanation and reason have failed

SOURCES: Based on material from the Tri-City Substance Abuse Coalition, cited in McMahon, 1993; Project Charlie, cited in Shoop and Edwards, 1994; and "Parenting skills . . . ," 2000.

(Lauer, 1973). According to a study by Public Agenda, a New York City research organization, many adults don't think much of today's children, either. Only 37 percent of the general public felt that today's children aged 6 to 12 will make the world a better place when they're adults. Half said that parents spoil their children and fail to discipline them, and only 22 percent felt that parents who are good role models are "very common" (Russell, 1997).

Despite such criticism, parents are not very different from parents in past generations. Since the 1950s, for example, parents have said that the most important quality they value in their children is the ability to think for themselves. Other important traits include obedience to established rules, hard work, and helping others (Alwin, 1988; "Raising 'em right," 1999). In fact, as you saw earlier, many mothers today are more likely to attend their children's school events than were their own mothers and to spend more time with their children, and larger numbers of fathers are more involved in raising their children than were their own fathers.

And, despite popular stereotypes, poor people are generally good parents. Regardless of where parents live or how much money they earn, many low-income parents scour their community for after-school programs,

church activities, and other opportunities to build their children's abilities, aspirations, and future success (Furstenberg et al., 1999). Many teenagers today are better educated and more ambitious than in the past, argue some observers, but are not getting the parental guidance they need to prepare for adulthood (Schneider and Stevenson, 1999). Nonetheless, many adults typically blame young people and not themselves for many social ills: "Adults always have—and always will—believe that youth is going to hell in a handbasket" and that "today's youth are always the worst" (Males, 1999; Robinson, 2000).

Another important issue is communication. By around ages 11 and 12, children start withholding private thoughts and feelings from their parents because they fear rejection. Parents are advised not to react to their children's ideas with sarcasm, putdowns, or scorn. Communication and respect should be reciprocal, however. The "bill of rights" for parents and children shown in *Table 11.4* makes it clear that both have many of the same rights. The biggest difference is that parental rights also include adult responsibilities.

Despite the general public's perception that parents are doing a bad job raising kids, many teenagers appreciate their parents. In one national survey, for example, 89 percent of teenagers aged 13 to 17 said their parents are interested in their concerns and 75 percent said their parents understand their problems. Most teenagers (94 percent) described their relationships with their mothers as "very happy" or "fairly happy," and 81 percent considered their relationships with their fathers as happy. Not all parent–teenager relationships are satisfying, of course. The same survey reported that 12 percent of the teenagers had witnessed domestic abuse at home and 17 percent were aware that a parent was using drugs (Hales, 1996).

Despite the stresses and time constraints of two-income families, most teenagers don't feel that their parents neglect them. In a recent national study, for example, Galinsky (1999) found that although 56 percent of the working parents thought their children wanted more time with them, only 10 percent of the children wanted more time with mom and about 16 percent wanted more time with dad. The majority felt that they had enough time with both parents. Similarly, a *Newsweek* poll found that 61 percent of teenagers felt they spent enough time with their parents and 15 percent said that they spent too much time with their parents (Begley, 2000).

Whether children feel that parents spend enough time with them or not, several writers note that the best way to raise responsible kids is to surround them with responsible adults. If parents have good interpersonal relationships, for example, children will have positive role models and develop good peer relations (Doyle and Markiewicz, 1996; Pittman, 1998). Parents aren't always good role models, however. Recently, for example, a father became enraged when his son took an elbow to the face during a 9- and 10-year old hockey game. An argument erupted between the fathers, and one (in front of his three sons) beat the other to death (Wingert and Lauerman, 2000). And parents who are sexually promiscuous or cohabit with a number of partners are outraged when their children don't abstain from sex or bear a child during their teenage years (Chapter 6).

Most important, parents are a child's major source of support. Parents' most significant contribution involves developing their youngsters' physical health, cognitive skills, and sense of socioemotional well-being.

Nonparental Child Care

The Reverend Jesse Jackson reportedly said, "Your children need your presence more than your presents." In 1993, a 15-year-old British boy went to court in an effort to force his mother to spend more time with him. Although such drastic measures are relatively rare, a number of parents are spending little time with their children. Much of the evidence comes from the research on absentee fathers, latchkey kids, and child care.

Absentee Fathers

Some believe (see Chapter 1) that one of the most serious problems facing families today is that the United States is becoming an increasingly fatherless society:

> *Tonight, about 40 percent of American children will go to sleep in homes in which their fathers do not live. Before they reach the age of eighteen, more than half of our nation's children are likely to spend at least a significant portion of their childhoods living apart from their fathers. . . . Never before have so many children grown up without knowing what it means to have a father. (Blankenhorn, 1995: 1)*

As you saw earlier, fathers play a critical role in nurturing babies and providing guidance for adolescents. Using national data, Amato and Rivera (1999) found a strong association between paternal involvement and children's behavior. Irrespective of the mother's involvement, white, black, and Latino fathers and stepfathers who reported spending a lot of time with their children (e.g., eating and playing together, engaging in activities away from home, helping with homework) had a positive effect on their children in terms of fewer problems at school and at home. We discuss the effects on children who do not see their nonresident fathers after a divorce or separation in Chapters 15 and 16. There are, however, millions of children born outside of marriage who also don't see their fathers.

Among unmarried fathers, 13 percent never see their children and another 21 percent see them only a few times a year (Jacobsen and Edmondson, 1994). Absentee fathers can have a tremendous negative impact on their children, from birth to young adulthood. Compared to children living with both biological parents, children with an absentee father are twice as likely to drop out of high school, more likely to spend time in juvenile correctional facilities, 20 to 42 percent more likely to suffer health problems, and more likely to have lower earnings in young adulthood. They are also more likely to be poor, and to have a higher probability themselves of experiencing a marital disruption, or to have a premarital birth, thereby repeating the cycle of single parenthood (Goulter and Minninger, 1993; Lino, 1994).

Such negative outcomes aren't due *only* to the lack of a father. Compared to children raised in single-mother households, for example, those raised in single-father homes are less well behaved in the classroom, are less successful at getting along with others, and put forth less effort in class. Thus, teenagers who have behavioral problems in school and in the community reflect the problems that arise from the absence of a second parent, male or female (Downey et al., 1998).

Millions of "latchkey kids" return from school every day to empty houses for two to four hours until an adult or other caretaker arrives. Most schools don't provide after-school care. In other cases, parents—especially single mothers—can't afford expensive after-school programs.

In addition, teenagers who don't get along with their fathers are at greater risk of engaging in deviant behavior regardless of family structure. Children living in two-parent families who have a fair or poor relationship with their father are at 68 percent higher risk of smoking, drinking, and using drugs compared to all teens living in a two-parent household. The average teen living in a household headed by a single mother is at 30 percent higher risk compared to all teens in a two-parent household ("Family relationships," 1999).

Latchkey Kids

The traditional family is changing to a family in which both parents are employed full time outside the home, creating a family type that has been referred to as **DEWKS**, or **dual-employed with kids.** The proportion of DEWKS families in the United States has increased from 33 percent of all families in 1976 to 64 percent in

1998 (Bachu, 1993; U.S. Census Bureau, 1999c). As a result, latchkey kids have become a growing concern.

There's nothing new about children being on their own at home. The phrase *latchkey children* originated in the early 1800s when youngsters who were responsible for their own care wore the key to their home tied to a string around their necks. Today the phrase **latchkey kids** generally refers to children who return home after school and let themselves in, with their own keys, to an empty house or apartment, where they are alone and unsupervised until their parents or another adult comes home.

The number of latchkey kids has almost doubled since the 1970s. According to a nationwide study, almost 3 million children (9.3 percent) care for themselves on a regular basis before or after school. About one in four children is completely alone after school. The average amount of time spent unsupervised by adults ranges from 47 minutes for children aged 5 to 7 to 1 hour and 15 minutes for children aged 11 and 12 (Hofferth et al., 2000). In another study, about 21 percent of children aged 6 to 12 are regularly without adult supervision when not in school (Capizanno et al., 2000). All these estimates of latchkey kids are probably low because (1) they do not include the children of women who are not in the labor force but who nevertheless spend some part of the day in unsupervised situations or (2) children who are left alone occasionally (Casper et al., 1994a).

Who are the children who are home alone? The older children are, the more likely they are to be latchkey kids. For example, whereas 1 percent of all 6-year-old children whose mothers were employed cared for themselves, 20 percent of 14-year-old children of working mothers are in this category.

Children of mothers who work full time are four times more likely to be latchkey kids than children whose mothers work part time. Suburban children are about twice as likely to be home alone as children living in either cities or rural areas. This may be because suburban parents feel that their neighborhoods are safe or because their neighbors have agreed to be called on in emergencies (Casper et al., 1994a). Socioeconomic status, race-ethnicity, and parents' work schedules have little effect on a family's decision to leave children to care for themselves (Capizanno et al., 2000):

- *Income:* Family income makes little difference in the use of self-care for 6- to 8-year old children, but self-care is more often used by 10- to 12-year-olds in higher-income (more than twice the federal poverty level; see Chapter 13) families.

- *Race and ethnicity:* White 10- to 12-year-olds are nearly twice as likely as their black and Latino peers to regularly spend time in self-care. There are few differences among racial and ethnic groups in the use of self-care for younger children.

■ *Parental work schedules:* Ten- to 12-year-old children whose parents work traditional hours are more likely to be in self-care than those who work nontraditional hours (such as evenings or midnight-to-morning shifts).

The similarity of latchkey children across social classes and ethnic groups may be due to the scarcity of services rather than costs. As you'll see in the next section, few child-care facilities exist to accommodate the millions of children who need care before or after school.

Many children enjoy being home alone. They like the independence of being by themselves. They watch television, play, study and do homework, read, and do some housework (Hofferth et al., 2000). Others, however, are frightened about being by themselves, don't structure their time, don't do their homework or appointed chores, or invite friends against house rules (Belle, 1999). Children who take care of themselves for 11 or more hours a week are nearly twice as likely to drink alcohol, smoke cigarettes, or use marijuana as are children who are under adult supervision (Richardson, 1989).

Child Care

About 80 percent of families include two working parents. Seventy percent of parents and child advocates feel that having one parent at home is the best child-care arrangement during the earliest years. Among mothers between the ages of 18 and 29, 80 percent prefer to be at home ("Necessary compromises . . . ," 2000). Being at home isn't possible for many parents because they have to work to support themselves and their children. As the number of divorces and working single parents grows, parents must make child-care arrangements. Mothers who work unusual hours or on weekends must often stitch together multiple arrangements. About 65 percent of parents juggle multiple child-care arrangements that include day-care centers, Head Start programs, and relatives, friends, and baby-sitters (Capizzano and Adams, 2000b; Capizzano et al., 2000).

Child-Care Patterns and Characteristics About 76 percent of children under age 5 with employed parents are in some form of nonparental care each week. Nationwide, in 1997, 62 percent of children were in only one child-care arrangement. Almost two out of five (38 percent) children in nonparental care had two or more child-care arrangements. The child-care arrangements vary due to such factors as the availability of certain types of child care, the costs of care, the ability of parents to pay for care, and the differences between work schedules and the hours of the child-care programs (Uttal, 1999; Capizzano and Adams, 2000b). Of the children under age 5 in child-care, 41 percent are in care for 35 or more hours per week (see *Figure 11.3*).

Before- and after-school programs and relatives are the most common child-care arrangements for 6- to 9-year-old children, with 21 percent of children in this age group in each of these forms of care while the mother is working. A significant percentage of 10- to 12-year-old children rely on relatives as their primary care provider (17 percent). However, only 10 percent

Some companies, such as Stride-Rite (a shoe manufacturer) in Cambridge, Massachusetts, have implemented innovative programs that combine elder care and child care.

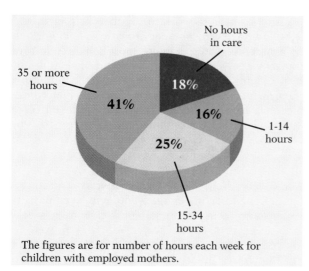

The figures are for number of hours each week for children with employed mothers.

FIGURE 11.3 **Hours Spent in Nonparental Care by Children Under Five (1997)**

SOURCE: Based on Capizzano and Adams, 2000a, Figure 1.

of these children are in before- and after-school programs (Capizzano et al., 2000).

As with children under age 5, the use of different types of care and the amount of time that school-age children spend in care vary widely across families and reflect a number of factors, including economic resources, parental preferences, and parents' information about different child-care options. In terms of family income, for example, 6- to 9-year-old children from lower-income or poverty-level families spend more time in their supervised primary child-care arrangements than do higher-income children (15.5 hours per week, as opposed to 12.3 hours per week). Children from higher-income families are more likely to live in neighborhoods that parents consider safe and thus let children care for themselves (Capizzano et al., 2000).

In terms of racial and ethnic backgrounds, black 6- to 9-year-old children are more likely to use before- and after-school programs while the mother is working than Latino children (27 percent, compared with 16 percent). Among 10- to 12-year-olds, white children are twice as likely as Latino children, and almost three times as likely as black children, to use self-care as the primary form of care (30 percent for whites, compared with 15 percent for Latinos and 11 percent for blacks). It is not clear how much the child-care and self-care patterns vary because of parental preferences, economic constraints, or other factors (Capizzano et al., 2000).

Effects of Child Care on Children Day care is a controversial issue. Revelations of sexual abuse by caregivers during the early 1990s made many parents fearful and suspicious. One study found that more

than six in ten parents were concerned about abuse and neglect in day-care centers, even though statistics show that children are more likely to be abused by relatives than by day-care workers ("Necessary compromises . . . ," 2000). Some estimate that there may be between 240 and 320 deaths a year in child-care facilities due to drowning, falls, or other neglect by caretakers (Pope, 1997).

In a survey of 220 facilities (including centers run by the federal government, for-profit and nonprofit companies, and private homes), the Consumer Product Safety Commission (1999) concluded that two of three child-care facilities had safety hazards that put children at risk. At 38 percent of the centers, children wore clothing with neck drawstrings, which can become caught in playground equipment and lead to strangulation. Twenty-four percent of the centers had unsafe playground surfaces, and 19 percent had cribs that contained soft bedding, which can smother children. Other dangers included poorly maintained playground equipment, loops on the cords of window blinds that can strangle a child, and failure to use child safety gates where necessary. In another study, the National Institute of Child Health and Human Development (NICHD) rated only 10 percent of day-care facilities for children aged 3 and under as "excellent." Nearly one-third were rated "good," 53 percent were ranked "fair," and 8 percent were deemed "poor" (Russell, 1999). Thus, parental concerns about unsafe and low-quality child-care centers are justified.

On the other hand, a number of studies show that a well-run day-care center has positive effects on children's social and cognitive development (Harvey, 1999; NICHD . . . , 1999a, 2000). In high-quality day care, even children from low-income families outscore more advantaged children on IQ tests by the time they enter kindergarten (Posner and Vandell, 1994; NICHD . . . , 1999b). A Gallup survey of working mothers with children under 18 found that many felt that child care offers young children numerous advantages; 77 percent said their children gained social skills and learned how to get along with other children, 72 percent said their children acquired better language skills, and 68 percent felt the children would be better prepared for school (Rubenstein, 1994).

The effect of high-quality educational child care in infancy persists into adulthood. A study of an all-day high-quality center in North Carolina compared the impact on children from low-income families who had received early intervention (such as enriching educational activities) from infancy through age 5 with children who had not received such intervention. Throughout their school years, the high-quality day-care group had better language and mathematical skills and higher academic achievement than their counterparts from the "regular" day-care group. The former were also more likely to attend college (Campbell and Ramey, 1999).

ASK YOURSELF

How Can I Find a Good Day-Care Program?

Here are some questions that will help you to evaluate the day-care programs you visit. Some are questions to ask of the administrators, teachers, and other staff, as well as of other parents. Others are questions to ask yourself, as you mull over the information you've gathered.

1. **What is the staff–child ratio?** The best programs have enough staff members on hand so that children get plenty of attention. Suggested staff–child ratios are 1 to 3 for infants, 1 to 10 for 5- and 6-year-olds, and 1 to 12 for children over 6.

2. **What is the staff turnover rate?** If half of the staff leaves every year it probably means that they are paid extremely low wages or feel that the program is not run well. Another warning signal is finding that parents remove their children at a high rate, apparently having arranged for care elsewhere.

3. **How do the staff and children look when you visit?** If the children seem unhappy, have runny noses, and seem passive, the center is probably ignoring such things as colds (which are easily spread) and is not providing meaningful activities for the children. If the staff seem distant or lackadaisical, they are probably not engaging kids in interesting projects.

4. **How well equipped is the facility?** There should be interesting indoor activities that give children a choice of projects, as well as ample playground space with swings, jungle gyms, and other exercise equipment. If there is no adjacent outdoor area, do the children go regularly to a park or playground where they can run, jump, climb, and swing? In addition, is the day-care facility clean, organized, and does it have a range of toys, books, materials, and activities?

5. **What are the safety regulations and hygienic practices?** Are children always accounted for when they arrive and leave? Are staff trained in first-aid? Do they use latex gloves when they change diapers or attend to a sick or bleeding child? What are the policies about children who take medications (for allergies, for example)?

6. **Is the director of the center willing to have you talk to other parents who utilize the child-care center?** If a center is run well, the director will be more than happy for you to talk to other parents. Beware of an evasive director (Skruck, 1994; see also Cadden, 1995, for a state-by-state evaluation of child care). The Taking It Further section at the end of this chapter provides Internet sites for accessing a wealth of information about day-care facilities.

Welfare reform has pushed at least a million preschoolers into mostly low-quality day care because mothers who participate in the mandated welfare-to-work programs don't have the finances to pay for high-quality child care. A study of child care for 2- to 4-year-olds in California, Connecticut, and Florida found that many of the preschoolers were in home-based care with few educational materials, little reading or storytelling, unclean facilities, and lots of television viewing. The adult care providers had only a high school diploma. The researchers concluded that children in low-quality facilities are behind in social and language development and will be unlikely to break out of poverty (Fuller and Kagan, 2000).

Those day-care centers with the best results are small and have high adult-to-child ratios (see the box "How Can I Find a Good Day-Care Program?"). Good child-care providers often quit, however, because they earn among the lowest wages—about $14,000 a year, less than pet groomers. Few receive health insurance,

and almost none receives retirement benefits (Baker, 1994). Consequently, 40 percent of day-care workers leave their jobs within a year (Ames, 1992). Top-notch day-care service that includes competent staff, high adult-to-child ratios, and staff stability is expensive—at least $200 a week. Because this is more than many families can afford, the lack of quality day care remains a serious problem.

Unlike the United States, many other Western countries offer high-quality child-care programs. Sweden has numerous government-financed day-care centers for the young children of working parents. Comprehensive day-care systems have characterized many European countries for years. For example, in France, Germany, and Italy most preschool children are in free full-day public programs. Many European countries routinely allow parents to leave work to care for sick children. Thus, there has been greater progress in meeting child-care needs in many European countries than in the United States, where "family values" are often celebrated (Kamerman, 1996).

Gay and Lesbian Parents and Children

It is estimated that 6 million to 14 million children in the United States have at least one gay parent (Kantrowitz, 1996). In most respects, lesbian and gay families are like heterosexual families: The parents must make a living, families face the usual disagreements about the use of space or money, and family members must develop problem-solving strategies (Laird, 1993; see also Chapters 5, 6, and 7). Gay and lesbian parents face the added burden of raising children who will often experience discrimination because of their parents' sexual orientation. It is for this reason and for fear of alienating their children that not all homosexual parents reveal their sexual orientation to their children, even though they may want to.

Disclosure to Children

Despite the anxiety of some homosexual parents, many children are generally accepting of gay or lesbian parents. If there is a strong parent–child bond, disclosure rarely undermines this relationship. Furthermore, disclosure may help to relieve family tensions. For example, parents may have been arguing about a partner's sexual orientation or may divorce because of it. Children often assume that they are somehow at fault when parents fight, and this tendency may be even stronger in children who do not know that a parent's homosexuality is the source of the difficulty. Children who are told the truth at an earlier age tend to have fewer problems with acceptance than do children who are told later on (Bozett, 1987).

Although most children are accepting, they may be ambivalent about disclosing to their friends that a parent is gay. Some try to hide the information from their peers or try to prevent them from seeing how their own home life differs from that of their friends:

> High school was the hardest. I was into all kinds of clubs, but I was afraid everything I had gained socially would disappear if anyone ever found out that while they went home after volleyball practice to their Brady Bunch dinners with Mom and Dad, I went home to two moms. My brother and I would never allow Mom and Barb to walk together or sit next to each other in a restaurant. We wouldn't have people spend the night; if we did have friends over, we would hide the gay literature and family pictures. (McGuire, 1996: 53)

In spite of the particular difficulties children in gay families face, their peer and other social relationships do not differ very much from those of children raised in heterosexual families. In a comprehensive summary of studies of gay parenting, for example, Patterson

(1992) concluded that the children raised in gay homes are just as well adjusted emotionally and do just as well in school as the children of heterosexual parents (see also Koepke et al., 1992; Okun, 1996). In fact, children raised by gay and lesbian parents may have some advantages. For example, teachers see the children as more responsive, and gay and lesbian parents tend to report fewer behavioral problems with their children than do parents of heterosexual children (Laird, 1993).

Sometimes gay and lesbian parents are stricter in setting limits on their children's behavior (Bigner and Jacobsen, 1989). This may reflect the additional pressures that homosexual parents experience as a result of their guilt over their sexuality or their fear that accusations of bad parenting can limit visitation or custody rights. Such fears are often justified. In some cases gay and lesbian parents have succeeded in getting visitation rights or have regained custody of their children only after appealing their cases to higher courts (Allen, 1997).

Parents with Gay and Lesbian Children

Anecdotal data suggest that many heterosexual parents have a problem accepting their children's homosexuality. The following reactions from heterosexual parents are not unusual:

> A male student had written to his parents announcing that he was homosexual and was living with his lover off campus. He immediately received a phone call in which his mother offered to pay the bill if he would go to a psychiatrist and get himself "cured." Another student went home and told her parents she had become a lesbian. The mother began to cry, and the father became furious. He told the daughter never to come home again, that she was not considered a member of the family any more. (LeMasters and DeFrain, 1989: 286)

Many parental reactions are initially negative because parents think that their children could be heterosexual if they wanted. Most Asian parents, for example, view homosexuality as a chosen lifestyle, "an undesirable indulgence of individual freedom in the United States" (Leonard, 1997: 148). A child who once was familiar now appears to be a stranger. Parents may also be concerned about becoming stigmatized themselves. Negative feelings are frequently followed with strong feelings of guilt and personal failure in their parenting roles. A common question is "Where did we fail?" Some parents may break off contact with their children, try to convince them to change their sexual preference, or ignore the issue. Others, however, and especially over time, accept the child's homosexuality (Barret and Robinson, 1990; Savin-Williams and Dubé, 1998).

CHOICES

The State of America's Children

Between 1950 and 1998, the overall annual death rate for U.S. children under the age of 15 declined substantially, primarily reflecting decreases in deaths associated with unintentional injuries, pneumonia, influenza, cancer, and congenital anomalies. During the same period, however, childhood homicide rates tripled and suicide rates quadrupled. Of 26 industrialized countries, the United States has the highest rates of childhood homicide, suicide, and firearm-related death. Between 1990 and 1995, in contrast, Hong Kong, the Netherlands, Singapore, Japan, and Kuwait reported *no* firearm-related deaths among children (Centers for Disease Control and Prevention, 1997b). The Children's Defense Fund (2000a: xxviii) reports a grim existence for many U.S. children:

Every 8 seconds	a high school student drops out.
Every 17 seconds	a child is arrested.
Every 40 seconds	a child is born into poverty.
Every 56 seconds	a child is born without health insurance.
Every minute	a child is born to a teen mother.
Every 2 minutes	a child is born at low birthweight (less than 5 lb., 8 oz.).
Every 4 minutes	a child is born to a mother who received late or no prenatal care.
Every 4 minutes	a child is arrested for drug abuse.
Every 7 minutes	a child is arrested for a violent crime.
Every 19 minutes	an infant dies.
Every 2 hours	a child or youth under 20 is killed by a firearm.
Every 2 hours	a child or youth under 20 is a homicide victim.
Every 4 hours	a child or youth under 20 commits suicide.
Every 19 hours	a young person under 25 dies from HIV infection.

Can we really improve the state of America's children? Certainly, according to many social analysts. There can be greater support for all families to raise kids successfully—employment opportunities for parents, quality health care, organized recreation, and safe streets (*Kids Count Data Book, 2000*). And a nation that ranks first in the world in defense expenditures should be able to fund many of the resources that parents need (Children's Defense Fund, 2000a).

Current Social Issues on Children's Well-Being

Despite the parenting flaws and societal limitations we discussed earlier (such as absentee fathers and inadequate child care), most people reach adulthood without serious mishaps. Millions of children, however, face tough odds of surviving or thriving because they live in poor households that generate myriad social and health problems (Rank and Hirschl, 1999; America's Children . . . , 2000). Compared to other industrialized countries, the United States ranks fairly low when it comes to children's health and well-being, as the box on "The State of America's Children" illustrates. This last section examines some of the risks that children face, and foster care, one of the responses for at-risk infants and children.

Children at Risk

Researchers have identified many factors that put children at risk of problems ranging from hyperactivity to becoming involved in crime. According to the U.S. Census Bureau (1997b), six of the most important risk factors between 1970 to 1996 were poverty, welfare dependence, absent parents, one-parent families, unwed mothers, and parents who did not graduate from high school. Although many people overcome these obstacles, others do not (Luster et al., 2000). Note, also, that the risk factors are usually interrelated.

- **Risk Factor 1: Poverty.** In 1998, 18 percent of American children under age 18 lived in families with incomes below the poverty level, up from 15 percent in 1970. Poor families have less money to invest in children's educational activities, which often means that children have to drop out of school and find a job to help care for younger siblings. Poverty also means that families have fewer resources to deal with stress, health problems, and family conflict (see Chapters 12 and 13).

- **Risk Factor 2: Welfare dependence.** In 1995, 15 percent of the nation's children were in households receiving cash assistance or food stamps. Many of those on welfare are teenage mothers and their children. Teenage females are more likely than older women who have out-of-wedlock children to drop out of high school or get a GED (which many employers see as inferior to a regular high school diploma), to compete less successfully for jobs, and to bear more children before age 30. By age 30, teen mothers receive over four times more in public assistance benefits than do women who delay childbearing (Hotz et al., 1997).

- **Risk Factor 3: Both parents are absent.** In 1999, 4 percent of children lived with neither parent compared to 3 percent in 1970. Some lived with grandparents or other relatives; others lived with nonrelatives, for example, as foster children. The number of children living with grandparents, with neither parent present, increased from less than 1 million in 1990 to almost 1.5 million in 1998. Grandparents often don't have the income or physical health to provide their charges with many resources (see Chapter 17).

- **Risk Factor 4: One-parent families.** In 1998, 28 percent of children lived in one-parent families, up from 12 percent in 1970. Many children in single-parent families, especially single-mother families, are resilient and function well despite risk factors. In fact, if the nonresident fathers are involved in child rearing but have problems themselves, they may provoke conflict and provide negative role models for their children (Thomas et al., 1996). Generally, however, the presence of only one parent is a handicap. There are fewer economic resources, for example, and single parents do not monitor and supervise their children as well as married or cohabiting parents (McLanahan and Sandefur, 1994).

- **Risk Factor 5: Unwed mothers.** In 1998, over 9 percent of children lived with a never-married mother, compared with fewer than 1 percent in 1970. A partner's economic contribution results in a 29 percent reduction in the proportion of children in cohabiting-couple families living in poverty, but they still fare poorly compared to children in married-couple families. Children in married-couple families are better off economically because of the higher education and income of their parents, rather than simply because they share a residence with two adults (Manning and Lichter, 1996).

- **Risk Factor 6: Parent who has not graduated from high school.** In 1998, 19 percent of children lived with a parent or guardian who had not graduated from high school, an improvement from 1970 when 38 percent of children had a nongraduate parent or guardian. However, since many of the better-paying manufacturing jobs that supported families in the past have vanished, a high school degree does not ensure staying out of poverty (see Chapters 1, 12, and 13).

As *Figure 11.4* shows, children who have been exposed to three or more risk factors are considerably more likely at ages 16 and 17 to experience two adverse outcomes—not being in school or not working (and becoming a teenage mother in the girl's case). Many teenage mothers may be nurturant and caring. In general, however, disadvantaged adolescent mothers must deal with numerous economic, social, and substance abuse problems that affect their relationships with their children (O'Hare, 1999). As a result, many teenage mothers tend to be less expressive and less likely to play or interact with their children and to have fewer positive attitudes toward their infants. They are also more likely to feel sad, tense and edgy, to worry about money, to lose control of their feelings, and to see infants as difficult to handle (Baranowski et al., 1990; Miller and Moore, 1990). Because many teenage fathers may be involved in drug use and other deviant behavior, they are unlikely to provide much financial support or fathering (Thornberry et al., 1997).

The family is one of the most powerful influences in an adolescent's life. Children who do not receive sufficient parental guidance, who are not supported emotionally by their parents, who live in high-conflict families, or who have drug-addicted parents are at increased risk of substance abuse, delinquency, and other social problems (Kimbrough, 1998).

Foster Care

The growth of poverty, child abuse (see Chapter 14), and parental neglect has resulted in a burgeoning of out-of-home placements for children. These placements include foster care, care by relatives, hospitalization,

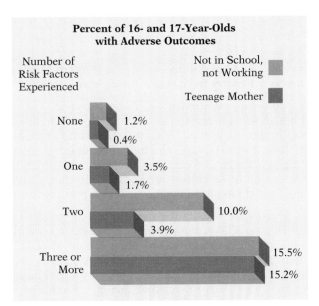

**Percent of 16- and 17-Year-Olds
with Adverse Outcomes**

Number of
Risk Factors
Experienced

Not in School,
not Working

Teenage Mother

None   1.2%
        0.4%

One   3.5%
        1.7%

Two   10.0%
        3.9%

Three or   15.5%
More   15.2%

FIGURE 11.4 **The More Risk Factors, The More
Likely Adverse Outcomes.** As the text discusses, the six
risk factors for children and adolescents include the
following: 1) poverty, 2) welfare dependence, 3) both
parents are absent, 4) one-parent families, 5) unwed
mothers, and 6) parent who has not graduated from high
school (U.S. Census Bureau, *America's Children at Risk,*
Census Brief (97-2), September 1997, p. 2).

residential treatment facilities, group homes (which
house a number of children under the auspices of a
charitable organization), and shelters for runaways.
The most common out-of-home placement for children
is the **foster home,** where a family raises children who
are not its own for a period of time but does not formally adopt them.

Nationally, the number of children in foster care
reached a record 547,000 in 1995, a 35 percent
increase since 1990. The number of children in foster
care as a result of parental abuse or neglect has
increased from 75,000 in 1963 to more than 200,000
in the early 1990s. Children who lose parents to AIDS
number from 72,000 to 125,000. Nearly 90 percent
of the children are black or Latino (Children's
Defense Fund, 2000a). Children born to mothers aged
16 to 17 are about one and one-half times more likely to be placed in foster care in the first five years of
their lives as are those born to mothers aged 20 to 21
(George and Lee, 1997). An estimated 40 to 80 percent of the families who become child-protective-
service cases have problems with alcohol or drugs
(Children's Defense Fund, 2000a). Many of the children from these households are placed in foster
homes.

Characteristics of Foster Homes In theory, foster
homes are supposed to provide short-term care until
the children can be adopted or returned to their biological parents. In reality, many children go through
multiple placements and remain in foster care until
late adolescence. Approximately 25 to 30 percent of
the children returned to their biological parents are
soon back in foster care. Children who are older or
have behavioral or emotional problems are the most
likely to bounce from home to home (Bartholet,
1999). Of the children in foster care, two-thirds are
black or Latino, nearly 45 percent enter care as babies
or toddlers, and nearly all have been neglected rather
than abused (Pascual, 1999/2000).

Problems of Foster Homes The typical foster
mother is paid very little and cares for a child who
no one else loves or parents. The mother is supervised by a social worker who is probably overworked
and often inaccessible, must deal with a variety of
people like teachers, police, judges, and medical staff,
and sometimes must face angry biological parents
who deny that they are incompetent or abusive
(Meyer, 1985).

Some children are closer to their foster families
than their biological parents and prefer to live with
their foster parents (Gardner, 1996). Others are never
able to adjust to a foster home (Fanshel et al., 1989).
If children have experienced more than one or two
placements and have been in foster care for more than
a few years, their self-esteem, self-confidence, and ability to forge satisfying relationships with peers may
erode (Kools, 1997). The solution, some propose, is to
move children as quickly as possible from foster care
to adoption (Bartholet, 1999).

Conclusion

As this chapter shows, there have been many *changes*
in raising children. Many fathers are more interested
in helping raise their children but there are more at-
risk children and a widespread need for quality day
care. Parents are faced with many *constraints* at both
the micro and macro levels. The most severe problems are generated by political and economic conditions. Even though the United States is one of the
wealthiest countries in the world, the number of
American children who live in poverty and are
deprived of basic health care and other services has
been increasing since 1980. Socioeconomic status,
race, ethnicity, and other factors often shape parental
choices. Gay and lesbian, minority, and working-
class parents, for example, have to struggle to raise
healthy children. In the next chapter we address the
unique constraints and choices that many racial-
ethnic families confront.

SUMMARY

1. Infants are not just passive recipients of care from their parents but play an active role in their own development and socialization. Parenting is not a "natural" process but a long-term, time-consuming task that parents must learn without any formal training but through trial and error.

2. Some of the major theories of child development and socialization are Mead's theory of the social self, Piaget's theory of cognitive development, and Erikson's psychosocial theory of development over the life cycle.

3. Many parents experience problems in raising children because they have unrealistic expectations and believe many well-entrenched myths about child development and child rearing.

4. Largely for economic reasons, adult children are staying in the home longer and are returning to their parents' homes, sometimes with their own children. Unless the children are chronically unemployed or have other severe problems like substance abuse, several generations living under the same roof do not have major conflicts.

5. Social scientists have identified three broad approaches to child rearing: authoritarian, permissive, and authoritative. Parenting styles vary across families, however. Some styles focus on changing the child, whereas others try to change a child's environment.

6. Corporal punishment is a controversial issue. Although some parents maintain that physical punishment is necessary, many educators argue that expressing love toward one's children, encouraging joint decision making, and creating special times with children are more successful methods of instilling discipline than spanking, slapping, or verbal putdowns.

7. Parents are usually the most important people in their children's lives, and most children see their parents as loving and supportive. Parenting can be stressful, however, if fathers are not involved in a constructive manner, if very young children are latchkey kids, and if child care is expensive, low quality, or otherwise inaccessible.

8. In general, gay and lesbian parenting is not different from heterosexual parenting. Some gay and lesbian parents fear disclosure of their sexual preference and feel more pressure to be successful as parents because they risk losing visitation or custody rights.

9. Many children face adverse outcomes such as not finishing high school, not working, and becoming teen parents. One response to such risks is to place children in out-of-home care, especially foster homes.

KEY TERMS

boomerang generation *285*
authoritarian approach *286*
permissive approach *287*

authoritative approach *287*
DEWKS *294*
latchkey kids *294*

foster home *301*

TAKING IT FURTHER

Parenting Resources

There are many great parenting Websites. This sample begins with a lighthearted perspective on child rearing and ends with some very pregnant sites.

Preparing for Parenthood offers humorous and serious information on anticipating and coping with parenthood.

www.sowashco.k12.mn.us/lake/pk/html/pfp.html

Welcome to Parent Soup! provides child-rearing advice and links to many parent discussion groups.

www.parentsoup.com

Family (the directory of regional activities for kids and families is unique).

www.family.go.com

CYFERNet provides practical, research-based information on children, youth, and families from the Cooperative Extension Services of universities in all 50 states.

http://www.cyfernet.org

The National Fatherhood Initiative encourages more effective fathering. I thought the "tips from fathers" section was especially interesting.

www.fatherhood.org

The National Child Care Information Center offers a wealth of information, including a link to *Child Care Resources on the Internet,* which then provides links to at least 100 sites on child-care issues.

www.nccic.org

And more . . . www.prenhall.com/benokraitis provides hundreds of sites on parenting newsletters from professional and government organizations, single-parenting sites, online journals, discussion groups about pregnancy and expectant parents, national parent information centers, sites targeted at fathers, children with disabilities, and resources for Latino families with young children.

CHAPTER 1

Racial and Ethnic Families: Strengths and Stresses

DATADIGEST

■ In 2000, **only 29 percent of Americans were satisfied with how well different groups in society get along with each other.** Looking at the country as a whole, 79 percent considered racial, religious, or ethnic tension as very serious or somewhat serious problems.

■ In 1998, **married-couple households across racial-ethnic groups** were as follows: 81 percent for whites, 82 percent for Asian and Pacific Islanders, 69 percent for Latinos, 65 percent for American Indians, and 47 percent for African Americans.

■ There are approximately **542 American Indian tribes** in the United States today. The largest is the Cherokee, with a population of 308,132; the smallest is the Siuslaw, with 44 people.

■ In 1996, the largest number of **people with Middle Eastern roots who immigrated to the United States** came from Pakistan (12,500), Iran (11,100), Iraq (5500), Lebanon (4400), Jordan (4400), Syria (3100), and Turkey (3100).

SOURCES: T.W. Smith, 2000; U.S. Census Bureau, 1999c.

WHAT do the following well-known people have in common: consumer advocate Ralph Nader, singer Paula Abdul, deejay Casey Kasem, heart surgeon Michael De Bakey, Heisman Trophy winner Doug Flutie, former Secretary of Health Donna Shalala, and Senator George Mitchell? All are Americans of Arab origin. Each has made a significant contribution to U.S. society, as have millions of other non-European Americans.

Chapter 3 discussed some of the history of white immigrants and families of color. This chapter focuses on contemporary African American, American Indian, Latino, and Asian families. We examine their changes in family structure, social and economic constraints, and family strengths. The chapter concludes with an exploration of marriage across racial and ethnic lines and raising biracial children. We begin with an overview of the growing diversity of American families.

The Increasing Diversity of U.S. Families

As you saw in Chapter 1, U.S. households are becoming more diverse in terms of racial and ethnic composition. Within the next 25 years, about one in three Americans will come from a non-European country. As the number and variety of immigrants increase, the ways we relate to each other may become more complex. Some people feel that immigrants should "blend" into U.S. society as soon as possible. Such blending in, or **acculturation,** is the process of adopting the language, values, beliefs, roles, and other characteristics of a host culture. Others argue that **cultural pluralism,** or maintaining aspects of immigrants' original cultures while living peacefully with the host culture—strengthens and renews U.S. society.

Changes in the Immigration Mosaic

The United States is essentially a country of immigrants. On average, 1 million immigrants enter the United States every year. Since the turn of the twentieth century, however, there has been a significant shift in many immigrants' country of origin (see *Figure 12.1*). In 1900, almost 85 percent of immigrants came from Europe; in 1997, Europeans made up only 17 percent of all new immigrants. Today's immigrants come primarily from Asia and Latin America. Most Asian immigrants come from China and the Philippines. Most Latin American immigrants come from Mexico. In addition, as you'll see shortly, there's a great deal of heterogeneity within the groups that the Census Bureau classifies as "Asian" or "Hispanic."

Today's proportion of foreign-born is small by historical standards. About 14 percent of the total U.S. population was foreign-born in 1920 compared to 8 percent in 1990, for example. Several major metropolitan areas (such as New York, Los Angeles, and Chicago) grew in the mid-1990s as immigrants replaced longtime residents who had left for other parts of the country ("Immigration fuels . . . ," 1998). It is not clear whether the native-born Americans in large cities are moving because of the increased concentration of immigrants, better economic prospects regardless of immigration, retirement, or a combination of these and other factors. Internal migrations, however, have recently ignited a resurgence of nativism.

Nativism, policies and practices that favor native-born citizens as opposed to immigrants, has surged and ebbed since 1798. In the past, anti-alien sentiments were directed at non-English-speaking Europeans (see the box "Stereotypes about European Immigrants" and the related text in Chapter 3). The targets of today's nativism, in contrast, tend to "wear

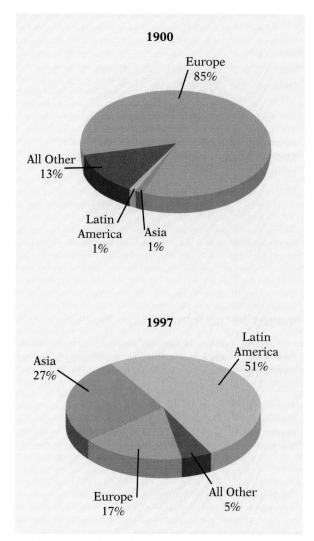

FIGURE 12.1 **Origins of U.S. Immigrants: 1900 and 1997.** In 1997, the largest number of legal immigrants in the "all other" category was 47,800 from Africa and 11,600 from Canada (Based on data in U.S. Department of Commerce, 1993, and Schmidley and Gibson, 1999).

Mexican, Central American, and Asian faces" (Perea, 1997: 2).

Immigrants usually suffer the worst discrimination during troubled economic times. These "inferior" immigrants are viewed as taking jobs, disrupting the employment opportunities of native-born Americans, and overloading schools and welfare systems (Feagin, 1997). Immigration opponents claim that the new arrivals are more likely than native-born Americans to be criminals, to bear children out of wedlock, and to have a variety of character flaws such as dishonesty and laziness (see Fukuyama, 1994). Some observers also suggest that as immigrants

improve their status and move out of cities or become more visible generally, middle-class suburbanites experience a rising level of discomfort by being exposed to "distant languages and alien cultures:"

> *I would argue that the increased visibility of new immigrants, the sight of veiled women in suburban supermarkets, the proliferation of mosques in large cities, the prevalent sound of Spanish in the streets, and the proliferation of small businesses with Korean, Indian, Arabic, and other ethnic advertising have aroused middle-class resentment in the 1990s similar to that observed nearly a century earlier. (Muller, 1997: 109)*

Not all Americans are nativists, of course. As the box "Diversity: Give Me Your Poor and Your Techies" shows, many U.S. groups have mixed feelings toward recent immigrants.

Race and Ethnicity Still Matter

Social scientists describe Latino, African, Asian, Middle Eastern, and American Indian families as minority groups. The most important characteristic of a **minority group** is its domination by a more powerful group. Numerically, a minority group can be larger than the majority, or dominant, group because the relative power of a minority group is more significant than its numbers. Louis Wirth (1945) explicitly defined a minority group in terms of its subordinate position. He went on to say that the people in such a group, "because of their physical or cultural characteristics, are singled out from others in the society in which they live for differential and unequal treatment."

What kinds of "physical and cultural characteristics" mark minority groups from a dominant group? Two of the most important are race and ethnicity. Racial physical characteristics, such as skin color or eye shape, are easily observed and mark racial groups for unequal treatment. *Ethnicity*—an individual's or group's cultural or national identity—can also be a basis for unequal treatment. As you saw in Chapter 3, many white European immigrants experienced considerable inequality when they came to the United States because of their ethnic roots.

A group that has both distinctive racial and cultural characteristics is referred to as a **racial-ethnic** group. African Americans, American Indians, Latinos, and Asian Americans are examples of racial-ethnic groups because both race and culture are central features of their heritage. Although Latinos can be of any race, most prefer terms that denote their cultural background. For example, *Neuyoricans* has been used to distinguish Puerto Ricans in New York from those in Puerto Rico, and *Chicanos* (*Chicanas* for women) is more likely to be used among Mexican Americans in the Southwest, West, and Midwest who support civil

MULTICULTURAL

Diversity: Give Me Your Poor and Your Techies

There has certainly been progress on some fronts. Latino and black middle classes have increased since the 1970s, for example (Chapter 13). And of the 4063 tech start-ups launched in Silicon Valley between 1995 and 1998, about 20 percent of the chief executive officers were of Chinese descent and 9 percent had Indian surnames (Lardnera, 2000).

The United States may be diverse in terms of race, ethnicity, and religion, but there's little evidence that cultural pluralism is one of our strengths. A 1997 public opinion poll found that 46 percent of Americans wanted immigration reduced or stopped. Almost 80 percent of the respondents were concerned that immigrants were overburdening the welfare system and increasing taxes (Martin and Midgely, 1999). Many people, especially blacks, feel that immigrants push native-born Americans out of many service and blue-collar jobs (Dunn, 1994; Becker, 2000).

In 1990, Congress created H-1B visas—six-year work permits for highly skilled overseas professionals employed by U.S. computer and software companies. Nearly 40 percent of these nonimmigrants entering with H-1B visas between 1993 and 1996 were from Asia and 17 percent were from India. Europe, led by the United Kingdom, contributed about 38 percent (Martin and Midgley, 1999).

Many of these workers, especially those from India, contend that their H-1B visas promote being "indentured servants." They claim, for example, that they are often at the mercy of "body shops," or recruiters, who collect large commissions on the workers' salaries. In addition, the workers are displaced by more recent (and cheaper) H-1B visa holders, pay U.S. immigration lawyers fees up to $25,000, receive only half of the salaries and none of the medical benefits they were promised, and are sued by powerful U.S. companies if they try to quit (Cohn and Roche, 2000).

Growth of the high-tech industries has produced numerous low-wage immigrant jobs. The Washington, D.C., suburbs, for example, comprise largely highly skilled government and business workers who have created a tremendous demand for people who will work for little pay, a demand filled almost exclusively by immigrants. Most of the immigrants, primarily from El Salvador and Mexico, are cooks, cleaners, nannies, and construction laborers. Even those with a high school or college education have little chance of upward mobility because automation has substantially eliminated middle-class jobs in finance, business services, and other non-manufacturing jobs (Suro, 1999). It's not surprising, then, that the poverty rate for people in immigrant households rose from 16 percent in 1979 to almost 22 percent in 1997. The poverty rate for persons in American-born households stayed relatively constant at about 12 percent (Camarota, 1999).

Although the poverty rates of immigrants reflect a low level of education and large family sizes, the poverty rate for immigrant-headed households has increased despite a booming economy. Because of few economic resources, many immigrants live in racially and ethnically segregated areas characterized by high rates of violence and alcohol availability, which creates unsafe neighborhoods (Alaniz et al., 1998).

rights movements among Hispanic-origin people. The term *Latino* originated in the West and Midwest. It has been adopted by groups that reject *Hispanic* as a government-imposed label that was recommended in 1973 by a task force on racial and ethnic categories (Cuello, 1997).

Race and ethnicity affect whether or not we and our family members will experience prejudice and discrimination. **Prejudice** is a negative *attitude*. It is suspicion, intolerance, or hatred of individuals and groups (usually minority groups) who are different from oneself in such things as race, national origin, or religion. **Discrimination** is *behavior*. It encompasses all sorts of actions that treat people unfairly on the basis of their race, national origin, or other characteristics. Discrimination ranges from social slights to the denial of jobs or decent salaries.

A recent survey asked respondents whether they had encountered any discrimination during the previous 30 days. Among blacks, 42 percent said they were discriminated against once (and 12 percent said it happened two or more times). Asians ranked second (31 percent) and then Latinos (16 percent). Only 13 percent of whites said they experienced discrimination because of race. The minority respondents complained of being followed around suspiciously or not being able to get the attention of salesclerks. Asians said they ran into the greatest unfair treatment at restaurants (Smith, 2000).

About 47 percent of blacks and Latinos own their homes. Nonetheless, several studies report that minorities still encounter mortgage lending discrimination, "racial steering" (where real estate agents steer minority clients to minority neighborhoods), and

Actor Danny Glover recently filed a discrimination complaint after a New York taxi refused to pick him up in a predominantly black neighborhood.

refusals for rental units ("New reports document . . . ," 1999; Heavens, 1999; Massey, 2000). Race and skin tone rather than social class play a major role in determining who gets a job and how much people are paid (Johnson and Farrell, 1995). These two issues, as we will see in the next chapter, have a big effect on families.

Although education and employment opportunities have improved since the mid-1960s, African Americans and other racial-ethnic families have to deal, often on a daily basis, with prejudice and discrimination. As this chapter shows, however, black, American Indian, Latino, and Asian American families also have strengths despite ongoing inequality. We now turn to a closer examination of each of these four groups.

African American Families

Contrary to what many people seem to think, there is no such thing as "the" African American family. They vary in terms of kinship structure, values, lifestyles, and social class (Allen and James, 1998). Yet profound stereotypes still exist (see the box on "The Ten Biggest Myths about the African American Family").

E. Franklin Frazier (1937) was one of the first sociologists to point out that there are several types of black family structures: those with matriarchal patterns; traditional families similar to those of middle-class whites; and families, usually of mixed racial origins, that have been relatively isolated from the main currents of African American life. Black family structures have changed and adapted to the pressures of society as a whole (Billingsley, 1992). Thus, when men become jobless, some nuclear families are replaced by extended families and augmented families in which nonrelatives such as fictive kin function as members of the household (see Chapter 1).

Family Structure

Black families have formed diverse households in response to societal changes. Some of these households, such as those involving stepparents and grandparents, will be examined in later chapters. We focus here on children living with one or both parents and on how the family is structured.

Black children have a greater likelihood of growing up with only one parent than do children in other racial-ethnic families. Although in 1998 almost 68 percent of all children under age 18 lived in two-parent homes, more black children lived in mother-only families than in any other type of household (see *Figure 12.2*). Mother-only households tend to be poorer than two-parent households. In 1999, for example, the median income of a black mother-only household was $19,133 compared to $50,758 for a two-parent household (U.S. Census Bureau, 1999b).

Husbands and Wives

Until the 1980s much attention focused on the alleged black matriarchy and the belief that black women had too much control and power in their families. In *Black Macho and the Myth of the Superwoman,* for example, Michele Wallace (1978) argued that the relationships between black men and women were deteriorating. In the late 1980s the movie *The Color Purple,* based on Alice Walker's novel, was criticized by many black men for depicting them as sadistic, exploitative, and brutal. In contrast, many black women felt the film realistically portrayed black women as supporting one another and their families.

Several studies show that many black families are happy with their marital lives. In a national representative sample of black husband-fathers, for example, Bowman (1993) found that 57 percent of the men were "very satisfied" with their family lives and 60 percent, 71 percent, and 77 percent primary providers, husbands, and fathers, respectively, felt that they had done "very well." In a study of 40 middle-income married-couple black families, 90 percent of the respondents reported being satisfied with their

CONSTRAINTS

The Ten Biggest Myths about the African American Family

There are many misconceptions about the African American family, most of which can be reduced to the following ten myths:

Myth 1. The bonds of the black family were destroyed during slavery. A number of historical studies have shown that most slaves lived in families headed by a father and a mother. Furthermore, large numbers of slave couples lived in long marriages, some for 30 years or more (Bennett, 1989).

Myth 2. The black family collapsed after emancipation. In 1865, the roads of the South were clogged with black men and women searching for long-lost wives, husbands, children, brothers, and sisters. Most freed slaves, some of them 80 to 90 years old, remained with their mates. Few renounced their slave vows, much less sought new partners (see Chapter 3).

Myth 3. The black family has always been a matriarchy characterized by domineering women and weak or absent men. Black America has produced a long line of extraordinary fathers, as well as many mothers and fathers working, loving, and living together (Billingsley, 1992; see also Chapter 3).

Myth 4. Most black families are poor and on welfare. Although 24 percent of African Americans live below the poverty level, in 1998 almost 26 percent of black families had annual incomes of $50,000 or more (U.S. Census Bureau, 1999c).

Myth 5. The major problem of black families is loose morals. In reality, black America has always condemned unrestrained sexual expression and has insisted on stable mating patterns. Children are valued—whether born in wedlock or out of wedlock (Hill et al., 1993).

Myth 6. Most black single-parent families are pathological. Compared to the obstacles they face, many single-parent families are remarkably resilient. They are raising children who graduate from college, who are highly motivated, and who become quite successful (Rhodes and Hoey, 1994). Although such films as *Boyz n the Hood* offer a realistic portrayal of some working-class black neighborhoods, these negative images should not be generalized to all black communities (Gaiter, 1994).

Myth 7. Black parents avoid work, fail to motivate their children, and teach them to rely on handouts. For most of the twentieth century, blacks were actually *more* likely to work than whites. Although black and white women participated in the labor force at nearly identical rates in the mid-1990s, black mothers have historically worked outside the home in larger proportions (see Chapter 3). Despite high unemployment, black men are only slightly less likely than white men to be in the work force—70 versus 76 percent (Thornton et al., 1992).

Myth 8. Black men can't sustain stable relationships. Many unmarried African American fathers maintain ties with their children and the mothers of their children. Some of these relationships last ten years or longer (Jarrett, 1994). Middle-class black fathers are often more family-oriented than middle-class white fathers (Staples, 1994).

Myth 9. Black families no longer face widespread job and housing discrimination. In a 1993 Gallup poll, almost 75 percent of white respondents said that "blacks have as good a chance as white people in my community to get any kind of job for which they are qualified" (C. G. Wheeler, 1993). In fact, qualified blacks are still less likely to be hired than their white counterparts (Thornton et al., 1992).

Myth 10. The African American family owes its survival to white generosity and government welfare. Most blacks survived because of the support of the extended family, house-rent parties, church suppers, and black schools and churches, not handouts or welfare. In fact, some observers note that the African American family has survived *in spite of* white paternalism and welfare.

spouses. When the spouses were asked to list the positive aspects of their marital relationships, they mentioned having a companion (34 percent), friendship (34 percent), mutual support (34 percent), and good communication (31 percent). In addition, the wives and husbands said they shared equally in the major decisions in the family such as what house or car to buy, which doctor to see, and children's curfews (McAdoo, 1993).

Black husbands are more likely than their white counterparts to share in the household chores (John and Shelton, 1997; Xu et al., 1997). The more egalitarian sharing of housework and child care probably reflects black husbands' willingness to "pitch in" because many of their wives are employed. Also, many grew up in families where mothers worked outside the home and many black men were "active participants" in domestic labor (Penha-Lopes, 1995).

The division of domestic work is not equal, however. Black married women are still more likely than men to do most of the traditional chores, such as cooking, cleaning, and laundry, and to be overworked. Some of the instability in black marriages, as in white marriages, has been a result of a conflict between the women's demands that men do more of the "traditionally female" domestic tasks (Hatchett, 1991).

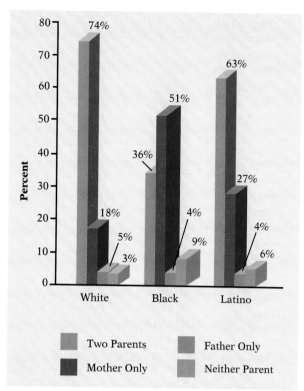

FIGURE 12.2 **Where Children Live, 1998**

SOURCE: Based on Lugaila, 1998.

Parents and Children

Although black families are often stereotyped as matriarchal, the egalitarian family pattern—where both men and women share equal authority—is a more common arrangement (McAdoo, 1993). One reason black husbands participate in child rearing is that, historically, this practice allowed women to take advantage of work opportunities that were generally not open to men, such as domestic labor and jobs in sweatshops and service industries (Jones, 1985).

Many black fathers make a conscious effort to be involved with their children because their own fathers were aloof. Others emulate fathers who participated actively in father–child activities. Still others are simply devoted to their kids:

> [My older son] and I do everything together. I learned to roller-skate so that I could teach him and then go skating together. I'm the one who picks him up from school. I'm one of his Sunday school teachers, so he spends Sundays with me at church while my wife stays at home with our two-month-old son. (Penha-Lopes, 1995: 187–188)

In a national study Toth and Xu (1999) found that black, white, and Latino fathers are very involved in

raising their children. Although the results indicate that there are more similarities than differences across the three groups, black and Latino fathers surpassed their white counterparts in such activities as monitoring, supervising their offspring's behavior, and teaching young children skills (such as reading and counting) and responsibility.

The close relationship between black parents and their children produces numerous advantages for the children. In a study of the intelligence scores of black and white 5-year-olds, for example, Brooks-Gunn et al. (1996) found that the home environment was critical in fostering a child's development. Even if the family was poor, when the parents—both black and white—provided warmth (as caressing, kissing, or cuddling the child) and stimulated the child's learning (as reading to the child at least three times a week), there were no differences between white and black children in terms of intelligence scores.

A national study found that black parents were more likely than their white and Latino counterparts to have someone in the family teach preschoolers letters, words, numbers, and songs. Black parents were also more likely to stress achievement in school to children about to enter kindergarten (Wagemaar and Coates, 1999). Black, Latino, and Asian American parents are more likely than white parents to emphasize that their children exercise self-control and succeed in school. This may reflect ethnic parents' concern that their children will have to work harder in school to overcome prejudice and discrimination (Julian et al., 1994; Thomas and Speight, 1999).

In another study, Jarrett (1995) found that low-income black families often buffered their children from the risks of getting involved in drugs and other problem behavior. The parents monitored the children's time and friendships and sometimes insisted that younger siblings act as "chaperones" by accompanying the older brother and sister to visits with boyfriends or girlfriends or to other community activities. Younger siblings can be bribed (or threatened) into silence, of course, but the parents felt that there would be fewer temptations if older brothers and sisters were responsible for the younger children.

Intact middle-class black families are very similar to their white counterparts in terms of parenting. If anything, the former are more flexible in family roles. Older children often help care for younger siblings. Black fathers also tend to be warm and loving toward their children and are involved in routine child-care activities, such as helping with homework and driving children to medical appointments (McAdoo, 1993).

According to Darrell Dawsey (1996: 112), a black journalist, "America makes shirking daddy duty easy," and some fathers are selfish and irresponsible in ignoring the children they sire. Some black men simply dump girlfriends who become pregnant because they don't want a love relationship or a long-term commitment, or

Family reunions, like this birthday celebration for John Garrett (seated, wearing white cap), of New Jersey, not only bring extended families together but also remind family members of their closeness and shared history.

don't have the money to support a child. Others may die young, be in jail, or, though not in jail, be involved in crime and drugs (Kaplan, 1997). Many fathers who are not married to the mother are often involved in parenting their children, however. Their involvement may vary from living with the child to visiting daily or seeing the child three to six times per week. Many of the fathers play with the child during visits, and they often feed, diaper, and baby-sit young children (Blackwell, 1991).

Black families are more likely than white or other racial-ethnic households to face violence or the threat of violence on an almost daily basis. In one poll, 75 percent of the black adults surveyed reported being pessimistic about their children's future. While they were concerned about such problems as poor educational opportunities, drug abuse, and out-of-wedlock teen births, three out of four black adults said they worried most that their children or other young people they know will become victims of violence (Fletcher, 1994).

Intergenerational Families

About one of five black children under 15 years old lives in extended families (see *Figure 11.2* in Chapter 11). Both black and white unwed mothers have a higher probability of living in an extended household than do their married counterparts (Furukawa, 1994). In some black households, and especially during emergencies, three generations often depend on one another for support (see Chapter 1).

Mothers of black teenage parents are especially important in helping adolescent mothers achieve educational and economic goals (Hogan et al., 1990; Dickerson, 1995). In low-income families, grandmothers'

child-care assistance is beneficial to the parenting of teenage mothers age 16 and younger. There may be mother–daughter tension for older teenage mothers, however, if the grandmothers are too involved in the grandchild's care or provide support, such as free room and board, only under specific conditions, such as not seeing the father of the baby or working to help repay the family's child-care support (East and Felice, 1996). There may also be tension and conflict if family members and relatives are unable to provide the financial assistance they had promised a teenage unmarried mother (Cramer and McDonald, 1996).

In a study of low-income black families that involved four and five generations of parents, children, and extended and fictive kin, Burton (1995b) found great diversity and complexity in intergenerational caregiving for adolescent mothers. The 14 caregiving patterns Burton uncovered included great-grandmothers, grandfathers, siblings, the child's biological father, and friends. Caregivers met the needs of family members across the life span in three ways. First, they helped socialize and parent the children of adolescent mothers. Second, they provided extensive instrumental aid (such as baby-sitting, financial assistance, and housing) and emotional support to adolescent, young-adult, midlife, and elderly family members. Finally, they met the daily needs, such as bathing and feeding, of family members who could not care for themselves, such as frail elderly parents, handicapped children, severely disabled midlife adults, or drug-addicted young adults.

What may appear to be a broken black home to outsiders may be a strong extended family network in which the female head receives a significant amount of aid from both male (father, grandfather, brother, uncle, cousin) and female (mother, grandmother, sister, aunt,

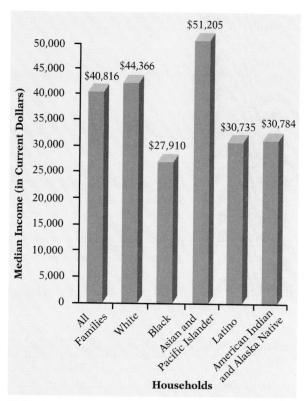

FIGURE 12.3 **Median Incomes of White and Racial-Ethnic Households, 1999.** The data for American Indian families are for 1990 (based on data in U.S. Bureau of the Census, 1999b, Table A).

and cousin) members. Black family members visit and contact one another frequently and emphasize special family occasions and rituals (see Jackson, 1991; Kim and McKenry, 1998). Such supportive family networks are most common in close-knit families, and they are prevalent in families of both low- and high-socioeconomic levels (Taylor et al., 1990; Hatchett and Jackson, 1993).

The Impact of the Economy on African American Families

As *Figure 12.3* shows, the median family incomes of African Americans are the lowest of all racial-ethnic households. Black unemployment rates are twice as high as those of whites (U.S. Census Bureau, 1999c). Joblessness has resulted in marital instability, high rates of out-of-wedlock births, and female-headed households. In addition, African Americans with little education who are lucky enough to find work are disproportionately employed in low-wage jobs. Typically, they work in industries that are sensitive to recessions, such as manufacturing and construction. Often, because of their uneven job histories, they are not covered by benefit

programs and seniority (Bowman, 1991). According to some writers, it is the high levels of poverty and unemployment among blacks that have led many black males to pursue illegal ways of making money. In 1999, for example, almost one in three (32 percent) black males in the 20–29 age group were incarcerated, on probation, or on parole (see Chapter 8).

Although the percentage of black families with incomes of $50,000 or higher has increased, middle-class blacks who have "made it" in professional and other white-collar jobs have fewer financial assets, such as stocks and bonds, than their white counterparts. According to Oliver and Shapiro (1997), the accumulation of black wealth has been limited by several factors. Black families inherit less wealth, for example, which includes not only stocks, bonds, houses, and other assets but also what economists term "human capital." That is, many middle-class black parents are less able to afford private schools, college, and other educational opportunities. Middle-class blacks also face institutional discrimination that affects all family members. Across all socioeconomic levels, for example, black and Latino applicants are twice as likely to be turned down for a loan than are whites with similar credit qualifications (Lach, 1999).

Despite these and other economic problems, a recent *Newsweek* poll found that there has been some progress for black families. Asked if their situation is better now than five years ago, whites and blacks agree equally (about 48 percent) that their situations have improved. Many African Americans are also optimistic about the future. When asked about life ten years from now, 71 percent of the black respondents felt that their family income will be better than now (compared to 59 percent for white respondents). In addition, 57 percent of black Americans (compared to 48 percent of whites) said they expect that the job opportunities for family members would be better than in 1999 ("Feeling better . . . ," 1999).

Strengths of the African American Family

Much of the research on black families prior to the mid-1980s emphasized "pathological families" and numerous social problems. Although the problems have not been solved, recent research and analysis have emphasized the diversity and strengths of the black family—strong kinship bonds, family members' ability to adapt their roles to outside pressures, a strong work orientation despite recessions and unemployment, a determination to succeed in education, and an unwavering spirituality that helps people cope with adversity (Hopson and Hopson, 1990; Taylor et al., 1990). Single-parent families headed by mothers, especially, show enormous fortitude and coping skills (Edin and Lein, 1997).

Sociologist Robert Hill feels that researchers and reporters emphasize the black family's failures but

Gaming profits from the Mystic Lake Casino, owned and operated by the Shakopee Mdewakanton Sioux Indians in Minnesota, have enabled them to endow a program in Native American Studies at Augsburg College and to support Indian arts and the American Indian Dance Theatre. The casino also provides jobs for non-Indians, who make up more than half of its employees.

neglect its successes. He maintains that the nation pays more attention to the two black families in ten that are on welfare than to the eight that are not (cited in Bock, 1997). Despite economic adversity, many African Americans see their families as cohesive, love their children whether they are born within or outside of marriage, provide a strong religious foundation, and teach their children to be proud of their cultural heritage. Other strengths include imbuing children with self-respect, teaching them how to be happy, and stressing cooperation in the family (Brissett-Chapman and Issacs-Shockley, 1997; St. Jean and Feagin, 1998). Despite disproportionately high rates of joblessness and drug trafficking, there are numerous self-help institutions (churches, voluntary associations, neighborhood groups, and extended family networks) that enhance the resilience of black families even in the poorest communities (Hill, 1998). (For a good review of the literature on the strengths of black families, see Littlejohn-Blake and Darling, 1993.)

American Indian Families

American Indians used to be called the "vanishing Americans." Since the 1980s, however, the American Indian population has "staged a surprising comeback" due to higher birth rates, a longer life expectancy, and better health services (Snipp, 1996). In 1998, an estimated 2.4 million American Indians, Eskimos, and Aleuts resided in the United States. They made up almost 1 percent of the total population and increased 14 percent since 1990 while the population as a whole grew only 8 percent (U.S. Census Bureau, 1998). A

Shoshoni observed that American Indians "were the first footprints on this continent" (White Eagle, 1996). Not every American Indian, Eskimo, and Aleut is actually native to America, however. In 1997, 6 percent (142,000) were foreign-born and three out of four arrived in the United States after 1980 (U.S. Census Bureau, 1998).

American Indians are probably the most heterogeneous group in America. A Comanche-Kiowa educator cautions, for example, that "lumping all Indians together is a mistake. Tribes of one nation are sovereign nations and are as different from another tribe as Italians are from Swedes" (Pewewardy, 1998: 71). Unfortunately, and except for economic discussions, there is still relatively little information on the diversity of contemporary American Indian families.

Family Structure

The values that have served American Indians from their earliest cultures have enabled them to maintain their families (Harrison et al., 1984). These values include a strong sense of tribalism and pride in their heritage. American Indian families speak 300 different languages and dialects, practice different religions and customs, and maintain different economies and political styles (Harjo, 1993). Together, these practices create hundreds of separate tribal loyalties.

The Census Bureau estimates that the number of American Indian households in the United States will climb from 726,702 in 1998 to 906,036 in 2010. About 74 percent of the nation's American Indian households consist of families. Of these families, 65 percent are maintained by married couples, 26 percent

Among many American Indian tribes, some people preserve traditional ways while others adopt the practices and products of the majority culture. These differences can be seen even within extended families.

by women with no husband present, and 9 percent by men with no wife present. Thus, the percentage of married American Indian couples is lower than white or Asian couples but higher than black couples (see Data Digest). The typical American Indian family is made up of 3.6 people, larger than the average 3.1 people for families of all races. In addition, the American Indian population is young, with an estimated median age of 27.4 years—about 8 years younger than the median for the population as a whole (U.S. Census Bureau, 1998).

In the past, the extended family was much closer, more organized, and more protective of other family members. Extended families are still important today, however, and are fairly common on American Indian reservations. Among the Hopi and Navajo, for example, aunts and uncles are important family members. Sometimes the father's brothers are called "fathers," and uncles and aunts refer to nieces and nephews as "son" or "daughter." There is a strong sense of support among extended family members. For example, it was not unusual during the 1970s for American Indian students to arrive at college laden with expensive items like rugs and jewelry given them by family members to be sold in case they needed money (Burgess, 1980).

Today, American Indians are more likely than white and Latino families to interact frequently with

an interconnected web of kin that includes siblings and extended kin. American Indians' frequent contact with family members may be due to a reliance on family and kin to buffer stressful emotional and economic circumstances (MacPhee et al., 1996). About half of the nation's American Indian households live outside metropolitan areas. The remainder is split about equally between the suburbs and the central cities of metropolitan areas (U.S. Census Bureau, 1998). If American Indian families are more isolated geographically and socially because of migration, supportive family networks may be especially important.

Parents and Children

Although the extent of nonmarital pregnancy among American Indians is not known, women aged 15 to 19 have lower birth rates than their black and Latino counterparts (Ventura, Curtin et al., 2000). Some limited evidence suggests that no stigma is attached to having children outside of marriage. Both urban and reservation women disapprove of abortion regardless of economic hardship (if the couple can't afford another child, for example) or marital status (if the woman is not married) (John, 1988).

Children are important family members. Parents spend considerable time and effort in making items for children to play with or to use in popular activities and ceremonies (such as costumes for special dances, looms for weaving, and tools for gardening, hunting, and fishing). In many tribes socialization continues to be the province of the clan, band, or tribe. Spiritual values are taught and emphasized in special rituals and ceremonies (Yellowbird and Snipp, 1994).

Many tribes teach children to show respect for authority figures by listening and not interrupting. As one tribal leader reportedly noted, "You have two ears and one mouth for a reason" (Gose, 1994). American Indian families emphasize such values as cooperation, sharing, personal integrity, generosity, harmony with nature, and spirituality—values quite different from the individual achievement, competitiveness, and drive toward accumulation emphasized by many in the white community (see Stauss, 1995).

Sometimes American Indian parents feel they are losing control over their children's behavior and development. Parents often complain that their children don't obey or listen to them and that the children are irresponsible and preoccupied with unproductive pastimes, such as hanging around with friends and drinking. Such concerns may be justified. According to a study by the Bureau of Indian Affairs, for example, in 1997 there were an estimated 375 youth gangs at reservations, up from 181 gangs in 1994. Some of the gang members have been convicted of homicide, robbery, and other crimes ("Youth gangs on rise . . . ," 1997).

Researchers posit that there is a relationship between American Indian adolescents' risk-taking behavior (such as using drugs and dropping out of school) and low family connectedness. That is, migration off reservations has weakened the extended family, a principal mechanism through which values are transmitted and accountability is learned and enforced (Machamer and Gruber, 1998). Child abuse and neglect may be one manifestation of weakened family ties. As *Table 12.1* shows, child abuse and neglect among American Indians is slightly higher than among black households, but twice as high as in Latino and white households and three times the rate for Asian children. Some of the reasons, as you'll see shortly, may reflect economic and substance abuse problems.

Elders and Grandparents

American Indian children are taught to respect their elders. Old age is a "badge of honor." To have grown old is to have done the right things and to have pleased your creator. Elders have traditionally occupied a central role in a family's decision making, and, because of the Indian emphasis on family unity and cooperation, they have expected family members and tribal officials to offer them assistance without having to ask for it (John, 1988). According to the Navajo, for example, the life cycle consists of three stages: "being cared for," "preparing to care for," and "assuming care of" (Bahr and Bahr, 1995). Thus, caring for each other and elderly family members is a cultural value passed on to children.

In their research on Navajo and Apache reservations, Bahr and Bahr (1995) found that many grandmothers and grandchildren depend on each other:

> Grandchildren may help their grandmothers gather cattails to harvest yellow pollen, "pick" worms to sell to fishermen, catch fish to help supplement the family diet, or make tortillas. The grandmothers encourage the children in their schoolwork, and many of the grandchildren help with household chores, chopping wood, sweeping floors and washing dishes. (p. 248)

Although many elders and grandparents are still primary providers of child care and teach children their tribal customs and values, their influence and responsibilities have become more limited. Bahr and Bahr (1995) found, for example, that grandmothers feel they cannot spend as much time with their grandchildren and teach them as much as they'd like because when the grandchildren are home from school, they often watch television. Other researchers have noted that the status and authority that grandparents enjoyed in the past may be undermined by deteriorating social and economic conditions that threaten the viability of the elders' roles in the extended family (Yellowbird and Snipp, 1994). For example, many young American Indians have left reservations in

TABLE 12.1

Child Abuse and Neglect in U.S. Households, 1995

Racial-ethnic group	Number of victims per 100,000 children age 14 or younger
All children	1724
American Indian	3343
Black	3323
White	1520
Latino	1254
Asian	479

NOTE: Rates were calculated on the number of children age 14 or younger because they account for at least 80 percent of the victims of child abuse and neglect.

SOURCE: Greenfeld and Smith, 1999, p. 15.

search of decent housing and better employment and educational opportunities (Bonnette, 1994).

As families move off reservations, some grandparents play the role of "cultural conservators" (Weibel-Orlando, 1990). Conservator grandparents try to have their grandchildren live with them whenever possible. By taking their grandchildren to church meetings, tribal hearings, dances in full regalia at powwows, and other reservation activities, the grandparents hope to familiarize their grandchildren with the American Indian way of life. Today many American Indian college students return to work or to teach on reservations or in other American Indian communities because "they long for mothers, fathers, sisters, brothers, and perhaps most of all, their grandparents" (Garrod and Larimore, 1997: xi).

Health and Economic Well-Being

Two significant issues that tribal leaders have begun to address are mental health problems, such as depression, and the physical and sexual abuse of children. Suicide rates are high among American Indians, especially among teenagers and men under the age of 40. Alcohol-related violence is another problem and is related to depression, high suicide rates, and crime (see the box "Some Facts and Fictions about American Indians and Alcohol Use").

Many American Indians believe that one of the reasons for the high rate of alcoholism, especially among the young, has been the gradual erosion of Indian culture. Urban American Indian children have a particularly hard time maintaining their cultural identity and often feel like outsiders in both the American Indian and white cultures. In response, hundreds

CONSTRAINTS

Some Facts and Fictions about American Indians and Alcohol Use

American Indians have forbidden the sale of alcohol on two-thirds of all reservations, but alcohol consumption remains a serious problem. The rate of alcohol-related deaths is almost four times higher among American Indians than the rest of the U.S. population (May, 1999). American Indians under age 35 are about ten times as likely to die from diseases directly associated with alcoholism (such as liver disease) as are other U.S. residents. American Indians are also about three times more likely to commit suicide due to alcohol use (Holden, 1996). In addition, more than half of violent crimes among American Indians involves drinking by both the victim and the offender (Greenfeld and Smith, 1999).

Although alcohol abuse is a problem in any community, May (1999) notes that there are many stereotypes and myths about "the drunken Indian." In reality,

- There is extreme variation in the prevalence of drinking from one tribal group to another.

- About 75 percent of the alcohol-related deaths are due to sporadic, binge drinking rather than to chronic alcoholism.
- Serious injuries due to alcohol (such as car accidents) often cause deaths because many Indians live in rural, western environments where medical care is far away or unavailable.
- Although the media have publicized that "one in three" Indian babies are born with fetal alcohol syndrome (FAS), the rates range from a high of 190 per 1000 children to a low of 1.3 per 1000 children, depending on the community's socioeconomic characteristics and drinking patterns.

According to many tribal leaders, several major beer companies have specifically targeted American Indians with their marketing strategies. The poorest reservations often accept sponsorship of annual tribal fairs and rodeos by major brewing companies. Besides sponsoring more than 40 pow-wows, parades, and other American

Indian cultural and sports events each year, brewers use more direct methods, including roadside billboards with such slogans as "You're in Indian Country: Switch to Schlitz," accompanied by pictures of Indian rodeo riders and feather-bedecked chiefs. American Indians who attend national conferences often find that the events have been partly underwritten by beer companies, which also promote their brands with an open bar and free mementos (Haiken, 1992).

Some Indian tribes, including the Cherokee Nation, have stopped accepting brewery money for cultural events. Tribal communities that try to prohibit alcohol sales run into obstacles, however. When the governing body of the Yakama Nation in Washington State passed a resolution to ban the sale and possession of alcohol on the reservation, they were met with protest. The owners of 48 businesses that sell alcohol—most of them non-Indians who own land within tribal boundaries—argued that they'd lose their businesses and that many American Indians would lose their jobs (Greene, 2000). The dispute continues as this book goes to press.

of programs nationwide are fighting addiction by reinforcing Indian cultural practices and values (see Holmstrom, 1997).

Some of these problems reflect worsening economic conditions. American Indians have higher unemployment rates than do other racial-ethnic families. On some reservations, unemployment rates have been as high as 90 percent (Harjo, 1993). Poverty rates are also very high; about one-third of all American Indian families live below the poverty level. About half of all American Indians own their homes (U.S. Census Bureau, 1998). Nationwide, however, more than 100,000 American Indian families are homeless or live in substandard housing (Hamilton, 1997). In 1990, 18 percent of households on reservations compared to 3 percent of American Indian households living off reservations and only 1 percent of households

nationally didn't have complete kitchen facilities, defined by the Census Bureau as containing a sink with piped water, a range or cookstove, and a refrigerator (Bonnette, 1995a). Only one-tenth of 1 percent of U.S. households nationally lacked complete indoor plumbing facilities (hot and cold piped water, a flush toilet, and a bathtub or shower) and lived in crowded conditions (more than one person per room) compared to 10 percent of households on reservations (Bonnette, 1995b).

Some tribes have become more "capitalistic" in eradicating poverty in their communities. Gaming, or the establishment of casinos on tribal lands, has resulted in the creation of jobs, economic stability, and political power (Gerdes et al., 1998). American Indians operate 124 gambling establishments in 24 states. A few, as in Connecticut and Wisconsin, are very lucrative and have created jobs, health clinics, new schools, sanitation systems, and services for the elderly (Holmstrom, 1994). Tribes in the Warm Springs Confederation, in central Oregon, own a power plant that brings in more than $3 million a year in sales to Pacific Power & Light, manage the reservation's timber, run an expensive vacation resort, and operate an apparel company that has manufactured clothing for Nike. The White Mountain Apaches of northern Arizona operate nine enterprises that generate over $45 million in revenue, including a ski resort, timber operations, and a plant that produces insulation and other materials for McDonnell Douglas's Apache helicopter (Serwer, 1993).

Strengths of the American Indian Family

American Indian family strengths include "relational bonding," a core behavior that is built on widely shared values such as respect, generosity, and sharing across the tribe, band, clan, and kin group. Harmony and balance include putting community and family needs above individual achievements. Another basis of strength is a spirituality that sustains the family's identity and place in the world (Stauss, 1995; Cross, 1998). Despite such obstacles as poverty and alcoholism, tribal leaders have implemented several strategies to improve American Indian children's self-identity and self-esteem and to empower families. The first tribal college was founded in 1968 on the Navajo reservation in Arizona. In 1997, there were 27 tribally controlled colleges in the United States, most of them two-year community colleges (Boyer, 1997). One of the achievements of the colleges has been a celebration of American Indian traditions and of the values that strengthen both the family and the community (Conover, 1997).

Latino Families

Latino families are a diverse group. Some trace their roots to the Spanish and Mexican settlers who established homes and founded cities in the Southwest before the arrival of the Pilgrims. Others are immigrants or children of immigrants who arrived in large numbers by the beginning of the twentieth century (see Chapter 3). Latino families have adapted differently to the surrounding white culture, depending on the economic and political realities they encountered.

The many different Spanish-speaking groups in the United States vary widely, but in this chapter we focus primarily on characteristics that Latino families share. Where possible, we will note intergroup variations. Keep in mind that people from Mexico, Ecuador, the Dominican Republic, or Spain are not all alike in their customs nor in their experiences in U.S. society.

Family Structure

Latino family households are less likely than white or Asian family households to be traditional two-parent families, and are more likely to be headed by single women with no spouse present (see *Table 12.2*). Like their white and African American counterparts, more Latino children are being raised in mother-only households because of divorce, out-of-wedlock births, or separation.

A combination of factors—such as attitudes about having children outside of marriage, immigration, and birth rates—affects the size of households. In 1998, Latino households were on average larger (3.9 persons) than white (3.0 persons) or black (3.4 persons) households (Casper and Bryson, 1998). Latino households are larger than those of other groups both because Latino families have more children and because more relatives live under the same roof. The share of Latino children living with two parents has declined, however, from 78 percent in 1970 to 63 percent in 1998 (Lugaila, 1998). Shifting social norms and economic changes have altered the structure of many Latino families. Men and women marry later, couples are more likely to divorce, women are more likely to work outside the home, and young children are less likely to be under the exclusive care of their parents (del Pinal and Singer, 1997). It appears, then, that many Latino families are becoming similar to most white families.

Economic Well-Being and Poverty

Many Latinos are successful. Although they make up only 5 percent of all firms in the United States, Latino-owned businesses grew 76 percent between 1987 and 1992 (from about 490,000 to 863,000). Central or South American Latinos owned about 21 percent, Mexican Americans owned half of these businesses, and Cuban Americans owned 12 percent. Because many Latino-owned businesses are in service and retail-trade industries, the average annual revenue is lower ($94,000) than that of the average U.S. company ($193,000). Nonetheless, Latino-owned businesses have increased at twice the rate of all businesses since 1987 (Salyers and Strang, 1996).

Like black families, middle-class Latino families have expanded. The proportion of Latino households earning more than $50,000 a year increased from 7 percent in 1972 to 23 percent in 1998. As *Figure 12.4* shows, nearly one-fourth of Latino families had incomes of $50,000 or more in 1998. Once again, however, there is a great deal of variation among Latino families. Among the most economically successful are the Cubans in southern Florida. In 1998, 37 percent of Cuban households earned more than $50,000 a year. In contrast, only 21 percent of Mexican American families earned this much.

TABLE 12.2

Characteristics of U.S. Family Households by Race and Ethnicity, 1996

Race-ethnic group	Family households (thousands)	Percent of family households		
		Married-couple families	Female-headed families	Male-headed families
Total population	69,597	77	18	5
Non-Hispanic	63,311	78	17	5
White	52,861	83	13	4
Black	7,871	46	47	7
Other non-Hispanic*	2,579	75	17	8
Hispanic	6,287	68	26	7
Mexican	3,815	72	21	7
Puerto Rican	742	51	42	8
Cuban	312	75	19	6
Central/South American	929	65	29	7
Other Hispanic	489	62	32	6

NOTE: Percentages may not add to 100 because of rounding.

*Includes Native American, Eskimo, Aleut, and Pacific Islander.

SOURCE: Based on U.S. Bureau of the Census, 1997a, 1997b.

Economic success and social mobility across Latino subgroups depend on a number of interrelated factors. Some of these factors include U.S. immigration policies and political relations with the country of origin, timing of migration, the skills that immigrants bring with them, and the deterioration of major metropolitan areas that are open to development. In the case of Cuban immigrants, for example, all of these variables were "just right." Perhaps one of the most important reasons for many Cuban Americans' success is that the U.S. government, hoping to weaken Fidel Castro's power, extended Cuban exiles a "generous welcome." Unlike any other Latino or non-Latino group of immigrants, the United States welcomed Cuban refugees and provided them with government subsidies, magnanimous refugee programs, scholarships for college students, and other resources (Suro, 1998). Many of the Cubans were middle or upper middle class and had human capital resources such as high educational levels and entrepreneurial skills, worked hard to develop rundown and abandoned Miami neighborhoods, and became politically active (Pérez, 1992).

In contrast, most other Latino immigrants received minimal welfare assistance from the U.S. government or have few human capital resources. In terms of the latter, for example, nearly 60 percent of the Latino immigrants in the Washington, D.C., area identify themselves as Central Americans, mainly Salvadorans, Guatemalans, and Nicaraguans. They tend to have low educational levels, and 40 percent can communicate only in Spanish (Rentería, 2000). In New York, Brazilians—with or without work papers—"are welcomed with open arms by many low-wage employers, be they the owners of chic Manhattan restaurants looking for dishwashers or harried career women in need of nannies to care for their children or immigrant entrepreneurs seeking seamstresses for their sweatshops" (Margolis, 1998: 46). Some Mexican American workers complain that Anglo bosses are happy to hire them because they work hard, but discard them after an injury instead of providing health care (Niemann et al., 1999).

This doesn't mean that all Cuban Americans are wealthy or even middle class and all other Latino groups are poor. As *Figure 12.5* shows, there is considerable variation among Latino subgroups. Mexican families are most likely to be poor, while Cubans are least likely. In 1998, for instance, 11 percent of all Cuban families lived below the poverty level and one of four Mexican American families had an annual income of at least $50,000 (U.S. Census Bureau,

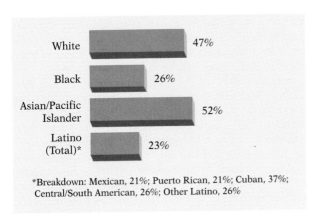

*Breakdown: Mexican, 21%; Puerto Rican, 21%; Cuban, 37%; Central/South American, 26%; Other Latino, 26%

FIGURE 12.4 **Families with Annual Incomes of $50,000 or More, 1995** (Based on U.S. Census Bureau, 1999c, Tables 51, 52, 55).

1999c; see *Figure 12.4*). In many cases, however, according to one Latino researcher, "The family that is doing the right thing is still falling behind. We have people working, people married and yet we see poverty increasing" (Fletcher, 1997).

Why do many Latino families have such low income and high poverty rates? Immigration tends to increase overall poverty rates. Even when Latinos (and Asians) are highly educated, many new immigrants find only low-paying jobs. They must make money to support their families, but they don't have time both for a job and for learning the language that would help them gain the accreditation they need to practice as doctors, lawyers, and accountants. Many immigrants who were professionals in their native land work at such low-paying jobs as delivering food for restaurants, cleaning buildings, and working as cashiers in stores ("Living humbled . . . ," 1996).

Other recent entrants have low educational levels. They tend to have fewer skills that employers want and fewer years of relevant work experience, and thus are likely to earn entry-level salaries in lower-skilled jobs (del Pinal and Singer, 1997). In 1997, 31 percent of Latinos aged 18 to 24 were high school dropouts (U.S. Census Bureau, 1999c). Some leave because they're failing, some to work to support their families. Others say they drop out because public schools marginalize them, disrespect their culture, and make them feel "like a dumb Mexican" (Headden, 1997).

Familism and Extended Families

Familism (see Chapter 3) is often seen as an important characteristic of many Latino families. In a recent national poll, for example, 82 percent of the Latinos compared to 67 percent of the general U.S. population said that relatives are more important than friends ("The ties that bind," 2000). Familism and the

strength of the extended family have traditionally provided emotional and economic support to many Latino households.

Familism The family is an important support system for emotional and economic help. Sharing and cooperation are key values (Markides et al., 1986). Some scholars suggest that familism is often a response to historical conditions of economic deprivation, and that many Mexican American families, for example, survive only because they have the support of earlier immigrants (Baca Zinn, 1994).

Many researchers who have relied on small samples or their own experiences have maintained that Latino families are more familistic than white families and that social support increases with each Latino generation living in the United States (see Hurtado, 1995, and Vega, 1995, for a summary of some of this literature). In contrast, Roschelle's (1997) study, based on a nationally representative sample, found that African American, Mexican American, Puerto Rican, and white families were about equally familistic. In fact, white women and men gave and received more childcare help and household assistance than did the other racial and ethnic groups.

Roschelle also found that participation in kin and nonkin networks does not occur equally within racial-ethnic groups but varies across socioeconomic status, country of birth, household structure, marital status, and the proximity of relatives. As socioeconomic status in racial and ethnic families increases, for example, so does the likelihood of a person's participation in social support networks that provide expressive aid (such as emotional support during times of crises)

FIGURE 12.5 **Who Are the Latino Poor?** About 1.7 million families, or 25 percent of all Latino-origin families, live below the poverty level. As you can see, the majority of the poor are Mexican. (Based on data from U.S. Census Bureau, 1999c, Table 55).

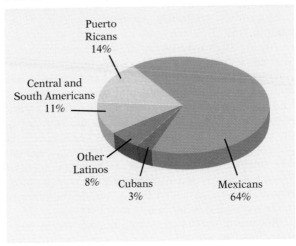

and instrumental assistance (such as helping with child care, grocery shopping, and housework). Thus, a lack of economic resources *erodes* rather than nourishes familism and support networks among white, black, and Latino families.

Familism varies, furthermore, by such variables as marital status and sex. Roschelle found, for example, that unmarried people, regardless of race or ethnic group, were less involved in family networks than their married counterparts. Women were more involved in kin and nonkin support because they were responsible for giving or receiving child-care help and household assistance.

The Extended Family Many Latino families include aunts and uncles, grandparents, cousins, in-laws, godparents, and even close friends (López, 1999). The extended family exchanges a wide range of goods and services, including child care, temporary housing, personal advice, nursing, and emotional support (Muller and Espenshade, 1985; DeBord and de Atiles, 1999). Some Mexicans have practiced a kind of "chain migration" in which those already in the United States find employment and housing for other kin who are leaving Mexico (Garcia, 1980; Ramirez and Arce, 1981). Especially among Mexican American families, two historical functions of the family have been to protect individuals from the hostilities of the dominant white society and to provide financial assistance. Some families have pooled their resources to buy a car or to provide a higher education for their children.

Typically, Latino grandparents are welcome to live with the family. It is not unusual for older Puerto Rican women to relocate to the mainland to help their adult children raise their families (Sanchez-Ayendez, 1988). In many Mexican American families, the elderly often have *placitas,* or "talks," with their children or grandchildren and are often actively engaged in passing on religious beliefs to the younger members of their families (Paz, 1993). Grandmothers, especially, are seen not as a burden but as a blessing because they serve as role models and often take care of the children while the parents are working (Carrasquillo, 1991).

Again, there may be variations by residence and social class. In a study of Mexican families in Texas, Williams (1990: 137) concluded that "the extended family has been disappearing, and among economically advantaged Mexican Americans in urban centers, the extended family is not central to the routines of everyday life." According to Abalos (1993), in very poor communities where the family has been decimated by unemployment, drugs, or AIDS, social agencies and community-based organizations have sometimes become the new extended family, taking the place of grandparents and other family members.

Acculturation can erode traditionally strong intergenerational ties. Even when they speak Spanish, for example, Mexican American grandchildren who are more acculturated than their grandparents report less frequent interaction and a decline of affection over time. Grandchildren whose cultural values more closely resemble those of their grandparents (such as celebrating Mexican holidays and marrying Mexican Americans) retain strong emotional ties and contact. Grandparents, however, report close relationships with both acculturated grandchildren and those who are more traditional. The researchers suggest that grandparents are "either insensitive or resilient to the invidious nature of a culture gap" because they emphasize intergenerational continuity while their acculturated grandchildren value intergenerational autonomy (Silverstein and Chen, 1999).

Among many recent immigrants, young children often have more responsibilities than native-born children. Because children tend to learn English faster than their parents, they frequently assume adult roles:

> I see a lot of situations where [Salvadoran and Guatemalan] parents will take a young child to get their gas installed, to ask why their services were shut off, to pay the bill. . . . So it's the children here who learn to read and write for their parents who brought them. . . . In that sense the children play a different role from other children because they are secretaries or assistants to their parents in order [for the family] to function. (Dorrington, 1995: 121)

Because children learn English quickly, they assimilate more quickly than their parents do. Such acclimation can be a source of tension between parents and children. Adolescents, for example, may want greater independence, whereas parents "want to keep a tight hand on what's happening to their children" (Dorrington, 1995: 122).

Machismo and Gender Roles

In Chapter 3 we defined *machismo* as a concept of masculinity that emphasizes such characteristics as dominance, assertiveness, pride, and sexual prowess. The last of these qualities has gotten more press than the others. Although some Latino men (like non-Latino men) pursue extramarital sexual relations, *machismo* encompasses manliness in a broader sense. *Machismo* includes such elements as courage, honor, respect for others, nurturing and guiding one's children, providing for one's family, and maintaining close ties with the extended family (Alvirez et al., 1981; Mayo, 1997). Among Puerto Rican males, according to De La Cancela (1994), *respeto* (a respect for authority, tradition and family) and *dignidad* (avoiding a loss of dignity in front of others) are central components of *machismo*. (See also the discussion of *marianismo*, the counterpart of *machismo*, in Chapter 6.)

Migrant families at the lower socioeconomic level, like this family in Texas, not uncommonly rely on their children to help in the often-backbreaking labor they perform on America's farmlands.

Some scholars contend that *machismo* has created a "ludicrous stereotype" because the concept has been misunderstood and misinterpreted in explaining Latino men and their domestic roles. In many Cuban American households, according to Bermúdez (1995: 101), *machismo* reflects a man's role as a provider and an "honorary" disciplinarian. Women, however, really govern the household: "It has been the Cuban woman who has taught values to the children, overseen their education, and offered the children the emotional support to deal with life's eventualities" (see also de Snyder, 1999). According to González (1996), there are many good role models among U.S. Latino men who participate in domestic work and child rearing but they are often overlooked in favor of the macho tough guy or the domineering husband and father.

On the other hand, some writers feel that *machismo* is deeply internalized in many Latino families. Women, they say, are often viewed as submissive, naive, and somewhat childlike (Becerra, 1988). After interviewing 200 Latinas, Flores (1994) concluded that "machismo is rampant within Latino marriages" and keeps women "in their place":

From the day a Latina starts her role as a wife, she is subjugated by **machismo.** *She carries out her household chores without any assistance from her husband. She prepares his meals, does his laundry and manages his household. When her husband gets home from work, she's always there to greet him with dinner ready. If she's employed, she'll rush home to take care of him. She is desperate for his approval. (p. 51)*

Other researchers also report that even wives who work outside the home are often assigned a status subordinate to that of men and are expected to follow traditional family roles. In a study of Puerto Rican families, for example, Toro-Morn (1998) found that working mothers were primarily responsible for the care of the home and the children. Women, not men, juggled both domestic and work schedules. And, in a study of Central American workers, Repak (1995) found that men in working-class households balked at sharing household responsibilities and child care even when women worked full time outside the home. The men expected their partners to do most of the cooking, cleaning, and caring for children because this represented the traditional gender roles in their country of origin.

If a woman holds a high-status or middle-class job, however, her husband may be less likely to exhibit *machismo* as the male-dominant stereotype. In her study of Mexican families, for example, Williams (1990) found that neither working-class nor professional women had egalitarian relationships with their husbands. Professional women, however, had an advantage over their working-class counterparts in exerting more influence and power in specific decision-making areas such as the discipline of children and the purchase of major items like cars. In another study of 20 two-earner, middle-class, Mexican American married couples, sharing housework was more likely if the wife earned as much as or more than her husband (Coltrane, 1996).

Strengths of the Latino Family

Despite their economic vulnerability, many Latino families have been resilient and adaptive. Family networks protect many family members' health and emotional well-being, and gender-role behaviors have been responsive to changing circumstances (Vega, 1995).

Many immigrants are demonstrating "incredible internal resources" in coping with economic hardship, learning a new language, and shaping their own solutions to the problems of family adjustment in a new environment (Dorrington, 1995). The ability of Latino families to transmit traditional values about familism has offset the negative impact of prejudice and discrimination, drug use, and other unhealthy risk-taking behavior among many adolescents (Brook et al., 1998; Randolph et al, 1998; Rodriguez and Kosloski, 1998; Strait, 1999; Quintana and Vera, 1999).

There was a strong "English-only" movement during the 1980s and 1990s that proposed English as the official language of the United States. Recently, however, bilingualism has been paying off economically. In 1996, for example, the U.S. Treasury Department agreed to pay 5 percent higher salaries to bilingual customs inspectors. The bilingual inspectors' language skills often forced them to do more work than their English-only co-workers in cities that had large numbers of Spanish-speaking travelers (Fiagome, 1996).

When George Bush ran for the presidency in 1992, he patronizingly referred to one of his grandchildren, George Prescott Bush, as "one of the little brown ones"—because the mother was born in Mexico. In the 2000 presidential campaign, however, George Bush's son, George W. Bush, peppered his speeches with Spanish phrases, wooed Latinos, and the "little brown one" campaigned for George W. Bush in flawless Spanish (Maceri, 2000). The growing Latino voting population might be very influential in changing some of the current stereotypes, prejudices, and discriminatory practices.

Asian American Families

Asian Americans include people from locations as disparate as India, Manchuria, and Samoa. They follow different religions, speak different languages, and even use different alphabets. The two broad groups that are well represented in the United States are those that originate from East/Southeast Asia—which includes China, Taiwan, the Koreas, Japan, Vietnam, Laos, Cambodia, and the Philippines—and South Asia, which includes India, Pakistan, Nepal, Bhutan, Sri Lanka, and Maldives (Shankar, 1998). Regardless of the country of origin, most Asian families feel pressure to adapt to U.S. culture. Some of these changes are in family structure, socialization practices, parent–child relationships, and intergenerational interaction.

Family Structure

Many factors affect Asian American family structure—the family's country of origin, the time of its arrival, current immigration policies, whether or not the family came from a land ravaged by war, and the parents' original socioeconomic status. For example, there are at least four different Vietnamese family patterns in the United States: the *nuclear family*, made up of a husband, wife, and children; the *extended family*, composed of a nuclear family, grandparents, and other relatives living together; the *broken family*, in which the father or mother and some children are in the United States and the rest of the family lives in Vietnam or died there; and the *one-person family*, which consists of the person who arrived in the United States alone and left a spouse, children, or parents in Vietnam (Tran, 1988).

Modern Chinese American families can be divided into two major types. The first type is the "ghetto or Chinatown Chinese." A dual-worker family, this type consists of the new immigrant Chinese family living in or near a Chinatown in one of the major metropolitan areas of the United States. Approximately half of these immigrants may be classified as working class, being employed as service workers, machine operators (such as sewing machines and presses), craftspeople, or laborers.

The second type is the middle-class, white-collar, or professional family that has moved from Chinatown into the surrounding urban areas and suburbs. These immigrant or American-born Chinese are more modern and cosmopolitan in orientation and view themselves as more American than Chinese (Wong, 1988). In most cases one parent, if not both, has a college degree and a professional or white-collar occupation.

Parents and Children

Major socialization values are very similar across most Asian American families (Min, 1995). There is an emphasis on group cooperation, filial piety, and obedience, as well as responsibility and obligation to the family. As in the Latino emphasis on familism, the Asian American family is more important than the individual. For example, the Vietnamese saying *mot giot mau dao hon ao nuoc la* ("one drop of blood is much more precious than a pond full of water") reflects the belief that family solidarity is more important than outside relationships. A Vietnamese can always depend on family or relatives in time of need and considers it a moral obligation to support the family and relatives (Tran, 1988). Even when extended kin don't live together, they may cooperate in running a common family business, pool income, and share certain domestic functions, such as meal preparation (Glenn and Yap, 1994).

Encouraging children to get good grades in school, maintaining discipline, being concerned about what others think, and conformity (not standing out in a deviant way) are also important in most Asian American families (Kitano, 1988). Some Asian families avoid seeking available social services, such as counseling and legal assistance, because going to an outsider for help or allowing someone outside the family to become aware of family problems is perceived as shameful and "losing face " (Fong, 1994).

Maturity is usually encouraged in Asian American children at a very young age. Aggressive behavior and sibling rivalry are not tolerated, for example, and older children are expected to serve as role models for younger children. When parents are involved with their children, much of their time is spent in academic-related activities. For example, in a study of Vietnamese, Chinese Vietnamese, and Lao families, Caplan et al. (1989, 1992) found that 45 percent of the parents help children with their homework, even though they may not speak English well enough to supervise the content of the work. The emphasis on academic achievement is depicted in the box "How to Be a Perfect Taiwanese Kid."

Some scholars explain the similarity of values as being grounded in cultural tradition, especially in religion. Many Asian American groups follow Confucianism, which teaches harmonious social relations, mutual benevolence between parents and children, and children's obedience to and reverence for parents, other adults, and the elderly. In the case of Indian Asians, traditional Hindu values regard marriage as a social duty toward the family and the community, emphasize family harmony and unity, and view kinship ties as of paramount importance over individual interests (Chekki, 1996).

Family relationships and socialization practices vary by social class and the degree of acculturation, however. For example, Korean parents whose children were born and raised in Korea tend to be authoritarian. They use punishment more and are not likely to give monetary rewards for positive reinforcement as often as younger, middle-class Korean immigrants do. Immigrants with more education, especially those with U.S. college or university degrees, have more liberal child-rearing practices. Like many middle-class U.S. parents, they tend to adopt more "democratic" methods of socialization in which both children's and adults' attitudes are given a hearing (Min, 1988).

Acculturation shapes other relationships between parents and children. In a study of immigrant Indian fathers, for example, Jain and Belsky (1997) found that the most acculturated fathers were more involved in such fathering roles as caretaking, including feeding, bathing, and comforting a distressed child; playing with and disciplining a child; or reading books to a child. Less acculturated fathers were less likely to be involved in any of these parenting roles. Lin and Liu (1993) also found a shift of emphasis in filial obligations among Chinese immigrant families in California. Although children were generous in providing resources for the well-being of their parents, they were reluctant to follow their parents' wishes in such areas as choosing marriage partners or general parental advice.

There is some evidence that gender-role socialization is still very traditional in many Asian American

Many Asian American families see education as the most important factor in getting ahead and being successful in U.S. society. Many parents, such as this Korean dad, often help their children with homework.

families. For example, Korean mothers who work outside the home expect girls, but not boys, to help with cooking and dishwashing. In terms of extracurricular activities, boys are encouraged to take up sports, whereas girls take music and art lessons (Min, 1988). Vietnamese parents expect obedience from all children, both sons and daughters. Parents enforce discipline more strongly among girls than among boys, however, even in the use of corporal punishment. These and other socialization differences exist because of the Vietnamese ideal of "the virtuous woman," which calls not only for passive obedience but also for living up to higher behavioral standards than are expected of men (Zhou and Bankston, 1998).

Husbands and Wives

In many Asian American families, males are valued more than females. Among Asian Indian and Chinese American families, for example, men are the heads of the household, the decision makers, the primary wage earners, and the disciplinarians. Women are typically subordinate to men rather than being regarded as equal partners (Segal, 1991; Yu, 1995). The role of the male as the authority figure may be changing, however. Large numbers of Asian American mothers are employed because a double income is necessary for economic survival. In some cases, a woman may work

MULTICULTURAL

"How to Be a Perfect Taiwanese Kid"

Many immigrants—Latino, Middle Eastern, and African—emphasize education as the route to upward mobility and success. The value of education is embodied in the Chinese proverb: "If you are planning for a year, sow rice; if you are planning for a decade, plant trees; if you are planning for a lifetime, educate people." For many Asian parents, securing a good education for their children is a paramount objective (see, for example, Zhou and Bankston, 1998; Hurh, 1998; Pollard and O'Hare, 1999).

By excelling in school, the child brings honor to the family. Educational and occupational successes further enhance the family's social status and ensure its economic well-being as well as that of the individual and his or her own family or the next generation (Chan, 1999). The following observations about how to be the perfect Taiwanese kid (Ng, 1998:42) from the first generation's perspective would apply to many other Asian American families as well:

1. Score 1600 on the SAT [Scholastic Aptitude Test].
2. Play the violin or piano on the level of a concert performer.
3. Apply to and be accepted by 27 colleges.
4. Have three hobbies: studying, studying, and studying.
5. Go to a prestigious Ivy League university and win a scholarship to pay for it.
6. Love classical music and detest talking on the phone.
7. Become a Westinghouse, Presidential, and eventually a Rhodes Scholar.
8. Aspire to be a brain surgeon.
9. Marry a Taiwanese-American doctor and have perfect, successful children (grandkids for *ahma* and *ahba!*).
10. Love to hear stories about your parents' childhood . . . especially the one about walking 7 miles to school without shoes.

---

outside the home to support the family while the man pursues educational or technical training for a skilled job (Kibria, 1994).

According to some Vietnamese husbands, more Vietnamese American families are breaking up because of the stress that results when wives must work to make ends meet. When women work, they become independent and no longer tolerate abuse or adultery by their mates: "Over here they say the hell with you and they leave" (Seaberry, 1991: B9). Similarly, third-generation Japanese men and women have greater economic equality, which means that women have more choices in finding partners, are less dependent on marriage, and may seek a divorce if the marriage is unhappy (Takagi, 1994).

In many other cases, however, working outside the home has not decreased the wife's homemaker role. For example, in many Vietnamese families, although both husband and wife work full time, the wife is expected to cook, clean the house, and take care of the children:

Mrs. Nguyen is employed by a local sewing factory, where she works 40 hours per week and often works overtime. Her husband, Mr. Nguyen, is a machinist employed by a local factory. He also works 40 hours per week. The couple has four children who are all of school age. Every morning, Mrs. Nguyen gets up early to cook breakfast . . . and prepares lunches for the children, her husband, and herself. In the evening, Mrs. Nguyen
hurries home to cook dinner. When she has to work overtime, her older daughter, a 16-year-old, prepares dinner for the family. Mr. Nguyen never knows what is going on in the kitchen, but he would become angry if dinner were not ready at 7:00 P.M. Mrs. Nguyen takes care of all domestic affairs, including controlling and planning the family budget. During the weekend, Mr. Nguyen spends most of his time working with the Vietnamese Catholic community (attending meetings or other social activities) while his wife stays home and cleans the house or works in the garden. (Tran, 1988: 292–93)

A number of studies show that Korean, Filipino, Hmong, and other Asian wives typically bear a heavy burden of double roles (Agbayani-Siewart, 1994; Chan, 1994; Bergano and Bergano-Kinney, 1997; Chen, 1999; Kim, 1999). Because a majority of wives and husbands adhere to traditional gender roles (see Chapter 4), working wives have to struggle alone to manage the household work unless they receive some help from their children or relatives. Furthermore, they bear the double roles regardless of length of residence in the United States (Hurh, 1998; Kim and Kim, 1998).

Also important among some recent immigrant families is the expansion of women's roles beyond such traditional work as child care and housework. For example, Vietnamese refugee women must often deal with social institutions outside the home, such as schools, hospitals, and welfare agencies. This "intermediary" role played by women is a potentially important source of power for wives in their relations with husbands (Kibria, 1994).

Intergenerational Relationships

What often keeps many new immigrant families together is tradition, religion, and cultural bonds brought with them from their homeland. As children become more assimilated, however, their attitudes about marriage and family life tend to become dissimilar from those of their parents.

In some Asian American families, American-born children are rapidly outnumbering family members who were born outside the United States. For example, in 1979, 22 percent of Asian Indians living in the United States and between 14 and 24 years of age had migrated from India, but nine years later only 13 percent of this group were foreign-born (Segal, 1991). Thus, growing numbers of Asian Indian children are first-generation American citizens. This creates the potential for greater generational and cultural conflicts.

Even families who have been in the United States a short time experience generational conflict. A social worker who worked with Vietnamese families noted that "the kids are completely American after 7 years in America. They want to date, they want to go out with their boyfriend, girlfriend. This idea never existed in Vietnam. So the older generation cannot stand this stuff. And the kids feel terribly upset when mother says, "Hey—you have to stay home" (cited in Gold, 1993: 311).

Intergenerational conflicts vary across groups in terms of length of residence, degree of acculturation, and self-identity (being "Japanese" versus "Japanese American," for example). In a study of Japanese Americans and Indo-Americans in California, for example, Kar et al. (1998) found that both Indo-American parents and their second-generation children reported that the single greatest source of conflict was over dating and marriage partners. Unlike the Japanese American respondents, Indo-American parents were concerned that their children were dating and would marry people with different religious and ethnic backgrounds.

Children's responses to intergenerational conflict vary. Many second-generation Filipino youth are college-educated and middle class and have integrated easily into U.S. society. Others, however, experience stress and alienation. They are unable to deal with parental pressure to excel academically or to major in college disciplines chosen by their parents. They feel that they can't communicate with their parents. When some of the children ventured to tell a parent about their thoughts, their lives, or their problems, the young people immediately regretted sharing the information: "Instead of the empathy, understanding, support and love that they had hoped for, they received a lecture, anger, disappointment, or emotional punishment." Filipino family ideology teaches that a child's problem that is revealed to an "outsider"—whether a friend, teacher, or counselor—would create gossip and bring shame (*hiya*) and embarrassment to the family because it implies that parents are doing a bad job of raising their children. Bottling problems up may lead to loneliness, depression, and suicidal thoughts (Wolf, 1997).

Some recent refugee families face even more serious problems. Unlike some of the educated elite who fled Vietnam in the mid-1970s, the second and third waves are poor, lack education, and are finding it harder to assimilate. If Southeast Asian teenagers don't speak much English, they may be rejected by their American counterparts and then rebel against Old World values. Vietnamese, Filipino, Asian Indian, and other teenagers may deal with conflict by engaging in premarital sex, using drugs, running away from home, or joining neighborhood gangs (Ungar, 1995; Bhattacharya, 1998; Alsaybar, 1999; Posadas, 1999).

Relationships with aging parents and grandparents also vary across Asian American subgroups. The ideal family myth, according to Ishii-Kuntz (1997), is that Asian Americans have great respect for their elderly family members. It has long been assumed that—because of the traditional value of filial responsibility—Asian American adults feel more obligated to their parents, provide more financial aid to their parents, and interact more frequently with their parents than do other racial-ethnic groups. In reality, Ishii-Kuntz's research shows, filial obligations vary quite a bit across Chinese, Japanese, and Korean families due to a number of structural and economic factors. For example, Korean American adults are more likely to provide emotional and financial support to their parents compared to their Chinese and Japanese counterparts, due in part to the recency of immigration for many elderly Koreans. Chinese American adults who have stable financial resources assist their elderly parents, whereas those who have few financial resources are unable to do so.

Some aging Cambodian refugees live in extended families because of economic reasons rather than choice. As one 63-year-old man observed, "I share this room with two people, my younger brother and one other. We have to live together to help each other out. I would like to live alone so I can have a bigger room and privacy, but no, I can't do it. No money, no space" (Becker and Beyene, 1999: 299). While many Asian grandparents transmit cultural values to their grandchildren, they can also create conflict by "meddling" or criticizing adult children and grandchildren who have become Americanized (Lessinger, 1995; Pettys and Balgopal, 1998).

As a group, Asian American families have maintained much of their cultural identity and have remained cohesive despite assimilation and intergenerational differences. Ironically, their ability to succeed despite historical discrimination and exclusion has created other problems: Their reputation for being a "model minority," for example, has both helped and hindered their progress.

The Model Minority: Fictions and Facts

Many Asian parents invest more resources in their children's education than their white counterparts despite comparable family incomes. The emphasis on education may reflect the fear that only a "safe" profession, such as being a doctor or engineer, will protect their children from future discrimination (Kao, 1995). The high percentage of Asian American students achieving academic success in the United States has prompted the media to stereotype Asian families as the "model minority."

Fictions about the Model Minority Although the median income of Asian American families compares favorably to that of other groups (see *Figure 12.4*), such figures are misleading because many Asian American households are larger than average and include more workers (Takagi, 1994). Thus, higher median incomes may often represent more persons working per family, not necessarily higher salaries. Furthermore, about 60 percent of all Asian Americans live in the three states that have both higher incomes and higher costs of living—California, Hawaii, and New York (O'Hare et al., 1994). This means that family expenditures are also high.

Many Asians arrive in the United States with few skills and low educational levels. Lumping all Asians together and treating them as a "model minority"

ignores many subgroups that are not doing well because of academic and economic difficulties. For example, only about 31 percent of the Hmong population compared to 88 percent of Japanese have graduated from high school. Among Pacific Islanders, the proportion with at least a high school diploma ranges from 64 percent for Tongans to 80 percent for Hawaiians (Bennett and Martin, 1995). In many colleges on the West Coast, there are more students enrolled in noncredit classes such as English as a Second Language (ESL) and vocational training than in academic courses for credit. Many students may have to wait as long as a year to get into the noncredit classes, and it typically takes them at least three years to complete the ESL sequence (Magner, 1993).

Income figures show that the most successful Asian Americans are those who speak English relatively well *and* have high educational levels (Hughey, 1990). Many recent immigrants who have top-notch credentials from their homeland often experience underemployment in the United States. That is, they work at much lower level jobs than those for which they are qualified. Because they do not know English very well, or are not qualified to take state accreditation exams (because they have not received their degree from a U.S. institution or because their residence or citizenship status makes them ineligible), many former doctors, accountants, and engineers work as janitors, assembly-line laborers, or waiters ("Living humbled . . . ," 1996; Jo, 1999). Foreign-born physicians have to pass stringent medical exams not required of native-born Americans because foreign-born medical training is often deemed inferior or less rigorous (Gamboa, 1995).

FIGURE 12.6 **Interracial and Interethnic Married Couples, 1998** (based on data in U.S. Census Bureau, 1999c, Table 65).

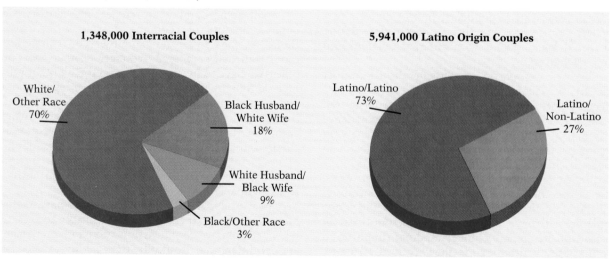

1,348,000 Interracial Couples

White/Other Race 70%
Black Husband/White Wife 18%
White Husband/Black Wife 9%
Black/Other Race 3%

5,941,000 Latino Origin Couples

Latino/Latino 73%
Latino/Non-Latino 27%

MULTICULTURAL

Dangers of the Model Minority Myth

In recent years, many scholars, especially Asian American scholars, have spent considerable energy debunking the stereotypical notion of Asian Americans as a "model minority." Peterson (1966: 21) first used the phrase "model minority" when he described Japanese Americans as an unparalleled success story:

By any criterion that we choose, the Japanese Americans are better than any other group in our society, including native-born whites. They have established this remarkable record, moreover, by their own almost totally unaided effort. Every attempt to hamper this progress resulted only in enhancing their determination to succeed.

Do (1999: 118–122) presents six dangers closely associated with the model minority image. Although Do is referring to Vietnamese Americans, the negative effects of the model minority myth apply to other Asian Americans as well.

Danger #1: The model minority image distorts and fails to acknowledge the differences within Asian American communities. Even though Vietnamese Americans, for example, share many cultural characteristics and customs, they are also a diverse group. The diversity lies in the time of their arrival to the United States, their degree of exposure to Western culture, education, social and economic status in Vietnam, English proficiency, and degree of support after arrival from social services, family, and the Vietnamese American community.

Danger #2: The model minority stereotype creates tension and antagonism within and across Asian American subgroups. If recently arrived immigrants aren't as successful as their predecessors, there must be something wrong with *them*. Other immigrants have done very well, after all.

Danger #3: Model minority images can lead to verbal and physical assaults. White supremacist groups, who resent many Asian Americans' educational and occupational accomplishments, often target Asian Americans in hate crimes that include homicide.

Danger #4: The model minority myth camouflages ongoing racial discrimination in U.S. society by blaming the victim. If some groups don't succeed, it must be their own fault rather than U.S. policies or racism.

Danger #5: As with any image or stereotype, the model minority image deprives members of that group of their individuality. Although many Asian American students are interested in teaching, social work, dance, and theater, they are often pressured to pursue careers in law, medicine, engineering, dentistry, computer science, or the biological sciences.

Danger #6: The model minority myth deprives individuals of necessary social services and monetary support. Asian Americans are typically excluded from corrective civil rights policies, such as affirmative action programs, because they are labeled as "achievers" (see Ancheta, 1998). For example, Filipino Americans living in California have often been denied consideration for special programs targeting "underrepresented" groups on campuses because they have generally not been seen as needing special assistance, as have black, Latino, and American Indian students (Posadas, 1999).

Some Korean doctors work as hospital orderlies and nurses' assistants because they can't support a family at the same time as they prepare for the English-language test and the medical exam in their field of specialization. Because of an oversupply in some medical professions in the United States, hundreds of Filipino pharmacists work as clerical, sales, and wage laborers. Even when Asian Americans are employed in professional jobs—such as architects, engineers, computer systems analysts, teachers, and pharmacists—they are not in the upper levels of management (Hope and Jacobson, 1995). The box "Dangers of the Model Minority Myth" describes some negative consequences of this image on Asian Americans and society at large.

Facts about the Model Minority There are two major reasons why many Asian American families have become successful. One is that the United States has typically screened immigrants and allowed entry primarily to those who are the "cream of the crop" in their own country. The other reason is that some Asian values and traditions are particularly compatible with American capitalistic values.

Some of the immigrants from many Asian countries represent highly skilled and well-educated people. For example, nearly 66 percent of the recent Filipino immigrants have been professionals, usually nurses and other medical personnel, and nearly two-thirds of all Asian Indian professionals in the United States have advanced degrees. Foreign-born professionals are willing to work the long hours demanded by public hospitals, and they are more likely than American-born medical personnel to work for lower salaries (Suro, 1994).

Second, many scholars argue, the mixture of Buddhist and Confucian values and traditions resembles traditional middle-class prerequisites for success in America. Both cultures emphasize hard work, education, achievement, self-reliance, sacrifice, steadfast purpose, and long-term goals. Asian and American traditions do differ in at least one important way, however. Whereas American values stress individualism, competition, and independence, Buddhist and Confucian traditions emphasize interdependence, cooperation, and pooling of resources (Caplan et al., 1989). Thus, for example, many Korean immigrants have been able to secure capital to start a small business through *kae* (or *kye*), a credit-rotation system in which about a dozen families donate $1000 or more to help a shopkeeper set up a new business (Yoon, 1997).

Once established in business, Asian store owners lead anything but leisurely lives. It is not unusual for small store owners who are husband-and-wife teams to work up to 137 hours a week. They try to keep their stores open as many hours as possible even when this puts them at risk of physical danger, for many of the stores are in slum areas and vulnerable to robberies (Bock, 1992).

Money pools like the *kae* are not limited to Koreans. According to Sun (1995), the rotating savings and credit organization is common to many ethnic groups in the Washington, D.C., area: Ethiopians call it *ekub,* Bolivians call it *pasanaqu* (from the Indian word that means to "pass from hand to hand"), and Cambodians call it *tong-tine.* All operate on the same basic principles: Organize a group of close friends; agree on how much and how often to pay into the kitty; and determine how the money will be apportioned, whether by lottery or need. The winner can use the funds to start a business, pay for a wedding, put down a deposit for a home, or pay for college tuition.

One of the most important catalysts in the success of the Asian American family has been its emphasis on education. During high school, many Indochinese students spend three hours per day on homework, two-and-a-half hours in junior high, and an average of two hours in grade school. In contrast, many U.S. students study about one and a half hours per day at both the junior and senior high school levels (Caplan et al., 1992). Among young adults (aged 16 to 24), Asian Americans are more likely than whites to be in school and less likely to be in the labor force. In 1990, 66 percent of Asian Americans in this age group were in school, compared to just 54 percent of whites (O'Hare and Felt, 1991). Even the poorest Asian American families are determined to succeed. All of a family's energies are often directed toward education as a means of upward mobility.

Strengths of the Asian American Family

As in the case of Latino families, researchers continuously emphasize that Asian American families vary significantly in terms of country of origin, when they immigrated, the ability to speak English, and other factors. Generally, however, the strengths of Asian American families include stable households where parents encourage children to remain in school and offer personal support that reduces stress against discrimination and leads to better emotional health (Barringer et al., 1993; Leonard, 1997). Although many traditional family characteristics are changing, many young adults such as Vietnamese Americans want to maintain the close-knit character of their family life that emphasizes cooperation, caring, and self-sacrifice (Kibria, 1994; Zhou and Bankston, 1998).

Interracial/Interethnic Marriages and Raising Biracial Children

As you saw in Chapter 7, the number of interracial and interethnic married couples has increased since the 1970s. This section looks at these marriages in greater detail and examines some of the issues involved in raising biracial children.

Interracial and Interethnic Marriages

Some sociologists and anthropologists have estimated that 75 to 90 percent of African Americans have white ancestors and about 1 percent of white Americans— millions of people—have black ancestors without knowing it (Davis, 1991). Most of this mixed ancestry is largely the result of slaveowners' and other white men's raping of black women during slavery (see Chapter 3). Laws against miscegenation (marriage or sexual relations between a man and a woman of different races) existed in America as early as 1661. It wasn't until 1967, in the U.S. Supreme Court's *Loving v. Virginia* decision, that antimiscegenation laws were overturned nationally.

Interracial and interethnic marriages, or exogamy, in the United States have increased slowly—from 0.7 percent in 1970 to about 5 percent of all married couples in 1998. Thus, 95 percent of all couples are married to someone of the same race or ethnicity. (See, however, in Labov and Jacobs, 1998, that some of the intermarriage figures aren't accurate because they don't consider the marriages of children who have mixed ancestry.) As *Figure 12.6* shows, of the almost 1.4 million interracial married couples in 1998, only 26 percent involved white and black unions. Such unions were more likely between a black man and a white woman (65 percent) than between a black woman and a white man (35 percent). In the same year, 27 percent of the married couples involved Latinos and non-Latinos. Latino women were more likely than Latino men to have a non-Latino spouse. And, of all Latino groups, Mexican men and women were the most likely to marry Mexicans rather than other Latinos or non-Latinos.

African Americans have the lowest interracial marriage rates (about 6 percent) and American Indians have the highest (about 74 percent) (Spain, 1999). Large numbers of American Indians are marrying people with black, Asian, Latino, or white backgrounds. About half of those who intermarry have white spouses (Yellowbird and Snipp, 1994; Bachu, 1996).

Asian men are more likely than Asian women to marry within their own group (78 percent versus 64 percent) and Asian-Anglo intermarriage (compared to marrying other Asians) accounts for an overwhelming proportion of out-marriage. There are variations across Asian groups and sexes, however. Japanese men are the most likely to out-marry, whereas Filipino, Asian Indian, Chinese, Korean, and Vietnamese men are more likely to marry within their racial and ethnic groups. Asian Indian and Chinese women are the least likely to marry within their own groups, whereas Japanese, Filipino, and Korean women are more likely to intermarry (Hwang et al., 1997).

Why have interracial and interethnic marriage rates increased? There are a number of reasons. As you saw in Chapter 7, dating and mating occur with people we see on a regular basis. A University of Michigan study found, for example, that the military, one of the most integrated of U.S. institutions, seems to encourage interracial marriage. White men who had served in the military were three times as likely to marry black women as were white men who had never served. White women who served were seven times more likely to marry outside their racial group than those who had never served ("Interracial marriages . . . ," 1997). And, in a study of black–white marriages in the Los Angeles area, Kouri and Lasswell (1993) found that the increased socioeconomic mobility of African Americans has provided greater opportunity for interracial contact through housing, schools, work, and leisure activities (see also Kalmijn, 1998).

Asian groups that are less likely to out-marry have a larger number of eligible partners who live in their communities, do not speak fluent English, and have lived in the United States a short time. In contrast, acculturation, a large pool of eligible partners with similar socioeconomic characteristics across Asian American groups, and a heightening racial awareness encourage marriage across Asian boundaries (Shinagawa and Pang, 1996). Among Japanese Americans, for example, intermarriage may be due to a shrinking number of eligible partners of Japanese origin or descent and to greater assimilation into American culture. Many families who have been in the country for four or five generations and have acculturated may be more accepting of intermarriage (Leon and Weinstein, 1991; Hwang et al., 1994).

There is also some evidence that interracial marriage is, at least for some white women, a means of upward mobility. Studying marriages between black men and white women in 33 states, Kalmijn (1993) found that in most of these unions the men were of higher status than the women. In another example, Asian American men and women with high socioeconomic status are more likely to marry other Asian Americans because they can compete successfully for the available marital partners. In contrast, those at lower socioeconomic levels "may be forced to settle for a less desirable choice outside of the group" (Hwang et al., 1997).

Some of the increase in interracial marriages also reflects changing attitudes. American approval of interracial marriage rose from 20 percent in 1968 to 57 percent in 2000 (Gallup and Newport, 1991; "Race relations in the U.S. . . . ," 2000). Although a growing number of people are deciding to intermarry, there is much evidence that such marriages, especially between whites and blacks, are often met with hostility, discrimination, and racist slurs (see Gaskins, 1999; O'Hearn, 1998; and Reddy, 1994). Recently, for example, a southern Ohio pastor refused to allow a wedding in his church when he learned that the white bride's groom was black ("Interracial wedding . . . ," 2000).

White Americans who reject racial intermarriage are not alone. Many African Americans of all social ranks disapprove of intermarriage, especially black-white marriages. With a significant shortage of marriageable black men, many black women feel betrayed or deserted when a black man marries a white woman. Some black activists feel that mixed marriages weaken black solidarity (see Chapter 7).

Asian American parents often encourage their children to marry within their own group to preserve "lineage purity" and to avoid a clash of values (about child rearing, hard work, and respect for elders, for example) that intermarriage with "mainstream America" often brings. Even if parents object to their children's marrying outside of their specific ethnic group, they are more accepting of marriages within Asian groups. As a Chinese American writer and artist explained, his mother's initial dismay that he was dating a non-Chinese person evaporated when she learned that he was seeing a Korean American woman. The mother saw Koreans as physically similar to the Chinese and felt that many of the values would be similar (Kibria, 1997).

Raising Biracial Children

In 1997, professional golfer Tiger Woods sparked a controversy when he told talk-show host Oprah Winfrey that he objected to being called an African American. He said he was "Cablinasian," a word he'd made up as a boy, because he was one-eighth Caucasian, one-fourth black, one-eighth American Indian, one-fourth Thai, and one-fourth Chinese. Many blacks were upset that Woods seemed to reject his African American roots, but Woods felt that he was embracing all parts of his multicultural heritage.

In a study of biracial adults, Funderberg (1994: 378) found that most of the 65 people she interviewed took on "the challenges of race and identity with determination and humor." Despite the respondents' optimism, many worry that biracial children will be rejected by both the white and black communities. Others, such as many black social workers, feel that parents who adopt biracial children are unlikely or unprepared to teach black children about their heritage (see Chapter 10).

Because there are no national data comparing the development of single-race and biracial children, it's impossible to know how biracial children fare. Several studies based on small and nonrandom samples suggest, however, that most biracial adolescents have positive self-concepts, high self-esteem, and about the same percentage of behavioral problems as their single-race peers (Gibbs and Hines, 1992; Field, 1996). Some researchers attribute the children's strong, positive, and confident sense of identity to parents who provide strong support from the extended family and friends, supply the child with identity-bolstering books and toys, instruct the child about what to say when the child's racial identity is questioned, and build connections to the black community or to a strong black family (Rosenblatt et al., 1995).

Anecdotal material and studies based on small samples suggest that biracial children experience ongoing conflict about their multicultural and biracial roots. Children with black and white parents or black and Asian parents, for example, may feel ambiguous loyalties to each heritage, a marginal status in both groups, or they may be accused of "talking like a honky" if they're raised in middle-class families (Maxwell, 1998;

Williams and Thornton, 1998; Berry, 2000). American Indian children who have interracial or interethnic roots report that they're often rejected by both groups, don't look "Indian enough" when they're recruited through affirmative action programs, or have been raised by parents who teach only a white worldview rather than mixed-heritage perspectives (D.D. Jackson, 1998; Mihesuah, 1998; Herring, 1999).

Parents of biracial children must often struggle with issues that same-race couples don't face. In the case of white women married to black men, for example, the mother may experience more stress because she is most likely to be the primary child caretaker and have to deal with the prejudices that others have about her children (Chan and Smith, 1995). As interracial marriages increase and more people know married couples and biracial children, however, the acceptance of biracial children may also increase (Min, 1995; Wilson and Jacobson, 1995).

Conclusion

The racial and ethnic composition of American families is *changing*. There has been an influx of immigrants from many non-European countries, and the growth of African American, American Indian, Asian American, and Latino families is expected to continue in the future. As this chapter has shown, there are many variations both between and among racial-ethnic families in terms of family structure, extended kinship networks, and parenting styles. This means that families have more *choices* outside of the traditional, white, middle-class family model. These choices are often steeped in *constraints,* however. Even middle-class racial-ethnic families confront stereotypes and discrimination on a daily basis. Because many children are bicultural, they must live in two worlds. Whether or not they will succeed largely depends on the economic resources of their families, an issue we examine in the next chapter.

SUMMARY

1. U.S. households are becoming more diverse in terms of racial and ethnic composition. Demographers project that—if current migration, immigration, and birth-rate trends continue—by 2050 almost half of the population in the United States will be nonwhite.

2. Latino, African, Asian, Middle Eastern, and American Indian families are considered minority groups. One of the most important characteristics of a minority group is its lack of economic and political power.

3. Black families are very heterogeneous in terms of lifestyle. They also vary in kinship structure, values,

and social class. Despite such variations, black families are surrounded by many myths.

4. Most racial and ethnic families emphasize the importance of extended families. White families are more likely than racial and ethnic families, however, to participate in kin support networks.

5. American Indian families are complex and diverse. American Indians speak different languages, practice different religions and customs, and maintain different economies and political styles. Because of

assimilation, however, a number of tribes have lost their language and customs during the last generation.

6. Latino families differ on a number of characteristics, including when they settled in the United States, where they came from, and how they adapted to economic and political problems.

7. Recent research has challenged many stereotypes about the Latino family. For example, family structure and dynamics vary greatly by social class and the degree of assimilation.

8. Asian American families are even more diverse than American Indian and Latino families. Asian American family structures vary depending on the family's origin, when the immigrants arrived, whether or not their homeland was ravaged by war, and the socioeconomic status of the parents.

9. Interracial and interethnic unions have been increasing slowly since 1967, when laws forbidding interracial marriages were overturned. Some of the reasons for the growing number of interracial marriages include proximity in school and workplaces, greater public acceptance, and a shrinking pool of eligible marriage partners among some groups.

10. The available data suggest that biracial children have positive self-concepts, high self-esteem, and about the same rate of behavioral problems as their single-race peers.

KEY TERMS

acculturation *305*
cultural pluralism *305*
nativism *305*

minority group *306*
racial-ethnic group *306*
prejudice *307*

discrimination *307*

TAKING IT FURTHER

Race and Ethnicity Resources on the Internet

The first site, **American Studies Web,** is very comprehensive, containing national and international materials on groups such as African Americans, Asian Americans, American Indians, and Latinos. The other URLs provide links to specific racial-ethnic groups.

American Studies Web

www.georgetown.edu/crossroads/asw/index.html

American Indian Resources

jupiter.lang.osaka-u.ac.jp/~krkvls/naindex.html

Asian Studies WWW Virtual Library

coombs.anu.edu.au/WWWVL-AsianStudies.html

Black/African Related Resources

www.sas.upenn.edu/African_Studies/Home_Page/
mcgee.html

Arab-American Affairs Homepage

www.arab-american-affairs.net

Hispanic / Latino American Minority Links

www.census.gov/pubinfo/www/hisphot1.html

Interracial Voice

www.webcom.com/~intvoice

And more . . . www.prenhall.com/benokraitis provides sites on teaching tolerance, minority health, civil rights legislation, and several hundred URLs on ethnic/ minority groups in the United States.

Families and Work:
Facing the Economic Squeeze

DATA DIGEST

■ From 1995 to 1998, the proportion of **families with incomes of $50,000 or more rose** about one-fifth, to 34 percent, while the proportion with incomes below $10,000 fell about one-sixth, to 13 percent.

■ In 1999, the **median income for all U.S. households was $40,816:** $51,205 for Asian and Pacific Islander households, $44,366 for white households, $30,735 for Latino households, and $27,910 for black households.

■ In 1998, **59 percent of dual-earner mothers of children 1 year of age or younger were in the labor force,** up from 31 percent in 1976.

■ In 1998, only **27 percent of households conformed to the traditional model** of a wage-earning father, a stay-at-home mother, and one or more children.

■ The **average number of vacation days a worker receives** after being on the job for one year varies widely—from 30 to 31 days in Denmark and Finland to 6 in Mexico. The average number of vacation days for employees in Canada, Japan, and the United States is 10 days.

SOURCES: U.S. Census Bureau, 1999b, 1999c; T.W. Smith, 1999; Bachu and O'Connell, 2000; Kennickell et al., 2000; "Who gets the most time off," 2000.

THE economy is changing and having a big impact on the family:

Cleveland cabbie Tom Ventura, 49, wishes he could see more of his three teenage sons, but to make up for slowing business he now drives 12 to 14 hours a day, six days a week. Some nights he arrives home at 11:30 and is back in the taxi by 5 A.M. His wife cannot take up much of the slack at home because she works 10 hours a day as a courier. . . . As a result, the Ventura boys get themselves off to school and often take care of supper on their own. "We can't afford the time to do the things we used to do," Ventura laments. "I'll send them to a ballgame instead of going with them. You can't do it as a family." (Boroughs et al., 1992: 60)

As Tom Ventura's experience illustrates, macroeconomic conditions affect individual families. You'll see in this chapter that many mothers are entering the labor force, parents are spending less time with their children, and family roles are changing as parents juggle domestic and job responsibilities.

Macroeconomic Changes That Affect the Family

Many families today feel that they are working harder than their parents did, just to maintain a modest standard of living. Many researchers agree: "Families seem to be in a situation where they have to run as fast as they can just to remain in the same place" (Zill and Nord, 1994: 11). Because of an increase in income inequality, poverty, and homelessness during the last 25 years, some families fell out of the race no matter how fast they ran, while a growing number of families have watched the race from their penthouses.

Unequal Income Distribution

The expansion in the U.S. economy during the last 25 years has not benefited all families. Instead, *income inequality* has increased since the late 1960s (Karoly, 1993). The rich have gotten richer and the poor have gotten poorer. According to the Center on Budget and Policy Priorities (Bernstein, McNichol et al., 2000), a nonpartisan research group, income inequality in the United States is greater than in any other Western, industrialized nation (see also Galbraith, 1998).

The Census Bureau uses several methods to measure income inequality. One of these methods is the share of combined household income, where households are ranked from lowest to highest on the basis of income and then divided into quintiles, or fifths. (The Gini index, another way of measuring income concentration, is described in U.S. Census Bureau, 1999b.) Census Bureau data as well as other studies on household incomes show that the rich are getting richer, the middle class is shrinking, and the working class is barely surviving.

The Rich Are Getting Richer The net worth of the typical family—the value of real estate, stocks and bonds, and other assets minus outstanding debts—

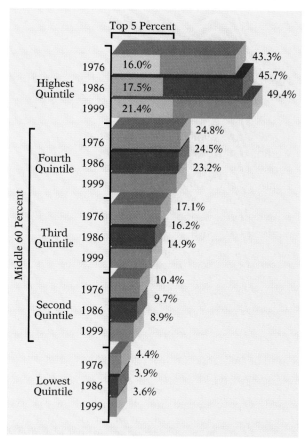

Top 5 Percent

Highest Quintile
1976   16.0%   43.3%
1986   17.5%   45.7%
1999   21.4%   49.4%

Fourth Quintile
1976   24.8%
1986   24.5%
1999   23.2%

Third Quintile
1976   17.1%
1986   16.2%
1999   14.9%

Second Quintile
1976   10.4%
1986   9.7%
1999   8.9%

Lowest Quintile
1976   4.4%
1986   3.9%
1999   3.6%

Middle 60 Percent

FIGURE 13.1 **Distribution of Household Income, 1976–1999.** (U.S. Census Bureau of the Current Population Reports, P60-209. 1999. *Money Income in the United States: 1999,* Tables B-3, C.)

increased from $59,700 in 1989 to $71,600 in 1998. While less than a third of families owned stock in 1989, for example, nearly half did so in 1998, either directly or through vehicles such as 401(k)-type retirement plans. The net worth of families with incomes under $25,000, which had been rising since 1989, turned downward between 1995 and 1998, however (Kennickell et al., 2000).

As *Figure 13.1* shows, the proportion of families both in the highest 20 percent and, within that group, in the top 5 percent has increased since 1976. The richest 20 percent of American households make nearly half of the nation's total family income, up from 44 percent in 1967 (U.S. Census Bureau, 1999b). The mean household incomes represent quite a range: lowest quintile, $9940; second quintile, $24,436; third quintile, $40,879; fourth quintile, $63,555; and highest quintile, $135,401. According to some economists, the Census Bureau figures of the highest quintile are conservative because the data don't include capital gains income—such as making a bundle after selling

"hot" stock (Shapiro et al., 2000). In fact, the boom on Wall Street during the late 1990s widened the income gap between the poorest and the most affluent families. The earnings for the poorest fifth of U.S. families rose less than 1 percent from 1988 to 1998 but increased 15 percent for the richest fifth (Bernstein, McNichol et al., 2000). In 1979, the average family income in the top 5 percent of the earnings distribution was more than ten times that of the bottom 20 percent. By 1999, the ratio had increased by 19 to 1 (Lardner, 2000b).

The Middle Class Is Shrinking According to two recent national polls, 61 percent of Americans identified themselves as "middle income" and 45 percent said they were "middle class" ("A middle-class nation," 1999). The middle class is not easy to define, however, because it encompasses a wide range of people—from professional workers at one end of the continuum to white-collar workers at the other—who may differ quite a bit on such variables as occupation, education, prestige, and lifestyle (see Zweig, 2000). For example, a new elementary school teacher may earn $23,000 a year, while a chemical engineer may have an entry salary of about $55,000 a year. Both are middle class because they have college degrees and hold professional jobs. However, the difference in these two professionals' salaries means considerably less access to better housing, recreation, retirement benefits, and other goods and services for the lower-paid worker.

Many politicians, economists, and journalists have been raving about the economic growth of the mid-1990s. Overall, U.S. workers report very high levels of satisfaction with their current jobs. In 1999, nearly nine in ten (89 percent) of workers said they were satisfied with their jobs, including more than half (55 percent) who said they were very satisfied (Harrison and Dautrich, 1999). According to many economists, however, middle-class workers have little to celebrate. Americans spend more time on the job than workers anywhere else in the industrialized world (see *Figure 13.2*). While the hours worked dropped in almost all of these countries since 1980, those for U.S. workers increased by 4 percent between 1980 and 1997. Americans now spend the equivalent of two additional 40-hour workweeks a year on the job compared with the Japanese, long viewed as a nation of "workaholics." In France, legislation was recently introduced to limit the workweek to 35 hours ("Working longer, working better?" 1999). U.S. workers also have fewer vacation days than their counterparts in many countries (see Data Digest).

While U.S. worker productivity rose by about 20 percent from 1989 to 1999, median real wages (adjusted for inflation) for men actually fell during this period and women saw only a 4 percent gain (Mishel et al., 2001). While most middle-class wages fell, the

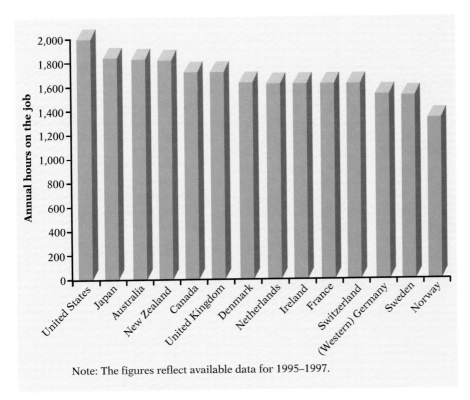

Note: The figures reflect available data for 1995–1997.

FIGURE 13.2 On-the-Job Hours in Industrialized Countries

Source: Based on "Working longer, working better?," International Labor Organization, 1999.

share of middle-income workers with some form of employer-provided health insurance (on their own or through their spouse) actually fell between 1989 and 1997. As a result, almost 30 percent of those in the middle had no health coverage (Schmitt, 1999). Less accessibility to health benefits and a decrease in the incomes of families in the middle 60 percent (see *Figure 13.1*) suggest that the middle class is shrinking.

The middle class has been shrinking for a number of reasons. Some suggest that the prosperity gap has increased because many people work in the "old economy" versus the "new economy." The old economy includes construction, transportation, manufacturing, wholesale and retail, health care, and education. All of these industries rely on personal services and selling physical products. In contrast, the new economy (software, computer and financial services, consulting, and Internet retailing) is based primarily on providing information. Because information technology exploded during the late 1990s, the argument goes, workers who have high-tech skills earn much higher wages (Mandel, 1999).

Others contend that the income gains from the new economy have gone, disproportionately, to those with high incomes. Since 1995, compensation for wages plus benefits per worker grew at an average rate of only 0.7 percent in the United States compared to 1.6 percent in Britain and 1.5 percent in Denmark (Mishel et al., 2001). In contrast to other countries, U.S. corporate mergers, buyouts, and downsizing have

dislodged hundreds of thousands of white-collar employees. Instead of investing the massive profits in wage increases, most corporations are spending more on productivity-enhancing equipment such as computers and the latest software (Boroughs, 1996).

In addition, only the most highly skilled workers are prospering in the new economy. As you saw in Chapter 12, service workers and teachers in high-tech communities have not enjoyed higher wages, even though they are in high demand. Often, also, middle-class families can't afford the housing costs. In Silicon Valley (northern California), for example, only 29 percent of the families can afford the median home priced at $421,000. Many middle-class jobs have also been converted to part-time, temporary, and contract work, which typically doesn't provide any health benefits (Bernstein, 2000; Rogers, 2000). While many already affluent middle-class families are reaping the financial benefits of the new economy, those in the third and second quintiles have stagnating or declining incomes.

The Working Class Is Barely Surviving While many middle-class households are managing to stay afloat, numerous working-class families are clinging to a sinking ship:

When Howard Hagen took early retirement from a steel mill 10 years ago, he was making $23 an hour. Today, his daughter, Nancy, makes $5.25 an hour selling advertising. On that, she supports her

CONSTRAINTS

Does Corporate Welfare Help Working-Class Families?

Business incentives take many forms: tax discounts, payroll rebates, cash grants, training funds, low-cost loans and leases, free buildings, and free land. A number of states, counties, and cities offer generous business incentives to companies and corporations with the understanding or promise that the incentives will create new jobs, especially among low-wage earners. Instead, corporations and high-income families have benefited from such largesse. For example,

- Between 1994 and 1996, the state of Maryland provided London Fog Industries Inc. with funds to train workers and low monthly rent. In addition, union employees agreed to cut the base hourly rate from $7.90 to $6.90 and to increase production quotas. In 1997, London Fog closed the plant and moved its production overseas where labor is cheaper. In 1999, and despite much public opposition, Maryland's governor provided Marriott International with $44 million in giveaways because the company threatened to move 3500 workers to Virginia if it did not receive tax breaks. There is no evidence that Marriott International has improved the wages of

the impoverished workers that live in Baltimore.

- BMW, a German company that assembles luxury cars in Greer, South Carolina, has never paid the state's 5 percent tax on corporate profits. BMW pays $1 a year to lease its $36 million piece of land. In addition, South Carolina taxpayers spent $40 million on a runway for BMW's planes and furnished millions more for BMW worker "training," including whitewater-rafting trips for executives. More than 200 other companies in South Carolina have received property tax discounts since 1997. To support crumbling schools and improve roads, the state has increased homeowner taxes and the taxes of established businesses.

- Sunlite Casual Furniture Company negotiated more than $8 million in state incentives for promising to create 900 jobs in Paragould, Arkansas. The jobs never materialized.

- Fruit of the Loom, a clothing manufacturer, obtained more than $10 million in tax breaks from Louisiana before it closed several plants there and laid off more than 4000 employees over a three-year period.

- Rite Aid Corporation laid off 600 employees and closed a West Virginia distribution center that received more than $2 million in low-cost loans.

- Fulcrum Direct, owner of children's playclothes, shut down in New Mexico and laid off 700 workers after costing the state $1 million in training funds.

Who profits from the corporate welfare packages that many states offer? Companies that can increase their profits, well-paid consultants hired by states who also represent businesses in incentives negotiations, and politicians who get credit for promising to bring low-paid jobs into poor and working-class neighborhoods (Hetrick, 1994; Henry, 1999; Hancock, 1999a, 1999b).

Finally, many U.S. corporations have been exporting white-collar and blue-collar jobs overseas. In 1994, for example, Motorola moved much of its software production to India. Multinational corporations, the majority of which are based in the United States, relocate to poor countries because of their low wages and weak environmental laws. The relocations result in laying off working-class workers but lower corporations' operating costs.

---

four children. . . . Her ex-husband, a plumber, works only sporadically and hasn't kept up his child support payments. Even with public help—Medicaid for the children, subsidies for her heating bills—her budget, like an old car, is constantly breaking down. . . . She buys clothes at thrift shops, and even a simple purchase like new tennis shoes requires a juggling act. "Every Friday night we went out for dinner," she remembers. "Now, when I take the kids to McDonald's, it's a big deal!" (Roberts, 1994: 32)

Most of the reasons for the dire financial predicament of working-class families, whose members range from skilled blue-collar workers to those who make

barely the minimum wage—are macro-level. First, technological changes have replaced many manual workers with machines. The so-called smokestack industries and assembly lines that employed many production workers have dwindled in number or have upgraded jobs that use robots or computerization.

Second, the entire industrial structure of the economy has changed. Many of the high-paying, goods-producing industries have been replaced by service industries that pay only a minimum wage. Between 1981 and 1989, the minimum wage of $3.35 an hour remained unchanged. The minimum wage—paid to 3 million Americans, over 60 percent of whom are adults (Ropers, 1991)—was raised to $3.80 an hour in 1990, to $4.25 in 1991, and to $5.15 in 1996. Social scientists point out that these increases will not raise millions of low-wage workers above the poverty line. Between 1970 and 1990, the minimum wage lost almost 40 percent of its real value because of inflation (Levine, 1994). Activists argue that businesses have a social responsibility to pay their workers a "living wage" (a wage they can live on). They say, also, that the hourly wage necessary to support a family of four on two incomes is close to $11 in many parts of the country and that the increased purchasing power would spur local economies. Opponents of living wage legislation maintain, however, that businesses will flee jurisdictions that require them to pay a living wage because they would go out of business or they would replace low-wage jobs with automated systems (Noguchi, 1999).

Third, many working-class families are barely surviving because a number of states place a higher priority on corporate welfare rather than family welfare. To attract new businesses and expand employment possibilities among low-wage earners, a number of counties and states have offered enticing tax incentives to corporations. According to some observers, however, the tax incentives have benefited big business rather than working-class families. The box "Does Corporate Welfare Help Working-Class Families?" examines this issue more closely.

Poverty

The **poverty line** is the minimal level of income that the federal government considers necessary for individuals' and families' basic subsistence. The poverty line is calculated by measuring such things as the annual cost of food that has the minimum nutrients and the cost of adequate housing. Poverty levels do not include the value of such noncash benefits as food stamps, medical services (such as Medicare and Medicaid), and public housing subsidies. The poverty line, which in 1999 was $17,029 for a family of four, changes every year. It reflects changes in the *Consumer Price Index,* an index of prices that measures the change in the cost of basic goods and services in comparison to a fixed base period.

Policy analysts disagree on the validity of official poverty statistics. Some feel that poverty rates are inflated because the amount of money needed for subsistence varies drastically by region. They also argue that revising poverty definitions to include more families would place greater demands on government programs. Others claim that the poverty level is unrealistically low and that it ignores the needs of single mothers who require affordable child care so they can work, as well as transportation costs to child-care centers and jobs (Bergmann, 1994). In 1996, for example, the poverty threshold for a family with one adult and two children was $12,646. To afford basics (food, clothing, shelter, utilities, and a small amount for other necessities) such a family needed between $20,000 and $40,000, depending on the region where they lived (Bernstein, Brocht, and Spade-Aguilar, 2000). Nevertheless, in 1999 more than 32 million people—almost 12 percent of the U.S. population—lived below the official government poverty line (see *Figure 13.3*).

Over half of unemployed husbands in poor married-couple families are ill or disabled, and the remainder are unable to find work, are going to school, or are retired (Lamison-White, 1997). Those who are

David Sadat of New York works full time at the Broadway 99 Cent Store in Harlem. After paying rent, he has little left to live on (see text). The number of full-time workers who live in poverty has climbed in the past 20 years.

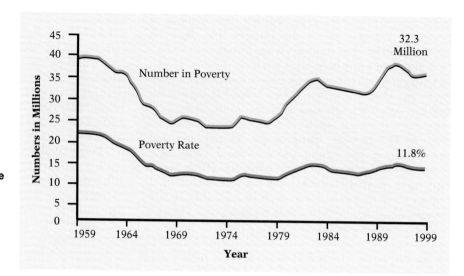

FIGURE 13.3   Poverty in the United States, 1959 to 1999.
Note: The data points represent the midpoints of the respective years.

SOURCES: Lamison-White, 1997; Figure 1; Dalaker and Proctor, 2000: Figure 1.

disproportionately poor are children, the elderly, women, and racial-ethnic families.

Children and the Elderly   In 1999, more than half of the nation's poor were either children under age 18 or older people age 65 and over. In 1998, almost 14 million children—nearly one out of every five—lived in poverty. Among elderly Americans, in contrast, the poverty rate (10.5 percent) has never been lower (Children's Defense Fund, 2000a). Children make up only 26 percent of the U.S. population but represent 37 percent of the poor (America's children . . . , 2000). People 65 and over account for 13 percent of the total population and 9 percent of the poor (Dalaker and Proctor, 2000). Although government programs for the elderly have kept up with the rate of inflation, since 1980 many welfare programs for children have been reduced or eliminated. About 40 percent of *all* children will experience poverty at some point in their lives because families move in and out of poverty over time (Kacapyr, 1998).

Children's economic well-being varies substantially by race-ethnicity, by state, and by type of family. Most children in poverty are white. However, the poverty rate of black and Latino children is much higher than the poverty rate of white children. In 1998, 10 percent of white children lived in poverty compared with 36 percent of black children and 34 percent of Latino children (America's children . . . , 2000). Longitudinal studies show that children who fare worst are those who face multiple risks, such as being born to young, never-married mothers living in economically depressed areas and on public assistance (Rexroat, 1994).

States vary considerably in median income and, consequently, economic resources for children. California, Mississippi, and Texas, for example, are the three poorest states in terms of median resources available to children, while New Jersey, Massachusetts, Minnesota, and Wisconsin rank at the top. In addition, children have few economic resources *within* states, depending on family living arrangements (Acs and Gallagher, 2000).

Women   Children's poverty rates reflect both living arrangements and whether any of the family members work. Single mothers and their children make up a large segment of the poor. As *Figure 13.4* shows, poverty rates are higher for people who live in single-female households than those who live in married-couple families (30 percent compared with 6 percent). Even with one or more workers, however, female-headed households are almost five times more likely to be poor as married-couple families. More than half of all children younger than 6 and living in female-headed households are poor (Dalaker and Proctor, 2000). As you saw in Chapter 11, children raised in poor households often suffer long-term negative effects, such as lower educational attainment, at-risk behavior, and cognitive developmental problems.

Researcher Diana Pearce (1978), who coined the term *the feminization of poverty* to describe the likelihood that female heads of households will be poor, believes that the official statistics tend to underestimate the number of poor women because many single mothers move in with relatives to save on housing costs. Two major reasons for the feminization of poverty are job and wage discrimination, which we touched on in Chapter 4 and will discuss further in this chapter.

Divorce also makes it more likely that women and mothers will be poor (Lino, 1995). Ex-husbands and absent fathers typically offer very little support to women and their children (see Chapter 15). The poorer the family is to begin with, the less likely it is that

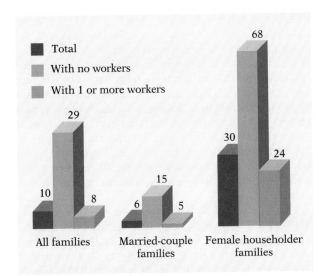

FIGURE 13.4   Poverty Rates by Family Type and Presence of Workers: 1999

SOURCE: Dalaker and Proctor, 2000, Figure 5.

the father will provide support after a divorce (Amott, 1993).

Unlike the United States, gender-linked poverty is almost nonexistent in many other industrialized countries. In Sweden, for example, few single mothers are poor because they have greater economic equality in the workplace. In the Netherlands, a generous welfare system provides benefits for all unemployed people, regardless of gender or marital status (Casper et al., 1994b). In 11 other industrialized countries, government assistance has reduced the number of children in poverty by at least half (O'Hare, 1996). These findings suggest that the public sector in other developed countries does more than the United States to lift children out of poverty.

Racial-Ethnic Families   Most poor people in the United States are white (68 percent). Most white people are not poor, however. As *Figure 13.5* shows, a greater percentage of racial-ethnic families are poor considering their numbers in the general population. For the first time ever, in 1996 the poverty figure for Latino families rose above the rate for black families. Many Latino families are poor even when both parents work full time, year-round (Gomez, 1993). During economic recessions, African Americans and Latinos are particularly vulnerable to layoffs because they often fall victim to "last hired, first fired" policies. (See Chapter 12 for a discussion of poverty across Latino subgroups.)

The Working Poor   Almost one-fifth of all full-time workers now fall into the category of the *working poor*. The U.S. Department of Labor defines the working poor as individuals who spend at least 27 weeks in the labor force (working or looking for work) but whose family or personal incomes falls below the official poverty level (Beers, 2000). For example,

> *Donna Chambers works at a job that sounds decent enough: assistant manager at the Broadway 99 Cent store in Harlem, N.Y. She puts in long hours—often six days a week.*
>
> *Yet the mother of two doesn't earn enough that she can always put food on the table: She frequently gets free groceries from food pantries. She has no health insurance. She's struggling to pay an outstanding medical bill . . . Another obstacle is the cost of living. Housing alone consumes most of Chambers's income, which averages $1,000 a month. "The rent is horrendous," she says. Her boss, David Sadat, says he, too, has barely enough to live on after paying rent. "It doesn't matter if you work full time. It's still not enough." (Francis, 2000a: 1, 9)*

Although many people think that the poor are simply looking for government handouts, during the late 1990s

- The majority of the working poor (63 percent) were full-time workers.
- Almost 3 percent of full-time employees were poor in 1998, most of ethnic origin, and the highest percentage since the early 1980s.
- About 74 percent of poor children live in working families who cannot make enough to escape poverty.

FIGURE 13.5   Percent of Families Living in Poverty, 1999. (Data from U.S. Census Bureau, 1999c, Tables 51, 52, 54, 55.)

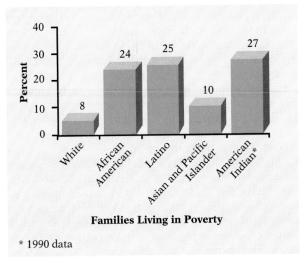

- Almost 38 percent of poor female householders worked, and almost 7 percent worked year-round, full time.
- Half of all children, most of whom are white, are in working-poor families and live with two parents (O'Hare and Schwartz, 1997; Barrington, 2000; Beers, 2000; Children's Defense Fund, 2000).

As these statistics indicate, the poor are not "a bunch of loafers and parasites," but working does not guarantee staying out of poverty. The greatest hardships are faced by two-parent working-poor families in rural areas where job opportunities are minimal, the poor are isolated socially, and social services and benefits are less available than in urban areas (Duncan, 1999).

Poverty in the Suburbs Of all people below the poverty level, over one-third live in the suburbs (O'Hare, 1996). Aging whites generally constitute the majority in poor suburbs, but these suburbs are beginning to house an increasing number of minorities and criminals who prey on the poor. Some of the poorest suburbs, like Ford Heights, Illinois, have unemployment rates of nearly 60 percent. These areas often attract only those industries that other communities reject, such as landfills. They tend to have minimal social and recreational services and are often mismanaged because they can't afford to hire professional managers. Without public transit systems, many of the poorest suburbanites are isolated and unable to commute to suburban or city jobs (McCormick and McKillop, 1989).

Programs for Poor Families What help is available for the poor? Not much. In 1996 Congress passed the Personal Responsibility and Work Opportunity Conciliation Act (PRWORA) that reformed the welfare system. PRWORA was targeted, almost entirely, at poor, mother-only families. The central feature of PRWORA was the replacement of Aid to Families with Dependent Children (AFDC) with block grants. The states set their own eligibility criteria and benefit levels. Three other important changes included the following: (1) Federal money cannot be used to provide cash assistance to unmarried women under the age of 18 or to children born to mothers who are already receiving assistance; (2) adults are expected to work after receiving welfare for two years; and (3) a family cannot receive cash assistance for more than two years.

PRWORA advocates are delighted that some families have left the welfare rolls. Critics argue, however, that PRWORA has scapegoated poor, unmarried mothers and their children instead of focusing on macro-level problems such as increasing economic inequality, diminishing jobs that don't provide decent wages and benefits, and growing poverty among young, two-parent families (Sidel, 1998). A recent study found, for example, that "welfare leavers" are entering the low end of the labor market, where they are working in much the same circumstances as near-poor and low-income mothers who have not recently been on welfare (Loprest, 1999). There are also non-profit organizations, such as community action groups, legal services, and community development agencies, that enable the poor to address social, legal, and economic issues at the local level but rarely help poor families to be upwardly mobile. We return to the issue of welfare and the recent welfare reform laws in Chapter 18.

Why does the United States, one of the wealthiest countries in the world, have such high poverty rates? In a classic article on poverty, sociologist Herbert Gans (1971) maintained that poverty and inequality have many functions: (1) They ensure that society's dirty work gets done; (2) the poor subsidize the middle and upper classes by working for low wages; (3) the poor buy goods and services that would otherwise be rejected (such as day-old bread, used cars, and the services of old, retired, or incompetent "professionals"); and (4) the poor absorb the costs of societal change and community growth (such as providing the backbreaking work that built railroads and cities in the nineteenth century and being pushed out of their homes by urban renewal and construction of expressways, parks, and stadiums). Unlike the United States, countries like Germany, Italy, and the Netherlands have less poverty because they have higher minimum wages, guaranteeing that full-time workers' children will not be poor.

Homeless Families

One of the most devastating consequences of poverty is homelessness. In 1987, the government estimated as many as 500,000 to 600,000 homeless people used shelter services at any one time during the year. In 1996, as the economy surged, the homeless estimate jumped to 842,000 people (Burt et al., 1999).

Families have been the fastest-growing group of homeless people. In 1996, families with children accounted for 34 percent of the homeless population; 84 percent were female and 16 percent were male. In terms of race and ethnicity, 39 percent were white, 43 percent were black, 15 percent were Latino, 3 percent were American Indian, and 1 percent of another race (Burt et al., 1999).

Although more than half of the homeless are members of minority groups, the homeless population in any one place reflects local and regional population trends. Major metropolitan areas on the East Coast have high proportions of homeless African Americans, whereas Minneapolis has many homeless American Indians. In western cities like Los Angeles and Phoenix the homeless include many Latinos, and in the Northwest, some cities report that most of their homeless are white (Baum and Burnes, 1993).

Why do people lose their homes? In general, homelessness is caused by a combination of factors, some of which are beyond individuals' or families' control. Poverty, lack of education, lack of marketable skills, unemployment, domestic violence, substance abuse, the inability of relatives and friends to provide social and economic support during crises, and the absence of affordable housing are among the most common causes of homelessness (Van Ry, 1993; Winkleby and Boyce, 1994). Young mothers with very young children are especially likely to become homeless (Rossi, 1994). The homeless also include teenage runaways escaping from family violence or incest (Whitbeck and Hoyt, 1999). In addition, men formerly employed in unskilled blue-collar jobs that have been eliminated may be unable to secure the training they need to move to new kinds of work.

Families' Efforts to Adapt to Changing Economic Trends

Across the country, many families are struggling to survive. They have adopted a variety of techniques, including taking low-paying jobs, moonlighting, working shifts, doing part-time work, and working overtime. If or when these tactics fail, they join the ranks of the unemployed.

Low-Wage Jobs, Moonlighting, and Shift Work

Researcher Marc Levine (1994) has described the United States as "a nation of hamburger flippers" because of the growing number of low-wage jobs. Measured in terms of buying power, hourly wages have actually declined 15 percent since 1973 and are now at mid-1960s' levels. An explosion of jobs in the information technology section has resulted in well-paid jobs for highly educated employees. But for others, especially low-income workers, a changing economy has meant layoffs, a loss of job security, and in some cases, lower wages and lack of health-care benefits. When corporations merge, workers at the lower-end jobs are the first to be laid off.

Family members have reacted to this economic decline in several ways. In 1998, 6 percent of all employed people held two or more jobs (U.S. Census Bureau, 1999c). Most are moonlighting to meet regular household expenses or to pay off debts (see *Figure 13.6*). Most multiple jobholders are not married, and women are slightly more likely than men are to hold two or more jobs. Men are more likely than women to add a part-time job to a full-time one; women are more likely to hold two part-time jobs (Uchitelle,

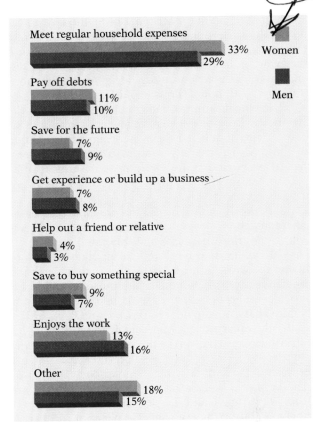

FIGURE 13.6   **Why Women and Men Have Multiple Jobs: 1997**

SOURCE: Based on data in U.S. Census Bureau, 1999c, Table 669.

1994). Black women and Latinas, as well as single-head-of-household mothers, are the most likely to moonlight to meet regular household expenses (Amott, 1993; U.S. Census Bureau, 1999c).

Not all of the moonlighting can be blamed on low wages, of course. Some middle-class professionals moonlight to pay off credit-card debt, buy a vacation home, or increase their salaries. High-tech workers, especially, are taking advantage of plentiful job opportunities that pay well for their skills. In many cases, however, and especially in midwestern rural areas that are far from metropolitan centers, holding down a second job is often a matter of economic survival (Wilkinson, 2000).

Parenting is especially difficult if mothers and fathers have unconventional work schedules. According to an AFL-CIO study, nearly half of all women who are married or living with someone say they work a different schedule than their spouse or domestic partner ("Working women," 2000). About one-fourth of two-earner couples work split shifts—one spouse working during the daytime, the other working evenings, nights, or weekends. The share of split-shift workers is higher among couples with preschool-age children than among other types of families. Mothers with only a high school diploma are especially likely to be locked into evening and night-shift jobs because they work as cashiers, nursing home aides, waitresses, and janitors—positions most likely to require non-standard work hours (Presser and Cox, 1997).

The globalization of industries means that workers are needed almost around the clock because business is being conducted somewhere almost every hour of the day. Because day care is so expensive, many two-income families are working split shifts so that parents can save money by taking turns at child-care tasks (see Chapter 11).

Shift work and evening shifts are almost twice as common among single parents (especially mothers) who can't afford day care and must find relatives to baby-sit while they work. Single mothers are more likely to work nonstandard hours than married women because grandmothers are the main child-care providers, and one-third of grandmothers caring for children have other paid jobs (Presser and Cox, 1997). Married women are also more likely to work at night, when their husbands are available to take care of the children. Off-hours child care after 6:00 P.M. can cost at least 50 percent more than regular day care (Gardner, 1995b). Thus, the lack of affordable child care forces both single and married mothers to work part time and during the evenings (Casper et al., 1994a).

Many husbands who work rotating evening shifts (six days on, three days off, for example) feel guilty and angry because the demands of their work limit their participation in family life. One father saw himself reliving a situation he had resented as a child:

> I always remember my father as sleeping during the day. Never seeing him because he'd be in bed. Then I'd hear him get up and go to work at night. I didn't see much of my father. I missed that. Now I feel guilty if I can't have it with my family. (Hertz and Charlton, 1989: 501)

When both parents work shifts, husbands and wives may rarely see each other or participate as a family with their children:

> My husband works a 9-to-5 shift, and I work from 6 P.M. until 2:30 A.M. We have done this for [12] years because with three kids, it helps save the cost of child care. I average four hours of sleep a night. My husband comes home after an eight-hour day of work, has dinner with the kids, helps with their homework, takes care of baths and reads them stories at bedtime. I wake up, get the kids off to school, clean the house, do the laundry, start dinner and prepare for another night of work. Since I also have a 3-year-old at home, going back to bed is out of the question. I barely see my older kids, and my husband [and] I have no social life. . . . I

have no time for myself, and neither does my husband. As soon as he walks in the door from work, I walk out. ("Night shift . . . ," 1996: 3D)

Too Little Work or Too Much

Many families face an economic dilemma: On the one hand, an increasing proportion of available jobs are only part time. On the other hand, some employees are required to work unwanted overtime.

Part-Time Jobs   In 2000, about 19 percent of all employed people worked part time (defined as working less than 35 hours a week). Of these part-timers, 38 percent were men and 62 percent were women. Although 75 percent of part-timers were "voluntary" because they didn't want to work more hours, 25 percent were involuntary because they wanted full-time employment (U.S. Department of Labor, 2000). The percentage of part-time employees, voluntary or not, is likely to increase because many employers don't pay health or other benefits.

In 1997 there was a strike of part-timers working for United Parcel Service (UPS). Despite many years of part-time work, they were not being offered full-time work with full benefits. UPS maintained that 50 percent of their approximately 115,000 part-time employees who were college students appreciated the money they could make while working odd hours and still attending school. They could work during the "short bursts" of three or four hours when the delivery schedule was the highest (Nifong, 1997). Most employees are not college students, however, and need full-time jobs to support themselves and their families, as well as the health care and paid vacations that are among the benefits offered many full-time workers. About 30 million part-timers have to pay for their own medical insurance, for example, even though most are working at minimum-wage jobs.

Overtime Demands   At the other extreme is the demand by some employers that experienced workers, especially those in production, work more overtime because this is cheaper than hiring and training new employees. The most common violation is failing to pay hourly wage earners time-and-a-half when they work more than 40 hours a week—or failing to pay anything at all for the extra hours. During the late 1990s, a number of employees filed class action suits against grocery chains, drugstores, poultry processors, and fast-food restaurants for unpaid overtime (Murr, 1998; Shatzkin, 2000).

Skilled and highly educated employees are especially likely to work long hours. Among those with professional, technical, or managerial jobs, more than 33 percent of men and 17 percent of women now put in 50-hour-plus weeks, compared with 20 percent of men and 7 percent of women in other occupations.

College graduates are four times more likely to work long hours than those with less than a high school degree. Some are compensated and some are not. Those working at least 50 hours a week are the most dissatisfied with the long hours because it curtails the time available for domestic tasks and family life (Jacobs and Gerson, 1998). Faced with high fringe benefits costs, many employers would rather have full-time workers put in more time than hire additional workers. Many also economize by using more part-timers who get few benefits.

Unemployment

The unemployed include such diverse groups as people who have been laid off or fired, have quit, or are about to begin a new job. Overall, more than half of the unemployed are people who have lost their jobs. Teenagers and adult blacks are two to three times more likely to be unemployed than adult white workers (U.S. Department of Labor, 2000). During the 1990s' economic expansion, however, many non-college-educated black men aged 16 to 24 and living in metropolitan areas experienced higher employment rates and earnings (Freeman and Rodgers, 1999).

Families living under the threat of unemployment have difficulties in communication and in problem solving, and relationships between spouses and with children suffer (Larson et al., 1994). Unemployment is often associated with marital and familial dissatisfaction, as well as with separation and divorce. Unemployed workers argue more frequently with their spouses and experience more family conflict that has negative effects on children's physical health, psychological well-being, and behavior (Voydanoff, 1991).

Some blue-collar male workers, after being laid off from fairly well-paying jobs in such smokestack industries as shipbuilding, coal mining, and steelmaking, are unwilling to take what work is available. Most new jobs for inexperienced people with less education are in traditionally "female" areas such as clerical work, sales, and personal service. Many men refuse to take such jobs both because of the low earnings and the traditional association of these jobs as "women's work": "For men, whether black, Latino or white, there are strong cultural and social norms about what is appropriate work" (Nasar, 1994: D15).

Another reason for unemployment is the phenomenon of the **discouraged worker,** or what some call the "hidden unemployed." The discouraged worker wants a job and has looked for work during the preceding year but has not searched recently because she or he believes that job-hunting efforts are futile. Why do people give up? Usually for one of the following reasons: They've found no work available in their area of expertise; they lack necessary schooling, training, or experience; they believe employers have rejected them as too young or too old; or they have experienced

other types of discrimination. Many young discouraged workers, including Latino males, may turn to illegal ways of making a living because they lack the skills and education that many employers seek (Soltero, 1996).

Finally, many experts feel that unemployment rates are misleading because they ignore the **underemployed worker.** The underemployed include workers who have part-time jobs but would rather be working full time, as well as those who accept jobs below their level of job experience and educational credentials. Women, particularly those with children, are more likely to suffer from underemployment than men because of problems in finding and being able to pay for good child-care services. Another large group of underemployed workers are professionals (engineers, physicists, and chemists)—especially men in their fifties—who were laid off during the 1990s and have jobs with much lower salaries and responsibility than in the past. Companies can hire two young college graduates for the price of a senior-level employee, and often do so.

New Economic Roles within Marriage

In Chapter 4 we examined the traditional male breadwinner—female homemaker roles. Although for many couples these traditional roles are evolving, if slowly, into more egalitarian arrangements, there are currently two variations on the traditional division of labor within marriage—the two-person single career and the stay-at-home dad.

The Two-Person Single Career

In the **two-person single career,** one spouse, typically the wife, participates in the partner's career behind the scenes without pay or direct recognition (Papanek, 1979). The wives of many college and university professors, for example, support their husbands' careers by entertaining faculty and students, doing library research, helping to write and edit journal articles or books, and grading exams.

Probably the best example of the gratifying aspects of such unpaid work is presidential first ladies, who have often enjoyed considerable power and influence behind the scenes. Rosalynn Carter, Nancy Reagan, and Barbara Bush all played more or less quiet roles in their husbands' presidencies, but Hillary Rodham Clinton was a visible promoter of some of President Clinton's domestic policies. Many middle-class homemakers are proud of their husbands' accomplishments and experience a sense of fulfillment by helping them out. Some wives, however, complain that a two-person career is very stressful and that they

There are many husband-wife businesses where both partners, such as these owners of a photo store, work together to support themselves and their families.

experience burnout as commonly as their high-powered husbands do. They are constantly involved in activities like entertaining and organizing fund-raising events besides running a household and raising their children.

Stay-at-Home-Dads

In a reversal of traditional roles, as in the TV sitcom *Daddio,* some husbands relinquish the role of breadwinner to their wives. Stay-at-home-dads (or *househusbands,* as they were called during the 1990s) are those rare men who stay home to care for the family and do the housework while their wives are the wage earners. Leaders of the father movement estimate (perhaps hopefully) that almost 2 million fathers care for preschoolers and children under 14 while mothers work. Many of these fathers work part time, and the wives still do much of the housework and child care during evenings and weekends. According to Lynne Casper, a Census Bureau demographer and statistician, only about 200,000 men have chosen to quit their jobs and raise their children full time (cited in Nakamura, 1999). Many of these fathers, moreover, have wives who earn more than they do, have greater job security, and better health benefits.

In addition, being a stay-at-home dad is usually a temporary role. Some get the role by default; they are unemployed or are not working because of poor health or a disability. Sometimes graduate students who are supported by their wives take on a modified housekeeping role, doing household chores between classes and studying at the library.

Recent experiential accounts suggest that being a full-time father is a mixed blessing. On the one hand, the fathers enjoy seeing a child crawl and take a first step. They also don't have to worry about the quality of day-care facilities. On the other hand, some stay-at-home-dads express concern that they are losing skills and their "professional place in line." Some feel unappreciated by their working wives, who may complain that the house is a mess or that people view them as "nonachievers" professionally (Baldauf, 2000; Gardner, 1999a).

Juggling Family and Work Roles

Surveys of adolescents and college students suggest that many young people expect to have a career and raise children simultaneously. In a nationwide study of college students, for example, nearly 75 percent of college freshmen said that being very well off financially was "very important" or "essential," and 73 percent felt the same way about raising a family. However, almost 32 percent of the men and 20 percent of the women said that "the activities of married women are best confined to the home and family" (data cited in *Chronicle of Higher Education,* 1998). Unless they have very high-paying jobs and expect equally high job security in the future, it's not clear how one-earner families can expect to be well off financially.

Women's Increasing Participation in the Labor Force

The high proportions of both high school and college women who say they expect to marry, have children, and work are right on target, for many will have to work to support themselves and their families. In fact, the widespread employment of mothers is often cited as one of the most dramatic changes in family roles

TABLE 13.1

Women and Men in the Labor Force during the Twentieth Century

Year	Percent of all Men and Women in the Labor Force — Men	Percent of all Men and Women in the Labor Force — Women	Women as a Percentage of All Workers
1890	84	18	17
1900	86	20	18
1920	85	23	20
1930	82	24	22
1940	83	28	25
1945	88	36	29
1947	87	32	27
1950	87	34	29
1960	84	38	33
1970	80	43	37
1980	78	52	42
1990	76	58	45
1998	75	60	46

SOURCE: U.S. Census Bureau, 1997b, Table 621; 1999c, Tables 650, 651.

degrees (67 percent) than for women who are high school graduates (58 percent) or who are not high school graduates (38 percent). This pattern suggests that women with more time invested in their educational careers return to work more rapidly because they have a greater job commitment, higher salaries and more work experience than do women with fewer years of schooling, and the resources to purchase child care services—especially if a husband is also employed (Bachu and O'Connell, 2000).

Why Do Women Work?

The two principal reasons why women work outside the home are the same reasons that men work: personal satisfaction and supporting themselves and their dependents. Studies have generally reported positive effects of work for both men and women (see Rosenfield, 1989, for a review of this literature). Work usually adds meaning to life. The opportunity to succeed at tasks and to be rewarded for competence enhances self-esteem, which, in turn, increases overall well-being. This is especially true for people who enjoy their work or who are employed in stimulating, rewarding jobs.

As you saw earlier, the purchasing power of the median U.S. income has declined since the mid-1980s. It is not surprising, then, that seven out of ten mothers are in the labor force (U.S. Census Bureau, 1999c). Although the need for a creative outlet motivates some women to work, in most cases women are employed because of economic necessity. The box "Variations in the Working Mother Role" examines motherhood and employment more closely.

during the twentieth century. Except for a brief period after the end of World War II, the numbers of working women have been increasing steadily since the turn of the century (see *Table 13.1*).

Women's labor force rates are expected to grow more rapidly than men's in the near future. By 2005, for example, the Bureau of Labor Statistics predicts that about 63 percent of women will be in the labor force compared with 74 percent of men. One reason is that female baby boomers are far more likely than their predecessors to have gone to college and to have more and better-paying work opportunities.

An even more dramatic change has been the increase of mothers in the labor force who have an infant at home (see Data Digest). Historically, black mothers with infants were more likely than any other group to be employed, but the gap is narrowing. As *Figure 13.7* shows, the majority of women with babies are going back to work within the child's first year of life, and the rates are very similar for white and black women.

Labor force participation rates are appreciably higher for women with graduate or professional degrees (74 percent) and for women with college

FIGURE 13.7 Percentage of Women with Newborns in the Labor Force, 1998

SOURCE: Based on Bachu and O'Connell, 2000: Table F.

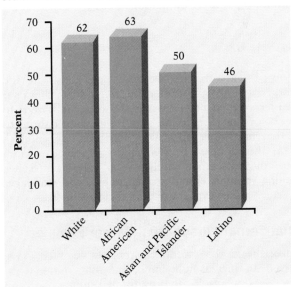

CHANGES ••

Variations in the Working Mother Role

Fewer women today have a choice between being full-time homemakers and working outside the home. Of Moen's (1992: 42–44) four categories of working mothers—captives, the conflicted, copers, and the committed—only members of the last group have fully chosen their roles.

- **Captives** would prefer to be full-time homemakers. These mothers may be single parents who are sole breadwinners, wives of blue-collar workers whose own incomes are insufficient to support the family, or middle-class wives who find two salaries necessary for a desired standard of living. Captives find their multiple responsibilities overwhelming and remain in the labor force reluctantly.

- **Conflicted** mothers feel that their employment is harmful to their children. They are likely to leave the labor force while their children are young, and many quit work when they can afford to do so. Conflicted mothers include many Latinas whose husbands support their wives' employment as long as the mothers continue to fulfill all housework and child-care duties despite their outside work, and who quit their jobs as soon as their husbands secure better-paying work (Segura, 1994).

- **Copers** are women with young children who choose jobs with enough flexibility to accommodate family needs. Some manage to reduce their daily or weekly working hours or leave the labor force for brief periods. As a result, they often must settle for minimally demanding jobs that offer lower wages and fewer benefits and, in the long run, forgo promotional opportunities, seniority advantages, and pay increases.

- **Committed** mothers have both high occupational aspirations and a strong commitment to marriage and family life. As the section on dual-earner families shows, however, mothers who can afford good child care and who are free to pursue career goals are still a minority.

Being more committed to work doesn't mean that women are less committed to their families. When the Families and Work Institute asked a national sample of adults whether or not they'd work outside the home "if you had enough money to live comfortably," only 15 percent of the women but 33 percent of the men said they'd work full time. Thirty-one percent of the women compared to 21 percent of the men said they would prefer to care for their families full time rather than working outside the home if this were an option (Whirlpool Foundation, 1995).

Dual-Earner Families

After 61 years of being the traditional housewife and mother, in the late 1990s the comic-strip character Blondie opened up a catering business and went to work for herself. Blondie's and Dagwood's shifts to dual-earner status reflect what has been happening in many U.S. families. In this section we look at several types of dual-earner families—dual-career marriages, trailing spouses, commuter marriages, and marriages in which wives earn more than their husbands.

Dual-Earner versus Dual-Career Families

Throughout the twentieth century, women have played an increasingly important role in the work force. As a result, the traditional home with an employed husband and wife keeping house and raising children has declined considerably (see Data Digest). Over the past 50 years, the proportion of married women in the work force has almost tripled. Families with a working wife have seen their incomes nearly triple, too. As *Figure 13.8* shows, in 1998 the median family incomes with wives in the labor force were almost 42 percent higher than those where wives were not in the labor force. The labor force figures include both dual-earner and dual-career families.

In **dual-earner couples**, both married partners are employed outside the home. Such couples are also referred to as *dual-income, two-income, two-earner,* or *dual-worker couples.* These employed couples make up 64 percent of all married couples (U.S. Census Bureau, 1999c). Despite their two incomes, and after taxes, dual-earner families are seldom affluent. Only a small fraction of such households has a significant amount of **discretionary income** (income that remains after such basic necessities as food, rent, utilities, and transportation have been paid for and that is then available for other purposes).

There is often little discretionary income because many dual-earner families consist of middle-age householders who are paying for their children's college, caring for their aging parents, and saving for their own retirement. Having two wage earners raises the family's standard of living, however. If the husbands' income is low or they are laid off, financial backing from their wives relieves some of the pressure on men to be successful providers. And in many ethnic groups that rely on unpaid family members' participation in creating a small business that will succeed, much of the discretionary income may be invested in the entrepreneurship (Wong, 1998; see also Chapter 12).

In **dual-career couples,** both marriage partners work in professional or managerial positions that require extensive training, a long-term commitment, and ongoing professional growth. Usually, but not always, dual-career partners earn incomes well above average. Only about 5 percent of dual-earner families are dual-career couples. Married women in such professions as law, medicine, high-level management, or college teaching remain a numerically small group among dual-earner couples as a whole. Because such women are less likely to have children, dual-career families with children make up an extremely small percentage of all dual-earner families. Although there are no hard data, only 1 to 2 percent of dual-career couples probably include children.

Both dual-career and dual-earner families experience stress, but the causes may be different. A common source of stress for dual-earner families is finding affordable child care. Ironically, many dual-earner mothers work as child-care providers or baby sitters for dual-career mothers who are able to pay for such services.

The most common source of stress for dual-career couples is the pressure caused by work or role overload, especially when the children are young. Both partners often feel the need to work intensely and competitively and have an urgency to achieve their career goals. As a result, they may experience guilt and frustration when they neglect their spouses and children. In addition, the role overload caused by multiple work and family responsibilities can lead to increased health risks; decreased productivity; increased tardiness, absenteeism, and turnover; and poor morale at work (Duxbury et al., 1994). On the positive side, dual-earner parents feel that they provide responsible adult role models for their children and that their children are more independent and less "needy" than they would be if both parents didn't work (Silberstein, 1992; Barnett and Rivers, 1996).

Trailing Spouses

By 1996, about 30 percent of U.S. companies had established programs or recruited outside firms to provide employment assistance for the **trailing spouse**— the partner who gives up his or her work and searches for another position in the location where a spouse has taken a job. Male trailing spouses—only 10 to 15 percent of cases—fall into five categories: (1) those who have been unable to find suitable employment in their present location; (2) those who are confident that they can take their profession anywhere, such as photographers, computer programmers, and engineers; (3) those who take genuine pride in their wives' accomplishment and try to accommodate them; (4) those who have blue-collar skills, such as construction workers, who are used to changing jobs and locations; and (5) those who are managers and executives but have been laid off and decided to relocate because

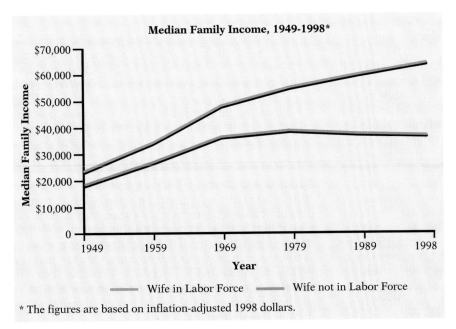

FIGURE 13.8   Median Family Income, 1949–1998

Source: U.S. Census Bureau, 2000, "Historical Income Tables—Families," Table F-7, www.census.gov/hhes/income/histinc/f07.html (accessed October 15, 2000).

Median Family Income, 1949-1998*

* The figures are based on inflation-adjusted 1998 dollars.

Ernestina Galindo owns and operates a factory in Austin, Texas, that makes Mexican foods such as tortillas.

their wives are climbing the corporate ladder (Cohen, 1994; "The big picture," 2000).

Income, however, is usually the best predictor of who the trailing spouse will be. As a wife's income increases, both in absolute terms and relative to the income of her husband, she tends to play a greater role in deciding whether or not the family will move. Typically, however, the husband's job has a greater influence because his income is usually higher than his wife's (Bielby and Bielby, 1992).

There are drawbacks to being the trailing spouse. Frame and Shehan (1994) found that moving was considerably harder on wives than husbands. Most husbands continued to perform similar tasks in new locations and maintained their contacts with colleagues through meetings and conferences. Wives, however, lost contact with friends; felt a lack of support from husbands who saw relocation as an important career step for them; were anxious about the children's adjustment to a new environment; and felt lonely and isolated. In addition, nearly 60 percent of the wives had been employed, and many felt anxiety over the loss of their jobs.

Relocating can be especially stressful because it is often a lateral job shift rather than a step up the career ladder. The number of relocations due to promotions dropped by one-third between 1987 and 1995, for example, and nearly half of the trailing spouses reported lower salaries in their new jobs after relocation. Sometimes an employee must relocate, even in a lateral career move, or lose her or his job. If there's a choice, however, 1 in 12 prospective transferees reject

an offer to relocate because moving may be too disruptive and stressful for all family members, especially children who must change schools (Capell, 1995).

The most recent wrinkle in the relocation/trailing spouse issue involves divorce and remarriage. If a divorced parent who has custody of a child (or children) remarries and decides to relocate as a trailing spouse, state laws may bar her or him from doing so. In Illinois, for example, the parent who wants to leave the state has to prove that relocation is in the best interest of the child and that the move won't damage the noncustodial parent–child relationship. In Missouri, it's illegal for a divorced parent to move, "even across the street," over an ex's objection (Downey, 2000). Although there are no national statistics on this topic, the high divorce and remarriage rates, as well as a booming economy that encourages moving to find better jobs, suggest that remarried couples who seek relocation might become more contentious in the future.

Commuter Marriages

In a **commuter marriage,** married partners live and work in different geographic areas and get together intermittently, such as over weekends. An estimated 2 million American couples have such long-distance marriages (U.S. Census Bureau, 1999c). In 1999, when Hillary Clinton announced that she'd establish residence in New York City and run for state senator, some media reporters felt that President Clinton and his wife's association reflected a typical commuter marriage because of the long-distance relationship. At least one journalist, however, was more astute. She noted that the Clintons didn't have young children, that both spent many days apart because of national and overseas engagements, and that, most importantly, they were hardly representative of the typical commuter marriage:

> *. . . unlike the president and first lady, most couples who work in separate cities can't call up a motorcade or military jet to get home whenever they want—or send the bill to taxpayers. And, unlike the president, most spouses left holding down the fort probably don't have cooks, gardeners, and other help to take care of all the household duties.*

Benefits and Costs There are several reasons why a couple may have a commuter marriage. If one partner (usually the wife) sees that relocation will have negative effects on her employment prospects, she may decide not to move. If both partners have a well-established career in different cities, neither may be willing to make major sacrifices after marriage. In addition, a commuter marriage may create less stress on the family because it avoids uprooting teenage children or elderly parents.

What are the advantages of commuter marriages? Long-distance couples feel that they can devote more attention to their work during the week and that they learn to appreciate and make the most of the time they have together. Each person is more independent and can take advantage of time alone to pursue hobbies or recreational interests that the other partner might not enjoy. As one writer noted, "She can watch all the foreign movies she wants and eat sushi for lunch and dinner. I can play Wiffle ball in the living room and clean the bathtub with a mop" (Justice, 1999: 12). Also, couples are forced to reexamine the quality of their relationship and to make changes to improve it.

Commuter marriages also have several costs, one of which is the sheer expense involved. Telephone bills, airplane flights, the costs of maintaining two housing units with utilities—all these can be very high. The commuting partner may feel isolated from community and social relationships. And one of the partners may become involved in extramarital relationships. Furthermore, the stay-at-home parent may become resentful that the weekend parent is not shouldering his or her responsibility in raising the children. If the couple has no children, decision making as to whether and when to have children and where the children will live may prove stressful (Belkin, 1985; Justice, 1999).

Coping with Commuter-Marriage Stress   The major dilemma for commuter couples is *role transition*. If a husband sees his family only every two weeks or so, for example, his wife and children may resent changing their lifestyles to suit his needs. Almost equally problematic is the *supersuccess syndrome,* in which partners feel guilty about their absences and seem driven to succeed at everything. Commuting wives may try to prepare family meals for the week to come; fathers may try extra hard to "mother" their children in their wives' absence (Winfield, 1985; Anderson and Spruill, 1993).

Not surprisingly, physical exhaustion is a common problem in commuter marriages. Many commuting partners work 14- to 18-hour days during the week, live in hotel rooms or small apartments, and subsist on TV dinners or deli sandwiches. Their spouses, on the other hand, often work equally long hours and have the added burden of child care. Besides feeling lonely, parents also report feeling helpless if something goes wrong at home. For example, one father said that the worst moment of the year was when he was paged— 800 miles from home—with the message that his daughter, 6, had stitches in her forehead after an accident at school (Stiehm, 1997).

Why Do They Do It?   Some commuter couples live apart to pursue careers. Partners in such marriages typically see their work as an integral part of their self-concept. For example, when Amy left her job to be with husband, Paul, in Los Alamos, she took a part-time job locally but soon felt as if she'd lost her "own

separate sphere." When encouraged by her husband to go back to the work she'd left, Amy said, "When I did, I found myself in love again with working on a newspaper" (Winfield, 1985: 41).

If jobs become less secure in a volatile economy while prices keep going up, financial security is an increasingly important factor in maintaining commuter marriages. As you saw earlier, many professional and high-skilled workers are working multiple jobs to save for the future (see *Figure 13.6*). Some of these jobs may involve living apart during part of the week or on weekends. In addition, racial-ethnic couples may feel that commuter marriages are the only possible route to occupational success. According to Jackson and her associates (2000), black dual-career commuter marriages are rising in response to exclusionary employment practices. Although black commuter marriages increase career options and social mobility, they also take a toll (very similar to those of their white counterparts) on the couple's interpersonal relationships, child–parent interactions, community life, and friendship networks.

When Wives Earn More

Although, overall, U.S. women still make only about 75 cents for each dollar that men make, 48 percent of working wives provide at least half of the household's income (Blank, 1997). Wives who earn more than their husbands typically work full time, year-round as professionals or managers. The majority has no children at home, and many have a college degree. Black women are more likely to outearn black men than are their white counterparts because they have a college degree and more job experience (Bianchi and Spain, 1996). In some cases women's reported higher incomes may be short term. For example, a wife's income may be higher only for a year or so because her husband has been laid off, on sick/disability leave, or is pursuing a degree in higher education (see Roberts, 1994).

Some anecdotal evidence suggests that a wife's higher earnings have a positive effect on the marriage; the husband may be relieved not to have to work late and is willing to take full responsibility for the children when the wife goes on business trips (Sandroff, 1994). In contrast to exchange and resource theories (see Chapters 2 and 9), there is little impact on marital power when wives in high-status occupations earn more than their husbands do. Instead, these couples ignore the income differences or minimize them by having joint bank accounts and contribute equally to joint expenses. Wives enjoy a more equitable division of labor in the home than their lower-income counterparts, but they often still bear the larger burden of domestic labor. They don't see this as unfair because they tend to judge their success as wives and mothers by how much they do around the house rather than how much they bring home. Fathers who contribute a smaller proportion of the family income are still seen as providers both because wives don't want to challenge such perceptions and because "providing is not just about money." Thus, gender, rather than the women's income or status, reinforces the husband's marital power (Tichenor, 1999).

The Effect of Work on Family Dynamics

Employment—whether in dual-earner families, dual-career marriages, or commuter marriages—affects the family in many ways. Most importantly, of course, work keeps most families out of poverty. Work roles also have an impact on the quality of a marriage, the division of household labor, and children's well-being.

Marital Quality and Family Life

Sociologist Arlie Hochschild (1997) studied a major U.S. corporation (which she called "Amerco") and concluded that employees prefer the office to home life. The office, Hochschild maintains, is orderly and predictable, where people get to socialize, feel competent, and relax with friends during breaks. In contrast, home life is usually stressful and frantic. One of her female respondents confessed, for example, that she worked a lot of overtime because "The more I get out of the house, the better I am" (p. 38). Because Hochschild interviewed only 130 people and at a family-friendly corporation that allows flexible hours and other benefits, her conclusions are interesting but not necessarily representative. The larger point, however, is that the workplace affects the family, and vice versa.

The impact of employment on marital and personal satisfaction depends largely on how each partner perceives and feels about the situation. Wives tend to be happy when they want to work and are employed and most dissatisfied when they want to work and cannot (Mirowsky and Ross, 1986; Segura, 1994). Husbands are happiest when both agree that the wife should work and least happy when their wives work against their wishes (Ulbrich, 1988).

Women's employment and income do *not* undermine marriage. To the contrary, marital discord significantly increases the likelihood that wives who are not employed will enter the labor force, work more hours per week, or seek more training (Rogers, 1999). If wives are unhappy in their marriages, the increased income may also increase the likelihood of wives' initiating a divorce at a later time (see Chapter 15).

When fathers work long hours in demanding high-status jobs, they may be less knowledgeable about their school-age children's experiences, especially if there is marital dissatisfaction and little communication between the working parents (Bumpus et al.,

Although this working mother provides her daughter with a good role model, if her husband is unemployed or if he earns less than his wife does, there may be stress and conflict in the family.

1999). If either partner has a job that carries high demands but little decision-making power, or if a job has poor working conditions, little chance for promotion, low earnings, long hours, poor interpersonal relationships, or the threat of job loss, it places a strain on the marriage (Hughes and Galinsky, 1994; Piokowski and Hughes, 1993).

A study of working-class fathers in dual-earner families found that positive work conditions such as having autonomy, good peer relations, and a supportive supervisor heightened the worker's self-esteem. Heightened self-esteem, in turn, increased the man's self-confidence and encouraged such positive parenting styles as having a positive attitude toward his children and of not using controlling behaviors such as nagging (Grimm-Thomas and Perry-Jenkins, 1994). On the other hand, and regardless of gender, job stress can be "buffered" by strong marital ties (Barnett, 1994; Grzywacz and Marks, 2000).

Division of Household Labor

As you saw in Chapters 4 and 9, many married mothers have decreased their hours of housework while married fathers have increased their household work. There are still disparities in the domestic roles of employed men and women, however (Thompson and Walker,

1991; Manke et al., 1994). Even if a family needs the money, overtime can create marital conflict because wives are dissatisfied with their spouses' minimal participation in household chores (Kluwer et al., 1996).

Much of the dissatisfaction may reflect the types of housework tasks that women and men do. According to Barnett and Shen (1997), for example, mothers in dual-earner families are more likely to experience anxiety and symptoms of depression because women spend more time on what the researchers call "low-schedule-control" housework, or jobs that must be done immediately to keep the household running smoothly, such as meal preparation, cleaning up after meals, buying the groceries, and doing the laundry. Men are more likely to perform household jobs that have a lower level of immediacy and greater control. There are times when the plumbing needs immediate attention, but most of the tasks labeled as "male" (such as looking after the car and making repairs around the home) do not have to be performed on a regular schedule and permit high control over whether, how, and when they need to be done. Barnett and Shen found that when men have many low-schedule-control tasks, they feel just as anxious and distressed as their wives do, regardless of other factors such as the number of children, education, occupational prestige, marital role quality, or number of hours in paid employment.

Working-class families, especially those where spouses are over age 40, may experience greater conflict over family work than their middle-class counterparts. Worn out from working one shift at home and one at work, wives may feel entitled to their husbands' full participation in domestic labor: "Sure, he helps me out. . . . He'll give the kids a bath or help with the dishes. But when I ask him. He doesn't have to ask me to go to work every day, does he? Why should I have to ask him?" (Rubin, 1994: 87). On the other hand, some men feel that their wives' complaints are unreasonable and unfair:

> The men, battered by economic uncertainty and by the escalating demands of their wives, feel embattled and victimized on two fronts—one outside the home, the other inside. Consequently, when their wives seem not to see the family work they do, when they don't acknowledge and credit it, when they fail to appreciate them, the men feel violated and betrayed. "You come home and you want to be appreciated a little. But it doesn't work that way, leastwise not here anymore," complains [a twenty-nine-year-old drill press operator]. (Rubin, 1994: 87–88)

If working-class (or other) men have jobs that are tedious or unrewarding, being expected to do low-schedule-control housework may create marital conflict. Moreover, since employed married men tend to

work longer hours than their full-time employed wives (Perry-Jenkins and Folk, 1994), their wives' demands to do more family work may seem especially oppressive.

The division of household labor varies not only by social class but also by occupational level and racial and national origin. As you saw in Chapter 12, black men are more likely than men of other races to cook, clean, and care for children. The greater participation in family work might reflect the historical exclusion of African American men from many jobs:

> "My mother worked six days a week cleaning other people's houses, and my father was an ordinary laborer, when he could find work, which wasn't very often," explains thirty-two-year-old Troy Payne, a black waiter and father of two children. "So he was home a lot more than she was, and he'd do what he had to do around the house. The kids all had to do their share, too. It seemed only fair, I guess." (Rubin, 1994: 92)

According to Perry-Jenkins and Folk (1994), the more resources a wife has, such as job status and income, the more likely it is that family work will be divided more equitably between marriage partners. In a study of Latino families, for example, Valdez and Coltrane (1993) found that wives who earned less money, worked fewer hours, held less prestigious jobs, had less education, or were much younger than their husbands were the most likely to feel responsible for all of the housework and child care. Asian and Latino men who are least likely to share in family work are those who live in ethnic neighborhoods where there is strong support for traditional gender roles, even when the wife works outside the home (Rubin, 1994).

Children's Well-Being

Managing parent–children relationships in the dual-earner family can be stressful:

> [In] an all too familiar scenario, Mother comes home exhausted, wanting support from Father; Father comes home irritable and . . . wanting to be left alone; neither can give the other the support he or she needs, and their interactions are tense and brief. Meanwhile, the children are demanding attention—the little one needs diapering, while the older one is watching television instead of doing his homework. . . . [And] dinner still needs to be prepared. (Piokowski and Hughes, 1993: 198)

Time and energy are precious commodities in many dual-earner families. Young families, especially, spend many years accommodating their child-rearing tasks to the demands of the workplace. Both dual-earner parents try to balance work and family life by making

CHOICES

Juggling Competing Demands in Dual-Earner Families

The strains in juggling work and family life are bound to affect a marriage sooner or later. Here are several strategies that some practitioners suggest for maintaining one's sanity and the well-being of all family members (Beck, 1988; Crosby, 1991b):

- **Emphasize the positive.** Concentrate on the benefits you get from having a job: personal fulfillment, an increased standard of living, an ability to provide more cultural and educational opportunities for your children, and greater equality between you and your spouse.
- **Set priorities.** Because conflicts between family and job demands are inevitable, you need some guiding principles for resolving clashes. For example, parents might take turns meeting such emergencies as staying at home with sick children.
- **Be ready to compromise.** Keep in mind that it is unrealistic to strive for perfection in both family and job responsibilities. Instead, aim for the best possible balance among your various activities, making

compromises when necessary. For example, you may have to spend a little less time with your children than you would like, or you may have to sacrifice an opportunity for advancement at work.

- **Separate your family and work roles.** Try to separate your roles. Many mothers, especially, feel guilty while at work because they are not with their children, and when they are, they feel guilty about not working on assignments they've brought home from the office. If you must work at home, set time limits for that work and spend the rest of the time fully with your family.
- **Be realistic about your standards.** Some people believe that their homes should be just as immaculate after they have children as before or when both spouses work instead of just one. You may need to adjust your standards and to accept some disorder.
- **Organize domestic duties.** Domestic overload can sometimes be resolved by dividing family work more equitably among spouses and children.

Many families find it useful to prepare a weekly or monthly job chart, in which everyone's assignments are clearly written down. It's also useful to rotate assignments, so that everyone gets to do both the "better" and the "worse" jobs.

- **Cultivate a sharing attitude with your spouse.** Sit down with your spouse periodically and discuss what you can do to help each other in your respective jobs both at home and at work. Home problems deserve as much respect and attention as do work problems. Many husbands and wives are relieved when their partners offer a sounding board or give advice or encouragement.
- **Try to maintain a balance between responsibilities and recreation.** Remember that if you are both working to improve your standard of living, you should use some of your extra income to relish life. If you spend all your psychological resources on job and home responsibilities, you will have little energy to do the things that will make your life more enjoyable.

---

trade-offs, such as taking on additional work when it's economically necessary to do so and sometimes missing family occasions or holidays. Others are scaling back in meeting the demands of high-powered jobs to maintain a sense of family (Becker and Moen, 1999; Milkie and Peltola, 1999).

Although parents may feel stressed, most children see their parents as loving and responsive. In a recent national study of children in the third through twelfth grades, for example, Galinsky (1999) asked the children to "grade" both their mothers and fathers on "making me feel important and loved." Most children (72 percent) gave their mothers an A and 67 percent gave their fathers an A. There was no difference in the grades the children gave where the mother was employed compared to those who stayed at home or between mothers who worked part time and those who worked full time.

Mothers' employment can have benefits for children, including increased financial resources and more egalitarian sex-role models (see Chapter 4). Still, many women feel guilty about returning to work after childbirth, and consequently they spend time with their children at the expense of their own sleep and leisure (Rubin and Riney, 1994). Recently, researchers have suggested that the important question is not how a mother's employment, per se, affects children but how the *quality of child care*—whether parental or nonparental—affects children's development.

Parents who are unsupportive, unresponsive, and inconsistent can have more damaging effects on a child than can nonparental child care that is sensitive, responsive, and supportive (Belsky, 1991). In addition, the father's role in dual-earner families is just as important in children's well-being as a mother's employment. Loving and respectful interaction patterns between spouses are important factors in shaping child development (Moorehouse, 1993).

Perhaps the greatest stressors for the dual-earner family are those created by work-related tensions. For example, when parents experience job stress and work-family role overload, they are more restrictive, they withdraw more, and they are less positive when interacting with their children. Parental job stress may also be associated with a child's poor academic achievement or behavioral problems in school, and it can also lead to child abuse (Piokowski and Hughes, 1993; Parcel and Menaghan, 1994). Suggestions for problems that families may encounter are offered in the box "Juggling Competing Demands in Dual-Earner Families."

Inequality in the Workplace

The issues we've discussed that confront dual-earner families are often compounded by workplace problems that are specifically gender related. Employed women are often romanticized by the media today, who present images of perfectly groomed women, briefcases in hand, chairing important meetings or flying across the country, cell phone in hand and laptop in action. In fact, the majority of working women have much less exciting jobs, and regardless of their occupations, face similar problems, including lack of promotion, wage discrimination, and sexual harassment. Although men are more likely to be the discriminators than the discriminated, they, too, may suffer wage discrimination and harassment. All of these issues affect the family's interpersonal and economic well-being.

The Mommy Track and the Daddy Penalty

In 1989, Felice Schwartz proposed differentiating women managers in business into two groups following two different tracks—the career-primary track and the career-and-family track. According to Schwartz, *career-primary women,* who sacrifice family and children for upward mobility, should be identified early and groomed for top-level positions alongside ambitious men. In contrast, *career-and-family women,* who are also valuable assets to a company, should be allowed to work part time and to spend more time at home. The latter option, quickly dubbed the **mommy track** by the media, was defined as a slower or even a sidetrack for women who wished to combine career with child rearing.

Some employers agreed with Schwartz's thesis, but many feminists argued that the mommy track concept gave employers reasons not to hire or promote talented women to high-level positions and that it perpetuated gender-role stereotypes. Critics also pointed out that the concept could well legitimize the actions of employers who were not yielding to pressures for paid parental leave, flextime, and child care (Ehrenreich and English, 1989).

These concerns are justified. Although women make up 46 percent of the work force (see *Table 13.1*), men still hold more than 95 percent of the top management jobs in the country's largest corporations. Only 7 percent of the 1315 board members at America's 100 biggest companies are women, and only about 3 percent of the 6502 corporate officers employed by the *Fortune* 500 companies are women (Wood, 1995). In 2000, only three women headed a *Fortune* 500 corporation. A survey of 100 Internet-related companies found that only 3 percent had female directors (McDonald, 2000). A study of 500 of the largest U.S. companies by Catalyst, a nonprofit women's research organization, found that only 12 percent of the corporate officers are women. Of those women, only 28 percent are in line jobs—positions that have responsibility for profit and loss. The rest of female corporate officers are in staff roles (such as human resources and public relations) that are important but don't lead to top jobs (Conlin and Zellner, 1999). Although there are some very successful women in business (such as Meg Whitman who built eBay into a multimillion-dollar online flea market), women received only 4 percent of the estimated $20 billion that venture capitalists invested in funding start-up companies (McDonald, 2000).

Furthermore, in what some see as a backhanded attempt to keep women out of the workplace, some corporations are penalizing the husbands of women who work outside the home, a phenomenon that the media called the **daddy penalty.** Fathers who are managers and professionals in dual-career families are paid lower salaries than their counterparts in traditional families where wives are full-time homemakers (Lewin, 1994).

In one study, Reitman and Schneer found that, after controlling for the number of hours that the men worked, their degree of experience, their fields of employment, and any interruptions to their careers, men whose wives stayed at home earned 25 percent more than those with working wives (cited in Harris, 1995). In another study, Stroh and Brett found that male managers at 20 *Fortune* 500 companies whose wives stayed home to care for the children received raises that were on average 20 percent larger than those given colleagues married to women who worked outside the home. All the researchers suggested that there is a corporate prejudice in favor of traditional families, and one described this prejudice as a "double whammy": "The dual-career wife earns less than she would if she were her husband, and her husband earns less than he would if she were not working" (quoted and reported in Harris, 1995: 27).

The Gender Gap in Wages

Women who worked full time, year-round in 1999 had a median income of $26,324 compared to $36,476 for men (U.S. Census Bureau, 1999b). In some cases, a

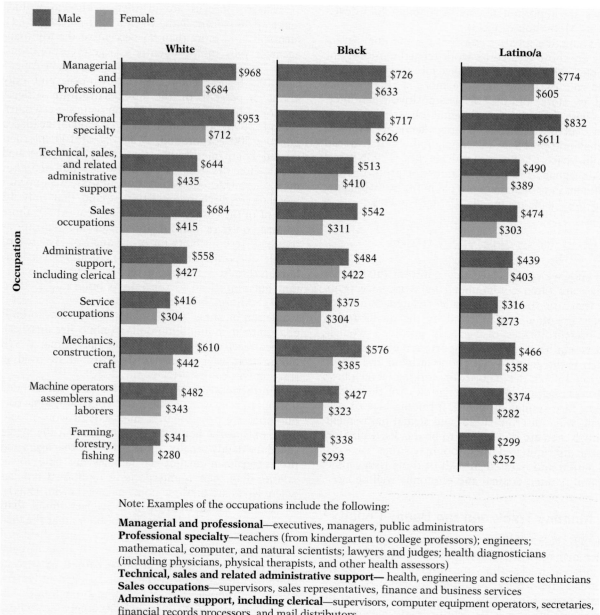

FIGURE 13.9 **Median Weekly Earnings of Full-Time Workers by Occupation Sex, and Race/Ethnicity, 1999**

SOURCE: Based on unpublished data, Bureau of Labor Statistics, Division of Labor Force Studies, 2000.

woman's income is lower than a man's, *even when the man doesn't work*, because many men who don't work still have income from unemployment, disability, pensions, and investments (Krafft, 1994). As *Figure 13.9* shows, men earn more than do women in *every* occupational category, and the earnings gap increases at the higher-paying managerial and professional levels. If we think about earnings as a ladder, men are on top—first white men, then black males, followed by Latinos. At the top of the bottom of the ladder are women, with Latinas faring worse than any of the other groups. We see, then, that sex *and* race intersect in the workplace (see also Browne, 1999).

The median annual income of female full-time wage and salary workers was only 72 percent that of men in 1999, down from the all-time high of 77 percent in 1997 (Berry, 1997; U.S. Census Bureau, 1999b). That is, women today are earning 74 cents for every male dollar. Compared to 1969, when women earned 59 cents for every dollar a man made, women have "made economic progress at roughly the rate of half a cent a year" (Goodman, 1999: 15A). The situation for many ethnic women is even worse. Although Asian Pacific American women earn 80 cents for every dollar that men earn, black women earn only 67 cents and Latinas 58 cents for every dollar that men earn. Over a lifetime of work, the average 25-year-old working woman will lose more than $523,000 to unequal pay. Families of working women lose $200 billion every year to the gender wage gap ("It's time for working women . . . ," 1998).

Many conservatives have an explanation for the gender wage gap:

> *Women have made enormous workplace gains, but they earn less because of their own choices, not because of discrimination. They choose to be teachers, or child-care providers, or mothers, even though they earn less. Then they compound the pay-gap by opting out of the labor force at times or by scaling back their career ambitions—and sometimes work schedules—for personal reasons. (Grimsley, 2000: E3)*

As this quote illustrates, we often hear that women's wages and salaries are lower than men's because many women are in low-paying jobs, choose low-paying occupations, or drop in and out of the job market.

Women who have children early in their lives are likely to experience wage penalties because their career interruptions occur during the critical period of building a career (Taniguchi, 1999). According to a number of studies, however, gender explains much of the earnings differential between women and men. That is, a wage gap remains after the researchers control for variables such as educational level, number of years in a job, seniority, marital status, number of children, and numerous other factors (see, for example, Menaghan and Parcel, 1991; Voydanoff, 1991; Blau and Ehrenberg, 1997; Hughes and Dodge, 1997; Goyette and Xie, 1999; Evans, 2000; "Summary of recent studies . . . ," 2000). As you can see from *Figure 13.10*, for example, male nurses, who make up

FIGURE 13.10 **Median Weekly Earnings in Traditionally Female Occupations, 1999.** Percent of women in each occupation: registered nurses (91 percent); elementary school teachers (83 percent); secretaries and office clerks (85 percent); health aides (89 percent); and cashiers (74 percent). (*Facts on Working Women . . .* 1996, Table 5; U.S. Bureau of the Census, 1997b, Table 645.)

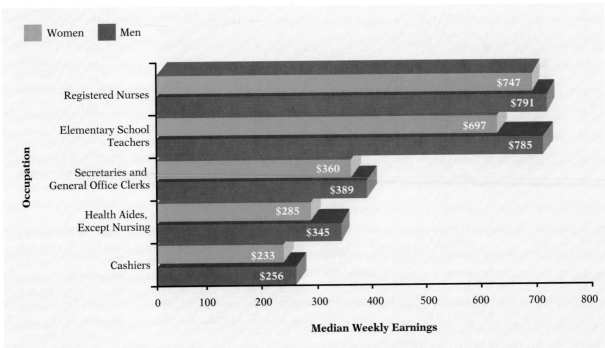

CROSSCULTURAL

Women as Cheap Labor around the World

A growing body of research shows that occupational sex segregation and wage disparities between men and women are the norm in most countries. U.S. corporations that locate plants in third world and other countries where labor in general is cheap are among the worst offenders, but national governments and businesses themselves practice much of this discrimination.

Five countries with the biggest wage disparities are Syria (60 percent), South Korea (54 percent), Japan (61 percent), Bangladesh (42 percent), and Russia (40 percent) (Neft and Levine, 1997). Two important factors contributing to these disparities are the limits placed on girls' education by parents and teachers and employers' discriminatory practices (Terrell, 1992).

In Kuwait, one of the wealthiest countries in the Middle East, Filipino maids normally put in exhausting 14-hour days as domestic servants and earn a monthly salary of about $150 (Prusher, 2000). The Philippine Overseas Employment Administration deploys hundreds of thousands of poor women to serve as domestic servants in middle- and upper-class homes in Europe, Japan, the Middle East, the United Kingdom, and the United States. Both the Philippine government and recruiting agencies reap tremendous profits from providing employers in these "host" countries with extremely cheap service workers who are often mistreated and work in appalling conditions (Chang, 2000; Gordy, 2000).

Even countries that promote women's rights in many areas still lag in the workplace. In Norway, for example, where women have considerable political clout, even though the prime minister is a woman who supports equal rights, and though women hold almost half the seats in the cabinet and parliament, "Norwegian women remain second-class citizens in the job market. They are hired last, fired first, denied equal pay for the same work as men and held back from promotions to top executive jobs" (Coleman, 1994: 58).

Although Maoist political slogans proclaimed that "women hold up half the sky" and the constitution of the People's Republic of China grants women a high status, Chinese women earn only 59 percent of what men earn (Neft and Levine, 1997). A delegate to the local National People's Congress who has spoken out against bias toward women noted that "women are always in the low-paying, dead-end jobs, like nurses, grade school teachers, nursery school teachers and street sweepers" ("A great leap . . . ," 1993: A24).

Undocumented or illegal Latina immigrants make up a large group of abused U.S. workers. In a survey by the Coalition for Immigration and Refugee Rights and Services, nearly half of a group of 400 undocumented women workers in the San Francisco area reported that employers abused them emotionally, physically, or sexually,

paid them less than their documented co-workers, or failed to pay them at all. Most of those surveyed worked as domestic servants or in stores, restaurants, or factories (Amott, 1993). The program director for the coalition said: "I have clients who work seven days a week, doing child care from 6 A.M. to 10 P.M. for $200 a month" (Chang, 1994: 260).

Multinational corporations that move their production units into countries with abundant and cheap labor may not always be the exemplary employers they appear to be. For example, although in 1994 the U.S. Council on Economic Priorities praised Levi Strauss, a U.S. company, for its "unprecedented commitment to non-exploitative work practices in developing countries," the company's jeans plant in Juarez, Mexico, which employed mostly women, was found guilty of many exploitative work conditions (Udesky, 1994). Rain that poured through a leaking roof caused sewing machine operators to get electric shocks. To sop up the water, managers would throw dirty toilet tissues and used sanitary napkins on the floor. "It smelled really bad, and there were no windows," one worker said. The U.S. owner that subcontracted with Levi Strauss and that abandoned the plant when these and other conditions were made public owed workers $400,000 in back wages.

---

only 7 percent of the profession, are earning more than the women who far outnumber them. The same is true in other traditionally female jobs. Since all of these occupations have been traditionally "female" for decades, it can't be argued that men earn more because of seniority, higher educational levels, or greater work experience.

Most employed women recognize that there's a gender wage gap. According to a recent national survey, for

example, 87 percent of the women said that unequal pay should be a top priority policy issue for women. Other important concerns included stronger affirmative action laws to provide more opportunities for women (80 percent), getting respect and recognition on the job (78 percent), a safe work environment (77 percent), retirement security (75 percent), and health insurance (75 percent). And regardless of race or ethnicity, income, educational level, age, or presence or absence of children in the home, 83 percent said that there should be paid leave ("Working women say . . . ," 2000).

Many women have tried to remedy the pay inequality. Throughout the 1990s, for example, women have filed *class action suits,* or legal proceedings brought by one or more persons but representing the interests of a larger group. In many of these lawsuits, the courts have ordered back pay, promotions, or job reinstatement in higher education institutions as well as businesses like Lucky Stores (a grocery store chain), Merrill Lynch and Salomon Smith Barney (financial institutions), and Home Depot USA Inc. (a large hardware retail corporation).

There is no country in the world where women's average earnings are equal to those of men. The size of the wage gap, however, varies enormously from one country to the next. Even within the same country there may be vast differences between urban and rural areas. As the box "Women as Cheap Labor around the World" shows, the United States is not the only nation that exploits women in the workplace.

Sexual Harassment

Sexual harassment was designated an illegal form of sex discrimination as early as 1964, in Title VII of the Civil Rights Act of 1964, and in the 1980 EEOC guidelines. According to the EEOC, the fastest-growing area of employment discrimination complaints is sexual harassment, with over 100,000 complaints filed with the EEOC between 1990 and 1999. Take the quiz in the box "Do You Recognize Sexual Harassment?" to see how attuned you are to what sexual harassment really is.

Sexual harassment, defined in Chapter 4, ranges from *verbal* behavior (such as pressures for dates or demands for sexual favors in return for hiring, promotion, or tenure), *nonverbal* behavior (such as indecent gestures and displaying posters, photos, or drawings of a sexual nature), to *physical* forms (such as pinching, touching, and rape or the threat of rape). Because harassing someone in the workplace, whether sexually or nonsexually, is a display of power, sexual harassment is usually perpetrated by a boss on a subordinate. Since men dominate positions of power in business and industry, it is far more likely that a harasser will be a man than a woman. The superior–subordinate relationship of perpetrator and victim also accounts for the fact that women often fail to report incidents of harassment. The women feel that nothing will be done and they'll lose their jobs if they complain.

Some people claim that there is a fine line between sexual harassment and flirting or simply giving a compliment. Wrong. If someone says "stop it" and the perpetrator does not stop, it is sexual harassment. Most people know—instinctively and because of the other person's reaction—when sexual attentions are unwelcome.

Sexual harassment can be very costly, both emotionally and financially, to victims, perpetrators, employers, corporations—indeed, to all of us. Victims of sexual harassment experience many emotional and behavioral problems that affect their families, including depression; changes in attitude toward sexual relationships or in sexual behaviors; irritability with family, friends, or co-workers; and/or alcohol and drug abuse (see Chapter 4).

Sexual harassment in the workplace is a widespread problem (see text). During the mid-1990s, hundreds of women reported sexual harassment at Aberdeen Proving Ground, Maryland, and other military bases. In 1997, an Army Captain pleaded guilty to adultery and other charges, was dismissed from the Army, and served four months in prison. In another case, a Staff Sergeant at Aberdeen was convicted on 18 counts of rape and other sexual harassment.

ASKYOURSELF

Do You Recognize Sexual Harassment?

Is it sexual harassment if:

	Yes	No
1. An employee is using e-mail to send sexual jokes to co-workers.	❏	❏
2. An employee continues to ask someone for dates despite the person's repeated refusals.	❏	❏
3. Employees tell bawdy jokes to friends who enjoy them in social, nonworkplace settings.	❏	❏
4. A male employee frequently brushes up against female employees "accidentally."	❏	❏
5. A male and female co-worker repeatedly talk about their respective sexual affairs and relationships during breaks around the office coffeepot.	❏	❏
6. A cashier in an eatery in the building greets each customer by calling him or her "Honey" or "Dearie."	❏	❏
7. A male supervisor tells a female employee that "You look very nice today."	❏	❏
8. Employees put up pornographic material on company bulletin boards or in lockers.	❏	❏
9. Employees or supervisors make frequent comments to co-workers on sexually printed material in the media (films, television, magazines).	❏	❏
10. At the end of a staff meeting, a male manager says to two female secretaries, "Why don't you two girls clean up this room."	❏	❏

(The answers to these questions are on page 359)

Is the Workplace Family-Friendly?

The mommy track, the daddy penalty, gender-related wage gaps, and sexual harassment can be devastating to workers and, consequently, to their families. Is there anything in the workplace that supports the family? Absolutely. Pregnancy discrimination laws give considerable protection to pregnant workers and their jobs, and family leave policies have made it easier to care for newborns and ill family members. On the other hand, provisions for child care and elder care still leave a great deal to be desired (see Chapters 17 and 18).

Pregnancy Discrimination Laws

The federal Pregnancy Discrimination Act of 1978 makes it illegal for employers with more than 15 workers to fire, demote, or penalize a pregnant employee. Some state laws extend this protection to companies with as few as four employees. In addition, many pregnant workers are now entitled to up to 12 weeks of unpaid, job-protected parental leave under the Family and Medical Leave Act (which we discuss shortly).

Despite all these protections, the EEOC reports that charges of pregnancy discrimination are increasing. Charges reached a six-year high in 1998, when nearly 4300 women filed complaints alleging that they were fired, demoted, or had some of their responsibilities taken away when their employers learned they were pregnant ("Pregnancy discrimination charges," 1999). According to the National Association of Working Women, this is just the tip of the iceberg. The EEOC figures don't reflect the complaints filed with state human rights commissions or lawsuits settled out of court. Further, only a fraction of the women who suffer pregnancy-related job discrimination ever take action because many do not know what their rights are.

Why are pregnancy discrimination reports increasing? More women are becoming aware of their rights and are willing to fight for them. In addition, pregnant workers are more vulnerable when a company downsizes. Pregnant women become "highly visible targets" because they are perceived as expensive employees, using more medical benefits than others and needing replacement with a temporary worker while on leave (Gilbert, 1994).

Family and Medical Leave Policies: Benefits and Limitations

One of the most important pieces of legislation for many families is the Family and Medical Leave Act (FMLA), which was introduced in Congress in 1985 and finally signed into law by President Clinton in 1993. This law allows eligible workers of employers with 50 or more employees to take up to 12 weeks of unpaid, job-protected annual leave—with continuation of health benefits—following the birth or adoption of a child, to care for a seriously ill family member, or to recover from their own serious illnesses. The box "A Tour through the Family and Medical Leave Act" provides a closer look at the rights for which an estimated 2 million employees are now eligible.

The most obvious benefit of family leave policies is that many employees will no longer lose their jobs because of sickness, childbirth, or parental leave. Further, most employees, except for the top 10 percent, are guaranteed their jobs or equivalent jobs when they return. The FMLA defines an "equivalent" position as one with the same pay, benefits, and working conditions, as well as "substantially similar" duties and responsibilities. Most important, because the act is law, employees don't have to depend on the supervisor's good will.

Unfortunately, the FMLA and other leave policies have several weaknesses. The biggest problem is that the 60 percent of U.S. employees who work in companies with fewer than 50 employees are not covered by the FMLA. Small companies are much less likely than companies with 50 or more employees to provide such employee benefits as health insurance, paid sick leave, and sickness insurance. Thus, millions of employees who already have limited benefits are ignored by the FMLA. In addition, because many women work in part-time, temporary positions, they are excluded from family leave policies (Trzcinski, 1994).

The FMLA is of little help to many parents because it involves unpaid time off and covers only major illnesses that typically require a hospital stay. In most cases, children don't need hospitalization but instead have frequent routine illnesses. Most important, and as we discussed at the beginning of this chapter, because low-paid, service jobs are expanding while higher-paid jobs are shrinking, many employees can't really afford to take unpaid leave.

Employees and employers may disagree about what constitutes an "equivalent" job or "substantially similar" responsibilities. Some women who returned after maternity leaves found that they were reassigned to positions with more clerical duties, fewer people to supervise, and less prestigious assignments (Saltzman, 1993). Does a person have an "equivalent" job if it involves driving an extra 30 minutes to work to an unfamiliar office and a less desirable location? Employers may label

• •

Answers to Do You Recognize Sexual Harassment?

Sources: Based on Langelan, 1993; Coolidge, 1998.

10. No, but it's a sexist comment.

9. Yes.

8. Yes, this creates a hostile work environment.

7. No.

6. No, if the comments are directed at both sexes and aren't intentionally derogatory or degrading.

5. No, if no one is around and the talk is consensual. It could be if a passerby finds such talk offensive.

4. Yes.

3. No.

2. Yes.

1. Repeated instances could meet the legal definition of sexual harassment if they create an offensive and hostile work environment.

CHOICES

A Tour through the Family and Medical Leave Act

Employees who know their rights under the Family and Medical Leave Act (FMLA) are more likely to take advantage of its benefits. Here is some basic information:

Who is covered?

Any employee is eligible who has worked at least 1250 hours during a 12-month period—roughly the equivalent of 25 hours a week—at a company or work site employing at least 50 people. However, although the highest-paid 10 percent of employees must be granted a leave like all others, this group is not guaranteed a job on return. If their absences cause "substantial and grievous economic injury" to their employers, they may be denied reinstatement. These well-paid employees must be notified when they request family leave that they may be out of a job when they are ready to return.

For what purposes is family and medical leave intended?

An employee may take family or medical leave for the birth or adoption of a child and to care for a newborn; to care for a spouse, child, or parent with a serious illness; and to recuperate from a serious illness that prevents an employee from working.

Who pays for the leave?

The employee pays for the leave. A company may require, or allow, employees to apply paid vacation and sick leave to the 12 weeks of family leave but does not have to pay workers who take leave. Employees must be given the same health benefits on return that they received before going on leave.

When should the employer be notified?

In foreseeable cases, such as a birth, adoption, or planned medical treatment, 30 days' oral or written notice is required. When that's impossible (for example, if a baby is born early), the employer must be notified as soon as possible, generally within one or two business days. Employers may ask for medical proof that a leave is needed.

Must the leave be taken all at once?

Leave need not be taken all at once. For example, it can be used to shorten the workweek, when an employee wants to cut back following the birth of a child. Medical leave can also be taken piecemeal, for example, to accommodate weekly appointments for chemotherapy treatments.

What if you feel your rights have been violated?

Any local or regional office of the U.S. Department of Labor's Wage and Hour Division, Employment Standards Administration, will accept complaints, which must be filed within two years of the alleged violation. Private lawsuits must also be filed within two years of the violation.

---

men who use flextime or paternity leave as not fully dedicated to their jobs or careers (Bailyn, 1993). And, with downsizing, "few [male] employees want to send a signal that they are less than 100 percent devoted to their jobs" (Saltzman, 1993: 66). In response, many men refuse paternity leave and instead use vacation days, sick days, or compensatory time off to spend time with their wives and newborns (Pleck, 1993).

In contrast, since 1989, 17 industrialized countries have provided between 12 and 72 weeks of *paid* parental leave (Ruhm and Teague, 1997). One of the most innovative solutions to the problem of negative male stereotyping with regard to paternity leave comes from Norway. Norwegian women now get 52 weeks of paid maternity leave—*but only if their husbands take off the first month, too*. If they don't, the wives' paid leave is cut in half: "The idea is to encourage

fathers to help with a baby from the beginning, in the belief that once they start, they will stay engaged in child rearing" (Coleman, 1994: 58).

Some policy analysts suggest that insurance, unemployment insurance to replace wages, and temporary disability insurance (TDI) could provide workers with paid leave for personal health matters or family needs. Some people don't like the idea of viewing pregnancy and childbirth as a "disability." Nonetheless, pregnancy often *is* disabling compared to pursuing one's everyday activities. Childbirth, also, and especially after a cesarean section, requires several months of recovery. Regardless of how we feel about TDI, Canada, Denmark, and several states (New Jersey, New York, Hawaii, California, and Rhode Island) have used TDI and other insurance to cover paid maternity leave (Wisensale, 2000).

Day Care for Dependents

One of the most serious problems facing families today is inadequate day care for young children, and increasingly families are confronting the need for day-care services for elderly parents as well. The absence of quality care for dependents creates many difficulties for working parents and keeps many mother-only households in poverty. We focus here on what industry, business, and government are doing to help families. In Chapter 18 we'll return to this topic to look at future prospects.

Child Care As you saw in Chapter 11, high costs, poor quality, and long waiting lists are just some of the obstacles that confront working parents who seek safe and reliable care for their children. According to Piokowski and Hughes (1993: 193), "The search for quality nonparental care for young children is daunting at best and can reach crisis proportions at worst, because our nation currently lacks a policy that ensures reliable, affordable, developmentally appropriate care for all children who need it."

The government and most employers are not dealing with these problems. Only a few companies have recognized that offering family benefits is good for business, and now provide some form of child-care assistance such as a company-run, on-site child-care center, access to a reputable child-care center near the company's facilities, and summer camps. One of the most popular issues of *Working Mother* magazine is its annual ranking of the 100 companies that offer the best

Sales representatives, like this mother, can often work from home, which enables them to interact more frequently with their children.

working conditions and benefits for working mothers. Major criteria in these rankings include competitive wages, opportunities for advancement, support for child care, and such family-friendly benefits as leave for childbirth, flextime, and job sharing. *Table 13.2* lists *Working Mother's* top ten companies for 2000.

TABLE 13.2

Ten Best U.S. Companies for Working Mothers

Name of Company	Years Ranked in Top 100*	Business/Industry
Allstate	10	Insures cars and homes
Bank of America (formerly NationsBank)	12	Fourth-largest U.S. banking company
Eli Lilly and Company	6	Pharmaceuticals
Fannie Mae	7	Financial services
Lincoln Financial Group	14	Diversified financial services
IBM	15	One of the world's largest computer manufacturers
Merrill Lynch & Co., Inc.	5	Financial services
Life Technologies, Inc.	5	Biotechnology
Novant Health, Inc.	1	Health-care consortium of hospitals and health care services
Prudential	11	Financial services

*Working Mother has been compiling this list for 15 years

Source: Based on *Working Mother*, "100 Best Companies for Working Mothers" (October, 2000): 60–170.

While *Working Mother* praises most of the companies for promoting women to executive ranks, the lower employees are on the organizational chart, the less likely they are to be included in family-friendly programs. In one U.S. Department of Labor study, over 22 percent of managers and professional workers but only 8 percent of blue-collar workers had been approved for flexible schedules (Saltzman, 1993).

Working at home, or telecommuting, is one of the newest modes of more flexible work styles. As the box "Working at Home: Still Not a Paradise" shows, telecommuting has both benefits and costs.

Some companies that tout child-care assistance actually do little more than provide a list of potential child-care providers in the area. Companies sometimes implement (and are applauded for) services that aren't useful. For example, many elderly family members don't live near their children and may be too frail to use company day-care services. Moreover, most companies charge for day-care services, and many low-wage workers are unable to pay even these reduced costs. Some innovative methods of monitoring children in day-care facilities are presented in Chapter 18.

Elder Care Elder-care services are rarely provided or even subsidized by business as yet, but some companies now offer employee seminars on a variety of elder-care topics, such as how to choose a nursing home or help elderly family members with financial matters. A Canadian company, Microchip Human Services in suburban Toronto, maintains a 24-hour computerized database service that employees from client companies can call toll free for detailed information on elder-care services anywhere in the country (Mergenbagen, 1994). Combining family and work is not impossible with a little help from enlightened businesses and the computer industry. So far, however, and as you'll see in Chapter 17, most of the elder care is provided by family members—especially women.

Conclusion

Because many families lack sufficient economic resources, they have very few *choices* in the workplace. Macro-level economic *changes* have created numerous *constraints* that often put the family in a catch-22 situation. Incomes have not kept up with the rate of inflation, so more household members have to

CHANGES

Working at Home: Still Not a Paradise

Personal computers, many analysts predicted, would help decrease the conflict between work and family roles. People could work at home, or *telecommute*—that is, work from home through computer hookups to a company office.

In 1997, more than 21 million persons did some work at home as part of their primary job. More than 70 percent of these people were in married-couple households, and women and men were about equally likely to work at home. The work-at-home rate for married parents was about the same as for married persons without children. White workers were more than twice as likely as blacks or Latinos to engage in some form of home-based work. Married parents were about as likely to work at home on a second job as mar-

ried persons without children. Single parents, however, and especially single mothers, had higher work-at-home rates than single workers without children ("Work at home . . . ," 1998).

On the positive side, many telecommuters spend less money on clothes, have a more flexible work schedule, and have reduced the cost of child care by working at home (Koncius, 1995). Some report that working at home brings the family closer together. A parent is available when a child returns after school and family members often become involved in the business tasks (Schafer, 1999).

On the negative side, some telecommuters miss their work friends and others feel that nothing replaces face-to-face communication (Allen and Moorman, 1997). Some telecommuters

resent having to maintain or fix complicated office equipment like computers or fax machines (Tanaka, 1997). Others worry that telecommuting might make them less visible to management when considering promotions and raises (Mogelonsky, 1995).

Telecommuting can decrease instead of increase the quality of family time. Some parents resent interruptions or distractions because of household chores, worry that job stress can't be left at the office, or find that it's hard to separate their family and business lives (Garland, 2000). Noise because of children, pets, and appliances may also decrease productivity and create stress. Finally, some people are concerned that the expenses for telecommuting may be screened more carefully by the Internal Revenue Service and increase the risks of audits (Allen and Moorman, 1997).

work. This cuts into family time and creates stress that can contribute to illness, absenteeism, and layoffs. The more successful employed women and men are, the more difficult it is for them to find time for family activities. But if men and women are not successful, they and their families have fewer choices in maintaining a decent standard of living. Many parents, and especially single mothers, can't afford child care because it is too expensive; but without child care, they can't get the training for jobs that will pull them out of poverty. Many of the same economic and political structures also have an impact on whether interpersonal relationships within the family are healthy or destructive, a topic we examine in the next chapter.

SUMMARY

1. Social class and economic resources play a major role in what happens to families. A small proportion of affluent families is getting richer, an increasing number of middle-class families is experiencing more employment instability, unemployment or underemployment, and the number of poor families is growing.

2. On the one hand, some scholars feel that poverty rates are exaggerated because they have been based on figures that overstate inflation and because they ignore noncash benefits from the government, such as food stamps, housing subsidies, and medical services. On the other hand, many feel that the proportion of the poor is underestimated because the amount of money needed for subsistence varies drastically by region and because the U.S. Census Bureau undercounts many of the poor.

3. The major programs for poor families include cash support; direct provision of necessities for food, shelter, and medical care; social services; and several community services. None of these programs has been very effective in helping families who want to get off welfare, however.

4. The country's homeless population has doubled every year since 1980. Although there are no exact figures, the estimates range from 3 million to 10 million homeless people. An estimated 34 percent of the homeless population includes families with children.

5. The expectations of many young people may be unrealistic and contradictory. Many adolescents and college students say that work is not a top priority; they also expect to have a house, several cars, state-of-the-art recreational equipment, and other amenities. Furthermore, more young men than young women expect the wife to stay home with the children instead of seeking a career.

6. Economic recessions and stagnant incomes have resulted in more dual-earner families. There is a great deal of variation in dual-earner families, however, in terms of social class and willingness to relocate or to have a commuter marriage.

7. Employment affects the family in many ways. Whether the results are positive or negative, work roles affect the duration and quality of a marriage, household labor, and children's well-being.

8. Employed women are frequently romanticized. In reality, and regardless of the occupation, most women face problems in sex-segregated workplaces, wage and pregnancy discrimination, and sexual harassment.

9. A landmark piece of legislation is the Family and Medical Leave Act. Although the law protects an employee's job during illness as well as maternity and paternity leave, the bill provides little or limited coverage to most families.

10. Due to economic changes and the increasing number of mothers with young children who must work, many families face serious problems in terms of child-care services and facilities. Furthermore, there is some evidence that such innovative employment options as working at home are not always as effective as many people had predicted.

KEY TERMS

poverty line 337
discouraged worker 343
underemployed worker 343
two-person single career 343

dual-earner couple 346
discretionary income 346
dual-career couple 347
trailing spouse 347

commuter marriage 348
mommy track 353
daddy penalty 353

TAKING IT FURTHER

Combining Family and Work More Effectively

The Internet offers a wide range of information on improving our working conditions and family life. A few sites include the following:

U.S. Department of Labor Home Page provides a cornucopia of data and practical information on employment, workplace illnesses, and employee benefits.

http://www.bls.gov

U.S. Department of Labor Women's Bureau Home Page offers statistics, advice on hiring someone to work in your home, and much data on women in the workplace.

http://www.dol.gov/dol/wb

The Families and Work Institute conducts policy and work site research on the changing work force and changing family/personal lives.

http://www.familiesandwork.org

The Center on Budget and Policy Priorities conducts research and analysis on a range of government work policies and programs, with an emphasis on those affecting low- and moderate-income families.

http://www.cbpp.org

Home Business Network provides networking tips and a newsletter for home-based businesses.

http://www.home-careers.com

And more . . . www.prenhall.com/benokraitis includes sites on the economic situation worldwide, reports on U.S. workers, homelessness, family finances, how to calculate your personal gender wage gap online, FMLA research, at-home dad resources, and more.

Family Violence and Other Crisis-Related Issues

DATA DIGEST

- Nationwide, between 1993 and 1998 **the rate of reported child abuse or neglect decreased** from 15.3 to 12.9 per 1000 children.

- As many as **3000 women are killed by their husbands or boyfriends each year.**

- An estimated 1.2 million American **women have been raped by their husbands** one or more times.

- Domestic violence incurs **medical expenses of at least $3 billion annually.** Businesses lose

another $100 million in sick leave, absenteeism, and nonproductivity.

- Each year, on average, between 1992 and 1997, a relative, intimate, or close acquaintance **injured about 36,000 persons age 65 or older and killed about 500.**

SOURCES: Laumann et al., 1994; Rand and Strom, 1997; Greenfeld and Snell, 1999; Klaus, 2000; U.S. Department of Health and Human Services, 2000.

RECENTLY a 3-year-old boy died after his father punched him several times in the stomach for jumping around and making too much noise during a televised football game. A mother repeatedly sexually assaulted her 6-year-old daughter with a toothbrush and a hairbrush, made the little girl eat her own feces, and finally killed her by smashing the girl's head against a cement wall. A computer specialist fatally stabbed his wife because the family started dinner without him.

Families can be warm, loving, and nurturing, but they can also be cruel and abusive. Family members are more likely than outsiders to assault or kill other family members. As Gelles (1997:12) observes, "That violence and love can coexist in a household is perhaps the most insidious aspect of family violence, because we grow up learning that it is acceptable to hit the people we love."

This chapter examines the different forms of violence among family members, explores several explanations for family violence, and discusses the benefits and limitations of prevention and intervention efforts. We then turn to such other problems in the family as the abuse of drugs and steroids, depression and suicide, eating disorders, and the early death of a family member.

Marital and Intimate Partner Violence

Violence in marriages may be physical or emotional. *Physical violence* includes such behaviors as throwing objects, pushing, grabbing, shoving, slapping, kicking, biting, hitting, beating, choking, threatening with a knife or gun, or using a knife or gun. *Emotional abuse* (which includes psychological and verbal abuse), equally

damaging, is more insidious. Scorn, criticism, ridicule, or neglect by loved ones can be emotionally crippling. Listen to a 33-year-old mother of two children: "He rarely says a kind word to me. He is always critical. The food is too cold or . . . too hot. The kids are too noisy. . . . I am too fat or too skinny. No matter what I do he says it isn't any good. He tells me I am lucky he married me 'cause no one else would have me" (Gelles and Straus, 1988: 68).

Marital and intimate partner violence is pervasive in U.S. society. According to a recent national survey, 25 percent of the women and about 7 percent of the men said they had been physically assaulted by a current or former spouse, cohabiting partner, or date at some time in their lifetime (Tjaden and Thoennes, 2000a). These numbers are probably conservative because violence is usually carried out in private and victims are often too ashamed or afraid to report it.

As *Figure 14.1* shows, female victimization by intimate partners decreased slightly between 1993 and 1998 but the numbers are still high and considerably higher than those for men. During the same period, women were five times more likely than men to experience violence by an intimate partner. In 1998, almost 85 percent of all attacks by intimate partners were against women (Rennison and Welchans, 2000). Thus, women are more likely to be assaulted by men they love or have loved than by strangers. Most victims of intimate homicide are killed by their spouses (see *Figure 14.2*). While the homicide victimization rates decreased by 75 percent for husbands, a wife's risk of being murdered by a spouse almost tripled between 1976 and 1995 (Puzone, 2000).

There may be several explanations for the overall decrease in spousal homicides and for the increase in wives' victimization rates. First, passage of no-fault divorce legislation in many states during the 1970s enhanced the ability to leave a marriage without

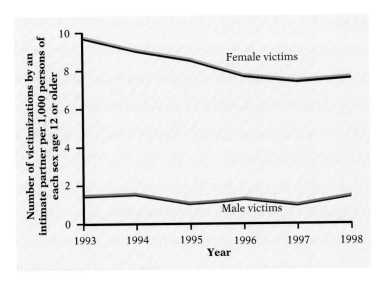

FIGURE 14.1   Rate of Violence by an Intimate Partner, by Gender, 1993–98

SOURCE: Rennison and Welchans, 2000: Figure 1.

seeking a partner's consent or providing reasons to a court (see Chapter 15). With fewer people getting and staying married, or even living together for long periods of time, there is less opportunity for killing each other. Second, many people have been postponing marriage (see Chapter 8). Because those aged 20 to 29 are the most likely to commit spousal homicide, delaying marriage contributes to the overall decline of spousal homicide rates. Third, the increased availability of shelters and legal assistance have provided many women options of leaving an abusive relationship before the violence becomes lethal (Dugan et al., 1999; see also Websdale, 1999).

Finally, women's increased educational and economic opportunities might help explain why wives' homicide rates have declined overall since 1976 and why the chances of being killed by a husband have increased. On the one hand, education and employment

provide women—across all racial and ethnic groups—with resources to leave an abusive relationship. On the other hand, these resources may result in an increased risk of a wife's murder if a husband feels threatened by her increased autonomy or his diminished role as a family's primary provider (Puzone, 2000).

Women can also be abusive (as you'll see shortly). Men's and women's experiences with violence in married and cohabiting relationships differ both qualitatively and quantitatively in several ways, however. Between 1993 and 1998, intimate partner violence made up 22 percent of violent crime against women compared to 3 percent against men (Rennison and Welchans, 2000; see also *Figure 14.1*). Men are more likely than women to engage in repeated and long-lasting violence against their partners and are far more likely to use lethal weapons like knives and guns (Tjaden and Thoennes, 2000b). Moreover, women are

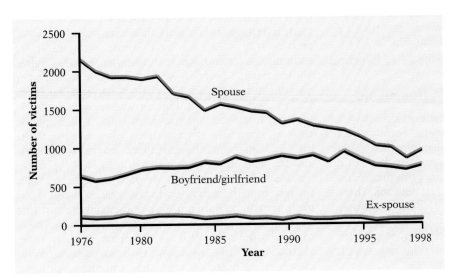

FIGURE 14.2   Homicides of Intimates by Relationship of Victim to the Offender, 1976–98

SOURCE: Rennison and Welchans, 2000: Figure 2.

TABLE 14.1

Risk Factors Associated with Domestic Violence

The couple reflects status disparities (especially if the woman's education level is higher than the partner's).

The couple is cohabiting rather than being married.

An adult caretaker physically assaulted either partner as a child.

The male partner is more likely to be the victim if his race and/or ethnicity differs from the woman's.

The husband is sadistic, aggressive, or obsessively jealous.

He has threatened, injured, or killed a family pet.

One or both spouses grew up seeing their father hit their mother.

One or both spouses are divorced and remarried or their current marriage is common-law.

The man is unemployed and the woman is employed.

The man is a high school dropout.

The total family income is below the poverty line.

The husband is under the age of 30.

Either or both spouses abuse alcohol and other drugs.

The husband has assaulted someone outside the family or has committed some other violent crime.

The family is socially isolated from neighbors, relatives, and the community.

SOURCES: Leonard and Senchak, 1993; Straus, 1993; Bachman, 1994; Gelles, 1995; Tjaden and Thoennes, 1999a; Hutchison, 1999; MacMillan and Gartner, 1999.

more likely to sustain serious and chronic physical injuries because they are usually smaller than their partners are or because they are attacked when they are pregnant and especially physically vulnerable (Wiist and McFarlane, 1998; Tjaden and Thoennes, 2000b).

Characteristics of the Violent Household

Table 14.1 lists a number of characteristics that are common to abusive intimate partners. Some reflect macro-level influences, such as unemployment and poverty. Others reflect micro-level factors, such as drug abuse. The more risk factors there are, both micro and macro, the more likely the violence. In addition, there are often complex relationships in abusive situations. For example, the combination of men in blue-collar status *and* heavy drinking *and* an attitude that violence against women is acceptable is associated with a high rate of wife abuse (Kantor and Straus, 1987).

Who batters? There is no typical profile of the batterer. As *Table 14.1* and other research suggest, however, both male and female abusers tend to be young, poor, black, unemployed, divorced or separated, use alcohol and other drugs, and have seen a father use violence to resolve conflict. Contrary to common wisdom, violence *does not occur only in lower socioeconomic families* but cuts across racial, ethnic, religious, and social class lines. Middle-class family violence is less visible, however, because such families are less likely to live in crowded housing where the neighbors call the police during fights. Moreover, their private family physicians are often reluctant to report injuries to the police or to social service agencies.

Husbands from higher socioeconomic levels also abuse their wives even though they often look and act like "normal" men. The attorney-husband of a 50-year-old Colorado woman appeared to be a pillar of the community. According to his wife of 28 years, however, he hit her, threw her down the stairs, and tried to run over her. "One night in Vail," she said, "when he had one of his insane fits, the police came and put him in handcuffs. . . . My arms were still red from where he'd trapped them in the car window, but somehow, he talked his way out of it" (Ingrassia and Beck, 1994: 29).

Women whose partners are jealous, controlling, or emotionally abusive are significantly more likely to report being raped, physically assaulted, and/or stalked by their partners regardless of other sociodemographic characteristics. Having a verbally abusive partner is the variable most likely to predict that a woman will be victimized by an intimate partner as part of a systematic pattern of dominance and control (Tjaden and Thoennes, 1999a).

Intimate Partner Violence, Race, and Ethnicity

Regardless of race or ethnicity, women report much higher victimization rates by intimate partners than do men. As *Figure 14.3* shows, however, there is considerable variation across racial-ethnic households. For example, American Indian women report the highest abuse rates (38 percent) while Asian American women report the lowest (15 percent). Black and American Indian men report the highest and most similar (12 percent) domestic violence rates. Mixed race (people who are biracial) victimizations of women are also high and similar to those of black women (30 percent and 29 percent, respectively).

National data on intimate partner violence should be interpreted cautiously for several reasons. First, there are still no data *within* ethnic-racial groups, such as possible variations within Latino and Asian American subgroups as well as American Indian tribes (Tjaden and Thoennes, 2000a). Second, some of the estimates are based on very small samples or different

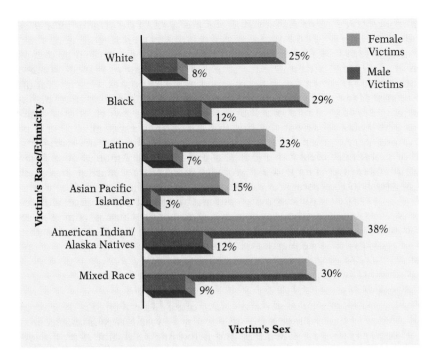

FIGURE 14.3 **Percent of Persons Victimized by an Intimate Partner in Lifetime, by Victim's Sex and Race/Ethnicity, 1998**

Source: Based on data in Tjaden and Thoennes, 2000a, Exhibits 6 and 7.

data collection methods. Among American Indians, for example, Bachman (1992) reported high rates of family violence compared to other ethnic groups. On the other hand, a recent study found that about one in six violent victimizations among American Indians involved an offender who was an intimate or family member, about the same as for victims of all races (Greenfeld and Smith, 1999). It's not clear whether the victimization rates differ because of self-reports by the respondents, variations in research designs, or other factors. Third, most of the national-level data don't control for socioeconomic variables. As a result, it's difficult to draw any conclusions, however tentative, about possible social class variations. Finally, much of domestic violence is not reported.

The last issue, underreporting, may be especially problematic in getting an accurate picture of intimate partner victimization rates across and within ethnic and racial groups. For example, Mexican American women who have not acculturated into U.S. society may not define wife rape as abuse because engaging in unwanted sexual relations (especially if the husband doesn't use force) avoids marital conflict and is part of the wife's sexual script (see Chapter 6). In addition, keeping silent about unwanted sex—whether in child sexual abuse, date rape, or marital relations—avoids bringing shame on themselves or their families (Lira and Koss, 1999). Asian American women, especially those who are recent immigrants and don't speak English, may not report marital violence because they fear deportation, being ostracized by their community, or don't know about or trust social service organizations that provide help (Huisman, 1996).

Despite these caveats, it's important to recognize that domestic violence among all racial-ethnic groups appears to be widespread. And women, much more than men, continue to be battered, maimed, or killed.

The Cycle of Domestic Violence

Lenore Walker (1978) proposed a "cycle theory of battering incidents" that is often used to explain the dynamics of marital abuse. According to Walker, a three-phase cycle begins with a tension-building phase that leads to the acute battering incident and ends with a period of calm that lasts until the cycle starts again.

Phase One: The Tension-Building Phase During the first phase of Walker's cycle, minor battering incidents occur, and the wife tries to prevent her husband's anger from escalating by catering to him or staying out of his way. At the same time, the battered wife often feels that her husband's abuse is justified: "When he throws the dinner she prepared for him across the kitchen floor she reasons that maybe she did overcook it, accidentally. As she cleans up his mess, she may think that he was a bit extreme in his reaction, but she is usually so grateful that it was a relatively minor incident that she resolves not to be angry with him" (p. 147). Although the wife hopes the situation will change, the tension typically escalates, the husband becomes more brutal, and the wife less able to defend herself.

Phase Two: The Acute Battering Incident Abusers are often described as having a Dr. Jekyll and Mr. Hyde personality where the rational and gentle

Dr. Jekyll changes, unpredictably, into an unreasonable and brutal Mr. Hyde. In the second phase Mr. Hyde emerges, exploding in rage and beating or otherwise abusing his wife. Some women who have lived with abuse for a long time actually anticipate this phase and trigger the violent incident to get it over with. They often deny the severity of their injuries and refuse to seek medical treatment. According to Walker, one woman who wanted to go to a family party with her husband and sensed that an acute battering incident was about to occur deliberately provoked it during the week so that by the weekend her husband would be pleasant for the party.

Phase Three: Calm   Mr. Hyde becomes the kindly Dr. Jekyll in the third phase, begging his wife's forgiveness and promising that he will never beat her again: "He manages to convince all concerned that this time he means it; he will give up drinking, dating other women, visiting his mother, or whatever else affects his internal anxiety state. His sincerity is believable" (p. 152). If his wife has been hospitalized because of her physical injuries, the husband often deluges her with flowers, candy, cards, and gifts. He may also get his mother, father, sisters, brothers, and other relatives to plead his case to his wife. They all build up her guilt by telling her that her husband would be destroyed if she left him and that a father should not be separated from his children. And because most battered women hold traditional values about love and marriage, the wife convinces herself that *this* time he will *really* change. Because he is now loving and kind, she identifies this "good man" as the one she loves. After a while, though, the calm, loving behavior gives way to battering incidents, and the cycle starts all over again.

Marital Rape

In 1991, England passed a law that made marital rape a criminal act. **Marital rape** (sometimes also referred to as "spousal rape" or "wife rape") is an act of violence in which a man forces his nonconsenting wife to engage in sexual intercourse. Raping a wife has been a crime in all states since 1993. About 32 states, however, grant a *marital-rape exemption*. That is, they do not prosecute a rape case if the man is actually living with the woman, married or not. Some states permit prosecution of a husband-rapist only if the rape occurred after one spouse filed for divorce or if the parties were not living together at the time of the rape (Russell, 1990). Even in those states where a husband can be charged for marital rape, a wife may have difficulty proving rape if she shows no visible signs of having been forced, such as bruises or broken bones.

In a recent national survey, 16 percent of American Indian women, 8 percent of white women and Latinas, 7 percent of black women, and 4 percent of Asian American women reported being raped by an intimate partner or husband (Tjaden and Thoennes, 2000a). One reason marital rape is so common is that it is still accepted by many people as a legitimate act. Although an estimated 15 percent of married women nationwide are raped by their spouses, very few report these crimes. A traditional wife, believing that she has no choice but to perform her "wifely duty," may accept the situation as normal, especially if her husband does not use a weapon or threaten her with physical harm (Michael et al., 1994). Among South Asian immigrants, women subjected to marital rape will rarely reveal the abuse. Consenting to marriage generally assumes consent to sexual intercourse with or without a woman's agreement because a woman's sexuality is perceived to be under a man's control within the marriage (Abraham, 2000).

Why Do Women Stay?

Battered wives are often described as dependent women who suffer from low self-esteem and feelings of inadequacy and helplessness. It's not clear, however, whether these characteristics reflect personality traits battered women possessed before they met the abusers, whether they are the result of the abuse, or a combination of both (Rathus and O'Leary, 1997).

Thus the obvious question: Why do these women stay? Despite the common tendency to think of abused women as passive punching bags, 87 percent of the abused wives and female partners seek help at various medical facilities that include hospital emergency rooms (Tjaden and Thoennes, 2000a). Many rely on family, friends, and shelters to leave batterers safely and permanently (Goetting, 1999). Some women, like one of my students, find the courage to leave only when they suddenly realize that the abusive relationship is harming their children:

> *John never laid a finger on his daughter but struck me in front of her. . . . I cringe to remember but at the time I chose to believe that what Sheri saw wasn't affecting her. One afternoon when I heard Sheri banging and yelling, I rushed to [her] room. . . . Sheri was hitting her doll and screaming four-letter words she often heard her father yell at me. She was just starting to talk, and that was what she was learning. That moment changed our lives forever. . . . I left John that night [and] . . . never went back. (Author's files)*

There is no single reason why some victims never try to leave an abusive relationship. There are multiple and overlapping explanations for a victim's staying with an abusive partner:

1. **Negative self-concept and low self-esteem.** Many battered women feel they have nothing to offer another person. Most batterers convince their

Hedda Nussbaum was the live-in lover of criminal attorney Joel Steinberg when he "adopted" infant Lisa (left). Six years later, battered beyond recognition by her "lover" (right), Hedda witnessed his arraignment for the murder of Lisa, whom he had begun to abuse as well. Doctors, teachers, and neighbors had noticed Lisa's bruises but did nothing. Late in 1987 Steinberg hit Lisa and left her lying on the floor, comatose. Lisa died three days later. Steinberg was convicted and jailed. Nussbaum, judged incapable of either harming or helping Lisa, began slowly to rebuild her life. She now spends much of her time on lecture circuits to help battered women.

partners that they are worthless, stupid, and disgusting: "Behind a closed door, a man calls a woman a 'slut' and a 'whore.' He tells her that she is too fat or too sexy or too frumpy, that she is 'a poor excuse for a mother,' a worthless piece of dirt" (Goode et al., 1994: 24). Such tyranny is effective because, in many cultures, a woman's self-worth still hinges on having a man. Women are often willing to pay any price to hold on to the relationship because they believe no one else could love them.

2. **Belief that the abuser will change.** One woman with a cheek still raw from her husband's beating said, "I'm still in love with him, and I know he's going to change as soon as he gets past these things that are troubling him." As we've said, our society has long nurtured the myth that women are responsible for changing men into kind and loving beings. Consider, for example, the message in the popular Walt Disney film *Beauty and the Beast.* The Beast turns into a prince only after Beauty stays with him and says she loves him despite his cruelty, threats, and breaking furniture—in a word, acting like a beast.

Or the women have romantic notions about what the relationships can do for themselves or their boyfriends. Rosen's (1996) research suggests, for example, that many women stay in violent relationships because they are seduced by the Cinderella fantasy. The Cinderella fantasy refers to the illusion that "a man can transform a woman's life, erase her insecurities, protect her from her fears, or save her from her problems" (p. 159). The woman believes that, sooner or later, the abuser will change and that she and Prince Charming will live "happily ever after."

3. **Economic hardship and homelessness.** Because many abused women do not work outside the home and have few marketable skills, they see no way to survive economically (Choice and Lamke, 1997). A social worker who works with welfare recipients points out that many men do not want their partners to become employed and independent. Some men, for example, frequently resort to violence to prevent women from completing employment-training programs or from entering the work force (Raphael, 1995).

A few years ago, an award-winning high school coach in Baltimore stabbed his wife ten times with a screwdriver, leaving her partially paralyzed. The wife pleaded with the judge not to send the husband to jail, even though he had violated a court order to stay away from her. Ironically, she wanted him to keep working so his health insurance could pay for treating her injuries; she had worked part time and had no medical benefits (Shatzkin, 1996).

Many batterers keep their wives in economic chains; nothing is in the woman's name—not checking or savings account, automobile, or home. Many abusers keep their victims isolated from friends and relatives, and as a result the women have no one to turn to. Moreover, those who might provide battered women a place to stay fear endangering their own families. Without resources, some abused women who do leave become homeless (Browne, 1993).

4. **Need for child support.** If leaving a husband or filing charges against him results in impairing his earning capacity, both the wife and children may lose his economic support. Many women believe that even an abusive husband (and father) is better than none. As one of my students, a former abused wife, once said in class, "This man brings in most of the family's income. Without him, you can't pay the rent, buy the groceries, or pay the electric bills. If he goes to jail, he'll probably lose his job. And then what will you and the kids do?"

5. **Fear of surviving alone in a hostile world.** Many women believe that if the people they love abuse them, so will everyone else. Strong cultural factors may also keep a woman from moving out of an abusive relationship. Among some Asian American communities, especially, and as you saw earlier, there is strong pressure not to bring shame or disgrace to the family by exposing such problems as domestic violence.

6. **A sense of shame or guilt.** Shame is common among battered wives because they know that many other women are not abused (Barnett and LaViolette, 1993). They often feel that somehow they have brought the violence on themselves. This is particularly likely if they have seen their mothers or grandmothers suffer similar treatment: "One woman whose bruises from her husband's beatings were clearly visible was told by her grandmother, 'You have to stop provoking him. You have two children, and the bottom line is you have nowhere to go. If he tells you to shut up, shut up'" (Goode et al., 1994: 27).

Thus a tradition is passed on. Women feel they are responsible for preventing male violence, and if they don't succeed, they believe that they must accept the consequences (Jones, 1993). Moreover, because some priests, ministers, and rabbis will remind a woman that she is married "for better or for worse," religious women may feel guilty and sinful for assuming that they have rights as human beings and for wanting to end the abusive relationship. *Table 14.2* lists the rights of battered women and men.

TABLE 14.2

The Rights of a Battered Spouse or Intimate Partner

I have the right to be angry over emotional or physical abuse.

I have the right to be free from fear or humiliation.

I have the right to have friends.

I have the right to privacy.

I have the right to express my thoughts and feelings.

I have the right to develop my talents and abilities.

I have the right to provide my children with a peaceful home.

I have the right to seek help.

I have the right to leave an abuser.

I have the right to prosecute an abuser.

I have the right to be happy.

SOURCE: Based on Fedders, 1990; A. Jones, 1994.

7. **Fear of the husband.** Fear is a *major* reason why women stay in abusive marriages. Husbands have threatened to kill their wives, their wives' relatives, and even the children if the wives try to run away. When I was doing research on domestic violence a few years ago, several directors of battered women's shelters said that it is not unusual for husbands to track down their families from as far away as 1000 miles and threaten violence to get them to return. And even when women go to court to protect themselves, they may find that a judge does not take domestic violence seriously. Consider this courtroom experience:

[The judge] took a few minutes to decide on the matter. . . . He said, "I don't believe anything that you're saying . . . because I don't believe that anything like this could happen to me. If I was you and someone had threatened me with a gun, there is no way that I would continue to stay with them. . . . Therefore, since I would not let that happen to me, I can't believe that it happened to you." When I left the courtroom that day, I felt very defeated, very defenseless, and very powerless and very hopeless. (Maryland Special Joint Committee, 1989: 3)

Such reactions by judges are not as dated as you might think. Some judges take domestic violence seriously, but others still view it as little more than "marital spats" (see Ptacek, 1999).

8. **The home becomes a prison.** Both emotional and physical abuse literally trap the battered woman in her home, which becomes a jail rather than a refuge, with little chance of escape. The battered wife is very much like a prisoner. Her husband is the ultimate authority and she is punished if she disagrees with him. She must follow his "house rules" about not leaving the house or even making phone calls without his permission. In some cases, he takes the phone with him when he leaves for work. She has no control over her body, is isolated from her friends and relatives, and is watched constantly (Avni, 1991; Cottle, 1994).

All these factors make it logical, rather than illogical, that most women stay in abusive relationships: "Staying may mean abuse and violence, but leaving may mean death. A bureaucracy may promise safety, but cannot ensure it. For many battered women, this is a risk they cannot take" (Englander, 1997: 149–150). The battered woman's inability to leave the abusive spouse has serious consequences not only for her own welfare but also for the welfare of her children. We will return to this issue later.

Women Who Abuse Men

In 1994, a highly publicized legal case brought attention to women's abuse of men. Lorena Bobbitt cut off her husband's penis with a kitchen knife, fled their apartment, and tossed the penis from her car window (doctors reattached the organ). Lorena Bobbitt claimed that she had acted impulsively after her husband had raped her and that he had repeatedly abused her during their five-year marriage. A jury of seven women and five men found her not guilty by reason of temporary insanity. When Lorena then charged John with marital rape, the jury acquitted him. A year later, however, John Bobbitt, who had begun appearing in pornographic films, was convicted of two domestic battery charges against a former fiancée and was ordered to serve 30 days in jail by a judge who called him a "bully."

Some researchers and journalists have argued that women hit men as often as men hit women and that husband abuse is the most underreported form of marital violence (Steinmetz, 1978; Pearson, 1997). Three reasons have been suggested to explain why men do not protect themselves: Many men believe that only a bully would hit a woman; others fear they might hurt their wives if they fight back. Finally, some husbands feel they could punish their wives by showing them the injuries they had inflicted and making the wives feel guilty.

According to (usually male) advocates for abused men, many men fail to report spousal assaults because "society simply doesn't take the issue seriously . . . [and] men who claim such abuse are deemed wimps and laughed at" (Hastings, 1994: 1D; see also Brooks, 1994). Although many wives strike their husbands, Gelles (1997: 92) maintains that there has been considerable rhetoric but "precious little scientific data" that women are as abusive as their husbands. He notes that data from studies of households where the police intervene in domestic violence "clearly indicate" that men are rarely the victims of assault and battery and that women are ten times more likely than men to be injured in domestic violence cases. In addition, battered men are less physically injured than battered women, less trapped than women because of greater economic resources, and can walk out of an abusive situation because, typically, women and not men, feel responsible for the children.

Violence against Children

In 1990, police in San Bernardino, California, followed up a telephone call from a neighbor and discovered a 12-year-old girl whose parents had kept her imprisoned in closets since the age of 2. The 4-foot-by-5-foot closet the girl was found in was littered with human waste and fast-food wrappers. The girl was barefoot and wore an oversized jogging suit that was soaked in urine. She was bruised from beatings allegedly administered by her father. Police said the girl's physical development appeared to have been so stunted by her decade-long ordeal that she looked about 7 years old.

The abuse—physical and psychological—of children is not a recent phenomenon. Among the Puritans, women were instructed to protect the children "if a man is dangerously cruel with his children in that he would harm either body or spirit" (Andelin, 1974: 52). And men were not the only offenders: In 1638, Dorothy Talbie "was hanged at Boston for murdering her own daughter, a child of 3 years old" (Demos, 1986: 79). In 1946, John Caffey's observations of unexplained fractures in children he had seen earlier led the pediatric radiologist to suggest the possibility that these children had been abused. And in what may have been the first formal paper on the subject, physician C. Henry Kempe and his colleagues published an article on the battered-child syndrome in 1962 in the *Journal of the American Medical Association*. Nevertheless, it is only in recent years that child abuse has become a major public issue.

Defining Child Abuse

Although I will use the older and more familiar term *child abuse* frequently throughout this section, I will also employ a newer term, *child maltreatment*. Both terms are often used interchangeably. Their definitions are similar, but the newer term puts more emphasis on emotional abuse and the failure of caretakers to provide a child with proper care. (For a comprehensive overview of child maltreatment, see Miller-Perrin and Perrin, 1999.)

Child abuse, as defined by the National Center on Child Abuse and Neglect and codified in Public Law 93–237 in 1974, is "the physical or mental injury, sexual abuse, negligent treatment, or maltreatment of a child under the age of 18 by a person who is responsible for the child's welfare under circumstances that indicate that the child's health or welfare is harmed or threatened thereby." **Child maltreatment** is characterized by a broad range of behaviors that place the child at serious risk, including physical abuse, sexual abuse, neglect, and emotional maltreatment.

Physical abuse, which refers to an ongoing pattern of physically injurious actions, includes beating with the hands or an object, scalding, severe physical punishments of various sorts, and a rare form of abuse called *Munchausen by proxy,* where an adult (usually a white, middle-class mother and educated in some aspect of medicine or nursing) will feign or induce illness in a child to attract medical attention and support for both her and her child. The motives for the feigned illness include the desire to be the center of attention; a dislike for the child; tangible rewards such as money, charitable donations, or life insurance; and the desire to attract the husband's attention. The mother may be needy and lonely or may have a psychiatric problem (Rosenberg, 1997; Parnell and Day, 1998).

Sexual abuse includes making a child watch sexual acts, fondling a child's genitals, forcing a child to engage in sexual acts for photographic or filmed pornography, and incest. This category also includes sexual assault on a child by a relative or a stranger.

Child neglect is the failure to provide basic caretaking obligations. Most recently, some clinicians have included stimulation neglect and language neglect under the child-neglect umbrella. In *stimulation neglect,* Cantwell (1997) includes parents who don't cuddle and talk to babies, who don't take their children to the park (or other recreational spots), and who don't play with or engage in activities that nourish a child's development.

Language neglect includes discouraging the child's communication skills, such as not encouraging an infant's babbling, not reading to a child, and commanding young children ("Put this here" or "Don't do that") instead of conversing with the child and eliciting a response ("Where do you think we should hang this picture?") (see Oates and Kempe, 1997). Neglectful caretakers are usually the child's parents, but this term may be applied as well to personnel in residential centers for children or foster-care homes.

Finally, *emotional maltreatment,* a recently recognized form of child victimization, includes such acts as belittlement, verbal abuse, terrorizing by threatening physical harm, and a caretaker's failure to nurture the child physically and emotionally. Verbal abusers devalue and reject their children with constant criticism, put-downs, and sarcasm, making him or her feel inferior or unacceptable (Briere, 1992; Brassard and Hardy, 1997). Other forms of emotional maltreatment include neglect by parents who focus on their own problems and ignore those of their children; who use guilt and other manipulations to control children's lives; who subject children to unpredictable mood swings due to alcoholism and other drug abuse; and who frequently demand that children assume adult caretaking responsibilities (Forward, 1990).

Rates of Child Abuse

Children represent one-quarter of U.S. crime victims (*Breaking the cycle . . . ,* 1999). Many of these victims are quite young. Law enforcement data indicate that 1 in 18 victims of violent crime is under age 12. In one-third of the sexual assaults reported to law enforcement, the victim is under age 12 (*Children as victims,* 2000).

Of the 2.8 million alleged cases of child abuse and neglect investigated by the U.S. Department of Health and Human Services (2000) in 1998, there were an estimated 903,000 cases nationwide, a decline for the last five years (see Data Digest). Some believe, however, that most maltreatment cases go unreported. More than 3.1 million cases were reported to child protective agencies in 1995, for example, but as many as 9 million children in the United States may suffer some form of neglect or abuse annually (Wiese and Daro, 1995; Kelley et al., 1997). As *Figure 14.4* shows, most child abuse is due to neglect or physical abuse. One or both parents maltreated almost 88 percent of the victims. The most common pattern of maltreatment was a child neglected by a mother (45 percent).

Victimization rates by race-ethnicity range from a low of 3.8 Asian/Pacific Islander victims per 1000 children to 20.7 African Americans (see *Figure 14.5*). While the differences in rates across groups appear large, there is some evidence that child abuse reporting may be more common in poor and black families (Ards et al., 1998). On the other hand, white, middle-class child abuse is often underreported. According to a study of children under age 3, for example, doctors misdiagnosed nearly a third of child-abuse cases with head trauma, even when the children were bruised, suffering seizures, or comatose. Doctors were twice as likely to miss abuse in two-parent families, compared with single-parent families, and in white families, compared with minority families. The researchers attributed the misdiagnoses to physicians' lack of training to recognize child abuse and to their being uncomfortable about casting suspicion on the parents (Jenny et al., 1999).

The maltreatment of children often results in murder. As *Figure 14.6* shows, in 21 percent of all murders committed within the family, children are the victims.

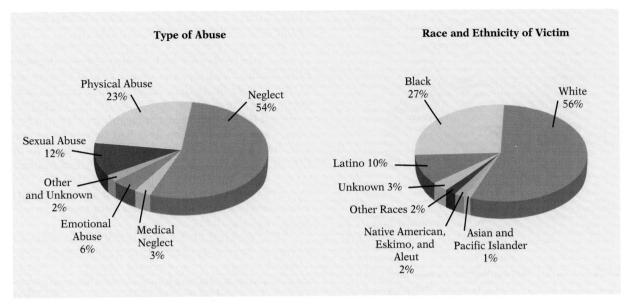

FIGURE 14.4 Child Maltreatment: 1998. These figures represent 903,000 confirmed child maltreatment cases in 1998. About 46 percent of the cases involved males and 54 percent involved female victims. The highest victmization rates were for children age 3 and under (U.S. Department of Health and Human Services, 2000, p. 4–4).

Homicide, usually due to beating, is the leading cause of death among children under the age of 1. When the child is under 2, the mother is most likely to be the murderer, but an estimated one-quarter to one-third of child murders are committed by single mothers' boyfriends (McCormick, 1994). In 1998, an estimated 1100 children died of abuse. Children under a year old accounted for 38 percent of the fatalities; almost 78 percent were not yet 5 years old. In 33 percent of the cases, the murder was committed by the mother, by the father in 11 percent of the cases, and by both parents in 21 percent of the cases (U.S. Department of Health and Human Services, 2000).

Between 1976 and 1997, parents and stepparents murdered nearly 11,000 children. Mothers and stepmothers committed about half of these murders. Mothers were responsible for a higher share of children killed during infancy while fathers were more likely to murder children age 8 and older (Greenfeld and Snell, 1999). A study of homicide records of children age 10 and younger in North Carolina found that the number of children who died at the hands of

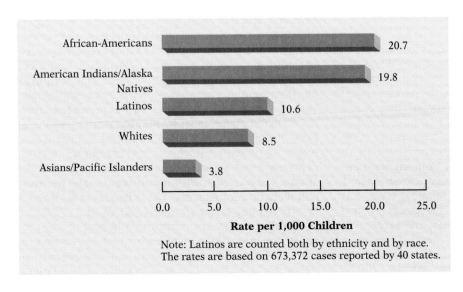

Note: Latinos are counted both by ethnicity and by race. The rates are based on 673,372 cases reported by 40 states.

FIGURE 14.5 Child Victimization Rates by Race and Ethnicity: 1998

Source: U.S. Department of Health and Human Services, 2000, Figure 4–5.

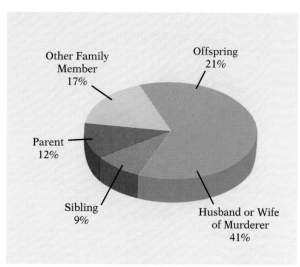

FIGURE 14.6 **Murder Victims in the Family.** In a study of 8,063 family homicides in the 75 largest U.S. urban areas, spouses were found to be the most frequent victims of family violence, and children made up the second largest group of victims. Among white spouse victims, 53 percent were wives, 47 percent husbands; among black spouse victims these percentages were 63 and 38, respectively. (Numbers may not add up to 100 because of rounding.) (Adapted from U.S. Department of Justice, Bureau of Justice Statistics, press release. 1994c. "Wives are the most frequent victims in family murders," July 10.)

parents or other caregivers was underreported by nearly 60 percent (Herman-Giddens et al., 1999). Experts from the National Center for Prosecution of Child Abuse believe that the number of child deaths from maltreatment may be as high as 5000 per year ("Child fatalities fact sheet," 2000).

Explaining Child Abuse

There are many reasons for child maltreatment. The biggest problem is parental substance abuse (Wiese and Daro, 1995). Other factors include the child's age and sex, the family's economic situation, the parents' marital status, and spousal abuse. One national study found that the older the children were, the more likely they were to be abused, and that children from larger families (with four or more children) experienced more abuse and neglect than did children from smaller families. Additional children, and especially closely spaced children in large families, mean additional tasks and responsibilities and more worry about finances (Belsky, 1993). According to the same study, 52 percent of abused children are female and 47 percent are male. Girls are more than six times as likely as boys to be the victims of sexual assaults and abuse (Snyder, 2000).

These differences reflect girls' greater vulnerability to sexual abuse, which we will discuss shortly.

Economic stress and poverty characterize most abusive homes (Drake and Pandey, 1996). Children from families with incomes under $15,000 a year are 26 times more likely than children from families with annual incomes above $30,000 to be abused or neglected (U.S. Department of Health and Human Services, 1996). Women who have had two or more children by the time they reach age 19 also tend to be abusive (Zuravin and DiBlasio, 1996). Teen mothers may be more abusive than older mothers due to a variety of factors such as substance abuse and inadequate information about a child's developmental needs (Gaudin et al., 1996).

Child maltreatment is also highly likely in homes where the wife is abused. Using national data, Ross (1996) found that the greater the amount of violence toward a spouse, the greater the probability of physical abuse of a child by the abusive spouse and that this relationship is stronger for husbands than for wives. Noting that 70 percent of wife beaters also physically abuse their children, Kurz (1993) posits that family violence, including child maltreatment, is a direct outcome of men's attempts to maintain control over the powerless members of the family—women and children.

The period just after divorce may make child maltreatment more likely because parental conflict and family tension are high (Baumrind, 1994). For example, the custodial parent may be changing residences, working longer hours, and experiencing more turmoil. Parents who are already stressed may react abusively to infants who, also affected by the parents' emotional state, become more irritable and harder to soothe.

Sexual Abuse and Incest

In the most conservative "guesstimates" based on reports to child protective agencies, 12 percent involved specific cases of sexual abuse (see *Figure 14.4*). Some research suggests, however, that sexual abuse rates are much higher than those reported to law enforcement agencies and child protective services. For example, a study of 582 southwestern American Indian tribal members found that 49 percent of the females and 14 percent of the males had experienced childhood sexual abuse, most by family members and relatives (Robin et al., 1997). In a study of Latinas in Los Angeles County, California, 33 percent of the respondents reported sexual abuse before age 18. Of the alleged perpetrators, 96 percent were male and over half were family members. The others were boyfriends or other young males (Romero and Wyatt, 1999).

Children who are victims of physical and sexual abuse are most likely to be maltreated by a father. In cases of sexual abuse, more than half (56 percent) of the victims are abused by male parents, male relatives, or other males (U.S. Department of Health and Human Services, 2000). Of the sexual abuse cases reported to child protective agencies, over one-fourth of children are sexually abused by a birth parent, one-fourth by nonbirth parents such as stepparents, and nearly one-half by relatives or acquaintances (U.S. Department of Health and Human Services, 1996). Most cases of reported incest are between fathers and daughters or stepfathers and stepdaughters. The rarest forms of sexual abuse, estimated to account for 1 percent of all cases, are between sons and fathers and sons and mothers (Masters et al., 1992).

The incest taboo, which forbids sexual intercourse between close blood relatives, is a cultural norm in almost all known societies, as noted in Chapter 1. In the United States, **incest** is defined by the law as sexual intercourse and/or marriage between members of the nuclear family, as well as between uncles and nieces, aunts and nephews, grandparents and grandchildren, and, often, first cousins and half-siblings. Moreover, there are strong social sanctions against sexual activity of any kind between such relatives.

Nevertheless, it has been estimated that as many as 17 percent of Americans have been involved in an incestuous relationship (Thornton, 1984). In one national survey, 15 percent of adults said they had been victims of unwanted sexual touching and intercourse as children (75 percent of those who had been sexually abused were women), and nearly 50 percent said they had never told anyone about the experience (Patterson and Kim, 1991). One of the effects of underreporting is that many people refuse to believe that incest is a serious problem (see the box "Myths and Facts about Incest").

Characteristics of Incestuous Adults

Although people who commit incest vary greatly in personality characteristics, studies have found some common traits. Sexual offenders often have low self-esteem and lack self-control. Incest offenders have been described as "narcissistic, uninhibited men who believe that their own sexual impulses must be fulfilled" (Hanson et al., 1994: 197).

Typically, a man who abuses his child or children starts when a child is between 8 and 12 years of age, although in some cases, the child is still in diapers. The father may select only one child (usually the oldest daughter) as his victim, but it is common for several siblings to be victimized, either sequentially or simultaneously over the years. According to some researchers, as long as children are nurtured almost exclusively by women, men are going to be likely to view their children—especially daughters—as sexual objects rather than as their flesh and blood to be cared for and nurtured (M. T. Erickson, 1993). They often intimidate victims with promises of physical retaliation against the victim and other family members. They threaten that they will be arrested or the family

More than 35 years after she was crowned Miss America, Marilyn Van Derbur disclosed that as a child she was sexually abused by her father.

will break up if the incest is reported. Children remain silent out of fear and guilt because they feel they are somehow responsible for the abuse.

Is Incest the Mother's Fault?

Many people blame mothers for the incest that occurs between fathers and daughters or between stepfathers and stepdaughters: "Why didn't her mother do something about it? She must have known that something was going on" or "She probably wasn't giving her husband enough sex." Let's look first at a typology of mothers in incestuous families and then consider what factors may prevent a mother from protecting her child.

In some cases the mother may be a *colluder*—selfish, irresponsible, or dysfunctional, and she sacrifices her daughter either intentionally or inadvertently (Jacobs, 1990). Whether she literally watches the behavior or fantasizes about it, she derives unconscious pleasure from it. In other cases, a mother may lose interest in sex, withdraw from her husband, and ignore the incestuous relationship that may develop between the husband and the daughter.

Sometimes the mother is seen as *dependent*—a helpless person who is suffering from a disabling condition like depression or a physical infirmity. She may

CONSTRAINTS

Myths and Facts About Incest

Forcing, coercing, or cajoling a child into incest or other sexual activities is one of the most devastating things an adult can do to a child. Although physical injury may not be severe or permanent, the psychological scars often last a lifetime. Yet, even when family members are aware of incestuous behavior within the family, most neither report nor try to stop it. Why? Because they believe in myths like the following:

• *Myth:* Children lie about incest.

Fact: Children rarely lie about incest. Most are too young to know about the sexually explicit acts they describe.

• *Myth:* Children fantasize about incest. Every daughter fantasizes a romantic relationship with her father; every son imagines a romantic relationship with his mother.

Fact: A child wants and needs love and caring, not incest.

• *Myth:* If a child is not coerced, it is not incest.

Fact: Whether a child has been verbally seduced or violently raped, the act of intercourse between blood relatives is incest and, in most states, a punishable crime.

• *Myth:* If the child experiences pleasurable feelings during the encounter, the incest is not harmful.

Fact: A child's physiological excitement as an automatic response to sexual manipulation is one of the most damaging effects of incest. It can cause confusion and feelings of guilt or complicity, and it can make it difficult, later in life, for the person to separate satisfying sexual experiences from the original incestuous one.

• *Myth:* The younger the victim, the less traumatic the incest.

Fact: Incest is traumatic at any age. People who are asked to recall incestuous experiences vividly describe feelings of pain and humiliation.

• *Myth:* Incest happens only in poor, disorganized, or unstable families.

Fact: Incest is more likely to be discovered in poor, disorganized, or unstable families because these families often come to the attention of social services. Incest occurs in many seemingly "normal" middle-class families.

• *Myth:* Fathers turn to their daughters for warmth and nurturance denied them by their wives.

Fact: The majority of men who are guilty of incest have gotten plenty of nurturance from their mothers, wives, and other women.

• *Myth:* Incest is usually punished by incarceration.

Fact: Perpetrators are rarely charged or imprisoned, largely because a child's testimony is seldom accepted as evidence of incest. In addition, solid physical evidence is rarely available because the event is not reported and investigated quickly enough.

• *Myth:* A daughter takes part in incest out of hatred for her mother.

Fact: A daughter is either forced or seduced into incest by the attacker. It is true, however, that the daughter sometimes blames her mother for not protecting her.

• *Myth:* A child can be seductive and thus is often responsible for the adult's sexual arousal.

Fact: Children are never responsible for either adults' sexual arousal or for their physical advances.

SOURCES: Tamarack, 1986; Faller, 1990; Adams et al., 1994.

have extremely low self-esteem and few problem-solving skills, and she may be psychologically maladjusted. As a result, the mother may have difficulty communicating (Reis and Heppner, 1993). Rather than dealing with marital problems with such a wife, or when efforts to deal with problems fail, the husband may distance himself from his wife and turn to his daughter for emotional and sexual gratification. The daughter may become a surrogate wife to her father and assume the mother's responsibilities in both homemaking and sex.

Finally, the mother may be largely a *victim* who fails to intervene in the father–daughter relationship because of her own victimization when she was a child. According to Jacobs (1990), this mother is accustomed to a situation in which the dominant male does whatever he wants.

Still, you might ask, how can a mother fail to protect her child from her own husband's sexual attacks? One reason may be that the general public has not been taught to recognize the symptoms of incest. Some mothers may not realize that incest is occurring. If a child shows unusual interest in sex, becomes rebellious, or withdraws, a mother may interpret such behavior as part of a developmental stage. She may blame the onset of adolescence or a response to other difficulties, such as school problems or peer interactions. One mother, for example, interpreted her 4-year-old daughter's resistance to her going to work as resentment rather than as fear of being left alone with the sexually abusive father (Elbow and Mayfield, 1991). Many women lack the resources that may be required to protect their children. Some mothers, like the colluders just described, ignore the problem.

The Impact of Violence on Children

At worst, the physically violent abuse of a child may lead to death. A child abused by a much bigger and stronger person often cannot withstand the blows, punches, kicks, and other forms of torture inflicted by an adult. Even children who survive severe violence are often left with brain injuries; infants who are shaken violently may suffer intracranial (within the brain) bleeding; abused infants may have feeding and sleeping disorders, fail to thrive or demonstrate persistent lethargy, hyperactivity, or irritability; and children who are neglected may have poor physical growth, including underdevelopment of the brain and consequent problems in intellectual and speech development.

Whether abuse is physical, emotional, or sexual, children often suffer from a variety of physiological, social, and emotional problems, including headaches, bed-wetting, chronic constipation, difficulty in communicating, learning disabilities, poor performance in school, and a variety of mental disorders. Children from violent families are often more aggressive and more difficult to handle than children from nonviolent families, and they also are more likely to be arrested for delinquency, adult criminality, or violent criminal behavior.

In a study of white and Mexican American children aged 9 to 15, the researchers found that parental conflict and violence in both married and divorced families placed the children at risk for problem behaviors. The behaviors included cheating, running away from home, bullying classmates and feeling worthless, depressed, and sad (Buehler et al., 1998). Long-term consequences of childhood victimization may also include mental health problems, educational difficulties, alcohol and drug abuse, and employment problems in adulthood (Darby et al., 1998; Esbensen et al., 1999; *Making a difference . . . ,* 1999; Osofsky, 1999; Hyman, 2000).

Adolescents who experience maltreatment are more likely than their nonabused counterparts to engage in early sexual activity, have unintended pregnancies, suffer emotional and eating disorders, abuse alcohol and other drugs, engage in delinquent behavior, and attempt suicide (Council on Scientific Affairs, 1993). A history of child abuse increases the likelihood of problems during adolescence that include engaging in violent delinquency, using drugs, performing poorly in school, displaying symptoms of mental illness, and (for girls) becoming pregnant. Childhood abuse is associated with an increased risk of at least 25 percent for each of these outcomes (Kelley et al., 1997). Incestuous

relationships in childhood often lead to lack of trust, fear of intimacy, and sexual dysfunctions in adulthood. *Table 14.3* summarizes some of the physical and behavioral signs that a child is being abused and needs protection.

Hidden Victims: Siblings and the Elderly

Violence between siblings and the abuse of elderly family members may be less common than the forms of domestic abuse we've discussed, but they are equally devastating. They are less visible largely because the authorities are rarely notified.

Sibling Abuse

Siblings' abuse of each other is so common it is almost normative. The available data show that physical, emotional, and sexual abuse between siblings is widespread (Wallace, 1996; Underwood and Patch, 1999).

Physical and Emotional Abuse Almost all young children hit a sibling occasionally. More than 80 percent of parents in one survey said that their children had engaged in at least one incident of sibling violence (such as kicking or punching) in the preceding year. Furthermore, whereas in the late 1970s only 0.3 percent of siblings used a knife or gun, by the late 1980s this number had increased to 3 percent. Thus every year in the United States more than 100,000 children may face brothers or sisters with lethal weapons (Gelles and Straus, 1988). Although most sibling abuse does not involve weapons, it is highly traumatic nonetheless. Wiehe and Herring (1991) describe various forms of sibling abuse:

- **Name-calling and ridicule** Name-calling is the most common form of emotional abuse among siblings, and ridicule is closely linked to it. Victims still remember being belittled about things like their height, weight, looks, intelligence, or athletic ability. One woman is still bitter because her brothers called her "fatso" and "roly-poly" during most of her childhood. Another woman said: "My sister would get her friends to sing songs about how ugly I was" (p. 29).
- **Degradation** Degrading people, or depriving them of a sense of dignity and value, can take many forms: "The worst kind of emotional abuse I experienced was if I walked into a room, my brother would pretend he was throwing up at the sight of me. As I got older, he most often would pretend I wasn't there and would speak as if I didn't exist, even in front of my father and my mother" (p. 35).

TABLE 14.3

Signs of Child Abuse

	Physical Signs	Behavioral Signs
Physical abuse	• Unexplained bruises (in various stages of healing), welts, human bite marks, bald spots • Unexplained burns, especially cigarette burns or immersion burns (glovelike) • Unexplained fractures, lacerations, or abrasions	• Self-destructive acts • Withdrawn and aggressive—behavioral extremes • Arrives at school early or stays late, as if afraid to be at home • Uncomfortable with physical contact • Chronic runaway (adolescents) • Complains of soreness or moves uncomfortably • Wears inappropriate clothing to cover bruises
Physical neglect	• Abandonment • Unattended medical needs • Lack of parental supervision • Consistent hunger, inappropriate dress, poor hygiene • Lice, distended stomach, emaciated	• Fatigue, listlessness, falling asleep • Steals food, begs from classmates • Reports that no caretaker is at home • Frequently absent or tardy • School dropout (adolescents)
Sexual abuse	• Torn, stained, or bloody underclothing • Pain or itching in genital area • Difficulty walking or sitting • Bruises or bleeding in external genitalia • Venereal disease • Frequent urinary or yeast infections	• Withdrawal, chronic depression • Excessive seductiveness • Role reversal, overly concerned for siblings • Lack of self-esteem • Massive weight change • Hysteria, lack of emotional control • Sudden school difficulties • Sex play; premature understanding of sex • Threatened by closeness, problems with peers • Promiscuity • Suicide attempts (especially adolescents)
Emotional maltreatment	• Speech disorders • Delayed physical development • Substance abuse • Ulcers, asthma, severe allergies	• Habit disorders (sucking, rocking) • Antisocial, destructive acts • Neurotic traits (sleep disorders, inhibition of play) • Swings between passive and aggressive behaviors • Delinquent behavior (especially adolescents) • Developmental delay

SOURCE: American Humane Association brochure.

■ **Promoting fear** Siblings may often use fear to control or terrorize their brothers or sisters. A woman in her forties said that her siblings would take her sister and her "out into the field to pick berries. When we would hear dogs barking, they would tell us they were wild dogs, and then they'd run away and make us find our own way home. We were only five or six, and we didn't know our way home" (p. 37).

■ **Torturing or killing a pet** The emotional impact on the child who loves, and is loved by, an animal that a sibling tortures or destroys can last for many years: "My second-oldest brother shot my little dog that I loved dearly. It loved me—only me. I cried by its grave for several days. Twenty years passed before I could care for another dog" (p. 39).

■ **Destroying personal possessions** Childhood treasures, such as favorite toys, can become instruments of emotional abuse: "My brother would cut out the eyes, ears, mouth, and fingers of my dolls and hand them to me" (p. 38).

Many children report that parents rarely take physical or emotional abuse by siblings seriously: "'You must have done something to deserve it,' parents might say. My parents seemed to think it was cute when [my brother] ridiculed me. Everything was always a joke to them. They laughed [at me]. Usually their reply was for me to quit complaining— 'You'll get over it'" (Wiehe and Herring, 1991: 22, 73).

Parents often promote sibling violence by treating children differently or having favorites. Parents may describe one child as the "smart one" or the "lazy one." Such labeling often inhibits sibling respect for each other and creates resentment. The preferred child may target a "less preferred" sibling for maltreatment, especially when parents aren't present. Also, a favored child may become abusive toward siblings because of his or her power and status in the family. A child's perception that she or he is less loved not only damages sibling relationships but also the child's self-image and self-worth (Caffaro and Conn-Caffaro, 1998).

Most parents view sibling violence as a normal part of growing up and may even unwittingly encourage competition rather than cooperation. However, statistics on family homicides reveal that about 10 percent of all murders in families are *siblicides*, killing one's sibling, and account for almost 2 percent of all murders (Dawson and Langan, 1994). The mean age of siblicide victims is 33 years, and the murder occurs during early and middle adulthood rather than adolescence as one might expect. Males are considerably more likely to be both the offenders (88 percent) and the victims (84 percent) in siblicide cases. The most common circumstance preceding a sibling homicide is some form of argument between the perpetrator and the victim (Underwood and Patch, 1999).

By not discouraging sibling violence, parents are sending the message that it's appropriate to resolve conflict through fighting. Children raised in such violent environments learn that aggression is acceptable not only between brothers and sisters but also later with their own spouses and children (Gelles, 1997).

Sexual Abuse A survey of college students found that 17 percent had had a sexual experience with a sibling before age 13. Moreover, 2 percent of the incidents involved force and approximately 6 percent threatened force (Greenwald and Leitenberg, 1989).

Sexual abuse by a sibling is rarely a one-time event. In most instances the episodes continue over time. They are often accompanied by physical and emotional abuse and may escalate. According to one woman,

> I can't remember exactly how the sexual abuse started but when I was smaller there was a lot of experimenting. [My brother] would do things to me like putting his finger in my vagina. Then, as I got older, he would perform oral sex on me. (Wiehe, 1997:72)

Many respondents said they were sexually abused by brothers who were baby-sitting (Wiehe and Herring, 1991). Some used trickery: "At about age ten my brother approached me to engage in 'research' with him. He told me he was studying breast-feeding in school and needed to see mine. He proceeded to undress me and fondle my breasts" (p. 52). Others threatened violence: "I was about twelve years old. My brother told me if I didn't take my clothes off, he would take his baseball bat and hit me in the head and I would die. I knew he would do it because he had already put me in the hospital. Then he raped me" (p. 55). Most children say nothing about sexual abuse, either because they are afraid of reprisal or because they think their parents won't believe them.

In most cases of sibling incest, older brothers molest younger sisters. Male and female roles in sibling incest families are often shaped by rigid gender stereotypes. Girls generally perceive themselves as less powerful than boys in sibling relationships. As a result of gender-based power differences in offender and victim roles, an older brother and a younger sister dyad is most at risk for sibling incest. As one adult woman explained,

> My brother was the hero of the family. He was the firstborn, and there was a great deal of importance placed on him being a male. My father tended to talk to him about the family business and ignore us girls. My mother would hang on every word [my brother] said. . . . If he ever messed up or did something wrong, my parents would soon forgive and forget. When I finally confronted them about Shawn molesting me as a teenager, at first they didn't believe me. Later, they suggested that I just get over it. (Caffaro and Conn-Caffaro, 1998: 53)

It's not a coincidence that most sibling-abuse cases involve boys as the perpetrators. Although girls and sisters are also abusive, our society is more likely to condone violence by boys as normal or masculine (Miedzian, 1991; see also Chapter 4).

Elder Abuse

Although many older people are able to relax in their later years, some have a much less idyllic existence. Their spouses or children abuse them. **Elder abuse** encompasses physical abuse (such as hitting or slapping), negligence (such as inadequate care), financial exploitation (such as borrowing money and not repaying it), psychological abuse (such as swearing at or blaming the elderly for one's problems), deprivation of such basic necessities as food and heat, isolation from friends and family, and failing to administer needed medications (Decalmer and Glendenning, 1993; Carp, 2000).

Social workers describe some horrific cases of elderly abuse or neglect. Some elderly die of starvation and their bodies aren't discovered for a year or more.

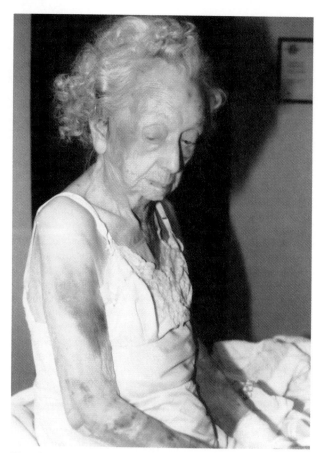

This 84 year-old-woman suffered continuous physical abuse by a caregiver in the older woman's home. When arrested, the caregiver claimed that the woman had fallen out of bed.

A 71-year-old woman was left in bed for so long that her bedsores became infested with maggots. Loved ones mistreat an estimated 5 percent of the elderly every year (see Data Digest). Some gerontologists refer to elder abuse as "the hidden iceberg" because only the tip of abuse cases is reported. Researchers suggest that elderly abuse may be ten times higher than the reported cases.

Baby boomers, now in their late-thirties to mid-fifties, are often referred to as the **sandwich generation** because they care not only for their own children but for their aging parents as well. The percentage of young workers who can support the elderly is expected to shrink considerably. As a result, there is increasing pressure on these children of aging parents who are living longer but who are in frail health and who often have minimal financial resources (Zal, 1992). Most people in the sandwich generation are remarkably adept at meeting the needs of both the young and the old, but those who are not may

abuse their children, their elderly parents and relatives, or both.

Characteristics of the Abused A recent study found that approximately 450,000 people (age 60 and over) in domestic settings were abused and/or neglected during 1996. The rates for different types of maltreatment included physical abuse, 62 percent; abandonment, 56 percent; emotional/psychological abuse, 54 percent; financial/material abuse, 45 percent; and neglect, 41 percent (Tatara, 1998).

Female elders were abused at a higher rate than males in all categories except abandonment. While making up about 58 percent of the total national elderly population in 1996, women were the victims in 76 percent of emotional/psychological abuse, 72 percent of physical abuse, 63 percent of financial/material exploitation, and 60 percent of neglect, the most frequent type of maltreatment. A majority of the victims of abandonment were men (62 percent) (Tatara, 1998). Elderly women are probably more likely than men to be abused because they live longer than men, are more dependent on caretakers because they have fewer economic resources, and because they may command less authority and power with family members (see Chapters 4 and 17).

Later in life, according to Garbarino (1989), the likeliest victims are middle- to lower-middle-class white women between 75 and 85 years of age who have suffered some form of physical or mental impairment. Moreover, if either or both the caretaker and the elderly person abuse alcohol and other drugs or if they have had a poor relationship, the likelihood of abuse increases (Decalmer and Glendenning, 1993).

Who Are the Abusers? Why Do They Do It? As *Figure 14.7* shows, adult children are the largest category of perpetrators (53 percent), followed by the victim's spouse (19 percent). Overall, men are the perpetrators of abuse and neglect in 53 percent of the cases. Only in cases of neglect are women slightly more frequent (52 percent) perpetrators than men. Those aged 41 to 59 are the most likely offenders (38 percent), followed by those age 40 and less (27 percent). About one-third of the perpetrators are elderly persons themselves. In terms of race and ethnicity, 84 percent of the victims are white, 8 percent black, 5 percent Latino, 2 percent Asian, and 0.4 percent American Indian (Tatara, 1998). I've suggested some of the macro-level stresses to which caregivers may be subjected; now we explore some micro-level reasons.

1. **Impairment of the caregiver** A 70-year-old "child" who cares for a 90-year-old parent—not uncommon today—may be frail, ill, or mentally disabled and thus unaware that he or she is being abusive or neglectful (Harris, 1990). In some cases caretakers are drug abusers who lack the resources to live elsewhere and they tyrannize their elderly parents.

2. **Impairment of the care recipient** Several studies have found that caregivers who are violent respond to the aggression of those in their care. Elderly people with dementias may pinch, shove, bite, kick, or strike their caregivers. Caregivers, especially spouses, are likely to hit back during such assaults (Coyne et al., 1993; Pillemer and Suitor, 1991). Children or spouses who know little about such debilitating diseases as Alzheimer's (see Chapter 17) or who don't have supportive networks to provide occasional relief from their caretaking activities experience strain and may become violent toward their elderly parents or relatives (Kilburn, 1996).

3. **Dependency of the older person or caregiver** Economic independence is often related to a sense of power and competence as well as self-esteem. Elderly people who live with their children because they are too poor to live on their own may also be impaired by incontinence, serious illness, or mental disabilities. They become physically as well as economically dependent on their caretakers. If the elderly are demanding or tyrannical, caregivers may feel angry or resentful.

   The dependency between the abuser and the victim is often mutual. Spouses, for example, may depend on each other for companionship (Wolf, 1996). In the case of children and parents, while the abuser may need the older person for money or housing, the older parent needs the abuser for help with chores or to alleviate loneliness (Baron and Welty, 1996). If the adult child is still depending on an elderly parent, she or he may strike out or maltreat as a compensation for the lack, or loss, of power (Gelles, 1997).

4. **Medical costs** Among middle-class families particularly, having to pay medical costs for an elderly relative may trigger abuse. Unlike working-class people, members of the middle class are not eligible for admission to public institutions, yet few can afford the in-home nursing care and service that upper-class families can provide. As a result, cramped quarters and high expenses increase the stress of caretakers.

Why Do the Elderly Tolerate Abuse? The elderly often tolerate abuse from family caretakers because they love the abusers, because they see no viable alternatives, because they are lonely, because they are afraid of depriving their grandchildren or of being deprived of contact with them, or because they have decided (unconsciously) to exchange submissiveness and passivity for the care they need (see Chapter 2 on exchange theory). Women who had abusive parents or who have been married to an abusive spouse are especially likely to accept assaults from caregivers as normal (Simons et al., 1993).

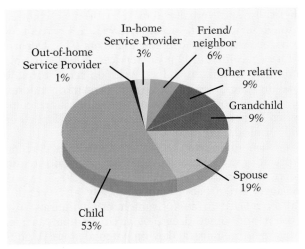

FIGURE 14.7 **Relationship of Perpetrators to Victims of Domestic Elder Abuse**

Source: Based on Tatara, 1998: Figure 4–9.

There are cultural variations in family members' definitions of elder abuse. Some aging Asian Americans might see their children's behavior as neglectful if sons don't fulfill their filial responsibilities to provide for parents' unmet needs, whether medical, transportational, financial, or emotional. If, for example, elderly Korean Americans expect sons to live up to filial obligations that include caring activities, infrequent contact might be viewed as neglectful. Similarly, if daughters-in-law don't live up to cultural expectations to perform filial services for parents-in-law, they might be seen as emotionally or psychologically abusive (Chang and Moon, 1997).

There are also cultural variations that help explain why older people tolerate abuse or neglect. For example, in a study of black, white, and Korean American women aged 60 to 75, Moon and Williams (1993) found that the Korean women were the least likely to report abuse. They didn't want to reveal "family shame" to others and they feared creating conflict among their children and relatives as a consequence of telling them about the abusive incidents. The women wanted to maintain peace in the family at the expense of their own suffering. Family harmony was more important to them than their own well-being (see Chapter 12).

Other Hidden Victims: Adolescents and Gay Families

Although family violence and child homicide decrease as children get older, the percentage of teenagers who are abused by their parents (or stepparents) is staggering. As you saw in Chapter 11, many parents are physically and verbally abusive with their children throughout the teen years. In 1995, 21 percent of teenagers were abused by their parents (U.S. Department of Health and Human Services, 1997). Forcible sodomy, sexual assaults with objects, forcible fondling, and incest affect up to 8 percent of children age 12 and younger. Most of these crimes are committed by parents or adult family members (Finkelhor and Ormrod, 2000).

When adolescents fail to live up to their parents' expectations, parents sometimes use physical force to assert their parental control (Gelles, 1997). Some teenagers strike back, both physically and verbally. Others rebel, run away from home, withdraw, use alcohol and other drugs, or even commit suicide. Because little empirical data on parental abuse of adolescents exists, there is minimal information on the dynamics between parents and adolescents that result in violence.

Another overlooked form of violence is abuse in gay and lesbian households. Researchers estimate that the incidence of battering in lesbian and gay couples is about the same as it is for heterosexual couples—occurring in approximately 25 to 33 percent of all couples (Brand and Kidd, 1986; Lundy, 1993).

Much of the abuse tends to be recurrent. Renzetti (1992), for example, found that 54 of the 100 respondents in her study of lesbian couples said that they experienced more than ten abusive incidents during the course of the relationship about which they were reporting. In almost 35 percent of the cases, the mother's partner abused the children. Farley's (1996) study of 288 gay and lesbian batterers referred for treatment reported that all of the men and women had been psychologically abused as children. About 93 percent of the males and 88 percent of the females said they had experienced physical abuse during childhood. Because treatment and support services for violent gay and lesbian households are practically nonexistent, children living in these families may be an especially high-risk group for future violence (see Leventhal and Lundy, 1999).

Explaining Family Violence

Why are families violent? Why is violence among family members so widespread? Several theories have been proposed to explain the origins of family violence, why most violence is perpetrated by men on women and children, and why this victimization of women and children has long been ignored. As we look at the explanations offered by patriarchy/male-dominance theory, psychological theories, social learning theory, resource theory, conflict theory, and exchange theory, we will also see how societal institutions—religion, the law, government, and politics—support family violence.

Patriarchy/Male-Dominance Theory

Family violence is found in societies around the world. According to a study by the World Bank, data from 35 countries showed that a quarter to more than half of the women surveyed reported having been physically abused by a present or former partner (Heise et al., 1994). The *patriarchy/male-dominance theory* maintains that in societies in which authority is held by men (see Chapter 1) and in which women and children are defined as the property of men, violence by men against women and children, particularly female children, will be more common. In such a society, men hold power, resources, and privilege and feel free to use women and children as sexual objects and as targets of physical abuse. Because of such societal values, neither women nor children are likely to challenge the abusive male (see Ollenburger and Moore, 1992):

Kate was involved in an incestuous relationship until she was 16. When she was 9, her father crept into her bedroom one night and "began fondling my genitals. I woke up because it was uncomfortable. I told him it hurt, so he stopped and explained my body to me. That was the first time anyone told me I had a vagina. My father was the household god—the absolute authority. All decisions went through him, and it didn't occur to me to question him." (Kinkead, 1977: 172)

Even professionals don't always view domestic violence as a problem. In a study of nursing students, for example, Coleman and Stith (1997) found that the students with traditional gender-role views (men should be aggressive and authoritarian and women should be passive and self-sacrificing) were less sympathetic to battered women than were students with more egalitarian gender-role attitudes.

Men may demonstrate their competence by acting "masculine," defined partly by showing contempt for anything feminine or for females in general. According to a number of scholars, as long as our culture encourages men to be controlling, dominant, competitive, and aggressive rather than nurturant, caring, and concerned for the welfare of others, they will continue to express their anger and frustration through violence and abuse against others (see, for example, Birns et al., 1994). And, as you can see from the box "Worldwide Male Dominance and Violence against Women and Children," other cultures face similar problems.

Even religious dogma and institutions reinforce female submissiveness and male violence. Studying abusive men in a treatment program, Brutz and Allen (1987) found that among Quakers the husbands who professed the greatest religious commitment were also the most likely to abuse their wives physically. Many of these men, as well as others from fundamentalist Christian sects, both blue-collar and middle-class men, cited

CROSSCULTURAL

Worldwide Male Dominance and Violence against Women and Children

Violence against women and girls includes physical, sexual, psychological, and economic abuse. It is often known as "gender-based" violence because it arises from women's subordinate status in society. Many cultures have beliefs, norms, and social institutions that legitimize and therefore perpetuate violence against women.

Worldwide, at least one of every three women has been beaten, coerced into sex, or otherwise abused in her lifetime. In Managua, Nicaragua, for example, intimate partners in the previous year physically abused 69 percent of women (Heise et al., 1999).

In many areas of the developing world, both laws and customs work against women who are victims of violent assaults by men. In Pakistan, for example, for a rapist to be punished, four religious Muslim male adults must testify in court that they witnessed vaginal penetration. If a victim cannot prove that the rape occurred, authorities often charge her with adultery (Okie, 1993). Because Muslim law and religious practice make women the property of their husbands, there are no sanctions against forcible intercourse with one's wife.

In Kenya and other African countries, societal beliefs and customs hold that within a marriage a wife must always consent to sex. Thus most Africans do not accept the notion that a husband can rape a wife.

Child rape—and rape in general—is a widespread problem in South Africa. According to police statistics, child rapes increased from 7559 in 1994 to almost 14,000 in 1996. About 83 percent of the rapists are friends, acquaintances, or relatives of the victims; 17 percent are the victim's father or stepfather. Because many husbands and boyfriends are unemployed, close living quarters and idle men at home alone with children increase the likelihood of child rape (Duke, 1997).

Even though India has legally abolished the institution of dowry, dowry-related violence is on the rise. More than 5000 women are killed annually by their husbands and in-laws, who burn them in "accidental" kitchen fires if their ongoing demands for dowry before and after marriage are not met. Sulfuric acid has emerged as a cheap and easily accessible weapon to disfigure and sometimes kill women and girls for reasons as varied as family feuds, inability to meet dowry demands, and rejection of marriage proposals. In Bangladesh, it is estimated that there are over 200 acid attacks each year ("Domestic violence . . . ," 2000).

In several countries, including Bangladesh, Egypt, Jordan, Lebanon, Pakistan, and Turkey, women are killed to uphold the "honor" of the family. Any reason—alleged adultery, premarital relationships (with or without sexual relations), rape, falling in love with a person of whom the family disapproves—is enough reason for a male member of the family to kill the woman concerned ("Domestic violence . . . ," 2000). From 1991 to 1996, Chinese police freed 88,000 kidnapped women and children who had been sold into slavery (Elliott, 1998).

In Thailand, a predominantly Buddhist population espouses family harmony and compassion, but there is also a high level of wife abuse. According to Hoffman et al. (1994), for example, 20 percent of the Bangkok married women they surveyed reported battering. The fact that 93 percent of battering husbands were employed full time pretty much rules out the idea that unemployment or poverty underlays the violence and strongly suggests that in this culture, at least, male dominance is a factor in wife abuse.

---

the Bible and their "natural patriarchal rights" to beat their wives if they did not submit to the husbands' rules.

Many wives of these men tolerated their husbands' abuse "because that's the way it's supposed to be." Others, whose pastors often supported their husbands' behavior, said that their relationship with God would make them strong enough to endure whatever their husbands might do (Shupe et al., 1987). Christian counseling centers may also reinforce wife battering by sending mixed messages:

> We were members of a strict Protestant denomination. . . . We talked to the counselor about . . . everything except the violence. Finally, I told him

> I was afraid of my husband. The counselor told me in front of my husband to be a better wife and mother, to pray harder, to be more submissive. He told my husband that he shouldn't hit me. When we got home, my husband only remembered the part about how I should be more submissive. (Barnett and LaViolette, 1993: 32)

Psychological Theories

Some researchers rely on psychological models to explain family violence. A *personality theory* of abuse maintains that the abuser's personality characteristics are the major determinants of family abuse. Some psychologists, for example, feel that abusers are borderline psychotics who have deep-seated feelings of powerlessness because they grew up with emotionally rejecting or absent fathers and only intermittently available mothers (Dutton and Golant, 1995). Such men never recover from these traumas, presumably, and engage in wife battering to claim some of the power they never experienced.

Some researchers attribute male domestic violence to men who had insecure attachments to parents, especially mothers, during childhood (see Chapter 5). If men with insecure attachment histories have unrealistic expectations about their partners' (especially wives') ability to fulfill their needs, the men may be unusually aggressive (Kesner et al., 1997). Other psychiatrists and psychologists note that a child's characteristics may also contribute to parental abuse. If, for example, a child is demanding, hyperactive, or moody, the child's personality may add to a parent's stress and increase the likelihood of a parent's abuse (Ammerman and Patz, 1996).

Social Learning Theory

You will recall from Chapter 2 that, according to social learning theory, we learn by observing the behavior of others. For most people the family is the first school of behavior, so to speak. But this does not mean that all children who witness abuse or are abused grow up to be violent themselves. Some people purposely seek to avoid the kind of violence to which they've been accustomed. However, studies indicate that continuous exposure to abuse and violence during childhood increases the likelihood that a person will be violent as an adult (McKay, 1994). Moreover, people learn and internalize social and moral justifications for abusive behavior. A child may grow up believing the explanation that "it's for your own good" is a legitimate reason for abnormal behavior (Gelles and Cornell, 1990).

So far, no one really knows whether, or how much, family violence is transmitted intergenerationally through modeling or imitation (see National Research Council, 1998, for a review of some of this literature). Modeling probably plays an important role in learning abusive behavior, but macro-level stressors such as unemployment exacerbate the probability of family violence. Furthermore, as you've seen in Chapter 4, cultural values—including television programs and movies—that demean, debase, and devalue women and children promote and reinforce abusive behavior. In a study of battered women and their children, Holden and Ritchie (1991) found that violent husbands were reported to be less involved in child rearing and to use more physical punishment. As long as men continue to dominate and abuse their wives and children, and as long as women continue to

nurture and comfort others, girls and boys will grow up believing that male violence and female nurturing are "the way it's supposed to be."

Jackson (1996) found that male and female cohabitors are more violent than spouses, even when both types of abusers grew up in similarly abusive families. Jackson suggests that if children growing up in married-couple households learned that abusive behavior is "normal," abuse will be seen as even more acceptable by cohabitors in nonlegal unions. Also, violence in nonmarried couples may be tolerated more than in married families because many cohabitors are more socially isolated than spouses are from families and relatives who might intervene in abusive relationships.

Resource Theory

From the perspective of resource theory (see Chapter 2), men usually command greater financial, educational, personal, and social resources than women do, so they have more power. Power can be positive or negative. In general, people who don't have these resources feel powerless and resort to force and violence. For example, a husband who wants to play the dominant role in the family but who has little education, holds a job low in prestige and income, and has poor communication skills may use violence to maintain his dominant position (Babcock et al., 1993). Many women cannot assert themselves against men simply because their resources are even fewer than those of their partners.

Resource theory also helps explain premarital violence. As we discussed in Chapter 7, violence is not uncommon in dating relationships. If a woman feels she has few resources to offer, she may be willing to date an abusive man just to have *someone*. Or, as you saw earlier, she may convince herself that she can reform the batterer. On the other hand, women who have more resources (such as money, a good job, or a college education) may be less willing to put up with the abuse.

Conflict Theory

Conflict theory, like resource theory and patriarchy/male-dominance theory, posits that groups with such resources as wealth, power, and prestige can impose their rules or their will over groups who lack these resources. Remember, though, that conflict theory is a macro theory. It examines the absence of resources through a wide-angle lens. Conflict theorists, therefore, argue that women and children are victimized in the family not only because they have few individual resources but also because societal institutions such as the legal system, religious organizations, and medical institutions rarely take violence against women and children seriously. As we will explore shortly, conflict theorists often support their positions with evidence that there is little institution-wide commitment to pre-venting or treating such violence.

Exchange Theory

According to exchange theory, both victimizers and victims tolerate or engage in violent behavior because they believe it offers them more benefits than costs. As we said earlier, victims may stay in an abusive rela-tionship because of economic benefits. Rewards for perpetrators include the release of anger and frustra-tion, as well as the accumulation of power and control.

Men who are employed and who are married to the women they assault are less likely to be violent against them again after an arrest. In contrast, men who are not married to the women they assault and are not employed become even more violent after being arrested and released (Sherman, 1992). From an exchange perspective, unemployed and unmarried men become more violent because they have little to lose: They don't care about being identified as a wife beater, they spend little time in jail, they don't have to worry about losing a job while in jail because they're already unemployed, and the women they abuse often take them back. Thus, abusive men are in control.

Violence also has costs. First, it's possible that the victim will hit back. Second, a violent assault could lead to arrest and/or imprisonment as well as a loss of status among family and friends. Finally, the abuser may break up the family (Gelles and Cornell, 1990). Remember, however, that if a patriarchal society con-dones violence against women and children and defines violence as an important resource, the costs will be minimal.

When researchers try to explain family violence, they rarely rely on only one theory because the reasons for our behavior, including violence, are complex. For example, men who have few resources when it comes to living up to a provider role are more violent toward their wives than men who earn a high income (resource theory). However, men who have average incomes but lower educational levels than their employed wives and earn less income may resort to violence. The men have less egalitarian expectations about decision making or explode when the wives pressure them to share more of the housework (patri-archy/male-dominance theory) (see Anderson, 1997). If we add personality variables and exchange factors into the stew, explaining family violence becomes even more complicated.

Intervening in Family Violence

Many clinicians, social workers, and health-care prac-titioners feel that families need help to prevent abuse before it starts. Until professionals and the public acknowledge that family violence is a serious problem,

however, effective intervention programs—prevention, treatment, rehabilitation, and legal services—will not be developed (Flynn, 1990).

Prevention and Treatment Programs

One of the most effective intervention programs has been the University of Rochester's effort to prevent child abuse by teenage mothers. In this program, nurs-es cultivate warm relationships with new teenage mothers by visiting them regularly in their homes from the onset of pregnancy until the child's second birth-day. The nurses not only show the young mothers how to care for their babies but how to play with them and talk to them. The nurses also help mothers find jobs and obtain benefits. According to Levine (1991), only 4 percent of the low-income teenage mothers who received this help neglected or abused their children, compared to 19 percent of the young women who were not part of the program. The program has also been successful with parents who were themselves abused as children.

There is some evidence that treatment programs help change some batterers' behavior, but the evalua-tion data are limited (Davis and Taylor, 1999). Since we are not going to eliminate sexism and the norms that legitimize violence overnight, our immediate con-cern must be to help victims of abuse recognize that they have rights. For example, filing assault charges against an intimate partner is often a powerful deter-rent to future violence (McFarlane, 2000).

Shelters are very important in providing a haven for abused women and children where they can avoid further injury or even death. A shelter can't work mir-acles, however. A basic requirement for a woman to feel safe in beginning a new life is to ensure that legal restraining orders placed on the assailant are enforced (Kurz, 1993). Many districts are training their police departments to take domestic violence restraining orders more seriously. Finally, women need economic support and encouragement in making the one deci-sion that can stop the violence—to leave the marriage or relationship permanently.

During the 1980s, a number of police departments in Minnesota, Wisconsin, North Carolina, Florida, Colorado, and Georgia experimented with arresting abusers (with and without warrants) to reduce future assaults. The results were mixed. Arrest deterred domestic violence primarily for white or Latino men who were married and employed. However, arrest escalated violence for black, unemployed, unmarried suspects (Schmidt and Sherman, 1993). Because poverty is increasing (see Chapter 13), some researchers suggest that there should be more effort in protecting victims from retaliation and ensuring their safety. If prosecution cases were handled quickly, for example, victims would be more likely to testify against the assailant. Sentencing should be swift and probation should be replaced by incarceration. Finally, victims should be protected after the abuser gets out of prison or violates probation or parole conditions (Hart, 1993).

Some states are implementing innovative programs to deter family violence. In Raleigh, North Carolina, for example, police officers, prosecutors, and judges prosecute an abuser without the victim's being in the courtroom. Such programs overcome stumbling blocks such as the victims' reluctance to press charges or testify against the assailants. The U.S. Department of Justice provides numerous resources in preventing and treating family violence (see, for example, Connelly, 1999; Shure, 1999; see also the "Taking It Further" section at the end of this chapter).

Barriers to Intervention

Many cases of domestic violence never come to the attention of protective service agencies. Even when they do, the penalties imposed on assailants are usually insignificant. In some large cities, fewer than 1 percent of those arrested for wife abuse spend any appreciable amount of time in jail (Hirschel and Hutchinson, 1992). According to reports produced at the beginning of O. J. Simpson's trial in mid-1994, Simpson's wife, Nicole, had called the police on eight separate occasions before he was finally arrested for the first time, in 1989, on battery charges. On the latter occasion the judge fined Simpson $200, ordered him to make a $500 donation to a battered women's shelter, and to perform 120 hours of community service, instead of sending Simpson to prison.

In a recent case in Baltimore, a husband returned home unexpectedly and found his wife in bed with another man. After drinking and arguing with his wife for several hours, the husband shot and killed her. The judge sentenced the husband to serve only 18 months, and remarked during the sentencing that "I seriously wonder how many married men . . . would have the strength to walk away without inflicting some corporal punishment" (Lyons and James, 1994: 1A). Do you think that if the situation had been reversed—the wife had found her husband in bed with another woman—the judge would have reacted in the same way?

The prospect of legal action in incest cases may encourage some mothers to see incest as a legal issue rather than as an emotional or private family matter. Some mothers worry that numerous interviews and possible court appearances will traumatize the abused child further. Although this is an understandable and legitimate concern, it overlooks the fact that the child has already been traumatized beyond anything the courts can do; and children generally realize that they are being helped. Many mothers, of course, have been intimidated by threats of violence or by actual physical abuse and thus are afraid for themselves as much as for the children. Such fear and

isolation may discourage reporting the perpetrator's abuse of the child (Elbow and Mayfield, 1991). Abuse requires macro-level remedies, including passing laws that protect victims rather than offenders, appropriating sufficient funds to investigate and prosecute abuse and neglect problems when they are reported, and providing quality child day care and educational and employment opportunities equally to women and men.

Although states require that abuse and neglect of the elderly be reported, these laws are not always taken seriously either. Many health providers are reluctant to testify in court because of the long waits and delays, loss of time from their practice, and potential indignity of attacks on their credentials and judgment. Physicians may be reluctant to get involved because of malpractice suits: "You say 'court' to a physician and he'll shudder. . . . They'd rather be spending their spare time volunteering in a clinic than testifying" (Rovner, 1991: 7). Some physicians feel that reporting family violence cases will require a lot of paperwork and that social services agencies will not respond or that the response will not improve the child's welfare. Laws and medical practices must be changed to support health-care providers who deal with family violence.

Legal Issues

In 1991, the governors of Maryland, Ohio and Washington pardoned a group of women who had been imprisoned for killing or assaulting partners who had abused them physically. The women were pardoned based on the defense of the **battered-woman syndrome,** defined as a condition reached by a woman who has experienced many years of physical abuse and who feels incapable of leaving (see also Walker, 2000). In a desperate effort to defend themselves, such women sometimes kill the abusers. Some people were very sympathetic and applauded the governors' decisions. One observer noted that because more than 1 million women are battered every year by their husbands or boyfriends, it is amazing so few kill their aggressors. Others disagreed that all of the women should have been pardoned. Because several women killed their husbands while they were asleep or had hired hit men to do the job, many people felt the women had gotten away with premeditated murder.

It remains to be seen whether the battered-woman syndrome will become institutionalized as a valid defense for women who kill abusers and whether this new legal option will discourage wife abuse. Approximately 750 cases of battered-woman syndrome appear before the courts every year, and in most instances, the murder is committed when the woman is threatened or attacked. Only about 25 percent of those accused of murdering an abusive partner are acquitted, however (Trafford, 1991).

Other Crises in Family Life

Although abuse and violence can destroy a family, other health-related problems can also become crises. For example, many families have to deal with long-term problems like drug abuse and the inappropriate use of steroids, depression and suicide, and eating disorders like anorexia and bulimia. The family may also have to cope with the death—sometimes sudden and unexpected—of young family members.

Drug Abuse and Steroids

In 1999, an estimated 7 percent of the U.S. population 12 years and older were illicit drug users. Seventy-five percent of illicit drug users consumed only marijuana or marijuana and another drug. Those with the lowest usage rates were college graduates, employed adults, people living in rural areas, and women. In terms of race-ethnicity, both for youth and the general population, American Indians had the highest rates and Asian Americans the lowest (see *Figure 14.8*).

Why are the adolescent illicit drug use rates so high? Although there are many reasons, such as poverty and peer pressure, parents play an important role in their children's drug use. Many middle-class parents, especially, rely on Ritalin and other drugs to "control" young children's behavior (Chapter 11). As you saw earlier in this chapter, children who experience domestic violence, including physical and sexual abuse, are more likely to use drugs and alcohol in adolescence and adulthood than their nonabused counterparts.

Although even the best parents can't prevent their children from trying drugs, many parents don't talk about drugs with their children. According to one national survey, for example, 35 percent of the parents but only 14 percent of teenagers aged 14 to 17 said that parents talk to teenagers about drugs "a lot" (Schultz, 2000). In a study of drug addicts in drug-treatment centers in four states, 20 percent of the respondents said that their parents had introduced them to drugs. The parent–teen drug sharing cut across racial lines (22 percent white, 18 percent black, 22 percent Latino) and was almost as pervasive in the suburbs (17 percent) as in the inner city (22 percent) (Baldauf, 2000). Parents increase children's chances of using alcohol by insisting that other kids, not theirs, drink or drink and drive instead of monitoring their children and promoting values that disapprove of adolescent drinking (Bogenschneider et al., 1998).

In addition to the drug use and addiction problems of adolescents, an estimated 20 percent of women use illicit drugs while pregnant, exposing half a million fetuses to potentially damaging substances every year (Lewis and Bendersky, 1995). Cocaine, particularly crack, the smokable form of the drug, is one of the drugs of choice among many pregnant women.

In 1988, one day after he set a world record in the 100-meter dash, Canadian sprinter Ben Johnson was stripped of his Olympic gold medal when it was discovered that he was using **steroids**—synthetic hormones, most often, testosterone. More recently, there was a cloud of suspicion about several athletes at the 2000 Olympic games in Sydney, Australia. When taken orally or injected, steroids increase the size and strength of muscles in just a few months. An estimated 2 million to 3 million Americans, most of them men, "gobble up the drugs like candy" (Fultz, 1991). An estimated 12 to 17 percent of adolescent males and 3 percent of adolescent females also take these drugs, mostly to improve their performance in sports, but often just to improve their appearance (Yesalis et al., 1997).

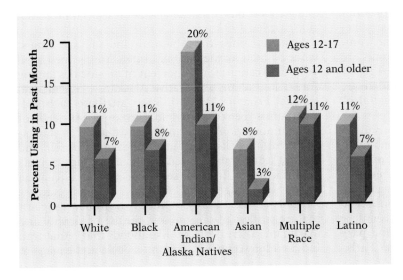

FIGURE 14.8   Illicit Drug Use, by Race/Ethnicity and Age, 1999

SOURCE: U.S. Department of Health and Human Services, 1999 Household Survey on Drug Abuse, 1999, Figures 5 and 6, www.samhsa.gov/oas/NHSDA/1999/Chapter 2.html (accessed October 19, 2000).

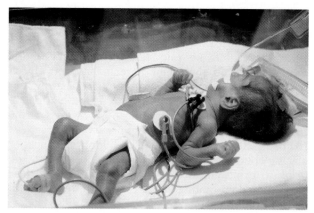

Many "crack babies" start life with severe handicaps compared to children who have not been exposed prenatally to drugs.

Steroids are dangerous. Many people who use them are unfamiliar with their side effects, which include a decrease in testosterone production, a possibly irreversible shrinkage of the testicles, disinterest in sex, acne, increased facial and body hair, early balding, strokes and heart attacks, reduced sperm counts, liver disorders, kidney disease, a sharp increase in aggression, and, with heavy usage, the possible development of psychosis. Teenagers run the particular risk of permanent damage to their reproductive and skeletal systems. Steroids may prevent one from reaching full height; for example, one 13-year-old who had taken steroids for two years stopped growing at five feet (Fultz, 1991).

Depression and Suicide

Two major problems for families, especially those with adolescents, are depression and suicide. Depressed children and adolescents frequently display the same symptoms that adults do, but young children may not be able to articulate their problems. Children are likely to exhibit such symptoms as agitation and complaints about poor sleep and phobias. Adolescents are more likely to exhibit such symptoms as feelings of hopelessness, excessive sleeping, irritability and anger, social withdrawal, weight change, and the use of alcohol and other drugs (Marbella, 1990).

Among adolescent girls, depression can lead to antisocial behavior. Girls who are depressed tend to be withdrawn, have limited interests, and suffer from low self-esteem. Rejected by many of their peers, they may gravitate toward other rejected youth who engage in deviant behavior. As a result, depressed adolescent girls are more likely than their nondepressed counterparts to be aggressive, assault other people, and participate in property crimes (Obeidallah and Earls, 1999).

Depression may lead to suicide, which is increasing as a major cause of teenage deaths. The suicide rate among adolescents between 15 and 19 years of age has increased to 11 per 100,000 population in that age group—triple the rate of the mid-1950s (U.S. Census Bureau, 1999c). Teenagers often exhibit problematic behaviors during normal maturation, but experts feel that when some of these behaviors form a consistent pattern, parents, friends, teachers, and relatives should seriously consider the possibility that the adolescent is planning suicide and should intervene. According to the Youth Suicide National Center, the most common suicide warning signs are the following:

- Withdrawal from family or friends
- Verbal expression of suicidal thoughts or threats, even as a joke
- Major personality change(s)
- Changes in sleeping or eating habits
- Drug or alcohol abuse or both
- Difficulty concentrating
- Violent or rebellious outbursts
- Running away
- Recent suicide of a relative or friend
- Rejection by a boyfriend or girlfriend
- Unexplained, sudden drop in quality of schoolwork or athletic endeavors
- Giving or throwing away prized possessions
- Showing a sudden lack of interest in one's friends or activities
- Extreme and sudden neglect of appearance
- Anorexia

No one knows for sure why people, including teenagers, commit suicide. For the most part, however, teenagers who commit suicide have long-term emotional problems. In more than 90 percent of cases of completed suicide, the person had shown evidence of a mental disorder or addiction to alcohol, crack, or other drugs. According to a national survey of teenagers, drug and alcohol abuse headed the list of reasons for teen suicide (Bezilla, 1993).

Suicide rates for American Indians are almost twice as high as the national rates. Young men aged 15 to 24 account for 64 percent of all suicides among American Indians and Native Alaskans ("Suicide and suicidal behavior," 2000). Some attribute such self-destructive behavior to acculturation. Instead of being moored in American Indian values that emphasize health, well-being, and longevity for self and family, acculturation often results in feelings of marginalization, a loss of self-respect, and alienation from both Anglo and American Indian cultures (Angell et al., 1997). Other researchers suggest that, regardless of age and sex, the use of alcohol and marijuana increases the likelihood that American Indian adolescents will commit suicide and engage in truancy, interpersonal violence, and gang activity (Potthoff et al., 1998).

A family environment that includes violence in the form of physical or sexual abuse may also contribute to the risk of suicide, regardless of ethnicity. Especially among young people, there may be such triggering events as the sudden death of a friend or interpersonal rejection (Moscicki, 1994). Sometimes if they are already depressed, teenagers may exaggerate problems like being dumped by a boyfriend or girlfriend way out of proportion. Males age 19 and younger account for eight in ten adolescent suicides ("Kids and guns," 2000). Many men, including adolescents, seem to have a harder time accepting breakups with their girlfriends (see Chapter 7). Thus, they may react violently against the women or commit suicide in a final desperate act.

Eating Disorders: Anorexia and Bulimia

When it comes to weight, U.S. children seem to react very differently depending on their sex. In a national study of 5- to 17-year-olds, the researchers concluded that about 11 percent of children are overweight (Freedman et al., 1999). And most of the overweight children aged 6 to 17 are boys. Being overweight can lead to a number of physical problems, such as fatty liver (a precursor to cirrhosis), sleep apnea problems (where excess flesh around the throat blocks the airway and causes loud snoring, fitful sleep, and a chronic lack of oxygen), and diabetes. Although these ailments afflict both sexes, women seem to be much more concerned about weight. Although girls are less likely to be overweight than boys, they endanger their lives and health "going thin" by being anorexic and/or bulimic.

Although physicians have known about anorexia nervosa since the 1870s, the general public knew little about the disease until the 1970s. In 1983, the death of 32-year-old popular singer Karen Carpenter as a result of heart failure caused by prolonged starvation generated interest in the disease. In 1994, former gymnast Christy Henrich died of "multiple organ system failure" that resulted from a history of both anorexia nervosa and bulimia. She was 22 and weighed 60 pounds. Henrich, who missed making the 1988 U.S. Olympic team by .118 of a point, became concerned about her weight later that year when, at a meet in Hungary, she overheard a judge say that she was too fat to make the Olympic team. At that time, she was 4 feet 11 and weighed 93 pounds (Lonkhuyzen, 1994).

Anorexia nervosa is an often intractable and dangerous eating disorder characterized by fear of obesity coupled with a distorted body image and the conviction that one is "fat"; significant weight loss (in people over 18 at least 25 percent of original body weight); and an absolute refusal to maintain weight within the normal limits for one's age and height. **Bulimia** is also an eating disorder, characterized by a

U.S. gymnast Christy Henrich performing during the 1988 Olympic trials, six years before her death from the effects of anorexia and bulimia.

cyclical pattern of eating binges followed by self-induced vomiting, fasting, excessive exercise, or the use of diuretics or laxatives.

According to the American Anorexia Bulimia Association, 7 million women and 1 million men between age 10 and the early 20s suffer from eating disorders. The association estimates that 15 percent of young women have "substantially disordered eating attitudes and behaviors," and that 1000 women die from anorexia every year. Girls who participate in competitive sports where body shape and size are a factor (ice skating, gymnastics, crew, dance) are three times more at risk for eating disorders ("Facts about eating disorders," 2000).

Both disorders have physical complications that can result in death. Anorexia may cause a slowing of the heartbeat, a loss of normal blood pressure, cardiac arrest, dehydration, skin abnormalities, hypothermia, lethargy, potassium deficiency, kidney malfunction, constipation, and the growth of fine silky body hair, termed *lanugo,* in an effort to conserve heat. Bulimia's binge-purge cycle can be devastating to health in many ways. It can cause fatigue, seizures, muscle cramps, an irregular heartbeat, and decreased bone density, which can lead to osteoporosis. Repeated vomiting can damage the esophagus and stomach, cause the salivary glands to swell, make the gums recede, and erode tooth enamel.

Most anorexics and bulimics are young white women of relatively high socioeconomic status who suffer from low self-esteem and a negative body image. These young women also tend to be perfectionistic in whatever they undertake (Szabò and Blanche, 1997). Their family histories often include eating disorders in other family members and abuse of such substances as

CHOICES

Coping with a Child's Death

When children die, they do not stop being their parents' children or their siblings' brothers or sisters. Most of us feel awkward and uncomfortable in helping family members and friends survive the death of a child. We don't know what to say or how to express our sympathy and personal sense of loss (James and Friedman, 1998; Silverman, 2000).

According to Zunin and Zunin (1991: 43–44), there are four key components in writing a thoughtful note.

You can change some of the wording if you didn't know the person who died:

1. **Acknowledge the loss.** For example, "Our family was deeply saddened when we heard that your son died."
2. **Express your sympathy.** "We are all thinking of you and send our heartfelt sympathy."
3. **Note special qualities of the deceased or the bereaved, or recount a memory about the**

deceased. "In the years we lived next door, your mother was the most wonderful neighbor! She was always warm, gracious, and ready to lend a hand. We feel fortunate to have known her."
4. **Close with a thoughtful word or phrase.** "With affection and deepest condolences." Or, if you know the family is religious, you may want to offer a spiritual message.

---

alcohol, marijuana, amphetamines, diet pills, or barbiturates. Girls who have experienced sexual abuse are also more likely to have severe eating disorder problems (DeGroot et al., 1992; Laws and Golding, 1996). Anorexic men include models, actors, gymnasts, and jockeys, as well as young men in nonprofessional sports training who are trying to keep their weight down during competitions (Seligmann and Rogers, 1994).

Anorexics and bulimics tend to equate body appearance with self-worth, and their preoccupation with body size and negative body image results in feeling inadequate (Kerr et al., 1991). Middle-school girls who reach puberty early, by the sixth grade, *and* who begin to date at that time may be at especially high risk for having negative body images and eating disorders (Smolak et al., 1993). Thompson (1996) suggests that eating disorders may also be a way of coping with racism. Some black and Latina women with eating disorders have been taught that thinness is important for middle-class standing. In a recent study of adolescents aged 12 to 16, however, Strauss (1999) found significant sex and racial differences in self-perception, desired weight and dieting. Adolescent white girls were significantly more likely to consider themselves overweight and to diet, even when their weight was normal, than black girls, black boys, and white boys.

Although women and girls are beginning to discard some of the worst stereotypical images associated with their traditional gender roles, dieting is still endemic (Rothblum, 1994). In a study of nearly 500 girls, some researchers found that up to 50 percent of 9-year olds and up to 80 percent of 10-year olds had a fear of fatness or were already dieting, even though only 15 percent were actually overweight (reported in Pertig, 1994). Kilbourne (1994: 402) notes that

women are conditioned to be terrified of fat: "Prejudice against fat people, especially against fat women, is one of the few remaining prejudices that are socially acceptable." Consequently, the most common explanation of anorexia and bulimia is that women are trying to live up to a cultural fixation that equates thinness with beauty and success:

> If I'm thin, I'll be popular. If I'm thin, I'll turn people on. If I'm thin, I'll have great sex. If I'm thin, I'll be rich. If I'm thin, I'll be admired. If I'm thin, I'll be sexually free. If I'm thin, I'll be tall. If I'm thin, I'll have power. If I'm thin, I'll be loved. If I'm thin, I'll be envied. (Munter, 1984: 230)

Several studies suggest that anorexics and bulimics become obsessed with living up to an image of beauty promoted by the media and fashion industry. For example, Heather Shaw and Eric Stice studied the eating habits of 238 female students at Arizona State University. They found that women who spent a lot of time reading popular women's magazines and watching television were significantly more likely to be dissatisfied with their physical appearance than were those who did not, and to display symptoms of eating disorders (cited in Vitousek and Manke, 1994). Other research suggests that anorexics and bulimics have greater difficulty in forming friendships and interpersonal relationships within their own families (Tiller et al., 1997).

Death and the Family

A death in the family typically distresses family members, but the death of a child can be shattering. It often results in what Knapp (1987) calls *shadow grief*—a grief that is never totally resolved. Shadow grief involves depression, a dull ache that never goes away, ongoing sadness, and a mild sense of anxiety. Many parents who have lost a child say that they have never since feared their own death. They often become much less involved in worldly achievements and much more concerned with cultivating and strengthening family relationships. Some fathers, for instance, become less interested in their jobs, less career motivated, less interested in making more money, and more involved in establishing better, more stable, and higher-quality relationships with other family members (Goodman et al., 1996).

Although the death of a child can strengthen a conjugal bond, it can also lead to separation or divorce when the grieving mother and father blame themselves or each other for not saving the child or when they cannot find solace through each other (Schwab, 1998; Gottlieb et al., 1996). As the box "Coping with a Child's Death" illustrates, family members and friends can be supportive and understanding, not intrusive, in helping people cope with a child's death.

Conclusion

Millions of U.S. families are experiencing many negative *changes*—for example, more domestic violence, more child abuse and neglect, more abuse of the elderly, and high drug abuse among middle-school children and teenagers. This does not mean that the situation is hopeless, however. As people become more informed about these and other problems, they have more *choices* in accessing supportive community resources and legal intervention agencies. These choices, however, are sometimes eclipsed by a number of *constraints*. Laws are not always enforced, our society still condones violence—especially male violence—and policy discussions of poverty and drug abuse rarely include the problem of family violence.

SUMMARY

1. People are more likely to be killed or assaulted by family members than by outsiders.

2. Although both men and women can be violent, wives and other intimate female partners suffer from abuse that results in much more serious physical and emotional damage than does husband or other intimate male partner abuse.

3. Battered wives have often been described as dependent women who suffer from low self-esteem and feelings of inadequacy and helplessness. It's not clear whether these characteristics reflect basic personality traits or are the result of battering and abuse.

4. Several factors help explain why women do not end abusive relationships: poor self-concept, a belief that the men they love will reform, economic hardship, a need for child support, doubt that they can get along alone, fear, shame and guilt, and being imprisoned in their homes.

5. There are four major categories of child abuse: physical abuse, sexual abuse, neglect, and emotional maltreatment. Factors that increase the likelihood that a child will be abused include being a female, being older (roughly 8 to 10 years old), having a stepfather, having a single mother who brings home boyfriends, and being poor.

6. Whether or not the abuse is sexual, many studies show that abused children suffer from a variety of physiological, social, and emotional problems. Some of these problems include difficulty communicating, increased aggression, learning disabilities, sleeping disorders, and poor performance in school. One of the major reasons for teenage runaways is family violence and abuse.

7. Much more physical and sexual abuse is perpetrated by siblings on each other and by family members on elderly relatives than is reported. Often the elderly are abused by adult children who are unable to take care of themselves because of drug abuse and other problems and with whom their elderly parents feel constrained to live.

8. The most influential theories that try to explain the reasons for family violence and female victimization are patriarchy/male-dominance theory, psychological theories, social learning theory, resource theory, conflict theory, and exchange theory.

9. One of the major reasons why effective programs have not been developed for the prevention and treatment of family violence is that many professionals and the public still do not see domestic violence as a serious problem.

10. Besides violence, families must grapple with other health-related issues, such as drug abuse. Parental drug abuse, the inappropriate use of steroids, depression and suicide, anorexia and bulimia, and a child's death also affect families.

KEY TERMS

marital rape *370*
child abuse *374*
child maltreatment *374*
incest *377*

elder abuse *381*
sandwich generation *382*
battered-woman syndrome *388*
steroids *389*

anorexia nervosa *391*
bulimia *391*

TAKING IT FURTHER

Family Violence: Prevention and Remedies

The **National Coalition against Domestic Violence** provides dozens of sites on women's shelters, counseling, legal aid, and other domestic violence resources.

www.ncadv.org

The **National Clearinghouse on Child Abuse and Neglect Information** focuses on the prevention, identification, and treatment of child abuse and neglect.

www.calib.com/nccanch

The **National Center on Elder Abuse** defines and illustrates the various types of abuse of the elderly and suggests agencies and hotline phone numbers established by federal, state, and local governments for seeking help.

www.gwjapan.com/NCEA

The **Bureau of Justice Statistics** provides statistics, data, and numerous reports related to domestic violence.

www.ojp.usdoj.gov

American Anorexia Bulimia Association, Inc., provides many services, including information, referrals and prevention programs.

www.aabainc.org

And more . . . www.prenhall.com/benokraitis provides sites to violence prevention centers, men's domestic violence homepages, legal sites, national research sources, and a test to evaluate if you or someone you know has eating disorders.

DATADIGEST •

- About 43 percent of all U.S. **first marriages are projected to end in divorce,** compared to two out of five marriages in Britain, Denmark, and Sweden and one in ten in France and other European countries.

- In 1998, **11 percent of African Americans, 10 percent of whites, 7 percent of Latinos, and 5 percent of Asian Americans** were divorced.

- Half of all divorces in the United States take place **during the first seven years of marriage;** the peak occurs about three years into the

marriage. Only 12 percent of all divorces are among couples married 20 years or longer.

- In 1998, almost 20 million children (28 percent of all children under 18 years of age) lived **with only one parent**—up from 5.8 million (9 percent of all children) in 1960.

- Of the **14 million custodial parents** in 1998, 7.9 million (56.3 percent) had some type of support agreement or award for their children.

SOURCES: Lugaila, 1998; U.S. Census Bureau, 1999c; Grall, 2000.

WHEN I was in college, during the mid-1960s, divorce was rare. The few friends whose parents were divorced were often described, in hushed tones, as "unfortunate children" and "poor dears," and their parents were frequently criticized as "disgraceful" and "selfish." As divorce rates climbed during the 1970s, however, marital dissolution became more commonplace. Statistically, nearly one out of every two students reading this chapter probably comes from a divorced home. During the 1960s it was common for marriage-and-family textbooks to describe divorce as deviant behavior. Today divorce is discussed as a normal event in a person's life course. Thus, both divorce rates and our reactions to divorce have changed dramatically within just one generation.

Just as divorce rates have increased, so have the rates of remarriage and redivorce (see Chapter 16). This means that family structures and relationships are more complex today than they were in the past. As this chapter will show, whether these changes produce costs, benefits, or both, separation and divorce often involve long-term processes and consequences.

Separation: Process and Outcome

A **separation** can mean several things. It may be a temporary "time-out" in a highly stressful marriage, in which the partners decide whether or not to continue their marriage. One person may move out of the home. Or partners may decide on a "trial separation" to see what living apart feels like. Physical separation can also be a permanent arrangement when religious beliefs preclude divorce. Or partners may seek a "legal

separation," that is, a temporary period of living apart that most states require before granting a divorce.

The Phases of Separation

Separation is usually a long and painful process that can be viewed as having four phases—preseparation, early separation, midseparation, and late separation (Ahrons and Rodgers, 1987). Whether a particular separation takes a long or a short time, and whether or not the partners go through all four phases, separation rarely happens overnight. Typically people may agonize for months or years before they make a final break.

During the *preseparation* phase, partners may fantasize about what it would be like to live alone, to escape from family responsibilities, or to form new sexual liaisons. Although the fantasies rarely become reality, they can make separation or divorce seem "sexy." In the later stages of the preseparation phase, the couple splits up after a gradual, emotional alienation. One partner who feels that a separation can be beneficial by ending the unhappiness of one or both partners initiates the separation. Even when couples are contemplating separation (or have already made the decision), they often maintain a public pretense that nothing is wrong. The couple may attend family and social functions together, and continue rituals like holding hands right up until the actual separation. Despite such outward appearances of tranquillity, however, separation is usually traumatic, especially for the person who is left. He or she may feel guilty for causing the separation and may also experience anxiety, fear of being alone, and panic about the future.

The *early separation* phase is beset with problems because our society does not have clear-cut rules for this process. Many questions, both serious and trivial, plague the newly separated couple: Who should move out? What should the partners tell their family and friends? Should the child's teacher be notified? Who gets the baseball season tickets? In addition, the partners may have very ambivalent feelings about the impending dissolution. They are confused and upset when their feelings vacillate—as they usually do—between love and hate, anger and sadness, euphoria and depression, and relief and guilt. Partners also must confront economic issues such as paying bills, buying the children's clothing, and splitting the old and the new expenses. Particularly problematic may be the question of the wife's economic survival. Even when employed outside the home, she typically earns considerably less than her spouse (see Chapter 13). As a result, she faces a lower standard of living. This is especially likely if the children live with her. Some partners get support from family and friends, but most must cope on their own.

In the *midseparation* phase, the harsh realities of everyday living set in. The pressures of maintaining two separate households and meeting the daily emotional and physical needs of the children mount, and stress intensifies. If family or friends don't or can't help, or if their help diminishes, the partners may feel overwhelmed, especially if there are additional stressors, such as illness, unexpected expenses, a dependent elderly parent, or difficulties at school or work.

Because of these problems, and especially when couples have been married at least ten years, people may experience "pseudo-reconciliation." That is, the earlier preseparation expectations or fantasies may be followed by a sense of loss when partners don't see their children, by guilt over abandoning the family, and by disapproval from parents, relatives, or friends. As a result, partners may move back in. This sort of second honeymoon, when partners feel less loneliness, fear, and guilt, rarely lasts. Soon the underlying problems that led to the separation in the first place surface again, conflicts reemerge, and the partners may separate once again (Everett and Everett, 1994).

During the *late separation* phase, partners must learn how to survive as singles again. This phase may be especially stressful for men who have been raised with traditional gender-role expectations. For example, many men report frustration and anger when they can't perform such routine tasks as ironing their shirts or preparing a favorite dish. Both partners must often deal with mutual friends who have a hard time with the separation. Some friends may avoid both partners because it threatens their perceptions of their own marriages. Others may take sides, which forces separating partners to develop new friends and relationships. Finally, and perhaps most important, partners must help their children deal with anxiety, anger, confusion, and sadness. We return to this topic later in the chapter.

On the positive side, separating partners may experience what Nelson (1994) calls "growth-oriented coping." In a study of separated women in Ontario, Canada, Nelson found that many separating women became more autonomous, furthered their education, and experienced an increase in confidence and a greater feeling of self-control.

Some Outcomes of Marital Separation

Not all separations end in divorce. Many low-income couples experience long-term separations without divorce because they may be unable to pay the necessary legal fees (Morgan, 1988). Higher family income typically increases the likelihood of divorce.

Racial-ethnic status also influences living apart. Several studies have found that blacks are more likely to live apart than whites for several reasons. African Americans are three times as likely as whites to be separated from their spouses because of military service (Rindfuss and Stephen, 1990). Second, blacks are more likely than whites to be convicted of a crime and, when convicted, to be incarcerated. Third, as we discussed in Chapter 12, because African American men are more likely to be unemployed than whites, some leave their families in search of jobs in other states.

Separation and Reconciliation Approximately 10 percent of all currently married couples (9 percent of white women and 14 percent of black women) in the United States have separated and reconciled (Wineberg and McCarthy, 1993). Using national data of black women who had a successful reconciliation in their first marriage, Wineberg (1996) found that a successful reconciliation varies by age at separation and whether or not the woman gave birth before marrying. Women separating after age 23 were substantially more likely to reconcile than their younger counterparts. Wineberg attributes this difference to older women being more mature, more willing to make the sacrifices necessary to reconcile, and having a greater incentive to reconcile because they have invested more in the marriage than women who separate before age 23. If there are children, both spouses may attempt a reconciliation because they have a strong commitment to the institution of marriage and "may exhaust all options to save the marriage" (p. 84). Although some couples reconcile, most separations end in divorce.

Separation and Divorce Divorce, the legal and formal dissolution of a marriage, is not new. The Code of Hammurabi, written almost 4000 years ago in ancient Mesopotamia, allowed the termination of a marriage. Among the nobility, especially, divorce was apparently as easy for women as for men:

> *If a woman so hated her husband that she has declared, "You may not have me," her record shall*

Divorced men, particularly if they've been married to traditional wives, often find it difficult to do mundane household chores.

be investigated at her city council; and if she was careful and was not at fault, even though her husband has been going out and disparaging her greatly, that woman, without incurring any blame at all, may take her dowry and go off to her father's house. (J. Monk, cited in Esler, 1994)

Marital dissolution is not a recent invention. Writing about the family in 1887, for example, Thwing and Thwing expressed alarm that divorce had been increasing since 1830 rather than being "a permanent and lifelong state" (cited in Reiss, 1971: 317).

During the early part of the twentieth century, a number of marriages ended by desertion, even though no legal divorce was ever obtained. Thus, the rising divorce rate reflects not only more dissolution of marriages but more legal dissolution. According to Brehm (1985), this change is an improvement: When a wife was deserted, she often had no idea whether her husband (deserters were more often male than female) would return. Moreover, a deserting husband rarely left his spouse any money or sent money later, which often put the wife and children in serious financial straits.

Divorce rates have increased in many countries, especially those in Europe. In the United States the divorce rate has risen gradually throughout the twentieth century (see *Figure 15.1*). The small peak during the late 1940s, the years following the end of World War II, has been attributed to divorces among people who had married impulsively before the men left for war and, when the men returned, found they had nothing in common, as well as to war-related family stress and disruption (Riley, 1991; Tuttle, 1993; see also Chapter 3). In the mid-1960s, divorce rates began

a steady climb. Since 1980, the divorce rate has plateaued and dropped slightly between 1995 and 1999 (National Center for Health Statistics, 1998, 2000). In effect, divorce rates are *lower* today than between 1975 and 1990. In addition, because family sizes have decreased (see Chapter 11), divorce affects fewer children now than in the past.

Most people want to marry and to stay married. In a recent nationwide survey, for example, 79 percent of the adults said that one of life's major goals was "having one marriage partner for life" (Rapaport, 2000). Despite such goals, divorce represents a painful milestone in many people's lives.

The Process of Divorce

Few divorces are spontaneous, spur-of-the-moment acts. The divorce process is usually spread over a long period during which two people gradually redefine, reorganize, and sometimes rebuild their relationship and their expectations of one another. In navigating this transition, many people go through a number of stages. One widely cited conceptualization is Bohannon's (1971) six "stations" of divorce—emotional, legal, economic, coparental, community, and psychic.

The *emotional divorce* begins before any legal steps are taken. One or both partners may feel disillusioned, unhappy, or rejected. They may irritate one another, but they remain in the marriage because they do not want to be alone, because they believe that divorce would hurt their children, or because they feel bound by their marriage vows "for better or for worse." Partners may be aloof or polite, despite their anger, or they may engage in overtly hostile

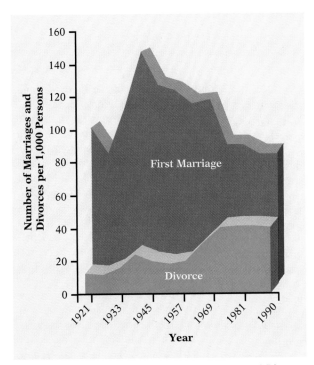

FIGURE 15.1 **Rates of First Marriage and Divorce, 1921–1990.** Each point on these curves represents a three-year average. These data represent women between the ages of 15 and 44 (Norton and Miller, 1992).

behavior, such as making sarcastic remarks or hurling accusations at each other.

In the *beginning phase* of the emotional divorce, partners feel disappointment in each other but hope that the marriage will improve (Kersten, 1990). During the *middle phase,* their feelings of hurt and anger increase as efforts to correct the situation seem unsuccessful. The partner who is more unhappy begins evaluating the rewards and costs of leaving the marriage. In the *end phase,* one of the partners stops caring and detaches emotionally from the other. Apathy and indifference replace loving, intimate feelings. Even when partners don't hate each other, it may be too late to rekindle the marriage:

> *I knew I was going to die if I didn't get out of this marriage. We couldn't talk. We buried our feelings until there was nothing between us except the shell of a life. I was depressed for a long time before I got the courage to leave. I think I must have been grieving for years. It was so sad. He is not a bad person. (Gold, 1992: 45)*

Some partners try to prolong the marriage: "They go to great lengths to set up roadblocks to ending the marriage, refusing to settle anything, including plans for their children" (P.M. Brown, 1995: 211). Others,

as we discuss later in this chapter, may use mediation and counseling to ward off the impending loss. Most seek legal advice to end the marriage.

The *legal divorce* is the formal dissolution of the marriage. During this stage, partners come to agreements on such issues as child custody and the division of property and other economic assets. In part because divorce is an adversarial procedure during which each partner's attorney tries to maintain the upper hand, the process is rarely trouble-free. For example, the partner who does not want the divorce may try to forestall the inevitable end of the marriage or to get revenge by making demands that the other spouse will find hard to accept, such as getting custody of the family dog.

Other issues may include **alimony**—monetary payments made by one ex-spouse to the other to support the latter's basic needs for survival—and especially **child support**—monetary payments by the noncustodial parent to the parent who has custody of the children to help pay child-rearing expenses. Partners often fail to agree on what is fair and equitable, however. They may use money to manipulate each other into making more concessions ("I'm willing to pay child support if you agree to sell the house and split the proceeds").

Even after a divorce is legal, partners may experience ambivalence: "Did I really do the right thing in getting a divorce?" "Should I have been satisfied with what I had?" "What if my family rejects me now that I'm divorced?" Such doubts are normal, but some clinicians caution divorcing parents not to reveal their ambivalence to their children, who may become confused or anxious or deny the reality of divorce and fantasize about reconciliation (Everett and Everett, 1994).

During the *economic divorce,* the partners may argue about who should pay past debts, property taxes, and unforeseen expenses for the children (such as dental braces). Thus, discussions and conflict over economic issues may continue even after the legal issues have been settled. In addition, partners may try to change child-support agreements or not make the required payments.

The *coparental divorce* involves the agreements between mother and father regarding legal responsibility for financial support of the children, the day-to-day care of the children, and the rights of both the custodial and noncustodial parents in spending time with the children. The amount of conflict during this period may be short-lived or long term, depending on how well the parents get along and whether or not children are caught in the middle of parental hostility.

Partners also go through a *community divorce,* when they inform friends, family, teachers, and others that they are no longer married. Relationships between grandparents and grandchildren often continue, but in-laws may sever ties. The partners may also replace old friendships with new ones, and they typically start dating again.

CHOICES

How You Relate Can Make All the Difference

Because divorcing partners are often angry, hurt, or bitter, many divorces are hostile and painful. As the following discussion of five styles of relating to each other suggests, the more civility partners can maintain in their postdivorce relationship, the more productive their relationships will be with each other and with their children (Ahrons and Rodgers, 1987; Gold, 1992).

Perfect Pals Some partners remain friends even after they have decided to divorce. A small group of divorced spouses share decision making and child rearing much as they did in marriage, and many feel that they are better parents after the divorce. These former spouses may even spend holidays together and maintain relationships with each other's extended families.

Cooperative Colleagues Although a sizable number of divorced spouses do not consider themselves good friends, they are able to cooperate. Working

together often takes effort, but these people accept their responsibilities as parents and believe it is their duty to make responsible decisions about their children. Cooperative parents want to minimize the trauma of divorce to their children and try to protect them from conflict. Such parents are willing to negotiate and compromise on some of their differences. They may also consult counselors and mediators to resolve impasses before going to court.

Angry Associates Anger is still an integral part of many relationships between divorced partners. These couples harbor bitter resentments about events in their past marriages as well as the divorce process. Some have long and heated battles over such things as custody, visitation rights, and financial matters. These battles may continue years after the divorce.

Fiery Foes Some divorced spouses are completely unable to coparent. Such partners are incapable of remembering

any good times in the marriage, and each clings to the wrongs done by the other. Children are caught in the middle of the bitter conflict and are expected to side with one parent and regard the other as the enemy. One parent, usually the father, sees the children less and less frequently over the years, and both parents blame each other for this declining contact. The divorces tend to be highly litigious; legal battles sometimes continue for years after the divorce, and the power struggle pervades the entire family.

Dissolved Duos Unlike the battling "fiery foes," the partners break off entirely with each other. Noncustodial parents may "kidnap" the children, or a partner may leave the geographic area where the family has lived. In some cases one partner, usually the man, actually disappears, leaving the other partner with the entire burden of reorganizing the family and the children with only memories and fantasies of the vanished parent.

Finally, the couple goes through a *psychic divorce,* in which the partners separate from each other emotionally. One or both may undergo a process of mourning. Some people never complete this stage because they can't let go of the pain, anger, and resentment, even after they remarry.

Not all couples go through all six of Bohannon's stages. Also, some couples may experience some stages, such as emotional and economic divorce, simultaneously. The important point is that divorce is a *process* that involves many people and not just the divorcing couple and takes time to complete. Moreover, because people differ, divorcing couples may respond to each other in varying ways, as the box "How You Relate Can Make All the Difference" illustrates.

Why Do People Divorce?

The reasons for divorce have generated thousands of books and articles. Researchers have collected an overwhelming amount of data suggesting that divorce

itself, as well as the rise in divorce rates, can be explained on three major levels: macro, or societal; demographic; and interpersonal. As you read this section keep in mind, as usual, that these various factors often overlap. As *Figure 15.2* shows, macro variables influence demographic variables, which in turn may cause specific marital problems, including divorce.

Macro-Level Reasons for Divorce

There are many macro-level reasons for the increase in divorce rates (see White, 1991, for a summary of some of the research findings). This section focuses on four important sources of change: social institutions, social integration, gender roles, and cultural values.

Social Institutions Changes in legal, religious, and family institutions have affected divorce rates. The increasing number of people entering the legal profession and the growth of free legal clinics has made divorce more accessible and cheaper. Interestingly, 76 percent of the adolescents surveyed in a national study said they thought that divorce rates were high because divorce laws are too lax (Bezilla, 1993). Adults, similarly, are reluctant to make divorce easier. In 1974, for example, a third thought that divorce laws should be liberalized. This number declined to 25 percent in 1998. Many people don't feel that unhappy couples should be trapped in a marriage (T.W. Smith, 1999).

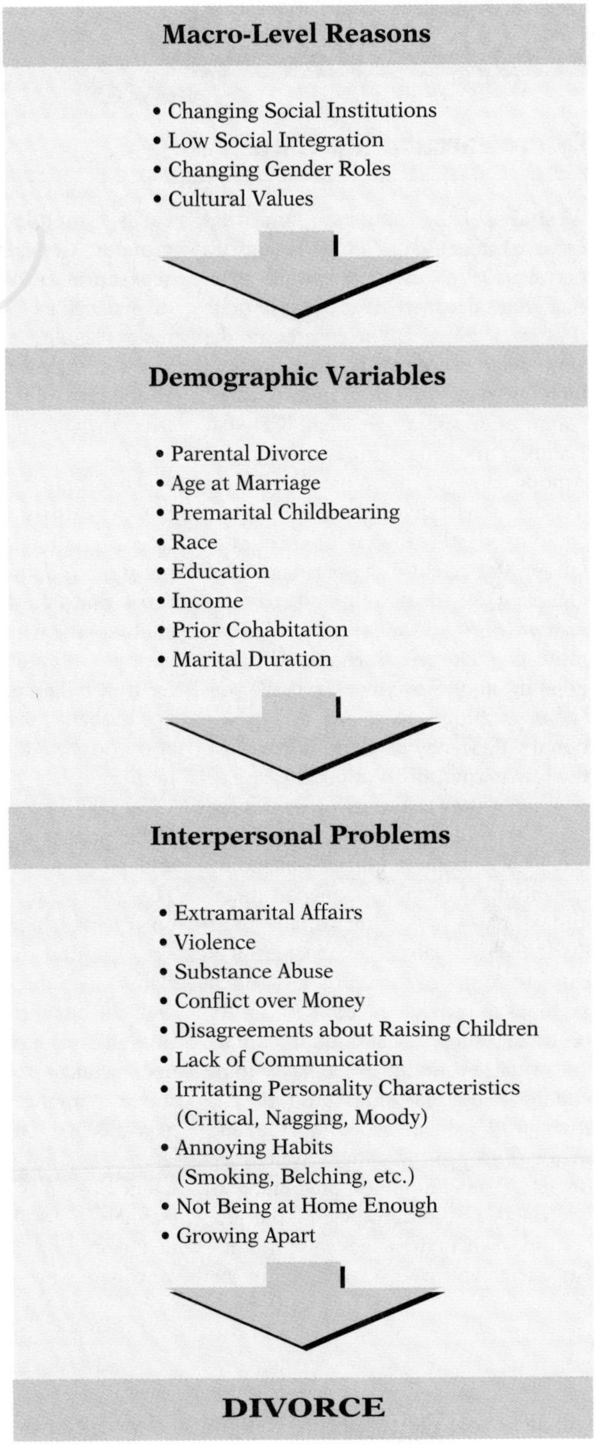

The question of whether the shift to **no-fault divorce**—the divorce process in which neither partner need establish the guilt or wrongdoing of the other—has led to a rise in the divorce rate continues to be debated. According to Balakrishnan and others (1987), no-fault divorce has increased the rate of marital dissolution in Canada and Australia. Similarly, some researchers claim that the switch from fault divorce law to no-fault divorce law "led to a measurable increase in the divorce rate" (Nakonezny et al., 1995; Rodgers et al., 1997). Others point out, however, that divorce rates started increasing in some states years before those states adopted no-fault legislation during the late 1960s and 1970s. In addition, there's little evidence that passage of no-fault laws increased divorce rates overall. Instead, no-fault laws simply ratified, symbolically, changes in values about marriage and divorce that had already occurred (Glenn, 1997b).

Regardless of how people feel about divorce, it's a thriving industry. Because domestic relations cases account for one-third of all civil lawsuits, divorce cases provide jobs for many lawyers, judges, and other employees of the legal system. If a divorcing couple has had a long-term marriage, accountants may spend several years disentangling property rights, accumulated marital property, and the rights of children still living at home. "Forensic accountants" may be asked to track down hidden assets in a contested divorce, and attorneys may hire appraisers, who can charge up to $50,000, to determine the value of jewelry, cars, boats, antiques, and businesses.

In child-custody dispute cases, attorneys may hire marriage counselors, psychologists, education specialists, medical personnel, clergy, social workers, and mediators (De Witt, 1994). Although not everyone who wants a divorce can afford all these services, their very availability may send the message that divorce is not only acceptable but that many professionals are ready to help.

Technological advances, such as Internet access, have also made marital dissolution more accessible than in the past. For example, in 1999 a Website in Britain, Desktop Lawyer (www.desktoplawyer.net), offered online divorce. For a fraction of attorneys' fees (about $85), Web users could download all the necessary legal forms to file for divorce. In the first ten weeks that the service was offered, 18,000 visitors filed for divorce via the site—6 percent of the United Kingdom's total divorce petitions for the period (Links, 1999). Critics, including the Catholic Church, said the service invited impulsiveness. Others contended:

Macro-Level Reasons

- Changing Social Institutions
- Low Social Integration
- Changing Gender Roles
- Cultural Values

Demographic Variables

- Parental Divorce
- Age at Marriage
- Premarital Childbearing
- Race
- Education
- Income
- Prior Cohabitation
- Marital Duration

Interpersonal Problems

- Extramarital Affairs
- Violence
- Substance Abuse
- Conflict over Money
- Disagreements about Raising Children
- Lack of Communication
- Irritating Personality Characteristics (Critical, Nagging, Moody)
- Annoying Habits (Smoking, Belching, etc.)
- Not Being at Home Enough
- Growing Apart

DIVORCE

FIGURE 15.2   Some Causes of Divorce

"You're not going to get divorced because it's on special offer" (O'Donnell et al., 1999: 8).

Religion plays a mixed role in divorce rates. On the one hand, people who claim that religion is very important in their lives are much less likely to divorce,

CROSSCULTURAL

Divorce around the World

A study of 27 nations found that divorce rates rose in 25 of the countries between 1950 and 1985 while marriage rates declined in 22 of the nations (Lester, 1996b). Divorce rates in the United States are two to three times as high as rates in other industrialized countries, such as Sweden, Canada, France, and the United Kingdom. Among developed countries, Russia has the highest divorce rate.

Some of the lowest divorce rates (about 20 percent of all marriages) are in Greece, Portugal, Italy, and Spain. In Eastern Europe, similarly, low divorce rates characterize Bulgaria, Croatia, Poland, and Slovenia (*The World's Women*, 2000). Religious and traditional values may account, in part, for the low marital dissolution rates.

One of the reasons divorce rates are rising around the world is that, since the 1970s, many countries—including Argentina, Australia, Canada, India, and Japan—have liberalized their divorce laws. Divorce is increasingly easy to obtain, men are less often required to provide their ex-wives with economic support, and both parents are often encouraged to have joint child custody (Fine and Fine, 1994).

In 1997, Ireland became the last major European country to legalize divorce. The Philippines, predominantly Roman Catholic, is one of the few countries where divorce is still prohibited, even though a marriage can be

easily annulled on psychological grounds. Chile, similarly, permits legal separation and annulment but not divorce. Since an annulled marriage never legally existed, however, the wives in these situations are not legally entitled to alimony or child support from their husbands (Neft and Levine, 1997).

Divorce is rare in the Muslim world, but the husband may obtain one unilaterally merely by repeating the phrase, "I divorce thee" to his wife three times in front of witnesses. In contrast, the wife who wants to divorce her husband must usually take the matter to a religious court and prove that her husband has had a harmful moral effect on the family or that he has failed to support her (Neft and Levine, 1997).

In 2000, however, a law took effect in Egypt that allows women to seek a unilateral, no-questions-asked divorce. The woman must return the husband's dowry (which can often be as modest as $30) and relinquish all financial claims, including alimony. Some argue that the new changes do not go far enough and that it will be difficult for poor women to return their dowries and to renounce financial rights (Elta-hawy, 2000). Others feel that the new law is a vast improvement in providing women even limited divorce rights (Schneider, 2000).

Divorce has become much simpler in China since the 1980 passage of

a law that allowed couples who had fallen out of love to separate formally. The divorce rate has gone up most sharply in urban centers, such as Beijing, where it rose from 2 percent of marriages in 1981 to 18 percent in 1992 (Walker, 1993). Some factors contributing to the rising divorce rate in China include Western television programs that depict extramarital sex; growing numbers, in urban areas, of well-educated women who are more likely to leave an unhappy marriage; and the growth of prostitution (see Lin-lin, 1993).

---

regardless of their specific religious denomination (Colasanto and Shriver, 1989). Having the same religion is also highly associated with marital stability (Lehrer and Chiswick, 1993). In fact, spouses who follow the same religion or who convert to a spouse's religion at marriage are more likely to reconcile after a separation. Religious similarity may be important in marital stability because it increases the commonality between partners' traditions, values, and sense of community (Wineberg, 1994).

Changes in the family as an institution have also had an effect on divorce. As we discussed in Chapter 1, the shift from a preindustrial to an industrial society altered some family functions. Family members became less dependent on one another for economic, recreational, and personal fulfillment because these and other needs could now be met by institutions outside the family. As more people moonlight or work evening and weekend shifts, for example, many family members spend less time together, especially in

BSC.0035 .HG Remember you're

"Remember, you're only middle aged once."

(*Modern Maturity,* May/June 2000, p. 12)

recreational activities (see Chapter 13). Nonstandard work schedules, as when parents have night and rotating shifts, increases physiological stress because parents don't get enough sleep when children are present. Fatigue, combined with demanding child-rearing responsibilities, may take a toll on the marriages (Presser, 2000). As the box "Divorce around the World" shows, nonindustrial societies are also experiencing increasing levels of marital dissolution.

Social Integration Emile Durkheim argued, at the turn of the twentieth century, that people who are integrated into a community are less likely to divorce, to commit suicide, or to engage in other self-destructive behavior. A number of contemporary social scientists contend, similarly, that **social integration**—the social bonds that people have with others and with the community at large—discourages divorce. For example, researchers have found that communities in which people hold similar values about marital roles and in which people stay in the same neighborhoods for long periods tend to have high integration and low divorce rates (Glenn and Shelton, 1985; Shelton, 1987). Similarly, low divorce rates characterize religious groups, such as Orthodox Jews, in which members feel a strong commitment to the group (Brodnar-Nemzer, 1986).

Social integration also helps explain the high divorce rates in the United States: The greater diversity of subcultures, languages, religious practices, and political organizations may decrease social integration. As workers are laid off and move to find other jobs or accept lateral career moves instead of being fired, relocation disrupts existing bonds between family, friends,

and neighbors (see Chapter 13). Remember, by the way, that none of these studies is claiming that all couples who stay married are happy. They are saying only that people who live in communities and societies that are more socially integrated are more likely to stay married.

Gender Roles Today women in the United States are twice as likely as men to seek divorce. It's not clear why women are more likely than men to file for divorce. It might be that some are escaping abusive marriages (see Chapter 14). For others, getting a divorce can increase the likelihood that a father who has abandoned his family can be tracked down for child-support payments. It might also be the case that women with more resources—those with college degrees, for example—are filing for divorce instead of living in an unhappy marriage (see Chapter 13).

Some of the research suggests that changing gender roles, especially employed women's growing economic independence, might be associated with an increase in divorce rates (Hiedemann et al., 1998). As you saw in Chapter 4, women are becoming more assertive of their needs and rights and expect their spouses to communicate with them and to share domestic tasks. If women are employed, they are more likely to leave unhappy relationships when these expectations are not met. Women who are economically self-sufficient may also be more likely to divorce husbands who have extramarital relationships. You'll recall from Chapter 6 that men engage in such relationships more frequently than women.

Some researchers suggest, however, that a woman's employment can have a stabilizing effect on a marriage.

A wife's income increases the family's financial security, which makes remaining married a more attractive alternative for both partners than becoming single again (Ono, 1998). Furthermore, women with a strong career orientation may postpone marriage, and getting married at a later age tends to decrease the risk of divorce (Greenstein, 1990).

Cultural Values American attitudes and beliefs about divorce have been changing. As you saw in Chapter 1, some researchers feel that Americans are emphasizing individual happiness rather than family commitments (see also Bellah et al., 1985; Whitehead, 1997). According to one family therapist, for example, a "narcissistic greed for personal happiness" is at the root of many divorces. As people pursue self-fulfillment, he contends, they betray their current spouses who love them (Pittman, 1999).

The women's movement during the late 1960s challenged traditional beliefs that women should stay in unhappy or abusive marriages. Throughout the 1970s and 1980s, many therapists and attorneys not only sent messages that "divorce is okay" but flooded the market with self-help books on how to get a divorce, how to cope with loneliness and guilt after a divorce, how to deal with child-custody disputes, and other legal issues. Television programs like *Divorce Court* (and its many recent variations) show viewers that divorce is not an anomaly but an everyday occurrence. Although there is still some stigma attached to divorce, for the most part, U.S. society now accepts it as normal.

Demographic Variables in Divorce

Many demographic variables help explain the divorce-prone couple. Among the factors that have elicited the greatest research are having divorced parents, the presence of children, age at marriage, premarital childbearing, race and ethnicity, and education (see also Amato and Rogers, 1997).

Parental Divorce If the parents of one or both partners in a marriage were divorced when they were children, the partners themselves are more likely to divorce (McLanahan and Bumpass, 1988). One reason for this may be that children of divorced parents tend to have lower educational attainment and to marry at younger ages, as we will discuss shortly. Because children of divorced parents are less able to afford college, they are more likely to marry early, and the younger partners are when they marry, the more likely they are to divorce (Saluter, 1994).

The effect of parental divorce varies, however, depending on gender and social class. Using national data, Keith and Finlay (1988) found that daughters of divorced parents had a higher probability of being divorced in both middle and lower socioeconomic

families. In contrast, sons of divorced parents run the same divorce risk *only if* they had lower social class backgrounds.

According to these researchers, when parents divorce, they may be less likely to encourage their daughters to continue their education after high school than their sons. They may also become more lax about checking out their daughters' dating partners. As a result, daughters may choose high-risk mates and at a young age. Sons from lower socioeconomic families may be unable to afford college. But because parents still tend to encourage higher education more often for sons than for daughters, many young men from middle-class families continue to enjoy the parents' economic resources, which allow them to go to college and to postpone marriage (Feng et al., 1999).

Presence of Children The relationship between the presence of children in a family and the likelihood that a couple will divorce varies according to the children's age and sex. Several studies have found that the presence of preschool children, especially firstborn children, increases marital stability. This may reflect the fact that some couples stay together "for the sake of the children." In addition, the presence of young children may make the divorce process more costly, both emotionally and financially.

Marital disruption is significantly more likely in families where children are 13 or older (Rankin and Maneker, 1985; Waite and Lillard, 1991). The risk of separation is relatively low when the youngest child is less than 3; it reaches a plateau as the youngest child passes through ages 7 to 12, peaks at the midteens, and drops sharply after age 17 (Heaton, 1990). Thus, whereas the presence of younger children appears to help hold marriages together, when children are older couples may have fewer incentives to stay together. Or they may purposely postpone divorce until their children are older. In some cases, problems with adolescent children exacerbate already strained marital relationships and the marriage may fall apart.

Several researchers suggest that marital disruption seems less likely when children are male rather than female (Katzev et al., 1994; Morgan et al., 1988). Because fathers play a more active role in raising sons than daughters—in such areas as rule setting and discipline—they are more involved in the family that has sons and are less likely to seek a divorce when problems arise. The researchers also posit that because boys continue to be more valued in U.S. society, mothers with sons may feel more satisfied in their marriages and less likely to consider separation from their spouses.

Age at Marriage Several studies have found that early age at marriage increases the chance of divorce (Balakrishnan et al., 1987; Thornton and Rodgers, 1987; Kurdek, 1993). In fact, early marriage may be the strongest predictor of divorce in the first five years of marriage (Martin and Bumpass, 1989). Couples who marry under age 18 are especially prone to divorce.

Why do young spouses often divorce? Sometimes if young couples are experiencing problems, parents and relatives who disapproved of the marriage may encourage divorce. In most cases, however, young couples are poorly prepared for marital responsibilities (Booth and Edwards, 1985). They are more unhappy than older spouses about their partners in terms of love, affection, sex, wage earnings, companionship, and faithfulness. They also complain that their spouses become angry easily, are jealous or moody, spend money foolishly, drink or use drugs, and get into trouble with the law.

Premarital Childbearing Women who conceive or give birth to a child *before* marriage have higher divorce rates after the first marriage than women who conceive or have a child *after* marriage (Norton and Miller, 1992). Divorce is especially likely among adolescents, who generally lack the education or income to maintain a stable family life (Wineberg, 1988; Martin and Bumpass, 1989). The effects may be especially negative for young black women. Teachman (1983) found that black women, marrying at age 16 or 17 after having had a child, had only a 38 percent chance of still being married 15 years later, compared to a 60 percent chance for white women under the same conditions. Other variables undoubtedly interact with early childbirth and divorce. For example, low educational attainment, high unemployment rates, and poverty increase separation and divorce rates (see also Chapters 12 and 13).

Race and Ethnicity When a national survey asked people whether divorce is acceptable or not, 66 percent of the general population felt it was acceptable compared to 57 percent of Latinos (Deane et al., 2000). Even though many Latinos feel that divorce is unacceptable, their divorce rates have been only slightly lower that those of white couples (see *Figure 15.3*).

One of the most consistent research findings is that blacks are more likely to divorce than any other racial-ethnic group. As *Figure 15.3* shows, divorce rates among African Americans have been more than 75 percent higher than divorce rates among either whites or Latinos since 1960, and since 1980 they have been nearly twice as high. These differences persist at all income, age, educational, and occupational levels (Rank, 1987; White, 1991).

Nearly half of the marriages among black women are expected to terminate by the end of 15 years, compared with 17 percent of marriages among white women. Not only are black women more likely to experience divorce, they do so sooner after marriage than their white counterparts. By the end of five years of first marriage, for example, 20 percent of black

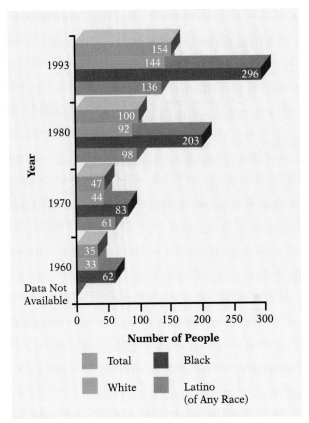

FIGURE 15.3 Divorce among Racial-Ethnic Groups, 1960–1993. The numbers shown are of divorced people per 1,000 married people (based on Saluter, 1994).

women are expected to divorce compared to only 6 percent of white women (Kposowa, 1998).

Being African American does not, of course, cause one to divorce. Other demographic, macro, and interpersonal factors are at work. One of the reasons for higher black marital dissolution rates is the higher rate of black teenage and premarital pregnancies. Women whose first birth is out of wedlock are more likely to separate than are those whose first birth occurred within marriage, and black women are more likely than white women to give birth outside of marriage. Thus, young black women face numerous obstacles to a lasting marriage. Compared to white women, they run a higher risk of teenage pregnancy, premarital pregnancy, early marriage, and separation or divorce (Garfinkel et al., 1994). Another reason for the high divorce rate among blacks is poverty. According to some scholars, because African Americans are disproportionately poor, they are more likely to face the many poverty-related stresses and strains that lead to divorce (Blackwell, 1991).

Finally, some researchers suggest that divorce may be more acceptable among African Americans. Divorce may be less strained because the community offers divorcing partners more social support (see Cherlin, 1998). In addition, black mothers report less difficulty than white mothers do in maintaining their parental authority. It may be that in preparing their children for the stresses of mainstream society—unemployment, poverty, racism, violence, crime—many African American mothers strengthen their authority as parents (McKenry and Fine, 1993).

Education and Income In a study of 11 nations, Lester (1996a) found an association between unemployment and a high divorce rate in nine of the countries. Such an association is not surprising because, as you saw in Chapters 13 and 14, unemployment and poverty increase family stress, violence, and disruption.

According to recent figures, Nevada has the highest U.S. divorce rate—8.5 compared to the national average of 4.2 per 1000 people. Aside from Nevada, which some refer to as the "quickie-divorce" capital of the United States, four so-called Bible belt states also had much higher divorce rates than the national average: 6.4 per 1000 in Tennessee, 6.1 in Arkansas, and 6.0 in Alabama and Oklahoma. (Data for California, Colorado, Indiana, and Louisiana were not available.) Why are the divorce rates so high in fundamentalist states that promote marriage and family values? Researchers suggest that low household incomes (Oklahoma ranks forty-sixth and Arkansas forty-seventh), as well as the tendency for couples to marry at younger ages than in other states, explain the high divorce rates. The lowest rates are in the Northeast (New Jersey, 3.1; Connecticut, 2.9; Massachusetts, 2.7; and New York, 2.5), which has relatively high household incomes. In addition, the northeastern states have large numbers of Roman Catholics whose church doesn't recognize divorce ("Bible belt wrestles . . . ," 1999).

In general, low educational attainment and low income (especially the father's) increase the possibility of divorce (Kurdek, 1993). A national study of men and women aged 25 to 34 found that people who had a bachelor's degree were less likely to divorce than those who had a high school education (Glick, 1984). Do people who have college degrees have more stable marriages because they're smarter? No. Rather, going to college postpones marriage for many couples, with the result that they are often more mature, more experienced, and more capable of dealing with personal crises when they marry. They also have better economic prospects, which lessens marital stress over financial problems.

The more education a man has, the less likely he is to divorce. The effects of educational attainment on women's likelihood of divorce are more complex. Even though a wife's higher education decreases the probability of divorce early in a marriage, it may increase her risk of divorce later in the marriage (Hiedemann et al., 1998). This finding may reflect changes over the life course, including a wife's employment, her rising income, her increased dissatisfaction if her husband does not share domestic and child-rearing tasks, and her greater freedom from household responsibilities after children leave the home.

Interpersonal Reasons for Divorce

Macro and demographic variables often affect interpersonal reasons for divorce. Some feel that the divorce rate has climbed due to greater longevity. Because we live longer than people did in the past, a married couple may spend a significantly longer period of time together, and there is a greater chance that over the years some partners may grate on each other's nerves.

Because people have fewer children, they have more time to focus on their relationship as a couple, both while the children are living at home and after they move out. And because they have more time to focus on the marital relationships, there is a greater chance that some marital partners will become disillusioned. Partners may have higher expectations about marriage. They may expect to be comforted, to be told that they are loved, or to be shown in other ways that they are appreciated and valued. Or couples may compare themselves with unrealistic models as portrayed in films and on television and feel that they *should* have higher expectations about marriage (see Chapter 1).

Interestingly enough, surveys do not show that "falling out of love" is the major reason for divorce. In a national study, Patterson and Kim (1991) found communication problems to be the major reason for divorce ("He doesn't understand who I am"; "She doesn't know me"). Infidelity ranked second, constant fighting third, emotional abuse fourth, and falling out of love fifth (see also Chapter 9). In an earlier study (Colasanto and Shriver, 1989), basic personality differences, or incompatibility, were reported as the leading cause of marital breakup in 47 percent of divorces. Women were much more likely than men (24 percent versus 6 percent) to cite alcohol or drug problems as the major reason for getting a divorce.

More recently, a study of 160 families found similar reasons for divorce. Both women (82 percent) and men (71 percent) reported that the major problems in their marriages arose from specific behaviors of their spouses that they found increasingly intolerable, such as not being respectful or supportive, spending too many evenings out with friends, and generally not being committed to family life. Other problems included extramarital affairs, substance abuse, arguments about money, a lack of communication, and disagreements about how to discipline children (Stewart et al., 1997; Amato and Rogers, 1997).

As you saw in Chapter 9, communication problems derail many marriages. Some researchers maintain that they can predict whether a newlywed couple will still be married four to six years later by observing not *what* they say but *how* they say it. Couples that last listen to each other respectfully even when they disagree, don't start discussions with accusatory statements ("You're lazy and never do anything around the house"), and use more positive than negative interaction (Gottman et al., 1998; Carrere and Gottman, 1999; Patz, 2000). Although enduring relationships may not be blissful, the communication may be peaceful or passionate, but it's not venomous.

Often, however, interpersonal factors, such as communication, reflect demographic or macro-level difficulties. In their study of black divorced men, for example, Lawson and Thompson (1999) found that financial strain created or exacerbated existing communication problems. As one divorced father explained: "I worked too much and spent little time at home. . . . It is ironic that my efforts to provide for my family made me vulnerable to charges of being distant and uncaring" (p. 65).

Consequences of Divorce

A popular film, at least among many women, was *The First Wives Club*, in which three middle-aged wives get revenge on their husbands for dumping them for younger girlfriends. Among other stereotypes, the husbands were presented as cads, the wives as innocent victims, and getting even was fun.

In real life, marital dissolution is usually an agonizing process for both women and men, across socioeconomic levels, and regardless of race or ethnicity. Divorce typically has a negative impact on child-free married couples as well, but this section focuses on married partners with children. In such cases, divorce has a significant effect in at least three areas of a couple's or family's life: both parents' and children's emotional and psychological well-being; economic and financial changes; and child-custody arrangements and the children's welfare.

Emotional and Psychological Effects

Despite today's greater acceptance of divorce, separated and divorced people sometimes feel stigmatized by family, friends, and co-workers (Gasser and Taylor, 1990; Kitson and Morgan, 1991). In a study by Gerstel (1987), many respondents said their friends often took sides, labeling one ex-spouse guilty and the other innocent. Many also believed that they were excluded from get-togethers with married couples. They felt others were afraid that their divorced status would "rub off on them," that their being sexually available was perceived as a threat by married friends. Divorced couples themselves felt that being married was normal and being divorced abnormal. Many put off telling colleagues for fear of being treated differently.

Although trashing wedding memorabilia may release some anger and hurt, it also suggests that the person has not come to terms with divorce and needs some physical sign to make it real.

Children may also be stigmatized by their parents' divorces. People's negative and often unconscious perceptions of children from divorced families can result in self-fulfilling prophecies:

If teachers, school principals, counselors, psychologists, social workers, and parents expect children from divorced families to have more than their share of problems, they may treat these children in ways that exacerbate, or even generate, these very problems. For example, compared with other children, teachers may call on children of divorce less often, give them fewer opportunities to display their competence, reward them less often for good behavior, or punish them more often. The possibility of a self-fulfilling prophecy should be of concern to all people who deal with children from divorced families. (Amato, 1991: 67)

ASKYOURSELF

Do You Know Someone with Divorce Hangover?

In a "healthy" divorce, ex-spouses must accomplish three tasks: letting go, developing new social ties, and, when children are involved, redefining parental roles (Everett and Everett, 1994). Often, however, divorced partners suffer from what Walther (1991) describes as "divorce hangover." They are unable to let go, develop new friendships, or reorient themselves as single parents.

In each of the following statements, put the name of someone you know who has just gone through a divorce in the blanks, and decide if the statement is true of that person. There is no scoring on this quiz, but if you agree that many of these statements describe your friend or acquaintance, you know someone with divorce hangover.

Sarcasm When someone mentions the ex-spouse, _____ is sarcastic or takes potshots at the former partner. The sarcasm may be focused on the marriage in particular or applied to all relationships: "All men leave the minute their wives turn forty" or "All women are just after their husbands' money."

Using the children _____ tries to convince the children that the divorce was entirely the other person's fault and may probe the children for information about the other parent.

Lashing out _____ may try to assert control in such ways as making unreasonable demands (for example, refusing joint custody) or blowing up at a friend because the ex-spouse was invited to a party.

Paralysis _____ can't seem to get back on track, starting back to school, getting a new job, becoming involved in new relationships, or finding new friends. Sometimes it's even hard for _____ to get up in the morning and go to work, clean the house, or return phone calls.

Holding on The ex-spouse's photograph still sits on _____'s piano, and clothing or other former possessions remain in view, keeping the ex-spouse's presence alive in _____'s daily life.

Throwing out everything Or _____ may throw away things of value—even jewelry, art, priceless collections—that are reminders of the ex-spouse. This may suggest just as much attachment as holding on.

Blaming and finding fault Everything that went wrong in the marriage or the divorce was someone else's fault, _____ maintains. The ex-spouse was responsible—or his or her family or friends, his or her lover, his or her kids, his or her job, his or her golf game, and so on.

Excessive guilt _____ feels guilty about the divorce regardless of which partner left the other. _____ buys the children whatever they want and gives in to the children's or the ex-spouse's demands, however unreasonable.

Living vicariously _____ may try to live through the children by pressuring them to succeed at things in which they have no interest or particular talent and may also latch on to friends who are more successful at work than _____ or more outgoing and at ease in social functions.

Dependency To fill the void left by the ex-spouse, _____ leans heavily on other people, particularly new romantic involvements.

Divorce can be devastating when it means a loss of emotional and sexual intimacy, identity as part of a couple, financial security, self-esteem, friends, possessions, predictability, and even a home. Confronting these symptoms of divorce hangover can help a divorced person recognize and begin to overcome these losses.

Some people feel anxious about "disgracing" their families and being objects of gossip or reproach. Others, however, feel that their family and friends are caring and supportive rather than curious or critical (Stewart et al., 1997).

The psychic divorce that we described earlier may continue for many years. Even when both partners know their marriage cannot be salvaged, they are often ambivalent. They may fluctuate between a sense of loss and a feeling of emancipation; they may have periods of depression punctuated with spurts of euphoria. The box "Do You Know Someone with Divorce Hangover?" examines some of the psychological adjustments the newly divorced face.

Economic and Financial Changes

Although both men and women undergo psychological adjustments after a divorce, one's sex has a dramatic impact on economic status. As one accountant noted, "The man usually walks out with the most valuable asset, earning ability, while the woman walks out with the biggest cash drain, the kids and house" (Gutner, 2000).

Most often this change reflects low educational attainment, which may restrict a woman to low-paying jobs in the service sector, or having a young child, which makes it difficult for a woman to find full-time employment and may limit her to part-time jobs that have more flexible hours (Smock, 1993). On the other hand, although many men are financially able to support their children and ex-wives, they don't do so, especially if they disagree with the child-custody arrangements (Finkel and Roberts, 1994).

Property Settlements and Alimony   In the past the law assumed that one partner was responsible for a marital breakup because of a transgression, such as adultery, desertion, or cruelty. In 1970, California became the first state to abolish the requirement of fault as the basis for marital dissolution, and *no-fault divorce* has been instituted in every state. The intent of the no-fault divorce statute was to change the adversarial nature of divorce and to reduce the long court battles and emotional trauma associated with establishing fault as grounds for divorce.

According to some observers, no-fault divorce has done more harm than good to many women. Because both partners are now treated as equals, each, theoretically at least, receives half of the family assets and the ex-wife is expected to support herself regardless of whether or not she has any job experience or work-related skills. In 1993, about 15 percent of divorced women were awarded alimony in their divorce settlements, but *only 3 percent actually received any payments*. Moreover, the average award in 1993 was only $7008 per year (personal communication, Bureau of the Census, February 1995). Thus, women who have been full-time housewives most of their lives and experience divorce in their forties or fifties are especially likely to become poor. If they have low educational levels and few marketable skills, alimony payments will not keep them out of poverty.

Despite the institution of the no-fault divorce and evidence that very few women receive substantial cash payments in a divorce, many people still believe that most women profit through divorce by high alimony payments. Dubbing this the "alimony myth," Weitzman (1985) suggests several reasons for its persistence. First, many people are not aware that alimony payments have been awarded in only a minority of divorce cases. Second, Weitzman says, alimony is often confused with child support and perceived simply as "money that divorced men have to pay." Third, the few women who do receive significant alimony are highly visible because their spouses are wealthy or celebrities.

Several studies show that women's economic health declines considerably after marital dissolution—about 30 percent during the first years of divorce (Peterson, 1996). Although young men, particularly minority men, may not be faring well economically themselves, women's postdivorce financial welfare is significantly lower than men's for all racial-ethnic groups (Smock, 1994). For example, in a national

In 1997, Lorna Wendt, the wife of a wealthy General Electric corporate executive, rejected a $10 million settlement after her husband of 32 years sought a divorce. Ms. Wendt went to court, arguing that she was worth more as a full-time homemaker because she had raised their children single-handedly, entertained her husband's business associates, and made numerous business-related trips in 40 countries to support her husband's career. The judge awarded her half of the marital estate—worth about $100 million. In 1998, Wendt founded the Institute for Equality in Marriage (www.equalityinmarriage.org) to help women in similar circumstances.

sample of Latino divorced men and women, Stroup and Pollock (1999) found that the average incomes for Latino married and divorced men were essentially equal. Latinas, in contrast, experienced a loss of about 24 percent of their income after a divorce. Those who were the most economically vulnerable included mothers with responsibilities for young children and who were employed in low-wage jobs.

Child Support Nearly 50 percent of all men neither see nor support their children after a divorce (Sorensen and Zibman, 2000). Many fathers have never provided any kind of help, including child-support payments and other forms of assistance like paying for clothes, buying presents, taking the children on vacations, paying for routine dental care or uninsured medical expenses, carrying medical insurance, helping the children with homework, and attending school events (Garfinkel et al., 1994). Two thirds of noncustodial fathers spend more on car payments than they do for child support (Kitson and Holmes, 1992).

In 1998, an estimated 14 million parents had custody of 22.9 million children under 21 years of age whose other parent lived elsewhere. Custodial mothers represented 85 percent of all custodial parents. Among all custodial mothers, 56 percent were white, 28 percent black, and 14 percent Latinas. The proportion of custodial parents and their children living below poverty decreased between 1993 and 1997 (Grall, 2000). Custodial mothers, however, were still three times as likely as custodial fathers to be poor (see *Figure 15.4*).

Only 56 percent of custodial parents had child-support agreements in 1998. The average amount of child support received by these custodial parents was $3622 a year—$3655 by custodial mothers and $3251

by custodial fathers. Besides financial payment, many noncustodial parents also provided noncash support. Over half of all custodial parents received such non-cash support as birthday, holiday, or other gifts (54 percent), clothes for the children (35 percent), food and groceries (23 percent), medical assistance other than health insurance (19 percent), or partial or full payments for child care or summer camp (10 percent) (Grall, 2000).

Even when child support is awarded, the payments vary. As *Figure 15.5* shows, for example, custodial mothers with the highest child-support payments tend to be white, divorced, and have some college education. In contrast, those with the lowest payments are black, have never been married, and are high school dropouts. These figures suggest that women with greater resources, such as a college degree, are able to collect more financial support, may have ex-husbands who can provide more support, or are more aggressive about getting court-ordered awards.

Although the annual child-support payments are small for all custodial mothers, the children of never-married parents fare the worst in getting economic support from fathers. Compared to divorced mothers, never-married mothers are significantly younger (under 20 years old), are less likely to have completed high school, and are more likely to be unemployed or not in the labor force (O'Connell, 1997). As state welfare programs continue to limit public cash assistance (Chapter 17), child-support orders that are well under the costs of raising children will impoverish poor families even further (Pirog et al., 1998).

Noncustodial parents (who are typically men) are more likely to pay full or partial child support when they have arrangements for joint child custody and visitation rights. About 85 percent of custodial parents

FIGURE 15.4 **Poverty Status of Custodial Parents: 1993–1997.**

SOURCE: Grall, 2000: Figure 2.

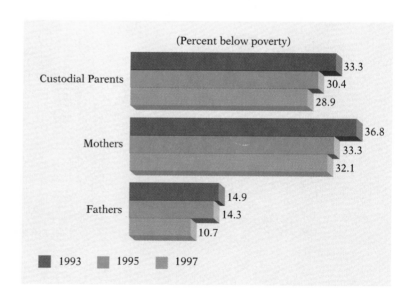

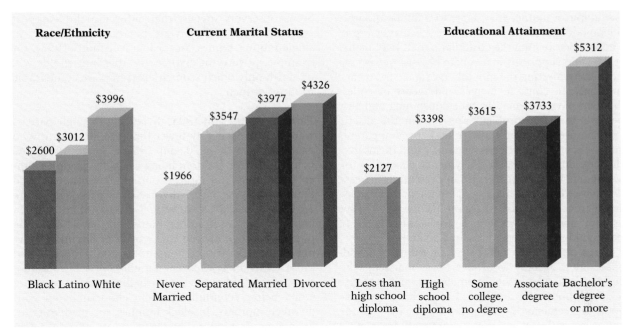

FIGURE 15.5 **Average Yearly Child Support Payments Received by Custodial Mothers: 1997**

Source: Based on Grall, 2000: Table B.

with these arrangements received full or partial support payments in 1998 compared to only 36 percent for those without either shared custody or visitation rights (Grall, 2000). There are also interpersonal and other micro variables that help explain why noncustodial parents, especially the majority of fathers, don't comply with child-support orders. According to Nuta (1986), for example, nonpaying fathers fall into four major categories:

1. *The parent in pain* may feel shut out of the family and distance himself physically and/or emotionally from his children. He may even rationalize his distancing ("She turned them against me"). Other fathers are angry if they feel that visitation rights are unfair.

2. *The overextended parent* is overburdened with financial obligations. Anxious to get out of his marriage as soon as possible, he may agree to pay more support than he can actually afford. He may remarry and, unable to support two families, fail to provide for the children of his first marriage. Or he may become ill and unemployed and thus be unable to meet the child-support payments.

3. *The vengeful parent* uses child support as a form of control. He may use nonpayment to change a visitation agreement or to punish his wife for initiating the divorce.

4. *The irresponsible parent,* representing the greatest number of child-support dodgers, simply does not take his parental duties seriously. He may expect others to take care of his family ("Welfare will pay" or "Her family has more money than I do"), or he may think that taking care of himself is more important than providing for his children. The irresponsible parent includes noncustodial parents with psychological and drug abuse problems who may not seek employment or hold on to a job (Dion et al., 1997).

In 1984, Congress passed the Child Support Enforcement Amendments that require states to deduct delinquent support from fathers' paychecks and tax returns. The Family Support Act of 1988 authorizes judges to use their discretion when support agreements cannot be met as, for example, when a father is unemployed and cannot pay child support. This act also mandates periodic reviews of award levels to keep up with the rate of inflation. Because many divorced fathers rarely provide for their children through means other than child support, court-ordered awards are often the only monetary contributions that many fathers make (Paasch and Teachman, 1991).

Court-ordered child support has several problems, however. Sometimes attorneys advise their clients to trade child-support payments for property settlements.

For example, a mother may agree to minimal monthly child-support payments in exchange for ownership of the house. Before long the custodial parent may realize that the child support is inadequate because she is having difficulty meeting the monthly mortgage payments. Going back to court to increase payments or collect delinquent payments may be time-consuming and very expensive. Another problem arises from the discretionary nature of the judicial system. Custodial parents in similar economic circumstances may find themselves with very different support payments depending on how capable their attorneys are in presenting the case and whether or not a judge is sympathetic to the custodial parent's financial situation (Wong, 1993; see Chisholm and Driedger, 1994, for a discussion of unpaid child-support payments in Canada).

States also vary a great deal in enforcing child-support laws. Fathers who have never married, who have less than a high school education, and who are black and poor are the least likely either to have support agreements or to meet them. In a study of noncustodial fathers, for example, Folse (1997) found that many Latino fathers (and compared, especially, to their white and black counterparts) want to maintain ties with their children. Their good intentions, however, are often stymied by child enforcement systems that penalize fathers who don't have steady employment. The divorced fathers in Folse's study also complained that child-support bureaucracies are sympathetic to mothers but ignore fathers. As a result, Folse suggests, even well-intentioned ethnic fathers may lose contact with their children after a divorce.

In addition, the bureaucracy that tracks a noncustodial parent's payments is lumbering and nonresponsive. If the noncustodial parent changes jobs often, for example, it is very difficult for employers to implement income withholding and disburse the payments for child support (Williams, 1994). When child support is routinely withheld from paychecks, there is a great deal of variation, even within a state, on how effectively court and child-support personnel enforce the withholding orders (Meyer and Bartfeld, 1996; Meyer et al., 1996). Fourteen states, for example, still have not computerized the child-support systems that track parents who owe money, even though the finances for this project were provided by Congress in 1988. Thus, many divorced mothers are powerless to collect child-custody awards.

As might be expected, ex-spouses who have good relationships with their former partners are more likely to receive court-ordered child-support awards than are those who do not. In Folse's study, noncustodial Latino fathers who had hostile relationships with their ex-wives accused them of often sabotaging the fathers' efforts to see their children. Good parental relationships appear critical in determining whether the children of divorced parents get economic and emotional assistance from their fathers (Garfinkel et al., 1994).

Some observers suggest that enforcing child-support payment laws will alleviate but not end poverty in single-mother homes. According to Amott (1993), for example, poverty in divorced-mother households will diminish only when women's earnings are comparable to those of men.

Family Income   In 1995, 87 percent of single parents were mothers, slightly fewer than the 90 percent who were mothers in 1970 and 1980 (Saluter, 1996). As you saw earlier, children living in never-married mother-only homes are more economically disadvantaged than those living with divorced mothers (see *Figure 15.5*). As *Table 15.1* shows, 38 percent of all children living in divorced-mother households live below the poverty level compared to 19 percent of children living in divorced-father households and 11 percent of those living in two-parent families. In white homes, especially, children living with divorced fathers fare much better economically than children living with divorced mothers. In black families, the median family income is reduced by at least 50 percent when children live with either a divorced mother or a divorced father rather than with both parents, and the percentage of children living below the poverty level increases dramatically in both divorced-father and divorced-mother homes.

Custody Issues

Children are often caught in the middle of custody battles:

> Mark, age eight: *"I don't think either one of them should get me. All they ever do is fight and yell at each other. I'd rather live with my grandma."*

> David, age five: *"Dad says he wants me there but every time we go over all he does is watch football and drink beer. I don't think he really wants us. I think he just says that to make Mommy mad."*

> Mary, age ten: *"I hate going to my dad's because every time I come back I get the third degree from Mom about what we did and who was there and whether Dad did anything wrong or anything that made us mad. I feel like a snitch."*

> Robin, age seven: *"Mom wants me to live with her and Dad wants me to live with him. But I want to live with both of them. Why do I have to choose? I just want us to be happy again."* (Everett and Everett, 1994: 84–85)

Custody   Custody refers to a court-mandated ruling as to which parent will have primary responsibility for the welfare and upbringing of a couple's children. Children live with a custodial parent, whereas they see the noncustodial parent according to specific visitation

TABLE 15.1

Living Arrangements of Children under Age 18, by Family Income, 1995

Race and Living Arrangement	Median Family Income	Percentage Below Poverty Level
All families		
Living with both parents	$46,195	11
Living with divorced mother	17,789	38
Living with divorced father	28,722	19
White families		
Living with both parents	47,048	10
Living with divorced mother	18,633	36
Living with divorced father	29,894	17
Black families		
Living with both parents	39,355	15
Living with divorced mother	15,662	47
Living with divorced father	16,784	38
Latino families		
Living with both parents	26,934	31
Living with divorced mother	11,926	58
Living with divorced father	30,111	35

SOURCE: Based on Saluter, 1996, Table 6.

schedules worked out in the custody agreement. Approximately 90 percent of all divorces are not contested but are settled out of court through negotiations. In about 72 percent of cases, the mother gets custody of the children; white husbands are more likely to be awarded custody than are black husbands (Clarke, 1995a).

According to a study of the Massachusetts courts, when men sue, they win either sole or joint custody more than 70 percent of the time (reported in Mansnerus, 1995). It is for this reason that divorce attorneys sometimes advise their male clients to wage an all-out battle for custody—even when they do not want it—simply as a bargaining chip in negotiations over child support. Mothers, afraid of losing custody, often agree to a modest alimony or child-support arrangement (Winner, 1996). Some mothers relinquish custody at the time of divorce or shortly thereafter for a variety of reasons: They feel they can't support the children financially, they experience emotional problems because life becomes tumultuous and mothers feel they're "falling apart," they want to avoid the threat of a legal custody fight, or they're in an abusive relationship with a mate who threatens to harm the children if the mother fights for custody (Herrerías, 1995).

There are three types of custody. In **sole custody** (about 81 percent of cases), one parent has sole responsibility for raising the child; the other parent has specified visitation rights. Parents may negotiate informally over such things as schedules or holidays, but if an agreement can't be reached, the legal custodian has the right to make the final decisions. In **split custody** (about 2 percent of cases), the children are divided between the parents either by gender—the mother gets the daughter(s) and the father gets the son(s)—or by choice—the children are allowed to choose the parent with whom they want to live. In **joint custody**, sometimes called *dual residence* (about 16 percent of cases), the children divide their time between both parents, who share in the decisions about their upbringing. In another 1 percent of cases, custody is awarded to someone other than the husband or wife, such as a relative (Clarke, 1995a). There are two types of joint custody: *joint legal custody*, which specifies that both parents are to share decision making on such issues as the child's education, health care, and religious training; and *joint physical custody*, which specifies how much time children will spend in each parent's home.

Joint Custody   Joint custody is a heated issue—a "politically charged minefield," according to one author (Mason, 1999)—because fathers' rights groups and many women are on opposite sides of the battlefield. Proponents advance several arguments. First, they maintain that men and women should have equal child-rearing responsibilities, both during marriage and after divorce. Second, many men say they want to care for their children and have formed such organizations as Fathers for Justice and Fathers United for Equal Justice to lobby in almost every state for joint-custody laws. Third, much research indicates that the relationship between a noncustodial father and his children is critical in the children's development (see Hetherington and Stanley-Hagan, 1997). Finally, a joint-custody arrangement lightens the responsibility of each parent and eases the economic burdens of parenting, particularly for mothers (Irving and Benjamin, 1991).

Opponents of joint custody, on the other hand, argue that it creates loyalty conflicts for children and exacerbates postdivorce conflicts between ex-spouses, who may disagree on child-rearing decisions (see Ferreiro, 1990, for a summary of the debates on whether or not joint custody should be mandated by state laws). As Maccoby and others (1991) point out, parents who argued a lot before they divorced are likely to continue, therefore, children may still have to deal with parental conflict. Critics of joint custody also maintain that this arrangement makes it possible for men who abused their wives or children before the divorce to continue the same behavior (Fineman, 1991).

Finally, some argue that joint custody does more harm than good. School attendance may be disrupted as children are shuttled between two homes and a school. In addition, even when fathers don't show up for scheduled visits or totally ignore their children, mothers who move out of state may lose custody of their children if they don't have the fathers' permission to move (Hoffman, 1995). The residential parent may feel that the nonresidential parent spoils the child(ren), uses "bad" language during the child's visitation, or does not provide an acceptable religious upbringing. The nonresidential parent, on the other hand, may feel that the residential parent argues about visitation times or changes plans on short notice. It is difficult, then, for many parents to assume coparenting outside of marriage (Wolchik et al., 1996).

If there is little interparental conflict, however, and both parents manage the separate households, set rules, and supervise their children, most adolescents adjust to joint legal custody with few problems (Buchanan et al., 1996; Braver and O'Connell, 1998). Joint legal custody also seems to work well if the custodial mother encourages coparental interaction and supports the father–child relationship after divorce. In these situations, joint legal custody facilitates divorced fathers' parenting role in two ways. It increases a father's sense of control and influence as a parent. It also allows fathers to maintain their legal authority as parents. These benefits increase both a father's satisfaction with his parenting performance and coparental interaction (Madden-Derdich and Leonard, 2000).

Controversial Issues about Joint Custody One of the most controversial issues during the mid-1990s was whether divorced working mothers are being punished in custody cases. Some mothers claim that they must choose between their child and their job. In Mississippi, for example, a flight attendant whose work took her away two nights a week had to let her daughter live with her ex-husband. The judge ruled that the ex-husband's job as a Federal Express courier provided him a more regular work schedule (Steinbach, 1995).

Some observers say that such cases are a minority because mothers get custody of children in most uncontested cases. When custody is contested, however, some feel that courts are applying a double standard: "Often, men are judged by the availability of other child care, from a second wife to a girlfriend, while women are evaluated based on their own, personal ability to be with a child, ignoring the presence of a grandmother or a babysitter" (Feldmann and Goodale, 1995: 18).

Gay parents face ongoing problems in being awarded custody and visitation rights. In many cases, judges assume that gay and lesbian households don't constitute a "family," even when the mother or father provides evidence of good parenting. Judges may deem gay and lesbian parents as "unfit" because of their sexual orientation and despite a child's preference to live with a gay rather than a heterosexual parent (Duran-Aydintug and Causey, 1996; Stein, 1996). Recently, however, courts in Maryland, Massachusetts, and New Jersey have ruled that ex-partners in gay and lesbian relationships can have similar visitation rights provided to divorced couples. In Maryland, the appeals court allowed visitation with a 5-year-old girl because it viewed the lesbian ex-partner as having a similar legal standing to a stepparent (Siegel, 2000).

How Does Divorce Affect Children?

The consequences of divorce vary and depend on a variety of factors. The absence of one parent can have serious effects on a child; a lower family income as a result of divorce can affect a child's educational opportunities and success in school; a child's relationship with the custodial spouse can influence his or her outcomes in a divorce; the child's age at the time of divorce influences his or her behavior; a child's gender seems to determine his or her responses to some degree; and the reactions of outsiders, like teachers, may have an impact on children's behavior. One of the most important influences on children's responses to their parents' divorce is the parents' behavior and the way they handle the divorce, as the box "Children of Divorce" demonstrates. The more civilized and mature the divorce, the easier it is on children.

Absent Fathers

This section could be called "The Absent Parent," but the fact is that the postdivorce single-father household from which the mother has totally disappeared is rare. In most sole-custody cases, it is the mothers who have custody and the fathers who get visitation rights. In a national study, Bianchi (1990) found that more than

CONTRAINTS

Children of Divorce

The way a divorcing couple deals with divorce may have long-term effects on the children. Interviewing adult children of divorce (sometimes called "ACODs") about their memories of their parents' divorce and their current behaviors and lifestyles, Fassel (1991) proposed five types of divorce and their subsequent effects on children:

The Disappearing Parent Suddenly, one parent leaves the home, and the children receive little explanation beyond "Your mother and I have been divorced today." Adults who recalled this situation often grew up suspicious of people, fearing that they too would leave them. Some tried to be perfect parents to avoid hurting their children in the ways they had been hurt.

The Surprise Divorce In this situation, parents often seemed close and open with each other, but without any warning, one filed for divorce. Adults recalled feeling shock and then bewilderment and anger that the parent who left disrupted what they had thought was a happy family. As they grow up, children may erect walls to protect themselves, becoming distant from friends and avoiding intimate relationships because they expect a partner, like the parent who left, to be unpredictable or undependable.

The Violent Divorce Spouse and sometimes child abuse as well causes many divorces. Children in such a setting don't learn how to handle anger because their role models could not handle it. The children often repress conflict for fear of violence, or they grow up believing that fighting is a way to test intimacy and to get a partner's attention.

The Late Divorce When parents stay together "for the children's sake," they often create an environment of veiled criticism and threats, unspoken anger, and even hatred. Many children in such homes learn to deny feelings just to survive, and some equate love with suffering in silence. Many are wary of commitment, which they equate with loss of freedom, and become cynical about the possibility of having a good relationship with anyone.

Protect-the-Kids Divorce Some well-intentioned parents may decide to protect their children by withholding information about the real reasons for their divorce. They don't accuse one another, they communicate well, and each listens respectfully as the other tells the children about the divorce. Sounds good? Not necessarily. In one case, a couple told their children that their father felt the need to explore, to

be free, to see the world. When, many years later, the children learned that their father was gay, they felt betrayed and angry.

How can divorcing couples avoid these negative outcomes for their children? Gold (1992) recommends "CPR" (a play on the abbreviation for cardiopulmonary resuscitation, which is an emergency procedure used to keep the heart and lungs going in an emergency like a heart attack):

Continuity Introduce all changes gradually, and try to maintain regular routines and child-rearing responsibilities as far as possible.

Protection Be civil with one another, and don't put your children in the middle of your conflicts. Preserve your children's relationships with both of you.

Reassurance Assure your children that you love them, that the divorce is not their fault, and that you will not abandon them. Tell your children about your plans for them to spend time with each of you; let them know about the possibility that they may have to move or change schools and give them warning ahead of time of any impending economic or financial changes.

---

60 percent of fathers either did not visit their children or did not visit them *and* had no telephone or mail contact with them over a one-year period. Even when fathers do see their children, they typically slack off or stop visiting after about two years (Loewen, 1988). One study found that even when the parents were separated but not yet divorced the average child had seen the father only six to eight days during the preceding month (Braver et al., 1991). Nonresident mothers are more likely than nonresident fathers to maintain contact with their children by letters, telephone calls, and extended visitations (Stewart, 1999).

Why do many fathers fail to take visitation rights seriously? For one thing, traditional cultural

expectations about child rearing and nurturing still emphasize the importance of mothers, not fathers (see Chapter 4). Also, when ex-spouses are engaged in continuing battles, fathers may try to avoid further conflict by not seeing their children. A third reason, according to some fathers, is that visitation is emotionally difficult for them or seems artificial. Finally, when a man forms new relationships or remarries, he may feel less committed to his children from an earlier marriage (Teyber and Hoffman, 1987; Loewen, 1988).

How important is a noncustodial father's involvement to his children's well-being? The findings are mixed. There is some evidence that the father's payment of child support benefits the children's educational

Divorced fathers can maintain close relationships with their children by seeing them as often as possible, setting rules, discussing problems, and providing guidance.

achievement. For example, children supported by such payments are more likely to finish high school and to enter college (Graham et al., 1994; Knox and Bane, 1994). Regular payments may also increase children's academic well-being because mothers, feeling more financially secure, are able to deal better with school-related problems (McLanahan et al., 1994). And when child-support payments are voluntary, fathers may have good relationships with their children and ex-spouses. The lack of parental conflict, which is ordinarily distressing and distracting, may help children focus on academic pursuits (Baydar and Brooks-Gunn, 1994).

There is less evidence that visits from a noncustodial father have beneficial effects on the child's emotional and behavioral well-being. Within a few years, children adapt to a father's absence, and some behavioral problems, especially among boys, decrease (Mott et al., 1997). Some children (and mothers) are better off having minimal contact with nonresident fathers if the fathers are abusive, fight with their ex-wives, or have other problems (King, 1994). For example, some fathers may abuse alcohol, some may be too depressed after a divorce to maintain meaningful ties with their children, some may feel that they are losing control over their children, and some may have developed closer relationships with new partners and their children (Aseltine and Kessler, 1993; Umberson and Williams, 1993).

Family counselors maintain, however, that it is important for children and fathers to maintain a close relationship after a divorce (Portes et al., 1992). Pruett (1987) suggests some specific steps that fathers can take to ensure the continuity of their relationship with their children:

1. A father should be guided by his child's developmental needs. For example, because toddlers' sense of time is different from adults' and their memories are shorter, it's better for a father to make frequent brief visits than long visits at greater intervals. On the other hand, older children who enjoy successful social and school activities need more visitation flexibility.

2. A father should live close to his children if at all possible, especially when they are young. Furthermore, whether or not he and his former wife are friendly, he should not give up seeing his children. He should be with his children whenever he can, whether he is changing their diapers or helping them with their homework.

3. A father should pay child support regularly. Skipping payments not only deprives the child of material things but lowers the father's self-respect. At the same time, a father should not overindulge his children; children of *all* ages expect a parent to establish limits for them.

4. A father should not cross-examine his children or dwell on the divorce. His job is to figure out how he and the children can fit into one another's lives and then make that happen.

Crisis need *not* spawn failure. Although divorce is often sad and difficult for both fathers and their children, the rewards are immeasurable when a father perseveres in maintaining a relationship with his children.

Parents as Peers

Divorced parents sometimes make the mistake of treating their children like peers. Particularly if the children are bright and verbal, a parent may see them as more mature than they really are. Mothers, who usually have custody, often share their feelings on a wide range of personal issues. They may express bitterness toward their ex-husbands, anger at men in general, or frustration over financial concerns or social isolation.

In response, children may console the parent and appear concerned and caring, but they may also feel anger, resentment, sadness, or guilt. According to a 15-year-old girl, for example,

Don't look to kids for emotional support. I was going through so much of my own emotional hell that my mom leaning on me was the last thing that

I wanted, and it made me very, very resentful of her. My mom tried to use me as her confidant for all the bad stuff my dad did to her, but she refused to see that he was still my dad, and I still loved him. (S. Evans, 2000: C4)

Children might manifest their anger and resentment through psychosomatic problems such as stomach pains, through sleeping or eating problems, through sexual or aggressive acting out, or through a use of drugs. They may be truant from school, exhibit a decline in academic performance, or run away. They may appear overcompliant with parental requests or simply withdraw (Devall et al., 1986; Glenwick and Mowrey, 1986).

Several researchers maintain that the mother–child "lean on me" relationship works well. For example, in a study of 58 first-year college students, Arditti (1999) concluded that mothers' leaning on children for emotional support and advice during and after a divorce contributed to a sense of equality, closeness, and friend status. And in a study of adolescents from divorced families, Buchanan et al. (1996) found that parents' confiding in their children had no negative effect on the adolescents unless the parent conveyed that she or he is weak and vulnerable and needs the adolescent to be strong, to be the caretaker.

Regardless of the message that parents think they're conveying to children, however, an especially sensitive or responsible child (often a girl) who is "parentified" during a divorce may find it difficult to focus on her (or his) own individual growth:

Many a time the only time Mom talked to Dad, and vice-versa, was through messages sent through me. Even my brother and sister saw the advantages in using me as a courier in getting the things they wanted. . . . I would feel an overwhelming sense of loneliness and desperation, as if no one understood me or would sympathize with my struggles to keep the peace and save the family. . . . I believe I went far away to college unconsciously, [but] once I was here, I suffered from guilt in abandoning my family duties. . . . [Now after three years] I still feel anger and sadness and loneliness when I see that it is once again my duty to restore the harmony in the family. (Brown and Amatea, 2000: 180)

The Effect of Age and Gender on Children's Well-Being

A study by the National Institute of Mental Health showed that children who were younger than 7 when their parents divorced were as adolescents three times more likely to be receiving psychological counseling and five times more likely to have been suspended or expelled from school than were adolescents of intact families (cited in Taylor, 1991). Children who do poorly in school or drop out have fewer occupational options and thus earn less as adults (Biblarz and Raftery, 1993). And some adolescents react to divorce by becoming more socially isolated; they disappear into their rooms, spend hours watching television, and jump at the chance to get out of the house. Others may react by becoming addicted to drugs or alcohol or by overeating, undereating, shoplifting, or becoming promiscuous (Walther, 1991).

Some studies have shown that teacher evaluations, often in the form of grades, are lower for children from single-parent families (Demo and Acock, 1988; Bianchi, 1990). It's not clear, however, whether these evaluations reflect behavioral problems due to parental divorce or, as we discussed earlier, to teachers' negative expectations of children from divorced families.

Divorce appears to affect sons and daughters differently. Boys, particularly those with absent fathers, tend to have lower levels of achievement in school, to have to repeat a grade in school, and to have difficulty getting along with peers and teachers (Bianchi, 1990). In general, young boys experience more behavioral and emotional problems, such as increased levels of aggression, heightened anxiety, dependency, and a tendency to withdraw or to be easily distracted.

Such reactions may reflect downward mobility rather than divorce: Economic hardship after divorce may create emotional stress for both mothers and children. Boys may respond behaviorally (arguments or anger) while girls manifest distress in less observable ways, such as becoming more anxious or depressed (Morrison and Cherlin, 1995; Simons et al., 1999). In what Wallerstein and Blakeslee (1989) call a "sleeper effect," girls' negative reactions to divorce may be delayed until adolescence or young adulthood. For example, one study found that women who were younger than 16 when their parents separated or divorced were 59 percent more likely to end up separated or divorced themselves compared to 32 percent of males (Glenn and Kramer, 1987).

There are more similarities than differences between the sexes, however. For example, in a study of young people aged 18 to 23 in divorced or separated families, Furstenberg and Teitler (1994) found that divorce appeared to produce similar effects for boys and girls. Both had a higher likelihood than children from intact families to drop out of high school, to have sex before age 17, and to cohabit; the girls were more likely to become pregnant before age 19.

Behavioral and Emotional Problems

Research findings on the short- and long-term effects of divorce on children's behavior and emotional and mental health are mixed and inconclusive. Children's

According to many studies (see text), it is not the divorce itself but parental conflict during and after a divorce that is most damaging to children.

responses are complex in terms of such variables as age, sex, and predivorce family relationships that gauge the impact of divorce.

Several national studies show that adult children of divorce report lower satisfaction in such areas as leisure activities, friendships, family life, and happiness (Glenn and Kramer, 1987; Glenn, 1991). In part because parents are able to exercise less supervision and control over children in single-parent households, adolescents of both sexes are more likely to engage in such deviant behavior as truancy, burglary, and alcohol and drug use (Thornberry et al., 1999). A study that assessed children at ages 7, 11, 16, and 23 concluded, however, that the negative emotional effects of parental divorce in young adulthood were minimal, that only a minority of young adults developed serious mental problems (such as depression or anxiety) as a result of parental divorce, and that only a small group needed "clinical intervention" in young adulthood. The most vulnerable young adults were those who experienced indirect effects of parental divorce such as conflict between the divorced parents, lower economic status, fewer schooling and career opportunities, and an absence of appropriate sex-role models (Chase-Lansdale et al., 1995).

Postdivorce problems are often explained in terms of social learning theories. That is, whereas girls had same-sex role models in their mothers, who are typically the custodial parents, boys had a harder time

adjusting to living without a same-sex parent. It may be, however, that preadolescent children are more upset by the presence of another man in the house than by the absence of their biological father, and they react negatively (Mott et al., 1997).

Some social scientists maintain that emotional problems, regardless of gender, are influenced not by family structure (divorced or intact) but by family process, including a lack of parental supervision, poor parent–child relationships, and open disagreements between custodial mothers and adolescents on issues such as clothes, friends, girlfriends or boyfriends, sexual behavior, and helping around the house (Buchanan et al., 1996; Demo and Acock, 1996a). If noncustodial fathers don't play the role of parent, mere contact or even sharing good times together may not contribute in a positive way to children's development (Amato, 1996). If, however, nonresident fathers play an authoritative role (such as listening to children's problems, giving advice, and working together on projects), fathers and children report a close relationship (Amato and Gilbreth, 1999).

Some researchers have questioned whether divorce creates new dilemmas or crystallizes long-standing family problems. In longitudinal studies of the effects of divorce on children between the ages of 11 and 16 in Great Britain and the United States, a team of researchers found that, especially for boys, the achievement and behavioral problems existed well before the separation and divorce occurred (Cherlin et al., 1991). Although divorce increases the risk of problems such as worrying about things and feeling unhappy, most children whose parents divorce don't experience these difficulties (Cherlin, 1999). In a study of American adolescents and young adults from divorced families, Furstenberg and Teitler (1994) also concluded that some of the processes that end in divorce begin long before marital disruption actually occurs. That is, partners who divorce are more likely to have poor parenting skills and high levels of marital conflict or to suffer from persistent economic stress.

Family structure and processes probably overlap in explaining negative divorce outcomes. Data from an 18-year intergenerational study show, for example, that it is not the divorce itself but parental attitudes during and after the divorce that affect children's behavior and their perceptions about family life. Parents who undergo a divorce may communicate negative attitudes to their children about marriage and may view cohabitation (and, consequently, premarital sex) as an attractive alternative to marriage (Axinn and Thornton, 1996). Some divorced parents may communicate sexually permissive values by expressing negative feelings about marriage and by engaging in sexual relations outside of marriage.

Simons (1996) maintains that family structure is a critical factor that increases children's risk for developmental problems in divorced families. He suggests, however, a "causal sequence" that incorporates both family structure and process: Marital dissolution increases the probability that a woman will experience economic pressures and psychological depression. This strain and emotional distress tend to reduce the quality of her parenting. Reductions in the quality of parenting, in turn, increase a child's risk for emotional and behavioral problems and poor developmental outcomes.

Simons and other researchers emphasize that children will not develop difficulties simply because their parents have divorced. Divorce is disruptive and increases the *chances* of negative consequences for both parents and children because it affects the life course in other ways. That is, if divorce interferes with continued schooling, this disadvantage cumulates through life, affecting occupational status, income, and economic well-being. People with low levels of educational attainment and high levels of economic hardship are more likely to have high levels of depression as adults and to experience unhappy or unstable interpersonal relationships (Ross and Mirowsky, 1999).

Helping Children Adjust during Divorce

Time and again, studies have shown that it is not divorce itself that is damaging to children but the *parental conflict* that becomes manifest not only before but during and after the divorce (Gabardi and Rosen, 1992; Booth and Amato, 1994; Forehand et al., 1994; Vandewater and Lansford, 1998). Children experience the greatest stress when they are put in the middle of their parents' struggle, as mentioned earlier, by trying to get children to side with them, using the children to get information about the other parent, or denigrating a former spouse (Buehler and Trotter, 1990; Massey, 1992; Cummings and Davies, 1994; Schaefer and DiGeronimo, 1999). According to researchers and clinicians, parents can lessen some of these negative effects:

■ Help prepare children for the actual physical separation by giving them some extra time beforehand and by being around to answer their questions. Explain what divorce is as clearly as you can to the children, including changes they can expect in their day-to-day experience, and be prepared to repeat this information several times for younger children.

■ Each parent should contribute to the explanation given the children, speaking for himself or herself, and the couple should agree ahead of time on what they will and will not say. Speak about yourself, your feelings, and your perspective without criticizing your spouse.

■ Reassure the children that you love them and that you will remain actively involved with them. Partners should emphasize that both parents will continue to love and care for the children and that the children will always be free to love both parents.

■ Don't be afraid to talk about your feelings. This can set the stage for open communication between parents and their children. You can discuss your unhappiness and even your anger, but if you blame the other parent you will force the children to take sides.

■ Modify what you say based on the children's ages. For example, younger children need more concrete examples to help them understand the nature of divorce.

■ Emphasize that the children are not responsible for problems between the parents. Point out that each of you is divorcing the other but not the children.

■ Give the children the news when they are together so that they can lean on one another for support, and encourage them to ask any questions that occur to them both then and later.

■ Make it clear that you have made the decision to divorce carefully, rationally, but regretfully. Expressing your sadness encourages children to cry and mourn without having to hide their feelings of loss from you or from themselves.

■ Reassure your children that they will continue to see their grandparents on both sides of the family.

■ Recognize the cries of help in your children's behavior during and after your divorce. For example, preschool children may regress to an earlier stage of their development and suck their thumbs or be afraid of the dark. They may lose their appetites and wake frequently during the night crying anxiously. Elementary school children may suddenly show a lack of interest in school or get poor grades in courses in which they previously excelled. Adolescents may "tell" you that you need to work constructively on your relationship with them if they suddenly begin to cut class, become verbally abusive or sexually irresponsible, defy curfew rules, or start using alcohol, cocaine, or other drugs.

■ Understand that the children's fundamental need for security has not changed. Your children need to feel, above all else, that Mom and Dad will always provide them with the emotional and physical security they need to develop into confident maturity. Their security does *not* depend on your income or where you live but on whether you and your ex-spouse demonstrate by your behavior that both of you are fully competent to weather the storms of change that divorce entails and to shelter them from these storms (Lansky, 1989; Greif, 1990).

■ It is critical for the noncustodial parent, usually the father, to maintain an ongoing relationship with the children. Noncustodial fathers who maintain stable, frequent visitation provide more advice to their children, and their adolescent children are more satisfied with the support of the absent parent and less likely to experience depression (Barber, 1994).

Amato (1993) suggests that children's outcomes following divorce could be enhanced by parents' maintaining or increasing resources and decreasing stressors. Major *resources* include parental support (emotional support, practical help, guidance, supervision, and role models), as well as parental socioeconomic resources. All parents can provide support. Some parents have more financial resources than others, of course, but nonresident fathers and nonresident mothers who do not support their children economically increase stress and decrease their children's opportunities to develop socially, emotionally, and cognitively. *Stressors* include interparental conflict that may precede and follow divorce and subsequent disruptive life changes that may include a lack of economic resources. Again, most divorced parents can minimize the stressors and maximize the resources to improve their children's short-term and long-term well-being.

Some Positive Outcomes of Divorce

Much of this chapter has addressed the debilitating effects of divorce on adults and their children. In response to such negative outcomes, some groups are proposing that no-fault divorce be eliminated and that divorce laws should be tougher (see the box "Should It Be Harder to Get a Divorce?"). Does divorce have any *positive* effects?

In a highly publicized book, *The Unexpected Legacy of Divorce,* Wallerstein and her colleagues (2000) advise parents to stay in unhappy marriages to avoid hurting their children. What many people don't realize is that such advice, although presumably well intentioned, is based on a clinical study of a small group of highly "dysfunctional" divorced families. In contrast, most divorced couples and their children adjust and function very well.

The major positive outcome of divorce is that it provides options to people in unsatisfactory marriages. Insofar as divorce does away with an unhappy, frustrating, and stressful situation, it may improve the mental and emotional health of both ex-spouses and their children. Divorced parents who take joint-custody arrangements seriously, who maintain good communication with their children and with each other, and who receive support from family, friends, and the larger community report being physically and mentally healthy (Golby and Bretherton, 1998).

In addition, parental separation is better for children, at least in the long run, than remaining in an intact family where there is continuous conflict (Demo and Acock, 1991). A divorce that causes minimal disruption to a child's life may offer fewer long-term risks than does a marriage that children perceive as unhappy. Divorce can offer both parents and children opportunities for personal growth, more gratifying relationships, and a more harmonious family situation (Hetherington et al., 1993).

Although men as a group tend to interpret their divorces more negatively than women do, both men and women cite gains after a divorce. Women, for example, enjoy their new-found freedom from overbearing husbands, have less money but like controlling what they have, take pride in learning to fix things around the house, and develop self-confidence as they take on economic roles or go back to school. Men have reported benefits such as spending more money on themselves or their hobbies, learning to manage a household, having more leisure time to themselves, and dating numerous partners (Riessman, 1990). As one author advises black men: "While the break-up may mean broken dreams, it doesn't have to mean broken homes. It may present fresh opportunities for men to reassess their lives and learn from their mistakes. And, perhaps, they won't stumble over the same rocks" (Hutchinson, 1994: 113).

Not surprisingly, adult children of divorce have less idealized views of marriage than do people who come from intact families. Although most adult children of divorce value marriage, they are more aware of its limitations and more accepting of alternatives to traditional family forms (Amato, 1988). Some social scientists suggest that children who grow up in father-absent homes may be less pressured to conform to traditional gender roles and may instead learn more androgynous roles that will help them be better parents in adulthood (Gately and Schwebel, 1992).

Gold (1992) and other clinicians have suggested that the positive effects of divorce can be increased if adults act like adults. For example, divorcing parents can make "divorce vows" that reinforce their commitment to their children:

■ I vow to continue to provide for our children's financial and emotional welfare.

■ I vow to place our children's emotional needs above my personal feelings about my former spouse.

■ I vow to be fair and honest about the divorce settlement.

C H A N G E S

Should It Be Harder to Get a Divorce?

In a recent *Time*/CNN poll, 61 percent of the respondents said it should be harder for married couples with young children to get a divorce (Kirn, 1997). High U.S. divorce rates and research show, as you've seen, that children of divorced parents have a greater likelihood of dropping out of school, getting into trouble with the law, and having children out of wedlock. As a result, many religious and political groups are considering eliminating "revolving-door marriages" by reforming no-fault divorce laws.

In 1997, for example, Louisiana passed a law that couples could sign a license for a "covenant marriage" that includes the line, "We understand that a covenant marriage is for life" (Banisky, 1997). Signing the license gives up the right to no-fault divorce. A couple promises to have counseling if the marriage falters, and can be divorced only for a limited number of reasons—including adultery, a felony conviction, abuse, and abandonment—

or after a two-year separation. The purpose of the optional covenant marriage license is to discourage divorce by making it more difficult to get. Here are a few arguments from both sides of this issue:

Make getting a divorce more difficult

- Simply discussing the covenant marriage option will force couples to consider their vows more seriously and to seek counseling.
- It's too easy to get a divorce.
- Couples break up over little things because a divorce is "no big deal."
- No-fault divorces disregard the interests of children of divorce.
- Ending no-fault divorce would give more rights to the partner who doesn't want a divorce.

Leave current divorce laws alone

- Covenant marriages could trap people whose spouses are alcoholics or

hurt low-income families with little means for counseling.
- Getting a divorce is difficult, complicated, expensive, and stressful.
- Many couples seek therapy to keep the marriage together and stay in destructive relationships for many years.
- Children fare worse in high-conflict two-parent families than in loving single-parent families.
- Ending no-fault divorce could keep children in high-conflict homes longer and make divorce even more adversarial.

What are other advantages in making divorce harder to get? What about the disadvantages? Should we make it harder to get a divorce? Harder to get married? Both? Leave things alone?

Sources: Galston, 1996; Leland, 1996; Shipley, 1997; Trafford, 1997.

- I vow to support the children's relationships with my former spouse and never to do anything that might compromise that relationship.

- I vow to deal with the issues in this divorce as constructively as I know how, so that we can all go forward.

Such vows may seem hokey. On the other hand, the vows might remind divorcing parents that continuous parental conflict is unhealthy for their children. According to one counselor, for example:

> The kids are hearing way too much about finances and child support payments and not getting enough care. They're so tuned into their parents' conflict and the financial situation that they lose the sense that they're valued and cared for. . . . Some children are so preoccupied with parental conflict that they become incapacitated, unable to

focus on any task. . . . I've seen kids in the schools that are so worried about their mothers or fathers that they sit in the classroom and do nothing. All their energy goes into worrying. (Suro, 1997: 12)

Counseling and Divorce Mediation

Increasingly, marital counseling helps families get through the process of divorce. When couples aren't convinced they want a divorce, therapists can help the couples reconcile.

Counseling can be useful for a number of reasons. Most importantly, therapists typically serve as impartial observers rather than favoring one side or the other (as attorneys do). Counselors can help parents recognize that a child is having a problem by being preoccupied with the parents' discord. Therapists can help divorcing parents build stronger relationships with their children. Family practitioners assist divorcing couples and families in a number of ways: They individualize treatment programs, assist nonresidential and custodial parents to coparent as effectively as possible, help children cope with fears such as losing the nonresidential parent permanently, provide information on remarriage and its potential impact on the child(ren) and ex-spouse, and organize a variety of support networks (Leite and McKenry, 1996).

Women who divorced at age 40 or older report that counselors helped them to understand why they were "dumped," to get rid of the guilt, and to learn to cope with the new situation. In other cases, therapy provides some of the women the strength to leave abusive or alcoholic husbands (Hayes et al., 1993).

Increasingly, many jurisdictions are ordering divorcing parents to attend educational seminars with professional counselors before going to court. The purpose of the sessions is not to convince parents to stay together but to teach them about their children's emotional and developmental needs during the divorce process. In other cases, the counseling is a preliminary step before meeting with a mediator.

Divorce mediation is a technique and practice, carried out by a person trained in the mediation of disputes, in which a divorcing couple is assisted in coming to an agreement. Some of the issues that are resolved include custody arrangements, child support and future college expenses, and the division of marital property (which might include a house, furniture, stocks, savings accounts, retirement accounts, pension plans, cars, and computers, and even other assets such as rental property and vacation homes, debts, medical expenses, and self-employment income). Although most mediators are either attorneys or mental health professionals, accountants and others are now seeking training in mediation to facilitate divorce agreements (De Witt, 1994).

Mediation will not eliminate the hurt caused by separation and divorce, but it can pave the way for the emotional healing and adjustment of both the couple and the children (see Hahn and Kleist, 2000, for a review of the conditions under which mediation is the most effective). First, mediation increases communication between spouses. It decreases the anger and does not force the children to choose sides in the divorce. Second, mediation reduces the conflict between spouses. When parents can resolve a dispute—whether it is over a weekend visitation schedule or the division of the proceeds of an employee stock plan—without screaming at each other or exchanging bitter looks, children benefit, and parents see they are capable of reaching an agreement.

Third, mediation creates a cooperative attitude between parents, sparing the child from being forced into the difficult role of a go-between (Kelly, 2000). Fourth, mediation generally reduces the time required to negotiate the divorce settlement. A mediation settlement typically takes two to three months; a divorce obtained through a court proceeding may take two or three years. Putting divorce behind them as quickly as possible is

even more important for children than it is for adults. Mediation also often helps parents adopt a stable schedule of visitation and reduces the potential for disputes.

Fifth, mediated agreements generally make it easier to accommodate changes as the children grow. As Jennifer or Sam change from a Saturday morning ballet lesson, at age 8, to Wednesday night driving lessons, at age 15, parents can negotiate schedule changes without resorting to costly and time-consuming requests for changes in court-imposed arrangements. Finally, mediation prevents children from being pawns or trophies in a divorce contest. The mediator's approach is "What arrangements are best for you, your spouse, and your children?" There is no room for the adversarial stance, "Which of you will win the children?" Mediation assumes that divorcing parents can work together to benefit both themselves and their children.

Dillon and Emery (1996) conducted a follow-up study of parents who pursued mediation versus traditional adversarial litigation for resolving child-custody disputes. Nine years after the settlements, the noncustodial parents (most of whom were fathers) who used mediation were more likely than the noncustodial parents who had opted for litigation to have been communicating about the children with the ex-spouses on a frequent basis, to have seen their children more often, and to have been more involved in child-related decisions. The researchers point out that parents who choose mediation over litigation are probably more interested in coparenting and more open to compromises. It might be the case, however, that if mediation were a required first step for *all* divorcing couples, greater cooperation between the parents and better relationships between parents and children would result.

Conclusion

The greater acceptance of divorce today has created *change* in family structures. Indeed, separation and divorce now seem to have become "an intrinsic feature of modern family life rather than a temporary aberration" (Martin and Bumpass, 1989: 49). As this chapter has shown, a large segment of the adult population flows in and out of marriage during the life course. This means that people have more *choices* in leaving an unhappy marriage. Often, however, parents fail to recognize that what are choices for them may be *constraints* for their children, who often feel at fault, guilty, and torn between warring parents. If parents handled divorces in more rational and civilized ways, by using mediation successfully, for example, many children would be spared the emotional pain and economic deprivation that they now must suffer. Some of the pain that both parents and children experience may become even greater after parents remarry, the topic of the next chapter.

SUMMARY

1. A separation can be temporary or permanent, or it can precede a divorce. In most cases, separation is a lengthy process involving four phases—preseparation, early separation, midseparation, and late separation.

2. Marital separation leads to one of three outcomes: divorce, long-term unresolved separation, or reconciliation. The outcomes of marital separation often vary by race and socioeconomic status.

3. Divorce rates increased rapidly during the 1970s, reached a plateau during the 1980s, and have decreased slightly during the 1990s. Whereas in the past many marriages ended because of death or desertion, today divorce is the most common reason for marital dissolution.

4. Women file for divorce nearly twice as often as men do. This may reflect women's desire to legalize men's emotional or physical absence. Also, employed women are more independent economically and thus less inclined to tolerate husbands' extramarital affairs or other unacceptable behavior.

5. Divorce is often a long, drawn-out process. In most divorces, people go through one or more of six stages: the emotional divorce, the legal divorce, the economic divorce, the coparental divorce, the community divorce, and the psychic divorce.

6. The many reasons for divorce include macro-level causes, such as changing gender roles; demographic variables, such as marriage at a young age; and such interpersonal factors as poor communication and infidelity.

7. Divorce has psychological, economic, and legal consequences. Although property settlements are common, few women receive alimony payments. Furthermore, because child-support awards are either rare or very low, many women and children plunge into poverty after a divorce.

8. There are several types of child custody—sole, split, and joint. Although most mothers receive sole custody, joint custody is becoming more common.

9. In the past, much research indicated that divorce had detrimental effects on children. More recently, however, researchers have suggested that some problems may actually have existed before the divorce. Other problems may be attributed to the absence of one parent, usually the father, or to the lack of parenting responsibilities assumed by a nonresidential father.

10. Divorce mediation has emerged as an alternative to the traditional adversarial approach common to the legal process. Mediated divorces tend to be less bitter, less protracted, and to offer each partner more input in child-custody decisions.

KEY TERMS

separation 396
divorce 397
alimony 399
child support 399

no-fault divorce 401
social integration 403
custody 412
sole custody 413

split custody 413
joint custody 413
divorce mediation 422

TAKING IT FURTHER

Divorce Help and Information on the Internet

The **Divorce Support Page** contains links to many divorce, custody, and mediation sites, as well as divorce laws and professionals for each state.

www.divorcesupport.com

The **Academy of Family Mediators** can refer you to a mediator in your area.

www.mediators.org

The **Human Development and Family Life Education Resource Center,** The Ohio State University, provides online bulletins on topics such as divorce and noncustodial fathers, guides for parents helping children with divorce, and a Website for adolescents whose parents are divorcing.

www.hec.ohio-state.edu/famlife/bulletin/bullmain.htm

Dads at a Distance suggests ideas and activities on how to strengthen long-distance relationships with children.

www.daads.com

Divorce Helpline is aimed at helping couples reduce conflict and stay out of court and includes materials to minimize the need for a lawyer.

www.divorcehelp.com

And more . . . www.prenhall.com/benokraitis provides sites for bulletin boards to post-divorce-related questions, lobby groups to reform divorce laws, state-by-state information on divorce, chat rooms, and academic resources about divorce.

Remarriage and Stepfamilies: Life after Divorce

DATADIGEST

- The U.S. Census Bureau estimates that **stepfamilies will outnumber traditional nuclear families by the year 2007.**

- **One out of three Americans** is now a stepparent, a stepchild, a stepsibling, or some other member of a stepfamily.

- Within three years of divorce, **75 percent of women and 83 percent of men remarry.** Over 50 percent of men and 33 percent of women remarry within one year.

- **Remarriage partners** are usually people whose previous marriages ended in divorce. In about

- 11 percent of remarriages, one or both partners have been widowed.

- In **more than 40 percent of U.S. marriages** in 1991, the partners had been married previously between one and four times.

- **Fewer than 5 percent of all remarried couples have three sets of children**—yours, mine, and ours.

SOURCES: Larson, 1992; Norton and Miller, 1992; Ahrons, 1994; Furukawa, 1994; Clarke, 1995a; Wineberg and McCarthy, 1998; Herbert, 1999.

EVEN with rising divorce rates, most people aren't disillusioned with marriage. Indeed, many divorced people remarry, and some more than once. New family relationships formed after divorce can become intricate. Listen to a woman who married a widower as she describes her multifaceted family relationships shortly before the marriage of her stepdaughter. Both had children from previous marriages:

> *Ed will be my stepson-in-law, but there's no simple way to state the relationships between his daughter, Amy, and me. . . . Amy becomes my husband's stepgranddaughter, his daughter's stepdaughter, his granddaughters' stepsister or his son-in-law's daughter. But to me, the linguistic link is truly unwieldy: my husband's stepgranddaughter, my stepdaughter's stepdaughter, my stepgrandchildren's stepsister!" (Borst, 1996, p. 16)*

Because not all remarried couples have children from previous marriages living with them, we'll discuss remarriage and stepfamilies separately; quite clearly, though, the two topics overlap.

This chapter presents an overview of important topics on remarried spouses and their children, including the prevalence and characteristics of remarriages and stepfamilies, their intricacy and varied structures, stepfamily development, key relationships in stepfamilies, and some characteristics of happy stepfamilies. Before describing courtship that precedes a remarriage, I'd like to define stepfamily and provide a general picture of the prevalence of remarriages in the United States.

What Is a Stepfamily? How Common Is Remarriage?

A **stepfamily** is a household in which there is an adult couple at least one of whom has a child from a previous marriage (Visher and Visher, 1988). Such terms as *blended family, reconstituted family,* and *binuclear family* are often used interchangeably with "stepfamily." Although I sometimes use "blended family" rather than "stepfamily," some researchers avoid using "blended" because it connotes an unrealistic expectation that families can become *truly* blended into one, which is often not the case. In addition, "reconstituted" and "binuclear" are awkward and are rarely used by family sociologists (Kelley, 1996).

Remember, also, that regardless of which term is used, a stepparent and stepchild do not have to live together all of the time or even part of the time to have a relationship and to share stepfamily membership (Ganong et al., 1995). Children's membership in two households is becoming increasingly common due to joint legal and physical custody (see Chapter 15). And, as you saw in the quote from Borst at the beginning of this chapter, both the remarried couple and their children may have several combinations of household membership and kinship.

Stepfamilies are formed through remarriage, but how frequent is remarriage? The U.S. rate of remarriage, the highest in the world, has been erratic. It peaked in the mid-1940s, continued in the 1950s and 1960s, and has declined steadily since about 1967 (see *Figure 16.1*). The rate is still high, however. Over 40 percent of all marriages are remarriages for one or

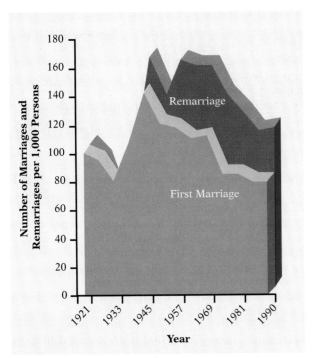

FIGURE 16.1   Rates of First Marriage and Remarriage, 1921–1990. These data are based on numbers of first marriages per 1,000 single women between the ages of 15 and 44 and the numbers of remarriages per 1,000 widowed or divorced women between the ages of 15 and 54 (Norton and Miller, 1992, p. 2).

both partners (Coleman and Ganong, 1991). In 20 percent of the marriages formed in 1990, both partners had been divorced at least once (Clarke, 1995b). More than 50 percent of today's youth are stepsons or stepdaughters. Many of these stepchildren have or will have half-siblings as well because 54 percent of women bear children in their remarriages (Wineberg, 1990).

The increase in divorce and remarriage rates has important implications for family structure and family roles. One demographer notes, for example, that while 70- to 85-year olds today have, on average, 2.4 biological children, by 2030 that group will average only 1.6 biological children. Since 1980, the ratio of biological children to stepchildren for people 70 to 85 has doubled, and is expected to rise by another 50 percent by 2030 (Wachter, 1997). This means that the baby boom generation (see Chapters 1, 3, and 13) will have to rely more on stepchildren and stepgrandchildren rather than biological children and biological grandchildren for caregiving when the boomers reach 70 to 85 and experience incapacitation. So, be nice to your steprelatives. (We examine aging and caregiving in the next chapter.)

Courtship after Divorce

Often partners start dating again even before the divorce is legally final. To insulate themselves from the pain of divorce, many people rush into another relationship: "It's not unusual to see women and men frantically dating in the first year after their separation, trying to fill the void with an intense new love or even with just another warm body" (Ahrons, 1994: 65).

If the partners are young and have not been married very long, reentering the "dating scene" will not be very difficult. Dating and courtship may be more awkward for older men and women or for those who have been married a long time because they may feel insecure about new dating patterns. For example, one of my friends, a woman who divorced after 12 years of marriage, wanted new relationships but was very anxious about dating: "Am I supposed to pay for myself when we go to dinner? Should I just meet him at the restaurant, or do men still pick women up? What if he wants to jump into bed after the first date?"

Although all dating couples—whether or not they have been married previously—often express similar concerns, people who have not been dating for many years are often more anxious. Divorced people tend not only to feel that their dating skills are "rusty" but also to be less self-confident in approaching new relationships because they believe they "failed" in their marriages. Both divorced men and women may avoid dating altogether or marry on the rebound. Some parents who date frequently may feel guilty about being unavailable to their children (Montgomery et al., 1992).

Custodial mothers sometimes rush into a new marriage because they want their children to have a father figure and male model. Men may see mothers as less attractive dating partners because they don't want parental responsibilities, however. Although some custodial parents delay dating because they believe it will further disrupt their children's lives, some research suggests that delaying dating may increase rather than decrease future problems. In a longitudinal study of 57 remarried stepfather families with children aged 9 to 13, Montgomery et al. (1992) found that the more time children spent in a single-parent household, the more likely it was that a stepfather and his stepchildren would experience difficulties in their relationships.

It appears this happens because daily family routines become more and more entrenched as time goes by, and changing accepted routines and rules may be especially stressful for young adolescents (Montgomery et al., 1992). It may be less disruptive for children to move into a remarriage household relatively quickly after a divorce than to establish a stable single-parent household only to have that stability disrupted by another transition. In addition, divorced mothers often rely on their children, especially their daughters, for emotional support. The closer this dependency becomes, the more difficult it may be for a daughter to accept the loss of her role as her mother's confidante and supporter (see Chapter 15).

Perhaps because of such constraints, many divorced couples have very short dating and engagement periods (see Data Digest). Dating couples spend only half as much time dating and courting before remarriage—a median of seven months of dating and two months of engagement—as they do before a first marriage (O'Flaherty and Eells, 1988). Surprisingly, divorced people rarely take steps to ensure a more successful remarriage. For example, in a study of men and women who were preparing for remarriage, Ganong and Coleman (1989) found that only about 50 percent discussed their children from a previous marriage. Fewer than 25 percent said that they talked about financial matters, and 13 percent said they did not discuss any substantive issues at all.

Some people may rush through the courtship process because they feel they are running out of time or are desperate for financial or child-rearing help. Others may feel that they do not need as much time to get to know each other because they have learned how to avoid past mistakes. As you'll see later in this chapter, high redivorce rates show that such assumptions are often wrong.

Remarriage: Characteristics, Process, and Satisfaction

Many factors affect people's decision to remarry. They include age, sex, race, income, educational level, and the marital status of potential partners. As this section shows, these variables often interact to explain remarriage rates.

Age, Sex, and Race

The average divorced woman who remarries is 33 years old, and the average divorced man is 35 (Clarke, 1995a). As one might expect, the average age for men and women divorcing from their second or third marriage is higher because people are older (see Data Digest). Typically, both men and women have been divorced for about four years before remarrying the first time. The average duration of first marriages is approximately eight years compared to between five and six years for second marriages. Third marriages end about two years sooner than second marriages (Clarke, 1995a). Each remarriage, then, has a shorter duration because of no-fault divorce laws (see Chapter 15) and other variables, such as partners' realizing that they can survive a divorce.

In addition, remarriage rates decline with age for both men and women. Some partners find someone with whom they're happy. Other remarried couples have fewer marital conflicts because they don't have young children who don't want a stepfather or stepmother or because the couple marries when the children are on their own. Still others, especially women, may stay with a husband because they feel that they have few prospective partners and don't want to be alone in their aging years.

Men remarry more quickly and more often than women do. Because divorced men rarely have custody of their children, they are usually freer to socialize and to date. As you saw in Chapter 7, they also have a larger pool of eligible partners: Society deems it more acceptable for an older man to marry a younger woman than for an older woman to marry a younger man (see Chapters 4, 8, and 9). The women most likely to remarry are those who married at a relatively young age, who have few marketable skills, and who want a family (Wu, 1994).

Whites are more likely to remarry than other racial-ethnic groups, and blacks are the least likely to remarry. In 1990, for example (and the most recent year for which such data are available), remarriage rates were higher for white women than for black women and Latinas in every age group, and especially between the ages of 30 and 49 (see *Figure 16.2*). Blacks are also more likely than other groups to separate without divorcing and to stay single longer after a divorce (Ganong and Coleman, 1994). In particular, black women with low socioeconomic status stand to gain little from marriage to the partners who are available to them (see Chapter 9).

In general, the more money a divorced man has, the more likely he is to remarry. In the marriage market, men tend to be "worth more" than women of the same age because they are usually financially better off (see Chapters 9 and 10). Divorced women, on the other hand, frequently have severe financial problems (see Chapter 15). It is not surprising, then, that women with low incomes and lower educational levels are more likely to remarry than divorced women who are older, highly educated, and financially independent (Ganong and Coleman, 1994). For many divorced women, the surest way to escape poverty is to remarry (Folk et al., 1992).

In his Canadian study, Wu (1994) found that men with high educational attainment were more likely to remarry than their female counterparts. Wu notes that although women with higher socioeconomic standing are more eligible remarriage candidates and are likely to attract more desirable marriage partners, they have less to gain from remarriage because they are often economically independent. Moreover, highly educated women have a smaller pool of eligible mates because they may be unwilling to marry someone from a lower socioeconomic level.

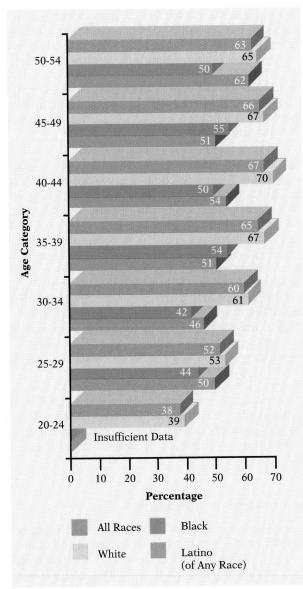

FIGURE 16.2 Women Who Remarried after Divorce, 1990. No percentages are gven for African American or Latina women in the 20 to 24 age category because the samples were too small. (Based on Norton and Miller, 1992, p. 3).

Marital Status

The majority of divorced men and women (61 percent) remarry other divorced people, 35 percent marry single men and women, and 4 percent marry widowed people (Wilson and Clarke, 1992). Widowers tend to remarry sooner than divorced men, probably because they have a more positive attitude toward married life, are economically secure, and have a large pool of marriage partners. Conversely, widows are slower to remarry. This may reflect the strong emotional attachment many

widows have to their deceased husbands. It may also reflect the fact that because widows are generally older than divorced women, they may be seen as less desirable by eligible men (Wu, 1994).

Among middle-aged widows, blacks and those with dependent children at home are less likely to remarry than whites or women who have no children (Smith et al., 1991). Some women, whether divorced or widowed, don't remarry because they "don't want to take care of a man at home" (see Chapter 9).

Other Variables

Other variables also affect remarriage decisions. For example, because the Catholic Church officially prohibits both divorce and remarriage, Catholics are less likely to remarry than Protestants (Wu, 1994). At the same time, the fact that the general divorce rate has been high for some time has created a large remarriage market for most people. Some people take advantage of this pool of eligible partners and remarry quickly. Others, especially men of higher socioeconomic status, may delay remarriage because there are many available women, many available younger women, and many younger women who exchange their youth and attractiveness for an older man's economic security (see Chapter 8).

How Do First Marriages and Remarriages Differ?

First marriages and remarriages differ in several important ways. The composition of the family tends to vary more in remarriages; role expectations are less defined; and family members in remarriages may be at different points in their life cycles. The combination of people from different original families, particularly the presence of children in remarriages, also creates certain kinds of problems. In addition, people who remarry may look specifically for partners who offer more than their first partners did.

Family Composition Remarriages often result in myriad new relationships and a dramatic change in family composition. Children may suddenly find themselves with **half-siblings**—brothers or sisters who share only one biological parent—stepsiblings, stepgrandparents, and a host of other relatives. As a result, the children's experiences may change radically. For example, they may have to share their biological parent's time, as well as their physical space, with stepsiblings. Listen to one 8-year-old:

We feel like guests in Jim's house. We are careful of what we do. It is like we are the intruders. And I feel very bad that we took Tommy's room. They fixed up a room for him in the basement, with posters and all, but he's still mad at us for taking his room. (Fishman and Hamel, 1981: 185)

Role Expectations The absence of normative role expectations for stepfamilies creates perplexing questions. For example, should stepparents have as much authority over children as the children's biological parents do? Should a noncustodial parent who has visitation rights have the same decision-making rights regarding his or her children as a custodial parent does? Should a child born to a remarriage have more legal rights than the stepchildren? And does the fact that few states have specific laws against marriage between stepchildren mean that such relationships are acceptable?

Life-Cycle Stages People who remarry sometimes find that they and their children are at different stages of the family life cycle. As a result, their goals may conflict with those of other family members. For example, a man with young adult children from his first marriage and who is planning for his retirement may marry a younger woman who is looking forward to starting a family. Or his new wife may be an older woman who has already raised her family and now looks forward to a career:

Claire and Sydney had been married for 4 years. Sydney had two adult children, ages 25 and 27, who had never lived with the couple, and Claire had a daughter who was 18 and in college. Sydney was a computer expert who had risen from working in the field as a technician to heading the marketing department for a large and successful electronics firm. He now had a month's vacation each year and looked forward to retirement in 10 years. Sydney wished to purchase a vacation home on a lake, as he had spent a number of years "dreaming about retiring there and fishing to his heart's content."

Claire, on the other hand, had gone to work at the telephone company to support herself and her daughter after her divorce. Now that she and Sydney were married, she had been able to return to school and study to be a nurse. She was employed at a local hospital, loved her work, and hoped to become a supervisor before long. She worked various shifts and had little time off. Claire's favorite way to relax was to read or knit . . . [but she also] liked to go dancing or to the movies in the evenings. Claire and Sydney worked out many of the stresses of their relationship arising from the joining of their two family groups, but they began to argue over weekend plans and future arrangements. (Visher and Visher, 1988: 161–62)

On the other hand, an older man may look forward to remarriage and a new set of biological children. If he's at the top of his career ladder and economically secure, for example, he has time to enjoy watching his "new" children grow up and participate in their upbringing. Also, the second (or third) wife who's much younger than he is might introduce the man to recreational activities (such as skiing or socializing with friends) that he missed during his first marriage because both spouses were struggling to pay bills and raise children.

Family Combinations Remarriage creates a unique set of issues because it combines people from at least two families. Imagine the transition process involved when a custodial mother marries a custodial father and the couple then decides to have their own children. Each partner's children from the former marriage may fear that new children will be loved more or receive more attention because they belong to both partners rather than just to one or the other. For their part, the parents may worry about dividing their attention among three sets of children so that none feels left out. To complicate matters further, ex-spouses and ex-grandparents may want to have input to the new family system—input that may not be welcomed by the remarried spouses.

Finally, remarriage partners sometimes seek someone who is more successful, more supportive, or more attractive than the ex-spouse. The box "Trophy Wives, Trophy Husbands in Remarriages" examines this phenomenon at the higher socioeconomic levels of American society.

Remarriage as a Process

Like divorce, remarriage is a process, but it is generally more complicated than divorce. For one thing, there are fewer social or legal guidelines for the remarried. If the husband's ailing mother wants to move in with her son, for example, should the second wife be willing to care for her? Or if the remarried couple didn't draw up a prenuptial agreement or a will and are killed in a car accident, should all of the children share in the estate, even though most of the estate came from one partner (Manners, 1993)? In addition, when problems arise that involve children from former marriages, should the remarried couple handle these issues? The children's biological parent or parents? Both biological and remarried partners?

The remarriage process may involve as many as six stages, similar to Bohannon's six stations of divorce (Goetting, 1982; see also Chapter 15). Like Bohannon's stages of divorce, the stages of remarriage aren't necessarily sequential, and not every couple goes through all of them or with the same intensity. If partners can deal successfully with each stage, they are more likely to emerge with a new identity as a couple.

CHANGES

Trophy Wives, Trophy Husbands in Remarriages

Fortune magazine ran a cover story on the "trophy wives" for whom, the story said, chief executive officers (CEOs) were trading in their loyal, self-sacrificing, matronly, child-rearing wives. The newer, younger, and flashier trophy wives were sexier and socially adept. They pampered their husbands and never criticized them, spent money on these men rather than hoarding it for "the children's education," and generally made the CEOs feel like kings of the castle.

According to the *Fortune* article, second wives were enticing for a number of reasons. They were younger and thinner than the first wife and bolstered the man's corporate image of being successful both professionally and sexually. Because many of these women were successful in their own right (many were well educated and had thriving small businesses of their own), they enhanced the man's status without overshadowing his success. The trophy wives also spent a lot of time on looking good. Nancy Brinker, 42, the third wife of Norman Brinker, 58, who founded the Steak and Ale and

Bennigan's restaurant chains and who was the CEO of Chili's restaurant chain, said, "I work out one hour a day at aerobics, I diet rigorously, and I play polo with my husband. . . . Norman likes me to look good" (Connelly, 1989: 54).

Unlike the first wife, who is busy caring for the children, the trophy wife has the time and connections to improve her husband's reputation: "She totes him to small dinner parties, opera galas, museum benefits, and auctions for worthy causes, having secured the invitations by serving on various committees and getting her husband to cough up something suitable in the way of a donation" (p. 54).

Most important, the trophy wife has the advantage of being glamorous, independent, and available because she is not saddled with the husband's children: "The CEO now wants a playmate, someone who is free to travel with him and have fun" (p. 61). The husband can play father when he wants to, rather than when he must. His children need not interfere in his or his trophy wife's economic or romantic life:

"Having pots of money may ease the burden of not being there because the CEO can afford to fly the kids out to see him and go on exciting vacations with them" (p. 61).

More recently, Finke (1994) has suggested that a handful of successful women are now seeking trophy husbands in *their* second or third marriage: "The basic criterion is this: No matter how successful a woman is in her profession, he is at least her equal, and maybe her better. He has three or more of the five attributes that tend to accompany achievement: fame, prestige, power, brains, and money" (pp. 37, 39). For example, when television news star Diane Sawyer married Academy Award–winning director Mike Nichols, the media circles claimed that "they hadn't so much wed as 'acquired' each other." Further, "Kennedy cousin Maria Shriver brought home perhaps the only thing she could find bigger than her famous family—Arnold Schwarzenegger" (p. 40).

Do trophy wives and trophy husbands characterize only the rich and celebrities? Or have such remarriages occurred among people you know?

Emotional Remarriage   The *emotional remarriage* is often a slow process in which a divorced person reestablishes a bond of attraction, commitment, and trust. Because many people feel inadequate after a divorce, this process often involves a fear that the new emotional investment will also lead to loss and rejection. These feelings may make the emotional remarriage a painful or volatile process.

Psychic Remarriage   Through the process of *psychic remarriage* people change their identities from individuals to couples once more. Because social status and personal identity are relatively independent of marital status for many men, a shift in marital status does not represent an extreme change in personal identity for them. Since the marital scene has traditionally been seen as the woman's domain, the identify shift for

a woman may be more difficult. For a traditional woman, the psychic remarriage represents the recovery of a valued identity as a wife. A nontraditional woman for whom the role of wife is less important, however, may worry about the loss of her highly valued independence and freedom.

Community Remarriage   People must often make changes in their community of friends when they remarry. This *community remarriage* may be a turbulent process because unmarried friends, especially friends of the opposite sex, are typically lost and replaced by married or remarried couples who are friends with both members of the new couple. During the community remarriage stage, close personal ties that were established after a divorce may be severed. Thus, although the community divorce represents reentrance into the

Filling the role of stepparent may be easier when stepchildren are grown than when they are very young.

"normal" world of a married couple's common friends, it may also mean the loss of valuable friendships.

Parental Remarriage The *parental remarriage* involves developing relationships between one partner and the children of the new spouse. If the children's other biological parent still plays an active role in their lives, the stepparent may have many hurdles to overcome. He or she cannot assume the role of either father or mother but must behave as a nonparent, deferring to the biological parent's rights. The stepparent and the biological parent generally share in making the residential, educational, financial, health, and moral decisions that affect the children. Because there are no guidelines for this formal cooperation, the parental remarriage stage can lead to confusion and frustration for parents and children.

In some families, biological nonresidential fathers may step aside as stepfathers move in. In their national study of different family forms, for example, Acock and Demo (1994) found that children in divorced families averaged three weeks per year staying with their nonresidential father, compared to a little more than one week per year for children in stepfamilies. If divorced fathers live close to their biological children, however, they maintain ties through telephone calls or visits. And the higher the father's educational level, the more likely he is to maintain close relationships with these children (Cooksey and Craig, 1998).

Another difficulty in this stage is that remarried couples often fail to work out their expectations of each other as marital partners before they have to take on major responsibilities within marriage, such as child rearing. Particularly when one or both partners have children from previous marriages, there may be little time to develop workable and comfortable marital relationships and to establish a primary husband–wife bond before the arrival of children. Instead, both marital and parental roles must be assumed simultaneously, and this may encourage the inappropriate involvement of children in marital dissension. For example, the biological parent's prior relationship to his or her child can threaten the establishment of a primary husband–wife bond. This, in turn, may detract from the integration of the new family unit.

Economic Remarriage The *economic remarriage* is the reestablishment of a marital household as an economically productive unit. The main problems in this stage stem from the existence of children from a former marriage. The economic behavior of the remarried couple and that of the ex-spouse(s) are often interrelated. For example, a biological father's child-support payments may become sporadic once a custodial mother has remarried. Many stepfamilies can't predict how much money will be available from month to month because of the uncertainty of such payments.

Another source of economic instability is the unpredictable nature of the needs of the husband's children, who typically live with their biological mother. The possibility of unexpected expenses, such as dentists' and doctors' fees, can cast a shadow over the biological father's remarriage. And there may be disagreements about the distribution of resources: If *his* daughter is taking ballet lessons, should he also pay for *her* son's tennis lessons? If the noncustodial parent is not honoring child-custody payments, should the stepparent provide the money for recreational, educational, and social expenses for the children?

Legal Remarriage   Remarriage does not mean that a person exchanges one family for another. Instead, she or he takes on an *additional* family. Because legal responsibilities have not been defined, people are left to struggle with many problems on their own (Ramsey, 1994). For example, the *legal remarriage* raises such questions as which wife deserves a man's life and accident insurance, medical coverage, retirement benefits, pension rights, and property holdings. Do these legal rights belong to the former wife, who played a major role in building the estate, or to the current wife? Which children should a remarried father support—especially in such high-priced endeavors as providing a college education—his, hers, or theirs?

State laws rarely recognize the rights or responsibilities of stepparents. State laws do not require that stepparents provide for their stepchildren, for example. If the marriage ends, the stepparent currently has no legal standing to ask for custody of visitation. Instead, the courts rule on such petitions one by one. Schools and other public institutions typically don't recognize the stepparent as a legitimate parent. School registration forms, field trip permission slips, and health emergency information are required or requested of biological parents, not stepparents. "The message, whether intended or not, has been that only biological parents count" (Herbert, 1999: 67). Even when there is a will, many state inheritance laws do not recognize the existence of stepchildren. In most states, stepchildren may have to go to court and battle biological children even when a stepparent has left the estate or other assets to a stepchild (Mason and Mauldon, 1996).

Goetting notes that each stage of remarriage may be further complicated if one or both partners is still adjusting to his or her divorce. Some people begin the stages of remarriage without having completed the stages of divorce.

How Satisfying Is Remarriage?

A popular song tells us that "love is better the second time around." But as you've seen, remarriages must often deal with more complicated issues than first marriages. Are second and third marriages more stable?

Marital Stability   The duration of second and third marriages is shorter than the duration of first marriages. A recent nationwide study suggests, however, that when age is factored in, second marriages may be more stable than first marriages. That is, the most stable marriages seem to be remarriages between people who were 45 years of age or older and in which *both* partners had been married before. Older couples may

choose their second mates more carefully, have more resources to make the marriage work, and/or are reluctant to divorce again (Clarke and Wilson, 1994).

Why, in general, do remarried people divorce? There are several possible reasons. People who marry for the first time during their teenage years are more likely to divorce after a second marriage (Wilson and Clarke, 1992). This may reflect a lack of problem-solving skills or immaturity in dealing with marital conflict. Booth and Edwards (1992) described the people most likely to divorce again as those who saw divorce as a remedy for marital dissatisfaction. They married for the first time as teens, and they often felt estranged from their parents and their spouse's parents. The researchers also noted that the presence of stepchildren was related to high redivorce rates. If a woman has a child between marriages, she is more likely to divorce. Intermarital birth (giving birth between marriages) may force a newly married couple to cope with an infant rather than devote time to their relationship (Wineberg, 1991).

Marital Quality   The data on marital satisfaction are mixed. Although people in first marriages reported greater satisfaction than did remarried spouses, the differences were "certainly not substantial" (Vemer et al., 1989). Reviewing the remarriage literature, Coleman and Ganong (1991) came to a similar conclusion, that there were very few differences between the two groups. If, especially, the remarried parents have a stable relationship and the mother feels that the children's life is going well, remarried mothers benefit psychologically from remarriage and are happier than divorced mothers (Demo and Acock, 1996b).

In other studies, remarried couples reported less marital satisfaction than their nondivorced first-marriage counterparts. The more negative interactions in remarried couples are probably due to the stress and change with the new marriage and forming the stepfamily. In the first few years of marriage, this effect could reflect deficient communication and problem-solving skills that resulted in a previous divorce. In remarriages that have lasted up to seven years, marital relationships may suffer due to the increased stress and dealing with the behavior problems of young adolescents (Bray, 1999).

Internal Family Dynamics   Besides family structure and composition, the internal dynamics of the remarried couple also affect marital satisfaction. According to Ihinger-Tallman and Pasley (1987), the instability of a remarriage may reflect failure in one of four main areas: commitment, cohesion, communication, and the maintenance of the family's boundaries.

People may fail to make a *commitment* to a remarriage because, having survived one divorce, they may feel that another divorce is a ready remedy for an unhappy marriage; thus they may exert less effort to make the remarriage work. They may be unwilling to invest the time and energy necessary to try to resolve problems. Or one or both partners may have personal and/or emotional problems. For example, alcoholics, drug users, those who are physically violent, or those who are emotionally unstable are more likely to move in and out of marriage repeatedly.

Achieving *cohesion,* or developing ties that hold the family together, requires time and effort. Merging two families is difficult because the members have no shared family history. To reduce conflict, family members may have to develop new rules (how many phone calls each member may make in an evening, or by what hour the children must be home) and redistribute resources (who may use the family car and when, or how much each child will receive as an allowance).

Communication is also important. Particularly if lack of communication was a problem in one or both partner's previous marriages, couples may have to break old habits and learn to interact with each other differently. Establishing effective communication may be especially difficult if children from a former marriage are part of the new family, in part because the couple has less time and privacy to cultivate new communication patterns.

Finally, remarried couples must deal with more *boundary-maintenance* issues than do people in first marriages. For example, people in remarriages often have to insulate themselves against undue interference from outside sources, such as ex-spouses and in-laws from the first marriage. Furthermore, as I have already noted, remarried couples have to spend more effort establishing boundaries with new family members and new relatives, especially if one of the partners is a custodial parent.

Stepfamilies Are Diverse and Complex

When a stepfamily is formed, new family networks emerge. These new networks are often traced through a **genogram,** or a diagram showing the biological relationships among family members. Look at *Figure 16.3.* This genogram presents a picture of the possible family systems when two people who have been married before and have children from previous marriages marry each other.

Stepfamilies can vary in terms of parent–child relationships. There are three common types of stepfamilies. In the **biological mother–stepfather family,** all the children are biological children of the mother and stepchildren of the father. In the **biological father–stepmother family,** all the children are biological children of the father and stepchildren of the mother. In the

FIGURE 16.3 **Stepfamily Networks.** Each set of parents of our target couple, Bill and Maria, are grandparents to at least two sets of children. For example, Maria's parents are the grandparents of her children with her former husband, Bob—Billy, Mario, and Linda—and of her child with Bill—Joy. Depending on the closeness of the relationship Bill maintains with his former wife, Althea, however, Maria's parents might play a grandparental role to Peter and Julian, Bill and Althea's boys, as well (Based on Everett and Everett, 1994, p. 132).

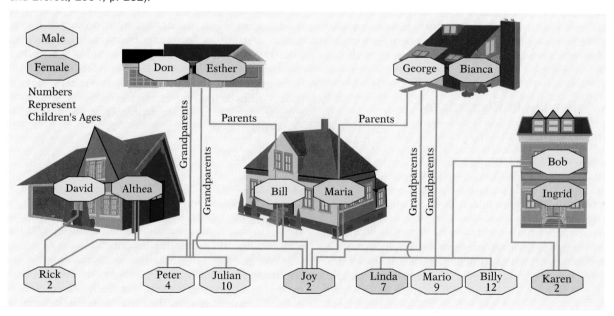

joint biological–stepfamily, at least one child is the biological child of both parents, at least one child is the biological child of only one parent and the stepchild of the other parent, and no other type of child is present.

Stepfamilies can get more complicated. The term *complex stepfamily* describes a family in which both adults have children from previous marriages. But there are even more intricate relationships. For example, in joint step-adoptive families and joint biological-step-adoptive families, at least one child is a biological child of one parent and a stepchild of the other parent and one or both parents have adopted at least one child. Nor does "complex stepfamily" take account of relationships among cohabitants, one or both of whom have been married before and have children from earlier relationships, even though such cohabitants often consider themselves stepfamilies. The concept of stepfamily could also be expanded to include the increasingly common situation in which an unmarried mother and her child move in with a man who is not the child's biological father (Cherlin and Furstenberg, 1994).

Gay and lesbian stepfamilies share the problems of all other stepfamilies, but these problems are often exacerbated by the parent's and stepparent's sexual orientation. Berger (1998) posits that lesbian and gay stepfamilies encounter "triple stigmatization." First, they are stigmatized for their homosexuality, which is viewed by many people as an immoral "lifestyle." Second, gay and lesbian stepfamilies are still seen as deficient compared to nuclear families. Last, gay parenthood is often stigmatized by the nonparental homosexual community, especially by gay men, because "the gay culture tends to emphasize primacy of the couple relationship" rather than parenting (p. 153).

Despite these obstacles, there is some evidence that lesbian stepfamilies are resilient and as diverse as heterosexual stepfamilies. According to Wright (1998), for example, lesbian stepfamilies reflect three distinct stepparent roles. In the *co-parent family,* the nonbiological mother is a helper and supporter of and consultant to the biological mother, an active parent of the children, and a dedicated and committed family member. The *stepmother family* parallels heterosexual stepmother families. That is, the lesbian stepmother does most of the traditional mothering kinds of tasks, but the biological mother (like the biological father in heterosexual families) retains most of the decision-making power. In the *co-mother family,* both mothers have equal rights and responsibilities in everyday decisions and child-rearing tasks.

Stereotypes about Stepfamilies

The myth of the evil stepmother, perpetuated in Western culture by such classic tales as *Cinderella* and *Snow White,* still exists (Ganong and Coleman, 1997;

"You're right, I should spend more time with the kids. Which ones are ours?"

Medical Economics/January 25, 1993.

Kheshgi-Genovese and Genovese, 1997). This myth, which presents stepmothers as cruel and unloving people who abuse or even try to get rid of their unwanted stepchildren, has had ripple effects over time so that many people have come to view the whole idea of the stepfamily with a jaundiced eye. In several studies, for example, college students had more negative evaluations of stepparents than of biological, adoptive, or widowed parents (Bryan et al., 1986; Schwebel et al., 1991). These negative images persist even though many stepmothers neither wish nor expect to replace the stepchild's mother (Orchard and Solberg, 1999).

In contrast, the more recent "myth of instant love" maintains not only that remarriage creates an instant family but that stepmothers will automatically love their stepchildren. In the *Sound of Music,* for example, Julie Andrews wins the affections of the von Trapp children within a few months. Remarried parents, especially women, expect instant love because—according to another myth, discussed in Chapter 11—mothering comes easily and naturally to all women (see Quick et al., 1994, for a summary of the research on negative images of stepmothers).

Members of a newly constituted family who confront both of these myths may experience considerable stress as they try to adapt to new personalities, new lifestyles, and new schedules and routines (Dainton, 1993). And considering the unrealistic views that people hold of the intact nuclear family (see the section on Myths about Marriage and the Family in Chapter 1), it is not surprising that the stepfamily suffers by comparison (Gamache, 1997).

One reason for the persistence of such negative attitudes is the limited knowledge most people have about stepfamilies. A study of marriage-and-family textbooks noted that the accounts were generally based not on empirical data but on clinical work with people in distress or on popular, self-help source materials. The latter have implied, however subtly, that stepfamilies are rarely successful (Nolan et al., 1984). A more recent article (Coleman et al., 1994) saw some improvement in textbook coverage of remarriage and stepfamilies but noted that the texts still focus largely on problems rather than on the potential strengths of stepfamilies or on the positive outcomes of such family mergers.

The power of myths and unsubstantiated beliefs can be seen in the fact that adults often enter relationships with stepchildren with unrealistic expectations. Many stepmothers have one of three common misconceptions about stepmothering: (1) The stepchildren will have little impact on the new marriage; (2) we will all be one big, happy family; or (3) we will both love our stepchildren as though they were our own (Burns, 1985).

A woman who grew up believing that a stepmother is inevitably bad may try to become a "super stepmom." She may be especially frustrated if her stepchildren rebel despite all her efforts and mothering. By the same token, a child who grew up with the same ideas about stepmothers may have negative expectations and refrain from developing a positive relationship. Thus, a self-perpetuating cycle is often set in motion. The children expect the stepmother to be nasty and will stay aloof. Their unpleasant behavior may cause the stepmother to become more demanding and critical (Berger, 1998).

Many men also have unrealistic expectations of their new families. According to Pill (1990), in 41 percent of stepfamilies in the study, one or both partners said that they had entered remarried life expecting that their stepfamily would become as close as a nuclear family. Many of the couples reported disappointment and astonishment when the everyday realities of stepfamily life were fraught with problems.

Characteristics of Stepfamilies

Stepfamilies may look like intact nuclear families because they are composed of married adults and children living in the same household. They differ from nondivorced families in many ways, however.

1. Stepfamilies have a complex structure.
It bears repeating that stepfamilies create new roles: stepparents, stepsiblings, half-siblings, stepgrandparents. It is important to recognize that this structure does not make stepfamilies better or worse than nuclear families; they are simply *different*. As *Figure 16.4* shows, the majority of

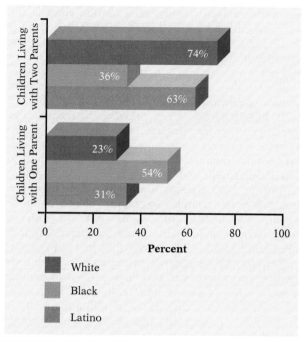

FIGURE 16.4 **Living Arrangements of Children Under 18 Years Old: 1998**

SOURCE: Based on Lugaila, 1998.

white and Latino children live with two parents. Many of these homes are stepfamilies. An estimated 23 percent of children live in married two-parent stepfamilies. This percentage rises to 30 percent if we include children who live with a cohabiting parent (Bumpass et al., 1995).

Stepfamilies offer the possibility for many different kinds of relationships, including relationships with uncles, aunts, and cousins. Ties between stepgrandparents and their stepgrandchildren range from no contact to close relationships, depending largely on the investment that stepgrandparents make (Cherlin and Furstenberg, 1994).

2. A stepfamily must cope with unique tasks.
The stepparent may struggle to overcome rejection because the children may still be grieving over the breakup of the biological family, or the stepparent may disagree with the biological parent about discipline and the enforcement of rules (Papernow, 1984).

One of the most common tasks is redefining, and sometimes renegotiating, family boundaries. This may include making "visiting" children feel welcome, as well as working out "turf" problems:

Consider the stepfamily in which the husband's three children rejoined the household every 3–4 days for a few days' time. The house was small,

It is important in stepfamilies to make sure that all the children receive love and attention. If signs of jealousy appear, both parents should listen to their children's concerns and try to understand.

and the mother's three children who lived in the household had to shift where they slept, where they put their clothes, and where they could go to relax or to be alone in order to make the available space accommodate the extra family members. Bedrooms became dormitories, and the continual chaos created tension and instability for everyone. (Visher and Visher, 1993: 241)

In such situations, it is not easy to develop clear and consistent rules about "property rights" so that there is a stable place for each family member.

3. Stepfamilies often experience more stress and conflict than nuclear families.

As the previous example illustrates, much of the stress in stepfamilies is caused by ambiguity and the "lack of fit" with cultural norms that, however unrealistic, define the "ideal" family. Ambiguity may decrease as family members adjust to new roles and lifestyles, and the sense that the family doesn't fit the ideal model may lose its intensity as family functioning improves.

A major source of tension is the fact that family members must adjust to each other all at once rather than gradually, as in a nuclear family. Stress may come from several sources. More people make more demands; parents may differ on how to discipline children; one partner may feel excluded from the relationship between her or his spouse and the spouse's biological children; or there may not be enough resources to meet the larger family's needs (Whitsett and Land, 1992).

4. It typically takes years, rather than months, to achieve satisfactory stepfamily integration.

The age and sex of the children, as well as the type of stepfamily (stepmother, stepfather, and children from both previous marriages), can affect adjustment. As the box "The Stepfamily Cycle" suggests, it may take as long as seven years (some say ten) for a couple to consolidate their family and to work as a team. And if they have a new baby, or if there are unexpected problems such as unemployment or a death in the family, the process may take even longer.

5. Important relationships may be cut off or end abruptly while others spring up overnight.

As you saw in Chapter 15, many fathers have no contact with their children after a divorce. Furthermore, siblings are sometimes split between parents and may rarely see one another. Children are especially distressed if a biological parent's wedding announcement comes as a surprise:

One divorced father awakened his children one morning, asked them to get dressed, and drove them to the courthouse where he married a woman they had only recently met. The children were shocked and felt betrayed that they were not allowed to know that their father was serious about this woman and wanted to marry her. The woman also had a child, so that by 10 P.M. these children went to bed in a house that now included a new stepmother and a new stepsister. The children were not happy about it. (Knox and Leggett, 1998: 184)

CHANGES

The Stepfamily Cycle

Clinician Patricia Papernow (1993: 70–231) divides the process of becoming a stepfamily into three major stages. The early stage is characterized by fantasies, confusion, and slowly getting to know the others; in the middle stage the family begins to restructure; and in the late stage the family achieves its own identity.

The Early Stages: Getting Started without Getting Stuck

Stage 1: Fantasy. Most remarrying couples start out not only with the fantasy that they will love the children of the person they love and be loved by them but that they will be welcomed into a ready-made family. They see themselves as filling empty spots for the children, for their spouses, and for themselves.

Children in new stepfamilies, too, have fantasies, a mixture of hope and fear. Some children still hope that their biological parents will reunite. Or they may fear losing or injuring one of their own parents if they come to love a stepparent.

Stage 2: Immersion. Chaos and confusion often characterize this stage. Familiarity and strangeness continually clash, but the problems are seen differently by biological parents, children, and stepparents. Stepparents may feel left out of the biological parent–child unit and may experience jealousy, resentment, and inadequacy.

The biological parent is often caught in the middle. Some exhaust themselves trying to meet everyone's needs and make the stepfamily work; others try to deny the difficulties. Particularly in the latter case, the children may feel lost and ignored. Some children respond with tears and angry outbursts; others withdraw.

Stage 3: Awareness. Members of the stepfamily get to know each other and "map the territory" of each family member. Stepparents can learn about the children's likes and dislikes, their friends, and their memories without trying to influence the children. Biological parents can articulate how much change his or her children can tolerate and to try to find the right balance between overprotecting children and asking too much of them. Children should be encouraged to look at the positive aspects of the stepfamily, such as the love both parents offer, or want to offer, them.

The Middle Stages: Restructuring the Family

Stage 4: Mobilization. It is in this critical stage that many stepfamilies fall apart. The stepparent's task is to identify a few important changes that matter (such as establishing family meetings to deal with difficult issues) and make a sustained effort to communicate these to other family members while respecting the biological unit. The biological parent's task is to voice the needs of her or his children and ex-spouse while supporting and empathizing with the stepparent's concerns. Children may voice their own needs to ease the pressures of their conflicting loyalties.

Stage 5: Action. In this stage, the stepfamily can begin to make larger moves to reorganize its structure by making some truly joint decisions about how the family will operate. The stepparent begins to play a more active role in the family, and the biological parent doesn't feel the pressure to be all things to all people. Both parents work together as a team in making decisions and carving time out for themselves.

The Later Stages: Solidifying the Stepfamily

Stage 6: Contact. In this stage, family members begin to interact more easily. There is less withdrawal and more recognition of each other's efforts when things go right. The stepparent has become a firm insider in the adult couple relationship, and has begun to forge a more intimate, authentic relationship with at least some of the stepchildren.

Stage 7: Resolution. Relationships begin to feel comfortable. The stepparent role is now well defined and solid. Stepparents become mentors to some of their stepchildren. Other stepparent–stepchild relationships have reached a mutually suitable distance. The adult stepcouple has become a sanctuary, a place to turn for empathy, support, and cooperative problem solving. The stepfamily finally has a sense of character and its own identity.

According to both researchers and clinicians, children should be given plenty of notice about an impending marriage. The new partner and the children should get to know each other over a year or two, go on vacations and have meals together, and just "hang around the house," getting to know each other (Bray and Kelly, 1998; Knox and Leggett, 1998).

6. **There are continual transitions instead of stability.** In a stepfamily, the cast of characters living in a household can change continuously. The boundaries between who is a member of a stepfamily and who is not are not always clear: Is the new spouse of a child's noncustodial parent a part of the child's family? And who decides this question?

Many families agree to "permeable boundaries" so that children can see both of their biological parents and can move easily between households, not only when they are still young but also when they are adults. If each adult child has parents who are divorced or remarried, there may be some difficulty in juggling individual needs, family traditions, and emotional ties among as many as four families.

7. **Stepfamilies are less cohesive than nuclear or single-parent households.**

Stepchildren often feel closer to biological parents than to stepparents. As children grow up, they may also feel alienated because of differential economic support (for example, if some children are supported during college and others are not), unequal favors (at least as they perceive them) bestowed by grandparents, and inheritance inequities.

8. **Stepfamilies need great flexibility in terms of their everyday behavior.**

Varying custody and residential arrangements require different daily or weekly routines. Moreover, within the household, the "expected" ways a family operates may not apply. For example, when one stepfamily with children from two former families found it beneficial for the children to eat separately from the adults and for the adults to spend Saturdays doing something without the children, they were labeled a "bad" stepfamily. Creativity and flexibility provide family members with the time and space—both physical and psychological—that they need to develop and grow.

The need for creativity and variety may decrease over time, but situations often arise (such as weddings, births, deaths, and holidays) that may require unusual solutions and arrangements. Should a noncustodial father who rarely visits his children pay for his daughter's wedding, or should her stepfather pay for it? Or, if both the biological and stepfather are important in a young woman's life, who should walk down the aisle with her at her wedding? Both of them?

9. **Stepfamily members must rid themselves of unrealistic expectations.**

Stepfamilies often compare themselves to biological families and have expectations that are idealized or naive. There is no reason why members of the family—aside from the newly married adults—should automatically feel any sort of familial relation to one another. They need to accept that it is physically and emotionally impossible for a stepfamily to try to mirror a biological family; there are simply too many players and too many new relationships. As you saw in the box on "The Stepfamily Cycle," stepfamilies must forge their own rules and identities.

Sometimes a new baby creates stress in a stepfamily, but when the children from former marriages are adolescents or young adults, family members often adapt well to the new relationships.

10. **There is no shared family history.**

The new stepfamily is a group of individuals who must develop meaningful, shared experiences. To do this, they must learn one another's patterns of communication (verbal and nonverbal) and interaction. New stepfamily members often speak of "culture shock": When their own behavioral patterns and those of others in the household are different, they sometimes feel as if they are in an alien environment. For example, mealtimes and the meals themselves may be different from the past.

One way to ease some of the strangeness is to mesh rituals. In one remarried family, when a major holiday was approaching, family members were asked to suggest favorite foods. By preparing and serving these dishes the new family honors the traditions of the previous families (Imber-Black and Roberts, 1993).

11. **There are many loyalty conflicts.**

Although questions of loyalty arise in all families, loyalty conflicts in stepfamilies are intensified. For example, suppose a child in the stepfamily feels closer to the noncustodial parent or to that parent's new spouse than to the biological and custodial

sexuality with stepchildren

parent or that parent's new spouse. Should these relationships be nurtured despite the resentment of the custodial parent or stepparent?

Furthermore, a newly remarried adult must make a sustained effort to maintain loyalty to a new spouse despite loyalty to biological children. For example, when Gwen, who had lived with her mother and stepfather for nine years and then lived on her own while attending college, came back home for a time, her mother felt conflicted:

Hugh [Gwen's stepfather] wants her to pay rent. I don't want her to. I feel that at this point in her life I would be a little more lenient than Hugh is. A lot of the difficulty is that she's been away for five years and now she's back in the fold. Hugh's a very rigid person—everything is preplanned and set up that way and that's the way you do it. I'm a little more loose. (Beer, 1992: 133)

Gwen's mother's task was to find ways to help her daughter that did not diminish her loyalty to her husband. Had her husband been as "loose" as she was, adjustment might have been easier for this stepfamily.

12. **Stepfamily roles are often ambiguous.**
On the one hand, a positive aspect of role ambiguity is that it provides freedom of choice: One may be able to choose among a variety of roles played with different children and adults. For example, a stepparent who is willing to be a friend to the children rather than a parent can serve as a mediator when there is conflict between the children and the biological, custodial parent. On the other hand, ambiguity creates problems because people don't know what's expected of them or what to expect from others. A partner may want a spouse who offers support, not mediation, when there are disagreements with the children.

The Dynamics of Merging Two Households

Besides dealing with role ambiguity, most stepfamilies encounter a number of tasks in merging two households after a remarriage. Some of the most common issues include a lack of institutional support, distributing family resources, integrating the children into the family, establishing discipline and authority, helping children adjust to the new family form, and developing intergenerational relationships.

Institutional Support The English language has fairly clear terms for defining relationships in intact families, such as "father," "mother," "brother," and "daughter." There are no words for many stepfamily relationships, however. For example, "my spouse's ex-spouse's new spouse" or "my stepsister's stepbrother"

require most people to stop and think for several minutes before they can understand what is meant (Beer, 1992).

Why is the lack of stepfamily terminology problematic? Suppose, for example, that a new wife's own children want to call their stepfather "Dad," but the stepfather's biological children, their security threatened, refuse to permit this? Bad feelings may result all around. Moreover, according to Beer (1992: 11), "It may be difficult to think clearly about a relationship when the words to describe it are inaccurate or when there is no word at all. Being unable to think clearly may make it more difficult to decide how to behave." In contrast to English, many other languages have specific terms for stepfamily members. In Spanish, for example, there's *padrastro* (stepfather), *madrastra* (stepmother), *hermanastro* (stepbrother), *hermanastra* (stepsister), *hijastra* (stepdaughter), and *hijastro* (stepson).

One stepmother was uncomfortable with her three young stepchildren's calling her by her first name (as her husband does) because it seemed impersonal and disrespectful. Here's her solution:

I did not want to confuse the children by asking them to call me "Mom," since they already have a mother. So, I came up with a name that worked—"Smom." It's now a year later, and the kids are completely comfortable calling me Smom. Even my husband's ex-wife calls me that. Sometimes, the kids have variations, like "Smommy" or "Smama." I'm happy, they're happy. (Ann Landers, 2000: C11)

The law is also inadequate in regulating or guiding families after remarriage. For example, most states prohibit sexual relations between siblings and between parents and children in nuclear, biological families but have no restrictions about sexual relations between members of a stepfamily—either between stepchildren or between a stepparent and a stepchild. As we discussed in Chapter 14, there is considerable research evidence that some stepfathers and male cohabitants abuse children sexually. An estimated 30 percent of all cases of adult–child sexual abuse involve a stepfather (Levine, 1990). Also, stepsiblings may drift into romantic relationships, which can lead to serious problems within the stepfamily. As the box "Dealing with Sexual Boundaries in the Stepfamily" suggests, one way to cope with such sexual problems is to prevent them in the first place.

Distributing Resources Financial matters are more complicated in stepfamilies than in first marriages. Financial planners and marriage experts are nearly unanimous in urging people who are planning a second marriage to spell out their financial obligations to each other in a legally binding prenuptial agreement.

CHOICES

Dealing with Sexual Boundaries in the Stepfamily

Only some states prohibit romantic relationships between nonbiologically related members of a stepfamily. The weakened incest taboo within the stepfamily makes rules less clear (Bloomfield and Kory, 1993), but sexual liaisons can create confusion, anger, and a sense of betrayal. Practitioners Emily and John Visher (1982: 162–66) offer the following suggestions to remarried partners for dealing with sexuality in the stepfamily:

- Be affectionate and tender but not passionate with each other when the children are with you. Teenagers are particularly sensitive to open displays of affection because of their own emerging sexuality. Be aware of this sensitivity and forgo the stolen kisses and embraces in the kitchen.
- Don't be sexually provocative. Walking around in undershorts or a bra and panties are guaranteed not to keep sexuality under control in your household, even when only younger children are around. Set a limit on teenagers' behaving in provocative ways. The first time a

teenager parades around the house scantily or inappropriately clad, for example, he or she should be told firmly to go back to his or her room and to dress properly. Be firm in setting limits for appropriate dress and behavior.
- Avoid roughhousing with children after they are 10 or 11 years old. This kind of behavior may become a physical turn-on between stepsiblings or between children and stepparents.
- Relinquish some forms of intimate behavior with children after they turn 10 or 11 years of age. For example, sitting on a stepfather's lap and showering him with kisses is inappropriate behavior for a teenage stepdaughter.
- If a teenager develops a crush on a stepparent, talk to him or her openly. Discuss the nature of crushes. Point out that the teen's affections are misplaced (for example, you're married to his or her parent). Suggest alternatives, such as schoolmates. Finally, make it clear that there is a big difference between feelings and behavior, that just

because people are attracted to others does not mean that they act on their impulses.
- When you and your partner are having an argument or there is some emotional distance between you, don't turn for emotional support to a younger person in the household. You may open the door to the expression of feelings of intimacy that ought not be encouraged. Instead, keep the lines of communication open between you and your partner.
- Rearrange the living space to cool off a sexual situation between stepsiblings. For example, avoid adjoining bedrooms and rearrange the bathroom sharing so that older children have both privacy and less temptation.
- Do not tolerate sexual involvement in your home. In one family, the adults asked the college-aged son to move out of the house because they were unwilling to accept his sexual relationship with his stepsister. Although stepparents can't control sexual attractions between stepsiblings, they can control what happens in their home.

The issues to be resolved include whether to share financial responsibility for children from previous marriages, how to divide up estates, whether to merge assets and liabilities, and how to divide property acquired before and after the marriage in case of divorce (Rowland, 1994; see also Appendix F).

The rules that control disposition of an estate vary from state to state, but almost everywhere, the spouse is entitled to a major share, from 25 to 50 percent. And no matter where you live, federal law says the spouse is the sole beneficiary of your company pension or profit-sharing plan, both of which may be the major portion of an estate. Unless there is a prenuptial agreement that allows a future spouse to waive his or her rights to a set share of an estate, children from a previous marriage may be practically disinherited even though this was not the intention of the parent (Spears, 1994). Moreover, biological children may

resent their inheritance being divided with stepsiblings (Cleaver, 1999).

Legal experts also advise setting up a trust fund to safeguard the biological children's or grandchildren's inheritance. Trusts allow parents to transmit gifts and inheritances to whomever they choose while they are alive or after their death. In addition, to minimize family friction, attorneys advise people to discuss their estate plans with those who are affected by them (Spears, 1994).

The partners must decide whether or not to pool their resources and how to do so. They may experience stress and resentment if there are financial obligations to a former family (such as custody awards, mortgage payments, or outstanding debts). There may also be conflict about whose children should be supported at college or how wills should be written (whether the common property should be divided equally between

Children may feel anger and hostility when a parent or stepparent must go to court over such things as support payments owed by a child's biological father.

the two families or among the children). Disagreements may range from seemingly petty issues like how much should be spent for relatives' birthday and wedding presents to drastically different attitudes about whether money should be saved or spent.

Because men typically have more economic resources than women do, stepfathers may have more decision-making power in the new family. Sometimes men use money to control the children's and spouse's behavior ("If you don't shape up, you can pay for your own car insurance next time"). This kind of manipulation creates hostility. The children of remarried fathers are typically at a financial disadvantage if they live with their biological mothers because the stepchildren living with their remarried father may receive more support, such as loans, money gifts, and health coverage (White, 1992; see also Aquilino, 1994). The loss of economic support can impoverish biological children and produce hostility.

Resources such as time, space, and affection must also be allocated and distributed equitably so that all family members feel content with the new living arrangements. Mothers with live-in stepchildren sometimes are angry about spending much of their time and energy on stepchildren, and they feel that they receive few rewards in the process:

> *I'd rather not have my stepsons. Mind you, I care for them and I am attached to them but I never set out to have children, and having someone else's children is a burden. I often resent it. At the same time, I wish they didn't have their mother so that way I would benefit at least from being a mother. But in my situation I have all the problems a mother has since they live here and none of the advantages, maybe less so with the younger one*

because he was so little when I moved in. (Ambert, 1986: 799)

While such difficulties of stepfamily life are common, Vinick (1997) found that stepmothers are often "carpenters for damaged relationships." They might reestablish estranged ties between their husbands and his biological children by urging their husbands to make phone calls or by calling themselves, sending invitations for visits and family get-togethers, and writing letters. Biological mothers can strengthen ties between their children and stepfathers by nudging them to spend time together. As one mother said, "I'd send them off to the movies or to a park. They had to form a relationship without me intervening" (Wolcott, 2000).

Blending Parent–Child Relationships Several national studies have found that children from stepfamilies show less emotional, social, and familial adjustment than children from intact nuclear families (see Ganong and Coleman, 1994, for a summary and review of some of this research). Studying families of different structures, Hetherington and Clingempeel (1992) found that almost three times as many children in single-mother and remarried households as in nondivorced households were described by their mothers as having serious behavioral problems.

In a longitudinal study, similarly, Hetherington and her colleagues (1999) found that being in a complex stepfamily, in contrast to a nonstepfamily, was associated with more problems in family relationships. These problems included parent–child conflict, a child's lower sense of social responsibility, and greater externalizing behavior (like acting out, antisocial behavior, noncompliance, and aggression). Such difficulties aren't inherent in becoming a stepfamily, however. Instead, they reflect negative experiences associated with parental divorce. Parental hostility teaches adolescents aggressive and antagonistic ways of dealing with conflict and disagreement. These patterns reflect adolescent difficulties in both divorced families and stepfamilies (Anderson et al., 1999).

Even if biological children have close ties with their families, children may be at greater risk for problem behavior if stepfathers are not supportive and do not monitor the child's behavior (Marsiglio, 1995; Mekos et al., 1996). Some of the problems, however, may reflect stepfamily-related characteristics rather than the stepfamily structure itself. Even though the family's economic resources increase after a remarriage, alternating residences during the school year increases the children's risk of dropping out of school or having more problems with school authorities than for children who live with both biological parents (Astone and McLanahan, 1994).

Relationships with stepchildren are more difficult for stepmothers than stepfathers (Lee et al., 1994;

MacDonald and DeMaris, 1996). Although stepfathers who don't monitor their stepchildren may have a negative effect on the children's behavior in the long run, stepmothers may be less likely to have good relationships with their stepchildren because the stepmother is more often the disciplinarian (Kurdek and Fine, 1993). If she is at home more of the time, she may be more involved in raising the stepchildren, and she is often expected to play a more active domestic role than is the father. Regardless of the parent's gender, relations between children and parents in both intact and remarried homes are more positive when the parents include the children in decision making and are supportive rather than always critical (Barber and Lyons, 1994; Crosbie-Burnett and Giles-Sims, 1994).

Establishing Discipline and Closeness

Even though many stepfathers are more permissive than stepmothers, two of the biggest problems in stepfamilies concern discipline and authority, especially in relationships between a stepfather and adolescents. Teenagers complain, "He's not my father and I don't have to listen to him." Stepfathers resent not being obeyed both because they consider themselves authority figures and because they may be working hard to support the family. Mothers may feel caught in the middle. Although they love their husbands, they may feel guilty for having married someone the children don't like, or they may disagree with the stepfather's disciplinary measures (Giles-Sims and Crosbie-Burnett, 1989).

Whether they intend it or not, when parents find themselves forming strong relationships with the children of a new partner, they may feel that they are betraying their biological children. Similarly, children may feel guilty if they find themselves liking a stepparent better than a biological parent because the stepparent is more fun, more understanding, or easier to get along with (Papernow, 1993).

Integrating a stepfamily that includes teenagers can be particularly difficult because adolescents begin to move away from their parents during puberty. If adolescent children have supportive relationships with friends, neighbors, and other relatives, their adjustment after a remarriage will be smoother (Quick et al., 1994). Finally, regardless of age, "visiting" children may feel awkward and uncomfortable, and if their visits are intermittent, they may not develop a sense of belonging or fitting in. As stated earlier, however, ensuring that each family member has stable physical space can lessen the alienation of "visitors."

Gender Differences in Children's Adjustment

Several studies have found that stepdaughter–stepfather relationships are more negative than are those between stepsons and stepparents of either sex. Even when stepfathers make friendly overtures, stepdaughters may withdraw (Vuchinich et al., 1991). One explanation for this distancing behavior is that daughters, who once had a privileged status in the family because they shared much of the authority in helping to raise younger children, may resent being replaced with someone with more power in the family (Fischman, 1988). The stepdaughter–stepfather relationship may also be more distant because the stepfather has made sexual overtures or behaved in other inappropriate ways toward the stepdaughter (see Chapter 14).

Whatever the reasons for the problems experienced by girls in remarried families, they are serious enough to cause adolescent girls to leave stepfamily households at an earlier age than do girls in single-parent or intact homes. Stepdaughters also leave earlier to establish independent or cohabiting households (Goldscheider and Goldscheider, 1993). In a British study, 23-year-olds were asked the main reason why they left their parental homes. Those who had lived in stepfamily households were substantially more likely than those who had lived in intact households to report that they left due to "friction at home" (Kiernan, 1992).

In many cases, the negative reactions of children (especially young children) are fairly short-lived. According to several national studies, stepmothers and stepchildren establish more positive relationships within a few years (Baydar, 1988; Hetherington and Clingempeel, 1992). Stepfathers, especially, need to be patient in establishing new relationships after a remarriage. In describing the gradual process of developing a relationship with the stepchild, one stepfather commented, "Brian is different now. At first he was reclusive and jealous and he saw me as infringing. It was a slow progression" (Santrock et al., 1988: 159). The box on "The Ten Commandments of Stepparenting" suggests some dos and don'ts for stepparents.

Intergenerational Relationships

Ties across generations, especially with grandparents and stepgrandparents, can be healthy and meaningful or disruptive and intrusive. After a divorce or during a remarriage, grandparents can provide an important sense of continuity to children when many other things are changing. Although many children typically do not become as attached to their new stepgrandparents as to their biological grandparents, they can resent new grandparents who seem to neglect or reject them:

One twelve-year-old girl in our practice became angry and aggressive toward her two new and younger stepsiblings following their first Christmas holiday together, even though she had been very loving with them before that. Several weeks later she revealed to her father that she was hurt and disappointed because the stepsiblings received twice as many gifts from their grandparents as she received in total from everyone in the family. (Everett and Everett, 1994: 140)

CHOICES

The Ten Commandments of Stepparenting

All families have to work at peaceful coexistence. Practitioners (Turnbull and Turnbull, 1983; Visher and Visher, 1996) offer the following advice to stepparents who want to increase family harmony.

1. *Provide neutral territory.* Most people have a strong sense of territoriality. Stepchildren may have an especially strong sense of ownership because some of their privacy may be invaded. If it is impossible to move to a new house where each child has a bedroom, provide a special, inviolate place that belongs to each child individually.

2. *Do not try to fit a preconceived role.* Be honest right from the start. Each parent has faults, peculiarities, and emotions, and the children will have to get used to these weaknesses. Children detect phoniness and will lose respect for any adult who is insincere or too willing to please.

3. *Set limits and enforce them.* One of the most difficult issues is discipline. Parents should work out the rules in advance and support each other in enforcing the rules. Rules can change as the children grow, but there should be agreement in the beginning on such

issues as mealtimes, bedtimes, resolving disagreements, and household responsibilities.

4. *Allow an outlet for the children's feelings for the biological parent.* The stepparent should not feel rejected if a child wants to maintain a relationship with a noncustodial biological parent. Children's affections for their biological parents should be supported so that the children do not feel disloyal.

5. *Expect ambivalence.* Children's feelings can fluctuate between love and hate, sometimes within a few hours. Ambivalence is normal in human relationships.

6. *Avoid mealtime misery.* Many families still idealize the family dinner hour as a time when family members have intelligent discussions and resolve problems. Although both parents should reinforce table manners, a less than blissful family mealtime should be ignored or sometimes avoided. Some suggested strategies include daily vitamins, getting rid of all junk foods, letting the children fix their own meals, eating out once in a while, and letting the father do some of the cooking.

7. *Do not expect instant love.* It takes time for emotional bonds to

be forged; sometimes this never occurs. Most children under 3 years of age adapt with relative ease. Children over age 5 may have more difficulty. Some children are initially excited at having a "new" mother or father but later find that the words "I hate you" are potent weapons. This discovery frequently coincides with puberty. A thick skin helps in these hurtful times.

8. *Do not accept all the responsibility; the child has some, too.* Children, like adults, come in all types and sizes. Some are simply more lovable than others. Like it or not, the stepparent has to take what he or she gets. That does not mean assuming all the guilt for a less than perfect relationship, however.

9. *Be patient.* The words to remember here are "things take time." The first few months, and often years, are difficult. The support and encouragement of other parents who have had similar experiences can be invaluable.

10. *Maintain the primacy of the marital relationship.* The couple must remember that the marital relationship is primary in the family. The children need to see that the parents get along together, can settle disputes, and most of all, will not be divided by the children.

Relations with paternal grandparents tend to lessen when a child lives with his or her mother after divorce and remarriage. When parents remarry, they tend to live further away, have fewer visits with grandparents, and make fewer telephone calls (Lawton et al., 1994). Such distanced behavior can decrease grandparent–stepgrandchild contact and closeness. Even maternal grandparents may visit less often, call less often, and not offer baby-sitting services to remarried daughters compared to married or divorced daughters (Spitze et al., 1994). Intergenerational relationships, then,

depend on how much effort both the remarried partners and steprelatives put into maintaining or forging close family ties.

Successful Remarriages and Stepfamilies

In a review of the stepfamily literature, Ihinger-Talman and Pasley (1997) caution against drawing pessimistic conclusions about children's adjustment in stepfamilies because many of the results are based on clinical samples rather than nonclinical populations. That is, we rarely hear about well-adjusted and happy families that don't need or seek therapeutic interventions. Even longitudinal studies based on national samples have found, however, as much of this chapter shows, that many stepfamilies encounter difficulties such as boundary issues, cohesiveness, and conflicting loyalties that biological families rarely face.

What makes a remarried family successful? In a review of the literature, Visher and Visher (1993) suggest that six characteristics are common to remarried families in which children and adults experience warm interpersonal relationships and satisfaction with their lives. Don't worry if you have a feeling of déjà vu; some of these characteristics are in fact the opposite of the problems we've discussed earlier. The major point to remember is that these traits can be achieved.

Some Characteristics of Successful Families

First, successful stepfamilies have developed *realistic expectations*. They have rejected the myth of instant love because they realize that trying to force a friendship or love simply doesn't work. In addition, they don't try to replicate the biological family because they accept the fact that the stepfamily structure is "under construction." Teenagers who are beginning to rebel against authority generally are particularly sensitive to adult supervision. As one teenager in a stepfamily put it, "Two parents are more than enough. I don't need another one telling me what to do" (Visher and Visher, 1993: 245).

Second, adults in successful stepfamilies *let children mourn their losses*. These adults are sensitive to children's feelings of sadness and depression. They also support the children in their expression of fear and anger, neither punishing the children nor taking these reactions as personal rejection. According to Crosbie-Burnett and Lewis (1993), black stepfamilies tend to focus more on nurturing and supporting a child than do white stepfamilies.

Third, the adults in well-functioning stepfamilies forge *a strong couple relationship*. This provides an atmosphere of stability because it reduces the children's anxiety about another parental breakup. It also provides children with a model of a couple who can work together effectively as a team and solve problems rationally (Kheshgi-Genovese and Genovese, 1997).

Fourth, *the stepparenting role proceeds slowly*. A stepparent is catapulted into a parenting role while a biological parent's relationship with a child develops over many years (see the discussion of achieved and ascribed status in Chapter 1). According to some researchers, one of the biggest mistakes that stepfathers make, usually with a wife's encouragement, is assuming an active parenting role too early in the

marriage and presuming an intimacy and authority that have not been earned. Although the stepfathers were caring, attentive, and loving, the children often reflected a spectrum of behaviors that included surliness, door slamming, loud shouting, and painful insults. The researchers concluded that during the first year or two of stepfamily life, the children were psychologically unprepared to accept both intimacy and authority from a stepfather (Bray and Kelly, 1998). Children might still be feeling the effects of "emotional divorce" (see Chapter 15) even if a biological parent has recovered.

Except when young children are present, the stepparent should take on a disciplinary role gradually. As one teenage girl stated, "My stepfather wasn't ever in my face, which was good, because I would have been mad if he had tried to discipline me" (Minton, 1995: 25). With teenagers, the biological parent should be the disciplinarian while the stepparent supports his or her behavior. In successful stepfamilies, adults realize that the relations between a stepparent and stepchildren can be quite varied—the stepparent may be a parent to some of the children, a companion to others, or just a good friend to all. And if there are no warm, interpersonal ties, it is enough that family members are tolerant and respectful of individual differences.

Here white stepfamilies can learn from the experiences of many African American families. In black families, "living in two cultures simultaneously [one white and one black] means that situations arise in which role expectations and definitions of self and family are ambiguous, or even in conflict" (Crosbie-Burnett and Lewis, 1993: 245). Thus, black adults are more likely to teach their children that there are several possible sets of behaviors, expectations, and roles.

Fifth, successful stepfamilies *develop their own rituals*. They recognize that there is more than one way to do the laundry, cook a turkey, or celebrate a birthday. It is not a matter of a right or a wrong way. Instead, successful remarried households may combine previous ways of sharing household tasks, develop new schedules of what to do together on the weekends, or try out several ways of sharing household tasks. The most important criteria are flexibility and a willingness to cooperate.

Finally, *well-functioning stepfamilies work out satisfactory arrangements between the children's households*. Adults don't have to like each other to be able to get along. In fact, it is useful for many adults to have a "business relationship" to work together during such family events as holidays, graduations, and weddings. Crosbie-Burnett and Lewis note that many black families have flexible and permeable familial boundaries so that children feel welcome in several households regardless of biological "ownership." In addition, community members, including fictive kin (see Chapter 2), share material and emotional resources in raising children.

The Rewards of Remarriage and Stepparenting

Couples often describe their remarriage as offering more benefits than their first marriage. Many feel they learned valuable lessons in their first marriage and that they have matured as a result of the experience. They feel they know each other better than they knew their former spouses, talk more openly and more freely about issues that concern them, and are less likely to suppress their real feelings to avoid causing pain. Successful remarried couples say they try harder, are more tolerant of minor irritations, and tend to be more considerate of each other's feelings than they were in the first marriage. Finally, they report enjoying the new interests and new friends a remarriage brings (Westoff, 1977).

Reactions from stepparents are more mixed. When Rosin (1987) asked stepfathers about the rewards they experienced, the responses ranged from one stepfather who felt that the rewards are "the same as the rewards of biological fathering" to another who said "none." In another study of 29 stepfamilies, nearly 33 percent of the couples said that living in a stepfamily required a continual and deliberate effort. One father wearily commented, "Stepfamily life is intense, and weekends feel like a workout!" Most were unprepared for the unrelenting nature of the demands placed on them (Pill, 1990: 190).

The quality of stepfamily relationships depends in part on the stepparents' role identity and those of their stepchildren. In one study, for example, 52 percent of the stepparents felt that "parent" was the ideal stepparent role but only 29 percent of the stepchildren felt this way. Instead, 40 percent of the stepchildren said the ideal stepparent role was "friend" (Fine et al., 1999). Such dissimilar perceptions and subsequent expectations might explain why stepparents' relationships with their stepchildren are tense.

Despite the ups and downs, a stepfamily provides members with opportunities that may be missing in an unhappy, intact family. Because children see happy adults, they have positive models of marriage (Rutter, 1994). When remarried partners are happy, children benefit from being in a satisfying household. A well-functioning stepfamily increases the self-esteem and well-being of divorced parents and provides children who have lost touch with noncustodial parents with a caring and supportive adult (Pill, 1990). In addition, the children's economic situation is often improved after a parent, especially a mother, remarries (Cherlin, 1992). As you saw in Chapter 15, many mother-custody families are plunged into poverty after a divorce.

One of the greatest benefits of remarriage and stepparenting is the opportunity to become more flexible and to learn patience. Family members learn to develop less rigid attitudes toward family issues and boundaries. Gender roles, for example, are less likely to be stereotypical because in well-functioning

Children in stepfamilies may often feel divided loyalties between their biological fathers, with whom they spend time periodically, their mothers, and their stepfathers.

stepfamilies, both parents typically earn money, write checks, do housework, and take care of the children (Kelley, 1992).

In many stepfamilies, the children benefit by having a more objective sounding board to discuss problems, and they may be introduced to new ideas, different perspectives, and a new appreciation for art, music, literature, sports, or other leisure activities (Ihinger-Tallman and Pasley, 1987). Finally, if stepsiblings live together, they get more experience in interacting, cooperating, and learning to negotiate with peers.

In some cases, children don't recognize the contributions of stepparents until they themselves are adults. One of my students, who admitted to being very rebellious and "a real pain" after her mother remarried, is now grateful that her stepfather didn't give up:

The best solution to mine and my stepfather's problems was age. As I am getting older and supporting myself more and more, I realize just how much my stepfather has done for me. Even though he is not my "real" dad, he is the only father I have known. He has provided me with food, clothes, an education, and a home. Growing up, I thought I had it so rough. I now realize that he's my friend. It's funny, but now I actually enjoy watching TV or a movie with my stepfather. (Author's files)

Conclusion

As this chapter shows, there is life after divorce. Of all the different marriage and family forms discussed in this textbook, stepfamilies are the most varied and complex. Thus, both children and adults must make many *changes* as the members adapt and work together. Despite high redivorce rates, remarriage and stepparenting give people more *choices* in establishing a well-functioning and satisfying family life. Although stepfamilies must deal with many *constraints* after a remarriage, there are also numerous rewards in establishing a new household.

SUMMARY

1. The most dramatic changes in family structure and composition are due to remarriage and the formation of stepfamilies. Over 40 percent of marriages are remarriages for one or both partners.

2. Dating and courtship patterns vary by age and gender. Most divorced people marry within three or four years after a divorce.

3. Remarriage rates vary by sex, race, age, socioeconomic status, and marital status. Men remarry more quickly than do women; remarriage rates are much higher for white women than for black women and Latinas; and women with low incomes and lower educational levels are the most likely to remarry.

4. Remarriage is a process that involves emotional, economic, psychic, community, parental, and legal aspects. Some of these phases occur independently of the existence of children, whereas others involve children.

5. There are several important differences between first marriages and remarriages. Some of these differences include the composition of the family, the children's experiences, stepfamily roles, life-cycle events, family goals and objectives, and family structure.

6. The research findings on remarriage and marital satisfaction are mixed, primarily because much of the research in this area is still recent and compares stepfamilies to first marriages.

7. Stepfamilies are very diverse in terms of parent–child relationships and their ties to biological families. Stepfamilies can have three "sets" of children under the same roof, which may result in strained living arrangements.

8. Stepfamilies still suffer from negative perceptions and stereotypes, even though much of the research shows that stepfamilies are similar to biological families in fulfilling basic family functions.

9. Although stepfamilies share many of the same functions as do intact nuclear families, there are a number of unique tasks in merging two households after a remarriage. Four of the most common issues are a lack of institutional support, the distribution of resources, the integration of children into the family, and intergenerational relationships.

10. Many couples who have remarried say they know each other better, communicate more openly, and are more considerate of each other's feelings than they were in their first marriage. Thus, although there are problems in remarriages, there are also many rewards.

KEY TERMS

stepfamily   *426*
half-sibling   *429*
genogram   *434*

biological mother–stepfather family *434*
biological father–stepmother family *434*

joint biological–stepfamily   *435*

TAKING IT FURTHER

Getting Information and Support on the Internet

The **Stepfamily Association of America** provides information, support, and articles on stepparenting.

www.stepfam.org

The **Children of Separation and Divorce Center, Inc.** describes itself as "an advocate and liaison for families in transition" and offers publications, parent seminars, newsletters, and suggestions for dealing with changes in family relationships.

www.divorceabc.com

The **Second Wives Club** serves stepmoms and second wives and offers a potpourri of resources that include articles, legal and practical advice. and finalizing custody arrangements.

www.secondwivesclub.com

The **Stepfamily Foundation** wants "to assist you to make this complex family work" and offers information on stepfamily research, counseling, and other resources.

www.stepfamily.org

The **American College of Trust and Estate Counsel** provides referrals for local lawyers who can draw up prenuptial agreements, trusts, and wills.

www.actec.org

And more . . . www.prenhall.com/benokraitis offers resource directories, sites for legal referrals, online information about stepparent adoptions, and URLs that suggest how stepfamily relations can be strengthened.

CHAPTER 17

Aging and Family Life: Grandparents, the Widowed, and Caregivers

DATADIGEST

- The percentage of the **U.S. population over age 65 has been increasing steadily**: 4 percent in 1900, 5 percent in 1920, 7 percent in 1940, 9 percent in 1960, and 13 percent in 2000. It is expected to grow to 20 percent by 2030.

- The **oldest old** (persons 85 years old and over) are a small but growing group. In 2000, it comprised 1.6 percent of the U.S. population compared to 0.6 percent in 1900.

- The **average life expectancy** was 47 years in 1900, 68 years in 1950, and rose to 76 years in 1991. In 1997, life expectancy was higher for women (79 years) than for men (74 years).

- The percentage of **racial-ethnic elderly age 65 and over** in the U.S. population will increase from 16 percent in 2000 to 25 percent in 2030, and to 32 percent by 2050.

- In what some call a **"global aging explosion,"** both industrialized and developing countries are expected by 2030 to have large percentages of people over 60 years old among their populations: Italy, 36 percent; the United States, 28 percent; Russia, 25 percent; China, 22 percent; Brazil, 17 percent; Mexico, 16 percent; and India, 13 percent.

SOURCES: Hobbs and Damon, 1996; "Older Americans, 2000 . . . ," 2000.

O N a sweltering June weekend in Springfield, Massachusetts, more than 600 over-50-year-old athletes from 11 states competed in 20 events, ranging from basketball to the pole vault, in the 1994 U.S. National Senior Sports Classic. The 73-year-old woman who jumped 8 feet to win the gold medal in the long jump also won golds in the high jump, the shot put, and the hammer throw. Another contender, 84 years old, had collected 205 gold and 23 silver medals in such events as discus, shot put, javelin, and the 1500-meter run since the Senior Games began in 1992 (Rohde, 1994).

What's more, the contestants in the Senior Games were youngsters compared to many other active older people. For example,

- Mieczyslaw Horszowski, the classical pianist, recorded a new album at age 99.
- At age 99, the twin sisters Kin Narita and Gin Kanie recorded a hit single in Japan and starred in a TV ad.
- At 97, Martin Miller of Indiana was working full time as a lobbyist for older citizens.
- At 91, Hulda Crooks climbed Mount Whitney, the highest mountain in the continental United States.
- Chef Julia Child tasted French food for the first time at the age of 37, was in her fifties when she became famous for her expertise in French cuisine (*Cooking with Julia Child* on television). In her eighties, she embarked on a new show in 1995 in which she plays host to famous chefs from around the world.
- In 1997, 94-year-old South Carolina Senator Strom Thurmond, who had served in Congress

more than 41 years, decided not to run for reelection in 2002 because he wasn't sure how his health would be at age 100.
- Before France's Jeanne Calment, the world's oldest living person, died at age 122, she took up fencing at 85, still rode a bicycle at 100, and released a rap CD at the age of 121.
- George Dawson, the grandson of slaves, learned to read at age 99 and co-authored a book at age 102 (see Dawson and Glaubman, 2000).

Are these people unusual? Probably. But as we continue into the twenty-first century, more older people are and will be similarly active and productive. As the numbers of older people continue to grow (see Data Digest), the later years can become increasingly more interesting and enjoyable. At the same time we must recognize that older family members must often deal with the death of loved ones, with their own health problems, and with both giving and receiving care. As this chapter shows, aging *does* result in changes for both older people and for their family and friends.

The Rise of Multigenerational Families

Despite the high incidence of illnesses like cancer and heart disease, more people are reaching age 65 than ever before, and American children born in 1990 have an average life expectancy of almost 76 years. Because many racial-ethnic groups in America have higher birth rates than whites, the numbers of elderly in these

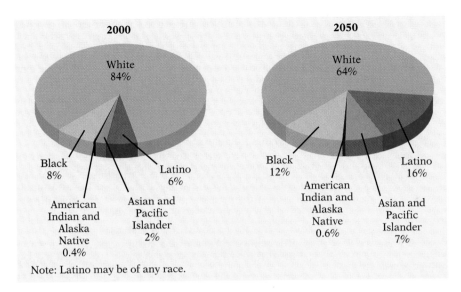

FIGURE 17.1   Population Age 65 and Older, by Race and Latino Origin, 2000 and 2050

SOURCE: "Older Americans 2000 . . . ," 2000, p. 4

groups are expected to grow at an even greater rate. As *Figure 17.1* shows, the ethnic population age 65 and over is expected to grow from 16 percent in 2000 to 36 percent in 2050.

One of the fastest-growing groups is people over 85, a population that has increased from 100,000 in 1900 to 4.3 million in 2000. By 2030, this group is expected to constitute almost 3 percent of the country's population ("Older Americans 2000 . . . ," 2000). In the same year, about 324,000 people will be centenarians, or people who are 100 years old or older: white, 62 percent; black, 13 percent; Latino, 15 percent; Asian, 8 percent; and American Indian/Eskimo/ Aleut, 3 percent (Krach and Velkoff, 1999).

While the numbers of older Americans are increasing, the proportion of young people is decreasing. As *Figure 17.2* shows, by the year 2030 there will be more elderly people in the United States than young people. As a result, the years of parent–child relationships will be prolonged. Many adult children will need to care for frail and elderly parents, and many young children will have not only great-grandparents but great-great-grandparents as well (Dellmann-Jenkins et al., 2000).

Aging: Changes in Health and Social Status

Gerontologists—scientists who study aging and the elderly—emphasize that the aging population should not be lumped into one group. There is a great deal of diversity among **later-life families,** that is, families that either are beyond the child-rearing years and have launched their children or childless families who are beginning to plan for retirement (Brubaker, 1991). Satisfaction with one's later life depends on a number of

factors, including personality, attitude toward life, income, social status, and, perhaps most important, the quality of one's health. We look first at the issue of health, then at the social status of the elderly, and finally at the societal stereotypes they must often confront.

Is Deterioration in Health Inevitable?

During the period 1994 to 1996, 72 percent of those age 65 and over reported being in good, very good, or excellent health. Among older men and women in every age group, blacks and Latinos were less likely to report good health than white persons. Even among those 85 or older, however, about half of black and

FIGURE 17.2   The Young and the Old: 1900 to 2030 (U.S. Special Committee on Aging et al., 1991: 9).

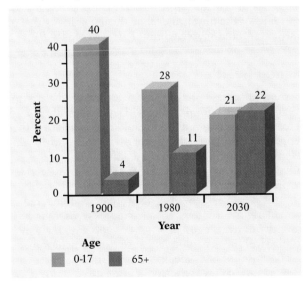

TABLE 17.1

Aging and Health

	Age			
	25	**45**	**65**	**85**
Maximum heart rate	100%	94%	87%	81%
Lung capacity	100%	82%	62%	50%
Muscle strength	100%	90%	75%	55%
Kidney function	100%	88%	78%	69%
Cholesterol level	198	221	224	206

SOURCE: Based on Begley et al., 1990: 44–48.

Latino people reported good to excellent health ("Older Americans 2000 . . . ," 2000).

Nevertheless, some physical decline across all age groups is normal and inevitable. Compared to 40 percent of adults between ages 18 and 64, approximately 80 percent of those 65 years of age and over are afflicted with one or more chronic diseases such as heart disorder and arthritis and diseases that affect the respiratory and digestive systems (Adams and Marano, 1995). As *Table 17.1* shows, people over 85 typically experience the most severe failure of lung capacity and muscle strength. Some older people are healthier than others, of course. During and after his flight in space in 2000, for instance, 77-year-old John Glenn's heart rate was better than those of astronauts half his age ("Glenn's health . . . ," 2000).

A gradual process of physical deterioration begins early in life and affects all body systems: Reflexes slow, hearing and eyesight dim, and stamina decreases. No matter how well tuned we keep our bodies, the parts eventually wear down. People age differently, depending on such things as lifestyle, inherited predisposition, and attitude toward life. A healthy diet and regular exercise can help many older people preserve their good health. According to exercise physiologists, at least half of the physical decline during aging is due to a sedentary and inactive lifestyle (Krucoff, 1999).

Mental Health

In some illnesses, physical changes can lead to emotional and behavioral changes. Depression affects 15 percent of Americans age 65 or older. It is believed that depression is caused by changes in the body's biochemistry bringing on thyroid disease, heart disease, kidney or liver dysfunction. **Depression** is characterized by pervasive sadness and other negative feelings like a sense of worthlessness. It is also often accompanied in the elderly by such physical symptoms as diarrhea, chest discomfort, nausea, or loss of appetite, for which no physical or physiological cause can be determined.

Because family members tend to interpret the "down" mood they see in an older relative as a reaction to the death of loved ones or to the loss of a job or good health, they may not recognize the signs of depression. Seven of the nine symptoms of depression listed in *Table 17.2*, including numbers 5 and 6 (depressed mood and loss of interest), must be present for at least a two-week period for a physician to diagnose major depression that should be treated. Among the elderly, about 85 percent of those diagnosed can be treated successfully with antidepressants (Henry, 1995).

In an open letter to the nation in 1994, former President Ronald Reagan disclosed that he had symptoms of Alzheimer's disease and hoped his announcement would promote more awareness of this illness. Before you continue reading, take the quiz "What Do You Know about Alzheimer's Disease?"

Alzheimer's disease is a progressive, degenerative disorder that attacks the brain and impairs memory, thinking, and behavior. Medical researchers believe that Alzheimer's is caused by proteins that kill nerve cells in the brain (Masur et al., 1994; Scinto et al., 1994). The disease afflicts about 4 million U.S. elderly—about 10 percent age 65 and older and nearly half of those over 85 (Alzheimer's Association, 2000). Alzheimer's requires round-the-clock care, costing about $26 billion yearly in medical expenses, absenteeism, the time of unpaid caregivers, and the patients' earning losses. Although Alzheimer's is incurable and irreversible, researchers are experimenting with a variety of medications and therapies to delay or prevent its onset (Cowley, 2000).

According to brain researchers, the neurons that store and process information are incredibly flexible and, unless interrupted by disease or injury, constantly replace and rearrange themselves, even into old age. Thus, most healthy elderly people do not experience cognitive decline with advancing age. Those who tend

TABLE 17.2

Symptoms of Depression

1. Changes in appetite and weight
2. Disturbed sleep
3. Motor retardation or agitation
4. Fatigue and loss of energy
5. Depressed or irritable mood
6. Loss of interest or pleasure in usual activities
7. Difficulty thinking or concentrating
8. Feelings of worthlessness, self-reproach, excessive guilt
9. Suicidal thoughts or attempts

SOURCES: Kaplan and Strawbridge, 1994; Henry, 1995.

ASK YOURSELF

What Do You Know about Alzheimer's Disease?

	True	False	Don't Know
1. Anyone who lives long enough will almost certainly get Alzheimer's disease.	☐	☐	☐
2. Alzheimer's is a form of insanity.	☐	☐	☐
3. At present there is no cure for Alzheimer's disease.	☐	☐	☐
4. A person with Alzheimer's experiences both mental and physical decline.	☐	☐	☐
5. The primary symptom of Alzheimer's disease is memory loss.	☐	☐	☐
6. If you are over 75, memory loss most likely indicates the beginning of Alzheimer's.	☐	☐	☐
7. Depression in an older person can sometimes look like Alzheimer's.	☐	☐	☐
8. Men are more likely to develop Alzheimer's than women.	☐	☐	☐
9. Alzheimer's disease is fatal.	☐	☐	☐
10. The majority of persons with Alzheimer's live in nursing homes.	☐	☐	☐
11. Aluminum is a significant cause of Alzheimer's disease.	☐	☐	☐
12. Alzheimer's disease can be diagnosed by a blood test.	☐	☐	☐
13. Alzheimer's patients become passive and withdrawn.	☐	☐	☐
14. Medicare covers nursing home costs for Alzheimer's patients.	☐	☐	☐
15. Medicines taken for high blood pressure can cause symptoms that look like Alzheimer's disease.	☐	☐	☐

(Answers are on page 454.)

---

to deteriorate have high levels of cardiovascular disease and diabetes, both of which are linked to obesity (Haan et al., 1999). In addition, mental and cognitive health are frequently associated with one's socioeconomic and social status.

Social Status of the Elderly

We often hear that the elderly no longer have the respect they enjoyed in "the good old days." Historians point out, however, that the elderly did not necessarily enjoy respect and deferential treatment in the past. In colonial America, for example, treatment of the elderly depended very much on the person's wealth and social class. Church fathers gave wealthy and successful men in their thirties seats in the front row, but poor men in their seventies occupied seats near the back (Demos, 1986). Elderly women were rarely treated with respect, primarily because many were poor and thus powerless.

It is probably true, however, that the status of the elderly has declined since the turn of the twentieth century. Grandparents' influence on their children and grandchildren is diminished because families often live far apart. And because divorce and remarriage rates are high, familial ties in many cases have become loosened. Grandparents may have to compete with stepgrandparents at family get-togethers, for example. Perhaps most important, whereas in many societies the elderly were once the source of all wisdom, contemporary advances in science, technology, and other areas have made some of the ideas of the elderly seem old-fashioned and outdated. Some widely read publications like *Parents* magazine have even questioned the effectiveness of "grandma" as a child-care provider. A recent article claimed that many professional caretakers have more training in child rearing than grandparents do and they take the job more seriously because it's work that's regulated by a state's licensing system (Ogintz, 1994).

Answers to What Do You Know about Alzheimer's Disease?

1. False. Alzheimer's occurs most often in the elderly, but it is a disease and not the inevitable consequence of aging.

2. False. Alzheimer's is a disease of the brain, but it is not a form of insanity.

3. True. There is no known cure for Alzheimer's. Research suggests that some currently experimental drugs may be successful in slowing the disease (Scinto et al., 1994).

4. True. Memory and cognitive decline are characteristic of the earlier stages of Alzheimer's disease; physical decline follows in the later stages.

5. True. This is the earliest sign of Alzheimer's disease.

6. False. Although Alzheimer's does produce memory loss, memory loss can be caused by other factors.

7. True. Depression can cause disorientation that looks like Alzheimer's.

8. False. Both sexes are equally likely to get Alzheimer's.

9. True. Alzheimer's produces mental and physical decline that is eventually fatal, but the course of the disease may run from a few years to as many as 20. On average, death occurs within eight years (DiBacco, 1994).

10. False. The early and middle stages of the disease usually do not require institutional care. Only a small percentage of those with the disease live in nursing homes, and most are over the age of 85 (Havemann, 1997b).

11. False. Although aluminum compounds have been found in the brain tissue of many Alzheimer's patients, these may simply be side effects of the disease. There is no evidence that using aluminum cooking utensils or foil causes Alzheimer's.

12. False. At present there is no blood test that can determine with certainty that a patient has Alzheimer's disease. Some recent studies do suggest that certain psychological tests may predict Alzheimer's disease among the healthy elderly (Masur et al., 1994).

13. False. Some Alzheimer's patients may become aggressive, physically violent, and combative with caretakers and others (Lyman, 1993).

14. False. Medicare generally pays only for short-term nursing home care after hospitalization, not for long-term care. Medicaid can pay for long-term nursing home care, but because it is a state-directed program for the medically indigent, coverage for Alzheimer's patients depends on state regulations and on the income of the patient and family.

15. True. Some antihypertensive medications can cause symptoms that resemble Alzheimer's.

In some cultures the elderly still maintain a position of some influence. Societies that do not emphasize self-reliance and independence are likely to give older people more power and privilege because the young depend on the old for approval and other rewards (Ishii-Kuntz and Lee, 1987). In addition, preindustrial societies that endorse *familism* and filial piety, characterized by absolute obedience to the elderly and a sacred duty to support one's parents in their old age, may be more likely to honor and respect the elderly (Cowgill, 1986). In these and many developing societies, older women, for example, enjoy more leisure because they delegate most of the work of the family to daughters or daughters-in-law, who defer to their knowledge and experience (Brown, 1992).

Stereotypes and Ageism

In our youth-oriented society many people dread growing old. Writer Betty Friedan admits that her reaction to turning 60 was anything but jubilant: "When my friends threw a surprise [birthday] party . . . I could have killed them all. Their toasts seemed [to be] . . . pushing me out of life . . . out of the race. Professionally, politically, personally, sexually . . . I was depressed for weeks" (Friedan, 1993: 13).

Some women, like actress Jane Fonda and others, try to resist aging through technological "fixes" like plastic surgery, cosmetic "disguises," and obsessive exercising. Others, like former First Lady Barbara Bush, have accepted their aging bodies and remain resolutely natural. Although Mrs. Bush admitted always wearing three strands of pearls to cover her "sagging neck," she refused to dye her hair because "people who worry about their hair all the time are boring." Mrs. Bush considers women who are slaves to the latest fashions as frivolous and narcissistic (Dinnerstein and Weitz, 1994).

In his classic book, *Why Survive? Being Old in America,* Butler (1975) coined the term **ageism** to refer to discrimination against people on the basis of age, particularly those who are old. Among other things, Butler pointed out the persistence of the "myth of senility"—the notion that if old people show forgetfulness, confusion, and inattention, they are senile. If a 16-year-old boy can't remember why he went to the refrigerator, we say he's "off in the clouds" somewhere or in

love, but if his 79-year-old grandfather forgets why he went to the refrigerator, we're likely to call him senile (Slade, 1985; see also Palmore, 1999, for examples of historical and current ageist humor). Saporta (1991) maintains that our language is full of ageist words and phrases that malign, stereotype, and generally disparage the old: "senior citizen," "old bat," "old bag," "old fart," "old fogey," "fossil," "old goat," "old hag," "deadwood," "old maid," "dirty old man," "crotchety," "over the hill." How many negative words do we have that demean young people or youth?

Although the data collected by gerontologists show otherwise, many people continue to believe that older Americans are less intelligent, less competent, and less active than younger people (see Levin, 1988). This view of the elderly is well illustrated by the experiment conducted by Patricia Moore, who wanted to know what it's like to be an older person in our society. As you can see from the box "Being Old in America," Moore found a strong and pervasive negative attitude toward the elderly.

However unintentionally, educators sometimes reinforce stereotypical attitudes. In a study of 27 undergraduate textbooks on marriage and family published between 1988 and 1993, for example, Stolley and Hill (1996) found that the aged received little coverage and were generally associated with specific "elderly" topics such as retirement and widowhood. According to the researchers, the elderly are rarely mentioned in chapters on gender, race, ethnicity, or sexuality.

The media also create and perpetuate negative images of aging. For instance, one study examined 100 top-grossing motion pictures spanning from the 1940s through the 1980s. The researchers concluded that ageist stereotypes were prevalent across the five decades in their portrayal of older people as unattractive, unfriendly, and having few positive outcomes compared to younger characters. The films were sexist as well as ageist in two ways: (1) They underrepresented older women (only 8 percent of the central

characters were females over age 35) and (2) they consistently depicted more negative images of older women than of older men. Compared to older men, for example, older females were portrayed as less friendly, less intelligent, sleazy, poor, and unattractive (Bazzini et al., 1997). Think about the films produced during the 1990s since this study was done. How many motion pictures use a double standard in the images of older women and older men?

One of the most common stereotypes is that older people become ill-tempered as they age. In fact, most research shows that people's personality characteristics remain stable over a lifetime (McCrea and Costa, cited in Belsky, 1988). If you're grumpy or unpleasant at 75, you were probably grumpy and unpleasant at 15, 35, and 55. Although work, marriage, and other life experiences do affect people, in general those who are depressed, hostile, anxious, and poorly adjusted in their twenties are likely to be depressed, hostile, anxious, and poorly adjusted in old age.

Contrary to the popular notion that the elderly become stubborn, Tyler and Schuller (1991) found that older people actually are more flexible than their younger counterparts. Older people have a larger repertoire of experiences, these researchers say, and they've developed ways of dealing with bureaucratic red tape and other daily problems. As a result, many older people realize that with a little patience they can often get what they want.

Some researchers suggest that as people age, they lose their cognitive ability to be more tolerant. As a result, they might think and express prejudicial or stereotypical thoughts (Von Hippel et al., 2000). On the other hand, some elderly people feel that they become less docile and subservient as they age. Thus, when older people "suddenly" seem stubborn and defiant, they may simply be shedding some long-term inhibitions:

One of the greatest thrills of being a woman of 70 is having the luxury to be open about what I

CONSTRAINTS

Being Old in America

With the help of a professional make-up artist, Patricia Moore, an industrial designer, put on latex wrinkles and a gray wig, wore splints under her clothes to stiffen her joints, and put plugs in her ears to dull her hearing. Putting baby oil in her eyes irritated them and blurred her vision. "The look was that of eyes with cataracts, as the baby oil would float on the surface of the eyeball" (Moore and Conn, 1985: 56). She used a special type of crayon, mixed with oil paint, to stain and discolor her teeth, and she gargled with salt to make her voice raspy (Ryan, 1993). Then she shuffled out into the world to find out what it's really like to be old in America.

Over a three-year period, Moore found dramatic differences between the way people reacted to "Young" and "Old" Pat Moore. For example, as Old Pat she went into a store to buy a typewriter ribbon. Ignoring her at first, the salesman finally approached her and was irritated when she was not sure what kind of ribbon she wanted and impatient when she fumbled with the clasp on her handbag. Wordlessly, he gave her her change and dropped the package on the counter instead of handing it to her. The next day, Young Pat, "sandy-blonde hair curled and falling on my shoulders, sunglasses and sandals," but wearing the same dress she had worn the day before, went to the same store to buy typewriter ribbon. This time the salesman smiled and immediately offered his assistance. When Pat pretended not to know what kind of ribbon she wanted, he was solicitous ("As long as you know it

when you see it, you're all right"), and when she fumbled with the clasp of the purse, saying, "Darn thing always gives me trouble," he was amiable ("Well, better for it . . . to take a little longer to open than to make it easy for the muggers and the pickpockets"). He chatted as he counted out her change and opened the door because "it sticks sometimes."

What impressed Pat Moore the researcher, almost as much as the negative attitudes and behavior she continued to encounter as Old Pat, was the way she accepted and internalized those negative responses. When she appeared to be 85 and people were more likely to push ahead of her in line, she didn't protest this behavior: "It seemed somehow . . . that it was okay for them to do this to the Old Pat Moore, since they were undoubtedly busier than I was

"Old Pat Moore."

anyway. . . . After all, little old ladies have plenty of time, don't they?"

Moore found that clerks assumed she was hard of hearing, that she would be slow in paying for purchases, or that she would "somehow become confused about the transaction. What it all added up to was that people feared I would be trouble, so they tried to have as little to do with me as possible. And the amazing thing is that . . . I absorbed some of their tacitly negative judgment about people of my age. It was as if, unconsciously, I was saying . . . 'You're right. I'm just a lot of trouble. I'm really not as valuable as all these other people, so I'll just get out of your way as soon as possible so you won't be angry with me. . . .' I think perhaps the worst thing about aging may be the overwhelming sense that everything around you is letting you know that you are not terribly important any more" (Moore and Conn, 1985: 75–76).

Patricia Moore as herself.

really think. When I was younger, I was so afraid of hurting people or worried about what they would think of me that I . . . kept my mouth shut. Now when I don't like something, I speak up. It's gotten me into trouble with my daughter and

sister, but I don't care. It's not that I try to be mean. . . . It's just that age has made me more truthful. And that's one of the reasons that I feel better about myself now than I have at any other time in life. (Belsky, 1988: 65–66)

Life in rural China has never been easy, and the government's current insistence that families support their elderly relatives has increased the economic burden for many people.

Retirement

Retirement is a recent phenomenon. Historians point out that many people who reached old age in colonial America worked well past the age of 65. Men in their seventies hauled grain, transported rugs, and tanned leather. One man still worked in the coal mines at the age of 102. Men over age 65 who were in government positions (such as governors and their assistants) or who were ministers typically retained their offices until death, and some women worked as midwives well into their seventies (Demos, 1986).

Retirement Is Longer   Because we have greater life expectancy today, we may well spend 20 percent of our adult life in retirement. We often hear that retirement is particularly difficult for men because the traditional male role calls for breadwinning and being "productive." Researchers have found, however, that health and financial security are the major determinants of retirees' satisfaction with life. When people are unhappy in retirement, it is more often because of health or income problems than the loss of the worker role (Gradman, 1994; Solomon and Szwabo, 1994). If retirement benefits do not keep up with inflation, or if the retiree is not covered by a pension plan, poverty can be just a few years away.

Although the overall poverty rate for U.S. citizens age 65 and older dropped from 35 percent in 1959 to 11 percent in 1998, there are large differences by marital status, sex and ethnicity. Fewer than 5 percent of married couples age 65 or older live in poverty compared to almost 18 percent of those who are not married ("Older Americans 2000 . . . ," 2000). And as *Figure 17.3* shows, older women are poorer than their male counterparts within each racial group, black elderly are poorer than whites or Latinos, and black women are the most likely to be poor.

The Financial Impact: Gender and Racial Differences

Retirement presents more financial problems to women than to men. **Social Security,** a public retirement pension system administered by the federal government, provides income support to over 90 percent of the elderly, but the benefits depend on how long people have been in the labor force and how much they have earned. Many women have had an uneven employment history because they have spent many years as homemakers and mothers or because periodically they have left jobs to raise children. Thus many women must continue to work at least part time after age 65 because their Social Security benefits are very low. (Chapter 18 examines the Social Security system more closely.)

Even if women have worked full time they have often been confined to low-paying jobs and their earnings have been lower than men's, even in comparable jobs. In 1997, for example, the average Social Security benefit was $660 a month for retired women workers and $848 for their male counterparts ("OASDI benefits . . . ," 1998). Such payments may seem adequate. Remember, however, that Medicare does not cover such expenses as dental care and dentures, over-the-counter drugs and most prescribed medicine, eyeglasses and eye examinations, hearing aids and hearing examinations, immunization shots, or custodial care in the home or long-term care in nursing homes. Many older people, as a result, spend 25 to 30 percent of their income for health care.

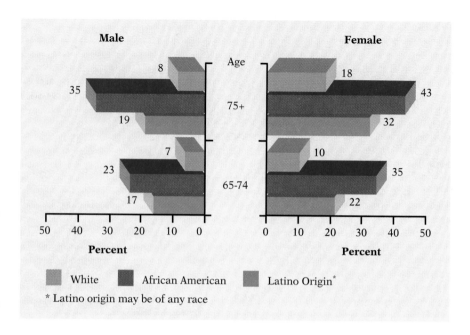

FIGURE 17.3 **Poverty Rates Are Highest for Elderly Black Women.** (From F. B. Hobbs and B. L. Damon, 1996. *65+ in the United States.* U.S. Bureau of the Census. Current Population Reports. Special Studies, P23-190. Washington, D.C.: Government Printing Office, Figure 4.9. Based on data from U.S. Bureau of the Census, *Poverty in the United States, 1992.* Current Population Reports, P60-185. Washington, D.C.: U.S. Government Printing Office, 1993, table 5).

Only 32 percent of women age 55 and older receive pension benefits compared to 55 percent of men. The average annual private sector benefit for women is $5200 compared to $11,800 for men ("Longer lives . . . ," 1996). In addition, women who divorce after fewer than ten years of marriage are not entitled to any of their husbands' benefits. As a result, after retirement many women are at a high risk of becoming dependent on public agencies or on their families for support (Gonyea, 1994).

Retirement has an especially devastating impact on black women. Many have worked in clerical or service positions that are low-paying and lack adequate pensions. If their husbands had low-paying jobs or a sporadic employment history because of recessions and discrimination, the husbands' benefits may also be inadequate. In one study, African American women over 65 said that work provided an alternative to welfare, and even highly educated black women reported working as long as possible to maintain the economic security of their families (Coleman et al., 1987).

Grandparenting

According to many gerontologists, grandparents are the cement, the glue that keeps the family close. In many families, grandparents represent stability and the continuity of family rituals and values. They often help their adult children in parenting activities by providing emotional support, encouragement, help with day-to-day parental needs (such as baby-sitting), and help in times of emergency or crisis, including illness and divorce (Szinovacz, 1998, provides a good summary of

grandparenting experiences across racial-ethnic families). No matter how strict they were with their own children, many grandparents often serve as family mediators, advocates for their grandchildren's point of view, and shoulders to cry on.

In general, today's grandparents are more affluent than grandparents of just a decade ago. Between 1980 and 1990, the median income of families headed by people age 65 and older increased by 22 percent, compared to only a 6 percent median income gain for families overall. Thus many are able to frequently buy their grandchildren gifts that range from small toys and items of clothing to expensive computers, sporting goods, and financial investments like stocks, bonds, or trust funds.

Over 25 percent of grandparents buy costly gifts, averaging more than $500 each, for their grandchildren. In addition, many grandparents give their adult children (who can't afford such expensive items) cameras and camcorders to capture their grandchildren's growing years (Brazil, 1998). With more money, more energy, and more leisure time than ever before, growing numbers of grandparents are taking advantage of tour packages designed specifically for grandparents and grandchildren.

Grandparenting Styles

Grandparents usually take great pleasure in their grandchildren. Their new grandparenting role gives their lives stability and provides them with new experiences. Not all grandparents feel the same, however. There are a number of different styles of grandparenting. In this section we look at five—remote, companionate, involved, advisory and cultural transmitters.

Remote In the *remote* relationship, the grandparents and grandchildren live far apart and see each other infrequently, maintaining a largely ritualistic, symbolic relationship. For example, grandparents who are "distant figures" may see their grandchildren only on holidays or special occasions. Such relationships may be cordial and benevolent but are also uninvolved and fleeting (Thompson and Walker, 1991). A recent American Association of Retired Persons (AARP) survey found that, nationally, only one in eight grandparents had little contact with a grandchild (Straw et al., 1999). Grandparents who both live far away and experience health problems are likely to be even less involved with their grandchildren (Field and Minkler, 1993).

Although they report feeling close to their great-grandchildren, great-grandparents often have remote relationships, either because they are in frail health, live far away, or feel that grandparents play a more authoritative role. Great-grandparents may also have difficulty adapting to new situations such as divorce and remarriage and often feel embarrassed, uncomfortable, or confused about great-grandchildren produced in cohabiting relationships. As one great-grandparent said, "I guess I have two or three great-grandchildren, depending on how you look at it. My grandson is living with someone and they have a child" (Doka and Mertz, 1988: 196).

Companionate The *companionate* style of grandparenting is the most common pattern. In a national survey, the Roper organization found that 90 percent of the grandparents said they saw their grandchildren at least once a month. About 66 percent talked to their grandchild by telephone at least once a month, 45 percent spent at least 100 hours a year taking care of their grandchildren, and 20 percent said they took their grandchildren on a trip, to see a movie or sports event, or to visit a museum once a month (reported in Waldrop, 1993). According to an AARP survey, more than eight out of ten grandparents had seen a grandchild and/or chatted on the phone in the previous month. About 54 percent of the grandmothers and 42 percent of the grandfathers saw their role as companion or friend (Straw et al., 1999).

Companionate grandparents often say that they love having their grandchildren with them and then remark, "And the best thing is that they go home!" According to satirist Erma Bombeck (1994: 8E), "Grandparenting is great. You can look at your grandchild with a diaper dragging on the floor and say to his mother, 'That kid is carrying a load! Change him!'" Companionate grandparents generally do not want to share parenting and tend to emphasize loving, playing, and having fun. Most often, when visiting, grandparents and grandchildren eat together, watch TV comedy, shop for clothes, play sports and attend church (Straw et al., 1999).

Love, intimacy, and companionship are just as important to older couples as to younger people.

Involved In a recent *Newsweek* poll of parents with children age 3 and under, 59 percent said the grandparents were very involved in their children's lives. About half of the parents reported that grandparents were also involved with grandchildren aged 6 to 17 (Hugick, 1999). In the *involved* grandparenting style, grandparents play an active role in raising their grandchildren. They may be spontaneous and playful, but they also exert substantial authority over their grandchildren, imposing definite—and sometimes tough—rules. According to a study of white and black working-class grandparents, grandmothers were more involved in teaching their grandchildren than were grandfathers. Black grandmothers, especially, said that they were concerned with teaching grandchildren sensitivity to others' feelings and the value of lifelong education (Watson and Koblinsky, 1997).

Involved grandparents are often younger than other types of grandparents and, frequently, they have welcomed their daughter(s) and grandchildren back home after a divorce. In other cases, grandparents, usually the grandmother, care for the grandchildren while the mother works. Involved grandparents include those who step in, occasionally or daily, to help manage a family crisis because the parent, usually a single mother, is young, poor, immature, or irresponsible in caring for the children (Oysterman et al., 1993).

Black grandparents, especially those who live in inner cities, often see themselves as family protectors against separation, divorce, drugs, and crime (Poe, 1992). But it's not only when there are problems that

Grandparents can often be excellent mentors to their grandchildren, encouraging and helping them with their studies and participating in other activities.

black grandparents are more involved with their grandchildren. For example, in a study of black and white grandfathers in a southeastern rural county, Kivett (1991) found that both groups provided warmth and affection. Black grandfathers, however, reported being closer to their grandchildren than their white counterparts. According to Kivett, black grandfathers are more likely to provide "unconditional love" because they see grandchildren as "holding the key to the future," whereas white grandfathers tend to emphasize the past and to see themselves as models for the younger generation.

Advisory   In the fourth, *advisory*, type of grandparenting, the grandparent serves as an adviser, or what Neugarten and Weinstein (1964) call a "reservoir of family wisdom." The grandfather, who may be the family patriarch, may act also as a financial provider, and grandmothers often play crucial advisory roles in their grandchildren's lives. Especially when the mother is very young, the maternal grandmother may help the "apprentice mother" make the transition to parenthood by supporting and mentoring her, but not replacing her in the parenting role. The grandmother provides emotional, financial, and child-care support until the "apprentice" shows that she is responsive to and responsible for the baby (Apfel and Seitz, 1991).

Many teenage grandchildren begin to break away from their families, including their grandparents. Sometimes the roles reverse at this stage, and teenage grandchildren may help their grandparents with errands or chores. Many adolescents, however, turn to their grandparents for advice or understanding. For example, a 17-year-old boy said: "With my grandpa

we discuss usually technical problems. But sometimes some other problems, too. He told me how to refuse to drink alcohol with other boys." A 16-year-old girl said that she and her grandmother go for walks and added, "I can tell her about everything" (Tyszkowa, 1993: 136).

Cultural Transmitters   Advisory grandparenting often overlaps with a fifth role where grandparents are *cultural transmitters* of values and norms. Among American Indian families, grandmothers may provide active parenting in the teaching and instruction of domestic chores, responsibility, and discipline that reflect tribal tradition. Grandfathers may transmit a knowledge of tribal history and cultural practices through storytelling (Woods, 1996).

Except for Japanese Americans, many of whom have lived in the United States for five generations (see Chapter 12), many recently arrived Asian immigrants live in extended families and are more likely to do so than Latinos. Between 20 percent (Chinese) and 39 percent (Asian Indians) of Asian Americans 55 years or older live with grandchildren. Such coresidence facilitates grandparents being "historians" who transmit values, ethnic heritage, and cultural traditions to their grandchildren even if there are English-language problems (Kamo, 1998). Chinese American grandparents, for example, help to develop their grandchildren's ethnic identity by teaching them Chinese, transmitting traditional practices and customs during holidays, and reinforcing cultural values. One mother commented, for instance, "My father taught [my children] well. Since he lived with us and had time to look after the children at home, he often told them to show filial piety towards their parents because parents worked very hard outside the home" (Tam and Detzner, 1998: 257).

Grandparents as Surrogate Parents

An emerging grandparenting role is that of surrogate, in which the grandparent provides regular care or replaces the parents in raising the grandchildren. As *Figure 17.4* shows, in 1997, 4 million children lived in a household headed by a grandparent, a 40 percent increase during the past decade. Contrary to the stereotype of the inner-city welfare mother who is raising her teenage daughter's baby, the majority of grandparent caregivers are white, between the ages of 50 and 64 and live in nonmetropolitan areas (Bryson and Casper, 1999).

The increase in grandchildren living with grandparents in these "skipped generations" homes is due to many factors: the growth in drug use among parents, teen pregnancy, divorce, the rapid rise of single-parent households, mental and physical illness, AIDS, child abuse and neglect, and the death or incarceration of parents (Roe et al., 1994; Carten and Fennoy, 1997; Bryson and Casper, 1999). According to Jendrek (1994), there are at least three categories of surrogate grandparents: custodial, living-with, and day-care grandparents.

Custodial Grandparents The *custodial* grandparents Jendrek interviewed had a legal relationship with their grandchildren through adoption, guardianship, or custody. Most did not view themselves as "taking the grandchild" away from the parent but believed they had taken legal action only when the situation became intolerable—for example, when the parent, usually the daughter, became an alcoholic or a drug addict and neglected or abandoned the grandchild. At age 75, actor George Kennedy and his wife, 68, adopted their 5-year-old granddaughter because the little girl's mother could not kick her drug habit. In other cases, grandparents might adopt a grandchild after the death of one or both parents.

Many grandparents are not eager to accept responsibility for their grandchildren. They do so, however, as a result of pressure from other family members, the judicial system, or out of a sense of loyalty and responsibility. For many grandparents, the new responsibility may mean that they must give up work to provide care, whereas others find they have little or no time for their usual activities or friends (Cox, 2000).

Living-with Grandparents *Living-with grandparents,* according to Jendrek, typically had the grandchild in their own home or, less commonly, lived in a home maintained by a grandchild's parent(s). Living-with grandparents took on these responsibilities either because their children had not yet moved out of the

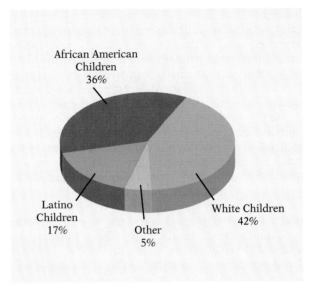

FIGURE 17.4 **Grandparents Raising Grandchildren, 1997**

SOURCE: Based on Bryson and Casper, 1999: Table 2.

house or because the latter could not afford to live on their own with their young children. These grandparents felt that they could provide the grandchild with an economically stable and loving environment, and preferred such an arrangement rather than allowing someone else to provide care.

In 75 percent of families with coresident grandparents and grandchildren, a grandparent maintains the household. A parent of the children maintains the remaining 25 percent of families with a grandparent or grandparents of the children living in the home. Half of the grandparent-maintained families (51 percent) have both a grandfather and a grandmother living with the grandchildren. A grandmother with no spouse present maintains most of the others (43 percent). A grandfather maintains only 6 percent alone. Over a third of the living-with grandparents are in "excellent" or "very good" health, often have at least a high school education, and are still in the labor force (Bryson and Casper, 1999).

Day-care Grandparents The *day-care grandparents* in Jendrek's study had assumed responsibility for the physical care of their grandchildren, usually their daughter's, until the parent(s) came home from work because of the high cost of quality day care. These grandparents were not casual baby-sitters, however. Some of the grandmothers even quit their part-time jobs to care for their grandchildren.

Some of the children in surrogate grandparent families are among the most needy and most emotionally damaged children in the United States (Sands and

Goldberg-Glen, 2000). In low-income areas, very few grandparents have reliable sources of support for their parenting roles. Although white, black, and Latino custodial parents often seek help from family members and formal services, becoming a primary caregiver often exacerbates already difficult economic circumstances (Roe and Minkler, 1998; Burnette, 1999). Although many grandmothers enjoy caring for grandchildren, they also experience stress and isolation, financial difficulties, and multiple roles that they hadn't anticipated in their later years (Rodgers and Jones, 1999). Providing care is especially stressful if the grandchildren have emotional or behavioral problems and if the grandparent, usually a grandmother, is a full-time surrogate and has few resources to meet the grandchild's needs (Fingerman, 1998; Bowers and Myers, 1999; Gattai and Musatti, 1999). The box "Grandparents as Silent Saviors" provides a closer look at grandparents as surrogate parents.

Grandparents and Their Children's Divorce

Divorce creates both opportunities and dilemmas for grandparents. Grandparents on the custodial side often deepen their relationships with children and grandchildren, especially when they provide financial assistance, a place to live, and help in child rearing, guidance, or advice. In contrast, grandparents on the noncustodial side typically have less access to the grandchildren. Many custodial parents move after the breakup, increasing the visiting distance. And troubled postdivorce relationships often result in a loss of contact between grandchildren and some of their grandparents because the mother feels a closer relationship to her genetic kin than to in-laws (Ganong and Coleman, 1999). One longitudinal study found that only 11 percent of ex-spouses had good relationships with each other's parents (Ambert, 1988).

If a custodial parent remarries, the noncustodial parent may drop out of the children's lives, making it awkward for the noncustodial grandparents to arrange visits with the grandchildren. However, if the custodial parent tries to maintain a relationship with the noncustodial grandparents so the children do not lose half of their family, and if the ex-spouses do not "bad-mouth" each other, children can have strong relationships with the noncustodial grandparents (Bray and Berger, 1990).

Many grandparent–grandchild relationships become closer after the parents divorce and/or remarry (Thomas, 1994). For example, if the mother gets custody of the children but has little or no child support, she may move in with her parents. Baby sitting while the mother works and generally being in close physical proximity to the grandchildren can foster a close emotional relationship between grandparent and grandchild. And grandparents can provide a safe haven for grandchildren whose divorcing parents are often so emotionally distraught that they do not recognize the children's fears and worries about the breakdown of their parents' marriage:

> *Last night I was reading and Penny came out of the bedroom and she was crying a bit and I said "come sit on gramma's lap" and we cuddled. She was upset because she had wet her bed, so I changed her. Her father had gone away and she is afraid her mother will be going away, too. So I talked to her and reassured her that her mother wouldn't go away. Then I asked her if she'd like to get into bed with gramma and she said "yes" and then went to sleep. (Gladstone, 1989: 71)*

The close relationship between grandchildren and grandparents often continues into the grandchildren's young adulthood. In a study of 704 college students who had at least one grandparent, the students from stepfamilies and single-parent families saw grandparents as playing a more active role in their families than did students from intact families. They reported that grandparents had important decision-making authority in the family, provided gifts or financial assistance, acted more like friends than authoritative elders, facilitated communication between the grandchildren and the parents, and helped parents in child rearing (Kennedy, 1990).

A divorce can create unexpected financial burdens for the grandparents, however. If grandparents anticipate being cut off from their grandchildren after the divorce, they may have to petition for visitation rights, thus incurring legal expenses. In other cases, parents may help children, especially daughters, to obtain a divorce. One father noted, for example, that "I'm at the age where a lot of my friends are retiring, and I'm spending all my retirement savings on attorneys" (Chion-Kenney, 1991: B5).

Grandparents' Visitation Rights

Whether an adult child is divorced or not, do grandparents have the right to visit a grandchild when the child's parents object? All 50 states have laws that say they do, if a judge decides visitation is in the best interest of the child. According to a 2000 U.S. Supreme Court ruling in a Washington state case, however, state judges may not force unwilling parents to grant visits to grandparents and other relatives. The controversial case stemmed from a dispute over visitation rights between the mother of two girls and the children's paternal grandparents. The grandparents petitioned the court for regular court-ordered visits with the children after their son, the father of the two girls, committed suicide.

CHANGES

Grandparents as Silent Saviors

Many grandparents have become the "silent saviors" (or "martyrs," according to some of my students) of grandchildren whose parents have abandoned them because of poverty, drug abuse, or other problems (Clemetson, 2000). Creighton describes one such family (1991: 85–86):

When the Richmond weather turns cold and bitter, 59-year-old May Toman and her two granddaughters pile blankets onto the worn living-room couch and chairs in their run-down row house. There, around an ancient gas burner, they sleep at night. The upstairs is without heat or electricity, and the leaky kitchen ceiling has already fallen in once. But May is afraid to complain for fear the landlord will raise her $110-a-month rent, a development that could leave them homeless. The girls—Shelly, 8, and Tabatha, 9—make do with thrift-shop clothing, and a steak dinner is a treat remembered for weeks.

Shelly's mother was only 17 when Shelly was born, and soon afterward she and Shelly's father began leaving the baby with friends or near friends, sometimes for long periods without contact. *For May, the final straw came when Shelly was 2. May found her alone in the yard one evening. She took Shelly home and called the Richmond Department of Social Services. After an investigation, May got legal custody.*

Several years later, May's son, Wayne, ran into marriage problems. When his wife left, he gave his daughter Tabatha, then 7, to his mother and his infant son to his mother-in-law. Tabatha's health had been neglected; her teeth were abscessed. May applied for custody and got it.

May, whom the girls call "Nanny," became their mother. May makes ends meet by taking in sewing and cutting corners. Up at 7, she walks the girls to school, then cleans house and grocery shops with food stamps. At 3, she meets the girls outside their brick school eight blocks away "so they know there's someone waiting."

One of Shelly's favorite pastimes is studying her baby album of herself and her mother smiling from behind plastic pages. The album ends abruptly when she is 2, and Shelly turns back to the first page to begin again. "I want to live with my mama in a big house," says Shelly, *"but I don't really think I'll ever get that." Shelly's mother lives across town and sees Shelly fairly often. But she has another child now, a year old, and says she does not have plans to take Shelly back soon.*

Tabatha says, "Well, my daddy lives in the neighborhood, but he can't take me right now. My mama used to call, which made me cry terribly, but she hasn't called now in a long time. She said she was going to send me a birthday card but she never did." Her father, Wayne, lives next door with two new children and their mother, and though in many ways he and Tabatha are close, he says, "I feel like Tabatha's better off with Nanny."

Although she loves her grandchildren, May is representative of many grandparents who had not anticipated raising their grandchildren. Even when a parent assumes some of the child-care responsibilities, many grandparents provide physical and emotional care but have little decision-making power. As one grandmother summed it up, "I've been feeling very hurt and self-pitying. . . . This is not what we had planned . . . and it's just not fair for this to happen to us."

The mother had since remarried and refused to permit what she considered to be excessive and time-consuming visitation with the grandparents. The trial judge in the case ordered the mother to turn over her children to the grandparents one weekend a month, a week during the summer, and for four hours on each of the girls' birthdays. That order was thrown out by the state supreme court, which ruled that parents have a fundamental right to raise their children without outside interference (except if the child faces harm). The U.S. Supreme Court agreed.

The case sparked considerable controversy. AARP and other groups argued, for example, that grandparents are part of an extended family and have a right to visitation despite parents' objections—especially when high divorce rates fragment a nuclear family. Others applauded the ruling for strengthening parental rights in deciding what's best for their children. Litigation is expected in the future because the U.S. Supreme Court didn't strike down grandparents' visitation privileges but said that third parties would have a higher burden of proof in seeking visitation rights over a parent's objections.

Relationships between Aging Parents and Adult Children

In many cases, adult children and aging parents live close enough to stay in touch on a daily basis. Lin and Rogerson (1995) found, for example, that 60 percent of parents age 60 and older have at least one child within ten miles. Geographic closeness is not the most critical factor that shapes intergenerational relationships, however. Divorced daughters with child custody have more contact than married daughters and often receive more help from parents. Sons, on the other hand, receive more baby-sitting help from their parents when they are married than in other situations (Spitze et al., 1994).

Adult daughters provide about the same amount of help to their parents whatever the parents' health, but sons tend to provide financial assistance only when parental health fails (Hamon, 1992). Another critical variable is the quality of family relationships. Regardless of their own marital status, both black and white adults are more likely to provide emotional and instrumental support (such as providing transportation and health care when parents are ill) if early family relationships were caring and loving (Chatters and Taylor, 1993). These strong and helpful relationships continue into the parents' seventies and eighties (Johnson, 1993).

Elderly parents generally try to avoid moving in with their children, primarily because they don't want to give up control of their own lives and lifestyles. In addition, they don't want to cause or to endure crowding and are reluctant to do the increased housework in a packed home. For many women, the "empty nest" is a relief. Some older parents feel that there would be a clash over different lifestyles or child-rearing ideas, as well as increased household expenses (Mancini and Blieszner, 1991). Finally, both younger and older generations value independence, and aging parents prefer to be both financially and emotionally self-sufficient.

There are advantages to multigenerational households, however. Such families exchange services and support on a regular basis: caring for family members during illness, giving money, providing gifts, running errands, preparing meals, taking care of children, giving advice on home management, cleaning the house and making repairs, giving advice on jobs, business matters, and expensive purchases, helping with transportation, counseling about life problems, and giving emotional support and affection (Mancini and Blieszner, 1991).

Rural elderly parents generally depend on their children for financial and emotional support more than do urban elderly parents. This is probably because the urban elderly typically have more resources and more access to resources, which makes them less dependent on their children. Even when formal support systems outside the family are available, the rural elderly still depend more on kinship networks. The older urban parents are the more likely they are to rely on their children for assistance (Dorfman and Mertens, 1990).

Contrary to what many of us might expect, it is often the needs and circumstances of adult children rather than those of their elderly parents that trigger dependent relationships. That is, coresidency is most likely among adult children who are unmarried and whose parents are in good health, under age 65, contribute to the family income, and often provide child care for their grandchildren while the parents work (Casper and Bryson, 1998; Bryson and Casper, 1999).

Death and Dying

Woody Allen once said, "It's not that I'm afraid to die. I just don't want to be there when it happens." Although people who are very old and in poor health sometimes welcome death, most of us have difficulty facing it, no matter what our age and physical condition. In this section we look first at several theories of how people deal with imminent death. Then we examine the kind of care available to the dying. Finally, we explore the ways survivors deal with their own loss and grief and console each other.

Dealing with Death and Dying

The way we deal with death depends on whether we are the medical personnel treating the ill patient, the relatives and friends of the patient, or the patient. Physicians and other medical staff, although many try to be compassionate, must often be more concerned with their patients' prognoses, that is, their realistic chances for survival. Patients and their loved ones, on the other hand, are generally concerned with getting the best possible treatment in the hope that the patients will survive. As a result, each has different perspectives on death and dying.

Health-Care Professionals Physicians and other health-care professionals often use the term *dying trajectory* to describe the manner in which a very ill person is expected to die. In a *lingering trajectory*—for example, death from a terminal illness like cancer—medical staffs do everything possible to treat the patient, but ultimately custodial care predominates. In contrast, the *quick trajectory* refers to the acute, crisis situation caused by a heart attack or a serious accident. Staff typically work feverishly to preserve the patient's life and well-being—and sometimes they are successful.

When the patient is elderly and suffering from a terminal illness like advanced cancer, health-care professionals and family members often perceive the course of dying and its treatment differently. For example, it is especially likely that overworked hospital staff who expect an elderly patient to have a lingering death will respond to the patient's requests more slowly, will place the patient in more remote wards, or even bathe and feed him or her less frequently. Family members, however, typically expect their elderly relatives to be treated as painstakingly as any other patient. Moreover, a patient's perceived social worth can influence care. For example, elderly

Family members in Chiba Prefecture, Japan, follow a Buddhist priest in a funeral procession. The daughter carries her father's photograph, the son his cremated remains.

patients in private hospitals or those with high socioeconomic status often receive better care than poor elderly patients or those in public hospitals (Hooyman and Kiyak, 1991).

Patients, Families, Friends   Among the several perspectives of the dying process from the point of view of those most deeply concerned—patients and their loved ones—probably the most well known is that of Elizabeth Kübler-Ross (1969). Based on work with 200 primarily middle-aged cancer patients, Kübler-Ross proposed five stages of dying: denial, anger, bargaining, depression, and acceptance. Her theory has been criticized by many. Some claim that the stages are not experienced by everyone or in the same order. Others point out that the stages do not apply to the elderly. Many practitioners believe, however, that Kübler-Ross's conception offers some useful ideas in understanding the psychology of most patients and families, regardless of age or specific illness:

Denial   In an effort to cope with the dreaded news that a loved one will die, many people simply refuse to believe it. Patients and their families may ask for more tests, change physicians, or try in other ways to stave off the inevitable.

Anger   When denial is no longer possible, people may become angry and sometimes project their anger onto medical staff or one another.

Bargaining   The dying person sometimes tries to forestall death by making a deal with God: "If I can just live until my daughter's college graduation, I'll make a large contribution to my church."

Depression   When the dying person recognizes that death is imminent, depression may set in. In *reactive depression,* patients experience sadness as a result of the various other losses that accompany illness and dying, such as the loss of hair during radiation therapy or the loss of functions such as the ability to walk unaided. *Preparatory depression* anticipates the loss of love objects; patients may give away prized belongings or spend extra time with family members.

Acceptance   When patients finally come to accept their approaching death, they may reflect on their lives and anticipate dying with quiet resignation.

In another model of dying among the elderly, Retsinas (1988) emphasizes the gradual acceptance of illness and dying. Whereas the middle-aged person facing death usually has one defined catastrophic illness, like heart disease or cancer, the illness and disabilities suffered by an elderly person may include such ailments as increasing visual and auditory problems, stroke, diabetes, and crippling arthritis. More accustomed to the sick role, many elderly have had to confront the possibility of death for many years.

In addition, says Retsinas, the process of aging involves a series of role redefinitions. For example, even before the onset of illness, elderly people may have to give up such activities as driving, gardening, or climbing stairs. Unlike the middle-aged person, the dying elderly person does not suddenly confront the loss of an active social role and related worries like the effects on the family of the loss of a person's earning power.

Moreover, rather than deny death the elderly may actually welcome it. Many have seen their spouses and friends die over the years, and unlike middle-aged people, the elderly may have already outlived most of the people who mattered to them. Elderly patients often view death as a natural part of nature's cycle, and they may even await death as an end to pain, sorrow, social isolation, dependency, and loneliness. In sum, Retsinas suggests that the elderly may not experience Kübler-Ross's stages of denial, anger, bargaining, and depression because they have been experiencing a "social death" over many years.

Hospice Care for the Dying

Taken from the medieval term that meant a place of shelter and rest for weary or sick travelers, a **hospice** is a place for the care of the dying that stresses the control of pain, giving patients a sense of security and companionship and trying to make them comfortable. Hospice care is implemented in a variety of settings—in patients' homes, in hospitals, or in other inpatient facilities.

In the hospice approach, both professional and lay workers work as a team in assessing and meeting the physical, psychosocial, and spiritual needs of both the patient and family members and in providing dying people with full and accurate information about their condition. Another important function is to develop supportive environments in which people can talk about their lives with sympathetic listeners. Hospice staff members work directly with family and friends to help them deal with their feelings and relate compassionately to the dying patient. Although some people prefer to care for a dying person at home, some practitioners warn that the in-home approach can be stressful for both family and friends and may severely strain a family's resources.

Coping with Someone's Death

The state of having been robbed, or deprived, by death of a loved person is called **bereavement,** and those close to the dead person are known as the *bereaved.* Bereavement takes on different expressions in different people, but grief and mourning are common reactions to the death of someone close.

The emotional response to loss, **grief** is seen by some as an entire process in which a variety of feelings—sadness, longing, bewilderment, anger, and loneliness—combine. The grieving process may extend over a year or more after the death of a loved one. **Mourning** is the customary outward expression of grief that varies among different social and cultural groups. Mourning ranges from normal grief to pathological melancholy that may include such reactions as physical or mental illness. Whether it's the death of a child, a parent, or grandparent, most people don't "recover"

and end mourning. Instead, they adapt, accommodate, and change (Silverman, 2000).

Some predict that parental deaths will hit babyboomers especially hard. By the time they turn 50, a quarter of the population typically lose their mothers and half lose their fathers. A parental death can be a serious trauma, frequently leading to depression, family conflict, or a midlife crisis because adult children realize that they're "next in line." Parents' death may be even tougher for baby boomers. They often live thousands of miles away from their families and have to commute for a parent's final moments or plan burials by long distance (McGinn and Halpert, 1998). Long-distance baby boomers may be especially vulnerable to funeral rip-offs. According to one consumer rights advocate, the $11 billion U.S. funeral industry is riddled with shoddy practices, greed, and insensitivity. For example, "professional service fees" amount on average to about 20 percent of the total funeral bill, but the consumer gets virtually nothing. Funeral homes inflate their prices wildly because they know their grief-stricken customers—especially those living far away—are unlikely to shop around (Carlson, 1998).

There are clusters or phases of grief (Hooyman and Kiyak, 1991). People generally respond initially with shock, numbness, and disbelief, followed by an all-encompassing feeling of sorrow. Recently bereaved elderly report more illnesses and an increased use of new medications, and usually rate their overall health more poorly.

In the intermediate stage of grief people often idealize loved ones who have died and may even actively search for them. For example, a widow may see her husband's face in a crowd. Recent widows or widowers may also feel guilty, regretting every lapse: "Why wasn't I more understanding?" "Why did we argue that morning?" Survivors may also become angry, blowing up at children and friends in a seemingly irrational way, and even the dead person may not escape their rage: "Why didn't he prepare me better for life on my own?" "Why didn't she take better care of her health?"

When people are hurt, they tend to lash out and to try to find a source of blame. Some people may displace their anger onto doctors and medical science for having failed to preserve life, even when they know that the death was inevitable (Belsky, 1988). When the grieving person finally accepts the loss and stops yearning for the deceased person, disorganization, anguish, and despair often follow. The person may feel aimless, without interest, purpose, or motivation, incapable of making decisions, and lacking in self-confidence.

The final stage of recovery and reorganization may not occur for as much as several years after the death, although many people begin to readjust and to reorganize their lives after about six months. For the elderly, grieving may be more complex than it is for younger people. Over a relatively brief period, and at

CHOICES

Helping Children Grieve

Because families are becoming increasingly complex and multigenerational, many children will experience the death not only of grandparents but also of great-grandparents, stepgrandparents, and other relatives. The following are some ways that Huntley (1991: 38–42) suggests for helping children grieve:

1. **Recognize that each child will grieve differently:** How children will grieve is influenced both by the responses of those close to them and by their relationship with the deceased. Moreover, children may have mixed emotions if the deceased was sometimes unloving or uncaring.

2. **Encourage questions:** When someone dies, children usually want to know what has happened and what will follow next. Tell them honestly what has occurred and explain what the word "dead" means. Don't be afraid to say "I don't know" when you don't know. If at any time you cannot deal with the children's questions (because you may be physically or emotionally exhausted, for example), tell them why you can't explain now and specify when you will be able to talk with them about the death.

3. **Encourage the expression of feelings:** Encourage children to show their emotions (Nolen-Hoeksema and Larson, 1999). Talk about other people's feelings as well. For example, if Grandma seems to be angry, explain that it is not because the children did anything wrong but because Grandma is upset that the doctors couldn't save Grandpa's life. Because children, like adults, vary in the degree to which they are comfortable expressing feelings, some may prefer to write down their thoughts, make an album of photos of the loved one, draw pictures or paint, or do some other kind of activity.

4. **Encourage participation in events following the death:** Tell the children about the events that will be taking place (wake, funeral, and burial). Explain that these rituals provide us with a way to say good-bye to the deceased, but don't force children to participate in these events if they are uncomfortable or are frightened by them. Instead, a child may prefer to commemorate the life of the deceased in his or her own way. For example, "If . . . Erin and her grandmother used to play under a particular tree at Grandma's house, then maybe Erin would like to plant a similar tree at home in her own backyard" (Huntley, 1991: 41).

5. **Try to maintain a sense of normalcy:** To restore some semblance of security, try to follow the children's normal routine as closely as possible. In the first few months following the death, try to avoid making any drastic changes, such as moving, unless it is absolutely necessary.

6. **Take advantage of available resources:** Schools, churches, or local hospitals sometimes have children's support groups. When children get together with other bereaved children, they become aware that they are not alone in their grief. Books written for children can be helpful, whether they are read by an adult to children or by the children themselves. When necessary, counselors who specialize in the area of grief and bereavement can help both you and your child. Increasingly, moreover, many people are finding a cyberspace network of caring, invisible supporters. The Internet is providing a new way for people to seek solace after the death of a loved one (see "Taking it Further" at the end of the chapter).

---

a time when their coping capacities and resources may be diminished, they often experience the deaths of many people who were important to them.

The intensity of a person's grief depends on a number of factors, including the quality of the lost relationship, the age of the deceased, and the suddenness of the death. For many people, no matter how private they may be in their grief, holidays are especially difficult because they are so connected to families and friends. People who are grieving may dread the normal festivities because everything—from cards and decorations to special meals and traditional music—may remind them of the loved one who has died. Counselors and therapists suggest that survivors not force themselves to participate in special family traditions if doing so is too painful (Thomas-Lester, 1994).

Adults sometimes don't realize that children may be confused or experience grief over a death. Parents may be so involved in their own loss that they overlook a child's attachment to the person who has died. Some *thanatologists*—social scientists who study death and grief—encourage parents and educators to talk about death with children openly and honestly (see the box "Helping Children Grieve") and to teach children how to deal with loss, especially the death of someone they love.

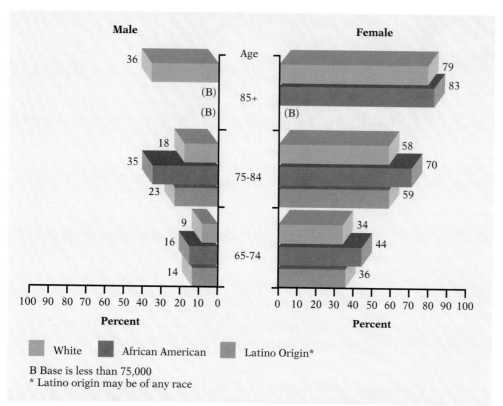

FIGURE 17.5 **Widowhood Is More Common for Elderly Women Than for Elderly Men** (percent of civilian noninstitutional population) (From F. B. Hobbs and B. L. Damon. 1996. *65+ in the United States.* U.S. Bureau of the Census. Current Population Reports, Special Studies, P23-190. Washington, D.C.: Government Printing Office, Figure 6-2. Based on U.S. Bureau of the Census, *Marital Status and Living Arrangements: March 1993,* Current Population Reports, P20-478. Washington, D.C.: U.S. Government Printing Office, 1994, table 1).

Being Widowed

The death of a spouse often means not just the loss of a life companion but the end of a whole way of life. Unfamiliar tasks—managing the finances, cooking meals, fixing the faucet—suddenly fall on the surviving spouse. Friendships may change or even end because many close relationships during marriage are based on being a couple. Other ties, such as relationships with in-laws, may weaken or erode.

As *Figure 17.5* shows, there are more widows than widowers in all categories age 65 and over for all races. At age 75 and over, over 66 percent of men are married (or remarried) and living with a spouse compared to only 27 percent of women (Lugaila, 1998). The numbers of elderly people living alone are expected to increase from 9 percent in 1990 to over 15 percent in 2020.

Most of those living alone will be women. Why? First, the life expectancy of women at age 65 now exceeds that of men of the same age by almost seven years. Second, married men have death rates two to three times higher than those of married women of the same age. Third, a wife is typically three or four years younger than her husband, which increases the likelihood that she will survive him. Fourth, widowers over age 65 are eight times as likely to remarry as are widows. As you saw in Chapter 7, social norms encourage the marriage of older men to younger women but discourage marriage between older women and younger men. Given the large pool of eligible women (those who are younger, widowed, divorced, or never married) and the shortage of men, it is easier for older men to remarry.

Facing Widowhood

Many recently widowed men and women exhibit such depressive symptoms as sadness, insomnia, appetite loss, weight loss, tearfulness, and self-dissatisfaction. Some longitudinal studies report that men and women experience similar physical and emotional difficulties

THE WIZARD OF ID   Brant parker and Johnny hart

© 1996 Creators Syndicate, Inc.

initially and, with time, do not differ much in their ability to cope with the loss of a spouse (Brubaker, 1991). In a study of recent widows, however, George Zubenko and Wendy Nuss (cited in Herman, 1992) noted several risk factors that might identify women likely to plunge into a protracted, major depression after the death of their husbands: never having worked outside the home, having had earlier psychiatric disorders, and believing that they had few friends and family to help them.

It is unclear whether widowhood is more difficult for women or men in the long run. Many researchers have found that adaptation to widowhood is related to income (see Brubaker, 1991, for a summary of the research on this topic). For both men and women, the financial situation is related to feelings of well-being. The emotional pain of losing a spouse coupled with the burden of the costs associated with a fatal illness can seem overwhelming.

Women who have been economically dependent on their husbands often find their incomes drastically reduced. If they are under 60 years of age and have never worked outside the home, they may experience the "widow's gap": Under present law, unless she is disabled, a widow is not eligible for Social Security benefits until she is 60. Moreover, some private pension plans provide no coverage for the spouse after the husband's death (Choi, 1992). Insurance benefits, when they exist, tend to be exhausted within a few years of the husband's death. Financial hardships may be especially great for a woman who cared for a spouse during a long illness or for the widow who depleted their joint resources during the spouse's institutionalization. Furthermore, many older widows have few opportunities to increase their income through paid employment.

Widowers' financial problems vary according to their educational and occupational levels. Men with high educational levels and higher-status jobs often have generous Social Security benefits, pension plans that are supplemented by employers, and investments

(such as stocks and bonds) that yield annual interest or can be sold. Not all widowers are so fortunate, of course. Children are sometimes surprised that they must provide for fathers who have worked all their lives and, the children assume, are well prepared for retirement (Burgess, 1988).

Social Isolation and Loneliness

Men more often complain of loneliness and seem to make slower emotional recoveries after the death of a spouse than do women, notwithstanding financial problems widows may have. They may be less comfortable expressing such emotions as grief because they have been less intimately involved in family and friendship roles throughout life. Their limited homemaking skills and experience may also contribute to feelings of helplessness and isolation (Anderson, 1984).

Many men have depended on their wives not only for emotional support and household maintenance but for arranging a social life as well. Consequently, men appear to "need" remarriage more than women do to restructure their lives. Whereas widows often have fewer resources than married women, they often have more time and more freedom to help friends and relatives (Gallagher and Gerstel, 1993; Bradsher, 1997). Thus, their ties with family and friends may grow stronger in widowhood.

Unlike women, many men have few confidants other than their wives. Thus, when their wives die, many men often find themselves alone in coping with their grief, without anyone to whom they can feel free to "bare their souls." In general, widowers tend to interact with others much less frequently than widows, and this pattern becomes more noticeable over time (Burgess, 1988), except among African Americans, where both widows and widowers may maintain contact with friends on an equally frequent basis (R. J. Taylor et al., 1993).

Besides being a healthy exercise, dancing is one way to be with people and, sometimes, to meet possible companions or mates. Square dancing and related forms of "country" dancing have become increasingly popular, especially among older adults.

Generally, widowhood increases social isolation for both women and men. Community affiliations such as church groups or social clubs may be important in coping with loneliness. Men are more depressed than women after a spouse's death, especially if they did not belong to any religious organization (Siegel and Kuykendall, 1990). Mental and physical impairments are higher for widowed persons of both sexes than they are for married persons of the same age. In addition, chronic illness, suicide, and death tend to be more common among widowed persons and particularly among men who don't have support systems (Hooyman and Kiyak, 1991).

Many widows and most widowers begin to date again within a few years after losing a mate. Friendship is the most important reason for dating. Like younger people, older people enjoy having friends and companions to share interests and on whom they can call in emergencies. As we discussed in Chapter 7, dating also prevents loneliness and isolation. Having a confidant is especially important for men who grew up during an era when it was considered unmasculine to have intimate relationships with one's children, other men, or female friends. Lovers play a crucial role because love, intimacy, and sexual activity continue to be an important part of life for the older person. And, finally, caregivers are important as providers of emotional and physical help in the event of accidents or illness.

Family Caregiving in Later Life

We often hear that adult children ignore their elderly parents and place them in institutions instead of caring for them themselves. In 1992, the media publicized the notion of "granny dumping"—abandoning an elderly person with Alzheimer's disease or some other form of mental disorder in a public place such as a shopping mall. Such cases are the exception, however.

Children today actually provide more care (and more difficult care) to more parents over much longer periods of time than they did in the so-called good old days. For example, fewer than 10 percent of family members who care for the frail elderly receive assistance from any formal services outside the home (Cox, 1993). If people who take care of ill or disabled family members were paid for their work, the bill would come to nearly $200 billion a year. This total dwarfs spending for formal home health care ($32 billion a year) and nursing home care ($83 billion a year) (Arno et al., 1999).

Who Provides Care?

A *sandwich generation,* you will recall from Chapter 13, is composed of midlife men and women who feel caught between meeting responsibilities to their own children as well as to their aging parents. According to Zal (1992: 1), "They find themselves tightly sandwiched between the needs and problems of their adolescent and young adult children, as they push toward independence, and their aging parents as they slowly slide into a more dependent role."

Just over 23 percent of all U.S. households provide care for an aging family member. About 73 percent of caregivers are female. The typical caregiver is a married woman in her mid-forties who works full time, is a high school graduate, and has an annual household income of $35,000. In terms of race-ethnicity, Asian (32 percent) and black households (29 percent) are more likely to include a caregiver than Latino households (29 percent) or white families (24 percent).

Unlike other groups, Asian caregivers are as likely to be male as female. And Asian and black caregivers are more likely than white and Latino caregivers to be involved in caring for more than one person ("Family caregiving . . . ," 1997).

There are several reasons for the racial-ethnic differences in caretaking. Much of the Latino population is young compared to the national population (see Chapters 1 and 12) and have fewer aging family members. Many Asian elderly may rely on family members for assistance because there is a strong sense of filial responsibility. In addition, some immigrants may rely on family members rather than formal agencies because of a lack of knowledge of services, language difficulties, and a lack of transportation to organizations that provide assistance (Tsai and Lopez, 1997; see also Chapters 12 and 14).

For many black families, caregiving is a "fact of life." It may be that they are better able to cope in this labor-intensive and time-consuming caregiving work because of more effective lifelong adaptive skills. Black elderly may also value and expect support from children more than do white elderly, even though blacks are more likely to receive assistance from formal agencies (Lee et al., 1998). In addition, many black families have developed informal support systems through black churches and other organizations that encourage caregiving to aging parents (Barker et al., 1998; Mui et al., 1998).

Midlife adults are not the only caregivers, however. In 1996, for example, 40 percent of women and 26 percent of men in their fifties and early sixties provided at least 100 hours of care for aging parents (Johnson and Lo Sasso, 2000). Spouses are most likely to care for aging or infirm partners, and one-third of the caregivers of the frail elderly are themselves over 65. As parents age, however, adult children provide more care and daughters outnumber sons as caretakers by more than three to one (Cox, 1993).

Family and Other Support Systems

The family is an important caregiving unit for the elderly. The fact that only 5 percent of the elderly are institutionalized—typically in nursing homes—shows that families are the primary source of assistance for frail, elderly people. Some formal support services exist, but they are often expensive or limited to elderly people who are ambulatory, who can take care of their own physical needs, and who do not suffer from mental illness.

Day Care for the Elderly One formal support service that is catching on across the United States is the day-care center for the elderly. This type of program is in the vanguard of efforts to keep elderly people out of nursing homes and in their own homes and communities as long as possible. Most centers are run by nonprofit

organizations, such as churches or government-funded senior centers. Increasingly, hospitals and nursing homes are also instituting day-care programs. In 1975, there were only 15 adult day-care centers, but by 1999 there were over 4000 (Field, 1999). Program providers estimate that 10,000 are needed.

Many centers provide transportation and some have medical personnel on staff. Some even offer overnight and weekend services. These centers provide needed respite for family caregivers, allowing them to work, run errands, or spend time with their children. For the aging participants, the centers offer structure, stimulation, social life, and a chance for renewed self-esteem.

The better centers offer a variety of programs, according to the level of care the older person needs. Clients may play bingo, volleyball, or other games, according to their physical capabilities. They attend picnics and lectures and sometimes join with preschoolers for activities like barbecues or finger painting. Most centers accept clients with mild to moderate mental difficulties. Some provide "pet therapy," in which elderly patients, especially those who are withdrawn, often open up to the affectionate behavior of pet dogs or cats (usually brought for visits by volunteers). Alzheimer's experts say the extra stimulation of a day-care center seems to help stave off some mental deterioration in these patients. Often the lighting, color schemes, furniture, and background music in the centers are chosen to have a calming effect, and many include fenced paths for patients who tend to wander. Some have exercise programs, showers, and beauty parlors run by local beauticians.

The day-care center's biggest problem is financial. In some states, Medicaid will cover fees for elderly people who meet income requirements. The middle-income group is the one that can't afford to participate. Attending five days a week can cost $700 or more a month—far more than the average Social Security check pays. Many long-term-care insurance providers now cover adult day-care expenses. Some for-profit groups, like ElderCare, Inc., charge $40 to $60 a day, and each center serves up to 75 people (Field, 1999).

Retirement Villages Older people have more options today in finding appropriate living arrangements. As the box "Housing Options for Older People" indicates, the range of available amenities and services includes home health care, housekeeping, meals, property maintenance, recreational facilities, and transportation. A growing number of retirement villages that serve black elderly are sprouting nationwide. Many are rooted in the black church (Chambers and Clemetson, 1999). Some retired educators are drawn to retirement communities that are located near colleges or universities. Such "academic villages" feature libraries and computer facilities, and provide

CHOICES

Housing Options for Older People

You saw in Chapter 8 (see the box "Senior Communes") that some older people are pooling their resources and establishing communal living arrangements. Besides such traditional possibilities as apartments and mobile homes, there are many other options:

Accessory apartment: Completely private living unit created in surplus space inside a single-family residence and rented either to outside tenants or to relatives.

Assisted-living facility: Residential long-term care environment in which residents have rooms, meals, help with activities of daily living, and some protective supervision or 24-hour care.

Board-and-care home: Similar to assisted living except on a smaller scale; more personal-care services are included.

Congregate housing: Specially planned, designed, and managed multi-unit rented housing, typically with self-contained apartments. Supportive services include communal meals, housekeeping, transportation, and social and recreational activities.

Continuing-care retirement community: Housing development planned, designed, and operated to provide a full range of accommodations and services for older adults, including independent living, congregate housing, assisted-living, and nursing home care.

Cooperative housing: Facility occupied by tenants who own shares of stock in the complex (but not the individual unit) and share costs of maintaining it in exchange for the right to occupy the unit.

ECHO (elder cottage housing opportunity): Separate, self-contained removable living unit placed on same property as and adjacent to an existing home as a residence for a relative or tenant. Such units meet the older person's desire for independence, privacy, and proximity to caretakers.

Foster-care home: Single-family residence in which nonrelated older people live with a foster family that provides meals, housekeeping, and personal care. Many foster families care for frail or disabled elderly.

Home sharing: Younger people seeking affordable housing live with seniors who have rooms to rent. Depending on the situation, tenants either pay low rent or do chores such as taking out the garbage or grocery shopping in exchange for rent.

Retirement community: Large, self-sufficient, age-segregated residential development containing owned and/or rental units. Support services and recreational amenities are often available.

Retirement hotel: Remodeled hotel or apartment complex that has been converted to residential units designed for independent older people. Hotellike services, such as housekeeping and messages, are provided.

Townhouse/condominium: Collection of individual living units owned by residents; includes common areas that are shared. The complex of units usually includes parking, a swimming pool, and recreation rooms.

SOURCES: *Modern Maturity*, 1993; Gilman, 1994; Quiason, 1997.

---

residents with lectures and seminars "on everything from humanities to international economics" (Vanderpool, 1999).

Caregiving Styles

Families care for their elderly members in different ways. According to Matthews and Rosner (1988), there are five primary types of family caregiving in later life.

The style that forms the backbone of the caregiving system is *routine help*. The adult child incorporates regular assistance to the elderly parent into his or her ongoing activities. For this system to work, a family member—generally one of the elderly person's children—is regularly available to do whatever needs to be done. Routine involvement may include a wide range of activities: household chores, checking to see the person is all right, providing outings, running errands, managing finances, and visiting.

In a second style, relatives serve as *backups*. Although one person may provide routine care to an aging parent, a brother or sister may step in when needed. For example, one sister explained, "I do what my sisters instruct me to do." She responded to her sisters' requests but did not initiate involvement. Another sibling was described as the "favorite child" and was called in primarily when a parent needed to be "convinced" to do something that the routine caregivers thought was necessary.

The *circumscribed style* of participation is highly predictable but carefully bounded. For example, one respondent said of her brother, "He gives a routine, once-a-week call." This call was important to the parent. The brother was not expected to increase his participation in providing parental care, however. Siblings who adopt this style can be counted on to help, but there are clear limits to what they can be called on to do. For example, in one family, a son who was a physician was relied on for medical advice or assistance but was not expected to assume any other responsibility.

In contrast to the first three types of caregiving, the *sporadic style* describes adult children who provide services to parents at their own convenience. For example, one daughter said, "We invite Mom to go along when we take trips." Another said, "My brother comes when he feels like it to take Mother out on Sunday, but it's not a scheduled thing." Some siblings don't mind this behavior but others resent brothers and sisters who avoid the most demanding tasks:

> [My sister and I] were always very close, and we're not now. I don't think she comes down often enough. . . . She calls, big deal: that's very different from spending three to four hours a day. . . . She does not wheel my mother to the doctor, she does not carry her to the car, she does not oversee the help. (Abel, 1991: 154)

The last style is *disassociation* from responsibility altogether. This behavior is quite predictable: Other sisters and brothers know that they cannot count at all on a sibling. In one family of three daughters, for example, the two younger sisters were routinely involved in helping their mother, whereas their older sister "is not included in our discussions or dealing with mother. . . . She doesn't do anything." Such children do not always disassociate themselves entirely from the family. In one case, the brother had broken off contact with his mother early in his life and consequently from parental care but not from contact with his siblings. His sister explained, "My brother has no interest at all and does not care about mother to any extent. The few times he comes into town, we deliberately don't discuss Mother with him" (Matthews and Rosner, 1988: 188–89).

The Satisfaction and Strain of Caregiving

Caregivers are not a homogeneous group. Some enjoy caregiving and believe that family relationships can be renewed or strengthened by helping elderly members. They see caregiving as a "labor of love" because of strong ties of affection that have always existed in the family (Saldana and Dassori, 1999).

For others, caregiving provides a feeling of being useful and needed. As one daughter said, "For me, that's what life's all about!" (Guberman et al., 1992: 601). Caring for parents may be especially gratifying when the work does not conflict with employment and when the provider is not caring for other family members or relatives (Gerstel and Gallagher, 1993). Even when there are responsibilities to one's own family, however, women often report that the caregiving enhanced their sense of self-worth and well-being, especially when family members assisted in the caregiving (Martire et al., 1997).

Often, however, caretaking creates stress and strain in families (Aranda and Knight, 1997; Dilworth-Anderson et al., 1999). Older people often need support at a time when their children's lives are complicated with many varied responsibilities. Families are often unprepared for the problems involved in caring for an elderly person. In general, daily routines are disrupted, caregivers are confined to the home, and parent–child conflict may increase. Parents who are cognitively impaired, who can't accomplish basic daily tasks of self-care, and/or who engage in disruptive behavior are clearly the most difficult to care for ("Family Caregiving . . . ," 1997).

Financial burdens include not only the direct costs of medical care but also such indirect costs as lost income or missed promotions. Funds for services to reduce caregivers' strains are limited. Women are more likely than men to quit their jobs or to decrease their work hours to provide care (Abel, 1991). Those who interrupt employment to be parental caregivers generally receive fewer retirement benefits for themselves.

Caregivers bear the emotional burdens of feeling alone, isolated, and without time for themselves. Rates of depression increase, especially among female caregivers, and distress may be intensified by the lack of information about and access to potential helping services. Even when support is available, the caregiver of the disabled, frail, or mentally ill elderly frequently faces many years of increasing dependence, decline, and demanding physical-care tasks (see Wilson, 1990).

Particularly when formal support services are unavailable or unknown, caregivers' feelings of isolation and strain may intensify. In some cases, stress may become severe enough to lead to family breakdown, neglect, or even abuse of the older person (see Chapter 14). In addition, an adult child may often have to forgo important social events and activities to meet caregiving needs. This may create additional strain and role conflict (Mui and Morrow-Howell, 1993; Saldana and Dassori, 1999).

Most often, it is a daughter or daughter-in-law who is responsible for organizing and providing care to an elderly family member. Married female caretakers get more financial and emotional support from their spouses and children than do never-married, divorced, or remarried female caregivers. Nonetheless, they often experience strain because of the competing demands from their spouses and children, on the one hand, and their elderly relative on the other (Brody et al., 1992). A troubled marital relationship may become more problematic with such added stress. Or, if female caretakers do not get support from their immediate family, they can fall into the "martyrdom trap" by making unreasonable demands on themselves (Couper and Sheehan, 1987).

For many women, caring for elderly relatives is not a single episode but continues throughout their life course, and dependence/independence issues may be replayed many times. The caregiving may be necessary for multiple elderly relatives and may be multilayered as a person's parents, in-laws, grandparents, and other elderly relatives require help sequentially or simultaneously. Given the discrepancy in life expectancy for men and women, inevitably many of these women will also care for dependent husbands in the future.

Conclusion

As this chapter has shown, there are many similarities in later-life families. Women tend to live longer, and men are more likely to remarry after being widowed. On the one hand, because of an increased life expectancy, many of us will have more *choices* in later life as to how we will spend our "golden years" and how we will play grandparenting roles. On the other hand, we will also face *constraints*, the most serious of which is how we will care for aging family members as longevity increases and health-related costs rise.

Another critical issue is how we will respond to the *changes* of an aging population that has diverse social, health, and financial needs. As we have discussed in earlier chapters, today's lifestyles vary greatly. Some people remain single, some marry but have no children, and some marry several times. These variations will probably continue as people age and the overall population ages. Conner (1992: 203) notes that "perhaps the biggest challenge for the future is to successfully meet the needs of our increasingly diverse population of senior citizens." Meeting family needs in the future is the focus of the last chapter.

SUMMARY

1. The aging of our society is occurring at an exceedingly rapid pace due to several factors: a decrease in fertility rates, an increase in life expectancy, and a faster growth of white and ethnic elderly populations.

2. Although there is great diversity in the aged population, people age 65 and over must confront such similar aging issues as accepting changes in health, dealing with stereotypes, and coping with mandatory retirement.

3. One of the biggest changes during the last two or three decades has been the rapid growth of the multi-generational family. Because families now often span three or four generations, the importance of the grandparent role has increased.

4. There are at least five styles of grandparenting: remote, companionate, involved, advisory, and cultural transmitters. These styles, and grandparents who act as surrogate parents, often reflect such factors as the grandparents' age, physical proximity, and relationships with their own children, especially daughters.

5. Adult children's divorce creates both opportunities and dilemmas for grandparents. Sometimes their relationships with grandchildren are strengthened, but sometimes, especially for in-laws, they increasingly lose touch.

6. All families must deal with the death of elderly parents. Physicians and other health-care professionals often view death in terms of the dying trajectory. Alternatively, the dying process can be understood from the point of view of the dying person and/or those who will survive the person.

7. Although many elderly parents and relatives die in hospitals and nursing homes, hospice care provides an alternative by making the patient more comfortable and by providing companionship, a sense of security, and control of pain.

8. On the average, women live nearly seven years longer than men. Although most women outlive their husbands, both widows' and widowers' coping strategies typically involve adapting to a change in income as well as dealing with loneliness and the emotional pain of losing a spouse.

9. Children today provide more care (and more difficult care) to more parents over much longer periods of time than ever before. As our population ages, more disabled and frail Americans will need long-term care.

10. Caregiving includes both family support systems and formal services such as day care for the elderly. There are several caregiving styles and all involve love as well as some degree of stress. For the most part, the primary caregivers are women.

KEY TERMS

gerontologist   *451*
later-life family   *451*
depression   *452*
Alzheimer's disease   *452*

ageism   *454*
Society Security   *457*
hospice   *466*
bereavement   *466*

grief   *466*
mourning   *466*

TAKING IT FURTHER

Aging on the Internet

There is an overwhelming number of aging-related resources on the Net. Here are a few URLs to whet your appetite:

Administration on Aging provides information on older persons and services for the elderly, numerous links, fact sheets, and other resources.

www.aoa.dhhs.gov

National Institute on Aging offers publications on health and aging topics and many links to caregiving sites.

www.nih.gov/nia

SeniorLaw Home Page includes materials on elder law, Medicare, Medicaid, estate planning, trusts, and the rights of the elderly and disabled.

www.seniorlaw.com

Senior Women.com offers many useful resources on grandparenting, politics, health, computers, a "letters from readers" column, and many links.

www.seniorwomen.com

Seniors-Site.com is fun. It provides a "unique, informative, interesting, and entertaining" Web site for adults over 50 and others. A site map includes links to advisers, pets, fitness, sex, and many other topics.

seniors-site.com

And more . . . www.prenhall.com/benokraitis gives dozens of URLs on national organizations for seniors, caregiver associations, home-care directories, health-related topics (such as Alzheimer's and vision loss), grief resources, health-care financing, and locating reputable funeral organizations.

The Family in the Twenty-first Century

476

DATADIGEST

- By 2010, **couples with children under age 18** are expected to make up 38 percent of all married-couple households, down from 47 percent in 1990.

- The **number of households headed by single mothers under age 25** is expected to increase by 44 percent, from 831,000 in 1995 to 1.2 million in 2010.

- The **number of single fathers** will grow an estimated 44 percent between 1990 and 2010, to 1.7 million; but it will remain less than 2 percent of all households.

- **One-person households,** 24 percent of all households in 1995, are expected to rise to 27 percent of all households in 2010.

- Between 1995 and 2010, **middle-aged householders are expected to increase greatly.** Householders aged 45 to 54 are expected to rise from 17 million to 25 million, a 45 percent increase; households headed by people between 55 and 64 are expected to rise from 12 million to 20 million, a 62 percent increase.

- The number of **elderly householders** grew 5 percent between 1995 and 2000, from 21.7 million to 22.8 million. This group is expected to increase another 14 percent in the following decade, to 26.1 million in 2010.

- **Social Security, Medicare, Medicaid, and federal retirement payments** amounted to about 30 percent of the U.S. budget in 1963. By 2003, these payments will be 72 percent of the federal budget.

Sources: Miller, 1995; Simpson, 1995; U.S. Census Bureau, 1999c.

IN considering the family of the twenty-first century, many observers assume that the dynamic processes that have shaped the family during the last two decades will continue to influence the family in the future. The idea that the family is an important institution has been a major theme throughout this book. In this chapter we consider, briefly, where the family is going in the future in six areas—family structure, racial-ethnic diversity, children's rights, health-related issues, economic concerns, and global aging.

Family Structure

In the future, it's likely that the variations in family structures will increase in number and forms. We will probably see more households that are multigenerational and composed of unrelated adults, as well as more stepfamilies with his, her, and their children. The high number of divorces and remarriages may mean that the elderly will be depending as much (or more) on "stepkin" as on biological kin to provide care (see Chapter 16). In 2030, the oldest baby boomers will be in their eighties. Whether or not stepkin will provide support to their elderly relatives will depend on geographic mobility and the degree to which stepparents form close relationships with their children. If society's attitude toward homosexuals becomes more positive and domestic partners acquire more legal rights, we may also see greater numbers of families headed by lesbian and gay parents.

Despite these changes, there is no evidence that marriage will be replaced. As you saw in earlier chapters, although many people are cohabiting and remaining single longer, about 93 percent of Americans marry at least once. Although many family functions have changed since the turn of the century (see Chapter 1), the family is still the primary group that provides the nurturance, love, and emotional sustenance that people need to be happy, healthy, and productive. Commuter marriages, increased work responsibilities, divorce, and other stressors aside, many Americans report that the family is one of the most important aspects of their lives (see Chapters 9 and 10).

Racial–Ethnic Diversity

One of the most striking changes in American society today, the growth of racially and ethnically diverse families, is expected to continue in the future. Factors such as immigration from abroad and higher fertility rates among African Americans and some Asian American and Latino groups contribute to this change. People of color currently account for 24 percent of the U.S. population and are expected to increase to 30 percent by 2020 (Population Reference Bureau, 1990).

One analyst has observed: "The question isn't really whether non-Hispanic whites will become a minority; it's a question of when" (Kate, 1997: 42). As minorities make up a larger share of the population and the labor force, they will have a greater impact on political, educational, and economic institutions. By 2025, for example, Latinos are expected to make up 48 percent of the population in New Mexico, 43 percent in California, 38 percent in Texas, and about 25 percent in Nevada and Florida.

Some expect that, as the Latino population increases, their political power will grow proportionately as well (Morgenthau, 1997). The twenty-first century may find young minorities working to support an older, white population. If older, white males continue to control the government and economy, such dominance, especially if current discrimination persists (Chapter 12), may increase racial-ethnic tension across generational lines.

Racial-ethnic communities will continue to grow and change in the twenty-first century. For example, whereas the most recent Asian Indian, Cambodian, and South American immigrants often live and work in interethnic areas of many large cities, Filipino and Korean American families have been moving to the suburbs and establishing communities where they have their own houses of worship and programs to teach their native languages to their children.

Children's Rights

In 1992, in an unprecedented lawsuit, an 11-year-old Florida boy asked a judge to "divorce" him from his parents. To protect the boy and his two younger brothers from their abusive, alcoholic father and neglectful mother, the children had been placed in the care of social service agencies for nearly two and a half years. During that time, the 11-year-old had lived in three foster homes and a boys' home. He chose to stay with the last foster family, a couple with eight children, who wanted to adopt him. The boy's mother and father, who were separated, tried to regain custody of their son. The mother's attorney argued that parents have the constitutional right to control the custody of their children. The boy's foster father, also an attorney, maintained that children have a right to pursue happiness. The judge ruled that his foster parents could adopt the boy. Some people would undoubtedly cite this case as another example of the American family in decline. Others might argue that the case illustrates the right of children to be part of a healthy, responsible, and loving household.

A national study of U.S. families concluded that the United States, the most prosperous nation on earth, is failing many of its children:

Although many children grow up healthy and happy in strong, stable families, far too many do not. They are children whose parents are too stressed and busy to provide caring attention and guidance. They are children who grow up without the material support and personal involvement of their mothers and fathers. They are children who are poor, whose families cannot adequately feed and clothe them and provide safe, secure homes. They are children who are victims of abuse and neglect at the hands of adults they love and trust, as well as those they do not even know. They are children who are born too early and too small, who face a lifetime of chronic illness and disability. They are children who enter school ill prepared for the rigors of learning, who fail to develop the skills and attitudes needed to get good jobs and become responsible members of adult society. They are children who lack hope for what their lives can become, who believe they have little to lose by dropping out of school, having a baby as an unmarried teenager, committing violent crimes, or taking their own lives. (National Commission on Children, 1991: vii–viii)

Such conclusions are well founded. Much of the research has shown not only that the United States has abandoned many of its children, but that the situation has been deteriorating since 1980 (see Chapters 11 and 13). Some scholars argue, moreover, that our children are being ignored because adults are investing more in themselves and their personal pursuits than in raising their children (see Chapter 1).

In 1999, almost 12 percent of children living below the poverty level experienced "moderate" or "severe" hunger ("*America's children . . . ,*" 2000). Scientific research indicates that hunger and undernutrition rob children of their potential. Biologists and neurologists have found that physical nourishment determines how many brain cells children develop. In addition, researchers also believe that stress activates hormones that can impair learning and memory and lead to intellectual and behavioral developmental problems (see Chapter 11).

Family Policy

About 17 million children in this country have absent fathers; each year 1 million children are born to unwed parents and another million are newly affected by divorce (Garry, 1997). **Family policy**—the measures taken by governmental bodies to achieve specific objectives relating to the family's well-being—has improved many of these children's lives. One bright spot, for example, is the future of child support. The first federal legislation to enforce the payment of child support was enacted in 1950, and additional bills were passed in 1965 and 1967, but the 1975 Office of Child Support Enforcement law was the first really significant piece of legislation in this area.

The new law not only requires all states to establish state offices of child-support enforcement but also provides federal reimbursement for nearly 75 percent

In 1992 Gregory Kingsley won the right to "divorce" his biological mother and to stay with his foster parents, who later adopted him.

of each state's enforcement costs. The 1975 act thus created the bureaucracy to enforce the private child-support obligation. Enacted nine years later, the 1984 Child Support Enforcement Amendments require states to adopt formulas and guidelines that the courts can use to determine child-support obligations. These amendments also require the states to withhold moneys equal to child-support obligations from wages and other income of noncustodial parents who are delinquent in their payments (Garfinkel et al., 1994).

In 1988, the Family Support Act strengthened the 1984 guidelines, requiring that judges provide a written justification for review by a higher court if they wish to depart from the state guidelines in any way. The act also requires that states review and update the child-support awards handled by the Office of Child Support Enforcement at least every three years. In addition, the legislation requires that by 1994 the states withhold funds for child-support payment in all cases, not just those that are delinquent. States have varied quite a bit in enforcing the latter requirement, however (see Chapter 15).

Courts are also becoming more "child-friendly" by recognizing children's rights. In 35 states, for example, statutes specifically mandate that trial judges consider the presence of domestic violence in child-custody disputes (Lehrman, 1996). Many divorcing women are afraid to testify against a batterer because they fear retaliation (see Chapter 14). Trial judges who take domestic violence seriously, however, are more likely to protect children from emotional and physical harm by *not* requiring joint physical and legal custody (see Chapter 15) and *not* awarding visitation rights to the violent parent.

Child Care and Parental Leave

Very few U.S. families, and especially those on welfare, can afford quality child-care services (see Chapter 13). Moreover, because mothers are much more likely than fathers to take time off from work to care for their children, women workers, as a group, fall permanently behind male workers in terms of pay, benefits, and seniority.

Women who are heads of households are even worse off. One national study found that nearly 23 percent of mothers between 21 and 29 years of age are out of the labor force because they can't afford child care. Because many of these mothers lack high school diplomas, they have difficulty competing in the labor market. And even for two employed parents, paying an average of $8540 per year per child for high-quality child care is more than most working-class or middle-class parents can afford (Gardner, 1995b).

Compared to those of other industrialized countries, the United States' record of child-care provisions has been abysmal. Congresswoman Pat Schroeder of Colorado once remarked, "Under our tax laws, a businesswoman can deduct a new Persian rug for her office but can't deduct most of her costs for child care. The deduction for a thoroughbred horse is greater than that for children" (Gibbs et al., 1990: 42).

In contrast to the U.S. system, 60 percent of child care in Japan is provided by the government, and both government and most companies offer monthly subsidies to parents with children (Shimomura, 1990). One of the most successful programs is in France, where parents can enroll their children in a variety of child-care centers, preschools, and special day-care homes run by the government. Tuition is free or minimal, adjusted according to the family income. Similar systems have been established in Denmark, Sweden, and other European countries (Neft and Levine, 1997).

In Belgium, Italy, and Denmark, at least 75 percent of children aged 3 to 5 are in some form of state-funded preschool programs, and in Germany, parents may deduct the cost of child care from their taxes. In Sweden, parents receive the equivalent of $1667 for each child in the form of a child-care subsidy, and local communities organize and maintain child-care centers for which parents pay about 10 percent of the actual cost (Herrstrom, 1990).

Many countries try to ensure children's rights by providing time for parenting, especially in families where both parents are employed. In over 30 developing countries, such as Angola and Ghana, parents have a paid infant-care leave (Frank and Zigler, 1996). Two major industrialized countries that do not mandate paid maternity leave are New Zealand and the United States (Neft and Levine, 1997). In the United States, the Family and Medical Leave Act passed in 1993 provides only unpaid leave and only to some employees (see Chapter 13).

A child-care center in Denmark, where more than three-quarters of children between 3 and 5 are in state-funded programs.

Unlike the United States, a number of developed nations provide generous parental leave benefits. The minimum childbirth-related leave among the European countries is three months in the Netherlands and a few other countries, sixteen weeks in France, six months in Canada, nine months to one year in Italy, one year in Denmark, one and one-half years in Sweden, and three years in Austria, Finland, France (with third and subsequent children), Germany, and Hungary. In Sweden, the parental leave can be shared equally by both parents. Sweden also is unique in providing a one-and-one-half-year job-protected leave and a cash benefit that covers 80 percent of wages for one year, three additional months at a minimum flat rate, and three more months as an unpaid leave. The benefit is available to either parent and can be prorated so that parents may use it to cover full-time, half-time, or three-quarter-time work while children are young. This enables parents to share child-care responsibilities during the first two years of the child's life (Kamerman, 1996).

In Austria, Canada, Denmark, Germany, Hungary, and Norway, fathers can share in some portion of the leave. In most of these countries the extended parental leave carries with it the right to a wage-related benefit, or a benefit is provided at a flat rate. In Finland, parents have a choice following the end of a one-year, fully paid parental leave. They can choose between a guaranteed, heavily subsidized place in a child-care center, a subsidy to help pay for in-home child care, or a cash benefit to provide support for an extended two-year parental leave at home to care for a child until her or his third birthday (Kamerman, 1996).

Because of the archaic parental leave policies in the United States, the lack of good child-care facilities, and the increased numbers of women entering the labor force or higher education institutions, battles over who should care for children will probably escalate. According to some researchers, such conflicts will decrease only when family policies take children and working parents seriously (see Leach, 1994).

Health-Related Issues

In some ways, many Americans are healthier. Smoking and alcohol consumption among youth have decreased. In 1974, for example, about half of those 12 to 17 years of age said they had tried cigarettes and alcohol. In 1999, 8 percent of eighth-graders, 16 percent of tenth-graders and 23 percent of twelfth-graders reported smoking cigarettes daily in the previous 30 days. In the same year, 31 percent of twelfth-graders, 26 percent of tenth-graders, and 15 percent of eighth-graders reported having at least five drinks in a row in the previous two weeks ("*America's children . . .,*" 2000). Thus, although smoking and drinking have decreased among young people since the 1970s, the rates are still high and may increase as children reach adulthood.

Among older Americans, consumption of red meat and eggs—two foods purportedly associated with stroke and heart disease—decreased greatly between 1970 and 1992 (Holmes, 1994; see also Bachman et al., 1997). Although a number of Americans are adopting healthier lifestyles, two health-related issues will probably have considerable impact on marriages and families in the coming years: HIV and AIDS and the growing concern over the lack of a national health-care system.

HIV and AIDS

We might expect that people, knowing that there is no cure for AIDS, would engage in casual sexual intercourse less often and with fewer partners and that they would use condoms. However, although some gay men have changed their patterns of sexual activity, there is little evidence that the threat of HIV-AIDS has changed sexual behavior among many heterosexuals. Adolescent males and females are unlikely to protect themselves; and not even college students or other people educated as to the risks of contracting AIDS are using condoms, even during casual sex (see Chapter 6). A recent study of HIV-infected people seeking treatment at hospitals found that about 40 percent of the men and women didn't tell their partners they were infected because doing so would be "too stressful," or they expressed fear of being rejected by their partners. The majority also didn't insist on the use of condoms (Stein, 1998).

HIV and AIDS will also affect multigenerational families. As the AIDS virus spreads, increasing numbers of children are being orphaned and will probably be cared for by foster parents, grandparents, or even great-grandparents (see Chapter 17).

National Health Care

The United States is one of the few industrialized countries that does not have national health insurance or a system that makes health care a right of all citizens. In 1999, 16 percent of the population had no health insurance. Despite the existence of programs such as Medicaid and Medicare, almost 33 percent of the poor had no health insurance of any kind. Among the poor, over 40 percent of Latinos and Asian Americans had no health insurance (see *Figure 18.1*).

Our chances of not having health insurance or having such coverage lapse depend on several factors. Women are slightly more likely than men to have health insurance because more of them live in families below the poverty line and, thus, qualify for Medicaid. Young adults aged 18 to 24 are more likely than any other group to have no health insurance because they have part-time jobs or low-paying jobs that offer no health benefits. Stable, full-time employment improves the chances that workers will have continuous coverage (Bennefield, 1995). According to one study (cited in Lief, 1997), about 12 percent of parents of uninsured children restrict their children's play because of fears of injuries.

The Canadian health-care system has received considerable attention from the U.S. news media. Among other appealing characteristics, there is little paperwork when seeing a doctor:

> Several years ago I moved from the United States to Canada, and a few months later I had my first experience with a nationalized health-care system.

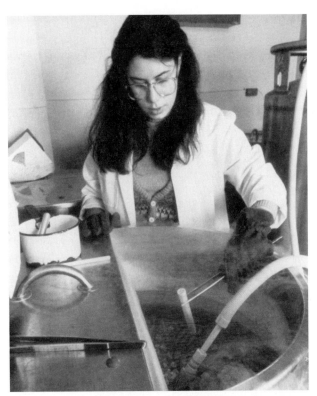

Some observers urge that laboratories like this one that freeze and store human sperm be regulated to screen out and dispose of samples that contain the genetic codes for diseases like AIDS or cystic fibrosis.

> After making my appointment with a physician who had been recommended to me by friends, I waited only a brief time to see the doctor and when we were finished I asked the receptionist whether there was anything I needed to do—I expected to pay a bill or fill out some forms or sign something. The receptionist seemed puzzled by my question and when I explained she said that there was nothing for me to do and that I could leave. (Klein, 1993)

Although often applauded as a model that the United States should adopt, the Canadian health-care system is not without its problems. Some observers point out that socialized medicine, as practiced in Canada and England, is most effective when health problems are relatively minor and people are able to wait for services. Also, high-tech resources such as sophisticated medical equipment are often scarce in these countries. Hundreds of physicians have reportedly left Canada, most for the United States, because increased government interventions cut their incomes and put restrictions on where and how doctors practice (Gottlieb, 1995).

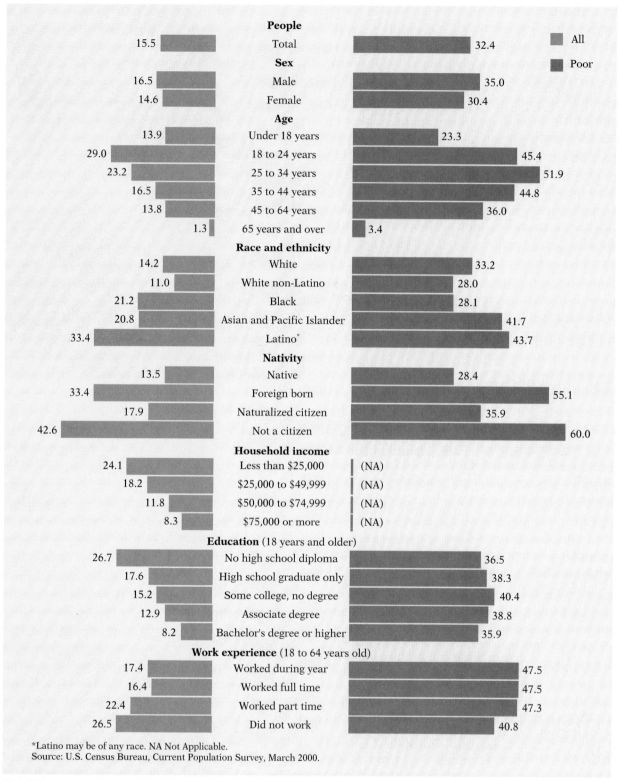

People

15.5 Total 32.4

Sex

16.5 Male 35.0
14.6 Female 30.4

Age

13.9 Under 18 years 23.3
29.0 18 to 24 years 45.4
23.2 25 to 34 years 51.9
16.5 35 to 44 years 44.8
13.8 45 to 64 years 36.0
1.3 65 years and over 3.4

Race and ethnicity

14.2 White 33.2
11.0 White non-Latino 28.0
21.2 Black 28.1
20.8 Asian and Pacific Islander 41.7
33.4 Latino* 43.7

Nativity

13.5 Native 28.4
33.4 Foreign born 55.1
17.9 Naturalized citizen 35.9
42.6 Not a citizen 60.0

Household income

24.1 Less than $25,000 (NA)
18.2 $25,000 to $49,999 (NA)
11.8 $50,000 to $74,999 (NA)
8.3 $75,000 or more (NA)

Education (18 years and older)

26.7 No high school diploma 36.5
17.6 High school graduate only 38.3
15.2 Some college, no degree 40.4
12.9 Associate degree 38.8
8.2 Bachelor's degree or higher 35.9

Work experience (18 to 64 years old)

17.4 Worked during year 47.5
16.4 Worked full time 47.5
22.4 Worked part time 47.3
26.5 Did not work 40.8

All

Poor

*Latino may be of any race. NA Not Applicable.
Source: U.S. Census Bureau, Current Population Survey, March 2000.

FIGURE 18.1   People Without Health Insurance by Selected Characteristics: 1999 (in percent)

SOURCE: Mills, 2000, Figure 2

While many U.S. citizens go to Canada for lower-cost pharmaceuticals, thousands of Canadians are coming to the United States, especially the Northeast, for cancer and other treatments. Because of financial problems, the Canadian government has closed 44 hospitals since 1995 and some hospitals have turned away ambulances citing overcrowding in the hospital wards. The Canadian government pays for treatment in the United States, including hotel and related costs (Walker, 1999). These problems suggest that the Canadian national health-care system isn't working as well as many people maintain.

Many Americans are ambivalent about national health-care coverage. About 88 percent, who already have health insurance, worry that a national plan might erode some of their existing benefits. According to a Gallup poll, for example, 54 percent of respondents feared they could end up with worse coverage than they have at present, and 38 percent believed that national reform would hurt the middle class more than any other income group (Saad, 1994). Ambivalence about helping the poor at the expense of the middle and working classes may increase in the future.

Economic Concerns

The vast majority of Americans' income comes from employment (rather than investments or inherited wealth, for example). However, the traditional assumption that holding a job will keep a person out of poverty or off welfare rolls is becoming increasingly shaky (see Chapters 12 and 13).

Poverty

Much research suggests that poverty, and especially child poverty, is not a compelling social issue in the United States. National reports have documented a high incidence of child poverty since 1909 (Jacobs and Davies, 1991). Moreover, the United States has higher child-poverty rates than many other industrialized countries: 1 out of 5 U.S. children lives in poverty compared to 1 out of 10 in Canada and Australia, 1 out of 25 in France, 1 out of 50 in Germany, and 1 out of 100 in Sweden (Danziger and Danziger, 1993).

According to some researchers, one of the reasons that the United States has high poverty rates is that it has never developed a *comprehensive* antipoverty agenda. Danziger and Danziger (1993), for example, suggest that an integrated set of policies would include many components: improved education and training, subsidies to working-poor families, greater access to health care and child care, expanded support services for children and their parents (such as youth development programs and decent housing), elimination of labor-market practices that discriminate against minorities and women, and provision of employment opportunities for those unable to find jobs (see Chapters 12 and 13).

Most important, child and family poverty could be alleviated if parents had jobs that paid enough. For example, a householder would have to earn $8.50 an hour (well above the $5.15 an hour minimum wage) and work full time, 52 weeks a year to have an annual gross salary (before taxes) of $17,600 to be above the $17,029 income level defined by the federal government as the poverty level for a family of four (in 1999). How many full-time jobs pay $8.50 an hour to people with a high school education or less? Very few.

Many families that don't have health care coverage must spend long hours in crowded waiting rooms of public clinics to receive medical treatment.

Welfare

Most Americans are recipients, either directly or indirectly, of some form of **welfare**—government aid to those who can't support themselves, generally because they are poor or unemployed. There are many programs, not called "welfare," that also help the middle classes and especially the rich. For example, the middle class can take advantage of student loans, expensive farm subsidies that pay farmers not to raise crops, and loans to veterans.

Corporate welfare is even greater. The federal government has directly subsidized the shipping industry, railroads, airlines, and exporters of iron, steel, textiles, paper, and other products. Since the late 1970s, the federal government has bailed out such companies as Chrysler Corporation, Penn Central, Lockheed, a number of petroleum companies, and hundreds of savings and loan banks when they declared bankruptcy because of fraud, bad investments, or widespread embezzlement (Eitzen and Baca Zinn, 1994).

Corporate welfare programs cost taxpayers about $10 billion in 1997. Some of the most egregious examples of corporate welfare include the Market Access Program. This program gives firms such as Campbell Soup, Ralston Purina, and Gallo Winery millions to promote their goods overseas instead of borrowing from banks for investments abroad. Critics of such "corporate welfare queens" note that corporate welfare programs are supported by both U.S. presidents and Congresses because the companies make large contributions to fund-raising by both Democrats and Republicans—up to $345 million for President Clinton from major technology companies alone, for example (Glassman, 1997). Because taxpayer dollars fund corporate welfare, there's less money available for financial assistance for poor, working-poor, and middle-class families.

In 1996, President Clinton signed the Personal Responsibility and Work Opportunity Reconciliation Act (PRWORA; also referred to as the "Welfare Reform Act") that turned control of federally financed welfare programs over to the states. The law converts AFDC (Aid to Families with Dependent Children) to a block grant, or a set amount of dollars, called Temporary Assistance to Needy Families (TANF) and has a five-year lifetime limit on benefits for welfare recipients.

Whether a family moves from state to state or goes off welfare and returns later, cash assistance cannot exceed five years. The law requires welfare recipients to work after receiving two years of benefits, to enroll in on-the-job or vocational training, or to do community service. Unmarried mothers under 18 years old are required to live with an adult and to attend school as a condition of receiving welfare. Poor, unemployed individuals between the ages of 18 and 50, who are not raising children, are limited to three

months of food stamps while unemployed during any three-year period.

Proponents of this law have argued that the best way to get people off welfare is to require them to work. Even if the work is low-paid, proponents maintain, job participation will give welfare recipients work experience, a job history, and require adults to contribute to their own support (Mead, 1996). Supporters of the new law also contend that eliminating entitlements, restricting cash assistance, and requiring work will fundamentally alter the employment and family patterns of current AFDC recipients (see Meyer and Cancian, 1997). A mother who doesn't receive AFDC benefits, many believe, will stop having babies out of wedlock or will marry the biological father because he will be the mother's primary (or only) source of financial support.

The welfare rolls have declined by 43 percent since 1996. Some states have spent much of the TANF money on job training and child care. Other states, however, have allegedly "stashed" the money away and/or have punished welfare recipients harshly for both minor and serious infractions. That is, many states have cut off checks to poor families not only because they have refused to work but also because they don't show up for appointments with social workers or fail to provide complete information on welfare forms ("Strict new rules . . . ," 1999; Kuttner, 2000).

Opponents of PRWORA maintain that the law will increase child poverty and punishes children for their parents' economic mistakes (Stevens, 1997). Others feel that the law is misguided. According to Harris (1996), for example, eliminating welfare without improving pay and benefits of the jobs that welfare recipients get keeps welfare families poor.

There is also no evidence, opponents argue, that welfare *causes* illegitimacy and single parenthood. The Netherlands, Germany, France, Sweden, and Denmark all have generous welfare programs for single mothers but lower proportions of families headed by single mothers than does the United States (Sandefur, 1996). In 1993, New Jersey was the first state in the nation to deny cash payments to mothers who had additional out-of-wedlock babies. These "family caps" have not reduced out-of-wedlock birth rates ("N.J. finds . . . ," 1997). Since many births to unmarried teenagers are unintended, there is no evidence that cutting welfare benefits will lower out-of-wedlock births.

Although millions of people have depended on welfare for survival, the median period of time over which a person has received welfare benefits throughout his or her lifetime is less than four years. About 30 percent of people have been on welfare for less than a year, and 70 percent have left the system within two years. About 20 percent have been welfare recipients for five or more years (Waldman et al., 1994). Furthermore, most children growing up in "welfare homes" have not themselves become dependent on welfare. If critics of the welfare system are successful in decreasing the aid to current welfare recipients without increasing jobs that provide a living, poverty levels will, in all likelihood, increase.

Although many states have cut their welfare rolls, there's no evidence that welfare leavers have lifted themselves out of poverty. According to some policy analysts, for example, most welfare leavers have entered the low end of the labor market where they are working in much the same circumstances as the near-poor and low-income mothers who have not recently been on welfare. Nearly a third of those who left welfare due to PRWORA had returned to welfare and were receiving benefits in 1997. And a sizable proportion (about 25 percent) of leavers are not working and have no partner working (Loprest, 1999).

Comparable Worth

A continuous problem, and one that contributes to women's and children's economic vulnerability, is the wage gap between women and men (see Chapter 13). The sex gap in pay stems from many factors, one of which is employment discrimination. Whatever their source, pay inequities have a negative impact on the family.

Comparable worth is a concept that calls for equal pay for both males and females doing work that requires comparable skill, effort, and responsibility and is performed under similar working conditions. Proponents argue that jobs can be measured in terms of such variables as required education, skills, experience, mental demands, and working conditions, and that the inherent worth of a job—for example, in terms of its importance to the society—can also be assessed. Assigning point values within these and other categories, several communities found that women were receiving much lower salaries than men, even though their jobs had high points. For example, a legal secretary was paid $375 a month less than a carpenter, but both received the same number of job evaluation points (U.S. Commission on Civil Rights, 1984).

Since 1984, a few states (for example, Minnesota, South Dakota, New Mexico, and Iowa) have raised women's wages after conducting comparable-worth studies. Although conservatives argue that these kinds of adjustments are too costly to achieve, proponents point out that the cost of implementing pay equity in Minnesota came to less than 4 percent of the state's payroll budget. A mid-1990s study found that the Minnesota law had improved women's wages in government by more than 10 percent, and a half dozen states now have similar pay-equity laws (Kleiman, 1993). Such pay adjustments have affected only public sector workers, however, because no U.S. law requires comparable worth in wages. In contrast, comparable-worth legislation has been enacted in half

Since the passage of the "Welfare Reform Act" in 1996 (see text), eligibility for food stamps was made stricter for some recipients, including able-bodied beneficiaries who are expected to work.

of the jurisdictions in Canada, a majority of which require that employers in both public and private sectors set job-pay levels in accordance with comparable-worth standards (Aman and England, 1997).

Global Aging

By 2000, almost 7 percent of the world's population was 65 years old or older. As *Figure 18.2* shows, in some countries, such as Belgium, France, Germany, Greece, Italy, Japan, and the United Kingdom, over 15 percent of the people are 65 years old and over. Such "world graying" is likely to affect both the young and the old. In the United States, for example, two emerging issues include the right to die and a competition for scarce resources.

Right-to-Die Issues

In 1994, the Netherlands legalized physician-assisted suicide under certain conditions. The patient must have made voluntary, deliberate, and repeated requests to die; the patient must be suffering with no prospect of

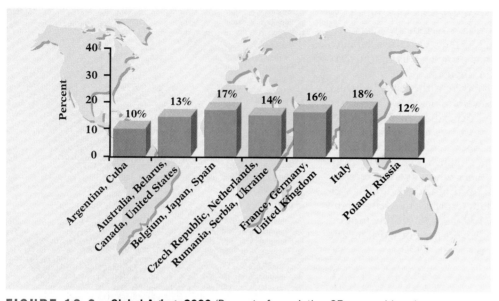

FIGURE 18.2 **Global Aging: 2000** (Percent of population 65 years old and over. Covers countries with 10 million or more population in 1997.) (Based on U.S. Bureau of the Census, 1997b, Table 1335).

relief; and the doctor must consult with colleagues before acting. Government figures estimate that in 1995 about 19 percent of all deaths in the Netherlands were assisted suicides. Most requests came from patients with AIDS or terminal cancer (Shapiro, 1997).

In the United States, legal, religious, and medical groups have taken a strong stand against assisted suicide. In 1994, however, voters supported a referendum in Oregon to legalize assisted suicide. The provisions of the Oregon proposal were as follows:

■ Right-to-die decisions were limited to competent adults who were terminally ill; children were not eligible.
■ The patient was required to make at least three requests to the physician, two orally and one in writing over the course of at least 15 days.
■ A second physician had to make an independent diagnosis of both terminal illness and of emotional competence.
■ If either physician felt the patient was not emotionally stable, the process was to be stopped and the patient was to be referred to a psychiatrist or clinical psychologist. The patient was to have the prescription filled and was to self-administer the drug. Patients not physically able to do this were not to be eligible for the "physician-aid-in-dying" process (Pridonoff, 1994).

The referendum passed, but was appealed. In 1997, the Supreme Court left it up to the states to decide the legality of doctor-aided suicide. Later that year, 60 percent of Oregon voters decided, a second time, to keep their Death with Dignity law. In the five months after voters approved the law, only two Oregonians were known to have used drugs prescribed under the law to commit suicide (Knickerbocker, 1998).

There is no evidence that the legalization of Oregon's 1997 Death with Dignity Act has triggered en masse physician-assisted suicides. According to Oregon health officials, 16 patients ingested lethal medications in 1998 and 27 did so in 1999. In 1999, the median age of those patients was 71 years, half were college graduates, all had health insurance, 21 were receiving hospice care, and 17 were dying of cancer. According to both physicians and family members, the patients requested assistance with suicide for several reasons, including loss of autonomy, loss of control of bodily functions, and a determination to control the manner of their death (Sullivan et al., 2000; see also Ganzini et al., 2000).

The right-to-die debate was triggered in 1990 when Jack Kevorkian, a physician, built a "suicide machine" to help people who suffered from chronic pain or terminal illnesses to kill themselves. He had been acquitted of second degree murder several times because he had provided lethal drugs to patients rather than administered them. In 1999, however, a Michigan judge sentenced Kevorkian to 10 to 25 years in prison because he had actually injected the drugs into the arm of a 52-year-old man suffering with Lou Gehrig's disease. Kevorkian will be eligible for parole in 2007.

Those opposed to the right-to-die movement argue, among other things, that the elderly may be pressured by caregivers to end their lives, that their acts may be due to feelings of guilt about being a burden, that they should be persuaded that much of their pain is treatable, and that physicians are responsible for extending rather than ending life (Veatch, 1995). Despite such opposition, many elderly and their families are becoming more vocal about a person's right to die in dignity, at home, and on his or her own terms. In 1992, a best-selling book was *Final Exit*, which describes how the elderly and terminally ill can commit suicide. Since then, several authors have addressed the right-to-die issue (see, for example, Kramer, 1993; Quill, 1993; Humphrey and Clement, 2000).

Such organizations as Choice in Dying, the Hemlock Society, and Concern for Dying have reported widespread interest in information on living wills. A **living will** is a legal document in which people can specify what, if any, life-support measures they wish in the case of serious illness and if or when they want to have such measures discontinued. Preparing such a document does not guarantee that its dictates will be followed, however. Physicians or hospitals may refuse to honor living wills if their policies support prolonging life at any cost, if family members contest the living will, or if there is any question about the patient's mental competence when the will was drawn up (Veatch, 1995). For these reasons and because state laws and policies vary widely, people who want living wills to be enforced should consult attorneys to minimize legal problems.

Such expressions of individual rights are bound to increase in the future. Because of their large numbers, baby boomers will undoubtedly be instrumental in challenging or promoting right-to-die laws.

Competition for Scarce Resources

When the Social Security Act was passed in 1935, life expectancy in the United States was just below 62 years, compared to around 76 years today. In the years ahead, the increasing numbers of older Americans will put a significant strain on the nation's health-care services and retirement-income programs.

According to Crenshaw (1992: 4), older people "are one of the largest and politically best organized groups in the nation." They vote in large numbers, follow issues carefully, and usually come well prepared to defend their positions during congressional hearings. The American Association of Retired Persons (AARP) is one of the most powerful advocates for the elderly. AARP has over 33 million members, more than $300 million in revenues, and more than 400,000 volunteers. Many other groups also lobby for older people, including the American Association of Homes for the Aging, the Gray Panthers, the National Association of Retired Federal Employees, the National Council of

This 70-year-old stonemason is laying the foundation for a fountain in a public park.

Senior Citizens, the National Council on the Aging, the Older Women's League, and the National Committee to Preserve Social Security and Medicare. It is not surprising, then, that the elderly have been successful in safeguarding and even increasing many of their benefits.

Although the elderly once had the highest poverty rates in the United States, they now have the lowest. Due in part to the growth of Social Security and Medicare (which claim about one-third of the federal budget), in 1998 about 11 percent of the elderly had incomes below the poverty line compared to more than a third in 1959 (see Chapter 17).

Some observers have charged that in a time of fiscal austerity older people have benefited at the expense of others, primarily children, because AFDC support has been cut while programs for the elderly have maintained their funding. There is an increasing chasm between the young and the old that reflects racial and ethnic differences. For example, projections for 2030 indicate that 41 percent of the children but only 24 percent of the old will be minorities. In the future, some speculate, the growing number of middle-aged minorities and parents with large numbers of children may resist increasing federal expenditures for a predominantly white, elderly population.

Remember, however, that although today's older people, as a group, are better off financially than previous generations, there are specific pockets of poverty. For example, the poverty rate for minority elderly is two to three times higher than for the white elderly

Unfortunately, Andrew, you — would still have to write thank-you notes even if Gramma and Grampa did have a modem.

© 1993 Chronicle Features

The *Quality Time* cartoon by Gail Machlis is reprinted by permission of Chronicle Features, San Francisco, California

(see Chapter 17). Poverty rates within the older population also increase dramatically with age. In 1992, about 15 percent of people age 65 and over were living in poverty, but nearly 20 percent of those age 85 or older were poor (Hobbs and Damon, 1996). Furthermore, the number of elderly who will be 85 or older is expected to triple by the year 2030, and much of the elderly population will have chronic health conditions that will increase the need for long-term care (Light, 1988).

Some Possible Solutions

Some feel that the competition for scarce resources between the young and the old can be lessened. For example, increasing the eligibility for old-age benefits from age 65 to age 70 can reduce the size of the elderly dependent population. Because, in general, people reaching age 65 now and in the future will be better educated and have more work-related skills than earlier cohorts, they are more likely to be productive employees. They may also offer an employer more skills than some young people, whose academic performance, as measured on standardized exams and college graduation, appears to have diminished.

Moreover, because the rates of adolescent criminal behavior, drug and alcohol use, out-of-wedlock births, and children living in poverty have increased, large

numbers of retirees in the year 2010 will be depending on a relatively small group of people in the labor force to support their Social Security and health-care benefits. Thus, some observers suggest, redefining "old age" would be beneficial to both the young and the old. If old age and mandatory retirement were pushed up to age 70 or higher, many productive older Americans could continue to work and contribute to Social Security. As a result, the burden of supporting an aging population would not fall wholly on younger workers.

Others have suggested combining the needs of the elderly and those of children. For example, a few companies have built day-care facilities at or near workplaces for the young and the old, where both generations can visit, talk, and forge friendships. Such programs can help fulfill reciprocal needs for the elderly to help children and for children to understand an older generation.

Conclusion

The family in the twenty-first century will be much more diverse in terms of racial and ethnic characteristics. It is difficult to predict whether this *change* will lead to greater cooperation or to conflict. Because the United States is the only country in the world with such a heterogeneous mix of cultural groups, there are no models for comparison. Optimists argue that cultural diversity is healthy and will strengthen communities.

Another expected but unprecedented change is the growth of a relatively "old" population that will have to rely on a generally less educated young population for its resources and health care. Given the increased health-care and economic problems of recent years, this new century may see more multigenerational households and greater numbers of adult children providing care to their aging parents.

The family in the twenty-first century will probably incorporate a wide variety of work roles and family roles. Because women's participation in the labor force is expected to increase, work and family functions will continue to overlap. The *constraints* posed by the need to balance domestic and work responsibilities are not expected to diminish, however. Consequently, women (and some men) may become more vocal in demanding family policies that put a higher priority on children, parenting, and the family.

Overall, families in the twenty-first century will continue to have more *choices* than they did in the past. Because divorce and remarriage are no longer uncommon, these options will probably become even more widespread in the future. In addition, as the technology improves eyeglasses, hearing aids, wheelchairs, and biomedical devices to strengthen or replace legs, arms, hearing, and eyesight, many older Americans will be able to live independently instead of depending on care from others (Longino, 1994).

SUMMARY

1. In the twenty-first century, some of the greatest changes will probably be in six areas: family structure, racial and ethnic diversity, children's rights, health-related issues, economics, and the needs of an aging population.

2. Family structures will continue to be diverse. Demographers predict that racial-ethnic diversity will increase because of increased immigration, as well as higher fertility rates among blacks and some Asian American and Latino families.

3. Children have few rights today. Except for an increase in child-support payments, there is little evidence that the economic and emotional well-being of most U.S. children will improve very much in the future. Our child-care and parental-leave policies, for example, are backward compared to those of all other developed countries. They are also paltry compared to those of some developing countries.

4. Health issues will probably be a major constraint on family life in the twenty-first century. Two of the dominant issues will be caring for HIV/AIDS patients and developing a national program that provides families with minimal health care.

5. There is little evidence that the economic problems of many families will decrease in the future. The United States has generous corporate welfare policies, whereas programs for the poor typically provide access to low-paying jobs that don't include health benefits and little opportunity for better wages.

6. As the world's population ages, right-to-die issues are becoming more prominent. In the United States, living wills are becoming more common, and some states are considering legalizing physician-assisted suicide.

7. In the future, there will probably be increased competition over resources between the young and the old. Because the elderly population is growing, is well organized, and has political clout, elderly issues may well be a higher priority than children's issues.

8. Overall, families in the twenty-first century will continue to have more choices than they did in the past, but there will also be many constraints.

KEY TERMS

family policy   478
welfare   484

comparable worth   485
living will   487

TAKING IT FURTHER

Families and the Future

IDB Population Pyramids, Census Bureau, allows you to obtain population pyramids by age and sex for a variety of countries for 1997, 2025, and 2050.

www.census.gov/ipc/www/idbpyr.html

Futurework, Department of Labor, provides information on technology and globalization and the role of the twenty-first-century workplace.

www.dol.gov/dol/asp/public/futurework/report.htm

The **National Committee on Pay Equity** offers information on pay-equity facts and activities throughout the United States and the world.

www.feminist.com/fairpay.htm

National Center for Policy Research on Women & Children examines policies and programs that address women's and children's economic and physical health.

www.cpr4womenandfamilies.org

Choice in Dying, the inventor of living wills in 1967, offers publications, services, and state-by-state "advance directives" on how to prepare instructions for future medical care.

www.choices.org

Several sites explain the **Personal Responsibility and Work Opportunity Reconciliation Act of 1996,** including the following:

www.urban.org
www.acf.dhhs.gov/news/welfare/wr/wr.htm

And more . . . www.prenhall.com/benokraitis provides sites on the future of children's health, analyses of welfare reform, aging around the world, and prospective changes in retirement.

APPALACHIAN A

APPENDIX A

Sexual Anatomy

The better you understand your own body, the more comfortable you may become with your sexuality. Also, remember that the word *intercourse* means "communication"; sexual intercourse is an activity in which two people communicate with each other through mutual bodily stimulation.

Female Anatomy

Collectively known as the **vulva** (Latin for "covering"), the external female genitalia consist of the mons veneris, labia majora, labia minora, clitoris, and vaginal and urethral openings. Figure A.1 shows these structures as well as the internal female reproductive organs.

The **mons veneris** (Latin for "mount of Venus," referring to the Roman goddess of love) is the soft layer of fatty tissue overlaying the area where the pubic bones come together. Because of the many nerve endings in the mons area, most women find gentle stimulation of the mons pleasurable. Below the mons are the **labia majora** (major, or larger, lips) and **labia minora** (minor, or smaller, lips), outer and inner elongated folds of skin that, in the sexually unstimulated state, cover and protect the *vaginal* and *urethral* openings. The labia majora extend from the mons to the hairless bit of skin between the vaginal opening and anus, called the **perineum**. Located at the base of the labia minora are **Bartholin's glands**, which, during prolonged stimulation, secrete a few drops of an alkaline fluid that help neutralize the normal acidity of the outer vagina (male sperm cannot survive in an acidic environment).

The **clitoris** (Greek for "hill" or "slope") develops from the same embryonic tissue as the penis and is extremely sensitive to touch. In fact, it is the only structure in either females or males whose only known function is to focus sexual sensations. Also highly sensitive are the labia minora, which meet at their upper end to form the **clitoral hood**, analogous to the male **foreskin** (or *prepuce*), hiding all but the tip, or **glans**, of the clitoris.

The area between the two labia minora is sometimes referred to as the **vestibular area** (Latin for "entrance hall") because it contains the entrance to the vagina. In

sexually inexperienced females, or "virgins," a thin membrane called the **hymen** may partially cover the opening to the vagina. The urethral opening, also located in this area between the clitoris and the vaginal opening, is the outlet of the **urethra**, which carries urine from the bladder out of the body.

The internal female reproductive system consists of the vagina, uterus, fallopian tubes, and ovaries. The **vagina** (Latin for "sheath") is an internal structure located behind the bladder and in front of the rectum. It serves not only to receive male sperm during sexual intercourse but as the passageway for a fully developed fetus at the time of birth.

The **uterus**, or womb, which holds and protects a developing fetus (see Appendix C), is connected to the vagina through its narrow end, called the **cervix**. The uterus has three layers: the innermost **endometrium**, in which a fertilized egg implants; a middle layer of muscles called the **myometrium**, which contract during labor; and

FIGURE A.1 **Side View of the Female Reproductive System** (adapted from Martini, 1955: 1078).

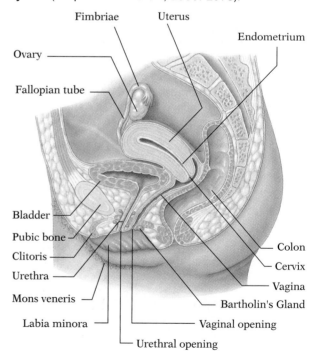

Appendix A is adapted from Bruce M. King, *Human Sexuality Today*, 3rd ed. (Upper Saddle River, NJ: Prentice Hall, 1999), pp. 25-42. Adapted by permission of Prentice Hall, Upper Saddle River, New Jersey.

an external cover called the **perimetrium**. Each month, after ovulation (see next paragraph), the endometrium thickens and becomes rich in blood vessels in preparation for the implantation of a fertilized egg. If fertilization does not occur, this tissue is sloughed off and discharged from the body as the menstrual flow.

Extending from each side of the uterus are the two fallopian tubes. The *fimbriae*, fingerlike structures at the end of each tube, brush against the **ovary**, which is the female sex gland. The ovaries, or gonads, are supported by ligaments on each side of the uterus and have two functions: to produce eggs (*ova*) and female hormones (*estrogen* and *progesterone*). Each month, in the process called *ovulation*, an egg is expelled from an ovary and picked up by the fimbriae, pulling it into one of the fallopian tubes. Fertilization, if it occurs, usually happens within the tube.

Male Anatomy

The external male genitalia are the penis and the scrotum. (The external and internal male reproductive organs are shown in Figure A.2.) The **penis**, which has both reproductive and excretory functions, consists of three parts: the body or shaft, the glans, and the root. Only the first two parts are visible. The *shaft* contains three parallel cylinders of spongylike tissue: two *corpora cavernosa*, or cavernous bodies, on top; and a *corpus spongiosum*, or "spongy body," on the bottom. The **glans** is the smooth, rounded end of the penis. The raised rim between the shaft and glans is the **corona**, the most sensitive to touch of any part of the penis. The **urethra**, which serves as a passageway for both urine and sperm, runs through the corpus spongiosum, and the urethral opening (*meatus*) is located at the tip of the glans.

The root of the penis is surrounded by two muscles (*bulbocavernous* and *ischiocavernosus*) that aid in both urination and ejaculation. (*Sphincter* muscles, which surround the urethra as it emerges from the bladder, contract during erection to prevent urine from mixing with semen.) The skin of the penis is very loose, to allow expansion during erection; unstimulated, the penis is about 3.75 inches long and 1.2 inches in diameter, but when erect it is about 6 inches long and 1.5 inches in diameter.

The sac located beneath the penis is called the **scrotum**. It holds the testicles outside of the body cavity to protect the sperm, which can be produced only at a temperature about 5° F lower than normal body temperature. For this reason the skin of the scrotum has many sweat glands that aid in temperature regulation.

The male internal reproductive system consists of the testicles, a duct system that transports sperm out of the body, the prostate gland, the seminal vesicles that produce the fluid in which the sperm are mixed, and Cowper's glands.

The **testes**, or testicles (the male gonads), have two functions: The testes produce sperm (*spermatozoa*) and male hormones (*testosterone* and other *androgens*). Millions of new sperm are produced each day in several hundred *seminiferous tubules*.

Once produced, sperm pass through a four-part duct system (*epididymus, vas deferens, ejaculatory duct,* and *urethra*) before being expelled from the penis during ejaculation. Although an average ejaculation of semen contains about 300 million sperm, most of the volume of the ejaculate is fluid from the prostate gland and seminal vesicles. Among other substances, the **seminal vesicles** secrete fructose, prostaglandins, and substances. The **prostate gland** also secretes these substances, as well as a substance (fibrinogenase) that causes semen to coagulate temporarily after ejaculation, thus helping to keep it in the vagina. **Cowper's glands** are two pea-sized structures located beneath the prostate. They secrete a few drops of alkaline fluid that may appear at the tip of the penis prior to orgasm. Cowper's secretion serves to neutralize the normal acidity of the urethra, protecting sperm as they pass through the penis during ejaculation. Because Cowper's secretion often contains sperm, withdrawal of the penis just before ejaculation is a very unreliable method of birth control.

FIGURE A.2   Side View of the Male Reproductive System (adapted from Martini, 1955: 1061).

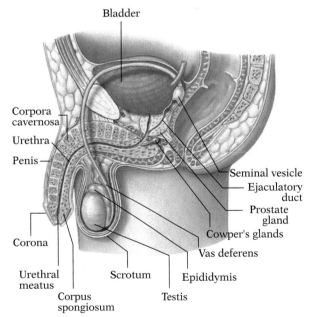

Bladder

Corpora cavernosa

Urethra

Penis

Corona

Urethral meatus

Corpus spongiosum

Scrotum

Testis

Epididymis

Vas deferens

Cowper's glands

Prostate gland

Ejaculatory duct

Seminal vesicle

APPENDIX B

Sexual Problems, Dysfunctions, and Treatment

There are many reasons for dissatisfaction with sex—poor general health, unhappiness with available sex partners, and not feeling loved by a partner. Most couples, at some time or other, may experience **sexual dysfunctions,** or conditions in which the ordinary physical responses of sexual function are impaired. Sometimes these problems are physiological, sometimes they are interpersonal, and sometimes they reflect a combination of both physiological and interpersonal factors. In general, serious sexual dysfunctions affect relatively small numbers of people.

Male Sexual Dysfunctions

Erectile dysfunction, or **impotence,** is the inability to attain or maintain an erection. It is a rare man who does not experience this problem at least once in his lifetime. Impotence can occur at any age and can assume many different forms. Typically, the male with erectile dysfunction has partial erections that are too weak to permit insertion in the vagina. Sometimes firm, erections quickly disappear when intercourse is attempted.

Impotence can have a negative effect on the female partner's self-esteem if she feels that she is not sexually desirable or is doing something wrong. Most continuing erectile dysfunctions—some estimates are as high as 86 percent—have an organic basis, such as circulatory problems, neurological disorders (due to multiple sclerosis or spinal-cord injury, for example), hormone imbalances, and infections or injuries of the penis, testes, urethra, or prostate gland. Diabetes, alcoholism, prescription medications (such as drugs for high blood pressure), and amphetamines, barbiturates, and narcotics can also cause erectile dysfunction.

Several other male dysfunctions are related to ejaculation. The most common of these dysfunctions is **premature ejaculation**—unintentional ejaculation before or while the male tries to enter his partner or soon after intercourse begins. An estimated 15 to 20 percent of all American men ejaculate prematurely on a regular basis. Whereas many female partners are understanding and accepting of the problem, others may feel angry, avoid sex, or seek another lover. Some men are not bothered, but others may question their masculinity. Some may experience heightened anxiety about performance, which, in turn, exacerbates the condition.

Many therapists believe that premature ejaculation is due to psychological factors. Others suggest that men who view women as sex objects are more likely to ejaculate prematurely, regardless of the woman's readiness. Other ejaculatory problems, such as the backward spurting of the semen into the bladder during orgasm, known as *retrograde ejaculation*, and ejaculation in the vagina only after a lengthy period and strenuous efforts (*retarded ejaculation*), or failure to ejaculate or achieve orgasm at all, may be caused by drug use, alcoholism, neurological disorders, or prescription medicines.

Female Sexual Dysfunctions

Approximately 2 to 3 percent of adult women are affected by **vaginismus,** or pain during penetration because of involuntary spasms of the muscles surrounding the outer third of the vagina. Vaginismus can be so severe that it prevents not only intercourse but even insertion of a finger or tampon. A woman's partner may deliberately avoid intercourse because vaginismus can be painful. Some men may become passive about sex, whereas others become impatient or openly hostile and may seek other sexual partners.

Vaginismus may have organic causes, such as poor vaginal lubrication, drugs that have a drying effect on the vagina (such as antihistamines, tranquilizers, or marijuana), diabetes, vaginal infections, or pelvic disorders. It can also reflect psychological difficulties, such as anxieties about intercourse, a fear of injury or harm to the internal organs, trauma (due to rape or abortion, for example), a strict religious upbringing in which sex was equated with sin, or fear of or hostility toward men. Such psychological problems are often treated by relaxation exercises followed by a gradual dilation of the vagina.

Another female sexual dysfunction is **anorgasmia**—the inability to reach orgasm. Anorgasmia, which used to be called frigidity, has several variations. In *primary anorgasmia*, a woman has never had an orgasm. In *secondary anorgasmia*, a woman who was regularly orgasmic at one time is no longer. And in *situational anorgasmia*, a woman is able to achieve orgasm only under certain circumstances, such as through masturbation.

Some anorgasmic women find that sex is satisfying and stimulating even though they have never experienced an orgasm. For others, the condition can lead to lowered self-esteem, a sense of futility, and depression. About 5 percent of cases of anorgasmia are attributed to organic causes. Orgasm can be blocked by severe chronic illness, diabetes, alcoholism, neurological problems, hormone deficiencies, pelvic disorders (due to infections, trauma, or scarring from surgery), or drugs (including narcotics, tranquilizers, and blood pressure medications). Other reasons for anorgasmia have an interpersonal basis. For example, women's most common sexual complaints include not getting enough sex because the partner gets tired too fast; intercourse does not last long enough; the partner is unskilled; the woman cannot readily lubricate because there is not enough foreplay; sex is boring ("same place, same time, same channel," according to one woman); or the timing is bad.

Finally, approximately 15 percent of adult women experience **dyspareunia,** or painful intercourse, several times a year. Another 1 to 2 percent are believed to have painful intercourse on a regular basis. Men, too, can experience dyspareunia (it is sometimes associated with problems of the prostate gland), but this disorder is believed to be much more common in women than in men. Like anorgasmia, female dyspareunia may be caused by any of a number of physical conditions, including poor vaginal lubrication, drugs, infections, diseases, and pelvic disorders.

Inhibited Sexual Desire

Both men and women can experience another common sexual problem, **inhibited sexual desire (ISD),** or a low interest in sex. Although the exact incidence of ISD is unknown, approximately 33 percent of the people who consult sex therapists do so because of ISD problems. It is important to remember that a low level of interest in sex is not uncommon. It creates a problem only when it becomes a source of personal distress. An extreme example of ISD is **sexual aversion,** in which people experience persistent or intense feelings of anxiety or panic in sexual situations and avoid sexual contact altogether. The causes of ISD are both organic and nonorganic. Organic factors include hormone deficiencies, alcoholism, kidney failure, drug abuse, and severe chronic illness. Nonorganic factors include fatigue, overwork, depression, and poor lovemaking skills.

Relationship Factors and Sexual Dysfunction

Personal and cultural factors play an important role in sexual expression. Many people do not realize that sex is not just a physiological response. Good or bad sex reflects the quality of our interpersonal relationships, especially in long-term situations. According to Wade and Cirese (1991), therapists typically encounter four interpersonal problems that are destructive to sexual relationships. The first is *anger and hostility.* Dissension and conflict are inevitable in any close relationship, but long-term resentments can sour erotic feelings and behavior. A second destructive problem in interpersonal relationships

is *boredom.* Boredom may be related specifically to sexual activity—it always takes place at the same time and in the same way—or it may reflect a general disinterest in the partner. Some people like sexual relations that are predictable; others become bored with predictability.

A second destructive problem in interpersonal relationships is *boredom.* Boredom may be related specifically to sexual activity—it always takes place at the same time and in the same way—or it may reflect a general disinterest in the partner. Some people like sexual relations that are predictable; others become bored with predictability.

Third, *conflicting sexual expectations* can also be harmful to the relationship. One partner may demand oral sex, for example, but the other may find this activity repulsive. Finally, *poor communication* is a constant problem in interpersonal relationships. Instead of saying what they want in sex, most people are reluctant to say anything, fearing to seem critical of the partner or to demand something they think the partner may not want to give. Suppressing their own needs may lead them to become angry and to strike out verbally at the partner ("You don't love me anymore"). Because many people find communicating about sex so difficult, they often deny the problem and allow it to fester.

Finally, *poor communication* is a constant problem in interpersonal relationships. Instead of saying what they want in sex, most people are reluctant to say anything, fearing to seem critical of the partner or to demand something they think the partner may not want to give. Suppressing their own needs may lead them to become angry and to strike out verbally at the partner ("You don't love me anymore"). Because many people find communicating about sex so difficult, they often deny the problem and allow it to fester.

Treating Sexual Problems

Because many sexual dysfunctions are caused by *organic* (physical or physiological) problems, a person experiencing such a dysfunction should first see a physician. If a thorough examination reveals no organic abnormalities, the physician may recommend that the person consult a psychiatrist or a psychotherapist. Be careful, however. Because sex therapy is largely an unregulated profession, people can offer their services with little more preparation than having attended a few workshops or reading a book. People seeking help should contact sex-therapy centers that are affiliated with universities, medical schools, or hospitals. They can also seek advice about qualified therapists from local medical societies, psychological associations, or family physicians. Even when a clinician is trained and competent, people should feel free to change to a therapist who may be better suited to their temperament and personality.

APPENDIX C

Conception, Pregnancy, and Childbirth

About midway through a woman's 28-day menstrual cycle, an *ovum*, or egg, is released into the abdominal cavity, where it is picked up by the *fimbriae* at the end of one of the fallopian tubes. The ovum takes three to seven days to move through the Fallopian tube to the uterus, and it is only during the first 24 hours after the egg leaves an ovary that it can be fertilized.

Conception

At orgasm during sexual intercourse, a man ejaculates into a woman's vagina 200 million to 400 million sperm, all of which attempt to pass through the cervix and uterus into the fallopian tubes. Only a few thousand live long enough, however, to complete the journey, and fewer than 50 reach the egg itself during its own journey through the tube. Because sperm can live for only 72 hours inside a woman's reproductive tract, the period during which conception can normally occur is extremely limited.

Conception takes place when one of the sperm penetrates the egg's surface. Within hours, spermatozoon (a single sperm cell) and ovum fuse to form a one-celled organism called a **zygote**, which contains the complete genetic code, or blueprint, for the new human life that has just begun. Shortly afterward, the zygote splits into two separate cells, then four, then eight, and so on. While this cell division continues, the organism journeys through the tube toward the uterus—a trip that transforms it into a hollow ball of cells called a **blastocyst**. At about 11 to 12 days after conception, the blastocyst, whose inner cell mass will become an embryo and whose outer layers will form structures to nourish and protect the growing fetus, burrows into the wall of the uterus in a process called **implantation**.

By about 14 days after conception, implantation is usually complete (see Figure C.1), and a series of connections between the mother and the **embryo**—the term for the developing organism after implantation—begins to form. The outer layers of the blastocyst begin to form the **placenta**, the organ that serves as a connection, or interface, between the infant's various systems and the

mother's. One layer forms the **umbilical cord**, which connects the developing baby with the placenta. The **amnion**, a thick-skinned sac filled with fluid that surrounds and protects the baby from sudden movements and changes in temperature, and the **chorion**, which develops into the lining of the placenta, begin to form.

Pregnancy

Pregnancy lasts an average of 260 to 270 days, or nine months. This time is divided into three-month periods called *trimesters*.

The First Trimester Women exhibit a varying number of symptoms during the first three months of pregnancy. Breasts may begin to enlarge and become tender. Veins may begin to show on the breasts, and the *areolas* (the darker rings surrounding the nipples) may turn dark. Nipples may also become larger. Urination may increase in frequency, and bowel movements may no longer be regular. Many women feel tired and run-down. One of the more common symptoms of pregnancy is nausea. Although it is called "morning sickness," it can occur at any time of the day.

In the first trimester, the developing baby undergoes a great deal of change (see Figure C.1). After implantation, cell division continues, and portions of the organism begin to differentiate in an orderly fashion. Growth in the unborn child occurs from the head downward and from the center outward. In the embryo, three inner cell layers will form specific parts of the body. The **ectoderm** forms the nervous system, skin, and teeth. The **mesoderm** forms the muscles, skeleton, and blood vessels. The **endoderm** forms the internal organs (such as lungs, liver, and digestive system).

In the third week of pregnancy, a central structure—the *neural tube*—becomes a dominant feature. This will become the central nervous system. By the end of the fourth week, the umbilical cord, heart, and digestive system begin to form. By eight weeks, all organs have begun to develop. The heart is pumping, and the stomach has begun to produce some digestive juices. From eight weeks until birth, the developing organism is called a **fetus**.

The Second Trimester In the fourth or fifth month of pregnancy, the movements of the fetus can be felt by its mother. The first experience of movement is called **quickening**. As her abdomen expands, red lines, or "stretch

Appendix C is adapted from Bruce M. King, *Human Sexuality Today*, 3rd edition (Upper Saddle River, NJ: Prentice Hall, 1999), Chapter 7. Copyright 1999. Adapted by permission of Prentice Hall, Upper Saddle River, New Jersey.

marks," may develop on the mother-to-be. The breasts begin to swell and may start to leak *colostrum,* a thick, sticky liquid that is produced before milk starts to flow. Water retention may cause swelling in the ankles, feet, and hands. Women may develop varicose veins and/or hemorrhoids. Morning sickness begins to diminish, which often brings an increase in appetite, and some women may experience heightened sexuality.

At this time, the fetus begins to make sucking motions with its mouth. In the fifth month, the fetus has a detectable heartbeat and will respond to sound. It also begins to show definite periods of sleep and wakefulness. In the sixth month, the fetus can open its eyes and will suck its thumb and respond to light. At the end of the second trimester, the fetus is almost a foot long and weighs well over a pound and a half.

The Third Trimester In the third trimester, walking, sitting, and rising become more difficult for the expectant mother, who may experience back pain as a result of the increasing burden she carries in her abdomen. The rapidly growing fetus puts pressure on the mother's bladder and stomach, often making urination more frequent. Indigestion, heartburn, gas, and constipation are also common complaints, and the active movements of the fetus may prevent restful sleep.

In the eighth month, the fetus's weight begins to increase dramatically. At the end of the eighth month, the fetus will weigh about 4 pounds and will be 16 to 17 inches long. From this point on, the fetus will gain about 0.5 pounds per week. In the ninth month, the fetus will grow to about 20 inches in length and weigh 7 to 7.5 pounds, but these measurements vary considerably. Shortly before birth (weeks or even hours before birth), the fetus will rotate its position so that its head is downward. This is called **lightening,** because once the fetus's head has lowered in the uterus, pressure on the mother's abdomen and diaphragm is greatly reduced.

Complications of Pregnancy

Teratogens are agents that can cross the placental barrier and harm a fetus, such as diseases, drugs, or environmental pollutants. Until recently the placenta was thought to be a perfect filter that kept out all harmful substances, but now we know that hundreds of teratogens can invade the fetus's small world. Three things determine the harm that can be caused by teratogens—the amount of the agent, the duration of time of exposure of the fetus, and the fetus's age. Each part of the fetus's body has a time, or *critical period,* when it is most susceptible to damage. Although teratogens should be avoided at all times, most body parts are maximally susceptible to damage during the first eight weeks of development.

Diseases Even the "weakened" disease organisms of certain vaccines can be harmful to a fetus if taken by the mother just before or during early pregnancy. Some strains of the flu, mumps, chicken pox, and other common diseases can also harm the fetus. One of the first teratogens to be discovered was the *rubella* virus, or "German measles." A fetus exposed to rubella may be born blind, deaf, and/or intellectually impaired. A woman can be safely inoculated against rubella any time up to three months before becoming pregnant. Most types of *sexually transmitted diseases* can also affect a fetus or newborn baby.

Toxemia of Pregnancy A pregnant woman can also have a disease called **toxemia of pregnancy,** referred to as *preeclampsia* in its early stages, whose symptoms include high blood pressure, excessive weight gain, swollen joints due to excessive water retention, and protein in the urine. In about 5 percent of cases, the disease advances to *eclampsia,* which is characterized by convulsions and coma. The cause of toxemia is unknown, but some researchers believe it is due to a parasitelike worm. A low-salt diet and bedrest are the usual treatments.

FIGURE C.1 **Prenatal Development** (adapted from Martini, 1995, Figure 29-4, p. 1114).

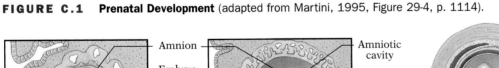

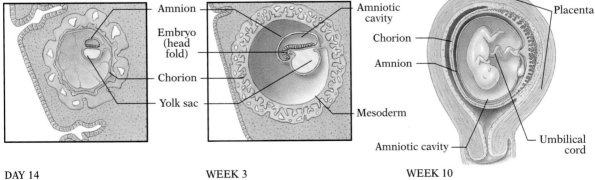

DAY 14　　　　　　WEEK 3　　　　　　WEEK 10

Rh Factor Most people's blood contains a protein called the **Rh factor**. If they do, they are "Rh positive"; if they don't, they are "Rh negative." The presence or absence of the Rh factor is determined genetically. In about 8 percent of pregnancies in the United States, the mother is negative and her baby is positive. Although this is not usually a dangerous situation in a first birth, antibodies may build up in the mother's blood and attack a second fetus who is also Rh positive. In order to prevent this, an injection should be given an Rh negative mother immediately after her first delivery to prevent the buildup of antibodies.

Smoking Cigarette smoking is associated with an increased risk of miscarriage, complications of pregnancy and labor, preterm birth, lower birth weight, and higher rates of infant mortality. It has also been associated with an increased risk that the placenta will separate from the uterus too soon, as well as with malformation of fetal organs such as the heart.

Alcohol The mother's use of alcohol during pregnancy can lead to physical deformities and/or mental retardation in the infant, a condition known as **fetal alcohol syndrome**, or **FAS** (see also Chapter 10). Alcohol can also cause the umbilical cord to collapse temporarily, cutting off oxygen to the fetus and causing a condition known as **minimal brain damage**, which has been associated with hyperactivity and learning disabilities. Even if a woman consumes only moderate amounts of alcohol, her baby still may develop health or emotional problems.

Other Drugs Many drugs—whether illegal, prescription, or over-the-counter—can cross the placental barrier. Women who are addicted to heroin (or methadone) while pregnant will give birth to infants who are addicted as well. These infants must go through withdrawal and typically show such symptoms as fevers, tremors, convulsions, and difficulty in breathing. Even moderate cocaine use by a mother can result in her baby exhibiting low birth weight. "Crack babies" have a variety of sensorimotor and behavioral deficits, including irritability and disorientation. In addition, commonly used drugs like antihistamines and megadoses of certain vitamins have proven to have harmful effects; for example, over-the-counter aspirin products taken in the last trimester can affect fetal circulation and cause complications during delivery.

Environmental Pollutants Substances like heavy metals (lead and cadmium, for example) in drinking water can cause damage to the fetus. Physical deformities and mental retardation have been found in children whose mothers ate mercury-contaminated fish. Radiation and x-rays are also powerful teratogens, especially in the first trimester. Exposure to x-rays has been linked to increased risk of leukemia.

Detecting Problems in Pregnancy The safest technique of examining the fetus in the womb for possible abnormalities is *ultrasound*, a "noninvasive" method in which sound waves are bounced off the fetus and the uterus. This technique is useful primarily in detecting structural problems. Other "invasive" techniques, those in which instruments are inserted into the womb or even the amniotic sac that holds the fetus, include *amniocentesis* and *chorionic villi sampling* (see Chapter 10), *celocentesis*, and *fetoscopy*. These methods can detect chromosomal problems, such as Down's syndrome, and certain diseases.

Childbirth

Labor is divided into three stages (see Figure C.2). In the initial, start-up stage, the woman's body prepares to expel the fetus from the uterus and into the outside world. This stage usually lasts from 6 to 13 hours. At this time, uterine contractions begin to push the baby downward toward the cervix, which undergoes **dilation**—widening—and **effacement**—thinning out. At first, contractions are far apart (one every 10 to 20 minutes) and last no more than 15 to 20 seconds, but eventually they begin to come closer together (1 to 2 minutes) and last longer (45 to 60 seconds or longer).

During labor, the thick layer of mucus that has plugged the cervix during pregnancy (to protect the developing baby from infection) is discharged, either as a bloody plug that pops out like a cork or a little at a time. In 10 percent of cases, the amniotic sac will also break before labor begins, and the fluid gushes out (the "water breaks"). Labor usually begins within a day after this happens. If not, most physicians will induce labor with drugs in order to prevent contact with the outside world from causing infection in the fetus. Physicians sometimes break the amniotic sac on purpose to speed up labor.

The last part of the first stage of labor is called the *transition phase*. It takes place when the cervix is almost fully dilated (8 to 10 centimeters). Contractions are severe, and the woman may feel nauseous, chilled, and very uncomfortable. The transition phase usually lasts 40 minutes or less, and it marks the end of the initial stage of labor and the beginning of the next.

The second stage of labor, which concludes with the actual birth, begins when the cervix is fully dilated and the fetus begins moving through the birth canal. Contractions during this stage of labor are accompanied by an intense desire to push or "bear down," and they cause the opening of the vagina to expand. This stage lasts from 30 to 80 minutes, on average. Just before delivery, physicians often use a surgical procedure called an **episiotomy**, in which they make an incision from the lower portion of the vagina through the perineum to avoid tearing.

Crowning usually gives the first sight of the fetus. In most cases, the crown of its head appears at the opening of the vagina. In 2 to 4 percent of cases, a fetus will try to come through the birth canal feet or buttocks first, referred to as a *breech birth*. Sometimes it is possible to turn the fetus, but often this situation requires a cesarean section (see next section). As the head is delivered, it is crucial to make sure the umbilical cord is not wrapped

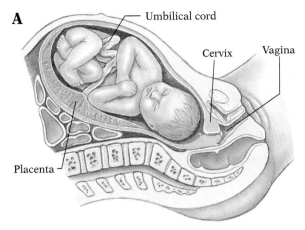

A

Umbilical cord

Cervix   Vagina

Placenta

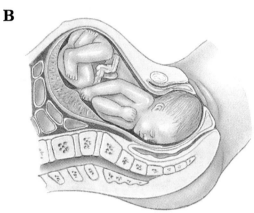

B

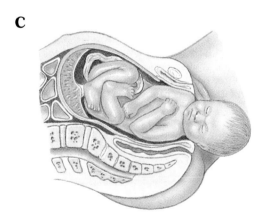

C

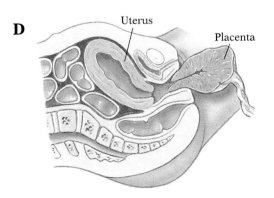

D

Uterus

Placenta

FIGURE C.2   The Stages of Labor. (A) The fetus is fully developed. (B) The first stage, dilation and effacement. (C) The second stage, expulsion. (D) The last stage, placenta detachment (adapted from Martini, 1995, Figure 29-12, p. 1130).

around the baby's neck. Suction is immediately applied to the baby's mouth and nose with a small rubber bulb to remove mucus so that the baby can breathe more easily. The head then turns, and the shoulders and the rest of the body come out rather quickly. A newborn will usually cry at birth. If not, the baby's back will be rubbed to start the baby breathing. The umbilical cord is clamped and cut about 1.5 inches from the baby's body; this stub will fall off in a few days, leaving what we call a *navel*.

In the third stage of labor the placenta detaches from the uterus and leaves the mother's body (along with other matter). Called the **afterbirth**, this stage usually lasts only 10 to 12 minutes. If even small pieces of the placenta stay in the uterus, infection and bleeding can occur. In this case, physicians use a procedure called *dilation* and *curettage*, or *D and C*, in which the cervix is dilated to allow access to the uterus, which is scraped clean. After the third stage of labor, the uterus normally contracts, returning eventually to its usual size.

Cesarean Section   A cesarean section, or *C-section*, involves the surgical delivery of a baby. In the past cesarean sections involved making a long vertical cut high on the abdomen through which the baby was delivered. Abdominal muscles run horizontally, however, so after these muscles have been cut, they are too weak to withstand the stress of labor in future pregnancies. Now physicians typically use a new type of incision that is horizontal and low on the abdomen (the "bikini cut"), which makes it possible to have normal (vaginal) deliveries in later pregnancies.

Prepared Childbirth   Prepared **childbirth** is the modern term for what was long called "natural childbirth"— techniques first used in the 1930s by a British physician, Grantly Dick-Read, and later expanded by the French physician Fernand Lamaze. On the theory that much of the pain and fear experienced by women during childbirth was the result of being in a strange environment, surrounded by strangers, and not knowing what was going to happen next, these and other medical professionals began to teach expectant mothers—and ultimately their partners as well—about pregnancy, labor, and birth. In addition, such physical methods as relaxation training and breathing techniques can help make labor easier.

Birth-control and Disease-prevention Techniques

There are three primary questions to ask yourself when you choose a contraceptive, or birth-control, technique. First, do you wish to prevent both pregnancy and the transmission of diseases like AIDS and other sexually transmitted diseases? As you will see, the methods that are most effective in preventing pregnancy are not always those that are most effective in protecting against disease. If you are single and dating different people, your need to protect yourself against disease is very great. If you are married and certain of your and your spouse's faithfulness, your concern about pregnancy may take priority. Second, if you wish to prevent pregnancy, do you want only to postpone it or to rule it out permanently? The most effective method of contraception—other than abstinence—is sterilization by surgical means and in most cases this is irreversible. Thus it is suitable only for those who are quite certain that they do not want (more) children. Third, do you need to consider such factors as religious restrictions? For example, the Catholic Church forbids artificial means of contraception. Your answers to these questions will help you sort through the various alternatives we discuss.

PROTECTION AGAINST DISEASE

Although spermicides that contain nonoxynol-9 not only kill sperm but have been shown to be effective against the bacteria and viruses that cause some STDs, spermicides reduce the risk of disease by only about 50 percent. The safest method of protection against disease is the latex rubber male condom used with a nonoxynol-9 spermicide.

PREVENTING PREGNANCY

The chart that follows provides information on the most common contraceptive methods, giving a general description as well as data on the effectiveness of each method, its particular advantages, and its possible side effects. Note that two figures are given for effectiveness. The first, labeled "With Perfect Use," is the rate at which pregnancy will occur if the method is used precisely as prescribed. The second, labeled "With Typical Use," allows for the fact that people often do *not* use these products as they are instructed to do; a woman may forget to take a pill, or a man may wait too late to put on a condom. In general, the chart moves from the most effective to the least effective methods; slight discrepancies in the progression of effectiveness rates reflect the desire to keep male and female methods (for example, male and female condoms) or related methods (the three different "fertility awareness" methods) together.

Appendix D is adapted from Bruce M. King, *Human Sexuality Today*, 3rd ed. (Upper Saddle River, NJ: Prentice Hall, 1999), Chapter 6. Copyright 1999. Adapted by permission of Prentice Hall, Upper Saddle River, New Jersey.

Method	Pregnancies per 100 Women in First Year of Continuous Use		Advantages	Problems
	With Perfect Use	With Typical Use		
Voluntary Sterilization: A **vasectomy** is a male sterilization technique in which the vas deferens is tied off and cut, preventing passage of sperm through the male's reproductive tract. A **tubal ligation** is the procedure by which a woman's Fallopian tubes are tied off or, more often, cut and tied. The procedure prevents passage of the egg, which simply disintegrates and is discharged during menstruation. The procedure is performed by **laparoscopy,** in which a long, tubelike instrument that transmits television pictures is inserted through a small incision; once the tubes are located, they are cauterized. Some doctors approach the fallopian tubes through the vagina (called a *culpotomy*).	0.1 for vasectomy; 0.2 for tubal ligation	0.2 for vasectomy; 0.4 for tubal ligation	Once done, many people report an increase in sexual desire because they no longer have to worry about pregnancy or contraceptive side effects; sexual relations can be completely spontaneous.	Surgical procedures always involve some risk, in part from the use of general anesthesia. Although it is sometimes possible to reverse vasectomy, and less often, a tubal ligation, sterilization should be considered permanent. Thus it should be used only by those who are quite sure they do not want any (or more) children.
Norplant: Norplant is a hormonal implant that offers contraceptive protection for up to 5 years. Six flexible silicone rubber tubes (or two rods), each about the size of a match, are inserted under the skin of the inside of a woman's arm, in a fanlike pattern. The tubes or rods contain levonorgestrel, a synthetic form of progesterone, that is slowly released over time and prevents pregnancy by inhibiting ovulation and thickening cervical mucus.	0.2	0.2	Believed by World Health Organization to be safer than the Pill because it contains no estrogen. Tubes can be removed at any time if a woman wants to conceive.	Spotting or irregular bleeding, weight gain, and headaches; less often, nervousness, dizziness, nausea, breast tenderness, and acne. However, more than 2/3 of users are very satisfied with this method.
Depo-Provera: Known as "the Shot," this injectable drug contains progestin. **Depo-Provera** works by preventing ovulation and lasts for 3 months. After discontinuation of the injections, it may take a woman from several months to a year to regain her fertility.	0.3	0.3	Avoids problem of pregnancy resulting from missing a daily dose, as with the Pill.	Initially thought to increase risk of several cancers, the drug is now approved by the World Health Organization. Some side effects are menstrual irregularities, fatigue and weakness, dizziness, and/or headaches.
The Pill: The most popular **Pill** combines synthetic estrogen and progesterone (progestins). It works by preventing ovulation, by inhibiting the buildup of the uterine lining necessary for implantation, and by keeping the cervical mucus thick and thus impeding the passage of sperm. A *minipill*, containing only progestin, has only the second and third of these actions and is for women who are breast-feeding or who cannot tolerate the side effects of the Pill's estrogen. Some combination pills try to adjust the levels of progestins to mimic "natural" hormonal phases of the menstrual cycle, but manufacturers don't agree on what is "natural." The Pill is taken for 21 days and then discontinued for 7 to permit menstrual bleeding.	0.1 (Pill); 0.5 (minipill)	0.3	May reduce risk of cancer of endometrium, benign breast tumors, ovarian cysts, rheumatoid arthritis, and pelvic inflammatory disease. Alleviates premenstrual syndrome and menstrual pain and reduces menstrual bleeding.	Cardiovascular problems, particularly in women who smoke, are over 35, or have diseases like diabetes or hypertension. May be less effective if antibiotics, analgesics, or tranquilizers are used at the same time. Backup methods must be used during the first month and whenever a woman forgets to take a pill.

Method	Pregnancies per 100 Women in First Year of Continuous Use		Advantages	Problems
	With Perfect Use	With Typical Use		
Intrauterine Device (IUD): The **intrauterine device,** or **IUD,** is a small, plastic or metal device (of various shapes and sizes) that is placed within the uterus by a doctor. IUDs work primarily by impeding the transit of sperm, and a copper or progesterone coating further impairs this passage. The copper-coated IUD is effective for up to 10 years. Insertion of an IUD requires dilation of the cervical opening, which may be uncomfortable or painful. Doctors must be certain that a woman is not pregnant and does not have a sexually transmitted disease at the time of insertion, and they must use proper sterilization procedures to avoid infection.	0.8 (copper); 1.5 (progesterone)	1.0 (copper); 2.0 (progesterone)	97% of women who use the IUD have a favorable opinion of it. Progesterone coating decreases menstrual blood loss and pain. The IUD permits spontaneity in sexual relations.	Today's IUDS are generally regarded as safe, although they may cause spotting, bleeding, and infection and are sometimes expelled. Some earlier IUDs—the Dalkon Shield in particular—were associated with serious cases of pelvic inflammatory disease.
Male Condom: The best **condom** is a thin sheath made of latex rubber or polyurethane[a] that fits over the penis and thus traps sperm. It also prevents contact between the man's and woman's skin and membranes, thus preventing the spread of sexually transmitted diseases. The condom should be put on *as soon as the penis is erect.* If the condom does not have a nipple tip, the man should leave a little extra space at the tip of the penis to catch the ejaculate. He should also hold the base of the condom as he withdraws after intercourse. Condoms can be used only once and should not be stored for long periods of time in a warm place (such as a wallet) or where they are exposed to light. For greatest effectiveness, condoms should be used with a spermicide.	Less than 1.0 with spermicide; 3.0 without spermicide	12.0	**Highly effective in reducing the spread of sexually transmitted diseases, including AIDS.** Putting on a condom takes less time than inserting any female device, and spermicide application is less messy.	Some men will not use condoms because they say they are allergic to rubber or that condoms reduce their sensitivity. Others complain about lack of spontaneity. These detractions are far outweighed by the high rate of effectiveness of this method in preventing both conception and disease.
Diaphragm: A **diaphragm** is a shallow rubber cup with a flexible rim that fits snugly between the pubic bone and the back of the cervix, sealing the entrance to the uterus and preventing the passage of sperm. The diaphragm must be fitted by a doctor or health-care worker, and refitting may be needed after pregnancy or weight changes of 10 pounds or more. For maximum effectiveness, it must be used with a spermicide and inserted no more than 2 hours before intercourse (lest the spermicide dissipate). More spermicide should be added (with an applicator) if intercourse is repeated during lovemaking. A diaphragm should be left in for 6 to 8 hours after intercourse to make sure no live sperm remain.	2.8–5.0	15.0	Offers some protection against gonorrhea and chlamydia. Is inexpensive, lasting for several years (but should be checked regularly for defects). Is associated with very few serious risks to fertility or general health.	Possible infection if left in for a prolonged period of time. Some couples feel that insertion (if not done until sex play has begun) takes away from the spontaneity of sexual activity.
Female Condom: The **female condom** is a 7-inch-long polyurethane pouch that is closed at one end, which is surrounded by a flexible metal rim, and open at the other, which is surrounded by a similar ring. The inner ring fits over the cervix, like a diaphragm, thus closing the entrance to the uterus; the outer ring covers part of the vulva. At present, the Reality Female condom is the only one on the U.S. market.	5.0–6.0	15.0	Thinner than male condoms, feels softer than rubber, and transfers heat. Some feel that it simulates bare-skin intercourse.	Much more expensive than male condom and, like it, can be used only once.

Method	Pregnancies per 100 Women in First Year of Continuous Use		Advantages	Problems
	With Perfect Use	With Typical Use		
Cervical Cap: The **cervical cap** is another barrier device designed to prevent passage of sperm from the vagina into the uterus. Made of latex rubber, it is smaller and more compact than a diaphragm and resembles a large rubber thimble. It should be used with spermicide, and it fits over the cervix by suction. It is especially useful for women whose vaginal muscles have been relaxed by childbearing. Insertion and removal of the cap are more difficult than for the diaphragm, but it is more comfortable and can be left in for 48 hours. Women should make sure after intercourse that the cap has not dislodged.	8.0–10.0[b]	18.0	May offer some protection against gonorrhea and chlamydia.	Possible infection with prolonged use due to long exposure to secretions trapped by the cap. Currently recommended only for women who have normal Pap smears lest it adversely affect cervical tissues.
Spermicides: Spermicides are chemicals that kill sperm (nonoxynol-9 or octoxinol-9). Used alone, spermicidal foams and suppositories are more effective than jellies and creams, but for maximum effectiveness any of these should be used with a physical barrier method (condom, diaphragm, etc.). Spermicides must be placed in the vagina shortly before intercourse begins. They lose their effectiveness over time, so new spermicide must be inserted before each time a woman has intercourse.	5.0	21.0	Spermicides reduce the risk of some STDs, including AIDS, by killing bacteria and viruses. They may also reduce the risk of cervical cancer.	Several studies have found that nonoxynol-9—containing spermicides—increase the risk of urinary tract infection. Some complain that they irritate the vagina or penis, detract from oral–genital sex, and interfere with spontaneity.
Withdrawal: In **withdrawal,** or *coitus interruptus,* the male withdraws his penis just before reaching orgasm and ejaculates outside his partner's vagina. However, because sperm are found in the fluid secreted by the Cowper's glands just before a man ejaculates, this method is highly unreliable.	4.0	19.0	The withdrawal method is better than no method at all.	Highly ineffective compared to other methods. Also, withdrawal may not be very physically or emotionally satisfying for either partner.
Fertility Awareness: Fertility awareness (*natural planning* or *rhythm*) is based on predicting ovulation and identifying "safe days" in a woman's menstrual cycle. A woman can become pregnant only during the first 24 hours or so after ovulation; after that, the egg is overly ripe, and a sperm can't fertilize it. There are three variations of this method. The **calendar method** uses a formula to calculate the unsafe period based on the length of a woman's menstrual cycles. According to the **basal body temperature method,** or **BBT,** a couple should abstain from having sexual intercourse from the end of menstruation until 2 to 4 days after a temperature rise is noted (a woman's basal body temperature rises 24 to 72 hours after ovulation by a few tenths of a degree Fahrenheit). The **Billings method** attempts to pinpoint the time of ovulation by noting changes in the consistency of a woman's cervical mucus, which changes from white (or cloudy) and sticky to clear and slippery (like that of an egg white) 1 or 2 days before ovulation. The *symptothermal* method combines the BBT and Billings methods.	9.0 for calendar method; 2.0 for BBT; 3.0 for Billings	20.0+ for calendar method; 20.0+ for BBT; 16.0+ for Billings	Rhythm methods are usually considered to be safer than other contraception techniques and are acceptable to most religious groups.	All rhythm methods may be frustrating because they involve fairly long periods of abstinence from sex. However, chemical testing kits that will pinpoint the time of ovulation accurately enough to serve as contraceptives may soon be available for home use. To be effective, a method will have to predict ovulation at least 4 to 5 days in advance. Current products available, which predict 12 to 36 hours in advance, are useful only for couples who *want* to conceive.

[a]Do *not* buy condoms made of lamb intestine. These "skins" are porous, and HIV and other viruses and bacteria may easily penetrate through the tiny holes.
[b]In those who have not yet given birth.

APPENDIX E

··

HIV/AIDS and Other Sexually Transmitted Diseases

Sexually transmitted diseases (once called *venereal diseases*, after the Roman goddess of love, Venus) are diseases that are spread either exclusively through sexual contact, like chlamydia, gonorrhea, herpes, and human papillomavirus infection (genital warts), or primarily through sexual activity but by other means as well, like HIV/AIDS, hepatitis B, syphilis, and trichomoniasis. The chart on the following pages provides information on the symptoms, causes, and means of transmission of these diseases, as well as their current forms of treatment and progress if left untreated. (STDs, with an emphasis on

HIV/AIDS, are also discussed in Chapter 6.) Although there are probably more than 20 known STDs, these 8 have the highest incidence and the most serious effects.

In the United States, there have been major outbreaks of STDs from time to time. The present epidemic situation can probably be attributed to several factors. First, the discovery of penicillin and other antibiotics about the time of World War II may have given some people a false sense of confidence, leading them to engage in sexual intercourse when previously they might have feared to do so. Second, the new feeling of sexual freedom given people by the arrival of the Pill and other reliable means of birth control may have lessened their attention to disease prevention. And third, because recent drug treatments have slowed the progression of HIV/AIDS, many people have become lax about using condoms (see Chapter 6).

---

*Appendix E is adapted from Bruce M. King, *Human Sexuality Today*, 2nd ed., (Englewood Cliffs, NJ: Prentice Hall, 1996), Chapter 5. Adapted by permission of Prentice Hall, Englewood Cliffs, New Jersey.

Disease/Symptoms	Incidence[a]	Cause	How Transmitted	Progress of Disease If Left Untreated	Current Treatments
Acquired Immune Deficiency Syndrome (AIDS): HIV may remain dormant for a time and then cause such flulike symptoms as diarrhea, fever, and other infections that linger on. In full-blown AIDS, diseases like lymphoma, Kaposi's sarcoma, and pneumocystis carinii pneumonia appear.	85,000+	*Human immuno-deficiency* virus, resident in semen, vaginal fluids, and blood.	Intimate sexual contact (anal or vaginal intercourse, occasionally oral sex); exposure to infected blood (sharing of needles among IV drug users); mother-to-fetus transmission through blood.	AIDS is terminal, but death can be postponed and the quality of life improved with treatment.	Four *antiretroviral drugs* slow progression of HIV infection: zidovudine (AZT), didanosine (DDI), zalcitabine (DDC), and stavudine (D4T). Since 1996, new drugs known as "protease inhibitors," used in combination with AZT and DDI, have been found to slow or reduce HIV in the bloodstream.
Chlamydia: In both men and women, irritation and burning of the urethra and a thin, clear discharge. However, many people have no symptoms in the initial stage.	4,000,000	*Chlamydia trachomatis* bacterium.	Sexual activity; contact between mucous membranes of infected person and those of another person.	In men, infection of prostate and epididymis and possible sterility. In women, *pelvic inflammatory disease* leading to increased risk of tubal pregnancy and/or sterility. Babies born to infected women may have eye, nose, or throat infections.	Tetracycline, doxycycline, or an erythromycin. Some doctors are using newer drugs like azithromycin.
Gonorrhea: Inflammation of urethra or vulva; discharge from penis or vagina; irritation during urination. Some men and many women show no initial symptoms.	800,000	*Neisseria gonorrhoeae* bacterium (often referred to as *gonococcus*).	Almost exclusively through intimate sexual contact.	In men, inflammation of prostate, seminal vesicles, bladder, and epididymis; severe pain and fever; possible sterility. In females, pelvic inflammatory disease with severe abdominal pain and fever; possible sterility. Baby born to infected mother may become blind.	Ceftriaxone followed by tetracycline or an erythromycin.
Hepatitis B: Poor appetite, diarrhea, fever, vomiting, pain, fatigue, jaundiced or yellow tinge of skin and eyes; dark urine.	50,000–1,000,000	HBC virus.	By infected blood or body fluids such as saliva, semen, and vaginal secretions. About half of U.S. cases are contracted sexually (commonest through anal sex); also by sharing drug-use needles, by blood transfusions, and by blood exchange between mother and fetus.	Serious, sometimes fatal, liver disease.	Interferon is effective in about a third of patients; 90% of patients recover, but up to 10% remain infected and become carriers, infecting others.
Herpes: *Prodrome stage*—tingling, burning, itching of skin that contacted virus; *vesicle stage*—fluid-filled blisters,	200,000–500,000	Herpes simplex virus Types I and II. I is thought to cause oral herpes, II to cause genital	Direct contact between infected site on one person and skin of another. One can get genital herpes from con-	Herpes is a leading cause of infectious blindness today. *Herpes encephalitis* is a rare disease of the brain that is often fatal. *Herpes meningitis*	No cure. Once you have herpes, the potential for another attack is always there. Acyclovir relieves

Disease/Symptoms	Incidence[a]	Cause	How Transmitted	Progress of Disease If Left Untreated	Current Treatments
flulike symptoms, painful urination; *crusting-over stage*—sores develop scales and form scabs.		herpes, but the symptoms and outcome of both types are the same.	tact with a blister on a partner's lip or oral herpes from a genital sore. People can spread their own herpes from one site to another (such as the eyes) by touch.	(inflammation of membranes covering brain and spinal cord) is also possible. In women, risks cancer of cervix. A baby may be infected during childbirth, suffering neurological, eye, skin, and internal organ damage.	symptoms and speeds healing during primary attack. Researchers are working on a herpes vaccine.
Human Papillomavirus Infection (also *genital warts*): Some people have symptoms that only a doctor can detect; others develop cauliflower-like warts that cause itching, irritation, or bleeding. In males, warts usually apear on penis, scrotum, or anus and sometimes in the urethra; in females, on the cervix and vaginal wall, vulva, and anus.	200,000–500.000	Human papilloma virus causes nongenital warts and other skin conditions; two types of HPV cause genital warts.	By sexual intercourse or sometimes oral-genital sex; highly contagious, and most common STD caused by viruses in the United States.	In women, HPV infection increases risk of cervical cancer. Cancer of penis occurs but is rare. Recurrence of symptoms of HPV infection is common (see Current Treatments Column).	No cure. External treatment with podophyllin (brand name Codylox); large warts may be removed surgically, internal ones by laser surgery. Cervical HPV infection is treated with cryotherapy (freezing). Vaccine to prevent HPV infection may be developed in the near future.
Syphilis: *Primary stage* begins with ulcerlike sore called *chancre,* usually on penis, cervix, lips, tongue, or anus, that is highly infectious but usually painless. Sore may disappear, but spirochete enters bloodstream and infection spreads throughout the body. In *secondary stage,* an itchless, painless rash spreads over the body; sores appear in moist areas around the genitals; other flu- and cold-like symptoms.	113,000	*Treponema pallidum* bacterium (referred to as the *spirochete*).	Majority of cases are transmitted by sexual contact. Spirochete can also pass directly into the bloodstream through a cut or scrape; thus one can get syphilis by merely touching the sores of an infected person.	If initial chancre is ignored it will disappear, but the person remains infected. In the third, *latent stage,* there are usually no symptoms although in about a third of victims large ulcers develop on skin and bones. In all cases bacteria continue their attack on the body's internal organs, particularly the heart, blood vessels, and brain and spinal cord. Deafness, paralysis, insanity, and death often result.	Spirochetes are easily eradicated with antibiotics; penicillin is still the most effective, although there are some indications that the bacterium may be becoming resistant to this agent.
Trichomoniasis: In women a heavy vaginal discharge with a foul odor accompanied by severe vaginal itching.	3,000,000+	One-celled protozoan, *Trichomonas vaginalis.*	Majority of cases are transmitted by sexual intercourse, but disease can be contracted from a wet toilet seat or by sharing towels (protozoan survives in urine and tap water for hours to days).	Can lead to adhesions in the fallopian tubes and sterility.	Metronidazole is the treatment of choice. However, this drug is under study as a possible carcinogen.

[a]Estimated new cases per year in the United States; based on 1995 data.

APPENDIX F

Premarital and Nonmarital Agreements

A premarital (also called a prenuptial or antenuptial) agreement is a contract between potential spouses that spells out the rights and expectations of the partners and determines how their property will be divided if they divorce. It specifies what is "yours, mine and ours."

Most lawyers agree that never-before-married young people with few assets don't need a premarital agreement, but such contracts are recommended for couples marrying for the first time later in life, especially if they have pursued careers and have accumulated assets, or remarry. While some lawyers think that preparing a premarital agreement creates distrust and may damage the marriage, many others believe such pacts help ensure a successful marriage because both partners (and their children, if any) know what to expect in case there is a divorce or death.

I begin with some of the standard issues, especially property rights, covered by legal contracts and lawyers (see, for example, Winer and Becker, 1993; Dorf et al., 1996). I also include some items that would not be legally enforceable but that might be useful for couples who are planning to marry, as well as those living together, that "how-to" books written by lawyers often omit.

Premarital Property

- Do the partners plan to keep or dispose of premarital property (such as houses and land)?
- If the premarital property is kept or sold, how will the real estate profits be divided between the partners?
- If the premarital property increases in value over time, will both partners share the income that is generated when the property is sold?

Assets, Liabilities, and Income

- What is the income of both partners? What about savings, stocks, and other assets?
- Have both partners seen each other's tax returns?
- Who will be responsible for filing tax returns? Who will pay the taxes? How will refunds be distributed?
- Who is responsible for paying a partner's debts (such as college loans, credit card balances, and bank loans)?
- Should both partners hold all property jointly? Or should income, rents, profits, interest, dividends, stock splits, bank accounts, and other assets also be held separately by each partner?

Business or Investment Partnerships

- Should a spouse be a business partner, especially in a family-owned business?
- In a privately held corporation, should a spouse inherit stock or receive stock as part of a divorce settlement?

Disposition of Marital Property

- In case of death or divorce, will marital property go to the partner or the deceased partner's children?
- Will the property be sold? If so, how will the partners share the profits?
- What happens to such personal property as clothing, jewelry, collections (art, coins, stamps, etc.), recreation or sports equipment, expensive tools or home maintenance equipment (such as lawn tractors)?

Life Insurance

- Do both partners have life insurance?
- What is the life insurance coverage? How much does each partner pay?
- Who is the beneficiary of the life insurance?
- Do both partners have documentation from the insurance company about the beneficiary?

Spousal Maintenance (Alimony)

- Will either partner receive alimony in case of divorce? If so, how much?
- Will alimony be paid in cash or through the disposition of property?
- Will alimony payments increase to keep up with inflation?
- How much should a spouse (typically a wife) be compensated if she has sacrificed her own career to support her husband's career or business?

Child Custody and Support

- If there is a divorce, who will have custody of the child(ren)?
- Will the custody be joint, split, or sole (see Chapter 15)?
- Who will be responsible for child support?
- What percentage of one's earnings is "reasonable" or "fair" for child support?

- Would both partners have the right to move to another state or country?
- Is either partner responsible for supporting children who attend college or trade schools after age 18?

Trusts and Wills

- If there are trust funds (such as leaving money or property to biological children), are these funds consistent with the terms of the will?
- Have all assets been listed in the will?
- Does the will list the beneficiaries of stock, bonds, and other income?
- Does the surviving partner have a right to live in the home even though she or he doesn't inherit the property?
- Does the surviving spouse have a right to choose a cemetery and burial decisions for the deceased partner?
- If the surviving spouse doesn't inherit the property, is there a monthly or annual allowance from the estate?

Although "lifestyle clauses" are not legally enforceable, they give partners a tool to disclose, examine, and specify expectations about their own and their partner's behavior. If people realize they cannot resolve major disagreements, they are preventing a future divorce by not getting married. Here are some topics that might be included in an informal nonmarital or premarital agreement:

Sex and Contraception

- What birth-control methods will be used? Are both partners willing to abort an unwanted fetus?
- How does each partner define "sex" (sexual intercourse, cuddling, fondling)?
- How often do partners expect to have sexual intercourse?
- Are there any sexual acts that are demeaning or offensive?
- What happens if a partner loses interest in sexual intercourse?
- How serious is infidelity? How does each partner define "infidelity"?

Having and Raising Children

- Do both partners want children? If so, how many and at what intervals?
- Is attending religious services important? If so, how often? Should current or future children have a religious upbringing?
- If the woman keeps her surname, will the children have the father's or the mother's surname?
- Who is responsible for disciplining children? Does discipline include spanking, slapping, or hitting?

- Who will do the housework? What chores will each person perform?

Relatives and Friends

- How important is it to maintain contact with one's parents, siblings, or other relatives? If they live far away, is there a limit on long-distance phone calls?
- Which partner's parent(s) should the couple visit, especially during the holidays?
- Is it important to celebrate relatives' birthdays, anniversaries, and other occasions? If so, who buys the cards and presents? Should there be a limit on gift-giving for births, birthdays, graduations, weddings, and other milestones?
- Can parents or other relatives live in the couple's home? Under what conditions and for how long?
- Who is responsible for caretaking an elderly or disabled parent or other relative?
- How important is socializing with friends? Is it acceptable for each partner to socialize with friends on her or his own? Can partners discuss their personal problems with friends or family members?

Financial Issues

- Should there be joint or separate savings and checking accounts? A combination?
- Can a partner do anything she or he wants with "his" or "her" separate checking or savings account?
- Who is responsible for paying the monthly bills?
- Who is responsible for preparing state and federal taxes?
- Do both partners agree that credit card debts are acceptable? If so, is there a limit on the amount of debt?
- Who decides whether and how much life insurance to buy? Who will be the beneficiaries?
- Who decides whether and when to invest in the stock market?
- If partners disagree about financial issues, how will the conflict be resolved?

GLOSSARY

abortion The artificially induced or natural expulsion of an embryo or fetus from the uterus.

acculturation The process of adapting to the language, values, beliefs, roles, and other characteristics of the host culture.

acquaintance rape Unwanted, forced sexual intercourse, often in a social context such as a party; the rapist may be a neighbor, friend of the family, co-worker, or a person the victim has just met.

acquired immunodeficiency syndrome (AIDS) A degenerative disease caused by a virus that attacks the body's immune system and makes it susceptible to a number of diseases such as pneumonia and cancer.

agape Love that is altruistic, self-sacrificing, and directed toward all humankind.

ageism Discrimination against people on the basis of age, particularly against those who are old.

alimony Monetary payments made by one ex-spouse to the other after a divorce to support the latter's basic needs for survival.

Alzheimer's disease A progressive, degenerative disorder that attacks the brain and impairs memory, thinking, and behavior.

amniocentesis A procedure performed in the twentieth week of pregnancy, in which a sample of the amniotic fluid is withdrawn by a needle inserted into the abdomen; the fluid is analyzed for possible genetic disorders and biochemical abnormalities in the fetus.

androgyny A blend of culturally defined male and female characteristics.

anorexia nervosa An often intractable and dangerous eating disorder characterized by fear of obesity, together with a distorted body image and the conviction that one is "fat," significant weight loss, and an absolute refusal to maintain weight within the normal limits for one's age and height.

artificial insemination An assisted reproductive technique in which male semen is introduced artificially into the vagina or uterus about the time of ovulation.

assisted reproductive technology (ART) A general term that includes all treatments and procedures that involve the handling of human eggs and sperm to produce a pregnancy.

attachment theory The notion that a warm, secure, and loving relationship is essential to human emotional growth and development.

authoritarian approach An approach to parenting that is demanding, controlling, and punitive; emphasizes respect for authority, work, order, and traditional family structure; often uses punitive, forceful measures to control behavior.

authoritative approach An approach to parenting that is demanding and controlling but supportive and responsive; encourages autonomy and self-reliance; generally uses positive reinforcement instead of punitive, repressive discipline.

baby boomer A person born in the post–World War II generation between 1946 and 1964.

battered woman syndrome A condition in which women who have experienced many years of physical abuse come to feel incapable of making any satisfactory change in their way of life; recently used as a defense in cases in which such women have murdered their abusive husbands.

bereavement The state of having been robbed, or deprived, by death of the presence of a loved one.

bigamy The act of marrying one person while still legally married to another.

biological father–stepmother family A family in which all the children are biological children of the father and stepchildren of the mother.

biological mother–stepfather family A family in which all the children are biological children of the mother and stepchildren of the father.

birth rate Refers to the number of live births per 1000 population.

bisexual A person who is sexually attracted to members of both sexes.

boomerang generation Young adults who move back into their parents' homes after living independently for a while.

bulimia An eating disorder characterized by a cyclical pattern of eating binges followed by self-induced vomiting, fasting, excessive exercise, or the use of diuretics or laxatives.

bundling A courting custom in American colonial times in which a young man and woman, both fully dressed, spent the night in bed together, separated by a wooden board.

child abuse According to Public Law 93-237, the physical or mental injury, sexual abuse, negligent treatment, or maltreatment of a child under the age of 18 by a person responsible for the child's welfare.

child maltreatment A wide range of behaviors that place the child at serious risk, including physical abuse, sexual abuse, neglect, and emotional mistreatment.

child support Monetary payments by the noncustodial parent to the parent who has custody of children to help pay the expenses of raising the children.

chlamydia A sexually transmitted bacterial infection that can contribute to infertility by triggering pelvic inflammatory disease. The symptoms of chlamydia often go unnoticed.

chorionic villi sampling A procedure in which some of the villi, or protrusions, of the membrane that surrounds the amniotic sac are removed by a catheter through the vagina and analyzed for abnormalities in the fetus.

clinical research The study of individuals or small groups of people who seek help for physical and/or social problems from mental health professionals.

cognitive development theory A theory positing that children learn by interacting with their environment and, using the processes of thinking, understanding, and reasoning, by interpreting and applying the information they gather.

cohabitation A living arrangement in which two people who are not related and not married share living quarters and usually have a sexual relationship.

common-law marriage A nonceremonial form of marriage, established by cohabitation and/or evidence of consummation (sexual intercourse).

commuter marriage A marriage in which partners live and work in separate geographic areas and get together intermittently.

compadrazgo A Mexican American family system in which close family friends are formally designated as godparents of a newborn, participate in the child's important rites of passage, and maintain continuing strong ties with their godchild.

comparable worth A concept that calls for equal pay for men and women who are doing work that involves comparable skill, effort, responsibility, and work conditions.

conflict-habituated marriage A marriage in which the partners fight both verbally and physically but do not believe that fighting is a reason for divorce.

conflict theory A macro-level sociological theory that examines the ways in which groups disagree and struggle over power and compete for scarce resources and that views conflict and its consequences as natural, inevitable, and often desirable.

contraception The prevention of pregnancy by behavioral, mechanical, or chemical means.

cultural pluralism This concept refers to maintaining aspects of immigrants' original cultures while living peacefully with the host culture.

cunnilingus Oral stimulation of a woman's genitals.

custody A court-mandated ruling as to which parent will have the primary responsibility for the welfare and upbringing of a child; the custodial parent cares for the child in her or his home, whereas the noncustodial parent may have specified visitation rights. *See also* joint custody.

daddy penalty A phenomenon in which men whose wives are employed outside the home are paid lower salaries than their counterparts whose wives are full-time homemakers.

date rape Unwanted, forced sexual intercourse in the context of a dating situation; victim and perpetrator may be on a first date or in a long-term dating relationship.

dating The process of meeting people socially for possible mate selection.

depression A mental disorder characterized by pervasive sadness and other negative emotions and that often also finds expression in physical symptoms such as diarrhea, chest discomfort, nausea, or loss of appetite for which no physical or physiological cause can be found.

developmental tasks Specific role expectations and responsibilities that must be fulfilled as people move through the family life cycle.

developmental theories Micro-level theories of marriage and the family that examine the ways in which family members accomplish developmental tasks as they move through the family life cycle.

devitalized marriage A marriage in which the partners are initially in love, spend time together, and have a satisfying sex life but in time find they are staying together out of duty; because they see no alternatives, they do not consider divorce.

DEWKS (dual-employed with kids) Term that describes a family in which both parents are employed full time outside the home.

discouraged worker An unemployed person who wants to work but who has recently given up the search for a position because of the belief that the job hunt is futile.

discretionary income Income remaining after essentials, such as rent or mortgage, food, utilities, and transportation costs, have been paid and that people can then spend as they please.

discrimination Behavior, often based on prejudice, that subjects members of minority groups, particularly, to unfair treatment, such as rejection of job applications and denial of housing opportunities.

divorce The legal and formal dissolution of a marriage.

divorce mediation The technique and practice in which a trained mediator helps a divorcing couple come to an agreement and resolve such issues as support, child custody, and the division of property.

dowry The money, goods, or property a woman in traditional societies brings to a marriage.

dual-career couple Marriage partners both of whom work in professional or managerial positions.

dual-earner couple Married partners both of whom work outside the home.

ecological theory A theoretical perspective that examines the interrelationship between individuals' and family roles and environmental settings.

elder abuse Physical abuse, negligence, financial exploitation, psychological abuse, deprivation of necessities like food and heat, isolation from friends and relatives, and failure to administer needed medications to people age 65 or older.

embryo transplant A procedure by which an embryo, or a fertilized egg, is implanted in the uterus of an infertile woman.

endogamy A cultural rule requiring that people marry and/or have sexual relations only within their own particular group.

endometriosis A condition in which endometrial tissue spreads outside the womb and attaches itself to other pelvic organs, such as the ovaries or the fallopian tubes.

engagement The formalization of a couple's decision to marry and the last step in the courtship process.

equity theory A theoretical perspective that seeks to explain how people perceive injustice and how they will react when they find themselves in unjust relationships.

eros Love based on beauty and physical attractiveness.

evaluation research Research that assesses the effectiveness of social programs in both the public and private sectors.

exogamy A cultural rule requiring that people marry outside of their particular group.

expressive role In structural-functional theory, the supportive and nurturing role of the wife or mother who must sustain and support the husband/father.

extended family A family in which two or more generations live together or in close proximity.

familism The notion that, within a given family, family relationships take precedence over the concerns of individual family members.

family Traditionally defined as a unit made up of two or more people who are related by blood, marriage, or adoption and who live together and form an economic unit. Defined in this book as an intimate environment in which (1) two or more people live together in a committed relationship; (2) the members see their identity as importantly attached to the group; and (3) the group shares close emotional ties and functions.

family life cycle A series of stages, each focusing on a different set of events, that the family goes through from the early days of a marriage to the death of one or both partners.

family of orientation The family into which a person is born.

family of procreation The family a person forms by marrying and having or adopting children.

family policy The measures taken by governmental bodies to achieve specific objectives relating to the family's well-being.

family systems theory A theoretical perspective that examines the daily functioning and interactions of family members with each other and the larger society.

fellatio Oral stimulation of a man's penis.

feminist theories Theoretical perspectives that analyze socially constructed expectations based on variables such as gender roles, social class, race, ethnicity, and sexual orientation.

fertility-enhancing drugs Drugs that stimulate ovaries to produce eggs.

fertility rate The number of births per year per 1000 women of childbearing age (15 to 44).

fetal alcohol syndrome (FAS) Physical deformities and/or mental retardation in an infant caused by the mother's excessive use of alcohol during pregnancy.

fictive kin Nonrelatives who are accepted as part of a family.

filter theory The theory that people in search of potential mates go through a process whereby they filter out eligible partners according to certain criteria and thus reduce the pool of eligibles to a relatively small number of candidates.

foster home A home in which a family raises a child or children who are not their own for a period of time but does not formally adopt them.

gamete intrafallopian transfer (GIFT) A variation of in vitro fertilization in which eggs and sperm are artificially inserted into a woman's fallopian tube.

gender The socially learned attitudes and behaviors that characterize a person of one sex or the other; based on differing social and cultural expectations of the sexes.

gender identity An individual's emotional and intellectual awareness of being either male or female.

gender roles Distinctive patterns of attitudes, behaviors, and activities that society prescribes for females and males.

gender-role stereotype The belief and expectation that women and men each display rigid, traditional gender-role characteristics.

gender schema theory The theory that children develop schema, or information-processing categories, that organize and guide their perceptions of cultural stimuli to develop a gender identity.

genogram A diagram of the biological relationships among family members.

gerontologist One who studies aging and the elderly.

grief The emotional response to loss.

half-sibling A brother or sister with whom one shares only one biological parent.

heterogamy Refers to dating or marrying someone from a social, racial, ethnic, religious, or age group different from one's own.

heterosexual A person who is sexually attracted to members of the opposite sex.

homogamy Refers to dating or marrying someone who possesses similar social characteristics such as ethnicity, race, religion, age, and social class.

homophobia Fear and hatred of homosexuality.

homosexual A person who is sexually attracted to persons of the same sex.

hormones Chemical substances secreted into the bloodstream by glands of the endocrine system.

hospice A place for the care of the dying that stresses the relief of pain, imparting a sense of security and companionship to dying patients, and making such patients comfortable.

human immunodeficiency virus (HIV) The virus that causes AIDS.

hypergamy Marrying or dating someone who is in a higher socioeconomic group than one's own.

identity bargaining A stage in the evolution of a marriage in which partners readjust their idealized expectations to the realities of their life together.

incest Sexual intercourse between family members who are closely related. *See also* incest taboo.

incest taboo Cultural norms and laws that forbid sexual intercourse between close blood relatives, such as brother and sister, father and daughter, or mother and son.

infertility The inability to conceive a baby after 12 months of unprotected sex.

instrumental role In structural-functional theory, the "breadwinner" role of the husband or father, who must be hardworking, tough, and competitive.

intracytoplasmic sperm injection (ICSD) A procedure that involves injecting sperm directly into an egg in a laboratory dish to produce a pregnancy.

intrinsic marriage A marriage that is inherently rewarding.

in vitro fertilization (IVF) An assisted reproduction technique in which eggs are surgically removed from a woman's ovaries, fertilized with sperm from the woman's husband or a donor, and then reimplanted in the woman's uterus.

joint biological-stepfamily A family in which at least one child is a biological child of both parents, at least one child is the biological child of one parent and the stepchild of the other parent, and no other "type" of child is present.

joint custody A custody arrangement in which the children divide their time between both parents; in *joint legal custody*, parents share decision making about the children's upbringing; in *joint physical custody*, the children live alternately and for specified periods in each parent's home.

kinship system A network of people who are related by marriage, blood, or adoption.

latchkey kids Children who return after school to an empty home and are alone and unsupervised until their parents or another adult arrives.

latent functions Functions that are not recognized or intended; present but not immediately visible.

later-life family A family that is beyond the years of child rearing and has launched the children or a childless family beginning to plan for retirement.

living will A legal document in which a person specifies what, if any, life-support measures she or he wishes to be provided with in the case of serious illness and if or when such measures should be discontinued.

ludus Love that is carefree and casual, "fun and games."

machismo A concept of masculinity that stresses such attributes as dominance, assertiveness, pride, and sexual prowess.

macro-level perspective A sociological perspective that focuses on large-scale patterns that characterize society as a whole.

male climacteric A "change of life" in men proposed by some as analogous to female menopause. More psychological than physiological, such a change affects only a small percentage of men and is not characterized by the cessation of reproductive capacity.

mania Love that is obsessive, jealous, and possessive.

manifest functions Functions that are recognized or intended and present in a clearly evident way.

marital burnout The gradual deterioration of love and, ultimately, the loss of an emotional attachment between marital partners.

marital·rape A violent act in which a nonconsenting woman is forced by her husband to engage in sexual activity.

marriage A socially approved mating relationship.

marriage market Courtship seen as a process in which prospective spouses compare the assets and liabilities of eligible partners and choose the best available mate.

marriage squeeze The term for the oversupply of female baby boomers, born between 1945 and 1964, in relation to eligible males.

married singles Married partners who continue to live together, may be good friends, and may be sexually intimate but who, in many ways, have drifted apart.

masturbation Sexual self-pleasuring that involves some form of direct physical stimulation.

matriarchy A familial relationship in which the authority is held by the oldest female, usually the mother. Women control cultural, political, and economic resources and, consequently, have power over men.

matrilineal A kinship system in which children trace their family descent through their mother's line and property is passed on to female heirs.

menopause The cessation of the menstrual cycle.

micro-level perspective A sociological perspective that focuses on small-scale patterns of social interaction in specific settings.

minority group A group of people who, because of their physical or cultural characteristics, are singled out from others in the society in which they live and may be subject to differential and unequal treatment.

mommy track A slower or even a side track in business along which women managers who wish to combine both career and child rearing are expected to move.

monogamy A marital or sexual relationship in which an individual is committed exclusively to one person.

mourning The customary outward expression of grief over the loss of a loved one that varies among different social and cultural groups.

nativism Refers to the policies and practices that favor native-born citizens versus immigrants.

no-fault divorce A divorce process in which neither partner need establish the guilt or wrongdoing of the other.

norm A culturally defined rule for behavior.

nuclear family A family made up of a wife, a husband, and their biological or adopted children.

observation A type of scientific investigation in which researchers collect data by systematically observing people in their natural surroundings.

open adoption An adoption process that encourages the sharing of information and contact between biological and adoptive parents during the adoption process and throughout the adopted child's life.

part-time/limited cohabitation A type of cohabitation into which people "drift" gradually.

passive-congenial marriage A marriage in which partners with minimal emotional investment and expectations of their union maintain independent spheres of interests and activities and derive satisfaction from relationships with others rather than from each other.

patriarchy A society or familial relationship in which the positions of power and authority—political, economic, legal, religious, educational, military, and domestic—are generally held by men.

patrilineal A kinship system in which children trace their family descent through their father's line and property is passed on to male heirs.

pelvic inflammatory disease (PID) An infection of the uterus that spreads to the fallopian tubes, ovaries, and surrounding tissues and produces scarring that blocks the fallopian tubes.

permissive approach An approach to parenting that is highly responsive and warm, not demanding but sometimes manipulative; this approach encourages freedom of expression, autonomy, and internal control.

petting Physical contact between males and females that produces erotic arousal without necessarily leading to sexual intercourse.

polygamy A form of marriage in which one woman or one man may have several spouses.

population Any well-defined group of people or things that a researcher wants to study.

POSSLQs "Persons of the opposite sex sharing living quarters"; a U.S. Census Bureau household category.

postpartum depression Depression experienced by some women soon after childbirth; thought to be at least partially caused by chemical imbalances.

poverty line The minimum income level determined by the federal government to be necessary for individuals' and families' basic subsistence.

power The ability to impose one's will on others.

pragma Love that is rational and based on practical considerations, such as compatibility and perceived benefits.

prejudice A negative attitude toward individuals and groups (often minority groups) who are different from oneself; based on suspicion, intolerance, and sometimes hatred.

premarital cohabitation Often a kind of trial marriage; a living arrangement in which a couple tests its relationship before making a final commitment.

primary group Important people, such as family members and close friends, characterized by close, long-lasting, intimate, and face-to-face interaction.

propinquity Geographic closeness.

qualitative research Refers to a data-collection process where researchers rely on observation and interviews and report their findings from the respondent's point of view.

quantitative research Refers to a data-collection process where researchers assign numbers to qualitative (i.e., nonnumeric) observations by counting and measuring attitudes or behavior.

racial-ethnic group A group of people with distinctive racial and cultural characteristics.

role Pattern of behavior attached to a particular status, or position, in society.

role conflict Frustration and uncertainty experienced by a person who is confronted with incompatible role requirements or expectations.

sample In science research, a group of people or things that is smaller than but representative of the population being studied.

sandwich generation Midlife men and women who feel caught between the need to care for both their own children and their aging parents.

secondary analysis Analysis of data that have been collected by other researchers.

secondary group Groups characterized by relatively impersonal and short-term relationships and where people work together on common tasks or activities.

self-disclosure Open communication in which one person offers his or her honest thoughts and feelings to another person in the hope that truly open communication will follow.

separation Separations are of several types: a temporary "time-out" while partners reassess their marriage; a "trial separation" during which a couple separate physically and evaluate the desirability of continuing their marriage; a permanent physical separation when one or both partners' religious faith precludes divorce; or a "legal separation," a temporary period of living apart required by most states before a divorce may be granted.

serial monogamy Marrying several people, one at a time; that is, marrying, divorcing, remarrying, divorcing again, and so on.

sex The biological—chromosomal, anatomical, hormonal, and other physical and physiological—characteristics with which we are born and that determine whether we are male or female.

sex ratio The proportion of men to women in a country or group.

sexual harassment Any unwelcome sexual advance, request for sexual favors, or other conduct of a sexual nature that makes a person uncomfortable and interferes with her or his work.

sexual orientation Refers to a preference for sexual partners of the same sex (homosexual), of the opposite sex (heterosexual), or of either sex (bisexual).

sexual response A person's physiological reaction to sexual stimulation.

sexually transmitted diseases (STDs) Diseases that are spread by contact with body parts or fluids that harbor what are usually bacterial or viral microorganisms. Most of the more than 20 currently prevalent STDs are spread exclusively by sexual contact.

sexual script Norms that specify what is acceptable and what is unacceptable sexual activity, identify eligible sexual partners, and define the boundaries of sexual behavior in time and place.

significant others People who play an important emotional role in a person's socialization.

social exchange theory A micro-level theory that proposes that the interaction between two or more people is based on the efforts of each to maximize rewards and minimize costs.

social integration The social bonds that people have with others and the community at large.

socialization The process of acquiring the language, accumulated knowledge, attitudes, beliefs, and values of one's society and culture and learning the social and interpersonal skills needed to function effectively in society.

social learning theory The notion that people learn attitudes and behaviors through interaction with the environment; learning may occur through reward and punishment or through imitation or role modeling.

Social Security A public retirement pension system administered by the federal government.

sole custody A type of custody in which one parent has exclusive responsibility for raising a child and the other parent has specified visitation rights.

split custody A custody arrangement in which children are divided between the parents, usually female children going to the mother, males to the father.

stepfamily A household in which there is an adult couple and at least one of the partners has a child from a previous marriage.

steroid A synthetic hormone, most often testosterone, that is taken to increase the size and strength of muscles.

storge Love that is slow-burning, peaceful, and affectionate.

structural-functional theory A macro-level theoretical perspective that examines the relationship between the family and the larger society as well as the internal relationships among family members.

substitute marriage A long-term commitment between two people without a legal marriage.

surrogacy An assisted reproduction technique in which a surrogate mother is either artificially inseminated by the husband of an infertile woman or is implanted with the woman's egg after it has been fertilized by the husband's sperm in vitro.

surveys Data-collection methods that systematically collect information from respondents either by a mailed or self-administered questionnaire or by a face-to-face or telephone interview.

symbolic interaction theory A micro-level theory that views everyday human interaction as governed by the symbolic communication of knowledge, ideas, beliefs, and attitudes.

theory A set of logically related statements that explain why a phenomenon occurs.

total marriage A marriage in which the partners participate in each other's lives at all levels and have few areas of tension or unresolved hostility.

trailing spouse A spouse who resigns from a position in order to search for another job in the location where her or his spouse has taken a position.

two-person single career An arrangement in which one spouse participates in the other's career behind the scenes without pay or direct recognition.

underemployed worker A worker who holds part-time jobs but would rather work full time or who accepts jobs below his or her level of expertise.

utilitarian marriage A marriage based on convenience.

vital marriage A marriage in which partners maintain a close relationship, resolve conflicts quickly through compromise, and often make sacrifices for each other.

welfare Government aid to those who can't support themselves, generally because they are poor or unemployed.

zygote intrafallopian transfer (ZIFT) A variation of in vitro fertilization in which a woman's eggs are fertilized by her husband's or a donor's sperm in vitro and are then transferred to the fallopian tube.

REFERENCES

· ·

A great leap back. 1993. *Baltimore Sun,* March 31, A24.

A middle-class nation. 1999. *Public Perspective* 10 (April/May): 13.

ABALOS, D. T. 1993. *The Latino family and the politics of transformation.* Westport, CT: Praeger.

ABBEY, A., L. ROSS, D. MCDUFFIE, AND P. MCAUSTIN. 1996. Alcohol and dating risk factors for sexual assault among college women. *Psychology of Women Quarterly* 20 (March): 147–69.

ABEL, E. K. 1991. *Who cares for the elderly? Public policy and the experiences of adult daughters.* Philadelphia: Temple University Press.

ABMA, J., A. CHANDRA, W. MOSHER, L. PETERSON, AND L. PICCINO. 1997. *Fertility, family planning, and women's health: New data from the 1995 National Survey of Family Growth.* Washington, DC: National Center for Health Statistics. Vital Health Statistics 23 (19).

ABMA, J., A. DRISCOLL, AND K. MOORE. 1998. Young women's degree of control over first intercourse: An exploratory analysis. *Family Planning Perspectives* 30 (January/February): 12–18.

Abortion now divides Americans as deeply as it ever has since 1973—and in the same proportions. 1998. *The Public Perspective* 9 (December/January): 31–34.

ABRAHAM, M. 2000. *Speaking the unspeakable: Marital violence among South Asian immigrants in the United States.* New Brunswick, NJ: Rutgers University Press.

ACKERMAN, D. 1994. *A natural history of love.* New York: Random House.

ACOCK, A. C., AND D. H. DEMO. 1994. *Family diversity and well-being.* Thousands Oaks, CA: Sage.

ACS, G., AND M. GALLAGHER. 2000. Income inequality among America's children. Series B, No. B-6. Urban Institute, Washington, DC. newfederalism.urban.org/pdf/anf_b6.pdf (accessed October 12, 2000).

ACUNA, R. 1988. *Occupied America: A history of Chicanos,* 3rd ed. New York: Harper & Row.

ADAMS, B. 1980. *The family.* Chicago: Rand McNally.

ADAMS, J. A., K. HARPER, S. KNUDSON, AND J. REVILLA. 1994. Examination findings in legally confirmed child sexual abuse: It's normal to be normal. *Pediatrics* 94 (September): 310–17.

ADAMS, P. F., and M. A. MARANO. 1995. *Current estimates from the National Health Interview Survey, 1994.* Vital Health Statistics Series 10, No. 193, December. Washington, DC: National Center for Health Statistics.

ADLER, J. 1996. Building a better dad. *Newsweek.* June 17, 58–64.

Adler, N. E., and J. M. Tschann. 1993. Conscious and preconscious motivation for pregnancy among female adolescents. In *The politics of pregnancy: Adolescent sexuality and public policy,* eds. A. Lawson and D. L. Rhode, 144–58. New Haven, CT: Yale University Press.

Adler, P. A., and P. ADLER. 1994. Observational techniques. In *Handbook of qualitative research,* eds. N. K. Denzin and Y. S. Lincoln, 377–92. Thousand Oaks, CA: Sage.

AGBAYANI-SIEWERT, P. 1994. Filipino American culture and family: Guidelines for practitioners.

Families in Society: The Journal of Contemporary Human Services 75 (September): 429–38.

AGBAYANI-SIEWART, P., AND L. JONES. 1997. Filipino American women, work and family: An examination of factors affecting high labor force participation. *International Social Work* 40 (October): 407–23.

AGUIRRE, A., JR., AND D. V. BAKER, eds. 2000. *Structured inequality in the United States: Discussions on the continuing significance of race, ethnicity, and gender.* Upper Saddle River, NJ: Prentice Hall.

AHRONS, C. 1994. *The good divorce: Keeping your family together when your marriage comes apart.* New York: HarperCollins.

AHRONS, C. R., AND R. H. RODGERS. 1987. *Divorced families: A multidisciplinary developmental view.* New York: Norton.

AHUVIA, A. C., AND M. B. ADELMAN. 1992. Formal intermediaries in the marriage market: A typology and review. *Journal of Marriage and the Family* 54 (May): 452–63.

AIDS rising again in San Francisco, sounding warning. 2000. *Baltimore Sun,* July 1, 3a.

AINSWORTH, M., ET AL. 1978. *Patterns of attachment: A psychological study of the strange situation.* Hillsdale, NJ: Lawrence Erlbaum Associates.

ALANIZ, M. L., R. S. CARTMILL, AND R N. PARKER. 1998. Immigrants and violence: The importance of neighborhood context. *Hispanic Journal of Behavioral Sciences* 20 (May): 155–74.

ALBAS, D., AND C. ALBAS. 1987. The pulley alternative for the wheel theory of the development of love. *International Journal of Comparative Sociology* 28 (3–4): 223–27.

ALDOUS, J. 1996. *Family careers: Rethinking the developmental perspective.* Thousand Oaks, CA: Sage.

ALDOUS, J., G. M. MULLIGAN, AND T. BIARNASON. 1998. Fathering over time: What makes the difference? *Journal of Marriage and the Family* 60 (November): 809–20.

ALIBHAI-BROWN, Y. 1993. Marriage of minds not hearts. *New Statesman & Society,* February 12, 28–29.

ALIGNE, C. A., AND J. J. STODDARD. 1997. Tobacco and children: An economic evaluation of the medical effects of parental smoking. *Archives of Pediatrics & Adolescent Medicine* 151 (July): 648–744.

ALLEN, K. R. 1997. Lesbian and gay families. In *Contemporary parenting: Challenges and issues,* ed. T. Arendell, 196–217. Thousand Oaks, CA: Sage.

ALLEN, K. R., AND R. S. PICKETT. 1987. Forgotten streams in the family life course: Utilization of qualitative retrospective interviews in the analysis of lifelong single women's family careers. *Journal of Marriage and the Family* 49 (August): 517–26.

ALLEN, K. S., AND G. F. MOORMAN. 1997. Leaving home: The emigration of home-office workers. *American Demographics* 19 (October): 57–61.

ALLEN, S. M., AND A. J. HAWKINS. 1999. Maternal gatekeeping: Mothers' beliefs and behaviors that inhibit greater father involvement in family

work. *Journal of Marriage and the Family* 61 (February): 199–212.

ALLEN, W. R., AND A. D. JAMES. 1998. Comparative perspectives on black family life: Uncommon explorations of a common subject. *Journal of Comparative Family Studies* 29 (Spring): 1–10.

ALMEIDA, R. V., ED. 1994. *Expansions of feminist family theory through diversity.* New York: Haworth Press.

ALSAYBAR, B. D. 1999. Deconstructing deviance: Filipino American youth gangs, "party culture," and ethnic identity in Los Angeles. *Amerasia Journal* 25 (Spring): 116–38.

ALTMAN, I., AND J. GINAT. 1996. *Polygamous families in contemporary society.* Cambridge: Cambridge University Press.

ALVARADO, D. 1991. Fathers' health and fetal harm. *Washington Post Health Supplement,* August 20, 6.

ALVIREZ, D., F. D. BEAN, AND D. WILLIAMS. 1981. The Mexican American family. In *Ethnic families in America: Patterns and variations,* 2nd ed., eds. C. H. Mindel and R. W. Habenstein, 269–92. New York: Elsevier.

ALWIN, D. F. 1988. From obedience to autonomy: Changes in traits desired in children, 1924–1978. *Public Opinion Quarterly* 52, 33–52.

Alzheimer's Association. 2000. Frequently asked questions. www.alz.org/people/faq.htm#howmany (accessed October 28, 2000).

AMAN, C. J., AND P. ENGLAND. 1997. Comparable worth: When do two jobs deserve the same pay? In *Subtle sexism: Current practices and prospects for change,* ed. N. V. Benokraitis, 297–314. Thousand Oaks, CA: Sage.

AMATO, P. R. 1988. Parental divorce and attitudes toward marriage and family life. *Journal of Marriage and the Family* 50 (May): 453–61.

AMATO, P. R. 1991. The "child of divorce" as a person prototype: Bias in the recall of information about children in divorced families. *Journal of Marriage and the Family* 53 (February): 59–69.

AMATO, P. R. 1993. Children's adjustment to divorce: Theories, hypotheses, and empirical support. *Journal of Marriage and the Family* 55 (February): 23–38.

AMATO, P. R. 1996. More than money? Men's contributions to their children's lives. Paper presented at the Men in Families Symposium, Pennsylvania State University.

AMATO, P. R., AND J. G. GILBRETH. 1999. Nonresident fathers and children's well-being: A meta-analysis. *Journal of Marriage and the Family* 61 (August): 557–73.

AMATO, P. R. AND F. RIVERA. 1999. Paternal involvement and children's behavior problems. *Journal of Marriage and the Family* 61 (May): 374–84.

AMATO, P. R., AND S. J. ROGERS. 1997. A longitudinal study of marital problems and subsequent divorce. *Journal of Marriage and the Family* 59 (August): 612–24.

AMBERT, A.-M. 1986. Being a stepparent: Live-in and visiting stepchildren. *Journal of Marriage and the Family* 48: 795–804.

AMBERT, A.-M. 1988. Relationships with former in-laws after divorce: A research note. *Journal of Marriage and the Family* 50 (August): 679–86.

AMBERT, A.-M. 1994. An international perspective on parenting: Social change and social constructs. *Journal of Marriage and the Family* 56 (August): 529-43.

AMBERT, A.-M. 1997. *Parents, children, and adolescents: Interactive relationships and development in context.* New York: Haworth Press.

American Association of University Women Educational Foundation. 1992. *How schools shortchange girls.* Washington, DC.

Americans on parenting. 1999. *Public Perspective* 10 (October/November): 18.

America's children: Key national indicators of wellbeing 2000. 2000. Washington, DC: Federal Interagency Forum on Child and Family Statistics.

AMES, K. 1992. Who's minding our children? *Newsweek,* June 6, 51.

AMES, K., WITH J. GORDON AND M. MASON. 1991. Savings plan for a generation. *Newsweek,* February 18, 71.

AMMERMAN, R. T., AND R. J. PATZ. 1996. Determinants of child abuse potential: Contribution of parent and child factors. *Journal of Clinical Child Psychology* 25 (September): 300–07.

AMOTT, T. 1993. *Caught in the crisis: Women and the U.S. economy today.* New York: Monthly Review Press.

ANCHETA, A. N. 1998. *Race, rights, and the Asian American experience.* New Brunswick, NJ: Rutgers University Press.

ANDELIN, H. 1974. *Fascinating womanhood: A guide to a happy marriage.* Santa Barbara, CA: Pacific Press.

ANDERS, G. 1994. The search for love goes on. *Washington Post,* September 19, D5.

ANDERSEN, M. L. 2000. *Thinking about women,* 4th ed. New York: Macmilan.

ANDERSON, C. A. AND K. E. DILL. 2000. Video games and aggressive thoughts, feelings, and behavior in the laboratory and in life. *Journal of Personality and Social Psychology* 78 (April): 772–90.

ANDERSON, E. 1999. *Code of the street: Decency, violence, and the moral life of the inner city.* New York: Norton.

ANDERSON, E. A., AND J. W. SPRUILL. 1993. The dual-career commuter family: A lifestyle on the move. *Marriage & Family Review* 19, (1–2): 121–47.

ANDERSON, E. R., S. M. GREENE, E. M. HETHERINGTON, AND W. G. CLINGEMPEL. 1999. The dynamics of parental remarriage: Adolescent, parent, and sibling influences. In *Coping with divorce, single parenting, and remarriage: A risk and resiliency perspective,* ed. E. M. Hetherington, 295–319. Mahwah, NJ: Lawrence Erlbaum Associates.

ANDERSON, J. 1990. *The single mother's book: A practical guide to managing your children, career, home, finances, and everything else.* Atlanta: Peachtree.

ANDERSON, K. L. 1997. Gender, status, and domestic violence: An integration of feminist and family violence approaches. *Journal of Marriage and the Family* 59 (August): 655–69.

ANDERSON, P. B., AND R. AYMAMI. 1993. Reports of female initiation of sexual contact: Male and female differences. *Archives of Sexual Behavior* 23 (August): 335–43.

ANDERSON, T. B. 1984. Widowhood as a life transition: Its impact on kinship ties. *Journal of Marriage and the Family* 46 (February): 105–14.

ANGELL, G. B., B. J. KURZ, AND G. M. GOTTFRIED. 1997. Suicide and North American Indians: A social constructivist perspective. *Journal of Multicultural Social Work* 6 (3/4): 1–26.

ANN LANDERS. 2000. *Washington Post,* May 9, C11.

ANSON, O. 1989. Marital status and women's health revisited: The importance of a proximate adult. *Journal of Marriage and the Family* 51, (February): 185–94.

ANSUINI, C. G., J. FIDDLER-WOITE, AND R. S. WOITE. 1996. The source, accuracy, and impact of initial sexuality information on lifetime wellness. *Adolescence* 31 (Summer): 283–89.

AOA factsheet—grandparents raising children. Administration on Aging. www.aoa.dhhs.gov/factsheets/Grandparents.pdf (accessed October 27, 2000).

APFEL, N. H., AND V. SEITZ. 1991. Four models of adolescent mother–grandmother relationships in black inner-city families. *Family Relations* 40 (October): 421–29.

AQUILINO, W. S. 1994. Impact of childhood family disruption on young adults' relationships with parents. *Journal of Marriage and the Family* 56 (May): 295–313.

AQUILINO, W. S. 1997. From adolescent to young adult: A prospective study of parent–child relations during the transition to adulthood. *Journal of Marriage and the Family* 59 (August): 670–86.

AQUILINO, W. S., AND K. R. SUPPLE. 1991. Parent-child relations and parents' satisfaction with living arrangements when adult children live at home. *Journal of Marriage and the Family* 53 (February): 13–27.

ARANDA, M. P., AND B. G. KNIGHT. 1997. The influence of ethnicity and culture on the caregiver stress and coping process: A sociocultural review and analysis. *The Gerontologist* 37 (3): 342–54.

ARDITTI, J. A. 1999. Rethinking relationships between divorced mothers and their children: Capitalizing on family strengths. *Family Relations* 48 (April): 109–19.

ARDS, S., C. CHUNG, AND S. L. MYERS JR. 1998. The effects of sample selection bias on racial differences in child abuse reporting. *Child Abuse & Neglect* 22 (February): 103–16.

ARENDELL, T. 1997. A social constructionist approach to parenting. In *Contemporary parenting: Challenges and issues,* ed. T. Arendell, 1–44. Thousand Oaks, CA: Sage.

ARENOFSKY, J. 1993. Childless and proud of it. *Newsweek,* February 8, 12.

ARIES, P. 1962. *Centuries of childhood.* New York: Vintage.

ARLISS, L. P. 1991. *Gender communication.* Upper Saddle River, NJ: Prentice Hall.

ARNO, P. S., C. LEVINE, AND M. M. MEMMOTT. 1999. The economic value of informal caregiving. *Health Affairs* 18 (March): 182–88.

ARNOLD, M., AND S. L. PAUKER. 1987. *The first year of marriage: What to expect, what to accept, and what you can change.* New York: Warner.

ARONSON, E. 1995. *The social animal,* 7th ed. New York: W. H. Freeman.

ASELTINE, R. H., JR., AND R. C. KESSLER. 1993. Marital disruption and depression in a community sample. *Journal of Health and Social Behavior* 34 (September): 237–51.

ASTONE, N. M., AND S. S. MCLANAHAN. 1994. Family structure, residential mobility, and school dropout: A research note. *Demography* 31 (November): 575–84.

At least 100 children a year leave U.S. to be adopted. 1997. *Baltimore Sun,* August 28, 10A.

Attitudes and characteristics of freshmen. 2000. *Chronicle of Higher Education Almanac* 47 (September): 28.

AUSTIN, A. 2000. More teens opt for plastic surgery. *Christian Science Monitor,* August 30, 14.

AVIS, J. M. 1985. The politics of functional therapy: A feminist critique. *Journal of Marital and Family Therapy* 11, (2): 127–38.

AVNA, J., AND D. WALTZ. 1992. *Celibate wives: Breaking the silence.* Los Angeles: Lowell House.

AVNI, N. 1991. Battered wives: The home as a total institution. *Violence and Victims* 6, (2): 137–49.

AXINN, W. G., AND A. THORNTON. 1993. Mothers, children, and cohabitation: The intergenerational effects of attitudes and behavior. *American Sociological Review* 58 (April): 233–46.

AXINN, W. G., AND A. THORNTON. 1996. The influence of parents' mutual dissolutions on children's attitudes toward family formation. *Demography* 33 (February): 66–81.

BABCOCK, J. C., J. WALTZ, N. S. JACOBSON, AND J. M. GOTTMAN. 1993. Power and violence: The relation between communication patterns, power discrepancies, and domestic violence. *Journal of Consulting and Clinical Psychology* 61, (1): 40–50.

BACA ZINN, M. 1994. Adaptation and continuity in Mexican-origin families. In *Minority families in the United States: A multicultural perspective,* ed. R. L. Taylor, 64–81. Upper Saddle River, NJ: Prentice Hall.

BACA ZINN, M. 1996. Family, feminism, and race in America. In *Race, class & gender: Common bonds, different voices,* eds. E. N. Chow, D. Wilkinson, and M. Baca Zinn, 169–83. Thousand Oaks, CA: Sage.

BACHMAN, J. G., K. N. WADSWORTH, P. M. O'MALLEY, L. D. JOHNSTON, AND J. E. SCHULENBERG. 1997. *Smoking, drinking, and drug use in young adulthood: The impacts of new freedoms and new responsibilities.* Hillsdale, NJ: Lawrence Erlbaum Associates.

BACHMAN, R. 1992. *Death and violence on the reservation: Homicide, family violence, and suicide in American Indian populations.* Westport, CT: Auburn House.

BACHMAN, R. 1994. *Violence against women: A national crime victimization survey report.* U.S. Department of Justice, Office of Justice Programs, Bureau of Justice Statistics. Fall.

BACHRACH, C. A., P. F. ADAMS, S. SAMBRANO, AND K. A. LONDON. 1990. Adoption in the 1980's. *Vital Health Statistics,* no. 181, January 5, advance data. Hyattsville, MD: National Center for Health Statistics.

BACHU, A. 1993. *Fertility of American women: June 1992.* U.S. Census Bureau, Current Population Reports P20-470. Washington, DC: U.S. Government Printing Office.

BACHU, A. 1996. *Fertility of American men.* U.S. Census Bureau, Population Division, Fertility Statistics Branch. Washington, DC: U.S. Government Printing Office.

BACHU, A., AND M. O'CONNELL. 2000. *Fertility of American women,* June 1998. U.S. Census Bureau, Current Population Reports P20-526. www.census.gov/prod/2000pubs/p20-526.pdf (accessed November 7, 2000).

BAEZCONDE-GARBANTI, L., AND C. J. PORTILLO. 1999. Disparities in health indicators for Latinas in California. *Hispanic Journal of Behavioral Sciences* 21 (August): 302–29.

BAGLEY, C. 1993. Transracial adoption in Britain: A follow-up study, with policy considerations. *Child Welfare* 72 (May/June): 285–300.

BAHR, K. S., AND H. M. BAHR. 1995. Autonomy, community, and the mediation of value: Comments on Apachean grandmothering, cultural change, and the media. In *American families: Issues in race and ethnicity,* ed. C. K. Jacobson, 229–60. New York: Garland.

BAILEY, J. M., D. BOBROW, M. WOLFE, AND S. MIKACH. 1995. Sexual orientation of adult sons of gay fathers. *Developmental Psychology* 31 (January): 124–29.

BAILEY, J. M., AND R. C. PILLARD. 1991. A genetic study of male sexual orientation. *Archives of General Psychiatry* 48 (December): 1089–96.

BAILEY, J. M., R. C. PILLARD, M. C. NEALE, AND Y. AGYEI. 1993. Heritable factors influence sexual orientation in women. *Archives of General Psychiatry* 50 (March): 217–23.

BAILYN, L. 1993. *Breaking the mold: Women, men, and time in the new corporate world.* New York: Free Press.

BAKER, L. 1994. Day-care disgrace. *The Progressive* (June): 26–27.

BAKER, M. 2000. Adolphus gets married; soon he'll meet his wife. *Christian Science Monitor,* February 15, 7.

BALAKRISHNAN, T. R., V. RAO, E. LAPIERRE-ADAMCYK, AND K. KROTKI. 1987. A hazard model analysis of the covariates of marriage dissolution in Canada. *Demography* 24, 395–406.

BALDAUF, S. 2000. More men forsake jobs to be full-time fathers. *Christian Science Monitor,* May 10, 1, 5.

BALDWIN, J. D., AND J. I. BALDWIN. 1989. The socialization of homosexuality and heterosexuality in a non-Western society. *Archives of Sexual Behavior* 18, (1): 13–29.

BANDURA, A., AND R. H. WALTERS. 1963. *Social learning and personality development.* New York: Holt, Rinehart & Winston.

BANISKY, S. 1994. Decline in abortions looks like a trend. *Baltimore Sun,* June 16, A1.

BANISKY, S. 1997. Altering the way to the altar. *Baltimore Sun,* October 20, 1A, 7A.

BANNER, L. W. 1984. *Women in modern America: A brief history,* 2nd ed. New York: Harcourt Brace Jovanovich.

BARAN, A., AND R. PANNOR. 1989. *Lethal secrets: The shocking consequences and unsolved problems of artificial insemination.* New York: Warner.

BARANOWSKI, M. D., G. L. SCHILMOELLER, AND B. S. HIGGINS. 1990. Parenting attitudes of adolescent and older mothers. *Adolescence* 25 (Winter): 781–90.

BARBER, B. K. 1994. Cultural, family, and personal contexts of parent–adolescent conflict. *Journal of Marriage and the Family* 56 (May): 375–86.

BARBER, B. L. 1994. Support and advice from married and divorced fathers: Linkages to adolescent adjustment. *Family Relations* 43 (October): 433–38.

BARBER, B. L., AND J. M. LYONS. 1994. Family processes and adolescent adjustment in intact and remarried families. *Journal of Youth and Adolescence* 23 (August): 421–36.

BARBER, J. S., AND W. G. AXINN. 1998a. Gender role attitudes and marriage among young women. *The Sociological Quarterly* 39 (Winter): 11–31.

BARBER, J., AND W. G. AXINN. 1998b. The impact of parental pressure for grandchildren on young people's entry into cohabitation and marriage. *Population Studies* 52 (July): 129–44.

BARKER, J. C., J. MORROW, AND L. S. MITTENESS. 1998. Gender, informal social support networks, and elderly urban African Americans. *Journal of Aging Studies* 12 (Summer): 199–222.

BARNES, G. M., A. S. REIFMAN, M. P. FARRELL, AND B. A. DINTCHEFF. 2000. The effects of parenting on the development of adolescent alcohol misuse: A six-wave latent growth model. *Journal of Marriage and the Family* 62 (February): 175–86.

BARNETT, O. W., AND A. D. LAVIOLETTE. 1993. *It could happen to anyone: Why battered women stay.* Thousand Oaks, CA: Sage.

BARNETT, R. C. 1994. Home-to-work spillover revisited: A study of full-time employed women in dual-earner couples. *Journal of Marriage and the Family* 56 (August): 647–56.

BARNETT, R. C., AND C. RIVERS. 1996. *She works, he works: How two-income families are happy, healthy, and thriving.* Cambridge, MA: Harvard University Press.

BARNETT, R. C., AND Y.-C. SHEN. 1997. Gender, high- and low-schedule-control housework tasks, and psychological distress: A study of dual-earner couples. *Journal of Family Issues* 18 (July): 403–28.

BARNEY, B. 1999. A preschool with snob appeal. *U.S. News & World Report,* September 13, 48.

BARON, S., AND A. WELTY. 1996. Elder abuse. *Journal of Gerontological Social Work* 25, (1–2): 33–57.

BARRECA, R. 1993. *Perfect husband (& other fairy tales): Demystifying marriage, men, and romance.* New York: Harmony.

BARRET, R. L., AND B. E. ROBINSON. 1990. *Gay fathers.* Lexington, MA: Lexington Books.

BARRET-DUCROCQ, F. 1991. *Love in the time of Victoria: Sexuality, class and gender in nineteenth-century London.* New York: Verso.

BARRETT, A. E. 1999. Social support and life satisfaction among the never married. *Research on Aging* 21 (January): 46–72.

BARRETT, M. B. 1989. *Invisible lives: The truth about millions of women-loving women.* New York: Morrow.

BARRINGER, H. R., R. W. GARDNER, AND M. J. LEVIN. 1993. *Asians and Pacific Islanders in the United States.* New York: Russell Sage Foundation.

BARRINGTON, L. 2000. Does a rising tide lift all boats? The Conference Board. www.conference-board.org/expertise/frames.cfm?main=about.cfm (accessed October 13, 2000).

BARROW, G. M. 1996. *Aging, the individual and society,* 6th ed. St. Paul, MN: West.

BARTH, R. P. 1997. Effects of age and race on the odds of adoption versus remaining in long-term out-of-home care. *Child Welfare* 76 (March–April): 285–308.

BARTHOLET, E. 1999. *Nobody's children: Abuse and neglect, foster drift, and the adoption alternative.* Boston: Beacon Press.

BASS, S. 1988. A lot of these affairs are never revealed. *New York Times,* December 19, C1.

BAUM, A. S., AND D. W. BURNES. 1993. *A nation in denial: The truth about homelessness.* Boulder, CO: Westview.

BAUMEISTER, R. F., AND S. R. WOTMAN. 1992. *Breaking hearts: The two sides of unrequited love.* New York: Guilford Press.

BAUMRIND, D. 1968. Authoritarian versus authoritative parental control. *Adolescence* 3, 255–72.

BAUMRIND, D. 1989. Rearing competent children. In *Child development today and tomorrow,* ed. W. Damon, 349–78. San Francisco: Jossey-Bass.

BAUMRIND, D. 1994. The social context of child maltreatment. *Family Relations* 43 (October): 360–68.

BAYDAR, N. 1988. Effects of parental separation and reentry into union on the emotional well-being of children. *Journal of Marriage and the Family* 50 (November): 967–81.

BAYDAR, N., AND J. BROOKS-GUNN. 1994. The dynamics of child support and its consequences for children. In *Child support and child well-being,* eds. I. Garfinkel, S. S. McLanahan, and P. K. Robins, 257–84. Washington, DC: Urban Institute Press.

BAYDAR, N., A. GREEK, AND J. BROOKS-GUNN. 1997. A longitudinal study of the effects of the birth of a sibling during the first 6 years of life.

Journal of Marriage and the Family 59 (November): 939–56.

BA-YUNUS, I. 1991. Muslims in North America: Mate selection as an indicator of change. In *Muslim families in North America,* eds. E. H. Waugh, S. M. Abu-Laban, and R. B. Qureshi, 232–55. Edmonton: University of Alberta Press.

BAZZINI, D. G., W. D. MCINTOSH, S. M. SMITH, S. COOK, AND C. HARRIS. 1997. The aging woman in popular film: Underrepresented, unattractive, unfriendly, and unintelligent. *Sex Roles* 36 (7/8): 531–43.

BECERRA, R. M. 1988. The Mexican American family. In *Ethnic families in America: Patterns and variations,* 3rd ed., eds. C. J. Mindel, R. W. Habenstein, and R. Wright, Jr., 141–59. New York: Elsevier.

BECK, A. T. 1988. *Love is never enough: How couples can overcome misunderstandings, resolve conflicts, and solve relationship problems through cognitive therapy.* New York: Harper & Row.

BECKER, G. S. 2000. Give me your yearning high-skilled professionals. *Business Week,* April 24, 30.

BECKER, G., AND Y. BEYENE. 1999. Narratives of age and uprootedness among older Cambodian refugees. *Journal of Aging Studies* 13 (Fall): 295–314.

BECKER, P. E., AND P. MOEN. 1999. Scaling back: Dual-earner couples' work-family strategies. *Journal of Marriage and the Family* 61 (November): 995–1007.

BEER, W. R. 1992. *American stepfamilies.* New Brunswick, NJ: Transaction.

BEERS, T. M. 2000. *A profile of the working poor, 1998.* U.S. Department of Labor, Bureau of Labor Statistics, stats.bls.gov/pdf/cpswp98.pdf (accessed October 12, 2000).

BEGLEY, S. 1998. The parent trap. *Newsweek,* September 7, 53–59.

BEGLEY, S. 2000. A world of their own. *Newsweek,* May 8, 53–59.

BEGLEY, S., WITH M. HAGER, AND A. MUIR. 1990. The search for the fountain of youth. *Newsweek,* March 5, 44–48.

BELCASTRO, P. A. 1985. Sexual behavior differences between black and white students. *Journal of Sex Research* 21, 56–57.

BELKIN, L. 1985. Affording a child: Parents worry as costs keep rising. *New York Times,* May 23, C1, C6.

BELL, R. R., AND K. COUGHEY. 1980. Premarital sexual experience among college females, 1958, 1968, and 1978. *Family Relations* 29, 353–57.

BELLAH, R. N., R. MADSEN, W. M. SULLIVAN, A. SWIDLER, AND S. M. TIPTON. 1985. *Habits of the heart: Individualism and commitment in American life.* Berkeley: University of California Press.

BELLE, D. 1999. *The after-school lives of children: Alone and with others while parents work.* Mahwah, NJ: Lawrence Erlbaum Associates.

BELSKY, J. 1991. Parental and nonparental child care and children's socioemotional development. In *Contemporary families: Looking forward, looking back,* ed. A. Booth, 122–40. Minneapolis, MN: National Council on Family Relations.

BELSKY, J. 1993. Etiology of child maltreatment: A developmental–ecological analysis. *Psychological Bulletin* 114 (November): 413–34.

BELSKY, J. K. 1988. *Here tomorrow: Making the most of life after fifty.* Baltimore: Johns Hopkins University Press.

BEM, S. L. 1975. Androgyny vs. the tight little lives of fluffy women and chesty men. *Psychology Today,* September, 58–62.

BEM, S. L. 1983. Gender schema theory and its implications for child development: Raising gender-schematic children in a gender-schematic society. *Signs* 8, 598–616.

BEM, S. L. 1993. *The lenses on gender: Transforming the debate on sexual inequality.* New Haven, CT: Yale University Press.

BENASSI, M. A. 1985. Effects of romantic love on perception of strangers' physical attractiveness. *Psychological Reports* 56 (April): 355–58.

BENJAMIN, E. 1998. Disparities in the salaries and appointments of academic women and men. American Association of University Professors, Washington, DC. www.aaup.org/Wrepup.htm (accessed January 1, 2001).

BENNEFIELD, R. 1995. Health insurance coverage— Who had a lapse between 1991 and 1993? *Statistical Brief SB/95–21,* August. U.S. Census Bureau, Washington, DC: U.S. Government Printing Office.

BENNETT, C. E., AND B. MARTIN. 1995. The nation's Asian and Pacific Islander population—1994. *Statistical Brief SB/95–24.* U.S. Census Bureau. Washington, DC: U.S. Government Printing Office.

BENNETT, L., JR. 1989. The 10 biggest myths about the black family. *Ebony* (November): 114–16.

BENNETT, N. G., A. K. BLANC, AND D. E. BLOOM. 1988. Commitment and the modern union: Assessing the link between premarital cohabitation and subsequent marital stability. *American Sociological Review* 53 (February): 127–38.

BENOKRAITIS, N. V. 1999. *Marriages and families: Changes, choices, and constraints,* 3rd ed. Upper Saddle River, NJ: Prentice Hall.

BENOKRAITIS, N. V., ED. 2000. *Feuds about families: Conservative, centrist, liberal, and feminist perspectives.* Upper Saddle River, NJ: Prentice Hall.

BENOKRAITIS, N. V., AND J. R. FEAGIN. 1995. *Modern sexism: Blatant, subtle, and covert discrimination,* 2nd ed. Upper Saddle River, NJ: Prentice Hall.

BENSON, J. M., AND M. J. HERRMANN. 1999. Right to die or right to life? *Public Perspective* 10 (June/July): 15–19.

BERELSON, B. 1983. The value of children: A taxonomical essay. In *Current issues in marriage and the family,* 3rd ed., ed. G. J. Wells, 159–67. New York: Macmillan.

BERGANO, A. L., AND B. L. BERGANO-KINNEY. 1997. Images, roles, and expectations of Filipino Americans by Filipino Americans. In *Filipino Americans: Transformation and identity,* ed. M. P. P. Root, 198–207. Thousand Oaks, CA: Sage.

BERGER, R. 1998. *Stepfamilies: A multi-dimensional perspective.* New York: Haworth Press.

BERGMAN, P. M. 1969. *The chronological history of the Negro in America.* New York: Harper & Row.

BERGMANN, B. 1994. The economic support of child-raising: Curing child poverty in the United States. *AEA Papers and Proceedings* 84 (May): 76–80.

BERK, B. R. 1993. The dating game. *Good Housekeeping* (September): 192, 220–21.

BERLIN, I. 1998. *Many thousands gone: The first two centuries of slavery in North America.* Cambridge, MA: Belknap Press of Harvard University.

BERMÚDEZ, A. G. 1995. The Cuban-American experience in exile. In *Educating for diversity: An anthology of multicultural voices,* ed. C. A. Grant, 97–109. Boston: Allyn & Bacon.

BERNARD, J. 1973. *The future of marriage.* New York: Bantam.

BERNHARD, L. A. 1995. Sexuality in women's lives. In *Women's health care: A comprehensive handbook,* eds. C. I. Fogel and N. F. Woods, 475–95. Thousand Oaks, CA: Sage.

BERNIER, J. C., AND D. H. SIEGEL. 1994. Attention-deficit hyperactivity disorder: A family and ecological systems perspective. *Families in Society: The Journal of Contemporary Human Services* (March): 142–50.

BERNSTEIN, A. 2000. Down and out in Silicon Valley. *Business Week,* March 27, 76–92.

BERNSTEIN, J., C. BROCHT, AND M. SPADE-AGUILAR. 2000. *How much is enough? Basic budgets for working families.* Washington, DC: Economic Policy Institute.

BERNSTEIN, J., E. C. MCNICHOL, L. MISHEL, AND R. ZAHRADNIK. 2000. Pulling apart: A state-by-state analysis of income trends. Center on Budget and Policy Priorities, Washington, DC. www.cbpp.org/1-18-00sfp.pdf (accessed October 12, 2000).

BERRY, C. 2000). It's time we rejected the racial litmus test. *Newsweek,* February 7, 13.

BERRY, G. L. 1998. Black family life on television and the socialization of the African American child: Images of marginality. *Journal of Comparative Family Studies* 29 (Summer): 233–42.

BERRY, J. M. 1997. Gap between pay of men, women may have expanded since 1993. *Washington Post,* September 16, C3.

BERRY, M. 1993. Adoptive parents' perceptions of, and comfort with, open adoption. *Child Welfare* 72 (May/June): 231–56.

BERSCHEID, E., K. DION, E. WALSTER, AND G. W. WALSTER. 1982. Physical attractiveness and dating choice: A test of the matching hypothesis. *Journal of Experimental Social Psychology* 1, 173–89.

BESHAROV, D. J. 1993. Teen sex. *American Enterprise* 4 (January): 52–59.

BETCHER, W., AND R. MACAULEY. 1990. *The seven basic quarrels of marriage: Recognize, defuse, negotiate, and resolve your conflicts.* New York: Villard.

BETCHER, W., AND W. POLLACK. 1993. *In a time of fallen heroes: The re-creation of masculinity.* New York: Atheneum.

BEZILLA, R. ed. 1993. *America's youth in the 1990s.* Princeton, NJ: George H. Gallup International Institute.

BHATTACHARYA, G. 1998. Drug use among Asian-Indian adolescents: Identifying protective/risk factors. *Adolescence* 33 (Spring): 169–84.

BIANCHI, S. 1990. America's children: Mixed prospects. *Population Bulletin* 45 (June): 3–41.

BIANCHI, S. M. 2000. Maternal employment and time with children: Dramatic change or surprising continuity? Presidential address to the Population Association of America, Los Angeles, March 24.

BIANCHI, S. M., AND D. SPAIN. 1996. Women, work, and family in America. *Population Bulletin* 51 (December).

BIBLARZ, T. J., AND A. E. RAFTERY. 1993. The effects of family disruption on social mobility. *American Sociological Review* 58 (February): 97–109.

Bible belt wrestles with high divorce rate. 1999. *Baltimore Sun,* November 14, 19A.

BIELBY, W. T., AND D. D. BIELBY. 1992. I will follow him: Family ties, gender-role beliefs, and reluctance to relocate for a better job. *American Journal of Sociology* 97 (March): 1241–67.

BIERNAT, M., AND C. B. WORTMAN. 1991. Sharing of home responsibilities between professionally employed women and their husbands. *Journal of Personality and Social Psychology* 60, (6): 844–60.

The big picture. 2000. *Business Week,* March 20, 10.

BIGNER, J., AND R. B. JACOBSEN. 1989. Parenting behaviors of homosexual and heterosexual fathers. *Journal of Homosexuality* 18, 173–86.

BILLER, H. B. 1993. *Fathers and families: Paternal factors in child development.* Westport, CT: Auburn House.

BILLINGSLEY, A. 1992. *Climbing Jacob's ladder: The enduring legacy of African-American families.* New York: Simon & Schuster.

BILLY, J. O. G., K. TANFER, W. R. GRADY, AND D. H. KLEPINGER. 1993. The sexual behavior of men in the United States. *Family Planning Perspectives* 25 (March): 52–60.

BIRD, C. E. 1999. Gender, household labor, and psychological distress: The impact of the amount and division of housework. *Journal of Health & Social Behavior* 40 (March): 32–45.

BIRNS, B. 1999. Attachment theory revisited: Challenging conceptual and methodological sacred cows. *Feminism & Psychology* 9 (February): 10–21.

BIRNS, B., M. CASCARDI, AND S.-L. MEYER. 1994. Sex-role socialization: Developmental influences on wife abuse. *American Journal of Orthopsychiatry* 64 (January): 50–59.

BISHOP, G. F., R. W. OLDENDICK, A. J. TUCHFARBER AND S. E. BENNETT. 1980. Pseudo-opinions on public affairs. *Public Opinion Quarterly* 44 (Summer): 198–209.

BISKUPIC, J. 1997. Appeals court upholds anti-gay-right measure. *Washington Post,* October 24, A3.

BLACKWELL, J. E. 1991. The black community: *Diversity and unity,* 3rd ed. New York: HarperCollins.

BLAIR, J. 1998. Softball rights: Life, liberty, and a nice flat field. *Christian Science Monitor,* April 28, 10

BLAIR, S. L. 1993. Employment, family, and perceptions of marital quality among husbands and wives. *Journal of Family Issues* 14 (June): 189–212.

BLAKE, J. 1989. *Family size and achievement.* Berkeley: University of California Press.

BLAKE, W. M., AND C. A. DARLING. 1994. The dilemmas of the African American male. *Journal of Black Studies* 24 (June): 402–15.

BLANC, A. K. 1987. The formation and dissolution of second unions: Marriage and cohabitation in Sweden and Norway. *Journal of Marriage and the Family* 49 (May): 391–400.

BLANCHARD, K. 1999–2000. Guy anxiety: What he's really nervous about. *Parents Expecting* 33 (Winter): 20–21.

BLANK, C. 1997. Women investing wisely. *American Demographics* 19 (August): 22–25.

BLANKENHORN, D. 1995. *Fatherless America: Confronting our most urgent social problem.* New York: HarperPerennial.

BLASKO, L. 2000. Blood and guts fly faster as video games get gorier. *Baltimore Sun,* June 19, 1C–2C.

BLAU, F. D., AND R. G. EHRENBERG, EDS. 1997. *Gender and family issues in the workplace.* New York: Russell Sage Foundation.

BLINN-PIKE, L. 1999. Why abstinent adolescents report they had not had sex: Understanding sexually resilient youth. *Family Relations* 48 (July): 295–301.

BLOOMFIELD, H. M., WITH R. P. KORY. 1993. *Making peace in your stepfamily: Surviving and thriving as parents and stepparents.* New York: Hyperion.

BLUESTONE, C. AND C. S. TAMIS-LEMONDA. 1999. Correlates of parenting styles in predominantly working- and middle-class African American mothers. *Journal of Marriage and the Family* 61 (November): 881–93.

BLUMSTEIN, P. 1976. Identity bargaining and self-conception. *Social Forces* 53 (3): 476–85.

BOCK, J. 1992. Battle brews over plan for new city liquor license. *Baltimore Sun*, March 2, B1, B6.

BOCK, J. 1997. Sociologist touts strengths of black families. *Baltimore Sun*, July 7, A2.

BODMAN, D. A., AND G. W. PETERSON. 1995. Parenting processes. In *Research and theory in family science*, eds. R. D. Day, K. R. Gilbert, B. H. Settles, and W. R. Burr, 205–25. Pacific Grove, CA: Brooks/Cole.

BODNAR, J. 1985. *The transplanted: A history of immigrants in urban America.* Bloomington: Indiana University Press.

BOERINGER, S. B., C. L. SHEHAN, AND R. L. AKERS. 1991. Social contests and social learning in sexual coercion and aggression: Assessing the contribution of fraternity membership. *Family Relations* 40 (January): 58–64.

BOGENSCHNEIDER, K. 1996. An ecological risk/protective theory for building prevention programs, policies, and community capacity to support youth. *Family Relations* 45 (April): 127–38.

BOGENSCHNEIDER, K., M.-Y. WU, M. RAFFAELLI, AND J. C. TSAY. 1998. "Other teens drink, but not my kid": Does parental awareness of adolescent alcohol use protect adolescents from risky consequences? *Journal of Marriage and the Family* 60 (May): 356–73.

BOGERT, C. 1994. Bringing back baby. *Newsweek*, November 21, 78–79.

BOHANNON, P. 1971. *Divorce and after*. New York: Doubleday.

BOLIG, R., P. J. STEIN, AND P. C. McKENRY. 1984. The self-advertisement approach to dating: Male–female differences. *Family Relations* 33 (October): 587–92.

BOMBECK, E. 1994. The art of grandmothering isn't lost. *Baltimore Sun*, February 24, 8E.

BONNETTE, R. 1994. Housing of American Indians on reservations—An overview. *Statistical Brief SB/94–32.* U.S. Census Bureau. Washington, DC: U.S. Government Printing Office.

BONNETTE, R. 1995a. Housing of American Indians on reservations—Equipment and fuels. *Statistical Brief SB/95–11.* U.S. Census Bureau. Washington, DC: U.S. Government Printing Office.

BONNETTE, R. 1995b. Housing of American Indians on reservations—Plumbing. *Statistical Brief SB/95–9.* U.S. Census Bureau. Washington, DC: U.S. Government Printing Office.

BOODMAN, S. G. 1992. Questions about a popular prenatal test. *Washington Post Health Supplement*, November 3, 10–13.

BOODMAN, S. G. 1995. The only child: Lonely or lucky? *Washington Post Health Supplement*, October 24, 10–13.

BOOTH, A., AND P. R. AMATO. 1994. Parental marital quality, parental divorce, and relations with parents. *Journal of Marriage and the Family* 56 (February): 21–34.

BOOTH, A., AND J. N. EDWARDS. 1985. Age at marriage and marital instability. *Journal of Marriage and the Family* 47 (February): 67–75.

BOOTH, A., AND J. N. EDWARDS. 1992. Starting over: Why remarriages are more unstable. *Journal of Family Issues* 13 (June): 179–94.

BOOTH, A., AND D. R. JOHNSON. 1994. Declining health and marital quality. *Journal of Marriage and the Family* 56 (February): 218–23.

BOR, J. 1995. Rise in multiple births a concern to physicians. *Baltimore Sun*, February 1, 1A, 10A.

BORDERS, L. D., L. K. BLACK, AND B. K. PASLEY. 1998. Are adopted children and their parents

at greater risk for negative outcomes? *Family Relations* 47 (July): 237–41.

BORGMAN, A. 1995. Adoptions abroad mix highs, lows. *Washington Post*, January 8, B3.

BORLAND, D. M. 1975. An alternative model of the wheel theory. *Family Coordinator* 24 (July): 289–92.

BOROUGHS, D. L. 1996. Winter of discontent. *U.S. News & World Report*, January 22, 47–54.

BOROUGHS, D. L., WITH D. HAGE, R. F. BLACK, AND R. J. NEWMAN. 1992. Love & money. *U.S. News & World Report*, October 19, 54–60.

BORST, J. 1996. Relatively speaking. *Newsweek*, July 29, 16.

BORZEKOWSKI, D. L. G., AND A. F. POUSSAINT. 1998. *Latino American Preschoolers and the media.* Philadelphia: University of Pennsylvania, Annenberg Public Policy Center.

Boston Women's Health Book Collective. 1992. *The new our bodies, ourselves: A book by and for women.* New York: Touchstone.

BOUSTANY, N. 1994. Matchmaker, matchmaker, find me some wives. *Washington Post*, September 5, A14.

BOWERS, B. F., AND B. J. MYERS. 1999. Grandmothers providing care for grandchildren: Consequences of various levels of caregiving. *Family Relations* 48 (July): 303–11.

BOWLBY, J. 1969. *Attachment and loss. Vol. 1. Attachment.* New York: Basic Books.

BOWLBY, J. 1984. *Attachment and loss. Vol 1, 2nd ed.* Harmondsworth, UK: Penguin.

BOWMAN, P. J. 1991. Joblessness. In *Life in black America*, ed. J. S. Jackson, 156–78. Thousand Oaks, CA: Sage.

BOWMAN, P. J. 1993. The impact of economic marginality among African American husbands and fathers. In *Family ethnicity: Strength in diversity*, ed. H. P. McAdoo, 120–37. Thousand Oaks, CA: Sage.

BOWMAN, P. J., and T. A. FORMAN. 1997. Instrumental and expressive family roles among African American fathers. In *Family life in black America*, eds. R. J. Taylor, J. S. Jackson, L. M. Chatters, 216–47. Thousand Oaks, CA: Sage.

BOYER, P. 1997. *Native American colleges: Progress and prospects.* San Francisco: Jossey-Bass.

Boys to men: Entertainment media, messages about masculinity. 1999. *Children Now.* www.childrennow.org/media/boystomen/index.html (accessed August 24, 2000).

BOZETT, F. W. 1987. *Gay and lesbian parents.* New York: Praeger.

BRADSHER, J. E. 1997. Older women and widowhood. In *Handbook on women and aging*, ed. J. M. Coyle, 418–29. Westport, CT: Greenwood Press.

BRADY, D. 1999. The Net is a family affair. *Business Week*, December 13, EB80–86.

BRADY, J. 1990. Why I [still] want a wife. *Ms.* (July/August): 17.

BRAND, P. A., AND A. H. KIDD. 1986. Frequency of physical aggression in heterosexual and female homosexual dyads. *Psychological Reports* 59 (December): 1307–13.

BRASSARD, M. R., AND D. B. HARDY. 1997. Psychological maltreatment. In *The battered child*, 5th ed., eds. M. E. Helfer, R. S. Kempe, and R. D. Krugman, 392–412. Chicago: The University of Chicago Press.

BRAUND, K. E. H. 1990. Guardians of tradition and handmaidens to change: Women's roles in Creek economic and social life during the eighteenth century. *American Indian Quarterly* 14 (Summer): 239–58.

BRAVER, S. H., S. H. WOLCHIK, I. N. SANDLER, B. S. FOGAS, AND D. ZVETINA. 1991. Frequency of visitation by divorced fathers: Differences in

reports by fathers and mothers. *American Journal of Orthopsychiatry* 6 (July): 448–54.

BRAVER, S. L., WITH D. O'CONNELL. 1998. *Divorced dads: Shattering the myths.* New York: Penguin Putnam.

BRAY, J. H. 1999. From marriage to remarriage and beyond: Findings from the developmental issues in Stepfamilies Research Project. In *Coping with divorce, single parenting, and remarriage: A risk and resiliency perspective*, ed. E. M. Hetherington, 253–71. Mahwah, NJ: Lawrence Erlbaum Associates.

BRAY, J. H., AND S. H. BERGER. 1990. Noncustodial father and paternal grandparent relationships in stepfamilies. *Family Relations* 39 (October): 414–19.

BRAY, J. H., AND J. KELLY. 1998. *Stepfamilies: Love, marriage, and parenting in the first decade.* New York: Broadway Books.

BRAZIL, J. 1998. You talkin' to me? *American Demographics* 20 (December): 55–59.

Breaking the cycle of violence: Recommendations to improve the criminal justice response to child victims and witnesses. 1999. Washington, DC: U.S. Department of Justice, Office of Justice Programs, Office for Victims of Crime.

BRECHER, E. M. 1984. *Love, sex, and aging.* New York: Little, Brown.

BREHM, S. S. 1985. *Intimate relationships.* New York: Random House.

BREHM, S. S. 1992. *Intimate relationships*, 2nd ed. New York: McGraw-Hill.

BREINES, W. 1992. *Young, white, and miserable: Growing up female in the fifties.* Boston: Beacon Press.

BRETSCHNEIDER, J. G., AND N. L. McCOY. 1988. Sexual interest and behavior in healthy 80- to 102-year olds. *Archives of Sexual Behavior* 17, (2): 109–29.

BRIERE, J. N. 1992. *Child abuse trauma: Theory and treatment of the lasting effects.* Thousand Oaks, CA: Sage.

BRIGGS, J. L. 1970. *Never in anger.* Cambridge, MA: Harvard University Press.

BRINES, J. 1994. Economic dependency, gender, and the division of labor at home. *American Journal of Sociology* 100 (November): 652–88.

BRINES, J., AND K. JOYNER. 1999. The ties that bind: Principles of cohesion in cohabitation and marriage. *American Sociological Review* 64 (June): 333–55.

Bringing up baby. 1999. *Public Perspective* 10 (October/November): 19.

BRINK, S. 1994. Too sick to be adopted? *U.S. News & World Report*, May 2, 66–69.

BRISSETT-CHAPMAN, S., AND M. ISSACS-SHOCKLEY. 1997. *Children in social peril: A community vision for preserving family care of African American children and youths.* Washington, DC: Child Welfare League of America.

BROCK, L. J., AND G. H. JENNINGS. 1993. Sexuality education: What daughters in their 30s wish their mothers had told them. *Family Relations* 42 (January): 61–65.

BRODERICK, C. B. 1988. To arrive where we started: The field of family studies in the 1930s. *Journal of Marriage and the Family* 50 (August): 569–84.

BRODERICK, C. B. 1993. *Understanding family process: Basics of family systems theory.* Thousand Oaks, CA: Sage.

BRODNAR-NEMZER, J. Y. 1986. Divorce and group commitment: The case of the Jews. *Journal of Marriage and the Family* 48 (May): 329–40.

BRODY, E. M., S. J. LITVIN, C. HOFFMAN, AND N. H. KLEBAN. 1992. Differential effects of daughters' marital status on their parent care experiences. *The Gerontologist* 32, (1): 58–67.

BRONFENBRENNER, U. 1979. *The ecology of human development: Experiments by nature and design.* Cambridge, MA: Harvard University Press.

BROOK, J. S., M. WHITEMAN, E. B. BALKA, P. T. WIN, AND M. D. GURSEN. 1998. Drug use among Puerto Ricans: Ethnic identity as a protective factor. *Hispanic Journal of Behavioral Sciences* 20 (May): 241–54.

BROOKE, J. 1994. Women in Colombia move to job forefront, *New York Times,* July 15, A6.

BROOKS, A. 1994. Sexism's bitterest trick. *New Scientist,* March 12, 48–49.

BROOKS, D. 2000. *Bobos in paradise: The new upper class and how they got there.* New York: Simon & Schuster.

BROOKS, G. R. 1995. *The centerfold syndrome: How men can overcome objectification and achieve intimacy with women.* San Francisco: Jossey-Bass.

BROOKS-GUNN, J., P. K. KLEBANOV, AND G. J. DUNCAN. 1996. Ethnic differences in children's intelligence test scores: Role of economic deprivation, home environment, and material characteristics. *Child Development* 67 (April): 396–408.

BROWN, B. B. 1999. "You're going out with *who?*" Peer group influences on adolescent romantic relationships. In *The development of romantic relationships in adolescence,* eds. W. Furman, B. B. Bradford, and C. Feiring, 291–329. New York: Cambridge University Press.

BROWN, D. 1997. Report shows dramatic decline in AIDS deaths. *Washington Post,* September 12, A3.

BROWN, D. 2000. Demographic shift noted in new cases of AIDS. *Washington Post,* January 14, A1, A15.

BROWN, J. K. 1992. Lives of middle-aged women. In *In her prime: New views of middle-aged women,* 2nd ed., eds. V. Kerns and J. K. Brown, 17–30. Urbana: University of Illinois Press.

BROWN, L. S. 1995. Lesbian identities: Concepts and issues. In *Lesbian, gay, and bisexual identities over the lifespan: Psychological perspectives,* eds. A. R. D'Augelli and C. J. Patterson, 3–23. New York: Oxford University Press.

BROWN, M. R. 1994. Whose eyes are these, whose nose? *Newsweek,* March 7, 12.

BROWN, N. M., AND E. S. AMATEA. 2000. *Love and intimate relationships: Journeys of the heart.* Philadelphia: Brunner/Mazel.

BROWN, P. M. 1995. *The death of intimacy: Barriers to meaningful interpersonal relationships.* New York: Haworth Press.

BROWN, R. A. 1994. Romantic love and the spouse selection criteria of male and female Korean college students. *Journal of Social Psychology* 134 (2): 183–89.

BROWN, S. L. 2000. Union transitions among cohabitors: The significance of relationship assessments and expectations. *Journal of Marriage and the Family* 62 (August): 833–46.

BROWN, S. L., AND A. BOOTH. 1996. Cohabitation versus marriage: A comparison of relationship quality. *Journal of Marriage and the Family* 58 (August): 668–78.

BROWN, S. S., AND L. EISENBERG, eds. 1995. *The best intentions: Unintended pregnancy and the well-being of children and families.* Washington, DC: National Academy Press.

BROWNE, A. 1993. Family violence and homelessness: The relevance of trauma histories in the lives of homeless women. *American Journal of Orthopsychiatry* 63 (July): 370–84.

BROWNE, I., ED. 1999. *Latinas and African American women at work.* New York: Russell Sage Foundation.

BROWNLEE, S., ET AL. 1994. The baby chase. *U.S. News & World Report,* December 5, 84–93.

BROWNLEE, S., AND S. SCHULTZ. 1999. Dying for sex. *U.S. News & World Report,* January 11, 62–65.

BROWNSWORTH, V. A. 1996. Tying the knot or the hangman's noose: The case against marriage. *Journal of Gay, Lesbian, and Bisexual Identity* 1 (January): 91–98.

BRUBAKER, T. H. 1991. Families in later life: A burgeoning research area. In *Contemporary families: Looking forward, looking back,* ed. A. Booth, 226–48. Minneapolis, MN: National Council on Family Relations.

BRUTZ, J. L., AND C. M. ALLEN. 1987. Religious commitment, peace activism, and marital violence in Quaker families. *Journal of Marriage and the Family* 48 (August): 491–502.

BRYAN, L. R., M. COLEMAN, AND L. H. GANONG. 1986. Person perception: Family structure as a cue for stereotyping. *Journal of Marriage and the Family* 48 (February): 169–74.

BRYSON, K., AND L. M. CASPER. 1999. Coresident grandparents and grandchildren, *Current Population Reports, P23-128,* U.S. Census Bureau. www.census.gov/prod/99pubs/p23-198.pdf (accessed October 28, 2000).

BUCHANAN, C. M., E. E. MACCOBY, AND S. M. DORNBUSCH. 1996. *Adolescents after divorce.* Cambridge, MA: Harvard University Press.

BUEHLER, C., A. KRISHNAKUMAR, G. STONE, C. ANTHONY, S. PEMBERTON, AND J. GERARD. 1998. *Journal of Marriage and the Family* 60 (February): 119–32.

BUEHLER, C., AND B. B. TROTTER. 1990. Nonresidential and residential parents' perceptions of the former spouse relationships and children's social competence following marital separation: Theory and programmed intervention. *Family Relations* 39 (October): 395–404.

BULCROFT, K., L. SMEINS, AND R. BULCROFT. 1999. *Romancing the honeymoon: Consummating marriage in modern society.* Thousand Oaks, CA: Sage.

BULCROFT, R. A., AND K. A. BULCROFT. 1993. Race differences in attitudinal and motivational factors in the decision to marry. *Journal of Marriage and the Family* 55 (May): 338–55.

BUMILLER, E. 1989. First comes marriage—then, maybe, love. In *Marriage and family in a changing society,* 3rd ed., ed. J. M. Henslin, 90–95. New York: Free Press.

BUMPASS, L., AND H.-H. LU. 2000. Trends in cohabitation and implications for children's family contexts in the United States. *Population Studies* 54 (March): 29–41.

BUMPASS, L. L., R. K. RALEY, AND J. A. SWEET. 1995. The changing character of stepfamilies: Implications of cohabitation and nonmarital childbearing. *Demography* 32 (August): 425–36.

BUMPASS, L. L., AND J. A. SWEET. 1989. National estimates of cohabitation. *Demography* 26 (November): 615–25.

BUMPASS, L. L., J. A. SWEET, AND A. CHERLIN. 1991. The role of cohabitation in declining rates of marriage. *Journal of Marriage and the Family* 53 (November): 913–27.

BUMPUS, M. F., A. C. CROUTER, AND S. M. MCHALE. 1999. Work demands of dual-earner couples: Implications for parents' knowledge about children's daily lives in middle childhood. *Journal of Marriage and the Family* 61 (May): 465–75.

Bureau of Labor Statistics. 1999. *Report on the American Workforce.* U.S. Department of Labor. stats.bls.gov/opub/rtaw/pdf/rtaw1999.pdf (accessed October 16, 2000).

BURGESS, B. J. 1980. Parenting in the Native-American community. In *Parenting in multicultural society,* eds. M. D. Fantini and R. Cardens. New York: Longman.

BURGESS, E. W., H. J. LOCKE, AND M. M. THOMES. 1963. *The family from institution to companionship.* New York: American Book Co.

BURGESS, J. K. 1988. Widowers. In *Variant family forms. Families in trouble* series, vol. 5, eds. C. S. Chilman, E. W. Nunnally, and F. M. Cox, 150–64. Beverly Hills, CA: Sage.

BURLESON, B. R., AND W. H. DENTON. 1997. The relationships between communication skill and marital satisfaction: Some moderating effects. *Journal of Marriage and the Family* 59 (November): 884–902.

BURNETTE, D. 1999. Social relationships of Latino grandparent caregivers: A role theory perspective. *The Gerontologist* 39 (February): 49–58.

BURNS, C. 1985. *Stepmotherhood: How to survive without feeling frustrated, left out, or wicked.* New York: Harper & Row.

BURR, C. 1996. *A separate creation: The search for the biological origins of sexual orientation.* New York: Hyperion.

BURR, W. R. 1995. Using theories in family science. In *Research and theory in family science,* eds. R. D. Day, K. R. Gilbert, B. H. Settles, and W. R. Burr, 73–90. Pacific Grove, CA: Brooks/Cole.

BURR, W. R., R. HILL, F. I. NYE, AND I. L. REISS, eds. 1979. *Contemporary theories about the family: Research-based theories,* vol. 2. New York: Free Press.

BURT, M. R., L. Y. ARON, T. DOUGLAS, J. VALENTE, E. LEE, AND B. IWEN. 1999. Homelessness: Programs and the people they serve. Urban Institute, Washington, DC. www.urban.org/housing/homeless/homelessness.pdf (accessed October 11, 2000).

BURTON, L. M. 1995a. Family structure and nonmarital fertility: Perspectives from ethnographic research. In *Report to Congress on out-of-wedlock childbearing,* 147–59. Hyattsville, MD: Centers for Disease Control and Prevention, National Center for Health Statistics.

BURTON, L. M. 1995b. Intergenerational patterns of providing care in African-American families with teenage childbearers: Emergent patterns in an ethnographic study. In *Adult intergenerational relations: Effects of societal change,* eds. V. L. Bengston, K. W. Schaie, and L. M. Burton, 79–96. New York: Springer.

BURTON, L. M., AND C. B. STACK. 1993. Conscripting kin: Reflections on family, generation, and culture. In *Family, self, and society: Toward a new agenda for family research,* eds. P. A. Cowan, D. Field, D. A. Hansen, A. Skolnick, and G. E. Swanson, 115–42. Hillsdale, NJ: Lawrence Erlbaum Associates.

BUSS, D. M. 1989. Sex differences in human mate preferences: Evolutionary hypotheses tested in 37 cultures. *Behavioral and Brain Sciences* 12 (March): 1–49.

BUSS, D. M., AND M. BARNES. 1986. Preferences in human mate selection. *Journal of Personality and Social Psychology* 50, no 3: 559–70.

BUSS, D. M., ET AL. 1990. International preferences in selecting mates: A study of 37 cultures. *Journal of Cross-Cultural Psychology* 21 (March): 5–47.

BUSS, D. M., R. J. LARSEN, AND D. WESTEN. 1996. Commentary: Sex differences in jealousy: Not gone, not forgotten, and not explained by alternative hypotheses. *Psychological Science* 7 (November): 373–75.

BUSSEY, K., AND A. BANDURA. 1992. Self-regulatory mechanisms governing gender development. *Child Development* 63 (October): 1236–50.

BUTLER, R. N. 1975. *Why survive? Being old in America*. New York: Harper & Row.

BUTLER, R. N., AND M. I. LEWIS. 1993. *Love and sex after 60*. New York: Ballantine.

BUTLER, S. 1999. In Japan, finally the women catch a break. *U.S. News & World Report*, July 5, 41.

BUYSSE, A. 1996. Adolescents, young adults and AIDS: A study of actual knowledge vs. perceived need for additional information. *Journal of Youth and Adolescence* 25 (April): 259–71.

CADDEN, V. 1995. Child care: How does your state rate? *Working Mother* (March): 21–32.

CAFFARO, J. V., AND A. CONN-CAFFARO. 1998. *Sibling abuse trauma: Assessment and intervention strategies for children, families, and adults*. New York: Haworth Press.

CAHN, S. K. 1994. *Coming on strong: Gender and sexuality in twentieth-century women's sports*. New York: Free Press.

CAMARILLO, A. 1979. *Chicanos in a changing society: From Mexican pueblos to American barrios in Santa Barbara and southern California, 1848–1930*. Cambridge, MA: Harvard University Press.

CAMAROTA, S. A. 1999. Importing poverty: Immigration's impact on the size and growth of the poor population in the United States. Center for Immigration Studies. www.cis.org/articles/poverty_study/index.html (accessed October 2, 2000).

CAMPBELL, F., AND C. RAMEY. 1999. *The Carolina abecedarian project*. www.fpg.unc.edu/~abc (accessed September 24, 2000).

CAMPBELL, J. R., C. M. HOMBO, AND J. MAZZEO. 2000. NAEP 1999 trends in academic progress: Three decades of student performance. nces.ed.gov/nationsreportcard/pubs/main1999/2000469.shtml (accessed August 27, 2000).

CAMPBELL, P. W. 1999. Researcher found guilty of misconduct. *Chronicle of Higher Education*, January 15, A34.

CAMPBELL, W. K. 1999. Narcissism and romantic attraction. *Journal of Personality and Social Psychology* 77 (December): 1254–70.

CAMPO-FLORES, B. AND Y. ROSENBERG. 2000. A return to wilding. *Newsweek*, June 26, 28.

CANADA, G. 1997. *Reaching up for manhood: Transforming lives of boys in America*. Boston: Beacon Press.

CANARY, D. J., W. R. CUPACH, AND S. J. MESSMAN. 1995. *Relationship conflict: Conflict in parent-child, friendship, and romantic relationships*. Thousand Oaks, CA: Sage.

CANCIAN, F. M. 1990. The feminization of love. In *Perspectives on the family: History, class, and feminism*, ed. C. Carlson, 171–85. Belmont, CA: Wadsworth.

CANNON, A. 1999. Sex, drugs, and sudden death. *U.S. News & World Report*, May 24, 73.

CANTWELL, H. B. 1997. The neglect of child neglect. In *The battered child*, 5th ed., eds. M. E. Helfer, R. S. Kempe, and R. D. Krugman, 347–73. Chicago: University of Chicago Press.

CAPELL, P. 1995. The stress of relocating. *American Demographics* 17 (November): 15–16.

CAPIZZANO, J., AND G. ADAMS. 2000a. The hours that children under five spend in child care: Variations across states. Urban Institute. newfederalism.urban.org/pdf/anf_b8.pdf (accessed September 27, 2000).

CAPIZZANO, J., AND G. ADAMS. 2000b. The number of child care arrangements used by children under five: Variation across states. Urban Institute. newfederalism.urban.org/pdf/anf_b12.pdf (accessed September 27, 2000).

CAPIZZANO, J., K. TOUT, AND G. ADAMS. 2000. Child care patterns of school-age children with employed mothers. Occasional Paper No. 41.

Urban Institute. newfederalism.urbanorg/pdf/occa41.pdf (accessed September 27, 2000).

CAPLAN, N., M. H. CHOY, AND J. K. WHITMORE. 1992. *Children of the boat people: A study of educational success*. Ann Arbor: University of Michigan Press.

CAPLAN, N., J. K. WHITMORE, AND M. H. CHOY. 1989. Culture, values, family life, and opportunity. In *The boat people and achievement in America: A study of family life, hard work, and cultural values*, 94–127. Ann Arbor: University of Michigan Press.

CARGAN, L., ed. 1991. *Marriage and families: Coping with change*, 3rd ed. Upper Saddle River, NJ: Prentice Hall.

CARGAN, L., AND M. MELKO. 1982. *Singles: Myths and realities*. Beverly Hills, CA: Sage.

CARLSON, L. 1998. *Caring for the dead: Your final act of love*. New York: Upper Access Book Publishers.

CARLSON, L. H., AND G. A. COLBURN, EDS. 1972. *In their place: White America defines her minorities, 1850–1950*. New York: Wiley.

CARP, F. M. 2000. *Elder abuse in the family: An interdisciplinary model for research*. New York: Springer.

CARPENTER, B. 1996. Investigating the next "Silent Spring." *U.S. News & World Report*, March 11, 50–52.

CARRASQUILLO, A. L. 1991. *Hispanic children and youth in the United States: A resource guide*. New York: Garland.

CARRERE, W., AND J. M. GOTTMAN. 1999. Predicting divorce among newlyweds from the first three minutes of a marital conflict discussion. *Family Process* 38 (Fall): 293–302.

CARRIER, J. M., AND S. O. MURRAY. 1998. Woman-woman marriage in Africa. In *Boy-wives and female husbands: Studies of African homosexualities*, eds. S. O. Murray and W. Roscoe, 255–66. New York: St. Martin's.

CARTEN, A. J., AND I. FENNOY. 1997. African American families and HIV/AIDS: Caring for surviving children. *Child Welfare* 76 (January–February): 107–25.

CARTER, S., AND J. SOKOL. 1993. *He's scared, she's scared: Understanding the hidden fears that sabotage your relationships*. New York: Delacorte.

CASEY, T. 1998. *Pride and joy: The lives and passions of women without children*. Hillboro, OR: Beyond Words Publishing.

CASLER, L. 1974. *Is marriage necessary?* New York: Human Sciences Press.

CASLER, W. 1993. *The lesbian sex book*. Boston: Alyson.

CASPER, L. M. 1997. *My daddy takes care of me! Fathers as care providers*. Current Population Reports P70-59. U.S. Bureau of the Census. Washington, DC: U.S. Government Printing Office.

CASPER, L. M., AND K. BRYSON. 1998. *Household and family characteristics: March 1998 (Update)*. Current Population Reports P20-515. www.census.gov/prod/3/98pubs/p20515u.pdf (accessed October 3, 2000).

CASPER, L. M., AND K. R. BRYSON. 1998. *Co-resident grandparents and their grandchildren: Grandparent maintained families*. Population Division Working Paper No. 26. U.S. Census Bureau. www.census.gov/population/www/documentation/twps0026/twps0026.html (accessed October 28, 2000).

CASPER, L. M., AND P. N. COHEN. 2000. How does POSSLQ measure up? Historical estimates of cohabitation. *Demography* 37 (May): 237–45.

CASPER, L. M., M. HAWKINS AND M. O'CONNELL. 1994a. *Who's minding the kids? Child care arrangements. Fall 1991*. Current Population

Reports. Bureau of the Census. Washington, DC: U.S. Government Printing Office.

CASPER, L. M., S. S. MCLANAHAN, AND I. GARFINKEL. 1994b. The gender-poverty gap: What we can learn from other countries. *American Sociological Review* 59 (August): 594–605.

CASSIDY, M. L., AND G. R. LEE. 1989. The study of polyandry: A critique and synthesis. *Journal of Comparative Family Studies* 20 (Spring): 1–11.

CASSIDY, S. 1993. A single woman: The fabric of my life. In *Single women: Affirming our spiritual journeys*, eds. M. O'Brien, and C. Christie, 35–48. Westport, CT: Bergin & Garvey.

CATALFO, P. 1994. Love at first link-up. *New Woman* 24 (March): 56, 58.

CATANIA, J. A., ET AL. 1992. Prevalence of AIDS-related risk factors and condom use in the United States. *Science*, November 13, 1101–06.

CATE, R. M., AND S. A. LLOYD. 1992. *Courtship*. Thousand Oaks, CA: Sage.

CATE, R. M., E. LONG, J. J. ANGERA, AND K. K. DRAPER. 1993. Sexual intercourse and relationship development. *Family Relations* 42 (April): 158–64.

CAVAN, R. S., AND K. H. RANCK. 1938. *The family and the Depression: A study of one hundred Chicago families*. Chicago: University of Chicago Press.

CEJKA, M. A. 1993. A demon with no name: Prejudice against single women. In *Single women: Affirming our spiritual journeys*, eds. M. O'Brien and C. Christie, 3–11. Westport, CT: Bergin & Garvey.

Center for Women Policy Studies. 1994. *Midlife & older women & HIV/AIDS*. Washington, DC: American Association of Retired Persons.

Centers for Disease Control and Prevention. 1996. *Sexually transmitted disease surveillance, 1995*. U.S. Department of Health and Human Services, Public Health Service, Division of STD Prevention, Atlanta. http://wonder.cdc.gov/rchtml/Convert/STD/CSTD3888.PCW.html (accessed November 15, 1997).

Centers for Disease Control and Prevention. 1997a. *1995 Assisted reproductive technology success rates: National summary and fertility clinic reports*. National Center for Chronic Disease Prevention and Health Promotion, Division of Reproductive Health, Atlanta. www.cdc.gov/nccdphp/drh/arts/index.htm (accessed January 15, 1998).

Centers for Disease Control and Prevention. 1997b. CDC Surveillance Summaries: Youth risk behavior surveillance. National college health risk behavior survey—United States, 1995. *Morbidity and Mortality Weekly Report* 46 (November 14): SS-6.

Centers for Disease Control and Prevention. 1998. *Trends in the HIV & AIDS epidemic*. Atlanta.

Centers for Disease Control and Prevention. 1999. Guidelines for national human immunodeficiency virus case surveillance, including monitoring for human immunodeficiency virus infection and acquired immunodeficiency syndrome. www.cdc.gov/epo/mmwr/preview/mmwrhtml/rr4813a1.htm#tab1 (accessed September 4, 2000).

CHADIHA, L. A., J. VEROFF, AND D. LEBER. 1998. Newlyweds' narrative themes: Meaning in the first year of marriage for African American and white couples. *Journal of Comparative Family Studies* 29 (Spring): 116–30.

CHAFE, W. H. 1972. *The American woman: Her changing social, economic, and political roles, 1920–1970*. New York: Oxford University Press.

CHALFIE, D. 1995. *The real Golden Girls: The prevalence and policy treatment of midlife and older people living in nontraditional households*.

Washington, DC: American Association of Retired Persons.

CHALKLEY, K. 1997. Female genital mutilation: New laws, programs try to end practice. *Population Today* 25 (October): 4–5.

CHAMBERS, V., AND L. CLEMETSON. 1999. A place they can call home. *Newsweek,* April 19, 58–59.

CHAN, A. Y., AND K. R. SMITH. 1995. Perceptions of marital stability of black–white intermarriages. In *American families: Issues in race and ethnicity,* ed. C. K. Jacobson, 369–86. New York: Garland.

CHAN, S., ED. 1994. *Hmong means free: Life in Laos and America.* Philadelphia: Temple University Press.

CHAN, S. 1999. Families with Asian roots. In *Developing cross-cultural competence: A guide for working with children and their families,* 2nd ed., eds. E. W. Lynch and M. J. Hanson, 251–344. Baltimore, MD: Paul H. Brookes.

CHANCE, P. 1988. The trouble with love. *Psychology Today* (February): 22–23.

CHANG, G. 1994. Undocumented Latinas: The new "employable mothers." In *Mothering: Ideology, experience, and agency,* eds. E. Glenn, E. Nakano, G. Chang, and L. R. Forcey, 259–85. New York: Routledge.

CHANG, G. 2000. *Disposable domestics: Immigrant women workers in the global economy.* Cambridge, MA: South End Press.

CHANG, J., AND A. MOON. 1997. Korean American elderly's knowledge and perceptions of elder abuse: A qualitative analysis of cultural factors. *Journal of Multicultural Social Work* 6 (1/2): 139–54.

CHAPMAN, A. B. 1994. *Entitled to good loving: Black men and women and the battle for love and power.* New York: Holt.

CHAPMAN, D. W., AND J. M. CLAFFEY. 1998. A new wealth of opportunities overseas. *Chronicle of Higher Education,* September 28, B6.

CHASE-LANSDALE, P. L., A. J. CHERLIN, AND K. E. KIERNAN. 1995. The long-term effects of parental divorce on the mental health of young adults: A developmental perspective. *Child Development* 66 (December): 1614–34.

CHATTERS, L. M., AND R. J. TAYLOR. 1993. Intergenerational support: The provision of assistance to parents by adult children. In *Aging in Black America,* eds. S. Jackson, L. M. Chatters, and R. J. Taylor, 60–83. Thousand Oaks, CA: Sage.

CHEKKI, D. A. 1996. Family values and family change. *Journal of Comparative Family Studies* 27 (Summer): 409–13.

CHEN, A. S. 1999. Lives at the center of the periphery, lives at the periphery of the center: Chinese American masculinities and bargaining with hegemony. *Gender & Society* 13 (October): 584–607.

CHERLIN, A. J. 1992. *Marriage, divorce, remarriage.* Cambridge, MA: Harvard University Press.

CHERLIN, A. J. 1998. Marriage and marital dissolution among black Americans. *Journal of Comparative Family Studies* 29 (Spring): 147–58.

CHERLIN, A. J. 1999. Going to extremes: Family structure, children's well-being, and social science. *Demography* 36 (November): 421–28.

CHERLIN, A. J., AND F. F. FURSTENBERG, JR. 1994. Stepfamilies in the United States: A reconsideration. *Annual Review of Sociology* 20, 359–81.

CHERLIN, A. J., F. F. FURSTENBERG, JR., P. L. CHASE-LANSDALE, K. E. KIERNAN, P. K. ROBINS, D. R. MORRISON, AND J. O. TEITLER. 1991. Longitudinal studies of effects of divorce on children in Great Britain and the United States. *Science,* June 7, 1386–89.

CHERRO, M. 1992. Quality of bonding and behavioral differences in twins. *Infant Mental Health Journal* 13 (Fall): 206–10.

CHESLER, P. 1988. *Sacred bond: The legacy of Baby M.* New York: Times Books.

CHEVAN, A. 1996. As cheaply as one: Cohabitation in the older population. *Journal of Marriage and the Family* 58 (August): 656–67.

Child abuse trial turns spotlight on polygamy. 1999. *Baltimore Sun,* April 21, 3a.

Child fatalities fact sheet. 2000. National Clearinghouse on Child Abuse and Neglect Information, Washington, DC. www.calib.com/nccanch/pubs/factsheets/fatality.htm (accessed October 18, 2000).

Child of misplaced embryo to return to genetic parents. 1999. *Baltimore Sun,* March 31, 15A.

Child welfare outcomes: 1998 annual report. 2000. Washington, DC: Department of Health and Human Services.

Children as victims. 2000. Washington, DC: U.S. Department of Justice, Office of Justice Pograms, Office of Juvenile Justice and Delinquency Prevention.

Children Now. 1998. A different world: Children's perceptions of race and class in the media, 1998. www.childrennow.org/redesigns/media/mc98/MC98page6.html (accessed August 24, 2000).

Children's Defense Fund. 1994. *The state of America's children yearbook 1994.* Washington, DC.

Children's Defense Fund. 1995. *The state of America's children yearbook 1995.* Washington, DC.

Children's Defense Fund. 2000a. *The state of America's children yearbook 2000.* Washington, DC.

Children's Defense Fund. 2000b. Where America stands. www.childrensdefense.org/facts_america98.html (accessed August 12, 2000).

CHION-KENNEY, L. 1991. Parents of divorce. *Washington Post,* May 6, B5.

CHISHOLM, P., AND S. D. DRIEDGER. 1994. Paying for the children of divorce. *Maclean's,* January 10, 36–37.

CHOI, N. G. 1992. Correlates of the economic status of widowed and divorced elderly women. *Journal of Family Issues* 12 (March): 38–54.

CHOICE, P., AND L. K. LAMKE. 1997. A conceptual approach to understanding abused women's stay/leave decisions. *Journal of Family Issues* 18 (May): 290–314.

CHRISTENSEN, A., AND J. L. SHENK. 1991. Communication, conflict, and psychological distance in nondistressed, clinical, and divorcing couples. *Journal of Consulting and Clinical Psychology* 59, 458–63.

CHRISTOPHER, F. S., AND R. M. CATE. 1984. Factors involved in premarital sexual decision-making. *Journal of Sex Research* 20, 363–76.

CHRISTOPHER, F. S., AND R. M. CATE. 1988. Premarital sexual involvement: A developmental investigation of relational correlates. *Adolescence* 23 (Winter): 793–804.

Chronicle of Higher Education. 1998. This year's freshmen: A statistical profile. January 16, A38–A39.

CLARK, J. M. 1999. *Doing the work of love: Men & commitment in same-sex couples.* Harriman, TN: Men's Studies Press.

CLARKBERG, M., R. M. STOLZENBERG, AND L. J. WAITE. 1995. Attitudes, values, and entrance into cohabitational versus marital unions. *Social Forces* 74 (December): 609–34.

CLARKE, J. W. 1990. *On being mad or merely angry: John W. Hinckley, Jr., and other dangerous people.* Princeton, NJ: Princeton University Press.

CLARKE, S. C. 1995a. Advance report of final divorce statistics, 1989 and 1990. *Monthly*

Vital Statistics Report 43, no. 9(S), March 22. Centers for Disease Control and Prevention.

CLARKE, S. C. 1995b. Advance report of final marriage statistics, 1989 and 1990. *Monthly Vital Statistics Report* 43, no. 12(S), July 14.

CLARKE, S. C., AND B. F. WILSON. 1994. The relative stability of remarriages: A cohort approach using vital statistics. *Family Relations* 43 (July): 305–10.

CLEAVER, J. Y. 1999. Good old dad. *American Demographics* 20 (June): 59–63.

CLEMENS, A. W., AND L. J. AXELSON. 1985. The not-so-empty-nest: The return of the fledgling adult. *Family Relations* 34 (April): 259–64.

CLEMENTS, M. 1994. Sex in America today. *Parade Magazine,* August 7, 4–7.

CLEMENTS, M. 1996. Sex after 65. *Parade Magazine,* March 17, 4–6.

CLEMETSON, L. 1999. Haunted by a painful history. *Newsweek,* February 22, 46–47.

CLEMETSON, L. 2000. Grandma knows best. *Newsweek,* June 12, 60–61.

CLIFT, E. 1996. A terrible, terrible trauma. *Newsweek,* September 30, 57.

COATES, D. L. 1999. The cultured and culturing aspects of romantic experience in adolescence. In *The development of romantic relationships in adolescence,* eds. W. Furman, B. B. Bradford, and C. Feiring, 330–63. New York: Cambridge University Press.

COCCO, M. 1998. Viagra is sign of double standard. *Baltimore Sun,* May 24, 41.

COHEN, C. E. 1994. The trailing-spouse dilemma. *Working Woman* (March): 69–70.

COHEN, P. N. 1999. Racial-ethnic and gender differences in returns to cohabitation and marriage: Evidence from the Current Population Survey. U.S. Census Bureau. www.census.gov/population/www/documentation/twps0035/twps0035.html (accessed August 8, 2000).

COHEN, T. F. 1993. What do fathers provide? Reconsidering the economic and nurturant dimensions of men as parents. In *Men, work, and family,* ed. J. C. Hood, 1–22. Thousand Oaks, CA: Sage.

COHN, D. 2000. Census complaints hit home. *Washington Post,* May 4, A9.

COHN, G., and W. F. ROCHE, JR. 2000. Indentured servants for high-tech trade. *Baltimore Sun,* February 21, 1A, 14A–15A.

COLAPINTO, J. 1997. The true story of John/Joan. *Rolling Stone* (December 11): 54–73, 92–97.

COLASANTO, D., AND J. SHRIVER. 1989. Middle-aged face marital crisis. *Gallup Report,* no. 284 (May): 34–38.

COLBURN, D. 1991. The way of the warrior. *Washington Post Health Supplement,* January 29, 10–12.

COLE, A. 1996. Yours, mine and ours. *Modern Maturity* (September/October): 12, 14–15.

COLEMAN, F. 1994. Political power is only half the battle. *U.S. News & World Report,* June 13, 58.

COLEMAN, J. U., AND S. M. STITH. 1997. Nursing students' attitudes toward victims of domestic violence as predicted by selected individual and relationship variables. *Journal of Family Violence* 12 (June): 113–38.

COLEMAN, L. M., T. C. ANTONUCCI, P. K. ADELMANN, AND S. E. CROHAN. 1987. Social roles in the lives of middle-aged and older black women. *Journal of Marriage and the Family* 49 (November): 761–71.

COLEMAN, M., AND L. H. GANONG. 1991. Remarriage and stepfamily research in the 1980s. In *Contemporary families: Looking forward, looking back,* ed. A. Booth, 192–207. Minneapolis, MN: National Council on Family Relations.

COLEMAN, M., L. H. GANONG, AND C. GOODWIN. 1994. The presentation of stepfamilies in marriage and family textbooks: A reexamination. *Family Relations* 43 (July): 289–297.

COLLETTE, L. 1993. Creating a separate space: Celibacy and singlehood. In *Single women: Affirming our spiritual journeys,* eds. M. O'Brien and C. Christie, 59–84. Westport, CT: Bergin & Garvey.

COLLIER, J. 1947. *The Indians of the Americas.* New York: Norton.

COLLINS, W. A., E. E. MACCOBY, L. STEINBERG, E. M. HETHERINGTON, AND M. H. BORNSTEIN. 2000. Contemporary research on parenting: The case for nature and nurture. *American Psychologist* 55 (February): 218–32.

COLLISON, M. N.-K. 1993. A sure-fire winner is to tell her you love her; women fall for it all the time. In *Women's studies: Thinking women,* eds. J. Wetzel, M. L. Espenlaub, M. A. Hagen, A. B. McElhiney, C. B. Williams, 228–30. Dubuque, IA: Kendall/Hunt.

COLTRANE, S. 1996. *Family man: Fatherhood, housework, and gender equality.* New York: Oxford University Press.

COLTRANE, S. 1998. *Gender and families.* Thousand Oaks, CA: Pine Forge Press.

COLTRANE, S., AND E. O. VALDEZ. 1993. Reluctant compliance: Work-family role allocation in dual-earner Chicano families. In *Men, work, and family,* ed. J. C. Hood, 151–75. Beverly Hills, CA: Sage.

CONLIN, M. 2000. Valley of no dolls. *Business Week,* March 6, 126, 129.

CONLIN, M., AND W. ZELLNER. 1999. The CEO still wears wingtips. *Business Week,* November 22, 85–90.

CONNELLY, H. 1999. *Children exposed to violence: Criminal justice resources.* Washington, DC: U.S. Department of Justice, Office of Justice Programs, Office for Victims of Crime.

CONNELLY, J. 1989. The CEO's second wife. *Fortune,* August 28, 53–62.

CONNER, K. A. 1992. *Aging America: Issues facing an aging society.* Upper Saddle River, NJ: Prentice Hall.

CONOVER, K. A. 1997. Tribal colleges: Gains for "underfunded miracles." *Christian Science Monitor,* May 21, 12.

Considering alternative lifestyles. 2000. *Public Perspective* 11 (January/February): 24–31.

Consumer Product Safety Commission. 1999. Be sure your child care setting is as safe as it can be. www.cpsc.gov/cpscpub/pubs/childcare.html (accessed September 28, 2000).

COOKSEY, E. C., AND P. H. CRAIG. 1998. Parenting from a distance: The effects of paternal characteristics on contact between nonresidential fathers and their children. *Demography* 35 (May): 187–200.

COOLIDGE, S. D. 1998. Harassment hits higher profile. *Christian Science Monitor,* March 2, B4–B5.

COOMBS, R. H. 1991. Marital status and personal well-being: A literature review. *Family Relations* 40 (January): 97–102.

COONEY, T. M., AND J. T. MORTIMER. 1999. Family structure differences in the timing of leaving home: Exploring mediating factors. *Journal of Research on Adolescence* 9 (4): 367–94.

COONTZ, S. 1992. *The way we never were: American families and the nostalgia trap.* New York: Basic Books.

COONTZ, S. 1997. *The way we really are: Coming to terms with America's changing families.* New York: Basic Books.

COOPER, C. R., AND R. G. COOPER, JR. 1992. Links between adolescents' relationships with their parents and peers: Models, evidence, and mechanisms. In *Family-peer relations: Modes of linkage,* eds. R. D. Parke and G. W. Ladd, 135–58. Hillsdale, NJ: Lawrence Erlbaum Associates.

COOPERMAN, A. 1997. No end in sight to a gruesome and widespread ritual. *U.S. News & World Report,* July 17, 51.

COOTE, A. 1991. Anatomy of a penis. *Cosmopolitan,* May 1, 86, 88, 90, 92.

Correspondence: Disclosure of authors' conflict of interest: A follow-up. 2000. *New England Journal of Medicine* 342 (February 24): 586–7.

COSE, E. 1993. *The rage of a privileged class.* New York: HarperCollins.

COSE, E. 1995. Black men & black women. *Newsweek,* June 5, 66–69.

COSE, E. 1999. Deciphering the code of the street. *Newsweek,* August 30, 33.

COTT, N. F. 1976. Eighteenth century family and social life revealed in Massachusetts divorce records. *Journal of Social History* 10 (Fall): 20–43.

COTT, N. F. 1977. *The bonds of womanhood.* New Haven, CT: Yale University Press.

COTT, N. F., AND E. H. PLECK, eds. 1979. *A heritage of her own: Toward a new social history of American women.* New York: Simon & Schuster.

COTTEN, S. R. 1999. Marital status and mental health revisited: Examining the importance of risk factors and resources. *Family Relations* 48 (July): 225–33.

COTTLE, T. J. 1994. Women who kill. *North American Review* 279 (May): 4–9.

Council on Scientific Affairs. 1993. Adolescents as victims of family violence. *JAMA,* October 20, 1850–56.

COUPER, D. P., AND N. W. SHEEHAN. 1987. Family dynamics for caregivers: An educational model. *Family Relations* 36, 181–86.

Couple wants to give gift of parenthood to childless. 1997. *Baltimore Sun,* December 25, 20A.

COWAN, C. P., AND P. A. COWAN. 1992. *When partners become parents: The big life change for couples.* New York: HarperCollins.

COWAN, C. P., AND P. A. COWAN. 2000. *When partners become parents: The big life change for couples.* Mahwah, NJ: Lawrence Erlbaum Associates.

COWAN, P. A., D. FIELD, D. A. HANSEN, A. SKOLNICK, AND G. E. SWANSON, eds. 1993. *Family, self, and society: Toward a new agenda for family research.* Hillsdale, NJ: Lawrence Erlbaum Associates.

COWELL, A. 1988. In Egypt, the in-laws still propose. *New York Times,* December 29, C1, C10.

COWELL, A. 1994. Cairo parley hits a new snag on migrants. *New York Times,* September 11, 10.

COWGILL, D. O. 1986. *Aging around the world.* Belmont, CA: Wadsworth.

COWHERD, K. 1994. State of the heart. *Baltimore Sun,* February 14, D1, D3.

COWLEY, G. 2000. Alzheimer's: Unlocking the mystery. *Newsweek,* January 31, 46–51.

COWLEY, G., WITH M. HAGER AND J. C. RAMO. 1993. The view from the womb. *Newsweek,* November 8, 64.

COWLEY, G., AND K. SPRINGEN. 1997. Multiplying the risks. *Newsweek,* December 1, 66.

COX, C. 1993. *The frail elderly: Problems, needs, and community responses.* Westport, CT: Auburn House.

COX, C. B., ED. 2000. *To grandmother's house we go and stay: Perspectives on custodial grandparents.* New York: Springer.

COYNE, A. C., W. E. REICHMAN, AND L. J. BERBIG. 1993. The relationship between dementia and elder abuse. *American Journal of Psychiatry* 150 (April): 643–46.

CRABB, P. B., AND D. BIELAWSKI. 1994. The social representation of material culture and gender in children's books. *Sex Roles* 30, (1/2): 69–79.

CRAMER, J. C., AND K. B. MCDONALD. 1996. Kin support and family stress: Two sides to early childbearing and support networks. *Human Organization* 55 (Summer): 160–69.

CRAWFORD, M. 1995. *Talking difference: On gender and language.* Thousand Oaks, CA: Sage.

CREIGHTON, L. L. 1991. Silent saviors. *U.S. News & World Report,* December 16, 80–89.

CREIGHTON, L. L. 1993. Kids taking care of kids. *U.S. News & World Report,* December 20, 26–33.

CRENSHAW, A. R. 1992. Assessing the political power of seniors. *Washington Post Family and Retirement Supplement,* April 29, 4–7.

CRENSHAW, A. R. 1994. For many, tax laws take the bliss out of wedded life. *Washington Post,* July 10, H1, H4.

CRISPELL, D. 1992. Myths of the 1950s. *American Demographics* (August): 38–43.

CRISPELL, D. 1993. Planning no family, now or ever. *American Demographics,* 6 (October): 23–24.

CRISPELL, D. 1996. Which good old days? *American Demographics* 9 (April): 35.

CRITTENDEN, D. 1999. *What our mothers didn't tell us: Why happiness eludes the modern woman.* New York: Simon & Schuster.

CROHAN, S. E. 1996. Marital quality and conflict across the transition to parenthood in African American and white couples. *Journal of Marriage and the Family* 58 (November): 933–44.

CROSBIE-BURNETT, M., AND E. A. LEWIS. 1993. Use of African-American family structures and functioning to address the challenges of European-American postdivorce families. *Family Relations* 42 (July): 243–48.

CROSBIE-BURNETT, M., AND J. GILES-SIMS. 1994. Adolescent adjustment and stepparenting styles. *Family Relations* 43 (October): 394–99.

CROSBY, J. F. 1991a. *Illusion and disillusion: The self in love and marriage,* 5th ed. Belmont, CA: Wadsworth.

CROSBY, F. J. 1991b. *Juggling: The unexpected advantages of balancing career and home for women and their families.* New York: Free Press.

CROSS, T. L. 1998. Understanding family resiliency from a relational world view. In *Resiliency in Native American and immigrant families,* eds. H. I. McCubbin, E. A. Thompson, A. I. Thompson, and J. E. Fromer, 143–57. Thousand Oaks, CA: Sage.

CROSSEN, C. 1994. *Tainted truth: The manipulation of fact in America.* New York: Simon & Schuster.

CROWELL, J. A., AND E. WATERS. 1994. Bowlby's theory grown up: The role of attachment in adult love relationships. *Psychological Inquiry* 5 (1): 31–34.

CUBER, J., AND P. HAROFF. 1965. *Sex and the significant Americans.* Baltimore: Penguin.

CUE, K. L., W. H. GEORGE, AND J. NORRIS. 1996. Women's appraisals of sexual-assault risk in dating situations. *Psychology of Women Quarterly* 20 (December): 487–504.

CUELLO, J. 1997. Latinos and Hispanics: A primer on terminology. Detroit, MI: Wayne State University, unpublished manuscript.

CUMMINGS, E. M., AND P. DAVIES. 1994. *Children and marital conflict: The impact of family dispute and resolution.* New York: Guilford Press.

CUNNINGHAM, J. D., AND J. K. ANTILL. 1995. Current trends in nonmarital cohabitation: In search of the POSSLQ. In *Under-Studied relationships: Off the beaten track,* eds. J. T. Wood and S. Duck, 148–72. Thousand Oaks, CA: Sage.

CURTIS, C. M., AND R. ALEXANDER, JR. 1996. The Multiethnic Placement Act: Implications for social work practice. *Child and Adolescent Social Work Journal* 13 (October): 401–10.

CURTIS, J. 1998. *Making and breaking families: The way ahead for parents and their children.* New York: Free Association Press.

CUSIMANO, M. 1997. Letters to the editor. *Baltimore Sun,* January 17, 12A.

CUTRONA, C. E. 1996. *Social support in couples: Marriage as a resource in times of stress.* Thousand Oaks, CA: Sage.

Cyberstalking. 2000. www.ncvc.org/special/cyber_stk.htm (accessed August 30, 2000).

Dads lacking on networks. 1999. *Baltimore Sun,* March 22, E1.

DAINTON, M. 1993. The myths and misconceptions of the stepmother identity: Descriptions and prescriptions for identity management. *Family Relations* 42 (January): 93–98.

DALAKER, J., AND B. D. PROCTOR. 2000. *Poverty in the United States: 1999.* U.S. Census Bureau, Current Population Reports: Consumer Income, P60-210. www.census.gov/prod/2000pubs/p60-210.pdf (accessed October 11, 2000).

DALSIMER, M. 1981. Bible communists: Female socialization and family life in the Oneida Community. In *Family life in America: 1620–2000,* eds. M. Albin and D. Cavallo, 30–46. New York: Revisionary Press.

DALY, K. J. 1999. Crisis of genealogy: Facing the challenges of infertility. In *The dynamics of resilient families,* eds. H. I. McCubbin, E. A. Thompson, A. I. Thompson, and J. A. Futrell, 1–40. Thousand Oaks, CA: Sage.

DANIELS, K. R. 1994. Adoption and donor insemination: Factors influencing couples' choices. *Child Welfare* 73 (January/February): 5–14.

DANZIGER, S. K., AND S. DANZIGER. 1993. Child poverty and public policy: Toward a comprehensive antipoverty agenda. *Daedalus* 122 (Winter): 57–84.

DARBY, P. J., W. D. ALLAN, AND J. C. REID. 1998. Analyses of 112 juveniles who committed homicide: Characteristics and a closer look at family abuse. *Journal of Family Violence* 13 (December): 365–74.

DARROCH, J. E., AND S. SINGH. 1999. *Why is teenage pregnancy declining? The roles of abstinence, sexual activity and contraceptive use.* New York: Alan Guttmacher Institute. www.agi-usa.org/pubs/or_teen_preg_decline.pdf (accessed September 1, 2000).

DAVIS, F. J. 1991. *Who is black?* University Park: Pennsylvania State University Press.

DAVIS, L. E., J. H. WILLIAMS, S. EMERSON, AND M. HOURD-BRYANT. 2000. Factors contributing to partner commitment among unmarried African Americans. *Social Work Research* 24 (March): 4–15.

DAVIS, P. W. 1994. The changing meanings of spanking. In *Troubling children,* ed. J. Best, 133–53. New York: Aldine de Gruyter.

DAVIS, P. W. 1996. Threats of corporal punishment as verbal aggression: A naturalistic study. *Child Abuse & Neglect* 20 (4): 289–304.

DAVIS, R. C., AND B.G. TAYLOR. 1999. Does batterers' treatment reduce violence? A synthesis of the literature. In *Women and domestic violence: An interdisciplinary approach,* ed. L. Feder, 69–93. New York: Haworth Press.

DAVIS, S. 1990. Men as success objects and women as sex objects: A study of personal advertisements. *Sex Roles* 23 (1/2): 43–50.

DAVIS-KIMBALL, J. 1997. Warrior women of the Eurasian steppes. *Archaeology* 50 (January): 44–48.

DAVIS-PACKARD, K. 2000. Why the number of teen mothers is falling. *Christian Science Monitor,* August 15, 1, 11.

DAWSEY, D. 1996. *Living to tell about it: Young black men in America speak their piece.* New York: Anchor.

DAWSON, G. , AND R. GLAUBMAN. 2000. *Life is so good.* New York: Random House.

DAWSON, J. M., AND P. A. LANGAN. 1994. *Murder in families.* Washington, DC: Bureau of Justice Statistics.

DAY, R. D. 1995. Family-systems theory. In *Research and theory in family science,* eds. R. D. Day, K. R. Gilbert, B. H. Settles, and W. R. Burr, 91–101. Pacific Grove, CA: Brooks/Cole.

DAY, R. D., G. W. PETERSON, AND C. MCCRACKEN. 1998. Predicting spanking of younger and older children by mothers and fathers. *Journal of Marriage and the Family* 60 (February): 79–94.

DEAN, C. R. 1991. Fighting for same-sex marriage. *Partners: Newsletter for gay and lesbian couples,* November/December.

DE ANGELIS, C. D. 2000. Women in academic medicine: New insights, same sad news. *New England Journal of Medicine* 342, February 10, 426–27.

DEANE, C., ET AL. 2000. Leaving tradition behind: Latinos in the great American melting pot. *Public Perspective* 11 (May/June): 5–7, 10.

DEATER-DECKARD, K., K. A. DODGE, AND G. S. PETTIT. 1996. Physical discipline among African American and European American mothers: Links to children's externalizing behaviors. *Developmental Psychology* 32 (November): 1065–72.

DEBORD, K. B., and J. T. R. DE ATILES. 1999. Latino parents: Unique preferences for learning about parenting. *Forum for Family and Consumer Issues* 4 (Spring): 1–10. www.ces.ncsu.edu/depts/fcs/pub/1999/latino.html (accessed March 14, 2000).

DECALMER, P., AND F. GLENDENNING, eds. 1993. *The mistreatment of elderly people.* Thousand Oaks, CA: Sage.

Deck the box. 1999. *American Demographics* 21 (November): 72.

DEGLER, C. 1981. *At odds: Women and the family in America from the Revolution to the present.* New York: Oxford University Press.

DEGROOT, J. M., S. KENNEDY, G. RODIN, AND G. MCVEY. 1992. Correlates of sexual abuse in women with anorexia nervosa and bulimia nervosa. *Canadian Journal of Psychiatry* 37 (September): 516–18.

DE LA CANCELA, V. 1994. "Coolin": The psychosocial communication of African and Latino men. In *African American males: A critical link in the African American family,* ed. D. J. Jones, 33–44. New Brunswick, NJ: Transaction.

DELAMATER, J., AND P. MCCORQUODALE. 1979. *Premarital sexuality: Attitudes, relationships, behavior.* Madison: University of Wisconsin Press.

DEL CASTILLO, R. G. 1984. *La familia: Chicano families in the urban Southwest, 1848 to the present.* Notre Dame, IN: University of Notre Dame Press.

DELISLE, S. 1997. Preserving reproductive choice: Preventing STD-related infertility in women. *Siecus Report* 25 (March): 18–21.

DELLMANN-JENKINS, M., M. BLANKEMEYER, AND O. PINKARD. 2000. Young adult children and grandchildren in primary caregiver roles to older relatives and their service needs. *Family Relations* 49 (April): 177–86.

DEL PINAL, J., AND A. SINGER. 1997. Generations of diversity: Latinos in the United States. *Population Bulletin* 52 (October). Washington, DC: Population Reference Bureau.

DEMARIS, A., AND W. MACDONALD. 1993. Premarital cohabitation and marital instability: A test of the unconventionality hypothesis. *Journal of Marriage and the Family* 55 (May): 399–407.

DEMO, D. H., AND A. C. ACOCK. 1988. The impact of divorce on children. *Journal of Marriage and the Family* 50 (August): 619–48.

DEMO, D. H., AND A. C. ACOCK. 1991. The impact of divorce on children. In *Contemporary families: Looking forward, looking back,* ed. A. Booth, 162–91. Minneapolis, MN: National Council on Family Relations.

DEMO, D. H., AND A. C. ACOCK. 1996a. Family structure, family process, and adolescent well-being. *Journal of Research on Adolescence* 6 (4): 457–88.

DEMO, D. H., AND A. C. ACOCK. 1996b. Singlehood, marriage, and remarriage. *Journal of Family Issues* 17 (May): 388–407.

DE MORAES, L. 1999. TV's open closet. *Washington Post,* March 3, C1, C3.

DEMOS, J. 1970. *A little commonwealth: Family life in Plymouth colony.* New York: Oxford University Press.

DEMOS, J. 1986. *Past, present, and personal: The family and the life course in American history.* New York: Oxford University Press.

DENHAM, S. A., S. M. RENWICK, AND R. W. HOLT. 1991. Working and playing together: Prediction of preschool social–emotional competence from mother–child interaction. *Child Development* 62 (April): 242–49.

DENSON, D. R., R. VOIGHT, AND R. EISENMAN. 1993. Factors that influence HIV/AIDS instruction in schools. *Adolescence* 28 (Summer): 309–13.

DERLEGA, V. J., S. METTS, S. PETRONIO, AND S. T. MARGULIS. 1993. *Self-disclosure.* Thousand Oaks, CA: Sage.

DE SNYDER, V. N. S. 1999. Latina women: Constructing a new vision from within. *Hispanic Journal of Behavioral Sciences* 21 (August): 229–35.

DESTEFANO, L., AND D. COLASANTO. 1990. Unlike 1975, today most Americans think men have it better. *Gallup Poll Monthly* (February): 25–36.

DESTENO, D. A., AND P. SALOVEY. 1996. Evolutionary origins of sex differences in jealousy? Questioning the "fitness" of the model. *Psychological Science* 7 (November): 367–72.

DEUTSCH, C. H. 1986. Prenuptial decrees up, prenuptial trust down. *New York Times,* November 19, C1, C16.

DEUTSCHL, F. M., J. B. LUSSIER, AND L. J. SERVIS. 1993. Husbands at home: Predictors of paternal participation in childcare and housework. *Journal of Personality and Social Psychology* 65 (6): 1154–66.

DEVALL, E., Z. STONEMAN, AND G. BRODY. 1986. The impact of divorce and maternal employment on pre-adolescent children. *Family Relations* 35 (January): 153–60.

DEVLIN, B., M. DANIELS, AND K. ROEDER. 1997. The heritability of IQ. *Nature* 388, July 31, 468–70.

DEVOR, H. 1997. *FTM: Female-to-male transsexuals in society.* Bloomington: Indiana University Press.

DE WITT P. M. 1993. In pursuit of pregnancy. *American Demographics* 6 (May): 48–54.

DE WITT, P. M. 1994. Breaking up is hard to do. *American Demographics,* reprint package 8–12.

DE WOLFF, M. S., AND M. H. VAN IJZENDOORN. 1997. Sensitivity and attachment: A meta-analysis on parental antecedents of infant attachment. *Child Development* 68 (August): 571–91.

DIAMOND, M., AND K. SIGMUNDSON. 1997. Sex reassignment at birth: Long-term review and clinical implications. *Archives of Pediatrics & Adolescent Medicine* 15 (March): 298–304.

DIAZ, R. M., E. S. MORALES, E. BEIN, E. DIHIN, AND R. A. RODRIGUEZ. 1999. Predictors of sexual risk in Latino gay/bisexual men: The role of demographic, developmental, social, cognitive, and behavioral variables. *Hispanic Journal of Behavioral Sciences* 21 (November): 480–501.

DIBACCO, T. V. 1994. Tracing the trail of Alzheimer's. *Washington Post Health Supplement,* November 29, 9.

DICKERSON, B. J. 1995. Introduction. In *African American single mothers: Understanding their lives and families,* ed. B. J. Dickerson, ix–xxx. Thousand Oaks, CA: Sage.

DIETZ, T. L. 1998. An examination of violence and gender role portrayals in video games: Implications for gender socialization and aggressive behavior. *Sex Roles* 38 (March): 425–42.

Differences within. 2000. *Public Perspective* 11 (May/June): 12.

DIGGS, N. B. 1998. *Steel butterflies: Japanese women and the American experience.* Albany: State University of New York Press.

DILL, K. E., AND J. C. DILL. 1998. Video game violence: A review of the empirical literature. *Aggression and Violent Behavior: A Review Journal* 3 (Winter): 407–28.

DILLER, L. H. 1998. *Running on Ritalin: A physician reflects on children, society, and performance in a pill.* New York: Bantam.

DILLON, P. A., AND R. E. EMERY. 1996. Divorce mediation and resolution of child custody disputes: Long-term effects. *American Journal of Orthopsychiatry* 66 (January): 131–40.

DILMAN, I. 1998. *Love: Its forms, dimensions, and paradoxes.* New York: St. Martin's.

DILWORTH-ANDERSON, P., L. M. BURTON, AND W. L. TURNER. 1993. The importance of values in the study of culturally diverse families. *Family Relations* 42 (July): 238–42.

DILWORTH-ANDERSON, P., S. W. WILLIAMS, AND T. COOPER. 1999. The contexts of experiencing emotional distress among family caregivers to elderly African Americans. *Family Relations* 48 (October): 391–96.

DINNERSTEIN, M., AND R. WEITZ. 1994. Jane Fonda, Barbara Bush and other aging bodies: Femininity and the limits of resistance. *Feminist Issues* 14 (Fall): 3–24.

DION, K., E. BERSCHEID, AND E. WALSTER. 1972. What is beautiful is good. *Journal of Personality and Social Psychology* 24, 285–90.

DION, M. R., S. L. BRAVER, S. A. WOLCHIK, AND I. N. SANDLER. 1997. Alcohol abuse and psychopathic deviance in noncustodial parents as predictors of child-support payment and visitation. *American Journal of Orthopsychiatry* 67 (January): 70–79.

Division of STD Prevention. 1999. *Sexually Transmitted Disease Surveillance, 1998.* Centers for Disease Control and Prevention. www.cdc.gov/nchstp/dstd/Stats_Trends/1998_Surv_Rpt_main_pg.htm (accessed September 2, 2000).

DO, D. D. 1999. *The Vietnamese Americans.* Westport, CT: Greenwood Press.

DOGAR, R. 1997. Here comes the billion-dollar bride. *Working Woman* (May): 33–35, 69–70.

DOKA, K. J., AND M. E. MERTZ. 1988. The meaning and significance of great-grandparenthood. *The Gerontologist* 28 (2): 192–96.

Domestic violence against women and girls. 2000. United Nations Children's Fund. www.unicef-icdc.org/pdf/domestic.pdf (accessed September 22, 2000).

DORF, P. A., J. E. LANDAU, AND M. R. SANDERS. 1996. *Effective family law practice in Maryland.* Eau Claire, WI: National Business Institute.

DORFMAN, L. T., AND C. E. MERTENS. 1990. Kinship relations in retired rural men and women. *Family Relations* 39, 166–73.

DORKENOO, E., AND S. ELWORTHY. 1992. *Female genital mutilation: Proposals for change.* London: Minority Rights Group.

DORRINGTON, C. 1995. Central American refugees in Los Angeles: Adjustment of children and families. In *Understanding Latino families: Scholarship, policy, and practice,* ed. R. E. Zambrana, 107–29. Thousand Oaks, CA: Sage.

DORTCH, S. 1994. What's good for the goose may gag the gander. *American Demographics* (May): 15–16.

DORTCH, S. 1995. Mature, active woman seeks educated, healthy man. *American Demographics* 17 (February): 11–12.

DORTCH, S. 1997. Chinese Yellow Pages. *American Demographics* 19 (October): 39.

DOUGLAS, J. D., AND F. C. ATWELL. 1988. *Love, intimacy, and sex.* Beverly Hills, CA: Sage.

DOWNEY, D. B., J. W. AINSWORTH-DARNELL, AND M. J. DUFUR. 1998. Sex of parent and children's well-being in single-parent households. *Journal of Marriage and the Family* 60 (November): 878–93.

DOWNEY, S. 2000. The moving-van wars. *Newsweek,* February 28, 53.

DOWNS, L. 1994. In Japan where mom knows best. *Washington Post Education Review,* April 3, 16.

DOYLE, A. B., AND D. MARKIEWICZ. 1996. Parents' interpersonal relationships and children's friendships. In *The company they keep: Friendship in childhood and adolescence,* eds. W. M. Bukowski, A. F. Newcomb, and W. W. Hartup, 115–36. New York: Cambridge University Press.

DRAKE, B., AND S. PANDEY. 1996. Understanding the relationships between neighborhood poverty and specific types of child maltreatment. *Child Abuse & Neglect* 20 (November): 1103–18.

DRISCOLL, A. K., G. K. HEARN, V. J. EVANS, K. A. MOORE, B. W. SUGLAND, AND V. CALL. 1999. Nonmarital childbearing among adult women. *Journal of Marriage and the Family* 61 (February): 178–86.

Drug cocktails encourage unsafe sex. 1999. *Baltimore Sun,* September 1, 9a.

DUCK, S. 1998. *Human relationships,* 3rd ed., Thousand Oaks, CA: Sage.

DUGAN, L., D. NAGIN, AND R. ROSENFELD. 1999. Explaining the decline in intimate partner homicide: The effects of changing domesticity, women's status, and domestic violence resources. *Homicide Studies* 3, 187–214.

DUKE, L. 1997. Rape stalks South Africa's children. *Washington Post,* January 14, A1, A26.

DUNBAR, R. 1995. Are you lonesome tonight? *New Scientist* 145, February 11, 26–31.

DUNCAN, C. M. 1999. *Worlds apart: Why poverty persists in rural America.* New Haven, CT: Yale University Press.

DUNEIER, M. 1992. *Slim's table: Race, respectability, and masculinity.* Chicago: University of Chicago Press.

DUNKIN, A. 2000. Adopting? You deserve benefits, too. *Business Week,* February 21, 160.

DUNN, A. 1994. In California, the numbers add up to anxiety. *New York Times,* October 30, 3.

DURAN-AYDINTUG, C., AND K. A. CAUSEY. 1996. Child custody determination: Implications for lesbian mothers. *Journal of Divorce & Remarriage* 25 (1/2): 55–74.

Dutch gays get equal marriage, divorce, adoption rights. 2000. *Baltimore Sun,* September 13, 19A.

DUTTON, D. G., AND S. K. GOLANT. 1995. *The batterer: A psychological profile.* New York: Basic Books.

DUVALL, E. M. 1957. *Family development.* Philadelphia: Lippincott.

DUXBURY, L., C. HIGGINS, AND C. LEE. 1994. Work-family conflict: A comparison by gender, family type, and perceived control. *Journal of Family Issues* 15 (September): 449–66.

EAGLY, A. H., AND W. WOOD. 1999. The origins of sex differences in human behavior. *American Psychologist* 54 (June): 408–23.

EARLE, A. M. 1899. *Child life in colonial days.* New York: Macmillan.

EAST, P. L., AND M. E. FELICE. 1996. *Adolescent pregnancy and parenting: Findings from a racially diverse sample.* Mahwah, NJ: Lawrence Erlbaum Associates.

ECCLES, J. S., J. E. JACOBS, AND R. D. HAROLD. 1990. Gender role stereotypes, expectancy effects, and parents' socialization of gender differences. *Journal of Social Issues* 40 (2): 183–201.

ECKEL, S. 1999. Single mothers, many faces. *American Demographics* 21 (May): 63–66.

ECKLAND, B. K. 1968. Theories of mate selection. *Eugenics Quarterly* 15 (1): 71–84.

EDER, D. with C. C. EVANS AND S. PARKER. 1995. *School talk: Gender and adolescent culture.* New Brunswick, NJ: Rutgers University Press.

EDIN, K., AND L. LEIN. 1997. *Making ends meet: How single mothers survive welfare and low-wage work.* New York: Russell Sage Foundation.

EDMONSTON, B. 1999. The 2000 census challenge. *Population Reference Bureau* 1 (February): 1.

EDWARDS, J. N., AND A. BOOTH. 1994. Sexuality, marriage, and well-being: The middle years. In *Sexuality across the life course,* ed. A. S. Rossi, 233–59. Chicago: University of Chicago Press.

EEOC obtains $1 million for low-wage workers who were sexually harassed at food processing plant. 2000. www.eeoc.gov/press/6-1-00.html (accessed August 26, 2000).

EEOC settles same-sex harassment suit for a half million dollars against major Colorado auto dealership. 2000. www.eeoc.gov/press/8-4-00.html (accessed August 26, 2000).

EGAN, T. 1999. The persistence of polygamy. *New York Times Magazine,* February 24, 51–55.

EHRENREICH, B., AND D. ENGLISH. 1989. Blowing the whistle on the "mommy track." *Ms.* (July/August): 56–58.

EHRENREICH, B., E. HESS, AND G. JACOBS. 1986. *Re-making love: The feminization of sex.* Garden City, NY: Anchor.

EHRHARDT, A. A. 1996. Editorial: Our view of adolescent sexuality—a focus on risk behavior without the developmental context. *American Journal of Public Health* 86 (November): 1523–25.

EITZEN, D. S., AND M. BACA ZINN. 1994. *Social problems,* 6th ed. Boston: Allyn & Bacon.

ELBOW, M., AND J. MAYFIELD. 1991. Mothers of incest victims: Villains, victims, or protectors? *Families in Society* 72 (February): 78–86.

ELIAS, Z., AND T. GOLDMAN. 1999. *How not to embarrass your kids.* New York: Warner.

ELLIOT, P., AND N. MANDELL. 1995. Feminist theories. In *Feminist issues: Race, class, and sexuality,* ed. N. Mandell, 3–31. Scarborough, Ont.: Prentice Hall Canada.

ELLIOTT, D. 1998. Trying to stand on two feet. *Newsweek,* June 29, 48–49.

ELLIS, A. 1963. *The origins and the development of the incest taboo.* New York: Lyle Stuart.

ELLIS, B. J., AND J. GARBER. 2000. Psychosocial antecedents of variation in girls' pubertal timing: Maternal depression, stepfather presence, and marital and family stress. *Child Development* 71 (March): 485–501.

ELLISON, C. G. 1997. Religious involvement and the subjective quality of family life among African Americans. In *Family life in black America*, eds. R. J. Taylor, J. S. Jackson, and L. M. Chatters, 117–31. Thousand Oaks, CA: Sage.

ELO, I. T., R. B. KING, AND F. F. FURSTENBERG, JR. 1999. Adolescent females: Their sexual partners and the fathers of their children. *Journal of Marriage and the Family* 61 (February): 74–84.

ELSHTAIN, J. B. 1988. What's the matter with sex today? *Tikkun: A Bimonthly Jewish Critique of Politics, Culture and Society* 3 (3): 42–43.

ELSHTAIN, J. B., E. AIRD, A. ETZIONI, W. GALSTON, M. GLENDON, M. MINOW, AND A. ROSSI. 1993. *A communitarian position paper on the family.* Washington, DC: Communitarian Network.

ELTAHAWY, M. 2000. Giving wives a way out. *U.S. News & World Report*, March 6, 35.

ENGLANDER, E. K. 1997. *Understanding violence.* Hillsdale, NJ: Lawrence Erlbaum Associates.

ENRICO, D. 1993. The male-order magazine. *Baltimore Sun*, May 13, 10E.

ERICKSON, M. T. 1993. Rethinking Oedipus: An evolutionary perspective of incest avoidance. *American Journal of Psychiatry* 150 (March): 411–16.

ERICKSON, R. J. 1993. Reconceptualizing family work: The effect of emotion work on perceptions of marital quality. *Journal of Marriage and the Family* 55 (November): 888–900.

ESBENSEN, F.-A., D. HUIZINGA, AND S. MENARD. 1999. Family context and criminal victimization in adolescence. *Youth & Society* 31 (December): 168–98.

ESLER, A. 1994. *The Western world: Prehistory to the present*, 3rd ed. Upper Saddle River, NJ: Prentice Hall.

ESPINOSA, P. 1997. The rich tapestry of Hispanic America is virtually invisible on commercial TV. *Chronicle of Higher Education*, October 3, B7–B8.

ESTESS, P. S. 1994. When kids don't leave. *Modern Maturity* (November–December): 56, 58, 90.

ETAUGH, C. E., AND M. B. LISS. 1992. Home, school, and playroom: Training grounds for adult gender roles. *Sex Roles* 26 (3/4): 129–47.

EVANS, C. 2000. Facts about female faculty: 1999–2000 AAUP faculty compensation survey. www.aaup.org/wsalrep.htm (accessed October 15, 2000).

EVANS, K. 2000. *The lost daughters of China: Abandoned girls, their journey to America, and the search for a missing past.* New York: Tarcher/Putnam.

EVANS, S. 2000. The children of divorce. *Washington Post*, May 9, C4.

EVERETT, C., AND S. V. EVERETT. 1994. *Healthy divorce.* San Francisco: Jossey-Bass.

EXTER, T. 1990. Entertaining singles. *American Demographics* (August): 6–7.

EYER, D. E. 1992. *Mother–infant bonding: A scientific fiction.* New Haven, CT: Yale University Press.

Facts about eating disorders. 2000. Harvard Eating Disorders Center. www.hedc.org/info.html (accessed October 20, 2000).

FADER, S. 1985. House power. *Working Woman* (December): 89–91.

FALLER, K. C. 1990. *Understanding child sexual maltreatment.* Beverly Hills, CA: Sage.

FALUDI, S. 1999. *Stiffed: The betrayal of the American man.* New York: Morrow.

Family caregiving in the U.S.: Findings from a national survey. 1997. National Alliance for Caregiving and American Association of Retired Persons. www.hedc.org/info.html (accessed October 20, 2000).

Family relationships. 1999. National Center on Addiction and Substance Abuse at Columbia University. www.casacolumbia.org/info-url 1940/info-url_show.htm?doc_id=20821 (accessed September 24, 2000).

FANSHEL, D., S. J. FINCH, AND J. F. GRUNDY. 1989. Modes of exit from foster family care and adjustment at time of departure of children with unstable life histories. *Child Welfare* 68 (July/August): 391–402.

FARAGHER, J. M. 1986. *Sugar Creek: Life on the Illinois prairie.* New Haven, CT: Yale University Press.

FARBER, B. 1964. *Family: Organization and interaction.* San Francisco: Chandler.

FARBER, B. 1972. *Guardians of virtue: Salem families in 1800.* New York: Basic Books.

FARLEY, N. 1996. A survey of factors contributing to gay and lesbian domestic violence. In *Violence in gay and lesbian domestic partnerships*, eds. C. M. Renzetti and C. H. Miley, 35–42. New York: Harrington Park Press.

FARRELL, D. M. 1997. Jealousy and desire. In *Love Analyzed*, ed. Roger E. Lamb, 165–88. Boulder, CO: Westview.

FASSEL, D. 1991. *Growing up divorced: A road to healing for adult children of divorce.* New York: Pocket Books.

FAUSTO-STERLING, A. 1985. *Myths of gender.* New York: Basic Books.

FEAGIN, J. R. 1997. Old poison in new bottles: The deep roots of modern nativism. In *Immigrants out! The new nativism and the anti-immigrant impulse in the United States*, ed. J. F. Perea, 13–43. New York: New York University Press.

FEAGIN, J. R., AND M. P. SIKES. 1994. *Living with racism: The black middle-class experience.* Boston: Beacon Press.

FEDDERS, C. 1990. In their own words. *Washington Post*, October 6, E5.

Feeling better about the future. 1999. *Newsweek*, June 7, 35.

FEENEY, J., AND P. NOLLER. 1996. *Adult attachment.* Thousand Oaks, CA: Sage.

FEHR, B. 1993. How do I love thee? Let me consult my prototype. In *Individuals in relationships*, ed. S. Duck, 87–120. Thousand Oaks, CA: Sage.

FEIN, E., AND S. SCHNEIDER. 1996. *The rules: Time tested secrets for capturing the heart of Mr. Right.* New York: Warner.

FELDMAN, H. 1931. *Racial factors in American industry.* New York: Harper & Row.

FELDMAN, S. S., E. CAUFFMAN, AND J. J. ARNETT. 2000. The (un)acceptability of betrayal: A study of college students' evaluations of sexual betrayal by a romantic partner and betrayal of a friend's confidence. *Journal of Youth and Adolescence* 29 (August): 499–523.

FELDMANN, L. 1997. The ethics of putting eggs on ice. *Christian Science Monitor*, October 20, 1, 18.

FELDMANN, L., AND G. GOODALE. 1995. Custody cases test attitudes of judges. *Christian Science Monitor*, March 3, 1, 18.

FENG, D., R. GIARRUSSO, V. L. BENGSTON, AND N. FRYE. 1999. Intergenerational transmission of marital quality and marital instability. *Journal of Marriage and the Family* 61 (May): 451–63.

FERNANDEZ, M. I. 1995. Latinas and AIDS: Challenges to HIV prevention efforts. In *Women at risk: Issues in the primary prevention of AIDS*, eds. A. O'Leary and L. S. Jemmott, 159–74. New York: Plenum Press.

FERREE, M. M. 1990. Beyond separate spheres: Feminism and family research. *Journal of Marriage and the Family* 52 (November): 866–84.

FERREIRO, B. W. 1990. Presumption of joint custody: A family policy dilemma. *Family Relations* 39 (October): 420–25.

Fetal alcohol syndrome. 2000. Centers for Disease Control and Prevention. www.cdc.gov/nceh/cddh/fas/fasfact.htm (accessed September 22, 2000).

FIAGOME, C. 1996. Bilingual job, higher pay. *Christian Science Monitor*, January 26, 3.

FIELD, A. 1999. The best old-age home may be at home. *Business Week*, November 22, 180–1.

FIELD, D., AND M. MINKLER. 1993. The importance of family in advanced old age: The family is "forever." In *Family, self, and society: Toward a new agenda for family research*, eds. P. A. Cowan, D. Field, D. A. Hansen, A. Skolnick, and G. E. Swanson, 331–52. Hillsdale, NJ: Lawrence Erlbaum Associates.

FIELD, L. D. 1996. Piecing together the puzzle: Self-concept and group identity in biracial black/white youth. In *The multiracial experience: Racial borders as the new frontier*, ed. M. P. P. Root, 211–26. Thousand Oaks, CA: Sage.

FIESTER, L. 1993. Teen survey sparks concern. *Washington Post*, February 2, 1, 3.

FINCHAM, F. D., AND T. N. BRADBURY. 1987. The assessment of marital quality: A reevaluation. *Journal of Marriage and the Family* 49 (November): 797–809.

FINE, G. A. 1993. Ten lies of ethnography: Moral dilemmas of field research. *Journal of Contemporary Ethnography* 22 (October): 267–94.

FINE, M. A., M. COLEMAN, AND L. H. GANONG. 1999. A social constructionist multi-method approach to understanding the stepparent role. In *Coping with divorce, single parenting, and remarriage: A risk and resiliency perspective*, ed. E. M. Hetherington, 273–94. Mahwah, NJ: Lawrence Erlbaum Associates.

FINE, M. A., AND D. A. FINE. 1994. An examination and evaluation of recent changes in divorce laws in five western countries: The critical role of values. *Journal of Marriage and the Family* 56 (May): 249–63.

FINEMAN, M. 1991. *The illusion of equality: The rhetoric and reality of divorce reform.* Chicago: University of Chicago Press.

FINGERMAN, K. L. 1998. The good, the bad, and the worrisome: Emotional complexities in grandparents' experiences with individual grandchildren. *Family Relations* 47 (October): 403–14.

FINK, D. 1992. *Agrarian women: Wives and mothers in rural Nebraska, 1880–1940.* Chapel Hill: University of North Carolina Press.

FINKE, N. 1994. Trophy husbands. *Working Woman* (April): 37, 39, 41, 88, 90–91.

FINKEL, J., AND P. ROBERTS. 1994. *The incomes of noncustodial fathers.* Washington, DC: Center for Law and Social Policy.

FINKELHOR, D., AND R. ORMROD. 2000. *Characteristics of crimes against juveniles.* Washington, DC: U.S. Department of Justice, Office of Justice Programs, Office of Juvenile Justice and Delinquency Prevention.

1st woman prepares to lead crew into space. 1999. *Baltimore Sun*, June 18, 4a.

FISCHMAN, J. 1988. Stepdaughter wars. *Psychology Today*, (November): 38–41.

FISHEL, E. 1987. Baby makes three. *Parents* (September): 73–76, 78.

FISHER, C. S., M. HOUT, M. S. JANKOWSKI, S. R. LUCAS, A. SWIDLER, AND K. VOSS. 1996. *Inequality by design: Cracking the bell curve myth.* Princeton, NJ: Princeton University Press.

FISHER, H. 1992. *Anatomy of love: The natural history of monogamy, adultery, and divorce.* New York: Norton.

FISHER, H. E. 1993. After all, maybe it's . . . biology. *Psychology Today* (March/April): 40–45, 82.

FISHMAN, B., AND B. HAMEL. 1981. From nuclear to stepfamily ideology: A stressful change. *Alternative Lifestyles* 4, 181–204.

FITZPATRICK, M. A., AND A. MULAC. 1995. Relating to spouse and stranger: Gender-preferential language use. In *Gender, power, and communication in human relationships*, eds. P. J. Kalbfleisch and M. J. Cody, 213–31. Hillsdale, NJ: Lawrence Erlbaum Associates.

FLANDERS, S. 1996. The benefits of marriage. *The Public Interest* 124 (Summer): 80–86.

FLETCHER, A. C., L. STEINBERG, AND E. B. SELLERS. 1999. Adolescents' well-being as a function of perceived interparental consistency. *Journal of Marriage and the Family* 61 (August): 599–610.

FLETCHER, M. A. 1994. Blacks pessimistic about children's future, poll finds. *Baltimore Sun*, May 27, 13A.

FLETCHER, M. A. 1997. Latinos see signs of hope as middle class expands. *Washington Post*, July 22, A8.

FLORES, B. R. 1994. *Chiquita's cocoon*. New York: Villard.

FLYNN, C. P. 1990. Relationship violence by women: Issues and implications. *Family Relations* 39 (April): 194–97.

FLYNN, C. P. 1994. Regional differences in attitudes toward corporal punishment. *Journal of Marriage and the Family* 56 (May): 314–24.

FOGEL, C. I., AND N. F. WOODS. 1995. Midlife women's health. In *Women's health care: A comprehensive handbook*, eds. C. I. Fogel and N. F. Woods, 79–100. Thousand Oaks, CA: Sage.

FOLBRE, N. 1994. *Who pays for the kids? Gender and the structures of constraint*. New York: Routledge.

FOLK, K. F., J. W. GRAHAM, AND A. H. BELLER. 1992. Child support and remarriage: Implications for the economic well-being of children. *Journal of Family Issues* 13, 142–57.

FOLSE, K. A. 1997. Hispanic fathers and the child support enforcement experience. *Journal of Multicultural Social Work* 6 (3/4): 139–58.

FONG, R. 1994. Family preservation: Making it work for Asians. *Child Welfare* 73 (July/August): 331–41.

FORD, C., AND E. BEACH. 1972. *Patterns of sexual behavior*. New York: Harper & Row. (Originally published 1951.)

FORD, P. 1999. Europe puts mute on kid ads. *Christian Science Monitor*, December 16, 1, 10.

FORD, P. 2000. Mummy and daddy spare rod—or go to court. *Christian Science Monitor*, February 2, 1, 10.

FOREHAND, R., B. NEIGHBORS, D. DEVINE, AND L. ARMISTEAD. 1994. Interparental conflict and parental divorce: The individual, relative, and interactive effects on adolescents across four years. *Family Relations* 43 (October): 387–93.

For-profit orphanages eligible for federal funds. 1997. *Baltimore Sun*, May 4, 11A.

FORWARD, S. 1990. *Toxic parents: Overcoming their hurtful legacy and reclaiming your life*. New York: Bantam.

FOSHEE, V. A., K. E. BAUMAN, AND G. F. LINDER. 1999. Family violence and the perpetuation of adolescent dating violence: Examining social learning and social control processes. *Journal of Marriage and the Family* 61 (May): 331–42.

FOSSETT, M. A., AND K. J. KIECOLT. 1993. Mate availability and family structure among African Americans in U.S. metropolitan areas. *Journal of Marriage and the Family* 55 (May): 288–302.

FOST, D. 1996. Child-free with an attitude. *American Demographics* 18 (April): 15–16.

FOX, G. L., C. BRUCE, AND T. COMBS-ORME. 2000. Parenting expectations and concerns of fathers and mothers of newborn infants. *Family Relations* 49 (April): 123–31.

FRAME, M. W., AND C. L. SHEHAN. 1994. Work and well-being in the two-person career: Relocation stress and coping among clergy husbands and wives. *Family Relations* 43 (April): 196–205.

FRANCIS, D. R. 2000a. The unsolved mystery of the gilded economy. *Christian Science Monitor*, June 30, 1, 9.

FRANCIS, D. R. 2000b. Will "marriage penalty" relief be left at the altar? *Christian Science Monitor*, May 6, 17.

FRANK, M., AND E. F. ZIGLER. 1996. Family leave: A developmental perspective. In *Children, families, and government: Preparing for the twenty-first century*, eds. E. F. Zigler, S. L. Kagan, and N. W. Hall, 117–31. New York: Cambridge University Press.

FRANZBLAU, S. H. 1999. Historicizing attachment theory: Binding the ties that bind. *Feminism & Psychology* 9 (February): 22–31.

FRAZIER, E. F. 1937. The impact of urban civilization upon Negro family life. *American Sociological Review* 2 (October): 609–18.

FRAZIER, E. F. 1939. *The Negro family in the United States*. Chicago: University of Chicago Press.

FREEDMAN, D. C. 1986. Wife, widow, woman: Roles of an anthropologist in a Transylvanian village. In *Women in the field: Anthropological experiences*, 2nd ed., ed. P. Golde, 333–58. Berkeley: University of California Press.

FREEDMAN, D. S., W. H. DIETZ, S. R. SRINIVASAN, AND G. S. BERENSON. 1999. The relation of overweight to cardiovascular risk factors among children and adolescents: The Bogalusa heart study. *Pediatrics* 103 (June): 1175–82.

FREEMAN, E. W., AND K. RICKELS. 1993. *Early childbearing: Perspectives of black adolescents on pregnancy, abortion, and contraception*. Beverly Hills, CA: Sage.

FREEMAN, R. B., AND W. M. RODGERS III. 1999. Area economic conditions and the labor market outcomes of young men in the 1990s expansion. *NBER Working Paper No. W7073*. papers.nber.org/papers/W7073 (accessed October 16, 2000).

FREIBERG, K. 1996. Rural Singles Directory strikes a match! *Farm Journal* 129 (January): 8.

FRENKIEL, N. 1990. Shape up or ship out. *Baltimore Sun*, May 2, 1F, 8F.

FRIED, M. 1998. *Taking time: Parental leave policy and corporate culture*. Philadelphia: Temple University Press.

FRIEDAN, B. 1963. *The feminine mystique*. New York: Norton.

FRIEDAN, B. 1993. *The fountain of age*. New York: Simon & Schuster.

FROMM, E. 1956. *The art of loving*. New York: Bantam.

FRUG, M. J. 1992. *Postmodern legal feminism*. New York: Routledge.

FUKUYAMA, F. 1993. Immigrants and family values. *Commentary* 95 (May): 26–32.

FUKUYAMA, F. 1994. Immigrants and family values. In *Arguing immigration: The debate over the changing face of America*, ed. N. Mills, 151–68. New York: Touchstone.

FULLER, B., AND S. L. KAGAN. 2000. Remember the children: Mothers balance work and child care under welfare reform. www-gse.berkeley.edu/research/PACE/PDF/GUPExSum.pdf (accessed September 28, 2000).

FULLILOVE, R. E., W. BARKSDALE, AND M. T. FULLILOVE. 1994. Teens talk sex: Can we talk back? In *Sexual cultures and the construction of adolescent identities*, ed. J. M. Irvine, 31–32. Philadelphia: Temple University Press.

FULTZ, O. 1991. 'Roid rage. *American Health*, May, 60–64.

FUNDERBURG, L. 1994. *Black, white, other*. New York: Morrow.

FURGATCH, V. 1995. It's time to remove all barriers to adoption across racial lines. *Christian Science Monitor*, September 12, 19.

FURSTENBERG, F. F. 1991. As the pendulum swings: Teenage childbearing and social concern. *Family Relations* 40 (April): 127–38.

FURSTENBERG, F. F., JR., AND J. O. TEITLER. 1994. Reconsidering the effects of marital disruption: What happens to children of divorce in early adulthood? *Journal of Family Issues* 15 (June): 173–90.

FURSTENBERG, F. F., JR., ET AL. 1999. *Managing to make it: Urban families and adolescent success*. Chicago: University of Chicago Press.

FURUKAWA, S. 1994. *The diverse living arrangements of children: Summer 1991*. U.S. Census Bureau, Current Population Reports, Series P70, No. 38. Washington, DC: U.S. Government Printing Office.

GABARDI, L., AND L. A. ROSEN. 1992. Intimate relationships: College students from divorced and intact families. In *Divorce and the next generation: Effects on young adults' patterns of intimacy and expectations for marriage*, ed. C. Everett, 25–56. New York: Haworth Press.

GABRIEL, T. 1997. Pack dating: For a good time, call a crowd. *New York Times*, January 5, 22.

GAGE, A. 1994. Marriage has its advantages, but taxes aren't one of them. *Washington Post*, March 13, H4.

GAITER, L. 1994. The revolt of the black bourgeoisie. *New York Times Magazine*, June 26, 42–43.

GALBRAITH, J. K. 1998. *Created unequal: The crisis in American pay*. New York: Free Press.

GALINSKY, E. 1999. *Ask the children: What American children really think about working parents*. New York: Morrow.

GALLAGHER, M. 1996. *The abolition of marriage: How we destroy lasting love*. Washington, DC: Regnery.

GALLAGHER, S. K., AND N. GERSTEL. 1993. Kinkeeping and friend keeping among older women: The effect of marriage. *The Gerontologist* 33 (5): 675–81.

GALLUP, G., JR., AND F. NEWPORT. 1990. Virtually all adults want children, but many of the reasons are intangible. *Gallup Poll Monthly* (June): 8–22.

GALLUP, G., JR., AND F. NEWPORT. 1991. For first time, more Americans approve of interracial marriage than disapprove. *Gallup Poll Monthly* (August): 60–62.

GALSTON, W. A. 1996. Divorce American style. *The Public Interest* (Summer): 12–26.

GAMACHE, S. J. 1997. Confronting nuclear family bias in stepfamily research. *Marriage & Family Review* 26 (1/2): 41–69.

GAMACHE, D. 1990. Domination and control: The social context of dating violence. In *Dating Violence: Young women in danger*, ed. B. Levy, 69–118. Seattle: Seal Press.

GAMBOA, E. 1995. "International medical graduates are tested every step of the way." In *Filipino American lives*, ed. Y. L. Espiritu, 127–42. Philadelphia: Temple University Press.

GANONG, L. H., AND M. COLEMAN. 1989. Preparing for remarriage: Anticipating the issues, seeking solutions. *Family Relations* 38 (January): 28–33.

GANONG, L. H., AND M. COLEMAN. 1992. Gender differences in self and future partner expectations. *Journal of Family Issues* 13, 55–64.

GANONG, L. H., AND M. COLEMAN. 1994. *Remarried family relationships.* Thousand Oaks, CA: Sage.

GANONG, L. H., AND M. COLEMAN. 1997. How society views stepfamilies. *Marriage & Family Review* 26 (1/2): 85–106.

GANONG, L. H., AND M. COLEMAN. 1999. *Changing families, changing responsibilities: Family obligations following divorce and remarriage.* Mahwah, NJ: Lawrence Erlbaum Associates.

GANONG, L., M. COLEMAN, AND M. FINE. 1995. Remarriage and stepfamilies. In *Research and theory in family science,* eds. R. D. Day, K. R. Gilbert, B. H. Settles, and W. R. Burr, 287–303. Pacific Grove, CA: Brooks/Cole.

GANS, H. J. 1971. The uses of poverty: The poor pay all. *Social Policy* (July/August): 78–81.

GANS, H. J. 1979. *Deciding what's news: A study of CBS Evening News, NBC Nightly News, Newsweek and Time.* New York: Pantheon.

GANZINI, L. H. D. NELSON, T. A. SCHMIDT, D. F. KRAEMER, M. A. DELORIT, AND M. A. LEE. 2000. Physicians' experiences with the Oregon Death with Dignity Act. *New England Journal of Medicine* 342 (February): 557–63.

GAOUETTE, N. 1998. When a college degree means a job serving tea. *Christian Science Monitor,* March 23, B4.

GARBARINO, J. 1989. The incidence and prevalence of child maltreatment. In *Family Violence,* eds. L. Ohlin and M. Tonry, 219–61. Chicago: University of Chicago Press.

GARBARINO, J. 1999. *Lost boys: Why our sons turn violent and how we can save them.* New York: Free Press.

GARCIA, M. T. 1980. La familia: The Mexican immigrant family, 1900–1930. In *Work, family, sex roles, language,* eds. M. Barrera, A. Camarillo, and F. Hernandez, 117–40. Berkeley, CA: Tonatiua-Quinto Sol International.

GARDNER, H. 1996. The concept of family: Perceptions of children in family foster care. *Child Welfare* 75 (March–April): 161–82.

GARDNER, M. 1994. A hidden fact of life for teens: Dating violence. *Christian Science Monitor,* June 30, 12.

GARDNER, M. 1995. Full-time dads launch nationwide group. *Christian Science Monitor,* August 29, 1, 12.

GARDNER, M. 1995. Parents who work shifts seek off-hours care. *Christian Science Monitor,* June 22, 6,12.

GARDNER, M. 1999a. Beyond Mr. Mom. *Christian Science Monitor,* December 22, 15–16.

GARDNER, M. 1999b. Body by Madison Avenue. *Christian Science Monitor,* November 24, 18–19.

GARDNER, M. 2000. Keeping Dad as part of the family picture. *Christian Science Monitor,* June 14, 13.

GARFINKEL, I., S. S. McLANAHAN, AND P. K. ROBINS, eds. 1994. *Child support and child well-being.* Washington, DC: Urban Institute Press.

GARLAND, E. 1999. An anthropologist learns the value of fear. *Chronicle of Higher Education,* May 7, B4–B5.

GARLAND, S. B. 2000. Work at home? First, get real. *Business Week,* September 18, 112, 116.

GARROD, A., AND C. LARIMORE, eds. 1997. *First person, first peoples: Native American college graduates tell their life stories.* Ithaca, NY: Cornell University Press.

GARRY, E. M. 1997. *Responsible fatherhood.* OJJDP Fact Sheet #73. U.S. Department of Justice, Office of Justice Programs, Office of Juvenile Justice and Delinquency Prevention, December.

GASKINS, P. F., ED. 1999. *What are you? Voices of mixed-race young people.* New York: Henry Holt and Company.

GASSER, R. D., AND C. M. TAYLOR. 1990. Role adjustment of single parent fathers with dependent children. *Family Relations* 40 (July): 397–400.

GATELY, D., AND A. I. SCHWEBEL. 1992. Favorable outcomes in children after parental divorce. In *Divorce and the next generation: Effects on young adults' patterns of intimacy and expectations for marriage,* ed. C. Everett, 57–78. New York: Haworth Press.

GATTAI, F. B., AND T. MUSATTI. 1999. Grandmothers' involvement in grandchildren's care: Attitudes, feelings, and emotions. *Family Relations* 48 (January): 35–42.

GAUDIN, J. M., JR., N. A. POLANSKY, A. C. KILPATRICK, AND P. SHILTON. 1996. Family functioning in neglectful families. *Child Abuse & Neglect* 20 (April): 363–77.

GAULIN, S. J. C., AND J. S. BOSTER. 1990. Dowry as female competition. *American Anthropologist* 92 (December): 994–1005.

GAYLIN, W. 1986. *Rediscovering love.* New York: Viking.

GAYLIN, W. 1992. *The male ego.* New York: Viking.

GECAS, V., AND M. A. SEFF. 1991. Families and adolescents: A review of the 1980s. In *Contemporary families: Looking forward, looking back,* ed. A. Booth, 208–25. Minneapolis, MN: National Council on Family Relations.

GEEASLER, M. J., L. L. DANNISON, AND C. J. EDLUND. 1995. Sexuality education of young children: Parental concerns. *Family Relations* 44 (April): 184–88.

GELLES, R. J. 1995. *Contemporary families: A sociological view.* Thousand Oaks, CA: Sage.

GELLES, R. J. 1997. *Intimate violence in families,* 3rd ed. Thousand Oaks, CA: Sage.

GELLES, R. J., AND C. P. CORNELL. 1990. *Intimate violence in families,* 2nd ed. Thousand Oaks, CA: Sage.

GELLES, R. J., AND M. A. STRAUS. 1988. *Intimate violence.* New York: Simon & Schuster.

GENOVESE, E. D. 1981. Husbands and fathers, wives and mothers, during slavery. In *Family life in America: 1620–2000,* eds. M. Albin and D. Cavallo, 237–51. St. James, NY: Revisionary Press.

GEORGE, R. M., AND B. J. LEE. 1997. Abuse and neglect of the children. In *Kids having kids: Economic costs and social consequences of teen pregnancy,* ed. R. A. Maynard, 205–30. Washington, DC: Urban Institute Press.

GERAGHTY, M. 1997. Hazing incidents at sororities alarm colleges. *Chronicle of Higher Education,* June 20, A37–A38.

GERBNER, G. 1993. Women and minorities on television. A report to the Screen Actors Guild and the American Federation of Radio and Television Artists. Mimeo. June.

GERDES, K., M. NAPOLI, C. PATTEA, AND E. SEGAL. 1998. The impact of Indian gaming on economic development. *Journal of Poverty* 4 (2): 17–30.

GERSON, K. 1997. The social construction of fatherhood. In *Contemporary parenting: Challenges and issues,* ed. T. Arendell, 119–53. Thousand Oaks, CA: Sage.

GERSTEL, N. 1987. Divorce and stigma. *Social Problems* 34 (April): 172–86.

GERSTEL, N., AND S. K. GALLAGHER. 1993. Kinkeeping and distress: Gender, recipients of care, and work-family conflict. *Journal of Marriage and the Family* 55 (August): 598–607.

GIBBS, J., AND A. HINES. 1992. Negotiating ethnic identity: Issues for black-white biracial adolescents. In *Racially mixed people in America,* ed. M. P. P. Root, 223–38. Thousand Oaks, CA: Sage.

GIBBS, N., J. JOHNSON, M. LUDTKE, AND M. RILEY. 1990. Shameful bequests to the next generation. *Time,* October 8, 42–46.

GIBSON, J. T. 1991. Disciplining toddlers. *Parents* (May): 190.

GILBERT, E. 1994. Pregnancy discrimination alert. *Working Mother* (June): 34–35.

GILES-SIMS, J., AND M. CROSBIE-BURNETT. 1989. Adolescent power in stepfather families: A test of normative-resource theory. *Journal of Marriage and the Family* 51 (November): 1065–78.

GILES-SIMS, J., M. A. STRAUS, AND D. B. SUGARMAN. 1995. Child, maternal, and family characteristics associated with spanking. *Family Relations* 44 (April): 170–76.

GILLIGAN, C. 1982. *In a different voice: Psychological theory and women's development.* Cambridge, MA: Harvard University Press.

GILLIS, J. R. 1996. *A world of their own making: Myth, ritual, and the quest for family values.* New York: Basic Books.

GILMAN, E. 1994. Matching the elderly with foster families. *New York Times,* February 20, D8.

GJERDINGEN, D. K., D. G. FROBERG, K. M. CHALONER, AND P. M. McGOVERN. 1993. Changes in women's physical health during the first postpartum year. *Archives of Family Medicine* 2 (March): 277–83.

GLADSTONE, J. W. 1989. Perceived changes in grandmother–grandchild relations following a child's separation or divorce. *The Gerontologist* 28 (1): 66–72.

GLASSMAN, J. E. 1997. The corporate welfare queens. *U.S. News & World Report,* May 19, 53.

GLAZER, N., AND D. P. MOYNIHAN. 1963. *Beyond the melting pot.* Cambridge, MA: MIT Press and Harvard University Press.

GLENN, E. N., WITH S. G. H. YAP. 1994. Chinese American families. In *Minority families in the United States: A multicultural perspective,* ed. R. L. Taylor, 115–45. Upper Saddle River, NJ: Prentice Hall.

GLENN, N. D. 1982. Interreligious marriage in the United States: Patterns and recent trends. *Journal of Marriage and the Family* 52: 818–31.

GLENN, N. D. 1991. Quantitative research on marital quality in the 1980s. In *Contemporary families: Looking forward, looking back,* ed. A. Booth, 28–41. Minneapolis, MN: National Council on Family Relations.

GLENN, N. D. 1996. Values, attitudes, and the state of American marriage. In *Promises to keep: Decline and renewal of marriage in America,* eds. D. Popenoe, J. B. Elshtain, and D. Blankenhorn, 15–33. Lanham, MD: Rowman & Littlefield.

GLENN, N. D. 1997a. A critique of twenty family and marriage and the family textbooks. *Family Relations* 46 (July): 197–211.

GLENN, N. D. 1997b. A reconsideration of the effect of no-fault divorce on divorce rates. *Journal of Marriage and the Family* 59 (November): 1023–30.

GLENN, N. D., AND K. B. KRAMER. 1987. The marriages and divorces of the children of divorce. *Journal of Marriage and the Family* 49 (November): 811–25.

GLENN, N. D., AND B. A. SHELTON. 1985. Regional differences in divorce in the United States. *Journal of Marriage and the Family* 47: 641–52.

Glenn's health in space in line with colleagues'. 2000. *Baltimore Sun,* January 29, 3A.

GLENWICK, D. S., AND J. D. MOWREY. 1986. When parent becomes peer: Loss of intergenerational boundaries in single parent families. *Family Relations* 35 (January): 57–62.

GLICK, P. C. 1984. Marriage, divorce and living arrangements: Prospective changes. *Journal of Family Issues* 5 (March): 7–26.

GODDARD, H. W. 1994. *Principles of parenting.* Auburn, AL: Auburn University, Department of Family and Child Development.

GOETTING, A. 1982. The six stations of remarriage: Developmental tasks of remarriage after divorce. *Family Relations* 31 (April): 231–22.

GOETTING, A. 1999. *Getting out: Life stories of women who left abusive men.* New York: Columbia University Press.

GOLBY, B. J., AND I. BRETHERTON. 1998. Resilience in postdivorce mother–child relationships. In *The dynamics of resilient families,* eds. H. I. McCubbin, E. A. Thompson, A. I. Thompson, and J. A. Futrell, 237–65. Thousand Oaks, CA: Sage.

GOLD, L. 1992. *Between love and hate: A guide to civilized divorce.* New York: Plenum Press.

GOLD, S. J. 1993. Migration and family adjustment: Continuity and change among Vietnamese in the United States. In *Family ethnicity: Strength in diversity,* ed. H. P. McAdoo, 306–16. Thousand Oaks, CA: Sage.

GOLDBERG, H. 1987. *The inner male: Overcoming roadblocks to intimacy.* New York: New American Library.

GOLDBERG, S. 1983. Parent–infant bonding: Another look. *Child Development* 54, 1355–82.

GOLDIN, C. 1997. Exploring the "present through the past": Career and family across the last century. *American Economic Review* 87 (May): 396–99.

GOLDSCHEIDER, F. K., AND J. DAVANZO. 1989. Pathways to independent living in early adulthood: Marriage, semiautonomy, and premarital residential independence. *Demography* 26 (November): 597–614.

GOLDSCHEIDER, F. K., AND C. GOLDSCHEIDER. 1993. *Leaving home before marriage: Ethnicity, familism, and generational relationships.* Madison: University of Wisconsin Press.

GOLDSCHEIDER, F. K., AND C. GOLDSCHEIDER. 1998. The effects of childhood family structure on leaving and returning home. *Journal of Marriage and the Family* 60 (August): 745–56.

GOLDSCHEIDER, F. K., AND L. LAWTON. 1998. Family experiences and the erosion of support for intergenerational coresidence. *Journal of Marriage and the Family* 60 (August): 623–32.

GOLDSCHEIDER, F. K., AND L. J. WAITE. 1986. Sex differences in the entry into marriage. *American Journal of Sociology* 92 (July): 91–109.

GOLDSTEIN, A. 1998. Legal procedure, hostile climate. *Washington Post,* January 22, A1, A8.

GOLOMBOK, S., AND R. FIVUSH. 1994. *Gender development.* New York: Cambridge University Press.

GOLOMBOK, S., AND F. TASKER. 1996. Do parents influence the sexual orientation of their children? Findings from a longitudinal study of lesbian families. *Developmental Psychology* 32 (1): 3–11.

GOMEZ, M. 1993. Breaking the cycle. *Hispanic* (August): 12.

GONYEA, J. G. 1994. The paradox of the advantaged elder and the feminization of poverty. *Social Work* 39 (January): 35–41.

GONZÁLEZ, R. 1996. *Muy macho: Latino men confront their manhood.* New York: Anchor.

GOODE, E. 1990. *Deviant behavior,* 3rd ed. Upper Saddle River, NJ: Prentice Hall.

GOODE, E., ET AL. 1994. Till death do them part? *U.S. News & World Report,* July 4, 24–28.

GOODE, W. J. 1963. *World revolution and family patterns.* New York: Free Press.

GOODMAN, E. 1992. A woman's place is in the paper. *Baltimore Sun,* April 7, 15A.

GOODMAN, E. 1993. A pill to make abortions private. *Baltimore Sun,* March 2, 11A.

GOODMAN, E. 1999. Equal pay an issue, again. *Baltimore Sun,* March 18, 15A.

GOODMAN, M., H. K. BLACK, AND R. L. RUBINSTEIN. 1996. Paternal bereavement in older men. *Omega* 33 (4): 303–22.

GOODSMITH, L. 2000. Taliban's yoke crushes women. *Baltimore Sun,* June 11, 1C, 4C.

GOPNIK, A. A., N. MELTZOFF, AND P. K. KUHL. 1999. *The scientist in the crib: Minds, brains, and how children learn.* New York: Morrow.

GORDON, L. H. 1993. Intimacy: The art of working out your relationships. *Psychology Today* 26 (September/October): 40–43, 79–82.

GORDY, M. 2000. A call to fight forced labor. *Parade Magazine,* February 20, 4–5.

GORMAN, C. 1995. Trapped in the body of a man? *Time,* November 13, 94–95.

GORMAN, E. H. 2000. Marriage and money. *Work & Occupations* 27 (February): 64–88.

GORMAN, J. C. 1998. Parenting attitudes and practices of immigrant Chinese mothers of adolescents. *Family Relations* 47 (January): 73–80.

GOSE, B. 1994. Spending time on the reservation. *Chronicle of Higher Education,* August 10, A30–A31.

GOSE, B. 1996. Public debate over a private choice. *Chronicle of Higher Education,* May 10, A45, A47.

GOTTLIEB, L. N., A. LANG, AND R. AMSEL. 1996. The long-term effects of grief on marital intimacy following an infant's death. *Omega* 33 (1): 1–19.

GOTTLIEB, S. 1995. Canada's health-care woes. *Christian Science Monitor,* May 31, 19.

GOTTMAN, J. M. 1982. Emotional responsiveness in marital conversations. *Journal of Communication* 32, 108–20.

GOTTMAN, J. M. 1994. *What predicts divorce? The relationships between marital processes and marital outcome.* Hillsdale, NJ: Lawrence Erlbaum Associates.

GOTTMAN, J. M., J. COAN, S. CARRERE, AND C. SWANSON. 1998. Predicting marital happiness and stability from newlywed interactions. *Journal of Marriage and the Family* 60 (February): 5–22.

GOULD, D. C., R. PETTY, AND H. S. JACOBS. 2000. For and against: The male menopause—does it exist? *British Medical Journal* 320 (March): 858–60.

GOULTER, B., AND J. MINNINGER. 1993. *The father-daughter dance: Insight, inspiration, and understanding for every woman and her father.* New York: Putnam's.

GOVE, W. R. 1984. Gender differences in mental and physical illness: The effects of fixed roles and nurturant roles. *Social Science and Medicine* 19, 77–84.

GOYETTE, K., AND Y. XIE. 1999. The intersection of immigration and gender: Labor force outcomes of immigrant women scientists. *Social Science Quarterly* 80 (June): 395–408.

GRADMAN, T. J. 1994. Masculine identity from work to retirement. In *Older men's lives,* ed. E. H. Thompson, Jr., 104–21. Thousand Oaks, CA: Sage.

GRADY, D. 1996. How to coax new life. *Time,* Special Issue (Fall): 37–39.

GRAHAM, E. 1996. Craving closer ties, strangers come together as family. *Wall Street Journal,* March 4, B1, B5.

GRAHAM, J. W., A. H. BELLER, AND P. M. HERNANDEZ. 1994. The effects of child support on educational attainment. In *Child support and child well-being,* eds. I. Garfinkel, S. S. McLanahan,

and P. K. Robins, 317–54. Washington, DC: Urban Institute Press.

GRAHAM, L. O. 1996. *Member of the club: Reflections on life in a racially polarized world.* New York: HarperCollins.

GRALL, T. 2000. Child support for custodial mothers and fathers, U.S. Census Bureau. www.census.gov/prod/2000pubs/p60-212.pdf (accessed October 20, 2000).

GRAY, H. M., AND V. FOSHEE. 1997. Adolescent dating violence: Differences between one-sided and mutually violent profiles. *Journal of Interpersonal Violence* 12 (February): 126–41.

GRAY, J. 1992. *Men are from Mars, women are from Venus.* New York: HarperCollins.

GRAY, M. R., AND L. STEINBERG. 1999. Unpacking authoritative parenting: Reassessing a multidimensional construct. *Journal of Marriage and the Family* 61 (August): 574–87.

GREELEY, A. 1994. Marital infidelity. *Society* (May/June): 9–13.

GREENBERG, J., AND M. RUHLEN. 1992. Linguistic origins of Native Americans. *Scientific American* 267: 94.

GREENBLATT, C. S. 1983. The salience of sexuality in the early years of marriage. *Journal of Marriage and the Family* 45 (May): 289–99.

GREENE, D. L. 2000. Tribe at war against alcohol. *Baltimore Sun,* April 17, 1A, 4A.

GREENFELD, L. A., AND S. K. SMITH. 1999. *American Indians and crime.* Washington, DC: U.S. Department of Justice, Office of Justice Programs.

GREENFELD, L. A., AND T. L. SNELL. 1999. *Women offenders.* Washington, DC: U.S. Department of Justice, Office of Justice Programs, Bureau of Justice Statistics.

GREENSTEIN, T. N. 1990. Marital disruption and the employment of married women. *Journal of Marriage and the Family* 52 (August): 657–76.

GREENSTEIN, T. N. 2000. Economic dependence, gender, and the division of labor in the home: A replication and extension. *Journal of Marriage and the Family* 62 (May): 322–35.

GREENWALD, E., AND H. LEITENBERG. 1989. Long-term effects of sexual experiences with siblings and nonsiblings during childhood. *Archives of Sexual Behavior* 18: 389–400.

GREENWALD, J. 1996. Barbie boots up. *Time,* November 11, 48–50.

GREER, G. 1999. *The whole woman.* New York: Knopf.

GREIDER, L. 2000. How not to be a monster-in-law. *Modern Maturity* (March/April): 57–59.

GREIF, G. L. 1990. *The daddy track and the single father.* Lexington, MA: Lexington Books.

GRIFFIN, M. D. 1995. African American households and community effects on economic deprivation. In *American families: Issues in race and ethnicity,* ed. C. K. Jacobson, 301–22. New York: Garland.

GRIMM-THOMAS, K., AND M. PERRY-JENKINS. 1994. All in a day's work: Job experiences, self-esteem, and fathering in working-class families. *Family Relations* 43 (April): 174–81.

GRIMSLEY, K. D. 2000. Panel asks why women still earn less. *Washington Post,* June 9, E3.

GRISWOLD, R. L. 1993. *Fatherhood in America: A history.* New York: Basic Books.

GROSS, J., WITH R. SMOTHERS. 1994. In prom dispute, a town's race divisions emerge. *New York Times,* August 15, A10.

GROVE, L. 2000. The reliable source. *Washington Post,* February 15, C3.

GROVES, E. R. 1928. *The marriage crisis.* New York: Longmans, Green.

GRUSON, L. 1985. Jewish singles groups play matchmakers to preserve the future of Judaism. *New York Times,* April 1, B1, B2.

GRZYWACZ, J. G., AND N. F. MARKS. 2000. Family, work, work-family spillover, and problem drinking during midlife. *Journal of Marriage and the Family* 62 (May): 336–48.

GUBERMAN, N., P. MAHEU, AND C. MAILLÉ. 1992. Women as family caregivers: Why do they care? *The Gerontologist* 32 (5): 607–17.

GUEST, J. 1988. *The mythic family.* Minneapolis, MN: Milkweed.

GUPTA, G. R. 1979. Love, arranged marriage and the Indian social structure. In *Cross-cultural perspectives of mate-selection and marriage,* ed. G. Kurian, 169–79. Westport, CT: Greenwood Press.

GUPTA, S. 1999. The effects of transitions in marital status on men's performance of housework. *Journal of Marriage and the Family* 61 (August): 700–11.

GUTMAN, H. 1976. The black family in slavery and freedom, 1750–1925. New York: Pantheon.

GUTMAN, H. G. 1983. Persistent myths about the Afro-American family. In *The American family in socio-historical perspective,* 3rd ed., ed. M. Gordon, 459–81. New York: St. Martin's.

GUTNER, T. 2000. Getting your fair share in a divorce. *Business Week,* May 29, 250.

GWARTNEY-GIBBS, P. A. 1986. The institutionalization of premarital cohabitation: Estimates from marriage license applications, 1970 and 1980. *Journal of Marriage and the Family* 48 (May): 423–34.

HAAG, P. S. 1999. *Voices of a generation: Teenage girls on sex, school, and self.* Washington, DC: American Association of University Women.

HAAN, M. N., L. SHEMANSKI, W. J. JAGUST, T. A. MANOLIO, AND L. KULLER. 1999. The role of APOE E4 in modulating effects of other risk factors for cognitive decline in elderly persons. *JAMA* 282, July 7, 40–46.

HAFFNER, D. W. 1993. Toward a new paradigm on adolescent sexual health. *SIECUS Report* 21 (2): 26–30.

HAFFNER, D. W. 1997. What's wrong with abstinence-only sexuality education programs? *SIECUS Report* 25 (April/May): 9–13.

HAFFNER, D. W. 1999. Facing facts: Sexual health for American adolescents. *Human Development & Family Life Bulletin* 4 (Winter): 1–3.

HAHN, B. A. 1993. Marital status and women's health: The effect of economic marital acquisitions. *Journal of Marriage and the Family* 55 (May): 495–504.

HAHN, R. A., AND D. M. KLEIST. 2000. Divorce mediation: Research and implications for family and couples counseling. *Family Journal* 8 (April): 165–71.

HAIKEN, M. 1992. Liquor ads targeted at Indians dismay some tribal leaders. *Washington Post Health Supplement,* September 22, 11–12.

HALES, D. 1996. How teenagers see things. *Parade Magazine,* August 18, 4–5.

HALEY, A. 1976. *Roots: The saga of an American family.* Garden City, NY: Doubleday.

Half of older Americans report they are sexually active; 4 in 10 want more sex, says new survey. 1998. National Council on Aging. www.ncoa.org/news/archives/sexsurvey.htm (accessed August 30, 2000).

HALL, C. C. I., AND M. J. CRUM. 1994. Women and "body-isms" in television beer commercials. *Sex Roles* 31 (September): 329–37.

HALPERN, C. T., K. JOYNER, AND C. SUCHINDRAN. 2000. Smart teens don't have sex (or kiss much either). *Journal of Adolescent Health* 26 (March): 213–225.

HALPERN, S. 1989. Infertility: Playing the odds. *Ms.* (January/February): 147–51, 154–56.

HAMER, D. H., S. HU, V. MAGNUSON, N. HU, AND A. M. L. PATTATUCCI. 1993. A linkage between DNA markers on the X chromosome and male sexual orientation. *Science,* July 16, 321–27.

HAMILTON, C. 1997. Indians to tackle housing crisis—on their own. *Christian Science Monitor,* August 8, 4–5.

HAMILTON, J. C. 1999. The ethics of conducting social-science research on the Internet. *Chronicle of Higher Education,* December 3, B6–B7.

HAMON, R. R. 1992. Filial role enactment by adult children. *Family Relations* 41 (January): 91–96.

HANCOCK, J. 1999a. A business bonanza paid by taxpayers. *Baltimore Sun,* October 10, 1A, 16A–17A.

HANCOCK, J. 1999b. S.C. pays dearly for added jobs. *Baltimore Sun,* October 12, 1A, 8A–9A.

HANNON, R., D. S. HALL, T. KUNTZ, S. VAN LAAR, AND J. WILLIAMS. 1995. Dating characteristics leading to unwanted vs. wanted sexual behavior. *Sex Roles* 33 (11/12): 767–83.

HANSON, M. J. 1998. Ethnic, cultural, and language diversity in intervention settings. In *Developing cross-cultural competence: A guide for working with children and their families,* 2nd ed., eds. E. W. Lynch and M. J. Hanson, 3–22. Baltimore: Paul H. Brookes.

HANSON, R. K., R. GIZZARELLI, AND H. SCOTT. 1994. The attitudes of incest offenders: Sexual entitlement and acceptance of sex with children. *Criminal Justice and Behavior* 21 (June): 187–202.

HANSON, S. L. 1996. *Lost talent: Women in the sciences.* Philadelphia: Temple University Press.

HAQ, F. 1996. Women, Islam and the state in Pakistan. *Muslim World* 86 (April): 158–75.

HARARI, S. E., AND M. A. VINOVSKIS. 1993. Adolescent sexuality, pregnancy, and childbearing in the past. In *The politics of pregnancy: Adolescent sexuality and public policy,* eds. A. Lawson and D. I. Rhode, 23–45. New Haven, CT: Yale University Press.

HAREVEN, T. K. 1984. Themes in the historical development of the family. In *Review of child development research,* Vol. 7, *The family,* ed. R. D. Parke, 137–78. Chicago: University of Chicago Press.

HARJO, S. S. 1993. The American Indian experience. In *Family ethnicity: Strength in diversity,* ed. H. P. McAdoo, 199–207. Thousand Oaks, CA: Sage.

HARMS, T. 1989. The 12 building blocks of discipline. *Parents* (August): 76–78, 81–82.

HARRIS, D. 1995. Salary survey: 1995. *Working Woman* (January): 25–34.

HARRIS, D. K. 1990. *Sociology of aging,* 2nd ed. New York: Harper & Row.

HARRIS, D. R., AND H. ONO. 2000. Intimate relationships between races more common than thought. www.umich.edu/~newsinfo/Releases/2000/Mar00/r032300a.html (accessed September 16, 2000).

HARRIS, J. R. 1998. *The nurture assumption: Why children turn out the way they do.* New York: Free Press.

HARRIS, K. M. 1996. The reforms will hurt, not help, poor women and children. *Chronicle of Higher Education,* October 4, B7.

HARRIS, L. 1996. The hidden world of dating violence. *Parade Magazine,* September 22, 4–6.

HARRIS, M. 1994. *Down from the pedestal: Moving beyond idealized images of womanhood.* New York: Doubleday.

HARRIS, M. 1996. Aggressive experiences and aggressiveness: Relationship to ethnicity, gender, and age. *Journal of Applied Social Psychology* 26: 843–70.

HARRISON, A., F. SERAFICA, AND H. McADOO. 1984. Ethnic families of color. In *Review of child development research,* Vol. 7, *The family,* ed. R. D. Parke, 329–71. Chicago: University of Chicago Press.

HARRISON, C., AND K. DAUTRICH. 1999. The modern American worker. *Public Perspective* 10 (August/September): 38–41.

HART, B. 1993. Battered women and the criminal justice system. *American Behavioral Scientist* 36 (May): 624–38.

HARTILL, L. 2000. For sale on international market—human sperm. *Christian Science Monitor,* January 13, 14.

HARTMAN, S. 1988. Arranged marriages live on. *New York Times,* August 10, C12.

HARVEY, E. 1999. Short-term and long-term effects of early parental employment on children of the National Longitudinal Survey of Youth. *Developmental Psychology* 35 (March): 445–59.

HASS, A. 1979. *Teenage sexuality: A survey of teenage sexual behavior.* New York: Macmillan.

HASTINGS, D. 1994. Battered men continue to have no place to go. *Baltimore Sun,* August 1, 1D, 5D.

HATCHER, R. A., ET AL. 1990. *Contraceptive technology 1990–1992,* 15th ed. New York: Irvington.

HATCHETT, S. J. 1991. Women and men. In *Life in black America,* ed. J. S. Jackson, 84–104. Thousand Oaks, CA: Sage.

HATCHETT, S. J., AND J. S. JACKSON. 1993. African American extended kin systems: An assessment. In *Family ethnicity: Strength in diversity,* ed. H. P. McAdoo, 90–108. Thousand Oaks, CA: Sage.

HATFIELD, E. 1983. What do women and men want from love and sex? In *Changing boundaries: Gender roles and sexual behavior,* eds. E. R. Allgeier and N. B. McCormick, 106–34. Mountain View, CA: Mayfield.

HATFIELD, E., AND R. L. RAPSON. 1996. *Love and sex: Cross-cultural perspectives.* Boston: Allyn & Bacon.

HATFIELD, E., AND S. SPRECHER. 1986. *Mirror, mirror . . . The importance of looks in everyday life.* Albany: State University of New York Press.

HAUBEGGER, C. 1999. The legacy of generation Ñ. *Newsweek,* July 12, 61.

HAVEMANN, J. 1997a. N.J. allows gays to adopt jointly. *Washington Post,* December 18, A1, A24.

HAVEMANN, J. 1997b. Nursing home alternatives gaining in popularity. *Washington Post,* January 24, A6.

HAWKE, D. F. 1988. *Everyday life in early America.* New York: Harper & Row.

HAYASHI, G. M., AND B. R. STRICKLAND. 1998. Long-term effects of parental divorce on love relationships: Divorce as attachment disruption. *Journal of Social & Personal Relationships* 15 (February): 23–38.

HAYES, C. L., D. ANDERSON, AND M. BLAU. 1993. *Our turn: The good news about women and divorce.* New York: Pocket Books.

HAYS, S. 1998. The fallacious assumptions and unrealistic prescriptions of attachment theory: A comment on parents' socioemotional investment in children. *Journal of Marriage and the Family* 60 (August): 782–95.

HAZAN, C., AND P. R. SHAVER. 1987. Conceptualizing romantic love as an attachment process. *Journal of Personality and Social Psychology* 52, 511–24.

HEADDEN, S. 1997. The Hispanic dropout mystery. *U.S. News & World Report,* October 20, 64–65.

HEATON, T. B. 1990. Marital stability throughout the child-rearing years. *Demography* 27 (February): 55–63.

HEATON, T. B., C. K. JACOBSON, AND K. HOLLAND. 1999. Persistence and change in decisions to remain childless. *Journal of Marriage and the Family* 61 (May): 531–39.

HEAVENS, A. J. 1999. Pervasive discrimination an ugly foe of community. *Baltimore Sun*, January 3, 8M.

HECHT, M. L., P. J. MARSTON, AND L. K. LARKEY. 1994. Love ways and relationship quality in heterosexual relationships. *Journal of Social and Personal Relationships* 11 (1): 25–43.

HEINTZ-KNOWLES, K. E., P. CHEN, P. MILLER, AND A. HAUFLER. 2000. *Fall colors II: Exploring the quality of diverse portrayals on prime time television.* www.childrennow.org/media/fall-colors-2k/fc2-2k.pdf (accessed August 24, 2000).

HEISE, L. L., WITH J. PITANGUY, AND A. GERMAIN. 1994. *Violence against women: The hidden burden.* Washington, DC: World Bank.

HEISE, L., M. ELLSBERG, AND M. GOTTEMOELLER. 1999. Ending violence against women. *Population Reports*, Series L. No. 11. Baltimore: Johns Hopkins University School of Public Health, Population Information Program. www.jhuccp.org/pr/l11/violence.pdf (accessed October 14, 2000).

HEISS, J. 1986. Family roles and behavior. In *Sex roles and social patterns*, eds. F. A. Boudreau, R. S. Sennott, and M. Wilson, 84–120. New York: Praeger.

HENDIN, H. 1982. *Suicide in America.* New York: Norton.

HENDRICK, C., AND S. HENDRICK. 1992a. *Liking, loving, and relating,* 2nd ed. Monterey, CA: Brooks/Cole.

HENDRICK, S., AND C. HENDRICK. 1992b. *Romantic love.* Thousand Oaks, CA: Sage.

HENDRICKSON, M. L. 1994. Couples should fight for a good marriage. *U.S. Catholic* 59 (April): 20–25.

HENDRIX, H. 1988. *Getting the love you want: A guide for couples.* New York: Henry Holt.

HENKEN, E. R., AND M. H. WHATLEY. 1995. Folklore, legends, and sexuality education. *Journal of Sex Education and Therapy* 21 (1): 46–61.

HENRY, K. 1999. Chapter 11 for London Fog. *Baltimore Sun*, September 28, 1A, 7A.

HENRY, S. 1995. America's hidden disease. *Parade Magazine*, February 12, 4–6.

HENSHAW, S. A. 1998. Unintended pregnancy in the United States. *Family Planning Perspectives* 30 (January/February): 24–29.

HENTON, J., R. CATE, S. LLOYD, AND S. CHRISTOPHER. 1983. Romance and violence in dating relationships. *Journal of Family Issues* 4, 467–82.

HERBERT, C. 1989. *Talking of silence: The sexual harassment of schoolgirls.* New York: Falmer.

HERBERT, W. 1999. When strangers become family. *U.S. News & World Report*, November 29, 58–67.

HERBERT, W., AND S. HAMMEL. 1999. Getting close, but not too close. *U.S. News & World Report*, March 22, 56–57.

HERDT, G. H., ED. 1984. *Ritualized homosexuality in Melanesia.* Berkeley: University of California Press.

HERMAN, D. L. 1989. The rape culture. In *Women: A feminist perspective*, 4th ed., ed. J. Freeman, 20–44. Mountain View, CA: Mayfield.

HERMAN, R. 1992. Depression in widows. *Washington Post Family and Retirement Supplement*, April 29, 10–11.

HERMAN-GIDDENS, M., G. BROWN, S. VERBIEST, P. J. CARLSON, E. G. HOOTEN, E. HOWELL, AND J. D. BUTTS. 1999. Underascertainment of child abuse mortality in the United States. *JAMA* 282 (August): 463–67.

HERN, W. M. 1992. Shipibo polygyny and patrilocality. *American Ethnologist* 19 (August): 501–22.

HEROD, A. 1993. Gender issues in the use of interviewing as a research method. *Professional Geographer* 45 (August): 305–17.

HERRERÍAS, C. 1995. Noncustodial mothers following divorce. *Marriage & Family Review* 20 (1/2): 233–55.

HERRING, R. D. 1999. Experiencing a lack of money and appropriate skin color: A personal narrative. *Journal of Counseling & Development* 77 (Winter): 25–27.

HERRSTROM, S. 1990. Sweden: Pro-choice on child care. *New Perspectives Quarterly* 7 (Winter): 27–30.

HERSHATTER, G. 1984. Making a friend: Changing patterns of courtship in urban China. *Pacific Affairs* 57 (Summer): 237–51.

HERTZ, R., AND J. CHARLTON. 1989. Making family under a shiftwork schedule: Air force security guards and their wives. *Social Problems* 36 (December): 491–507.

HETHERINGTON, E. M., AND W. G. CLINGEMPEEL. 1992. Coping with marital transitions: A family systems perspective. *Monographs of the Society for Research in Child Development* 57, 2–3, serial no. 227.

HETHERINGTON, E. M., S. H. HENDERSON, AND D. REISS. 1999. *Adolescent siblings in stepfamilies: Family functioning and adolescent adjustment.* Malden, MA: Society for Research in Child Development.

HETHERINGTON, E. M., AND K. M. JODL. 1994. Stepfamilies as a setting for child development. In *Stepfamilies: Who benefits? Who does not?* eds. A. Booth and J. Dunn, 55–79. Mahwah, NJ: Erlbaum.

HETHERINGTON, E. M., T. C. LAW, AND T. G. O'CONNOR. 1993. Divorce: Challenges, changes, and new chances. In *Normal family processes*, 2nd ed., ed. F. Walsh, 208–34. New York: Guilford Press.

HETHERINGTON, E. M., AND M. M. STANLEY-HAGAN. 1997. The effects of divorce on fathers and their children. In *The role of the father in child development*, ed. M. E. Lamb, 191–211. New York: Wiley.

HETRICK, R. 1994. London Fog workers swallow pride, cuts. *Baltimore Sun*, September 27, A1, A14.

HEYN, D. 1997. *Marriage shock: The transformation of women into wives.* New York: Villard.

HIEDEMANN, B., O. SUHOMLINOVA, AND A. M. O'RAND. 1998. Economic independence, economic status, and empty nest in midlife marital disruption. *Journal of Marriage and the Family* 60 (February): 219–31.

HILL, R. B. 1998. Understanding black family functioning: A holistic perspective. *Journal of Comparative Family Studies* 29 (Spring): 15–25.

HILL, R. B., ET AL. 1993. *Research on the African-American family: A holistic perspective.* Westport, CT: Auburn House.

HINSCH, B. 1990. *Passions of the cut sleeve: The male homosexual tradition in China.* Berkeley: University of California Press.

HIRSCHEL, J. D., AND I. W. HUTCHISON III. 1992. Female spouse abuse and the police response: The Charlotte, North Carolina, experiment. *Journal of Criminal Law & Criminology* 83 (1): 73–119.

HITE, S. 1987. *Women and love: A cultural revolution in progress.* New York: Knopf.

HIV/AIDS Surveillance Report. 1997. 9:1. Atlanta, GA: Centers for Disease Control and Prevention.

HIV/AIDS Surveillance Report. 2000. Table 6: HIV infection cases by age group, exposure category, and sex. www.cdc.gov/hiv/stats/hasr1102/table6.htm (accessed September 3, 2000).

HOBART, C. W. 1958. The incidence of romanticism during courtship. *Social Forces* 36 (May): 362–67.

HOBBS, F. B., AND B. L. DAMON. 1996. *65+ in the United States.* U.S. Census Bureau. Current Population Reports, Special Studies, P23–190. Washington, DC: U.S. Government Printing Office.

HOCHSCHILD, A. R. 1997. *The time bind: When work becomes home and home becomes work.* New York: Metropolitan Books.

HOCHSCHILD, A., WITH A. MACHUNG. 1989. *The second shift: Working parents and the revolution at home.* New York: Penguin.

HOCKSTADER, L. 1995. For women, new Russia is far from liberating. *Washington Post*, September 1, A25, A 31.

HOFFERTH, S. L., Z. JANKUNIENE, AND P. D. BRANDON. 2000. Self-care among school-age children. University of Michigan, Institute for Social Research, unpublished paper.

HOFFMAN, J. 1995. Divorced fathers make gains in battles to increase rights. *New York Times*, April 26, B1, B5.

HOFFMAN, K. L., D. H. DEMO, AND J. N. EDWARDS. 1994. Physical wife abuse in a non-Western society: An integrated theoretical approach. *Journal of Marriage and the Family* 56 (February): 131–46.

HOGAN, D. P., L.-X. HAO, AND W. L. PARISH. 1990. Race, kin networks, and assistance to mother-headed families. *Social Forces* 68, 797–812.

HOJAT, M., R. SHAPURIAN, H. NAYERAHMADI, M. FARZANEH, D. FOROUGHI, M. PARSI, AND M. AZIZI. 1999. Premarital sexual, child rearing, and family attitudes of Iranian men and women in the United States and in Iran. *Journal of Psychology: Interdisciplinary & Applied* 133 (January): 19–31.

HOLDEN, C. 1996. Health of Native Americans. *Science* 273 (September 27): 1805.

HOLDEN, G. W., P. C. MILLER, AND S. D. HARRIS. 1999. The instrumental side of corporal punishment: Parents' reported practices and outcome expectancies. *Journal of Marriage and the Family* 61 (November): 908–19.

HOLDEN, G. W., AND K. L. RITCHIE. 1991. Linking extreme marital discord, child rearing, and child behavior problems: Evidence from battered women. *Child Development* 62, 311–27.

HOLLAND, D. C., AND M. A. EISENHART. 1990. *Educated in romance: Women, achievement, and college culture.* Chicago: University of Chicago Press.

HOLMAN, T. B., AND W. R. BURR. 1980. Beyond the beyond: The growth of family theories in the 1970s. *Journal of Marriage and the Family* 42 (November): 729–41.

HOLMAN, T. B., J. H. LARSON, AND S. L. HARMER. 1994. The development and predictive validity of a new premarital assessment instrument: The preparation for marriage questionnaire. *Family Relations* 43 (January): 46–52.

HOLMES, S. A. 1994. A generally healthy America emerges in a census report. *New York Times*, October 13, B13.

HOLMSTROM, D. 1994. Gambling ventures reverse poverty for only some Indians. *Christian Science Monitor*, July 8, 3.

HOLMSTROM, D. 1997. Indian traditions help "drunk town" shed its image. *Christian Science Monitor*, July 14, 10–11.

HOLMSTROM, D. 2000. United we stand. *Christian Science Monitor*, July 26, 11–15.

HONEY, M. 1984. *Creating Rosie the Riveter: Class, gender, and propaganda.* Amherst: University of Massachusetts Press.

HONG, S.-M., AND S. FAEDDA. 1994. Ranking of romantic acts by an Australian sample. *Psychological Reports* 74, 471–74.

HOON, S. J. 1993. Farming for brides. *Far Eastern Economic Review*, March 4, 24.

HOOYMAN, N. R., AND H. A. KIYAK. 1991. *Social gerontology: A multidisciplinary perspective*, 2nd ed. Boston: Allyn & Bacon.

HOPE, T. L., AND C. K. JACOBSON. 1995. Japanese American families: Assimilation over time. In *American families: Issues in race and ethnicity*, ed. C. K. Jacobson, 145–75. New York: Garland.

HOPSON, D. P., AND D. S. HOPSON. 1990. *Different and wonderful: Raising black children in a race-conscious society*. New York: Prentice Hall.

HORTON, H. D., AND N. J. BURGESS. 1992. Where are the black men? Regional differences in the pool of marriageable black men in the United States. *National Journal of Sociology* 6 (Summer): 3–19.

HORWITZ, A. V., AND H. R. WHITE. 1998. The relationship of cohabitation and mental health: A study of a young adult cohort. *Journal of Marriage and the Family* 60 (May): 505–14.

HORWITZ, A. V., H. R. WHITE, AND S. HOWELL-WHITE. 1996. Becoming married and mental health: A longitudinal study of a cohort of young adults. *Journal of Marriage and the Family* 58 (November): 895–907.

HOSLEY, C. A., AND R. MONTEMAYOR. 1997. Fathers and adolescents. In *The role of the father in child development*, ed. M. E. Lamb, 162–78. New York: Wiley.

HOTZ, V. J., S. W. MCELROY, AND S. G. SANDERS. 1997. The impacts of teenage childbearing on the mothers and the consequences of those impacts for government. In *Kids having kids: Economic costs and social consequences of teen pregnancy*, ed. R. A. Maynard, 55–94. Washington, DC: Urban Institute Press.

HOUSEKNECHT, S. K., AND J. SASTRY. 1996. Family "decline" and child well-being: A comparative assessment. *Journal of Marriage and the Family* 58 (August): 726–39.

HOWARD, J. A., AND J. A. HOLLANDER. 1997. *Gendered situations, gendered selves: A gender lens on social psychology*. Thousand Oaks, CA: Sage.

HOWE, R. F. 1991. Fertility doctor accused of using his own sperm. *Washington Post*, November 20, A1, A38.

HUDAK, M. A. 1993. Gender schema theory revisited: Men's stereotypes of American women. *Sex Roles* 28 (5/6): 279–92.

HUDSON, J. W., AND L. F. HENZE. 1969. Campus values in mate selection: A replication. *Journal of Marriage and the Family* 31 (November): 772–75.

HUGHES, D., AND M. A. DODGE. 1997. African American women in the workplace: Relationships between job conditions, racial bias at work, and perceived job quality. *American Journal of Community Psychology* 25 (October): 581–99.

HUGHES, D. L., AND E. GALINSKY. 1994. Gender, job and family conditions, and psychological symptoms. *Psychology of Women Quarterly* 18, 251–70.

HUGHEY, A. M. 1990. The incomes of recent female immigrants to the United States. *Social Science Quarterly* 71 (June): 383–90.

HUGICK, L. 1999. Taking credit where it's due. *Public Perspective* 10 (October/November): 10–14.

HUISMAN, D. A. 1996. Wife battering in Asian American communities. *Violence against Women* 2 (September): 260–83.

HUMPHRY, D., AND M. CLEMENT. 2000. *Freedom to die: People, politics, and the right-to-die movement*. New York: St. Martin's/Griffin.

HUNT, J. 1991. Ten reasons not to hit your kids. In *Breaking down the wall of silence: The liberating experience of facing painful trust*, ed. A. Miller, 168–71. Meridian, NY: Dutton.

HUNT, M. M. 1969. *The affair: A portrait of extramarital love in contemporary America*. New York: World.

HUNTLEY, T., ED. 1991. *Helping children grieve: When someone they love dies*. Minneapolis, MN: Augsburg Press.

HUPKA, R. B. 1991. The motive for the arousal of romantic jealousy: Its cultural origin. In *The psychology of jealousy and envy*, ed. P. Salovey, 252–70. New York: Guilford Press.

HURH, W. M. 1998. *The Korean Americans*. Westport, CT: Greenwood Press.

HURTADO, A. 1995. Variations, combinations, and evolutions: Latino families in the United States. In *Understanding Latino families: Scholarship, policy, and practice*, ed. R. E. Zambrana, 40–61. Thousand Oaks, CA: Sage.

HUSTON, M., AND P. SCHWARTZ. 1995. The relationships of lesbians and of gay men. In *Understudied relationships: Off the beaten track*, eds. J. T. Wood and S. Duck, 89–121. Thousand Oaks, CA: Sage.

HUTCHINSON, E. O. 1994. *Black fatherhood. II: Black women talk about their men*. Los Angeles: Middle Passage Press.

HUTCHINSON, M. K., AND T. M. COONEY. 1998. Patterns of parent–teen sexual risk communication: Implications for intervention. *Family Relations* 47 (April): 185–94.

HUTCHISON, I. W. 1999. The effect of children's presence on alcohol use by spouse abusers and their victims. *Family Relations* 48 (January): 57–65.

HUTTER, M. 1988. *The changing family: Comparative perspectives*, 2nd ed. New York: Macmillan.

HWANG, S.-S., R. SAENZ, AND B. F. AGUIRRE. 1994. Structural and individual determinants of outmarriage among Chinese-, Filipino-, and Japanese-Americans in California. *Sociological Inquiry* 64 (November): 396–414.

HWANG, S.-S., R. SAENZ, AND B. E. AGUIRRE. 1997. Structural and assimilationist explanations of Asian American intermarriage. *Journal of Marriage and the Family* 59 (August): 758–72.

HYDE, J. S. 1996. Where are the gender differences? Where are the gender similarities? In *Sex, power, conflict: Evolutionary and feminist perspectives*, eds. D. M. Buss and N. M. Malamuth, 107–18. New York: Oxford University Press.

HYMAN, B. 2000. The economic consequences of child sexual abuse for adult lesbian women. *Journal of Marriage and the Family* 62 (February): 199–211.

HYMAN, M. 1999. The "babe factor" in women's soccer. *Business Week*, July 26, 118.

IHINGER-TALLMAN, M., AND K. PASLEY. 1987. *Remarriage*. Beverly Hills, CA: Sage.

IHINGER-TALLMAN, M., AND K. PASLEY. 1997. Stepfamilies in 1984 and today—A scholarly perspective. *Marriage & Family Review* 26 (1/2): 19–40.

IKONOMIDOU, C., P. BITTIGAU, M. J. ISHIMARU, D. F. WOZNIAK, C. KOCH, K. GENZ, M. T. PRICE, V. STEFOVSKA, F. HÖRSTER, T. TENKOVA, K. DIKRANIAN, AND J. W. OLNEY. 2000. Ethanol-induced apoptotic neurodegeneration and fetal alcohol syndrome. *Science* 287, February 11, 1056–60.

IMBER-BLACK, E., AND J. ROBERTS. 1993. Family change: Don't cancel holidays! *Psychology Today* 26 (March/April): 62, 64, 92–93.

Immigrant visas issued to orphans coming to the U.S.: Top countries of origin. 2000. U.S. State Department. travel.state.gov/orphan_numbers. html (accessed September 23, 2000).

Immigration fuels cities' growth. 1998. *Baltimore Sun*, January 1, 10A.

IMPOCO, J., WITH M. BENNEFIELD, K. POLLACK, R. BIERCK, K. SCHMIDT, AND S. GREGORY. 1996. TV's frisky family values. *U.S. News & World Report*, April 15, 58–62.

INGRASSIA, M., AND M. BECK. 1994. Patterns of abuse. *Newsweek*, July 4, 26–33.

INGRASSIA, M., AND K. SPRINGEN. 1994. She's not Baby Jessica anymore. *Newsweek*, March 21, 60–65.

Institute for Philosophy and Public Policy. 1989. *Surrogate Motherhood* 9 (Winter): 1–5.

Interracial marriages rising, study of Census data says. 1997. *Baltimore Sun*, March 26, 3A.

Interracial wedding barred in Ohio. 2000. *Baltimore Sun*, July 11, 3A.

IRVING, H. H., AND M. BENJAMIN. 1991. Shared and sole-custody parents: A comparative analysis. In *Joint custody and shared parenting*, 2nd ed., ed. J. Folberg, 114–31. New York: Guilford Press.

ISHII-KUNTZ, M. 1993. Japanese fathers: Work demands and family roles. In *Men, work and family*, ed. J. C. Hood, 45–67. Thousand Oaks, CA: Sage.

ISHII-KUNTZ, M. 1997. Intergenerational relationships among Chinese, Japanese, and Korean Americans. *Family Relations* 46 (October): 23–32.

ISHII-KUNTZ, M., AND G. R. LEE. 1987. Status of the elderly: An extension of the theory. *Journal of Marriage and the Family* 49 (May): 413–20.

Italy promises pensions for housewives. 1996. *Baltimore Sun*, August 11, 18A.

It's time for working women to earn equal pay. 1998. AFL-CIO. www.aflcio.org/women/equalpay.htm (accessed October 16, 2000).

IWAO, S. 1993. *The Japanese women: Traditional image and changing reality*. New York: Free Press.

JACKLIN, C. N., AND L. A. BAKER. 1993. Early gender development. In *Gender issues in contemporary society*, eds. S. Oskamp and M. Costanzo, 41–57. Thousand Oaks, CA: Sage.

JACKSON, A. P., R. P. BROWN, AND K. E. PATTERSON-STEWART. 2000. African Americans in dual-career commuter marriages: An investigation of their experiences. *Family Journal: Counseling and Therapy for Couples and Families* 8 (January): 22–36.

JACKSON, A. P., P. GYAMFI, J. BROOKS-GUNN, AND M. BLAKE. 1998. Employment status, psychological well-being, social support, and physical discipline practices of single black mothers. *Journal of Marriage and the Family* 60 (November): 894–902.

JACKSON, D. D. 1998. "This hole in our heart": Urban Indian identity and the power of silence. *American Indian Culture and Research Journal* 22 (4): 227–54.

JACKSON, J. S., ED. 1991. *Life in black America*. Thousand Oaks, CA: Sage.

JACKSON, N. A. 1996. Observational experiences of intrapersonal conflict and teenage victimization: A comparative study among spouses and cohabitors. *Journal of Family Violence* 11 (September): 191–203.

JACKSON, S. A. 1998. "Something about the word": African American women and feminism. In *No middle ground: Women and radical protest*, ed., K. M. Blee, 38–50. New York: New York University Press.

JACOBS, F. H., AND M. W. DAVIES. 1991. Rhetoric or reality? Child and family policy in the United States. *Social Policy Report* 5 (4): 1–25.

JACOBS, J. A., AND K. GERSON. 1998. Who are the overworked Americans? *Review of Social Economy* 56 (Winter): 442–59.

JACOBS, J. L. 1990. Reassessing mother blame in incest. *Signs* 15 (Spring): 500–14.

JACOBSEN, L., AND B. EDMONDSON. 1994. Father figures. *American Demographics, Parenting Reprint Package,* 31–37.

JACOBSON, N. S., AND M. E. ADDIS. 1993. Research on couples and couples therapy: What do we know? Where are we going? *Journal of Clinical and Consulting Psychology* 61 (1): 85–93.

JACOBY, S. 1999. Great sex. *Modern Maturity* (September–October): 41–45, 91.

JAIMES, M. A., WITH T. HALSEY. 1992. American Indian women: At the center of indigenous resistance in contemporary North America. In *The state of Native America: Genocide, colonization, and resistance,* ed. M. A. Jaimes, 311–44. Boston: South End Press.

JAIN, A., AND J. BELSKY. 1997. Fathering and acculturation: Immigrant Indian families with young children. *Journal of Marriage and the Family* 59 (November): 873–83.

JAMES, A. D. 1998. What's love got to do with it? Economic viability and the likelihood of marriage among African American men. *Journal of Comparative Family Studies* 29 (Summer): 373–86.

JAMES, J. W., AND R. FRIEDMAN. 1998. *The grief recovery handbook: The action program for moving beyond death, divorce, and other losses.* New York: HarperPerennial.

JANEWAY, E. 1981. Incest: A rational look at the oldest taboo. *Ms.* (November): 81.

JANKOWIAK, W. R., AND E. F. FISCHER. 1992. A cross-cultural perspective on romantic love. *Ethnology* 31 (April): 149–55.

JARRETT, R. L. 1994. Living poor: Family life among single parent, African-American women. *Social Problems* 41 (February): 30–49.

JARRETT, R. L. 1995. Growing up poor: The family experiences of socially mobile youth in low-income African American neighborhoods. *Journal of Adolescent Research* 10 (January): 111–35.

JARRETT, R. L., AND L. M. BURTON. 1999. Dynamic dimensions of family structure in low-income African American families: Emergent themes in qualitative research. *Journal of Comparative Family Studies* 30 (Spring): 177–87.

JARRETT, W. H. 1985. Caregiving within kinship systems: Is affection really necessary? *The Gerontologist* 25 (1): 5–10.

JAYAKODY, R., L. M. CHATTERS, AND R. J. TAYLOR. 1993. Family support to single and married African American mothers: The provision of financial, emotional, and child-care assistance. *Journal of Marriage and the Family* 55 (May): 261–76.

JEMMOTT, J. B., III, AND K. L. ASHBY. 1989. Romantic commitment and the perceived availability of opposite-sex persons: On loving the one you're with. *Journal of Applied Social Psychology* 19 (14): 1198–211.

JEMMOTT, L. S., V. CATAN, A. NYAMAATHI, AND J. ANASTASIA. 1995. African American women and HIV-risk-reduction issues. In *Women at risk: Issues in the primary prevention of AIDS,* eds. A. O'Leary and L. S. Jemmott, 131–57. New York: Plenum Press.

JENDREK, M. P. 1994. Grandparents who parent their grandchildren: Circumstances and decisions. *The Gerontologist* 34 (2): 206–16.

JENNY, C., K. P. HYMEL, A. RITZEN, S .E. REINERT, AND T. C. HAY. 1999. Analysis of missed cases of abusive head trauma. *JAMA* 281 (February): 621–26.

JERROME, D. 1994. Time, change and continuity in family life. *Aging and Society* 14 (March): 1–27.

JHALLY, S. 1995. Image-based culture: Advertising and popular culture. In *Gender, race and class in media: A text-reader,* eds. G. Dines and J. M. Humez, 77–87. Thousand Oaks, CA: Sage.

JO, M. H. 1999. *Korean immigrants and the challenge of adjustment.* Westport, CT: Greenwood Press.

JOHN, D., AND B. A. SHELTON. 1997. The production of gender among black and white women and men: The case of household labor. *Sex Roles* 36 (February): 171–93.

JOHN, R. 1988. The Native American family. In *Ethnic families in America: Patterns and variations,* 3rd ed., eds. C. H. Mindel, R. W. Habenstein, and R. Wright, Jr., 325–66. New York: Elsevier.

JOHNSON, A. G. 1997. *The gender knot: Unraveling our patriarchal legacy.* Philadelphia: Temple University Press.

JOHNSON, B. K. 1996. Older adults and sexuality: A multidimensional perspective. *Journal of Gerontological Nursing* 22 (February): 6–15.

JOHNSON, C. L. 1993. The prolongation of life and the extension of family relationships: The families of the oldest old. In *Family, self, and society: Toward a new agenda for family research,* eds. P. A. Cowan, D. Field, D. A. Hansen, A. Skolnick, and G. E. Swanson, 317–30. Hillsdale, NJ: Lawrence Erlbaum Associates.

JOHNSON, D. 1991. Polygamists emerge from secrecy, seeking not just peace but respect. *New York Times,* April 9, A22.

JOHNSON, E. M., AND T. L. HUSTON. 1998. The perils of love, or why wives adapt to husbands during the transition to parenthood. *Journal of Marriage and the Family* 60 (February): 195–204.

JOHNSON, J. H., JR., AND W. C. FARRELL, JR. 1995. Race still matters. *Chronicle of Higher Education,* July 7, A48.

JOHNSON, L. 1996. Some rural Chinese women seek greater role in society. *Baltimore Sun,* October 12, 10A.

JOHNSON, R. 1985. Stirring the oatmeal. In *Challenge of the heart: Love, sex, and intimacy in changing times,* ed. J. Welwood. Boston: Shambhala.

JOHNSON, R. W., AND A. T. LO SASSO. 2000. Parental care at midlife: Balancing work and family responsibilities near retirement, The Retirement Project, No. 9, Urban Institute. www.urban.org/retirement/briefs/9/BRIEF9.PDF (accessed October 28, 2000).

JOHNSON, S., AND H. E. MARANO. 1994. Love: The immutable longing for contact. *Psychology Today* (March/April): 33–37, 64ff.

JONES, A. 1994. *Next time, she'll be dead: Battering and how to stop it.* Boston: Beacon.

JONES, A., AND S. SCHECHTER. 1992. *When love goes wrong: What to do when you can't do anything right.* New York: HarperCollins.

JONES, C. 1994. Living single. *Essence* (May): 138–40.

JONES, E. F., J. D. FORREST, N. GOLDMAN, S. HENSHAW, R. LINCOLN, J. I. ROSOLL, C. F. WESTOFF, AND D. WULF. 1986. *Teenage pregnancy in industrialized countries.* New Haven, CT: Yale University Press.

JONES, J. 1985. *Labor of love, labor of sorrow: Black women, work and the family from slavery to the present.* New York: Basic Books.

JONES, R. K. 1993. Female victim perceptions of the causes of male spouse abuse. *Sociological Inquiry* 63 (August): 351–61.

JONES, W. H., AND M. P. BURDETTE. 1994. Betrayal in relationships. In *Perspectives on close relationships,* eds. A. L. Weber and J. H. Harvey, 243–62. Boston: Allyn & Bacon.

JOSSELSON, R. 1992. *The space between us: Exploring the dimensions of human relationships.* San Francisco: Jossey-Bass.

JULIAN, T. W., P. C. McKENRY, and M. W. McKELVEY. 1994. Cultural variations in parenting: Perceptions of Caucasian, African-American, Hispanic, and Asian-American parents. *Family Relations* 43 (January): 30–37.

JUSTICE, G. 1999. We're happily married and living apart. *Newsweek,* October 18, 12.

KABACOFF, R. I. 1998. Gender differences in organizational leadership: A large study sample, Management Research Group. www.mrg.com/articles/Gender_Paper_1998.pdf (accessed August 28, 2000).

KACAPYR, E. 1998. How hard are hard times? *American Demographics* 20 (February): 30–32.

KAFFMAN, M. 1993. Kibbutz youth: Recent past and present. *Journal of Youth and Adolescence* 22 (December): 573–604.

KALMIJN, M. 1993. Trends in black/white intermarriage. *Social Forces* 72 (September): 119–46.

KALMIJN, M. 1998. Intermarriage and homogamy: Causes, patterns, trends. *Annual Review of Sociology* 24: 395–421.

KALMIJN, M. 1999. Father involvement in childrearing and the perceived stability of marriage. *Journal of Marriage and the Family* 61 (May): 409–21.

KAMARA, C. H. 1998. *Guinea means woman: Guinea's national efforts in the fight against female genital mutilation.* London: Rainbow Press.

KAMERMAN, S. B. 1996. Child and family policies: An international overview. In *Children, families, and government: Preparing for the twenty-first century,* eds. E. F. Zigler, S. L. Kagan, and N. W. Hall, 31–48. New York: Cambridge University Press.

KAMO, Y. 1990. Husbands and wives living in nuclear and stem family households in Japan. *Sociological Perspectives* 33 (3): 397–417.

KAMO, Y. 1998. Asian grandparents. In *Handbook on grandparenthood,* ed. M. E. Szinovacz, 97–112. Westport, CT: Greenwood Press.

KAMO, Y., AND E. L. COHEN. 1998. Division of household work between partners: A comparison of black and white couples. *Journal of Comparative Family Studies* 29 (Spring): 131–45.

KANALEY, R. 2000. Women closing gap in Net use, report finds. *Baltimore Sun,* May 15, 1C–2C.

KANE, E. W., AND L. J. MACAULAY. 1993. Interviewer gender and gender attitudes. *Public Opinion Quarterly* 57 (Spring): 1–28.

KANIN, E. G., K. R. DAVIDSON, AND S. R. SCHECK. 1970. A research note on male-female differentials in the experience of heterosexual love. *Journal of Sex Research* 6 (February): 64–72.

KANN, L., S. A. KINCHEN, B. I. WILLIAMS, J. G. ROSS, R. LOWRY, J. A. GRUNBAUM, AND L. J. KOLBE. 2000. Youth risk behavior surveillance—United States, 1999. CDC Surveillance Summaries, June. *Morbidity and Mortality Weekly Report* 49 (no. SS-5).

KANN, L., C. W. WARREN, W. A. HARRIS, J. L. COLLINS, B. I. WILLIAMS, J. G. ROSS, AND L. J. KOLBE. 1996. Youth risk behavior surveillance—United States, 1995. CDC Surveillance Summaries, September 27, 1996. *Morbidity and Mortality Weekly Report* 45 (no. SS-4).

KANTOR, G. K., AND M. A. STRAUS. 1987. The "drunken bum" theory of wife beating. *Social Problems* 34 (June): 213–30.

KANTOR, R. M. 1970. Communes. *Psychology Today* (July): 53–57, 78.

KANTROWITZ, B. 1996. Gay families come out. *Newsweek,* November 4, 51–57.

KANTROWITZ, B., AND P. WINGERT. 1999. The science of a good marriage. *Newsweek,* April 19, 52–57.

KAO, G. 1995. Asian Americans as model minorities? A look at their academic performance. *American Journal of Education* 103 (February): 121–59.

KAPLAN, D. A., WITH S. D. LEWIS AND J. HAMMER. 1993. Is it torture or tradition? *Newsweek,* December 20, 124.

KAPLAN, E. B. 1997. *Not our kind of girl: Unraveling the myths of black teenage motherhood.* Berkeley: University of California Press.

KAPLAN, G. A., AND W. J. STRAWBRIDGE. 1994. Behavioral and social factors in healthy aging. In *Aging and quality of life,* eds. R. P. Abeles, H. C. Gift and M. G. Ory, 57–78. New York: Springer.

KAPLAN, H. S. 1979. *Disorders of sexual desire.* New York: Brunner/Mazel.

KAPRIO, J., M. KOSKENVUO, AND H. RITA. 1987. Mortality after bereavement: A prospective study of 95,647 widowed persons. *American Journal of Public Health* 77, 283–87.

KAR, S. B., A. JIMENEZ, K. CAMPBELL, AND F. SZE. 1998. Acculturation and quality of life: A comparative study of Japanese-Americans and Indo-Americans. *Amerasia Journal* 24 (Spring): 129–42.

KARANJA, W. W. 1987. "Outside wives" and "inside wives" in Nigeria: A study of changing perceptions of marriage. In *Transformations of African marriage,* eds. D. Parkin and D. Nyamwaya, 247–61. Manchester, England: Manchester University Press.

KARASIK, S. 2000. More latchkey kids means more trouble: High-risk behavior increases when parents are gone. www.apbnews.com/safetycenter/family/2000/04/14/sitter0414_01.html (accessed September 28, 2000).

KARNEY, B. R., AND T. N. BRADBURY. 1995. The longitudinal course of marital quality and stability. *Psychological Bulletin* 118 (July): 3–34.

KAROLY, L. A. 1993. The trend in inequality among families, individuals, and workers in the United States: A twenty-five year perspective. In *Uneven tides: Rising inequality in America,* eds. S. Danziger and P. Gottschalk, 19–97. New York: Russell Sage Foundation.

KASS, L. R. 1997. The end of courtship, *The Public Interest,* no. 126 (Winter): 39–63.

KATE, N. T. 1997. What if . . . whites become a minority? *American Demographics* 19 (December): 42.

KATE, N. T. 1998. How many children? *American Demographics* 20 (March): 35.

KATZEV, A. R., R. L. WARNER, AND A. C. ACOCK. 1994. Girls or boys? Relationship of child gender to marital instability. *Journal of Marriage and the Family* 56 (February): 89–100.

KAUFMAN, M. 1993. *Cracking the armour: Power, pain and the lives of men.* New York: Viking/Penguin.

KAYSER, K. 1993. *When love dies: The process of marital disaffection.* New York: Guilford Press.

KEITH, P. M., S. KIM, AND R. B. SCHAFER. 2000. Informal ties of the unmarried in middle and later life: Who has them and who does not? *Sociological Spectrum* 20 (April–June): 221–38.

KEITH, V. M. 1997. Life stress and psychological well-being among married and unmarried blacks. In *Family life in black America,* eds. R. J. Taylor, J. S. Jackson, L. M. Chatters, 95–116. Thousand Oaks, CA: Sage.

KEITH, V. M., AND B. FINLAY. 1988. The impact of parental divorce on children's educational attainment, marital timings, and likelihood of divorce. *Journal of Marriage and the Family* 50 (August): 797–809.

KELLEY, B. T., T. P. THORNBERRY, AND C. A. SMITH. 1997. *In the wake of childhood maltreatment.* U.S. Department of Justice, Office of Justice Programs, Office of Juvenile Justice and Delinquency Prevention, August.

KELLEY, P. 1992. Healthy stepfamily functioning. *Families in Society: Journal of Contemporary Human Services* 73 (December): 579–87.

KELLEY, P. 1996. Family-centered practice with stepfamilies. *Families in Society: The Journal of Contemporary Human Services* 77 (November): 535–44.

KELLY, G. F. 1994. *Sexuality today: The human perspective,* 4th ed. Guilford, CT: Dushkin.

KELLY, J. B. 2000. Children's adjustment in conflicted marriage and divorce: A decade review of research. *Journal of the American Academy of Child & Adolescent Psychiatry* 39 (August): 963–73.

KEMP, S. AND J. SQUIRES, EDS. 1997. *Feminisms.* New York: Oxford University Press.

KENDALL, D. 1999. *Sociology in Our Times,* 2nd ed. Belmont, CA: Wadsworth.

KENEN, R. H. 1993. *Reproductive hazards in the workplace: Mending jobs, managing pregnancies.* New York: Haworth Press.

KENNEDY, G. E. 1990. College students' expectations of grandparent and grandchild role behaviors. *The Gerontologist* 30 (1): 43–48.

KENNICKELL, A. B., M. STARR-MCCLUER, AND B. J. SURETTE. 2000. Recent changes in U.S. family finances: Results from the 1998 survey of consumer finances. *Federal Reserve Bulletin* 40 (January): 1–29

KENRICK, D. T., G. E. GROTH, M. R. TROST, AND E. K. SADALLA. 1993. Integrating evolutionary and social exchange perspectives on relationships: Effects of gender, self-appraisal, and involvement level on mate selection criteria. *Journal of Personality and Social Psychology* 64 (6): 951–69.

KEPHART, P. 1996. Money can't buy them love. *American Demographics* 18 (February): 23–24.

KEPHART, W. M. 1987. *Extraordinary groups: An examination of unconventional lifestyles,* 3rd ed. New York: St. Martin's.

KEPHART, W. M., AND W. W. ZELLNER. 1991. *Extraordinary groups: An examination of unconventional lifestyles,* 4th ed. New York: St. Martin's.

KERCKHOFF, A. C., AND K. E. DAVIS. 1962. Value consensus and need complementarity in mate selection. *American Sociological Review* 27 (June): 295–303.

KERN, S. 1992. *The culture of love: Victorians to moderns.* Cambridge, MA: Harvard University Press.

KERR, J. K., R. L. SKOK, AND T. F. MCLAUGHLIN. 1991. Characteristics common to females who exhibit anorexic or bulimic behavior: A review of the current literature. *Journal of Clinical Psychology* 47 (November): 846–53.

KERSTEN, K. K. 1990. The process of marital disaffection: Interventions at various stages. *Family Relations* 39 (July): 257–65.

KESNER, J. E., T. JULIAN, AND P. C. MCKENRY. 1997. Application of attachment theory to male violence toward female intimates. *Journal of Family Violence* 12 (June): 211–28.

KHESHGI-GENOVESE, Z., AND T. A. GENOVESE. 1997. Developing the spousal relationship within stepfamilies. *Families in Society: The Journal of Contemporary Human Services* 78 (May–June): 255–64.

KHOO, S.-E. 1987. Living together as married: A profile of de facto couples in Australia. *Journal of Marriage and the Family* 49 (February): 185–91.

KIBRIA, N. 1994. Vietnamese families in the United States. In *Minority families in the United States: A multicultural perspective,* ed. R. L. Taylor, 164–76. Upper Saddle River, NJ: Prentice Hall.

KIBRIA, N. 1997. The construction of "Asian American": Reflections on intermarriage and ethnic identity among second-generation Chinese and Korean Americans. *Ethnic and Racial Studies* 20 (July): 523–44.

Kids and guns. 2000. Washington, DC: U.S. Department of Justice, Office of Justice Programs, Office of Juvenile Justice and Delinquency Prevention.

Kids count data book: State profiles of child well-being. 2000. Baltimore, Annie E. Casey Foundation.

KIECOLT, K. J., AND M. A. FOSSETT. 1997. The effects of mate availability on marriage among black Americans: A contextual analysis. In *Family life in black America,* eds. R. J. Taylor, J. S. Jackson, L. M. Chatters, 63–78. Thousand Oaks, CA: Sage.

KIECOLT-GLASER, J. K., L. D. FISHER, P. OGROCKI, AND J. C. STOUT. 1987. Marital quality, marital disruption, and the immune function. *Psychosomatic Medicine* 49 (January–February): 13–34.

KIEFER, F. 2000. Commuter marriages test more Americans. *Christian Science Monitor,* January 7, 1, 4.

KIERNAN, K. E. 1992. The impact of family disruption in childhood on transitions made in young adult life. *Population Studies* 46, 213–34.

KILBOURNE, J. 1994. Still killing us softly: Advertising and the obsession with thinness. In *Feminist perspectives on eating disorders,* eds. P. Fallon, M. A. Katzman, and S. C. Wooley, 395–418. New York: Guilford Press.

KILBOURNE, J. 1999. *Deadly persuasion: Why women and girls must fight the addictive power of advertising.* New York: Free Press.

KILBURN, J. C., JR., 1996. Network effects in caregiver to care-recipient violence: A study of caregivers to those diagnosed with Alzheimer's disease. *Journal of Elder Abuse & Neglect* 8 (1): 69–80.

KIM, E. 1999. Sexual division of labor in the Korean American family. Paper presented at the annual National Council on Family Relations meetings, Washington, DC, November.

KIM, H. K., AND P. C. MCKENRY. 1998. Social networks and support: A comparison of African Americans, Asian Americans, Caucasians, and Hispanics. *Journal of Comparative Family Studies* 29 (Summer): 313–36.

KIM, K. C, AND S. KIM. 1998. Family and work roles of Korean immigrants in the United States. In *Resiliency in Native American and immigrant families,* eds. H. I. McCubbin, E. A. Thompson, A. I. Thompson, and J. E. Fromer, 225–42. Thousand Oaks, CA: Sage.

KIMBROUGH, R. J. 1998. Treating juvenile substance abuse: The promise of juvenile drug courts. *Juvenile Justice* 5 (December): 11–19.

KIMMEL, M. S., AND M. A. MESSNER. 1995. *Men's lives,* 3rd ed. New York: Allyn & Bacon.

KINDLON, D. J., WITH T. BARKER, AND M. THOMPSON. 1999. *Raising Cain: Protecting the emotional life of boys.* New York: Random House.

KING, P., AND K. HAMILTON. 1997. Bringing kids all the way home. *Newsweek,* June 16, 60–65.

KING, V. 1994. Nonresident father involvement and child well-being: Can dads make a difference? *Journal of Family Issues* 55 (March): 78–96.

KING, W. 1996. "Suffer with them till death": Slave women and their children in nineteenth-century America. In *More than chattel: Black women and slavery in the Americas*, eds. D. B. Caspar and D. C. Hine, 147–68. Bloomington: Indiana University Press.

KINKEAD, G. 1977. The family secret. *Boston Magazine* (October): 100.

KINSEY, A. C., W. B. POMEROY, AND C. E. MARTIN. 1948. *Sexual behavior in the human male*. Philadelphia: Saunders.

KINSEY, A. C., W. B. POMEROY, C. E. MARTIN, AND P. H. GEBHARD. 1953. *Sexual behavior in the human female*. Philadelphia: Saunders.

KIRBY, D., ET AL. 1994. School-based programs to reduce sexual risk behaviors: A review of effectiveness. *Public Health Reports* 109 (May/June): 339–60.

KIRN, W. 1997. The ties that bind. *Time*, August 18, 48–50.

KISSMAN, K., and J. A. ALLEN. 1993. *Single-parent families*. Beverly Hills, CA: Sage.

KITANO, H. H. L. 1988. The Japanese American family. In *Ethnic families in America: Patterns and variations*, 3rd ed., eds. C. H. Mindel, R. W. Habenstein, and R. Wright, Jr., 258–75. New York: Elsevier.

KITSON, G. C., AND L. A. MORGAN. 1991. The multiple consequences of divorce. In *Contemporary families: Looking forward, looking back*, ed. A. Booth, 150–61. Minneapolis, MN: National Council on Family Relations.

KITSON, G. C., WITH W. M. HOLMES. 1992. *Portrait of divorce: Adjustment to marital breakdown*. New York: Guilford Press.

KITZINGER, S. 1989. *The crying baby*. New York: Penguin.

KIVETT, V. R. 1991. Centrality of the grandfather role among older rural black and white men. *Journal of Gerontology: Social Sciences* 46 (5): S250–58.

KLAUS, M., AND J. KENNELL. 1976. *Maternal-infant bonding*. St. Louis, MO: Mosby.

KLAUS, P. A. 2000. *Crimes against persons age 65 or older, 1992–97*. Washington, DC: U.S. Department of Justice, Office of Justice Programs.

KLEIMAN, C. 1993. Comparable pay could create jobs. *Orlando Sentinel*, October 13, C5.

KLEIN, D. M., AND J. M. WHITE. 1996. *Family theories: An introduction*. Thousand Oaks, CA: Sage.

KLEIN, J. D. 1997. The national longitudinal study on adolescent health: Preliminary results, great expectations. *JAMA* 278 (September 10): 864–66.

KLEIN, R. 1993. Personal correspondence.

KLINETOB, N. A., AND D. SMITH. 1996. Demand-withdraw communication in marital interaction: Tests of interspousal contingency and gender role hypotheses. *Journal of Marriage and the Family* 58 (November): 945–58.

KLINKENBERG, D., AND S. ROSE. 1994. Dating scripts of gay men and lesbians. *Journal of Homosexuality* 26 (4): 23–35.

KLITSCH, M. 1994. Decline in fertility among Japanese women attributed not to contraceptive use but to late age at marriage. *Family Planning Perspectives* 26 (May/June): 137–38.

KLUWER, E. S., J. A. M. HEESINK, AND E. VAN DE VLIERT. 1996. Marital conflict about the division of household labor and paid work. *Journal of Marriage and the Family* 58 (November): 958–69.

KNAPP, M. L., AND J. A. HALL. 1992. *Nonverbal communication in human interaction*, 3rd ed. New York: Holt, Rinehart & Winston.

KNAPP, R. J. 1987. When a child dies. *Psychology Today*, July, 60–65.

KNICKERBOCKER, B. 1998. Oregon escalates its heated right-to-die debate. *Christian Science Monitor*, April 8, 4.

KNICKERBOCKER, B. 2000. Forget crime—but please fix the traffic. *Christian Science Monitor*, February 16, 3.

KNOX, D., WITH K. LEGGETT. 1998. *The divorced dad's survival book: How to stay connected with your kids*. New York: Insight Books.

KNOX, D. H., JR., AND M. J. SPORAKOWSKI. 1968. Attitudes of college students toward love. *Journal of Marriage and the Family* 30 (November): 638–42.

KNOX, D., C. SCHACHT, AND M. E. ZUSSMAN. 1999. Love relationships among college students. *College Student Journal* 33 (March): 149–51.

KNOX, D., M. E. ZUSMAN, C. BUFFINGTON, AND G. HEMPHILL. 2000. Interracial dating attitudes among college students. *College Student Journal* 34 (March): 69–71.

KNOX, V. W., AND M. J. BANE. 1994. Child support and schooling. In *Child support and child well-being*, eds. I. Garfinkel, S. S. McLanahan, and P. K. Robins, 285–316. Washington, DC: Urban Institute Press.

KOEPKE, L., J. HARE, AND P. B. MORAN. 1992. Relationship quality in a sample of lesbian couples with children and child-free lesbian couples. *Family Relations* 41 (April): 224–49.

KOHLBERG, L. 1969. Stage and sequence: The cognitive-developmental approach to socialization. In *Handbook of socialization theory and research*, ed. D. A. Goslin, 347–480. Chicago: Rand McNally.

KOHN, A. 1991. The spoiled child. *Ladies Home Journal* (May): 78.

KONCIUS, J. 1995. At home, at work. *Washington Post Home Supplement*, October 19, 9, 20–21.

KOOLS, S. M. 1997. Adolescent identity development in foster care. *Family Relations* 46 (July): 263–71.

KOONIN, L. M., L. T. STRAUSS, C. E. CHRISMAN, M. A. MONTALBANO, L. A. BARTLETT, AND J. C. SMITH. 1999. Abortion surveillance—United States, 1996. CDC Surveillance Summaries, July 30. *Morbidity and Mortality Weekly Report* 48 (no. SS-4).

KOSS, M. P. AND S. I. COOK. 1993. Facing the facts: Date and acquaintance rape are significant problems for women. In *Current controversies on family violence*, eds. R. J. Gelles and D. R. Losede, 104–19. Thousand Oaks, CA: Sage.

KOURI, K. A., AND M. LASSWELL. 1993. Black-white marriages: Social change and intergenerational mobility. *Marriage and Family Review* 19 (3/4): 241–55.

KPOSOWA, A. J. 1998. The impact of race on divorce in the United States. *Journal of Comparative Family Issues* 29 (Fall): 529–48.

KRACH, C. A., AND V. A. VELKOFF. 1999. *Centenarians in the United States*. U.S. Bureau of the Census, Current Population Reports, Series P23-199RV. www.census.gov/prod/99pubs/p23-199.pdf (accessed June 12, 2000).

KRAFFT, S. 1994. Why wives earn less than husbands. *American Demographics* 16 (January): 16–17.

KRAMER, H. 1993. *Conversations at midnight: Coming to terms with dying and death*. New York: Morrow.

KRANCE, M. 1993. Conquest. In *Reinventing love: Six women talk about lust, sex, and romance*, eds. L. Abraham, L. Green, M. Krance, J. Rosenberg, J. Somerville, and C. Stoner, 159–61. New York: Plume.

KREITER, S. R., AND D. P. KROWCHUK. 1999. Gender differences in risk behaviors among adolescents who experience date fighting. *Pediatrics* 104 (December): 1286–92.

KRICH, J. 1989. Here come the brides: The blossoming business of imported love. In *Men's lives*, eds. M. S. Kimmel and M. A. Messner, 382–92. New York: Macmillan.

KRISHNAN, V. 1998. Premarital cohabitation and marital disruption. *Journal of Divorce & Remarriage* 28: 157–70.

KROKOFF, L. J. 1987. The correlates of negative affect in marriage: An exploratory study of gender differences. *Journal of Family Issues* 8 (March): 111–35.

KRUCOFF, C. 1999. Setting standards for seniors. *Washington Post*, July 20, 28.

KRUEGER, R. A. 1994. *Focus groups: A practical guide for applied research*, 2nd ed. Thousand Oaks, CA: Sage.

KÜBLER-ROSS, E. 1969. *On death and dying*. New York: Macmillan.

KUNKEL, D., K. M. COPE, W. J. M. FARINOLA, E. BIELY, E. ROLLIN, AND E. D. DONNERSTEIN. 1999. Sex on TV: A biennial report to the Kaiser Family Foundation. Washington, DC: Henry J. Kaiser Family Foundation. www.kff.org (accessed September 3, 2000).

KURDEK, L. A. 1993. Predicting marital dissolution: A 5-year prospective longitudinal study of newlywed couples. *Journal of Personality and Social Psychology* 64 (2): 221–42.

KURDEK, L. A. 1994. Areas of conflict for gay, lesbian, and heterosexual couples: What couples argue about influences relationship satisfaction. *Journal of Marriage and the Family* 56 (November): 923–24.

KURDEK, L. A. 1998. Relationship outcomes and their predictors: Longitudinal evidence from heterosexual married, gay cohabiting, and lesbian cohabiting couples. *Journal of Marriage and the Family* 60 (August): 553–68.

KURDEK, L. A., AND M. A. FINE. 1993. The relation between family structure and young adolescents' appraisals of family climate and parenting behavior. *Journal of Family Issues* 14, 279–90.

KURZ, D. 1993. Physical assaults by husbands: A major social problem. In *Current controversies on family violence*, eds. R. J. Gelles and D. R. Loseke, 88–103. Thousand Oaks, CA: Sage.

KUSHNER, E. 1997. *Experiencing abortion: A weaving of women's words*. New York: Haworth Press.

KUTTNER, R. 2000. The states are ending welfare as we know it—but not poverty. *Business Week*, June 12, 36.

KYMAN, W. 1995. The first step: Sexuality education for parents. *Journal of Sex Education and Therapy* 21 (3): 153–57.

LABOV, T., AND J. A. JACOBS. 1998. Preserving multiple ancestry: Intermarriage and mixed births in Hawaii. *Journal of Comparative Family Studies* 29 (Autumn): 481–502.

LACH J. 1999. Lending inequalities. *American Demographics* 21 (November): 11–12.

LADD, E. C. 1999. Everyday life: How are we doing? *Public Perspective* 10 (April/May): 1, 7.

LADD, G. W., K. D. LE STEUR, AND S. M. PROFILET. 1993. Direct parental influences on young children's peer relations. In *Learning about relationships*, ed. S. Duck, 152–83. Thousand Oaks, CA: Sage.

LAFFERTY, E. 1999. Ruling against anti-abortion website raises storm in US over rights. *The Irish Times*. courses.cs.vt.edu/~cs3604/lib/Freedom.of.Speech/Nuremburg.Irish.Times.html (accessed September 24, 2000).

LAFRANCHI, H. 1997. Girls who find new roles in Mexico also face danger. *Christian Science Monitor*, June 4, 1, 6.

Laird, J. 1993. Lesbian and gay families. In *Normal family processes*, 2nd ed., ed. F. Walsh, 282–330. New York: Guilford Press.

Lakoff, R. T. 1990. *Talking power: The politics of language*. New York: Basic Books.

Lakshmanan, I. A. R. 1997. Marriage? Think logic, not love. *Baltimore Sun*, September 22, 2A.

Lamison-White, L. 1997. *Poverty in the United States: 1996*. U.S. Census Bureau, Current Population Reports, Series P60–198. Washington, DC: U.S. Government Printing Office.

Landale, N. S. 1989. Agricultural opportunity and marriage: The United States at the turn of the century. *Demography* 26 (May): 203–18.

Landale, N. S., and S. E. Tolnay. 1991. Group differences in economic opportunity and the timing of marriage. *American Sociological Review* 56 (February): 33–45.

Landry, D., J. L. Kaeser, and C. L. Richards. 1999. Abstinence promotion and the provision of information about contraception in public school district sexuality education policies. *Family Planning Perspectives* 31 (November/December): 280–86.

Laner, M. R. 1989. Competitive vs. noncompetitive styles: Which is most valued in courtship? *Sex Roles* 20 (3/4): 165–72.

Langelan, M. J. 1993. *Back off! How to confront and stop sexual harassment and harassers*. New York: Simon & Schuster.

Lansky, V. 1989. *Vicki Lansky's divorce book for parents*. New York: New American Library.

Lantz, H. R. 1976. *Marital incompatibility and social change in early America*. Beverly Hills, CA: Sage.

Lardner, J. 2000a. Give us your wired elite! *U.S. News & World Report*, July 10, 34–36.

Lardner, J. 2000b. The rich get richer. *U.S. News & World Report*, February 21, 39–43.

Larimer, M. E., A. R. Lydum, and A. P. Turner. 1999. Male and female recipients of unwanted sexual contact in a college student sample: Prevalence rates, alcohol use, and depression symptoms. *Sex Roles* 40 (February): 295–308.

LaRossa, R. ed. 1984. *Family case studies: A sociological perspective*. New York: Free Press.

LaRossa, R. 1986. *Becoming a parent*. Thousand Oaks, CA: Sage.

LaRossa, R., and D. C. Reitzes. 1993. Symbolic interactionism and family studies. In *Sourcebook of family theories and methods: A contextual approach*, eds. P. G. Boss, W. J. Doherty, R. LaRossa, W. R. Schumm, and S. K. Steinmetz, 135–63. New York: Plenum Press.

Larson, J. 1992. Understanding stepfamilies. *American Demographics* (July): 36–40.

Larson, J. H. 1988. The marriage quiz: College students' beliefs in selected myths about marriage. *Family Relations* 37 (January): 3–11.

Larson, J. H., S. M. Wilson, and R. Beley. 1994. The impact of job insecurity on marital and family relationships. *Family Relations* 43 (April): 138–43.

Larson, R., and M. H. Richards. 1994. *Divergent realities: The emotional lives of mothers, fathers, and adolescents*. New York: Basic Books.

Larzelere, R. E., P. R. Sather, W. N. Schneider, D. B. Larson, and P. L. Pike. 1998. Punishment enhances reasoning's effectiveness as a disciplinary response to toddlers. *Journal of Marriage and the Family* 60 (May): 388–403.

Lasch, C. 1977. *Haven in a heartless world: The family besieged*. New York: Basic Books.

Lasch, C. 1978. *The culture of narcissism*. New York: Norton.

Laslett, P. 1971. *The world we have lost*, 2nd ed. Reading, MA: Addison-Wesley.

Lasswell, T. E., and M. E. Lasswell. 1976. I love you but I'm not in love with you. *Journal of Marriage and Family Counseling* 2 (July): 211–24.

Lauer, J., and R. Lauer. 1985. Marriages made to last. *Psychology Today* (June): 22–26.

Lauer, R. H. 1973. *Perspectives on social change*. Boston: Allyn & Bacon.

Laumann, E. O., J. H. Gagnon, R. T. Michael, and S. Michaels. 1994. *The social organization of sexuality: Sexual practices in the United States*. Chicago: University of Chicago Press.

Laumann, E. O., A. Paik, and R. C. Rosen. 1999. Sexual dysfunction in the United States: Prevalence and predictors. *JAMA* 281 (February): 537–44.

Laursen, B., and L. A. Jensen-Campbell. 1999. The nature and functions of social exchange in adolescent romantic relationships. In *The development of romantic relationships in adolescence*, eds. W. Furman, B. B. Bradford, and C. Feiring, 50–74. New York: Cambridge University Press.

Lavee, Y., and D. H. Olson. 1993. Seven types of marriage: Empirical typology based on research. *Journal of Marital and Family Therapy* 19 (October): 325–40.

Lawrence, S. V. 1994. Family planning, at a price. *U.S. News & World Report*, September 19, 56–57.

Laws, A., and J. M. Golding. 1996. Sexual assault history and eating disorder symptoms among white, Hispanic, and African-American women and men. *American Journal of Public Health* 86 (April): 579–82.

Lawson, A. 1988. *Adultery: An analysis of love and betrayal*. New York: Basic Books.

Lawson, E. J., and A. Thompson. 1999. *Black men and divorce*. Thousand Oaks, CA: Sage.

Lawton, L., M. Silverstein, and V. Bengston. 1994. Affection, social contact, and geographic distance between adult children and their parents. *Journal of Marriage and the Family* 56 (February): 57–68.

Lazarus, A. A. 1985. *Marital myths*. San Luis Obispo, CA: Impact.

Leach, P. 1994. *Children first: What our society must do—and is not doing—for our children today*. New York: Knopf.

Lederer, W. J., and D. D. Jackson. 1968. *The mirages of marriage*. New York: Norton.

Lee, G. R., C. W. Peek, and R. T. Coward. 1998. Race differences in filial responsibility expectations among older parents. *Journal of Marriage and the Family* 60 (May): 404–12.

Lee, J. A. 1973. *The colors of love*. Upper Saddle River, NJ: Prentice Hall.

Lee, J. A. 1974. The styles of loving. *Psychology Today* (October): 46–51.

Lee, V. E., D. T. Burkan, H. Zimiles, and B. Ladewski. 1994. Family structure and its effects on behavioral and emotional problems in young adolescents. *Journal of Research on Adolescence* 4, 405–37.

Leerhsen, C., and E. Schaefer. 1989. Pregnancy + alcohol = problems. *Newsweek*, July 31, 57.

Leff, L. 1994. Becoming woman: At 15, Hispanic girls celebrate rite of passage. *Washington Post*, February 6, B1, B8.

Legato, M. J. 1998. Research on the biology of women will improve health care for men, too. *Chronicle of Higher Education*, May 15, B4–B5.

Lehr, S. T., C. DiLorio, W. N. Dudley, and J. A. Lipana, 2000. The relationship between parent–adolescent communication and safer sex behaviors in college students. *Journal of Family Nursing* 6 (May): 180–96.

Lehrer, E. L., and C. U. Chiswick. 1993. Religion as a determinant of marital stability. *Demography* 30 (August): 385–404.

Lehrman, F. 1996. Factoring domestic violence into custody cases. *Trial* 32 (February): 32–39.

Leite, R., and P. C. McKenry. 1996. Putting nonresidential fathers back into the family portrait. *Human Development and Family Life Bulletin* 2 (Autumn). www.hec.ohio-state.edu/famlife/index.htm (accessed February 3, 1998).

Leitenberg, H., M. J. Detzer, and D. Srebnik. 1993. Gender differences in masturbation and the relation of masturbation experience in preadolescence and/or early adolescence to sexual behavior and sexual adjustment in young adulthood. *Journal of Social Behavior* 22 (April): 87–98.

Lejeune, C., and V. Follette. 1994. Taking responsibility: Sex differences in reporting dating violence. *Journal of Interpersonal Violence* 9 (March): 133–45.

Leland, J. 1996. Tightening the knot. *Newsweek*, February 19, 72–73.

Leland, J. 2000. Shades of gay. *Newsweek*, March 20, 45–9.

LeMasters, E. E., and J. DeFrain. 1989. *Parents in contemporary America: A sympathetic view*, 5th ed. Belmont, CA: Wadsworth.

Lemieux, R. and J. L. Hale. 1999. Intimacy, passion, and commitment in young romantic relationships: Successfully measuring the triangular theory of love. *Psychological Reports* 85 (October): 497–503.

Leon, J. J., and M. G. Weinstein. 1991. The varieties of other Caucasian intramarriage in Hawaii: 1987. *Journal of Comparative Family Studies* 22 (Spring): 75–83.

Leon, J. J., J. L. Philbrick, F. Parra, E. Escobedo, and F. Malgesini. 1994. Love-styles among university students in Mexico. *Psychological Reports* 74, 307–10.

Leonard, K. E., and M. Senchak. 1993. Alcohol and premarital aggression among newlywed couples. *Journal of Studies on Alcohol*, Suppl. 11, 96–108.

Leonard, K. I. 1997. *The South Asian Americans*. Westport, CT: Greenwood Press.

Leppard, W., S. M. Ogletree, and E. Wallen. 1993. Gender stereotyping in medical advertising: Much ado about something? *Sex Roles* 29, (11/12): 829–37.

Leslie, L. A., T. L. Huston, and M. P. Johnson. 1986. Parental reactions to dating relationships: Do they make a difference? *Journal of Marriage and the Family* 48 (February): 57–66.

Less is more. 1999. *Public Perspective* 10 (October/November): 19.

Lessinger, J. 1995. *From the Ganges to the Hudson: Indian immigrants in New York City*. Boston,: Allyn & Bacon.

Lester, D. 1996a. The impact of unemployment on marriage and divorce. *Journal of Divorce & Remarriage* 25, (3/4): 151–53.

Lester, D. 1996b. Trends in divorce and marriage around the world. *Journal of Divorce & Remarriage* 25 (1/2): 169–71.

Levant, R. F., with G. Kopecky. 1995. *Masculinity reconstructed: Changing the rules of manhood—at work, in relationships, and in family life*. New York: Dutton.

LeVay, S. 1993. *The sexual brain*. La Jolla, CA: MIP Press.

Leventhal, B., and S. E. Lundy, eds. 1999. *Same-sex domestic violence: Strategies for change*. Thousand Oaks, CA: Sage.

Levesque, R. J. R. 1993. The romantic experience of adolescents in satisfying love relationships. *Journal of Youth and Adolescence* 11 (3): 219–50.

LEVIN, W. C. 1988. Age stereotyping. *Research on Aging* 10 (March): 134–48.

LEVINE, A. 1990. The second time around: Realities of remarriage. *U.S. News & World Report,* January 29, 50–51.

LEVINE, A. 1991. The biological roots of good mothering. *U.S. News & World Report,* February 25, 61.

LEVINE, M. V. 1994. A nation of hamburger flippers? *Baltimore Sun,* July 31, 1E, 4E.

LEVINE, R. V. 1993. Is love a luxury? *American Demographics* (February): 27, 29.

LEVY, J. A. 1994. Sex and sexuality in later life stages. In *Sexuality across the life course,* ed. A. S. Rossi, 287–309. Chicago: University of Chicago Press.

LEVY-SCHIFF, R. 1994. Individual and contextual correlates of marital change across the transition to parenthood. *Developmental Psychology* 30 (4): 591–601.

LEWIN, T. 1994. Men whose wives work earn less, studies show. *New York Times,* October 12, A1, A21.

LEWIS, M. 1997. *Altering fate: Why the past does not predict the future.* New York: Guilford Press.

LEWIS, M., AND M. BENDERSKY, EDS. 1995. *Mothers, babies, and cocaine: The role of toxins in development.* Hillsdale, NJ: Lawrence Erlbaum Associates.

LIBBON, R. P. 1999. Datadog. *American Demographics* 21 (December): 25.

LIBBON, R. P. 2000. MediaChannels. *American Demographics* 21 (February): 29.

LICHT, J. 1995. Marriages that endure. *Washington Post Health Supplement,* October 31, 18–20.

LICHTER, S. R., L. S. LICHTER, AND S. ROTHMAN. 1991. *Watching America.* Upper Saddle River, NJ: Prentice Hall.

LIEBOWITZ, S. W., D. C. CASTELLANO, AND I. CUELLAR. 1999. Factors that predict sexual behavior among young Mexican American adolescents: An exploratory study. *Hispanic Journal of Behavioral Sciences* 21 (November): 470–79.

LIEF, L. 1997. Kids at risk. *U.S. News & World Report,* April 28, 66–70.

LIGHT, P. C. 1988. *Baby boomers.* New York: Norton.

LIGHTFOOT-KLEIN, H. 1989. *Prisoners of ritual: An odyssey into female genital circumcision in Africa.* New York: Haworth Press.

LIN, C., AND W. T. LIU. 1993. Intergenerational relationships among Chinese immigrant families from Taiwan. In *Family ethnicity: Strength in diversity,* ed. H. P. McAdoo, 271–86. Thousand Oaks, CA: Sage.

LIN, G., AND P. A. ROGERSON. 1995. Elderly parents and the geographic availability of their adult children. *Research on Aging* 17 (September): 303–09.

LINDBERG, L. D., S. BOGGESS, L. PORTER, AND S. WILLIAMS. 2000. *Teen risk-taking: A statistical portrait.* Washington, DC: Urban Institute. www.urban.org/family/TeenRiskTaking.pdf (accessed September 4, 2000).

LINDSEY, L. L. 1997. *Gender roles: A sociological perspective,* 3rd ed. Upper Saddle River, NJ: Prentice Hall.

LINKS, S. H. 1999. Easy escape from the ties that bind. *The Times* (London), November 8. www.thetimes.co.uk (accessed October 20, 2000).

LINLIN, P. 1993. Matchmaking via the personal advertisements in China versus in the United States. *Journal of Popular Culture* 27 (Summer): 163–70.

LINO, M. 1994. Income and spending patterns of single-mother families. *Monthly Labor Review* (May): 29–37.

LINO, M. 1995. The economics of single parenthood: Past research and future directions. *Marriage & Family Review* 20 (1/2): 99–114.

LINO, M. 2000. *Expenditures on children by families: 1999 annual report.* U.S. Department of Agriculture, Center for Nutrition Policy and Promotion, Miscellaneous Publication No. 1528-1999. www.usda.gov:80/cnpp/Crc/crc1999.PDF (accessed September 23, 2000).

LIPS, H. M. 1991. *Women, men, and power.* Mountain View, CA: Mayfield.

LIPS, H. M. 1993. *Sex & gender: An introduction,* 2nd ed. Mountain View, CA: Mayfield.

LIRA, L. R., AND M. P. KOSS. 1999. Mexican American women's definitions of rape and sexual abuse. *Hispanic Journal of Behavioral Sciences* 21 (August): 236–65.

LITTLEJOHN-BLAKE, S. M., AND C. A. DARLING. 1993. Understanding the strengths of African American families. *Journal of Black Studies* 23 (June): 460–71.

LITWACK, E., AND P. MESSERI. 1989. Organizational theory, social supports, and mortality rates: A theoretical convergence. *American Sociological Review* 54, 49–66.

LIU, P., AND C. S. CHAN. 1996. Lesbian, gay, and bisexual Asian Americans and their families. In *Lesbians and gays in couples and families: A handbook for therapists,* eds. J. Laird and R.-J. Green, 137–54. San Francisco: Jossey-Bass.

LIVELY, K. 1996. The "date-rape drug." *Chronicle of Higher Education,* June 28, A29.

Living humbled, unhappy lives. 1996. *Baltimore Sun,* May 23, 2A.

LLOYD, S. A. 1991. The dark side of courtship: Violence and sexual exploitation. *Family Relations* 40 (January): 14–20.

LLOYD, S. A., AND B. C. EMERY. 2000. *The dark side of courtship: Physical and sexual aggression.* Thousand Oaks, CA: Sage.

LOCK, M. 1993. *Encounters with aging: Mythologies of menopause in Japan and North America.* Berkeley: University of California Press.

LOEWEN, J. W. 1988. Visitation fatherhood. In *Fatherhood today: Men's changing role in the family,* eds. P. Bronstein and C. P. Cowan, 195–213. New York: Wiley.

Longer lives, less cash. 1996. *U.S. News & World Report,* August 12, 14.

LONGINO, C. F., JR. 1994. Myths of an aging America. *American Demographics* (August): 36–42.

LONKHUYZEN, L. V. 1994. Female gymnasts prone to eating disorders. *Baltimore Sun,* July 29, C1, C3.

LOOMIS, L. S., AND N. S. LANDALE. 1994. Nonmarital cohabitation and childbearing among black and white American women. *Journal of Marriage and the Family* 56 (November): 949–62.

LÓPEZ, R. A. 1999. *Las comadres* as a social support system. *Affilia* 14 (Spring): 24–41.

LOPREST, P. 1999. Families who left welfare: Who are they and how are they doing? Washington, DC: Urban Institute. newfederalism.urban.org/pdf/discussion99-02.pdf (accessed October 14, 2000).

LORD, M. G. 1994. *Forever Barbie: The unauthorized biography of a real doll.* New York: Morrow.

LUEPNITZ, D. A. 1988. *Family therapy interpreted.* New York: Basic Books.

LUGAILA, T. A. 1998. Marital status and living arrangements: March 1998 (Update), Current Population Reports, P20-514, U.S. Census Bureau. www.census.gov/prod/99pubs/p20514.pdf (accessed August 8, 2000).

LUKEMEYER, A., M. K. MEYERS, AND T. SMEEDING. 2000. Expensive children in poor families: Out-of-pocket expenditures for the care of disabled and chronically ill children in welfare families. *Journal of Marriage and the Family* 62 (May): 399–415.

LUNDY, S. E. 1993. Abuse that dare not speak its name: Assisting victims of lesbian and gay domestic violence in Massachusetts. *New England Law Review* 28 (Winter): 272–311.

LUPTON, D., AND L. BARCLAY. 1997. *Constructing fatherhood: Discourses and experiences.* Thousand Oaks, CA: Sage.

LUSTER, T., L. BATES, H. FITZGERALD, M. VANDENBELT, AND J. P. KEY. 2000. Factors related to successful outcomes among preschool children born to low-income adolescent mothers. *Journal of Marriage and the Family* 62 (February): 133–46.

LYE, D. N., AND T. J. BIBLARZ. 1993. The effects of attitudes toward family life and gender roles on marital satisfaction. *Journal of Family Issues* 14 (June): 157–88.

LYMAN, K. A. 1993. *Day in, day out with Alzheimer's: Stress in caregiving relationships.* Philadelphia: Temple University Press.

LYNN, D. B. 1969. *Parental and sex role identification: A theoretical formulation.* Berkeley, CA: McCutchen.

LYNN, M., AND M. TODOROFF. 1995. Women's work and family lives. In *Feminist issues: Race, class, and sexuality,* ed. N. Mandell, 244–71. Scarborough, Ont.: Prentice Hall Canada.

LYNXWILER, J., AND D. GAY. 1994. Reconsidering race differences in abortion attitudes. *Social Science Quarterly* 75 (March): 67–84.

LYONS, S., AND M. JAMES. 1994. Man gets 18-month term for killing unfaithful wife. *Baltimore Sun,* October 18, 1A, 12A.

MACCOBY, E. E. 1990. Gender and relationships: A developmental account. *American Psychologist* 45 (4): 513–20.

MACCOBY, E. E., C. E. DEPNER, AND R. H. MNOOKIN. 1991. Co-parenting in the second year after divorce. In *Joint custody and shared parenting,* 2nd ed., ed. J. Folberg, 132–52. New York: Guilford Press.

MACDONALD, W. L., AND A. DEMARIS. 1996. The effects of stepparents' gender and new biological children. *Journal of Family Issues* 17 (1): 5–25.

MACER, D. R. J. 1994. Perception of risks and benefits of in vitro fertilization, genetic engineering and biotechnology. *Social Science & Medicine* 38 (January): 23–33.

MACERI, D. 2000. Bush's *español: Un poco* goes far. *Christian Science Monitor,* August 4, 11.

MACFARQUHAR, E., ET AL. 1994. The war against women. *U.S. News & World Report,* March 28, 42–48.

MACHAMER, A. M., AND E. GRUBER. 1998. Secondary school, family, and educational risk: Comparing American Indian adolescents and their peers. *Journal of Educational Research* 91 (July/August): 357–69.

MACKLIN, E. 1974. Cohabitation in college: Going very steady. *Psychology Today,* November, 53–59.

MACMILLAN, R., AND R. GARTNER. 1999. When she brings home the bacon: Labor-force participation and the risk of spousal violence against women. *Journal of Marriage and the Family* 61 (November): 947–58.

MACPHEE, D., J. FRITZ, AND J. MILLER-HEYL. 1996. Ethnic variations in personal social networks and parenting. *Child Development* 67 (6): 3278–95.

MADDEN-DERDICH, D. A., AND S. A. LEONARD. 2000. Parental role identity and fathers' involvement in coparental interaction after divorce: Fathers' perspectives. *Family Relations* 49 (July): 311–18.

MAGGIO, R. 1992. *The Beacon book of quotations by women.* Boston: Beacon Press.

MAGNER, D. K. 1993. College's Asian enrollment defies stereotype. *Chronicle of Higher Education,* February 10, A34.

MAIER, T. 1998. *Dr. Spock: An American life.* New York: Harcourt Brace.

MAJORS, R., AND J. M. BILLSON. 1992. *Cool pose: The dilemmas of black manhood in America.* New York: Lexington Books.

MAKINEN, J. 1997. Love amid the laundry. *Washington Post,* May 15, D1, D5.

Making a difference for juveniles. 1999. Washington, DC: U.S. Department of Justice, Office of Justice Programs, Office of Juvenile Justice and Delinquency Prevention.

MALES, M. 1999. For adults, "today's youth" are always the worst. www.latimes.com/news/opinion/19991120/t000106131.html (accessed November 22, 1999).

MANCINI, J. A., AND R. BLIESZNER. 1991. Aging parents and adult children: Research themes in intergenerational relations. In *Contemporary families: Looking forward, looking back,* ed. A. Booth, 249–64. Minneapolis, MN: National Council on Family Relations.

MANDEL, M. J. 1999. The prosperity gap. *Business Week,* September 27, 89–102.

MANKE, B., B. L. SEERY, A. C. CROUTER, AND S. M. MCHALE. 1994. The three corners of domestic labor: Mothers', fathers', and children's weekday and weekend housework. *Journal of Marriage and the Family* 56 (August): 657–68.

MANN, S. A., M. D. GRIMES, A. A. KEMP, AND P. J. JENKINS. 1997. Paradigm shifts in family sociology? Evidence from three decades of family textbooks. *Journal of Family Issues* 18 (May): 315–49.

MANNERS, J. 1993. The perils of a second marriage. *Money,* January, 108–20.

MANNING, C. 1970. *The immigrant woman and her job.* New York: Ayer.

MANNING, W. D. 1993. Marriage and cohabitation following premarital conception. *Journal of Marriage and the Family* 55 (November): 839–50.

MANNING, W. D., AND D. T. LICHTER. 1996. Parental cohabitation and children's economic well-being. *Journal of Marriage and the Family* 58 (November): 998–1010.

MANNIS, V. S. 1999. Single mothers by choice. *Family Relations* 48 (April): 121–28.

MANSNERUS, L. 1995. The divorce backlash. *Working Woman* (February): 38–45, 70.

MARBELLA, J. 1990. A chorus of opinions on what love's got to do with it. *Baltimore Sun,* February 14, 1F, 5F.

MARCUS, D. L., A. MULRINE, AND K. WONG. 1999. How kids learn. *U.S. News & World Report,* September 13, 44–52.

MARCUS, E. 1990. Justice Department rape statistics called unrealistically low. *Washington Post,* September 30, A9.

MARDER, D. 2000. A helping hand down the aisle. *Baltimore Sun,* January 23, 1n, 5n.

MARGOLIS, M. L. 1998. *An invisible minority: Brazilians in New York City.* Boston: Allyn & Bacon.

MARKIDES, K. S., J. S. BOLDT, AND L. A. RAY. 1986. Sources of helping and intergenerational solidarity: A three generation study of Mexican Americans. *Journal of Gerontology* 41, 506–11.

MARKIDES, K. S., J. ROBERTS-JOLLY, L. A. RAY, S. K. HOPPE, AND L. RUDKIN. 1999. Changes in marital satisfaction in three generations of Mexican Americans. *Research on Aging* 21 (January): 36–45.

MARKS, A. 2000. Vermont launches revolution by allowing same-sex unions. *Christian Science Monitor,* April 27, 2.

MARKS, N. F. 1996. Flying solo at midlife: Gender, marital status, and psychological well being. *Journal of Marriage and the Family* 58 (November): 917–32.

MARKS, S. R. 1986. *Three corners: Exploring marriage and the self.* Lexington, MA: Heath.

MARKSTROM-ADAMS, C. 1991. Attitudes on dating, courtship, and marriage: Perspectives on in-group relationships by religious minority and majority adolescents. *Family Relations* 40 (January): 91–98.

The marriage movement: A statement of principles. 2000. www.marriagemovement.org/html/report.html (accessed August 2, 2000).

Married adults still in the majority. 1999. U.S. Census Bureau. www.census.gov/Press-Release/www/1999/cb99-03.html (accessed September 12, 2000).

MARSIGLIO, W. 1993. Adolescent males' orientation toward paternity and contraception. *Family Planning Perspectives* 25 (January/February): 22–31.

MARSIGLIO, W., ED. 1995. *Fatherhood: Contemporary theory, research, and social policy.* Thousand Oaks, CA: Sage.

MARSIGLIO, W., AND D. DONNELLY. 1991. Sexual relations in later life: A national study of married persons. *Journal of Gerontology* 46, (November): S338–S344.

MARSIGLIO, W., AND R. A. GREER. 1994. A gender analysis of older men's sexuality. In *Older men's lives,* ed. E. H. Thompson, 122–40. Thousand Oaks, CA: Sage.

MARTIN, A. 1993. *The lesbian and gay parenting handbook: Creating and raising our families.* New York: HarperPerennial.

MARTIN, C. L. 1990. Attitudes and expectations about children with nontraditional and traditional gender roles. *Sex Roles* 22 (February): 151–65.

MARTIN, P., AND E. MIDGLEY. 1999. Immigration to the United States. *Population Bulletin* 54 (June): 1–44.

MARTIN, P. Y., AND R. A. HUMMER. 1993. Fraternities and rape on campus. In *Violence against women.* eds. P. B. Bart and E. G. Moran, 114–31. Thousand Oaks, CA: Sage.

MARTIN, T. C., AND L. L. BUMPASS. 1989. Recent trends in marital disruption. *Demography* 26 (February): 37–51.

MARTIRE, L. M., M. P. STEPHENS, AND M. M. FRANKS. 1997. Multiple roles of women caregivers: Feelings of mastery and self-esteem as predictors of psychosocial well-being. *Journal of Women & Aging* 9, (1/2): 117–31.

Maryland Special Joint Committee. 1989. *Gender bias in the courts.* Annapolis: Administrative Office of the Courts, May.

MARZOLLO, J. 1993. *Fathers & babies: How babies grow and what they need from you from birth to 18 months.* New York: HarperCollins.

MASON, C. A., A. M. CAUCE, AND N. GONZALES. 1997. Parents and peers in the lives of African-American adolescents: An interactive approach to the study of problem behavior. In *Social and emotional adjustment and family relations in ethnic minority families,* eds., R. D. Taylor and M. C. Wang, 85–98. Mahwah, NJ: Lawrence Erlbaum Associates.

MASON, M. A. 1999. *Custody wars: Why children are losing the legal battle and what we can do about it.* New York: Basic Books.

MASON, M. A., AND J. MAULDON. 1996. The new stepfamily requires a new public policy. *Journal of Social Issues* 52 (3): 11–27.

MASSEY, D. 2000. Housing discrimination 101. *Population Today* 28 (August/September): 1, 4.

MASSEY, L. 1992. What is really the best interest of the child? *Legal Assistant Today* (November/December): 140–41.

MASTEKAASA, A. 1994. Marital status, distress, and well-being: An international comparison. *Journal of Comparative Family Studies* 25 (Summer): 183–205.

MASTERS, W. H., V. E. JOHNSON, AND R. C. KOLODNY. 1986. *On sex and human loving.* Boston: Little, Brown.

MASTERS, W. H., V. E. JOHNSON, AND R. C. KOLODNY. 1992. *Human sexuality,* 4th ed. New York: HarperCollins.

MASUR, D. M., M. SLIWINSKI, AND H. A. CRYSTAL. 1994. Neuropsychological prediction of dementia and the absence of dementia in healthy elderly persons. *Neurology* 44 (August): 1427–33.

MATANOSKI, G. 1994. Different means of artificial insemination can give childless couples hope. *Baltimore Sun,* July 26, 3D.

MATE-KOLE, C., M. FRESCHI, AND A. ROBIN. 1990. A controlled study of psychological and social change after surgical gender reassignment in selected male transsexuals. *British Journal of Psychiatry* 157 (August): 261–64.

MATHES, V. S. 1981. A new look at the role of women in Indian society. In *The American Indian: Past and present,* 2nd ed., ed. R. L. Nichols, 27–33. New York: Wiley.

MATHEWS, T. J., AND S. J. VENTURA. 1997. Birth and fertility rates by educational attainment: United States, 1994. *Monthly Vital Statistics Report* 45 (10), suppl. Hyattsville, MD: National Center for Health Statistics.

MATHIAS, B. 1992. Yes, Va. (Md. & D.C.), there are happy marriages. *Washington Post,* September 22, B5.

MATHIAS, B. 1997. No longer just a member of the wedding. *Washington Post,* March 18, C5.

MATTHAEI, J. A. 1982. *An economic history of women in America: Women's work, the sexual division of labor, and the development of capitalism.* New York: Schocken.

MATTHEWS, S. H., AND T. T. ROSNER. 1988. Shared filial responsibility: The family as the primary caregiver. *Journal of Marriage and the Family* 50 (February): 185–95.

MATTHIAS, R. E., J. E. LUBBEN, K. A. ATCHISON, AND S. O. SCHWEITZER. 1997. Sexual activity and satisfaction among very old adults: Results from a community-dwelling Medicare population survey. *The Gerontologist* 17 (1): 6–14.

MATTOX, W. 1994. The hottest valentines. *Washington Post,* February 13, C5.

MAXWELL, A. 1998. Not all issues are black or white: Some voices from the offspring of cross-cultural marriages. In *Cross-Cultural marriage: Identity and choice,* eds. R. Breger and R. Rosanna, 209–26. New York: Berg.

MAY, E. T. 1995. *Barren in the promised land: Childless Americans and the pursuit of happiness.* New York: Basic Books.

MAY, P. A. 1999. The epidemiology of alcohol abuse among American Indians: The mythical and real properties. In *Contemporary Native American cultural issues,* ed., D. Champagne, 227–44. Walnut Creek, CA: AltaMira Press.

MAYER, C. E. 1999. For a generation in denial, a fountain of youth products. *Washington Post,* May 6, A1, A16.

MAYNARD, M. 1994. Methods, practice and epistemology: The debate about feminism and research. In *Researching women's lives from a feminist perspective,* eds. M. Maynard and J. Purvis, 10–26. London: Taylor & Francis.

MAYNARD, R. A., ED. 1997. *Kids having kids: Economic costs and social consequences of teen pregnancy.* Washington, DC: Urban Institute Press.

MAYO, Y. 1997. Machismo, fatherhood, and the Latino family: Understanding the concept. *Journal of Multicultural Social Work* 5 (1/2): 49–61.

MAYS, V. M., L. M. CHATTERS, AND S. D. COCHRAN. 1998. African American families in diversity: Gay men and lesbians in family networks. *Journal of Comparative Family Studies* 29 (Spring): 73–88.

MCADOO, J. L. 1986. Black fathers' relationships with their preschool children and the children's development of ethnic identity. In *Men in families,* eds. R. A. Lewis and R. E. Salt, 159–68. Thousand Oaks, CA: Sage.

MCADOO, J. L. 1993. Decision making and marital satisfaction in African American families. In *Family ethnicity: Strength in diversity,* ed. H. P. McAdoo, 109–19. Thousand Oaks, CA: Sage.

MCCABE, M. P. 1984. Toward a theory of adolescent dating. *Adolescence* 19 (Spring): 159–70.

McCaughey septuplets celebrate their second birthday. 1999. *Baltimore Sun,* November 19, 23A.

MCCORMICK, J. 1994. Why parents kill. *Newsweek,* November 14, 31–34.

MCCORMICK, J., AND P. MCKILLOP. 1989. The other suburbia: An ugly secret in America's suburbs: Poverty. *Newsweek,* June 26, 22–24.

MCCOY, E. 1986. Your one and only. *Parents,* October, 118–21, 236.

MCDADE, K. 1995. How we parent: Race and ethnic differences. In *American families: Issues in race and ethnicity,* ed. C. K. Jacobson, 283–300. New York: Garland.

MCDONALD, K. A. 1999. Studies of women's health produce a wealth of knowledge on the biology of gender differences. *Chronicle of Higher Education,* June 25, A19, A22.

MCDONALD, M. 2000. A start-up of her own. *U.S. News & World Report,* May 15, 34–42.

MCELROY, W., ED. 1991. *Freedom, feminism, and the state: An overview of individualist feminism.* New York: Holmes & Meier.

MCELVAINE, R. S. 1993. *The great depression: America, 1929–1941.* New York: Times Books.

MCFARLANE, J. 2000. Women filing assault charges on an intimate partner: Criminal justice outcome and future violence experienced. *Violence against Women* 6 (April): 396–408.

MCFARLANE, M., S.S. BULL, AND C.A. RIETMEIJER. 2000. The Internet as a newly emerging risk environment for sexually transmitted diseases. *JAMA* 284 (July 26): 443–46.

MCGILL, M. 1985. *The McGill report on male intimacy.* New York: Holt, Rinehart & Winston.

MCGINN, D., AND J. E. HALPERT. 1998. Final farewells. *Newsweek,* December 14, 60–62.

MCGINNIS, T. 1981. *More than just a friend: The joys and disappointments of extramarital affairs.* Upper Saddle River, NJ: Prentice Hall.

MCGOLDRICK, M., AND J. GIORDANO. 1996. Overview: Ethnicity and family therapy. In *Ethnicity and family therapy,* 2nd ed., eds. M. McGoldrick, J. Giordano, and J. K. Pearce, 1–27. New York: Guilford Press.

MCGOLDRICK, M., M. HEIMAN, AND B. CARTER. 1993. The changing family life cycle: A perspective on normalcy. In *Normal family processes,* 2nd ed., ed. F. Walsh, 405–43. New York: Guilford Press.

MCGONAGLE, K. A., R. C. KESSLER, AND I. H. GOTLIB. 1993. The effects of marital disagreement style, frequency, and outcome on marital disruption. *Journal of Social and Personal Relationships,* 10 (August): 385–404.

MCGUINESS, T., AND L. PALLANSCH. 2000. Competence of children adopted from the former

Soviet Union. *Family Relations* 49 (October): 457–64.

MCGUIRE, M. 1996. Growing up with two moms. *Newsweek,* November 4, 53.

MCINTYRE, J. 1981. The structure-functional approach to family study. In *Emerging conceptual frameworks in family analysis,* eds. F. I. Nye and F. M. Berardo, 52–77. New York: Praeger.

MCKAY, M. M. 1994. The link between domestic violence and child abuse: Assessment and treatment considerations. *Child Welfare* 73 (January–February): 29–39.

MCKENRY, P. C., AND M. A. FINE. 1993. Parenting following divorce: A comparison of black and white single mothers. *Journal of Comparative Family Studies* 24 (Spring): 99–111.

MCKINLAY, J. B., AND H. A. FELDMAN. 1994. Age-related variation in sexual activity and interest in normal men: Results from the Massachusetts male aging study. In *Sexuality across the life course,* ed. A. S. Rossi, 261–85. Chicago: University of Chicago Press.

MCLANAHAN, S., AND L. BUMPASS. 1988. Intergenerational consequences of family disruption. *American Journal of Sociology* 94 (July): 130–52.

MCLANAHAN, S., AND G. SANDEFUR. 1994. *Growing up with a single parent: What hurts, what helps.* Cambridge, MA: Harvard University Press.

MCLANAHAN, S. S., J. A. SELTZER, T. L. HANSON, AND E. THOMSON. 1994. Child support enforcement and child well-being: Greater security or greater conflict? In *Child support and child well-being,* eds. I. Garfinkel, S. S. McLanahan and P. K. Robins, 239–56. Washington, DC: Urban Institute Press.

MCLANE, D. 1995. The Cuban-American princess. *New York Times Magazine,* February 26, 42–43.

MCLAUGHLIN, D. K., D. T. LICHTER, AND G. M. JOHNSTON. 1993. Some women marry young: Transitions to first marriage in metropolitan and nonmetropolitan areas. *Journal of Marriage and the Family* 55 (November): 827–38.

MCMAHON, T. 1993. *It works for us! Proven child-care tips from experienced parents across the country.* New York: Pocket Books.

MCNAMARA, R. P., M. TEMPENIS, AND B. WALTON. 1999. *Crossing the line: Interracial couples in the South.* Westport, CT: Greenwood Press.

MCPHARLIN, P. 1946. *Love and courtship in America.* New York: Hastings House.

MEAD, L. M. 1996. Work requirements can transform the system. *Chronicle of Higher Education,* October 4, B6.

MEAD, M. 1935. *Sex and temperament in three primitive societies.* New York: Morrow.

MEKOS, D., E. M. HETHERINGTON, AND D. REISS. 1996. Sibling differences in problem behavior and parental treatment in nondivorced and remarried families. *Child Development* 67 (October): 2148–65.

MELTZER, N., ED. 1964. *In their own words: A history of the American Negro, 1619–1865.* New York: Crowell.

MENAGHAN, E. G., AND T. L. PARCEL. 1991. Parental employment and family life. In *Contemporary families: Looking forward, looking back,* ed. A. Booth, 361–80. Minneapolis, MN: National Council on Family Relations.

MENDELSOHN, K. D., L. Z. NIEMAN, K. ISAACS, S. LEE, AND S. P. LEVISON. 1994. Sex and gender bias in anatomy and physical diagnosis text illustrations. *JAMA,* October 26, 1267–70.

MERGENBAGEN, P. 1994. Job benefits get personal. *American Demographics* 16 (September): 30–38.

MERGENBAGEN, P. 1996. The reunion market. *American Demographics* 18 (April): 30–34, 52.

MERKLE, E. G., AND R. A. RICHARDSON. 2000. Digital dating and virtual relating: Conceptualizing computer mediated romantic relationships. *Family Relations* 49 (April): 187–92.

MERTEN, D. E. 1996. Going-with: The role of a social form in early romance. *Journal of Contemporary Ethnography* 24 (January): 462–84.

METTS, S. 1994. Relational transgressions. In *The dark side of interpersonal communication,* eds. W. R. Cupach and B. H. Spitzberg, 217–39. Hillsdale, NJ: Lawrence Erlbaum Associates.

MEYER, C. H. 1985. A feminist perspective on foster family care: A redefinition of categories. *Child Welfare* 64 (May/June): 249–58.

MEYER, D. R., AND J. BARTFELD. 1996. Compliance with child support orders in divorce cases. *Journal of Marriage and the Family* 58 (February): 201–12.

MEYER, D. R., J. BARTFELD, I. GARFINKEL, AND P. BROWN. 1996. Child support reform: Lessons from Wisconsin. *Family Relations* 45 (January): 11–18.

MEYER, D. R., AND M. CANCIAN. 1997. Life after welfare. *Population Today* 25 (July/August): 4–5.

MEYER, J. 1990. Guess who's coming to dinner this time? A study of gay intimate relationships and the support for those relationships. In *Homosexuality and family relations,* eds. F. W. Bozett and M. B. Sussman, 59–82. New York: Harrington Park Press.

MIALL, C. 1986. The stigma of involuntary childlessness. *Social Problems* 33 (April): 268–82.

MIALL, C. E. 1987. The stigma of adoptive parent status: Perceptions of community attitudes toward adoption and the experience of informal social sanctioning. *Family Relations* 36 (January): 34–39.

MICHAEL, R. T., J. H. GAGNON, E. O. LAUMANN, AND G. KOLATA. 1994. *Sex in America: A definitive study.* Boston: Little, Brown.

MIEDZIAN, M. 1991. *Boys will be boys: Breaking the link between masculinity and violence.* New York: Anchor.

MIELL, D., AND R. CROGHAN. 1996. Examining the wider context of social relationships. In *Social interaction and personal relationships,* eds. D. Miell and R. Dallos, 267–318. Thousand Oaks, CA: Sage.

MIHESUAH, D. A. 1998. American Indian identities: Issues of individual choices and development. *American Indian Culture and Research Journal* 22 (2): 193–226.

MILKIE, M. A., AND P. PELTOLA. 1999. Playing all the roles: Gender and the work-family balancing act. *Journal of Marriage and the Family* 61 (May): 476–90.

MILKMAN, R. 1976. Women's work and the economic crisis: Some lessons from the great depression. *Review of Radical Political Economics* 8 (Spring): 73–97.

MILLER, B. 1995. Household futures. *American Demographics* 17 (March): 4, 6.

MILLER, B. C. 1986. *Family research methods.* Beverly Hills, CA: Sage.

MILLER, B. C. 1995. Risk factors for adolescent nonmarital childbearing. In *Report to Congress on out-of-wedlock childbearing,* 217–21. Hyattsville, MD: Centers for Disease Control and Prevention, National Center for Health Statistics.

MILLER, B. C., AND K. A. MOORE. 1990. Adolescent sexual behavior, pregnancy, and parenting: Research through the 1980s. *Journal of Marriage and the Family* 52 (November): 1025–44.

MILLER, K. S., R. FOREHAND, AND B. A. KOTCHICK. 1999. Adolescent sexual behavior in two ethnic minority samples: The role of family variables. *Journal of Marriage and the Family* 61 (February): 85–98.

MILLER, L. F., AND J. E. MOORMAN. 1989. Married-couple families with children. In *Studies in marriage and the family,* Bureau of the Census, Current Population Reports, Series P-23, No. 162, 27–36. Washington, DC: U.S. Government Printing Office.

MILLER, W. L., AND B. F. CRABTREE. 1994. Clinical research. In *Handbook of qualitative research,* eds. N. K. Denzin and Y. S. Lincoln, 340–52. Thousand Oaks, CA: Sage.

MILLER-PERRIN, C. L., AND R. D. PERRIN. 1999. *Child maltreatment: An introduction.* Thousand Oaks, CA: Sage.

MILLS, R. J. 2000. Health insurance coverage, 1999. U.S. Census Bureau, P60-211. www.census.gov/prod/2000pubs/p60-211.pdf (accessed October 28, 2000).

MIN, P. G. 1988. The Korean American family. In *Ethnic families in America: Patterns and variations,* 3rd ed., eds. C. H. Mindel, R. W. Habenstein, and R. Wright, Jr., 199–229. New York: Elsevier.

MIN, P. G., ED. 1995. *Asian Americans: Contemporary trends and issues.* Thousand Oaks, CA: Sage.

MINDEL, C. H., R. W. HABENSTEIN, AND R. WRIGHT, JR., EDS. 1988. *Ethnic families in America: Patterns and variations,* 3rd ed. New York: Elsevier.

MINTON, L. 1995. Stepfamilies. *Parade Magazine,* February 26, 24–25.

MINTZ, S., AND S. KELLOGG. 1988. *Domestic revolution: A social history of American family life.* New York: Free Press.

MIRANDE, A. 1985. *The Chicano experience: An alternative perspective.* Notre Dame, IN: University of Notre Dame Press.

MIROWSKY, J., AND C. E. ROSS. 1986. Social patterns of distress. *Annual Review of Sociology* 12, 23–45.

MISHEL, L., J. BERNSTEIN, AND J. SCHMITT. 2001. *The state of working America 2000–2001.* Ithaca, NY: Cornell University Press.

MITCHELL, B. A., AND E. M. GEE. 1996. "Boomerang kids" and midlife parental marital satisfaction. *Family Relations* 45 (October): 442–48.

MITTELSTADT, M. 1994. Hispanics seek higher, more positive profile on television. *Baltimore Sun,* September 7, D1, D5.

Modern Maturity. 1993. Which living arrangement is for you? April/May, 32–33.

MOEN, P. 1992. *Women's two roles: A contemporary dilemma.* Westport, CT: Auburn House.

MOFFITT, R. A. 1995. The effect of the welfare system on nonmarital childrearing. In *Report to Congress on out-of-wedlock childbearing,* 167–73. Hyattsville, MD: Centers for Disease Control and Prevention, National Center for Health Statistics.

MOGELONSKY, M. 1995. Myths of telecommuting. *American Demographics* 17 (June): 15–16.

MOGELONSKY, M. 1996. The rocky road to adulthood. *American Demographics* 18 (May): 26–35, 56.

MOHR, J. 1981. The great upsurge of abortion, 1840–1880. In *Family life in America: 1620–2000,* eds. M. Albin and D. Cavallo, 119–30. St. James, NY: Revisionary Press.

Moms: Mum's not the word. 1999. *Population Today* 27 (September): 3.

MONEY, J., AND A. A. EHRHARDT. 1972. *Man & woman, boy & girl.* Baltimore: Johns Hopkins University Press.

MONTAGU, A. 1974. *The natural superiority of women.* London: Collier Macmillan.

MONTGOMERY, M. J., AND G. T. SORELL. 1997. Differences in love attitudes across family life stages. *Family Relations* 46 (January): 55–61.

MONTGOMERY, M. J., E. R. ANDERSON, E. M. HETHERINGTON, AND W. G. CLINGEMPEEL. 1992. Patterns of courtship for remarriage: Implications for child adjustment and parent–child relationships. *Journal of Marriage and the Family* 54 (August): 686–98.

MOON, A., AND O. WILLIAMS. 1993. Perceptions of elder abuse and help-seeking patterns among African-American, Caucasian American, and Korean-American elderly women. *The Gerontologist* 33 (3): 386–95.

MOORE, J., AND H. PACHON. 1985. *Hispanics in the United States.* Upper Saddle River, NJ: Prentice Hall.

MOORE, K. A. 1995. Nonmarital childbearing in the United States. In *Report to Congress on out-of-wedlock childbearing,* v–xxii. Hyattsville, MD: Centers for Disease Control and Prevention, National Center for Health Statistics.

MOORE, K. A., A. R. PAPILLO, S. WILLIAMS, J. JAGER, AND F. JONES. 1999. *CTS facts at a glance.* Washington, DC: Child Trends.

MOORE, K. A., AND N. Q. SNYDER. 1994. *Facts at a glance.* Brochure. Washington, DC: Child Trends.

Moore, P., with C. P. Conn. 1985. *Disguised.* Waco, TX: Word Books.

MOOREHOUSE, M. J. 1991. Linking maternal employment patterns to mother–child activities and children's school competence. *Developmental Psychology* 27 (March): 295–303.

MOOREHOUSE, M. J. 1993. Work and family dynamics. In *Family, self, and society: Toward a new agenda for family research,* eds. P. A. Cowan, D. Field, D. A. Hansen, A. Skolnick, and G. E. Swanson, 265–86. Hillsdale, NJ: Lawrence Erlbaum Associates.

MORALES, E. 1996. Gender roles among Latino gay and bisexual men: Implications for family and couple relationships. In *Lesbians and gays in couples and families: A handbook for therapists,* eds. J. Laird and R.-J. Green, 272–97. San Francisco: Jossey-Bass.

MORELL, C. M. 1994. *Unwomanly conduct: The challenges of intentional childlessness.* New York: Routledge.

MORGAN, D. I., ED. 1993. *Successful focus groups: Advancing the state of the art.* Thousand Oaks, CA: Sage.

MORGAN, L. A. 1988. Outcomes of marital separation: A longitudinal test of predictors. *Journal of Marriage and the Family* 50 (May): 493–98.

MORGAN, P. D. 1998. *Slave counterpoint: Black culture in the eighteenth-century Chesapeake & lowcountry.* Chapel Hill: University of North Carolina Press.

MORGAN, S. P., O. N. LYE, AND G. A. CONDRAN. 1988. Sons, daughters, and the risk of marital disruption. *American Journal of Sociology* 94 (July): 110–29.

MORGAN, W. L. 1939. *The family meets the depression: A study of a group of highly selected families.* Westport, CT: Greenwood Press.

MORGENTHAU, T. 1997. The face of the future. *Newsweek,* January 27, 58–60.

MORIN, R. 1994. How to lie with statistics: Adultery. *Washington Post,* March 6, C5.

MORRISON, D. R., AND A. J. CHERLIN. 1995. The divorce process and young children's well-being: A prospective analysis. *Journal of Marriage and the Family* 57 (August): 800–12.

MORSE, S. 1995. Why girls don't like computer games. *AAUW Outlook* 88 (Winter): 14–17.

MOSBY, L., AND A. W. RAWLS. 1999. Troubles in interracial talk about discipline: An examination of African American child rearing. *Journal of Comparative Family Studies* 30 (Summer): 489–522.

MOSCICKI, E. K. 1994. Gender differences in completed and attempted suicides. *Annals of Epidemiology* 4 (March): 152–58.

MOSHER, S. W. 2000. "Land of the setting sun." Population Research Institute, PRI Weekly News Briefing Archives, June 14. www.pop.org/briefings/settingsun.htm (accessed September 23, 2000).

MOSHER, W. D., AND W. F. PRATT. 1991. Fecundity and infertility in the United States: Incidence and trends. *Fertility and Sterility* 56 (August): 192–93.

MOSHER, W. D., AND W. F. PRATT. 1993. *AIDS-related behavior among women 15–44 years of age: United States, 1988 and 1990.* U.S. Department of Health and Human Services, Centers for Disease Control and Prevention, December 22.

Motherhood today—A tougher job, less ably done. 1997. Pew Research Center for the People & the Press. www.people-press.org/momrpt.htm (accessed October 5, 1997).

Mothers work. 2000. *Public Perspective* 11 (July/August): 23.

MOTT, F. L., L. KOWALESKI-JONES, AND E. G. MENAGHAN. 1997. Paternal absence and child behavior: Does a child's gender make a difference? *Journal of Marriage and the Family* 59 (February): 103–18.

MOUNT, S. L., AND J. L. PAPILLO. 1999. A study of 10,296 pediatric and adolescent papanicolaou smear diagnoses in northern New England. *Pediatrics* 103 (March): 539–45.

MOWRER, E. R. 1972. War and family solidarity and stability. In *The American family in World War II,* ed. R. A. Abrams, 100–06. New York: Arno Press and New York Times. (Originally published in *Annals of the American Academy of Political and Social Science* 229 [September 1943].)

MOYNIHAN, D. P., ED. 1970. *Toward a national urban policy.* New York: Basic Books.

MUEHLENHARD, C. L., S. DANNOFF-BURG, AND I. G. POWCH. 1994. Is rape sex or violence? Conceptual issues and implications. In *Sex, power, conflict: Evolutionary and feminist perspectives,* eds. D. M. Buss and N. M. Malamuth, 119–37. New York: Oxford University Press.

MUEHLENHARD, C. L., AND M. A. LINTON. 1987. Date rape and sexual aggression in dating situations: Incidence and risk factors. *Journal of Counseling Psychology* 34 (2): 186–96.

MUI, A. C., AND N. MORROW-HOWELL. 1993. Sources of emotional strain among the oldest caregivers: Differential experiences of siblings and spouses. *Research on Aging* 15 (March): 50–69.

MUI, A. C., N. G. CHOI, AND A. MONK. 1998. *Long-term care and ethnicity.* Westport, CT: Auburn House.

MULLER, T. 1997. Nativism in the mid-1990s: Why now? In *Immigrants out! The new nativism and the anti-immigrant impulse in the United States,* ed. J. F. Perea, 105–18. New York: New York University Press.

MULLER, T., AND T. J. ESPENSHADE. 1985. *The fourth wave: California's newest immigrants.* Washington, DC: Urban Institute Press.

MUNCY, R. LEE. 1988. Sex and marriage in utopia. *Society* 25 (January/February): 46–48.

MUNTER, C. 1984. Fat and the fantasy of perfection. In *Pleasure and danger: Exploring female sexuality,* ed. C. Vance, 225–31. Boston: Routledge & Kegan Paul.

MURDOCK, G. P. 1967. Ethnographic atlas: A summary. *Ethnology* 6, 109–236.

MURPHY, M. 1999. How women took over the news. *TV Guide,* October 9, 16–23.

MURPHY, M., K. GLASER, AND E. GRUNDY. 1997. Marital status and long-term illness in Great Britain. *Journal of Marriage and the Family 59* (February): 156–64.

MURR, A. 1998. Pay? How about a pizza? *Newsweek,* April 20, 42–43.

MURRAY, C. 1994. Does welfare bring more babies? *American Enterprise 5* (January/February): 52–59.

MURSTEIN, B. I. 1974. *Love, sex, and marriage through the ages.* New York: Springer.

MURSTEIN, B. I., JR., R. MERIGHI, AND S. A. VYSE. 1991. Love styles in the United States and France: A cross-cultural comparison. *Journal of Social and Clinical Psychology 10* (Spring): 37–46.

MYERS, G. 1996. Why women pay more. *American Demographics 18* (April): 40–41.

MYERS, S. M., AND A. BOOTH. 1999. Marital strains and marital quality: The role of high and low locus of control. *Journal of Marriage and the Family 61* (May): 423–36.

NAJAB, B. 1997. In Iran, respected and protected as a woman. *Baltimore Sun,* June 9, 13A.

NAKAMURA, D. 1999. Dads who rock the cradle. *Washington Post,* March 16, 7.

NAKONEZNY, P. A., R. D. SHULL, AND J. L. RODGERS. 1995. The effect of no-fault divorce law on the divorce rate across the 50 states and its relation to income, education, and religiosity. *Journal of Marriage and the Family 57* (May): 477–88.

NANCE, J. 1975. *The gentle Tasaday.* New York: Harcourt Brace Jovanovich.

NARDI, P. M., AND D. SHERROD. 1994. Friendship in the lives of gay men and lesbians. *Journal of Social and Personal Relationships 11* (May): 185–99.

NASAR, S. 1994. More men in prime of life spend less time working. *New York Times,* December 1, D1, D15.

NASS, G. D., R. W. LIBBY, AND M. P. FISHER. 1981. *Sexual choices: An introduction to human sexuality.* Belmont, CA: Wadsworth.

National Center for Health Statistics. 1998. Births, marriages, divorces and deaths for June 1997. *Monthly Vital Statistics Report 46,* no. 6. Hyattsville, MD: National Center for Health Statistics.

National Center for Health Statistics. 2000. Centers for Disease Control and Prevention. Births, marriages, divorces, and deaths: Provisional data for September 1999. www.cdc.gov/nchs/data/nvs48_15.pdf (accessed August 11, 2000).

National Commission on Children. 1991. *Beyond rhetoric: A new agenda for children and families.* Washington, DC: U.S. Government Printing Office.

National Research Council. 1993. *Losing generations: Adolescents in high-risk settings.* Washington, DC: National Academy Press.

National Research Council. 1998. *Violence in families: Assessing prevention and treatment programs.* Washington, DC: National Academy Press.

Necessary compromises: How parents, employers, and children's advocates view child care today. 2000. Public Agenda Online. www.publicagenda.org/specials/childcare/childcare.htm (accessed September 29, 2000).

NEFT, N., AND A. D. LEVINE. 1997. *Where women stand: An international report on the status of women in over 140 countries, 1997–1998.* New York: Random House.

NELSON, G. 1994. Emotional well-being of separated and married women: Long-term follow-up study. *American Journal of Orthopsychiatry 64* (January): 150–60.

NEUFELD, J., J. R. MCNAMARA, AND M. ERTL. 1999. Incidence and prevalence of dating partner abuse and its relationship to dating practices. *Journal of Interpersonal Violence 14* (February): 125–37.

NEUGARTEN, B. L., AND K. K. WEINSTEIN. 1964. The changing American grandparents. *Journal of Marriage and the Family 26* (May): 199–204.

NEUMAN, W. L. 1994. *Social research methods: Qualitative and quantitative approaches,* 2nd ed. Boston: Allyn & Bacon.

NEVILLE, L. 1997. Database: Heart trouble. *U.S. News & World Report,* February 10, 16.

New reports document discrimination against minorities by mortgage lending institutions. 1999. U.S. Department of Housing and Urban Development. www.hud.gov/pressrel/newsconf/menu.html (accessed October 2, 2000).

New York Times. 1994. Court lets landlord refuse unmarried couple. May 29, A3.

NEWPORT, F. 1996. Americans generally happy with their marriages. *Gallup Poll Monthly* (September): 18–22.

Newsweek. 2000. Newsweek.com live vote. May 8, 6.

NG, F. 1998. *The Taiwanese Americans.* Westport, CT: Greenwood Press.

NICHD Early Child Care Research Network. 1999a. Child care and mother–child interaction in the first 3 years of life. *Developmental Psychology 35* (November): 1399–461.

NICHD Early Child Care Research Network. 1999b. Child outcomes when child care center classes meet recommended standards for quality. *American Journal of Public Health 89* (July): 1072–77.

NICHD Early Child Care Research Network. 2000. Characteristics and quality of child care for toddlers and preschoolers. *Journal of Applied Developmental Science* (in press).

NICOLOSI, A., ET AL. 1994. The efficiency of male-to-female and female-to-male sexual transmission of the human immunodeficiency virus—a study of 730 stable couples. *Epidemiology 5* (November): 570–75.

NIE, N. H., AND L. ERBRING. 2000. Internet and society: A preliminary report. www.stanford.edu/group/siqss/Press_Release/Preliminary_Report-4-21.pdf (accessed August 4, 2000).

NIEMANN, Y. F., J. ROMERO, J. ARREDONDO, AND V. RODRIGUEZ. 1999. What does it mean to be "Mexican"? Social construction of an ethnic identity. *Hispanic Journal of Behavioral Sciences 21* (February): 47–60.

NIFONG, C. 1997. How part-timers fare in US economy. *Christian Science Monitor,* August 14: 4.

Night shift puts serious dent in family life. 1996. Ann Landers column. *Baltimore Sun,* December 9, 3D.

NIKKAN, J., AND L. FURMAN. 2000. *Our boys speak: Adolescent boys write about their inner lives.* New York: St. Martin's.

NIMKOFF, M. F. 1961. Marriage. In *The encyclopedia of sexual behavior,* vol. 2, eds. A. Ellis and A. Abarbanel, 663–71. New York: Hawthorn Books.

1997 Assisted reproductive technology success rates: National summary and fertility clinic reports. 1999. Centers for Disease Control and Prevention. www.cdc.gov/nccdphp/drh/art97/pdf/art97.pdf (accessed September 21, 2000).

N.J. finds welfare "family cap" fails to reduce additional births. 1997. *Baltimore Sun,* September 12, A3.

NOCK, S. L. 1995. A comparison of marriages and cohabiting relationships. *Journal of Family Issues 16* (January): 53–76.

NOCK, S. L. 1998. *Marriage in men's lives.* New York: Oxford University Press.

NOGUCHI, Y. 1999. Working for a living wage. *Washington Post,* October 4, 19–20.

NOLAN, J., M. COLEMAN, AND L. GANONG. 1984. The presentation of stepfamilies in marriage and family textbooks. *Family Relations 33,* 559–66.

NOLEN-HOEKSEMA, S., AND J. LARSON. 1999. *Coping with loss.* Mahwah, NJ: Lawrence Erlbaum Associates.

NOLLER, P. 1984. *Nonverbal communication and marital interaction.* New York: Pergamon Press.

NOLLER, P., AND M. A. FITZPATRICK. 1993. *Communication in family relationships.* Upper Saddle River, NJ: Prentice Hall.

NONNEMAKER, L. 2000. Women physicians in academic medicine: New insights from cohort studies. *New England Journal of Medicine 342,* February 10, 399–405.

NORTON, A. J., AND L. F. MILLER. 1992. *Marriage, divorce, and remarriage in the 1990's.* U.S. Census Bureau, Current Population Reports, P23–180. Washington, DC: U.S. Government Printing Office.

NOWINSKI, J. 1993. *Hungry hearts: On men, intimacy, self-esteem, and addiction.* New York: Lexington Books.

NURIUS, P. S., J. NORRIS, L. A. DIMEFF, AND T. L. GRAHAM. 1996. Expectations regarding acquaintance sexual aggression among sorority and fraternity members. *Sex Roles 35* (7/8): 427–44.

NUTA, V. R. 1986. Emotional aspects of child support enforcement. *Family Relations 35* (January): 177–82.

NYE, F. I. 1988. Fifty years of family research, 1937–1987. *Journal of Marriage and the Family 50* (May): 305–16.

NYE, F. I., AND F. M. BERARDO, EDS. 1981. *Emerging conceptual frameworks in family analysis.* New York: Praeger.

NYMAN, L. 1995. The identification of birth order personality attributes. *Journal of Psychology: Interdisciplinary and Applied 129* (January): 51–60.

OASDI benefits, Table 1.B3: Number and average monthly benefit in current-payment status for adult beneficiaries by type of benefit, sex, and age, September 1997. ftp://ftp.ssa.gov/pub/statistics/1b3 (accessed March 15, 1998).

OATES, R. K., AND R. S. KEMPE. 1997. Growth failure in infants. In *The battered child,* 5th ed., eds. M. E. Helfer, R. S. Kempe, and R. D. Krugman, 374–91. Chicago: University of Chicago Press.

OBEIDALLAH, D. A., AND F. J. EARLS. 1999. *Adolescent girls: The role of depression in the development of delinquency.* U.S. Department of Justice, Office of Justice Programs, National Institute of Justice. Washington, DC.

O'CONNELL, M. 1997. Children with single parents—how they fare. *Census Brief,* CENBR/97-1. U.S. Census Bureau, September. Washington, DC: U.S. Government Printing Office.

O'DONNELL, P., S. STEVENSON, V. S. STEFANAKOS, AND K. PERAINO. 1999. Click and split. *Newsweek,* November 22, 8.

O'FLAHERTY, K. M., AND L. W. EELLS. 1988. Courtship behavior of the remarried. *Journal of Marriage and the Family 50* (May): 499–506.

OGBURN, W. F. 1927. Eleven questions concerning American marriages. *Social Forces 5,* 5–12.

OGGINS, J., J. VEROFF, AND D. LEBER. 1993. Perceptions of marital interaction among black and white newlyweds. *Journal of Personality and Social Psychology* 65 (September): 494–511.

OGINTZ, E. 1994. Is Grandma always the best baby-sitter? *Parents*, September, 139.

O'HARE, W. 1996. A new look at poverty in America. *Population Bulletin* 51 (September). Washington, DC: Population Reference Bureau.

O'HARE, W., AND J. SCHWARTZ. 1997. One step forward, two steps back. *American Demographics* 19 (September): 53–56.

O'HARE, W. P. 1999. *Teen childbearing in America's largest cities.* A KIDS COUNT Working Paper. Baltimore: The Annie E. Casey Foundation.

O'HARE, W. P., AND J. C. FELT. 1991. *Asian Americans: America's fastest growing minority group.* Washington, DC: Population Reference Bureau.

O'HARE, W. P., W. H. FREY, AND D. FOST. 1994. Asians in the suburbs. *American Demographics* 16 (May): 32–38.

O'HEARN, C. C., ED. 1998. *Half and half: Writers on growing up biracial and bicultural.* New York: Pantheon Books.

O'KELLY, C. G., AND L. S. CARNEY. 1986. *Women and men in society: Cross-cultural perspectives on gender stratification,* 2nd ed. Belmont, CA: Wadsworth.

OKIE, S. 1993. The boys "only wanted to rape them." *Washington Post,* February 17, A24.

OKIE, S. 1997. Immigration law arouses adopters' opposition. *Washington Post Health Supplement,* July 1, 7.

OKIN, S. M. 1997. Families and feminist theory: Some past and present issues. In *Feminism and families,* ed. H. L. Nelson, 13–26. New York: Routledge.

OKUN, B. F. 1996. *Understanding diverse families: What practitioners need to know.* New York: Guilford Press.

OLDENBURG, D. 1996. Guys and dolls. *Washington Post,* December 13, C5.

OLDENBURG, D. 1999. Sperm banks online: Going too far? *Washington Post,* November 18, C4.

Older Americans 2000: Key indicators of well-being. 2000. Federal Interagency Forum on Aging-Related Statistics. www.agingstats.gov/chartbook2000/OlderAmericans2000.pdf (accessed October 28, 2000).

OLECK, J. 2000. The kids are not all right. *Business Week,* February 14, 74, 78.

OLIVER, M. B., AND C. SEDKIDES. 1992. Effects of sexual permissiveness on desirability of partner as a function of low and high commitment to relationship. *Social Psychology Quarterly* 55 (3): 321–33.

OLIVER, M. L., AND T. M. SHAPIRO. 1997. *Black wealth/white wealth: A new perspective on racial inequality.* New York: Routledge.

OLLENBURGER, J. C., AND H. A. MOORE. 1992. *A sociology of women: The intersection of patriarchy, capitalism and colonization.* Upper Saddle River, NJ: Prentice Hall.

OLSON, M. R., AND J. A. HAYNES. 1993. Successful single parents. *Families in Society: The Journal of Contemporary Human Services* 74 (May): 259–67.

O'MARA, R. 1997. Who am I? *Baltimore Sun,* June 29, 1J, 4J.

$1.3 million settlement in EEOC racial and sexual harassment suit against Foster Wheeler constructors. 2000. Equal Employment Opportunity Commission, Washington, DC. www.eeoc.gov/press/1-7-00.html (accessed August 26, 2000).

ONO, H. 1998. Husbands' and wives' resources and marital dissolution. *Journal of Marriage and the Family* 60 (August): 674–89.

ORCHARD, A. L., AND K. B. SOLBERG. 1999. Expectations of the stepmother's role. *Journal of Divorce & Remarriage* 31 (1/2): 107–23.

ORDOÑEZ, R. Z. 1997. Mail-order brides: An emerging community. In *Filipino Americans: Transformation and identity,* ed. M. P. Root, 121–42. Thousand Oaks, CA: Sage.

ORENSTEIN, P. 1994. *Schoolgirls: Young women, self-esteem, and the confidence gap.* New York: Doubleday.

ORENSTEIN, P. 1995. Looking for a donor to call dad. *New York Times Magazine,* June 16, 26–35, 42–58.

ORNISH, D. 1998. *Love & survival: The scientific basis for the healing power of intimacy.* New York: HarperCollins.

OROPESA, R. S., D. T. LICHTER, AND R. N. ANDERSON. 1994. Marriage markets and the paradox of Mexican American nuptiality. *Journal of Marriage and the Family* 56 (November): 889–907.

OSGOOD, N. J. 1985. *Suicide in the elderly.* Rockville, MD: Aspen Systems Corporation.

OSHERSON, S. 1992. *Wrestling with love: How men struggle with intimacy with women, children, parents and each other.* New York: Fawcett Columbine.

OSMOND, M. W., AND B. THORNE. 1993. Feminist theories: The social construction of gender in families and society. In *Sourcebook of family theories and methods: A contextual approach,* eds. P. G. Boss, W. J. Doherty, R. LaRossa, W. R. Schumm, and S. K. Steinmetz, 591–623. New York: Plenum Press.

OSOFSKY, J. D. 1999. The impact of violence on children. *Domestic Violence and Children* 9 (Winter): 33–49.

O'SULLIVAN, L. F., AND E. S. BYERS. 1993. Eroding stereotypes: College women's attempts to influence reluctant male sexual partners. *Journal of Sex Research* 30 (August): 270–82.

O'SULLIVAN, L. F., B. JARAMILLO, D. MOREAU, AND H. F. L. MEYER-BAHLBURG. 1999. Mother–daughter communication about sexuality in a clinical sample of Hispanic adolescent girls. *Hispanic Journal of Behavioral Sciences* 21 (November): 447–69.

OVERHOLSER, G. 1996. Front page story: Women. *Washington Post,* April 21, C6.

OYSTERMAN, D., N. RADIN, AND R. BENN. 1993. Dynamics in a three-generational family: Teens, grandparents, and babies. *Developmental Psychology* 29 (3): 564–73.

PAASCH, K. M., AND J. D. TEACHMAN. 1991. Gender of children and receipt of assistance from absent fathers. *Journal of Family Issues* 12 (December): 450–66.

PADILLA, E. R., AND K. E. O'GRADY. 1987. Sexuality among Mexican Americans: A case of sexual stereotyping. *Journal of Personality and Social Psychology* 52 (1): 5–10.

PAGLIA, C. 1990. *Sexual personae: Art and decadence from Nefertiti to Emily Dickinson.* New Haven, CT: Yale University Press.

PALMORE, E. B. 1999. *Ageism: Negative and positive.* New York: Springer.

PAMUK, E., D. MAKUC, K. HECK, C. REUBEN, AND K. LOCHNER. 1998. *Socioeconomic status and health chartbook: Health, United States, 1998.* Hyattsville, MD: National Center for Health Statistics.

PAN, E. 2000. Why Asian guys are on a roll. *Newsweek,* February 21, 50–51.

PAPANEK, H. 1979. Family status production. *Signs* 4, 775–81.

PAPERNOW, P. L. 1984. The stepfamily cycle: An experiential model of stepfamily development. *Family Relations* 33, 355–63.

PAPERNOW, P. L. 1993. *Becoming a stepfamily: Patterns of development in remarried families.* San Francisco: Jossey-Bass.

PARCEL, T. L., AND E. G. MENAGHAN. 1994. *Parents' jobs and children's lives.* New York: Aldine de Gruyter.

Parenting skills: 21 tips & ideas to help you make a difference. 2000. Office of National Drug Control Policy. Washington, DC: National Clearinghouse for Alcohol and Drug Information.

PARKE, R. D. 1996. *Fatherhood.* Cambridge, MA: Harvard University Press.

PARKER, S. 1996. Full brother–sister marriage in Roman Egypt: Another look. *Cultural Anthropology* 11 (August): 362–76.

PARNELL, T. F., AND D. O. DAY, EDS. 1998. *Munchausen by proxy syndrome.* Thousand Oaks, CA: Sage.

PARSONS, T., AND R. F. BALES. 1955. *Family, socialization and interaction process.* Glencoe, IL: Free Press.

PASCUAL, P. 1999/2000. More foster families, fewer children entering care. *Advocasey* 1 (Fall/Winter): 4–7, 9–10.

PATNER, M. M. 1990. Between mothers and daughters: Pain and difficulty go with the territory. *Washington Post,* November 8, C5.

PATTERSON, C. J. 1992. Children of lesbian and gay parents. *Child Development* 63 (October): 1025–43.

PATTERSON, J., AND P. KIM. 1991. *The day America told the truth: What people really believe about everything that really matters.* Upper Saddle River, NJ: Prentice Hall.

PATZ, A. 2000. Will your marriage last? *Psychology Today* 33 (January/February): 58–63.

PAZ, J. J. 1993. Support of Hispanic elderly. In *Family ethnicity: Strength in diversity,* ed. H. P. McAdoo, 177–83. Thousand Oaks, CA: Sage.

PEARCE, D. 1978. The feminization of poverty: Women, work, and welfare. *Urban and Social Change Review* 11, 28–36.

PEARSON, J. C. 1985. *Gender and communication.* Dubuque, IA: Wm. C. Brown.

PEARSON, P. 1997. *When she was bad: Violent women and the myth of innocence.* New York: Viking/Penguin.

PEAVY, L., AND U. SMITH. 1994. *Women in waiting in the westward movement: Life on the home frontier.* Norman: University of Oklahoma Press.

PEELE, S., WITH A. BRODSKY. 1976. *Love and addiction.* New York: New American Library.

PENHA-LOPES, V. 1995. "Make room for daddy": Patterns of family involvement among contemporary African American men. In *American families: Issues in race and ethnicity,* ed. C. K. Jacobson, 179–99. New York: Garland.

PEPLAU, A. 1993. Lesbian and gay relationships. In *Psychological perspectives on lesbian and gay male experiences,* eds. L. D. Garnets and D. C. Kimmel, 395–419. New York: Columbia University Press.

PEREA, J. F. 1997. Introduction. In *Immigrants out! The new nativism and the anti-immigrant impulse in the United States,* ed. J. F. Perea, 1–10. New York: New York University Press.

PÉREZ, L. 1992. Cuban Miami. In *Miami now! Immigration, ethnicity, and social change,* eds. G. J. Grenier and A. Stepick III, 83–108. Gainesville: University Press of Florida.

PERKINS, F., T. LUSTER, F. A. VILLARRUEL, AND S. SMALL. 1998. An ecological, risk-factor examination of adolescents' sexual activity in three ethnic groups. *Journal of Marriage and the Family* 60 (August): 660–73.

PERRY, S. K. 1996. *Fun time, family time.* New York: Avon Books.

PERRY-JENKINS, M., AND K. FOLK. 1994. Class, couples, and conflict: Effects of the division of labor on assessments of marriage in dual-earner families. *Journal of Marriage and the Family* 56 (February): 165–80.

PERTIG, J. 1994. A weighty problem. *American Health* (January/February): 82.

PESSAR, P. R. 1995. *A visa for a dream: Dominicans in the United States.* Boston: Allyn & Bacon.

PETERSEN, W. 1966. Success story, Japanese American style. *New York Times Magazine,* January 6, 20ff.

PETERSON, J. L., J. J. CARD, M. B. EISEN, AND B. SHERMAN-WILLIAMS. 1994. Evaluating teenage pregnancy prevention and other social programs: Ten stages of program assessment. *Family Planning Perspectives* 26 (May): 116–20, 131.

PETERSON, R. 1996. A re-evaluation of the economic consequences of divorce. *American Sociological Review* 61 (June): 528–36.

PETTYS, G. L., AND P. R. BALGOPAL. 1998. Multi-generational conflicts and new immigrants: An Indo-American experience. *Families in Society: The Journal of Contemporary Human Services* 79 (July–August): 410–22.

PEWEWARDY, C. 1998. Fluff and feathers: Treatment of American Indians in the literature and the classroom. *Equity & Excellence in Education* 31 (April): 69–76.

PHILLIPS, L. E. 1999. Love, American style. *American Demographics* 21 (February): 56–57.

PIAGET, J. 1950. *The psychology of intelligence.* London: Routledge & Kegan Paul.

PIAGET, J. 1954. *The construction of reality in the child.* New York: Basic Books.

PILL, C. J. 1990. Stepfamilies: Redefining the family. *Family Relations* 39 (April): 186–92.

PILLEMER, K. A., AND D. FINKELHOR. 1988. The prevalence of elder abuse: A random sample survey. *The Gerontologist* 28, 51–57.

PILLEMER, K., AND J. J. SUITOR. 1991. Will I ever escape my child's problems? Effects of adult children's problems on elderly parents. *Journal of Marriage and the Family* 53 (August): 585–94.

PIÑA, D. L., AND V. L. BENGSTON. 1993. The division of household labor and wives' happiness: Ideology, employment, and perceptions of support. *Journal of Marriage and the Family* 55 (November): 901–12.

PIOKOWSKI, C. S., AND D. HUGHES. 1993. Dual-earner families in context: Managing family and work systems. In *Normal family processes,* 2nd ed., ed. F. Walsh, 185–207. New York: Guilford Press.

PIORKOWSKI, G. K. 1994. *Too close for comfort: Exploring the risks of intimacy.* New York: Plenum Press.

PIPHER, M. 1994. *Reviving Ophelia: Saving the selves of adolescent girls.* New York: Ballantine.

PIROG, M.A., M. E. KLOTZ, AND K. V. BYERS. 1998. Interstate comparisons of child support orders using state guidelines. *Family Relations* 47 (July): 289–95.

PITTMAN, F. 1989. *Private lives: Infidelity and the betrayal of intimacy.* New York: Norton.

PITTMAN, F. 1999. *Grow up! How taking responsibility can make you a happy adult.* New York: Golden Books.

PLECK, J. H. 1990. American fathering in historical perspective. In *Perspectives on the family: History, class, and feminism,* ed. C. Carlson, 377–89. Belmont, CA: Wadsworth.

PLECK, J. H. 1993. Are "family-supportive" employer policies relevant to men? In *Men, work, and family,* ed. J. C. Hood. Thousand Oaks, CA: Sage.

PLECK, J. H. 1997. Paternal involvement: Levels, sources, and consequences. In *The role of the father in child development,* ed. M. E. Lamb, 66–103. New York: Wiley.

PLOTNICK, R. D. 1993. The effect of social policies on teenage pregnancy and childbearing. *Families in Society: The Journal of Contemporary Human Services* 74 (June): 324–28.

PLOTNIKOFF, D. 1994. Sexism and bias pollute cyberspace. *Baltimore Sun,* August 24, 6D.

POE, L. M. 1992. *Black grandparents as parents.* Berkeley, CA: L. M. Poe.

POLIT, D. F., AND T. FALBO. 1987. Only children and personality development: A quantitative review. *Journal of Marriage and the Family* 49 (May): 309–25.

POLK, N. 1988. Matchmaking as a retirement career. *New York Times,* October 23, 29.

POLLACK, W. 1998. *Real boys: Rescuing our sons from the myths of boyhood.* New York: Henry Holt.

POLLARD, K. M., AND W. P. O'HARE. 1999. America's racial and ethnic minorities. *Population Bulletin* 54 (September): 1–48.

POMFRET, J. 2000. Among Chinese, a low-key gay liberation. *Washington Post,* January 24, A1, A18.

POPE, J. R., H. G. R. OLIVARDIA, AND J. BOROWIECKI. 1999. Evolving ideals of male body image as seen through action toys. *International Journal of Eating Disorders* 26 (July): 65–72.

POPE, V. 1997. Day-care dangers. *U.S. News & World Report,* August 4, 31–37.

POPENOE, D. 1996. *Life without father: Compelling new evidence that fatherhood and marriage are indispensable for the good of children and society.* New York: Free Press.

POPENOE, D., AND B. D. WHITEHEAD. 1999. *Should we live together? What young adults need to know about cohabitation before marriage.* The National Marriage Project. New Brunswick, NJ: Rutgers, the State University of New Jersey.

Population Reference Bureau. 1990. *America in the 21st century: Social and economic support systems.* Washington, DC.

PORTES, P. R., S. C. HOWELL, J. H. BROWN, S. EICHENBERGER, AND C. A. MAS. 1992. Family functions and children's postdivorce adjustment. *American Journal of Orthopsychiatry* 62 (October): 613–17.

POSADAS, B. M. 1999. *The Filipino Americans.* Westport, CT: Greenwood Press.

POSNER, J. K., AND D. L. VANDELL. 1994. Low-income children's after-school care: Are there beneficial effects of after-school programs? *Child Development* 65 (April): 440–56.

POTTHOFF, S. J., L. H. BEARINGER, C. L. SHAY, N. CASSUTO, R. W. BLUM, AND M. D. RESNICK. 1998. Dimensions of risk behaviors among American Indian youth. *Archives of Pediatrics & Adolescent Medicine* 152 (February): 157–63.

POWELL, E. 1991. *Talking back to sexual pressure.* Minneapolis, MN: CompCare.

PRAGER, K. J. 1995. *The psychology of intimacy.* New York: Guilford Press.

Pregnancy discrimination charges. 2000. U.S. Equal Employment Opportunity Commission. www.eeoc.gov/stats/pregnanc.html (accessed August 26, 2000).

PRESSER, H. B. 2000. Nonstandard work schedules and marital instability. *Journal of Marriage and the Family* 62 (February): 93–110.

PRESSER, H., AND A. COX. 1997. The work schedules of low-educated American women and welfare reform. *Monthly Labor Review* 120 (April): 25–35.

PRICE, J. A. 1981. North American Indian families. In *Ethnic families in America: Patterns and variations,* 2nd ed., eds. C. H. Mindel and R. W. Habenstein, 245–68. New York: Elsevier.

PRIDONOFF, J. A. 1994. Is the right-to-die movement a danger? *Washington Post Health Supplement,* October 18, 19.

PRIETO, Y. 1992. Cuban women in New Jersey: Gender relations and change. In *Seeking common ground: Multidisciplinary studies of immigrant women in the United States,* ed. D. Gabaccia, 185–201. Westport, CT: Greenwood Press.

Primary HIV infection associated with oral transmission. 2000. Centers for Disease Control and Prevention. www.cdc.gov/hiv/pubs/facts/oralsexqa.htm (accessed September 3, 2000).

PRUETT, K. D. 1987. *The nurturing father: Journey toward the complete man.* New York: Warner.

PRUSHER, I. R. 2000. Housemaids' woes spur Kuwait to review labor law. *Christian Science Monitor,* May 30, 1, 9.

PTACEK, J. 1999. *Battered women in the courtroom: The power of judicial response.* Boston: Northeastern University Press.

Public Perspective. 1994. American Youth Culture: A Roper Center Review 5 (May/June): 21–24.

PURVIS, A. 1990. The sins of the fathers. *Time,* November 26, 90–92.

PURVIS, A. 1997. Joni, no longer blue. *Time,* April 21, 101.

PUZONE, C. A. 2000. National trends in intimate partner homicide: United States, 1976–1995. *Violence against Women* 6 (April): 409–26.

PYKE, K. D. 1994. Women's employment as a gift or burden? Marital power across marriage, divorce, and remarriage. *Gender and Society* 8 (March): 73–91.

QUEEN, S. A., R. W. HABENSTEIN, AND J. S. QUADAGNO. 1985. *The family in various cultures,* 5th ed. New York: Harper & Row.

QUIASON, M. 1997. Home sharing makes living easier all around. *Christian Science Monitor,* September 23, 15.

QUICK, B. 1992. Tales from the self-help mill. *Newsweek,* August 31, 14.

QUICK, D. S., P. C. MCKENRY, AND B. M. NEWMAN. 1994. Stepmothers and their adolescent children: Adjustment to new family roles. In *Stepparenting: Issues in theory, research, and practice,* eds. K. Pasley and M. Ihinger-Tallman, 119–25. Westport, CT: Greenwood Press.

QUILL, T. E. 1993. *Death and dignity: Making choices and taking charge.* New York: Norton.

QUINDLEN, A. 2000. Sexual assault, film at eleven. *Newsweek,* July 3, 68.

QUINN, J. B. 1993. What's for dinner, Mom? *Newsweek,* April 5, 1993, 68.

QUINN, J. B. 1999. Forget the marriage penalty, it's singles who suffer at tax time. *Baltimore Sun,* September 5, 2D.

QUINN, W., AND M. ODELL. 1998. Predictors of marital adjustment during the first two years. *Marriage & Family Review* 27 (1/2): 113–30.

QUINTANA, S. M., AND V. M. VERA. 1999. Mexican American children's ethnic identity, understanding of ethnic prejudice, and parental ethnic socialization. *Hispanic Journal of Behavioral Sciences* 21 (November): 387–404.

QURESHI, R. B. 1991. Marriage strategies among Muslims from South Asia. In *Muslim families in North America,* eds. E. H. Waugh, M. Abu-Laban, and R. B. Qureshi, 185–211. Edmonton: University of Alberta Press.

Race relations in U.S. seen to be gradually improving. 2000. *Baltimore Sun,* July 11, 6A.

Raising 'em right. 1999. *Public Perspective* 10 (October/November): 21.

RALEY, R. K., AND J. BRATTER. 2000. Not even if you were the last person on earth! How marital search constraints affect the likelihood of marriage. Department of Sociology, University of Texas at Austin, unpublished paper.

RAMIREZ, O., AND C. H. ARCE. 1981. The contemporary Chicano family: An empirically based review. In *Explorations in Chicano psychology,* ed. A. Baron, 3–28. New York: Praeger.

RAMSEY, S. H. 1994. Stepparents and the law: A nebulous status and a need for reform. In *Stepparenting: Issues in theory, research and practice,* eds. K. Pasley and M. Ihinger-Tallman, 217–37. Westport, CT: Greenwood Press.

RAMU, G. N. 1989. Patterns of mate selection. In *Family and marriage: Cross-cultural perspectives,* ed. K. Ishwaran, 165–78. Toronto: Wall & Thompson.

RAND, M. R., AND K. STROM. 1997. *Violence-related injuries treated in hospital emergency departments.* NCJ-156921. U.S. Department of Justice, Bureau of Justice Statistics, Special Report, August.

RANDLE, W. 1998. So far from home. *Essence* (September): 76, 176.

RANDOLPH, W. 1996. *Waking the tempests: Ordinary life in the new Russia.* New York: Simon & Schuster.

RANDOLPH, W. M., C. STROUP-BENHAM, S. A. BLACK, AND K. S. MARKIDES. 1998. Alcohol use among Cuban-Americans, Mexican-Americans, and Puerto Ricans. *Alcohol Health & Research World* 22 (4): 265–69.

RANK, M. R. 1987. The formation and dissolution of marriages in the welfare population. *Journal of Marriage and the Family* 49 (February): 15–20.

RANK, M. R. AND T. A. HIRSCHL. 1999. The economic risk of childhood in America: Estimating the probability of poverty across the formative years. *Journal of Marriage and the Family* 61 (November): 1058–67.

RANKIN, R. P., AND J. S. MANEKER. 1985. The duration of marriage in a divorcing population: The impact of children. *Journal of Marriage and the Family* 47 (February): 43–52.

RAPAPORT, J. 2000. Good life goals. *Christian Science Monitor,* July 6, 14.

RAPHAEL, J. 1995. Welfare women, violent men. *Christian Science Monitor,* April 20, 20.

RATHUS, J. H., AND K. D. O'LEARY. 1997. Spouse-specific dependency scale: Scale development. *Journal of Family Violence* 12 (June): 159–68.

RAWLINGS, S. W. 1994. *Household and Family Characteristics: March 1993.* U.S. Census Bureau, Current Population Reports, P20–477. Washington, DC: U.S. Government Printing Office.

RAYBECK, D., S. DORENBOSCH, M. SARAPATA, AND D. HERRMAN. 2000. The quest for love and meaning in the personals. Unpublished paper.

RAYMOND, C. 1990. Studies of abortion's emotional effects renew controversial scholarly debate. *Chronicle of Higher Education,* February 2, A6, A7.

REDDY, M. T. 1994. *Crossing the color line: Race, parenting, and culture.* New Brunswick, NJ: Rutgers University Press.

REGAN, P. C., AND E. BERSCHEID. 1999. *Lust: What we know about human sexual desire.* Thousand Oaks, CA: Sage.

REID, J. 1993. Those fabulous '50s. *Utne Reader* 55 (January): 18–19.

REIMER, S. 1999. Sex questions show how little our kids know. *Baltimore Sun,* September 9, 1e, 4e.

REINISCH, J. M., WITH R. BEASLEY. 1990. *The Kinsey Institute new report on sex: What you must know to be sexually literate.* New York: St. Martin's.

REIS, S. D., AND P. P. HEPPNER. 1993. Examination of coping resources and family adaptation in mothers and daughters of incestuous versus nonclinical families. *Journal of Counseling Psychology* 40 (1): 100–08.

REISBERG, L. 1999. To help Latino students, a college looks to parents. *Chronicle of Higher Education,* January 15, A43–A44.

REISBERG, L. 2000. 10% of students may spend too much time online. *Chronicle of Higher Education,* June 16, A43.

REISS, I. 1960. Toward a sociology of the heterosexual love relationship. *Marriage and Family Living* 22 (May): 139–45.

REISS, I. L. 1971. The family system in America. New York: Holt, Rinehart & Winston.

REISS, I. L., AND G. R. LEE. 1988. *Family systems in America,* 4th ed. New York: Holt, Rinehart & Winston.

RENN, J. A., AND S. L. CALVERT. 1993. The relation between gender schemas and adults' recall of stereotyped and counterstereotyped televised information. *Sex Roles* 28 (7/8): 449–59.

RENNISON, C. M., AND S. WELCHANS. 2000. *Intimate partner violence.* Washington, DC: U.S. Department of Justice, Office of Justice Programs, Bureau of Justice Statistics.

RENTERÍA, R. A. 2000. A vibrant Latino presence in Washington, DC. *Footnotes* 28 (May/June): 1, 41.

RENZETTI, C. M. 1992. Violent betrayal: *Partner abuse in lesbian relationships.* Thousand Oaks, CA: Sage.

RENZETTI, C. M., AND D. J. CURRAN. 1995. *Women, men, and society,* 3rd ed. Boston: Allyn & Bacon.

REPAK, T. A. 1995. *Waiting on Washington: Central American workers in the nation's capital.* Philadelphia: Temple University Press.

RETSINAS, J. 1988. A theoretical reassessment of the applicability of Kübler-Ross's stages of dying. *Death Studies* 12 (3): 207–16.

REXROAT, C. 1994. *The declining economic status of black children.* Washington, DC: Joint Center for Political and Economic Studies.

RHEINGOLD, H. L. 1969. The social and socializing infant. In *Handbook of socialization theory and research,* ed. D. A. Goslin, 779–90. Chicago: Rand McNally.

RHODES, W. A., AND K. HOEY. 1994. *Overcoming childhood misfortune: Children who beat the odds.* Westport, CT: Praeger.

RICE, G., C. ANDERSON, N. RISCH, AND G. EBERS. 1999. Male homosexuality: Absence of linkage to microsatellite markers at Xq28. *Science* 284 (April 23): 665–67.

RICHARDSON, D. 1993. *Women, motherhood and childrearing.* New York: St. Martin's.

RICHARDSON, J. 1989. Substance use among eighth grade students who take care of themselves after school. *Pediatrics* 84, September 6, 556–66.

RICHEY, W. 1997. Girls, boys, sports, and fairness. *Christian Science Monitor,* October 3, 1, 4.

RIESSMAN, C. K. 1990. *Divorce talk: Women and men make sense of personal relationships.* New Brunswick, NJ: Rutgers University Press.

RIGGS, D. S., AND M. B. CAULFIELD. 1997. Expected consequences of male violence against their female dating partners. *Journal of Interpersonal Violence* 12 (April): 229–40.

RILEY, G. 1991. *Divorce: An American tradition.* Lincoln: University of Nebraska Press.

RINDFUSS, R. R., AND E. H. STEPHEN. 1990. Marital noncohabitation: Absence does not make the heart grow fonder. *Journal of Marriage and the Family* 52 (February): 259–70.

RINDFUSS, R. R., AND A. VANDENHEUVEL. 1990. Cohabitation: A precursor to marriage or an alternative to being single? *Population and Development Review* 16 (December): 703–26.

RINGLE, K. 1999. Unamicable partners. *Washington Post,* March 15, C1, C7.

ROBERTS, D. F., U. G. FOEHR, V. J. RIDEOUT, AND M. BRODIE. 1999. *Kids & media @ the new millennium.* Washington, DC: Kaiser Family Foundation.

ROBERTS, L. J. 2000. Fire and ice in marital communication: Hostile and distancing behaviors as predictors of marital distress. *Journal of Marriage and the Family* 62 (August): 693–707.

ROBERTS, L., AND L. J. KROKOFF. 1990. A time-series analysis of withdrawal, hostility, and displeasure in satisfied and dissatisfied marriages. *Journal of Marriage and the Family* 52 (February): 95–105.

ROBERTS, S. V. 1994. The blue-collar blues. *U.S. News & World Report,* November 7, 32.

ROBIN, R. W., B. CHESTER, J. K. RASMUSSEN, J. M. JARANSON, AND D. GOLDMAN. 1997. Prevalence, characteristics, and impact of childhood sexual abuse in a southwestern American Indian tribe. *Child Abuse & Neglect* 21 (August): 769–87.

ROBINSON, E. 1994. Furor over fertility options. *Washington Post Health Supplement,* January 11, 6.

ROBINSON, J. P., AND G. GODBEY. 1997. *Time for life: The surprising ways Americans use their time.* University Park: Pennsylvania State University Press.

ROBINSON, J. P., AND G. GODBEY. 1999. *Time for life: The surprising ways Americans use their time,* 2nd ed. University Park: Pennsylvania State University Press.

ROBINSON, M. J. 2000. Americans' history. *Public Perspective* 11 (March/April): 5–9.

ROBINSON, R. B., AND D. I. FRANK. 1994. The relation between self-esteem, sexual activity, and pregnancy. *Adolescence* 29 (Spring): 27–35.

RODBERG, G. 1999. Woman and man at Yale. www.culturefront.org/culturefront/magazine/99/spring/article.5.html (accessed August 29, 2000).

RODGERS, A. Y., AND R. L. JONES. 1999. Grandmothers who are caregivers: An overlooked population. *Child and Adolescent Social Work Journal* 16 (December): 455–66.

RODGERS, J. L., P. A. NAKONEZNY, AND R. D. SHULL. 1997. The effect of no-fault divorce legislation on divorce rates: A response to a reconsideration. *Journal of Marriage and the Family* 59 (November): 1026–30.

RODGERS, K. A. 1999. Parenting processes related to sexual risk-taking: Behaviors of adolescent males and females. *Journal of Marriage and the Family* 61 (February): 99–109.

RODGERS, W. L., AND A. THORNTON. 1985. Changing patterns of first marriage in the United States. *Demography* 22, 265–79.

RODRIGUEZ, J. M., AND K. KOSLOSKI. 1998. The impact of acculturation on attitudinal familism in a community of Puerto Rican Americans. *Hispanic Journal of Behavioral Sciences* 20 (August): 375–90.

ROE, K. M, M. MINKLER, AND R.-S. BARNWELL. 1994. The assumption of caregiving: Grandmothers raising the children of the crack cocaine epidemic. *Qualitative Health Research* 4 (August): 281–303.

ROE, K. M., AND M. MINKLER. 1998. Grandparents raising grandchildren: Challenges and responses. *Generations* 22 (Winter): 25–32.

ROGERS, J. K. 2000. *Temps: The many faces of the changing workplace.* Ithaca, NY: Cornell University Press.

ROGERS, M. F. 1999. *Barbie culture.* Thousand Oaks, CA: Sage.

ROGERS, S. J. 1999. Wives' income and marital quality: Are there reciprocal effects? *Journal of Marriage and the Family* 61 (February): 123–32.

ROHDE, D. 1994. Golden-aged athletes go for the gold. *Christian Science Monitor,* July 8, 10–11.

ROHLFING, M. E. 1995. "Doesn't anybody stay in one place anymore?" An exploration of the under-studied phenomenon of long-distance relationships. In *Under-studied relationships: Off the beaten track,* eds. J. T. Wood and S. Duck, 173–96. Thousand Oaks, CA: Sage.

ROHNER, R. P., S. L. BOURQUE, AND C. A. ELORDI. 1996. Children's perceptions of corporal punishment, caretaker acceptance, and psychological adjustment in a poor, biracial southern community. *Journal of Marriage and the Family* 58 (November): 842–52.

ROIPHE, K. 1993. *The morning after: Sex, fear, and feminism on campus.* Boston: Little, Brown.

Roman Catholic college dismisses gay dean. 1997. *Chronicle of Higher Education,* October 31, A8.

Romance writers of America. 2000. www.rwanational.com (accessed August 30, 2000).

ROMERO, G. J., AND G. E. WYATT. 1999. The prevalence and circumstances of child sexual abuse among Latina women. *Hispanic Journal of Behavioral Sciences* 21 (August): 351–67.

ROMPF, E. L. 1993. Open adoption: What does the "average person" think? *Child Welfare* 72 (May/June): 219–30.

RONFELDT, H. M., R. KIMERLING, AND I. ARIAS. 1998. Satisfaction with relationship power and the perpetration of dating violence. *Journal of Marriage and the Family* 60 (February): 70–78.

Roper Organization. 1990. *The 1990 Virginia Slims Opinion Poll: A 20-year perspective of women's issues.* Storrs: University of Connecticut Press.

Roper Starch Worldwide, Inc. 1994. *Teens talk about sex: Adolescent sexuality in the 90s.* New York: Sexuality Information and Education Council of the United States.

Roper Starch Worldwide, Inc. 1996. *The 1995 Virginia Slims Opinion Poll.* Storrs: The Roper Center, University of Connecticut.

Roper Youth Report. 1999. Who's going to stay home with the kids? Nearly 2 in 5 teen girls say it will be their husbands. www.roper.com/news/content/news156.htm (accessed August 25, 2000).

ROPERS, R. H. 1991. *Persistent poverty: The American dream turned nightmare.* New York: Plenum Press.

ROSCHELLE, A. R. 1997. *No more kin: Exploring race, class, and gender in family networks.* Thousand Oaks, CA: Sage.

ROSCOE, B., M. S. DIANA, AND R. H. BROOKS II. 1987. Early, middle, and late adolescents' views on dating and factors influencing partner selection. *Adolescence* 22 (Spring): 59–68.

ROSE, S., AND I. H. FRIEZE. 1993. Young singles' contemporary dating scripts. *Sex Roles* 28 (May): 499–509.

ROSEN, B. C. 1982. *The industrial connection: Achievement and the family in developing societies.* New York: Aldine.

ROSEN, K. H. 1996. The ties that bind women to violent premarital relationships: Processes of seduction and entrapment. In *Family violence from a communication perspective,* eds. D. D. Cahn and S. A. Lloyd, 151–76. Thousand Oaks, CA: Sage.

ROSEN, K. H., AND S. M. STITH. 1993. Intervention strategies for treating women in violent dating relationships. *Family Relations* 42 (October): 427–33.

ROSENBERG, D. A. 1997. Unusual forms of child abuse. In *The battered child,* 5th ed., eds. M. E. Helfer, R. S. Kempe, and R. D. Krugman, 413–30. Chicago: University of Chicago Press.

ROSENBERG, J. 1993. Just the two of us. In *Reinventing love: Six women talk about lust, sex, and romance,* eds. L. Abraham, L. Green, M. Krance, J. Rosenberg, J. Somerville, and C. Stoner, 301–307. New York: Plume.

ROSENBLATT, P. C. 1994. *Metaphors of family systems theory: Toward new constructions.* New York: Guilford Press.

ROSENBLATT, P. C., T. A. KARIS, AND R. D. POWELL. 1995. *Multiracial couples: Black & white voices.* Thousand Oaks, CA: Sage.

ROSENBLATT, P. C., AND R. A. PHILLIPS, JR. 1975. Family articles in popular magazines: Advice to writers, editors, and teachers of consumers. *Family Coordinator* 24 (July): 267–71.

ROSENFIELD, S. 1989. Sex differences in depression: Do women always have higher rates? *Journal of Health and Social Behavior* 30, 77–91.

ROSENTHAL, C. J. 1985. Kinkeeping in the familial division of labor. *Journal of Marriage and the Family* 47 (November): 965–74.

ROSENZWEIG, P. M. 1992. *Married and alone: The way back.* New York: Plenum Press.

ROSIN, M. B. 1987. *Stepfathering: Stepfathers' advice on creating a new family.* New York: Simon & Schuster.

ROSS, C. E., AND J. MIROWSKY. 1999. Parental divorce, life-course disruption, and adult depression. *Journal of Marriage and the Family* 61 (November): 1034–45.

ROSS, C. E., J. MIROWSKY, AND K. GOLDSTEIN. 1991. The impact of the family on health: The decade in review. In *Contemporary families: Looking forward, looking back,* ed. A. Booth. Minneapolis, MN: National Council on Family Relations.

ROSS, S. M. 1996. Risk of physical abuse to children of spouse abusing parents. *Child Abuse & Neglect* 20 (July): 589–98.

ROSSI, P. H. 1994. Troubling families: Family homelessness in America. *American Behavioral Scientist* 37 (January): 342–95.

ROTHBLUM, E. D. 1994. I'll die for the revolution, but don't ask me not to diet: Feminism and the continuing stigmatization of obesity. In *Feminist perspectives on eating disorders,* eds. P. Fallon, M. A. Katzman, and S. C. Wooley, 53–76. New York: Guilford Press.

ROTHBLUM, E. D., AND K. A. BREHONY, EDS. 1993. *Boston marriages: Romantic but asexual relationships among contemporary lesbians.* Amherst: University of Massachusetts Press.

ROTHMAN, B. K. 1984. *Hands and hearts: A history of courtship in America.* New York: Basic Books.

ROTHMAN, B. K. 1989. Women, health, and medicine. In *Women: A feminist perspective,* 4th ed., ed. J. Freeman, 76–86. Mountain View, CA: Mayfield.

ROTHMAN, B. K. 1999. The potential cost of the best genes money can buy. *Chronicle of Higher Education,* June 11, A52.

ROTHMAN, E. K. 1983. Sex and self-control: Middle-class courtship in America, 1770–1870. In *The American family in social-historical perspective,* 3rd ed., ed. M. Gordon, 393–410. New York: St. Martin's.

ROTHMAN, S. M. 1978. *Women's proper place: A history of changing ideals and practices, 1870 to the present.* New York: Basic Books.

ROVNER, S. 1991. Battered wives: Centuries of silence. *Washington Post Health Supplement,* August 20, 7.

ROWE, D. C. 1994. *The limits of family influence: Genes, experience, and behavior.* New York: Guilford Press.

ROWE, J., AND R. KAHN. 1997. *Successful aging.* New York: Pantheon.

ROWLAND, M. 1994. Love and money the second time around. *Working Woman* (August): 22, 24.

ROYLANCE, F. D. 1997. Hopkins researcher punished. *Baltimore Sun,* April 30, 1B, 4B.

RUBENSTEIN, C. 1994. The confident generation. *Working Mother* (May): 38–45.

RUBIN, L. B. 1983. *Intimate strangers: Men and women together.* New York: Harper & Row.

RUBIN, L. B. 1985. *Just friends: The role of friendship in our lives.* New York: Harper & Row.

RUBIN, L. B. 1994. *Families on the fault line: America's working class speaks about the family, the economy, race, and ethnicity.* New York: HarperCollins.

RUBIN, R. M., AND B. J. RINEY. 1994. *Working wives and dual-earner families.* Westport, CT: Praeger.

RUBIN, Z. 1973. *Liking and loving.* New York: Holt, Rinehart & Winston.

RUHM, C. J., AND J. L. TEAGUE. 1997. Parental leave policies in Europe and North America. In *Gender and family issues in the workplace,* eds. F. D. Blau and R. G. Ehrenberg, 133–56. New York: Russell Sage Foundation.

Runzheimer International. 1997. Runzheimer analyzes daycare costs nationwide. www.runzheimer.com/091597.htm (accessed January 15, 1998).

RUSSELL, C. 1997. What's wrong with kids? *American Demographics* 19 (November): 12–16.

RUSSELL, C. 1999. Only 10% of day care is rated excellent. *Washington Post,* February 23, 8–9.

RUSSELL, D. E. H. 1990. *Rape in marriage.* Bloomington: Indiana University Press.

RUSSELL, K., M. WILSON, AND R. HALL. 1992. *The color complex: The politics of skin color among African Americans.* New York: Harcourt Brace Jovanovich.

RUSSO, N. F., J. D. HORN, AND S. TROMP. 1993. Childspacing intervals and abortion among blacks and whites: A brief report. *Women & Health* 20 (3): 43–51.

RUST, B. 2000. Walking the plain talk. *Advocasey* (Spring/Summer): 1–11.

RUTTER, V. 1994. Lessons from stepfamilies. *Psychology Today* (May): 30–33, 60ff.

RYAN, M. 1993. Undercover among the elderly. *Parade Magazine,* July 18, 8.

RYAN, M. P. 1983. *Womanhood in America: From colonial times to the present,* 3rd ed. New York: Franklin Watts.

SAAD, L. 1994. Public has cold feet on health care reform. *Gallup Poll Monthly* (August): 2–5.

SABBAGH, S. 1996. Introduction: The debate on Arab women. In *Arab women: Between defiance and restraint,* ed. S. Sabbagh, xi–xxvii. Brooklyn, NY: Olive Branch Press.

SADKER, M., AND D. SADKER. 1994. *Failing at fairness: How America's schools cheat girls.* New York: Scribner's.

SAFER, J. 1996. *Beyond motherhood: Choosing a life without children.* New York: Pocket Books.

SAFILIOS-ROTHSCHILD, C. 1977. *Love, sex, and sex roles.* Upper Saddle River, NJ: Prentice Hall.

SAGARIN, E. 1963. *Incest: The nature and origin of the taboo* together with A. Ellis *The origins and the development of the incest taboo.* New York: Lyle Stuart.

ST. JEAN, Y., AND J. R. FEAGIN. 1998. *Double burden: Black women and everyday racism.* Armonk, NY: M. E. Sharpe.

ST. JEAN, Y., AND R. E. PARKER. 1995. Disapproval of interracial unions: The case of black females. In *American families: Issues in race and ethnicity,* ed. C. K. Jacobson, 341–51. New York: Garland.

SALDANA, D. H., AND A. M. DASSORI. 1999. When is caregiving a burden? Listening to Mexican

American women. *Hispanic Journal of Behavioral Sciences* 21 (August): 283–301.

SALTZMAN, A. 1993. Family friendliness. *U.S. News & World Report,* February 22, 59–66.

SALTZMAN, A. 1999. From diapers to high heels. *U.S. News & World Report,* July 26, 57–58.

SALUTER, A. F. 1994. *Marital status and living arrangements: March 1993.* U.S. Census Bureau, Current Population Reports, Series P20–478. Washington, DC: U.S. Government Printing Office.

SALUTER, A. F. 1996. *Marital status and living arrangements: March 1995 (Update).* U.S. Census Bureau, Department of Commerce, Economics and Statistics Administration.

SALUTER, A. F., AND T. A. LUGAILA. 1998. *Marital status and living arrangements: March 1996.* U.S. Census Bureau, Current Population Reports, P20–496. www.census.gov/population/www/socdemo/ms-la.html (accessed April 29, 1998).

SALYERS, E., AND V. STRANG. 1996. Hispanic-owned businesses: Reaching new heights. *Statistical Brief* SB/96-4. U.S. Census Bureau. Washington, DC: U.S. Government Printing Office.

SANCHEZ, R. 1999. Abortion foes' Internet site on trial. *Washington Post,* January 15, A3.

SANCHEZ-AYENDEZ, M. 1988. The Puerto Rican American family. In *Ethnic families in America: Patterns and variations,* 3rd ed., eds. C. J. Mindel, R. W. Habenstein, and R. Wright, Jr., 173–98. New York: Elsevier.

SANDAY, P. R. 1990. *Fraternity gang rape: Sex, brotherhood, and privilege on campus.* New York: New York University Press.

SANDAY, P. R. 1996. *A woman scorned: Acquaintance rape on trial.* New York: Doubleday.

SANDEFUR, G. 1996. Welfare doesn't cause illegitimacy and single parenthood. *Chronicle of Higher Education,* October 4, B7–B8.

SANDER, J. 1991. *Before their time: Four generations of teenage mothers.* New York: Harcourt Brace Jovanovich.

SANDROFF, R. 1994. When women make more than men. *Working Woman* (January): 39–41, 87–88.

SANDS, R. G., AND R. S. GOLDBERG-GLEN. 2000. Factors associated with stress among grandparents raising their children. *Family Relations* 49 (January): 97–105.

SANTELLI, J. S., L. D. LINDBERG, J. ABMA, C. S. McNEELEY, AND M. RESNICK. 2000. Adolescent sexual behavior: Estimates and trends from four nationally representative surveys. *Family Planning Perspectives* 32(4): 156–65, 194.

SANTROCK, J. W., K. A. SITTERLE, AND R. A. WARSHAK. 1988. Parent–child relationships in stepfather families. In *Fatherhood today: Men's changing role in the family,* eds. P. Bronstein and C. P. Cowan, 144–65. New York: Wiley.

SAPOLSKY, R. 2000. It's not "all in the genes." *Newsweek,* April 10, 68.

SAPORTA, S. 1991. Miscellany: Old maid and dirty old man: The language of ageism. *American Speech* 66 (Fall): 333–34.

SARCH, A. 1993. Making the connection: Single women's use of the telephone in dating relationships with men. *Journal of Communications* 43 (Spring): 128–44.

SARNOFF, I., AND S. SARNOFF. 1989. The dialectic of marriage. *Psychology Today* (October): 54–57.

SAVAGE, H., AND P. FRONCZEK. 1993. *Who can afford to buy a house in 1991?* U.S. Census Bureau, Housing and Household Economic Statistics Division. Washington, DC: U.S. Government Printing Office.

SAVIN-WILLIAMS, R. C., AND E. M. DUBÉ. 1998. Parental reactions to their child's disclosure of a gay/lesbian identity. *Family Relations* 47 (January): 7–13.

SCARF, M. 1987. *Intimate partners: Patterns in love and marriage.* New York: Random House.

SCHAEFER, C. E., AND T. F. DiGERONIMO. 1999. *How to talk to teens about really important things: Specific questions and answers and useful things to say.* San Francisco: Jossey-Bass.

SCHAFER, S. 1999. At-home business, with pleasure. *Washington Post,* October 4, A1, A4.

SCHECTER, S., AND A. GANELY. 1995. *Domestic violence: A national curriculum for family preservation practitioners.* San Francisco: Family Violence Prevention Fund.

SCHMIDLEY, D. A., AND C. GIBSON. *Profile of the foreign-born population in the United States: 1997.* 1999. U.S. Census Bureau, Current Population Reports, Series P23-195. Washington, DC: U.S. Government Printing Office.

SCHMIDT, J. D., AND L. W. SHERMAN. 1993. Does arrest deter domestic violence? *American Behavioral Scientist* 36 (May): 601–09.

SCHMITT, J. 1999. Middle-class workers have little to celebrate. *Baltimore Sun,* September 6, 11A.

SCHNEIDER, B., AND D. STEVENSON. 1999. *The ambitious generation: America's teenagers, motivated but directionless.* New Haven, CT: Yale University Press.

SCHNEIDER, H. 2000. Egyptian women given faster route to divorce. *Washington Post,* April 14, A16–A17.

SCHOEN, R., AND R. M. WEINICK. 1993. Partner choice in marriages and cohabitations. *Journal of Marriage and the Family* 55 (May): 408–14.

SCHOETTLER, C. 1994. Government study indicates breakdown in traditional family life in Britain. *Baltimore Sun,* January 27, 6A.

SCHRECK, L. 1999. Adolescent sexual activity is affected more by mothers' attitudes and behavior than by family structure. *Family Planning Perspectives* 31 (July): 200–01.

SCHROF, J. M. 1994. A lens on matrimony. *U.S. News & World Report,* February 21, 66–69.

SCHROF, J. M. 1999. Who's guilty? *U.S. News & World Report,* May 17, 60–62.

SCHROF, J. M., with B. WAGNER. 1994. Sex in America. *U.S. News & World Report,* October 17, 75–81.

SCHULMAN, K. A., ET AL. 1999. The effect of race and sex on physicians' recommendations for cardiac catheterization. *New England Journal of Medicine* 340 (February 25): 618–26.

SCHULTZ, S. 2000. Talk to kids about drugs? Parents just don't do it. *U.S. News & World Report,* February 7, 56–57.

SCHUMM, W. R., AND M. A. BUGAIGHIS. 1986. Marital quality over the marital career: Alternative explanations. *Journal of Marriage and the Family* 48 (February): 165–68.

SCHUSTER, M. A., R. M. Bell, AND D. E. KANOUSE. 1996. The sexual practices of adolescent virgins: Genital sexual activities of high school students who have never had vaginal intercourse. *American Journal of Public Health* 86 (November): 1570–76.

SCHWAB, R. 1998. A child's death and divorce: Dispelling the myth. *Death Studies* 22 (July/August): 445–68.

SCHWARTZ, F. N. 1989. Management women and the new facts of life. *Harvard Business Review* 89 (January–February): 65–76.

SCHWARTZ, J. 1998. Pregnant smokers pass potent carcinogen to womb, study finds. *Washington Post,* August 24, A10.

SCHWARTZ, P. 1994. *Peer marriage: Love between equals.* New York: Free Press.

SCHWEBEL, A. I., M. A. FINE, AND M. A. RENNER. 1991. A study of perceptions of the stepparent role. *Journal of Family Issues* 12 (March): 43–57.

SCINTO, L., ET AL. 1994. A potential noninvasive neurobiological test for Alzheimer's disease. *Science,* November 11, 1051–54.

SCOTT, D. C. 1994. Child abductions: Mexico's hidden problems. *Christian Science Monitor,* June 30, 6.

SCOTT, D., AND B. WISHY, EDS. 1982. *America's families: A documentary history.* New York: Harper & Row.

SEABERRY, J. 1991. Household life's all in the family for Asians, Hispanics in D.C. area. *Washington Post,* September 8, B1, B9.

SECCOMBE, K. 1991. Assessing the costs and benefits of children: Gender comparisons among childfree husbands and wives. *Journal of Marriage and the Family* 53 (February): 191–202.

Seek spouse in India? Take out an ad. 1989. *Baltimore Sun,* June 7, F6.

SEFF, M. A. 1995. Cohabitation and the law. *Marriage & Family Review* 21 (3/9): 141–68.

SEGAL, J. 1989. 10 myths about child development. *Parents,* July, 81–84, 87.

SEGAL, L., AND Z. SEGAL. 1991. Does spanking work? *Parents* (March): 188.

SEGAL, U. A. 1991. Cultural variables in Asian Indian families. *Families in Society* 72 (April): 233–42.

SEGURA, D. A. 1994. Working at motherhood: Chicana and Mexican immigrant mothers and employment. In *Mothering: Ideology, experience, and agency,* eds. E. N. Glenn, G. Chang, and L. R. Forcey, 211–33. New York: Routledge.

SEITER, E. 1993. *Sold separately: Children and parents in consumer culture.* New Brunswick, NJ: Rutgers University Press.

SELBY, H. 1995. Gay couples find joy as parents. *Baltimore Sun,* January 3, B1, B3.

SELIGMANN, J., AND P. ROGERS. 1994. The pressure to lose. *Newsweek,* May 2, 60–61.

The Sentencing Project. 2000. Facts about prisons and prisoners. www.sentencingproject.org (accessed September 14, 2000).

SERWER, A. E. 1993. American Indians discover money is power. *Fortune,* April 19, 136–42.

SETER, J. 1994. U.S. concerns: Bride burnings, infanticide. *U.S. News & World Report,* February 14, 6.

Sex and America's teenagers. 1994. New York: Alan Guttmacher Institute.

Sexual harassment charges EEOC & FEPAs combined: FY 1992-FY 1999. 1999. www.eeoc.gov/stats/harass.html (accessed August 26, 2000).

SHAABAN, B. 1995. The muted voices of women interpreters. In *Faith and freedom: Women's human rights in the Muslim world,* ed. M. Afkhami, 61–77. Syracuse, NY: Syracuse University Press.

SHANKAR, R. 1998. South Asian identity in Asian America. In *A part, yet apart,* eds., L. D. Ahankar and R. Srikanth, ix–xv. Philadelphia: Temple University Press.

SHAPIRO, I., R. GREENSTEIN, AND W. PRIMUS. 2000. An analysis of new IRS income data. Center on Budget and Policy Priorities, Washington, DC. www.cbpp.org/9-4-00inc.pdf (accessed October 13, 2000).

SHAPIRO, J. L. 1987. The expectant father. *Psychology Today* (January): 36–39.

SHAPIRO, J. P. 1997. Death rights. *U.S. News & World Report,* January 13, 21–27.

SHAPIRO, L. 1990. Guns and dolls. *Newsweek,* May 28, 57–65.

SHATZKIN, K. 1996. Battered wife wants husband to keep job. *Baltimore Sun,* December 7, A1, A4.

SHATZKIN, K. 1999. A better message on teen pregnancy. *Baltimore Sun,* November 9, 1A, 8A.

SHATZKIN, K. 2000. Perdue violated wage statute. *Baltimore Sun,* February 29, C1.

SHAVER, P., C. HAZAN, AND D. BRADSHAW. 1988. Love as attachment. In *The psychology of love,* eds. R. J. Sternberg and M. L. Barnes, 68–99. New Haven, CT: Yale University Press.

SHEA, J. A., AND G. R. ADAMS. 1984. Correlates of romantic attachment: A path analysis study. *Journal of Youth and Adolescence* 13 (1): 27–44.

SHEARER, L. 1990. Too much television = too much fat. *Parade Magazine,* May 27, 13.

SHELTON, B. A. 1987. Variations in divorce rates by community size: A test of the social integration explanation. *Journal of Marriage and the Family* 49 (November): 827–32.

SHELTON, B. A., AND D. John. 1993. Ethnicity, race, and difference: A comparison of white, black, and Hispanic men's household labor time. In *Men, work, and family,* ed. J. C. Hood, 131–50. Thousand Oaks, CA: Sage.

SHENON, P. 1994. A Chinese bias against girls creates surplus of bachelors. *New York Times,* August 16, A1, A8.

SHERMAN, L. 1992. *Policing domestic violence: Experiment and dilemmas.* New York: Free Press.

SHIMOMURA, M. 1990. Japan: Too much mommysan. *New Perspectives Quarterly* 7 (Winter): 24–27.

SHINAGAWA, L. H., AND G. Y. PANG. 1996. Asian American panethnicity and intermarriage. *Amerasia Journal* 22 (Spring): 127–52.

SHIPLEY, S. 1997. Making vows last longer in Louisiana. *Christian Science Monitor,* July 1, 14.

SHOOP, R. J., AND D. L. EDWARDS. 1994. *How to stop sexual harassment in our schools: A handbook and curriculum guide for administrators and teachers.* Boston: Allyn & Bacon.

SHUPE, A., W. A. Stacey, AND L. R. HAZLEWOOD. 1987. *Violent men, violent couples.* Lexington, MA: Lexington Books.

SHURE, M. B. 1999. *Preventing violence the problem-solving way.* Washington, DC: U.S. Department of Justice, Office of Justice Programs, Office of Juvenile Justice and Delinquency Prevention.

SIDEL, R. 1998. *Keeping women and children last: America's war on the poor.* New York: Penguin.

SIEGEL, A. F. 2000. Court rules lesbian ex can seek visitation. *Baltimore Sun,* May 3, 1A, 7A.

SIEGEL, J. M., AND D. H. KUYKENDALL. 1990. Loss, widowhood, and psychological distress among the elderly. *Journal of Consulting and Clinical Psychology* 58 (5): 519–24.

SIGNORIELLI, N., D. MCLEOD, AND E. HEALY. 1994. Gender stereotypes in MTV commercials: The beat goes on. *Journal of Broadcasting & Electronic Media* (Winter): 91–101.

SILBERSTEIN, L. R. 1992. *Dual-career marriage: A system in transition.* Hillsdale, NJ: Lawrence Erlbaum Associates.

SILVERMAN, P. R. 2000. *Never too young to know: Death in children's lives.* New York: Oxford University Press.

SILVERSTEIN, M., AND X. CHEN. 1999. The impact of acculturation in Mexican American families on the quality of adult grandchild–grandparent relationships. *Journal of Marriage and the Family* 61 (February): 188–98.

SIMMONS, A. M. 1998. Here beauty is measured in pounds. *Baltimore Sun,* October 24, 2a.

SIMMONS, C. H., A. VON KOLKE, AND H. SHIMIZU. 1986. Attitudes toward romantic love among American, German, and Japanese students. *Journal of Social Psychology* 126 (June): 327–36.

SIMON, R. J. 1993. *The case for transracial adoption.* Washington, DC: American University Press.

SIMON, R. J., AND H. ALTSTEIN. 2000. *Adoption across borders: Serving the children in transracial and intercountry adoptions.* Lanham, MD: Rowman & Littlefield.

SIMONS, R. L., & ASSOCIATES. 1996. *Understanding differences between divorced and intact families: Stress, interaction, and child outcome.* Thousand Oaks, CA: Sage.

SIMONS, R. L., C. JOHNSON, J. BEAMAN, AND R. D. CONGER. 1993. Explaining women's double jeopardy: Factors that mediate the association between harsh treatment as a child and violence by a husband. *Journal of Marriage and the Family* 55 (August): 713–23.

SIMONS, R. L., C. JOHNSON, AND R. D. CONGER. 1994. Harsh corporal punishment versus quality of parental involvement as an explanation of adolescent maladjustment. *Journal of Marriage and the Family* 56 (August): 591–607.

SIMONS, R. L., K.-H. LIN, L. C. GORDON, R. D. CONGER, AND F. O. LORENZ. 1999. Explaining the higher incidence of adjustment problems among children of divorce compared with those in two-parent families. *Journal of Marriage and the Family* 61 (November): 1020–33.

SIMPSON, A. 1995. The Social Security pie: Save a piece for the kids. *Christian Science Monitor,* March 10, 19.

SKRUCK, K. 1994. 10 keys to quality. *Working Mother* (August): 40–42.

SLADE, M. 1985. Treating parents as children. *New York Times,* May 13, C5.

SLOANE, L. 1987. Prenuptial agreements. *New York Times,* June 13, 34.

SMALL, M. F. 1995. *What's love got to do with it? The evolution of human mating.* New York: Anchor/Doubleday.

SMALL, S. A., AND D. KERNS. 1993. Unwanted sexual activity among peers during early and middle adolescence: Incidence and risk factors. *Journal of Marriage and the Family* 55 (November): 941–52.

SMALL, S., AND D. RILEY. 1990. Toward a multidimensional assessment of work spillover into family life. *Journal of Marriage and the Family* 52 (August): 51–62.

SMITH, K. E., AND A. BACHU. 1999. Women's labor force attachment patterns and maternity leave: A review of the literature, Population Division Working Paper No. 32, U.S. Bureau of the Census, Washington, DC. www.census.gov/population/www/documentation/twps0032/twps0032.html (accessed November 10, 2000).

SMITH, K. R., C. D. ZICK, AND G. J. DUNCAN. 1991. Remarriage patterns among recent widows and widowers. *Demography* 28 (August): 361–74.

SMITH, L. 1993. Perimenopause. *Baltimore Sun,* December 14, 1D, 5D.

SMITH, T. W. 1994. Can money buy you love? *Public Perspective* 5 (January/February): 33–34.

SMITH, T. W. 1999. The emerging 21st century American family. www.norc.uchicago.edu/online/emerge.htm (accessed August 12, 2000).

SMITH, T. W. 2000. *Taking America's pulse II: A survey of intergroup relations,* survey conducted for the National Conference for Community and Justice and Bank of America. fdncenter.org/pnd/20000516/003375.html (accessed October 2, 2000).

SMITH, W. L. 1999. *Families and communes: An examination of nontraditional lifestyles.* Thousand Oaks, CA: Sage.

SMOCK, P. J. 1993. The economic costs of marital disruption for young women over the past two decades. *Demography* 30 (August): 353–71.

SMOCK, P. J. 1994. Gender and the short-run economic consequences of marital disruption. *Social Forces* 73 (September): 243–62.

SMOCK, P. J. 2000. Cohabitation in the United States: An appraisal of research themes, findings, and implications. *Annual Review of Sociology* 26, 1–20.

SMOCK, P. J., AND W. D. MANNING. 1997. Cohabiting partners' economic circumstances and marriage. *Demography* 34 (August): 331–41.

SMOLAK, L., M. P. LEVINE, AND S. GRALEN. 1993. The impact of puberty and dating on eating problems among middle school girls. *Journal of Youth and Adolescence* 22 (August): 355–68.

SNIPP, C. M. 1996. A demographic comeback for American Indians. *Population Today* 24 (November): 4–5.

SNYDER, H. N. 2000. *Sexual assault of young children as reported to law enforcement: Victim, incident, and offender characteristics.* Washington, DC: U.S. Department of Justice, Office of Justice Programs.

SOCARIDES, C. W. 1995. *Homosexuality: A freedom too far.* Phoenix, AZ: Adam Margrave Books.

SOLOMON, K., AND P. A. SZWABO. 1994. The work-oriented culture: Success and power in elderly men. In *Older men's lives,* ed. E. Thompson, Jr., 42–64. Thousand Oaks, CA: Sage.

SOLTERO, J. M. 1996. *Inequality in the workplace: Underemployment among Mexicans, African Americans, and whites.* New York: Garland.

SOMERS, M. D. 1993. A comparison of voluntarily childfree adults and parents. *Journal of Marriage and the Family* 55 (August): 643–50.

SOMERVILLE, F. P. L. 1994. Their faith offers better feminism. Muslim women say—rights with protection. *Baltimore Sun,* February 15, 4B.

SOMMER, M. 1994. Welcome cribside, Dad. *Christian Science Monitor,* June 28, 19.

SOMMERS, C. 1989. Philosophers against the family. In *Vice and virtue in everyday life: Introductory readings in ethics,* eds. C. Sommers and F. Sommers, 728–54. New York: Harcourt Brace Jovanovich.

SOMMERS, C. H. 2000. *The war against boys: How misguided feminism is harming our young men.* New York: Simon & Schuster.

SORENSEN, E., AND C. ZIBMAN. 2000. Child support offers some protection against poverty, Urban Institute, Washington, DC. newfederalism. urban.org/pdf/b10.pdf (accessed October 21, 2000).

SORENSON, T. 1981. A follow-up study of operated transsexual males. *Acta Psychiatrica Scandinavica* 63, 486–503.

SOUTH, S. J. 1993. Racial and ethnic differences in the desire to marry. *Journal of Marriage and the Family* 55 (May): 357–70.

SOWELL, T. 1996. Love and other four-letter words. *Forbes,* January 1, 64.

SPAIN, D. 1999. *America's diversity: On the edge of two centuries.* Washington, DC: Population Reference Bureau.

SPAKE, A. 1998. Adoption gridlock. *U.S. News & World Report,* June 22, 30–37.

SPEARE, JR., A., AND R. AVERY. 1993. Who helps whom in older parent–child families? *Journal of Gerontology: Social Sciences* 48 (2): S64-S73.

SPEARS, G. 1994. Estate-planning musts for blended families. *Kiplinger's Personal Finance Magazine* 48 (December): 91–96.

SPENCER, R. F., AND J. D. JENNINGS. 1977. *The Native Americans: Ethnology and backgrounds of the North American Indians.* New York: Harper & Row.

SPICHER, C. H., AND M. A. HUDAK. 1997. Gender role portrayal on Saturday morning cartoons: An update. Paper presented at the American

Psychological Association meetings, Chicago, August 18.

SPIEKER, S. J., N. C. LARSON, AND L. GILCHRIST. 1999. Developmental trajectories of disruptive behavior problems in preschool children of adolescent mothers. *Child Development* 70 (March): 443–58.

SPITZE, G., J. R. LOGAN, G. DEANE, AND S. ZERGER. 1994. Adult children's divorce and intergenerational relationships. *Journal of Marriage and the Family* 56 (May): 279–93.

SPRECHER, S. 1999. "I love you more today than yesterday": Romantic partners' perceptions of changes in love and related affect over time. *Journal of Personality and Social Psychology* 76 (January): 46–53.

SPRECHER, S., A. BARBEE, AND P. SCHWARTZ. 1995. "Was it good for you, too?": Gender differences in first sexual intercourse experiences. *Journal of Sex Research* 32 (1): 3–15.

SPRECHER, S., AND K. MCKINNEY. 1993. *Sexuality.* Thousand Oaks, CA: Sage.

SPRECHER, S., K. MCKINNEY, AND T. L. ORBUCH. 1991. The effect of current sexual behavior on friendship, dating, and marriage desirability. *Journal of Sex Research* 28 (August): 367–408.

SQUIER, D. A., AND J. S. QUADAGNO. 1988. The Italian American family. In *Ethnic families in America: Patterns and variations,* 3rd ed., eds. C. J. Mindel, R. W. Habenstein, and R. Wright, Jr., 109–37. New York: Elsevier.

SQUIRES, S. 1995. What to do when your child asks about sex. *Washington Post Health Supplement,* September 12, 10–13.

Stalking. 2000. www.ncvc.org/SPECIAL/stalking. htm (accessed August 30, 2000).

STAMP, G. H. 1994. The appropriation of the parental role through communication during the transition to parenthood. *Communication Monographs* 61 (June): 89–112.

STANFIELD J. M., II, ED. 1993. *A history of race relations research: First-generation recollections.* Thousand Oaks, CA: Sage.

STANGER, J. D. 1997. Television in the home: *The 1997 study of parents and children.* Philadelphia: University of Pennsylvania, Annenberg Public Policy Center.

STANNARD, D. E. 1979. Changes in the American family: Fiction and reality. In *Changing images of the family,* eds. V. Tufte and B. Myerhoff, 83–98. New Haven, CT: Yale University Press.

STAPINSKI, H. 1999. Y not love? *American Demographics* 21 (February): 63–68.

STAPLES, R. 1988. The black American family. In *Ethnic families in America: Patterns and variations,* 3rd ed., eds. C. H. Mindel, R. W. Habenstein, and R. Wright, Jr., 303–24. New York: Elsevier.

STAPLES, R. 1994. *The black family: Essays and studies,* 5th ed. Belmont, CA: Wadsworth.

STARK, E. 1993. A quickie guide to prenups for Trump, Gates—and you. *Money* (June): 17.

STARRELS, M. E. 1994. Gender differences in parent-child relations. *Journal of Family Issues* 15 (March): 148–65.

STAUSS, J. H. 1995. Reframing and refocusing American Indian family strengths. In *American families: Issues in race and ethnicity,* ed. C. K. Jacobson, 105–18. New York: Garland.

STEIL, J. M. 1997. *Marital equality: Its relationship to the well-being of husbands and wives.* Thousand Oaks, CA: Sage.

STEIN, M. D. 1998. Sexual ethics: Disclosure of HIV-positive status to partners. *Archives of Internal Medicine* 158, February 9, 253–57.

STEIN, P. J., ED. 1981. *Single life: Unmarried adults in social context.* New York: St. Martin's.

STEIN, T. J. 1996. Child custody and visitation: The rights of lesbian and gay parents. *Social Service Review* 70 (September): 435–50.

STEINBACH, A. 1995. Custody wars. *Baltimore Sun,* March 13, 1D–2D.

STEINMETZ, S. 1978. The battered husband syndrome. *Victimology* 2, (3/4): 499–509.

STEPHENS, W. N. 1963. *The family in cross-cultural perspective.* New York: Holt, Rinehart & Winston.

STERK-ELIFSON, C. 1994. Sexuality among African-American women. In *Sexuality across the life course,* ed. A. S. Rossi, 99–126. Chicago: University of Chicago Press.

STERLING, A. J. 1992. *What really works with men.* New York: Warner.

STERNBERG, R. J. 1986. A triangular theory of love. *Psychological Review* 93 (2): 119–35.

STERNBERG, R. J. 1988. *The triangle of love.* New York: Basic Books.

STETS, J. E. 1993a. Control in dating relationships. *Journal of Marriage and the Family* 55 (August): 673–85.

STETS, J. E. 1993b. The link between past and present intimate relationships. *Journal of Family Issues* 14 (June): 236–60.

STETS, J. E., AND M. A. PIROG-GOOD. 1990. Interpersonal control and courtship aggression. *Journal of Social and Personal Relationships* 7 (August): 371–94.

STEVENS, G. V. 1997. A retreat on children's well-being. *Christian Science Monitor,* August 22, 18.

STEWART, A. J., A. P. COPELAND, N. L. CHESTER, J. E. MALLEY, AND N. B. BARENBAUM. 1997. *Separating together: How divorce transforms families.* New York: Guilford Press.

STEWART, S. D. 1999. Nonresident mothers' and fathers' social contact with children. *Journal of Marriage and the Family* 61 (November): 894–907.

STIEHM, J. 1997. Marriage long-distance style. *Baltimore Sun,* July 7, 1A, 6A.

STILLARS, A. L. 1991. Behavioral observation. In *Studying interpersonal interaction,* eds. B. M. Montgomery and S. Duck, 197–218. New York: Guilford Press.

STINNETT, N., AND J. DEFRAIN. 1985. *Secrets of strong families.* Boston: Little, Brown.

STOCKEL, H. H. 1991. *Women of the Apache nation.* Reno: University of Nevada Press.

STODDART, T., AND E. TURIEL. 1985. Housework: It isn't going to go away. *Philadelphia Inquirer,* September, 1, 11, 14.

STOLBA, A., AND P. R. AMATO. 1993. Extended single-parent households and children's behavior. *Sociological Quarterly* 34 (3): 543–49.

STOLLEY, K. S., AND A. E. HILL. 1996. Presentations of the elderly in textbooks on marriage and family. *Teaching Sociology* 24 (January): 34–45.

STONE, A. 1993. Financial fitness for unmarried couples. *Business Week,* June 21, 162–63.

STONE, R., AND C. WASZAK. 1992. Adolescent knowledge and attitudes about abortion. *Family Planning Perspectives* 24 (March/April): 52–57.

STRAIT, S. C. 1999. Drug use among Hispanic youth: Examining common and unique contributing factors. *Hispanic Journal of Behavioral Sciences* 21 (February): 89–103.

STRASBURGER, V. C. 1997. Tuning in to teenagers. *Newsweek,* May 19, 18–19.

STRATTON, J. L. 1981. *Pioneer women: Voices from the Kansas frontier.* New York: Simon & Schuster.

STRAUS, M. A. 1993. Identifying offenders in criminal justice research on domestic assault. *American Behavioral Scientist* 36 (May): 587–600.

STRAUS, M. A., AND C. FIELD. 2000. Psychological aggression by American parents: National data on prevalence, chronicity, and severity. Paper presented at the meeting of the American Sociological Association, Washington, DC, August 15. www.unh.edu/frl/cts27G1.pdf (accessed September 24, 2000).

STRAUS, M. A., AND J. H. STEWART. 1999. Corporal punishment by American parents: National data on prevalence, chronicity, severity, and duration, in relation to child and family characteristics. *Clinical Child and Family Psychology Review* 2 (June): 55–70.

STRAUS, M. A., AND C. L. YODANIS. 1996. Corporal punishment in adolescence and physical assaults on spouses in later life: What accounts for the link? *Journal of Marriage and the Family* 58 (November): 825–41.

STRAUSS, R. S. 1999. Self-reported weight status and dieting in a cross-sectional sample of young adolescents. *Archives of Pediatrics & Adolescent Medicine* 153 (July): 741–47.

STRAW, G., L. O'CONNOR, AND D. GANN. 1999. The AARP grandparenting survey: The sharing and caring between mature grandparents and their children, American Association of Retired Persons. research.aarp.org/general/grandpsurv. pdf (accessed October 28, 2000).

Strict new rules help pare recipients from welfare rolls. 1999. *Baltimore Sun,* March 29, 7A.

STROUP, A. L., AND G. E. POLLOCK. 1999. Economic consequences of marital dissolution for Hispanics. *Journal of Divorce & Remarriage* 30 (1/2): 149–66.

STROUSE, J. S., N. BUERKEL-ROTHFUSS, AND E. C. J. LONG. 1995. Gender and family as moderators of the relationship between music video exposure and adolescent sexual permissiveness. *Adolescence* 30 (Fall): 505–21.

SUGG, D. K. 2000. Subtle signs of heart disease in women are often missed. *Baltimore Sun,* January 25, 1A, 13A.

Suicide and suicidal behavior. 2000. National Center for Injury Prevention and Control. www. cdc.gov/ncipc/pub-res/FactBook/suicide.htm (accessed October 19, 2000).

SULLIVAN, A. D., K. HEDBERG, AND D. W. FLEMING. 2000. Legalized physician-assisted suicide in Oregon—the second year. *New England Journal of Medicine* 342 (February): 598–604.

SULLOWAY, F. J. 1996. *Born to rebel: Birth order, family dynamics, and creative lives.* New York: Pantheon.

Summary of recent studies on the wage gap between men and women professors. 2000. American Association of University Professors, Washington, DC. www.aaup.org/wstudy.htm (accessed October 15, 2000).

SUN, L. H. 1995. Traditional money pools keep immigrants afloat. *Washington Post,* February 17, A1, A22.

SURO, M. D. 1997. Child-friendly divorce: Counselors try to keep kids together when families fall apart. *Washington Post Health Supplement,* August 26, 10–12, 15.

SURO, R. 1994. Study of immigrants finds Asians at top in science and medicine. *Washington Post,* April 18, A6.

SURO, R. 1998. *Strangers among us: How Latino immigration is transforming America.* New York: Knopf.

SURO, R. 1999. Crossing the high-tech divide. *American Demographics* 21 (July): 55–60.

SWAIN, S. O. 1992. Men's friendships with women: Intimacy, sexual boundaries, and the informant role. In *Men's friendships,* ed. P. M. Nardi, 153–72. Thousand Oaks, CA: Sage.

SWAN, S. H., E. P. ELKIN, AND L. FENSTER. 1997. Have sperm densities declined? A reanalysis of global trend data. *Environmental Health Perspectives* 105 (November): 1228–33.

SWEDLUND, A. C. 1993. Review of *Anatomy of love: The natural history of monogamy, adultery, and divorce* by H. E. Fisher (New York: Norton, 1992). *American Anthropologist* 95 (December): 1053–54.

SWINFORD, S. P., A. DeMARIS, S. A. CERNKOVICH, AND P. G. GIORDANO. 2000. Harsh physical discipline in childhood and violence in later romantic involvements: The mediating role of problem behaviors. *Journal of Marriage and the Family* 62 (May): 508–19.

SWISHER, P. N., H. A. MILLER, AND W. I. WESTON. 1990. *Family law: Cases, materials and problems.* New York: Matthew Bender.

SWISS, D. J., AND J. P. WALKER. 1993. *Women and the work/family dilemma: How today's professional women are finding solutions.* New York: Wiley.

SWOBODA, F. 2000. Big 3 extend benefits to domestic partners. *Washington Post,* June 6, A1, A22.

SZABÒ, X. P., AND M. J. T. BLANCHE. 1997. Perfectionism in anorexia nervosa. *American Journal of Psychiatry* 154 (January): 132.

SZAPOCZNIK, J., AND R. HERNANDEZ. 1988. The Cuban American family. In *Ethnic families in America: Patterns and variations,* 3rd ed., eds. C. J. Mindel, R. W. Habenstein, and R. Wright, Jr., 160–72. New York: Elsevier.

SZEGEDY-MASZAK, M. 1993. Dating passages. *New Woman* 23 (March): 85–88.

SZINOVACZ, M. E., ED. 1998. *Handbook on grandparenthood.* Westport, CT: Greenwood Press.

SZYMANSKI, L. A., A. S. DEVLIN, J. C. CHRISLER, AND S. A. VYSE. 1993. Gender role and attitudes toward rape in male and female college students. *Sex Roles* 29 (1/2): 37–57.

Taboo no more: Workplace romances. 2000. *Christian Science Monitor,* February 14, 14.

TAKAGI, D. Y. 1994. Japanese American families. In *Minority families in the United States: A multicultural perspective,* ed. R. L. Taylor, 146–63. Upper Saddle River, NJ: Prentice Hall.

TAKAYAMA, H. 1990. The main track at last. *Newsweek,* January 22, 50–51.

TAM, V. C.-W., AND D. F. DETZNER. 1998. Grandparents as a family resource in Chinese-American families: Perceptions of the middle generation. In *Resiliency in Native American and immigrant families,* eds. H. I. McCubbin, E. A. Thompson, A. I. Thompson, and J. E. Fromer, 243–64. Thousand Oaks, CA: Sage.

TAMARACK, L. I. 1986. Fifty myths and facts about incest. In *Sexual abuse of children in the 1980s: Ten essays and an annotated bibliography,* ed. B. Schlesinger. Buffalo, NY: University of Toronto Press.

TAN, C. L.-L. 2000. The brave new world of TV dating. *Baltimore Sun,* August 6, 3F.

TANAKA, J. 1997. There's no place like home, unless it's the office. *Newsweek,* July 7, 14.

TANAKA, Y. 1994. Tokyo's marriage bureau sifts many for elusive few. *Baltimore Sun,* February 24, 2A.

TANIGUCHI, H. 1999. The timing of childbearing and women's wages. *Journal of Marriage and the Family* 61 (November): 1008–19.

TANNEN, D. 1990. *You just don't understand: Women and men in conversation.* New York: Ballantine.

TANUR, J. M. 1994. The trustworthiness of survey research. *Chronicle of Higher Education,* May 25, B1–B3.

TATARA, T. 1998. The national elder abuse incidence study. The National Center on Elder Abuse and the American Public Humane Services Association. www.aoa.gov/abuse/report/main-pdf.htm (accessed October 19, 2000).

TAVRIS, C. 1992. *The mismeasure of woman.* New York: Simon & Schuster.

TAYLOR, K., J. L. LESIAK, J. CARROLL, AND W. J. LESIAK. 1993. Kindergartners' responses to males in nontraditional roles: A replication of Styer (1975). *Psychological Reports* 72 (June): 1179–83.

TAYLOR, P. 1991. Therapists rethink attitudes on divorce: New movement to save marriages focuses on impact on children. *Washington Post,* January 29, A1, A6.

TAYLOR, R. J., L. M. CHATTERS, M. B. TUCKER, AND E. LEWIS. 1990. Developments in research on black families: A decade review. *Journal of Marriage and the Family* 52 (November): 993–1014.

TAYLOR, R. J., V. M. KEITH, AND M. B. TUCKER. 1993. Gender, marital, familial, and friendship roles. In *Aging in black America,* eds. J. S. Jackson, L. M. Chatters and R. J. Taylor, 49–68. Thousand Oaks, CA: Sage.

TEACHMAN, J. D. 1991. Contributions to children by divorced fathers. *Social Problems* 38 (August): 358–70.

TEACHMAN, J. D. 1983. Marriage, premarital fertility, and marital dissolution: Results for blacks and whites. *Journal of Family Issues* 4, 105–28.

TEACHMAN, J. D., AND K. A. POLONKO. 1990. Cohabitation and marital stability in the United States. *Social Forces* 69 (September): 207–20.

TEACHMAN, J. D., J. THOMAS, AND K. PAASCH. 1991. Legal status and the stability of coresidential unions. *Demography* 26 (November): 571–86.

Teen sex and pregnancy. 1999. Guttmacher Institute. www.agi-usa.org/pubs/fb_teen_sex.html (accessed August 12, 2000).

TEFFT, S. 1995. A rush to rock the cradle—of girls. *Christian Science Monitor,* August 2, 1, 8.

TENNESEN, M. 1993. Are there dating services for seniors? *Modern Maturity* (April–May): 84.

TERESI, D. 1994. How to get a man pregnant. *New York Times Magazine,* November 27, 54–55.

TERRELL, K. 1992. Female–male earnings differentials and occupational structure. *International Labour Review* 131 (4–5): 387–403.

TEYBER, E., AND C. D. HOFFMAN. 1987. Missing fathers. *Psychology Today* (April): 36–69.

THOMAS, A. J., AND S. L. SPEIGHT. 1999. Racial identity and racial socialization attitudes of African American parents. *Journal of Black Psychology* 25 (May): 152–70.

THOMAS, G., M. P. FARRELL, AND G. M. BARNES. 1996. The effects of single-mother families and nonresident fathers on delinquency and substance abuse in black and white adolescents. *Journal of Marriage and the Family* 58 (November): 884–94.

THOMAS, J. L. 1994. Older men as fathers and grandfathers. In *Older men's lives,* ed. E. H. Thompson, Jr., 197–217. Thousand Oaks, CA: Sage.

THOMAS, W. I., AND F. ZNANIECKI. 1927. *The Polish peasant in Europe and America,* vol. 2. New York: Knopf. (Originally published 1918 by the University of Chicago Press.)

THOMAS-LESTER, A. 1994. Carrying on: A joyless time for the grieving. *Washington Post,* December 15, D5.

THOMPSON, B. W. 1996. "A way outa no way": Eating problems among African American, Latina, and white women. In *Race, class, & gender: Common bonds, different voices,* eds. E. N.-L. Chow, D. Wilkinson, and M. B. Zinn, 52–69. Thousand Oaks, CA: Sage.

THOMPSON, L., AND A. J. WALKER. 1991. Gender in families. In *Contemporary families: Looking forward, looking back,* ed. A. Booth, 76–102. Minneapolis, MN: National Council on Family Relations.

THOMPSON, L., AND A. J. WALKER. 1995. The place of feminism in family studies. *Journal of Marriage and the Family* 57 (November): 847–65.

THOMSON, E. 1997. Couple childbearing desires, intentions, and births. *Demography* 34 (August): 343–54.

THOMSON, E., S. S. McLANAHAN, AND R. B. CURTIN. 1992. Family structure, gender, and parental socialization. *Journal of Marriage and the Family* 54 (May): 368–78.

THORNBERRY, T. P., C. A. SMITH, AND G. J. HOWARD. 1997. Risk factors for teenage fatherhood. *Journal of Marriage and the Family* 59 (August): 505–22.

THORNBERRY, T. P., C. A. SMITH, C. RIVERA, D. HUIZINGA, AND M. STOUTHAMER-LOEBER. 1999. *Family disruption and delinquency.* Washington, DC: U.S. Department of Justice, Office of Justice Programs, Office of Juvenile Justice and Delinquency Prevention.

THORNE, 1982. Feminist rethinking of the family: An overview. In *Rethinking the family: Some feminist questions,* eds. B. Thorne and M. Yalom, 1–24. New York: Longman.

THORNE, B. 1993. *Gender play: Girls and boys in school.* New Brunswick, NJ: Rutgers University Press.

THORNTON, A. 1991. Influence of the marital history of parents on the marital and cohabitational experiences of children. *American Journal of Sociology* 96 (January): 868–94.

THORNTON, A., AND W. RODGERS. 1987. The influence of individual and historical time on marital dissolution. *Demography* 24 (February): 1–22.

THORNTON, A., L. YOUNG-DeMARCO, AND F. GOLDSCHEIDER. 1993. Leaving the parental nest: The experience of a young white cohort in the 1980s. *Journal of Marriage and the Family* 5 (February): 216–29.

THORNTON, E. 1994. Video dating in Japan. *Fortune,* January 24, 12.

THORNTON, J. 1984. Family violence emerges from the shadows. *U.S. News & World Report,* January 23, 66.

THORNTON, J., AND D. WHITMAN WITH D. FREEDMAN. 1992. Whites' myths about blacks. *U.S. News & World Report,* November 9, 41–44.

TICHENOR, V. J. 1999. Status and income as gendered resources: The case of marital power. *Journal of Marriage and the Family* 61 (August): 638–60.

The ties that bind. 2000. *Public Perspective* 11 (May–June): 10.

TIGER L. 1999. *The decline of males.* New York: Golden Books.

TILLER, J. M., G. SLOANE, U. SCHMIDT, N. TROOP, M. POWER, AND J. L. TREASURE. 1997. Social support in patients with anorexia nervosa and bulimia nervosa. *International Journal of Eating Disorders* 21 (January): 31–38.

Time. 1997. Women of the house, June 16, 20.

TJADEN, P., AND N. THOENNES. 2000a. *Extent, nature, and consequences of intimate partner violence: Findings from the National Violence against Women Survey.* Washington, DC: U.S. Department of Justice, Office of Justice Programs.

TJADEN, P., AND N. THOENNES. 2000b. Prevalence and consequences of male-to-female and female-to-male intimate partner violence as measured by the National Violence against Women Survey. *Violence against Women* 6 (February): 142–61.

TJADEN, P., N. THOENNES, AND C. J. ALLISON. 1999. Comparing violence over the life span in samples of same-sex and opposite-sex cohabitants. *Violence and Victims* 14 (Winter): 413–25.

TORO-MORN, M. I. 1995. Gender, class, family, and migration. *Gender & Society* 9 (December): 712–26.

TORO-MORN, M. I. 1998. The family and work experiences of Puerto Rican women migrants in Chicago. In *Resiliency in Native American and immigrant families,* eds. H. I. McCubbin, E. A. Thompson, A. I. Thompson, and J. E. Fromer, 277–94. Thousand Oaks, CA: Sage.

TOSA, M. 1998. *Barbie: Four decades of fashion, fantasy, and fun.* New York: Abrams.

TOTH, J. 1992. Study of runaways finds lives of abuse. *Baltimore Sun,* January 2, 3A.

TOTH, J. F., JR., AND X. XU. 1999. Ethnic and cultural diversity in fathers' involvement: A racial/ethnic comparison of African American, Hispanic, and white fathers. *Youth & Society* 31 (September): 76–99.

TOUSIGNANT, M. 1994. Bogged down in Bucharest. *Washington Post,* October 26, B1, B5.

TRAFFORD, A. 1991. Why battered women kill: Self-defense, not revenge, is often the motive. *Washington Post Health Supplement,* February 26, 6.

TRAFFORD, A. 1997. Getting tough on divorce not the same as getting real. *Washington Post Health Supplement,* August 26, 6.

TRAN, T. V. 1988. The Vietnamese American family. In *Ethnic families in America: Patterns and variations,* 3rd ed., eds. C. H. Mindel, R. W. Habenstein, and R. Wright, Jr., 276–302. New York: Elsevier.

TRAVIS, R., AND V. KOHLI. 1995. The birth order factor: Ordinal position, social strata, and educational achievement. *Journal of Social Psychology* 135 (August): 499–508.

TREAS, J. 1999. Diversity in American families. In *A nation divided: Diversity, inequality, and community in American families,* eds. P. Moen, D. Dempster-McCain, and H. A. Walker, 245–59. Ithaca, NY: Cornell University Press.

TREAS, J., AND D. GIESEN. 2000. Sexual infidelity among married and cohabiting Americans. *Journal of Marriage and the Family* 62 (February): 48–60.

TRENT, K. 1994. Family context and adolescents' expectations about marriage, fertility, and nonmarital childbearing. *Social Science Quarterly* 75 (June): 319–39.

TRIMBLE, J. E., AND B. MEDICINE. 1993. Diversification of American Indians: Forming an indigenous perspective. In *Indigenous psychologies,* eds. U. Kim and J. W. Berry, 133–51. Newbury Park, CA: Sage.

TROTTER, R. J. 1986. Failing to find the father-infant bond. *Psychology Today* (February): 18.

TRUMBULL, D. A., AND D. RAVENEL. 1999. Spare the rod? New research challenges spanking critic. *Family Policy,* Family Research Council, January 22.

TRUMBULL, M. 1995. Demographics, computers multiply Asian-language media in the US. *Christian Science Monitor,* July 24, 13.

TRZCINSKI, E. 1994. Family and medical leave, contingent employment, and flexibility: A feminist critique of the U.S. approach to work and family policy. *Journal of Applied Social Sciences* 18 (Fall/Winter): 71–87.

TSAI, D. T., AND R. A. LOPEZ. 1997. The use of social supports by elderly Chinese immigrants. *Journal of Gerontological Social Work* 29 (1): 77–94.

TUCKER, M. B., AND R. J. TAYLOR. 1989. Demographic correlates of relationship status among black Americans. *Journal of Marriage and the Family* 51 (August): 655–65.

TUCKER, M. B., AND R. J. TAYLOR. 1997. Gender, age, and marital status as related to romantic involvement among African American singles. In *Family life in black America,* eds. R. J. Taylor, J. S. Jackson, L. M. Chatters, 79–94. Thousand Oaks, CA: Sage.

TUCKER, M. B., R. J. TAYLOR, AND C. MITCHELL-KERNAN. 1993. Marriage and romantic involvement among aged African Americans. *Journal of Gerontology: Social Sciences* 48 (3): S128–S132.

TUCKER, R. K. 1992. Men's and women's ranking of thirteen acts of romance. *Psychological Reports* 71, 640–42.

TUCKER, S. K. 1989. Adolescent patterns of communication about sexually related topics. *Adolescence* 24 (Summer): 269–78.

TULLER, D. 1994. Men, women respond differently to jealousy. *San Francisco Chronicle,* June 24, A17.

TURNBULL, S. K., AND J. M. TURNBULL. 1983. To dream the impossible dream: An agenda for discussion with stepparents. *Family Relations* 32, 227–30.

TURNER, C. F., L. KU, S. M. ROGERS, L. D. LINDBERG, J. H. PLECK, AND F. L. SONENSTEIN. 1998. Adolescent sexual behavior, drug use, and violence: Increased reporting with computer survey technology. *Science* 280, May 8, 867–73.

TURNER, J. S., AND L. RUBINSON. 1993. *Contemporary human sexuality.* Upper Saddle River, NJ: Prentice Hall.

TUROW, J., AND L. NIR. 2000. The Internet and the family 2000: The view from parents, the view from kids. Annenberg Public Policy Center, University of Pennsylvania. http://appcpenn. org/finalrepor_fam.pdf (accessed August 13, 2000).

TUTTLE, W. M., JR., 1993. *Daddy's gone to war: The Second World War in the lives of America's children.* New York: Oxford University Press.

TV Guide cover story should look at the numbers before they cheer journalistic gender parity. www.fair.org/activism/tv-guide-women.html (accessed August 27, 2000).

TWITCHELL, J. B. 1987. *Forbidden partners: The incest taboo in modern culture.* New York: Columbia University Press.

TYLER, T. R., AND R. A. SCHULLER. 1991. Aging and attitude change. *Journal of Personality and Social Psychology* 61 (5): 689–97.

TYSON, A. S. 2000. "Family values" come to the tax code. *Christian Science Monitor,* February 7, 1, 5.

TYSZKOWA, M. 1993. Adolescents' relationships with grandparents: Characteristics and developmental transformations. In *Adolescence and its social worlds,* eds. S. Jackson and H. Rodriguez-Tomé, 121–43. East Sussex, UK: Lawrence Erlbaum Associates.

TZENG, O. C. S. 1993. *Measurement of love and intimate relations: Theories, scales, and applications for love development, maintenance, and dissolution.* Westport, CT: Praeger.

U. of Cal. settles with infertility patients. 1997. *Chronicle of Higher Education,* August 1, 11.

U.S. Census Bureau. 1997a. *Household and family characteristics: March 1996.* Detailed tables for Current Population Reports, P20-495. Washington, DC: U.S. Government Printing Office.

U.S. Census Bureau. 1999b. *Money income in the United States: 1999.* Current Population Reports, P60-209. www.census.gov/prod/ 2000pubs/p60-209.pdf (accessed October 4, 2000).

U.S. Census Bureau. 1993. *Poverty in the United States: 1992.* Current Population Reports, Series P60-185. Washington, DC: U.S. Government Printing Office.

U.S. Census Bureau. 1997b. *Money income in the United States: 1996 (With separate data on valuation of noncash benefits).* Current Population Reports, P60-197. Washington, DC: U.S. Government Printing Office.

U.S. Census Bureau. 1997c. *Statistical abstract of the United States, 1997,* 117th ed. Washington, DC: U.S. Government Printing Office.

U.S. Census Bureau. 1998. Census Bureau Facts for features. www.census.gov/Press-Release/ cb98ff13.html (accessed October 5, 2000).

U.S. Census Bureau. 1999a. Table MS-2: Estimated median age at first marriage, by sex. www. census.gov/population/socdemo/ms-la/tabms-2.txt (accessed August 5, 2000).

U.S. Census Bureau. 1999c. *Statistical abstract of the United States, 1999,* 119th ed. Washington, DC: U.S. Government Printing Office.

U.S. Commission on Civil Rights. 1984. *Comparable worth: Issues for the 80's,* vol. 1. Washington, DC: U.S. Government Printing Office.

U.S. Department of Health and Human Services. 1996. National Center on Child Abuse and Neglect. *Third national incidence study of child abuse and neglect: Final report* (NIS-3). Washington, DC: U.S. Government Printing Office.

U.S. Department of Health and Human Services. 1997. National Center on Child Abuse and Neglect. *Child maltreatment 1995: Reports from the states to the National Child Abuse and Neglect Data System.* Washington, DC: U.S. Government Printing Office.

U.S. Department of Health and Human Services. 2000. *Child maltreatment 1998: Reports from the states to the National Child Abuse and Neglect Data System.* Washington, DC: U.S. Government Printing Office.

U.S. Department of Justice. Bureau of Justice Statistics. 1997. Criminal offenders statistics. www.ojp.usdoj.gov/bjs/crimoff/htm#summary (accessed January 2, 1998).

U.S. Department of Labor. 2000. *The employment situation: September 2000.* www.bls.gov/news. release/pdf/empsit.pdf (accessed October 16, 2000).

U.S. Senate Special Committee on Aging, American Association of Retired Persons, Federal Council on the Aging, and U.S. Administration on Aging. 1991. *Aging America: Trends and projections, 1991.* Washington, DC: Department of Health and Human Services.

UCHITELLE, L. 1994. Moonlighting plus: 3-job families on the rise. *New York Times,* August 16, D1, D18.

UDESKY, L. 1994. Sweatshops behind the labels. *The Nation,* May 16, 665–68.

UDRY, J. R. 1993. The politics of sex research. *Journal of Sex Research* 30 (May): 103–10.

ULBRICH, P. M. 1988. The determinants of depression in two-income marriages. *Journal of Marriage and the Family* 50 (February): 121–31.

UMBERSON, D., AND C. L. WILLIAMS. 1993. Divorced fathers: Parental role strain and psychological distress. *Journal of Family Issues* 14 (September): 378–400.

UNDERWOOD, R. C., AND P. C. PATCH. 1999. Siblicide: A descriptive analysis of sibling homicide. *Homicide Studies* 3 (November): 333–48.

UNGAR, S. J. 1995. *Fresh blood: The new American immigrants.* New York: Simon & Schuster.

UNICEF. 1994. *The progress of nations.* New York.

United Nations Children's Fund. 2000. *The state of the world's children 1998.* www.unicef.org (accessed August 12, 2000).

UPCHURCH, M., C. S. ANESHENSEL, C. A. SUCOFF, AND L. LEVY-STORMS. 1999. Neighborhood and family contexts of adolescent sexual activity. *Journal of Marriage and the Family* 61 (November): 920–33.

Utah legislature bans gay student clubs in high schools. 1996. *Baltimore Sun,* April 19, 5A.

UTTAL, L. 1999. Using kin for child care: Embedment in the socioeconomic networks of extended families. *Journal of Marriage and the Family* 61 (November): 845–57.

VALDEZ, E. O., AND S. COLTRANE. 1993. Work, family, and the Chicana: Power, perception, and equity. In *The employed mother and the family context,* ed. J. Frankel, 153–79. New York: Springer.

VAN BIEMA, D. 1997. Sparse at seder? *Time,* April 26, 67.

VAN GELDER, L., AND P. R. BRANDT. 1996. *The girls next door: Into the heart of lesbian America.* New York: Simon & Schuster.

VAN RY, M. 1993. *Homeless families: Causes, effects, and recommendations.* New York: Garland.

VANCE, E. B., AND N. N. WAGNER. 1976. Written descriptions of orgasm: A study of sex differences. *Archives of Sexual Behavior* 5: 87–98.

VANDERPOOL, T. 1999. Retirement communities for the PhD set. *Christian Science Monitor,* November 22, 3.

VANDEWATER, E. A., AND J. E. LANSFORD. 1998. Influences of family structure and parental conflict on children's well-being. *Family Relations* 47 (October): 233–330.

VEATCH, R. M. 1995. Death and dying. In *Ethics applied,* eds. M. L. Richardson and K. K. White, 215–43. New York: McGraw-Hill.

VEEVERS, J. 1980. *Childless by choice.* Toronto: Butterworth.

VEGA, W. A. 1995. The study of Latino families: A point of departure. In *Understanding Latino families: Scholarship, policy, and practice,* ed. R. E. Zambrana, 3–17. Thousand Oaks, CA: Sage.

VEMER, E., M. COLEMAN, L. H. GANONG, AND H. COOPER. 1989. Marital satisfaction in remarriage: A meta-analysis. *Journal of Marriage and the Family* 51 (August): 713–25.

VENTURA, S. J., C. A. BACHRACH, L. HILL, K. KAYE, P. HOLCOMB, AND E. KOFF. 1995. The demography of out-of-wedlock childbearing. In *Report to Congress on out-of-wedlock childbearing,* v–xxii. Hyattsville, MD: Centers for Disease Control and Prevention, National Center for Health Statistics.

VENTURA, S. J., S. C. CURTIN, AND T. J. MATHEWS. 2000. Variations in teenage birth rates, 1991-98: National and state trends. *National Vital Statistical Reports* 48, April 24, Centers for Disease Control and Prevention. www.cdc.gov/nchs/data/nvs48_6.pdf (accessed September 22, 2000).

VENTURA, S. J., J. A. MARTIN, S. C. CURTIN, T. J. MATHEWS, AND M. M. PARK. 2000. Births: final data for 1998. *National Vital Statistical Reports* 48, March 28, Centers for Disease Control and Prevention. www.cdc.gov/nchs/data/nvs48_3.pdf (accessed September 22, 2000).

VENTURA, S. J., S. C. MOSHER, S. C. CURTIN, J. C. ABMA, AND S. HENSHAW. 2000. Trends in pregnancies and pregnancy rates by outcome: Estimates for the United States, 1976–96. National Center for Health Statistics, *Vital Health Statistics,* 21 (56).

VENTURA, S. J., K. D. PETERS, J. A. MARTIN, AND J. D. MAURER. 1997. Births and deaths: United States, 1996. *Monthly Vital Statistics Report*

46 (1), Suppl. 2. Hyattsville, MD: National Center for Health Statistics.

VERBRUGGE, L. 1979. Marital status and health. *Journal of Marriage and the Family* 41 (May): 267–85.

VICK, K. 1998. Letter from Lagos: Abiola: A man of many parts and many wives, *Washington Post,* July 14, A9, A11.

VINICK, B. H. 1997. Stepfamilies in later life: What happens to intergenerational relationships? Paper presented at the American Sociological Association Annual Meeting, Toronto.

VINOVSKIS, M. A., AND S. M. FRANK. 1997. Parenting in American society: A historical overview of the colonial period through the 19th century. In *Contemporary parenting: Challenges and issues,* ed. T. Arendell, 45–67. Thousand Oaks, CA: Sage.

VISHER, E., AND J. VISHER. 1982. *How to win as a stepfamily.* New York: Dembner.

VISHER, E. B., AND J. S. VISHER. 1988. *Old loyalties, new ties: Therapeutic strategies with stepfamilies.* New York: Brunner/Mazel.

VISHER, E. B., AND J. S. VISHER. 1993. Remarriage families and stepparenting. In *Normal family processes,* 2nd ed., ed. F. Walsh, 235–53. New York: Guilford Press.

VISHER, E. B., AND J. S. VISHER. 1996. *Therapy with stepfamilies.* New York: Brunner/Mazel.

VITOUSEK, K., AND F. MANKE. 1994. Personality variables and disorders in anorexia nervosa and bulimia nervosa. *Journal of Abnormal Psychology* 103 (February): 137–74.

VOBEJDA, B. 1997. Abortion rate in U.S. off sharply. *Washington Post,* December 5, A3.

VOGLER, C., AND J. PAHL. 1994. Money, power and inequality within marriage. *Sociological Review* 42 (May): 263–88.

VON HIPPEL, W., L. A. SILVER, AND M. E. LYNCH. 2000. Stereotyping against your will: The role of inhibitory ability in stereotyping and prejudice among the elderly. *Personality & Social Psychology Bulletin* 26 (May): 523–59.

VOYDANOFF, P. 1991. Economic distress and family relations. In *Contemporary families: Looking forward, looking back,* ed. A. Booth, 429–45. Minneapolis, MN: National Council on Family Relations.

VUCHINICH, S. 1987. Starting and stopping spontaneous family conflicts. *Journal of Marriage and the Family* 49 (August): 591–601.

VUCHINICH, S., E. M. HETHERINGTON, R. A. VUCHINICH, AND W. G. CLINGEMPEEL. 1991. Parent–child interaction and gender differences in early adolescents' adaptation to stepfamilies. *Developmental Psychology* 27 (4): 618–26.

WACHTER, K. W. 1997. Kinship resources for the elderly. *Philosophical Transactions: Biological Sciences* 352 (December 29): 1811–17.

WADE, C., AND S. CIRESE. 1991. *Human sexuality,* 2nd ed. New York: Harcourt Brace Jovanovich.

WAGEMAAR, T. C., AND R. D. COATES. 1999. Race and children: The dynamics of early socialization. *Education* 120 (Winter): 220–36.

WAGNER, B. 1998. Who has abortions. *U.S. News & World Report,* August 19, 8.

WAITE, L. J., ED. 2000. *The ties that bind: Perspectives on marriage and cohabitation.* New York: Aldine de Gruyter.

WAITE, L. J., AND L. A. LILLARD. 1991. Children and marital disruption. *American Journal of Sociology* 96 (January): 930–53.

WALCZAK, L., ET AL. 2000. The politics of prosperity. *Business Week,* August 7, 96–108.

WALDMAN, S., ET AL. 1994. Welfare booby traps. *Newsweek,* December 12, 34–35.

WALDROP, J. 1993. The grandbaby boom. *American Demographics* 15 (September): 4.

WALKER, A. J. 1996. Couples watching television: Gender, power, and the remote control. *Journal of Marriage and the Family* 58 (November): 813–23.

WALKER, J. 1990. Genetic parents win custody of baby: California judge also denies surrogate mother visitation rights. *Washington Post,* October 23, A4.

WALKER, L. 1978. Treatment alternatives for battered women. In *The victimization of women,* eds. J. R. Chapman and M. Gates, 143–74. Beverly Hills, CA: Sage.

WALKER, L. E. A. 2000. *The battered woman syndrome,* 2nd ed. New York: Springer.

WALKER, P. V. 1996. The Public Health Service's Office of Research Integrity has found a physician guilty of scientific misconduct. *Chronicle of Higher Education,* May 17, A33.

WALKER, P. V. 1997. 2 lawsuits may change handling of research-misconduct charges. *Chronicle of Higher Education,* June 6, A27–A28.

WALKER, R. 1999. Canada rethinks its Medicare. *Christian Science Monitor,* December 14, 1, 8.

WALKER, T. 1993. Chinese men embrace divorce. *World Press Review* 40 (October): 48.

WALKER, W. D., R. C. ROWE, AND V. L. QUINSEY. 1993. Authoritarianism and sexual aggression. *Journal of Personality and Social Psychology* 65 (5): 1036–45.

WALLACE, H. 1996. *Family violence: Legal, medical, and social perspectives.* Boston: Allyn & Bacon.

WALLACE, M. 1978. *Black macho and the myth of the superwoman.* New York: Routledge.

WALLER, W. 1937. The rating and dating complex. *American Sociological Review* 2 (October): 727–34.

WALLERSTEIN, J., AND S. BLAKESLEE. 1989. *Second chances: Men, women and children a decade after divorce.* New York: Ticknor & Fields.

WALLERSTEIN, J. S., AND S. BLAKESLEE. 1995. *The good marriage: How and why love lasts.* Boston: Houghton Mifflin.

WALLERSTEIN, J. S., J. M. LEWIS, AND S. BLAKESLEE. 2000. *The unexpected legacy of divorce: A 25 year landmark study.* New York: Hyperion.

WALSH, A. 1991. *The science of love: Understanding love and its effects on mind and body.* Buffalo, NY: Prometheus Books.

WALSH, E. O., M. E. GAZALA, AND C. HAM. 2000. The truth about the digital divide. www.forrester.com/ER/Research/Brief/0,1317,9208,FF.html (accessed August 4, 2000).

WALSH, F., ED. 1993. *Normal family processes,* 2nd ed. New York: Guilford Press.

WALSTER, E., E. BERSCHEID, AND G. W. WALSTER. 1973. New directions in equity research. *Journal of Personality and Social Psychology* 25 (2): 151–76.

WALTHER, A. N. 1991. *Divorce hangover.* New York: Pocket Books.

WALZER, S. 1998. *Thinking about the baby: Gender and transitions into parenthood.* Philadelphia: Temple University Press.

WANG, P. 1993. What every woman should know about stockbrokers. *Money* (June): 14–16.

Want ad proves a woman's worth is never done. 1997. Ann Landers column. *Baltimore Sun,* September 20, 3D.

WARD, L. M. 1995. Talking about sex: Common themes about sexuality in the prime-time television programs children and adolescents view most. *Journal of Youth and Adolescence* 24 (October): 595–615.

WARD, S. K., K. CHAPMAN, E. COHN, S. WHITE, AND K. WILLIAMS. 1991. Acquaintance rape and the college social scene. *Family Relations* 40 (January): 65–71.

WATKINS, S. C. 1996. Helping students use sociology to study the family. *Chronicle of Higher Education,* October 11, A72.

WATKINS, T. H. 1993. *The great depression: America in the 1930s.* New York: Little, Brown.

WATSON, J. A., AND S. A. KOBLINSKY. 1997. Strengths and needs of working-class African-American and Anglo-American grandparents. *International Journal of Aging and Human Development* 44 (2): 149–65.

WATSON, K. W. 1997. Bonding and attachment in adoptions: Towards better understanding and useful definitions. *Marriage & Family Review* 25 (3/4): 159–73.

WATSON, T., J. P. SHAPIRO, J. IMPOCO, AND T. M. ITO. 1996. Is there a "gay gene"? *U.S. News & World Report,* November 13, 93–96.

WEATHERFORD, D. 1986. *Foreign and female: Immigrant women in America, 1840–1930.* New York: Schocken.

WEBER, L., T. HANCOCK, AND E. HIGGINBOTHAM. 1997. Women, power, and mental health. In *Women's health: Complexities and differences,* eds., S. B. Ruzek, V. L. Olesen, and A. E. Clarke, 380–96. Columbus: Ohio State University Press.

WEBSDALE, N. 1999. *Understanding domestic homicide.* Boston: Northeastern University Press.

WECHSLER, H. 1995. *Binge drinking on American college campuses: A new look at an old problem.* Boston: Harvard School of Public Health.

WEIBEL-ORLANDO, J. 1990. Grandparenting styles: Native American perspectives. In *The cultural context of aging,* ed. J. Sokolovsky, 109–25. Westport, CT: Greenwood Press.

WEIL, B. E. AND P. WINTER. 1993. *Adultery: The forgivable sin.* New York: Birch Lane Press.

WEINBERG, M. S., C. J. WILLIAMS, AND D. W. PRYOR. 1994. *Dual attraction: Understanding bisexuality.* New York: Oxford University Press.

WEINGARTEN, T., AND M. HOSENBALL. 1999. A fertile scheme. *Newsweek,* November 8, 78–79.

WEIR, F. 2000. Adoptions stalled: Reform or red tape? *Christian Science Monitor,* June 16, 1, 8.

WEISS, C. H. 1998. *Evaluation research: Methods for assessing program effectiveness,* 2nd ed. Upper Saddle River, NJ: Prentice Hall.

WEISS, R. 1997. Research violates Georgetown ban. *Washington Post,* January 15, A3.

WEISS, R. 2000. Limited pay for egg donors advised. *Washington Post,* August 4, A5.

WEISSMAN, R. X. 1999a. *Los niños* go shopping. *American Demographics* 21 (May): 37–39.

WEISSMAN, R. X. 1999b. That magical night. *American Demographics* 21 (May): 80.

WEITZMAN, L. J. 1985. *The divorce revolution: The unexpected social and economic consequences for women and children in America.* New York: Free Press.

WELLMAN, B. 1997. The road to utopia and dystopia on the information highway. *Contemporary Sociology* 26 (July): 445–49.

WELTER, B. 1966. The cult of true womanhood: 1820–1860. *American Quarterly* 18 (2): 151–74.

WENNERAS, C., AND A. WOLD. 1997. Nepotism and sexism in peer review. *Nature* 387 (May): 341–43.

WEST, C., AND D. H. ZIMMERMAN. 1987. Doing gender. *Gender and Society* 1 (June): 125–51.

WESTOFF, L. A. 1977. *The second time around: Remarriage in America.* New York: Viking.

What works? 1999. *Public Perspective* 10 (October/November): 23.

WHATLEY, M. H. 1994. Keeping adolescents in the picture: Construction of adolescent sexuality in textbook images and popular films. In *Sexual cultures and the construction of adolescent identities,* ed. J. M. Irvine, 183–205. Philadelphia: Temple University Press.

WHEELER, C. G. 1993. 30 years beyond "I have a dream." *Gallup Poll Monthly,* October, 2–8.

WHEELER, L. 1998. Excavation reveals slaves as entrepreneurs. *Washington Post,* October 13, B3.

WHIPPLE, E. E., AND C. A. RICHEY. 1997. Crossing the line from physical discipline to child abuse: How much is too much? *Child Abuse & Neglect* 21 (May): 431–44.

Whirlpool Foundation. 1995. *Women: The new providers.* Benton Harbor, MI.

Whirlpool Foundation. 1996. *Women: Setting new priorities.* Benton Harbor, MI.

WHITAKER, D., J. MILLER, AND S. KIM. 2000. Parent-adolescent discussions about sex and condoms: Impact on peer influences of sexual risk behavior. *Journal of Adolescent Research* 15 (March): 251–73.

WHITBECK, L. B., AND D. R. HOYT. 1999. *Nowhere to grow: Homeless and runaway adolescents and their families.* New York: Aldine de Gruyter.

WHITBECK, L. B., K. A. YODER, D. R. HOYT, AND R. D. CONGER. 1999. Early adolescent sexual activity. *Journal of Marriage and the Family* 61 (November): 934–46.

WHITE, G. L., AND P. E. MULLEN. 1989. *Jealousy: Theory, research, and clinical strategies.* New York: Guilford Press.

WHITE, J. W., AND J. A. HUMPHREY. 1994. Women's aggression in heterosexual conflicts. *Aggressive Behavior* 20 (3): 195–202.

WHITE, J. W., AND M. P. KOSS. 1991. Courtship violence: Incidence in a national sample of higher education students. *Violence and Victims* 6 (4): 247–56.

WHITE, L. 1992. The effect of parental divorce and remarriage on parental support for adult children. *Journal of Family Issues* 13 (June): 234–50.

WHITE, L. K. 1991. Determinants of divorce. In *Contemporary families: Looking forward, looking back,* ed. A. Booth, 150–61. Minneapolis, MN: National Council on Family Relations.

WHITE EAGLE, J. 1996. What is the definition of a true Native American? *Indian Country Today,* November 18–25, A5.

WHITEFORD, LINDA M., AND L. GONZALEZ. 1995. Stigma: The hidden burden of infertility. *Social Science and Medicine* 40 (January): 27–36.

WHITEHEAD, B. D. 1996. The decline of marriage as the social basis of childrearing. In *Promises to keep: Decline and renewal of marriage in America,* eds. D. Popenoe, J. B. Elshtain, and D. Blankenhorn, 3–14. Lanham, MD: Rowman & Littlefield.

WHITEHEAD, B. D. 1997. *The divorce culture.* New York: Knopf.

WHITEHEAD, M. B., WITH L. SCHWARTZ-NOBEL. 1989. *A mother's story: The truth about the Baby M case.* New York: St. Martin's.

White majority fading in Calif. 2000. *Baltimore Sun,* July 4, 4a.

WHITSETT, D., AND H. LAND. 1992. The development of a role strain index for stepparents. *Families in Society: The Journal of Contemporary Human Services* 73 (January): 14–22.

WHITTELSEY, F. C. 1993. *Why women pay more: How to avoid marketplace perils.* Washington, DC: Center for Study of Responsive Law.

Who gets the most time off? 2000. *Christian Science Monitor,* July 3, 12.

WHYTE, M. K. 1990. *Dating, mating, and marriage.* New York: Aldine de Gruyter.

WICKRAMA, K. A. S., F. O. LORENZ, R. D. CONGER, AND G. H. ELDER, JR. 1997. Marital quality and physical illness: A latent growth curve analysis. *Journal of Marriage and the Family* 59 (February): 143–55.

WIEHE, V. R. 1997. *Sibling abuse: Hidden physical, emotional, and sexual trauma,* 2nd ed. Thousand Oaks, CA: Sage.

WIEHE, V. R., WITH T. HERRING. 1991. *Perilous rivalry: When siblings become abusive.* Lexington, MA: Lexington Books.

WIESE, D., AND D. DARO. 1995. *Current trends in child abuse reporting and fatalities: The results of the 1994 annual fifty state survey.* Chicago: National Committee to Prevent Child Abuse.

WIIST, W. H., AND J. MCFARLANE. 1998. Severity of spousal and intimate partner abuse to pregnant Hispanic women. *Journal of Health Care for the Poor & Underserved* 9 (August): 248–61.

WILKIE, J. R., M. M. FERREE, AND K. S. RATCLIFF. 1998. Gender and fairness: Marital satisfaction in two-earner couples. *Journal of Marriage and the Family* 60 (August): 577–94.

WILKINSON, T. 2000. Midwest by moonlight: Low pay means two jobs. *Christian Science Monitor,* August 16, 1, 5.

WILLIAMS, B. L. 1994. Reflections on family poverty. *Families in Society: The Journal of Contemporary Human Services* 75 (January): 47–50.

WILLIAMS, N. 1990. *The Mexican American family: Tradition and change.* New York: General Hall.

WILLIAMS, T. K., AND M. C. THORNTON. 1998. Social construction of ethnicity versus personal experience: The case of Afro-Amerasians. *Journal of Comparative Family Studies* 29 (Summer): 255–84.

WILLIAMS, W. M. 1998. Do parents matter? Scholars need to explain what research really shows. *Chronicle of Higher Education,* December 11, B6–B7.

WILLIS, S. L., AND J. D. REID, EDS. 1999. *Life in the middle: Psychological and social development in middle age.* San Diego, CA: Academic Press.

WILSON, B. F., AND S. C. CLARKE. 1992. Remarriages: A demographic profile. *Journal of Family Issues* 13 (June): 123–41.

WILSON, D. S., AND C. K. JACOBSON. 1995. White attitudes toward black and white interracial marriage. In *American families: Issues in race and ethnicity,* ed. C. K. Jacobson, 353–67. New York: Garland.

WILSON, G. 1990. The consequences of elderly wives caring for disabled husbands: Implications for practice. *Social Work* 35 (September): 417–21.

WILSON, R. 1999. An MIT professor's suspicion of bias leads to a new movement for academic women. *Chronicle of Higher Education,* December 3, A16–A18.

WILSON, R. 2000. U. of Rhode Island admits that its engineering school was hostile to women. *Chronicle of Higher Education,* April 14, A28.

WILSON, W. J. 1987. *The truly disadvantaged: The inner city, the underclass and public policy.* Chicago: University of Chicago Press.

WINEBERG, H. 1988. Duration between marriage and first birth and marital stability. *Social Biology* 35 (Spring): 91–102.

WINEBERG, H. 1990. Childbearing after remarriage. *Journal of Marriage and the Family* 52 (February): 31–38.

WINEBERG, H. 1991. Intermarital fertility and dissolution of the second marriage. *Social Science Quarterly* 75 (January): 62–65.

WINEBERG, H. 1994. Marital reconciliation in the United States: Which couples are successful?

Journal of Marriage and the Family 56 (February): 80–88.

WINEBERG, H. 1996. The prevalence and characteristics of blacks having a successful marital reconciliation. *Journal of Divorce & Remarriage* 25 (1/2): 75–86.

WINEBERG, H., AND J. MCCARTHY. 1993. Separation and reconciliation in American marriages. *Journal of Divorce & Remarriage* 20, 21–42.

WINEBERG, H., AND J. MCCARTHY. 1998. Living arrangements after divorce: Cohabitation versus remarriage. *Journal of Divorce & Remarriage* 29 (1/2): 131–46.

WINER, E. L., AND L. BECKER, EDS. 1993. *Premarital and marital contracts: A lawyer's guide to drafting and negotiating enforceable marital and cohabitation agreements.* Chicago: American Bar Association.

WINFIELD, F. E. 1985. *Commuter marriage: Living together, apart.* New York: Columbia University Press.

WINGERT, P., AND J. F. LAUERMAN. 2000. Parents behaving badly. *Newsweek,* July 24, 48–49.

WINKLEBY, M. A., AND W. T. BOYCE. 1994. Health-related risk factors of homeless families and single adults. *Journal of Community Health* 19 (February): 7–23.

WINNER, K. 1996. *Divorced from justice: The abuse of women and children by divorce lawyers and judges.* New York: Regan Books.

WINTON, C. A. 1995. *Frameworks for studying families.* Guilford, CT: Dushkin.

WIRTH, L. 1945. The problem of minority groups. In *The science of man in the world crisis,* ed. R. Linton, 347–72. New York: Columbia University Press.

WISENSALE, S. 2000. Paid leave offers balance. *Baltimore Sun,* March 17, 11A.

WITT, G. E. 1998. Vote early and often. *American Demographics* 20 (December): 23.

WOLCHIK, S. A., A. M. FENAUGHTY, AND S. L. BRAVER. 1996. Residential and nonresidential parents' perspectives on visitation problems. *Family Relations* 45 (April): 230–37.

WOLCOTT, J. 2000. Finding Mrs. Right (and all the little Rights). *Christian Science Monitor,* February 23, 15–17.

WOLF, D. L. 1997. Family secrets: Transnational struggles among children of Filipino immigrants. *Sociological Perspectives* 40 (3): 457–82.

WOLF, R. S. 1996. Elder abuse and family violence: Testimony presented before the U.S. Senate Special Committee on aging. *Journal of Elder Abuse & Neglect* 8 (1): 81–96.

WOLFE, L. 1981. *The Cosmo report.* New York: Arbor House.

WOLFE, S. M. 1991. *Women's health alert.* Reading, MA: Addison-Wesley.

WOLFSON, E. 1996. Why we should fight for the freedom to marry: The challenges and opportunities that will follow a win in Hawaii. *Journal of Gay, Lesbian, and Bisexual Identity* 1 (1): 79–89.

WOLL, S. B., AND P. YOUNG. 1989. Looking for Mr. or Ms. Right: Self-presentation in videodating. *Journal of Marriage and the Family* 51 (May): 483–88.

Woman gives birth using her dead husband's sperm. 1999. *Baltimore Sun,* March 27, 5A.

Women's Leadership Fund. 1999. Study finds differences in newspaper coverage of female and male candidates. www.womensleadershipfund.org/press/index.html (accessed August 24, 2000).

WONG, B. 1998. *Ethnicity and entrepreneurship: The new Chinese immigrants in the San Francisco Bay area.* Boston: Allyn & Bacon.

WONG, M. G. 1988. The Chinese American family. In *Ethnic families in America: Patterns and variations,* 3rd ed., eds. C. H. Mindel, R. W. Habenstein, and R. Wright, 230–57. New York: Elsevier.

WONG, P. 1993. *Child support and welfare reform.* New York: Garland.

WOOD, D. B. 1995. States' bid to change workplace hire laws leaves women split. *Christian Science Monitor,* April 7, 1, 4.

WOOD, J. T. 1994. *Gendered lives: Communication, gender, and culture.* Palo Alto, CA: Mayfield.

WOODARD, E. H., IV, AND N. GRIDINA. 2000. *Media in the home: The fifth annual survey of parents and children, 2000.* Philadelphia: University of Pennsylvania, Annenberg Public Policy Center.

WOODS, R. D. 1996. Grandmother roles: A cross cultural view. *Journal of Instructional Psychology* 23 (December): 286–92.

WOODWARD, K. L., AND K. SPRINGEN. 1992. Better than a gold watch. *Newsweek,* August 24, 71.

Work at home in 1997. 1998. Bureau of Labor Statistics, Labor Force Statistics from the Current Population Survey. ftp://146.142.4.23/pub/news.release/homey.txt (accessed October 14, 2000).

Working longer, working better? 1999. International Labour Organization. www.ilo.org/public/english/bureau/inf/magazine/31/work.htm (accessed October 11, 2000).

Working women say . . . 2000. AFL-CIO. www.aflcio.org/women/survey1.htm (accessed October 15, 2000).

Working women: Equal pay—Ask a working woman. 2000. AFL-CIO. www.aflcio.org/women/survey1.htm (accessed October 15, 2000).

The World's Women 2000: Trends and Statistics. 2000. New York: United Nations.

WRIGHT, C. I., AND L. S. FISH. 1997. Feminist family therapy: The battle against subtle sexism. In *Subtle sexism: Current practices and prospects for change,* ed. N. V. Benokraitis, 201–15. Thousand Oaks, CA: Sage.

WRIGHT, J. 1997. Motherhood's gray area. *Washington Post,* July 29, E5.

WRIGHT, J. M. 1998. *Lesbian step families: An ethnography of love.* New York: Haworth Press.

WU, L. L. 1996. Effects of family instability, income, and income instability on the risk of a premarital birth. *American Sociological Review* 61 (June): 386–406.

WU, Z. 1994. Remarriage in Canada: A social exchange perspective. *Journal of Divorce & Remarriage* 21 (3/4): 191–224.

WU, Z., AND M. S. POLLARD. 2000. Economic circumstances and the stability of nonmarital cohabitation. *Journal of Family Issues* 21 (April): 303–28.

XU, X., C. D. HUDSPETH, AND S. ESTES. 1997. The effects of husbands' involvement in child rearing activities and participation in household labor on marital quality: A racial comparison. *Journal of Gender, Culture, and Health* 2 (3): 171–93.

YAMANI, M. 1998. Cross-cultural marriage within Islam: Ideals and reality. In *Cross-cultural marriage: Identity and choice.* R. Breger and R. Rosanna, eds., 153–69. New York: Berg.

YELLOWBIRD, M., AND C. M. SNIPP. 1994. Native American families. In *Minority families in the United States: A multicultural perspective,* ed. R. L. Taylor, 179–201. Upper Saddle River, NJ: Prentice Hall.

YESALIS, C. E., C. K. BARSUKIEWICZ, AND M. S. BAHRKE. 1997. Trends in anabolic-androgenic steroid use among adolescents. *Archives of Pediatrics & Adolescent Medicine* 151 (December): 1197–207.

YOKOTA, F., AND K. M. THOMPSON. 2000. Violence in G-rated animated films. *JAMA* 283 (May 24/31): 2716–20.

YOON, I.-J. 1997. *On my own: Korean businesses and race relations in America.* Chicago: University of Chicago Press.

YOSHIHAMA, M., A. L. PAREKH, AND D. BOYINGTON. 1991. Dating violence in Asian/Pacific communities. In *Dating violence: Young women in danger,* ed. B. Levy, 184–95. Seattle, WA: Seal Press.

Youth gangs on rise at Indian reservations. 1997. *Baltimore Sun,* September 18, 6A.

YU, Y. 1995. Patterns of work and family: An analysis of the Chinese American family since the 1920s. In *American families: Issues in race and ethnicity,* ed. C. K. Jacobson, 131–44. New York: Garland.

ZABIN, L. S., AND S. C. HAYWARD. 1993. *Adolescent sexual behavior and childbearing.* Thousand Oaks, CA: Sage.

ZABIN, L. S., M. B. HIRSH, E. A. SMITH, R. STREET, AND J. B. HARDY. 1986. Evaluation of a pregnancy prevention program for urban teenagers. *Family Planning Perspectives* 18, 119–26.

ZABLOCKI, B. 1980. *Alienation and charisma: A study of contemporary American communes.* New York: Free Press.

ZAL, H. M. 1992. *The sandwich generation: Caught between growing children and aging parents.* New York: Plenum Press.

ZAPLER, M. 1995. States may be next battleground for human-embryo research. *Chronicle of Higher Education,* January 20, A24.

ZHOU, B. 1994. New childless families in China. *Beijing Review,* January 31–February 6, 24–25.

ZHOU, J.-N., M. A. HOFMAN, AND D. F. SWAAB. 1995. A sex difference in the human brain and its relation to transsexuality. *Nature* 378 (November 2): 68–70.

ZHOU, M., AND C. L. BANKSTON III. 1998. *Growing up American: How Vietnamese children adapt to life in the United States.* New York: Russell Sage Foundation.

ZHU, B.-P., R. T. ROLFS, B. E. NANGLE, AND J. M. HORAN. 1999. Effect of the interval between pregnancies on perinatal outcomes. *New England Journal of Medicine* 340 (February 25): 589–94.

ZILL, N., AND C. W. NORD. 1994. *Running in place: How American families are faring in a changing economy and an individualistic society.* Washington, DC: Child Trends.

ZIMBALIST, A. 2000. Backlash against Title IX: An end run around female athletes. *Chronicle of Higher Education,* March 3, B9–B10.

ZITO, J. M., D. J. SAFER, S. DOS REIS, J. F. GARDNER, M. BOLES, AND F. LYNCH. 2000. Trends in the prescribing of psychotropic medications to preschoolers. *JAMA* 283, February 23, 105–1030.

ZUNIN, L. M., AND H. S. ZUNIN. 1991. *The art of condolence: What to write, what to say, what to do at a time of loss.* New York: Harper-Collins.

ZURAVIN, S. J., AND F. A. DIBLASIO. 1996. The correlates of child physical abuse and neglect by adolescent mothers. *Journal of Family Violence* 11 (June): 149–66.

ZURAWIK, D. 1996. Shows sexploit "family hour." *Baltimore Sun,* December 11, 1E, 5E.

ZWEIG, M. 2000. *The working class majority: America's best kept secret.* Ithaca, NY: Cornell University Press.

PHOTO CREDITS ••

NAME INDEX

Gupta, S., 229
Gutman, H., 58
Gutner, T., 408
Gwartney-Gibbs, P. A., 204

Haag, P. S., 100
Haan, M. N., 453
Haas, L., 209
Haffner, D. W., 141, 142, 145, 148
Hage, D., 357
Hager, M., 285
Hahn, B. A., 227
Hahn, R. A., 422
Haiken, M., 316
Hales, D., 293
Haley, A., 57
Hall, C. C. I., 82, 87
Halpern, C. T., 150
Halpern, S., 252, 260
Hamer, D. H., 133
Hamilton, C., 316
Hamilton, J. C., 38
Hamon, R. R., 464
Hancock, J., 336
Hannon, R., 187
Hanson, M., 28
Hanson, R. K., 377
Hanson, S. L., 84
Haq, F., 101
Harari, S. E., 51
Hareven, T. K., 63
Harjo, S. S., 313, 316
Harms, T., 291
Harris, D. K., 205, 212, 353, 382
Harris, D. R., 204
Harris, J.R., 79
Harris, K. M., 484
Harris, L., 187, 188
Harris, M., 91
Harrison, A., 313
Harrison, C., 334
Hart, B., 388
Hartill, L., 259
Hartman, S., 176
Harvey E., 296
Hass, A., 140, 142
Hastings, D., 373
Hatcher, R. A., 272
Hatchett, S. J., 309, 312
Hatfield, E., 118, 124, 127, 135, 174
Haubegger, C., 21
Havemann, J., 257, 454
Hawke, D. F., 51
Hayashi, G. M., 121
Hayes, C. L., 422
Hays, S., 112
Haynes, J. A., 313
Hayward, S. C., 287
Hazan, C., 111, 112
Headden, S., 319
Heaton, T. B., 404
Heavons, A. J., 308
Hecht, M. L., 125
Heintz-Knowles, K., 90
Heise, L. L., 384, 385
Heiss, J., 212
Hendin, H., 117
Hendrick, C., 116, 118, 201
Hendrick, S., 116, 118, 201
Hendrickson, M. L., 241
Hendrix, H., 127
Henken, E. R., 140

Henry, K, 336
Henry, S., 452
Henshaw, S., 245
Henton, J., 187
Herbert, C., 137
Herbert, W., 426, 434
Herdt, G. H., 132
Herman, D. L., 118
Herman, R., 469
Herman-Giddens, M. E., 376
Hern, W. M., 7
Herod, A., 40
Herrerias, C., 413
Herring, T., 379, 381
Herrstrom, S., 479
Hershatter, G., 184
Hertz, R., 342
Hess, E., 142
Hetherington, E. M., 284, 413, 420, 442, 443
Hetrick, R., 336
Heyn, D., 232
Hiedemann, B., 403, 406
Hill, R. B., 36, 309, 312, 313
Hinsch, B., 132
Hirschel, J. D., 388
Hite, S., 148
HIV/AIDS Surveillance Report, 160, 162
Hobart, C. W., 117, 118
Hobbs, F. B., 450, 458, 468, 488
Hochschild, A., 94, 350
Hockstader, L., 102
Hofferth, S. L., 294, 295
Hoffman, J., 414, 415
Hoffman, K., 385
Hogan, D. P., 311
Hojat, M., 135
Holden, C., 316
Holden, G. W., 289, 386
Holland, D. C., 200
Holman, T. B., 37, 224
Holmes, S. A., 480
Holmstrom, D., 21, 316, 317
Honey, M., 67
Hong, S. M., 127
Hoon, S. J., 185
Hooyman, N. R., 465, 466, 470
Hope, T. L., 327
Hopson, D. P., 312
Hopson, D. S., 312
Horton, H. D., 200
Horwitz, A. V., 227
Hosley, C. A., 283
Hotz, V. J., 300
Houseknecht, S. K., 15, 16
Hout, M., 361, 363
Howard, J. A., 74
Howe, R. F., 258
Hudak, M. A., 81, 88
Hudson, J., 178
Hughes, D. L., 350, 351, 353, 355, 361
Hughey, A. M., 326
Hugick, L., 93
Huisman, D. A., 369
Humphry, D., 487
Hunt, J., 290
Hunt, M. M., 155
Huntley, T., 467
Hupka, R. B., 122
Hurh, W., 324
Hurtado, A., 319
Huston, M., 170, 210

Huston, T. L., 191
Hutchinson, E.,420
Hutchinson, M. K., 140
Hutchison, I. W., 368, 413
Hutter, M., 23
Hwang, S.- S., 329
Hyde, J. S., 135
Hyman, B., 379
Hyman, M., 84

Ihinger-Tallman, M., 433, 444, 446
Ikonomidou, C., 248
Imber-Black, E., 439
Impoco, J., 131
Ingrassia, M., 368
Institute for Philosophy and Public Policy, 262
Irving, H. H., 414
Ishii-Kuntz, M., 288, 454
Iwao, S., 102

Jacklin, C. N., 283
Jackson, A. P., 287, 349
Jackson, D. D., 13, 330
Jackson, J. S., 312
Jackson, N. A., 386
Jackson, S. A., 33
Jacobs, F. H., 484
Jacobs, G., 134
Jacobs, J. A., 328, 343
Jacobs, J. L., 378
Jacobsen, L., 293
Jacobson, C. K., 271
Jacobson, N. S., 240, 368, 386
Jacoby, S., 154
Jager, J., 265, 268
Jaimes, M. A., 55
Jain, A., 323
James, J. W., 468
Janeway, E., 4
Jankowiak, W. R., 126
Jarrett, R. L., 33, 36, 309, 310
Jarrett, W. H., 123, 310
Jayakody, R., 231
Jemmott, J. B., III, 120
Jemmott, L. S., 160
Jendrek, M. P., 460, 461
Jenny, C., 374
Jerrome, D., 35
Jhally, S., 21
Jo, M. H., 326
John, D., 231, 309
John, R., 54, 56, 314, 315
Johnson, A. G., 77
Johnson, B. K., 155
Johnson, C. L., 289, 383, 463
Johnson, D., 8
Johnson, E. M., 249, 278
Johnson, J. H., Jr., 308
Johnson, L., 101
Johnson, R., 107
Johnson, R. W., 471
Johnson, S., 111
Johnson, V. E., 143, 145, 146, 148, 149, 252, 253, 377
Jones, A., 122, 123
Jones, C., 201
Jones, E. F., 267
Jones, F., 265, 268
Jones, J., 58, 59, 310
Jones, R. K., 371
Jones, W. H., 239

Josselson, R., 109
Julian, T., 289, 310
Justice, G., 349

Kabacoff, R. I., 73
Kacapyr, E., 338
Kaffman, M., 212
Kalmijn, M., 278, 329
Kamara, C. H., 137
Kamerman, S. B., 297
Kamo, Y., 231, 267
Kanaley, R., 20
Kane, E. W., 40
Kanin, E. G., 118
Kann, L., 131, 149, 150, 151, 187
Kantor, G. K., 367
Kantor, R. M., 211
Kantrowitz, B., 240, 298
Kao, G., 326
Kaplan, D. A., 136, 137
Kaplan, E. B., 311
Kaplan, G. A., 453
Kaplan, H. S., 146
Kaprio, J., 227
Kar, S. B., 325
Karanja, W. W., 9
Karasik, S., 282
Karney, B. R., 234
Karoly, L. A., 333
Kass, L. R., 121
Kate, N. T., 246, 479
Katzev, A. R., 431
Kaufman, M., 92
Kayser, K., 228, 229
Keith, P. M., 202
Keith, V. M., 227
Kelley, B. T, 366, 376, 379
Kelley, P., 426, 446
Kelly, G. F., 144
Kelly, J. B., 422
Kemp, S., 32
Kendall, D., 93
Kenen, R. H., 254
Kennedy, G. E., 462
Kennickell, A. B., 333, 334
Kenrick, D. T., 182
Kephart, P., 106
Kephart, W. M., 9, 213
Kerckhoff, A. C., 173
Kern, S., 220
Kerr, J. K., 392
Kersten, K. K., 399
Kesner, J. E., 386
Kheshgi-Genovese, Z., 435, 445
Khoo, S.-E., 207
Kibria, N., 324, 325, 328, 329
Kiecolt, K. J., 175
Kiecolt-Glaser, J. K., 117
Kiernan, K. E., 417, 443
Kilbourne, J., 87
Kilburn, J. C., Jr., 383
Kim, E., 231, 324
Kim, H. K., 312
Kim, K. C., 231, 324
Kimbrough, R. J., 300
Kimmel, M. S., 83
Kindlon, D. J., 100
King, P., 256
King, V., 415
King, W., 59
Kinkead, G., 385
Kinsey, A. C., 132, 145, 156, 157
Kirby, D., 142

SUBJECT INDEX

Bigamy, 3
  Mormon Church, 7–8
Billings method, contraception, 501
Biological theories:
  gender differences, 75
  love, 118
  sexual orientation, 139
Biracial children, 329–30
  concerns about, 330
Birth control. see Contraception
Birth control pill, 499
Birth defects, and prenatal testing, 285
Birthing rooms, 267
Birth order, and personality, 284
Birth rate:
  and educational background, 271
  meaning of, 270
  in U.S., 270–71
Bisexuality:
  cross cultural view, 140
  identity development, 140–41
  meaning of, 139
Blame, in communication, 256
Blank slate concept, human development, 279
Blastomere analysis before implantation (BABI), 263–64
Bobbitt, Lorena, 373
Books, gender role stereotypes, 85
Boomerang generation, 251
Brain, chemistry and love, 118
Breadwinner fathers, 278
Brown, Louise, 280
Bulimia, 391–92
Bundling, 51
Burnout, marital, 246, 247

Calendar method, contraception, 501
Canada, national health care, 481, 483
Caregiving:
  rewards of, 473
  strain of, 473–74
  styles of, 472–73
Caring, and love, 116–17
Case-studies, 40–41
  pros/cons of, 41
Catholic marriages, 2
Census Bureau, 43
  definition of family, 3
Ceremonial marriage, 2, see also, Marriage
Cervical cap, 501
Cesarean section, 267, 497
Chiefs, American Indian women as, 55
Child abuse, 373–79
  definition of, 374
  forms of, 374
  and later functioning, 281, 379
  prevalence of, 374–76
  risk factors, 376
  sexual abuse, 374, 376–79
  signs of, 380
Childbirth, 267, 496–97
  afterbirth, 497
  birthing rooms, 267
  cesarean section, 497
  labor, stages of, 496–97

prepared childbirth, 497
Child care, 246–48
  abuse and neglect in, 296
  day care centers, 296–97
  safety in, 296
  by fathers, 278–279
  global view, 297, 479–80
  by mothers, 246–48
  by relatives, 246–47, 295–96
  at workplace, 361
Child development:
  Erikson's psychosocial theory, 279–281
  impact of parents on, 291–93
  Mead's theory of social self, 279, 280
  myths, 281–282
  Piaget's cognitive development, 279, 280
Child labor, Industrial Revolution era, 62
Childlessness, decisions about, 270–72
Child maltreatment, meaning of, 374
Child neglect, aspects of, 374
Children: see also Family; Parenthood; Parenting; specific developmental periods (eg. Adolescents)
  adoption of, 275–78
  as adults. see Adult children
  African American, 308, 310–11
  American Indians, 54–56
  at-risk, 299–300
  attachment, 113–16
  child abuse, 373–79
  child care, 246–48, 295–97
  and cohabitation, 287
  in colonial era, 52–53
  communication with, 292
  development theories, 279–281
  discipline of, 288–91
  divorce effects on, 414–20
  foster care, 300–1
  during Great Depression, 66
  homosexual, 298
  of homosexual parents, 298
  Industrial Revolution era, 61–62
  infant mortality rate, 13
  inner resources needed, 291
  kids/parents rights, 292
  latchkey kids, 294–95
  Mexican Americans, 59
  in phase of marriage, 251
  poverty, 338
  reactions to conflict, 281
  and remarriage, 429–30, 434–35
  sexual abuse of, 374, 376–79
  as source of conflict, 259
  World War II era, 68
Child support, 399, 410–12
  legal enforcement, 411–12, 478–79
  non-compliance of fathers, 278, 411
Child Support Enforcement Amendments, 411, 478–79
Child well-being, 15–16
China:
  adoptees from, 277

cohabitation in, 226
contraceptive policies, 267
divorce in, 402
homosexuality/bisexuality in, 140
marriage squeeze, 214
mate selection, 199–200
personal ads, 201
status of women, 78, 101
Chlamydia, 172, 503
  and infertility, 252
Chorionic villus sampling, 263, 496
Christian Action Network, 46
Cigarette smoking, pregnancy complications, 496
Cinderella fantasy, 371
Circumcision, female, 78, 144, 145–46
Civil Rights Act of 1964, Title VII, 357
Civil rights movement, and family changes, 21
Clinical research, 40–41
  case-studies, 41
  pros/cons of, 41
Clinton, Bill, 155
Clocksprings theory, love, 118–19
Cognitive developmental theory:
  concepts in, 80–81
  gender roles, 80–81
  Piaget's theory, 279, 280
Cohabitation, 2–3, 221–26
  benefits of, 223–24
  and children, 223, 287
  disadvantages of, 224–25
  and future marital success, 225
  global view, 19, 226
  increase in, 19, 221
  legal aspects, 225–26
  part-time/limited cohabitation, 222
  premarital cohabitation, 222
  substitute marriage, 222
  violent behavior, 386
Colonial era, family in, 50–54
  African Americans, 56–59
  children, 52–53
  courtship, 180
  economic roles, 52
  family structure, 50
  regional variations, 54
  roles of husbands/wives, 51–52
  sexuality, 51, 180
  social class, 54
Commitment, and love, 117, 119–20
Common-law marriage, 3
Communal households, 229–31
  examples of, 229–30
  senior communes, 230
Communication:
  approach/avoidance in, 255–56
  with children, 292
  communication problems, types of, 256–57
  gender differences, 104, 253–56
  and gender roles, 254–55
  good communication, aspects of, 252, 261–62
  of men, 254
  self-disclosure in, 252–53
  and sexual problems, 493

of women, 254
Communitarians, 14
Commuter marriage, 348–49
  pros/cons of, 348–49
  stress of, 349
Compadrazgo, 60
Companionate
  family, 65
  grandparent, 459
  marriage, 242
Companionship:
  dating, 180–81
  marriage, 212–13
Comparable worth, meaning of, 485
Computer assisted telephone interviewing (CATI), 38–39
Computer-dating services, 186
  global view, 199, 200
Computers, and family changes, 20
Conception, process of, 494
Concrete operational stage, Piaget's theory, 280
Condom, 500
Conflict, 258–60
  adult children, 286
  children's reactions, 281
  common sources of, 258–59
  coping methods, 259–60
  fair fighting, rules for, 261
  family therapy, 260
  vs. good communication, 261–62
  meaning of, 258
  stepfamilies, 437, 441–42
Conflict-habituated marriage, 239–40
Conflict theory, 32
  family violence, 386–87
Consumers, sex discrimination, 103
Consummation, 3
Contempt, signs of, 257
Contraception, 266–68
  birth control pill, 20, 499
  cervical cap, 501
  condom, 500
  Depo-Provera, 499
  diaphragm, 500
  and family changes, 20
  female condom, 500
  fertility awareness, 501
  global view, 288–89
  intrauterine device (IUD), 500
  Norplant, 499
  spermicides, 501
  sterilization, 499
  withdrawal method, 501
Controlling behavior:
  in dating relationships, 200–201, 202
  in love, 129, 196
Cooley, Charles Horton, 6
Corporal punishment, 289–290,
Corporate welfare, 484
Courtship. see Dating; Mate selection
Criticism, 256–57
Cross-cultural view: see also Ethnic/racial minorities; racial and ethnic groups
  abortion, 270
  adolescent sex, 162

social class, 191–92
in traditional societies, 197, 198
in transitional societies, 199–200
values, 192
warning signs, 196
Matriarchy, 4
African Americans, 58
Matrilocal residence, 9
Media. *see* specific media forms
Mediation, divorce mediation, 421–22
Medicaid, 471
Medicare, 487
Menopause, 165–66
global view, 166
post-menopause pregnancy, 262
signs of, 165
Men's roles:
colonial era, 51–52
domestic tasks, 99–101, 246–49
European immigrants, 61, 62–64
full-time fathers, 101
Great Depression, 66
in home, 99–101
Industrial Revolution era, 61
instrumental role, 31, 82–83
Mexican Americans, 59–61
1950s, 68–69
in patriarchy, 4, 77–78
Promise Keepers, 22, 34
sexual scripts, 142–43
slave males, 58
stereotypes, 74
traditional, pros/cons of, 96–98
Merchant class, 54
Meritor Savings Bank v. Vinson, 102
Mexican Americans, 59–61
birth rate, 270–71
children, 60
European influences on, 61
family structure, 60
male/female roles, 59–60
Mexico, status of women, 107
Micro-level view, family changes, 18–19
Microsystem, 30–31
Middle adulthood:
family in, 251–52
male climacteric, 166
menopause, 165–66
parenthood in, 272–73, 284
sexuality in, 165–66
Middle class:
African Americans, 312
Latinos, 317–18
shrinking of, 334–35
Middle Eastern families, 18
Military:
sexual harassment in, 102
women in combat, 102
Million Mom March, 22
Minimal brain damage, 496
Minority group: *see also*
Ethnic/racial minorities;
specific minority and ethnic groups
meaning of, 306

Miscegenation, 2
Misogyny, meaning of, 203
Model minority, Asian Americans, facts/fictions, 327–8
Mommy track, 353
Money pools, of ethnic groups, 328
Monogamy:
meaning of, 8
serial monogamy, 8
Moonlighting, 341
Mormons:
family structure, 8
intermarriage, 190–91
polygamy, 7–8, 229
Morocco, status of women, 78, 106
Mortality rate:
of infants, 13
Mothers:
and adolescents, 283
feelings of expectant mothers, 267
–infant attachment, 113–16, 268–69
role expectations, 277–78
sexual abuse of children, 377–79
employed, 15
Mourning, meaning of, 466
Movies:
oral sex in, 156
sexual information from, 150–51
MTV, gender stereotypes, 94–95
Multiethnic Placement Act of 1994, 255
Munchausen by proxy, 374
Mundugumors, 76
Muslims. *see* Islam
Myths:
about African Americans, 309
about child development, 281–282
about family, 10–13
as providing love, 13
as perfect, 13–13
about marriage and family, 10–13
about the past, 11–12
about incest, 378
about self-sufficient families, 12–13
about sexual response, 160
about singlehood, 220
about stepfamilies, 435–36
about what is natural in families, 12
dysfunctional, 10
functional, 10

Nativism, 305–6
Nature–nurture issue, gender roles, 76–79
Neglect of children, aspects of, 374
Neolocal residence, 9
Netherlands, assisted suicide, 485–86
Netrodin, 285
New Guinea, homosexuality among Sambia, 140
Newlyweds, phase of marriage, 250–51

Newspapers, gender role stereotypes, 87
Nigeria
polygynous marriages, 9
status of women, 78
No-fault divorce, 401, 409
Non-ceremonial marriage, 2, *see also*, Common-law marriage
Nonparticipant observation, 41, 42
Norms, and marriage, 2
Norplant, 499
Norway, status of women, 78
Nostalgia, family-related, 11–12
Nuclear family, 4

Objects, women as, 142–43
Observation, 41–43
participant and nonparticipant, 41, 42
pros/cons of, 42
Older persons. *see* Aging; Late adulthood
Oneida, group marriage among, 9, 229
Only children:
characteristics of, 284–85
famous onlies, 284
Open adoption, 277
Oral sex, 156–57
African Americans, 156
in movies, 156
prevalence of, 156
Orgasm, 158–59
dysfunction of, 492–93
compared to ejaculation, 158
gender differences, 159
Orphanages, for-profit types, 277
Out-of-wedlock births, 286–87
see also Teen pregnancy
absentee fathers, 293–94
at-risk children, 300
and educational level, 287
ethnic/racial minorities, 286–87
increase in, 286–87
Outside wife, 9–10
Overtime, work, 342–43
Ovulation, failure of, 252

Pack dating, 183–84
Pakistan, status of women, 78
Parenthood: *see also* Fathers;
Mothers; Pregnancy
benefits/costs of, 266–67
birthing choices, 267
childfree decision, 292–93
expectant fathers, feelings of, 269–70
expectant mother, experiences of, 267
fathers, feelings of, 269–70
father's role, 278–279
infertility, 252–54
lifestyle changes, 275
mother–infant bonding, 268–69
mother's role, 276–277
new parents, 275–76, 278
older parents, 272–73, 284
postponing, 271–72
reactions to pregnancy, 266
role strain, 276–279

Parenting:
absentee fathers, 293–94
adolescents, 281–85, 292–93
adult children in home, 285–86
and birth order, 284–85
child care, 295–96
racial/ethnic differences in, 283–84
Parenting roles:
contemporary, 276–77
internalizing, 275–76
homosexual parents, 298
latchkey kids, 294–95
only children, 284–85
in stepfamilies, 444
Parenting styles:
authoritarian parenting, 286–87
authoritative parenting, 287
discipline, 288–91
to influence children, 287–88
permissive parenting, 287
to shape environment, 288
and social class, 286–87
Participant observation, 41, 42
Part-time jobs, 342
Part-time/limited cohabitation, 222
Passive-congenial marriage, 240
Patriarchy:
male aggression, 77–78
meaning of, 4
Patriarchy/male-dominance theory, family violence, 384–85
Patrilocal residence, 9
Peers:
and adolescent sex, 162
and gender role socialization, 84–85
sexual information from, 150
and sexual violence, 204
Pelvic inflammatory disease (PID), 172
infertility, 252
Pergonol, 285
Permanent availability model, mate selection, 192–93
Permissive parenting, 287
Personal ads, 185–86
in China, 201
pros/cons of, 185
Personality theory, family violence, 385–86
Personal Responsibility and Work Opportunity Reconciliation Act (PRWORA), 484–85
Petting, 156
Physical attractiveness:
mate selection, 189–90, 213
in personal ads, 185
unrequited love, 129–30
Physical punishment, of children, *see also* Corporal punishment, 289–90
Physicians, American Indian women as, 55
Piaget's cognitive theory, 279, 280
stages in, 280
Pioneer era, family hardships, 11
Placenta, 494
Play, gender role socialization, 83–84